NAVE'S
COMPACT TOPICAL BIBLE

NAVE'S
COMPACT TOPICAL BIBLE

ZondervanPublishingHouse
Academic and Professional Books
Grand Rapids, Michigan

A Division of HarperCollins*Publishers*

Requests for information should be addressed to:
Zondervan Publishing House
Academic and Professional Books
Grand Rapids, Michigan 49530

Library of Congress Catalog Card Number 72-83885

ISBN 0-310-48991-1

Printed in the United States of America

94 95 96 97 98 99 00 01 02 /BP/ 10 9 8 7 6 5 4 3 2 1

PREFACE

The *Nave's Compact Topical Bible* is a compact yet comprehensive reference tool for Bible students and teachers.

What is a topical Bible? A topical Bible is an organization of scripture verses by subjects or topics — even though the topic itself may not be among the words found in the text.

How does a topical Bible differ from a concordance? A concordance offers only references to *exact* words found in various texts: a topical Bible offers *a complete reference to the concepts as well as the words* found throughout the Bible.

How can a topical Bible help Bible study? All texts relating to a given topic are listed — and organized — in one location. Cross-references are provided for ease in finding similar topics, synonyms and various spellings — for comparisons.

How many Scripture references are there in this compact topical Bible? There are well over 100,000 references included under close to 7,000 various topics. Some verses are referred to as many as thirty times — according to the number of subjects a verse contains. This, therefore, is a comprehensive subject index to the entire Bible.

On what larger volume is this compact volume based? This topical Bible is a compact edition of *The New Nave's Topical Bible: Expanded and Revised,* the largest and most extensive topical Bible ever made available, edited by Edward Viening, with assistance received from the study Bible edited by Orville J. Nave. Also, the compiler wishes to thank his wife, Hazel, who worked while he studied, watched while he worked, and patiently typed and edited the material compiled here.

How does this compact volume differ from the mother book? First: all scripture verses previously printed in full have been deleted and only the references given—making it more compact. Second: many topics have been further subdivided and organized into numerous subtopics (over 25,000 subtopics in all)—making subjects and concepts easier to locate. Third: approximately 100 additional topics have been added to this volume—making it more comprehensive.

What additional help does his book offer? Proper names, places, objects and events are defined, thereby performing the services of a Bible dictionary. Various uses of subjects are given with biblical illustrations and applications, providing teachers and preachers with practical, natural outlines on every conceivable biblical theme.

Here, then is one of the most comprehensive and best organized topical Bibles ever published—*The Nave's Compact Topical Bible*.

THE PUBLISHERS

Abbreviations of the Names of the Books of the Bible

Ge	=Genesis
Ex	=Exodus
Le	=Leviticus
Nu	=Numbers
De	=Deuteronomy
Jos	=Joshua
J'g	=Judges
Ru	=Ruth
1Sa	=I Samuel
2Sa	=II Samuel
1Ki	=I Kings
2Ki	=II Kings
1Ch	=I Chronicles
2Ch	=II Chronicles
Ezr	=Ezra
Ne	=Nehemiah
Es	=Esther
Job	=Job
Ps	=Psalms
Pr	=Proverbs
Ec	=Ecclesiastes
Song	=Song of Solomon
Isa	=Isaiah
Jer	=Jeremiah
La	=Lamentations
Eze	=Ezekiel
Da	=Daniel
Ho	=Hosea
Joe	=Joel
Am	=Amos
Ob	=Obadiah
Jon	=Jonah
Mic	=Micah
Na	=Nahum
Hab	=Habakkuk
Zep	=Zephaniah
Hag	=Haggai
Zec	=Zechariah
Mal	=Malachi
M't	=Matthew
M'k	=Mark
Lu	=Luke
Joh	=John
Ac	=Acts
Ro	=Romans
1Co	=I Corinthians
2Co	=II Corinthians
Ga	=Galatians
Eph	=Ephesians
Ph'p	=Philippians
Col	=Colossians
1Th	=I Thessalonians
2Th	=II Thessalonians
1Ti	=I Timothy
2Ti	=II Timothy
Tit	=Titus
Ph'm	=Philemon
Heb	=Hebrews
Jas	=James
1Pe	=I Peter
2Pe	=II Peter
1Jo	=I John
2Jo	=II John
3Jo	=III John
Jude	=Jude
Re	=Revelation

Other Abbreviations

I Macc	= I Maccabees
II Macc	= II Maccabees
ASV	= American Standard Version
AV	= Authorized Version
KJV	= King James Version
RV	= Revised Version
RSV	= Revised Standard Version
Marg.	= Margin

A

AARON. Lineage of (Ex 6:16-20; Jos 21:4, 10; 1Ch 6:2, 3; 23:13). Marriage of (Ex 6:23). Children of (Ex 6:23, 25; 1Ch 6:3; 24:1, 2). Descendants of (Ex 6:23, 25; 1Ch 6:3-15, 50-53; 24).

Meets Moses in the wilderness and is made spokesman for Moses (Ex 4:14-16, 27-31; 7:1, 2). Inspiration of (Ex 12:1; Le 10:8; 11:1; 13:1; 15:1; Nu 2:1; 4:1, 17; 18:1; 19:1; 20:12). Commissioned as a deliverer of Israel (Ex 6:13, 26, 27; Jos 24:5; 1Sa 12:8; Ps 77:20; 105:26; Mic 6:4). Summoned to Sinai with Nadab, Abihu, and seventy elders (Ex 19:24; 24:1, 9, 10).

Priesthood of (Ex 28:1; 29:9; Nu 17; 18:1; Ps 99:6; Heb 5:4). Consecration of, to the priesthood (Ex 28; 29; Le 8). Enters upon the priestly office (Le 9). See Priest, High. Descendants of, ordained priests forever (Ex 28:40-43; 29:9; Nu 3:3; 18:1; 1Ch 23:13; 2Ch 26:18).

Judges Israel in the absence of Moses (Ex 24:14). Makes the golden calf (Ex 32; Ac 7:40; De 9:20, 21). Rod of, buds (Nu 17; Heb 9:4); preserved (Nu 17; Heb 9:4). Murmured against, by the people (Ex 5:20, 21; 16:2-10; Nu 14:2-5, 10; 16:3-11, 41; 20:2; Ps 106:16). Places pot of manna in the ark (Ex 16:34). With Hur supports the hands of Moses during battle (Ex 17:12). His benedictions upon the people (Le 9:22; Nu 6:23). Forbidden to mourn the death of his sons Nadab and Abihu (Le 10:6, 19). Intercedes for Miriam (Nu 12:11, 12). Stays the plague by priestly intercession (Nu 16:46-48). Jealous of Moses (Nu 12:1). His presumption, when the rock is smitten (Nu 20:10-12). Not permitted to enter Canaan (Nu 20:12, 23-29). Age of, at death (Ex 7:7; Nu 33:38, 39). Death and burial of (Nu 20:27, 28; De 10:6; 32:50).

Character of (Ps 106:16).

AARONITES, descendants of Aaron who helped David (1Ch 12:27).

AB, the fifth month of the Hebrew year (Nu 33:38).

And Aaron the priest went up into mount Hor at the commandment of the LORD, and died there, in the fortieth year after the children of Israel were come out of the land of Egypt, in the first *day* of the fifth month (Nu 33:38).

ABADDON (ruin). In Job 31:12 it means "ruin;" in Job 26:6; Pr 15:11; 27:20, "Sheol;" in Job 28:22, "death;" in Re 9:11, "Apollyon" who reigns over the infernal regions.

ABAGTHA, chamberlain of King Ahasuerus (Es 1:10).

ABANA, a river of Damascus (2Ki 5:12).

ABARIM (those beyond), either a region E of the Jordan or a mountain range NW of Moab (Nu 27:12). See NEBO 2.

ABBA (Aramaic for **father**), (M'k 14:36; Ro 8:15; Ga 4:6).

ABDA (probably **servant of God**). 1. Father of Adoniram (1Ki 4:6). 2. A Levite (Ne 11:17).

ABDEEL (servant of God), father of Shelemiah (Jer 36:26).

ABDI (probably **servant of God**). 1. A Levite, the father of Kish and grandfather of Ethan (1Ch 6:44; 2Ch 29:12). 2. A son of Elan (Ezr 10:26).

ABDIEL (servant of God), a Gadite chief (1Ch 5:15).

ABDON (probably **servant, service,** or **servile**). 1. A judge of Israel (J'g 12:13-15).

2. Son of Shashak (1Ch 8:23, 28).

3. Son of Jeiel of Gibeon (1Ch 8:30; 9:35, 36).

4. An official of King Josiah (2Ch 34:20; called Achbor in 2Ki 22:12).

ABDON (City), a Levitical city in Asher (Jos 21:30; 1Ch 6:74).

ABED-NEGO (servant of Nego), called also Azariah, a Jewish captive in Babylon (Da 1:6-20; 2:17, 49; 3:12-30).

ABEL. Son of Adam. History of (Ge 4:1-15, 25). References to the death of (M't 23:35; Lu 11:51; Heb 11:4; 12:24; 1Jo 3:12).

ABEL (meadow). 1. A city in Ammon (2Sa 20:14, 18). 2. In 1Sa 6:18 KJV "the great stone of Abel" should probably be "stone."

ABEL-BETH-MAACHAH, a town in Naphtali (2Sa 20:15). Sheba fled there from King David (2Sa 20:14-22). Ben-hadad later seized it (1Ki 15:20) and Tiglath-pileser captured it (2Ki 15:29).

ABEL-CHERAMIM (meadow of vineyards), a place in Ammon, east of the Jordan, to which Jephthah pursued the Ammonites (J'g 11:33).

ABEL-MAIM (meadow of waters), variant of Abel-beth-maachah (2Ch 16:4).

ABEL-MEHOLAH (meadow of dancing), a town probably in the Jordan valley (J'g 7:22; 1Ki 4:12). Probably Elisha's birthplace (1Ki 19:16).

ABEL-MIZRAIM (meadow or **mourning of Egypt),** place where the Israelites mourned for Jacob (Ge 50:11).

ABEL-SHITTIM (See Shittim.)

ABEL THE GREAT. In 1Sa 6:18 "the great stone of Abel" (KJV) should be "the great stone," as in ASV and the RSV.

ABETTING (See Complicity.)

ABEZ, town in Issachar (Jos 19:20).

ABI, the mother of King Hezekiah, spoken of also as the daughter of Zechariah. A contraction of Abijah (2Ki 18:2; 2Ch 29:1).

ABIA, a variant for Abijah.

ABIAH. 1. Wife of Hezron (1Ch 2:24). 2. Son of Samuel (1Sa 8:1-5; 1Ch 6:28).

ABI-ALBON, called also Abiel. One of David's heroes (2Sa 23:31; 1Ch 11:32).

ABIASAPH (the father gathers), a Levite son of Korah (Ex 6:24).

ABIATHAR (father of abundance). 1. High priest. Called Ahimelech in 2Sa 8:17; 1Ch 24:3, 6, 31, and Abimelech (1Ch 18:16). Son of Ahimelech (1Sa 22:20). Escapes to David from the vengeance of Saul, who slew the priests in the city of Nob (1Sa 22:20-23, with 6:19). Consults the ephod for David (1Sa 22:10; 23:9; 30:7). Associate high priest with Zadok in the reign of David (2Sa 15:35; 20:25; 1Ki 4:4; 1Ch 15:11), but called Ahimelech and father of Abiathar (2Sa 8:17; 1Ch 18:16). Loyal to David when Absalom rebelled; leaves Jerusalem with the ark of the covenant, but is directed by David to return with the ark (2Sa 15:24-29). Aids David by sending his son from Jerusalem to David with secret information concerning the counsel of Ahithophel (2Sa 15:35, 36; 17:15-22; 1Ki 2:26). Supports Adonijah's pretensions to the throne (1Ki 1:7). Thrust out of office by Solomon (1Ki 2:26, 27, with 1Sa 2:31-35).

2. See Ahimelech.

ABIB (an ear of corn), called also Nisan. First month in the Jewish calendar (Ex 12:2). Passover instituted, and Israelites depart from Egypt in (Ex 23:15; De 16:1). Tabernacle set up in (Ex 40:2, 17). Israelites arrive at the wilderness of Zin in (Nu 20:1). Enter Canaan in (Jos 4:19). Jordan's overflow in (1Ch 12:15).

ABIDA (the father knows), appears as Abidah in KJV (Ge 25:4). A son of Midian and grandson of Abraham and Keturah (Ge 25:4; 1Ch 1:33).

ABIDAH, a descendant of Abraham (Ge 25:4).

ABIDAN (the father is judge), a prince of the tribe of Benjamin chosen to represent his tribe in the wilderness of Sinai (Nu 1:11; 2:22). He was present at the dedication of the tabernacle (Nu 7:60, 65).

ABIEL (the father is God, or **God is father).** 1. The grandfather of Saul and Abner (1Sa 9:1; 14:51).

2. One of David's mighty men (1Ch 11:32), also called Abi-Albon (2Sa 23:31).

ABIEZER (father of help). 1. Called also Jeezer, progenitor of the Abiezrites (Nu 26:30; Jos 17:2; J'g 6:34; 8:2).

2. One of David's heroes (2Sa 23:27; 1Ch 11:28; 27:12).

ABIGAIL (father is rejoicing). 1. The wife of Nabal, and, after his death, of David (1Sa 25:3, 14-44; 27:3; 2Sa 2:2), to whom she bore his second son, Chileab (2Sa 3:3, or Daniel, as in 1Ch 3:1).

2. A sister of David, daughter of Nahash, and mother of Amasa, commander of David's army (2Sa 17:25; 1Ch 2:16).

ABIHAIL (the father is strength). 1. A Levite, the father of Zuriel (Nu 3:25).

2. The wife of Abishur (1Ch 2:29).

3. A Gadite who lived in Gilead of Bashan (1Ch 5:14).

4. The wife of Rehoboam, king of Judah. A daughter of Eliab, David's eldest brother (2Ch 11:18).

5. The father of Queen Esther (Es 2:15; 9:29).

ABIHU (the father is he). Son of Aaron (Ex 6:23; Nu 3:2). Summoned by God to Sinai (Ex 24:9). Called to the priesthood (Ex 28:1). Death of (Le 10:1, 2; Nu 26:61). Died childless (Nu 3:4).

ABIHUD (the father is majesty), son of Bela, the eldest son of Benjamin (1Ch 8:3).

ABIJAH (Jehovah is Father). 1. The wife of Judah's grandson Hezron (1 Ch 2:24).

2. The seventh son of Becher the son of Benjamin (1Ch 7:8).

3. The second son of the prophet Samuel. Appointed a judge by his father; he became corrupt (1Sa 8:2; 1Ch 6:28).

4. A descendant of Aaron. The ancestral head of the eighth of the 24 groups into which David had divided the priests (1Ch 24:10).

5. A son of Jeroboam I of Israel (1Ki 14:1-18). He died from illness when still a child, in fulfillment of a prediction by the prophet Ahijah.

6. King of Judah, the son and successor of Rehoboam. He made war on Jeroboam in an effort to recover the ten tribes of Israel. Prosperity tempted him to multiply wives and to follow the evil ways of his father. He reigned three years (2Ch 12:16; 13; 14:1).

7. A priest of Nehemiah's time (Ne 10:7; 12:4, 17).

8. The mother of Hezekiah (2Ch 29:1), called Abi in 2Ki 18:2.

9. A chief of the priests who returned from Babylon with Zerubbabel (Ne 12:4, 7).

ABIJAM, called also Abijah and Abia. King of Judah (1Ki 14:31; 15:1; 2Ch 12:16). History of (1Ki 15:1-8; 2Ch 11:22; 13). Succeeded by Asa (1Ki 15:8; 2Ch 14:1).

ABILENE, (probably **meadow),** a Roman province in Palestine (Lu 3:1).

ABIMAEL (God is Father), the ninth of the 13 sons or descendants of Joktan, who was descended from Shem (Ge 10:28; 1Ch 1:22).

ABIMELECH (probably either **the father is king** or **the father of a king).** 1. A Philistine king of Gerar, near Gaza (Ge 20:1-18).

2. A second king of Gerar, probably the son of the one mentioned in 1, at whose court Isaac tried to pass off his wife Rebekah as his sister (Ge 26:1-11).

3. The son of Gideon by a concubine (J'g 8:31; 9:1-57).

4. A Philistine king mentioned in the title of Psalm 34, who very likely is the same as Achish, king of Gath (1Sa 21:10-22:1), with whom David sought refuge when he fled from Saul.

5. A priest in the days of David, a son of Abiathar (1Ch 18:16); also called Ahimelech (LXX and in 1Ch 24:6).

6. See Achish; Ahimelech.

ABINADAB (father is generous). 1. A Levite, in whose house the ark of God rested twenty years (1Sa 7:1, 2; 2Sa 6:3, 4; 1Ch 13:7).

2. Son of Jesse (1Sa 16:8; 17:13).

3. Called also Ishui, son of Saul (1Sa 14:49; 31:2).

4. Father of one of Solomon's purveyors. Called in *R. V.* Ben-Abinadab (1Ki 4:11).

ABINOAM (the father is pleasantness), the father of Barak (J'g 4:6; 5:12).

ABIRAM (the father is exalted). 1. An Israelite who conspired with Dathan against Moses and Aaron (Nu 16; 26:9, 10; De 11:6; Ps 106:17).

2. Son of Hiel (1Ki 16:34).

ABISHAG (the father wanders), a Shunamite woman who looked after David in his old age (1Ki 1:3, 15; 2:17ff).

ABISHAI. Son of Zeruiah, David's sister (1Ch 2:16). One of David's chief men (2Sa 23:18). Seeks Saul's life (1Sa 26:6-8). Pursues and slays Abner (2Sa 2:24; 3:30). Defeats the Edomites (1Ch 18:12); the Ammonites (2Sa 10:10, 14). Seeks the life of Shimei (2Sa 16:9; 19:21). Leads a division of David's army against Absalom (2Sa 18:2, 5). Overthrows Sheba (2Sa 20:1-22). Saves David from being slain by a Philistine (2Sa 21:17). Obtains water from the well of Bethlehem for David (1Ch 11:15-20).

ABISHALOM (1Ki 15:2, 10). See Absalom.

ABISHUA (perhaps **the father is salvation** or **noble).** 1. The son of Phinehas the priest (1Ch 6:4, 5, 50; Ezr 7:5).

2. A Benjamite of the family of Bela (1Ch 8:4).

ABISHUR (the father is a wall), a man of Judah, the son of Shammai (1Ch 2:28, 29).

ABITAL (the father is dew), one of the wives of David (2Sa 3:4; 1Ch 3:3).

ABITUB (the father is goodness), a Benjamite, son of Shaharaim and Hushim (1Ch 8:8-11).

ABIUD, son of Zerubbabel (M't 1:13).

ABLUTION (Ex 19:10, 14; M't 15:2; M'k 7:2-5, 8, 9; Lu 11:38; Heb 9:10). Of priests (Ex 29:4; 30:18-21; 40:12, 31, 32; Le 8:6; 16:4, 24, 26, 28; Nu 19:7-10, 19; 2Ch 4:6).

Of burnt offerings (Le 1:9, 13; 9:14; 2Ch 4:6). Of the dead (Ac 9:37). Of infants (Eze 16:4). Of the face (M't 6:17); feet (Ge 18:4; 19:2; 24:32; 43:24; Ex 30:19, 21; 40:31; J'g 19:21; 2Sa 11:8; Song 5:3; Lu 7:38, 44; Joh 13:5; 1Ti 5:10); hands (Ex 30:18-21; 40:30-32). Of the hands, as a token of innocency (De 21:6; Ps 26:6; M't 27:24).

For defilement: Of lepers (Le 14:8, 9); those having bloody issue (Le 15:5-13); those having eaten that which died (Le 17:15, 16).

Traditional forms of, not observed by Jesus (Lu 11:38, 39).

Figurative: Of baptism (Ac 22:16). Of believers (1Co 6:11; Tit 3:5; Heb 1:3; 9:14; 2Pe 1:9; 1Jo 1:7, 9). Of bodies (Heb 10:22). Of the Church (Eph 5:26). Of conscience (Heb 9:14; 10:22). Of hands (Ps 73:13; Jas 4:8). Of heart (Ps 73:13; Pr 20:9; Jas 4:8). Of leaven (1Co 5:7). Of robes (Re 7:14; 22:14).

Of sin, corporate (Ps 79:9; Isa 1:16, 18; 4:3, 4; Da 12:10; Zec 13:1; Joh 13:8; 2Co 7:1; Re 1:5). Of sin, general (Pr 16:6). Of sin, personal (Ps 51:2; 65:3; Pr 20:9; Joh 13:8; 2Pe 1:9; 1Jo 1:7, 9).

By Christ, work and blood of (Eph 5:26; Tit 3:5, 6; Heb 1:3; 9:14; 1Jo 1:7; Re 1:5; 7:14). See Defilement; Purification; Regeneration.

ABNER (the father is a lamp), son of Ner. Cousin of Saul (1Sa 14:50, 51, with 1Sa 9:1). Captain of the host (1Sa 14:50; 17:55; 26:5, 14). Dedicated spoils of war to the tabernacle (1Ch 26:27, 28). Loyalty of, to the house of Saul (2Sa 2:8-32). Alienation of, from the house of Saul (2Sa 3:6-21). Murdered by Joab; David's sorrow for (2Sa 3:27-39).

ABOMINATION. God's law regarding: Idolatry (De 7:25; 27:15; 32:16); sorcery and necromancy (De 18:10, 11); offering seed to Molech (Le 18:21), or children in sacrifice (De 18:10); the hire of a whore and price of a dog as a consecrated gift (De 23:18). Incest (Le 18:6-18); lying with a woman in her menses (Le 18:19); adultery (Le 18:20); sodomy (Le 18:22; 20:13); bestiality (Le 18:23); wearing clothes of opposite sex (De 22:5); remarriage of defiled wife (De 24:4). Unjust weights and measures (De 25:13-16; Pr 11:1; 20:10, 23).

Actions and attitudes: False pride (Pr 6:17; 16:5); false witness (Pr 6:19; 17:15); lying (Pr 6:17, 19; 12:22); mischievousness, *i.e.* evil (Pr 6:18); murder (Pr 6:17); perverseness (Pr 3:32; 11:20); wicked imaginations, *i.e.* mind (Pr 6:18; 15:26; 21:27); wickedness (Pr 8:7).

People, types: False witness (Pr 6:19; 17:15); scorner (Pr 24:9); trouble maker (Pr 6:19); unjust (Pr 29:27).

Of wicked: Prayer (Pr 28:9); sacrifice (Pr 15:8; 21:27); thoughts (Pr 15:26); way (Pr 15:9).

Body, figurative: Eyes (Pr 6:17); feet (Pr 6:18); hands (Pr 6:17); heart (Pr 6:18; 11:20; 16:5); lips (Pr 8:7; 12:22); thoughts, *i.e.* mind (Pr 6:18; 15:26; 21:27); tongue (Pr 6:17).

ABOMINATION OF DESOLATION, a term used to describe an utterly abhorrent and loathsome abomination (Da 9:27; 11:31; 12:11).

Many scholars hold that Jesus' prophecy that His followers would see the abomination of desolation, spoken of by Daniel the prophet, standing in the Holy Place (M't 24:15) was fulfilled when Jerusalem was destroyed in the year A.D. 70.

ABORTION. Punishment for (Ex 21:22-25). As a judgment (Ho 9:14). Of animals, caused by thunder (Ps 29:9).

ABRAHAM, called also Abram. Son of Terah (Ge 11:26, 27). Marries Sarah (Ge 11:29). Dwells in Ur, but removes to Haran (Ge 11:31; Ne 9:7; Ac 7:4) and Canaan (Ge 12:4, 5, 6; Ac 7:4).

Divine call of (Ge 12:1-3; Jos 24:3; Ne 9:7; Isa 51:2; Ac 7:2, 3; Heb 11:8). Canaan given to (Ge 12:1, 7; 15:7-21; Eze 33:24). Dwells in Beth-el (Ge 12:8). Sojourns in Egypt (Ge 12:10-20; 26:1). Deferring to Lot, chooses Hebron (Ge 13; 14:13; 35:27). Dwells in Gerar (Ge 20; 21:22-34).

Defeats Chedorlaomer (Ge 14:5-24;

Heb 7:1). Is blessed by Melchizedek (Ge 14:18-20; Heb 7:1-10).

God's covenant with (Ge 15; 17:1-22; Mic 7:20; Lu 1:73; Ro 4:13; 15:8; Heb 6:13, 14; Ga 3:6-18, 29; 4:22-31). Called Abraham (Ge 17:5; Ne 9:7). Circumcision of (Ge 17:10-14, 23-27). Angels appear to (Ge 18:1-16; 22:11, 15; 24:7). His questions about the destruction of the righteous and wicked in Sodom (Ge 18:23-32). Witnesses the destruction of Sodom (Ge 19:27, 28). Ishmael born to (Ge 16:3, 15). Dwells in Gerar; deceives Abimelech concerning Sarah, his wife (Ge 20). Isaac born to (Ge 21:2, 3; Ga 4:22-30). Sends Hagar and Ishmael away (Ge 21:10-14; Ga 4:22-30).

Trial of his faith in the offering of Isaac (Ge 22:1-19; Heb 11:17; Jas 2:21). Sarah, his wife, dies (Ge 23:1, 2). He purchases a place for her burial, and buries her in a cave (Ge 23:3-20). Marries Keturah (Ge 25:1). Provides a wife for Isaac (Ge 24).

Children of (Ge 16:15; 21:2, 3; 25:1-4; 1Ch 1:32-34). Testament of (Ge 25:5, 6). Wealth of (Ge 13:2; 24:35; Isa 51:2). Age of, at different periods (Ge 12:4; 16:16; 21:5; 25:7). Death (Ge 15:15; 25:8-10). In Paradise (M't 8:11; Lu 13:28; 16:22-31).

Friend of God (Isa 41:8; 2Ch 20:7; Jas 2:23). Piety of (Ge 12:7, 8; 13:4, 18; 18:19; 20:7; 21:33; 22:3-13; 26:5; Ne 9:7, 8; Ro 4:16-18; 2Ch 20:7; Isa 41:8; Jas 2:23). A prophet (Ge 20:7). Faith of (Ge 15:6; Ro 4:1-22; Ga 3:6-9; Heb 11:8-10, 17-19; Jas 2:21-24) Unselfishness of (Ge 13:9; 21:25-30). Independence of, in character (Ge 14:23; 23:6-16).

Ancestors of, idolatrous (Jos 24:2). How regarded by his descendants (M't 3:9; Lu 13:16, 28; 19:9; Joh 8:33-40, 52-59).

ABRAHAM'S BOSOM was a Jewish symbol of blessedness after death (Lu 16:22, 23).

ABRAM (See Abraham.)

ABRECH (probably an Egyptian word meaning **to kneel),** (Ge 41:43, ASV margin, RSV margin).

ABRONAH, in KJV Ebronah. Place where the Israelites camped (Nu 33:34, 35).

ABSALOM, called also Abishalom. Son of David by Maacah (2Sa 3:3; 1Ch 3:2) Beauty of (2Sa 14:25). Slays Amnon (2Sa 13:22-29). Flees to Geshur (2Sa 13:37, 38). Is permitted by David to return to Jerusalem (2Sa 14:1-24). His demagogism (2Sa 15:2-6, 13); conspiracy (2Sa chapters 15-17); death and burial (2Sa 18:9-17). David's mourning for (2Sa 18:33; 19:1-8). Children of (2Sa 14:27; 18:18; 1Ki 15:2; 2Ch 11:20). Pillar of (2Sa 18:18).

ABSTEMIOUSNESS. Admonished (Pr 23:1-3). Instances of: Daniel and his Hebrew companions (Da 1:8-16); John the Baptist (M't 11:18). See Abstinence; Temperance.

ABSTINENCE, TOTAL. *From intoxicating beverages.* Admonished: (Pr 23:20, 31, 32); Aaron and priesthood (Le 10:8-10; Eze 44:21); Nazarites (Nu 6:3-4); Manoah's wife, *i.e.* Samson's mother (J'g 13:4, 13, 14); kings and princes (Pr 31:4, 5); John the Baptist (Lu 1:15).

Instances of: Israelites in the wilderness (De 29:6). Samson (J'g 16:17, w 13:3-5, 13, 14; Nu 6:3, 4). Daniel (Da 1:8, 12). Rechabites (Jer 35:6-14). John the Baptist (M't 11:18; Lu 1:15; 7:33). See Temperance.

ABUNDANCE. Entrance (2Pe 1:11). From God: Grace (2Co 9:8); joys (Ps 36:8); life (Joh 10:10); power (Eph 3:20); provisions, *i.e.* needs (Le 26:5; De 30:9; Ps 132:15; Pr 3:10; Isa 30:23; Eze 36:30; Am 9:13; Zec 8:12; Ph'p 4:19).

ABYSS means, in the NT, **the nether world, prison of disobedient spirits** (Lu 8:31; Re 9:1, 2, 11; 11:7; 17:8; 20:1-3), or **the world of the dead** (Ro 10:7). The word does not occur in the KJV, but is translated **bottomless pit** in Revelation, or **deep** in Luke.

ACACIA WOOD, used in the construction of the tabernacle (Ex 25:5, 10; 26:15; 30:1; 36:20; 37:1, 10).

ACCAD, a city conquered by Nimrod (Ge 10:10).

ACCEPTED OF GOD. Children of Israel (Ex 28:38; Eze 20:40; 43:27). David (2Sa 24:23). Job (Job 42:9). Believers: righteous and reverential (Ac 10:35); diligent (2Co 5:9); through Christ (Eph 1:6).

ACCEPTED TIME. The time favorable for seeking God: when forgiven (Ps 32:6); when in trouble (Ps 69:13); today, *i.e.* now (Ps 95:7; Isa 49:8; 2Co 6:2).

ACCESS TO GOD, Is of God (Ps 65:4). Is by Christ (Joh 10:7, 9; 14:6; Ro 5:2; Eph 2:13; 3:12; Heb 7:19, 25; 10:19; 1Pe 3:18). Is by the Holy Ghost (Eph 2:18). Obtained through faith (Ac 14:27; Ro 5:2; Eph 3:12; Heb 11:6). Follows upon reconciliation to God (Col 1:21, 22). In prayer (De 4:7; M't 6:6; 1Pe 1:17). See Prayer. In His temple (Ps 15:1; 27:4; 43:3; 65:4). To obtain mercy and grace (Heb 4:16). A privilege of saints (De 4:7; Ps 15; 23:6; 24:3, 4). Saints have, with confidence (Eph 3:12; Heb 4:16; 10:19, 22). Vouchsafed to repenting sinners (Ho 14:2; Joe 2:12). See Repentance. Saints earnestly seek (Ps 27:4; 42:1, 2; 43:3; 84:1, 2). The wicked commanded to seek (Isa 55:6; Jas 4:8). Urge others to seek (Isa 2:3; Jer 31:6). Promises connected with (Ps 145:18; Isa 55:3; M't 6:6; Jas 4:8). Blessedness of (Ps 16:11; 65:4; 73:28). Typified (Le 16:12-15, with Heb 10:19-22). Exemplified (*Moses,* Ex 24:2; 34:4-7).

ACCESSORY (See Complicity.)

ACCHO, called also Ptolemais, a town of Phenicia (J'g 1:31; Ac 21:7).

ACCOMPLICE (See Complicity.)

ACCOUNTABILITY (See Responsibility.)

ACCURSED, what so called (De 21:23; Jos 6:17, 18; 7:1, 11, 15; 1Ch 2:7; Isa 65:20; Ro 9:3; 1Co 12:3; Ga 1:8).

ACCUSATION, FALSE. Forbidden (Ex 23:1, 7; Le 19:16; Lu 3:14; Tit 2:3).

Consolation for falsely accused (M't 5:11; 1Pe 4:14).

Instances of: Against Joseph by Potiphar's wife (Ge 39:7-20); against Joseph's brothers by Joseph (Ge 42:9-14); against Moses by Korah (Nu 16:1-3, 13); against the prophet Ahimelech by Saul (1Sa 22:11-16); against Abner by Joab (2Sa 3:24-27); against Job by Satan (Job 1:9, 10; 2:4, 5); against David (Ps 41:5-9) by the princes of Ammon (2Sa 10:1-4; 1Ch 19:1-4); against Elijah by Ahab (1Ki 18:17, 18); against Naboth by Jezebel (1Ki 21:1-14); against Jews, returned under Ezra (Ezr 4:6-16; Ne 6:5-9); against Jeremiah (Jer 26:8-11; 37:13-15; 43:1-4); against Amos (Am 7:10, 11); against Mary (M't 1:19); against Jesus (M't 9:34; 10:25; 12:2-14; 26:59-61; M'k 3:22; 14:53-65; Lu 23:2; Joh 18:30); against Stephen (Ac 6:11, 13); against Paul (Ac 17:7; 21:27-29; 24:1-9, 12, 13; 25:1, 2, 7; Ro 3:8); against Paul and Silas (Ac 16:19-21).

In last days (2Ti 3:3).

See Conspiracy; Evidence; False Witness; Persecution; Speaking, Evil; Talebearing.

ACELDAMA, or Akeldama, **(the field of blood),** (M't 27:8), the field purchased with the money which Judas received for betraying Christ (Ac 1:18, 19).

ACHAIA, a region of Greece. Paul visits (Ac 18; 19:21; Ro 16:5; 1Co 16:15; 2Co 1:1). Benevolence of the Christians in (Ro 15:26; 2Co 9:2; 11:10).

ACHAICUS. A Corinthian Christian who visited Paul at Ephesus (1Co 16:17-19).

ACHAN, sin and punishment of (Jos 7; 22:20; 1Ch 2:7).

ACHAR (trouble). The same as Achan (1Ch 2:7).

ACHAZ (See Ahaz.)

ACHBOR (mouse). 1. Father of a king of Edom (Ge 36:38, 39; 1Ch 1:49).

2. A messenger of King Josiah (2Ki 22:12, 14; called Abdon in 2Ch 34:20).

3. Father of Elnathan (Jer 26:22; 36:12, 15).

ACHIM (Jehovah will establish). A descendant of Zerubbabel (M't 1:14). Ancestor of Christ.

ACHISH. King of the Philistines, called also Abimelech. David escapes to (1Sa 21:10-15; 27; 28:1, 2; 29; 1Ki 2:39, 40).

ACHMETHA, ancient Ecbatana, modern Hamadan, capital of Media (Ezr 6:2).

ACHOR, a valley near Jericho, where Achan was stoned (Jos 7:24-26; 15:7; Isa 65:10; Ho 2:15).

ACHSA (See Achsah).

ACHSAH, Caleb's daughter (Jos 15:16-19; J'g 1:9-13). Called Achsa (1Ch 2:49).

ACHSHAPH, a city (Jos 11:1) which Joshua captured with its king (Jos 12:7, 20). It is named as being on the border of the lot assigned to Asher (Jos 19:24, 25).

ACHZIB (a lie). 1. A city of Judah (Jos 15:44) perhaps Tell el-Beida, southwest of Adullam. Called Chezib (Ge 38:5) and Chozeba (1Ch 4:22). See Mic 1:14.

2. A town in Asher (J'g 1:31; Jos 19:29) on the coast north of Accho.

ACRE, the amount of land a pair of oxen could plow in a day (1Sa 14:14; Isa 5:10).

ACROPOLIS, the upper or higher city, citadel, or castle of a Greek municipality, especially the high rocky promontory in Athens where the treasury of the city and its finest temples were located.

ACROSTIC, a literary device by which the first letter of each line of poetry forms either a word or the successive letters of the alphabet. An outstanding example is the 119th Psalm, in which each successive set of eight verses begins with a different letter of the Hebrew alphabet. The effect is not apparent in the English translation, but the Hebrew letters are given between the lines in order to preserve the construction.

ACROSTIC POETRY (See Poetry.)

ACTIONS AT LAW, duty of defendant (M't 5:40). See Adjudication; Arbitration.

ACTIVITY, EVIL. Of sinners in general (Pr 1:16; 4:16; 6:18; Isa 59:7; Mic 2:1; 7:3; Ro 3:15). Of Pharisees (M't 23:15). Of Paul in persecuting the church (Ac 9:2; 26:11; Ga 1:13; Ph'p 3:6). Of busybodies in the church, stirring up strife (2Th 3:11; 1Ti 5:13; 1Pe 4:15). Of Satan (1Pe 5:8).

ACTS OF THE APOSTLES. The NT book which gives the history of early Christianity from the ascension of Christ to the end of Paul's imprisonment in Rome. It is a selection of the deeds and words of the apostles illustrating the progress of the church in the first century. The traditional author is Luke, "the beloved physician" (Col 4:14). The place of writing is not stated, but since the book ends abruptly with Paul awaiting trial in Rome, it was probably written there shortly after the latest event mentioned, about A. D. 62. Acts emphasizes the missionary growth of the church among the Gentiles, and the work of the Holy Spirit. Outline: 1. The origins of the church in Jerusalem (1:1-8:3). 2. The transition from the Jewish to the Gentile ministry, including the preaching to Samaria (ch. 8), the conversion of Paul (ch. 9), and the beginning of Gentile work in Caesarea (ch. 10) and Antioch (11, 12). 3. The missionary journeys of Paul (13-28).

ADADAH, a city in Judah (Jos 15:22).

ADAH (ornament or **morning).** 1. Wife of Lamech (Ge 4:19, 20, 23). 2. Wife of Esau (Ge 36:2, 4, 10, 12, 16).

ADAIAH (Jehovah has adorned). 1. A man of Boscath (2Ki 22:1). 2. A Levite (1Ch 6:41-43). 3. Son of Shimshi (1Ch 8:1, 21). 4. A Levite (1Ch 9:10-12). 5. Father of a man who helped make Joash king (2Ch 23:1). 6. A man who married a foreign wife during the exile (Ezr 10:29). 7. Another man who did the same thing (Ezr 10:34). 8. A descendant of Judah (Ne 11:5). 9. A Levite (Ne 11:12).

ADALIA, son of Haman (Es 9:8).

ADAM (of the ground). 1. The first man. Creation of (Ge 1:26-28; 2:7; 1Co 15:45; 1Ti 2:13). History of, before he sinned (Ge 1:26-30; 2:16-25). Temptation and sin of (Ge 3; Job 31:33; Isa 43:27; Ho 6:7; Ro 5:14-21; 1Ti 2:14). Subsequent history of (Ge 3:20-24; 4:1, 2, 25; 5:1-5). His death (Ge 5:5). Progenitor of the human race (De 32:8; Mal 2:10). Brought sin into the world (1Co 15:22, 45). Type of Christ (Ro 5:14).

2. A name of Christ (1Co 15:45, 47).

ADAM (red, or **made),** a city in the Jordan valley where the Israelites entered the promised land (Jos 3:16).

ADAMAH (red ground), a city of Naphtali (Jos 19:36). Location disputed.

ADAMANT, a flint (Eze 3:9; Zec 7:12). See Diamond.

ADAMI (earthy), a place on the border of Naphtali (Jos 19:33).

ADAR. 1. Twelfth month in Jewish calendar (Ezr 6:15; Es 3:7; 8:12; 9:1).

2. A place on the S border of Judah (Jos 15:3). Rendered Addar in ASV and RSV.

ADBEEL (languishing for God), son of Ishmael (Ge 25:13; 1Ch 1:29).

ADDAN, called also Addon, uncertain whether person or town (Ezr 2:59; Ne 7:61).

ADDAR (threshing floor). 1. Son of Bela, grandson of Benjamin (1Ch 8:3). Called Ard in Genesis 46:21 and Numbers 36:40; counted as a son of Benjamin and head of a family in the tribe.

2. In ASV and RSV for Adar of KJV.

ADDER, a venomous serpent (Ge 49:17; Ps 58:4; 91:13; 140:3; Pr 23:32).

ADDI (my witness, or **adorned),** an ancestor of Joseph, the husband of Mary (Lu 3:28).

ADDON, the same place as Addan (Ne 7:61).

ADER (a flock), a son of Beriah, grandson of Shaharaim, a Benjaminite (1Ch 8:15).

ADIEL (ornament of God). 1. A descendant of Simeon (1Ch 4:36).

2. A priest, son of Jahzerah (1Ch 9:12).

3. Father of Azmaveth, who was supervisor of David's treasuries (1Ch 27:25). Perhaps the same as No. 2.

ADIN (delicate, or **ornament).** 1. One whose family returned from exile with Zerubbabel (Ezr 2:15; Ne 7:20).

2. One whose posterity came back with Ezra (Ezr 8:6).

3. The name of a family sealing the covenant (Ne 10:16).

ADINA (ornament), one of David's military officers (1Ch 11:42).

ADINO (his adorned one). A Tachmonite, one of David's valiant men (2Sa 23:8 KJV).

ADITHAIM (double ornaments), a city of Judah (Jos 15:36).

ADJUDICATION AT LAW. To be avoided (Pr 17:14; 20:3; 25:8-10; M't 5:25, 40; Lu 12:58).

See Actions at Law; Arbitration; Compromise; Courts; Justice; Litigation.

ADJURATION. The noun does not occur in the Bible, but the verb "adjure" is often found in both Testaments (1Sa 14:24; 1Ki 22:16; M'k 5:7). In every case, an appeal in the most impressive manner is meant.

ADLAI (justice of Jehovah), father of Shaphat, who oversaw David's cattle (1Ch 27:29).

ADMAH (red earth), a city near Gomorrah and Zeboim (Ge 10:19) with a king (Ge 14:2, 8); destroyed with Sodom and Gomorrah (De 29:23 w Ge 19:24-28; See Ho 11:8).

ADMATHA (unrestrained), a prince of Persia and Media (Es 1:14).

ADMONITION (See Wicked, Warned.)

ADNA (pleasure). 1. A son of Pahath-moab who had married a foreign wife during the exile (Ezr 10:30).

2. A priest, head of his father's house in the days of Joiakim (Ne 12:12-15).

ADNAH (pleasure). 1. A Manassite who joined David at Ziklag (1Ch 12:20).

2. A man of Judah who held high military rank under Jehoshaphat (2Ch 17:14).

ADONI-BEZEK (lord of lightning), king of Bezek (J'g 1:4-7).

ADONIJAH (my Lord is Jehovah). 1. Son of David and Haggith (2Sa 3:4; 1Ki 1:5, 6; 1Ch 3:2). Usurpation of, and downfall (1Ki 1). Executed by Solomon (1Ki 2:13, 25).

2. A Levite (2Ch 17:8).

3. A chieftain who with Nehemiah sealed the covenant (Ne 10:14-16).

4. See Adonikam.

ADONIKAM (my Lord has arisen), called also Adonijah, a Jew who returned with Ezra from Babylon (Ezr 2:13; Ne 7:18; 10:16).

ADONIRAM (my Lord is exalted), called also Adoram, a tax-gatherer (2Sa 20:24; 1Ki 4:6; 5:14; 12:18).

ADONI-ZEDEK, ADONI-ZEDEC (KJV) **(lord of righteousness),** Amorite king of Jerusalem who with four other kings was defeated in battle and slain by Joshua at Gibeon (Jos 10:1-27).

ADOPTION, *Explained* (2Co 6:18).

Of Children. Instances of: Of one born in Abram's house (Ge 15:3); of Joseph's sons (Ge 48:5, 14, 16, 22); of Moses (Ex 2:5-10; Ac 7:21; Heb 11:24); of Esther (Es 2:7).

Spiritual adoption. Of Israel (Ex 4:22, 23; Nu 6:27; De 14:1; 26:18; 27:9; 28:10; 32:5, 6; 2Ch 7:14; Isa 63:8, 16; Jer 3:19; 31:9, 20; Ho 1:9, 10; 11:1; Ro 9:4); of Solomon (2Sa 7:14; 1Ch 22:10; 28:6).

Of the righteous (Pr 14:26; Isa 43:1-6; 63:8, 16; M't 5:9, 45; 12:50; 13:43; Lu 6:35; Joh 11:52; Ro 9:8, 26; 2Co 6:17, 18; Eph 2:19; Ph'p 2:15; Heb 12:6, 7, 9; 1Jo 3:1, 2, 10; 4:4; Re 21:17).

Of the Gentiles. Promised (Ho 3:23; Ro 9:24-26; Eph 3:6); through the Gospel (Eph 3:6); by faith in Christ (Joh 1:12, 13; Ga 3:26, 29; Eph 1:5; 3:6, 15; Heb 2:10, 11, 13); testified to by the Holy Spirit (Ro 8:14-17, 19, 21, 29; Ga 4:5-7).

Means of Adoption. According to promise (Ro 9:8; Ga 3:29; Eph 3:6); by faith (Joh 1:12, 13; Ga 3:7, 26); by God's grace (Eze 16:3-6; Ro 4:16, 17; Eph 1:5, 6, 11); through Christ (Joh 1:12, 13; Ga 4:4, 5; Eph 1:5; Heb 2:10, 11, 13); through the gospel (Eph 3:6); by predestination (Ro 8:29).

Role of the Holy Spirit. Witnessed to by the Spirit (Ro 8:16); led by the Spirit as evidence of (Ro 8:14); Spirit received (Ro 8:15; Ga 4:6).

Results. God is Father-Redeemer (Isa 63:16); disciplined by the Father (De 8:5; 2Sa 7:14; Pr 3:11, 12; Heb 12:5-11); recipient of God's longsuffering mercy (Jer 31:1, 19, 20); the new birth (Joh 1:12, 13); a new name (Nu 6:27; Isa 62:2; Ac 15:17); a new inheritance (M't 13:43; Ro 8:17); become brethren of Christ (Joh 20:17; Heb 2:11, 12); safety (Pr 14:26).

A new life style: Confidence in God (M't 6:25-34); desire for God's glory (M't 5:16); following God (Eph 5:1); holiness (2Co 6:17, 18; 7:1; Ph'p 2:15); likeness to God (M't 5:44, 45, 48); a love of peace (M't 5:9); an avoidance of ostentation (M't 6:1-4); a forgiving spirit (M't 6:14); a spirit of prayer (M't 7:7-11); a merciful spirit (Lu 6:35, 36).

A new future: Gathered together in one by Christ (Joh 11:52); final consummation (Ro 8:19, 23; 1Jo 3:2).

ADORAIM, a fortress in Judah (2Ch 11:9).

ADORAM. 1. Officer over the tribute (2Sa 20:24).

2. See Adoniram.

ADORNING, *Physical:* Ornaments, wearing of (Ex 33:4; Isa 3:18; Jer 3:32; 4:30; Eze 16:11; 23:40). Bracelets (Ge 24:22; 38:18; Ex 35:22; Nu 31:50; 2Sa 1:10). Chains, used as ornaments (Ge 41:42; Pr 1:9; Eze 16:11; Da 5:29). Earrings (Ge 24:22; 35:4; Ex 32:2; 35:22; Nu 31:50; J'g 8:24; Job 42:11; Pr 25:12; Eze 16:12; Ho 2:13). Rings, for the fingers (Ge 41:42; Ex 35:22; Es 3:10; 8:8; Isa 3:21; Lu 15:22).

Jewels: General references to (Ge 24:53; Ex 3:22; 35:22; Nu 31:50; Isa 6:10). Discarded (Ge 35:4; Ex 33:4; 1Pe 3:3). Brought as offerings to God (Ex 35:22; Nu 31:50).

Spiritual: General references to (Ps 45:13; Pr 1:9; 4:9; Song 1:10; Isa 61:10; 1Pe 3:4; Re 21:2). The robe of righteousness (Job 29:14; Ps 132:16; Isa 52:1; 61:10; Zec 3:4; M't 22:11; Lu 15:22). White raiment, the heavenly garment (M't 17:2; Re 3:5; 3:18; 4:4; 7:9; 19:8).

ADRAMMELECH (Adar is king). 1. Name given to Adar, the god brought to Samaria from Assyria by the Sepharvites (2Ki 17:31). 2. Son of Sennacherib, whom he slew (2Ki 19:37; Isa 37:38).

ADRAMYTTIUM, a port city of Mysia, in the Roman province of Asia (Ac 27:2).

ADRIA, same as Adriatic Sea, a body of water between Italy on the W and Dalmatia, Macedonia and Achaia on the E (Ac 27:27).

ADRIEL, Saul's son-in-law (1Sa 18:19; 2Sa 21:8, 9).

ADULLAM (refuge). 1. A cave near the Dead Sea. David takes refuge in (1Sa 22:1; 2Sa 23:13; 1Ch 11:15. See titles of Psalms 57 and 142).

2. An ancient city of Canaan (Ge 38:1; Jos 12:15; 15:35; 2Ch 11:7; Ne 11:30; Mic 1:15).

ADULLAMITE, used of Hirah, Judah's friend (Ge 38:1, 12, 20).

ADULTERY. *Defined* (M't 5:28, 32; 19:9; M'k 10:11, 12; Lu 16:18; Ro 7:3).

Fatal consequences of (Pr 2:16-19; 5:3-22; 6:24-33; 7:5-23; 9:13-18; 22:14 23:27). Law concerning wife accused of (Nu 5:11-30; De 22:13-19). Moral corruption by (Jer 3:1; 5:7, 8; Ho 4:1, 2, 11). Repugnant to righteous (Job 31:1, 9-12; Eze 18:5, 6, 9). Source: The heart (M't 15:19; M'k 7:21); the flesh (Ga 5:19).

Figurative (Jer 3:2; Eze 16:15, 16; Ho 1).

Forbidden (Ex 20:14; Le 18:20; 19:29; De 5:18; 23:17; Pr 31:3; M't 5:27; 19:18; M'k 10:19; Lu 18:20; Ac 15:20, 29; Ro 13:9, 13; 1Co 5:9-11; 6:13-18; 10:8; Eph 4:17-19; 5:3; Col 3:5; 1Th 4:3-5, 7; 1Ti 1:10; Jas 2:11).

Forgiveness of (J'g 19:1-4; Joh 8:10, 11).

Impenitence in (Pr 30:18-20; Isa 57:3, 4; Jer 7:9, 10; Ro 1:28, 29, 32; 2Co 12:21; 1Pe 4:3, 4; Re 9:21).

Instances of. Sodomites (Ge 19:5-8; Jude 7). Lot (Ge 19:31-38). Shechem (Ge 34:2). Reuben (Ge 35:22). Judah (Ge

38:1-24). Potiphar's wife (Ge 39:7-12). The Levite's concubine (J'g 19:2). The Gibeahites (J'g 19:22-25). Gilead (J'g 11:1). Samson (J'g 16:1). Sons of Eli (1Sa 2:22). David (2Sa 11:1-5). Amnon (2Sa 13:1-20). Absalom (2Sa 16:22). Israelites (Ex 32:6, 25; Jer 23:10; 29:23; Eze 22:9-11; 33:26; Ho 7:4). Herod (M't 14:3, 4; M'k 6:17, 18; Lu 3:19). Samaritan woman (Joh 4:17, 18). The woman brought to Jesus in the temple (Joh 8:4-11). Corinthians (1Co 5:1-5). Heathen (Eph 4:17-19; 1Pe 4:3). Apostates (2Ti 3:6).

Penalties for. Curses (Nu 5:11-30; De 27:20, 22, 23; Job 24:15-18). Death (Ge 20:3, 7; 26:11; 38:24; Le 19:20-22; 20:10-12; 21:9; De 22:20-27; 2Sa 12:14; Eze 23:45, 47, 48; Joh 8:4, 5). Divine judgments (2Sa 12:10-12; Jer 29:22, 23; Eze 16:38-41; Mal 3:5; 1Co 10:8; Heb 13:4; 2Pe 2:9, 10, 14; Re 2:20-22; 18:9, 10). Exclusion from kingdom of God (1Co 6:9, 10; Ga 5:19, 21; Eph 5:5, 6; Jude 7; Re 21:8; 22:15). Excommunication (1Co 5:1-13; Eph 5:11, 12). Fines (Ex 22:16, 17; De 18:19, 28, 29).

See Fornication; Idolatry; Lasciviousness; Rape; Sensuality; Sodomy; Whore; Whoredom.

ADUMMIM (red spots), a pass (Jos 15:7; 18:17), on the road between Jerusalem and Jericho. On the north border of Judah and the south border of Benjamin. Convincingly held to be the scene of Jesus' parable of the Good Samaritan (Lu 10:30-35).

ADVENT (See Jesus, Second Coming of; Millennium.)

ADVERSARY, an enemy, personal, national, or supernatural (Ex 23:22; M't 5:25).

ADVERSITY (See Afflictions.)

ADVICE (See Counsel.)

ADVOCATE (helper, Paraclete), the Holy Spirit, or Comforter in KJV (Joh 14:16, 26; 15:26); Jesus Christ (1Jo 2:1).

AENEAS, a paralytic, healed at Lydda by Peter (Ac 9:32-35).

AENON (springs), a place near Salim where John the Baptist baptized (Joh 3:22, 23).

AEON, a word meaning a period of time (Heb 9:26), generally translated "world" (Ro 12:2; 2Ti 4:10), or "age(s)" (Eph 2:7; Col 1:26).

AFFECTIONS. Should be supremely set upon God (De 6:5; M'k 12:30). Should be set upon the commandments of God (Ps 19:8-10; 119:20, 97, 103, 167); upon the house and worship of God (1Ch 29:3; Ps 26:8; 27:4; 84:1, 2); upon the people of God (Ps 16:3; Ro 12:10; 2Co 7:13-16; 1Th 2:8); upon heavenly things (Col 3:1, 2). Should be zealously engaged for God (Ps 69:9; 119:139; Ga 4:18). Christ claims the first place in (M't 10:37; Lu 14:26). Enkindled by communion with Christ (Lu 24:32). Blessedness of making God the object of (Ps 91:14). Should not grow cold (Ps 106:12, 13; M't 24:12; Ga 4:15; Re 2:4). Of saints, supremely set on God (Ps 42:1; 73:25; 119:10). Of the wicked, not sincerely set on God (Isa 58:1, 2; Eze 33:31, 32; Lu 8:13). Carnal, should be mortified (Ro 8:13; 13:14; 1Co 9:27; Col 3:5; 1Th 4:5). Carnal affections crucified in saints (Ro 6:6; Ga 5:24). False teachers seek to captivate (Ga 1:10; 4:17; 2Ti 3:6; 2Pe 2:3, 18; Re 2:14, 20). Of the wicked, are unnatural and perverted (Ro 1:31; 2Ti 3:3; 2Pe 2:10).

AFFLICTED. Exhorted to pray (Jas 5:13). Help for (Job 22:29; Isa 58:6, 7; Lu 10:30-37; 1Ti 5:10). Prayer for (Jas 5:14, 15). Rewards of service to (Isa 53:10; M't 25:34-45). Sympathy with (Job 6:14; M't 25:34-40).

Duty to. Bear in mind (Heb 13:3); comfort (Job 16:5; 29:25; 2Co 1:4; 1Th 4:18); pity (Job 6:14); pray (Ac 12:5; Ph'm 1:16, 19; Jas 5:14-16); protect (Ps 82:3; Pr 22:22; 31:5); relieve (Job 31:19, 20; Isa 58:10; Ph'm 1:14; 1Ti 5:10); sympathize (Ro 12:15; Ga 6:2).

AFFLICTED SAINTS. God is with (Ps 46:5, 7; Isa 43:2). God is a refuge and strength to (Ps 27:5, 6; Isa 25:4; Jer 16:19; Na 1:7). God comforts (Isa 49:13; Jer 31:13; M't 5:4; 2Co 1:4, 5; 7:6). God preserves (Ps 34:20). God delivers (Ps 34:4, 19; Pr 12:13; Jer 39:17, 18). Christ is with (Joh 14:18). Christ supports (2Ti 4:17; Heb 2:18). Christ comforts (Isa 61:2; M't 11:28-30; Lu 7:13; Joh 14:1; 16:33). Christ preserves (Isa 63:9; Lu 21:18). Christ delivers (Re 3:10). Should praise God (Ps 13:5, 6; 56:8-10; 57:6, 7; 71:20-23). Should imitate Christ (Heb 12:1-3; 1Pe 2:21-23). Should imitate the prophets (Jas 5:10). Should be patient (Lu 21:19; Ro 12:12; 2Th 1:4; Jas 1:4; 1Pe 2:20). Should be resigned (1Sa 3:18;

2Ki 20:19; Job 1:21; Ps 39:9). Should not despise chastening (Job 5:17; Pr 3:11; Heb 12:5). Should acknowledge the justice of their chastisements (Ne 9:33; Job 2:10; Isa 64:5-7; La 3:39; Mic 7:9). Should avoid sin (Job 34:31, 32; Joh 5:14; 1Pe 2:12). Should trust in the goodness of God (Job 13:15; Ps 71:20; 2Co 1:9). Should turn and devote themselves to God (Ps 116:7-9; Jer 50:3, 4; Ho 6:1). Should keep the pious resolutions made during affliction (Ps 66:13-15). Should be frequent in prayer (Ps 50:15; 55:16, 17. [See Affliction, Prayer under]). Should take encouragement from former mercies (Ps 27:9; 2Co 1:10). Examples of afflicted saints. *Joseph* (Ge 39:20-23; Ps 105:17-19). *Moses* (Heb 11:25). *Eli* (1Sa 3:18). *Nehemiah* (Ne 1:4). *Job* (Job 1:20-22). *David* (2Sa 12:15-23). *Paul* (Ac 20:22-24; 21:13). *Apostles* (1Co 4:13; 2Co 6:4-10).

AFFLICTION, *Consolation Under:* God is the Author and Giver of (Ps 23:4; Ro 15:5; 2Co 1:3; 7:6; Col 1:11; 2Th 2:16, 17). Christ is the Author and Giver of (Isa 61:2; Joh 14:18; 2Co 1:5). The Holy Ghost is the Author and Giver of (Joh 14:16, 17; 15:26; 16:7; Ac 9:31). Promised (Isa 51:3, 12; 66:13; Eze 14:22, 23; Ho 2:14; Zec 1:17). Through the Holy Scriptures (Ps 119:50, 76; Ro 15:4). By ministers of the gospel (Isa 40:1, 2; 1Co 14:3; 2Co 1:4, 6). Is abundant (Ps 71:21; Isa 66:11). Is strong (Heb 6:18). Is everlasting (2Th 2:16). Is a cause of praise (Isa 12:1; 49:13). Pray for (Ps 119:82). Saints should administer to each other (1Th 4:18; 5:11, 14). Is sought in vain from the world (Ps 69:20; Ec 4:1; La 1:2). To those who mourn for sin (Ps 51:17; Isa 1:18; 40:1, 2; 61:1; Mic 7:18, 19; Lu 4:18). To the troubled in mind (Ps 42:5; 94:19; Joh 14:1, 27; 16:20, 22). To those deserted by friends (Ps 27:10; 41:9-12; Joh 14:18; 15:18, 19). To the persecuted (De 33:27). To the poor (Ps 10:14; 34:6, 9, 10. To the sick (Ps 41:3). To the tempted (Ro 16:20; 1Co 10:13; 2Co 12:9; Jas 1:12; 4:7; 2Pe 2:9; Re 2:10). In prospect of death (Job 19:25. 26; Ps 23:4; Joh 14:2; 2Co 5:1; 1Th 4:14; Heb 4:9; Re 7:14-17; 14:13). Under the infirmities of age (Ps 71:9, 18).

Prayer Under: Exhortation to (Jas 5:13). That God would consider our trouble (2Ki 19:16; Ne 9:32; Ps 9:13; La 5:1). For the presence and support of God (Ps 10:1; 102:2). That the Holy Spirit may not be withdrawn (Ps 51:11). For divine comfort (Ps 4:6; 119:76). For mitigation of troubles (Ps 39:12, 13). For deliverance (Ps 25:17, 22; 39:10; Isa 64:9-12; Jer 17:14). For pardon and deliverance from sin (Ps 39:8; 51:1; 79:8). That we may be turned to God (Ps 80:7; 85:4-6; Jer 31:18). For divine teaching and direction (Job 34:32; Ps 27:11; 143:10). For increase of faith (M'k 9:24). For mercy (Ps 6:2; Hab 3:2). For restoration to joy (Ps 51:8, 12; 69:29; 90:14, 15). For protection and preservation from enemies (1Ki 19:19; 2Ch 20:12; Ps 17:8, 9). That we may know the causes of our trouble (Job 6:24; 10:2; 13:23, 24). That we may be taught the uncertainty of life (Ps 39:4). That we may be quickened (Ps 143:11).

AFFLICTIONS. God appoints (2Ki 6:33; Job 5:6, 17; Ps 66:11; Amos 3:6; Mic 6:9). God dispenses as He will (Job 11:10; Isa 10:15; 45:7). God regulates the measure of (Ps 80:5; Isa 9:1; Jer 46:28). God determines the continuance of (Ge 15:13, 14; Nu 14:33; Isa 10:25; Jer 29:10). God does not willingly send (La 3:33). Man is born to (Job 5:6, 7; 14:1). Saints appointed to (1Th 3:3). Consequent upon the fall (Ge 3:16-19). Sin produces (Job 4:8; 20:11; Pr 1:31). Sin visited with (2Sa 12:14; Ps 89:30-32; Isa 57:17; Ac 13:10, 11). Often severe (Job 16:7-16; Ps 42:7; 66:12; Joh 2:3; Re 7:14). Always less than we deserve (Ezr 9:13; Ps 103:10). Frequently terminate in good (Ge 50:20; Ex 1:11, 12; De 8:15, 16; Jer 24:5, 6; Eze 20:37). Tempered with mercy (Ps 78:38, 39; 106:43-46; Isa 30:18-21; La 3:32; Mic 7:7-9; Na 1:12). Saints are to expect (Joh 16:33; Ac 14:22). Of saints, are comparatively light (Ac 20:23, 24; Ro 8:18; 2Co 4:17). Of saints, are but temporary (Ps 30:5; 103:9; Isa 54:7, 8; Joh 16:20; 1Pe 1:6; 5:10). Saints have joy under (Job 5:17; Jas 5:11). Of saints, end in joy and blessedness (Ps 126:5, 6; Isa 61:2, 3; M't 5:4; 1Pe 4:13, 14). Often arise from the profession of the gospel (M't 24:9; Joh 15:21; 2Ti 3:11, 12). Exhibit the love and faithfulness of God (De 8:5; Ps 119:75; Pr 3:12; 1Co 11:32; Heb 12:6, 7; Re 3:19).

Made Beneficial: In promoting the glory of God (Joh 9:1-3; 11:3, 4; 21:18, 19). In exhibiting the power and faithfulness of God (Ps 34:19, 20; 2Co 4:8-11). In teaching us the will of God (Ps 119: 71; Isa 26:9; Mic 6:9). In turning us to God (De 4:30, 31; Ne 1:8, 9; Ps 78:34; Isa 10:20, 21; Ho 2:6, 7). In keeping us from again departing from God (Job 34:31, 32; Isa 10:20; Eze 14:10, 11). In leading us to seek God in prayer (J'g 4:3; Jer 31:18; La 2:17-19; Ho 5:14, 15; Joh 2:1). In convincing us of sin (Job 36:8, 9; Ps 119:67; Lu 15:16-18). In leading us to confession of sin (Nu 21:7; Ps 32:5; 51:3, 5). In testing and exhibiting our sincerity (Job 23:10; Ps 66:10; Pr 17:3). In trying our faith and obedience (Ge 22:1, 2 w Heb 11:17; Ex 15:23-25; De 8:2, 16; 1Pe 1:7; Re 2:10). In humbling us (De 8:3, 16; 2Ch 7:13, 14; La 3:19, 20; 2Co 12:7). In purifying us (Ec 7:2, 3; Isa 1:25, 26; 48:10; Jer 9:6, 7; Zec 13:9; Mal 3:2, 3). In exercising our patience (Ps 40:1; Ro 5:3; Jas 1:3; 1Pe 2:20). In rendering us fruitful in good works (Joh 15:2; Heb 12:10, 11). In furthering the gospel (Ac 8:3, 4; 11:19-21; Ph'p 1:12; 2Ti 2:9, 10; 4:16, 17). Exemplified, *Joseph's brethren* (Ge 42:21). *Joseph* (Ge 45:5, 7, 8). *Israel* (De 8:3, 5). *Josiah* (2Ki 22:19). *Hezekiah* (2Ch 32:25, 26). *Manasseh* (2Ch 33:12). *Jonah* (Jon 2:7). *Prodigal son* (Lu 15:21).

Of the Wicked: God is glorified in (Ex 14:4; Eze 38:22, 23). God holds in derision (Ps 37:13; Pr 1:26, 27). Are multiplied (De 31:17; Job 20:12-18; Ps 32:10). Are continual (Job 15:20; Ec 2:23; Isa 32:10). Are often sudden (Ps 73:19; Pr 6:15; Isa 30:13; Re 18:10). Are often judicially sent (Job 21:17; Ps 107:17; Jer 30:15). Are for examples to others (Ps 64:7-9; Zep 3:6, 7; 1Co 10:5-11; 2Pe 2:6). Are ineffectual of themselves, for their conversion (Ex 9:30; Isa 9:13; Jer 2:30; Hag 2:17). Their persecution of saints, a cause of (De 30:7; Ps 55:19; Zec 2:9; 2Th 1:6). Impenitence is a cause of (Pr 1:30, 31; Eze 24:13; Am 4:6-12; Zec 7:11, 12; Re 2:21, 22). Sometimes humble them (1Ki 21:27). Frequently harden (Ne 9:28, 29; Jer 5:3). Produce slavish fear (Job 15:24; Ps 73:19; Jer 49:3, 5). Saints should not be alarmed at (Pr 3:25, 26). Exemplified. *Pharaoh and the Egyptians* (Ex 9:14, 15; 14:24, 25). *Ahaziah* (2Ki 1:1-4). *Gehazi* (2Ki 5:27). *Jehoram* (2Ch 2:12-19). *Uzziah* (2Ch 26:19-21). *Ahaz* (2Ch 28:5-8, 22).

AFTERWARDS (Ps 73:24; Pr 20:17; 29:11; M't 25:11; Joh 13:36; 1Co 15:46; Ga 3:23; Heb 12:11, 17).

AGABUS, a prophet living in Jerusalem who prophesied a world-wide famine (Ac 11:27-30) and warned Paul he would be arrested in Jerusalem (Ac 21:10, 11).

AGAG. 1. King of Amalek (Nu 24:7). 2. Another king of Amalek. Saul spared him when he should have killed him (1Sa 15).

AGAGITE, Haman is thus called (Es 3:1, 10; 8:5; 9:24).

AGAPE, a word meaning "love" and "lovefeasts," which were followed by the Lord's Supper (1Co 11:20-34).

AGAR, name of Sarai's handmaid (Ga 4:24, 25). See Hagar.

AGATE, a precious stone (Ex 28:19; Isa 54:12; Eze 27:16). See Minerals.

AGE, OLD (See Old Age.)

AGED, gospel invitation to (M't 20:5, 6). See Old Age.

AGEE, father of Shammah (2Sa 23:11).

AGENCY. *In Salvation of Men* (Job 33:14-30; Ps 8:2; M't 4:19; 5:13-16; Lu 1:17; 5:10; 10:17; 15:16; 1Co 1:26-29; 1Th 2:4; 1Ti 1:11; 6:20; Jas 5:20).

In Executing Judgments (Ge 3:15; 1Sa 15:18; 2Sa 7:14; 2Ki 9:6, 7; 19:25, 26; 2Ch 22:7; Ps 17:13, 14; Isa 10:5, 6; 13:5; 41:15; Jer 27:8; 51:20-23).

AGONY (anguish), occurs only in Lu 22:44, of Jesus' agony in Gethsemane.

AGORA (market place), in ancient cities the town meeting place, where the public met for the exchange of merchandise, information, and ideas ("Streets" M'k 6:56; Ac 17:17).

AGRAPHA (unwritten things), sayings ascribed to Jesus transmitted to us outside of the canonical Gospels. The number is not large, and most are obviously apocryphal or spurious. They are found in the NT outside the Gospels, ancient manuscripts of the NT, patristic literature, papyri, and apocryphal gospels.

AGRICULTURE or HUSBANDRY. The cultivation of the earth (Ge 3:23). The occupation of man before the fall

(Ge 2:15). Rendered laborious by the curse on the earth (Ge 3:17-19). Man doomed to labor in, after the fall (Ge 3:23). Contributes to the support of all (Ec 5:9). The providence of God to be acknowledged in the produce of (Jer 5:24; Ho 2:8).

Requires: Wisdom (Isa 28:26). Diligence (Pr 27:23-27; Ec 11:6). Toil (2Ti 2:6). Patience in waiting (Jas 5:7). Diligence in, abundantly recompensed (Pr 12:11; 13:23; 28:19; Heb 6:7).

Persons Engaged in, Called: Tillers of the ground (Ge 4:2). Husbandmen (2Ch 26:10). Laborers (M't 9:37; 20:1). Peace favorable to (Isa 2:4; Jer 31:24). War destructive to (Jer 50:16; 51:23). Patriarchs engaged in (Ge 4:2; 9:20). The labor of, supposed to be lessened by Noah (Ge 5:29, with Ge 9:20). The Jews loved and followed (J'g 6:11; 1Ki 19:19; 2Ch 26:10). Soil of Canaan suited to (Ge 13:10; De 8:7-9). Climate of Canaan favorable to (De 11:10, 11).

Was Promoted Amongst the Jews, by: Allotments to each family (Nu 36:7-9). The right of redemption (Le 25:23-28). Separation from other nations (Ex 33:16). The prohibition against usury (Ex 22:25). The promises of God's blessing on (Le 26:4; De 7:13; De 11:14, 15).

Enactments to Protect: Not to covet the fields of another (De 5:21). Not to move landmarks (De 19:14; Pr 22:28). Not to cut down crops of another (De 23:25). Against the trespass of cattle (Ex 22:5). Against injuring the produce of (Ex 22:6). Often performed by hirelings (1Ch 27:26; 2Ch 26:10; M't 20:8; Lu 17:7). Not to be engaged in during the Sabbatical year (Ex 23:10, 11). Produce of, often blasted because of sin (Isa 5:10; 7:23; Jer 12:13; Joe 1:10, 11). Grief occasioned by the failure of the fruits of (Joe 1:11; Am 5:16, 17). Produce of, exported (1Ki 5:11; Eze 27:17).

Operations in: Hedging (Isa 5:2, 5; Ho 2:6). Plowing (Job 1:14). Digging (Isa 5:6; Lu 13:8; 16:3). Manuring (Isa 25:10; Lu 14:34, 35). Harrowing (Job 39:10; Isa 28:24). Gathering out the stones (Isa 5:2). Sowing (Ec 11:4; Isa 32:20; M't 13:3). Planting (Pr 31:16; Isa 44:14; Jer 31:5). Watering (De 11:10; 1Co 3:6-8). Weeding (M't 13:28). Grafting (Ro 11:17-19, 24). Pruning (Le 25:3; Isa 5:6; Joh 15:2). Mowing (Ps 129:7; Am 7:1). Reaping (Isa 17:5). Binding (Ge 37:7; M't 13:30). Gleaning (Le 19:9; Ru 2:3). Stacking (Ex 22:6). Threshing (De 25:4; J'g 6:11). Winnowing (Ru 3:2; M't 3:12). Storing in barns (M't 6:26; 13:30).

Beasts Used in: The ox (De 25:4). The ass (De 22:10). The horse (Isa 28:28).

Implements of: The plow (1Sa 13:20). The harrow (2Sa 12:31). The mattock (1Sa 13:20; Isa 7:25). The sickle (De 16:9; 23:25). The pruninghook (Isa 18:5; Joe 3:10). The fork (1Sa 13:21). The ax (1Sa 13:20). The teethed threshing instrument (Isa 41:15). The flail (Isa 28:27). The cart (1Sa 6:7; Isa 28:27, 28). The shovel (Isa 30:24). The sieve (Am 9:9). The fan (Isa 30:24; M't 3:12).

Illustrative of the: Culture of the Church (1Co 3:9). Culture of the heart (Jer 4:3; Ho 10:12).

AGRIPPA I, known in history as King Herod Agrippa I, and in the NT as Herod. He was the grandson of Herod the Great and ruled over the whole of Palestine from A. D. 40 to 44. He slew James to please the Jews and intended to do the same to Peter (Ac 12:2-4). He died in A.D. 44.

AGRIPPA II, known in history as King Herod Agrippa II and in the NT as Agrippa. He was the son of Agrippa I, and ruled over only a small part of his father's territory. Paul appeared before him and Festus, as recorded in Ac 25:23-26:32. He died in A.D.100.

AGUE (Le 26:16.)

AGUR (gatherer), the author or "collector" of the wise sayings in Pr 30. He is named as the son of Jakeh (Pr 30:1).

AHA, a term of derision (Ps 35:21; 40:15; 70:3; Eze 25:3; 26:2; 36:2).

AHAB. 1. King of Israel (1Ki 16:29). Marries Jezebel (1Ki 16:31). Idolatry of (1Ki 16:30-33; 18:18, 19; 21:25, 26); other wickedness of (2Ki 3:2; 2Ch 21:6; 22:3, 4; Mic 6:16). Reproved by Elijah; assembles the prophets of Baal (1Ki 18:17-46). Fraudulently confiscates Naboth's vineyard (1Ki 21). Defeats Benhadad (1Ki 20). Closing history and death of (1Ki 22; 2Ch 18). Succeeded by his son, Ahaziah (1Ki 22:40). Prophecies against (1Ki 20:42; 21:19-24; 22:19-28;

2Ki 9:8, 25, 26). Sons of, murdered (2Ki 10:1-8).

2. A false prophet (Jer 29:21, 22).

AHARAH, called also Ehi, and Ahiram, and Aher, son of Benjamin (Ge 46:21; Nu 26:38; 1Ch 7:12; 8:1).

AHARHEL, a son of Harum, founder of a family enrolled in the tribe of Judah (1Ch 4:8).

AHASAI (my protector), a priest who lived in Jerusalem (Ne 11:13).

AHASBAI, father of Eliphelet, one of David's heroes (2Sa 23:34. See Ur, 1Ch 11:35).

AHASUERUS. 1. Father of Darius the Mede (Da 9:1). 2. King of Persia mentioned in the book of Esther. There is much evidence that he was Xerxes, who reigned from 486 to 465 B. C. The Ahasuerus of Ezra 4:6 is probably also this same Xerxes, although sometimes identified with Cambyses, son of Cyrus.

AHAVA, a river of Babylon (Ezr 8:15, 21, 31).

AHAZ (he has grasped). 1. King of Judah, son and successor of Jotham (2Ki 15:38; 16:1; 2Ch 27:9; 28:1). Idolatrous abominations of (2Ki 16:3, 4; 2Ch 28:2-4, 22-25). Kingdom of, invaded by the kings of Syria and Samaria (2Ki 16:5, 6; 2Ch 28:5-8). Robs the temple to purchase aid from the king of Assyria (2Ki 16:7-9, 17, 18; 2Ch 28:21). Visits Damascus, obtains a novel pattern of an altar, which he substitutes for the altar in the temple in Jerusalem and otherwise perverts the forms of worship (2Ki 16:10-16). Sundial of (2Ki 20:11; Isa 38:8). Prophets in the reign of (Isa 1:1; Ho 1:1; Mic 1:1). Prophecies concerning (Isa 7:13-25). Succeeded by Hezekiah (2Ki 16:20).

2. Son of Micah and great-grandson of Jonathan (1Ch 8:35; 9:41, 42).

AHAZIAH (Jehovah hath grasped). 1. King of Judah. Called Azariah and Jehoahaz (2Ch 21:17; 25:23). History of (1Ki 8:25-29; 9:16-29). Gifts of, to the temple (2Ki 12:18). Brethren of, slain (2Ki 10:13, 14). Succeeded by Athaliah (2Ch 22:10-12).

2. King of Israel. History of (1Ki 22:40, 49, 51-53; 2Ch 20:35-37; 2Ki 1). Succeeded by Jehoram (2Ki 3:1).

AHBAN, a man of Judah, of the house of Jerahmeel (1Ch 2:29).

AHER, a Benjamite (1Ch 7:12). See Aharah.

AHI. 1. Chief of the Gadites in Gilead (1Ch 5:15).

2. A man of Asher, son of Shamer (1Ch 7:34).

AHIA (See Ahimelech.)

AHIAH. 1. Grandson of Phinehas (1Sa 14:3, 18).

2. One of Solomon's scribes (1Ki 4:3).

3. A Benjamite (1Ch 8:7).

See Ahijah.

AHIAM (mother's brother), one of David's heroes (2Sa 23:33). Called also Sacar (1Ch 11:35).

AHIAN, son of Shemidah (1Ch 7:19).

AHIEZER. 1. Captain of the tribe of Dan (Nu 1:12; 2:25, 26). Contributes to the tabernacle (Nu 7:66-71).

2. One of David's valiant men (1Ch 12:3).

AHIHUD (brother is majesty). 1. A prince of Asher, assists in allotting the land of Canaan among the tribes (Nu 34:27).

2. A son of Bela (1Ch 8:7).

AHIJAH (brother of Jehovah), called also Ahiah. 1. Son of Bela (1Ch 8:7).

2. Son of Jerahmeel (1Ch 2:25).

3. A priest in Shiloh, probably identical with Ahimelech, mentioned in 1Sa 22:11. Was priest in Saul's reign (1Sa 14:3, 18). Slain (1Sa 22:11-19).

4. One of David's heroes (1Ch 11:36). Called also Eliam (2Sa 23:34).

5. A Levite who was treasurer in the tabernacle (1Ch 26:20).

6. Son of Shisha (1Ki 4:3).

7. A prophet in Shiloh (1Ki 11:29-39).

8. Father of Baasha (1Ki 15:27, 33; 2Ki 9:9).

9. An Israelite, who subscribed to the covenant of Nehemiah (Ne 10:26).

AHIKAM (my brother has risen up), son of Shaphan (2Ki 22:12-14; 25:22; 2Ch 34:20; Jer 26:24; 39:14; 40:5-16; 41:1-18; 43:6).

AHILUD (a child's brother), father of Baana (1Ki 4:12); and of Jehoshaphat (2Sa 8:16; 20:24; 1Ki 4:3; 1Ch 18:15).

AHIMAAZ (brother of anger). 1. Father in law of king Saul (1Sa 14:50).

2. Son of Zadok, the high priest. Loyal to David (2Sa 15:36; 17:17-20; 18:19-33; 1Ch 6:8, 9, 53).

3. One of Solomon's 12 commissary

officers (1Ki 4:15). He married Basemath, the daughter of Solomon. Some suggest that he should be identified with the son of Zadok.

AHIMAN (my brother is a gift). 1. One of the three giant sons of Anak seen in Mount Hebron by the spies (Nu 13:22). The three sons, Sheshai, Ahiman, and Talmai, were driven by Caleb from Hebron (Jos 15:14) and killed (J'g 1:10).

2. A Levite gatekeeper (1Ch 9:17).

AHIMELECH (brother of a king). 1. Saul's high priest who helped David by giving him the shewbread and Goliath's sword. Upon hearing this, Saul ordered the death of Ahimelech and the other priests with him (1Sa 21-22). Abiathar, son of Ahimelech, escaped.

2. Son of Abiathar, and grandson of Ahimelech (2Sa 8:17; 1Ch 18:16; 24:6).

3. A Hittite who, with Abishai, was asked to accompany David to Saul's camp (1Sa 26:6).

AHIMOTH (brother of death), son of Elkanah (1Ch 6:25), descendant of Kohath and a Levite.

AHINADAB, son of Iddo (1Ki 4:14).

AHINOAM (my brother is delight). 1. Wife of King Saul (1Sa 14:50).

2. One of David's wives, a Jezreelitess (1Sa 25:43), who lived with him at Gath (27:3). She and Abigail were captured by the Amalekites at Ziklag (30:5), but rescued by David (30:18). Ahinoam bore Amnon, David's first son (2Sa 3:2).

AHIO (brotherly). 1. A Levite, who drove the cart bearing the ark (2Sa 6:3, 4; 1Ch 13:7).

2. A Benjamite (1Ch 8:14).

3. Son of Jehiel (1Ch 8:31; 9:37).

AHIRA (brother of evil), prince captain of the tribe of Naphtali (Nu 1:15; 2:29; 7:78, 83; 10:27).

AHIRAM (brother of height, exalted brother), son of Benjamin (Nu 26:38). See Aharah.

AHIRAMITE (of the family of Ahiram), (Nu 26:38).

AHISAMACH (my brother supports), a Danite, the father of Aholiab (Ex 31:6; 35:34; 38:23).

AHISHAHAR (brother of dawn), a descendant of Benjamin through Jediael and Bilhan (1Ch 7:10).

AHISHAR (my brother has sung), an official over Solomon's household (1Ki 4:6).

AHITHOPHEL (brother of folly). One of David's counsellors (2Sa 15:12; 1Ch 27:33). Joins Absalom (2Sa 15:31, 34; 16:15, 20-23; 17:1-23). Probably referred to by David in Ps 55:12-14. Suicide of (2Sa 17:1-14, 23).

AHITUB (brother of goodness). 1. High Priest, father of Ahiah (1Sa 14:3; 22:9, 11, 12, 20).

2. Father of Zadok (2Sa 8:17; 1Ch 18:16).

3. Ruler of the house of God (1Ch 9:11; Ne 11:11).

4. The Ahitub mentioned in 1Ch 6:8, 11, 12, is probably identical with the last described above, or else he is confused with Azariah (2Ch 31:10).

AHLAB (fat or **fruitful),** a town of Asher from which the Israelites were not able to drive the inhabitants (J'g 1:31).

AHLAI (O would that!). 1. The father of Zabad, one of David's soldiers (1Ch 11:41).

2. A daughter of Sheshan who married her father's Egyptian slave Jarha. They had a son Attai (1Ch 2:31-35).

AHOAH (brotherly), a son of Bela (1Ch 8:4), from whom is derived the term "Ahohite" (2Sa 23:9, 28; 1Ch 11:12). Called also Ahiah (1Ch 8:7), and Ira (1Ch 7:7).

AHOHITE, a patronymic given to the descendants of Ahoah: Dodo (2Sa 23:9), Zalmon (23:28), and Ilai (1Ch 11:29).

AHOLA (See Aholah.)

AHOLAH (tent woman), in God's parable to Ezekiel (Eze 23) a woman who represents Samaria, and with her sister Aholibah (Jerusalem) was accused of being unfaithful to Jehovah.

AHOLIAB (father's tent), an artificer of the tabernacle (Ex 31:6; 35:34; 36:1, 2; 38:23).

AHOLIBAH, an imaginary character, typical of idolatry (Eze 23:4, 5, 36, 44).

AHOLIBAMAH (tent of the high place). 1. One of Esau's three wives (Ge 36:2, 18, 25). Also called Judith the daughter of Beeri (Ge 26:34).

2. An Edomite duke (Ge 36:41; 1Ch 1:52), probably so named from the district of his possession.

AHUMAI, son of Jahath (1Ch 4:2).

AHURA MAZDA, the all wise spirit in

the dualistic system of Zoroastrianism. Darius the Great, Xerxes (the Biblical Ahasuerus), and Artaxerxes were zealous worshipers of Ahura Mazda, held to be the creator of the worlds, greatest of the gods and source of all good.

AHUZAM (possessor), son of Ashur (1Ch 4:6).

AHUZZATH (possession), a "friend" of Abimelech, who made a peace treaty with Isaac at Beersheba after they saw that the Lord had blessed him (Ge 26:23-33).

AI (ruin). 1. A royal city of the Canaanites. Conquest and destruction of (Jos 7; 8). Rebuilt (Ezr 2:28). Called also Aija (Ne 11:31); and Aiath (Isa 10:28). Population of (Jos 8:25).

2. A city of the Ammonites (Jer 49:3).

AIAH (falcon). 1. A Horite (Ge 36:24; 1Ch 1:40).

2. The father of Rizpah, Saul's concubine (2Sa 3:7; 21:8).

See Ajah.

AIATH, feminine form of the city Ai (Isa 10:28).

AIJA, another form of Ai (Ne 11:31).

AIJALON (See Ajalon.)

AIJELETH SHAHAR (hind of the morning), a musical term which probably indicated the sprightly movement of the music set to Ps 22. See Title.

AIN. 1. A city of Simeon (Jos 19:7; 15:32; 21:16; 1Ch 4:32). Called also Ashan (1Ch 6:59). Possibly identical with En-Rimmon (Ne 11:29).

2. A landmark on the northern boundary of Palestine (Nu 34:11).

AIN FESHKA, oasis on the W side of the Dead Sea, S of Khirbet Qumran.

AIN KAREM, a Hebrew phrase meaning "the vineyards of Engedi" (Song 1:14).

AIN KARIM, a village in the hill country of Judea.

AJAH (falcon), called also Aiah. 1. A Horite (Ge 36:24; 1Ch 1:40).

2. Father of Rizpah (2Sa 3:7; 21:8-11).

AJALON. 1. A city of Dan (Jos 19:42). Assigned to the Levites (Jos 21:24; 1Sa 14:31; 1Ch 6:69). Amorites of, not exterminated (J'g 1:35).

2. A city of Zebulun (J'g 12:12).

3. A city of Judah (2Ch 28:18; 11:10).

4. A valley (Jos 10:12).

AKAN, a Horite (Ge 36:27). Called also Jaakan (De 10:6); and Jakan (1Ch 1:42).

AKELDAMA (See Aceldama.)

AKHENATON (he who is beneficial to Aton), the name chosen by Amenhotep IV (1377-1360 B.C.), ruler in the Eighteenth Dynasty of Egypt, when he changed the religion of his country, demanding that all worship only the sun god under the name Aton.

AKKAD (See Accad.)

AKKUB (pursuer). 1. Son of Elioenai (1Ch 3:24).

2. A Levite who founded a family of Temple porters (1Ch 9:17).

3. The head of a family of the Nethinim (Ezr 2:45).

4. A Levite who helped expound the Law (Ne 8:7).

AKRABBIM, a chain of hills in the south of Palestine (Nu 34:4; Jos 15:3; J'g 1:36).

ALABASTER. A white stone. Vessels made of (M't 26:7; M'k 14:3; Lu 7:37).

ALAMETH (concealment). 1. A son of Becher and grandson of Benjamin (1Ch 7:8).

2. Variant of Alemeth (KJV, ASV), son of Jehoadah or Jarah (1Ch 8:36; 9:2).

ALAMMELECH (oak of a king), a town of Asher (Jos 19:26).

ALAMOTH. A musical term (1Ch 15:20). Inscription to Ps 46. See Music.

ALEMETH (concealment). 1. A Levitical city (1Ch 6:60). See Almon.

2. Son of Jehoadah (1Ch 8:36); or of Jarah (1Ch 9:42).

ALEXANDER (man-defending). 1. Son of Simon who bore the cross of Jesus (M'k 15:21).

2. A relative of the high priest, present at the defense of Peter and John (Ac 4:6).

3. A Jew of Ephesus (Ac 19:33).

4. A copper-smith (1Ti 1:20; 2Ti 4:14).

ALEXANDER THE GREAT. Son of Philip, King of Macedon. Lived from 356-323 B.C. He conquered the civilized world from Greece eastward to India. Described in Da 8.

ALEXANDRA, wife of Aristobulus, King of the Jews (105-104 B. C.).

ALEXANDRIA. A city of Egypt (Ac 6:9). Ships of (Ac 27:6; 28:11). Apollos born in (Ac 18:24).

ALGUM, called also Almug, trees of Ophir and Lebanon (1Ki 10:11, 12; 2Ch 2:8; 9:10, 11).

ALIAH (See Alvah.)

ALIAN (See Alvan.)

ALIENS, strangers, heathen. To be treated with justice (Ex 22:21; 23:9; Le 19:33, 34; De 1:16; 10:19; 24:14, 17; 27:19; Jer 7:6; 22:3; Eze 22:29; Mal 3:5). Religious privileges of (Ex 12:48, 49; Nu 9:14; 15:14, 15). Kindness to Edomites, enjoined (De 23:7). Jews authorized to purchase, as slaves (Le 25:44, 45); and to take usury from (De 15:3; 23:20); not permitted to make kings of (De 17:15). Forbidden to eat the passover (Ex 12:45). Partially exempt from Jewish law (De 14:21). Numerous in times of David and Solomon (2Sa 22:45, 46; 2Ch 2:17; 15:9). Oppressed (Eze 22:29). Rights of (Nu 35:15; Jos 20:9; Eze 47:22, 23). David's kindness to (2Sa 15:19, 20). Hospitality to, required by Jesus (M't 25:35, 38, 43).

See Gleaning; Heathen; Hospitality; Inhospitableness; Proselyte; Strangers.

ALL THINGS. Commanded (M't 7:12; 28:20; 1Co 13:7; 16:14; Eph 4:15; 5:20; Ph'p 2:14; Col 3:14; 1Th 5:21; 2Ti 4:5; Tit 2:7). General references to (Ps 8:6; Jer 17:9; M't 19:26; 21:22; M'k 9:23; Ro 8:28, 32; 1Co 3:21; 9:25; 2Co 5:17; Ph'p 3:8; 1Ti 4:8).

ALLEGORY. Of the trees seeking a king (J'g 9:8-15). Messiah's kingdom represented under, of the wolf and the lamb dwelling together (Isa 11:6-8). Wilderness to blossom as the rose (Isa 35). The two covenants (Ga 4:24). See Parable; Symbol.

ALLELUIA (praise ye Jehovah), a word used by the writers of various psalms to invite all to join them in praising God (104:35; 105:45; 106:1, 48; 111:1; 112:1; 113:1, 9; 115:18; 116:19; 117:2; 135:1, 21; first and last vs. of Ps 146 to 150). The term Alleluia in Re 19:1, 3, 4, 6 is borrowed from these Psalms.

ALLIANCES. Forbidden (Ex 23:32; 34:12; De 7:2, 3; 13:6, 8; Jos 23:6, 7; J'g 2:2; Ezr 9:12; Pr 1:10, 15; 2Co 6:14-17; Eph 5:11). Lead to idolatry (Ex 34:15, 16; Nu 25:1-8; De 7:4; J'g 3:5-7; Re 2:20). Have led to murder and human sacrifice (Ps 106:37, 38). Provoke the anger of God (De 7:4; 31:16, 17; 2Ch 19:2; Ezr 9:13, 14; Ps 106:29, 40; Isa 2:6). Provoke God to leave men to reap the fruits of them (Jos 23:12, 13; J'g 2:1-3). Are ensnaring (Ex 23:33; Nu 25:18; De 12:30; 13:6; Ps 106:36). Are enslaving (2Pe 2:18, 19). Are defiling (Ezr 9:1, 2). Are degrading (Isa 1:23). Are ruinous to spiritual interests (Pr 29:24; Heb 12:14, 15; 2Pe 3:17). Are ruinous to moral character (1Co 15:33). Are a proof of folly (Pr 12:11). Children who enter into, bring shame upon their parents (Pr 28:7). Evil consequences of (Pr 28:19; Jer 51:7). The wicked are prone to (Ps 50:18; Jer 2:25). The wicked tempt saints to (Ne 6:2-4). Sin of, to be confessed, deeply repented of, and forsaken (Ezr 10). Involve saints in their guiltiness (2Joh 9-11; Re 18:4). Involve saints in their punishment (Nu 16:26; Jer 51:6; Re 18:4). Unbecoming in those called saints (2Ch 19:2; 2Co 6:14-16; Ph'p 2:15). Exhortations to shun all inducements to (Pr 1:10-15; 4:14, 15; 2Pe 3:17). Exhortations to hate and avoid (Pr 14:7; Ro 16:17; 1Co 5:9-11; Eph 5:6, 7; 1Ti 6:5; 2Ti 3:5). A call to come out from (Nu 16:26; Ezr 10:11; Jer 51:6, 45; 2Co 6:17; 2Th 3:6; Re 18:4). Means of preservation from (Pr 2:10-20; 19:27). Blessedness of avoiding (Ps 1:1). Blessedness of forsaking (Ezr 9:12; Pr 9:6; 2Co 6:17, 18). Saints grieve to meet with, in their intercourse with the world (Ps 57:4; 120:5, 6; 2Pe 2:7, 8). Saints grieve to witness in their brethren (Ge 26:35; Ezr 9:3; 10:6). Saints hate and avoid (Ps 26:4, 5; 31:6; 101:7; Re 2:2). Saints deprecate (Ge 49:6; Ps 6:8; 15:4; 101:4, 7; 119:115; 139:19). Saints are separate from (Ex 33:16; Ezr 6:21). Saints should be circumspect when undesignedly thrown into (M't 10:16; Col 4:5; 1Pe 2:12). Pious parents prohibit, to their children (Ge 28:1). Persons in authority should denounce (Ezr 10:9-11; Ne 13:23-27). Punishment of (Nu 33:56; De 7:4; Jos 23:13; J'g 2:3; 3:5-8; Ezr 9:7, 14; Ps 106:41, 42; Re 2:16, 22, 23). Exemplified. *Solomon* (1Ki 11:1-8). *Rehoboam* (1Ki 12:8, 9). *Jehoshaphat* (2Ch 18:3; 19:2; 20:35-38). *Jehoram* (2Ch 21:6). *Ahaziah* (2Ch 22:3-5). *Israelites* (Ezr 9:1, 2). *Israel* (Eze 44:7). *Judas Iscariot* (M't 26:14-16). Examples of avoiding.

Man of God (1Ki 13:7-10). *Nehemiah* (Ne 6:2-4; 10:29-31). *David* (Ps 101:4-7; 119:115). *Jeremiah* (Jer 15:17). *Joseph of Arimathea* (Lu 23:51). *Church of Ephesus* (Re 2:6). Examples of forsaking. *Israelites* (Nu 16:27; Ezr 6:21, 22; 10:3, 4, 16, 17). *Sons of the Priests* (Ezr 10:18, 19). Examples of the judgments of God against. *Korah* (Nu 16:32). *Ahaziah* (2Ch 22:7, 8). *Judas Iscariot* (Ac 1:18).

ALLON (oak). 1. Son of Jedaiah (1Ch 4:37).

2. A city of Naphtali (Jos 19:33).

ALLON-BACHUTH, place where Rebekah was buried (Ge 35:8).

ALLOY, of metals (Isa 1:25).

ALMIGHTY (meaning uncertain). LXX *pantokrator*, **all powerful.** Used 57 times with *'el, Kúrios, Theós* for identification (Ge 17:1), invocation (Ge 28:3), description (Eze 10:5), praise (Re 4:8).

ALMODAD (the beloved), first-mentioned of Joktan's 13 sons (Ge 10:26; 1Ch 1:20).

ALMON, Levitical city of Benjamin (Jos 21:18). Called Alemeth (1Ch 6:60).

ALMOND, a tree. Fruit of (Ge 43:11). Aaron's rod of the (Nu 17:8). Bowls of candlestick in the tabernacle fashioned after the nuts of the (Ex 25:33, 34; 37:19, 20).

Figurative Use of: Ec 12:5; Jer 1:11.

ALMON-DIBLATHAIM. Camping place of Israelites (Nu 33:46, 47). Probably identical with Beth-diblathaim (Jer 48:22), and with Diblath (Eze 6:14).

ALMS. Enjoined (De 15:7-11; M't 5:42; 19:21; Lu 12:33; 2Co 9:5-7; Ga 2:10; 1Ti 6:18; Heb 13:16). To be given without ostentation (M't 6:1-4; Ro 12:8); freely (2Co 9:6, 7). Withholding, not of love (1Jo 3:17). Solicited by the unfortunate (Joh 9:8; Ac 3:2).

See Beneficence; Gifts; Giving; Liberality; Poor.

Instances of Giving: Zaccheus (Lu 19:8). Dorcas (Ac 9:36). Cornelius (Ac 10:2). The early Christians (Ac 2:44, 45; 4:34-37; 6:1-3; 11:29, 30; 24:17; Ro 15:25-28; 1Co 16:1-4; 2Co 8:1-4; 9:1; Heb 6:10).

ALMUG (See Algum.)

ALOES. Used as perfume (Ps 45:8; Pr 7:17; Song 4:14). In embalming the dead (Joh 19:39). Lign-aloes (Nu 24:6).

ALOTH, a district mentioned in 1Ki 4:16.

ALPHA, a title of Christ (Re 1:8, 11; 21:6; 22:13). Compare Isa 41:4; 44:6; 48:12.

ALPHAEUS. 1. Father of James (M't 10:3; M'k 3:18).

2. Father of Levi (M'k 2:14).

3. Possibly Cleophas, husband of the Mary at the cross (Joh 19:25 cf. M'k 15:40), as Cleophas and Alphaeus are of Semitic derivation. Unlikely the Cleopas of the Emmaus road (Lu 24:18) since Cleopas was a common Greek name.

ALTAR OF BURNT-OFFERING, THE. Dimensions of (Ex 27:1; 38:1). Horns on the corners of (Ex 27:2; 38:2). Covered with brass (Ex 27:2). All its vessels of brass (Ex 27:3; 38:3). A network grate of brass placed in (Ex 27:4, 5; 38:4). Furnished with rings and staves (Ex 27:6, 7; 38:5-7). Made after a divine pattern (Ex 27:8).

Called: The brazen altar (Ex 39:39; 1Ki 8:64). The altar of God (Ps 43:4). The altar of the Lord (Mal 2:13). Placed in the court before the door of the tabernacle (Ex 40:6, 29). Sanctified by God (Ex 29:44). Anointed and sanctified with holy oil (Ex 40:10; Le 8:10, 11). Cleansed and purified with blood (Ex 29:36, 37). Was most holy (Ex 40:10). Sanctified whatever touched it (Ex 29:37). All sacrifices to be offered on (Ex 29:38-42; Isa 56:7). All gifts to be presented at (M't 5:23, 24). Nothing polluted or defective to be offered on (Le 22:22; Mal 1:7, 8). Offering at the dedication of (Nu 7).

The Fire Upon: Came from before the Lord (Le 9:24). Was continually burning (Le 6:13). Consumed the sacrifices (Le 1:8, 9). Sacrifices bound to the horns of (Ps 118:27). The blood of sacrifices put on the horns and poured at the foot of (Ex 29:12; Le 4:7, 18, 25; 8:15).

The Priests: Alone to serve (Nu 18:3, 7). Derived support from (1Co 9, 13). Ahaz removed and profaned (2Ki 16:10-16). The Jews condemned for swearing lightly by (M't 23:18, 19). A type of Christ (Heb 13:10).

ALTAR OF INCENSE. Dimensions of (Ex 30:1, 2; 37:25). Covered with gold (Ex 30:3; 37:26). Top of, surrounded with a crown of gold (Ex 30:3; 37:26). Had four rings of gold under the crown for the staves (Ex 30:4; 37:27). Staves of, covered with gold (Ex 30:5). Called the golden altar (Ex 39:38). Placed before the veil in the outer sanctuary (Ex 30:6; 40:5, 26). Said to be before the Lord (Le 4:7; 1Ki 9:25). Anointed with holy oil (Ex 30:26, 27). The priest burned incense on, every morning and evening (Ex 30:7, 8). No strange incense nor any sacrifice to be offered on (Ex 30:9). Atonement made for, by the high priest once every year (Ex 30:10; Le 16:18, 19). The blood of all sin offerings put on the horns of (Le 4:7, 18).

Punishment for: Offering strange fire on (Le 10:1, 2). Unauthorized offering on (2Ch 26:16-19). Covered by the priests before removal from the sanctuary (Nu 4:11). A type of Christ (Re 8:3; 9:3).

ALTARS. Designed for sacrifice (Ex 20:24). To be made of earth, or unhewn stone (Ex 20:24, 25; De 27:5, 6). Of brick, hateful to God (Isa 65:3). Natural rocks sometimes used as (J'g 6:19-21; 13:19, 20). Were not to have steps up to them (Ex 20:26). For idolatrous worship, often erected on roofs of houses (2Ki 23:12; Jer 19:13; 32:29). Idolaters planted groves near (J'g 6:30; 1Ki 16:32, 33; 2Ki 21:3). The Jews not to plant groves near (De 16:21). For idolatrous worship, to be destroyed (Ex 34:13; De 7:5). Probable origin of inscriptions on (De 27:8).

Mentioned in Scripture: Of Noah (Ge 8:20). Of Abraham (Ge 12:7, 8; 13:18; 22:9). Of Isaac (Ge 26:25). Of Jacob (Ge 33:20; 35:1, 3, 7). Of Moses (Ex 17:15; 24:4). Of Balaam (Nu 23:1, 14, 29). Of Joshua (Jos 8:30, 31). Of the temple of Solomon (2Ch 4:1, 19). Of the second temple (Ezr 3:2, 3). Of Reubenites. E of Jordan (Jos 22:10). Of Gideon (J'g 6:26, 27). Of the people of Israel (J'g 21:4). Of Samuel (1Sa 7:17). Of David (2Sa 24:21, 25). Of Jeroboam at Bethel (1Ki 12:33). Of Ahaz (2Ki 16:10-12). Of the Athenians (Ac 17:23). For burnt-offering (Ex 27:1-8). For incense (Ex 30:1-6). Protection afforded by (1Ki 1:50, 51). Afforded no protection to murderers (Ex 21:14; 1Ki 2:18-34).

AL-TASCHITH. Title of Ps 57-59; 75. (See Music).

ALTRUISM (disinterested benevolence). *Jesus inculcates:* By precept (M't 20:26, 27; 23:11; M'k 9:35; 10:43-45; Lu 22:26, 27; Joh 13:4-17; Ac 20:35). By example (Joh 13:4-17); came to serve (M't 20:28; Ph'p 2:7); went about doing good (Ac 10:38); pleased not self (Ro 15:3); became poor for others (2Co 8:9).

Paul inculcates: By precept, to help the weak (Ac 20:33-35; Ro 15:1, 2); to promote the welfare of others (1Co 10:24, 33; Ga 6:1, 2, 10; Ph'p 2:4-9). By example, became servant of all (1Co 9:19-22; 2Co 4:5); made many rich (2Co 6:10).

Motives inspiring to: Love of neighbor (Lu 10:25-37). To save men (1Co 9:22). For Jesus' sake (2Co 4:5). Example of Jesus (2Co 8:9; Ph'p 2:3-8).

See Alms; Beneficence; Charitableness; Duty of Man to Man; Liberality; Love.

ALUSH, camping place of the Israelites (Nu 33:13).

ALVAH. Duke of Edom (Ge 36:40). Called Aliah (1Ch 1:51).

ALVAN. Son of Shobal (Ge 36:23). Called Alian (1Ch 1:40).

AMAD, a town of Asher (Jos 19:26).

AMAL, son of Helem (1Ch 7:35).

AMALEK. Son of Eliphaz (Ge 36:12; 1Ch 1:36). Probably not the ancestor of the Amalekites mentioned in time of Abraham (Ge 14:7).

AMALEKITES, THE. Descent of (Ge 36:12, 16).

Character of: Wicked (1Sa 15:18). Oppressive (J'g 10:12). Warlike and cruel (1Sa 15:33). Governed by kings (1Sa 15:20, 32). A powerful and influential nation (Nu 24:7). Possessed cities (1Sa 15:5).

Country of: In the south of Canaan (Nu 13:29; 1Sa 27:8). Extended from Havilah to Shur (1Sa 15:7). Was the scene of ancient warfare (Ge 14:7). Part of the Kenites dwelt amongst (1Sa 15:6). Were the first to oppose Israel (Ex 17:8). Discomfited at Rephidim, through the intercession of Moses (Ex 17:9-13). Doomed to utter destruction for opposing Israel (Ex 17:14, 16; De 25:19). Their utter destruction foretold (Nu 24:20). Presumption of Israel punished by (Nu 14:45). United with Eglon against Israel (J'g 3:13). Part of their possessions taken by Ephraim (J'g 5:14, w J'g 12:15). With Midian, oppressed Israel (J'g 6:3-5).

Saul: Overcame, and delivered Israel (1Sa 14:48). Commissioned to destroy

(1Sa 15:1-3). Massacred (1Sa 15:4-8). Condemned for not utterly destroying (1Sa 15:9-26; 28:18). Agag, king of, slain by Samuel (1Sa 5:32, 33). Invaded by David (1Sa 27:8, 9). Pillaged and burned Ziklag (1Sa 30:1, 2). Pursued and slain by David (1Sa 30:10-20). Spoil taken from, consecrated (2Sa 8:11, 12). Confederated against Israel (Ps 83:7). Remnant of, completely destroyed during the reign of Hezekiah (1Ch 4:41-43).

AMAM. A city of Judah (Jos 15:26). Probably situated within the district assigned afterward to Simeon (Jos 19:1-9).

AMANA, AMANAH (See Abana.)

AMANA (constant (?) **),** a mountain near Lebanon (Song 4:8), whence flow the Amana springs (2Ki 5:12, marg.).

AMANUENSIS (Jer 36:4; 45:1).

AMARANTHINE (fadeth not away), an inheritance (1Pe 1:4), glory (1Pe 5:4). From amaranth, a flower which when picked does not wither; the unfading flower of the poets.

AMARIAH. 1. Two Levites (1Ch 6:7, 52; 23:19; 24:23).

2. Chief priest in the reign of Jehoshaphat (2Ch 19:11).

3. A high priest, father of Ahitub (1Ch 6:11; Ezr 7:3).

4. A Levite, who assisted in distributing temple gifts (2Ch 31:15-19).

5. Son of Hizkiah (Zep 1:1).

6. Father of Zechariah (Ne 11:4).

7. A priest, returned from exile (Ne 10:3; 12:2). Probably identical with one mentioned in Ne 12:13.

8. A returned exile. Divorces his idolatrous wife (Ezr 10:42).

AMARNA, TELL EL (the hill amarna), the modern name for the ancient capital of Amenhotep IV (c. 1387-1366 B. C.), where in 1887 a large number of clay tablets containing the private correspondence between the ruling Egyptian Pharaohs and the political leaders in Palestine were discovered.

AMASA. 1. Nephew of David (2Sa 17:25; 1Ch 2:17). Joins Absalom (2Sa 17:25). Returns to David, and is made captain of the host (2Sa 19:13). Slain (2Sa 20:8-12; 1Ki 2:5, 32).

2. Son of Hadlai (2Ch 28:12).

AMASAI. 1. A Levite and ancestor of Samuel (1Ch 6:25, 35).

2. Leader of a body of men disaffected toward Saul, who joined David (1Ch 12:18).

3. A priest and trumpeter (1Ch 15:24).

4. A Levite of the Kohathites (2Ch 29:12).

AMASHAI, priest in Nehemiah's time (Ne 11:13).

AMASIAH, a captain under Jehoshaphat (2Ch 17:16).

AMAZIAH (whom Jehovah strengthens). 1. A Levite (1Ch 6:45).

2. King of Judah. History of (2Ki 14; 2Ch 25).

3. An idolatrous priest at Bethel (Am 7:10-17).

4. Father of Joshah (1Ch 4:34).

AMBASSADORS. Sent by Moses to Edom (Nu 20:14); to the Amorites (Nu 21:21); by Gibeonites to the Israelites (Jos 9:4); Israelites to various nations (J'g 11:12-28); Hiram to David (2Sa 5:11); and Solomon (1Ki 5:1); Benhadad to Ahab (1Ki 20:2-6); Amaziah to Jehoash (2Ki 14:8); Ahaz to Tiglath (2Ki 16:7); Hoshea to So (2Ki 17:4); Sennacherib through Rabshakeh to Hezekiah (2Ki 19:9); Berodach to Hezekiah (2Ki 20:12; 2Ch 32:31); Zedekiah to Egypt (Eze 17:15).

Other references to (Pr 13:17; Isa 18:2; 30:4; 33:7; 36:11; 39:1, 2; Lu 14:32).

Figurative: Job 33:23; Ob 1; 2Co 5:20; Eph 6:20.

AMBER, used only to describe the color of divine glory (Eze 1:4, 27; 8:2).

AMBITION. *Worthy* (1Ti 3:1). *Worldly* (Jas 4:1, 2; 1Jo 2:16); cursed (Isa 5:8; Heb 2:9); false accusation against Moses (Nu 16:13); insatiable (Hab 2:5, 6, 9); parable illustrating (2Ki 14:9); perishable (Job 20:6, 7; Ps 49:11-13); rebuked by Jesus (M't 16:26; 18:1-3; 20:20-28; 23:5-7, 12; M'k 9:33-37; 10:35-45; 12:38, 39; Lu 9:25, 46-48; 11:43; 22:24-30; Joh 5:44); temptation by Satan (M't 4:8-10; Lu 4:5-8).

Instances of: Lucifer (Isa 14:12-15); Eve (Ge 3:5, 6); Aaron and Miriam (Nu 16:3-35); Abimelech (J'g 9:1-6); Absalom (2Sa 15:1-13; 18:18); Haman (Es 5:9-13); disciples of Jesus (M't 18:1-3; 20:20-24; M'k 9:33-37; 10:35-45; Lu 9:46-48; 22:24-30); Diotrephes (3Jo 9, 10).

Disappointed: Ahithophel (2Sa 17:23); Adonijah (1Ki 1:5); Haman (Es 6:6-9).

AMBUSH. *Instances of:* At Ai (Jos 8:2-22); Shechem (J'g 9:25, 34); Gibeah (J'g 20:29-41). Near Zemaraim (2Ch 13:13).

By Jehoshaphat (2Ch 20:22). See Armies.

Figurative: Jer 51:12.

AMEN (confirm, support). A word used to reinforce a statement (Nu 5:22; De 27:12-26; Ne 5:13; 2Co 1:20; Re 1:18; 22:20). Used in prayer (1Ki 1:36; 1Ch 16:36; Ne 8:6; Ps 41:13; 72:19; 89:52; 106:48; Jer 28:6; M't 6:13; 1Co 14:16; Re 5:14; 19:4). A title of Christ (Re 3:14).

AMETHYST, a precious stone (Ex 28:19; 39:12; Re 21:20).

AMI or **AMON,** a servant of Solomon (Ezr 2:57), called Amon in Ne 7:59.

AMINADAB (See Amminadab.)

AMITTAI (faithful), father of Jonah (2Ki 14:25; Jon 1:1).

AMMAH (mother, beginning), a hill around Gibeon (2Sa 2:24).

AMMI (my people), symbolic name given to Israel (Ho 2:1).

AMMIEL (my kinsman is God). 1. The son of Gemali and spy sent out by Moses (Nu 13:12).

2. The father of Machir, of Lodebar (2Sa 9:4, 5; 17:27).

3. The father of Bath-sheba, one of David's wives (1Ch 3:5). Called also Eliam (2Sa 11:3).

4. The sixth son of Obed-edom who, with his family, was associated with the Tabernacle porters (1Ch 26:5).

AMMIHUD (my kinsman is glorious). 1. The father of Elishama, chief of Ephraim (Nu 1:10; 2:18; 7:48, 53); and son of Laadan (1Ch 7:46).

2. A man of Simeon and father of Shemuel (Nu 34:20).

3. A Naphtalite whose son, Pedahel, also assisted in the division of the land (Nu 34:28).

4. Father of Talmai and king of Geshur. Absalom fled to Talmai after he slew his brother Amnon (2Sa 13:37).

5. Son of Omri, father of Uthai (1Ch 9:4).

AMMIHUR (See Ammihud.)

AMMINADAB (my people is willing or **my kinsman is generous).** 1. A Levite. Aaron's father-in-law (Ex 6:23).

2. A prince of Judah (Nu 1:7; 2:3; 7:12, 17; 10:14; Ru 4:19, 20; 1Ch 2:10; M't 1:4; Lu 3:33).

3. A son of Kohath, son of Levi (1Ch 6:22). Perhaps the same as No. 1.

4. A Kohathite who assisted in the return of the ark from the house of Obed-edom (1Ch 15:10, 11).

AMMINADIB (See Amminadab.)

AMMISHADDAI (an ally is the Almighty), father of Abiezer, captain of the tribe of Dan in Moses' time (Nu 1:12; 2:25; 7:66, 71; 10:25).

AMMIZABAD (my kinsman hath endowed), son of Benaiah, third of David's captains (1Ch 27:6).

AMMON (a people). Ammon or Benammi is the name of one of the sons of Lot borne to him by his youngest daughter in the neighborhood of Zoar (Ge 19:38).

AMMONITES. Descendants of Benammi, one of the sons of Lot (Ge 19:38). Character of (J'g 10:6; 2Ki 23:13; 2Ch 20:25; Jer 27:3, 9; Eze 25:3, 6; Am 1:13; Zep 2:10). Territory of (Nu 21:24; De 2:19; Jos 12:2; 13:10, 25; J'g 11:13).

Israelites forbidden to disturb (De 2:19, 37). Excluded from the congregation of Israel (De 23:3-6). Confederate with Moabites and Amalekites against Israel (J'g 3:12, 13). Defeated by the Israelites (J'g 10:7-18; 11:32, 33; 12:1-3; 1Sa 11; 2Sa 8:12; 10; 11:1; 12:26-31; 17:27; 1Ch 18:11; 20:1-3; 2Ch 20; 26:7, 8; 27:5). Conspire against the Jews (Ne 4:7, 8).

Solomon takes wives from (1Ki 11:1; 2Ch 12:13; Ne 13:26). Jews intermarry with (Ezr 9:12; 10:10-44; Ne 13:23).

Kings of: Baalis (Jer 40:14; 41:10); Hanun (2Sa 10; 1Ch 19), Nahash (1Sa 11; 2Sa 10:1, 2; 1Ch 19:1, 2).

Idols of: Milcom (2Ki 23:13); Molech. See Molech. Prophecies concerning (Isa 11:14; Jer 9:25, 26; 25:15-21; 27:1-11; 49:1-6; Eze 21:20, 28-32; 25:1-11; Da 11:41; Am 1:13-15; Zep 2:8-11).

AMNESTY. For political offenses: To Shimei (2Sa 19:16-23); to Amasa (2Sa 19:13, with 17:25).

AMNON. 1. Son of David (2Sa 3:2; 1Ch 3:1. Incest of, and death (2Sa 13).

2. Son of Shimon (1Ch 4:20).

AMOK, priest who returned with Zerubbabel from exile (Ne 12:7, 20).

AMON. 1. Governor of the city of Samaria (1Ki 22:26; 2Ch 18:25).

2. King of Judah (2Ki 21:18-26; 2Ch 33:21-25; Zep 1:1; M't 1:10).

3. Ancestor of one of the families of the Nethinim (Ne 7:59). Called Ami (Ezr 2:57).

AMON, a city thought by most scholars to be the same as No (Jer 46:25). It was the capital of Egypt. Thebes is the Greek name.

AMORITES (mountain dwellers). Descendants of Canaan (Ge 10:15, 16; 1Ch 1:13, 14). Were giants (Am 2:9). Smitten by Chedorlaomer and rescued by Abraham (Ge 14).

Territory of (Ge 14:7; Nu 13:29; 21:13; De 1:4, 7, 19; 3:8, 9; Jos 5:1; 10:5; 12:2, 3; J'g 1:35, 36; 11:22); given to descendants of Abraham (Ge 15:21; 48:22; De 1:20; 2:26-36; 7:1; Jos 3:10; J'g 11:23; Am 2:10); allotted to Reuben, Gad, and Manasseh (Nu 32:33-42; Jos 13:15-21); conquest of (Nu 21:21-30; Jos 10:11; J'g 1:34-36).

Chiefs of (Jos 13:21). Wickedness of (Ge 15:16; 2Ki 21:11; Ezr 9:1). Idolatry of (J'g 6:10; 1Ki 21:26). Judgments denounced against (Ex 23:24; 33:2; 34:10, 11; De 20:17, 18). Hornets sent among (Jos 24:12). Not exterminated (J'g 1:34-36; 3:1-3, 5-8; 1Sa 7:14; 2Sa 2:2; 1Ki 9:20, 21; 2Ch 8:7). Intermarry with Jews (Ezr 9:1, 2; 10:18-44). Kings of (Jos 10:3-26).

AMOS (burden-bearer). A prophet (Am 1:1). Forbidden to prophesy in Israel (Am 7:10-17). Vision of (Am 8:2).

AMOZ, father of Isaiah (2Ki 19:2, 20; 20:1; Isa 1:1; 13:1).

AMPHIPOLIS (a city pressed on all sides), city of Macedonia not far from Philippi. Paul passed through it (Ac 17:1).

AMPLIAS, ASV, RSV, Ampliatus, a Christian to whom Paul sent a greeting (Ro 16:8).

AMRAM (people exalted). 1. Father of Moses (Ex 6:18, 20; Nu 26:58, 59; 1Ch 6:3, 18; 23:12, 13). Head of one of the branches of Levites (Nu 3:19, 27; 1Ch 26:23). Age of, at death (Ex 6:20).

2. Son of Bani (Ezr 10:34).

3. Son of Dishon (1Ch 1:41). ASV, RSV have Hamran.

AMRAPHEL, king of Shinar (Ge 14:1, 9).

AMULET, anything worn as a charm against evil, disease, witchcraft, etc (Isa 3:20; Jer 8:17).

AMUN (See Amon.)

AMUSEMENTS AND WORLDLY PLEASURES. Belong to the works of the flesh (Ga 5:19, 21); are transitory (Job 21:12, 13; Heb 11:25); vain (Ec 2:11); choke the word of God in the heart (Lu 8:14); formed a part of idolatrous worship (Ex 32:4, 6, 19, with 1Co 10:7; J'g 16:23-25).

Lead to rejection of God (Job 21:12-15); poverty (Pr 21:17); disregard of the judgments and works of God (Isa 5:12; Am 6:1-6); terminate in sorrow (Pr 14:13); lead to greater evil (Job 1:5; M't 14:6-8); the wicked seek for happiness in (Ec 2:1, 8).

Indulgence in, a proof of folly (Ec 7:4); a characteristic of the wicked (Isa 47:8; Eph 4:17, 19; 2Ti 3:4; Tit 3:3; 1Pe 4:3); a proof of spiritual death (1Ti 5:6); an abuse of riches (Jas 5:1, 5); wisdom of abstaining from (Ec 7:2, 3); shunned by the primitive saints (1Pe 4:3).

Abstinence from, seems strange to the wicked (1Pe 4:4); denounced by God (Isa 5:11, 12); exclude from the kingdom of God (Ga 5:21); punishment of (Ec 11:9; 2Pe 2:13); renunciation of, exemplified by Moses (Heb 11:25).

See Dancing; Games; Pleasure, Worldly; Worldliness.

AMZI. 1. A descendant of Merari and of Levi, and progenitor of Ethan, whom David set over the service of song (1Ch 6:44-46).

2. Ancestor of Adaiah, a priest in the second Temple (Ne 11:12).

ANAB (grapes), a city of the Anakim, taken by Joshua (Jos 11:21). It fell to Judah (Jos 15:50). SE of Debir, SW of Hebron. It retains its ancient name.

ANAH. 1. Daughter of Zibeon and mother of Aholibamah, Esau's wife (Ge 36:2, 14, 25).

2. Son of Seir, duke of Edom (Ge 36:20, 29; 1Ch 1:38).

3. Son of Zibeon (Ge 36:24; 1Ch 1:40, 41). Called also Beeri (Ge 26:34).

ANAHARATH, city on the border of Issachar (Jos 19:19). Modern en-Naura.

ANAIAH (Jehovah has answered). 1. A prince or priest who assisted in the reading of the law to the people (Ne 8:4).

2. A Jew who, with Nehemiah, sealed the covenant (Ne 10:22). Nos. 1 and 2 may be the same person.

ANAK (long necked), descendant of Arba (Jos 15:13) and ancestor of the Anakim (Nu 13:22, 28, 33).

ANAKIM, The. Descent of (Nu 13:22; Jos 15:13).

Were Called: The sons of Anak (Nu 13:33). The sons of the Anakim (De 1:28). The children of the Anakims (De 9:2). Divided into three tribes (Jos 15:14). Inhabited the mountains of Judah (Jos 11:21). Hebron, chief city of (Jos 14:15 w Jos 21:11). Of gigantic strength and stature (De 2:10, 11, 21). Israel terrified by (Nu 14:1, w Nu 13:33). Hebron a possession of, given to Caleb for his faithfulness (Jos 14:6-14). Driven from Hebron by Caleb (Jos 15:13, 14). Driven from Kirjath-sepher or Debir by Othniel (Jos 15:15-17; J'g 1:12, 13). Almost annihilated (Jos 11:21, 22).

ANAMIM, a tribe descended from Mizraim (Ge 10:13; 1Ch 1:11).

ANAMMELECH, an Assyrian idol (2Ki 17:31).

ANAN (cloud), a Jew, returned from Babylonian captivity (Ne 10:26).

ANANI, a descendant of David (1Ch 3:24).

ANANIAH (Jehovah is a protector). 1. Son of Maaseiah (Ne 3:23; 8:4).

2. Town of Benjamin (Ne 11:32).

ANANIAS (Jehovah has been gracious). 1. High priest, before whom Paul was tried (Ac 23:2-5; 24:1; 25:2).

2. A covetous member of church at Jerusalem. Falsehood and death of (Ac 5:1-11).

3. A Christian in Damascus (Ac 9:10-18; 22:12-16).

ANARCHY. *In Israel* (Isa 3:5-8). *In the early church:* Warned against (Ga 5:13, 14); insubordinate members hostile to authority (2Pe 2:10-19; Jude 8-13).

ANAT or **ANU,** Babylonian-Assyrian god of the sky, first named in a triad with Bel and Ea.

ANATH, father of Shamgar (J'g 3:31).

ANATHEMA (anything devoted). A thing devoted to God becomes His and is therefore irrevocably withdrawn from common use (Le 27:28, 29; Ro 9:3; 1Co 12:3; 16:22; Ga 1:9).

ANATHEMA MARANATHA. The words were formerly interpreted as a double imprecation, but are now believed to have no necessary connection.

ANATHOTH. 1. A Levitical city in Benjamin (Jos 21:18; 1Ch 6:60). Abiathar confined in (1Ki 2:26). Birthplace of Jeremiah (Jer 1:1; 32:7-12); of Abiezer (2Sa 23:27); of Jehu (1Ch 12:3). Prophecies against (Jer 11:21-23). Inhabitants of, after Babylonian captivity (Ezr 2:23; Ne 7:27).

2. Son of Becher (1Ch 7:8).

3. A Jew, who returned from Babylon (Ne 10:19).

ANATOMY, human (Job 10:11).

ANCHOR (Ac 27:29, 30). *Figurative:* Heb 6:19.

ANCIENT OF DAYS, an appellation of Jehovah (Da 7:9, 13, 22).

ANCIENTS. This word (except in one instance—1Sa 24:13) renders a Hebrew word which should always be translated "old men" or "elders."

ANDREW (manly). An apostle. A fisherman (M't 4:18). Of Bethsaida (Joh 1:44). A disciple of John (Joh 1:40). Finds Peter, his brother, and brings him to Jesus (Joh 1:40-42). Call of (M't 4:18; M'k 1:16). His name appears in the list of the apostles in M't 10:2; M'k 3:18; Lu 6:14. Asks the Master privately about the destruction of the temple (M'k 13:3, 4). Tells Jesus of the Greeks who sought to see him (Joh 12:20-22). Reports the number of loaves at the feeding of the five thousand (Joh 6:8). Meets with the disciples after the Lord's ascension (Ac 1:13).

ANDRONICUS, kinsman of Paul (Ro 16:7).

ANEM, a Levitical city (1Ch 6:73).

ANER. 1. A Canaanitish chief and brother of Mamre (Ge 14:13, 24).

2. A Levitical city of Manasseh (1Ch 6:70).

ANGEL. *One of the Holy Trinity:* Trinitarian authorities interpret the Scriptures cited under this topic as referring to Christ, who according to this view was the divine presence in the wilderness. Called Angel (Ac 7:30, 35); Mine Angel (Ex 32:34); Angel of God (Ex 14:19; J'g 13:6; 2Sa 14:17, 20); Angel of the Lord (Ex 3:2; J'g 2:1); Angel of his Presence (Isa 63:9).

ANGELS. Created by God and Christ (Ne 9:6; Col 1:16). Worship God and Christ (Ne 9:6; Ph'p 2:9-11; Heb 1:6). Are ministering Spirits (1Ki 19:5; Ps 68:17; 104:4; Lu 16:22; Ac 12:7-11; 27:23; Heb 1:7, 14). Communicate the will of God and Christ (Da 8:16, 17; 9:21-23; 10:11; 12:6, 7; M't 2:13, 20; Lu 1:19, 28; Ac 5:20; 8:26; 10:5; 27:23; Re 1:1). Obey the will of God (Ps 103:20; M't 6:10). Execute the purposes of God (Nu 22:22; Ps 103:21; M't 13:39-42; 28:2; Joh 5:4; Re 5:2). Execute the judgments of God (2Sa 24:16; 2Ki 19:35; Ps 35:5, 6; Ac 12:23; Re 16:1). Celebrate the praises of God (Job 38:7; Ps 148:2; Isa 6:3; Lu 2:13, 14; Re 5:11, 12; 7:11, 12). The law given by the ministration of (Ps 68:17; Ac 7:53; Heb 2:2).

Announced: The conception of Christ (M't 1:20, 21; Lu 1:31). The birth of Christ (Lu 2:10-12). The resurrection of Christ (M't 28:5-7; Lu 24:23). The ascension and second coming of Christ (Ac 1:11). The conception of John the Baptist (Lu 1:13, 36). Minister to Christ (M't 4:11; Lu 22:43; Joh 1:51). Are subject to Christ (Eph 1:21; Col 1:16; 2:10; 1Pe 3:22). Shall execute the purposes of Christ (M't 13:41; 24:31). Shall attend Christ at his second coming (M't 16:27; 25:31; M'k 8:38; 2Th 1:7). Know and delight in the gospel of Christ (Eph 3:9, 10; 1Ti 3:16; 1Pe 1:12). Ministration of, obtained by prayer (M't 26:53; Ac 12:5, 7). Rejoice over every repentant sinner (Lu 15:7, 10). Have charge over the children of God (Ps 34:7; 91:11, 12; Da 6:22; M't 18:10). Are of different orders (Isa 6:2; 1Th 4:16; 1Pe 3:22; Jude 9; Re 12:7). Not to be worshiped (Col 2:18; Re 19:10; 22:9). Are examples of meekness (2Pe 2:11; Jude 9). Are wise (2Sa 14:20). Are mighty (Ps 103:20). Are holy (M't 25:31). Are elect (1Ti 5:21). Are innumerable (Job 25:3; Heb 12:22).

Fallen: Job 4:18, M't 25:41; 2Pe 2:4; Jude 6; Re 2:9.

ANGEL OF THE CHURCHES (Re 1:20; 2:1, 8, 12, 18; 3:1, 7, 14).

ANGER. Forbidden (Ec 7:9; M't 5:22; Ro 12:19). A work of the flesh (Ga 5:20). A characteristic of fools (Pr 12:16; 14:29; 27:3; Ec 7:9).

Connected With: Pride (Pr 21:24). Cruelty (Ge 49:7; Pr 27:3, 4). Clamor and evil-speaking (Eph 4:31). Malice and blasphemy (Col 3:8). Strife and contention (Pr 21:19; 29:22; 30:33). Brings its own punishment (Job 5:2; Pr 19:19; 25:28). Grievous words stir up (J'g 12:4; 2Sa 19:43; Pr 15:1). Should not betray us into sin (Ps 37:8; Eph 4:26). In prayer be free from (1Ti 2:8). May be averted by wisdom (Pr 29:8). Meekness pacifies (Pr 15:1; Ec 10:4). Children should not be provoked to (Eph 6:4; Col 3:21). Be slow to (Pr 15:18; 16:32; 19:11; Tit 1:7; Jas 1:19). Avoid those given to (Ge 49:6; Pr 22:24). Justifiable, Exemplified. *Our Lord* (M'k 3:5). *Jacob* (Ge 31:36). *Moses* (Ex 11:8; 32:19; Le 10:16; Nu 16:15). *Nehemiah* (Ne 5:6; 13:17, 25). Sinful, Exemplified. *Cain* (Ge 4:5, 6). *Esau* (Ge 27:45). *Simeon and Levi* (Ge 49:5-7). *Moses* (Nu 20:10, 11). *Balaam* (Nu 22:27). *Saul* (1Sa 20:30). *Ahab* (1Ki 21:4). *Naaman* (2Ki 5:11). *Asa* (2Ch 16:10). *Uzziah* (2Ch 26:19). *Haman* (Es 3:5). *Nebuchadnezzar* (Da 3:13). *Jonah* (Jon 4:4). *Herod* (M't 2:16). *Jews* (Lu 4:28). *High Priest* (Ac 5:17; 7:54).

ANGER OF GOD, THE. Averted by Christ (Lu 2:11, 14; Ro 5:9; 2Co 5:18, 19; Eph 2:14, 17; Col 1:20; 1Th 1:10). Is averted from them that believe (Joh 3:14-18; Ro 3:25; 5:1). Is averted upon confession of sin and repentance (Job 33:27, 28; Ps 106:43-45; Jer 3:12, 13; 18:7, 8; 31:18-20; Joe 2:12-14; Lu 15:18-20). Is slow (Ps 103:8; Isa 48:9; Jon 4:2; Na 1:3). Is righteous (Ps 58:10, 11; La 1:18; Ro 2:6, 8; 3:5, 6; Re 16:6, 7). The justice of, not to be questioned (Ro 9:18, 20, 22). Manifested in terrors (Ex 14:24; Ps 76:6-8; Jer 10:10; La 2:20-22). Manifested in judgments and afflictions (Job 21:17; Ps 78:49-51; 90:7; Isa 9:19; Jer 7:20; Eze 7:19; Heb 3:17). Cannot be resisted (Job 9:13;14:13; Ps 76:7; Na 1:6). Aggravated by continual provocation (Nu 32:14). Specially reserved for the day of wrath (Zep 1:14-18; M't 25:41; Ro 2:5, 8; 2Th 1:8; Re 6:17; 11:18; 19:15).

Against: The wicked (Ps 7:11; 21:8, 9; Isa 3:8; 13:9; Na 1:2, 3; Ro 1:18; 2:8; Eph 5:6; Col 3:6). Those who forsake him (Ezr 8:22; Isa 1:4). Unbelief (Ps 78:21, 22; Joh 3:36; Heb 3:18, 19). Impenitence (Ps 7:12; Pr 1:30, 31; Isa 9:13, 14; Ro 2:5). Apostacy (Heb 10:26, 27).

Idolatry (De 29:20, 27, 28; 32:19, 20, 22; Jos 23:16; 2Ki 22:17; Ps 78:58, 59; Jer 44:3). Sin, in saints (Ps 89:30-32; 90:7-9; 99:8; 102:9, 10; Isa 47:6). Extreme, against those who oppose the gospel (Ps 2:2, 3, 5; 1Th 2:16). Folly of provoking (Jer 7:19; 1Co 10:22). To be dreaded (Ps 2:12; 76:7; 90:11; M't 10:28). To be deprecated (Ex 32:11; Ps 6:1; 38:1; 74:1, 2; Isa 64:9). Removal of, should be prayed for (Ps 39:10; 79:5; 80:4; Da 9:16; Hab 3:2). Tempered with mercy to saints (Ps 30:5; Isa 26:20; 54:8; 57:15, 16; Jer 30:11; Mic 7:11). To be borne with submission (2Sa 24:17; La 3:39, 43; Mic 7:9). Should lead to repentance (Isa 42:24, 25; Jer 4:8). Exemplified against, *The old world* (Ge 7:21-23). *Builders of Babel* (Ge 11:8). *Cities of the plain* (Ge 19:24, 25). *Egyptians* (Ex 7:20; 8:6, 16, 24; 9:3, 9, 23; 10:13, 22; 12:29; 14:27). *Israelites* (Ex 32:35; Nu 11:1, 33; 14:40-45; 21:6; 25:9; 2Sa 24:1, 15). *Enemies of Israel* (1Sa 5:6; 7:10). *Nadab* (Le 10:2). *The Spies* (Nu 14:37). *Korah* (Nu 16:31, 35). *Aaron and Miriam* (Nu 12:9, 10). *Five Kings* (Jos 10:25). *Abimelech* (J'g 9:56). *Men of Bethshemesh* (1Sa 6:19). *Saul* (1Sa 31:6). *Uzzah* (2Sa 6:7). *Saul's family* (2Sa 21:1). *Sennacherib* (2Ki 19:28, 35, 37).

ANIAM (lament of the people), a son of Shemidah, a Manassehite (1Ch 7:19).

ANIM, a city of Judah (Jas 15:20).

ANIMALS. *Creation of* (Ge 1:24, 25; 2:19; Jer 27:5). Food of (Ge 1:30). Named (Ge 2:20). Ordained as food for man (Ge 9:2, 3; Le 11:3, 9, 21, 22; De 14:4-6, 9, 11, 20). God's care of (Ge 9:9, 10; De 25:4; Job 38:41; Ps 36:6; 104:11, 21; 145:15, 16; 147:9; Jon 4:11; M't 6:26; 10:29; Lu 12:6, 24; 1Co 9:9). Under the curse (Ge 3:14; 6:7, 17). Suffer under divine judgments sent upon man (Jer 7:20; 12:4; 21:6; Eze 14:13, 17, 19-21; Joe 1:18-20). Two of every sort preserved in the ark (Ge 6:19, 20; 7:2, 9, 14, 15; 8:19). Seven clean, of every sort, preserved in the ark (Ge 7:2, 3). Suffered the plagues of Egypt (Ex 8:17; 9:9, 10, 19; 11:5). Perish at death (Ec 3:21). Possessed of devils (M't 8:31, 32; M'k 5:13; Lu 8:33). Clean and unclean (Ge 7:2, 8; 8:20; Le 7:21; 11; 20:25; De 14:3-20; Ac 10:11-15; 1Ti 4:3-5).

God's control of (Ps 91:13; Lu 10:19). Instruments of God's will (Ex 8; 10:4-15, 19; Nu 21:6; 22:28; Jos 24:12; Joe 1:4). Belong to God (Ps 50:10-12). Sent in judgment (Le 26:22; Nu 21:6, 7; De 8:15; Eze 5:17; 14:15; Re 6:8). Nature of (Job 41; Ps 32:9; Jas 3:7). Habits of (Job 12:7, 8; 37:8; 39; 40:20, 21; Ps 29:9; 104:20-25; Isa 13:21, 22; 34:14). Breeding of (Ge 30:35-43; 31:8, 9). Instincts of (De 32:11; Job 35:11; 39; 40:15-24; Ps 104:11-30; Pr 6:5-8; 30:25-28; Isa 1:3; Jer 2:24; 8:7; La 4:3; M't 24:28). Abodes of (Job 24:5; 37:8; 39:5-10, 27-29; Ps 104:20, 22, 25; Isa 34:14, 15; Jer 2:24; 50:39; M'k 1:13.

Cruelty to: Of Balaam to his ass (Nu 22:22-33). Houghing horses (2Sa 8:4; 1Ch 18:4).

Kindness to: (De 25:4; Pr 12:10; 1Ti 5:18). In relieving the overburdened (Ex 23:5; De 22:4). In rescuing from pits (M't 12:11; Lu 13:15; 14:5). In feeding (Ge 24:32; 43:24; J'g 19:21).

Instances of: Jacob in erecting booths for his cattle (Ge 33:17). People of Gerar in providing tents for cattle (2Ch 14:15).

Laws concerning: Sabbath rest for (Ex 20:10; De 5:14).

Treatment of vicious (Ex 21:28-32, 35, 36). Penalty for injury of (Ex 21:33, 34). Hybridizing of, forbidden (Le 19:19). Working of (De 22:10). Mother birds and their young (De 22:6, 7).

Names of: Apes (1Ki 10:22). Asses, beasts of burden (Ge 22:3; Nu 22:28; De 22:10; J'g 5:10; 10:4; 1Sa 9:3; M't 21:2). Bears (1Sa 17:34; 2Sa 17:8; 2Ki 2:24; Pr 17:12; 28:15; Isa 11:7). Behemoth (Job 40:15). Boars (Ps 80:13). Bullocks, as offerings (Ex 29:11, 36; Le 4:4; Nu 15:8; 1Ki 18:33; 2Ch 13:9; Ezr 6:17; Ps 66:15). Calves (Ge 18:7; 1Sa 28:24; Am 6:4; Lu 15:23). Camels (Ge 12:16; 30:43; Le 11:4; J'g 6:5; 1Sa 30:17; 1Ch 5:21; Job 1:3; M't 19:24; 23:24). Cattle (Ge 1:25; 31:18; Ex 9:4; 20:10; Nu 32:1; Jos 14:4; Eze 39:18; Am. 4:1). Chameleon (Le 11:30). Conies, rock rabbits (Le 11:5; Ps 104:18; Pr 30:26). Deer (De 14:5; 2Sa 2:18; 22:34; 1Ch 12:8; Ps 42:1; Pr 5:19; 6:5; Isa 35:6; Jer 14:5). Dogs (De 23:18; 1Ki 14:11; 22:38; Ps 59:6; Pr 26:17; Ec 9:4; Lu 16:21). Dragons (De 32:33; Ps 91:13; Isa 34:13; Jer 9:11; 51:37; Mic 1:8; Mal 1:3). Dromedaries, used as beasts of burden (1Ki 4:28; Es 8:10; Isa 60:6; Jer 2:23). Elephants (1Ki 10:22; Job 40:15). Ferret (Le 11:30). Foxes (J'g 15:4; Ne 4:3; Ps 63:10; Song 2:15; M't 8:20). Goats, as offerings (Ge 15:9; Le 4:24; 16:15; J'g 13:19; 2Ch 29:23). Greyhound (Pr 30:31). Hare (Le 11:6). Heifers, offered as sacrifices (Ge 15:9; Nu 19:2; De 21:3; Heb 9:13). Horses (De 17:16; 2Ki 23:11; Job 39:19; Ps 32:9; 33:17; Isa 31:1). Kine (Ge 32:15; De 7:13; 1Sa 6:7). Lambs, for offerings (Ex 29:39; Le 3:7; 4:32; 5:6; Nu 6:12). Leopards (Song 4:8; Isa 11:6; Jer 5:6; 13:23; Ho 13:7; Hab 1:8). Lions, General references to (J'g 14:5; 1Sa 17:34; 1Ki 13:24; Da 6:19). Characteristics of (De 33:22; J'g 14:18; 2Sa 17:10; Job 10:16; Ps 17:12; Pr 30:30; Isa 31:4; Na 2:12). Lizards (Le 11:30). Mice (Le 11:29; 1Sa 6:4; Isa 66:17). Mules (2Sa 13:29; 18:9; 1Ki 1:33; Ps 32:9; Zec 14:15). Oxen, laws concerning (Ex 21:28; 22:1; 23:4; Le 17:3; De 5:14; 22:1; 25:4; Lu 13:15; 1Co 9:9; 1Th 5:18). Pygarg (De 14:5). Rams, used in sacrifices (Ge 15:9; 22:13; Ex 29:15; Le 5:15; Nu 5:8). Sheep (Ge 4:4; 30:32; De 18:4; 32:14; 2Ch 7:5; 15:11; Job 1:3; 42:12; M't 12:11). Swine (Le 11:7; Isa 65:4; 66:17; M't 7:6; 8:30; Lu 15:15; 2Pe 2:22). Unicorn (Nu 23:22; De 33:17; Job 39:9; Ps 29:6; Isa 34:7). Vipers, poisonous serpents (Job 20:16; Isa 30:6; 59:5). Weasel (Le 11:29). Wolves, a type of the wicked (M't 7:15; 10:16; Joh 10:12; Ac 20:29).

ANISE, a seed, used as a condiment (M't 23:23).

ANKLET, an ornament for the ankles worn by women.

ANNA (grace), a widow and prophetess who at the age of 84 recognized Jesus as the Messiah when He was brought into the Temple (Lu 2:36-38).

ANNAS, associate high priest with Caiaphas (Lu 3:2; Joh 18:13, 19, 24; Ac 4:6).

ANNUAL FEASTS. *Instituted by Moses.* Designated as: Solemn feasts (Nu 15:3; 2Ch 8:13; La 2:6; Eze 46:9). Set feasts (Nu 29:39; Ezr 3:5). Appointed feasts (Isa 1:14). Holy convocations (Le 23:4). First and last days were Sabbatic (Le 23:39, 40; Nu 28:18-25; 29:12, 35; Ne 8:1-18). Kept with rejoicing (Le 23:40; De 16:11-14; 2Ch 30:21-26; Ezr 6:22; Ne 8:9-12, 17; Ps 122:4; Isa 30:29; Zec 8:19). Divine protection given during (Ex 34:24).

All males were required to attend (Ex 23:17; 34:23; De 16:16; Eze 36:38; Lu 2:41, 42; Joh 4:45; 7). Aliens permitted to attend (Joh 12:20; Ac 2:1-11). Attended by women (1Sa 1:3, 9; Lu 2:41). Observed: By Jesus (M't 26:17-20; Lu 2:41, 42; 22:15; Joh 2:13, 23; 5:1; 7:10; 10:22). By Paul (Ac 20:6, 16; 24:11, 17).

Of New Moon (Nu 10:10; 28:11-15; 1Ch 23:31; 2Ch 31:3; Ezr 3:5). Traffic at time of, suspended (Am 8:5).

The Passover: Institution of (Ex 12:3-49; 23:15-18; 34:18; Le 23:4-8; Nu 9:2-5, 13, 14; 28:16-25; De 16:1-8, 16; Ps 81:3, 5). Design of (Ex 12:21-28).

Special passover, for those who were unclean, or on journey to be held in second month (Nu 9:6-12; 2Ch 30:2-4). Lamb killed by Levites, for those who were ceremonially unclean (2Ch 30:17; 35:3-11; Ezr 6:20). Strangers authorized to celebrate (Ex 12:48, 49; Nu 9:14).

Observed at place designated by God (De 16:5-7). With unleavened bread (Ex 12:8, 15-20; 13:3, 6; 23:15; Le 23:6; Nu 9:11; 28:17; De 16:3, 4; M'k 14:12; Lu 22:7; Ac 12:3; 1Co 5:8). Penalty for neglecting to observe (Nu 9:13).

Reinstituted by Ezekiel (Eze 45: 21-24).

Observation of: Renewed, by the Israelites on entering Canaan (Jos 5:10, 11). By Hezekiah (2Ch 30:1). By Josiah (2Ki 23:22, 23; 2Ch 35:1, 18). After return from captivity (Ezr 6:19, 20). Observed by Jesus (M't 26:17-20; Lu 22:15; Joh 2:13, 23; 13). Jesus when twelve years old, in the temple at time of (Lu 2:41-50). Jesus crucified at time of (M't 26:2; M'k 14:1, 2; Joh 18:28). Lord's supper ordained at (M't 26:26-28; M'k 14:12-25; Lu 22:7-20). The lamb of, a type of Christ (1Co 5:7).

Prisoners released at, by the Romans (M't 27:15; M'k 15:6; Lu 23:16, 17; Joh 18:39). Peter imprisoned at time of (Ac 12:3).

Christ called, Our Passover (1Co 5:7).

Pentecost: Called, Feast of Weeks (Ex 34:22; De 16:10). Feast of Harvest (Ex 23:16). Day of First Fruits (Nu 28:26). Day of Pentecost (Ac 2:1; 20:16; 1Co 16:8).

Institution of: (Ex 23:16; 34:22; Le 23:15-21; Nu 28:26-31; De 16:9-12, 16).

Holy Ghost given to the apostles on the day of (Ac 2).

Of Purim: Instituted to commemorate the deliverance of the Jews from the plot of Haman (Es 9:20-32).

Of Tabernacles, called also Feast of Ingathering: Instituted (Ex 23:16; 34:22; Le 23:34-43; Nu 29:12-40; De 16:13-16). Design of (Le 23:42, 43). The law read in connection with, every seventh year (De 31:10-12; Ne 8:18).

Observance of. After the captivity (Ezr 3:4; Ne 8:14-18). By Jesus (Joh 7:2, 14). Observance of, omitted (Ne 8:17). Penalty for not observing (Zec 14:16-19).

Jeroboam institutes an idolatrous feast to correspond to, in the eighth month (1Ki 12:32, 33; 1Ch 27:11).

Of Trumpets: When and how observed (Le 23:24, 25; Nu 29:1-6). Celebrated after the captivity with joy (Ne 8:2, 9-12).

ANOINTING. Of the body (De 28:40; Ru 3:3; Es 2:12; Ps 92:10; 104:15; 141:5; Pr 27:9, 16; Ec 9:8; Song 1:3; 4:10; Isa 57:9; Am 6:6; Mic 6:15). Of guests (2Ch 28:15; Lu 7:46); the sick (Isa 1:6; M'k 6:13; Lu 10:34; Jas 5:14; Re 3:18); the dead (M't 26:12; M'k 14:8; 16:1; Lu 23:56). Of Jesus, as a token of love (Lu 7:37, 38, 46; Joh 11:2; 12:3). Omitted in mourning (2Sa 12:20; 14:2; Isa 61:3; Da 10:3). God preserves those who receive (Ps 18:50; 20:6; 89:20-23). Saints receive (Isa 61:3; 1Jo 2:20).

In Consecration: Of High Priests (Ex 29:7, 29; 40:13; Le 6:20; 8:12; 16:32; Nu 35:25; Ps 133:2).

Of Priests: (Ex 28:41; 30:30; 40:15; Le 4:3; 8:30; Nu 3:3).

Of Kings: (J'g 9:8, 15); Saul (1Sa 9:16; 10:1; 15:1); David (1Sa 16:3, 12, 13; 2Sa 2:4; 5:3; 12:7; 9:21; 1Ch 11:3). Solomon (1Ki 1:39; 1Ch 29:22); Jehu (1Ki 19:16; 2Ki 9:1-3, 6, 12). Hazael (1Ki 19:15); Joash (2Ki 11:12; 2Ch 23:11); Jehoahaz (2Ki 23:30); Cyrus (Isa 45:1).

Of Prophets: (1Ki 19:16).

Of the Tabernacle: (Ex 30:26; 40:9; Le 8:10; Nu 7:1); altars of (Ex 30:26-28; 40:10; Le 8:11; Nu 7:1); vessels of (Ex 30:27, 28; 40:9, 10; Le 8:10, 11; Nu 7:1).

Jacob's Pillar: at Beth-el (Ge 28:18; 31:13; 35:14). See Dedication.

Figurative: Of Christ's kingly and priestly office (Ps 45:7; 89:20; Isa 61:1; Da 9:24; Lu 4:18; Ac 4:27; 10:38; Heb 1:9). Of spiritual gifts (2Co 1:21; 1Jo 2:20, 27).

Typified: (Ex 40:13-15; Le 8:12; 1Sa 16:13; 1Ki 19:16).

Symbolical: Of Jesus (M't 26:7-12; Joh 12:3-7).

ANOINTING OIL. Formula of, given by Moses (Ex 30:22-25, 31-33).

See Oil; Ointment.

ANT (Pr 6:6-8; 30:25).

ANTEDILUVIANS. Worship God (Ge 4:3, 4, 26). Occupations of (Ge 4:2, 3, 20-22). Arts of (Ge 4:2, 3, 20-22; 6:14-22). Enoch prophesies to (Jude 14, 15). Noah preaches to (2Pe 2:5). Wickedness of (Ge 6:5-7). Destruction of (Ge 7:1, 21-23; Job 22:15-17; M't 24:37-39; Lu 17:26, 27; 2Pe 2:5).

See Flood.

Longevity of, See Longevity.

Giants among, See Giants.

ANTELOPE (See Deer.)

ANTHROPOMORPHISMS, figures of speech which attribute human forms acts, and affections to God.

Forms: Arm (Ps 89:13); body or form (Nu 11:25); ear (Ps 34:15); eye (Ch 16:9); hands (Isa 1:15); mouth (Ps 33:6); voice (Eze 1:24, 28); wings (Ps 36:7; 57:1). See terms for human forms, *figurative.*

Intellectual Facilities: Knowing (Ge 18:17-19). Memory (Isa 43:26; 63:11); assisted by tokens (Ge 9:16). Reason (Isa 1:18). Remembering (Ge 19:29; Ex 2:24). Understanding (Ps 147:5). Will (Ro 9:19).

Acts: Breathing (Ps 33:6); fainting not (Isa 40:28); grasping, with hand (Ps 35:2); hearing (Ge 2:25; Ps 94:9); laughing (Ps 2:4; 37:13; 59:8; Pr 1:26); resting (Ge 2:2, 3, 19; Ex 20:11; 31:17; De 5:14; Heb 4:4, 10); seeing (Ge 18:21; Ex 14:24; Ps 94:9); sleeping (Ps 44:23; 78:65; 121:4); speaking (Ge 18:33; Nu 11:25; Ps 33:6); standing (Ps 35:2); walking (Ge 3:8; Le 26:12; De 23:14; Job 22:14; Hab 3:15).

Affections and Emotions: Amazement (Isa 59:16; 63:5; M'k 6:6); grief (Ge 6:6; J'g 10:16; Ps 95:10; Heb 3:10, 17); jealousy (Ex 20:5; 34:13, 14; Nu 25:11; De 29:20; 32:16, 21; 1Ki 14:22; Ps 78:58;

79:5; Isa 30:1, 2; 31:1, 3; Eze 16:42; 23:25; 36:5, 6; 38:19; Zep 1:18; 3:8; Zec 1:14; 8:2; 1Co 10:22); swearing an oath (Isa 62:8; Heb 6:16, 17; 7:21, 28). See Oaths; Anger of God.

ANTICHRIST (M't 24:5, 23, 24, 26; M'k 13:6, 21, 22; Lu 21:8; 2Th 2:3-12; 1Jo 2:18, 22; 4:3; 2Jo 7). To be destroyed (Re 19:20; 20:10, 15).

ANTI-LEBANON (See Lebanon.)

ANTIOCH. 1. A city of Syria. Disciples first called Christians in (Ac 11:19-30). Church in (Ac 13:1; 14:26, 27). Barnabas and Paul make second visit to (Ac 14:26-28). Dissension in church of (Ac 15:22, w verses 1-35). Paul and Peter's controversy at (Ga 2:11-15).

2. A city of Pisidia. Persecutes Paul (Ac 13:14-52; Ac 14:19-22; 18:22; 2Ti 3:11).

ANTIOCHUS (withstander). 1. Antiochus III, the Great (223-187 B. C.), king of Syria; gained control of Palestine in 198 B. C.

2. Antiochus IV (Epiphanes), son of Antiochus III (175-163 B.C.); his attempt to Hellenize the Jews led to the Maccabean revolt.

3. Antiochus V (Eupator), son of the above; after a brief reign he was slain.

ANTIPAS, a contraction of Antipater. 1. An early Christian martyr of Pergamum (Re 2:13).

2. Herod Antipas, son of Herod the Great, he ruled Galilee and Perea from 4 B. C. to A. D. 39. See Herod.

ANTIPATER (See Herod.)

ANTIPATRIS, a city in Samaria (Ac 23:31).

ANTITYPE, that which is represented by a type.

ANTONIA, TOWER OF, a fortress castle connected with the Temple at Jerusalem, built by Herod the Great. It was garrisoned by Roman soldiers who watched the temple area (Ac 21:30ff).

ANTOTHIJAH, son of Shashak, a Benjamite (1Ch 8:24, 25).

ANTOTHITE, inhabitant of Anathoth (1Ch 11:28; 12:3).

ANUB, son of Coz of the tribe of Judah (1Ch 4:8).

ANVIL, the word occurs in several senses in the OT; only once with the meaning of "anvil" (Isa 41:7).

ANXIETY. Forbidden (M't 6:25-34; Lu 12:11, 12, 22-28; 1Co 7:32; Ph'p 4:6; 1Pe 5:7).

Unavailing (Ps 39:6; 127:6; M't 6:27; Lu 12:25, 26). Proceeds from unbelief (M't 6:26, 28-30; Lu 12:24, 27, 28). Martha rebuked for (Lu 10:40, 41).

Remedy for (Ps 37:5; 55:22; Heb 13:5; 1Pe 5:6, 7).

See Care, Worldly.

APE, in Solomon's zoological collections (1Ki 10:22; 2Ch 9:21).

APELLES, a disciple in Rome (Ro 16:10).

APHARSACHITES, Ezr 5:6; 6:6.

APHARSATHCHITES, colonists in Samaria who protested to Darius against the rebuilding of the Temple in Jerusalem (Ezr 4:9; 5:6; 6:6).

APHARSITES, Samaritans who protested the rebuilding of the Temple in Jerusalem (Ezr 4:9).

APHEK (strength, fortress). 1. A city of the tribe of Asher (Jos 19:30). Called Aphik (J'g 1:31).

2. A city of the tribe of Issachar. Philistines defeat Israelites at (1Sa 4:1-11). Saul slain at (1Sa 29:1, w chapter 31). Probably the same mentioned in Jos 12:18 as a royal city of the Canaanites.

3. A city between Damascus and Palestine. Benhadad defeated at (1Ki 20:26-30).

APHEKAH, a city in the mountains of Judah (Jos 15:53).

APHIAH, ancestor of Saul (1Sa 9:1).

APHIK (See Aphek.)

APHRAH, a city (Mic 1:10). Perhaps identical with Ophrah (1Ch 4:14).

APHSES, a governor of the temple (1Ch 24:15).

APOCALYPSE (See Apocalyptic Literature.)

APOCALYPTIC LITERATURE. There are two types, canonical and uncanonical. The first includes Daniel and Revelation which give revelations of the secret purposes of God, the end of the world, and the establishment of God's Kingdom on earth. The second appeared between c. 200 B. C. and A. D. 200 and also purports to give revelations of the last times, the salvation of Israel, the last judgment, and the hereafter. Outstanding apocalypses are I Enoch, Jubilees, Assumption of Moses, Second Esdras, Apocalypse of Baruch, Second Enoch. The Testaments of the Twelve Prophets, the Psalms of Solomon (17th and 18th), and the Sibylline Oracles are also usually included in a discussion of apocalyptic literature. Certain characteristics mark them. They deal with the future; imitate the visions of the prophets; are written under the names of OT worthies; use symbolism; are Messianic.

APOCRYPHA (hidden, spurious). Books and chapters interspersed among the canonical books of the OT in the Vulgate, but not found in the Hebrew OT. The Roman Catholic Church received as canonical at the Council of Trent (1546) all of these books except I and II Esdras and the Prayer of Manasseh. From the time of Luther Protestants have rejected their canonicity. They include: I and II Esdras, Tobit, Judith, Additions to the Book of Esther, The Wisdom of Solomon, Ecclesiasticus, Baruch, Epistle of Jeremiah. The Prayer of Azariah and the Song of the Three Young Men, Susanna, Bel and the Dragon, The Prayer of Manasseh, I and II Maccabees.

APOLLONIA, a city of Macedonia (Ac 17:1).

APOLLOS. An eloquent Christian convert at Corinth (Ac 18:24-28; 19:1; 1Co 1:12; 3:4-7). Refuses to return to Rome (1Co 16:12). Paul writes Titus about (Tit 3:13).

APOLLYON, angel of the bottomless pit (Re 9:11).

APOSTASY. Described (De 13:13, 32; 32:15; Isa 65:11, 12; M't 12:45; Lu 11:24-26; Ac 7:39-43; 1Ti 4:1-3; 2Ti 3:6-9; 4:3, 4; Heb 3:12; 2Pe 2:15-22; Jude 8). Foretold (M't 24:12; 2Th 2:3; 1Ti 4:1-3; 2Ti 3:1-9; 4:3, 4; 2Pe 2:1).

Admonitions against (M't 24:4, 5; M'k 13:5, 6; Heb 3:12; 2Pe 3:17; 2Jo 8; Jude 4-6).

Caused by persecution (M't 13:20, 21; 24:9-12; M'k 4:5-17; Lu 8:13); by worldliness (2Ti 4:10). No remedy for (Heb 6:4-8; 10:26-29). Punishment (1Ch 28:9; Isa 1:28; 65:12-15; Jer 17:5, 6; Eze 3:20; 18:24, 26; 33:12, 13, 18; Zep 1:4-6; Joh 15:6; 2Th 2:11, 12; Heb 10:25-31, 38, 39; 2Pe 2:17, 20-22; Jude 6).

Instances of: Israelites (Ex 32; Nu 14; Ac 7:39-43); Saul (1Sa 15:26-29; 18:12; 28:15, 18); Amaziah (2Ch 25:14, 27); disciples (Joh 6:66); Judas (M't 26:14-16; 27:3-5; M'k 14:10, 11; Lu 22:3-6, 47, 48; Ac 1:16-18); Hymanaeus and Alexander (1Ti 1:19, 20); Phygellus and Hermogenes (2Ti 1:15).

See Antichrist; Backsliding; Backsliding of Israel; Backsliders; Reprobacy; Reprobates.

APOSTATES. Described (De 13:13; Heb 3:12). Persecution tends to make (M't 24:9, 10; Lu 8:13). A worldly spirit tends to make (2Ti 4:10). Never belonged to Christ (1Jo 2:19). Saints do not become (Ps 44:18, 19; Heb 6:9; 10:39). It is impossible to restore (Heb 6:4-6). Guilt and punishment of (Zep 1:4-6; Heb 10:25-31, 39; 2Pe 2:17, 20-22). Cautions against becoming (Heb 3:12; 2Pe 3:17). Shall abound in the latter days (M't 24:12; 2Th 2:3; 1Ti 4:1-3). Exemplified. *Amaziah* (2Ch 25:14, 27). *Professed disciples* (Joh 6:66). *Hymenaeus and Alexander* (1Ti 1:19, 20).

APOSTLE, an appellation of Jesus (Heb 3:1).

APOSTLES. A title distinguishing the twelve disciples, whom Jesus selected to be intimately associated with himself (Lu 6:13).

Names of: Now the names of the twelve apostles are these; The first, Simon, who is called Peter, and Andrew his brother; James *the son* of Zebedee, and John his brother; Philip, and Bartholomew; Thomas, and Matthew the publican; James *the son* of Alphaeus, and Lebbaeus, whose surname was Thaddaeus; Simon the Canaanite, and Judas Iscariot, who also betrayed him (M't 10:2-4; See M'k 3:16-19; Lu 6:13-16; Ac 1:13, 26).

Selection of (M't 4:18-22; 9:9, 10; 10:2-4; M'k 3:13-19; Lu 6:13-16; Joh 1:43).

Commission of (M't 10; 28:19, 20; M'k 3:14, 15; 6:7-11; 16:15; Lu 9:1-5; 22:28-30; Joh 20:23; 21:15-19; Ac 1; 2; 10:42). Unlearned (M't 11:25; Ac 4:13). Miraculous power given to (M't 10:1; M'k 3:15; 6:7; 16:17; Lu 9:1, 2; 10:9, 17; Ac 2:4, 43; 5:12-16; 1Co 14:18; 2Co 12:12). Authority of (See Commission of, above, and M't 16:19; 18:18; 19:28).

Inspiration of (M't 10:27; 16:17-19; Lu 24:45; Ac 1:2; 13:9). Duties of (See Commission of, above and Lu 24:48; Joh 15:27; Ac 1:8, 21, 22; 2:32; 3:15; 4:33; 5:32; 10:39-41; 13:31; 2Pe 1:16, 18; 1Jo 1:1-3). See Ministers.

Moral state of, before Pentecost (M't 17:17; 18:3; 20:20-22; Lu 9:54, 55). Slow to receive Jesus, as Messiah (M't 14:33). Forsake Jesus (M'k 14:50).

Fail to comprehend the nature and mission of Jesus, and the nature of the kingdom he came to establish (M't 8:25-27; 15:23; 16:8-12, 21, 22; 19:25; M'k 4:13; 6:51, 52; 8:17, 18; 9:9, 10, 31, 32; 10:13, 14; Lu 9:44, 45; 18:34; 24:19, 21; Joh 4:32, 33; 10:6; 11:12, 13; 12:16; 13:6-8; 14:5-9, 22; 16:6, 17, 18, 32; 20:9; 21:12; Ac 1:6).

See Barnabas; Matthias; Ministers; Paul.

False: 2Co 11:13; Re 2:2.

See Teachers, False.

APOSTROPHE, to death and the grave (Ho 13:14; 1Co 15:55).

APOTHECARY, a compounder of drugs (Ex 30:25, 35; 37:29; 2Ch 16:14; Ne 3:8). Ointment of (Ec 10:1).

APPAIM, son of Nadab (1Ch 2:30, 31).

APPAREL (See Dress.)

APPEAL. Paul makes, to Caesar (Ac 25:10, 11, 21-27; 26:32; 28:19).

See Change of Venue; Courts, Superior and Inferior.

APPEAL TO GOD, to witness (Ge 31:50; De 30:19; J'g 11:10; 1Sa 12:5; Job 16:19; Ro 1:9; 2Co 1:23; Ph'p 1:8; 1Th 2:5).

APPEARANCES of God to men (Ge 12:7; 17:1; 18:1; 26:2; 35:9; Ex 3:16; 1Ki 3:5; 9:2; 2Ch 3:1).

APPEARING (See Eschatology.)

APPELLATIO, the judicial process of appealing to a higher magistrate, as Paul did in Festus' court (Ac 25:1-12).

APPETITE. Kept in subjection (Pr 23:1, 2; Da 1:8-16; 1Co 9:27).

See Temperance.

APPHIA, a Christian at Colosse (Ph'm 2).

APPIAN WAY, an ancient Roman road on which Paul traveled (Ac 28:13-16).

APPII FORUM, a market town in Italy (Ac 28:15).

APPIUS, MARKET OF (See Appii Forum.)

APPLE, a fruit (Pr 25:11; Song 2:3, 5; 7:8; 8:5; Joe 1:12).

APPLE OF THE EYE, the eyeball; symbolizing that which is precious and protected (De 32:10; Ps 17:8; Pr 7:2; La 2:18; Zec 2:8).

APRON (See Dress.)

AQABAH, GULF OF, the eastern arm of the Red Sea, where Solomon's seaport was located (1Ki 9:26).

AQUEDUCT, a channel made of stone to convey water to places where the water is to be used. Many fine Roman aqueducts survive.

AQUILA (eagle), a Jewish Christian, a tentmaker by trade, who with his wife Priscilla labored with Paul at Corinth and was of help to Apollos and many others (Ac 18:2, 18, 26; Ro 16:3, 4; 1Co 16:19; 2Ti 4:19).

AR, a city of Moab (Nu 21:15; De 2:9, 18, 24, 29). Destruction of (Nu 21:26-30; Isa 15:1).

ARA, son of Jether (1Ch 7:38).

ARAB, a city of Judah (Jos 15:52).

ARABAH (desert plain), name applying to the rift running from Mt. Hermon to the Gulf of Aqabah. It is a narrow valley of varying breadth and productivity. The Israelites made stops there in their wilderness wanderings, and Solomon got iron and copper from its mines (De 1:1, 7; 11:30; Jos 3:16; 1Sa 23:24; Jer 39:4).

ARABIA (steppe). Tributary to Solomon (2Ch 9:14), and Jehoshaphat (2Ch 17:11). Exports of (Eze 27:21). Prophecies against (Isa 21:13; Jer 25:24). Paul visits (Ga 1:17).

ARABIANS. Pay tribute to Solomon (2Ch 9:14); to Jehoshaphat (2Ch 17:11). Invade and defeat Judah (2Ch 21:16, 17; 22:1). Defeated by Uzziah (2Ch 26:7). Oppose Nehemiah's rebuilding the walls of Jerusalem (Ne 2:19; 4:7). Commerce of (Eze 27:21). Gospel preached to (Ac 2:11; Ga 1:17). Prophecies concerning (Isa 21:13-17; 42:11; 60:7; Jer 25:24).

ARAD. 1. A city on the S. of Canaan (Nu 21:1; 33:40). Subdued by Joshua (Jos 12:14; J'g 1:16).

2. Son of Beriah (1Ch 8:15).

ARAH. 1. An Asherite (1Ch 7:39).

2. Father of a family that returned from exile (Ezr 2:5; Ne 7:10).

3. Jew whose granddaughter became

the wife of Tobiah the Ammonite (Ne 6:18).

ARAM. 1. Son of Shem (Ge 10:22, 23).

2. Son of Kemuel, Abraham's nephew (Ge 22:21).

3. An Asherite (1Ch 7:34).

4. In KJV, for the Greek form of Ram (M't 1:3, 4, ASV, RSV), called Arni in ASV, RSV of Lu 3:33.

5. Place in Gilead (1Ch 2:23).

6. The name of Syria (Nu 23:7), and usually so designated (2Sa 8:5; 1Ki 20:20; Am 1:5). The Aramaean people spread from Phoenicia to the Fertile Crescent, and were closely related to Israel, with whom their history was intertwined.

ARAMAIC, a Semitic language, closely related to Hebrew, which developed various dialects and spread to all of SW Asia. Aramaic portions in the OT are (Da 2:4-7:28; Ezr 4:8-6:18; 7:12-26; Jer 10:11). Aramaic words occur in the NT (M'k 5:41; 15:34; M't 27:46; Ro 8:15; Ga 4:6; 1Co 16:22). Aramaic was the colloquial language of Palestine from the time of the return from the exile.

ARAN, son of Dishan (Ge 36:28; 1Ch 1:42).

ARARAT, name applied to Armenia (2Ki 19:37; Isa 37:38) and to its mountain range (Ge 8:4). Noah's ark is supposed to have rested on Mt. Ararat (Ge 8:4). The region is now part of Turkey.

ARATUS, Greek poet from whom Paul quotes in Ac 17:28. He lived c. 270 B.C.

ARAUNAH. A Jebusite from whom David bought a site for an altar (2Sa 24:16-24). Called also Ornan (1Ch 21:15-25).

ARBA, giant ancestor of Anak (Jos 14:15; 15:13; 21:11).

ARBATHITE, a native of Beth-arabah (2Sa 23:31; 1Ch 11:32).

ARBITE, one of David's mighty men (2Sa 23:35).

ARBITRATION. *Instances of:* The two harlots before Solomon (1Ki 3:16-28). Urged by Paul, as a mode of action for Christians (1Co 6:1-8).

See Court.

ARCH (See Architecture.)

ARCHAEOLOGY. Study of the material remains of the past by excavating ancient buried cities and examining their remains, deciphering inscriptions, and evaluating the language, literature, art, architecture, monuments, and other aspects of human life and achievement. Biblical archaeology is concerned with Palestine and the countries with which the Hebrews and early Christians came into contact. Modern archaeology began with Napoleon's expedition to Egypt, on which many scholars accompanied him to study Egyptian monuments (1798), and with the work of Edward Robinson in Palestine (1838, 1852). Discoveries of great importance which throw much light upon the Patriarchal Period are the Mari Tablets, the Nuzi Tablets, the Tell-el Amarna Tablets, and the Ras Shamra Tablets. The discovery of the Dead Sea Scrolls and the excavation of Qumran are the most recent archaeological finds of importance. Archaeology is of great help in better understanding the Bible, in dealing with critical questions regarding the Bible, and in gaining an appreciation of the ancient world.

ARCHANGEL (1Th 4:16; Jude 9). See Angel.

ARCHELAUS, son of Herod the Great; he ruled over Judea, Samaria, and Idumea from 4 B. C. to A. D. 6 (M't 2:22).

ARCHERS, hunters or warriors with bow and arrow, weapons universally used in ancient times (Ge 21:20; J'g 5:11; 1Sa 20:17-42; Isa 21:17). "Arrow" is often used figuratively (Job 6:4; Jer 9:8), as is also "bow" (Ps 7:12; 64:3).

ARCHERY. Practiced by Ishmael (Ge 21:20); Esau (Ge 27:3); Jonathan (1Sa 20:20, 36, 37); sons of Ulam (1Ch 8:40); Philistines (1Sa 31:1-3; 1Ch 10:3); Persians (Isa 13:17, 18); people of Kedar (Isa 21:17); Syrians (1Ki 22:31-34); Israelites (2Sa 1:18; 1Ch 5:18; 12:2; 2Ch 14:8; 26:14; Ne 4:13; Zec 9:13); Lydians (Jer 46:9).

In war (Ge 49:23; J'g 5:11; 1Sa 31:3; Isa 22:3; Jer 4:29; 5:3; Zec 10:4).

See Arrow; Armies; Bow; War.

ARCHEVITES, colonists in Samaria who complained to the king of Persia about the Jews' rebuilding of Jerusalem (Ezr 4:9).

ARCHI, perhaps the name of a clan in Ephraim (Jos 16:2).

ARCHIPPUS (master of the horse), an

office bearer in the church at Colosse (Col 4:17; Ph'm 2).

ARCHITE, member of a clan in Ephraim (Jos 16:2; 1Ch 27:33).

ARCHITECTURE. The materials of architecture in antiquity were wood, clay, brick (formed of clay, whether sun-baked or kiln-fired), and stone. The determining factor in the choice of material used was local availability. The homes of the poor had no artistic distinction. The wealthy and the nobility, however, adorned their palatial homes ornately with gold and ivory. Architectural remains—temples, city gates, arches, ziggurats, pyramids—survive intact in great abundance, and archaeology has uncovered the foundations of countless buildings. Each country had its own distinctive style of architecture. No architecture has surpassed that of Greece, although the temple of Solomon and the one rebuilt by Herod were universally admired.

ARCTURUS, constellation of (Job 9:9; 38:32).

ARD. 1. Son of Benjamin (Ge 46:21).

2. Son of Bela (Nu 26:40).

ARDITE, descendant of Ard (Nu 26:40).

ARDON, son of Caleb (1Ch 2:18).

ARELI, founder of the Arelite tribal family (Ge 46:16; Nu 26:17).

AREOPAGITE, a member of the Areopagus (Ac 17:34).

AREOPAGUS (hill of Ares). 1. The rocky hill of the Greek god of war Ares on the Acropolis at Athens.

2. The name of a council which met on Mars' Hill. In NT times it was primarily concerned with morals and education. Paul was brought before it (Ac 17:19).

ARETAS (virtuous), a Nabataean king, father-in-law of Herod Antipas (2Co 11:32).

ARGOB (heap, region of clods). 1. A region in Bashan taken by the Israelites under Moses (De 3:4) and given to the half-tribe of Manasseh (De 3:13).

2. 2Ki 15:25 refers either to a place or a person. The Heb. text is uncertain.

ARIDAI, son of Haman killed by the Jews (Es 9:9).

ARIDATHA, another son of Haman killed by the Jews (Es 9:8).

ARIEH, either a person or a place. The text is uncertain (2Ki 15:25).

ARIEL (lion of God). 1. Leader under Ezra (Ezr 8:16, 17).

2. In 2Sa 23:20 and 1Ch 11:22 the KJV, ASV, and RSV have varying readings because of the uncertainty of the text.

3. Figurative name for Jerusalem (Isa 29:1, 2, 7).

ARIMATHEA, home of Joseph who buried Jesus in his own tomb (M't 27:57; M'k 15:43; Lu 23:51; Joh 19:38). Its location is in doubt, but it is conjectured to be Ramathaim-zophim, c. 20 miles NW of Jerusalem.

ARIOCH. 1. King of Ellasar (Ge 14:1, 9).

2. Captain of Nebuchadnezzar's guard (Da 2:14, 15, 24, 25).

ARISAI, son of Haman (Es 9:9).

ARISTARCHUS (best ruler), a Thessalonian traveling companion of Paul (Ac 19:29; 20:4; 27:2; Col 4:10; Ph'm 24).

ARISTOBULUS (best counselor), a Roman Christian greeted by Paul (Ro 16:10).

ARK. Noah's. Directions for building of (Ge 6:14-16). Noah and family preserved in (Ge 6:18; 7:8; M't 24:38; Heb 11:7; 1Pe 3:20). Animals saved in (Ge 6:19, 20; 7:1-16).

ARK, of bulrushes (Ex 2:3).

ARK OF THE COVENANT, THE. Dimensions of (Ex 25:10; 37:1). Entirely covered with gold (Ex 25:11; 37:2). Surrounded with a crown of gold (Ex 25:11). Furnished with rings and staves (Ex 25:12-15; 37:3-5). Tables of testimony alone placed in (Ex 25:16, 21; 1Ki 8:9, 21; 2Ch 5:10; Heb 9:4). Mercy-seat laid upon (Ex 25:21; 26:34). Placed in the Holy of Holies (Ex 26:33; 40:21; Heb 9:3, 4). The pot of manna and Aaron's rod laid up before (Heb 9:4 w Ex 16:33, 34; Nu 17:10). A copy of the law laid in the side of (De 31:26). Anointed with sacred oil (Ex 30:26). Covered with the veil by the priests before removal (Nu 4:5, 6).

Was Called the: Ark of God (1Sa 3:3). Ark of God's strength (2Ch 6:41; Ps 132:8). Ark of the covenant of the Lord (Nu 10:33). Ark of the testimony (Ex 30:6; Nu 7:89). A symbol of the presence and glory of God (Nu 14:43, 44; Jos 7:6; 1Sa 14:18, 19; Ps 132:8). Esteemed the glory of Israel (1Sa 4:21, 22). Was holy

(2Ch 35:3). Sanctified its resting-place (2Ch 8:11). The Israelites inquired of the Lord before (Jos 7:6-9; J'g 20:27; 1Ch 13:3).

Was Carried: By priests or Levites alone (De 10:8; Jos 3:14; 2Sa 15:24; 1Ch 15:2). Before the Israelites in their journeys (Nu 10:33; Jos 3:6). Sometimes to the camp in war (1Sa 4:4, 5). Profanation of, punished (Nu 4:5, 15; 1Sa 6:19; 1Ch 15:13). Protecting of, rewarded (1Ch 13:14). Captured by the Philistines (1Sa 4:11).

Miracles Connected With: Jordan divided (Jos 4:7). Fall of the walls of Jericho (Jos 6:6-20). Fall of Dagon (1Sa 5:1-4). Philistines plagued (1Sa 5:6-12). Manner of its restoration (1Sa 6:1-18). At Kirjath-jearim twenty years (1Sa 7:1, 2). Removed from Kirjath-jearim to the house of Obed-edom (2Sa 6:1-11). David made a tent for (2Sa 6:17; 1Ch 15:1). Brought into the city of David (2Sa 6:12-15; 1Ch 15:25-28). Brought by Solomon into the temple with great solemnity (1Ki 8:1-6; 2Ch 5:2-9). A type of Christ (Ps 40:8; Re 11:19).

ARKITES, descendants of Canaan (Ge 10:17; 1Ch 1:15).

ARM. Figurative, of divine providence (Ex 6:6; 15:16; De 4:34; 5:15; 7:19; 9:29; 11:2; 26:8; 33:27; 1Ki 8:42; 2Ki 17:36; 2Ch 6:32; Ps 77:15; 89:10, 13, 21; 98:1; 136:12; Song 2:6; Isa 33:2; 40:10, 11; 51:5, 9; 52:10; 53:1; 59:16; 62:8; 63:5, 12; Jer 21:5; 27:5; 32:17; Eze 20:33; Lu 1:51; Ac 13:17).

See Anthropomorphisms.

ARMAGEDDON (Mount Megiddo), a word found only in Re 16:16, for the final battleground between the forces of good and evil. Located on the S rim of Esdraelon, the scene of many decisive battles in the history of Israel (J'g 5:19, 20; 6:33; 1Sa 31; 2Ki 23:29, 30).

ARMENIA, a region in Western Asia (2Ki 19:37; Jer 51:27). Assassins of Sennacherib take refuge in (Isa 37:38).

ARMIES. Who of the Israelites were subject to service in (Nu 1:2, 3; 26:2; 2Ch 25:5); who were exempt from service in (Nu 1:47-50; 2:33; De 20:5-9; J'g 7:3). Enumeration of Israel's military forces (Nu 1:2, 3; 26:2; 1Sa 11:8; 2Sa 18:1, 2; 24:1-9; 1Ki 20:15; 2Ch 25:5). Levies for (Nu 31:4; J'g 20:10). Compulsory service in (1Sa 14:52). See Cowardice.

How officered: Commander-in-chief (1Sa 14:50; 2Sa 2:8; 8:16; 17:25; 19:13; 20:23); generals of corps and divisions (Nu 2:3-31; 1Ch 27:1-22; 2Ch 17:12-19); captains of thousands (Nu 31:14, 48; 1Sa 17:18; 1Ch 28:1; 2Ch 25:5); of hundreds (Nu 31:14, 48; 2Ki 11:15; 1Ch 28:1; 2Ch 25:5); of fifties (2Ki 1:9; Isa 3:3). See Cavalry; Chariots.

Rendezvous of: Methods employed in effecting: Sounding a trumpet (Nu 10:9; J'g 3:27; 6:34; 1Sa 13:3, 4); cutting oxen in pieces, and sending the pieces throughout Israel (1Sa 11:7). Refusal to obey the summons, instance of (J'g 21:5-11, w J'g 20).

Tactics: Camp and march (Nu 2). March in ranks (Ex 13:18 [marg.]; 1Ch 12:33; Joe 2:7). Move, in attack, in three divisions (J'g 7:16; 9:43; 1Sa 11:11; 13:17, 18; 2Sa 18:2; Job 1:17). Flanks called wings (Isa 8:8). See Strategy.

Orders delivered with trumpets (2Sa 2:28; 18:16; 20:1, 22; Ne 4:18, 20).

Stratagems: Ambushes, at Ai (Jos 8:2-22); Shechem (J'g 9:25, 34); Gibeah (J'g 20:29-43); Zemaraim (2Ch 13:13). By Jehoshaphat (2Ch 20:22). Reconnaissances: Of Jericho (Jos 2:1-24); Ai (Jos 7:2, 3); Beth-el (J'g 1:23, 24); Laish (J'g 18:2-10). Night attacks (Ge 14:15; J'g 7:16-22). Decoy (Jos 8:4-22; J'g 20:29-43; Ne 6). Delay (2Sa 17:7-14). Celerity of action: Abraham, in pursuit of Chedorlaomer (Ge 14:14, 15). Joshua, against the Amorites (Jos 10:6, 9); the confederated kings (Jos 11:7). David's attack upon the Philistines (2Sa 5:23-25). Forced marches (Isa 5:26, 27). Sieges (Jer 39:1); of Jericho (Jos 6); Samaria (2Ki 6:24-33; 7); Jerusalem (2Ki 25:1-3).

"Engines" used (2Ch 26:15; Jer 6:6 [marg.]; Eze 26:9). Fortifications (J'g 9:31; 2Sa 5:9; 2Ki 25:1; 2Ch 11:11; 26:9; Ne 3:8; 4:2; Isa 22:10; 25:12; 29:3; 32:14; Jer 6:6; 32:24; 33:4; 51:53; Eze 4:2; 17:17; 21:22; 26:8; 33:27; Da 11:15, 19; Na 2:1; 3:14).

Standards (Nu 2:2, 3, 10, 17, 18, 25, 31, 34; 10:14, 18, 22, 25). Uniforms of (Eze 23:6, 12; Na 2:3). Standing armies (1Sa 13:2; 1Ch 27; 2Ch 1:14; 17:12-19; 26:11-15).

Religious ceremonies attending: Seeking counsel from God before battle (Nu

27:21; J'g 1:1; 1Sa 14:19, 37-41; 23:2-12; 30:8; 2Sa 2:1; 5:19, 23; 1Ki 22:7-28; 2Ki 3:11-19; 1Ch 14:10, 14; Jer 37:7-10); sacrifices (1Sa 13:11, 12); purifications (Nu 31:19-24); prophets prophesy before (2Ch 20:14-17); holiness enjoined (De 23:9); officers consecrate themselves to God (2Ch 17:16). Army choir and songs (2Ch 20:21, 22). Ark taken to battle (Jos 6:6, 7, 13; 1Sa 4:4-11).

Divine assistance to: When Aaron and Hur held up Moses' hands (Ex 17:11, 12); in siege of Jericho (Jos 6); sun stands still (Jos 10:11-14); Gideon's victory (J'g 7); Samaria's deliverances (1Ki 20; 2Ki 7); Jehoshaphat's victories (2Ki 3; 2Ch 20); angel of the Lord smites the Assyrians (2Ki 19:35).

Determine royal succession (2Sa 2:8-10; 1Ki 16:16; 2Ki 11:4-12).

Composed of insurgents (1Sa 22:1, 2). Mercenaries (2Sa 10:6; 1Ch 19:6, 7; 2Ch 25:5, 6). Confederated (Jos 10:1-5; 11:1-5; J'g 1:3; 2Sa 10:6, 15, 16, 19; 1Ki 15:20; 22:1-4; 2Ki 16:9; 18:19-21; 1Ch 19:6, 7; 2Ch 16:2-9; 18:1, 3; 20:1; 22:5; 28;16, 20; Ps 83:1-12; Isa 7:1-9; 8:9-12; 54:15). Exhorted before battle (De 20:1-9). Battle shouts (J'g 7:18; 1Sa 17:20, 52). Triumphs of, celebrated: With songs (J'g 5; 1Sa 18:6, 7); music (2Ch 20:28); dancing (1Sa 18:6, 7).

Rewards for meritorious conduct: The general offers his daughter in marriage (Jos 15:16, 17); king offers his daughter (1Sa 17:25; 18:17-28), promotion (2Sa 23:8-39; 1Ch 11:6, 10-47); share the spoils (Nu 31:25-47).

Children instructed in military arts (2Sa 1:18).

Insubordination in, punished, Achan (Jos 7). Check roll-call (1Sa 14:17; Nu 31:48, 49).

Panics (Isa 30:17); among the Midianites (J'g 7:21); Philistines (1Sa 14:15-19); Syrians (2Ki 7:7-15). Soldiers destroy each other to escape captivity (1Sa 14:20; 31:4-6).

Champions fight instead of (1Sa 17:8-53; 2Sa 2:14-17; 21:15-22). Confidence in vain (Ps 33:16; 44:6). Escort duty performed by (2Ki 1:9; Ac 23:23, 24, 31-33).

Roman army: Captains [*R.V.* marg.; military tribunes] of (Ac 22:24-29); centurions (M't 8:5, 8; 27:54; Lu 7:2; 23:47; Ac 10:1, 7, 22; 21:32; 22:26; 23:17, 23; 24:23; 27:1, 11, 43; 28:16). Divided into "bands" ([*R.V.* marg., cohorts]. Ac 10:1; 27:1).

For other than armies of the Israelites and Romans, see Amalekites; Assyria; Babylon; Egyptians; Midianites; Persia, Syria.

For commissaries of, see Commissary.

For weapons used, see Armor.

See Ambush; Cavalry; Fort; Garrison; Herald; Hostage; Navy; Reconnaissance; Siege; Soldiers; Spies; Standard; Strategy; Truce; War.

Figurative: De 33:2; 2Ki 6:17; Ps 34:7; 68:17; Re 9:16.

ARMLET, BRACELET, an ornament usually for the upper arm, worn by both men and women (Ex 35:22; Nu 31:50; 2Sa 1:10; Isa 3:20).

ARMONI (belonging to the palace), a son of Saul by his concubine Rizpah, slain by the Gibeonites to satisfy justice (2Sa 21:8-11).

ARMOR. The equipment of a soldier (1Sa 13:22; Jer 46:3, 4; Eph 6:14-17).

Defensive: Helmet (1Sa 17:5, 38; 2Ch 17:17; 26:14; Jer 46:4; Eze 23:24). Breastplate (Re 9:9-17). Coat of mail (1Sa 17:5, 38; 1Ki 22:34; 2Ch 18:33). Greave, protection for the leg (1Sa 17:6). Shield (2Sa 1:21; 8:7; 1Ki 10:16, 17; 14:27; 2Ch 9:16; 26:14; Ne 2:3).

Offensive: Bows (Ge 21:16, 20). Made. of steel [*R.V.* brass] (2Sa 22:35; Job 20:24; Ps 18:34). Of wood (Eze 39:9). David instructed the Israelites in the use of, by writing war song to (2Sa 1:18). Arrows (1Sa 31:3; 2Sa 22:15; 1Ki 22:34; 2Ki 19:32; 2Ch 17:17; Ps 7:13; Isa 22:3; Jer 51:3).

Battle ax (Jer 51:20). Dart, a light javelin (Nu 25:7; 1Sa 18:10; 2Sa 18:14; Job 41:29). Javelin, a heavy lance (Eze 39:9). Used, by Goliath (1Sa 16:6). By Saul (1Sa 18:11; 19:9, 10).

Sling, used for throwing stones (Pr 26:8). David slays Goliath with (1Sa 17:40-50). Dexterous use of (J'g 20:16). Used in war (J'g 20:16; 2Ki 3:25; 2Ch 26:14).

Sword, used by Gideon (J'g 7:20). By Peter (M't 26:51; Joh 18:10). David's army equipped with (1Ch 21:5).

Figurative (Ro 13:12; 2Co 6:7; 10:4; Eph 6:11-17; 1Th 5:8).

ARMOR-BEARER, an attendant who

carried a soldier's equipment. Of Abimelech (J'g 9:54); Jonathan (1Sa 14:6, 7, 12, 14, 17); Saul (1Sa 16:21; 31:6); Goliath (1Sa 17:7); Joab (2Sa 18:15).

ARMORY. A place for the storage of armor (Ne 3:19; Song 4:4; Isa 22:8; 39:2). In different parts of the kingdom (1Ki 10:17; 2Ch 11:12).

See Jerusalem.

Figurative: Jer 50:25.

ARMY. In Israel males (except Levites) were subject to military duty at the age of 20 (Nu 1:3, 17). Army divisions were subdivided into thousands and hundreds, with respective officers (Nu 31:14). Until Israel got its first king it had no standing army, but whenever there was need God raised up men of special ability to save the country from its enemies. Down to the time of Solomon Israel's armies were composed mostly of footmen (1Sa 4:10); later horsemen and chariots were added (2Sa 8:4; 1Ki 10:26, 28, 29). The Roman army was composed of legions divided into cohorts, maniples, and centuries (Ac 10:1; 21:31).

ARNAN, patronymic of a family descended from David (1Ch 3:21).

ARNON. A river emptying into the Dead Sea from the east. Boundary between Moabites and Amorites (Nu 21:13, 14, 26; 22:36; De 2:24, 36; 3:8, 16; Jos 12:1). Fords of (Isa 16:2). Miracles at (Nu 21:14).

AROD, son of Gad (Nu 26:17).

ARODI, descendants of Arod (Ge 46:16).

AROER (poor, naked). 1. A city of the Amorites in the valley of the river Arnon (De 4:48). Conquered by Israelites (De 2:36; 3:12; J'g 11:26). Taken by Hazael (2Ki 10:33).

2. A city built, or, probably more correctly, rebuilt, by the Gadites (Nu 32:34; Jos 13:25). Jephthah smites the Ammonites at (J'g 11:33).

3. A city in Judah (1Sa 30:28). Birthplace of two of David's heroes (1Ch 11:44).

ARPAD, called also Arphad. A fortified city of Syria, perhaps identical with Arvad (2Ki 18:34; 19:13). Idols of (Isa 36:19).

ARPHAD (See Arpad.)

ARPHAXAD, son of Shem (Ge 10:22; 11:10-13; 1Ch 1:17, 18, 24; Lu 3:36).

ARREST. Of Jesus (M't 26:57; M'k 14:46; Lu 22:54; Joh 18:12); apostles (Ac 5:17, 18; 6:12); Paul and Silas (Ac 16:19); Paul (Ac 21:30). Paul authorized to arrest Christians (Ac 9:2).

See Extradition; Prison; Prisoners.

ARROGANCE. Talk no more so exceeding proudly; let *not* arrogancy come out of your mouth: for the LORD *is* a God of knowledge, and by him actions are weighed (1Sa 2:3).

Pride, and arrogancy, and the evil way, and the froward mouth, do I hate (Pr 8:13).

I will cause the arrogancy of the proud to cease, and will lay low the haughtiness of the terrible (Isa 13:11).

See Pride.

ARROWS. Deadly and destructive weapons (Pr 26:18). Called shafts (Isa 49:2). Sharp (Ps 120:4; Isa 5:28). Bright and polished (Isa 49:2; Jer 51:11). Sometimes poisoned (Job 6:4). Carried in a quiver (Ge 27:3; Isa 49:2; Jer 5:16; La 3:13).

Discharged: From a bow (Ps 11:2; Isa 7:24). From engines (2Ch 26:15). At a mark for amusement (1Sa 20:20-22). At the beasts of the earth (Ge 27:3). Against enemies (2Ki 19:32; Jer 50:14). With great force (Nu 24:8; 2Ki 9:24). Fleetness of, alluded to (Zec 9:14). The ancients divined by (Eze 21:21).

Illustrative: Of Christ (Isa 49:2). Of the word of Christ (Ps 45:5). Of God's judgment (De 32:23-42; Ps 7:13; 21:12; 64:7; Eze 5:16). Of severe afflictions (Job 6:4; Ps 38:2). Of bitter words (Ps 64:3). Of slanderous tongues (Jer 9:8). Of false witnesses (Pr 25:18). Of devices of the wicked (Ps 11:2). Of young children (Ps 127:4). Of lightnings (Ps 77:17, 18; Hab 3:11). (Broken), of destruction of power (Ps 76:3). (Falling from the hand), of the paralyzing power (Eze 39:3).

ARSON (Ps 74:7, 8). Law concerning (Ex 22:6).

Instances of: By Samson (J'g 15:4, 5); Absalom (2Sa 14:30); Zimri (1Ki 16:18).

ARTAXERXES. 1. A Persian king, probably identical with Ahasuerus. Prohibits the rebuilding of Jerusalem (Ezr 4:7-24).

2. King of Persia. Decrees of, in behalf of the Jews (Ezr 7; Ne 2; 5:14).

ARTEMAS, a companion of Paul (Tit 3:12).

ARTEMIS, the Greek goddess of hunting, corresponding to the Roman Diana. Her largest and most famous temple was at Ephesus; it was regarded as one of the wonders of the ancient world (Ac 19:23-41).

ARTIFICER (See Occupations.)

ARTILLERY (1Sa 20:40). See Arms.

ARTISANS (See Occupations.)

ARTS AND CRAFTS. Apothecary or perfumer (Ex 30:25, 35). Armorer (1Sa 8:12). Baker (Ge 40:1; 1Sa 8:13). Brick-maker (Ge 11:3; Ex 5:7, 8, 18). Brazier (Ge 4:22; 2Ti 4:14). Blacksmith (Ge 4:22; 1Sa 13:19). Carver (Ex 31:5; 1Ki 6:18). Carpenter (2Sa 5:11; M'k 6:3). Calker (Eze 27:9, 27). Confectioner (1Sa 8:13). Dyer (Ex 25:5). Embroiderer (Ex 35:35; 38:23). Embalmer (Ge 50:2, 3, 26). Engraver (Ex 28:11; Isa 49:16; 2Co 3:7). Founder (J'g 17:4; Jer 10:9). Fuller (2Ki 18:17; M'k 9:3). Gardener (Jer 29:5; Joh 20:15). Goldsmith (Isa 40:19). Husbandman (Ge 4:2; 9:20). Mariner (Eze 27:8, 9). Mason (2Sa 5:11; 2Ch 24:12). Musician (1Sa 18:6; 1Ch 15:16). Potter (Isa 64:8; Jer 18:3; La 4:2; Zec 11:13). Refiner of metals (1Ch 28:18; Mal 3:2, 3). Ropemaker (J'g 16:11). Silversmith (Ac 19:24). Stonecutter (Ex 20:25; 1Ch 22:15). Ship-builder (1Ki 9:26). Smelter of metals (Job 28:2). Spinner (Ex 35:25; Pr 31:19). Tailor (Ex 28:3). Tanner (Ac 9:43; 10:6). Tent-maker (Ge 4:20; Ac 18:3). Weaver (Ex 35:35; Joh 19:23). Wine-maker (Ne 13:15; Isa 63:3). Writer (J'g 5:14).

ARUBOTH, a district laid under tribute to Solomon's commissariat (1Ki 4:10).

ARUMAH, place near Shechem where Abimelech lived (J'g 9:41).

ARVAD, island off the coast of Phoenicia (Eze 27:8, 11). Its people were descended from Ham (Ge 10:18).

ARVADITES, descendants of Canaan (Ge 10:18; 1Ch 1:16; Eze 27:8, 11).

ARZA, a steward of Elah (1Ki 16:9).

ASA (healer). 1. King of Judah (1Ki 15:8-24; 1Ch 3:10; 2Ch 14; 15; 16; M't 1:7).

2. A Levite (1Ch 9:16).

ASADIAH, ancestor of Baruch (Baruch 1:1).

ASAHEL (whom God made). Nephew of David, and one of his captains (2Sa 2:18-24, 32; 3:27; 23:24; 1Ch 2:16; 11:26; 27:7).

2. A Levite, commissioned by Jehoshaphat to teach the law to Judah (2Ch 17:8).

3. A Levite, who had charge of tithes (2Ch 31:13).

4. Father of Jonathan (Ezr 10:15).

ASAHIAH (whom Jehovah made), an officer of King Josiah (2Ki 22:12-20; 2Ch 34:20-28).

ASAIAH (whom Jehovah made). 1. A Simeonite (1Ch 4:36).

2. Levite in the time of David (1Ch 6:30).

3. A Shilonite (1Ch 9:5).

4. Chief Levite in David's day who helped bring the ark to Jerusalem (1Ch 15:6, 11).

ASAPH. 1. Father of Joah (2Ki 18:18; Isa 36:3, 22).

2. Son of Berachiah. One of the three leaders of music in David's organization of the tabernacle service (1Ch 15:16-19; 16:5-7; 25:1-9; 2Ch 5:12; 35:15; Ne 12:46). Appointed to sound the cymbals in the temple choir (1Ch 15:17, 19; 16:5, 7). A composer of sacred lyrics (2Ch 29:13-30). See titles of Ps 50 and 73-83, inclusive. Descendants of, in the temple choir (1Ch 25:1-9; 2Ch 20:14; 29:13; Ezr 2:41; 3:10; Ne 7:44; 11:22).

3. A Levite, whose descendants dwelt in Jerusalem after the exile (1Ch 9:15).

4. A Kohath Levite (1Ch 26:1).

5. Keeper of forests (Ne 2:8).

ASAREEL, son of Jehaleleel (1Ch 4:16).

ASARELAH. One of the temple choir (1Ch 25:2, 14); probably identical with Azareel.

ASCENSION OF CHRIST, THE. Prophecies respecting (Ps 24:7; 68:18, w Eph 4:7, 8). Foretold by Himself (Joh 6:62; 7:33; 14:28; 16:5; 20:17). Forty days after His resurrection (Ac 1:3). Described (Ac 1:9). From Mount Olivet (Lu 24:50; w M'k 11:1; Ac 1:12). While blessing His disciples (Lu 24:50). When He had atoned for sin (Heb 9:12; 10:12). Was triumphant (Ps 68:18). Was to supreme power and dignity (Lu 24:26; Eph 1:20, 21; 1Pe 3:22). As the Forerunner of His people (Heb 6:20). To intercede (Ro 8:34; Heb 9:24). To send the Holy Ghost (Joh 16:7; Ac 2:33). To receive gifts for men (Ps 68:18, w Eph 4:8-11). To prepare a place for His people (Joh 14:2). His second coming shall be in like manner as (Ac 1:10, 11).

Typified: Le 16:15 with Heb 6:20; Heb 9:7, 9, 12.

ASCETICISM, a philosophy that leads to severe austerities in subordinating the body to the control of the moral attributes of the mind. Extreme application of, rebuked by Jesus (M't 11:19; Lu 7:34); by Paul (Col 2:20-23; 1Ti 4:1-4, 8).

See Stoicism.

Instances of the practice of: John the Baptist (M't 11:18; Lu 7:33). Those who practiced celibacy "for the kingdom of heaven's sake" (M't 19:12).

ASENATH, wife of Joseph and mother of Manasseh and Ephraim (Ge 41:45, 50; 46:20).

ASER (See Asher.)

ASH, a tree (Isa 44:14).

ASHAN, a Levitical city of Judah, later of Simeon (Jos 15:42; 19:7; 1Ch 4:32; 6:59).

See Ain.

ASHBEA, a descendant of Shelah (1Ch 4:21).

ASHBEL, son of Benjamin (Ge 46:21; Nu 26:38; 1Ch 8:1).

ASHCHENAZ (See Ashkenaz.)

ASHDOD (stronghold). A city of the Philistines (Jos 13:3; 1Sa 6:17; Am 3:9). Anakim inhabit (Jos 11:22). Assigned to Judah (Jos 15:47). Dagon's temple in, in which was deposited the ark (1Sa 5). Conquest of, by Uzziah (2Ch 26:6); by Tartan (Isa 20:1). People of, conspire against the Jews (Ne 4:7, 8). Jews intermarry with (Ne 13:23, 24). Prophecies concerning (Jer 25:20; Am 1:8; 3; Zep 2:4; Zec 9:6). Called Azotus (Ac 8:40).

ASHDODITES (people of Ashdod).

ASHDOTH-PISGAH, the water courses flowing from Mount Pisgah (De 3:17; 4:49; Jos 12:3; 13:20).

ASHER (happy). 1. Son of Jacob, by Zilpah (Ge 30:13; 35:26; 49:20; Ex 1:4; 1Ch 2:2). Descendants of (Ge 46:17; Nu 26:44-47).

2. Tribe of: Census of, by families (Nu 1:40, 41; 26:44-47; 1Ch 7:40; 12:36). Station of, in camp (Nu 2:25, 27). Prophecies concerning by Moses (De 33:24, 25); by John (Re 7:6). Allotment to, of land in Canaan (Jos 19:24-31; Eze 48:2). Upbraided by Deborah (J'g 5:17). Summoned by Gideon (J'g 6:35; 7:23). Join Hezekiah (2Ch 30:11).

3. A city of Shechem (Jos 17:7; 1Ki 4:16).

ASHERAH. 1. Canaanite goddess.

2. Images of the goddess Asherah, whose worship was lewd (Ex 34:13; 1Ki 16:29-33).

ASHES. Uses of, in purification (Nu 19:9, 10, 17; Heb 9:13). A symbol of mourning (2Sa 13:19; Es 4:1, 3). Sitting in (Job 2:8; Isa 58:5; Jer 6:26; Eze 27:30; Jon 3:6; Lu 10:13). Repenting in (Job 42:6; Da 9:3; Jon 3:6; M't 11:21; Lu 10:13). Disguises of (1Ki 20:38, 41).

ASHIMA, an idol (2Ki 17:30).

ASHKELON, called also Askelon. One of the five chief cities of the Philistines (Jos 13:3). Captured by the people of Judah (J'g 1:18). Samson slays thirty men of (J'g 14:19). Emerods (tumors, *R.V.*) of (1Sa 6:17). Prophecies concerning (Jer 25:20; 47:5, 7; Am 1:8; Zep 2:4, 7; Zec 9:5).

ASHKENAZ, called also Ashchenaz. Son of Gomer (Ge 10:3; 1Ch 1:6). Descendants of (Jer 51:27).

ASHNAH, name of two towns in Judah (Jos 15:33, 43).

ASHPENAZ, a prince in Nebuchadnezzar's court (Da 1:3).

ASHRIEL (See Asriel.)

ASHTAROTH. 1. Plural form of Ashtoreth, which see.

2. The capital city of Bashan (De 1:4; Jos 9:10). Giants dwell at (Jos 12:4). Allotted to Manasseh (Jos 13:31; 1Ch 6:71). Possibly identical with Ashteroth Karnaim, mentioned in Ge 14:5).

ASHTEROTH KARNAIM, an ancient city of Palestine taken by Chedorlaomer (Ge 14:5).

ASHTORETH. An idol of the Philistines, Zidonians, and Phenicians. Probably identical with queen of heaven (Jer 7:18). Worshipped by Israelites (J'g 2:13; 10:6; 1Sa 7:3, 4; 12:10; 1Ki 11:5, 33; 2Ki 23:13). Temple of (1Sa 31:10). High places of, at Jerusalem, destroyed (2Ki 23:13).

ASHUR, son of Hezron (1Ch 2:24; 4:5).

ASHURBANIPAL (Ashur creates a son), king of Assyria, reigned from 688-626 B. C.; great lover of learning—his library (over 22,000 tablets) survives.

ASHURITES (possibly Geshurites), (2Sa 2:9; Eze 27:6).

ASHURNASIRPAL II, ruthless king of Assyria, reigned early in 9th cent. B. C.

ASHVATH, son of Japhlet (1Ch 7:33).

ASIA. Inhabitants of, in Jerusalem, at Pentecost (Ac 2:9; 21:27; 24:18). Paul and Silas forbidden by the Holy Ghost to preach in (Ac 16:6). Gospel preached in, by Paul (Ac 19; 20:4). Paul leaves (Ac 20:16). Churches of (1Co 16:19; Re 1:4, 11).

ASIARCHS (chiefs of Asia), civil and priestly officials of the Roman province of Asia chosen yearly to preside over the national games and theatrical displays (Ac 19:31).

ASIEL, grandfather of Jehu (1Ch 4:35).

ASKELON (See Ashkelon.)

ASNAH, descendants of, return to Jerusalem (Ezr 2:50).

ASNAPPER, a noble Assyrian prince, who colonized the cities of Samaria after the Israelites were taken captive to Assyria (Ezr 4:10).

See Samaria.

ASP. A venomous serpent (De 32:33; Job 20:14, 16; Isa 11:8; Ro 3:13). Venom of, illustrates the speech of the wicked (Ps 140:3; Ro 3:13); injurious effects of wine (De 32:33; Pr 23:32). Deprived of venom, illustrates conversion (Isa 11:8, 9).

ASPATHA, son of Haman (Es 9:7).

ASPHALTUM (See Slime.)

ASRIEL. 1. Descendant of Manasseh (Nu 26:31; Jos 17:2).

2. Son of Manasseh, Ashriel (1Ch 7:14).

ASS, DOMESTIC. Unclean (Le 11:2, 3, 26, w Ex 13:13).

Described as: Not devoid of instinct (Isa 1:3). Strong (Ge 49:14). Fond of ease (Ge 49:14, 15). Often fed on vine-leaves (Ge 49:11). Formed a part of patriarchal wealth (Ge 12:16; 30:43; Job 1:3; 42:12).

Was Used: In agriculture (Isa 30:6, 24). For bearing burdens (Ge 42:26; 1Sa 25:18). For riding (Ge 22:3; Nu 22:2). In harness (Isa 21:7). In war (2Ki 7:7, 10). Governed by a bridle (Pr 26:3). Urged on with a staff (Nu 22:23, 27). Women often rode on (Jos 15:18; 1Sa 25:20). Persons of rank rode on (J'g 10:3, 4; 2Sa 16:2). Judges of Israel rode on white (J'g 5:10). Young, most valued for labor (Isa 30:6, 24). Trusty persons appointed to take care of (Ge 36:24; 1Sa 9:3; 1Ch 27:30). Often taken unlawfully by corrupt rulers (Nu 16:15; 1Sa 8:16; 12:3). Latterly counted an ignoble creature (Jer 22:19).

Laws Respecting: Not to be coveted (Ex 20:17). Fallen under a burden, to be assisted (Ex 23:5). Astray, to be brought back to its owner (Ex 23:4; De 22:1). Astray, to be taken care of till its owner appeared (De 22:2, 3). Not to be yoked with an ox (De 22:10). To enjoy the rest of the Sabbath (De 5:14). First-born of, if not redeemed, to have its neck broken (Ex 13:13; 34:20). Christ entered Jerusalem on (Zec 9:9; Joh 12:14).

Miracles Connected With: Mouth of Balaam's opened to speak (Nu 22:28; 2Pe 2:16). A thousand men slain by Samson with a jaw-bone of (J'g 15:19). Water brought from the jaw-bone of (J'g 15:19). Not torn by a lion (1Ki 13:28). Eaten during famine in Samaria (2Ki 6:25).

ASS, WILD. Inhabits wild and solitary places (Job 39:6; Isa 32:14; Da 5:21). Ranges the mountains for food (Job 39:8). Brays when hungry (Job 6:5). Suffers in time of scarcity (Jer 14:6).

Described as: Fond of liberty (Job 39:5). Intractable (Job 11:12). Unsocial (Ho 8:9). Despises his pursuers (Job 39:7). Supported by God (Ps 104:10, 11).

Illustrative of: Intractableness of natural man (Job 11:12). The wicked in their pursuit of sin (Job 24:5). Israel in their love of idols (Jer 2:23, 24). The Assyrian power (Ho 8:9). The Ishmaelites (Ge 16:12).

ASSASSINATION. David's abhorrence of (2Sa 4:9-12). Laws prohibiting (De 27:24).

Instances of: Of Eglon, by Ehud (J'g 3:15-22); Abner, by Joab (2Sa 3:27); Ish-bosheth, by the sons of Rimmon (2Sa 4:5-7); Amnon, by Absalom (2Sa 13:28, 29); Amasa, by Joab (2Sa 20:9, 10); Joash, by his servants (2Ki 12:20); Sennacherib, by his sons (2Ki 19:37; Isa 37:38).

ASSAULT AND BATTERY. Laws concerning (Ex 21:15, 18, 19, 22-27; De 17:8-12; M't 5:39; Lu 6:29). Damages and compensation for (Ex 21:18, 19, 22).

The Smiting of Jesus: Prophecies of (Isa 50:6; La 3:30). The attacks upon (M't 26:67; 27:30; M'k 14:65; Lu 22:63; Joh 19:3).

See Stripes; Stoning.

ASSHUR, son of Shem, and ancestor of the Assyrians (Ge 10:11, 22; 1Ch 1:17; Eze 32:22).

See Assyria.

ASSHURIM, descendants of Dedan (Ge 25:3).

ASSIR (captive). 1. Son of Korah (Ex 6:24; 1Ch 6:22).

2. Son of Ebiasaph (1Ch 6:23, 37).

3. Son of Jeconiah (1Ch 3:17).

ASSOCIATION—SEPARATION. Evil, warnings concerning (Ex 23:2; 34:12; Ps 1:1; Pr 4:14; 24:1; 1Co 5:11; 2Co 6:14).

Results of (Nu 33:55; 1Ki 11:2; 2Ch 19:2; Pr 28:7; Joh 18:18; 18:25; 1Co 15:33).

Companionship (Ps 119:63; Pr 2:20; 13:20; 2Th 3:14).

Contact, personal (2Ki 10:15; M't 9:25; M'k 9:27; Ac 3:7; 9:41).

With Christ (M't 9:20; 14:34-36; M'k 3:10; Lu 6:19).

With impurity (Le 5:2; 15:11; Nu 19:13; Isa 52:11; 2Co 6:17; Col 2:21).

Separation, From unclean (Le 13:5, 21, 33, 46; Nu 5:3).

From heathen (Ex 33:16; Le 20:26; Nu 23:9; De 7:2; Jos 23:7; J'g 2:2; Ezr 9:12; 10:11; Jer 15:19).

From evil associations (Isa 52:11; Joh 15:19; Ac 2:40; Eph 5:11; 2Th 3:6).

Final (M't 13:30, 49; 25:32; Lu 16:26; 17:34).

ASSOS, a seaport in Mysia (Ac 20:13, 14).

ASSURANCE. Produced by faith (Eph 3:12; 2Ti 1:12; Heb 10:22). Made full by hope (Heb 6:11, 19). Confirmed by love (1Jo 3:14, 19; 4:18). Is the effect of righteousness (Isa 32:17). Is abundant in the understanding of the gospel (Col 2:2; 1Th 1:5).

Saints Privileged to Have, of: Their election (Ps 4:3; 1Th 1:4). Their redemption (Job 19:25). Their adoption (Ro 8:16; 1Jo 3:2). Their salvation (Isa 12:2). Eternal life (1Jo 5:13). The unalienable love of God (Ro 8:38, 39). Union with God and Christ (1Co 6:15; 2Co 13:5; Eph 5:30; 1Jo 2:5; 4:13). Peace with God by Christ (Ro 5:1). Preservation (Ps 3:6, 8; 27:3-5; 46:3). Answers to prayer (1Jo 3:22; 5:14, 15). Continuance in grace (Ph'p 1:6). Comfort in affliction (Ps 73:26; Lu 4:18, 19; 2Co 4:8-10, 16-18). Support in death (Ps 23:4). A glorious resurrection (Job 19:26; Ps 17:15; Ph'p 3:21; 1Jo 3:2). A kingdom (Heb 12:28; Re 5:10). A crown (2Ti 4:7, 8; Jas 1:12). Give diligence to attain to (2Pe 1:10, 11). Strive to maintain (Heb 3:14, 18). Confident hope in God restores (Ps 42:11). Exemplified. *David* (Ps 23:4; 73:24-26). *Paul* (2Ti 1:12; 4:18).

ASSYRIA. Antiquity and origin of (Ge 10:8-11). Situated beyond the Euphrates (Isa 7:20). Watered by the river Tigris (Ge 2:14).

Called: The land of Nimrod (Mic 5:6). Shinar (Ge 11:2; 14:1). Asshur (Ho 14:3). Nineveh, chief city of (Ge 10:11; 2Ki 19:36). Governed by kings (2Ki 15:19, 29).

Celebrated for: Fertility (2Ki 18:32; Isa 36:17). Extent of conquests (2Ki 18:33-35; 19:11-13; Isa 10:9-14). Extensive commerce (Eze 27:23, 24). Idolatry, the religion of (2Ki 19:37).

As a Power, Was: Most formidable (Isa 28:2). Intolerant and oppressive (Na 3:19). Cruel and destructive (Isa 10:7). Selfish and reserved (Ho 8:9). Unfaithful (2Ch 28:20, 21). Proud and haughty (2Ki 19:22-24; Isa 10:8). An instrument of God's vengeance (Isa 7:18, 19; 10:5, 6). Chief men of, described (Eze 23:6, 12, 23). Armies of, described (Isa 5:26-29).

Invaded Israel (2Ki 15:19). Bought off by Menahem (2Ki 15:19, 20).

Tiglath-pileser King of: Ravaged Israel (2Ki 15:29). Asked to aid Ahaz against Syria (2Ki 16:7, 8). Took money from Ahaz, but did not strengthen him (2Ch 28:20, 21). Conquered Syria (2Ki 16:9).

Shalmaneser King of: Reduced Israel to tribute (2Ki 17:3). Was conspired against by Hoshea (2Ki 17:4). Imprisoned Hoshea (2Ki 17:4). Carried Israel captive (2Ki 17:5, 6). Re-peopled Samaria from Assyria (2Ki 17:24).

Sennacherib King of: Invaded Judah (2Ki 18:13). Bought off by Hezekiah (2Ki 18:14-16). Insulted and threatened Judah (2Ki 18:17-32; 19:10-13). Blasphemed the Lord (2Ki 18:33-35). Prayed against by Hezekiah (2Ki 19:14-19). Reproved for pride and blasphemy (2Ki 12:20-34; Isa 37:21-29). His army destroyed by God (2Ki 19:35). Assassinated by his sons (2Ki 19:36). Condemned for oppressing God's people (Isa 52:4). Manasseh taken captive to (2Ch 33:11). The re-peopling of Samaria from, completed by Asnapper (Ezr 4:10). Idolatry of, brought into Samaria (2Ki 17:29). Judah condemned for trusting to (Jer 2:18, 36). Israel condemned for trusting to (Ho 5:13; 7:11; 8:9). The Jews condemned for following the idolatries of (Eze 16:28; 23:5, 7). The greatness, extent, duration, and fall of, illustrated (Eze 31:3-17).

Predictions Respecting: Conquest of the Kenites by (Nu 24:22). Conquest of Syria by (Isa 8:4). Conquest and captivity of Israel by (Isa 8:4; Ho 9:3; 10:6; 11:5). Invasion of Judah by (Isa 5:26; 7:17-20; 8:8; 10:5, 6, 12). Restoration of Israel from (Isa 27:12, 13; Ho 11:11; Zec 10:10). Destruction of (Isa 10:12-19; 14:24, 25; 30:31-33; 31:8, 9; Zec 10:11). Participation in the blessings of the gospel (Isa 19:23-25; Mic 7:12).

ASTARTE (See Ashtaroth, Ashtoreth.)

ASTONISHMENT, Christ causes (M't 13:54; 15:31; 22:22, 33; M'k 2:12; 4:41; 7:37; 10:24; Lu 2:48; 4:22, 26; 8:25).

ASTROLOGERS, those who try to find out the influence of the stars upon human affairs and of foretelling events by their positions and aspects (Da 2:27; 4:7; 5:7, 11; Isa 47:12, 13).

ASTROLOGY, Isa 47:13; Jer 10:1, 2; Da 1:20; 2:27; 4:7; 5:7.

See Astronomy; Sorcery.

ASTRONOMY. *Phenomena concerning the universe:* God the creator of (Job 9:6-9; 26:7, 13; 37:18; Ps 8:3; 136:5-9; Isa 40:22, 26). God the ruler of (Job 38:31-33; Ps 63:33; Eze 32:7, 8; Am 5:8). Immeasurable (Jer 31:37; 33:22). Laws of, permanent (Ec 1:5; Jer 31:35, 36). Declares God's glory (Ps 19:1-6). Destruction of (Isa 34:4; M't 24:35; 2Pe 3:10; Re 6:12-14; 21:1).

Celestial phenomena: Fire from heaven, on the cities of the plain (Ge 19:24, 25); on the two captains and their fifties (2Ki 1:10-14); on the flocks and servants of Job (Job 1:16). Staying of the sun and moon (Jos 10:12-14). Hail on the Egyptians (Ex 9:22-34). Darkness, on the Egyptians (Ex 10:21-23); at crucifixion of Christ (M't 27:45; Lu 23:44, 45). Pillar of cloud and fire (Ex 13:21, 22; 14:19, 24; 40:38; Nu 9:15-23; Ps 78:14). Thunder and lightning on Mt. Sinai (Ex 19:16, 18; 20:18). Signs in the sun, moon and stars (Joe 2:30, 31; Isa 13:10); foretold by Jesus as part of His second coming (M't 24:29, 35; M'k 13:24, 25; Lu 21:25; Ac 2:19, 20); in the final judgments (Re 8:10-12; 9:1, 2; 10:1, 2; 12:3, 4; 13:13; 16:8, 9; 19:11-14).

Constellations (Isa 13:10); glory of (1Co 15:41); sun seemingly rotating (Ex 1:5); wandering (Jude 3); the serpent (Job 26:13); Orion and Pleides (Job 9:9; 38:31; Am 5:8).

See Constellations; Eclipse; Heaven; Meteorology; Moon; Stars; Sun.

ASUPPIM, storehouses at the S gate of the Temple (1Ch 26:15, 17; Ne 12:25).

ASYNCRITUS, a disciple at Rome (Ro 16:14).

ATAD, the place where the sons of Jacob mourned for their father (Ge 50:10, 11).

ATARAH, wife of Jerahmeel (1Ch 2:26).

ATAROTH (crowns), called also Atroth.
1. A city E of Jordan (Nu 32:3, 34).

2. A city, or possibly two different cities, of Ephraim (Jos 16:2, 5, 7; 18:13).

3. A city of Judah (1Ch 2:54). Called Atrothbeth-Joab.

4. A city of Gad (Nu 32:35).

ATAROTH-ADAR, called also Ataroth-Addar. See Ataroth, 2.

ATER. 1. A descendant of Hezekiah, who returned from Babylon (Ezr 2:16; Ne 7:21).

2. A porter (Ezr 2:42; Ne 7:45).

3. An Israelite, who subscribed to Nehemiah's covenant (Ne 10:17).

ATHACH, a city of Judah (1Sa 30:30).

ATHAIAH, son of Uzziah (Ne 11:4).

ATHALIAH. 1. Wife of Jehoram, king of Judah (2Ki 8:18, 26; 11:1-3, 12-16, 20; 2Ch 22:10-12; 23:12-15, 21).

2. Son of Jehoram (1Ch 8:26).

3. Father of Jeshaiah (Ezr 8:7).

ATHEISM. Instances of (Ps 10:4; 14:1, 53:1). Arguments against (Job 12:17-25; Ro 1:19, 20).

See God; Faith; Unbelief.

ATHENS, a city of Greece (Ac 17:15-34; 1Th 3:1).

ATHLAI, a son of Bebai (Ezr 10:28).

ATOMS OF MATTER (Pr 8:26).

ATONEMENT. For tabernacle and furniture (Le 16:15-20, 33). In consecration of the Levites (Nu 8:21). For those defiled by the dead (Nu 6:11). Made for houses (Le 14:53).

For sin, see below.

By meat offerings (Le 5:11-13); by jewels (Nu 31:50); by money (Ex 30:12-16; Le 5:15, 16; 2Ki 12:16); by incense (Nu 16:46-50); by animals, see below; by Jesus, see below.

Day of: Time of (Ex 30:10; Le 23:27; 25:9; Nu 29:7). How observed (Ex 30:10; Le 16:2-34; 23:27-32; Nu 29:7-11; Heb 5:3; 9:7).

Made by Animal Sacrifices: In the blood shed (Le 17:11); in burnt offerings (Le 1:4; 4:13-21; 12:6-8; Nu 15:22-28; 28:27-31; 29); in trespass offerings (Le 5:6-10; 6:7; 14:12-32); in sin offerings (Ex 29:36; Le 4:20, 22-35; 9:7; 10:17; 16:6-34; Nu 28:22; 29). Forgiveness of sins through (Le 5:10; 19:22).

Made by Jesus: Through His blood shed (Lu 22:20; 1Co 1:23; Eph 2:13-15; Heb 9:12-15, 25, 26; 12:24; 13:12, 20, 21; 1Jo 5:6; Re 1:5; 5:9; 7:14; 12:11). Through His death (Ro 3:24-26; 5:11-15; 1Th 1:10; Heb 13:12; 1Jo 2:2; 3:5; 4:10; Re 5:6, 9; 13:8). Typified in passover lamb (Ex 12:5, 11, 14; 1Co 5:7); in sacrifices (Ex 24:8; Le 16:30, 34; 17:11; 19:22; Heb 9:11-28); compare (Ge 4:4 w Heb 11:4; Ge 22:2 w Heb 11:17, 19; Ex 12:5, 11, 14 w 1Co 5:7; Ex 24:8 w Heb 9:10; Le 16:30, 34 w Heb 9:7, 12, 28; Le 17:11 w Heb 9:22).

Divinely inspired (Lu 2:30, 31; Ga 4:4, 5; Eph 1:3-12, 17-22; 2:4-10; Col 1:19, 20; 1Pe 1:20; Re 13:8). A mystery (1Co 2:7; 1Pe 1:8-12). Once for all (Heb 7:27; 9:24-28; 10:10, 12, 14; 1Pe 3:18). Vicarious (Isa 53:4-12; M't 20:28; Joh 6:51; 11:49-51; Ga 3:13; Eph 5:2; 1Th 5:9, 10; Heb 2:9; 1Pe 2:24).

For reconciliation (Da 9:24-27; Ro 5:1-21; 2Co 5:18-21; Eph 2:16, 17; Col 1:20-22; Heb 2:17). For remission of sins (Zec 13:1; M't 26:28; Lu 22:20; 24:46, 47; Joh 1:29; Ro 4:25; 1Co 15:3; Ga 1:3, 4; Eph 1:7; Col 1:14; Heb 1:3; 10:1-20; 1Jo 1:7; 3:5). For redemption (M't 20:28; Ac 20:28; Ga 3:13; 1Ti 2:6; Heb 9:12; Re 5:9).

See Blood; Jesus, Death of, Mission of, Sufferings of; Redemption; Salvation.

ATONEMENT, DAY OF, a Hebrew festival, instituted by Moses, and held on the 10th day of the 7th month, involving abstinence from labor, fasting, penitence and sacrifice for sin. The day marked the only entry of the high priest into the Holy of Holies (Le 16).

ATROPHY, of the hand (M't 12:10-13).

ATROTH, town built by Gadites E of Jordan (Nu 32:35).

ATTAI. 1. A Gadite warrior (1Ch 12:11).

2. Son of Rehoboam (2Ch 11:20).

3. Grandson of Sheshan (1Ch 2:35, 36).

ATTALIA, a seaport of Pamphylia (Ac 14:25).

ATTORNEY, employed (Ac 24:1, 2). See Lawyer.

ATTRIBUTES OF GOD (See God.)

AUGUSTUS, a title of Roman emperors (Lu 2:1; Ac 25:21, 25; 27:1).

AUL, obsolete variant of awl; a sharp piercing tool (Ex 21:6; De 15:17).

AVA, called also Ivah. A district near Babylon (2Ki 17:24; 18:34; 19:13. See Ezr 4:9).

AVARICE. A root of evil (1Ti 6:10). Insatiable Ec 4:7, 8; 5:10, 11). Forbidden in bishops (1Ti 3:2, 3; Tit 1:7).

Instances of: Descendants of Joseph (Jos 17:14-18).

See Covetousness; Rich; Riches.

AVEN (vanity). 1. "The plain of the Sun" (Am 1:5).

2. Another name for On (Eze 30:17).

3. Beth-aven (Ho 10:8).

AVENGER OF BLOOD. *Premosaic:* Edict of God (Ge 9:5, 6); Cain fears (Ge 4:14, 15); Lamech fears (Ge 4:24).

Mosaic Law Concerning: Given by God (Nu 35:19-29); De 19:4-13); city of refuge from (Jos 20:1-9); set aside by David (2Sa 14:4-11).

Figurative: (Ps 8:2; 44:16; Ro 13:4; 1Th 4:6).

See Homicide.

AVIM. 1. A city of Benjamin (Jos 18:23).

2. A tribe in southern Palestine. See Avites.

AVITES. 1. A nation in southern part of Canaan (De 2:23; Jos 13:3).

2. Colonists of Samaria (2Ki 17:31).

AVITH, capital city of the Edomites (Ge 36:35; 1Ch 1:46).

AWAKENINGS, REFORMS. General references (1Ki 18:39; 2Ch 30:11; Ezr 10:1; Lu 3:10; Joh 4:39; Ac 2:41; 8:6; 9:35; 11:21; 13:48; 18:8; 19:18).

Reforms: Asa (1Ki 15:12). Jehu (1Ki 10:27). Jehoiada (2Ki 11:18). Josiah (2Ki 23:4). Jehoshaphat (2Ch 19:3). Hezekiah (2Ch 31:1). Manasseh (2Ch 33:15). Ezra (Ezr 10:3). Nehemiah (Ne 13:19).

AWL, a tool (Ex 21:6; De 15:17). See Aul.

AX. An implement (De 19:5; 1Sa 13:20, 21; 2Sa 12:31; Ps 74:5, 6). Elisha causes to swim (2Ki 6:5, 6). Battle-ax (Eze 26:9).

Figurative: Jer 46:22; 51:20; M't 3:10.

AXLETREE, part of a wheeled vehicle (1Ki 7:32, 33).

AZAL, a place near Jerusalem (Zec 14:5).

AZALIAH, father of Shaphan (2Ki 22:3; 2Ch 34:8).

AZANIAH, father of Jeshua (Ne 10:9).

AZARAEL (See Azareel.)

AZAREEL (God is helper). 1. An Aaronite of the family of Korah (1Ch 12:6).

2. A musician in the temple (1Ch 25:18); Called Uzziel.

3. A Danite prince (1Ch 27:22).

4. A son of Bani (Ezr 10:41).

5. A priest (Ne 11:13; 12:36).

AZARIAH (Jehovah hath helped). 1. Man of Judah (1Ch 2:8).

2. King of Judah. See Uzziah.

3. Son of Jehu (1Ch 2:38).

4. Son of Ahimaaz (1Ch 6:9).

5. Levite (1Ch 6:36).

6. Son of Zadok (1Ki 4:2).

7. High priest (1Ch 6:10).

8. Son of Nathan (1Ki 4:5).

9. Prophet (2Ch 15:1-8).

10. Sons of King Jehoshaphat (2Ch 21:2).

11. Son of Jehoram (2Ch 22:6).

12. Son of Jeroham (2Ch 23:1).

13. Son of Johanan (2Ch 28:12).

14. Levite (2Ch 29:12).

15. High priest (2Ch 26:16-20).

16. Son of Hilkiah (1Ch 6:13, 14).

17. Opponent of Jeremiah (Jer 43:2).

18. Jewish captive of Babylon (Da 1:7).

19. Son of Maaseiah (Ne 3:23).

20. Levite (Ne 8:7).

21. Priest (Ne 10:2).

22. Prince of Judah (Ne 12:32, 33).

AZAZ (strong), father of Bela (1Ch 5:8).

AZAZEL (scapegoat). Word of uncertain meaning found only in Le 16:8, 10, 26 in connection with one of the goats chosen for the service of the Day of Atonement. It has been interpreted both personally and impersonally as meaning 1) an evil spirit, 2) removal, 3) devil.

AZAZIAH (Jehovah is strong). 1. A harper in the temple (1Ch 15:21).

2. Father of Hoshea (1Ch 27:20).

3. Overseer in temple (2Ch 31:13).

AZBUK, father of Nehemiah (Ne 3:16).

AZEKAH, a town of Judah (Jos 10:10, 11; 15:35; 1Sa 17:1; 2Ch 11:9; Ne 11:30; Jer 34:7).

AZEL, a Benjamite (1Ch 8:37, 38; 9:43, 44).

AZEM, a city in the S of Judah. Called also Ezem (Jos 15:29; 19:3; 1Ch 4:29).

AZGAD (fate is hard). 1. Ancestor of certain captives who returned from Babylon (Ezr 2:12; Ne 7:17).

2. A returned exile (Ezr 8:12).

3. A chief who signed Nehemiah's covenant (Ne 10:15).

AZIEL (God is my strength), a temple musician (1Ch 15:20).

AZIZA (strong), son of Zattu (Ezr 10:27).

AZMAVETH (death is strong). 1. One of David's heroes (2Sa 23:31).

2. Benjamite (1Ch 12:3).

3. David's treasurer (1Ch 27:25).

4. Descendant of Jonathan (1Ch 8:36).

5. Place N of Anathoth (Ezr 2:24; Ne 12:29).

AZMON (strong), a place on the S of Canaan (Nu 34:4, 5; Jos 15:4).

AZNOTH-TABOR, a town in Naphtali (Jos 19:34).

AZOR, ancestor of Jesus (M't 1:13, 14). Perhaps identical with Azrikam (1Ch 3:23).

AZOTUS (See Ashdod.)

AZRIEL (God is help). 1. A chief of Manasseh (1Ch 5:24).

2. Father of Jerimoth (1Ch 27:19).

3. Father of Seriah (Jer 36:26).

AZRIKAM (my help has arisen). 1. Son of Neraiah (1Ch 3:23).

2. Son of Azel (1Ch 8:38; 9:44).

3. A Levite (1Ch 9:14; Ne 11:15).

4. Governor of the house of Ahaz (2Ch 28:7).

AZUBAH (forsaken). 1. Mother of Jehoshaphat (1Ki 22:42; 2Ch 20:31).

2. Wife of Caleb (1Ch 2:18, 19).

AZUR, father of Jaazaniah (Eze 11:1).

AZZAH, a city of the Philistines. See Gaza.

AZZAN (strong), father of Paltiel (Nu 34:26).

AZZUR (helped). 1. An Israelite, who sealed Nehemiah's covenant (Ne 10:17).

2. A Gibeonite (Jer 28:1).

B

BAAL (lord, possessor, husband). 1. An idol of the Phoenicians, god of the sun. Wickedly worshiped by the Israelites in the time of the judges (J'g 2:10-23; 1Sa 7:3, 4); by the kingdom of Israel (2Ki 17:16; Jer 23:13; Ho 11:2; 13:1); under Ahab (1Ki 16:31-33; 18:18; 19:18); Jehoram (2Ki 3:2); by the Jews (2Ki 21:3; 2Ch 22:2-4; 24:7; 28:2; 33:3). Jeremiah expostulates against the worship of (Jer 2:8, 23; 7:9).

Altars of, destroyed by Gideon (J'g 6:25-32); by Jehoiada (2Ki 11:18); by Josiah (2Ki 23:4, 5).

Prophets of, slain by Elijah (2Ki 18:4). All worshipers of, destroyed by Jehu (2Ki 10:18-25).

2. A Benjamite (1Ch 8:30; 9:36).

3. A Reubenite (1Ch 5:5).

4. A city in the tribe of Simeon (1Ch 4:33). Called Baalath-beer (Jos 19:8).

BAALAH. 1. A city in the S of Judah (Jos 15:29). Apparently identical with Balah (Jos 19:3); and Bilhah (1Ch 4:29).

2. A city in the N of Judah called also Kirjath-jearim. See Kirjath-jearim.

3. A mountain in Judah (Jos 15:11). Probably identical with Mount Jearim.

BAALATH, a city of Dan (Jos 19:44; 1Ki 9:18; 2Ch 8:6).

BAALATH-BEER (See Baal, no. 4.)

BAALBEK (city of Baal), city of Coele-Syria, c. 40 miles NW of Damascus, famous for its ruins.

BAAL-BERITH. A god of the Shechemites (J'g 9:4). Worshiped by Israelites (J'g 8:33). Called Berith (J'g 9:46).

BAALE OF JUDAH, town on N border of Judah, same as Baalah and Kiriath-baal and Kirjath-jearim (2Sa 6:2; 1Ch 13:6).

BAAL-GAD (Gad is Baal). A city of the Canaanites (Jos 11:17; 12:7; 13:5). Probably identical with Baal-hermon (J'g 3:3; 1Ch 5:23).

BAAL-GUR (See Gur-baal.)

BAAL-HAMON (Baal of Hamon), a place where Solomon had a vineyard Song 8:11). Its location is unknown. Called Hammon (Jos 19:28).

BAAL-HANAN (Baal is gracious) 1. The son of Achbor and king of Edom (Ge 36:38; 1Ch 1:49).

2. An official under David (1Ch 27:28).

BAAL-HAZOR (Baal of Hazor), where Absalom had a sheep-range and where he brought about the death of Amnon in revenge for the outrage upon his sister (2Sa 13:23).

BAAL-HERMON (Baal of Hermon). 1. A city near Mount Hermon (1Ch 5:23). Identical with Baal-gad, which see.

2. A mountain of Lebanon (J'g 3:3).

BAALI (my lord), name often given to Jehovah by Israel (Ho 2:16).

BAALIM, plural form of Baal (J'g 2:11; 1Sa 7:4; Ho 2:13, 17; 11:2). See Baal.

BAALIS, king of the Ammonites (Jer 40:14).

BAAL-MEON. A city of the Reubenites (Nu 32:38; 1Ch 5:8; Eze 25:9). Called Beth-meon (Jer 48:23); Beth-baal-meon (Jos 13:17); Beon (Nu 32:3).

BAAL-PEOR (Baal of Peor), an idol of Moab (Nu 25:3, 5; De 4:3; Ps 106:28; Ho 9:10).

BAAL-PERAZIM (Baal of the breaking through). A place in the valley of Rephaim (2Sa 5:20; 1Ch 14:11). Called Perazim (Isa 28:21).

BAAL-SHALISHA (Baal of Shalisha), a place near Gilgal (1Sa 9:4; 2Ki 4:42).

BAAL-TAMAR (Baal of the palm tree), a place near Gibeah (J'g 20:33).

BAAL-ZEBUB (Baal, or lord of flies), name under which Baal was worshiped by the Philistines of Ekron (2Ki 1:2, 3, 6).

BAAL-ZEPHON (lord of the north), a place near which the Israelites encamped just before they crossed the Red Sea (Ex 14:2, 9; Nu 33:7). The site is unknown.

BAANA (son of oppression). 1. Son of Ahilud (1Ki 4:12).

2. Father of Zadok (Ne 3:4).

BAANAH (son of oppression). 1. A captain of Ish-bosheth's army (2Sa 4:2, 5, 6, 9).

2. Father of Heleb (2Sa 23:29; 1Ch 11:30).

3. A chief Jew of the exile (Ezr 2:2; Ne 7:7; 10:27).

4. The name is spelled Baana. Son of Hushai (1Ki 4:16).

BAARA (the burning one), wife of

Shaharaim (1Ch 8:8). Called Hodesh.

BAASEIAH (the Lord is bold), an ancestor of Asaph, the musician (1Ch 6:40).

BAASHA (boldness), king of Israel (1Ki 15:16-22, 27-34; 16:1-7; 21:22; 2Ki 9:9; 2Ch 16:1-6; Jer 41:9).

BABBLER, a sarcastic epithet applied to Paul (Ac 17:18).

BABBLING, condemned (1Ti 6:20; 2Ti 2:16).

BABEL, a city in the plain of Shinar. Tower built, and tongues confused at (Ge 11:1-9).

BABES. In the mouths of, is praise perfected (M't 21:16). A symbol of the guileless (Ps 8:2; M't 11:25; Lu 10:21); of the children of the kingdom of heaven (M't 18:2-6; M'k 10:15; Lu 18:17).

Figurative: Of weak Christians (Ro 2:20; 1Co 3:1; Heb 5:13; 1Pe 2:2).

See Children; Parents.

BABYLON. Origin of (Ge 10:8, 10, marg.). Origin of the name (Ge 11:8, 9).

Was Called: Land of the Chaldeans (Eze 12:13). Land of Shinar (Da 1:2; Zec 5:11). Land of Merathaim (Jer 50:1, 21). Desert of the sea (Isa 21:1, 9). Sheshach (Jer 25:12, 26). Lady of kingdoms (Isa 47:5). Situated beyond the Euphrates (Ge 11:31 w Jos 24:2, 3). Formerly a part of Mesopotamia (Ac 7:2). Founded by the Assyrians and a part of their empire (2Ki 17:24, w Isa 23:13). Watered by the rivers Euphrates and Tigris (Ps 137:1; Jer 51:13). Composed of many nations (Da 3:4, 29). Governed by Kings (2Ki 20:12; Da 5:1). With Media and Persia divided by Darius into one hundred and twenty provinces (Da 6:1). Presidents placed over (Da 2:48; 6:2). Babylon the chief province of (Da 3:1).

Babylon the Capital of: Its antiquity (Ge 11:4, 9). Enlarged by Nebuchadnezzar (Da 4:30). Surrounded with a great wall and fortified (Jer 51:53, 58). Called the golden city (Isa 14:4). Called the glory of kingdoms (Isa 13:19). Called beauty of Chaldees (Isa 13:19). Called the city of merchants (Eze 17:4). Called Babylon the great (Da 4:30).

Remarkable for: Antiquity (Jer 5:15). Naval power (Isa 43:14). Military power (Jer 5:16; 50:23). National greatness (Isa 13:19; Jer 51:41). Wealth (Jer 50:37; 51:13). Commerce (Eze 17:4). Manufacture of garments (Jos 7:21). Wisdom of senators (Isa 47:10; Jer 50:35).

Inhabitants of: Idolatrous (Jer 50:38; Da 3:18). Addicted to magic (Isa 47:9, 12, 13; Da 2:1, 2). Profane and sacrilegious (Da 5:1-3). Wicked (Isa 47:10).

As a Power Was: Arrogant (Isa 14:13, 14; Jer 50:29, 31, 32). Secure and self-confident (Isa 47:7, 8). Grand and stately (Isa 47:1, 5). Covetous (Jer 51:13). Oppressive (Isa 14:4). Cruel and destructive (Isa 14:17; 47:6; Jer 51:25; Hab 1:6, 7). An instrument of God's vengeance on other nations (Jer 51:7; Isa 47:6). Languages spoken in (Da 1:4; 2:4). Armies of, described (Hab 1:7-9).

Represented by: A great eagle (Eze 17:3). A head of gold (Da 2:32, 37, 38). A lion with eagle's wings (Da 7:4). Ambassadors of, sent to Hezekiah (2Ki 20:12). Figure of a woman (Re 17).

Nebuchadnezzar King of: Made Jehoiakim tributary (2Ki 24:1). Besieged Jerusalem (2Ki 24:10, 11). Took Jehoiachin captive to Babylon (2Ki 24:12, 14-16; 2Ch 36:10). Spoiled the temple (2Ki 24:13). Made Zedekiah king (2Ki 24:17). Besieged and took Jerusalem (2Ki 24:20). Besieged and took Jerusalem (2Ki 25:1-4). Burned Jerusalem (2Ki 25:9, 10). Took Zedekiah captive to Babylon (2Ki 25:7, 11, 18-21; 2Ch 36:20). Spoiled and burned the temple (2Ki 25:9, 13-17; 2Ch 36:18, 19). Revolt of the Jews from, and their punishment illustrated (Eze 17). The Jews exhorted to be subject to, and settle in (Jer 27:17; 29:1-7). Treatment of the Jews in (2Ki 25:27-30; Da 1:3-7). Grief of the Jews in (Ps 137:1-6). Destroyed by the Medes (Da 5:30, 31). Restoration of the Jews from (2Ch 36:23; Ezr 1; 2:1-67). The gospel preached in (1Pe 5:13). A type of Antichrist (Re 16:19; 17:5).

Predictions Respecting: Conquests by (Jer 21:3-10; 27:2-6; 49:28-33; Eze 21:19-32; 29:18-20). Captivity of the Jews by (Jer 20:4-6; 22:20-26; 25:9-11; Mic 4:10). Restoration of the Jews from (Isa 14:1-4; 44:28; 48:20; Jer 29:10; 50:4, 8, 19). Destruction of (Isa 13; 14:4-22; 21:1-10; 47; Jer 25:12; 50; 51). Perpetual desolation of (Isa 13:19-22; 14:22, 23;

Jer 50:13, 39; 51:37). Preaching of the gospel in (Ps 87:4).

BACA (balsam tree), unknown valley of Palestine (Ps 84:6); refers figuratively to an experience of sorrow turned into joy.

BACHRITES, a family of Ephraim, called Becherites in ASV, RSV (Nu 26:35), descendants of Becher (called Bered in 1Ch 7:20).

BACKBITING. Evil of (Ps 15:1-3; Pr 25:23; Ro 1:28, 30; 1Co 12:20).

See Accusation, False; Slander; Speaking, Evil.

BACKSLIDERS. *Described as:* Blind (2Pe 1:9; Re 3:17); godless (2Jo 9); idolaters (1Co 10:7); lukewarm (Re 3:15, 16); murmurers (Ex 17:7; 1Co 10:10); forsaking God (Jer 17:3); tempting Christ (1Co 10:9); forsaking God's covenant (Ps 78:10, 11; Pr 2:17); turned aside to evil (Ps 125:5; 1Ti 5:15); unfit for God's kingdom (Lu 9:62).

God's forbearance with (De 32:5, 6, 26, 27; Ezr 9:10, 14; Isa 42:3).

God's solicitude for (De 32:28, 29; Ps 81:13, 14; Isa 1:4-9, 21, 22; 65:2, 3; Jer 2:5, 11-13, 17, 31, 32; 18:13-15; 50:6; Ho 6:4-11; 11:1-4, 7-9; M't 23:37).

Warnings to (De 4:25-28; 28:58, 59; 29:18; 31:16-18; 1Ki 9:6-9; 2Ch 7:19-22; Jer 7:13-34; 11:9-17; M'k 9:50).

Corrective judgments upon (De 32:16-25; 1Ki 8:33; 2Ch 7:19-22; Ne 9:26-30; Job 34:26, 27; Isa 50:1; Jer 8:1-22; Eze 22:18-22; Ho 8:14; 9:1-17).

Called to repentance (Isa 30:9, 15; 31:6; Jer 3:4-7, 12-14, 21, 22; 4:14; 6:16; Ho 14:1; Mal 3:7; Re 2:4, 5, 20-22; 3:2, 3, 18, 19).

Promises to Penitent (Ho 14:4). Of finding the Lord (De 4:29-31; 2Ch 15:2-4). Of spiritual enlightenment (Isa 29:24; Jer 3:14-19; Ho 6:3). Of restoration (De 30:1-10; Pr 24:16; Isa 57:18, 19; Ho 14:4; Zec 10:6). Of temporal prosperity (Le 26:40-42; De 30:1-5, 7-10; Job 22:23-30).

Return of (Jer 31:18, 19; 50:4, 5; Ho 3:5; Jon 2:4).

Punishment of: By temporal loss (De 28:15-68; Ezr 8:22; Jer 13:24, 25; Eze 15; Am 2:4-6). By being overthrown by enemies (Nu 14:43; De 4:27, 28; J'g 2:12-15; 2Ki 18:11, 12; 2Ch 29:6-8; Ps 78:40-43, 56-64). By being forsaken of God (2Ch 24:20; Isa 2:6; Jer 6:30; 12:7; 14:7, 10; 15:1; Ho 4:6, 10). By bearing the fruits of their sin (Pr 14:14; Eze 11:21; 16:43; 23:35).

Instances of: Saul (1Sa 15:11, 26-28). Solomon (1Ki 11:4-40; Ne 13:26). Amon (2Ki 21:22, 23). Rehoboam (2Ch 12:1, 2). Joash (2Ch 24:24). Amaziah (2Ch 25:27). Jonah (Jon 1:3). Disciples of Jesus (Joh 6:66). Peter (M't 26:69-75). Corinthian Christians (1Co 5:1-8). Galatians (Ga 1:6, 3:1; 4:9-11; 5:6, 7). Hymenaeus and Alexander (2Ti 1:15). Demas (2Ti 4:10). Churches of Asia (2Ti 1:15; Re 2:4; 3:2, 3, 15-18).

See Apostasy; Backsliding; Church, Backslidden; Reprobacy.

BACKSLIDING. Is turning from God (1Ki 11:9). Is leaving the first love (Re 2:4). Is departing from the simplicity of the gospel (2Co 11:3; Ga 3:1-3; 5:4, 7). God is displeased at (Ps 78:57, 59). Warnings against (Ps 85:8; 1Co 10:12). Guilt and consequences of (Nu 14:43; Ps 125:5; Isa 59:2, 9-11; Jer 5:6; 8:5, 13; 15:6; Lu 9:62). Brings its own punishment (Pr 14:14; Jer 2:19). A haughty spirit leads to (Pr 16:18). Proneness to (Pr 24:16; Ho 11:7). Liable to continue and increase (Jer 8:5; 14:7). Exhortations to return from (2Ch 30:6; Isa 31:6; Jer 3:12, 14, 22; Ho 6:1). Pray to be restored from (Ps 80:3; 85:4; La 5:21). Punishment of tempting others to the sin of (Pr 28:10; M't 18:6). Not hopeless (Ps 37:24; Pr 24:16). Endeavor to bring back those guilty of (Ga 6:1; Jas 5:10, 20). Sin of, to be confessed (Isa 59:12-14; Jer 3:13, 14; 14:7-9). Pardon of, promised (2Ch 7:14; Jer 3:12; 31:20; 36:3). Healing of, promised (Jer 3:22; Ho 14:4). Afflictions sent to heal (Ho 5:15). Blessedness of those who keep from (Pr 28:14; Isa 26:3, 4; Col 1:21-23). Hateful to saints (Ps 101:3).

Instances of Israel's Backsliding: At Meribah (Ex 17:1-7); when Aaron made the golden calf (Ex 32); after Joshua's death (J'g 2); during Asa's reign (2Ch 15); Hezekiah's reign (2Ch 30:2-12).

BAD COMPANY (See Company, Evil.)

BADGER. [*R. V.*, Seal or Porpoise.] Skins of, used for covering of tabernacle (Ex 25:5; 26:14; 35:7, 23; 36:19; 39:34; Nu 4:6, 8, 10, 11, 12, 14, 25). For shoes (Eze 16:10). [*R. V.*, Sealskin.]

BAG, sack or pouch made for holding

anything. Many kinds are mentioned in Scripture (De 25:13; 2Ki 5:23; M't 10:10; "scrip").

BAGPIPE a musical instrument (Da 3:5).

BAHURIM, a village between the fords of the Jordan and Jerusalem (2Sa 3:16; 16:5; 17:18; 19:16; 1Ki 2:8).

BAIL (See Surety; Creditor; Debt; Debtor.)

BAJITH (house), a place of idolatrous worship in Moab (Isa 15:2).

BAKBAKKAR (investigator), a Levite (1Ch 9:15).

BAKBUK (bottle), the founder of a family of Nethinim who returned from the Captivity with Zerubbabel (Ezr 2:51; Ne 7:53).

BAKBUKIAH (flask, or perhaps, **the Lord pours out),** a name occuring three times in Nehemiah (11:17; 12:9, 25), a Levite in high office in Jerusalem right after the Exile.

BAKER (1Sa 8:13; Jer 37:21; Ho 7:4, 6). Pharaoh's chief baker (Ge 40).

See Bread.

BALAAM (devourer), son of Beor. From Mesopotamia (De 23:4). A soothsayer (Jos 13:22). A prophet (Nu 24:2-9; 2Pe 2:15, 16). Balak sends for, to curse Israel (Nu 22:5-7; Jos 24:9; Ne 13:2; Mic 6:5). Anger of, rebuked by his ass (Nu 22:22-35; 2Pe 2:16). Counsel of, an occasion of Israel's corruption with the Midianites (Nu 31:16; Re 2:14, 15). Covetousness of (2Pe 2:15; Jude 11). Death of (Nu 31:8; Jos 13:22).

BALAC (See Balak.)

BALAH, a city of Simeon (Jos 19:3). Called Bilhah (1Ch 4:29).

BALAK (devastator), king of Moab (Nu 22:4; Jos 24:9; J'g 11:25; Mic 6:5). Tries to bribe Balaam to curse Israel (Nu 22:5-7, 15-17).

See Balaam.

BALANCES. Used for weighing (Job 31:6; Isa 40:12, 15; Eze 5:1). Money weighed with (Isa 46:6; Jer 32:10). Must be just (Le 19:36; Pr 16:11; Eze 45:10). False balance used (Ho 12:7; Am 8:5; Mic 6:11); an abomination (Pr 11:1; 20:23).

Figurative: Job 6:2; 31:6; Ps 62:9; Isa 40:12; Da 5:27; Re 6:5.

BALD LOCUST (See Insects.)

BALDNESS (Le 13:40, 41). A judgment (Isa 3:24; Jer 47:5; 48:37; Eze 7:18). Artificial, a sign of mourning (Isa 22:12; Jer 16:6; Eze 27:31; 29:18; Am 8:10; Mic 1:16). Artificial, as an idolatrous practice, forbidden (Le 21:5; De 14:1).

Instances of: Elisha (2Ki 2:23).

BALL, playing at (Isa 22:18).

BALM, a medicinal balsam (Ge 37:25; 43:11; Jer 8:22; 46:11; 51:8; Eze 27:17).

BAMAH, a high place (Eze 20:29).

BAMOTH. A camping place of the Israelites (Nu 21:19, 20). Called Bamoth-baal, a city of Reuben (Jos 13:17).

BANI (posterity). 1. Gadite (2Sa 23:36).

2. Levite (1Ch 6:46).

3. Descendant of Judah (1Ch 9:4).

4. Levite (Ne 3:17).

5. Levite (Ne 9:4).

6. Levite (Ne 11:22).

7. Levite (Ne 10:13).

8. Man who signed covenant (Ne 10:14).

9. Ancestor of Jews who returned from captivity (Ezr 10:29).

10. Descendant of a Bani (Ezr 10:38).

BANISHMENT (Ezr 7:26). Of Adam and Eve, from Eden (Ge 3:22-24). Of Cain, to be "a fugitive and vagabond" (Ge 4:14). Of Jews, from Rome (Ac 18:2). Of John, to Patmos (Re 1:9).

See Exile.

BANK. A primitive kind of banking was known in ancient times. Israelites could not charge each other interest (Ex 22:25), but could charge Gentiles (De 23:20).

BANNER. Banners, ensigns, or standards were used in ancient times for military, national, and ecclesiastical purposes very much as they are today (Nu 2:2; Isa 5:26; 11:10; Jer 4:21).

BANQUET. Social feasting was common among the Hebrews. There were feasts on birthdays (Ge 40:20), marriages (Ge 29:22), funerals (2Sa 3:35), grape-gatherings (J'g 9:27), sheep-shearing (1Sa 25:2, 36), sacrifices (Ex 34:15), and on other occasions. Often a second invitation was sent on the day of the feast (Lu 14:17). Guests were welcomed with a kiss (Lu 7:45) and their feet were washed (Lu 7:44). Banquets were often enlivened with music, singing, and dancing (Lu 15:23-25).

BAPTISM. As administered by John (M't 3:5-12; Joh 3:23; Ac 13:24; 19:4).

Sanctioned by Christ's submission to it (M't 3:13-15; Lu 3:21). Adopted by Christ (Joh 3:22; 4:1, 2). Appointed an ordinance of the Christian church (M't 28:19, 20; M'k 16:15, 16). To be administered in the name of the Father, the Son, and the Holy Ghost (M't 28:19). Water, the outward and visible sign in (Ac 8:36; 10:47). Regeneration, the inward and spiritual grace of (Joh 3:3, 5, 6; Ro 6:3, 4, 11). Remission of sins, signified by (Ac 2:38; 22:16). Unity of the Church effected by (1Co 12:13; Ga 3:27, 28). Confession of sin necessary to (M't 3:6). Repentance necessary to (Ac 2:38). Faith necessary to (Ac 8:37; 18:8). There is but one (Eph 4:5). *Administered to:* Individuals (Ac 8:38; 9:18). Households (Ac 16:15; 1Co 1:16). Emblematic of the influences of the Holy Ghost (M't 3:11; Tit 3:5). Typified (1Co 10:2; 1Pe 3:20, 21).

Baptism With the Holy Ghost. Foretold (Eze 36:25). Is through Christ (Tit 3:6). Christ administered (M't 3:11; Joh 1:33). Promised to saints (Ac 1:5; 2:38, 39; 11:16). All saints partake of (1Co 12:13). Necessity for (Joh 3:5; Ac 19:2-6). Renews and cleanses the soul (Tit 3:5; 1Pe 3:20, 21). The Word of God instrumental to (Ac 10:44; Eph 5:26). Typified (Ac 2:1-4).

BAR, an Aramaic word meaning "son"; in the NT used as a prefix (M't 16:17).

BARABBAS (son of the father), a prisoner released by Pilate (M't 27:16-26; M'k 15:7-15; Lu 23:18-25; Joh 18:40; Ac 3:14).

BARACHEL (God blesses), a Buzite, whose son Elihu was the last of Job's friends to reason with him (Job 32:2, 6).

BARACHIAH. Called also Berechiah, father of Zechariah (Zec 1:1, 7). Called Barachias in M't 23:35.

BARAK (lightning), Israelite who defeated Sisera at the command of Deborah the judge (J'g 4, 5; Heb 11:32).

BARBARIAN, a foreigner (Ac 28:2-4; Ro 1:14; 1Co 14:11; Col 3:11).

See Stranger.

BARBER (Eze 5:1).

BARIAH, son of Shechaniah (1Ch 3:22).

BAR-JESUS (son of Jesus), a false prophet (Ac 13:6).

BAR-JONA (son of Jonah), surname of Peter (M't 6:17).

BARKOS, a Jew whose descendants returned from exile (Ezr 2:53; Ne 7:55).

BARLEY. A product of Egypt (Ex 9:31); Palestine (De 8:8; 1Ch 11:13; Jer 41:8). Fed to horses (1Ki 4:28). Used in offerings (Nu 5:15; Eze 45:15). Traffic in (2Ch 2:10; Ho 3:2). Tribute in (2Ch 27:5). Priests estimated value of (Le 27:16; 2Ki 7:1; Re 6:6). Absalom burns Joab's field of (2Sa 14:30).

Loaves of (Joh 6:9, 13).

BARN (2Ki 6:27; Job 39:12; Pr 3:10; Joe 1:17; Hag 2:19; M't 6:26; 13:30; Lu 12:18, 24).

See Garner.

BARNABAS (son of consolation), called also Joses. A prophet (Ac 13:1). An apostle (Ac 14:14). A Levite who gave his possessions to be owned in common with other disciples (Ac 4:36, 37). Goes to Tarsus to find Paul, brings him to Antioch (Ac 11:25, 26). Accompanies Paul to Jerusalem (Ac 11:30). Returns with Paul to Antioch (Ac 12:25). Goes with Paul to Seleucia (Ac 13); to Iconium (Ac 14:1-7). Called Jupiter (Ac 14:12-18). Goes to Derbe (Ac 14:20). Is sent as a commissioner to Jerusalem (Ac 15; Ga 2:1-9). Disaffected towards Paul (Ac 15:36-39). Is reconciled to Paul (1Co 9:6). Piety of (Ac 11:24). Devotion of, to Jesus (Ac 15:26).

BARREL, an earthen jar (1Ki 17:12, 14, 16; 18:33).

BARRENNESS, sterility of women. A reproach (Ge 30:22, 23; 1Sa 1:6, 7; 2:1-11; Isa 4:1; Lu 1:25). Miraculously removed. Instances of: Sarai (Ge 17:15-21); Rebecca (Ge 25:21); Manoah's wife (J'g 13); Hannah (1Sa 1:6-20); Elisabeth (Lu 1:5-25). Sent as a judgment (Ge 20:17, 18).

See Childlessness.

BARSABAS (son of Sabas). 1. Surname of Joseph (Ac 1:23).

2. Judas (Ac 15:22).

BARTER (See Commerce.)

BARTHOLOMEW (son of Tolmae), one of the apostles (M't 10:3; M'k 3:18; Lu 6:14; Ac 1:13).

BARTIMAEUS (son of Timaeus), a blind man (M't 20:29-34; M'k 10:46-52; Lu 18:35-43).

BARUCH (blessed). 1. An amanuensis of Jeremiah (Jer 32:12-16; 36:4-32; 43:3-6; 45:1, 2).

2. Son of Labai (Ne 3:20; 10:6).

3. A descendant of Pharez (Ne 11:5).

BARUCH, BOOK OF, Jewish apocryphal book found in the LXX, purporting to be a treatise by Jeremiah's scribe Baruch to Jewish exiles in Babylon.

BARZILLAI (made of iron). 1. A friend of David (2Sa 17:27-29; 19:31-39; 1Ki 2:7; Ezr 2:61; Ne 7:63).

2. Father of Adriel (2Sa 21:8).

3. A priest (Ezr 2:61; Ne 7:63).

BASE FELLOWS (sons of Belial) (De 13:13; 1Sa 2:12; 10:27; 25:17; 30:22; 1Ki 21:10; 2Ch 13:7).

BASEMATH (See Bashemath.)

BASHAN (smooth, fertile land). A region E of the Jordan and N of Arnon (Ge 14:5). Og, king of (Jos 13:12). Allotted to the two and one half tribes, which had their possession E of the Jordan (Nu 32:33; De 3:10-14; Jos 12:4-6; 13:29-31; 17:1). Invaded and taken by Hazael, king of Syria (2Ki 10:32, 33). Retaken by Jehoash (2Ki 13:25). Fertility and productiveness of (Isa 33:9; Jer 50:19; Na 1:4). Forests of famous (Isa 2:13; Eze 27:6; Zec 11:2). Distinguished for its fine cattle (De 32:14; Ps 22:12; Eze 39:18; Am 4:1; Mic 7:14).

See Argob; Ashtaroth; Edrei; Jair.

BASHAN-HAVOTH-JAIR, group of unwalled towns in the NW part of Bashan (Nu 32:41; De 3:14; Jos 13:30).

BASHEMATH (fragrant). 1. Wife of Esau (Ge 26:34).

2. Ishmael's daughter (Ge 36:3, 4, 13, 17). Called Mahalath in Ge 28:9.

3. Solomon's daughter, called Basmath (1Ki 4:15).

BASIN. Made of gold (1Ki 7:50; 1Ch 28:17; 2Ch 4:8, 22; Ezr 1:10; 8:27); of brass (Ex 27:3; 38:3; 1Ki 7:45).

See Tabernacle, Furniture of.

BASKET (Ge 40:16, 17; Ex 29:3, 23, 32; Le 8:2; Nu 6:15; De 26:2; 28:5, 17; 2Ki 10:7). Received the fragments after the miracles of the loaves (M't 14:20; 15:37; 16:9, 10). Paul let down from the wall in (Ac 9:25; 2Co 11:33).

BASMATH, daughter of Solomon (1Ki 4:15).

BASON (See Basin.)

BASTARD (child of incest), bastards and their descendants to the 10th generation were excluded from the assembly of the Lord (De 23:2); had no claim to paternal care or the usual privileges and discipline of legitimate children.

Instances of: Ishmael (Ge 16:3, 15; Ga 4:22); Moab and Ammon (Ge 19:36, 37); Jephthah (J'g 11:1); David's child by Bath-sheba (2Sa 11:2-5).

Figurative: Zec 9:6; Heb 12:8.

BAT (Le 11:19; De 14:18; Isa 2:20).

BATH, a Hebrew measure for liquids, containing about eight gallons, three quarts (1Ki 7:26, 38; Ezr 7:22; Isa 5:10; Eze 45:10, 11, 14).

BATH, BATHING, BATHE. Bathing for physical cleanliness or refreshment is not often mentioned in the Bible, where most references to bathing are to partial washing. Bathing in the Bible stands chiefly for ritual acts—purification of ceremonial defilement (Ex 30:19-21; Le 16:4, 24; M'k 7:3, 4).

BATH-RABBIM (daughter of multitudes), a gate in the city of Heshbon (Song 7:4).

BATH-SHEBA (daughter of Sheba), wife of Uriah and later wife of David. Called Bath-shua (1Ch 3:5). Adultery of (2Sa 11:2-5). Solomon's mother (1Ki 1:11-31; 2:13-21; 1Ch 3:5).

BATH-SHUA. 1. In KJV Ge 38:2 and 1Ch 2:3 have "daughter of Shua."

2. In 1Ch 3:5, the mother of Solomon. Probably a scribal error for Bath-sheba.

BATTERING-RAM (2Sa 20:15; Eze 4:2; 21:22).

BATTERY (See Assault and Battery.)

BATTLE. Shouting in (J'g 7:20; 1Sa 17:20). Priests in (2Ch 13:12). Prayer before: By Asa (2Ch 14:11); by Jehoshaphat (2Ch 20:3-12).

See Armies; War.

BATTLE OF LIFE. Ancient Heroes: Joshua (Jos 11:23). Gideon (J'g 7:14). Jonathan (1Sa 14:6). David (1Sa 17:45). Elisha (2Ki 6:17). Jehoshaphat (2Ch 20:20). The Spiritual Conflict: An inward battle (Ro 7:23). Spiritual weapons (2Co 10:4). Invisible foes (Eph 6:12). Young soldiers enlisted (1Ti 1:18). A fight of faith (1Ti 6:12). Demands entire consecration (2Ti 2:4). The Soul's Enemies: (Ps 86:14; Jer 2:34; 18:20; Eze 13:18; 22:25; Lu 22:31; Eph 6:12; 1Pe 5:8). Weapons and Armor: (1Sa 17:45; 2Co 10:4; Eph 6:17; Heb 4:12; Re 12:11). Divine Protection: Promised to believers (2Ch 16:9; Ps 34:7; 91:4; 125:2; Zec 2:5; Lu 21:18). Examples of: (Ge 35:5; Ex 14:20; 2Ki 6:17; Ezr 8:31; Da 6:22; Re 7:3). The Victory: (Isa 53:12; M't 12:20; Joh 16:33; 1Co 15:24; Re 3:21; 6:2; 17:14).

BATTLE-AX (Jer 51:20).

BATTLEMENTS, on roofs of houses (De 22:8); on walls (Jer 5:10).

BAVAI, man who helped rebuild walls of Jerusalem (Ne 3:18).

BAY TREE (Ps 37:35).

BAZLITH, called also Bazluth, one of the Nethinim (Ezr 2:52; Ne 7:54).

BDELLIUM, fragrant gum or resin listed with precious stones (Ge 2:12; Nu 11:7).

BEACON (Isa 30:17; Jer 6:1). See Ensign; Standard.

BEALIAH (Jehovah is Lord), a Benjamite soldier who joined David at Ziklag (1Ch 12:5).

BEALOTH. 1. A town in Judah (Jos 15:24).

2. A locality in north Israel (1Ki 4:16, Aloth KJV).

BEAM, large long piece of timber prepared for use for house (1Ki 7:3) or weaver's loom (J'g 16:14). Used in figurative sense by Jesus (M't 7:3; Lu 6:41).

BEAN (2Sa 17:28; Eze 4:9).

BEAR, THE. Inhabits woods (2Ki 2:24).

Described as: Voracious (Da 7:5). Cunning (La 3:10). Cruel (Am 5:19). Often attacks men (2Ki 2:24; Am 5:19). Attacks the flock in the presence of the shepherd (1Sa 17:34). Particularly fierce when deprived of its young (2Sa 17:8; Pr 17:12). Growls when annoyed (Isa 59:11). Miraculously killed by David (1Sa 17:36, 37).

Illustrative of: God in His judgments (La 3:10; Ho 13:8). The natural man (Isa 11:7). Wicked rulers (Pr 28:15). The kingdom of the Medes (Da 7:5). The kingdom of Antichrist (Re 13:2).

BEARD. Worn long by Aaron (Ps 133:2); Samson (J'g 16:17); David (1Sa 21:13; Eze 5:1). Shaven by Egyptians (Ge 41:14). Untrimmed in mourning (2Sa 19:24). Plucked (Ezr 9:3). Cut (Isa 7:20; 15:2; Jer 41:5; 48:37). Lepers required to shave (Le 13:29-33; 14:9). Idolatrous practice of marring, forbidden (Le 19:27; 21:5). Beards of David's ambassadors half shaven by the king of the Amorites (2Sa 10:4).

BEAST. 1. A mammal, not man, distinguished from birds and fishes (Ge 1:29, 30).

2. A wild, as distinguished from a domesticated animal (Le 26:22; Isa 13:21, 22).

3. Any of the inferior animals, as distinguished from man (Ps 147:9; Ec 3:19).

4. Apocalyptic symbol of brute force—sensual, lawless, and God-opposing (Da 7; Re 13:11-18).

BEATEN WORK, of metals (Ex 25:18; 37:17, 22; Nu 8:4).

BEATING, as a punishment (Ex 5:14; De 25:3; M'k 13:9; Ac 5:40; 16:22, 37; 18:17; 21:32; 22:19).

See Assault; Punishment.

BEATITUDES (blessedness), a word not found in the English Bible, but meaning either (1) the joys of heaven, or (2) a declaration of blessedness. Beatitudes occur frequently in the OT (Ps 32:1, 2; 41:1). The Gospels contain isolated beatitudes by Christ (M't 11:6; 13:16; Joh 20:29), but the word is most commonly used of those in M't 5:3-11 and Lu 6:20-22, which set forth the qualities that should characterize His disciples.

BEAUTY. Vanity of (Ps 39:11; Pr 6:25; 31:30; Isa 3:24; Eze 16:14; 28:17). Consumeth away (Ps 39:11; 49:14).

Instances of: Sarah (Ge 12:11). Rebekah (Ge 24:16). Rachel (Ge 29:17). Joseph (Ge 39:6). Moses (Ex 2:2; Heb 11:23). David (1Sa 16:12, 18). Bathsheba (2Sa 11:2). Tamar (2Sa 13:1). Absalom (2Sa 14:25). Abishag (1Ki 1:4). Vashti (Es 1:11). Esther (Es 2:7).

Spiritual: 1Ch 16:29; Ps 27:4; 29:2; 45:11; 90:17; 110:3; Eze 16:14; Zec 9:17.

BEAUTY AND BANDS, the staves, broken (Zec 11:7).

BEBAI, the name of three Jews whose descendants came from exile (Ezr 2:11; 8:11; 10:28; Ne 7:16; 10:15).

BECHER (young camel). 1. Son of Benjamin (Ge 46:21; 1Ch 7:6, 8).

2. Son of Ephraim (Nu 26:35). Called Bered (1Ch 7:20).

BECHORATH (the first birth), son of Aphiah (1Sa 9:1).

BED. Made of wood (Song 3:7-9); of iron (De 3:11); of ivory (Am 6:4); of gold and silver (Es 1:6). Used at meals (Am 6:4). Exempt from execution for debt (Pr 22:27). Perfumed (Pr 7:17).

Figurative: Ps 139:8.

BEDAD (alone), father of Hadad (Ge 36:35).

BEDAN (son of judgment). 1. One of the deliverers of Israel (1Sa 12:11), possibly identical with Abdon.

2. Son of Ullam (1Ch 7:17).

BEDEIAH (servant of Jehovah), a son of Bani who had taken a foreign wife (Ezr 10:35).

BEE. In Palestine (De 1:44; J'g 14:8; Ps 118:12; Isa 7:18). Called by hissing (Isa 7:18).

See Honey.

BEELIADA (the Lord knows), son of David (1Ch 14:7). Called Eliada (2Sa 5:16; 1Ch 3:8).

BEELZEBUB. The prince of devils (M't 10:25; 12:24, 27; M'k 3:22; Lu 11:15, 18, 19). Messengers sent to inquire of, by Ahaziah (2Ki 1:2).

See Baal-zebub.

BEELZEBUL (See Baal-zebub).

BEER (a well). 1. A station of the Israelites (Nu 21:16-18).

2. A town in the tribe of Judah (J'g 9:21).

BEERA, son of Zophah (1Ch 7:37).

BEERAH, a Reubenite (1Ch 5:6).

BEER-ELIM, a city of Moab (Isa 15:8).

BEERI (belonging to the well). 1. A Hittite (Ge 26:34). See Anah.

2. Father of Hosea (Ho 1:1).

BEER-LA-HAI-ROI (the well of the living one who sees me), a well, probably near Kadesh, where the Lord appeared to Hagar (Ge 16:7, 14) and where Isaac lived for some time (Ge 24:62; 25:11).

BEEROTH (wells). 1. A station of the Israelites. Aaron died at (De 10:6). See Bene-jaakan.

2. A city of the Hivites (Jos 9:17; 18:25; 2Sa 4:2; Ezr 2:25; Ne 7:29).

BEER-SHEBA (the seventh well). 1. The most southern city of Palestine (J'g 20:1). Named by Abraham, who dwelt there (Ge 21:31-33; 22:19). The dwelling place of Isaac (Ge 26:23). Jacob went out from, toward Haran (Ge 28:10). Sacrifices offered at, by Jacob when journeying to Egypt (Ge 46:1). In the inheritance of Judah (Jos 15:20, 28; 2Sa 24:7). Afterward assigned to Simeon (Jos 19:2, 9; 1Ch 4:28). Two sons of Samuel were judges at (1Sa 8:2). Became a seat of idolatrous worship (Am 5:5; 8:14).

2. Well of, belonged to Abraham and Isaac (Ge 21:25, 26).

3. Wilderness of, Hagar miraculously sees a well in (Ge 21:14-19). An angel fed Elijah in (1Ki 19:5, 7).

BEESH-TERAH, a Levitical city (Jos 21:27). Called Ashtaroth (1Ch 6:71).

BEETLE, authorized as food (Le 11:22).

BEGGARS. Set among princes (1Sa 2:8). Not the seed of the righteous (Ps 37:25). The children of the wicked (Ps 109:10; Pr 20:4; Lu 16:3).

Instances of: Bartimaeus (M'k 10:46); Lazarus (Lu 16:20-22); the blind man (Joh 9:8); the lame man (Ac 3:2-5).

See Poor.

BEHEADING. Execution by: of John (M't 14:10; M'k 6:27); of James (Ac 12:2); of the martyrs (Re 20:4).

See Punishment.

BEHEMOTH, an amphibious animal (Job 40:15).

BEKAH, a half shekel, about 31 cents (Ex 38:26).

BEL (lord), a Babylonian god (Isa 46:1; Jer 50:2; 51:44).

BELA (destruction). 1. A city called also Zoar (Ge 14:2, 8).

2. King of Edom (Ge 36:32, 33; 1Ch 1:43, 44).

3. Son of Benjamin (Nu 26:38, 40; 1Ch 7:6, 7; 8:1, 3). Called Belah (Ge 46:21).

4. Son of Azaz (1Ch 5:8).

BELIAL, not a proper noun in the OT, but a word meaning "worthlessness," "wickedness," "lawlessness" (De 13:13; J'g 19:22; 1Sa 25:25). Personified in 2Co 6:15.

BELIEVER (See Righteous.)

BELIEVING (See Faith.)

BELL. Attached to the hem of the priest's robe (Ex 28:33, 34; 39:25, 26). On horses (Zec 14:20).

BELLOWS, used with the furnace of the founder (Jer 6:29).

BELLY, used figuratively for the seat of the affections (Job 15:2, 35; 20:20; Ps 44:25; Pr 18:20; 20:27, 30; Hab 3:16; Joh 7:38; Tit 1:12).

BELOVED DISCIPLE, John spoken of as (Joh 13:23; 19:26; 20:2; 21:7, 20).

BELSHAZZAR (may Bel protect the King), king of Babylon (Da 5:1-30).

BELTESHAZZAR (may Bel protect his life), name given Daniel (Da 1:7).

See Daniel.

BEN (son), a Levite (1Ch 15:18).

BEN-ABINADAB (See Abinadab.)

BENAIAH (Jehovah has built). 1. Son of Jehoiada, commander of the Cherethites and Pelethites (2Sa 8:18; 1Ki 1:38). A distinguished warrior (2Sa 23:20-23; 1Ch 11:22-25; 27:5, 6). Loyal to Solomon (1Ki 1:2; 4:4).

2. An Ephraimite, and distinguished warrior (2Sa 23:30; 1Ch 11:31; 27:14).

3. A Levitical musician (1Ch 15:18, 20; 16:5).

4. A priest (1Ch 15:24; 16:6).

5. Son of Jeiel (2Ch 20:14).

6. A Levite in time of Hezekiah (2Ch 31:13).

7. A chief of the Simeonites (1Ch 4:36).

8. Father of Pelatiah (Ezr 11:1, 13).

9. Son of Parosh (Ezr 10:25).

10. Son of Pahath-moab (Ezr 10:30).

11. Son of Bani (Ezr 10:35).

12. Son of Nebo (Ezr 10:43).

BEN-AMMI (son of my people), son of one of Lot's daughters; progenitor of Ammonites (Ge 19:38).

BENCH, of ivory (Eze 27:6).

BEN-DEKAR (See Dekah.)

BENE-BERAK (sons of lightning), a city of Dan (Jos 19:45).

BENEDICTIONS. Divinely appointed (De 10:8; 21:5; Nu 6:23-26). By God, upon creatures He had made (Ge 1:22); upon man (Ge 1:28); upon Noah (Ge 9:1, 2).

Instances of: By Melchizedek, upon Abraham (Ge 14:19, 20; Heb 7:7). By Bethuel's household, upon Rebekah (Ge 24:60). By Isaac, upon Jacob (Ge 27:23-29, 37; 28:1-4); upon Esau (Ge 27:39, 40). By Jacob, upon Pharaoh (Ge 47:7-10); upon Joseph's sons (Ge 48); upon his own sons (Ge 49). By Moses, upon the tribes of Israel (De 33). By Aaron (Le 9:22, 23); by half the tribes who stood on mount Gerizim (De 11:29, 30; 27:11-13; Jos 8:33). By Joshua, upon Caleb (Jos 14:13); upon the Reubenites and Gadites, and half tribe of Manasseh (Jos 22:6, 7). By Naomi, upon Ruth and Orpah (Ru 1:8, 9). By the people, upon Ruth (Ru 4:11, 12). By Eli, upon Elkanah (1Sa 2:20). By David, upon the people (2Sa 6:18); upon Barzillai (2Sa 19:39). By Araunah, upon David (2Sa 24:23). By Solomon, upon the people (1Ki 8:14, 55-58; 2Ch 6:3). By Simeon, upon Jesus (Lu 2:34). By Jesus (Lu 24:50).

Levitical, Forms of: On this wise ye shall bless the children of Israel, saying unto them, The LORD bless thee, and keep thee; The LORD make his face shine upon thee, and be gracious unto thee: The LORD lift up his countenance upon thee, and give thee peace (Nu 6:23-26).

Apostolic (Ro 1:7; 15:5, 13, 33; 16:20; 1Co 1:3; 16:23; 2Co 1:2; 13:14; Ga 1:3; 6:16, 18; Eph 1:2; 6:23, 24; Ph'p 1:2; 4:23; Col 1:2; 1Th 1:1; 5:23; 2Th 1:2; 3:16, 18; 1Ti 1:2; 6:21; 2Ti 1:2; 4:22; Tit 3:15; Ph'm 3, 25; Heb 13:20, 21, 25; 1Pe 1:2; 5:10, 11, 14; 2Pe 1:2-4; 2Jo 3; Jude 2; Re 22:21).

BENEFACTOR (Lu 22:25).

BENEFICENCE. Enjoined (Le 25:35-43; De 15:7-15, 18; Pr 3:27, 28; 25:21, 22; M't 5:42; 19:21; 25:35-45; M'k 10:21; Lu 3:11; Ro 15:27; 1Co 13:3; 16:1-3; 2Co 8:7-15, 24; 9:1-15; Ga 2:10; 1Ti 5:8, 16; Heb 13:16; Jas 2:15, 16; 1Jo 3:17).

Blessed (Ps 41:4; Pr 22:9). Rewarded (Ps 112:9; Pr 11:25; 28:27; Isa 58:6-11; Eze 18:5-9; M't 19:21; M'k 9:41; 10:21; Heb 6:10).

Examples (M't 25:35-45; Ac 11:29, 30; Ro 15:25-27; 2Co 8:1-15; Ph'p 4:10-18; 1Ti 6:18).

See Alms; Liberality; Poor, Duties to; Rich; Riches.

Instances of: The old man of Gibeah (J'g 19:16-21). Boaz (Ru 2). The returned exile Jews (Ne 5:8-12; 8:10, 11). Job (Job 29:11-17; 31:16-23). The Temanites (Isa 21:14). The good Samaritan (Lu 10:33-35). Zacchaeus (Lu 19:8). The first Christians (Ac 2:44-46; 4:32-37). Cornelius (Ac 10:2, 4). Onesiphorus (2Ti 1:16-18).

See Alms; Poor, Duties to.

BENE-JAAKAN. A tribe that gave its name to certain wells in the wilderness (Nu 33:31, 32). Called Beeroth (De 10:6).

BENEVOLENCE. See Alms; Beneficence; Charitableness; Liberality; Love.

BEN-GEBER [*R.V.,* 1Ki 4:13]. See Geber.

BEN-HADAD (son of Hadad). 1. King

of Syria (1Ki 15:18-20; 2Ch 16:2-4).

2. A king of Syria, who reigned in the time of Ahab, son of Ben-hadad I (1Ki 20; 2Ki 5; 6; 7; 8:7-15).

3. Son of Hazael and king of Syria (2Ki 13:3, 24, 25; Am 1:4).

BEN-HAIL (son of strength), a prince of Judah (2Ch 17:7).

BEN-HANAN (son of grace), a son of Shimon (1Ch 4:20).

BEN-HUR. (See Hur.)

BENINU, a Levite (Ne 10:13).

BENJAMIN (son of my right hand). 1. Son of Jacob by Rachel (Ge 35:18, 24; 46:19). Taken into Egypt (Ge 42-45). Prophecy concerning (Ge 49:27). Descendants of (Ge 46:21; Nu 26:38-41).

2. *Tribe of:* Census of, at Sinai (Nu 1:37); in the plain of Moab (Nu 26:41). Clans of (Nu 26:38-40; 1Ch 7:6-12; 8). Position of, in camp and march (Nu 2:18, 22). Moses' benediction upon (De 32:12). Allotment in the land of Canaan (Jos 18:11-28). Reallotment (Eze 48:23). Did not exterminate the Jebusites (J'g 1:21). Join Deborah in the war against Sisera (J'g 5:14). Territory of, invaded by the Ammonites (J'g 10:9). Did not avenge the crime of the Gibeonites against the Levite's concubine, the war that followed (J'g 19; 20). Saul, the first king of Israel, from (1Sa 9:1, 17; 10:20, 21). Its rank in the time of Samuel (1Sa 9:21). Jerusalem within the territory of (Jer 6:1). A company of, joins David at Ziklag (1Ch 12:1, 2, 16). Not enrolled by Joab when he took a census of the military forces of Israel (1Ch 21:6). Loyal to Ish-bosheth, the son of Saul (2Sa 2:9, 15, 31; 1Ch 12:29). Subsequently joins David (2Sa 3:19; 19:16, 17). Loyal to Rehoboam (1Ki 12:21; 2Ch 11:1). Military forces of, in the reign of Asa (2Ch 14:8); of Jehoshaphat (2Ch 17:17). Skill in archery and as slingers of stones (J'g 3:15; 20:16; 1Ch 8:40; 12:2). Return to Palestine from the exile in Babylon (Ezr 1:5). Saints of, seen in John's vision (Re 7:8). Paul, of the tribe of (Ro 11:1; Ph'p 3:5).

See Israel.

3. Grandson of Benjamin (1Ch 7:10).

4. A son of Harim (Ezr 10:32); probably identical with the man mentioned in Ne 3:23.

5. A Jew who assisted in purifying the wall of Jerusalem (Ne 12:34).

6. A gate of Jerusalem (Jer 20:2; 37:13; 38:7; Zec 14:10).

BENO (his son), a descendant of Merari (1Ch 24:26, 27).

BEN-ONI (son of my sorrow), name given Benjamin by Rachel (Ge 35:18).

BEN-ZOHETH, son of Ishi (1Ch 4:20).

BEON, a place E of Jordan, probably same as Baal-meon (Nu 32:3, 38), which see.

BEOR. 1. Father of Bela (Ge 36:32; 1Ch 1:43).

2. Father of Balaam (Nu 22:5). Called Bosor (2Pe 2:15).

BEQUESTS (See Wills.)

BERA (gift), king of Sodom, defeated by Chedorlaomer in the days of Abraham (Ge 14:2, 8).

BERACHAH (a blessing). 1. An Israelite, who joined David at Ziklag (1Ch 12:3).

2. A valley in the S of Judah, where the Israelites blessed the Lord for a victory (2Ch 20:26).

BERACHAH, VALLEY OF (valley of blessing), the location where Jehoshaphat assembled his forces to offer praise to God for victory over the Ammonites and Moabites (2Ch 20:26). Between Bethlehem and Hebron.

BERACHIAH (See Berechiah.)

BERAIAH, son of Shimhi (1Ch 8:21).

BEREA, a city in the S of Macedonia (Ac 17:10, 13; 20:4).

BEREAVEMENT. From God (Ex 2:29; Ho 9:12). Mourning in, forbidden to Aaron, on account of his son's wickedness (Le 10:6); and to Ezekiel, for his wife (Eze 24:16-18).

Instances of: Abraham, of Sarah (Ge 23:2). Jacob, of Joseph (Ge 37:34, 35). Joseph, of his father (Ge 50:1, 4). The Egyptians, of their firstborn (Ex 12:29-33). Naomi, of her husband (Ru 1:3, 5, 20, 21). David, of his child by Bath-sheba (2Sa 12:15-23); of Absalom (2Sa 18:33; 19:4).

Resignation in: Job (Job 1:18-21); David (2Sa 12:22, 30); Solomon (Ec 7:2-4); Christians (1Th 4:13-18).

See Affliction, Comfort in; Resignation in. See also Resignation.

BERECHIAH (Jehovah blesses). 1. Father of Asaph (1Ch 15:17, 23). Called Berachiah (1Ch 6:39).

2. A warrior of Ephraim (2Ch 28:12).

3. A brother of Zerubbabel (1Ch 3:20).

4. Son of Asa (1Ch 9:16).

5. Son of Iddo (Zec 1:1, 7).

6. Son of Meshezabeel (Ne 3:4, 30; 6:18).

BERED (to be cold). 1. A town in the S of Palestine (Ge 16:14).

2. A son of Shuthelah (1Ch 7:20); probably same as Becher (Nu 26:35).

BERI (wisdom), son of Zophah (1Ch 7:36).

BERIAH (gift, evil). 1. Son of Asher (Ge 46:17; Nu 26:44, 45; 1Ch 7:30).

2. Son of Ephraim (1Ch 7:20-23).

3. A Benjamite (1Ch 8:13).

4. Son of Shimei (1Ch 23:10, 11).

BERIITES, a people mentioned only once in the Bible (Nu 26:44). Descended from Beriah, who, in turn, was from the tribe of Asher (Ge 46:17).

BERITES (choice young men), mentioned only in 2Sa 20:14. During the revolt of Sheba, responding to his call, these people followed him.

BERITH (See Baal-berith.)

BERNICE, daughter of Agrippa (Ac 25:13, 23; 26:30).

BERODACH-BALADAN (See Merodach-baladan.)

BEROTHAH (well), part of the northern boundary of Canaan (Eze 47:16).

BEROTHAI, a city of Zobah (2Sa 8:8).

BERYL (yellow jasper). A precious stone (Song 5:14; Eze 1:16; 10:9). Set in the breastplate (Ex 28:20; 39:13). John saw, in the foundation of the new Jerusalem (Re 21:20).

BESAI (down trodden), one of the Nethinim (Ezr 2:49; Ne 7:52).

BESODEIAH (in the council of Jehovah), father of Meshullam (Ne 3:6).

BESOM (broom), a word signifying the punishment that was to be meted out to Babylon (Isa 14:23).

BESOR, a brook near Gaza (1Sa 30:9, 10, 21).

BESTIALITY. Whosoever lieth with a beast shall surely be put to death (Ex 22:19).

Neither shalt thou lie with any beast to defile thyself therewith: neither shall any woman stand before a beast to lie down thereto: it *is* confusion (Le 18:23).

And if a woman approach unto any beast, and lie down thereto, thou shalt kill the woman, and the beast: they shall surely be put to death; their blood *shall be* upon them (Le 20:16).

See Sodomy.

BETAH (confidence), a city belonging to Hadadezer (2Sa 8:8).

BETEN (hollow), a city of Asher (Jos 19:25).

BETH (house), the name by which the second letter of the Hebrew alphabet is known. The Hebrew uses it also for the number two. It is the most common OT word for house.

BETHABARA (house of the ford). A city E of the Jordan (J'g 7:24). John testifies to Christ's messiahship, and baptizes at (Joh 1:28); Jesus at (Joh 10:39-42).

BETH-ANATH (the temple of Anath), a fortified city of Naphtali (Jos 19:38; J'g 1:33).

BETH-ANOTH (the house of Anoth), a city in Judah (Jos 15:59).

BETHANY (house of unripe figs). A village on the eastern slope of the Mount of Olives (Joh 11:18). Mary, Martha, and Lazarus dwell at (Lu 10:38-41). Lazarus dies and is raised to life at (Joh 11). Jesus attends a feast in (M't 26:6-13; Joh 12:1-9). The colt on which Jesus made His triumphal entry into Jerusalem obtained at (M'k 11:1-11). Jesus sojourns at (M't 21:17; M'k 11:11, 12, 19).

BETH-ARABAH (house of the desert). A city in the valley of the Dead Sea (Jos 15:6, 61; 18:22). Called Arabah (Jos 18:18).

BETH-ARAM. A fortified city of Gad (Jos 13:27). Probably identical with Beth-haran (Nu 32:36).

BETH-ARBEL (house of Arbel), a city spoiled by Shalman (Ho 10:14).

BETH-AVEN (house of vanity), a place on the mountains of Benjamin (Jos 7:2; 18:12; 1Sa 13:5; 14:23; Ho 4:15; 5:8; 10:5).

BETH-AZMAVETH (house of the strong one of death). A town of Benjamin (Ne 7:28). Called Azmaveth (Ne 12:29; Ezr 2:24).

BETH-BAAL-MEON (house of Baal-Meon). A place in the tribe of Reuben (Jos 13:17). Called Baal-meon (Nu 32:38; Eze 25:9); and Beon (Nu 32:3);

and Beth-meon (Jer 48:23). Subdued by the Israelites (Nu 32:3, 4). Assigned to the Reubenites (Jos 13:17).

BETH-BARAH (house of the ford), a place E of Jordan (J'g 7:24).

BETH-BIREI (house of my creator), a town of Simeon (1Ch 4:31).

See Beth-lebaoth.

BETH-CAR (house of sheep), a place W of Mizpeh (1Sa 7:11).

BETH-DAGON (house of Dagon). 1. A city of Judah (Jos 15:41).

2. A city of Asher (Jos 19:27).

BETH-DIBLATHAIM (house of a double cake of figs). A city of Moab (Jer 48:22). Called Almondiblathaim (Nu 33:46).

BETH-EL (house of God). 1. A city N of Jerusalem. The ancient city adjacent to, and finally embraced in, was called Luz (Jos 18:13; J'g 1:23-26). Abraham establishes an altar at (Ge 12:8; 13:3, 4). The place where Jacob saw the vision of the ladder (Ge 28:10-22; 31:13; Ho 12:4); and builds an altar at (Ge 35:1-15). Deborah dies at (Ge 35:8). Conquered by Joshua (Jos 8:17, w chapter 12:16); by the house of Joseph (J'g 1:22-26). Allotted to Benjamin (Jos 18:13, 22). Court of justice held at, by Deborah (J'g 4:5); by Samuel (1Sa 7:16).

Tabernacle at, and called House of God (J'g 20:18, 31; 21:2). Jeroboam institutes idolatrous worship at (1Ki 12:25-33; 2Ki 10:29). Idolatry at (Jer 48:13; Am 4:4). Shalmanezer sends a priest to (2Ki 17:27, 28). Prophecies against the idolatrous altars at (1Ki 13:1-6, 32; 2Ki 23:4, 15-20; Am 3:14). The school of prophets at (2Ki 2:3). Children of, mock Elisha (2Ki 2:23, 24). People of, return from Babylon (Ezr 2:28; Ne 7:32). Prophecies against (Am 5:5).

2. A city in the S of Judah (1Sa 30:27).

3. A mountain (1Sa 13:2).

BETH-EMEK (house of the valley), a city of Asher (Jos 19:27).

BETHER (separation), mountains of (Song 2:17).

BETHESDA (house of grace), a spring-fed pool in Jerusalem (Joh 5:1-16) into which the sick went for healing.

BETH-EZEL (a house adjoining), a town of Judah (Mic 1:11).

BETH-GADER (house of the wall). A place in Judah (1Ch 2:51). Probably identical with Geder (Jos 12:13); and with Gedor in Jos 15:58.

BETH-GAMUL (house of recompense), a city of Moab (Jer 48:23).

BETH-HACCEREM (house of the vineyard), a mountain in Judah (Ne 3:14; Jer 6:1).

BETH-HAGGAN. A garden house (2Ki 9:27). Probably identical with En-gannim (Jos 19:21).

BETH-HANAN (See Elon-beth-hanan.)

BETH-HARAN (house of the mountaineer). A fortified city E of Jordan (Nu 32:36). Probably identical with Beth-aram (Jos 13:27).

BETH-HOGLA (house of a partridge), a place on the border of Judah (Jos 15:6; 18:19, 21).

BETH-HORON (place of a hollow). Two ancient cities of Canaan, near which Joshua defeated the Amorites (Jos 10:10, 11; 16:3, 5; 18:13; 1Sa 13:18; 1Ch 7:24). Solomon builds (1Ki 9:17; 2Ch 8:5). Taken from Judah by the ten tribes (2Ch 25:13).

BETH-JESHIMOTH (house of desert). A place in Moab (Jos 12:3; 13:20; Eze 25:9). Called Beth-jesimoth (Nu 33:49).

BETH-JOAB (See Ataroth.)

BETH-LE-APHRAH (house of dust), a town, site unknown; "in the house of Aphrah roll thyself in the dust" (Mic 1:10).

BETH-LEBAOTH (house of lionesses). A town of Simeon (Jos 19:6). Called Lebaoth (Jos 15:32), and Beth-birei (1Ch 4:31).

BETHLEHEM (house of bread). A city SW of Jerusalem (J'g 17:7; 19:18). Called Ephratah and Ephrath (Ge 48:7; Ps 132:6; Mic 5:2), and Bethlehem-judah (J'g 17:7-9; 19:1, 18; Ru 1:1; 1Sa 17:12). Rachel dies and is buried at (Ge 35:16, 19; 48:7). The city of Boaz (Ru 1:1, 19; 2:4; 4). Taken and held by the Philistines (2Sa 23:14-16). Jeroboam converts it into a military stronghold (2Ch 11:6). The city of Joseph (M't 2:5, 6; Lu 2:4). Birthplace of Jesus (Mic 5:2; M't 2; Lu 2:4, 15). Herod slays the children of (M't 2:16-18).

2. A town of Zebulun, six miles W of

Nazareth (Jos 19:15). Israel judged at (J'g 12:10).

BETH-MAACHAH, a city of Manasseh (2Sa 20:14, 15, 18; 2Ki 15:29).

BETH-MARCABOTH (the house of chariots). A town of Simeon (Jos 19:5; 1Ch 4:31). Probably identical with Madmannah (Jos 15:31).

BETH-MEON, a city of Moab (Jer 48:23), same as Beth-baal-meon (Jos 13:17).

BETH-NIMRAH (house of leopard). A fenced city E of Jordan (Jos 13:27). Called Nimrah (Nu 32:3).

BETH-PALET (house of escape). A city in Judah (Jos 15:27). Called Beth-phelet (Ne 11:26).

BETH-PAZZEZ, a town of Issachar (Jos 19:21).

BETH-PEOR (house of Peor). A place in the tribe of Reuben (De 3:29; 4:46; 34:6). Near the burial place of Moses (Jos 13:20).

BETHPHAGE (house of unripe figs), a village on the Mount of Olives (M't 21:1; M'k 11:1; Lu 19:29).

BETH-PHELET (See Beth-palet.)

BETH-RAPHA, son of Eshton (1Ch 4:12).

BETH-REHOB (house of Rechob). A place in Dan (J'g 18:28; 2Sa 10:6). Called Rehob.

BETHSAIDA (house of fishing). 1. A city of Galilee. The city of Philip, Andrew, and Peter (Joh 1:44; 12:21). Jesus visits (M'k 6:45); cures a blind man in (M'k 8:22); prophesies against (M't 11:21; Lu 10:13).

2. Desert of, E of the sea of Galilee, Jesus feeds five thousand people in (M't 14:13; M'k 6:32; Lu 9:10).

BETH-SHAN (See Beth-shean.)

BETH-SHEAN (house of quiet). A city of Manasseh (Jos 17:11; 1Ch 7:29). Not subdued (J'g 1:27). Bodies of Saul and his sons exposed in (1Sa 31:10, 12). Called Beth-shan (1Sa 31:10, 12; 2Sa 21:12). District of, under tribute to Solomon's commissariat (1Ki 4:12).

BETH-SHEMESH (house of the sun). 1. A sacerdotal city of Dan (Jos 21:16; 1Sa 6:15; 1Ch 6:59). On the northern border of Judah (Jos 15:10; 1Sa 6:9, 12). In later times transferred to Judah (2Ki 14:11). Mentioned in Solomon's commissary districts (1Ki 4:9). Amaziah taken prisoner at (2Ki 14:11-13; 2Ch 25:21-23). Retaken by the Philistines (2Ch 28:18). Called Ir-shemesh (Jos 19:41).

2. A city near Jerusalem (Jos 19:22).

3. A fortified city of Naphtali (Jos 19:38; J'g 1:33).

4. An idolatrous temple (Jer 43:13).

BETH-SHITTAH (house of the acacia), a place near the Jordan (J'g 7:22).

BETH-TAPPUAH (house of apples), a town of Judah (Jos 15:53).

BETHUEL (abode of God), son of Nahor, father of Rebekah (Ge 22:22, 23; 24:15, 24; 25:20; 28:2, 5).

BETHUL. A city of Simeon (Jos 19:4). Called Chesil (Jos 15:30), and Bethuel (1Ch 4:30).

BETH-ZUR (house of rock), a town in Judah (Jos 15:58; 1Ch 2:45; 2Ch 11:7; Ne 3:16).

BETONIM, a town of Gad (Jos 13:26).

BETRAYAL. Of Jesus (M't 26:14-16, 45-50; M'k 14:10, 11; Lu 22:3-6; 22:47, 48; Joh 13:21). Of others, foretold (M't 20:18; 24:10). Of David, by Doeg (1Sa 22:9, 10, w chapter 21:1-10). Of cities (J'g 1:24, 25).

See Confidence Betrayed.

BETROTHAL. Of Jacob (Ge 29:18-30). Exempts from military duty (De 20:7). A quasi marriage (M't 1:18; Lu 1:27).

Figurative: Isa 62:4; Ho 2:19, 20; 2Co 11:2.

See Marriage.

BETTING, by Samson (J'g 14:12-19).

BEULAH (married), poetic name for restored Israel (Isa 62:4).

BEZAI. 1. Head of a Jewish family, which returned from Babylon (Ezr 2:17; Ne 7:23).

2. A family that sealed the covenant with Nehemiah (Ne 10:18).

BEZALEEL (in the shadow of God). 1. A divinely inspired mechanic and master workman, who built the tabernacle (Ex 31:2; 35:30-35; 36:1; 37:1; 38:1-7, 22).

2. Son of Pahath-moab (Ezr 10:30).

BEZEK (scattering, sowing). 1. Residence of Adoni-bezek (J'g 1:5).

2. A rendezvous of Israel under Saul (1Sa 11:8).

BEZER (strong). 1. A city of refuge, E of the Jordan (De 4:43; Jos 20:8; 21:36; 1Ch 6:78).

2. Son of Zophah (1Ch 7:37).

BIBLE, THE. General references to (2Sa 22:31; Ps 12:6; 119:9, 50; 147:15; M'k 12:24; Lu 8:11; Eph 6:17). The Book of the Ages (Ps 119:89; M't 5:18; 24:35; 1Pe 1:25). Food for the Soul (De 8:3; Job 23:12; Ps 119:103; Jer 15:16; 1Pe 2:2). Divinely Inspired (Jer 36:2; Eze 1:3; Ac 1:16; 2Ti 3:16; 2Pe 1:21; Re 14:13). Precepts Written in the Heart (De 6:6; 11:18; Ps 119:11; Lu 2:51; Ro 10:8; Col 3:16). Furnishes a Light (Ps 19:8; 119:105, 130; Pr 6:23; 2Pe 1:19). Loved By the Saints (Ps 119:47, 72, 82, 97, 140; Jer 15:16). Mighty in Its Influence: A devouring flame (Jer 5:14); A crushing hammer (Jer 23:29); A life-giving force (Eze 37:7); A saving power (Ro 1:16); A defensive weapon (Eph 6:17); A probing instrument (Heb 4:12). Blessings to Those Who Reverence It (Jos 1:8; Ps 19:11; M't 7:24; Lu 11:28; Joh 5:24; 8:31; Re 1:3). Purifies the Life (Ps 119:9; Joh 15:3; 17:17; Eph 5:26; 1Pe 1:22). Written With a Purpose (Joh 20:31; Ro 15:4; 1Co 10:11; 1Jo 5:13). The Standard of Faith (Pr 29:18; Isa 8:20; Joh 12:48; Ga 1:8; 1Th 2:13). Its Words Sacred (De 4:2; 12:32; Pr 30:6; Re 22:19). The Study of It Enjoined (De 17:19; Isa 34:16; Joh 5:39; Ac 17:11; Ro 15:4). Contains Seed-Corn for the Sower (Ps 126:6; M'k 4:14, 15; 2Co 9:10). Absolutely Trustworthy (1Ki 8:56; Ps 111:7; Eze 12:25; M't 5:18; Lu 21:33). Profitable for Instruction (De 4:10; 11:19; 2Ch 17:9; Ne 8:13; Isa 2:3). Ignorance of, Perilous (M't 22:29; Joh 20:9; Ac 13:27; 2Co 3:15).

BICHRI (first-born), father of Sheba (2Sa 20:1).

BIDKAR, Jehu's captain (2K 9:25).

BIER (2Sa 3:31; Lu 7:14).

BIGAMY (See Polygamy.)

BIGOTRY. Exhibited, in self-righteousness (Isa 65:5; M'k 2:16; Lu 15:2; 18:9-14); in intolerance (Lu 9:49, 50; Ac 18:12, 13).

Rebuke of (Ac 10:28, 45). Paul's argument against (Ro 3:1-23; 4:1-25).

Instances of: Joshua (Nu 11:27-29). Jews, with Samaritans (Joh 4:9, 27); with Jesus (Lu 4:28; 7:39; 11:38, 39; 15:22; 19:5-7; Joh 5:18); with the blind man (Joh 9:29-34); with Paul (Ac 21:28, 29; 22:22). John (M'k 9:38-40; Lu 9:49, 50). James and John (Lu 9:51-56). The early Christians (Ac 10:45; 11:2, 3; 15:1-10, 24; Ga 2:3-5). Paul (Ac 9:1, 2; 22:3, 4; 26:9-11; Ga 1:13, 14; Ph'p 3:6).

See Intolerance, Religious; Persecution; Uncharitableness.

BIGTHA, chamberlain of Ahasuerus (Es 1:10).

BIGTHAN, a conspiring Persian courtier (Es 2:21-23; 6:2).

BIGVAI (fortunate). 1. Man who returned from the captivity (Ezr 2:2; Ne 7:19).

2. Ancestor of family that returned from the captivity (Ezr 2:14; Ne 7:19).

3. Probably the same as 2 (Ezr 8:14).

BILDAD, one of Job's friends (Job 2:11; 8:1; 18:1; 25:1).

BILEAM. A town of Manasseh (1Ch 6:70). Called Ibleam (Jos 17:11); Gath-rimmon (Jos 21:25).

BILGAH (cheerfulness). 1. One of the chiefs of the sacerdotal courses in the temple (1Ch 24:14).

2. A priest (Ne 12:5, 18), perhaps identical with Bilgai (Ne 10:8).

BILGAI, a priest (Ne 10:8).

BILHAH (foolish). 1. Rachel's servant, bears children by Jacob (Ge 29:29; 30:3, 4; 37:2). Mother of Dan and Naphtali (Ge 30:1-8; 35:25; 46:23, 25). Reuben's incest with (Ge 35:22; 49:4).

2. A place in the land of Simeon (1Ch 4:29). Called Balah (Jos 19:3); and Baalah (Jos 15:29).

BILHAN (foolish). 1. A Horite chief (Ge 36:27; 1Ch 1:42).

2. A Benjamite (1Ch 7:10).

BILL OF DIVORCE (See Divorce.)

BILSHAN, a Jew of the captivity (Ezr 2:2; Ne 7:7).

BIMHAL, son of Japhlet (1Ch 7:33).

BINDING AND LOOSING. The carrying of a key or keys was a symbol of the delegated power of opening and closing. The apostles were given power to bind and to loose. Peter loosed the feet of the lame man at the Gate Beautiful (Ac 3:1-10) and Paul bound the sight of Bar-Jesus (Ac 13:8-11).

BINEA, a descendant of King Saul (1Ch 8:37; 9:43).

BINNUI (built). 1. A Jew of the captivity (Ne 7:15). Called Bani (Ezr 2:10).

2. A Levite of the captivity (Ne 3:24; 12:8; 10:9).

3. Father of Noadiah (Ezr 8:33).

4. Son of Pahath-moab (Ezr 10:30).
5. Son of Bani (Ezr 10:38).

BIRDS. Creation of, on the fifth creative day (Ge 1:20-30). Man's dominion over (Ge 1:26, 28; 9:2, 3; Ps 8:5-8; Jer 27:6; Da 2:38; Jas 3:7). Appointed for food (Ge 9:2, 3; De 14:11-20). What species were unclean (Le 11:13-20; De 14:12-19).

Used for sacrifice, see Dove; Pigeon. Divine care of (Job 38:41; Ps 147:9; M't 10:29; Lu 12:6, 24). Songs of, at the break of day (Ps 104:12; Ec 12:4; Song 2:12). Domesticated (Job 41:5; Jas 3:7). Solomon's proverbs of (1Ki 4:33). Nests of (Ps 104:17; M't 8:20; 13:32). Instincts of (Pr 1:17). Habits of (Job 39:13-18, 26-30). Migrate (Jer 8:7).

Mosaic law protected the mother from being taken with the young (De 22:6, 7). Cages of (Jer 5:27; Re 18:2).

See Snares.

Figurative: Isa 16:2; 46:11; Jer 12:9; Eze 39:4.

Symbolical: Da 7:6.

See Bittern; Chicken; Cormorant; Crane; Cuckoo; Dove; Eagle; Falcon; Glede; Hawk; Hen; Heron; Kite; Lapwing; Night Hawk; Osprey; Ossifrage; Ostrich; Owl; Partridge; Peacock; Pelican; Pigeon; Quail; Raven; Sparrow; Stork; Swallow; Swan; Vulture.

BIRSHA, a king of Gomorrah (Ge 14:2-10).

BIRTH. Pangs in giving (Ps 48:6; Isa 13:8; 21:3; Jer 4:31; 6:24; 30:6; 31:8). Giving, ordained to be in sorrow (Ge 3:16).

See Abortion; Children.

BIRTHDAY. Celebrated by feasts (Ge 40:20; M't 14:6). Cursed (Job 3; Jer 20:14, 18).

BIRTHRIGHT. Belonged to the first-born (De 21:15, 16). Entitled the first-born to a double portion of inheritance (De 21:15-17); royal succession (2Ch 21:3). An honorable title (Ex 4:22; Ps 89:27; Jer 31:9; Ro 8:29; Col 1:15; Heb 1:6; 12:23; Re 1:5).

Sold by Esau (Ge 25:29-34; 27:36, w 25:33; Heb 12:16; Ro 9:12, 13). Forfeited by Reuben (1Ch 5:1, 2). Set aside: That of Manasseh (Ge 48:15-20); Adonijah (1Ki 2:15); Hosah's son (1Ch 26:10).

See Firstborn.

BIRZAVITH, a descendant of Asher (1Ch 7:31).

BISHLAM, a Samaritan who obstructed the rebuilding of the temple at Jerusalem (Ezr 4:7-24).

BISHOP (overseer), same as elder or presbyter (1Ti 3:1; 4:14; Tit 1:5, 7); an overseer (Ac 20:17, 28; 1Pe 5:2); ruler (Ro 12:8). A title of Jesus (1Pe 2:25). See Elder.

BIT, part of a bridle (Ps 32:9; Jas 3:3).

BITHIAH (daughter of Jehovah), daughter of Pharaoh and wife of Mered of Judah (1Ch 4:18).

BITHRON (rough country), a district bordering on the Jordan (2Sa 2:29).

BITHYNIA, a Roman province in Asia Minor (Ac 16:7; 1Pe 1:1).

BITTER HERBS, eaten symbolically with the passover (Ex 12:8; Nu 9:11).

BITTER WATER. At Marah (Ex 15:23). A ceremonial water used by the priest (Nu 5:18-27).

BITTERN [*R. V.*, Porcupine], (Isa 14:23; 34:11; Zep 2:14).

BITTERNESS of spirit (De 32:32; Jer 4:18; Ac 8:23; Ro 3:14; Eph 4:31; Heb 12:15; Jas 3:14).

BITUMEN [marg. *R. V.*, slime], an inflammable mineral (Ge 11:3; 14:10; Ex 2:3).

See Petroleum.

BIZJOTHJAH (contempt of Jehovah), a town in Judah (Jos 15:28). Called Bizjothjah-baalah (Jos 15:32); Baalath-beer (Jos 19:8); and Balah (Jos 19:3).

BIZTHA, a Persian chamberlain (Es 1:10).

BLACKNESS. *Figurative:* Job 30:30; Joe 2:6. Blackness of darkness (Jude 13).

See Color, Symbolical.

BLACKSMITH (See Smith.)

BLAIN, an inflammatory abscess (Ex 9:9, 10).

BLASPHEMY. Reproaching God (2Ki 19:22; 2Ch 32:19; Ps 73:9, 11; 74:18; 139:20; Pr 30:9; Isa 5:19; 8:21, 22; 37:23; 45:9; 52:5; Eze 35:12, 13; Da 7:25; M't 10:25). Defying God (Isa 29:15, 16; 36:15-21; 37:10; Eze 8:12; 9:9; Mal 3:13, 14). Denying God's word (Jer 17:5). Speaking lies against God (Ho 7:13). Imputing ignorance to God (Ps 10:11, 13; Isa 40:27); unrighteousness to God (Jer 20:7; Eze 18:25; 33:17-20). Exalting oneself above God (Da 11:36,

37; 2Th 2:4). Calling Jesus accursed (1Co 12:3; Jas 2:7).

Occasioned by sins of believers (2Sa 12:14; Ro 2:24).

Foretold by Peter (2Pe 3:3, 4); by John (Re 13:1, 5, 6; 16:9, 11, 21; 17:3).

Forbidden (Ex 20:7; 22:28; Le 19:12; 22:32; Jas 3:10; 5:12).

Against the Holy Spirit (M't 12:31, 32; M'k 3:29, 30; Lu 12:10).

Punishment for (Le 24:10-16; Isa 65:7; Heb 10:29).

Instances of: The depraved son of Shelomith (Le 24:10-16). David's enemies (2Sa 12:14). Rabshakeh in the siege of Jerusalem (2Ki 18:22-26, 32-35; 19; Isa 36:15-20; 37:10-36). Israel (Eze 20:27, 28). Paul (1Ti 1:13). Early Christians (Ac 26:11); Hymenaeus and Alexander (1Ti 1:20). Ephesians (Re 2:9).

False accusations of: Against Naboth (1Ki 21:13). Against Jesus (M't 9:3; 26:65; M'k 2:7; 14:58; Lu 5:21; 22:70, 71; Joh 5:18; 10:33; 19:7). Against Stephen (Ac 6:11, 13).

Prophecy of (Re 13:1, 5, 6; 16:9, 11, 21; 17:3).

Instances of: The depraved son of Shelomith, who, in an altercation with an Israelite, cursed God (Le 24:10-16). Of the Israelites, in murmuring against God (Nu 21:5, 6). infidels, who used the adultery of David as an occasion to blaspheme (2Sa 12:14). Shimei, in his malice toward David (2Sa 16:5). Rabshakeh, in the siege of Jerusalem (2Ki 18:22; 19; Isa 36:15-20; 37:10-33). Job's wife, when she exhorted Job to curse God and die (Job 2:9). Peter, when accused of being a disciple of Jesus (M't 26:74; M'k 14:71). The revilers of Jesus, when He was crucified (M't 27:40-44, 63). The early Christians, persecuted by Saul of Tarsus compelled to blaspheme the name of Jesus (Ac 26:11; 1Ti 1:13). Two disciples, Hymenaeus and Alexander, who were delivered unto Satan that they might learn not to blaspheme (1Ti 1:20). Man of sin (2Th 2:3, 4) Backslidden Ephesians (Re 2:9).

False Indictments for: Of Naboth (1Ki 21:13); Jesus (M't 26:65; M'k 14:58; Lu 22:70, 71; Joh 19:7); Stephen (Ac 6:11, 13). Jesus falsely accused of, previous to his trial (M'k 2:7; Lu 5:21).

BLASTING. Blight (1Ki 8:37). Sent as a judgement (De 28:22; 2Ki 19:7; Isa 37:7; Am 4:9; Hag 2:17).

Figurative: Ex 15:8; 2Sa 22:16; Job 4:9; Ps 18:15.

BLASTUS, one of Herod's officers (Ac 12:20).

BLEMISH, a physical deformity. Debarred sons of Aaron from exercise of priestly offices (Le 21:17-23). Animals with, forbidden to be used for sacrifice (Le 22:19-25).

Figurative: Eph 5:27; 1Pe 1:19.

BLESSING. For blessing before eating, see Prayer, Thanksgiving and Prayer Before Taking Food. See also Benedictions.

BLESSINGS, SPIRITUAL. *From God* (De 33:25-27; Ps 18:28-36; 29:11; 37:6, 17, 24, 39; 63:8; 66:8, 9; 68:19, 28, 35; 84:5, 11; Isa 40:11, 29, 31; 41:10, 13, 16; Ac 3:19; 1Co 2:9; Ph'p 4:13; Jas 1:17; Jude 24).

Guidance (Ex 33:16; Ps 23:2, 3; 119:102; Isa 40:11; 58:11).

Sanctification (Ex 31:13; Le 21:8; Isa 1:25; 4:3, 4; 6:6, 7; 1Jo 1:9; Jude 1).

The perfecting of salvation (2Co 1:21; Ph'p 1:6; 2:13; 4:19; Col 1:11, 12; 1Th 5:24; Heb 13:20, 21; 1Pe 1:5; 2Pe 1:2-4).

The earnest of the Spirit (2Co 1:22; 5:5).

Peace (Isa 26:12; 57:19; Mal 4:2; Ph'p 4:7).

From Christ (Joh 1:16; Ro 1:7; 16:20; 1Co 1:3; 16:23; 2Co 1:2; 13:14; Ga 1:3; 6:16, 18; Eph 1:2; 6:23, 24; Ph'p 1:2; 4:23; 1Th 5:28; 2Th 1:2; 3:16, 18; 1Ti 1:2; 2Ti 1:2; Ph'm 3, 25; 2Pe 1:1; 2Jo 1:3).

Contingent upon obedience: Divine favor (Ex 19:5; Jer 7:23); mercy (Ex 20:6; De 5:10, 16; 7:9; 1Ki 8:23; 2Ch 30:9); holiness (De 28:9; 30:1-3, 6; Col 1:22, 23); eternal salvation (M't 10:22; 24:13; M'k 13:13; Heb 3:6, 14; 10:36; Re 2:10).

See Contingencies; Faithfulness; Regeneration; Salvation.

BLESSINGS, TEMPORAL. *From God* (Ps 136:25).

Rain (De 11:14; 28:12; Job 37:6; 38:25-27; Ps 68:9; 135:7; 147:8; Jer 10:13; 14:22; 51:16; Joe 2:23; Am 4:7; Zec 10:1; M't 5:45; Ac 14:17).

Seed time and harvest (Ge 8:22; Le

25:20-22; 26:4, 5; Ps 107:35-38; Isa 55:10; Jer 5:24; Eze 36:30; Mal 3:11; Ac 14:17).

Food and clothing (Ge 9:1-3; 28:20, 21; De 8:3-4; 10:18; 29:5; Ru 1:6; 2Ch 31:10; Ps 65:9; 68; 81:16; 104:14, 15, 27, 28; 111:5; 132:15; 145:15, 16; 146:7; Ec 2:24; 3:13; Isa 33:15, 16; Joe 2:26; M't 6:26, 30-33; Lu 12:22-31; Joh 6:31).

Preservation of life (De 4:4, 40; 5:33; 7:15; Ps 21:4; 3:6; 91:16; 103:2-5; Da 6:20, 22).

Children (Ps 113:9; 127:3-5).

Prosperity (Ge 24:56; 26:24; 49:24, 25; Nu 10:29; De 8:7-10, 18; 1Sa 2:7, 8; 1Ch 29:12, 14, 16; 2Ch 1:12; Ezr 8:22; Ps 147:13, 14; Ec 5:19; Isa 30:23; Ho 2:8).

National greatness (Ge 22:17; 26:3, 4; De 1:10; 7:13, 14; 15:4, 6; 26:18, 19; 32:13, 14; Job 12:23; Ps 69:35, 36; Isa 51:2; Jer 30:19; Eze 36:36-38; Da 5:18); social peace (Le 26:6; 1Ch 22:9); victory over enemies (Ex 23:22; Le 26:6-9; De 28:7; Ps 44:3); worldly honors (2Sa 7:8, 9; 1Ch 17:7, 8).

Exemplified to: Noah, at the time of the flood (Ge 7:1); Abraham (Ge 24:1); Isaac (Ge 26:12-24, 28); Jacob (Ge 35:9-15). Israelites, in Egypt (Ex 11:3); in the wilderness, supplying water (Ex 17:1-7; Nu 20:10, 11; Ps 78:15-20; 105:41); manna (Ex 16:14, 31; Nu 11:7-9; Ne 9:15; Ps 78:23, 24); quails (Nu 11:31-33; Ps 78:23-30; 105:40). To David (2Sa 5:10; 1Ch 14:17); Obed-edom (2Sa 6:11); Solomon (1Ki 3:13; 1Ch 29:25; 2Ch 1:1); Elijah, fed by ravens (1Ki 17:2-7); by an angel (1Ki 19:5-8). To the widow of Zarephath (1Ki 17:12-16). Hezekiah prospered (2Ki 18:6, 7; 2Ch 32:29); restored to health (2Ki 20:1-7); Asa (2Ch 14:6, 7); Jehoshaphat (2Ch 17:3-5; 20:30); Uzziah (2Ch 26:5-15); Jotham (2Ch 27:6); Job (Job 1:10; 42:10, 12); Daniel (Da 1:9).

Prayer for: Rain (1Ki 8:36; 2Ch 6:27); plentiful harvests (Ge 27:28; De 26:15; 33:13-16); daily bread (M't 6:11; Lu 11:3); prosperity (Ge 28:3, 4; 1Ch 4:10; Ne 1:11; 3Jo 2); providential guidance (Ge 24:12-14, 42-44; Ro 1:10; 1Th 3:11).

Instances of prayer for: Abraham (Ge 15:2-4); Abraham's servant (Ge 24:12); Laban (Ge 24:60); Isaac (Ge 25:21); Hannah (1Sa 1:11); Elijah (1Ki 17:20, 21; 18:42, 44; Jas 5:17, 18); Ezra (Ezr 8:21-23); Nehemiah (Ne 1:11; 2:4; 6:9).

Contingent upon obedience: Longevity (Ex 20:12; De 4:40; 5:16; 1Ki 3:14; Pr 3:1, 2). Deliverance from enemies (Ex 23:22; Le 26:6-8; De 28:7; 30:1-4; Pr 16:7; Jer 15:19-21). Prosperity (Le 26:3-5; De 7:12-14; 15:4, 5; 28:2-12; 29:9; 30:1-5, 9-20; Jos 1:8; 1Ki 2:3, 4; 9:3-9; 1Ch 22:13; 28:7, 8; 2Ch 7:17-22; 26:5; 27:6; 31:10; Job 36:11; Isa 1:19; Jer 7:3-7; 11:1-5; 12:16; 17:24-27; 22:4, 5, 15, 16; Mal 3:10-12). Favors to children (De 4:1, 40; 5:29; 7:9; 12:25, 28). Pre-eminent honors (De 28:1, 13; Zec 3:7). Averted judgments (Ex 15:26; De 7:15).

See God, Goodness of, Providence of; Prosperity.

BLIND. Cruelty to, forbidden (Le 19:14; De 27:18). Hated by David (2Sa 5:8).

See Blindness.

BLINDNESS. Disqualified for priestly office (Le 21:18). Of animals, disqualified for a sacrifice (Le 22:22; De 15:21; Mal 1:8). Miraculously inflicted upon the Sodomites (Ge 19:11); Syrians (2Ki 6:18-23); Saul of Tarsus (Ac 9:8, 9); Elymas (Ac 13:11). Sent as a judgment (De 28:28).

Miraculous healing of (M't 9:27-30; 11:5; 12:22; 21:14); of Bartimaeus (M't 20:30-34; M'k 10:46-52); a man of Bethsaida (M'k 8:22-25); man born blind (Joh 9:1-7).

Instances of: Isaac (Ge 27:1). Jacob (Ge 48:10). Eli (1Sa 4:15). Ahijah (1Ki 14:4).

Spiritual: Instances (De 29:4; Job 5:14; Isa 29:10-12; 56:10; 59:10; Jer 2:8; 5:21; 9:3; Eze 12:2; Ro 11:8); foretold (Isa 60:2; Ro 2:4; 11:10).

Manifested: In Ignorance: Of God (Ex 5:2; Isa 1:3; Jer 4:22; Ho 4:1, 6; Joh 7:28; 15:21; 16:2, 3; 17:25; Ac 17:23; 1Co 1:18-21; 2:8, 14, 15; 15:34; Ga 4:8; Eph 4:17-19; 1Th 4:4, 5; 1Jo 4:8; 3Jo 11). Of Christ (M't 16:3, 9; Lu 23:34; Joh 1:5, 10; 4:10, 11, 15, 22; 8:15, 19, 27, 33, 42, 43, 52-57; 9:29-39; Ac 3:14, 17; Ro 11:7, 8, 25; 1Pe 1:14; 1Jo 3:1, 6). Of the Holy Spirit (Joh 14:17; Ac 19:2). Of the Scriptures (M't 22:29; M'k 12:24; Ac 13:27; 2Co 3:14, 15; Heb 5:11, 12; 2Pe 3:16). Of moral truth (De 32:28; Pr

4:19; 28:5; Isa 5:13; Da 12:10; M't 15:14, 16; 16:3, 9; 23:19, 24, 26; M'k 7:18; Lu 6:39; 12:48, 57; 2Ti 3:7; Jude 10). Of the way of salvation (Lu 19:42; Joh 3:4; 6:52, 60; 2Pe 1:9; 1Jo 1:6, 8; 2:4, 9, 11; Re 3:17). Of God's ways (Ps 95:10; Jer 5:4; 8:7-9; Mic 4:12).

In Unbelief (Ps 14:1, 4; Isa 15:1; M'k 16:14; Joh 12:35, 38; Ac 28:25, 27; 2Co 4:3, 4, 6; 2Th 2:11, 12).

In Insensibility (De 29:4; J'g 16:20; Pr 7:7-23; 17:16; Isa 6:9, 10; 42:18-20; 44:18-20; 48:8; Jer 16:10; Ho 7:11; M't 6:23; 13:13-15; M'k 4:11, 12; 6:52; 8:18; Lu 8:10; Joh 12:40; Ac 28:25-27).

In Presumption (Ps 10:5, 6; 94:7, 8; Isa 28:10-15; 40:21, 27, 28; Jer 8:8, 9; Am 9:10).

In Perversity (Job 21:14, 15; Pr 1:7, 22, 29, 30; 13:18; 19:2, 3; Isa 5:20; 26:10, 11; Jer 9:3, 6; Eze 12:2, 3; Ho 5:4; M't 21:32; M'k 3:5; Lu 11:52; Joh 3:19; Ro 1:19-23, 28-31).

In Hypocrisy (Tit 1:15, 16).

Consequences of (Pr 10:21; 14:12; Isa 27:11; Ho 4:6, 14; 2Th 1:8).

Remedy for (Isa 9:2; 25:7; 35:5; 42:6, 7; Lu 4:18; Joh 8:12; Ac 26:18; 2Co 4:6; Eph 5:8; Col 1:13; 1Pe 2:9).

See Affliction, Obduracy in; Man, Ignorance of; God, Providence of, Misunderstood.

BLOOD. Is the life (Ge 9:4; Le 17:11, 14; 19:16; De 12:23; M't 27:4, 24). Forbidden to be used as food (Ge 9:4; Le 3:17; 7:26, 27; 17:10-14; 19:26; De 12:16, 23; 15:23; Eze 33:25; Ac 15:20, 29; 21:25). Plague of (Ex 7:17-25; Ps 78:44; 105:29).

Sacrificial: Sprinkled on altar and people (Ex 24:6-8; Eze 43:18, 20). Sprinkled on door posts (Ex 12:7-23; Heb 11:28). Without shedding of, no remission (Heb 9:22).

Of Sin Offering: Sprinkled seven times before the veil (Le 4:5, 6, 17); on horns of the altar of sweet incense, and at the bottom of the altar of burnt offering (Ex 30:10; Le 4:7, 18, 25, 30; 5:9; 9:9, 12). Of bullock of sin offering, put on the horns of the altar (Ex 29:12; Le 8:15); poured at the bottom of the altar (Ex 29:12; Le 8:15). See Offerings.

Of Trespass Offering: Sprinkled on the altar (Le 7:2). See Offerings.

Of Burnt Offering: Sprinkled round about, and upon the altar (Ex 29:16; Le 1:5, 11, 15; 8:19; De 12:27). See Offerings. Used for cleansing of leprosy (Le 14:6, 7, 17, 28, 51, 52). See Offerings.

Of Peace Offering: Sprinkled about the altar (Le 3:2, 8, 13; 9:19). Blood of the ram of consecration put on tip of right ear, thumb, and great toe of, and sprinkled upon, Aaron and his sons (Ex 29:20, 21; Le 8:23, 24, 30). See Offerings.

Blood of the Covenant: (Ex 24:5-8; Zec 9:11; M't 26:28; Heb 9:18, 19, 22; 10:29; 13:20). See Offerings.

Of Atonement: Sprinkled on mercy seat (Le 16:14, 15, 18, 19, 27; 17:11).

Figurative: Of victories (Ps 58:10); of oppression and cruelty (Hab 2:12); of destruction (Eze 35:6); of guilt (Le 20:9; 2Sa 1:16; Eze 18:13); of judgments (Eze 16:38; Re 16:6).

Of Jesus: Shed on the Cross (Joh 19:18, 34). Atoning (M't 26:28; M'k 14:24; Lu 22:20; Ro 3:24, 25; 5:9; Eph 2:13, 16; Heb 10:19, 20; 12:24; 13:20; 1Jo 5:6, 8). Redeeming (Ac 20:28; Eph 1:7; Col 1:14, 20; Heb 9:12-14; 1Pe 1:18, 19; Re 1:5; 5:9; 7:14). Sanctifying (Heb 10:29; 13:12).

Justification through (Ro 3:24, 25; 5:9). Victory through (Re 12:11). Eternal life by (Joh 6:53-56).

Typified by the blood of sacrifices (Heb 9:6-28). Symbolized by the wine of the Eucharist (1Co 10:16; 11:25).

See Atonement; Jesus, Mission of, Sufferings of.

BLOOD, AVENGER or **REVENGER OF.** One who took it upon himself to avenge the blood of a slain kinsman. This was often done in ancient Israel and is done among primitive peoples today (Ge 9:6; Nu 35:6).

BLOOD, ISSUE OF (See Diseases.)

BLOODY SWEAT (See Diseases.)

BLUE (See Color.)

BLUSHING, with shame (Ezr 9:6; Jer 6:15; 8:12).

BOANERGES (sons of thunder), surname of the sons of Zebedee (M'k 3:17).

BOAR, WILD (Ps 80:13). See Swine.

BOASTING. Folly of (Ps 49:6-9; Pr 27:1; Isa 10:15; Jas 4:16). Deceitful (Pr 20:14; 25:14). Of the wicked (Ps 52:1; 94:4; Ro 1:30). Of the tongue (Jas 3:5).

Forbidden (Jer 9:23).

Spiritual (Ps 52:1; 94:4; Ro 3:27; 11:17-21; 1Co 1:29; 4:6, 7; 2Co 10:12-18; Eph 2:8-10).

Instances of: Goliath (1Sa 17). Benhadad (1Ki 20:10). Amaziah (2Ch 25:17-20). Sennacherib (2Ki 18:19, 28-35; 19:8-13; Isa 10:8-15). The disciples (Lu 10:17, 20).

BOAT (See Ship.)

BOAZ. 1. An ancestor of Jesus (M't 1:5; Lu 3:32). History of, Ruth (chapters 2-4).

2. One of the brazen pillars of the temple (1Ki 7:21; 2Ch 3:17).

BOAZ AND JACHIN (See Temple.)

BOCHERU, son of Azel (1Ch 8:38; 9:44).

BOCHIM, a place W of Jordan, near Gilgal (J'g 2:1, 5).

BODY. Called: House (2Co 5:1); house of clay (Job 4:19); golden bowl (Ec 12:6); earthen vessel (2Co 4:7); tabernacle (2Pe 1:13); temple of God (1Co 3:16, 17; 6:19); member of Christ (1Co 6:15).

Corruptible (Job 17:14; 1Co 15:53, 54). To be consecrated to God (Ro 12:1). To be kept unto holiness (1Co 6:13-20).

Resurrection of (1Co 15:19-54; Ph'p 3:21). See Resurrection.

Spiritual (1Co 15:42-44; 2Co 5:1-4).

BOHAN, a Reubenite (Jos 15:6; 18:17).

BOIL, a tumor. Plague of Egyptians (Ex 9:9, 10; De 28:27, 35); of the Philistines [*R. V.*, tumors], (1Sa 5:6, 9; 1Sa 6:5). Of Hezekiah, healed (2Ki 20:7; Isa 38:21). Of Job (Job 2:7, 8). Levitical ceremonies prescribed for (Le 13:18-23).

BOILING POT, parable of (Eze 24:3-5).

BOLDNESS, OF THE RIGHTEOUS. Exemplified (Pr 28:1; Ac 18:26; 19:8; Heb 13:6); in prayer (Heb 4:16; 10:19; 1Jo 3:21, 22; 5:14, 15).

Inspired, by fear of the Lord (Pr 14:26); by faith in Christ (Eph 3:12).

Instances of, in Prayer: Abraham (Ge 18:23-32). Moses (Ex 33:12-18). In the day of judgment (1Jo 2:18; 4:17). Its effect on others (Ac 4:13).

See Courage.

BOLSTER, a pillow (Ge 28:11, 18; 1Sa 19:13).

BOLT, FIERY (Hab 3:5).

BOND, to keep the peace (Ac 17:9).

BONDAGE, of Israelites in Egypt (Ex 1:14; 2:23; 6:6); in Persia (Ezr 9:9).

See Emancipation; Servant.

BONDMAN (See Servant.)

BONES. Vision of the dry (Eze 37:1-14). None of Christ's broken (Ps 34:20; Joh 19:36).

BONNET, a turban. Worn by priests (Ex 28:40; 29:9; 39:28; Le 8:13; Eze 44:18); by women (Isa 3:20).

See Dress.

BOOK. Genealogies kept in (Ge 5:1). Law of Moses written in (Nu 5:23; De 17:18; 31:9, 24, 26; 2Ki 22:8). Topography of Palestine, recorded in (Jos 18:9).

Chronicles of the times kept in: By Jasher (Jos 10:13; 2Sa 1:18); Samuel, Nathan, and Gad (1Sa 10:25; 1Ch 29:29); Iddo (2Ch 12:15; 13:22); Isaiah (2Ch 26:22; 32:32; Isa 8:1). Of the kings of Judah and Israel: Of David (1Ch 27:24); Solomon (1Ki 11:41); Jehu (2Ch 20:34); of other kings (2Ch 24:27; 16:11; 25:26; 27:7; 28:26; 35:27; 36:8); of the kings of Israel (1Ki 14:19; 2Ch 20:34; 33:18). Other records kept in (Ezr 4:15; 6:1, 2; Es 6:1; 9:32; Jer 32:12; Ac 19:19).

Prophecies written in, by Jeremiah (Jer 25:13; 30:2; 45:1; 51:60, 63; Da 9:2). Other prophecies written in (2Ch 33:18, 19). Lamentations written in (2Ch 35:25). Numerous (Ec 12:12). Eating of (Jer 15:16; Eze 2:8-10; 3:1-3; Re 10:2-10). Of magic (Ac 19:19).

Paul's left at Troas (2Ti 4:13).

Made in a roll (Jer 36:4; Zec 5:1). Sealed (Isa 29:11; Da 12:4; Re 5:1-5).

Kirjath-jearim was called Kirjath-sepher, which signifies a city of books (Jos 15:15, 16; J'g 1:11, 12).

Figurative: Of Life: Names, of righteous written in (Ex 32:32; Da 12:1; Lu 10:20; Ph'p 4:3; Heb 12:23; Re 3:5; 21:27); of wicked blotted out of (Ex 32:33; Re 22:18, 19); of wicked not written in (Re 13:8; 17:8; 20:15).

Of Remembrance (Ps 56:8; 139:16; Mal 3:16; Re 20:12).

BOOTH. Made of boughs (Jon 4:5); made for cattle (Ge 33:17); watchmen (Job 27:18; Isa 1:8; 24:20). Prescribed for the Israelites to dwell in, during the Feast of Tabernacles, to celebrate their wanderings in the wilderness (Le 23:40-43; Ne 8:15, 16).

BOOTY. Spoils of war. Property and persons were sometimes preserved, and sometimes completely destroyed (Jos

6:18-21; De 20:14, 16-18). Abraham gave a tenth (Ge 14:20); David ordered that booty be shared with baggage guards (1Sa 30:21-25).

BOOZ (See Boaz.)

BORING THE EAR, a token of servitude for life (Ex 21:6).

BORROWING. Dishonesty in (Ps 37:21). Obligations in (Ex 22:14, 15). Distress from (Ne 5:1-5; Pr 22:7). Compassion toward debtors enjoined (Ne 5:6-13). Christ's rule concerning (M't 5:42).

See Lending; Interest.

Instances of: Israelites from the Egyptians (Ex 3:22; 11:2; 12:35).

Borrowing trouble (see Trouble, Borrowing.)

BOSCATH (See Bozkath.)

BOSOM. In Scripture the word is generally used in an affectionate sense (Isa 40:11; Joh 1:18). Sometimes it is almost synonymous with "heart" (Ec 7:9; Ps 35:13).

BOSOR (See Beor; Bozrah.)

BOSS, of a shield (Job 15:26).

BOTANICAL GARDENS, park, probably (Ec 2:5, 6, w 1Ki 4:33; 10:22).

BOTANY. Laws of nature in the vegetable kingdom uniform in action (M't 7:16-18, 20; Lu 6:43, 44; 1Co 15:36-38; Ga 6:7). Lily, beauty of (M't 6:28, 29). He that soweth sparingly shall reap also sparingly (2Co 9:6).

See Algum; Almond; Aloe; Anise; Apple; Ash; Balm; Barley; Bay; Bean; Box; Bramble; Bulrush; Camphire; Cane; Cassia; Cedar; Chestnut; Cinnamon; Cockle; Coriander; Corn; Cucumber; Cummin; Cypress; Date; Ebony; Elm; Fig Tree; Fir Tree; Fitch; Flag; Flax; Frankincense; Galbanum; Gall; Garlic; Gopherwood; Gourd; Grass; Hazel; Heath; Hemlock; Husk; Hyssop; Juniper; Leeks; Lentile; Lily; Mallow; Mandrake; Melon; Millet; Mint; Mulberry; Mustard; Myrrh; Myrtle; Nettle; Nut; Oak; Olive; Onion; Palm; Pine; Pomegranate; Poplar; Reed; Rose; Rue; Rye; Saffron; Shittim; Spikenard; Stacte; Sycamine; Sycamore; Tare; Teil; Thistle; Thorn; Thyine; Vine; Wheat; Willow; Wormwood.

BOTCH (See Boil.)

BOTTLE (Ge 21:14). Made of skins (Jos 9:4, 13; Job 32:19; Ps 119:83; M't 9:17; M'k 2:22; Lu 5:37, 38); of clay (Isa 30:14; Jer 19:1, 10; 48:12). Used as a lachrymatory (Ps 56:8).

See Pitcher.

BOTTOMLESS PIT (See Abyss.)

BOUNDARY STONES. Stones used to mark the boundary of property (Jos 13:21); to remove them was forbidden (De 27:17).

BOW. *A Weapon* (Ge 21:16, 20); Made of brass (2Sa 22:35; Job 20:24; Ps 18:34); of wood (Eze 39:9). Used in war (Isa 13:18; La 2:4; Eze 39:3). Used by the Elamites (Jer 49:35). David instructed the Israelites in the use of, by writing war song to (2Sa 1:18). Used in hunting. See Archery; Arrow.

Figurative: Ge 49:24; Job 16:13; 29:20; Ps 78:57; La 3:12; Ho 1:5; Hab 3:9; Re 6:2.

Rainbow: A token from God (Ge 9:8-16). A simile of God's glory (Eze 1:28). Symbolic (Re 4:3; 10:1).

BOWELS. Diseased (2Ch 21:15-20). Judas', gushed out (Ac 1:18).

Figurative: Of the sensibilities (Ge 43:30; 1Ki 3:26; Job 30:27; Ps 22:14; Song 5:4; Jer 4:19; 31:20; La 1:20; Ph'p 1:8; 2:1; Col 3:12; 1Jo 3:17).

See Heart.

BOWING, in worship (2Ch 7:3). See Worship, Attitudes in.

BOWL. Made of gold: For the tabernacle (Ex 25:29; 37:16); temple (1Ki 7:50; 1Ch 28:17; 2Ch 4:8); of silver (Nu 4:7; 7:13, 19, 25, 31, 37, 43, 49, 55, 61, 67, 73, 79, 84). Stamped "Holiness to the Lord" (Zec 14:20, 21).

See Basin.

Figurative: Ec 12:6.

BOX. For oil (2Ki 9:1-3). Made of alabaster (M't 26:7; M'k 14:3; Lu 7:37).

BOX TREE (Isa 41:19; 60:13).

BOXING. *Figurative:* 1Co 9:26 .

BOZEZ, a rock near Gibeah (1Sa 14:4).

BOZKATH, a city of Judah (Jos 15:39; 2Ki 22:1).

BOZRAH (sheepfold). 1. A city of Edom (Ge 36:33). Sheep of (Mic 2:12). Prophecies concerning (Isa 34:6; 63:1; Jer 49:13, 22; Am 1:12).

2. A town of Moab (Jer 48:24).

BRACELET. Present of (Ge 24:22). Worn by women (Ge 24:30; Isa 3:19); by men (Ge 38:18, 25). Dedicated to the tabernacle (Ex 35:22; Nu 31:50). Taken as spoils (Nu 31:50; 2Sa 1:10).

Figurative: Eze 16:11.

BRAMBLE (Isa 34:13; Lu 6:44). Allegory of (J'g 9:14, 15).

BRANCH, *Figurative* (Pr 11:28; Ho 14:6; Isa 60:21; Joh 15:2-5). Pruning of (Isa 18:5; Da 4:14; Joh 15:6; Ro 11:17, 21). Fruitless, cut off (Joh 15:2, 6). A title of Christ (Ps 80:15; Isa 4:2; 11:1; Jer 23:5; 33:15; Zec 3:8; 6:12). Symbolic name of Joshua (Zec 6:12).

See Grafting.

BRASS, or more probably Copper. Smelted (Eze 22:20; Job 28:2). A mineral of Canaan (De 8:9; Jos 22:8); of Syria (2Sa 8:8). Tyrians traded in (Eze 27:13). Abundance of, for the temple (1Ki 7:47; 1Ch 22:14). Articles made of: altar, vessels, and other articles of the tabernacle and temple (Ex 38:28-31; 1Ki 7:14-47; Ezr 8:27); cymbals (1Ch 15:19); trumpets (1Co 13:1); armor (1Sa 17:5, 6; 2Ch 12:10); bows, see Bows; fetters (J'g 16:21; 2Ki 25:7); gates (Ps 107:16; Isa 45:2); bars (1Ki 4:13); idols (Da 5:4; Re 9:20); mirrors (Ex 38:8); household vessels (M'k 7:4); money (M't 10:9; M'k 12:4 [marg.]).

Workers in: Tubal-cain (Ge 4:22); Hiram (1Ki 7:14); Alexander (2Ti 4:14).

See Brazier; Copper; Molding.

Figurative: Le 26:19; De 33:25; Isa 48:4; Jer 1:18; Eze 1:7; Da 2:32, 39; 7:19; 10:6; Zec 6:1; Re 1:15.

BRAVERY (See Boldness; Courage.)

BRAY, to pound (Pr 27:22).

BRAZEN SEA (See Laver.)

BRAZEN SERPENT. Made by Moses for the healing of the Israelites (Nu 21:9). Worshiped by Israelites (2Ki 18:4). A symbol of Christ (Joh 3:14, 15).

BRAZIER. 1. An artificer in brass and copper (Ge 4:22; 2Ti 4:14).

2. A utensil used for warming houses (Jer 36:22-24).

BREAD. Called the Staff of Life (Eze 4:16; 5:16; 14:13).

Kinds of: Bread of affliction (1Ki 22:27; Ps 127:2; Ho 9:4; Isa 30:20); leavened (Le 7:13; 23:17; Ho 7:4; Am 4:5; M't 13:33); unleavened (Ge 19:3; Ex 29:2; J'g 6:19; 1Sa 28:24).

Made of wheat flour (Ex 29:2; 1Ki 4:22; 5:11; Ps 81:16); manna (Nu 11:8); meal (1Ki 17:12); barley (J'g 7:13).

How Prepared: Mixed with oil (Ex 29:2, 23); honey (Ex 16:31); with leaven, or ferment, see leavened, in paragraph above, also see Leaven. Kneaded (Ge 18:6; Ex 8:3; 12:34; 1Sa 28:24; 2Sa 13:8; Jer 7:18; Ho 7:4). Made into loaves (1Sa 10:3; 17:17; 25:18; 1Ki 14:3; M'k 8:14); cakes (2Sa 6:19; 1Ki 17:12); wafers (Ex 16:21; 29:23); cracknels (1Ki 14:3). Baked in ovens (Ex 8:3; Le 2:4; 7:9; 11:35; 26:26; Ho 7:4); in pans (Le 2:5, 7; 2Sa 13:6-9); on hearths (Ge 18:6); on coals (1Ki 19:6; Isa 44:19; Joh 21:9).

Made by men (Ge 40:2); women (Le 26:26; 1Sa 8:13; Jer 7:18). Traffic in (Jer 37:21; M'k 6:37).

Sacrificed (Le 21:6, 8, 17, 21, 22; 22:25; 1Sa 2:36; 2Ki 23:9). By idolaters (Jer 7:18; 44:19).

See Shewbread; Offerings.

Figurative: Isa 55:2; 1Co 10:17; 2Co 9:10. Christ (Joh 6:32-35).

Symbolical: Of the body of Christ (M't 26:26; Ac 20:7; 1Co 11:23, 24).

BREASTPLATE. 1. For high priest (Ex 25:7). Directions for the making of (Ex 28:15-30). Made by Bezaleel (Ex 39:8, 21). Freewill offering of materials for (Ex 35:9, 27). Worn by Aaron (Ex 29:5; Le 8:8).

2. Armor for soldiers (Re 9:9, 17).

Figurative: For he put on righteousness as a breastplate, and an helmet of salvation upon his head (Isa 59:17).

Stand therefore, having your loins girt about with truth, and having on the breastplate of righteousness (Eph 6:14).

But let us, who are of the day, be sober, putting on the breastplate of faith and love; and for an helmet the hope of salvation (1Th 5:8).

BREATH. Of life (Ge 2:7; 7:22; Ac 17:25). Of God (2Sa 22:16; Job 4:9: 15:30; 33:4; 37:10; Ps 18:15; 33:6; Isa 30:33).

Figurative: Eze 37:9.

BREECHES, for the priests (Ex 28:42; 39:28; Le 6:10; 16:4; Eze 44:18).

BRETHREN, kindred of Christ (M't 12:46; 13:55; M'k 3:31; Joh 2:12; 7:3, 5; 1Co 9:5; Ga 1:19).

BRIBERY (Ps 26:9, 10; Pr 15:27; Isa 33:15, 16).

Corrupts conscience (Ex 23:8; De 16:18, 19; Ec 7:7). Perverts justice (1Sa 8:1, 3; 12:3; Pr 17:23; 28:21; Isa 1:23; 5:22, 23; Eze 22:12; Am 5:12; Mic 7:3).

Destroys national welfare (Pr 29:4). Profanes God (Eze 13:19).

Denunciation against (Job 15:34; Eze 22:12, 13). Punishment for (De 27:35; Am 2:6).

Instances of: Delilah (J'g 16:5). Samuel's sons (See above). The false prophet, Shemaiah (Ne 6:10-13). Ben-hadad (1Ki 15:19). Haman bribes Ahasuerus to destroy the Jews (Es 3:9). Chief priests bribe Judas (M't 26:15; 27:3-9; M'k 14:11; Lu 22:5). Soldiers bribed to declare that the disciples stole the body of Jesus (M't 28:12-15). Felix seeks a bribe from Paul (Ac 24:26).

BRICK. Used in building: Babel (Ge 11:3); cities in Egypt (Ex 1:11, 14); houses (Isa 9:10); altars (Isa 65:3). Made by Israelites (Ex 5:7-19; 2Sa 12:31; Jer 43:9; Na 3:14).

BRICK-KILN (Jer 43:9; Na 3:14). Captives tortured in (2Sa 12:31).

BRIDE. Presents to (Ge 24:53). Maids of (Ge 24:59, 61; 29:24, 29). Ornaments of (Isa 49:18; 61:10; Jer 2:32; Re 21:2).

Figurative: Ps 45:10-17; Eze 16:8-14; Re 19:7, 8; 21:2, 9; 22:17.

BRIDECHAMBER (See Wedding.)

BRIDEGROOM. Ornaments of (Isa 61:10). Exempt from military duty (De 24:5). Companions of (J'g 14:11). Joy with (M't 9:15; M'k 2:19, 20; Lu 5:34, 35).

Parable of (M't 25:1-13; Song 4:7-16).

Figurative: Eze 16:8-14.

BRIDGE. The word is not found in the English Bible. Bridges were hardly known among the Israelites, who generally crossed streams by a ford (Ge 32:22) or a ferry (2Sa 19:18).

BRIDLE (Ps 32:9; Pr 26:3; Re 14:20).

Figurative: 2Ki 19:28; Ps 39:1; Jas 1:26.

See Bit.

BRIER. *Figurative:* Isa 5:6; 55:13; Eze 2:6; 28:24.

BRIGANDINE, a coat of mail (Jer 46:4; 51:3).

BRIMSTONE, Fire and, rained upon Sodom (Ge 19:24; Lu 17:29). In Palestine (De 29:23).

Figurative: Job 18:15; Ps 11:6; Isa 30:33; Eze 38:22; Re 9:17, 18; 14:10; 19:20; 21:8.

BRONZE, an alloy of copper and tin. The word is not found in Scripture, but probably the "steel" used for making metallic bows was really bronze (2Sa 22:35; Job 20:24). (See Brass.)

BROOK (See River.)

BROTH (J'g 6:19, 20; 2Ki 4:38; Isa 65:4). Symbolical (Eze 24:5).

BROTHEL (See High Place.)

BROTHER. Signifies a relative (Ge 14:16; 29:12); neighbor (De 23:7; J'g 21:6; Ne 5:7); any Israelite (Jer 34:9; Ob 10); mankind (Ge 9:5; M't 18:35; 1Jo 3:15); companion (2Sa 1:26; 1Ki 13:30; 20:33). Love of (Pr 17:17; 18:24; Song 8:1). Unfaithful (Pr 27:10). Reuben's love for Joseph (Ge 37:21, 22). Joseph's, for his brethren (Ge 43:30-34; 45:1-5; 50:19-25).

A fraternal epithet, especially among Christians. Instituted by Christ (M't 12:50; 25:40; Heb 2:11, 12). Used by disciples (Ac 9:17; 21:20; Ro 16:23; 1Co 7:12; 2Co 2:13); Peter (1Pe 1:22). Used among the Israelites (Le 19:17; De 22:1-4).

Brother's widow, law concerning Levirate marriage of (De 25:5-10; M't 22:24; M'k 12:19; Lu 20:28).

BROTHERLY KINDNESS. See Brother; Charitableness; Fellowship; Fraternity; Friendship; Love.

BROTHERS OF OUR LORD. James, Joses, Simon, and Judas are called the Lord's brothers (M't 13:55); He also had sisters (M't 13:56); Joh 7:1-10 states that his brothers did not believe in him. There are differences of opinion as to whether the "brothers" were full brothers, cousins, or children of Joseph by a former marriage.

BRUISED REED (2Ki 18:21; Isa 42:3; Eze 29:6).

BUCKET (Nu 24:7; Isa 40:15).

BUCKLER (See Shield.)

BUILDER, of the tabernacle. See Bezaleel; Master Workman.

Figurative: Ps 118:22; M't 21:42; Ac 4:11; 1Pe 2:7; Heb 11:10.

See Carpenter.

BUILDING. *Figurative:* 2Co 5:1.

BUKKI. 1. Son of Abishua (1Ch 6:5, 51; Ezr 7:4).

2. A prince of Dan (Nu 34:22).

BUKKIAH, a Levite (1Ch 25:4, 13).

BUL, the eighth month (November). The temple completed in (1Ki 6:38). Jeroboam institutes an idolatrous feast in, to correspond with the Feast of Tabernacles (1Ki 12:32, 33; 1Ch 27:11).

BULL, wild, caught in nets (Isa 51:20). Blood of, in sacrifice (Heb 9:13; 10:4).

See Bullock; Offerings.

BULLOCK, OR OX (Synonymous terms *A. V.*). Uses of; For sacrifice (Ex 29:3, 10-14, 36; Le 4:8, 16; Nu 7:87, 88; 28:11-31; 29); plowing (1Sa 14:14; 1Ki 19:19; Pr 14:4; Isa 32:20; Jer 31:18); treading out corn (De 25:4); with wagons (Nu 7:3-8; 2Sa 6:3-6).

Laws concerning: Trespass by (Ex 21:28-36); theft of (Ex 22:1-10); rest for (Ex 23:12); not to be muzzled when treading grain (De 25:4; 1Co 9:9; 1Ti 5:18); not to be yoked with an ass (De 22:10).

Twelve brazen, under the molten sea in Solomon's temple (1Ki 7:25; 2Ch 4:4; Jer 52:20).

See Bull; Cattle.

Symbolical: Eze 1:10; Re 4:7.

BULRUSH [papyrus, *R. V.*], Moses' ark of (Ex 2:3). Boats made of (Isa 18:2).

Figurative: Ps 48:13; Isa 26:1.

BULWARK (De 20:20; 2Ch 26:15; Ec 9:14).

Figurative: Ps 48:13; Isa 26:1.

BUNAH, son of Jerahmeel (1Ch 2:25).

BUNNI. 1. A Levite, a teacher with Ezra (Ne 9:4).

2. Ancestor of Shemaiah (Ne 11:15).

3. A family of Jews (Ne 10:15).

BURDEN. *Figurative:* Of oppressions (Isa 58:6; M't 23:4; Lu 11:46; Ga 6:2). Of the prophetic message (Isa 13:1; 15:1; 17:1; 19:1).

BURGLARY (See Theft.)

BURIAL. Rites of (Jer 34:5). Soon after death (De 21:23; Jos 8:29; Joh 19:38-42; Ac 5:9, 10). With spices (2Ch 16:14; M'k 16:1; Lu 23:56). Bier used at (2Sa 3:31; Lu 7:14). Attended by relatives and friends: Of Jacob (Ge 50:5-9); Abner (2Sa 3:31); child of Jeroboam (1Ki 14:13); the son of the widow of Nain (Lu 7:12, 13); Stephen (Ac 8:2).

Lack of, a disgrace (2Ki 9:10; Pr 30:17; Jer 16:4; 22:19; Eze 39:15). Directions given about, before death, by Jacob (Ge 49:29, 30); Joseph (Ge 50:25). Burial of Gog (multitude) requiring 7 months (Eze 39:12, 13).

BURYING PLACES: Bought by Abraham (Ge 23; 25:9). Prepared by Jacob (Ge 50:5); Asa (2Ch 16:14); Joseph (M't 27:60). On hills (2Ki 23:16; Jos 24:33). In valleys (Jer 7:32).

Family (Ge 47:30; 49:29; Ac 7:16). Of kings (1Ki 2:10; 2Ch 32:33); a place of honor (2Ch 24:16, 25; 21:20). For poor and strangers (Jer 26:23; M't 27:7).

Tombs: In houses (1Sa 25:1; 1Ki 2:34); in gardens (2Ki 21:18, 26; Joh 19:41); in caves (Ge 23:9); under trees. Deborah's (Ge 35:8); King Saul's (1Sa 31:13).

Closed with stones (M't 27:60, 66; Joh 11:38; 20:1). Sealed (M't 27:66). Marked with pillars: Rachel's (Ge 35:20), and inscriptions (2Ki 23:17). Painted and garnished (M't 23:27, 29). With shelves (Isa 14:15). Demoniacs dwelt in (M't 8:28). Any who touched, were unclean (Nu 19:16, 18; Isa 65:4). Refused to the dead (Re 11:9). Robbed (Jer 8:1).

See Cremation; Dead, The; Death; Elegy; Grave; Mourning.

Figurative: Isa 22:16; Ro 6:4; Col 2:12.

BURNING, as a punishment. (See Punishment.)

BURNING-BUSH (Ex 3:2-5; Ac 7:30).

BURNT OFFERING (See Offerings, Burnt.)

BUSHEL, about one peck (M't 5:15; M'k 4:21; Lu 11:33).

BUSINESS LIFE. Virtues: Diligence (Pr 10:4; 13:4; 22:29; 2Pe 3:14). Fidelity (Ge 39:6; 2Ch 34:11, 12; Ne 13:13; Da 6:4; 1Co 4:2; Heb 3:5). Honesty (Le 19:35, 36; De 25:15; Pr 11:1; Ro 12:17; 13:8). Industry (Ge 2:15; Pr 6:6, 10:5; 12:11; 13:11; 20:13; Ro 12:11). Giving of just weights (Le 19:36; De 25:13; Pr 11:1; 16:11; 20:10; Eze 45:10; Mic 6:11). Integrity (Ps 41:12; Pr 11:3; 19:1; 20:7). Vices Found in: Breach of trust (Le 6:2; Song 1:6; Eze 16:17; Lu 16:12). Dishonesty (De 25:13; Pr 11:1; 20:14; 21:6; Ho 12:7). Extortion (Isa 10:2; Eze 22:12; Am 5:11; M't 18:28; 23:25; Lu 3:13). Fraud (Le 19:13; M'k 10:19; 1Co 6:8). Unjust gain (Pr 16:8; 21:6; 22:16; Jer 17:11; 22:13; Eze 22:13; Jas 5:4). Slothfulness (Pr 18:9; 24:30, 31; Ec 10:18; 2Th 3:11; Heb 6:12).

BUSYBODY (Pr 26:17; 1Ti 5:13; 2Th 3:11, 12).

Injunction against (Le 19:16; 1Pe 4:15).

See Talebearer; Speaking, Evil.

BUTLER. Pharaoh's, imprisoned and released (Ge 40; 1Ki 10:5; 2Ch 9:4; Ne 1:11; 2:1).

BUTTER (Ge 18:8; De 32:14; J'g 5:25; 2Sa 17:29; Job 20:17; Isa 7:15, 22). Made by churning (Pr 30:33).

BUZ. 1. Son of Nahor (Ge 22:21).

2. Father of Jahdo (1Ch 5:14).

BUZI, father of Ezekiel (Eze 1:3).

BYBLOS (See Gebal.)

BYWAYS, literally "crooked paths," travelled to avoid danger (J'g 5:6).

C

CAB, a dry measure containing about two quarts (2Ki 6:25).

See Measure.

CABBON, a place in Judah (Jos 15:40).

CABINET, heads of departments in government. David's (2Sa 8:15-18; 15:12; 20:23-26; 1Ch 27:32-34); Solomon's (1Ki 4:1-7); Hezekiah's (Isa 36:3); Artaxerxes' (Ezr 7:14).

See Counsellor; Minister, Prime.

CABUL. 1. A city in the N of Palestine (Jos 19:27).

2. Name given by Hiram to certain cities in Galilee (1Ki 9:13).

CAESAR. 1. Augustus (Lu 2:1).

2. Tiberius (Lu 3:1; 20:22).

3. Claudius (Ac 11:28).

4. Nero (Ph'p 4:22).

CAESAREA. A seaport in Palestine. Home of Philip (Ac 8:40; 21:8); Cornelius, the centurion (Ac 10:1, 24); Herod (Ac 12:19-23); Felix (Ac 23:23, 24). Paul conveyed to, by the disciples to save him from his enemies (Ac 9:30); by Roman soldiers to be tried by Felix (Ac 23:23-35).

CAESAREA PHILIPPI, a city in the N of Palestine; visited by Jesus (M't 16:13; M'k 8:27; Lu 9:18).

CAGE, for birds, unclean (Jer 5:27; Re 18:2).

CAIAPHAS. High priest (Lu 3:2); son-in-law of Annas (Joh 18:13). Prophesies concerning Jesus (Joh 11:49-51; 18:14). Jesus tried before (M't 26:2, 3, 57, 63-65; Joh 18:24, 28). Peter and other disciples accused before (Ac 4:1-22).

CAIN. 1. Son of Adam (Ge 4:1). Jealousy and crime of (Ge 4:3-15; Heb 11:4; 1Jo 3:12; Jude 11). Sojourns in the land of Nod (Ge 4:16). Children and descendants of (Ge 4:17, 18).

2. A city of Judah (Jos 15:57).

CAINAN. 1. Called also Kenan. Son of Enos (Ge 5:9-15; 1Ch 1:2; Lu 3:37).

2. Son of Arphaxad (Lu 3:36).

CAKES, mentioned (J'g 7:13; 2Sa 6:19; 1Ki 17:12; 19:6; Ho 7:8).

CALAH, an ancient city of Assyria (Ge 10:11, 12).

CALAMUS. A sweet cane of Palestine (Song 4:14; Eze 27:19). An ingredient of the holy ointment (Ex 30:23; Isa 43:24). Commerce in (Jer 6:20; Eze 27:19).

CALCOL, son of Zerah (1Ch 2:6).

CALDRON, in the tabernacle (1Sa 2:14); temple (2Ch 35:13; Jer 52:18, 19).

Figurative: Eze 11:3-11.

CALEB (dog). One of the two survivors of the Israelites permitted to enter the land of promise (Nu 14:30, 38; 26:63-65; 32:11-13; De 1:34-36; Jos 14:6-15). Sent to Canaan as a spy (Nu 13:6). Brings favorable report (Nu 13:26-30; 14:6-9). Assists in dividing Canaan (Nu 34:19). Life of, miraculously saved (Nu 14:10-12). Leader of the Israelites after Joshua's death (J'g 1:11, 12). Age of (Jos 14:7-10). Inheritance of (Jos 14:6-15; 15:13-16). Descendants of (1Ch 4:15).

CALEB-EPHRATAH, a place near Beth-lehem (1Ch 2:24).

CALENDAR. In Bible time was reckoned solely on astronomical observations. Days, months, and years were determined by the sun and moon. 1. Days of the week were not named by the Jews, but were designated by ordinal numbers. Jewish day began in the evening with the appearance of the first stars. Days were subdivided into hours and watches. Hebrews divided nights into three watches (Ex 14:24; J'g 7:19; La 2:19). 2. Egyptians had a week of 10 days. The seven-day week is of Semitic origin (the Creation account), and ran consecutively irrespective of lunar or solar cycles. This was done for man's physical and spiritual welfare. The Biblical records are silent regarding the observance of the Sabbath day from creation to the time of Moses. Sabbath observance was either revived or given special emphasis by Moses (Ex 16:23; 20:8). 3. The Hebrew month began with the new moon. Before the exile months were designated by numbers. After the exile names adopted from the Babylonians were used. Synchronized Jewish sacred calendar: 1. Nisan (March-April) (7). 2. Iyyar (April-May) (8). 3. Sivan (May-June) (9). 4. Tammuz (June-July) (10). 5. Ab (July-August) (11). 6. Elul (August-September) (12). 7. Tishri (September-October) (1). 8. Heshavan (October-November) (2). 9. Kislev (November-December) (3). 10. Tabeth (December-January) (4). 11. Shebat (January-February) (5). 12. Adar (February-March) (6). 4. The Jewish calendar had two concurrent years, the sacred year, beginning in the spring with the month Nisan, and the civic year, beginning with Tishri, numbered in parentheses above. The sacred year was instituted by Moses, and consisted of lunar months of 29-½ days each, with an intercalary month, called Adar Sheni, every 3 years. Every 7th year was a sabbatical year for the Jews—a year of solemn rest for landlords, slaves, beasts of burden, and land, and freedom for Hebrew slaves. Every 50th year was a Jubilee year, observed by family reunions, canceled mortgages, and return of lands to original owners (Le 25:8-17).

CALF. Offered in sacrifice (Mic 6:6). Golden, made by Aaron (Ex 32; De 9:16; Ne 9:18; Ps 106:19; Ac 7:41).

Images of, set up in Beth-el and Dan by Jeroboam (1Ki 12:28-33; 2Ki 10:29). Worshiped by Jehu (2Ki 10:29). Prophecies against the golden calves at Beth-el (1Ki 13:1-5, 32; Jer 48:13; Ho 8:5, 6; 10:5, 6, 15; 13:2; Am 3:14; 4:4; 8:14). Altars of, destroyed (2Ki 23:4, 15-20).

"Calves of the lips," a metaphor signifying worship (Ho 14:2).

CALKERS (Eze 27:9, 27).

CALL, *Personal:* By Christ (Isa 55:5; Ro 1:6); by his Spirit (Re 22:17); by his works (Ps 19:2, 3; Ro 1:20); by his ministers (Jer 35:15; 2Co 5:20); by his gospel (2Th 2:14). Is from darkness to light (1Pe 2:9). Addressed to all (Isa 45:22; M't 20:16). Most reject (Pr 1:24; M't 20:16). Effectual to saints (Ps 110:3; Ac 13:48; 1Co 1:24). Not to many wise (1Co 1:26). To repentance (Isa 55:1).

To saints, is of grace (Ga 1:6; 2Ti 1:9); according to the purpose of God (Ro 8:28; 9:11, 23, 24); without repentance (Ro 11:29); high (Ph'p 3:14); holy (2Ti 1:9); heavenly (Heb 3:1); to fellowship with Christ (1Co 1:9); to holiness (1Th 4:7); to a prize (Ph'p 3:14); to liberty (Ga 5:13); to peace (1Co 7:15; Col 3:15); to glory and virtue (2Pe 1:3); to the eternal glory of Christ (2Th 2:14; 1Pe 5:10); to eternal life (1Ti 6:12).

Partakers of, justified (Ro 8:30); walk worthy of (Eph 4:1; 2Th 1:11); blessedness of receiving (Re 19:9); is to be made sure (2Pe 1:10); praise God for (1Pe 2:9); illustrated (Pr 8:3, 4; M't 23:3-9).

Rejected (Jer 6:16; M't 22:3-7).

Rejection of, leads to judicial blindness (Isa 6:9, w Ac 28:24-27; Ro 11:8-10); delusion (Isa 66:4; 2Th 2:10, 11); withdrawal of the means of grace (Jer 26:4-6; Ac 13:46; 18:6; Re 2:5); temporal judgments (Isa 28:12; Jer 6:16, 19; 35:17; Zec 7:12-14); rejection by God (Pr 1:24-32; Jer 6:19, 30); condemnation (Joh 12:48; Heb 2:1-3; 12:25); destruction (Pr 29:1; M't 22:3-7).

To Special Religious Duty: Abraham (Ge 12:1-3; Isa 51:2; Heb 11:8). Moses (Ex 3:2, 4, 10; 4:1-16; Ps 105:26; Ac 7:34, 35). Aaron and his sons (Ex 4:14-16; 28:1; Ps 105:26; Heb 5:4). Joshua (Nu 27:18, 19, 22, 23; De 31:14, 23; Jos 1:1-9). Gideon (J'g 6:11-16). Samuel (1Sa 3:4-10). Solomon (1Ch 28:6, 10). Jehu (2Ki 9:6, 7; 2Ch 22:7). Cyrus (Isa 45:1-4). Amos (Am 7:14, 15). Apostles (M't 4:18-22; 9:9; M'k 1:16, 17; 2:14; 3:13-19; Lu 5:27; 6:13-16; Joh 15:16). The rich young ruler (M'k 10:21, 22). Paul (Ac 9:4-6, 15, 16; 13:2, 3; Ro 1:1; 1Co 1:1; 2Co 1:1; Ga 1:1, 15, 16; Eph 1:1; Col 1:1; 1Ti 1:1; 2Ti 1:1). To all believers (Ro 8:30; 1Co 1:2, 9, 24; 1Th 2:11, 12; 2Th 2:13, 14; 2Ti 1:9; Heb 3:1, 2, 7, 8; 1Pe 5:10; 2Pe 1:3, 10; Jude 1; Re 17:14).

See Ministers, Call of; Backsliders; Seekers.

CALLING, THE CHRISTIAN (1Co 1:26; Eph 1:18; 4:1; Ph'p 3:14; 1Th 2:12; 2Th 2:14; 2Ti 1:9; Heb 3:1; 1Pe 5:10; 2Pe 1:10).

CALNEH, called also Canneh and Calno, a city of Assyria (Ge 10:10; Isa 10:9; Eze 27:23; Am 6:2).

CALNO, city which tried to resist the Assyrians (Isa 10:9).

CALVARY (skull), called also Golgotha, place where Jesus was crucified (M't 27:33; M'k 15:22; Lu 23:33; Joh 19:17).

CAMEL, herds of (Ge 12:16; 24:35; 30:43; 1Sa 30:17; 1Ch 27:30; Job 1:3, 17; Isa 60:6).

Docility of (Ge 24:11). Uses of: For riding (Ge 24:10, 61, 64; 31:17); posts

(Es 8:10, 14; Jer 2:23); drawing chariots (Isa 21:7); for carrying burdens (Ge 24:10; 37:25; 1Ki 10:2; 2Ki 8:9; 1Ch 12:40; Isa 30:6); for cavalry (1Sa 30:17); for milk (Ge 32:15). Forbidden as food (Le 11:4). Hair of, made into cloth (M't 3:4; M'k 1:6).

Ornaments of (J'g 8:21, 26). Stables for (Eze 25:5).

CAMEL'S HAIR, mentioned only in M't 3:4 and M'k 1:6, where it is said that John the Baptist wore a garment of camel's hair. Such garments are still used in the Near East.

CAMON, place where Jair was buried (J'g 10:5).

CAMP, of the Israelites about the tabernacle (Nu 2; 3).

See Itinerary.

CAMPHIRE (Henna, *R.V.*), a shrub bearing fragrant flowers, not related to camphor (Song 1:14; 4:13).

CANA. Marriage at (Joh 2:1-11). Nobleman's son healed at (Joh 4:46, 47). Nathanael's home at (Joh 21:2).

CANAAN. 1. Son of Ham (Ge 9:18, 22, 25-27). Descendants of (Ge 10:6, 15; 1Ch 1:8, 13).

2. Land of (Ge 11;31; 17:8; 23:2). Called The Sanctuary (Ex 15:17); Palestine (Ex 15:14); Land of Israel (1Sa 13:19); of the Hebrews (Ge 40:15); of the Jews (Ac 10:39); of Promise (Heb 11:9); Holy Land (Zec 2:12); Lord's Land (Ho 9:3); Immanuel's Land (Isa 8:8); Beulah (Isa 62:4).

Promised to Abraham and his seed (Ge 12:1-7; 13:14-17; 15:18-21; 17:8; De 12:9, 10; Ps 105:11); renewed to Isaac (Ge 26:3). Extent of: According to the promise (Ge 15:18; Ex 23:31; De 11:24; Jos 1:4; 15:1); after the conquest by Joshua (Jos 12:1-8); in Solomon's time (1Ki 4:21, 24; 2Ch 7:8; 9:26). Prophecy concerning, after the restoration of Israel (Eze 47:13-20).

Fertility of (De 8:7-9; 11:10-13). Fruitfulness of (Nu 13:27; 14:7, 8; Jer 2:7; 32:22). Products of: Fruits (De 8:8; Jer 40:10, 12); mineral (De 8:9). Exports of (Eze 27:17).

Famines in (Ge 12:10; 26:1; 47:13; Ru 1:1; 2Sa 21:1; 1Ki 17). See Famine.

Spies sent into, by Moses (Nu 13:17-29). Conquest of, by the Israelites (Nu 21:21-35; De 3:3-6; Jos 6-12; Ps 44:1-3). Divided by lot among the twelve tribes and families (Nu 26:55, 56; 33:54; 34:13); by Joshua, Eleazar and a prince from each tribe (Nu 34:16-29; 35:1-8; Jos 14-19). Divided into twelve provinces by Solomon (1Ki 4:7-19). Into two kingdoms, Judah and Israel (1Ki 11:29-36; 12:16-21). Roman provinces of (Lu 3:1; Joh 4:3, 4).

CANAANITE, SIMON THE, one of the 12 apostles (M't 10:4).

CANAANITES. Eleven nations, descended from Canaan (Ge 10:15-19; De 7:1; 1Ch 1:13-16). Territory of (Ge 10:19; 12:6; 15:18; Ex 23:31; Nu 13:29; 34:1-12; Jos 1:4; 5:1); given to the Israelites (Ge 12:6, 7; 15:18; 17:8; Ex 23:23; De 7:1-3; 32:49; Ps 135:11, 12).

Wickedness of (Ge 13:13; Le 18:25, 27, 28; 20:23). To be expelled from the land (Ex 33:2; 34:11). To be destroyed (Ex 23:23, 24; De 19:1; 31:3-5). Not expelled (Jos 17:12-18; J'g 1:1-33; 3:1-3). Defeat the Israelites (Nu 14:45; J'g 4:1-3). Defeated by the Israelites (Nu 21:1-3; Jos 11:1-16; J'g 4:4-24); by the Egyptians (1Ki 9:16). Chariots of (Jos 17:18).

Isaac forbidden by Abraham to take a wife from (Ge 28:1). Judah marries a woman of (Ge 38:2; 1Ch 2:3). The exile Jews take wives from (Ezr 9:2).

Prophecy concerning (Ge 9:25-27).

CANANAEN, the description of Simon "the Zealot" in M't 10:4. Cananaen is Aramaic for Zealot. KJV has "Canaanite," but this is wrong.

CANDACE, queen of Ethiopia (Ac 8:27).

CANDIDATE. Refuses to make promises (2Ch 10:3-16). Electioneering by, instance of, Absalom (2Sa 15:1-6).

CANDLE. Revised version and commentators substitute lamp for candle throughout the Scriptures.

See Lamp.

CANDLESTICK. Of the Tabernacle: Made after divine pattern (Ex 25:31-40; 37:17-24; Nu 8:4). Place of (Ex 26:35; 40:24, 25; Heb 9:2). Furniture of (Ex 25:38; 37:23; Nu 4:9, 10). Burned every night (Ex 27:20, 21). Trimmed every morning (Ex 30:7). Carried by Kohathites (Nu 4:4, 15). Called The Lamp of God (1Sa 3:3).

Of the Temple: Ten branches of (1Ki

7:49, 50). Of gold (1Ch 28:15; 2Ch 4:20). Taken with other spoils to Babylon (Jer 52:19).

Symbolical: Zec 4:2, 11; Re 1:12, 13, 20; 2:5; 11:4.

CANE, probably the sweet calamus (Isa 43:24; Jer 6:20).

CANKER (gangrene), a word that may mean "cancer" (2Ti 2:17).

CANKERWORM, sent as a judgment (Joe 1:4; 2:25; Na 3:15, 16).

CANNEH (See Calneh.)

CANNIBALISM (Le 26:29; De 28:53-57; 2Ki 6:28, 29; Jer 19:9; La 2:20; 4:10; Eze 5:10).

CANONICITY. By the canon is meant the list of the books of the Bible accepted by the Christian church as genuine and inspired. The Protestant canon includes 39 books in the OT and 27 in the New. The Roman Catholic canon has 7 more books and some additional pieces in the OT. The Jews have the same OT canon as the Protestants. The OT canon was formed before the time of Christ, as is evident from Josephus (Against Apion 1:8), who wrote c. A. D. 90. We know very little of the history of the acceptance of the OT books as canonical. There is much more documentary evidence regarding the formation of the NT canon. The Muratorian Canon (c. A. D. 170), which survives only as a fragment, lists most of the NT books. Some of the books were questioned for a time for various reasons, usually uncertainty of authorship, but by the end of the 4th century our present canon was almost universally accepted, and this was done not by arbitrary decree of bishops, but by the general consensus of the church.

CANTICLES (See Song of Solomon.)

CAPERNAUM (village of Nahum). A city on the shore of the Sea of Galilee. Jesus chose, as the place of his abode (M't 4:13; Lu 4:31). Miracles of Jesus performed at (M't 9:1-26; 17:24-27; M'k 1:21-45; 2; 3:1-6; Lu 7:1-10; Joh 4:46-53; 6:17-25, 59).

His prophecy against (M't 11:23; Lu 10:15).

CAPHTOR, place from which the Philistines originally came (Am 9:7), probably from the island of Crete.

CAPHTORIM, people of Caphtor (Ge 10:14; De 2:23; 1Ch 1:12; Jer 47:4; Am 9:7).

CAPITAL PUNISHMENT (See Punishment.)

CAPITAL AND LABOR. Strife between (M't 21:33-41; M'k 12:1-9; Lu 20:9-10).

See Employee; Employer; Master; Rich, The; Servant.

CAPPADOCIA, easternmost province of Asia Minor (Ac 2:9; 1Pe 1:1).

CAPTAIN. Commander-in-chief of an army (De 20:9; J'g 4:2; 1Sa 14:50; 1Ki 2:35; 16:16; 1Ch 27:34). Of the tribes (Nu 2). Of thousands (Nu 31:48; 1Sa 17:18; 1Ch 28:1). Of hundreds (2 Ki 11:15). See Centurion. Of fifties (2Ki 1:9; Isa 3:3). Of the guard (Ge 37:36; 2Ki 25:8). Of the ward (Jer 37:13).

Signifying any commander (1Sa 9:16; 22:2; 2Ki 20:5); leader (1Ch 11:21; 12:34; 2Ch 17:14-19; Joh 18:12).

David's captains, or chief heroes (2Sa 23; 1Ch 11; 12). King appoints (1Sa 18:13; 2Sa 17:25; 18:1).

Angel of the Lord, called (Jos 5:14; 2Ch 13:12). Christ called (Heb 2:10).

See Armies.

CAPTIVE. Prisoner of war (Ge 14:12; 1Sa 30:1, 2). Cruelty to: Putting to death (Nu 31:9-20; De 20:13; 21:10; Jos 8:29; 10:15-40; 11:11; J'g 7:25; 8:21; 21:11; 1Sa 15:32, 33; 2Sa 8:2; 2Ki 8:12; Jer 39:6); twenty thousand, by Amaziah (2Ch 25:11, 12); ripping women with child (2Ki 8:12; 15:16; Am 1:13); tortured under saws and harrows (2Sa 12:31; 1Ch 20:3); blinded (J'g 16:21; Jer 39:7); maimed (J'g 1:6, 7); ravished (La 5:11-13; Zec 14:2); enslaved (De 20:14; 2Ki 5:2; Ps 44:12; Joe 3:6); robbed (Eze 23:25, 26); confined in pits (Isa 51:14). Other indignities to (Isa 20:4).

Kindness to (2Ki 25:27-30; Ps 106:46). Advanced to positions in state (Ge 41:39-45; Es 2:8; Da 1).

CAPTIVITY. Of the Israelites foretold (Le 26:33; De 28:36); of the ten tribes (2Ki 17:6, 23, 24; 18:9-12).

Of Judah in Babylon, prophecy of (Isa 39:6; Jer 13:19; 20:4; 25:2-11; 32:28); fulfilled (2Ki 24:11-16; 25; 2Ch 36; Jer 52:28-30). Jews return from (Ezr 2; 3; 8).

Israelites in, promises to (Ne 1:9).

As a judgment (Ezr 5:12; 9:7; Isa 5:13; Jer 29:17-19; La 1:3-5; Eze 39:23, 24).

Figurative: Isa 61:1; Ro 7:23; 1Co 9:27; 2Co 10:5; 2Ti 2:26; 3:6. "Captivity led captive" (J'g 5:12; Ps 68:18; Eph 4:8).

CARAVAN, company of travelers united together for a common purpose or for mutual protection and generally equipped for a long journey, especially in desert country or through foreign and presumably hostile territory (Ge 32; 33; 1Sa 30:1-20).

CARBUNCLE. A precious stone (Isa 54:12; Eze 28:13). One of the precious stones set in breast-plate (Ex 28:17; 39:10).

CARCAS, a Persian chamberlain (Es 1:10).

CARCASE (ASV and modern English, **carcass),** the dead body of a man or beast. Jews were ceremonially unclean if they touched a carcass (Le 11:8-40; Nu 6:6, 7; 9:10; De 14:8).

CARCHEMISH, a Babylonian city on the Euphrates, against which the king of Egypt made war (2Ch 35:20; Isa 10:9; Jer 46:2).

CARE. *Worldly* (Ps 39:6; 127:2; Ec 4:8; M't 6:25-34; 13:22; M'k 4:19; Lu 8:14; 12:27; 14:18, 19; 21:34; 1Co 7:32, 33; Ph'p 4:6; 2Ti 2:4).

Unavailing (Ps 39:6; 127:2; M't 6:27; Lu 12:25, 26); proceeds from unbelief (M't 6:26, 28-30; Lu 12:24, 27, 28); Martha rebuked for (Lu 10:40, 41).

Remedy for (Ps 37:5; 55:22; Pr 16:3; Jer 17:7, 8; M't 6:26-34; Lu 12:22-32; Ph'p 4:6, 7; Heb 13:5; 1Pe 5:6, 7).

Instances of: Martha (Lu 10:40, 41). Certain ones who desired to follow Jesus (M't 8:19-22; Lu 9:57-62).

See Anxiety; Carnal Mindedness; Rich; Riches; Worldliness.

CAREAH (See Kareah.)

CARMEL (garden). 1. A fertile and picturesque mountain in Palestine (Song 7:5; Isa 33:9; 35:2; Jer 46:18; 50:19; Am 1:2). Forests of (2Ki 19:23). Caves of (Am 9:3; Mic 7:14). An idolatrous high place upon; Elijah builds an altar upon, and confounds the worshipers of Baal, putting to death four hundred and fifty of its prophets (1Ki 18:17-46). Elisha's abode in (2Ki 2:25; 4:25).

2. A city of Judah (Jos 15:55). Saul erects a memorial at (1Sa 15:12). Nabal's possessions at (1Sa 25:2). King Uzziah, who delighted in agriculture, had vineyards at (2Ch 26:10).

CARMELITE, native of Judaean Carmel (1Sa 27:3; 1Ch 11:37).

CARMI. 1. Son of Reuben (Ge 46:9; Ex 6:14).

2. Son of Hezron (1Ch 4:1). Called Chelubai (1Ch 2:9, and Caleb).

3. Father of Achan (Jos 7:1, 18; 1Ch 2:7).

CARNAL MINDEDNESS. Is in conflict, with the inward man (Ro 7:14-22); with the Holy Spirit (Ga 5:17). Is at enmity with God (Ro 8:6-8; Jas 4:4). In the children of wrath (Eph 2:3). To be crucified (Ro 8:13; Ga 5:24). Excludes from kingdom of God (Ga 5:19-21). Reaps corruption (Ga 6:8).

See Care, Worldly; Riches; Sin, Fruits of; Worldliness.

CARPENTRY. Building the ark (Ge 6:14-16). Tabernacle, and furniture of (Ex 31:2-9). See Tabernacle. David's palace (2Sa 5:11). Temple (2Ki 12:11; 22:6). See Temple. Making idols (Isa 41:7; 44:13). Carpenters (Jer 24:1; Zec 1:20); Joseph (M't 13:55); Jesus (M'k 6:3).

See Carving; Master Workman.

CARPET (Pr 31:22).

CARPUS, a Christian at Troas (2Ti 4:13).

CARRIAGE, baggage (1Sa 17:22; Isa 10:28).

CARSHENA, a Persian prince (Es 1:14).

CART (1Sa 6:7-14; 2Sa 6:3; Isa 28:27, 28).

See Wagon.

CARVING. Woodwork of the temple was decorated with carvings of flowers, cherubim, and palm trees (1Ki 6:18, 29, 32, 35; Ps 74:6). Beds decorated with (Pr 7:16). Idols manufactured by (De 7:5; Isa 44:9-17; 45:20; Hab 2:18, 19). Persons skilled in: Bezaleel (Ex 31:5); Hiram (1Ki 7:13-51; 2Ch 2:13, 14).

CASIPHIA, a place in the Persian empire (Ezr 8:17).

CASLUHIM, a people whose progenitor was a son of Mizraim (Ge 10:14; 1Ch 1:12).

CASSIA. An aromatic plant, probably cinnamon (Ps 45:8; Eze 27:19). An ingredient of the sacred oil (Ex 30:24).

CASTING (See Molding.)

CASTING LOTS (Le 16:8; Nu 26:55; Jos 18:10; 1Sa 14:41; Es 3:7; Pr 16:33; 18:18; Jon 1:7; M't 27:35; Ac 1:26).

CASTLE. A tower (Ge 25:16; Nu 31:10; 1Ch 11:5, 7; 2Ch 17:12; 27:4; Ac 21:34, 37; 23:10, 16, 32). Bars of (Pr 18:19). For the doctrine, "The house is my castle," see De 24:10, 11.

See Fort; Tower.

CASTOR AND POLLUX, name of a ship (Ac 28:11).

CATACOMBS, subterranean burial places used by the early church. Most are in Rome, where they extend for 600 miles.

CATERPILLAR. Sent as a judgment (1Ki 8:37; Ps 78:46; 105:34; Jer 51:27; Joe 1:4; 2:25).

CATHOLIC EPISTLES, term applied to the Epistles of James, Peter, John, and Jude, probably because most of them are not addressed to individual churches or persons, but to the universal church.

CATHOLICITY. Liberality of religious sentiment.

Inculcated: In Christ's reproof of John (M'k 9:38-41; Lu 9:49, 50); Peter's vision of the sheet and visit to Cornelius (Ac 10:1-48); Paul's commission (Ro 1:1-7, 14-16); Paul's rebuke of Jewish exclusiveness (Ro 3:20-31; 4:1-25); judgment of apostolic church (Ac 15:1-31); unity of believers (Ro 5:1, 2; Ga 3:27, 28; Eph 2:14-17; Col 3:11-15); gifts of Holy Spirit to Gentiles as well as to Jews (Ac 10:44-48; 11:17, 18).

See Heathen; Strangers.

Instances of: Solomon, in his prayer (1Ki 8:41-43). Paul, in recognizing devout heathen (Ac 13:16, 26, 42, 43). Peter (Ac 10:34, 35). Rulers of the synagogue at Salamis, permitting the Apostles to preach (Ac 13:5).

CATTLE, of the bovine species. Used for sacrifice (1Ki 8:63). See Heifer; Offerings. Sheltered (Ge 33:17). Stall-fed (Pr 15:17).

Gilead adapted to the raising of (Nu 32:1-4), and Bashan (Ps 22:12; Eze 39:18; Am 4:1).

See Animals; Bull; Bullock; Cow; Heifer; Kine; Offering.

CAUL. 1. Probably the upper lobe of the liver. Burnt with sacrifice (Ex 29:13, 22; Le 3:4, 10, 15; 4:9; 7:4; 8:16, 25; 9:10, 19).

2. Netted caps (Isa 3:18).

CAUSE (See Actions at Law.)

CAUTION (See Expediency; Prudence.)

CAVALRY. Mounted on horses (Ex 14:23; 1Sa 13:5; 2Sa 8:4; 1Ki 4:26; 2Ch 8:6; 9:25; 12:3; Isa 30:16; 31:1; Jer 4:29; Zec 10:5; Re 9:16-18); on camels (1Sa 30:17).

See Armies.

CAVE. Used as a dwelling: By Lot (Ge 19:30); Elijah (1Ki 19:9); Israelites (Eze 33:27); saints (Heb 11:38). Place of refuge (Jos 10:16-27); J'g 6:2; 1Sa 13:6; 1Ki 18:4, 13; 19:9, 13). Burial place (Ge 23:9-20; 25:9; 49:29-32; 50:13; Joh 11:38).

Of Adullam (1Sa 22:1; 2Sa 23:13; 1Ch 11:15). En-gedi (1Sa 24:3-8).

CEDAR. Valuable for building purposes (Isa 9:10). David's ample provision of, in Jerusalem, for the temple (2Ch 1:15; 22:4). Furnished by Hiram, king of Tyre, for Solomon's temple (1Ki 5:6-10; 9:11; 2Ch 2:16). Used in rebuilding the temple (Ezr 3:7); in David's palace (2Sa 5:11; 1Ch 17:1); in Solomon's palace (1Ki 7:2); for masts of ships (Eze 27:5); in purifications (Le 14:4, 6, 49-52; Nu 19:6).

Figurative: Ps 72:16; 92:12; Isa 2:13; 14:8; Jer 22:7; Eze 31:3; Zec 11:2.

CEDRON. Called also Kidron. Brook of, running S under the eastern wall of Jerusalem (1Ki 2:37; Ne 2:15; Jer 31:40). Idols destroyed on the banks of: By Asa (1Ki 15:13); Josiah (2Ki 23:6, 12); Hezekiah (2Ch 29:16).

Its channel changed by Hezekiah (2Ch 32:4).

CEILING (KJV and ERV "cieling"), in 1Ki 6:15 the reference is to the walls of the Temple.

CELESTIAL PHENOMENA. Fire from heaven, on the cities of the plain (Ge 19:24, 25); on the two captains and their fifties (2Ki 1:10-14); on the flocks and servants of Job (Job 1:16). Hail, on the Egyptians (Ex 9:22-34).

Darkness, on the Egyptians (Ex 10:22, 23); at the crucifixion of Jesus (M't 27:45; Lu 23:44, 45). Pillar of cloud and fire (Ex 13:21, 22; 14:19, 24; 40:38; Nu 9:15-23; Ps 78:14). Thunder and lightning on Mt. Sinai (Ex 19:16, 18; 20:18).

Sun stood still (Jos 10:12, 13).

Prophecy of darkening of sun, moon, and stars (Joe 2:30, 32; M't 24:29; Lu 21:25; Ac 2:19, 20).

See Astronomy.

CELIBACY. Deplored by Jephthah's daughter (J'g 11:38). Not obligatory (1Co 7:1-9, 25, 26; 9:5; 1Ti 4:1-3). Practiced for kingdom of heaven's sake (M't 19:10-12; 1Co 7:32-40; Re 14:1, 4).

CELLAR, for wine (1Ch 27:27). Oil (1Ch 27:28).

CENCHREA, a city of Corinth (Ac 18:18; Ro 16:1).

CENSER. Used for offering incense (Le 16:12; Nu 4:14; 16:6, 7, 16-18, 46; Re 8:3). For the temple, made of gold (1Ki 7:50; 2Ch 4:22; Heb 9:4). Those which Korah used were converted into plates (Nu 16:37-39). Used in idolatrous rites (Eze 8:11).

Symbolical: Re 8:3, 5.

CENSORIOUSNESS (See Uncharitableness; Speaking, Evil; Charitableness.)

CENSUS. Numbering of Israel by Moses (Ex 38:26; Nu 1; 3:14-43; 26); by David (2Sa 24:1-9; 1Ch 21:1-8; 27:24).

A poll tax to be levied at each (Ex 30:12-16; 38:26).

Of the Roman Empire, by Caesar (Lu 2:1-3).

CENTURION. A commander of one hundred soldiers in the Roman army (M'k 15:44, 45; Ac 21:32; 22:25, 26; 23:17, 23; 24:23). Of Capernaum, comes to Jesus in behalf of his servant (M't 8:5-13; Lu 7:1-10). In charge of the soldiers who crucified Jesus, testifies, "Truly this was the Son of God" (M't 27:54; M'k 15:39; Lu 23:47).

See Cornelius; Julius.

CEPHAS (See Peter.)

CEREMONIAL WASHING. The Mosaic law, relative to ablutions, stresses that sin defiles. To keep this great truth constantly before the Israelites, specific ordinances concerning washings were given to Moses. The purpose was to teach, by this object lesson, that sin pollutes the soul, and that only those who were cleansed from their sins could be pure in the sight of the Lord (Heb 9:10; 10:22).

Of garments (Ex 19:10, 14). Of priests (Ex 29:4; 30:18-21; 40:12, 31, 32; Le 8:6; 16:4, 24, 26, 28; Nu 19:7-10, 19; 2Ch 4:6). Of burnt offerings (Le 1:9, 13; 9:14; 2Ch 4:6). Of the hands (M't 15:2; M'k 7:2-5; Lu 11:38). Of the feet (1Ti 5:10).

For defilement (Le 11:24-40). Of lepers (Le 13:6; 14:9). Of those having bloody issue (Le 15:5-13). Of those having eaten, or touched, that which died (Le 11:25, 40; 17:15, 16).

Traditional forms of, not observed by Jesus (Lu 11:38, 39). See Ablution; Defilement; Purification.

CESAR (See Caesar.)

CESAREA (See Caesarea.)

CESAREA PHILIPPI (See Caesarea Philippi.)

CHAFF, *Figurative:* Job 21:18; Ps 1:4; 35:5; Isa 17:13; Da 2:35; Ho 13:3; M't 3:12; Lu 3:17.

CHAINS. Used as ornaments. Worn by princes (Ge 41:12; Da 5:7, 29). Worn on ankles (Nu 31:50; Isa 3:19); on the breastplate of high priest (Ex 28:14; 39:15). As ornaments on camels (J'g 8:26). A partition of, in the temple (1Ki 6:21; 7:17).

Used to confine prisoners (Ps 68:6; 149:8; Jer 40:4; Ac 12:6, 7; 21:33; 28:20; 2Ti 1:16).

See Fetters.

Figurative: Ps 73:6; Pr 1:9; La 3:7; Eze 7:23-27; Jude 6; 2Pe 2:4; Re 20:1.

CHALCEDONY, a precious stone (Re 21:19).

CHALCOL, called also Calcol. Son of Nahor (1Ki 4:31; 1Ch 2:6).

CHALDEA, the southern portion of Babylonia. Often used interchangeably with Babylon, as the name of the empire founded in the valley of the Euphrates. Abraham a native of (Ge 11:28, 31; 15:7). Founded (*R.V.*, destroyed) by the Assyrians (Isa 23:13). Character of its people (Hab 1:6).

See Babylon; Chaldeans.

CHALDEAN ASTROLOGERS (See Wise Men.)

CHALDEANS, learned and wise men of the east (Da 1:4; 2:2; 4:7; 5:7; Jer 50:35).

CHALDEES, people of Chaldea.

CHALK (Isa 27:9).

CHAMBERING, acts of illicit intercourse (Ro 13:13).

CHAMBERLAIN, an officer of a king (2Ki 23:11; Es 1:10-15; 2:3-21; 4:4, 5; Ac 12:20; Ro 16:23).

CHAMBERS OF IMAGERY, rooms in the Temple where 70 elders of Israel worshiped idols with incense (Eze 8:12).
CHAMELEON, forbidden as food (Le 11:30).
CHAMOIS, a species of antelope (De 14:5).
CHAMPAIGN, a flat, open country (De 11:30).
CHAMPIONSHIP. Battles were decided by. *Instances of:* Goliath and David (1Sa 17:8-53). Young men of David's and Abner's armies (2Sa 2:14-17). Representatives of the Philistines' and David's armies (2Sa 21:15-22).
CHANAAN (See Canaan.)
CHANCELLOR, a state officer (Ezr 4:8, 9, 17).
See Cabinet.
CHANGE OF VENUE. Granted Paul (Ac 23:17-35). Declined by Paul (Ac 25:9, 11).
CHANGERS OF MONEY, men who exchanged one currency for another at a premium (M't 21:12; M'k 11:15; Joh 2:14, 15).
CHAPITER, head of a pillar (Ex 36:38; 1Ki 7:16-42; 2Ki 25:17; 2Ch 4:12, 13; Jer 52:22).
CHAPMAN, a peddler (2Ch 9:14).
CHARACTER. *Of Saints:* Attentive to Christ's voice (Joh 10:3, 4); blameless and harmless (Ph'p 2:15); bold (Pr 28:1); contrite (Isa 57:15; 66:2); devout (Ac 8:2; 22:13); faithful (Re 17:14); fearing God (Mal 3:16; Ac 10:2); following Christ (Joh 10:4, 27); godly (Ps 4:3; 2Pe 2:9); guileless (Joh 1:47); holy (De 7:6; 14:2; Col 3:12); humble (Ps 34:2; 1Pe 5:5); hungering for righteousness (M't 5:6); just (Ge 6:9; Hab 2:4; Lu 2:25); led by the Spirit (Ro 8:14); liberal (Isa 32:8; 2Co 9:13); loathing themselves (Eze 20:43); loving (Col 1:4; 1Th 4:9); lowly (Pr 16:19); meek (Isa 29:19; M't 5:5); merciful (Ps 37:26; M't 5:7); new creatures (2Co 5:17; Eph 2:10); obedient (Ro 16:19; 1Pe 1:14); poor in spirit (M't 5:3); prudent (Pr 16:21); pure in heart (M't 5:8; 1Jo 3:3); righteous (Isa 60:21; Lu 1:6); sincere (2Co 1:12; 2:17); steadfast (Ac 2:42; Col 2:5); taught of God (Isa 54:13; 1Jo 2:27); true (2Co 6:8); undefiled (Ps 119:1); upright (1Ki 3:6; Ps 15:2); watchful (Lu 12:37); zealous of good works (Tit 2:14).
See Righteous, Described.
Of the Wicked: Abominable (Re 21:8); alienated from God (Eph 4:18; Col 1:21); blasphemous (Lu 22:65; Re 16:9); blinded (2Co 4:4; Eph 4:18); boastful (Ps 10:3; 49:6); conspiring against saints (Ne 4:8; 6:2; Ps 38:12); corrupt (M't 7:17; Eph 4:22); covetous (Mic 2:2; Ro 1:29); deceitful (Ps 5:6; Ro 3:13); delighting in the iniquity of others (Pr 2:14; Ro 1:32); despising saints (Ne 2:19; 4:2; 2Ti 3:3, 4); destructive (Isa 59:7); disobedient (Ne 9:26; Tit 3:3; 1Pe 2:7); enticing to evil (Pr 1:10-14; 2Ti 3:6); envious (Ne 2:10; Tit 3:3); evildoers (Jer 13:23; Mic 7:3); fearful (Pr 28:1; Re 21:8); fierce (Pr 16:29; 2Ti 3:3); foolish (De 32:6; Ps 5:5); forgetting God (Job 8:13); fraudulent (Ps 37:21; Mic 6:11); froward (Pr 21:8; Isa 57:17); glorying in their shame (Ph'p 3:19); hard-hearted (Eze 3:7); hating the light (Job 24:13; Joh 3:20); heady and high-minded (2Ti 3:4); hostile to God (Ro 8:7; Col 1:21); hypocritical (Isa 29:13; 2Ti 3:5); ignorant of God (Ho 4:1; 2Th 1:8); impudent (Eze 2:4); incontinent (2Ti 3:3); infidel (Ps 10:4; 14:1); loathsome (Pr 13:5); lovers of pleasure, not of God (2Ti 3:4); lying (Ps 58:3; 62:4; Isa 59:4); mischievous (Pr 24:8; Mic 7:3); murderous (Ps 10:8; 94:6; Ro 1:29); prayerless (Job 21:15; Ps 53:4); persecuting (Ps 69:26; 109:16); perverse (De 32:5); proud (Ps 59:12; Ob 3; 2Ti 3:2); rebellious (Isa 1:2; 30:9); rejoicing in the affliction of saints (Ps 35:15); reprobate (2Co 13:5; 2Ti 3:8; Tit 1:16); selfish (2Ti 3:2); sensual (Ph'p 3:19; Jude 19); sold under sin (1Ki 21:20; 2Ki 17:17); stiff-hearted (Eze 2:4); stiff-necked (Ex 33:5; Ac 7:51); uncircumcised in heart (Jer 9:26); unclean (Isa 64:6; Eph 4:19); unjust (Pr 11:7; Isa 26:18); unmerciful (Ro 1:31); ungodly (Pr 16:27); unholy (2Ti 3:2); unprofitable (M't 25:30; Ro 3:12); unruly (Tit 1:10); unthankful (Lu 6:35; 2Tim 3:2); untoward (Ac 2:40); unwise (De 32:6).
See Wicked, Described.
Good (Pr 22:1; Ec 7:1). Defamation of, punished (De 22:13-19). Revealed in countenance (Isa 3:9).
Stability of (Ps 57:7; 108:1; 112:7; M'k 4:20; 2Th 3:3). Exhortations to (1Co 7:20; 15:58; 16:13; Eph 4:14, 15;

Ph'p 1:27; 4:1; Col 1:23; 1Th 3:8; 2Th 2:15; Heb 3:6, 14; 10:23; 13:9; 1Pe 5:9; 2Pe 3:17; Re 3:11). Reward of (M't 10: 22; Jas 1:25). Fixedness of (Re 22:11).

Instances of Firmness: Joseph (Ge 39:7-12). Moses (Heb 11:24-26). Joshua (Jos 24:15). Daniel (Da 1:8; 6:10). Three Hebrews (Da 3:16-18). Pilate (Joh 19:22). Peter and John (Ac 4:19, 20). Paul (Ac 20:22-24; 21:13, 14).

See Decision; Stability.

Instability of (Pr 27:8; Jer 2:36; Ho 6:4; 7:8; 10:2; M't 13:19-22; M'k 4:15-19; Lu 8:5-15; 2Pe 2:14; Re 2:4). Warnings against (Pr 24:21, 22; Lu 9:59-62; Eph 4:14; Heb 6:4-6; 13:9; Jas 1:6-8; 4:8; 2Pe 2:14).

Instances of Instability: Reuben (Ge 49:3, 4). Pharaoh (Ex 8:15, 32; 9:34; 14:5). Israelites (Ex 32:8; J'g 2:17-19; 2Ch 11:17). Saul (1Sa 18:19). Solomon (1Ki 11:4-8). Rehoboam (2Ch 12:1). Pilate (Joh 18:37-40; 19:1-6). Demas (2Ti 4:10).

CHARASHIM (craftsmen), valley of (1Ch 4:14; Ne 11:35).

CHARCHEMISH, CARCHEMISH, Hittite capital on the Euphrates.

CHARGE, delivered to ministers. (See Ministers.)

CHARGER, a dish. Dedicated to the tabernacle (Nu 7:13, 19, 25, 31, 37, 43, 49, 55, 61, 67, 73, 79, 84, 85). John Baptist's head carried on (M't 14:8, 11).

CHARIOT. For war (Ex 14:7, 9, 25; Jos 11:4; 1Sa 13:5; 1Ki 20:1, 25; 2Ki 6:14; 2Ch 12:2, 3; Ps 20:7; 46:9; Jer 46:9; 47:3; 51:21; Joe 2:5; Na 2:3, 4; 3:2). Wheels of Pharaoh's, providentially taken off (Ex 14:25).

Commanded by captains (Ex 14:7; 1Ki 9:22; 22:31-33; 2Ki 8:2). Made of iron (Jos 17:18; J'g 1:19). Introduced among Israelites by David (2Sa 8:4). Imported from Egypt by Solomon (1Ki 10:26-29). Cities for (1Ki 9:19; 2Ch 1:14; 8:6; 9:25). Royal (Ge 41:43; 46:29; 2Ki 5:9; 2Ch 35:24; Jer 17:25; Ac 8:29). Drawn by camels (Isa 21:7; Mic 1:13).

Traffic in (Re 10:13). Kings ride in (2Ch 35:24; Jer 17:25; 22:4). Cherubim in Solomon's temple mounted on (1Ch 28:18).

Figurative: Chariots of God (Ps 68:17; 104:3; 2Ki 6:17; Isa 66:15; Hab 3:8; Re 9:9).

Symbolical: Zec 6:1-8; 2Ki 2:11, 12.

CHARISM. An inspired gift, bestowed on the apostles and early Christians (M't 10:1, 8; M'k 16:17, 18; Lu 10:1, 9, 17, 19; Ac 2:4; 10:44-46; 19:6; 1Co 12).

See Miracles; Tongues.

CHARITABLENESS. Encouraged (Pr 10:12; 17:9). Enjoined (M't 5:23, 24; 7:1-5; 18:21, 22; Lu 6:36-42; 17:3, 4; Joh 7:24; Ro 14:1-23; 15:1, 2; 1Co 4:5; 10: 28-33; 16:14; 2Co 2:7; Ga 6:1; Eph 4:32; Col 3:13, 14; 1Ti 1:5; 4:12; 2Ti 2:22; Jas 2:13; 4:11, 12; 1Pe 3:9). Described (1Co 13).

Covers sins (Pr 10:12; 17:9; 19:11; 1Pe 4:8). Pleases God (M't 6:14, 15; 18:23-35).

See Love; Uncharitableness.

CHARITY (See Alms; Beneficence; Liberality; Love.)

CHARMERS AND CHARMING (Isa 19:3; Jer 8:17). Prohibited (De 18:11). Of serpents (Ps 58:4, 5; Jer 8:17).

See Sorcery.

CHARRAN (See Haran.)

CHASTISEMENT, FROM GOD. A blessing (Job 5:17; Ps 94:12, 13; Heb 12:11). Corrective (De 11:2-9; 2Sa 7:14, 15; 2Ch 6:24-31; 7:13, 14; Job 33:19; 34:31; Ps 73:14; 118:18; 119:67, 75; Isa 57:16-18; Jer 24:5, 6; 46:28; 1Co 11:32).

Inflicted for sins (Le 26:28; Ps 89:32; 107:10-12, 17; Isa 40:2; Jer 30:14; La 1:5; Ho 7:12; 10:10; Am 4:6). Administered in love (De 8:5; Pr 3:11, 12; Heb 12:5-10; Re 3:19).

Penitence under (Ps 106:43, 44; 107:10-13, 17-19; Isa 26:16; Jer 31:18, 19). Impenitence under (Isa 42:45; Jer 2:30; Hag 2:17).

Prayer to be spared from (Ps 6:1; 38:1 107:23-31). Vicariously borne by Jesus (Isa 53:4, 5).

See Afflictions; Judgments; Punishment; Wicked, Punishment of.

CHASTITY. Enjoined (Ex 20:14; Pr 2:10, 11, 16-22; 5:3-21; 6:24, 25; 7:1-5; 31:3; M't 5:27-32; Ac 15:20; Ro 13:13; 1Co 6:13-19; 7:1, 2, 7-9, 25, 26, 36, 37; Eph 5:3; Col 3:5; 1Th 4:3, 7).

Instances of: Joseph (Ge 39:7-20). Boaz (Ru 3:6-13). Job (Job 31:1, 9-12). Paul (1Co 7). The redeemed (Re 14:1-5).

See Continence.

CHEATING (See Dishonesty.)

CHEBAR, a river of Mesopotamia (Eze

1:1, 3; 3:15, 23; 10:15, 22; 43:3).

CHEDORLAOMER, king of Elam (Ge 14:1-16).

CHEERFULNESS (See Contentment.)

CHEESE (1Sa 17:18; 2Sa 17:29; Job 10:10).

CHELAL, son of Pahath-moab (Ezr 10:30).

CHELLUH, son of Bani (Ezr 10:35).

CHELUB (Caleb). 1. A descendant of Caleb (1Ch 4:11).

2. Father of Ezri (1Ch 27:26).

CHELUBAI. Son of Hezron (1Ch 2:9). Called Caleb.

CHEMARIM, a term descriptive of idolatrous priests (2Ki 23:15; Ho 10:5; Zep 1:4).

CHEMOSH, an idol of the Moabites and Ammonites (1Ki 11:7, 33; 2Ki 23:13; Jer 48:7, 13, 46); and Amorites (J'g 11:24).

CHENAANAH. 1. Father of the false prophet Zedekiah (1Ki 22:11, 24; 2Ch 18:10, 23).

2. Brother of Ehud (1Ch 7:10).

CHENANI, a Levite (Ne 9:4).

CHENANIAH. 1. A Levite (1Ch 15:22, 27).

2. An Izharite (1Ch 26:29).

CHEPHAR-HAAMMONAI, a town of Benjamin (Jos 18:24).

CHEPHIRAH, a city of the Hivites (Jos 9:17; 18:26; Ezr 2:25; Ne 7:29).

CHERAN, a Horite (Ge 36:26; 1Ch 1:41).

CHERETHITES. A Philistine tribe, which adhered to David, and with the Pelethites formed his bodyguard (1Sa 30:14, 16; 2Sa 8:18; 15:18; 20:7, 23: 1Ki 1:38, 44; 1Ch 18:17; Eze 25:16; Zep 2:5). Solomon's escort at his coronation (1Ki 1:38).

CHERITH, a brook near Jericho (1Ki 17:3-7).

CHERUB, name of a place or person (Ezr 2:59; Ne 7:61).

CHERUBIM. Eastward of the garden of Eden (Ge 3:24).

In the tabernacle (Ex 25:18-20; 37:7-9). Ark rested beneath the wings of (1Ki 8:6, 7; 2Ch 5:7, 8; Heb 9:5). Figures of, embroidered on walls of tabernacle (Ex 26:1; 36:8), and on the veil (Ex 26:31; 36:35).

In the temple (1Ki 6:23-29; 2Ch 3:10-13). Figures of, on the veil (2Ch 3:14); walls (1Ki 6:29-35; 2Ch 3:7); lavers (1Ki 7:29, 36).

In Ezekiel's vision of the temple (Eze 41:18-20, 25).

Figurative: Eze 28:14, 16.

Symbolical: Eze 1; 10.

CHESALON, a landmark in the N boundary of Judah (Jos 15:10).

CHESED, son of Nahor (Ge 22:22).

CHESIL. A town in the S of Palestine (Jos 15:30). Probably identical with Bethul (Jos 19:4); and Bethuel (1Ch 4:30).

CHEST, for money (2Ki 12:9; 2Ch 24:8-11).

CHESTNUT TREE (Ge 30:37; Eze 31:8).

CHESULLOTH. A city of Issachar (Jos 19:18). Probably identical with Chisloth-tabor and Tabor (1Ch 6:77).

CHEZIB. Birthplace of Shelah (Ge 38:5); probably identical with Chozeba (1Ch 4:22), and Achzib (Jos 15:44).

CHICKENS (M't 23:37); broods her young (Lu 13:34).

CHIDING. Cain chides God (Ge 4:13, 14). Pharaoh chides Abraham, for calling his wife his sister (Ge 12:18, 19). Abimelech chides Abraham for a like offense (Ge 20:9, 10). Abimelech chides Isaac for similar conduct (Ge 26:9, 10). Isaac and Laban chide each other (Ge 31:26-42). Jacob chides Simeon and Levi for slaying Hamor and Shechem (Ge 34:30). Reuben chides his brethren for their treatment of Joseph (Ge 42:22). Israelites chide Moses and tempt God (Ex 17:7). Deborah chides Israel in her epic (J'g 5:16-23). David chides Joab for slaying Abner (2Sa 3:28-31). Joab chides David for lamenting the death of Absalom (2Sa 19:5-7).

Jesus chides his disciples on account of their unbelief (M't 8:26; 14:31; 16:8-11; 17:17; M'k 4:40; Lu 8:25); for slowness of heart (M't 15:16; 16:8, 9, 11; M'k 7:18; Lu 24:25; Joh 14:9); for sleeping in Gethsemane (M't 26:40; M'k 14:27); for forbidding children to be brought to him (M't 19:14; M'k 10:14; Lu 18:16).

CHIDON. Place where Uzza was stricken to death (1Ch 13:9). Called Nachon's threshing floor (2Sa 6:6).

CHILDBEARING, an expression found only in 1Ti 2:15, a verse of uncertain meaning.

CHILDLESSNESS. A reproach (Ge 16:2; 29:32; 30:1-3, 13; 1Sa 1:6; Isa 4:1; Lu 1:25).

See Barrenness.

CHILDREN. *A Blessing* (Ge 5:29; 30:1; Ps 127:3-5; Pr 17:6). The gift of God (Ge 4:1, 25; 17:16, 20; 22:17; 28:3; 29:32-35; 30:2, 6, 17-20, 22-24; 35:5; 48:9, 16; Ru 4:13; Job 1:21; Ps 107:38, 41; 113:9; 127:3). Promised to the righteous (De 7:12, 14; Job 5:25; Ps 128:2-4, 6). Given in answer to prayer, to Abraham (Ge 15:2-5; 21:1, 2); to Isaac (Ge 25:21); to Leah (Ge 30:17-22); to Rachel (Ge 30:22-24); to Hannah (1Sa 1:9-20); to Zacharias (Lu 1:13).

In Infancy: Circumcision of, see Circumcision. Dedicated to God, Samson (Jg 13:5, 7); Samuel (1Sa 1:24-28); Jesus (Lu 2:22). Nurses for (Ex 2:7-9; Ru 4:16; 2Sa 4:4; 2Ki 11:2; Ac 7:20). Treatment of (Eze 16:4-6; Lu 2:7, 12). Weaning of (Ge 21:8; 1Sa 1:22; 1Ki 11:20; Ps 131:2; Isa 28:9).

In Early Childhood: Amusements of (Job 21:11; Zec 8:5; M't 11:16, 17; Lu 7:31, 32). Early piety of, Samuel (1Sa 2:18; 3); Jeremiah (Jer 1:5-7); John the Baptist (Lu 1:15, 80); Jesus (Lu 2:40, 46, 47, 52). Taught to walk (Ho 11:3). Tutored (2Ki 10:1; Ac 22:3; Ga 3:24; 4:1, 2). See Tutor.

God's Care Of (Ex 22:22-24; De 10:18; 14:29; Job 29:12; Ps 10:14, 17, 18; 27:10; 68:5; 146:9; Jer 49:11; Ho 14:3; Mal 3:5). Blessed by Jesus (M't 19:13-15; M'k 10:13-16; Lu 18:15-17). Intercessional sacrifices in behalf of (Job 1:5).

Commandments to: To honor and obey parents (Ex 20:12; Le 19:3, 32; De 5:16; Pr 1:8, 9; 6:20-23; 23:22; M't 15:4; 19:9; M'k 10:19; Lu 18:20; Eph 6:1-3; Col 3:20; 1Ti 3:4). To seek wisdom (Pr 4:1-11, 20-22; 5:1, 2; 8:32, 33; 27:11). To praise the Lord (Ps 148:12, 13). To remember their Creator (Pr 23:26; Ec 12:1). To obey the commandments (Ps 119:9; Pr 3:1-3; 6:20-25). To be pure (Ec 11:9, 10; La 3:27; 1Ti 4:12; 2Ti 2:22; Tit 2:6). See Young Men.

Miracles on behalf of: Raised from the dead, by Elijah (1Ki 17:17-23); by Elisha (2Ki 4:17-36); by Jesus (M't 9:18, 24-26; M'k 5:35-42; Lu 7:13-15; 8:49-56). Healing of (M't 15:28; 17:18; M'k 7:29, 30; 9:23-27; Lu 8:42-56; 9:38-42; Joh 4:46-54).

Prayer in behalf of: For healing (2Sa 12:16). For divine favor (Ge 17:18). For spiritual wisdom (1Ch 22:12; 29:19). For sins (Job 1:5).

Promises and assurances to: Divine instruction (Isa 54:13). Long life to the obedient (Ex 20:12; De 5:16; Pr 3:1-10; Eph 6:2, 3). Love and peace (Pr 8:17, 32; Isa 40:11; 54:13); from Jesus (M't 18:4, 5, 10; 19:14, 15; M'k 9:37; 10:16; Lu 9:48; 18:15, 16). Joy to parents of wise (Pr 23:15, 16, 24, 25; 29:3). Sins forgiven (1Jo 2:12, 13); and eternal redemption (Ac 2:39).

Of the righteous, blessed of God: In escaping judgments (Ge 6:18; 7:1; 19:12, 15, 16; Le 26:44, 45; 1Ki 11:13; 2Ki 8:19; Pr 11:21; 12:7). In temporal prosperity (Ge 12:7; 13:15; 17:7, 8; 21:13; 26:3, 4, 27; De 4:37; 10:15; 12:28; 1Ki 15:4; Ps 37:26; 102:28; 112:2, 3; Pr 13:22). In divine mercy (Ps 103:17, 18; Pr 3:33; 20:7; Isa 44:3-5; 65:23; Jer 32:39; Ac 2:39; 1Co 7:14).

Parental Relationships: Love of, for parents: Ruth (Ru 1:16-18); Jesus (Joh 19:26, 27). Counsel of parents to (1Ki 2:1-4; 1Ch 22:6-13; 28:9, 10, 20). Of ministers (1Ti 3:4; Tit 1:6).

Instruction of: The law (De 6:6-9; 11:19, 20; 31:12, 13; Jos 8:35; Ps 78:1-8). The fear of the Lord (Ps 34:11). The providence of God (Ex 10:2; 12:26, 27; 13:8-10, 14-16; De 4:9, 10; Joe 1:3). Righteousness (Pr 1:1-4; 22:6; Isa 28:9, 10; 38:19). The Scriptures (Ac 22:3; Eph 6:4; 2Ti 3:15). False (M'k 7:9-13). See Instruction; Tutor; Young Men.

Correction and punishment: By chastening (Pr 19:18; 23:13; 19:17; Eph 6:4 w Col 3:2). By reproof (Pr 29:15). By the rod (Pr 13:24; 22:15; 23:13, 14; 29:15). By death (Ex 21:15, 17; Le 20:9; De 21:21; 27:16; Pr 20:20; 22:15; 30:17; M't 15:4; M'k 7:10).

Differences and partiality: Differences made between male and female (Le 12). Partiality of parents, Rebekah for Jacob (Ge 27:6-17); Jacob for Joseph (Ge 37:3, 4). Partiality among, forbidden (De 21:15-17).

Death and mistreatment: Death, as a judgment upon parents: firstborn of Egypt (Ex 12:29; Nu 8:17; Ps 78:5); sons of Eli (1Sa 3:13, 14); sons of Saul (1Sa 28:18, 19); David's child by Uriah's wife (2Sa 12:14-19). Eaten, see Cannibalism. Edict to murder: of Pharaoh (Ex 1:22); of Jehu (2Ki 10:1-8); of Herod (M't 2:16-18). Caused to pass through fire (2Ki 16:3; 17:7; Jer 32:35; Eze 16:21). Sacrificed (2Ki 17:31; Eze 16:20, 21). Sold for debt (2Ki 4:1; Ne 5:5; Job 24:9; M't 18:25). Sold in marriage, law concerning (Ex 21:7-11). Instance of, Leah and Rachel (Ge 29:15-30).

Religious Involvement: Attend divine worship (Ex 34:23; Jos 8:35; 2Ch 20:13; 31:16; Ezr 8:21; Ne 8:2, 3; 12:43; M't 21:15; Lu 2:46). Entitled to enjoy religious privileges (De 12:12, 13). Bastard excluded from privilege of congregation (De 23:2; Heb 12:8).

Covenant involvement: Bound by covenants of parents (Ge 17:9-14). Share benefits of parents' covenant privileges (Ge 6:18; 12:7; 13:15; 17:7, 8; 19:12; 21:13; 26:3-5, 24; Le 26:44, 45; Isa 65:23; 1Co 7:14). Involved in guilt of parents (Ex 20:5; 34:7; Le 20:5; 26:39-42; Nu 14:18, 33; 1Ki 16:12; 21:29; Job 21:19; Ps 37:28; Isa 14:20, 21; 65:6, 7; Jer 32:18; Da 6:24). Not punished for parents' sake (2Ki 14:6; Jer 31:29, 30; Eze 18:1-30).

Character of: Known by conduct (Pr 20:11). Future state (M't 18:10; 19:14). Status of minors (Ga 4:1, 2). Alienated: Ishmael, to gratify Sarah (Ge 21:9-15). Adopted, see Adoption; Parents.

Good: Have Lord's presence (1Sa 3:19). Blessed of God (Pr 3:1-4; Eph 6:2, 3). Honor the aged (Job 32:6, 7). Honor father (Mal 1:6). A joy to parents (Pr 10:1; 15:20; 23:24; 29:3, 17). Keep the law (Pr 28:7). Know the scriptures (2Ti 3:15). Love parents (Ge 46:29). Obey parents (Ge 28:7; 47:30; Pr 13:1); which pleases God (Col 3:20). Attend to parental teaching (Pr 13:1). Partake of God's promises (Ac 2:39). Extol the Saviour (M't 21:15, 16 w Ps 8:2). Take care of parents (Ge 45:9-11; 47:12; M't 15:5). Wise (Ec 4:13).

Good: Illustrative of conversion (M't 18:3); of a teachable spirit (M't 18:4). Symbolic of regenerated (M't 18:2-6, 10; 19:14, 15; M'k 9:36, 37; 10:13-16; Lu 9:46-48; 18:15, 17).

Good: Instances of filial. Shem and Japheth (Ge 9:23). Isaac (Ge 22:6-12). Esau (Ge 28:6-9). Jacob (Ge 28:7). Judah (Ge 44:18-34). Joseph (Ge 45:9-13; 46:29; 47:11, 12, 29, 30; 48:12; 50:1-13). Moses (Ex 15:2; 18:7). Jephthah's daughter (J'g 11:36-39). Ruth (Ru 1:15-17). Samuel (1Sa 2:26; 3:10). Saul (1Sa 9:5). David (1Sa 22:3, 4; Ps 71:5, 17). Solomon (1Ki 2:19, 20; 3:3-13). Abijah (1Ki 14:13). Obadiah (1Ki 18:12). Jehoshaphat (1Ki 22:43; 2Ch 17:3).

Good: Instances of. The captive maid (2Ki 5:2-4). Jewish children (2Ch 20:13; Ne 8:3; 12:43). Josiah (2Ch 34:1-3). Job (Job 29:4). Elihu (Job 32:4-7). Jeremiah (Jer 1:5-7). The Rechabites (Jer 35:18, 19). Daniel and the three Hebrews (Da 1:8-20). Children in the temple (M't 21:15). John (Lu 1:80). Jesus (Lu 2:51, 52). Timothy (2Ti 1:5; 3:15).

Wicked: Disrespectful, to parents (De 27:16; Pr 15:20; 20:20; 30:11; Eze 22:7; Mic 7:6; Job 19:18; 2Ki 2:23); to the aged (Job 30:1, 12; Isa 3:5). Disobedient to parents (De 21:18-21; Pr 13:1; 15:5; 30:13; Ro 1:30; 2Ti 3:2). Defraud parents (Pr 28:7, 24). Disgrace parents (Pr 10:1; 17:2, 21, 25; 19:13, 26; 23:22). Betray parents (M'k 13:12). Depraved (Ge 8:21; Job 12:26; 20:11; Ps 144:7, 8, 11; Jer 3:25; 9:17, 18; 32:30).

Wicked: Instances of. Canaan (Ge 4:25). Lot's daughters (Ge 19:14, 30-38). Ishmael (Ge 21:9). Eli's sons (1Sa 2:12, 22-25). Samuel's sons (1Sa 8:3). Absalom (2Sa 15). Adonijah (1Ki 1:5). Abijan (1Ki 15:3). Ahaziah (1Ki 22:52). Children at Bethel (2Ki 2:23, 24), Samaritan's descendants (2Ki 17:41). Adrammelech and Sharezer (2Ki 19:37; 2Ch 32:31). Amon (2Ki 21:21).

See Babies; Young Men.

CHILDREN OF GOD (See Righteous.)

CHILEAB. A son of David (2Sa 3:3). Called Daniel (1Ch 3:1).

CHILION, son of Elimelech and Naomi; married Orpah (Ru 1:2-5; 4:9, 10).

CHILMAD, merchants of (Eze 27:23).

CHIMHAM, a Gileadite (2Sa 19:37, 38, 40; Jer 41:17).

CHIMNEY (Ho 13:3).

CHINESE. Sinim in Isa 49:12 is believed by many authorities to be a reference to the Chinese.

CHINNERETH. Called also Chinneroth, Cinnereth and Cinneroth. 1. A district in the N of Palestine (Jos 11:2; 1Ki 15:20).

2. A city in Naphtali (Jos 19:35).

3. The sea of (Nu 34:11; Jos 12:3; 13:27).

See Galilee, Sea of.

CHINNEROTH (See Chinnereth.)

CHIOS, an island W of Smyrna (Ac 20:15).

CHISLEU, ninth month in the Israelitish calendar (Ezr 10:9; Ne 1:1; Jer 36:22).

CHISLON, father of Eldad (Nu 34:21).

CHISLOTH-TABOR. A place on the border of Zebulun (Jos 19:12). Called Tabor (1Ch 6:77). Probably same as Chesulloth (Jos 19:18).

CHITTIM. Descendants of Javan (Ge 10:4). Probably inhabited islands of the Mediterranean (Isa 23:1, 12; Jer 2:10). Their commerce (Eze 27:6). Prophecies concerning (Nu 24:24; Da 11:30).

CHIUN, called also Remphan, a god of the Phoenicians (Am 5:26; Ac 7:43).

CHLOE, a Christian of Corinth (1Co 1:11).

CHOICE. Between life and death (De 30:19, 20). Between God and false gods (Jos 24:15-18). Between judgments, by David (2Sa 24:12-14; 1Ch 21:11-13). Between God and Baal (1Ki 18:21, 39, 40). Of Moses (Heb 11:24, 25).

See Contingencies; Blessings, Contingent on Obedience.

CHOIR. Leaders of (1Ch 25:2-6; Ne 12:42). Presided over by chief musician (Ps 4; Hab 31:9). Instructed by teachers (1Ch 15:22, 27; 25:7, 8).

In the tabernacle (1Ch 6:31-47). Composed of singers and instrumentalists (1Ch 15:16-21; 25:1-7; 2Ch 5:12, 13; 23:13; Isa 38:20). Mixed choirs (2Ch 35:15, 25; Ezr 2:64, 65). Sang, every morning and evening (1Ch 9:33; 23:5, 30); during offering of sacrifices (1Ch 16:41, 42; 2Ch 29:27, 28); at restoration of the temple (Ezr 2:41; 3:10, 11); at the dedication of the wall of Jerusalem (Ne 12:27-30). Detailed from the army to sing praises to God as a military stratagem (2Ch 20:21).

See Music.

CHOOSING (See Choice.)

CHOR-ASHAN. A town in Judah (1Sa 30:30). Perhaps identical with Ashan (Jos 15:42).

CHORAZIN, denunciation against (M't 11:21; Lu 10:13).

CHORUSES (See Music.)

CHOSEN, OR ELECTED. Few (M't 20:16). Called (1Pe 2:9; Re 17:14).

See Foreknowledge; Predestination.

CHOZEBA, a city of Judah (1Ch 4:22). See Chezib; Achzib.

CHRIST (See Jesus, The Christ.)

CHRISTIAN. Believers called (Ac 11:26; 26:28; 1Pe 4:16).

See Righteous.

CHRISTIANITY. The word does not occur in the Bible, but was first used by Ignatius, in the first half of the 2nd century. It designates all that which Jesus Christ brings to men of faith, life, and salvation.

CHRISTMAS, the anniversary of the birth of Christ, and its observance; celebrated by most Protestants and by Roman Catholics on Dec. 25; by Eastern Orthodox churches on Jan. 6; and by the Armenian church on Jan 19. The first mention of its observance on Dec. 25 is in the time of Constantine, c. A. D. 325. The date of the birth of Christ is not known. The word Christmas is formed of Christ plus Mass, meaning a religious service in commemoration of the birth of Christ. It is not clear whether the early Christians thought of or observed Christmas, but once introduced the observance spread throughout Christendom. Some Christian bodies disapprove of the festival.

CHRONICLES, I and II. Heb. name is "The words (affairs) of the days," meaning "The annals." Jerome first entitled them "Chronicles." Originally they formed a single composition, but were divided into I and II Chronicles in the LXX, c. 150 B. C. They stand last in the Heb. canon. Ancient tradition and modern scholarship suggest that they were written by Ezra some time c. 450 B. C. The work consists of 4 parts: genealogies, to enable the Jews to establish their lines of family descent (1Ch 1-9); the kingdom of David, as a pattern for the ideal theocratic state (1Ch 10:29); the glory of Solomon (2Ch 1-9); the history of the southern kingdom (2Ch 10-36).

CHRONOLOGY, NEW TESTAMENT.

In ancient times historians were not accustomed to record history under exact dates, but were satisfied when some specific event was related to the reign of a noted ruler or a famous contemporary. Our method of dating events in reference to the birth of Christ was started by Dionysius Exiguus, a monk who lived in the 6th century. The birth of Christ may be dated in the latter part of the year 5 B. C., as it is known that Herod the Great died in 4 B. C., and according to the gospels Jesus was born some time before the death of the king. Luke gives the age of Jesus at his baptism as "about thirty years" (3:23). This would bring the baptism at c. A. D. 26 or 27. Since Herod began the reconstruction of the temple in 20 B. C., the "forty and six years" mentioned by the Jews during the first Passover of Jesus' public ministry (Joh 2:13-22), brings us to A. D. 27 for this first Passover. The ministry of John the Baptist began about the middle of A.D. 26. The time of the crucifixion is determined by the length of the ministry of Jesus. Mark's gospel seems to require at least 2 years. John's gospel explicitly mentions 3 Passovers (2:23; 6:4; 11:55). If the feast of 5:1 is also a Passover, as seems probable, then the length of the ministry of Jesus was full three years and a little over. This places the crucifixion at the Passover of A. D. 30. As for the Apostolic Age the chronological data are very limited and uncertain. The death of Herod Agrippa I, one of the fixed dates of the NT, is known to have taken place in A. D. 44. This was the year of Peter's arrest and miraculous escape from prison. The proconsulship of Gallio was between 51 and 53, and this would bring the beginning of Paul's ministry at Corinth to c. A. D. 50. The accession of Festus as governor, under whom Paul was sent to Rome, probably took place c. 59, 60.

The following chronological table is regarded as approximately correct:

Birth of Jesus	5 B. C.
Baptism of Jesus	late A. D. 26 or early 27
First Passover of Ministry	27
Crucifixion of Jesus	30
Conversion of Saul	34 or 35
Death of Herod Agrippa I	44
Epistle of James	before 50
First Missionary journey	48-49
Jerusalem Conference	49 or 50
Second Missionary journey	begun spring 50
Paul at Corinth	50-52
I and II Thessalonians from Corinth	51
Galatians from Corinth (?)	early 52
Arrival of Gallio as Proconsul	May 52
Third Missionary journey	begun 54
Paul at Ephesus	54-57
I Cor. from Ephesus	spring 57
II Cor. from Macedonia	fall 57
Romans from Corinth	winter 57-58
Paul's arrest at Jerusalem	Pentecost 58
Imprisonment at Caesarea	58-60
On Island of Malta	winter 60-61
Arrival at Rome	spring 61
Roman Imprisonment	61-63
Colossians, Philemon, Ephesians	summer 62
Philippians	spring 63
Paul's release and further work	63-65
I Timothy and Titus	63
Epistle to the Hebrews	64
Synoptic Gospels and Acts	before 67
I and II Peter from Rome	64-65
Peter's death at Rome	65
Paul's second Roman imprisonment	66
II Timothy	66
Death at Rome	late 66 or early 67
Epistle of Jude	67-68
Writings of John	before 100
Death of John	98-100

CHRONOLOGY, OLD TESTAMENT. The chronology of the OT presents many complex and difficult problems. Often the data are completely lacking, and where they exist, they are not adequate or plain. Even where the data are abundant, the exact meaning is not immediately clear, and there are therefore many interpretations possible. For the period from the creation to the Deluge the only Biblical data are the ages of the patriarchs in the genealogical tables of Genesis 5 and 7:11. Extra-Biblical sources for this period are almost completely lacking. For the period from the Deluge to Abraham we are again dependent upon the genealogical data in the Bible. The numbers vary in the Masoretic text, the LXX, and the Samaritan Pentateuch. The construction of an absolute chronology from Adam to Abraham is not now possible on the basis of the available data. The patriarchs may be dated c. 2100-1875; the Exodus c. 1445 B. C.; the beginning of the conquest of Canaan c. 1405. An accurate chronology of the period of the judges is impossible, as the length of the period is unknown, and a number of the judges undoubtedly exercised control at the same time. The United Monarchy began c. 1050 B. C.; the Divided Monarchy in 931 B. C. The kingdom of Israel went into the Assyrian captivity c. 722 B. C.; and the kingdom of Judah into the Babylonian captivity in 586 B. C. Judah returned from the Babylonian captivity in 538 B. C. Nehemiah returned to Babylon in 433 B. C.

CHRYSOLYTE, a precious stone (Re 21:20).

CHRYSOPRASUS, a precious stone (Re 21:20).

CHUB, a people who were an ally tribe to Egypt, and probably inhabited Africa (Eze 30:5).

CHUN, a Syrian city (1Ch 18:8). See Betah; Berothai.

CHURCH, PLACE OF WORSHIP. *Called:* Courts (Ps 65:4; 84:2, 10; 92:13; 96:8; 100:4; 116:19; Isa 1:12; 62:9; Zec 3:7). Holy Oracle (Ps 28:2). Holy Place (Ex 28:29; 38:24; Le 6:16; 10:17; 14:13; 16:2-24; Jos 5:15; 1Ki 8:8; 1Ch 23:32; 2Ch 29:5; 30:27; 35:5; Ezr 9:8; Ps 24:3; 46:4; 68:17; Ec 8:10; Isa 57:15; Eze 41:4; 42:13; 45:4; M't 24:15; Ac 6:13; 21:28; Heb 9:12, 25). Holy Temple (Ps 5:7; 11:4; 65:4; 79:1; 138:2; Jon 2:4, 7; Mic 1:2; Hab 2:20; Eph 2:21; 3:17). House of God (Ge 28:17, 22; Jos 9:23; J'g 18:31; 20:18, 26; 21:2; 1Ch 9:11; 24:5; 2Ch 5:14; 22:12; 24:13; 33:7; 36:19; Ezr 5:8, 15; 7:20, 23; Ne 6:10; 11:11; 13:11; Ps 42:4; 52:8; 55:14; 84:10; Ec 5:1; Isa 2:3; Ho 9:8; Joe 1:16; Mic 4:2; Zec 7:2; M't 12:4; 1Ti 3:15; Heb 10:21; 1Pe 4:17). House of the Lord (Ex 23:19; 34:26; De 23:18; Jos 6:24; J'g 19:18; 1Sa 1:7, 24; 2Sa 12:20; 1Ki 3:1; 6:37; 7:40; 8:10, 63; 10:5; 2Ki 11:3, 4, 15, 18, 19; 12:4, 9, 10, 13, 16; 16:18; 20:8; 23:2, 7, 11; 25:9; 1Ch 6:31; 22:1, 11, 14; 23:4; 26:12; 2Ch 8:16; 26:21; 29:5, 15; 33:15; 34:15; 36:14; Ezr 7:27; Ps 23:6; 27:4; 92:13; 116:19; 118:26; 122:1, 9; 134:1; Isa 2:2; 37:14; Jer 17:26; 20:1, 2; 26:2, 7; 28:1, 5; 29:26; 35:2; 36:5, 6; 38:14; 41:5; 51:51; La 2:7; Eze 44:4; Hag 1:2; Zec 8:9). House of Prayer (Isa 56:7; M't 21:13; M'k 11:17; Lu 19:46). My Father's House (Joh 2:16; 14:2). Sanctuary (Ex 25:8; Le 19:30; 21:12; Nu 3:28; 4:12; 7:9; 8:19; 10:21; 18:1, 5; 19:20; 1Ch 9:29; 22:19; 24:5; 28:10; 2Ch 20:8; 26:18; 29:21; 30:8, 19; Ne 10:39; Ps 20:2; 28:2; 63:2; 68:24; 73:17; 74:3, 7; 77:13; 78:69; 150:1; Isa 16:12; 63:18; La 2:7, 20; 4:1; Eze 5:11; 42:20; 44:5, 27; 45:3; 48:8, 21; Da 8:11, 13, 14; 9:17, 26; 11:31; Heb 8:2; 9:1, 2). Tabernacle (Ex 26:1; Le 26:11; Jos 22:19; Ps 15:1; 61:4; 76:2; Heb 8:2, 5; 9:2, 11; Re 13:6; 21:3). Temple (1Sa 1:9; 3:3; 2Ki 11:10, 13; Ezr 4:1; Ps 5:7; 11:4; 27:4; 29:9; 48:9; 68:29; Isa 6:1; Mal 3:1; M't 4:5; 23:16; Lu 18:10; 24:53). Zion (Ps 9:11; 48:11; 74:2; 132:13; 137:1; Isa 35:10; Jer 31:6; 50:5; Joe 2:1, 15).

Edifices: See Synagogue; Tabernacle; Temple.

Nature: Instituted by divine authority (Ex 25:8, 9; De 12:11-14). Holy (Ex 30:26-29; 40:9; Le 8:10, 11; 16:33; 19:30; 21:12; 26:2; Nu 7:1; 8:19; 1Ki 9:3; 1Ch 29:3; 2Ch 3:8; Isa 64:15; Eze 23:39; 43:12). Should be reverenced (Le 19:30; 26:2). Figurative (1Co 3:17).

Note: No place in scripture does the word "church" identify a place of worship, but rather a group (or body) of believers.

CHURCH, THE BODY OF BELIEVERS. *Note:* Church here encompasses organized bodies of believers in both testaments. In the O.T., the church was a group of "gathered together" Hebrew believers, a congregation. In the N.T., the church (technically) was a group of "called out" Christian believers, the true Church.

Called: In the O.T., the Congregation or Congregation of Israel (Ex 12:3, 6, 19, 47; 16:1, 2, 9, 10, 22; Le 4:13, 15; 10:17; 24:14); Zion (2Ki 19:21, 31; Ps 9:11; 48:2, 11, 12; 74:2; 132:13; 137:1; Isa 35:10; 40:9; 49:14; 51:16; 52:1, 2, 7, 8; 60:14; 62:1, 11; Jer 31:6; 50:5; La 1:4; Joe 2:1, 15; see also Ro 9:33; 11:26; 1Pe 2:16); Daughter of Zion (Isa 62:11; Zec 9:9; see also M't 21:5; Joh 12:15). In the N.T., Church (M't 16:18; 18:17; Ac 2:47;

7:38; 20:28; 1Co 11:18; 14:19, 23, 28, 33, 34; 15:9; Ga 1:13; Eph 1:22; 1Ti 3:15).

Described as: Assembly of the Saints (Ps 89:7). Assembly of the Upright (Ps 111:1). Body of Christ (1Co 12:27; Eph 1:22, 23; 4:12; Col 1:24). Branch of God's planting (Isa 60:21). Bride (Ga 6:16). Bride of Christ (Re 21:9). Christ's body (Ro 12:5; 1Co 12:12, 27; Eph 1:22, 23; 4:12; Col 1:24). Church of God (Ac 20:28). Church of the Living God (1Ti 3:15). Church of the Firstborn (Heb 12:23). City of the Living God (Heb 12:22). Congregation of Saints (Ps 149:1). Congregation of the Lord's Poor (Ps 74:19). Dove (Song 2:14; 5:2). Family in Heaven and Earth (Eph 3:15). Flock of God (Eze 34:15; 1Pe 5:2). Fold of Christ (Joh 10:16). General Assembly of the Firstborn (Heb 12:23). The God of Jacob (Isa 2:3). Golden Candlestick (Re 1:20). God's Building (1Co 3:9). God's Husbandry (1Co 3:9). God's Heritage (Joe 3:2; 1Pe 5:3). Habitation of God (Eph 2:22). Heavenly Jerusalem (Ga 4:26; Heb 12:22). Holy City (Re 21:2). Holy Mountain (Zec 8:3). Holy Hill (Ps 2:6; 15:1). House (Heb 3:6). House of God (1Ti 3:15; Heb 10:21). House of Christ (Heb 3:6). Household of God (Eph 2:19). Inheritance (Ps 28:9; Isa 19:25); Israel of God (Ga 6:16). Joy of the Whole World (Ps 48:1, 2, 11-13). King's Daughter (Ps 45:13). Kingdom of God (M't 6:33; 12:28; 19:24; 21:31). Kingdom of Heaven (M't 3:2; 4:17; 5:3, 10, 19, 20; 10:7). His Kingdom (Ps 103:19; 145:12; M't 16:28; Lu 1:33). My Kingdom (Joh 18:36). Thy Kingdom (Ps 45:6; 145:11, 13; M't 6:10; Lu 23:42). Lamb's Bride (Eph 5:22-32; Re 22:17). Lamb's Wife (Re 19:7-9; 21:9). The Lord's Portion (De 32:9). Lot of God's Inheritance (De 32:9). Mount Zion (Heb 12:22). Mountain of the Lord's House (Isa 2:2). New Jerusalem (Re 21:2). Pillar and Ground of the Truth (1Ti 3:15). Place of God's Throne (Eze 43:7). Pleasant Portion (Jer 12:10). River of Gladness (Ps 46:4, 5). Sanctuary of God (Ps 114:2). Sister of Christ (Song 4:12; 5:2). Sought out, a city not forsaken (Isa 62:12). Spiritual House (1Pe 2:5). Spouse of Christ (Song 4:12; 5:1). Strength and Glory of God (Ps 78:61). Temple of God (1Co 3:16, 17). Temple of the Living God (2Co 6:16). Vineyard (Jer 12:10; M't 21:41).

List of N.T. Churches: Antioch (Ac 13:1). Asia (1Co 16:19; Re 1:4). Babylon (1Pe 5:13). Cenchrea (Ro 16:1). Caesarea (Ac 18:22). Cilicia (Ac 15:41). Corinth (1Co 1:2). Ephesus (Eph 1:22; Re 2:1). Galatia (Ga 1:2). Galilee (Ac 9:31). Jerusalem (Ac 15:4). Joppa (Ac 9:42). Judea (Ac 9:31). Laodicea (Re 3:14). Pergamos (Re 2:12). Philadelphia (Re 3:7). Samaria (Ac 9:31). Sardis (Re 3:1). Smyrna (Re 2:8). Syria (Ac 15:41). Thessalonica (1Th 1:1). Thyatira (Re 2:18).

Evil Conditions of: Backslidden (Re 2:1-5, 12-25; 3:1-4, 14-20; see Backsliders, Backsliding). Barren (M't 21:19, 20; M'k 11:13, 14; Lu 13:6-9). Corrupt (Isa 5:1-7; M't 21:33-46; M'k 12:1-12; Lu 20:9-19). Corruption in (Ho 4:9; Mic 3:1-4, 9, 11; M't 21:33-41; 23:2-7, 13-33; 26:14-16, 59-68; M'k 12:1-12; 14:10, 11; Lu 22:3-6). Dissensions in (1Co 1:11-13; 3:3, 4; 11:18, 19; 2Co 12:20, 21). Divisions in, to be shunned (Ro 16:17; 1Co 1:10; 3:3). Persecution of (Ac 8:1-3; 1Co 15:9; 1Th 2:14, 15; see Persecution).

God's Care for: Clothed in righteousness (Re 19:8). Defended by God (Ps 89:18; Isa 4:5; 49:25; M't 16:18). Edified by the Word (Ro 12:6; 1Co 14:4, 13; Eph 4:15, 16; Col 3:16). Is glorious (Ps 45:13; Eph 5:27). Growth of continuous (Ac 2:47; 5:14; 11:24). Harmonious fellowship (Ps 133; Joh 13:34; Ac 4:32; Ph'p 1:4; 2:1; 1Jo 3:4). Indwelt by God (Ps 132:14). Loved (see below). Not to be despised (1Co 11:22). Privileges of (Ps 36:8; 87:5). Provides leaders (Jer 3:15; Eph 4:11, 12). Punishment for defiling (1Co 3:17). Safe under God's care (Ps 46:1, 2, 5). Triumphant (Ga 4:26; Heb 12:22, 23; Re 3:12; 21:3, 10).

Loved: By God (Isa 27:2, 3; 43:1-7; 49:14-17; Jer 3:14, 15; 13:11). By Christ (Joh 10:8, 11, 14; Eph 5:25-32; Re 3:9). By believers (Ps 84:1, 2; 87:7; 102:14; 137:5; 1Co 12:25; 1Th 4:9). Manifested, by prayer for (Ps 122:6; Isa 62:6); by distress at misfortunes of (Ps 137:1-6; Isa 22:4; Jer 9:1; 14:17; 51:50, 51; La 2:11; 3:48-51); by joy at prosperity of (Isa 66:10, 13, 14); by zeal for (Isa 58:12; 62:1, 6, 7).

New Testment Church: Beneficence of (see Beneficence; Giving; Liberality). Christ, the head of (Ps 118:22, 23; Isa 28:16; 33:22; 55:4; M't 12:6, 8; 21:42, 43; 23:8, 10; M'k 2:28; 12:10; Lu 6:5; 20:17, 18; Joh 13:13; 15:1-8; Ac 2:36; Ro 8:29; 9:5; 1Co 3:11; 11:3; 12:5; Eph 1:10, 22, 23; 2:20-22; 4:15; 5:23-32; Col 1:13, 18; 2:10, 19; 3:11; Heb 3:3, 6; 1Pe 2:7; Re 1:13; 2:1-28; 3:1, 7; 5:6; 21:22, 23; 22:16; see Jesus, Kingdom of). Communism in (Ac 4:32). Decrees of (Ac 15:28, 29; 16:4). Design of (Ro 3:2; 9:4; Eph 2:20-22; 1Ti 3:15). Discipline (see Discipline below). Diversity of callings in (1Co 12:5, 28; Eph 4:11, 12). Divinely established or instituted (M't 16:15-18; Eph 2:20-22; 1Th 1:1; 2Th 1:1; 1Ti 3:15); founded on the Lordship of Christ (M't 16:18). Duty (see Responsibilities below). Edification, by teachers (Eph 4:11, 12); by public worship (Col 3:16; Heb 10:25). Government (see below). Growth of, rapid (Ac 2:41, 47; 4:4; 5:14; 6:7; 9:35; 11:21, 24; 14:1; 19:17-20); predicted (Isa 2:2; Eze 17:22-24; Da 34:35). Holiness of (2Co 11:2; Eph 5:27; 2Pe 3:14; Re 19:8). Loved (see above). Membership in (M't 12:50; 19:14; M'k 10:14; Lu 18:16; Joh 15:5, 6; Ac 2:41, 47; 4:4; 5:14; 9:35, 42; 11:21; Ro 12:4, 5; 1Co 3:11-15; 12:12-28; Eph 4:25; 5:30; Ph'p 4:3; Re 21:27). Militancy of (Song 6:10; Ph'p 2:25; 2Ti 2:3; 4:7; Ph'm 2). Mission of (see below). Pastoral care of (Ac 20:28). Responsibilities (see below). Unity of (Ps 133:1; Joh 10:16; 17:11, 21-23; Ro 12:4, 5; 1Co 10:17; 12:5, 12-27; Ga 3:26-28; Eph 1:10; 2:14-21; 3:6, 15; 4:4-6, 12-16, 25; Col 3:11, 15). Union of, with Christ (Joh 15:1-7; Ro 11:17; 2Co 11:2; Eph 5:30, 32; Re 19:7; 21:9). Worship, to be attended (Heb 10:25); to be conducted orderly (Ec 5:1, 3; 1Co 11:4, 5, 33; 14:26, 33, 40; 1Ti 3:15).

Discipline: In the Mosaic institution (Ge 17:14; Ex 12:15; 30:33, 37, 38; Le 7:27; 17:8, 9; 19:5-8; 20:18; 22:3; Nu 9:13; 15:31; 19:13, 20; De 13:12-18; 17:2-13; 19:16-21; 21:1-9, 18-21; 22:13-29; Ezr 10:7, 8).

Discipline: In the Christian Church: Design of, to save the soul (M't 18:15; 1Co 5:1-13; 2Th 3:14); to warn others (1Ti 5:20); to preserve sound doctrine (Ro 16:17; Ga 5:10; 1Ti 1:19, 20; Tit 1:13). Exercised, with kindness (2Co 2:6-11; Ga 6:1; Jude 22, 23); with forbearance (Ro 15:1-3). Reasons, for heresy (1Ti 6:3-5; Tit 3:10, 11; 2Jo 10, 11); for immorality (M't 18:17, 18; 1Co 5:1-7, 11-13; 2Th 3:6); for schism (Ro 16:17). By reproof (2Co 7:8; 10:1-11; 13:2, 10; 1Th 5:14; 2Th 3:15; 1Ti 5:1, 2; 2Ti 4:2; Tit 2:15). Witnesses required in (M't 18:16; 2Co 13:1; 1Ti 5:19).

Government: Of the Mosaic institution (De 17:8-13). Of the Christian Church: Authority, of apostles (M't 16:19; Joh 20:23; Ac 1:15, 23-26; 5:1-11; 1Co 7:17; 11:2, 33, 34; Ga 2:9); of apostolic council (Ac 15:1-31; 16:4, 5); of congregation (1Co 16:3, 16; Jude 22, 23). Leadership by, apostles (see above); bishops or overseers (1Ti 3:1-7); deacons (Ac 6:2-6; 1Ti 3:8-13); elders (Ac 14:23; 20:17, 28; 1Ti 5:1, 17, 22; Tit 1:5; Jas 5:14, 15; 1Pe 5:1-3); prophets and teachers (Ac 13:1, 3, 5; 1Ti 4:14; 2Ti 1:6). Obedience to rulers (Heb 13:17, 24).

Mission of: To be custodians of the oracles of God (Ro 3:2; 9:4). To bring, peace (Ps 22:27-31; Isa 2:3-5; 11:6-9; 52:1, 2, 7, 8; 61:1-3; 65:25); spiritual enlightenment (Isa 2:3; 29:18, 19; Joe 2:26-32; Hab 2:14; Ac 2:16-21); moral transformation (Isa 4:2-6; 32:3, 4, 15-17; 35:1, 2, 5-7; 44:3-5; 55:10-13; Zep 3:9). To be the salt and light of the world (M't 5:13).

Responsibilities and duties: Of believers to leaders, to encourage (1Co 16:10, 11); To esteem (Ph'p 2:29; 1Th 5:12, 13; 1Ti 5:17); to imitate the example of (1Co 11:1; Ph'p 3:17; 2Th 3:7; Heb 13:7; 1Pe 5:3); to obey (Heb 13:17); to receive (Ph'p 2:29); to reimburse (1Co 9:7-23; 2Co 12:13; Ga 6:6; Ph'p 4:10-18; 2Th 3:7-9; 1Ti 5:17, 18); to seek instruction from (Mal 2:7). Of leaders, to feed believers (Ac 20:28).

Prophecies Concerning: Its universality (Ge 12:3; Isa 2:2; 40:5; 42:3, 4; 45:23; 52:10, 15; 54:1-5; 56:7, 8; 59:19; 60:1, 3-9; 66:12, 19, 23; Jer 3:17; 4:2; 16:19; 31:7-9, 34; 33:22; Da 2:35, 45; 7:13, 14, 18, 22, 27; Am 9:11, 12; Zep 2:11; Zec 9:1, 10; 14:6-9, 16; Mal 1:11; M't 8:11; Joh 10:16; Re 11:15; 15:4). Its prosperity (Ps 72:7-11, 16, 19; 86:9; 102:15, 16, 18; 132:15-18; Isa 4:2-6; 25:6-8; 33:20, 21;

49:6-18; 51:3-8; 52:1, 2, 7, 8, 10, 15; 54:1-5, 11-14; 55:5, 10-13; 60:1-9, 19, 20; 61:1-11; 62:2, 3, 12; 65:18, 19, 23-25; 66:12, 19, 23; Jer 31:34; Eze 17:22-24; 34:26, 29-31; 47:3-12; Joe 2:26-32; Am 9:11, 12; Mic 4:3, 4; 5:2, 4, 7; Hab 2:14; Zep 3:9; Hag 2:7-9; Zec 2:10, 11; 6:15; 8:20-23). Its perpetuality (Isa 9:7; 33:20; Da 7:14, 27; M't 16:18; Eph 1:10; Heb 12:23, 24, 27, 28; Re 5:10, 13, 14; 11:15; 12:10; 15:4; 20:4-6; 21:9-27; 22:1-5). See Jesus, Kingdom of.

State: Relationship of Church and State. Ecclesiastical Power Superior to Civil: Appoints kings (1Sa 10:1); directs administration (1Sa 15:1-4); reproves rulers (1Sa 15:14-35); withdraws support and anoints a successor (1Sa 16:1-13; 2Ki 9:1-26; 11:4-12); attempted usurpation of ecclesiastical functions by civil authorities reproved (1Sa 13:8-14; 2Ch 26:16-21). State Superior to Church: evident, in David's appointments (1Ch 23; 24; 25; 2Ch 35:4); in Solomon's power (1Ki 2:26, 27; 5; 6; 7; 8); in Hezekiah reorganizing temple service (2Ch 31:2-19); Jeroboam subverting the Jewish religion (1Ki 12:26-33); in Manasseh subverting and restoring the true religion (2Ch 33:2-9, 15-17); in Jehoash supervising the repairs of the temple (2Ki 12:4-18); in Ahaz transforming the altars (2Ki 16:10-16); in Josiah exercising the function of a priest (2Ch 34:29-33). State Favorable to the Church: Cyrus, in proclamation to restore the temple (2Ch 36:22, 23; Ezr 1:1-11); Darius, in edict to further restoration of the temple (Ezr 6:1-14); Artaxerxes, in exempting religious institution from taxes (Ezr 7:24).

See Ecclesiasticism; Jesus, Kingdom of; Ministers; Usurption, in Ecclesiastical Affairs.

CHURNING (Pr 30:33). See Butter.

CHUSHAN-RISHATHAIM, king of Mesopotamia (J'g 3:8-10).

CHUZA, Herod's steward (Lu 8:3).

CILICIA. Maritime province of Asia Minor. Jews dwell in (Ac 6:9). Churches of (Ac 15:23, 41; Ga 1:21).

Sea of (Ac 27:5).

CINNAMON. A spice (Pr 7:17; Song 4:14; Re 18:13). An ingredient of the sacred oil (Ex 30:23).

CINNERETH (See Chinnereth; Galilee, Sea of.)

CIRCUMCISION. Institution of (Ge 17:10-14; Le 12:3; Joh 7:22; Ac 7:8; Ro 4:11). A seal of righteousness (Ro 2:25-29; 4:11). Performed on all males on the eighth day (Ge 17:12, 13; Le 12:3; Ph'p 3:5). Rite of, observed on the Sabbath (Joh 7:23). A prerequisite of the privileges of the passover (Ex 12:48). Child named at the time of (Ge 21:3, 4; Lu 1:59; 2:21). Neglect of, punished (Ge 17:14; Ex 4:24). Neglected (Jos 5:7). Covenant promises of (Ge 17:4, 14; Ac 7:8; Ro 3:1; 4:11; 9:7-13; Ga 5:3). Necessity of, falsely taught by Judaizing Christians (Ac 15:1). Paul's argument against the continuance of (Ro 2:25, 28; Ga 6:13). Characterized by Paul as a yoke (Ac 15:10). Abrogated (Ac 15:5-29; Ro 3:30; 4:9-11; 1Co 7:18, 19; Ga 2:3, 4; 5:2-11; 6:12; Eph 2:11, 15; Col 2:11; 3:11).

Instances of: Abraham (Ge 17:23-27; 21:3, 4). Shechemites (Ge 34:24). Moses (Ex 4:25). Israelites at Gilgal (Jos 5:2-9); John the Baptist (Lu 1:59). Jesus (Lu 2:21). Paul (Ph'p 3:5). Timothy (Ac 16:3).

Figurative: Ex 6:12; De 10:16; 30:6; Jer 4:4; 6:10; 9:26; Ro 2:28, 29; 15:8; Ph'p 3:3; Col 2:11; 3:11.

A designation of the Jews (Ac 10:45; 11:2; Ga 2:9; Eph 2:11; Col 4:11; Tit 1:10); of Christians (Ph'p 3:3).

CIS (See Kish.)

CISTERN, an artificial reservoir dug in the earth or rock for the collection and storage of water from rain or spring (Pr 5:15; Ec 12:6; Isa 36:16; Jer 2:13). Cisterns were a necessity in Palestine with its long, dry, rainless summers. Empty cisterns were sometimes used as prisons (Ge 37:22; Jer 38:6; Zec 9:11).

Figurative: 2Ki 18:31; Pr 5:15; Ec 12:6. See Wells.

CITIES. Ancient (Ge 4:17; 10:10-12). Fortified (Nu 32:36; De 9:1; Jos 10:20; 14:12; 2Ch 8:5; 11:10-12; 17:2, 19; 21:3; Isa 23:11). Gates of, see Gates. Designated as: Royal (Jos 10:2; 1Sa 27:5; 2Sa 12:26; 1Ch 11:7); treasure (Ge 41:48; Ex 1:11; 1Ki 9:19; 2Ch 8:4; 16:4; 17:12); chariot (2Ch 1:14; 8:6; 9:25); merchant (Isa 23:11; Eze 17:4; 27:3).

Town clerk of (Ac 19:35). Government of, by rulers (Ne 3:9, 12, 17, 18: 7:2). See Government.

Suburbs of (Nu 35:3-5; Jos 14:4).

Watchmen of (See Watchman).

Figurative: Heb 11:10, 16; 12:22; 13:14.

CITIES OF REFUGE, six cities set apart by Moses and Joshua as places of asylum for those who had accidentally committed manslaughter. There they remained until a fair trial could be held. If proved innocent of willful murder, they had to remain in the city of refuge until the death of the high priest (Nu 35; De 19:1-13; Jos 20).

CITIES OF THE PLAIN, cities near the Dead Sea, including Sodom, Gomorrah, Admah, Zeboiim, and Zoar. Lot lived in Sodom (Ge 13:10-12). They were destroyed because of their wickedness (Ge 19). They were probably at the S end of the Dead Sea, and it is believed that the sea covers the site.

CITIZENS. *Duties of:* Honor rulers (Ex 22:28; Nu 27:20; Job 34:18; Pr 16:14, 15; 24:21; 25:6, 7, 15; Ec 10:4, 20; Ac 23:5; 1Pe 2:17). Pray for rulers (Ezr 6:10; 1Ti 2:1, 2). Promote peace (Jer 29:7). Obey the law (Ezr 7:26; 10:8; Ec 8:2-4; Ac 19:35-41; Ro 13:1-7; Tit 3:1; 1Pe 2:13-16). Pay taxes (M't 17:24-27; 22:17-21; M'k 12:14-17; Lu 20:22-25; Ro 13:5-7).

Rights of: Public vindication when falsely accused (Ac 16:37). Protection from mob violence (Ac 19:36-41). Fair trial (Ac 22:25-29; 24:18, 19; 25:5, 10, 11, 16).

Loyal, Instances of: Israelites (Jos 1:16-18; 2Sa 3:36, 37; 15:23, 30; 18:3; 21:17; 1Ch 12:38). David (1Sa 24:6-11; 26:6-16; 2Sa 1:14). Hushai (2Sa 17:15, 16). David's soldiers (2Sa 18:12, 13; 23;15, 16). Joab (2Sa 19:5, 6). Barzillai (2Sa 19:32). Jehoiada (2Ki 11:4-12). Isaiah (Isa 22:4). Jeremiah (La 1-5). Mordecai (Es 2:21-23).

Wicked and Treasonable (Pr 17:11; 19:10, 12; 20:2; 2Ti 3:1-4; 2Pe 2:10; Jude 8). *Instances of:* Miriam and Aaron (Nu 12:1-11). Korah, Dathan and Abiram (Nu 16:1-35; 26:9). Shechemites (J'g 9:1-6, 22-25, 46-49). Ephraimites (J'g 12:1-4). Israelites (1Sa 10:27; 1Ki 12:16-19). Absalom (2Sa 15:10-13). Ahithophel (2Sa 15:12; 17:1-4). Sheba (2Sa 20:1, 2). Adonijah (1Ki 1:5-7). Jeroboam (1Ki 11:14-26; 12:20; 2Ch 13:5-9). Baasha (1Ki 15:27). Zimri (1Ki 16:9, 10). Jozochar and Jozabud (2Ki 12:19-21; 14:5). Shallum (2Ki 15:10). Menahem (2Ki 15:14). Pekah (2Ki 15:25). Hoshea (2Ki 15:30). Sons of Sennacherib (2Ki 19:37; 2Ch 32:21). Ishmael (Jer 40:14-16; 41). Bigthan and Teresh (Es 2:21). Jews (Eze 17:12-20). Barabbas (M'k 15:7). Theudas and 400 (Ac 5:36, 37). An Egyptian (Ac 21:38).

Figurative: Eph 2:19; Ph'p 3:20.

CITY OF DAVID. 1. Jebusite stronghold of Zion captured by David and made by him his royal residence (2Sa 5:6-9).

2. Bethlehem, the home of David (Lu 2:4).

CIVIL DAMAGES (See Damages.)

CIVIL ENGINEERING (Jos 18:9; Job 28:9-11).

CIVIL SERVICE. School for (Da 1:3-21). Appointment in, on account of merit (Ge 39:1-6; 41:38-44; 1Ki 11:28; Es 6:1-11; Da 1:7, 17-21; 6:1-3; M't 25:14, 15, 23-30; Lu 19:12-27). Corruption in (Ne 5:15; Da 6:4-17; M'k 15:15; Ac 24:26). Reform in (Ne 4:14, 15). Influence in (1Ki 1:5-40; 2Ki 4:13; M't 20:20-23; M'k 10:35).

CLAIRVOYANCE (1Sa 28:13, 14; 2Ki 6:15-17).

See Sorcery.

CLAUDA, an island near Crete (Ac 27:16).

CLAUDIA, a female disciple (2Ti 4:21).

CLAUDIUS, 4th Roman emperor (41-54). He banished all Jews from Rome (Ac 18:2). The famine foretold by Agabus took place in his reign (Ac 11:28).

CLAUDIUS LYSIUS, a Roman military officer (Ac 21:31-40; 22:23-30). Sends Paul to Felix (23:10-35).

CLAY, Man formed from (Job 33:6). Seals made of (Job 38:14). Used by potter (Isa 29:16; 41:25; 45:9). Blind man's eyes anointed with (Joh 9:6).

Figurative: Job 4:19; Ps 40:2; Isa 45:9; 64:8; Jer 18:6; Ro 9:21.

Symbolical: Da 2:33-41.

CLAY TABLETS, were made of clay which, while still wet, had wedge-shaped letters imprinted on them with a stylus, and then were kiln-fired or sun-dried.

They were made of various shapes, and were often placed in a clay envelope. Vast quantities have been excavated in the Near East. The oldest go back to 3000 B. C.

CLEAN AND UNCLEAN ANIMALS. See Animals. Of Birds, see Birds. Of Fish, see Fish. Of Insects, see Insects.

CLEANLINESS. Taught by frequent ablutions.

(See Ablution; Purification).

Regulation relating to, in camp (De 23:12-14).

Figurative: Ps 51:7, 10; 73:1; Pr 20:9; Isa 1:16; Eze 36:25; 1Jo 1:7, 9; Re 1:5.

CLEANSING (See Ablution.)

CLEANTHES, Greek Stoic philosopher of 3rd century B. C. whose poem, *Hymn to Zeus*, is quoted by Paul (Ac 17:28).

CLEMENCY. Of David toward disloyal subjects: Shimei (2Sa 16:5-13; 19:16-23); Amasa (2Sa 19:13, w 2Sa 17:25).

Divine, see God, Longsuffering of, and Mercy of.

CLEMENT, a disciple at Philippi (Ph'p 4:3).

CLEOPAS, a disciple to whom Jesus appeared after his resurrection (Lu 24:18).

CLEOPHAS, husband of one of the Marys (Joh 19:25).

CLERGYMAN (See Minister.)

CLERK, town (Ac 19:35).

CLOAK, Paul's left at Troas (2Ti 4:13).

Figurative: Joh 15:22; 1Pe 2:16.

CLOSET, private room or storage closet (Lu 12:3). Used as a place for prayer (M't 6:6).

CLOTH (M't 9:16; 27:59; M'k 14:51).

CLOTHING, of the Israelites, waxed not old (De 8:4; 29:5; Ne 9:21).

See Dress.

CLOUD. *Pillar of, with Fire:* Symbolic of the Lord's presence (Ex 13:21, 22; 16:20; 19:9, 16; 24:16-18; 33:9, 10; 34:5; Le 16:2; Nu 11:25; 12:5, 10; 14:10; 16:19, 42; De 31:15; 1Ki 8:10, 11; 2Ch 7:1-3; M't 17:5; Lu 9:34, 35; 1Co 10:1; see Isa 6:1, 4). A guide to Israel (Ex 14:19, 24; 40:36-38; Nu 9:15-23; 10:11, 12, 33-36; De 1:33; Ne 9:12, 19; Ps 78:14; 105:39; Isa 4:5). In Isaiah's prophecy (Isa 4:5). In Ezekiel's vision (Eze 10:3, 4, 18, 19; 11:22, 23).

Figurative: Jer 4:13; Ho 6:4; 13:3.

Symbolical: Re 14:14.

CLOUT (See Dress.)

CNIDUS, a city in Asia Minor (Ac 27:7).

COAL. The Bible never refers to true mineral coal, which has not been found in Palestine proper. The references are always either to charcoal or to live embers of any kind. Hebrews usually used charcoal for warmth or cooking (Isa 47:14; Joh 18:18; 21:9).

Figurative: Pr 25:22.

Symbolical: Isa 6:6, 7; 2Sa 14:7.

COAL OIL (See Oil.)

COAT OF MAIL (1Sa 17:5, 38; 1Ki 22:34; 2Ch 18:33).

COCK (See Birds.)

COCKATRICE, a fabulous serpent.

Figurative: Isa 11:8; 14:29; 59:5; Jer 8:17.

COCK CROWING (M't 26:34, 74, 75; M'k 13:35; 14:30, 68, 72).

COCKLE, a general term for obnoxious plants (Job 31:40).

COELE SYRIA (hollow Syria), name for that part of Syria that lay between the Lebanon and Anti-Lebanon Mts.

COERCION. *Religious:* Penalty for (Ex 22:20). Oath against (2Ch 15:12-15). Instance of (Da 3:2-6, 29; 6:26-27).

See Bigotry; Intolerance.

COFFER, a chest (1Sa 6:8, 11, 15; Eze 27:24).

See Treasury.

COFFIN (Ge 50:26).

See Burial.

COIN (See Money.)

COL-HOZEH, father of Baruch (Ne 11:5).

COLLAR (See Dress.)

COLLECTION, of money, for the poor.

See Alms; Beneficence; Giving; Liberality.

COLLEGE, second quarter of the city of Jerusalem (2Ki 22:14; 2Ch 34:22).

See School.

COLLOP, slice of meat or fat (Job 15:27).

COLLUSION. In Sin (Le 20:4, 5).

See Complicity; Connivance.

COLONIZATION. Of conquered countries and people (2Ki 17:6, 24; Ezr 4:9, 10).

COLORS, FIGURATIVE AND SYMBOLIC.

Black: Of affliction (Job 3:5; Ps 107:10, 11; 143:3; Isa 9:19; 24:11). Of calamity (Isa 5:30; 8:22; 50:3; Joe 2:6, 10; 3:14, 15; Na 2:10). Of day of wrath (Zep 1:14, 15). Of death (Job 10:20-22; Am 5:8). Of the abode of the lost (M't 8:12; 22:13; 25:30; 2Pe 2:4; Jude 13; Re 16:10).

Blue: Of deity (Ex 25:3, 4; 26:1; 28:28, 37; 38:18; 39:1-5, 21, 24, 29, 31; Nu 4:5-12; 15:38-40; 2Ch 2:7, 14; 3:14). Of royalty (Es 8:15; Eze 23:6). Predominant color in drapery and furnishings of the tabernacle, and vestments of the priests (Ex 24:10; Jer 10:9; Eze 1:26; 10:1).

Crimson, Red, Purple and Scarlet: Of iniquity (Isa 1:18; Re 17:3, 4; 18:12, 16). Of prosperity (2Sa 1:24; Pr 31:21; La 4:5). Of conquest (Isa 63:2; Na 2:3; Re 12:3). Of royalty (J'g 8:26; Da 5:7, 16, 29; M't 27:28). Types and shadows of the atonement (Ex 25:3-5; 26:1, 14, 31, 36; 27:16; 28:4-6, 8, 15, 31, 33, 37; 35:5-7, 23-25, 35; 36:8, 19, 35, 37; 38:23; 39; Le 14:4, 6, 49-52; Nu 4:7, 8, 13; 19:2, 5, 6; Isa 63:1-3; Heb 9:19-23).

White: Of Holiness (Le 16:4, 32; Ps 51:7; Ec 9:8; Isa 1:18; Da 7:9; 11:35; 12:10; M't 17:1, 2; 28:2, 3; M'k 9:3; Re 1:13, 14; 2:17; 3:4, 5, 18; 4:4; 6:2, 11; 7:9, 13, 14; 15:6; 19:8, 11, 14; 20:11). Choir singers arrayed in white (2Ch 5:12).

COLOSSE, a city of Phrygia (Col 1:2, 7, 8).

COLOSSIANS, BOOK OF, epistle written by Paul in prison; although he does not say where (Col 4:3, 10, 18), most likely in Rome, c. A. D. 62. It was written to combat a serious Judaic-Gnostic error. Outline:

1. Salutation and thanksgiving (1:1-8).
2. Doctrinal section (1:9-2:5).
3. Practical exhortations (2:6-4:6).
4. Concluding salutations (4:7-18).

COLT, ridden by Jesus (M't 21:2, 5, 7; M'k 11:2; Joh 12:15).

COMFORT (See Affliction, Consolation in; Righteous, Promises to.)

COMFORTER (See God, Grace of; Holy Spirit.)

COMMANDMENT, used in the English Bible to translate a number of Heb. and Gr. words meaning law, ordinance, statute, word, judgment, precept, saying, charge, etc.

COMMANDMENTS AND STATUTES, OF GOD.

Admonishing Against: Backsliding (De 8:11-17; 28:18; Eze 33:12, 13, 18; Lu 9:62; 1Co 10:12; Heb 3:12, 13; 12:15; 2Pe 2:20, 21). Conspiracy (Ex 23:1, 2). Hypocrisy (M't 6:1-5, 16; Lu 20:46, 47; 1Pe 2:1). Lusts (Pr 31:3; Ro 13:13, 14; Ga 5:16; 1Pe 2:11). Oppression of foreigners (Ex 22:21; 23:9; De 24:14; Zec 7:10). Popular corruption (Ex 23:2). Reviling rulers (Ex 22:28; Ac 23:5).

Concerning: Children, enjoining obedience to parents (Pr 6:20; Eph 6:1-3; Col 3:20; see Enjoining Reverence for Parents below). Debtors' protection (De 24:10, 12, 13). Father's concern for children (Eph 6:4; Col 3:21). Husband's love for wife (Eph 5:23; Col 3:19); honor for wife (1Pe 3:7). Indissolubility of marriage (Ge 2:24; M't 19:6; M'k 10:9; 1Co 7:1-16). Judges' justice in court (De 1:16). Lost property (Ex 23:4; De 22:1-3). Man's supremacy over animals (Ge 9:2). Masters', equity (Col 4:1); humane treatment of servants (Eph 6:9). Ministers (Ac 20:31; 1Ti 1:4; 3:2-13; 4:12-16; 5:20-22; 2Ti 2:1-3, 14-16, 22-24; Tit 1:5-9; 2:1-10, 15; 1Pe 5:2, 3); faithfulness (Col 4:17; 1Ti 6:11, 12, 14; 2 Ti 1:8, 13); fortitude (2Ti 2:3); foolish questions (2Ti 2:3); sanctification (2Ti 2:4, 5); strife (2Ti 2:24). Places of public worship (De 12:11). Restitution (Ex 21:30-36; 22:1-15; Le 6:4, 5; 24:18; Nu 5:7). Servants' obedience (Eph 6:5-8; Col 3:22-25; Tit 2:9, 10; 1Pe 2:18, 19). Soldiers' obedience (Eph 5:22; Col 3:18; 1Pe 3:1-4). Vicious animals (Ex 21:28-32, 35, 36). Wives' obedience (Eph 5:22; Col 3:18; 1Pe 3:1-4). Women (Eph 5:22, 24; Tit 2:3-5; 1Pe 3:1-3). Young men's parental obedience (Pr 6:20; 23:22).

The Decalogue (Ex 20:3-17; De 5:6-21). See Decalogue; Tables.

Enjoining: Abhorrence, of the abominations of the wicked (De 7:25, 26); of evil (Ro 12:9-21). Abiding in Christ (Joh 15:4, 9; 1Jo 2:28). Abstinence from evil (1Th 5:22). Accord with Christ, and concord with one another (Ph'p 2:2-5). Admonition and encouragement (1Th 5:14). Altruistic service (M't 20:26; M'k 9:35; 10:42-45; Lu 22:26; Joh 13:14; Ro 15:1, 2; 1Co 10:24; Ga 6:10; Ph'p 2:3, 4). Assistance to the distressed (Ps 82:4; Pr 24:11).

Building a sanctuary (Ex 25:8).

Casting anxiety upon the Lord (1Pe 5:7). Charitableness (M't 18:10; Lu 6:37, 38; Ro 14:1-3, 13, 19). Chastity (Pr 5:15-19; M't 5:27, 28). Cheerfulness (Ec 9:7-9). Choice of wise men for rulers (Ex 18:21; De 1:13). Christian graces (2Co 13:11; Col 3:12-17; 2Ti 2:22). Christian tolerance toward the weak (Ro 15:1). Confession of sin (Nu 8:12; Jas 5:16). Contentment (Lu 3:14; Heb 13:5). Courage (De 31:6, 7; Jos 1:6, 7, 9; 1Ki 2:2, 3; 1Ch 28:20; Ne 4:14; Jer 1:8; Eze 2:6). Cross-bearing (M't 16:24; M'k 8:34).

Destruction of idols (Ex 23:24; 34:13; Nu 33:52; De 7:25; 12:13). Diligence (Ec 9:10; 11:6). Diligence in business (Pr 27:23). Discipleship (M't 19:21; M'k 10:21; Lu 18:22). Discipline of disorderly church members (2Th 3:6). Discipline of children (M't 19:14; M'k 10:14; Lu 18:16, 17). Discreet conduct (Ro 12:17; Eph 4:1-3; 5:15, 16; Ph'p 1:27; 4:5; 1Pe 2:11, 12). Doing all to the glory of God (1Co 10:31; Col 3:17, 23).

Equity of servants (Col 4:1). Establishing, and providing for the ordination of, a holy ministry (Ex 28:1-3; 40:12-15; Le 8:1-13). Esteem for pastors (1Th 5:12, 13; 1Ti 5:17; Heb 13:7). Evangelism (M't 28:19).

Faith (Ex 14:13; 2Ch 20:20; Ps 37:3, 5; 62:8; 115:9, 11; Pr 3:5; Isa 26:4; 50:10; Jer 49:11; M'k 1:15; 5:36; 11:22; Joh 6:29; 12:36; 14:1, 11; 20:27); in Christ (1Jo 3:23). Faithfulness, of ministers (Col 4:17; 1Ti 6:11, 12, 14; 2Ti 1:8, 13); to friends (Pr 27:10). Family support (1Ti 5:8). Fear of God (Le 19:14, 32; 25:17; De 6:13; 10:12, 20; 13:4; Jos 24:14; 1Sa 12:24; 2Ki 17:39; Pr 3:7; 23:17; 24:21; Ec 12:13; Isa 8:13; 1Pe 2:17). Fidelity, in wedlock (Ge 2:24; M't 19:6; M'k 10:8; 1Co 7:10, 11); to God (1Sa 12:20; M't 22:21); to God and government (M't 22:21; M'k 12:17; Lu 20:25); to vows (Nu 30:2; De 23:21-23; Ps 50:14; Ec 5:4). Forbearance (Eph 4:2; Col 3:13). Forgiveness (M't 18:22; M'k 11:25; Lu 17:3, 4; Ro 12:14; Eph 4:32; Col 3:13). Fortitude under persecution (M't 10:26-28; M'k 13:9, 11-13; 2Ti 2:3; Re 2:10). Fraternal reproof (M't 18:15-17; Lu 17:3, 4). Fruits of righteousness (Lu 3:11, 14).

Gentleness (Tit 3:2). Godliness (Eph 5:1). Golden Rule, in conduct (M't 7:12; Lu 6:31). Good works (1Pe 3:10). Growth in grace (Heb 6:1; 2Pe 1:5-8; 3:18; Jude 20, 21).

Heed, to instruction (Pr 4:10; 19:20; 22:17); to parental instruction (Pr 1:8; 23:22); to the truth (M't 11:15; M'k 4:9; Re 2:7). Helpfulness (1Co 10:24; Ga 6:1, 2; Ph'p 2:4; 1Th 5:11). Holiness (Ex 22:31; 30:29; Le 11:44; 20:7, 25, 26; 21:7; Nu 15:40; De 18:13; Jos 7:13; Isa 1:16, 17; Jer 6:16; Am 5:14, 15; 1Co 5:7; 2Co 7:1; Eph 4:22-32; Col 3:5, 8, 9; 1Th 4:3-7; 2Ti 2:19, 22; Heb 12:14; Jas 1:21; 4:8; 1Pe 1:13-16; 2:11, 12; 3:15; 3Jo 11). Holiness in ministers (Le 21:6; Nu 8:14, 15). Honesty (Le 19:35, 36; De 25:13-16; 1Th 4:12); in service (1Co 4:2; Eph 6:5-7; Col 3:22, 23; Tit 2:9, 10); in office (Lu 3:13). Honor, to civil rulers (1Pe 2:17); to wife (1Pe 3:7). Hospitality (Ro 12:13; Heb 13:2; 1Pe 4:9). Humane treatment of servants (Eph 6:9). Humility (Ro 12:16; Ph'p 2:3; Jas 4:10; 1Pe 3:8; 5:6, 7).

Imitation of Christ (Ro 13:14; Col 2:6, 7). Industry (Pr 6:6; Eph 4:28; 1Th 4:11; 2Th 3:12). Influence for righteousness (M't 5:16; Ph'p 2:15).

Joyfulness (Ro 12:12; Ph'p 3:1; 4:4; 1Th 5:16). Justice (Le 19:15; Isa 56:1; Zec 7:9, 10; Joh 7:24); in courts (De 1:17; 25:1, 2); to, and love for, foreigners (Le 19:33, 34; 24:22).

Keeping the Sabbath holy (Ex 16:29; 20:8; 31:12-16; 35:2, 3; Le 19:3, 30; 26:2; De 5:12). Kindness (Pr 3:27, 28; Eph 4:32; Col 3:12; 1Th 5:15); to animals (De 25:4); to enemies (Ex 23:4, 5; Pr 25:21; Ro 12:20).

Labor (Ex 20:9; 35:2; De 5:13). Laying up treasure in heaven (M't 6:20). Liberality (Pr 3:9; Ec 11:1; M't 5:42; Lu 6:30; 12:33; 34:2; 2Co 8:7; Heb 13:16); in God's service (Mal 3:10); in support of religion (De 15:19; 16:17); toward house of God (Ex 22:29; 30:12-16; 34:26; 35:4-9); to the poor (Le 19:9, 10; 23:22; De 15:7-15; 24:19-21; Ro 12:13; Heb 13:16; 1Jo 3:17). Love, for enemies (M't 5:44; Lu 6:27-29; Ro 12:14, 15); for foreigners (Le 19:34; De 10:19); for God (De 6:5; 10:12; 11:1, 8, 13; 30:16; Jos 22:5; 23:11; M't 22:37; M'k 12:30; Lu 10:27); for man (Le 19:18, 33, 34; M't 19:19; 22:39; M'k 12:31; Lu 10:27; Joh 13:34; 15:12, 17; Ro 12:9, 10; 13:8-10; 1Co 16:14; Ga 5:14; Eph 5:2; Col 3:14; 1Th 3:12; 4:9; Heb 13:1; Jas 2:8; 1Pe

2:17; 3:8; 4:8; 1Jo 3:11, 18, 23; 4:7, 21; 2Jo 5); for wife (Eph 5:23; Col 3:19). Loving truth and pèace (Zec 8:19).

Manliness (1Co 16:13, 14). Manly gravity (1Co 14:20; Tit 2:2). Meekness (M't 5:39, 40; Lu 6:29; Eph 4:2; Col 3:12; Tit 3:2). Mercy (Pr 3:3; Zec 7:9, 10; Lu 6:36). Mercy to debtors (De 24:6).

Oaths in God's name (De 6:13; 10:20). Obedience (Le 18:4, 5, 26, 30; 19:19, 37; 20:8, 22; 22:31; 25:18; Nu 15:40; De 4:1, 6, 23, 40; 5:32, 33; 6:17, 18; 7:11; 8:1, 6; 10:12, 13; 11:1, 8, 13, 32; 12:28, 32; 13:4; 27:1, 10; 29:9; 30:2, 8, 16; 1Sa 15:1; 1Ki 2:2, 3; 2Ki 17:37, 38; 1Ch 28:20; Pr 3:6; 4:20, 21; 5:7; 7:1-14; Ec 12:13; Joh 13:15); of children (Pr 6:20; Eph 6:1-3; Col 3:20); of servants (Eph 6:5-8; Col 3:22-25; Tit 2:9, 10; 1Pe 2:18, 19); of soldiers (De 20:3; Lu 3:14); of wives (Eph 5:22; Col 3:18; 1Pe 3:1-4); of young men (Pr 6:20; 23:22); to Christ as Lord (1Pe 3:15); to civil government (Ec 8:2; M'k 12:17; Lu 20:25; Ro 13:1, 7; Tit 3:1; 1Pe 2:13); to God's law (De 11:8, 13, 32; 30:16; Jos 22:5; 2Ki 17:37, 38; 1Ch 28:8); to parents (Pr 6:20; Eph 6:1-3; Col 3:20). Orderly conduct of divine worship (1Co 14:26-33).

Patience (Jas 1:4; 5:7-9); under afflictions (Pr 3:11); under tribulations (Ro 12:12; Jas 1:2-4; 1Pe 4:1). Peaceableness (Ro 12:18; Col 3:15; 1Th 4:11; Heb 12:14). Perfection (Ge 17:1; M't 5:48). Praise (Ps 146 to 150. See Praise). Prayer (Jer 33:3; M't 7:7-11; Lu 11:9-13; Ph'p 4:6; Col 4:2; 1Th 5:17, 18; 1Ti 2:8); for more laborers in the Lord's vineyard (M't 9:38); for rulers (1Ti 2:1, 2). Prayerfulness (Lu 22:40; Ro 12:12; 1Th 5:17). Preparation for the Sabbath (Ex 16:23). Preparedness (M't 24:44; 25:13 w vs 1-12; 1Th 5:8). Propagation of children (Ge 9:1, 7). Propriety in worship (1Co 14:26-33, 40). Prudence (Col 4:5); in guests (Pr 23:1, 2); in speech (Ec 5:2, 6; 7:21; 10:20). Public instruction in the word of God (De 31:10-13). Public worship (Ex 34:23; De 12:5-7, 11-14, 17, 18, 26, 27; 16:16). Pure conversation (Eph 4:29; 1Pe 3:10). Purity (2Co 7:1; Eph 5:1-4; 1Ti 5:22; Heb 13:4); in family of a minister (Le 21:9); of thought (Ph'p 4:8).

Quietness (1Th 4:11).

Rebuke of sin (Le 19:17; Eph 5:11). Reconciliation between brethren (M't 5:23-25). Regard for consciences of others (1Co 10:28). Regulated enjoyments (Ec 11:9, 10). Religious instruction of children (De 4:9; 6:7-9; 11:19, 20; 32:46; Eph 6:14). Remembrance, of God in youth (Ec 12:1); of God's mercies (De 5:15; 8:2); of the law (De 6:6-9; 11:18; 32:46; 1Ch 16:15). Renunciation of sources of temptation (M't 5:29, 30: 18:8. 9; M'k 9:43-48). Repentance (Pr 1:23; Eze 33:11; Mal 3:7; M't 3:2; 7:13, 14; M'k 1:15; Ac 2:38; 17:30; Re 3:19). Reproof of the erring (1Ti 5:20). Resistance of evil (Jas 4:7). Respect for religious instruction (1Th 5:20). Rest on the Sabbath (Ex 20:10; 23:12; 34:21; 35:2, 3; Le 23:3, 24; De 5:14). Restraint of temper (Ec 7:9; Eph 4:26, 31; Jas 1:19). Returning good for evil (M't 5:4; 1Co 6:7; 1Pe 3:9). Reverence, for God's house (Le 19:30; 26:2; Ec 5:1); for holy places (Ex 3:5; Jos 5:15; Ac 7:33); for parents (Ex 20:12; Le 19:3, 30; 20:9; De 5:16; Pr 23:22; M't 15:4; 19:19; Lu 18:20; Eph 6:1, 2); for the aged (Le 19:32). Right conduct (De 6:18; Pr 4:26, 27; Ph'p 1:27; Jas 1:19). Righteousness (Ex 23:7; Eze 45:9; Ho 12:6; Lu 13:24; Ro 13:7, 8). Rulers to study God's law (De 17:18-20).

Secrecy in giving alms (M't 6:3). Seeking, the Lord (1Ch 16:11; Isa 55:6; Am 5:4, 6); the kingdom of God (M't 6:33; Lu 12:31). Self-denial (M't 16:24; M'k 8:34; 10:21; Lu 9:23; 18:22; Ro 15:2). Self-discipline (M't 5:29, 30; M'k 9:45-48). Self-examination (2Co 13:5). Service for God (Ex 23:25; De 6:13; 10:12, 20). Simplicity in worship (M't 6:7). Six days of labor, and one day of rest (Ex 20:9-11; 35:2). Sobermindedness (Tit 2:6). Sobriety (1Th 5:8; 1Pe 1:13; 4:7; 5:8, 9). Social peace (1Th 5:13). Spiritual diligence (Ro 12:11; 13:12; Heb 4:11; 2Pe 1:10; 3:14). Spirituality (Ga 5:16). Steadfastness (De 13:8, 10; Ro 12:21; 1Co 15:58; 16:13; Ga 5:1; Eph 6:11, 13, 14, 18; Ph'p 1:27; 4:1; 1Th 5:21; 2Th 2:15; 2Ti 1:13; 1Pe 1:13; Jude 21; Re 3:11). Steadfastness in prayer (Ro 12:12; Eph 6:18; 1Th 5:17). Submission, to God (2Ch 30:8; Pr 3:11; Jas 4:7); to fraternal counsel (Eph 5:21). Suffering, one for another (1Jo 3:16-17). Sympathy (Ro 12:15; Heb 13:3; 1Pe 3:8). Support of ministers (De 12:19; Ga 6:6; 1Ti 5:17, 18).

Thankfulness (De 8:10; Col 3:15). Thanksgiving (Eph 5:4, 20; Ph'p 4:6; Col 3:17; 1Th 5:17, 18; 1Ti 2:1; Heb 13:15). Tithing (De 12:6; 14:22). Truthfulness (Pr 3:3; Zec 8:16, 17, 19; Eph 4:25).

Various Christian duties (Ro 12:6-8; Eph 6:10-20; Jas 4:8-11; 5:7-9, 12, 14; 1Pe 1:13-17; 2:11-25; 3:8, 9, 15; 4:7-15; 5:5-8; 2Pe 1:5-7).

Watchfulness (Pr 4:23; M't 24:42, 44; 25:13; M'k 13:35-37; Lu 12:35-40; 21:36; 1Co 16:13, 14; Eph 5:15; Ph'p 3:2; Col 4:2; 1Th 5:6; 1Pe 5:8, 9; Re 3:2); against backsliding (De 4:9; 8:11; 11:16, 28; 2Pe 3:17); against covetousness (De 15:9; Lu 12:15); against false Christs (M't 24:23-26; M'k 13:21-23; Lu 17:23). Wholehearted service (Jos 22:5; 24:14; 1Sa 12:24; 1Ch 28:9; Ec 9:10). Wisdom (Pr 3:21; 4:5, 13; 5:1; 8:5, 6, 32, 33; 23:12, 23); in speech (Pr 23:9; 26:4, 5; Col 4:6). Wise self-restraint (Ec 7:16, 18, 21). Witnessing for Christ (M'k 5:19; 1Pe 3:15). Worship (Ge 35:1; Ex 20:24; Re 19:10; 22:9); social (Eph 5:19; Col 3:16).

Zeal for righteousness (Joh 6:27; 1Co 15:58); for the faith (Jude 3); in one's calling (Ro 12:6-8).

Fixing Penalty for: Adultery (Le 20:10; 21:9; 1Co 6:9, 10; Ga 5:19, 21). Arson (Ex 22:6).

Bestiality (Ex 22:19; Le 20:13, 15, 16). Blasphemy (Le 24:16).

Carnality (Le 19:20). Contempt of authority (De 17:12). Criminal neglect to safeguard life (Ex 21:28-36). Cursing parents (Ex 21:17; Le 20:9).

Destruction of neighbor's property (Le 24:18). Disobedience (Nu 15:30, 31).

False Witness (De 19:18, 19). Fornication (Ac 15:20; 1Co 6:18; 10:8).

Idolatry (Le 20:2-5; De 17:5); propagandism of idolatry (De 13:5, 9, 10, 15). Impenitence (Le 23:29). Incest (Le 20:11, 12, 14, 17, 19-21).

Laziness (2Th 3:10). Loss of borrowed property (Ex 22:14, 15); of property held in trust (Ex 22:7, 13).

Manstealing (Ex 21:16; De 24:7). Murder (Ex 21:12; Le 24:17; Nu 35:31; De 19:11-13).

Personal injury (Ex 21:18-27; Le 24:19, 20).

Sabbath breaking (Ex 31:14; 35:2). Seduction (Ex 22:16).

Theft (Ex 22:1-4). Trespass (Ex 22:5).

Untimely cohabitation (Le 20:18).

Witchcraft (Ex 22:18; Le 20:27).

Forbidding: Adultery (Ex 20:14; Le 18:20; De 5:18; M't 5:27; 19:18; Lu 18:20; Ro 13:9; 1Co 10:8). Anxiety (M't 6:25-34; 10:19-23; Lu 12:11, 22-32; Joh 14:27; Ph'p 4:6). Association, with evil company (Pr 1:10-19); with harlots (Pr 2:16; 5:3-21; 6:20, 24-26; 7:1-27; 23:26-28).

Bestiality (Le 18:23; 20:13, 15, 16). Boasting (De 9:4). Bribe taking (Ex 23:8; De 16:19; 27:25).

Causeless strife (Pr 3:30). Change in God's law (De 4:2; 12:32). Class, distinction (Ex 23:3; Le 19:15; Nu 15:29; De 16:19); legislation (Le 24:22). Company with winebibbers (Pr 23:20). Conformity to the world (Le 20:23). Contention (Ro 13:13; Ph'p 2:14; 2Ti 2:14; Tit 3:2). Corrupt conversation (Eph 4:29; 5:4; Col 3:8). Covetousness (Ex 20:17; De 5:21; 7:25, 26; Lu 12:15; Ro 13:9; Eph 5:3; Col 3:5; 1Ti 6:10, 11; Heb 13:5).

Dishonesty in business (Le 19:13, 35; 25:14; De 25:13-15; M'k 10:19). Divorce (1Co 7:10, 11 w M't 5:32; 19:9; M'k 10:11, 12; Lu 16:18). Drunkenness (Ro 13:13; Eph 5:18).

Envy (Pr 3:31; 23:17; 24:1, 19; Ro 13:13; 1Pe 2:1). Evil speech (Ps 34:13; Pr 4:24; 30:10; Tit 3:2; 1Pe 3:10). Evil, to a neighbor (Ex 20:16; Le 19:13, 16; Pr 3:29).

False, dealing (Le 6:1-5; 19:11); swearing (Le 19:12); witness (Ex 20:16; 23:1; Le 19:16; De 5:20; Pr 24:28; M't 19:18; Lu 18:20). Falsehood (Le 19:11; Eph 4:25; Col 3:9). Fellowship with the wicked (Pr 1:10-15; 4:14, 15; Ro 16:17; 1Co 5:9-11; 2Co 6:14, 17; Eph 5:11; 2Th 3:6; 2Ti 3:5). Foolish, unlearned questions (2Ti 2:23). Fraud (Le 19:11, 13, 35; 1Th 4:6).

Giving cause for stumbling (1Co 8:9; 10:32). Grudge (Le 19:18).

Haste for riches (Pr 23:4); in litigation (Pr 25:8, 9). Hatred (Le 19:17; Eph 4:31; Col 3:8). Heed to false teachers (De 13:1-18).

Idolatry (Ex 20:3-5, 23; Le 18:21; 20:2-5; 26:1; De 4:16-19, 23; 5:7-9; 6:14; 13:2, 3; 16:21, 22; Jos 24:14; 2Ki 17:35;

Eze 20:18; 1Co 10:7; 1Jo 5:21). Impure marriages (Le 21:7). Incest (Le 18:6; 20:11, 12, 14, 17, 19-21; De 22:30). Indulgence in wine (Pr 23:31; Eph 5:18; Tit 2:3). Injustice (Ex 23:2, 3; Le 19:15; 25:17; De 16:19); to foreigners (Ex 12:49; 22:21; Le 19:33, 34; De 1:16; 24:14, 17); to the poor (Ex 23:6). Intolerance (M'k 9:39; Lu 9:49, 50). Invidious respect of persons (Jas 2:1-9).

Labor on Sabbath (Ex 20:10; 23:12; 34:21; 35:2, 3; Le 23:3; De 5:14). Lasciviousness (Pr 31:3; Ro 13:13; Eph 4:17-39; 5:3; 1Th 4:2-6; 2Ti 2:22). Lawlessness (De 12:8). Laziness (2Th 3:10). Love of the world (1Jo 2:15).

Malice (Le 19:17, 18; Eph 4:31; Col 3:8; 1Pe 2:1). Malicious mischief (Le 19:14). Meddling (1Pe 4:15). Murder (Ex 20:13; De 5:17; M't 5:21; 19:18; Ro 13:9; Jas 2:11; 1Pe 4:15). Murmuring (1Co 10:10; Ph'p 2:14; Jas 5:9).

Offerings with blemish, which implied, in its teaching purpose, the forbidding of insincere or imperfect service of God (Le 1:3, 10; 3:1, 6; 4:3, 23, 28, 32; 5:15, 18; 6:6; 9:2, 3; 22:18-22; De 15:21; 17:1). Oppression (Le 19:13; Pr 22:22); of the poor (De 24:14); of widows and orphans (Ex 22:22-24; Jer 22:3; Zec 7:10). Ostentation in giving, in fasting, and in prayer (M't 6:1, 5, 6, 17, 18).

Perjury (Le 19:12). Perversion of justice (De 16:19, 20; 24:17). Prejudice (Ex 23:3). Profane swearing (M't 5:34-36; Jas 5:12). Profaning God's name (Ex 20:7; Le 18:21; 19:12; 21:6; 22:32; De 5:11). Prostitution of a daughter (Le 19:29). Putting a neighbor's life in peril by false witness (Le 19:16).

Removal of landmarks (De 19:14; Pr 22:28; 23:10). Resistance (M't 5:39). Retaliation (Le 19:18; Pr 24:29; M't 5:38-42; Ro 12:17; 1Th 5:15; 1Pe 3:9). Robbery (Le 19:13; Pr 22:22).

Sabbath breaking (Ex 31:14; Jer 17:21, 22). Self-confidence (Pr 3:5, 7). Self-esteem (Ro 12:3). Self-praise (Pr 27:2). Selfishness (1Co 10:24; Ph'p 2:4). Strife (2Ti 2:24). Sodomy (Le 18:22; 20:13).

Taking of interest (Ex 22:25; Le 25:35, 37). Talebearing (Le 19:16). Theft (Ex 20:15; Le 19:11; De 5:19; M't 19:18; Lu 18:20; Ro 13:9; Eph 4:28; 1Pe 4:15).

Uncharitable judgments (M't 7:1-5; Lu 6:37, 42; Ro 14:1-3, 13). Uncharitableness (Pr 24:17; M't 18:10). Unholy ambition (Ph'p 2:3). Unrighteous anger (M't 5:22). Unrighteous judgments (Le 19:15). Use of strong drink by priests (Le 10:9).

Vain repetitions in prayer (M't 6:7, 8). Various vices (Ro 13:12, 13; Ga 5:19-21; Eph 4:28-31; 5:3-6, 11, 18; Col 3:5, 8, 9; 1Th 4:3-6; 5:15, 22; 1Ti 3:3, 8; 6:17; 2Ti 3:2-5; Tit 2:3, 10; Heb 13:5; Jas 1:21; 2:11; 4:11; 5:9, 12; 1Pe 2:11; 3:9; 4:3).

Witchcraft (Le 19:26, 31; 20:6). Withholding a servant's wages (Le 19:13). Worldliness (M't 6:19; Ro 12:2; 1Jo 2:15); of ministers (2Ti 2:4, 5).

Implied: Enjoining an exact conscience (M't 6:22-24). Against self-righteousness (M't 7:3).

Precepts of Jesus, Stated or implied (M't 5:16, 22-24, 27-48; 6:1-4, 6-8, 16-25, 31-34; 7:1-29; 10:5-42; 16:24; 18:8-10, 15-17, 21, 22; 19:16-19; 20:25-28; 22:21, 34-40; 24:42-51; 25:34-46; M'k 6:7-11; 8:34; 9:35-50; 10:9-12, 17-22; 11:22; 12:17; 13:33-37; Lu 6:27-42; 10:28-37; 12:12-31; 13:24; Joh 7:24; 13:34, 35; 14:11, 15, 23, 24; 15:2-14, 17, 20-22).

Prescribing: Law of evidence (De 17:6; 19:15). Number of stripes in punishment (De 25:3). Priestly benedictions (Nu 6:23-26). Stimulants for the perishing (Pr 31:6).

Warning: The rich (1Ti 6:17-19).

Warning against: Covetousness (Lu 12:15). False teachers (M't 7:15; Eph 5:6, 7; Col 2:8). Love of money (Heb 13:5). Quenching the Spirit (1Th 5:19). Sensuality (Pr 6:24, 25). Sinful indulgence (Lu 21:34). Sinning against the Holy Spirit (Eph 4:30; 1Th 5:19). Temptations (Pr 1:10-15; 19:27).

See Adultery; Children; Citizen; Homicide; Instruction; Ministers; Obedience, Enjoined; Servants; Theft; Wife; Women; etc.

COMMANDMENTS AND STATUTES, OF MEN. Traditions (Isa 29:13; Ro 14:1-6, 10-23; Ga 1:14; Col 2:8; 1Ti 4:1-3). Rejected by Jesus (M't 15:2-20; M'k 7:2-23).

COMMERCE. Laws concerning (Le 19:36, 37; 25:14, 17). Carried on by means of caravans (Ge 37:25, 27; Isa 60:6); ships (1Ki 9:27, 28; 10:11; 22:48; Ps 107:23-30; Pr 31:14; Re 18:19). Conducted in fairs (Eze 27:12, 19; M't 11:16). Of the Arabians (Isa 60:6; Jer 6:20; Eze 27:21-24); Egyptians (Ge 42:2-34); Ethiopians (Isa 45:14); Ishmaelites (Ge 37:27, 28); Israelites (1Ki 9:26-28; Neh 3:31-32; Eze 27:17); Ninevites (Nah 3:16); Syrians (Eze 27:16, 18); Tyrians (2Sa 5:11; 1Ki 5:6; Isa 23:8; Eze 27; 28:5); Zidonians (Isa 23:2; Eze 27:8); Babylonians (Re 18:3, 11-13); Jews (Eze 27:17). From Tarshish (Jer 10:9; Eze 27:25).

Evil practices connected with (Pr 29:14; Eze 22:13; Ho 12:7).

Articles of: Apes (1Ki 10:22); balm (Ge 37:25); blue cloth (Eze 27:24); brass (Eze 27:13; Re 18:12); cinnamon (Re 18:13); corn (1Ki 5:11; Eze 27:17); cattle (Eze 27:21); chest of rich apparel (Eze 27:24); chariots (1Ki 10:29; Re 18:13); clothes for chariots (Eze 27:20); embroidery (Eze 27:16, 24); frankincense (Jer 6:20; Re 18:13); gold (1Ki 9:28; 10:22; 2Ch 8:18; Isa 60:6; Re 18:12); honey (Eze 27:17); horses (1Ki 10:29; Eze 27:14; Re 18:13); ivory (1Ki 10:22; 2Ch 9:21; Eze 27:15; Re 18:12); iron and steel (Eze 27:12, 19); land (Ge 23:13-16; Ru 4:3); lead (Eze 27:12); linen (1Ki 10:28; Re 18:12); oil (1Ki 5:11; Eze 27:17); pearls (Re 18:12); peacocks (1Ki 10:22); perfumes (Song 3:6); precious stones (Eze 27:16, 22; 28:13, 16; Re 18:12); purple (Eze 27:16; Re 18:12); sheep (Re 18:13); slaves (Ge 37:28, 36; De 24:7); silk (Re 18:12); silver (1Ki 10:22; 2Ch 9:21; Re 18:12); sweet cane (Jer 6:20); thyine wood (Re 18:12); timber (1Ki 5:6, 8); tin (Eze 27:12); wheat (Re 18:13); white wool (Eze 27:18); wine (2Ch 2:15; Eze 27:18; Re 18:13); bodies and souls of men (Re 18:13).

Transportation of passengers (Jon 1:3; Ac 21:2; 27:2, 6, 37).

See Merchant; Tarshish; Trade; Traffic.

COMMISSARY. For armies, cattle driven with (2Ki 3:9). See Armies. For royal households (2Ki 4:7-19, 27, 28).

COMMITMENT. Through the word of truth (Joh 1:17). Unto the Lord (Pr 16:3; 1Co 1:2; 2Co 7:1; 1Pe 1:15, 16).

COMMONWEALTH. *Figurative:* Ph'p 3:20.

COMMUNION. With God (Ps 16:7; Joh 14:23; 2Co 6:16; 1Jo 1:3). With Christ (Joh 14:23; 1Jo 1:3; Re 3:20). With the Spirit (Joh 14:16-18; 2Co 13:14; Ga 4:6; Ph'p 2:1, 2). See Fellowship.

Instances of: Enoch (Ge 5:22, 24). Noah (Ge 6:9, 13-22; 8:15-17). Abraham (Ge 12:1-3, 7; 17:1, 2; 18:1-33; 22:1, 2, 11, 12, 16-18). Hagar (Ge 16:8-12). Isaac (Ge 26:2, 24); in dreams (Ge 28:13, 15; 31:3; 35:1, 7; 46:2-4). Moses (Ex 3; 4:1-17; 33:9, 11; 34:28-35; Nu 12:8). Joshua (Jos 6:11-24; 7:10-15). Gideon (J'g 6:11-24). Solomon (1Ki 3:5-14; 2Ch 1:7-12).

Of Saints: Unity (Ps 119:63; 133:1-3; Am 3:3; Joh 17:20, 21; 1Co 10:16, 17; 12:12, 13). Enjoined (Ro 12:15; 2Co 6:14-18; Eph 4:1-3; 5:11; Col 3:16; 1Th 4:18; 5:11, 14; Heb 3:13; 10:24, 25; Jas 5:16). Exemplified (1Sa 23:16; Ps 55:14; Mal 3:16; Lu 22:32; 24:17, 32; Ac 2:42; 1Jo 1:3, 7). See Eucharist; Fellowship.

COMMUNISM. Christian (Ac 2:44, 45; 4:32, 34-37; 5:1-10).

COMPANY. *Evil:* Perils of (Ge 19:14, 15; Nu 16:21-26; 33:55; J'g 2:1-3; 2Ch 19:2; Ezr 9:14; Ps 50:18; 106:35, 36; Pr 13:20; Ho 7:5, 8, 9; Mic 6:16). Seductive (Pr 12:11, 26; 16:29; Ec 9:18; M't 24:12; 1Co 15:33; 2Pe 2:7, 8, 18). Shunned by the righteous (Ps 6:8; 26:4, 5, 9; 28:3; 31:6; 84:10; 101:4, 7; 119:115; 120:5-7; 139:19-22: 141:4; Pr 14:7; 17:12; Jer 9:2; 15:17; Ho 4:17; Re 2:2). Warnings against (Ge 49:6; 2Sa 23:6, 7; Pr 2:11, 12, 16, 19; 4:14, 15; 5:8; 9:6; 20:19; 22:5, 10, 24, 25; 23:6, 20; 24:1; 28:7, 19; 29:24; 1Ti 6:5).

Forbidden (Ex 23:2, 32, 33; 34:12-15; Le 18:3; 20:23; De 7:2-4; 12:30; Jos 23:6-13; Pr 1:10-15; Isa 8:11, 12; Jer 51:6, 45; Ro 16:17, 18; 1Co 5:6, 9-11; 2Co 6:14-17; Ga 5:9; Eph 5:6, 7, 11; 2Th 3:6; 1Ti 5:22; 2Ti 3:4, 5; 2Jo 10, 11; Re 18:4).

See Example; Influence, Evil.

Good (Ps 1:1; 15; Pr 13:20). See Communion, of Saints; Example; Fellowship; Influence, Good.

COMPASSES, CARPENTER'S (Isa 44:13).

COMPASSION, *Of God:* (See God, Mercy of.)

Of Christ (See Jesus, Compassion of.)

COMPEL, as used by Jesus in Lu 14:23 does not mean physical force, but zeal and moral urgency.

COMPLAINT (See Murmuring.)

COMPLICITY. Warnings against (Ps 50:18; Pr 29:24; Ro 1:32; 2Jo 10, 11).

Instances of: Sarah, in deceiving, Pharaoh (Ge 12:11-19); Abimelech (Ge 20:2-5, 11-14). Rebekah, in deceiving Isaac (Ge 27:5-17). The elders and nobles of Jezreel, in stoning Naboth (1Ki 21:7-14). Jews who opposed building the temple (Ne 6:10-19). Daughter of Herodias, in death of John the Baptist (M't 14:8; M'k 6:25). Pilate, in death of Christ (M't 27:17-26; M'k 15:9-15; Lu 23:13-25; Joh 19:13-16). Paul, in death of Stephen (Ac 7:58).

See Collusion; Connivance; Conspiracy.

COMPROMISE. *Before Litigation:* Enjoined, by Solomon (Pr 25:8-10); by Christ (M't 5:25, 26; Lu 12:58, 59).

See Adjudication; Arbitration; Court; Justice.

CONANIAH (Jehovah has founded). 1. Levite (2Ch 31:12, 13).

2. Another Levite (2Ch 35:9).

CONCEALMENT, EXPOSURE. Concealment of Sin: Ge 3:8; Jos 7:21; Pr 28:13; Isa 29:15; 30:1. Secret Sins: Warning against (2Ki 17:9; Job 24:16; Ps 19:12; 90:8; Eze 8:12; Eph 5:12). Called works of darkness (Job 24:14; Pr 7:8, 9; Joh 3:20; Ro 13:12; Eph 5:11; 1Th 5:7). Exposure of Sin: Inevitable (Nu 32:23; Job 20:27; Pr 26:26; Ec 12:14; Lu 12:2; 1Co 4:5). Rendered Doubly Certain (Job 10:14; 14:16; Jer 16:17; Eze 11:5; Ho 7:2; Am 5:12).

CONCEIT. Of the foolish (Pr 12:15; 26:5, 12, 16; 28:26; Ro 1:22). Of the rich (Pr 28:11). Of the self-righteous (Ps 36:2; Lu 18:11, 12).

Warnings against (Pr 3:5, 7; 23:4; Isa 5:21; Jer 9:23; Ro 11:25; 12:16; 1Co 3:18; Ga 6:3).

See Hypocrisy; Pride; Self-Exaltation.

CONCEPTION. *Miraculous:* By Sarah (Ge 21:1, 2); Rebekah (Ge 25:21); Rachel (Ge 30:22); Manoah's wife (J'g 13:3-24); Hannah (1Sa 1:19, 20); Elisabeth (Lu 1:24, 25, 36, 37, 58); Mary (M't 1:18, 20; Lu 1:31-35).

CONCISION (mutilation, cutting), circumcision that is wholly ceremonial and without regard for its spiritual significance (Ph'p 3:2).

CONCUBINAGE. *Laws Concerning:* (Ex 21:7-11; Le 19:20-22; De 21:10-14). Concubines might be dismissed (Ge 21:9-14). Called Wives (Ge 37:2; J'g 19:3-5). Children of, not heirs (Ge 15:4; 21:10).

Practiced by Abraham (Ge 16:3; 25:6; 1Ch 1:32). Nahor (Ge 22:23, 24); Jacob (Ge 30:4); Eliphaz (Ge 36:12); Gideon (J'g 8:31); a Levite (J'g 19:1); Caleb (1Ch 2:46-48); Manasseh (1Ch 7:14); Saul (2Sa 3:7); David (2Sa 5:13; 15:16); Solomon (1Ki 11:3); Rehoboam (2Ch 11:21); Abijah (2Ch 13:21); Belshazzar (Da 5:2).

See Marriage: Polygamy.

CONCUPISCENCE, intense longing for what God would not have us to have (Ro 7:8; Col 3:5; 1Th 4:5).

CONDEMNATION, SELF (See Self-condemnation.)

CONDESCENSION, OF GOD. In reasoning with his creatures: Sets forth his reasons for sending the flood (Ge 6:11-13). Enters into covenant with Abraham (Ge 15:1-21; 18:1-22). Indulges Abraham's intercession for Sodom (Ge 18:23-33). Warns Abimelech in a dream (Ge 20:3-7). Reasons with Moses (Ex 4:2-17). Sends flesh to the Israelites in consequence of their murmuring (Ex 16:12). Indulges Moses' prayer to behold his glory (Ex 33:18-23). Indulges Gideon's tests (J'g 6:36-40). Reasons with Job (Job 38; 39; 40; 41). Invites sinners, saying, "Come now, and let us reason together" (Isa 1:18-20). Expostulates with backsliding Israel (Isa 41:21-24; 43:1-19; 65:1-16; Jer 3:1-15; 4:1-31; 7:1-34; Eze 18:25-32; 33:10-20; Ho 2; Mic 6:1-9; Mal 3:7-15). In his care, for man (Ps 8:4-6; 144:3); for the world (Ps 113:5, 6); in redemption (Isa 45:11; Joh 3:16; Ro 5:8; Heb 2:11; 6:17, 18; 1Jo 4:10, 19).

Of Christ (Lu 22:27; Joh 13:5; 14; 2Co 8:9; Ph'p 2:7, 8; Heb 2:11).

CONDOLENCE. *Instances of:* David, to Hanun (2Sa 10:2). King of Babylon, to Hezekiah (2Ki 20:12, 13). The three friends of, to Job (Job 2:11). Jesus, to Mary and Martha (Joh 11:23-35).

See Affliction, Comfort in; Sympathy.

CONDUCT, CHRISTIAN. Believing God (M'k 11:22; Joh 14:11, 12). Fearing God (Ec 12:13; 1Pe 2:17). Loving God (De 6:5; M't 22:37). Following God (Eph 5:1; 1Pe 1:15, 16). Obeying God

(Lu 1:6; 1Jo 5:3). Rejoicing in God (Ps 33:1; Hab 3:18). Believing in Christ (Joh 6:29; 1Jo 3:23). Loving Christ (Joh 21:15; 1Pe 1:7, 8). Following the example of Christ (Joh 13:15; 1Pe 2:21-24). Obeying Christ (Joh 14:21; 15:14).

Living: To Christ (Ro 14:8; 2Co 5:15). Unto righteousness (Mic 6:8; Ro 6:18; 1Pe 2:24). Soberly, righteously, and godly (Tit 2:12).

Walking: Honestly (1Th 4:12). Worthy of God (1Th 2:12). Worthy of the Lord (Col 1:10). In the Spirit (Ga 5:25). After the Spirit (Ro 8:1). In newness of life (Ro 6:4). Worthy of our vocation (Eph 4:1). As children of light (Eph 5:8). Rejoicing in Christ (Ph'p 3:1; 4:4). Loving one another (Joh 15:12; Ro 12:10; 1Co 13; Eph 5:2; Heb 13:1). Striving for the faith (Ph'p 1:27; Jude 3). Putting away all sin (1Co 5:7; Heb 12:1). Abstaining from all appearance of evil (1Th 5:22). Perfecting holiness (M't 5:48; 2Co 7:1; 2Ti 3:17). Hating defilement (Jude 23). Following after that which is good (Ph'p 4:8; 1Th 5:15; 1Ti 6:11). Overcoming the world (1Jo 5:4, 5). Adorning the gospel (M't 5:16; Tit 2:10). Showing a good example (1Ti 4:12; Tit 2:7; 1Pe 2:12). Abounding in the work of the Lord (1Co 15:58; 2Co 8:7; 1Th 4:1). Shunning the wicked (Ps 1:1; 2Th 3:6). Controlling the body (1Co 9:27; Col 3:5). Subduing the temper (Eph 4:26; Jas 1:19). Submitting to injuries (M't 5:39-41; 1Co 6:7). Forgiving injuries (M't 6:14; Ro 12:20). Living peaceably with all (Ro 12:18; Heb 12:14). Visiting the afflicted (M't 25:36; Jas 1:27). Doing as we would be done by (M't 7:12; Lu 6:31). Sympathizing with others (Ga 6:2; 1Th 5:14). Honoring others (Ps 15:4; Ro 12:10). Fulfilling domestic duties (Eph 6:1-8; 1Pe 3:1-7). Submitting to authorities (Ro 13:1-7). Being liberal to others (Ac 20:35; Ro 12:13). Being contented (Ph'p 4:11; Heb 13:4). Blessedness of maintaining (Ps 1:1-3; 19:9-11; 50:23; M't 5:3-12; Joh 15:10).

CONDUIT, a channel for conveying water from its source to the place where it was delivered (2Ki 20:20; Isa 7:3).

CONEY (Le 11:5; De 14:7; Ps 104:18; Pr 30:26).

CONFECTION, a compound of perfume or medicine (not sweetmeats) (Ex 30:35).

CONFECTIONARY, a perfumer; found only in 1Sa 8:13.

CONFEDERACIES. *Instances of:* Of kings (Ge 14:1, 2; Jos 10:1-5; 11:1-5; 1Ki 20:1).

See Alliances.

CONFESSION, to acknowledge one's faith in anything, as in the existence and authority of God, or the sins of which one has been guilty (M't 10:32; Le 5:5; Ps 32:5); to concede or allow (Joh 1:20; Ac 24:14; Heb 11:13); to praise God by thankfully acknowledging Him (Ro 14:11; Heb 13:15).

CONFESSION. *Of Christ:* In baptism (Ac 19:4, 5; Ga 3:27). Unto salvation (M't 10:32; Lu 12:8; Ro 10:9-11).

Inspired by the Holy Spirit (1Co 12:3; 1Jo 4:2, 3). Fellowship with the Father through (1Jo 2:23; 4:15).

Timid believers deterred from (Joh 12:42, 43). Those refusing to make, rejected (M't 10:33; M'k 8:38; Lu 12:9; 2Ti 2:12). Hypocritical (M't 7:21-23; Lu 13:26; 1Jo 1:6; 2:4).

Enjoined (2Ti 1:8). Exemplified (M't 3:11; 14:33; 16:16; Joh 1:15-18; 6:29; 9:22-38; 11:27; Ac 8:35-37; 9:20; 18:5; Ro 1:16).

Of Sin: See Sin, Confession of.

CONFIDENCE. *In Man:* Warned against (Jer 9:4; 12:6; Mic 7:5).

Betrayed: Joshua, by the Gideonites (Jos 9:3-15). Eglon, by Ehud (J'g 3:15-23). Sisera, by Jael (J'g 4:17-22). Samson, by Delilah (J'g 16:17-20). Ahimelech, by David (1Sa 21:1-9). Abner, by Joab (2Sa 3:27). Amasa, by Joab (2Sa 20:9, 10). Worshippers of Baal, by Jehu (2Ki 10:18-28). See Betrayal.

False: See False Confidence.

In God: (Ps 118:8; Pr 3:26; 14:26; Ac 28:31; Eph 3:12; Heb 3:16; 10:35; 1Jo 2:28; 3:21; 5:14). See Faith.

CONFISCATION. Of property: By David, that of Mephibosheth (2Sa 16:4). By Ahab, of Naboth's vineyard (1Ki 21:7-16). By Ahasuerus, of Haman's house (Es 8:1). As a penalty (Ezr 10:8).

CONFLAGRATIONS (Ge 19:28; Jos 6:24; 8:20; 11:13; J'g 18:27; 1Sa 30:1; 1Ki 9:16; 2Ch 36:19; Job 1:16).

CONFUSION, of tongues (Ge 11:1-9).

CONGESTION (Le 13:28; De 28:22).

CONGREGATION, OF ISRAEL. Collective term for God's chosen in the O.T., or an assembly of the people summoned for a definite purpose (1Ki 8:65); either the whole assembly, or a part (Nu 16:3; Ex 12:6; 35:1; Le 4:13).

Often considered in a non-technical sense, as a gathering of believers or chosen, the church of the O.T. For that purpose, see Church, The Body of Believers.

CONIAH (See Jehoiachim).

CONNIVANCE. Judged (Le 20:4; 1Sa 3:11-13). Result (Pr 10:10).

CONONIAH, name of two Israelites (2Ch 31:12, 13; 35:9).

CONQUESTS of the heathen by Israel (Jos 6:20; 8:24; 10:28, 29; 11:8, 23; 12:7; J'g 1:8; 3:30; 4:16; 8:28; 9:45; 11:33).

CONSCIENCE. Guide (Ps 51:3; Pr 20:12; M't 6:22, 23; Lu 11:33-36; Ro 2:14, 15; 7:18, 22; 2Co 5:11). Approves (Job 27:6; Pr 21:2; Ac 23:1; 24:16; Ro 9:1; 1Co 4:4; 2Co 1:12; 1Ti 1:5, 19; 3:9; 2Ti 1:3; Heb 13:18; 1Pe 2:19; 3:16, 21; 1Jo 3:20, 21). Struggle with (Job 15:21, 24; Ps 51:3; M't 6:22, 23; Lu 11:33-36; Ro 7:15-23). Purged (Heb 9:14; 10:22). See Honesty; Integrity.

Of another, to be respected (Ro 14:2-20; 1Co 8:7-13; 10:27-32; 2Co 4:2).

Instances of Faithful: Pharaoh, when he took Sarah into his harem (Ge 12:18, 19). Abimelech, when he took Sarah for a concubine (Ge 26:9-11). Jacob, in his care of Laban's property (Ge 31:39); in his greeting of Esau (Ge 33:1-12). Joseph, with Potiphar's wife (Ge 39:7-12). Nehemiah, with taxes (Ne 5:15). Daniel, with the king's meat (Da 1:8). Peter, in his preaching (Ac 4:19, 20; 5:29).

Corrupt (M't 6:23; Lu 11:34; Joh 16:2, 3). Dead (Pr 16:25; 30:20; Jer 6:15; Am 6:1-6; Ro1:21-25; Eph 4:17-19). Defiled (Tit 1:15). Seared (1Ti 4:2).

Guilty (Job 15:21, 24; Ps 51:1-14; 73:21; Pr 28:1; Isa 59:9-14; M't 14:1, 2; 27:3-5; M'k 6:14, 16; Joh 8:9; Ac 2:37; 1Ti 4:2; Tit 1:15; Heb 9:14; 10:26, 27). See Blindness, Spiritual.

Instances of Guilty: Adam and Eve, after they sinned (Ge 3:7, 8). Jacob, after defrauding Esau (Ge 33:1-12). Joseph's brethren (Ge 42:21; 44:16). Pharaoh, after the plagues (Ex 9:27). Micah, after stealing (J'g 17:2). David, for his indignity to Saul (1Sa 24:5); for his adultery, and murder of Uriah (Ps 32; 38; 40:11, 12; 51); for numbering Israel (2Sa 24:10; 1Ch 21:1-8). The old prophet of Bethel (1Ki 13:18, 29-32). The lepers of Samaria (2Ki 7:8-10). Jonah (Jon 1:12). Herod, for beheading John the Baptist (M't 14:2; Lu 9:7). Peter, after denying the Lord (M't 26:75; M'k 14:72; Lu 22:62). Judas (M't 27:3-5). The accusers of the women taken in adultery (Joh 8:9).

CONSCIENCE MONEY (J'g 17:2; 2Ki 12:16; M't 27:3-5).

See Money.

CONSCIENTIOUSNESS (See Integrity.)

CONSCRIPTION, of soldiers (1Sa 14:52).

CONSECRATED THINGS, laws regarding (Le 27; Nu 18:8-32).

See Firstborn; Firstfruits.

CONSECRATION. Of Aaron, see Aaron. Of priests, see Priests. Of the altar, see Altar. Of the temple, see Temple, Dedication of. See also Offerings.

Enjoined (Ex 32:29). Personal (Ps 51:17; M't 13:44-46; Ro 6:13, 16, 19; 12:1; 2Co 8:5). Conditional (Ge 28:20-22; 2Sa 15:7, 8).

Instances of: Cain and Abel (Ge 4:4-7). Abraham, of Isaac (Ge 22:9-12). Jephthah, of his daughter (J'g 11:30-40). Hannah, of Samuel (1Sa 1:11, 24-28). David consecrates the water (2Sa 23:16; 1Ch 11:18). Zichri, of himself (2Ch 17:16).

See Dedication; Offerings.

CONSISTENCY. Encouraged (Ne 5:9; M't 6:24; Lu 16:13; Ro 14:22; 1Co 10:21).

See Deceit; Expediency; Hypocrisy; Inconsistency; Obduracy; Prudence.

CONSOLATION (See Affliction, Consolation in; Holy Spirit.)

CONSPIRACY. Law against (Ex 23:1, 2).

Instances of: Joseph's brethren, against Joseph (Ge 37:18-20). Miriam and Aaron, against Moses (Nu 12; 14:4; 16:1-35). Abimelech, against Gideon's sons (J'g 9:1-6). Gaal, against Abimelech (J'g 9:23-41). Delilah, against Samson (J'g 16:4-21). Abner, against Ish-bosheth (2Sa 3:7-21). Of Absalom (2Sa 15:10-13).

Of Jeroboam (1Ki 14:2). Of Baasha (1Ki 15:27). Of Zimri (1Ki 16:9). Of Jezebel, against Naboth (1Ki 21:8-13). Of Jehu (2Ki 9:14-26). Of Jehoiada (2Ki 11:4-16). Of servants, against Joash (2Ki 12:20).

People in Jerusalem, against Amaziah (2Ki 14:19). Shallum, against Zachariah (2Ki 15:10). Pekahiah (2Ki 15:23-25). Pekah (2Ki 15:30). Amon (2Ki 21:23). Sennacherib (2Ki 19:37). Amaziah (2Ch 25:27). Ahasuerus (Es 2:21-23). Jeremiah (Jer 18:18). Daniel (Da 6:4-17). Shadrach, Meshach, and Abed-nego (Da 3:8-18).

Against Jesus (Jer 11:9, 19; M't 12:14; 21:38-41; 26:3, 4; 27:1, 2; M'k 3:6). Paul (Ac 18:12; 23:12-15).

Falsely accused of: Jonathan (1Sa 22:8).

CONSTANCY. In obedience (Ps 119:31, 33). In friendship (Pr 27:10). Under suffering (M't 5:12; Heb 12:5; 1Pe 4:12-16). In prayer (Lu 18:1; Ro 12:12; Eph 6:18; Col 4:2; 1Th 5:17). In beneficence (Ga 6:9). In profession (Heb 10:23).

Instances of: Ruth (Ru 1:14); Jonathan (1Sa 18:1; 20:16); Priscilla and Aquila (Ro 16:3, 4).

See Character: Stability.

CONSTELLATIONS (Isa 13:10). The serpent (Job 26:13). Orion (Job 9:9; Am 5:8).

See Astronomy.

CONSTITUTION. *Agreement Between the Ruler and the People.* King enjoined to study and conform to Mosaic law (De 17:18-20). Made by David (2Sa 5:3; 1Ch 11:3). Made for Joash (2Ch 23:2, 3, 11). Made by Zedekiah, proclaiming liberty (Jer 34:8-11). King of Medes and Persians bound by (Da 6:12-15).

CONSUMPTION (Le 26:16; De 28:22).

CONTEMPT, Sin of (Job 31:13, 14; Pr 14:21). Folly of (Pr 11:12). A characteristic of the wicked (Pr 18:3; Isa 5:24; 2Ti 3:3).

Forbidden Towards: Parents (Pr 23:22). Christ's little ones (M't 18:10). Weak brethren (Ro 14:3). Young ministers (1Co 16:11). Believing masters (1Ti 6:2). The poor (Jas 2:1-3). Self-righteousness prompts to (Isa 65:5; Lu 18:9, 11). Pride and prosperity prompt to (Ps 123:4). Ministers should give no occasion for (1Ti 4:12). Of ministers, is a despising of God (Lu 10:16; 1Th 4:8).

Towards the Church: Often turned into respect (Isa 60:14). Often punished (Eze 28:26). Causes saints to cry unto God (Ne 4:4; Ps 123:3).

The Wicked Exhibit Towards: Christ (Ps 22:6; Isa 53:3; M't 27:29). Saints (Ps 119:141). Authorities (2Pe 2:10; Jude 8). Parents (Pr 15:5, 20). The afflicted (Job 19:18). The poor (Ps 14:6; Ec 9:16). Saints sometimes guilty of (Jas 2:6).

Exemplified: Hagar (Ge 16:4). Children of Belial (1Sa 10:27). Nabal (1Sa 25:10, 11). Michal (2Sa 6:16). Sanballat (Ne 2:19; 4:2, 3). False teachers (2Co 10:10).

CONTENTION (See Strife.)

CONTENTMENT. Desirable (Pr 14:14; 15:13, 15, 30; 16:8; 17:1, 22; 30:8; Ec 2:24; 4:6; 5:12; 6:9). Enjoined (Ps 37:7; Ec 9:7-9; Lu 3:14; 1Co 7:17, 20-24; Ga 5:26; 1Ti 6:6-8; Heb 13:5).

Instances of: Esau (Ge 33:9). Barzillai (2Sa 19:33-37). The Shunammite (2Ki 4:13). David (Ps 16:6). Paul (Ph'p 4:11, 12).

See Affliction, Resignation in; Resignation.

CONTINENCE. Vow of (Job 31:1). Enjoined (M't 5:27, 28; Ro 13:13; 1Co 7:1-9, 25-29, 36-38; Col 3:5; 1Ti 4:12; 5:1, 2).

Instances of: Joseph (Ge 39:7-12). Uriah (2Sa 11:8-13). Boaz (Ru 3:6-13). Joseph, husband of Mary (M't 1:24, 25). Eunuchs (M't 19:12). Paul (1Co 7:8; 9:27). Saints (Re 14:1, 4, 5).

See Chastity.

CONTINENTS (Ge 1:9, 10; Job 26:7, 10; 28:8-11; 38:4-18; Ps 95:5; 104:5-9; 136:6; Pr 8:29; 30:4).

See Geology.

CONTINGENCIES, *In Divine Government of Man.* Conditional Rewards (Ge 4:7; 18:19; Ex 19:5; Le 26:3-4; De 7:12; 11:26, 27; 30:15, 16, 19; 1Ki 3:14; 1Ch 28:7; 2Ch 26:5; Job 36:11; Jer 11:4; 18:9, 10; 22:4, 5; M't 19:17; 23:37; Joh 14:23; 15:7; Col 1:22, 23; Heb 3:17; Re 22:17).

Conditional Punishment (Ge 2:16, 17; 3:3; Le 26:14-16; De 11:28; 30:15, 19; 1Ki 3:14; 20:42; Job 36:12; Jer 12:17; 18:8; Eze 33:14-16; Jon 3:10; M'k 11:26; Joh 9:41; 15:6; 2Th 2:8-11; Re 2:22; 3:3).

Instances of choice: Joshua (Jos 24:15). David (2Sa 24:12-14). Jesus (M't 26:39).

See Blessings, Contingent upon Obedience; Predestination; Will.

CONTRACTS. Binding force of (Jos 9:19; Pr 6:1-5; M't 20:1-16; Ga 3:15). Penalty for breach of (Le 6:1-7).

Dissolved: By mutual consent (Ex 4:18); by blotting out (Col 2:14). Ratified: By giving presents (Ge 21:25-30; 1Sa 18:4); by consummating in the presence of the public at the gates of the city (Ge 23:17, 18; Ru 4:1-11); by erecting a heap of stones (Ge 31:44-54); by oaths (Ge 26:3, 28, 31; Jos 9:15, 20; 1Ch 16:16; Heb 6:16, 17); by joining hands (Pr 6:1; 11:21; 17:18; 22:26); with salt (Nu 18:19); by taking of the shoe (Ru 4:6-8); by written instrument (Jer 32:10-15); by boring servant's ear (Ex 21:2-6).

Instances of: Between Abraham and Abimelech, concerning wells of water (Ge 21:25-32); violated (Ge 26:15). Between Laban and Jacob, for Laban's daughter (Ge 29:15-20, 27-30); violated (Ge 29:23-27); regarding sharing flocks and herds (Ge 30:28-34); violated (Ge 30:27-43; 31:7). Between Joshua and Gibeonites (Jos 9:3-9, 15-19). Between Solomon and Hiram (1Ki 5:8-12; 9:11).

See Covenants; Fraud; Land; Vows.

CONTRITION (See Repentance; Sin, Confession of.)

CONVENTION, for counsel (Pr 15:22).

CONVERSATION, a word often used in the KJV to signify conduct or manner of life, especially with respect to morals.

Profane, forbidden (M't 5:37; Jas 5:12). Corrupt, forbidden (Eph 4:29; Col 3:8).

Edifying, enjoined (Eph 4:29; Col 4:6). Men judged by (M't 12:36, 37).

See Speaking.

CONVERSION (a turning), a turning, which may be literal or figurative, ethical or religious, either from God, or, more frequently, to God. It implies a turning from and a turning to something, and is therefore associated with repentance (Ac 3:19; 26:20) and faith (Ac 11:21). On its negative side it is turning from sin, and on its positive side it is faith in Christ (Ac 20:21). Although it is an act of man, it is done by the power of God (Ac 3:26). In the process of salvation, it is the first step in the transition from sin to God.

CONVERTS. "Wayside" (M't 13:4, 19). "Stony ground" (M't 13:5, 20, 21); "Choked" (M't 13:7, 22). "Good ground" (M't 13:8, 23; Lu 8:4-15).

See Backsliders; Proselytes; Revivals.

Instances of: Ruth (Ru 1:16). Nebuchadnezzar (Da 4). The mariners with Jonah (Jon 1:5, 6, 9, 14, 16). Ninevites (Jon 3). Gadarenes (Lu 8:35-39). The Samaritans (Joh 4:28-42). The thief on the cross (Lu 23:39-43). At Pentecost, three thousand (Ac 2:41). Post-pentecostal (Ac 4:4). The eunuch (Ac 8:35-38). Saul of Tarsus (Ac 9:3-18). Sergius Paulus (Ac 13:7, 12; 26:12-23). Cornelius (Ac 10). Jews and Greeks at Antioch (Ac 13:43). Lydia (Ac 16:14, 15). Jailer (Ac 16:27-34). Greeks (Ac 17:4, 12).

Zealous: Instances of: Nebuchadnezzar (Da 3:29; 4:1-37). Andrew (Joh 1:40, 41). Philip (Joh 1:43-45). The woman of Samaria (Joh 4:28, 29). The man possessed of demons (Lu 8:39). The blind men (M't 9:31; Joh 9:8-38). The dumb man (M'k 7:36).

CONVEYANCE. *Of Land* (See Land.)

CONVICTION, OF SIN. To convince or prove guilty. The first stage of repentance. The word "conviction" itself does not appear in the KJV.

Produced, by dreams (Job 33:14-17); by visions (Ac 9:3-9); by adversity (Job 33:18-30; La 1:20; Lu 15:17-21); by the gospel (Ac 2:37; 1Co 14:24, 25); by conscience (Joh 8:9; Ro 2:15); by the Holy Spirit (Joh 16:7-11); by God (De 28:65-67; Ps 38:1-22; 51:1-4, 7-17).

Instances of: Adam and Eve, after their disobedience (Ge 3:8-10). Cain, after he slew Abel (Ge 4:13). Joseph's brothers, because of their cruelty to him (Ge 42:21, 22; 44:16; 45:3; 50:15-21). Pharaoh, after the plague, of hail (Ex 9:27, 28); of locusts (Ex 10:16, 17); after the death of the firstborn (Ex 12:31).

The Israelites, after worshipping the golden calf and being rebuked (Ex 33:4); after the death of ten spies and their sentence (Nu 14:39, 40); after murmuring against God and being bitten by the serpents (Nu 21:7); after being judged for disobedience (De 28:65-67; Eze

33:10); in the last days (Eze 7:16-18, 25, 26).

Saul, after sparing Agag and the best of the spoils (1Sa 15:24). David, after the pestilence sent because he numbered the people (1Ch 21:8, 30); after his sin with Bathsheba (2Sa 12-13; Ps 51:1-17); in penitential Psalms (Ps 31:10; 38:1-22; see Psalms, Penitential). Widow of Zarephath, when her son died (1Ki 17:18). Job, in his distress (Job 40:4, 5).

Isaiah, after his vision of God's throne (Isa 6:5). Belshazzar, after the handwriting on the wall (Da 5:6). Darius, when Daniel was in the lions' den (Da 6:18). Mariners, after casting Jonah into the sea (Jon 1:16). Ninevites, at the preaching of Jonah (Jon 3; M't 12:41; Lu 11:32). Jonah, in the fish's belly (Jon 2).

Herod, when he heard of the fame of Jesus (M't 14:2; M'k 6:14; Lu 9:7). Jews, who condemned woman taken in adultery (Joh 8:9). Judas, after his betrayal of Jesus (M't 27:3-5). Peter, after the large catch of fish (Lu 5:8). Paul, on the way to Damascus (Ac 9:4-18). Felix, under the preaching of Paul (Ac 24:25). Philippian jailer, after the earthquake (Ac 16:29, 30).

See Penitents; Remorse; Repentance; Sin, Confession of; Wicked.

CONVOCATION, a religious festival during which no work could be done (Nu 10:2; Isa 1:13; 4:5).

COOKING. A kid might not be seethed in the mother's milk (De 14:21). Spice used in (Eze 24:10). Ephraim, a cake unturned (Ho 7:8). In the temple (Eze 46:19-24).

See Bread; Oven.

COOS (summit), island off the coast of Caria in S Asia Minor (Ac 21:1).

COPING, parapet on house roof (1Ki 7:9).

COPPER, incorrectly translated brass (De 8:9).

See Brass.

COPPERSMITH. The word should be rendered "worker in brass" (2Ti 4:14).

COPULATION. Forbidden between persons near of kin (Le 18:6-16). During menses (Le 15:19; 18:19); with animals.

See Adultery; Lasciviousness; Sodomy.

COR. A measure for liquids and solids, containing ten ephahs, or baths, and equal to the homer (Eze 45:14). Rendered measure in 1Ki 4:22; 5:11; 2Ch 2:10; 27:5; Ezr 7:22; Lu 16:7.

See Measures.

CORAL, ranked by Hebrews with precious stones (Job 28:18; Eze 27:16).

CORBAN (an offering), an offering, bloody or unbloody, made to God (Le 1:2, 3; 2:1; 3:1; Nu 7:12-17; M'k 7:11).

CORD. Ancient uses of: In casting lots (Mic 2:5); fastening tents (Ex 35:18, 39:40; Isa 54:2); leading or binding animals (Ps 118:27; Ho 11:4); hitching to cart or plough (Job 39:10); binding prisoners (J'g 15:13); measuring ground (2Sa 8:2; Jos 17:14; Ps 78:55; Am 7:17; Zec 2:1); worn on the head as a sign of submission (1Ki 20:31).

Figurative: Of spiritual blessings (Ps 16:6). Of sin (Pr 5:22). Of life (Ec 12:6). Of friendship (Ec 4:12; Ho 11:4).

Symbolical Uses of: Token in mourning (1Ki 20:31-33; Job 36:8). Signifying an inheritance (Jos 17:14).

CORIANDER, a spice (Ex 16:31; Nu 11:7).

CORINTH (ornament), a city of Achaia. Visited: By Paul (Ac 18; 2Co 12:14; 13:1; with 1Co 16:5-7; and 2Co 1:16); Apollos (Ac 19:1); Titus (2Co 8:16, 17; 12:18). Erastus, a Christian of (Ro 16:23; 2Ti 4:20).

Church of: Schism in (1Co 1:12; 3:4). Immoralities in (1Co 5; 11). Writes to Paul (1Co 7:1). Alienation of, from Paul (2Co 10). Abuse of ordinances in (1Co 11:22; 14). Heresies in (1Co 15:12; 2Co 11). Lawsuits in (1Co 6). Liberality of (2Co 9). Paul's letters to (1Co 1:2; 16:21-24; 2Co 1:1, 13).

CORINTHIANS, First and Second Epistles. I Corinthians was written by the Apostle Paul in Ephesus on his 3rd missionary journey (Ac 19; 1Co 16:8, 19), probably in 56 or 57. He had previously written a letter to the Corinthians which has not come down to us (1Co 5:9), and in reply had received a letter in which he was asked a number of questions. Paul had also heard of factions in the church from the servants of Chloe (1:11). These circumstances led to the writings of I Corinthians. Outline: 1. Factions in the church (1-4). 2. Incestuous marriage (5). 3. Disputes of Christians brought before heathen courts (6). 4. Phases of the subject of marriage (7). 5. Meat offered to idols (8-10). 6. Head coverings for women; proper observance of the Lord's Supper (11). 7. Spiritual gifts (12-14). 8. Resurrection of the body (15). 9. Collection for the poor of Jerusalem; closing remarks (16).

II Corinthians was written by Paul somewhere in Macedonia on his 3rd missionary journey as a result of a report concerning the church brought to him by Titus. Outline: 1. Some thoughts on the crisis through which the church has just passed (1-7). 2. Collection for the poor (8, 9). 3. Defense of Paul's ministry against the attacks of his enemies and a vindication of his apostleship (10-13).

CORMORANT, a bird forbidden as food (Le 11:17; De 14:17; Isa 34:11; Zep 2:14).

CORN. A general term applied to all grains. In valleys (Ps 65:13; M'k 4:28). A product of Egypt (Ge 41:47-49); Palestine (De 33:28; Eze 27:17). Parched (Ru 2:14; 1Sa 17:17; 25:18; 2Sa 17:28). Ground (2Sa 17:19). Eaten by the Israelites (Jos 5:11, 12). Shocks of, burnt (J'g 15:5). Heads of, plucked by Christ's disciples (M't 12:1). Mosaic laws concerning (Ex 22:6; De 23:25).

Figurative: Ps 72:16; Ho 14:7; Joh 12:24. Symbolical (Ge 41:5).

See Barley; Barn; Bread; Firstfruits; Gleaning; Harvest; Reaping; Rye; Threshing; Tithes; Wheat.

CORNELIUS (of a horn), Roman centurion stationed at Caesarea, and the first Gentile convert (Ac 10, 11).

CORNERSTONE (Job 38:6). See Stone.

Figurative: Ps 144:12. Of Christ (Ps 118:22; Isa 28:16; M't 21:42; M'k 12:10; Lu 20:17; Ac 4:11; 1Co 3:11; Eph 2:20; 1Pe 2:6).

CORNET, a wind instrument with a curved horn, the sound being a dull monotone (1Ch 15:28; Ps 98:6; Da 3:5, 10, 15; Ho 5:8).

CORPORAL PUNISHMENT (See Punishment.)

CORPULENCY. *Instances of:* Eglon (J'g 3:17); Eli (1Sa 4:18).

CORRECTION. See Affliction, Design of; Chastisement; Children, Correction of; Parents; Punishment; Scourging.

CORRUPTION. *Physical Decomposition:* Le 22:25. After death (Ge 3:19; Job 17:14; 21:26; 34:15; Ps 16:10; 49:9; 104:29; Ec 3:20; 12:7; Jon 2:6; Ac 2:27, 31; 13:34-37; 1Co 15:42, 50).

Figurative: Of sin (Isa 38:17; Ro 8:21; Ga 6:8; 2Pe 1:4; 2:12, 19). Mount of (2Ki 23:13).

Judicial: See Court; Government; Judge.

Ecclesiastical: See Church, Corrupt; Ministers.

Political: See Bribery; Civil Service; Government; Politics.

COSAM, ancestor of Christ (Lu 3:28).

COSMETICS, any of the various preparations used for beautifying the hair and skin (2Ki 9:30; Jer 4:30; Eze 23:40).

COTTON, originally designated muslin or calico; later included linen (Es 1:6; Isa 19:9).

COUCH, a piece of furniture for reclining, but sometimes only a rolled-up mat (Am 6:4; M't 9:6).

COULTER, a plowshare (1Sa 13:19-21).

COUNCIL. 1. Group of people gathered for deliberation (Ge 49:6; 2Ki 9:5).

2. The Jewish Sanhedrin (M't 26:59; Ac 5:34) and lesser courts (M't 10:17; M'k 13:9).

COUNSEL. Wisdom in (Ex 18:14-23; Pr 1:5; 11:14; 15:22; 19:20; 20:18; 24:6). The wise profit by (Pr 1:5; 9:9; 12:15; 27:9). Rejected, by Rehoboam (1Ki 12:8-16); by rich young ruler (M't 19:22). Consequences of rejecting divine (Pr 1:24-32).

See Prudence.

COUNSELLOR. A wise man, versed in law and diplomacy (1Ch 27:32, 33). Ahithophel was, to David (2Sa 16:23; 1Ch 27:33); to Absalom (2Sa 16:23). Was member of the Sanhedrin at Jerusalem (M'k 15:43; Lu 23:50, 51). A title of Christ (Isa 9:6).

COUNTENANCE. Angry (Pr 25:23). Cheerful (Job 29:24; Ps 4:6; 21:6; 44:3; Pr 15:13; 27:17). Fierce (De 28:50; Da 8:23). Guilty (Ge 4:5; Isa 3:9). Health indicated in (Ps 42:11; 43:5). Pride in (2Ki 5:1; Ps 10:4). Reading of (Ge 31:2, 5). Sad (1Sa 1:18; Ne 2:2, 3; Ec 7:3; Eze 27:35; Da 1:15; 5:6). Transfigured (Ex 34:29-35; Lu 9:29; 2Co 3:7, 13).

See Face.

COUNTRY, *Love of.* By Israelites in

exile (Ne 1:1-11; 2:1-20; 5:1-18; Ps 137:1-6). See Church; Congregation of Israel; Patriotism.

COURSE OF PRIESTS AND LEVITES. David divided the priests and Levites into 24 groups, called courses in Lu 1:8, each with its own head (1Ch 24:1ff). Each course officiated a week at a time.

COURAGE. Of righteous (Pr 28:1; 2Ti 1:7).

Exhortations to (Ps 31:24; Isa 51:7, 12-16; Eze 2:6; 3:9; M't 10:28; Lu 12:4; 1Co 16:13; Ph'p 1:27, 28).

Enjoined: Upon, Joshua (De 31:7, 8, 22, 23, Jos 1:1-9); the Israelites (Le 26:6-8; Jos 23:6; 1Ch 19:13; 2Ch 32:7, 8; Isa 41:10; 51:7, 12-16); Solomon (1Ch 22:13; 28:20); Asa (2Ch 15:1-7); the disciples (M't 10:26, 28; Lu 12:4); Paul (Ac 18:9, 10); other Christians (1Co 16:13; Ph'p 1:27, 28). By Jehoshaphat, upon judicial and executive officers (2Ch 19:11).

Instances of the Courage of Conviction: Abraham, in leaving his fatherland (Ge 12:1-9); in offering Isaac (Ge 22:1-14). Gideon, in destroying the altar of Baal (J'g 6:25-31). Ezra, in undertaking the perilous journey from Babylon to Palestine without a guard (Ezr 8:22, 23).

The Jews, in returning answer to Tatnai (Ezr 5:11). The three Hebrews, who refused to bow down to the image of Nebuchadnezzar (Da 3:16-18). Daniel, in persisting in prayer, regardless of the edict against praying (Da 6:10). Peter and John, in refusing to obey men, rather than God (Ac 4:19; 5:29).

See Ministers, Courage of; Reproof.

Instances of Personal Bravery: Joshua and Caleb, in advising that Israel go at once and possess the land (Nu 13:30; 14:6-12). Othniel, in smiting Kirjath-sepher (Jos 15:16, 17). Gideon, in attacking the confederate armies of the Midianites and Amalekites with three hundred men (J'g 7:7-23). Deborah, in leading Israel's armies (J'g 4). Jael, in slaying Sisera (J'g 4:18-22). Agag, in the indifference with which he faced death (1Sa 15:32, 33). David, in slaying Goliath (1Sa 17:32-50); in entering into the tent of Saul, and carrying away Saul's spear (1Sa 26:7-12). David's captains (2Sa 23). Joab, in reproving King David (2Sa 19:5-7). Nehemiah, in refusing to take refuge in the temple (Ne 6:10-13). Esther, in going to the king to save her people (Es 4:8, 16; 5-7).

Joseph of Arimathaea, in caring for the body of Jesus (M'k 15:43). Thomas, in being willing to die with Jesus (Joh 11:16). Peter and other disciples (Ac 3:12-26; 4:9-13, 19, 20, 31). The apostles, under persecution (Ac 5:21, 29-32). Paul, in going to Jerusalem, despite his impressions that bonds and imprisonments awaited him (Ac 20:22-24; 24:14, 25).

See Boldness of the Righteous; Ministers; Reproof, Faithfulness in; Cowardice.

COURT. *Ecclesiastical* (1Ch 26:29-32; 2Ch 19:8-11; M't 18:15-18; Joh 20:23). See Church, Discipline in.

Civil: Held, outside the camp (Le 24:14); at the tabernacle (Nu 27:2); at the gates of the city (De 21:19; 22:15; 25:7; Jos 20:4; Ru 4:1; Zec 8:16); under a palm tree (J'g 4:5). Circuit (1Sa 7:15-17).

Composition of, and mode of procedure (Ex 18:25, 26; De 1:15-17; 17:9; Ru 4:2-5; 1Ch 26:29; 2Ch 19:8-11; M't 26:54-71; M'k 14:53, 55-65; 15:1; Lu 22:50-71; Joh 18:13-28; Ac 5:17-21, 25-28, 34, 38-41). Accused spoke in his own defense (Jer 26:11-16; M'k 15:3-5; Ac 4:8-12, 18-20; 5:29-32; 7:1-56; 23:1-7; 26:1-32; see Appeal; Punishment; Witness). Superior and Inferior (Ex 18:21-26; 24:14; De 1:15-17; 17:8-13; 2Ch 19:5-10).

Justice required of (Ex 23:2, 3, 6-8; De 1:16, 17; 25:1; 27:19; 2Ch 19:5-10; Ac 25:16). Sentence of, final and obligatory (De 17:8-12). Contempt of (De 17:8-13; Mic 5:1; Ac 23:1-5). See Judge; Justice.

Corrupt (Pr 17:15; 29:26; Isa 1:23; 5:23; 10:1, 2; Mic 3:11; 7:3; Zep 3:3; M't 26:59-62; 27:18-26; M'k 14:53-65; 15:10; Ac 4:15-18; 6:11-14; 24:26, 27; see Bribery).

See Judge; Justice; Priest, Judicial function of.

Of the Tabernacle (Ex 27:9, 12, 16-19; 35:17, 18; 38:9, 15-20, 31; 39:40; 40:8, 33; Le 6:16, 26; Nu 3:26, 37; 4:26).

Of the Temple (1Ch 28:12; 2Ch 4:9;

6:13; 23:5; 33:5). The inner court (1Ki 6:36; 7:12). The middle court (1Ki 8:64; 2Ch 7:7).

COURTESY (See Manners.)

COURTSHIP. Ancient customs of: Suitor visited the maid (J'g 14:7); women proposed marriage (Ru 3:9-13).

See Marriage.

COVENANT. Blood of (Ex 24:8; see Blood of Covenant). Book of (Ex 24:7). The Mosaic Law called a covenant (Ex 34:28).

Of God with Men: Salt an emblem of (Le 2:13; Nu 18:19; 2Ch 13:5). Confirmed with an oath (Ge 22:16; 26:3; 50:24; Ex 34:27, 28; Nu 32:11; Ps 89:35; 105:9; Lu 1:73; Heb 6:13, 17, 18). Binding (Le 26; Jer 11:2, 3; Ga 3:15). Everlasting (Ge 8:20-22; 9:1-17; Ps 105:8, 10; Isa 54:10; 61:8). God faithful to (Le 26:44, 45; De 4:31; 7:8, 9; J'g 2:1; 1Ki 8:23; Ps 105:8-11; 106:45; 111:5; Mic 7:20). Repudiated by God on account of Jew's idolatry (Jer 44:26, 27; Heb 8:9). Broken by the Jews (Jer 22:9; Eze 16:59; Heb 8:9). Punishment for breaking (Le 26:25-46).

Instances of: The Sabbath (Ex 31:16). The ten commandments (Ex 34:28; De 5:2, 3; 9:9). With Adam (Ge 2:16, 17); Noah (Ge 6:18; 8:16; 9:8-17); Abraham (Ge 12:1-3; 15; 17:1-22; Ex 6:4-8; Ps 105:8-11; Ro 9:7-13; Ga 3; see Circumcision); Isaac (Ge 17:19); Jacob (Ge 28:13-15); Israelites, to deliver them from Egypt (Ex 6:4-8). Phinehas (Nu 25:12, 13); Israel, to destroy Amalek (Ex 17:14-16); at Horeb (Ex 34:27; De 5:2, 3); in Moab (De 29:1-15); Levites (Ne 13:29; Mal 2:4, 5); David (2Sa 7:12-16; 1Ch 17:11-14; 2Ch 6:16); David and his house (2Sa 23:5; Ps 89:20-37; Jer 33:21); God's people (Isa 55:3; 59:21). To be confirmed (Ge 9:27).

Of Man with God: Jacob (Ge 28:20-22). Joshua (Jos 24:25). Absalom (2Sa 15:7, 8). Jehoiada and Joash (2Ki 11:17). Josiah (2Ki 23:3). Asa (2Ch 15:12-15). Nehemiah (Ne 9:38; 10). Israelites (Ex 24:3, 7; 19:8; De 5:27; 26:17; Jer 50:5). See Vows.

Of Men with Men: Sacred (Jos 9:18-21; Ga 3:15). Binding (Jos 9.18-20; Jer 34:8-21; Eze 17:14-18; Ga 3:15); on those represented as well (De 29:14, 15). Breach of, punished (2Sa 21:1-6; Jer 34:8-22; Eze 17:13-19). National, see Alliances.

Ratified: By giving the hand (Ezr 10:19; La 5:6; Eze 17:18); loosing the shoe (Ru 4:7-11); writing and sealing (Ne 9:38; Jer 32:10-12); giving presents (Ge 21:27-30; 1Sa 18:3, 4); making a feast (Ge 26:30); erecting a monument (Ge 31:45, 46, 49-53); offering a sacrifice (Ge 15:9-17; Jer 34:18, 19); salting (Le 2:13; Nu 18:19; 2Ch 13:5); taking an oath (Ge 21:23, 24; 25:33; 26:28-31; 31:53; Jos 2:12-14; 14:9; see Oath). See Contracts; Vows.

Instances of: Abraham and Abimelech (Ge 21:22-32). Abimelech and Isaac (Ge 26:26-31). Jacob and Laban (Ge 31:44-54). Jonathan and David (1Sa 18:3, 4; 20:16, 42; 2Sa 21:7). Jews with each other, to serve God (2Ch 15:12-15; Ne 10:28-32). King Zedekiah and his subjects (Jer 34:8). Ahab with Benhadad (1Ki 20:34). Subjects with sovereign (2Ch 23:1-3, 16).

New Covenant, or Second Covenant: Prophecy concerning (Jer 31:31-34; w Heb 8:4-13). Abolishes Mosaic legalism in favor of Messianic grace (2Co 3:6-17). Purchased or ratified by the blood of Jesus (M't 26:28; M'k 14:24; Lu 22:20; 1Co 11:25). Jesus the mediator (Heb 12:18-24). Everlasting (Heb 13:20).

COVERING THE HEAD. Symbolic of woman's submission to man (1Co 11:3); in the form of a veil or covering (1Co 11:6, 13). In ancient Greece, only immoral women appeared publicly with their heads "shorn or shaven" (1Co 11:5, 6), therefore Christian women should not disregard social convention to the degradation of their testimony (1Co 11:15).

COVETOUSNESS. Idolatry (Col 3:5). Insatiable (Pr 1:19; 21:26; Ec 1:8; 4:8; 5:10, 11; Isa 56:11). Root of evil (1Ti 6:9-11). Tends to poverty (Pr 11:24, 26; 22:16). Gains of, unstable (Job 20:15; Pr 23:4-6; Jer 17:11). Debars, from sacred office (Ex 18:21; 1Ti 3:3; Tit 1:7, 11; 1Pe 5:2); from kingdom of God (M't 19:23, 24; 22:25; Lu 18:24, 25; 1Co 6:10; Eph 5:3, 5; Ph'p 3:18, 19). Denounced (Ps 10:3; Pr 1:19; Isa 5:8; Jude 11).

Warnings against (De 15:9, 10; Pr 1:19; 15:27; Ho 4:18; Hab 2:5-9; M't 6:19-21, 24, 25, 31-33; 13:22; 16:26; M'k

4:19; 7:21-23; Lu 8:14; 12:15-21; Joh 6:26, 27; 1Co 5:11; 1Th 2:5; 1Ti 6:5-8; 2Ti 3:2, 5; Heb 13:5; Jas 4:2; 1Jo 2:15-17). Commandments against (Ex 20:17; De 5:21; Ro 13:9; Col 3:2; 1Ti 3:8). Prayer against (Ps 119:36).

Reproof for (Ne 5:7; Isa 1:23; Jer 6:13; 22:17; Eze 33:31; Ho 10:1; Mic 2:2; 3:11; 7:3; Hag 1:6; Ro 1:29). Punishment for (Ex 18:21; Job 31:24, 25, 28; Isa 57:17; Jer 8:10; 51:13; Eze 22:12, 13; Col 3:5, 6; 2Pe 2:3, 14-17).

See Avarice; Rich; Riches; Worldliness.

Instances of: Eve, in desiring the forbidden fruit (Ge 3:6). Lot, in choosing the plain of the Jordan (Ge 13:10-13). Laban, in giving Rebekah to be Isaac's wife (Ge 24:29-51); in deceiving Jacob when he served him seven years for Rachel (Ge 29:15-30); in deceiving Jacob in wages (Ge 31:7, 15, 41, 42). Jacob, in defrauding Esau of his father's blessing (Ge 27:6-29); in defrauding Laban of his flocks and herds (Ge 30:35-43); in buying Esau's birthright (Ge 25:31). Balaam, in loving the wages of unrighteousness (2Pe 2:15, w Nu 22). Achan, in hiding the treasure (Jos 7:21). Eli's sons, in taking the flesh of the sacrifice (1Sa 2:13-17). Samuel's sons, in taking bribes (1Sa 8:3). Saul, in sparing Agag and the booty (1Sa 15:8, 9). David, of Bathsheba (2Sa 11:2-5). Ahab, in desiring Naboth's vineyard (1Ki 21:2-16). Gehazi, in taking a gift from Naaman (2Ki 5:20-27). Jews, in exacting usury of their brethren (Ne 5:1-11); in keeping back the portion of the Levites (Ne 13:10); in building fine houses while the house of the Lord lay waste (Hag 1:4-9); in following Jesus for the loaves and fishes (Joh 6:26). Money changers in the temple (M't 21:12, 13; Lu 19:45, 46; Joh 2:14-16). The rich young ruler (M't 19:16-22). The rich fool (Lu 12:15-21). Judas, in betraying Jesus for thirty pieces of silver (M't 26:15, 16; M'k 14:10, 11; Lu 22:3-6; Joh 12:6). The unjust steward (Lu 16:1-8). The Pharisees (Lu 16:14). Simon Magus, in trying to buy the gift of the Holy Ghost (Ac 8:18-23). The sorcerers, in filing complaint against Paul and Silas (Ac 16:19). Demetrius, in raising a riot against Paul and Silas (Ac 19:24, 27). Felix, in hoping for a bribe from Paul (Ac 24:26). Demas, in forsaking Paul for love of the world (2Ti 4:10).

See Avarice; Bribery; Rich; Riches.

COW. Used for draught (1Sa 6:7-12; Ho 10:11). Milk of, used for food. (See Milk; Cattle; Kine.)

Figurative: Am 4:1.

COWARDICE. Described (Jos 7:5). Disqualifies for military service (De 20:8; J'g 7:3). From God (Jos 23:10); inflicted as judgment (Le 26:36, 37; De 32:30). Rebuke for (Isa 51:12, 13).

Cause of adversity (Pr 29:25). Caused, by adversity (Job 15:24; 18:11); by wickedness (Pr 28:1).

See Courage.

Instances of: Adam, in attempting to shift responsibility for his sin upon Eve (Ge 3:12). Abraham, in calling his wife his sister (Ge 12:11-19; 20:2-12). Isaac, in calling his wife his sister (Ge 26:7-9). Jacob, in flying from Laban (Ge 31:31). Aaron, in yielding to the Israelites when they demanded an idol (Ex 32:22-24). The ten spies (Nu 13:28, 31-33). Israelites, in fearing to attempt the conquest of Canaan (Nu 14:1-5; De 1:26-28); in the battle with the people of Ai (Jos 7:5); to meet Goliath (1Sa 17:24); to fight with the Philistines (1Sa 13:6, 7). Twenty thousand of Gideon's army (J'g 7:3). Ephraimites (Ps 78:9). Ephraimites and Manassehites (Jos 17:14-18). Amoritish kings (Jos 10:16). Canaanites (Jos 2:11; 5:1). Samuel, fearing to obey God's command to anoint a king in Saul's stead (1Sa 16:2). David, in fleeing from Absalom (2Sa 15:13-17). Nicodemus, in coming to Jesus by night (Joh 3:1, 2). Joseph of Arimathaea, secretly a disciple (Joh 19:38). Parents of the blind man, who was restored to sight (Joh 9:22). Early converts among the rulers (Joh 12:42, 43). Disciples, in the storm at sea (M't 8:26; M'k 4:38; Lu 8:25); when they saw Jesus walking on the sea (M't 14:25; M'k 6:50; Joh 6:19); when Jesus was apprehended (M't 26:56). Peter, in denying the Lord (M't 26:69-74; M'k 14:66-72; Lu 22:54-60; Joh 18:16, 17, 25, 27). Pilate, in condemning Jesus, through fear of the people (Joh 19:12-16). Guards of the sepulcher of Jesus (M't 28:4). The Philippian jailer (Ac 16:27). Peter and other Christians, at Antioch (Ga 2:11-14). False teachers (Ga 6:12). Companions of Paul (2Ti 4:16).

COZ, father of Anub (1Ch 4:8).

COZBI, daughter of Zur (Nu 25:15, 18).

CRACKNEL, a biscuit or cake, hard baked (1 Ki 14:3).

CRAFTINESS. *Instances of:* Satan, in the temptation of Eve (Ge 3:1-5). Jacob, in purchase of Esau's birthright (Ge 25:31-33); obtaining Isaac's blessing (Ge 27:6-29); in management of Laban's flocks and herds (Ge 30:31-43). Gibeonites, in deceiving Joshua and the Israelites into a treaty (Jos 9:3-15). Sanballat, in trying to deceive Nehemiah into a conference (Ne 6). Jews, in seeking to entangle the Master (M't 22:15-17, 24-28; M'k 12:13, 14, 18-23; Lu 20:19-26); in seeking to slay Jesus (M't 26:4; M'k 14:1).

CRAFTSMAN (See Art; Master Workman.)

CRANE, an amphibious bird (Isa 38:14; Jer 8:7).

CREATION. The Bible clearly teaches that the universe, and all matter, had a beginning, and came into existence through the will of the eternal God (Ge 1, 2). The Bible gives no information as to how long ago the original creation of matter occurred, or the first day of creation began, or the sixth day ended. It appears that God ceased His creative activity after the sixth day and now rests from His labors. The Bible does not support the view that everything now existing has come into its present condition as a result of natural development. God determined that plants and animals were to reproduce "after their kind." The Scriptures do not say how large a "kind" is, and nothing in the Bible denies the possibility of change and development within the limits of a particular "kind." The two creation accounts in Ge 1, 2 supplement each other. Ge 1 describes the creation of the universe as a whole; while Ge 2 gives a more detailed account of the creation of man and says nothing about the creation of matter, light, heavenly bodies, plants and animals, except to refer to the creation of animals as having taken place at an earlier time.

CREATOR. Creator of the Natural Universe, God as (Ge 1:1; Ne 9:6; Job 26:7; Ps 102:25; Ac 14:15; Heb 11:3). Creator of Man, God as (Ge 1:26; 2:7; 5:2; De 4:32; Job 33:4; Ps 8:5; 100:3; Isa 51:13; Mal 2:10; Ac 17:28). Holy Spirit as (Ge 1:2; Job 26:13; 33:4; Ps 104:30).

CREATURE, that which has been created (Ro 1:25; 8:39; Heb 4:13).

CREATURE, LIVING, symbolical figure presented first in Eze 1:5ff, and again in Re 4:6-9; 5:6, 8, 11; 6:1, 3, 5-7 ASV. The living creatures in Revelation are somewhat modified from those in Ezekiel's vision.

CREDITOR. *Mosaic laws concerning:* Manumission of debtor-servants (Ex 21:2-6). Must return pawned raiment (Ex 22:25-27; De 24:10-13). Must not take, widows raiment for pledge (De 24:17); nor millstones (De 24:6). Must not extort interest of the poor (Le 25:35-37; De 15:2, 3; 23:19, 20). Must not oppress neighbor (Le 25:14-17).

Christ's injunctions to: M't 5:42; Lu 6:34.

Oppression by: Seizing debtor's, personal property (Job 22:6; 24:3, 10; Pr 22:26, 27); houses (Job 20:18-20). Imprisoning debtor (M't 5:25, 26; 18:28-35; Lu 12:58, 59). Enslaving debtor's children (2Ki 4:1; Ne 5:1-13; Job 24:9).

Merciful: Ps 112:5; M't 18:23-27; Lu 7:41-43.

See Debt; Debtor; Jubilee; Surety.

CREDULITY (Ge 3:6; Jos 9:14; Pr 14:15; 1Jo 4:1).

CREED, a succinct statement of faith epitomizing the basic tenets of religious faith. Such passages as M't 16:16 and 1Ti 3:16 give the Biblical foundation for the Christian creed. There are three ancient creeds: the Apostles' Creed, the Nicene Creed, and the Athanasian Creed. The Reformers also prepared creeds.

CREEK, modern translations use "bay" for the KJV "creek" in Ac 27:39, identified as St. Paul's Bay, c. 8 miles NW of the town of Zaletta on the island of Malta.

CREEPING THINGS. A general term for animals (Ge 1:26; Le 11:20-23, 29-31, 42; Ps 104:20, 25; Ro 1:23). Unclean (Le 5:2; 11:20, 29-44; De 14:19). Clean (Le 11:21, 22). Uses of, in idolatrous worship (Eze 8:10).

CREMATION (Jos 7:25; 1Sa 31:12; 2Ki 23:20; Am 2:1; 6:10). See Burial.
CRESCENS (increasing), a disciple with Paul at Rome (2Ti 4:10).
CRETE, CRETAN, an island in the Mediterranean, 165 miles long, 6-35 miles wide, forming a natural bridge between Europe and Asia Minor. It was the legendary birthplace of Zeus. Paul and Titus founded a church there (Tit 1:5-14). The Cretans in the OT are called Cherethites (1Sa 30:14; Eze 25:16). Cretans were in Jerusalem on the Day of Pentecost (Ac 2:11). According to Paul they were not of a high moral character (Tit 1:12).
CRIB, rack for the feeding of domestic livestock (Job 39:9; Pr 14:4; Isa 1:3; Lu 2:7).
CRIME. Some lists (Eze 22:8-12, 27-30; Ho 4:1, 2; M't 15:19; M'k 7:21, 22; Ro 1:24, 29-32; 3:14-18; 13:9; 1Co 5:11; Ga 5:19-21).
See individual listings of various crimes or sins. See also Punishment.
CRIMINALS. Released at feasts (M't 27:15, 21; M'k 15:6; Lu 23:17). Confined in prisons (Ge 39:20-23; Ezr 7:26; Ac 4:3; 12:4, 5; 16:19-40); in dungeons (Ge 40:15; 41:14; Ex 12:29; Isa 24:22; Jer 37:16; 38:10; La 3:53, 55).
Cruelty to. See Scourging; Stoning; Mocking.
Punishment of. See various crimes, such as Adultery, Arson, Homicide, etc. See also Punishments.
CRIMINATION (See Self-Crimination.)
CRIMSON, brilliant red dye obtained from a bug (2Ch 2:7, 14; Jer 4:30; Isa 1:18).
CRISPING PIN, pin for curling the hair (Isa 3:22).
CRISPUS, former ruler of Jewish synagogue at Corinth, converted by Paul (Ac 18:8; 1Co 1:14).
CRITICISM, Unjust. (See Uncharitableness.)
CROCODILE (See Dragon.)
CROP, pouch-like enlargement in gullet of many birds in which food is partially prepared for digestion (Le 1:16).
CROSS. Jesus crucified on (M't 27:32; M'k 15:21; Lu 23:26; Ac 2:23, 36; 4:10; 1Co 1:23; 2:2, 8; Eph 2:16; Ph'p 2:8; Col 1:20; 2:14; Heb 12:2). Borne by Simon (M't 27:32; M'k 15:21; Lu 23:26); by Jesus (Joh 19:17). Death on, a disgrace (Ga 3:13).
Figurative: Of duty (M't 10:38; 16:24; M'k 8:34; 10:21; Lu 9:23; 14:27). Of Christ's vicarious death (1Co 1:17, 18; Ga 5:11; 6:14; Ph'p 3:18).
See Crucifixion; Self-Denial.
CROSS-QUESTIONING (Pr 20:5).
See Witness.
CROW (See Birds.)
CROWN. Prescribed for priests (Ex 29:6; 39:30; Le 8:9). Worn by kings (2Sa 1:10; 12:30; 2Ki 11:12; Es 6:8; Song 3:11; Re 6:2); by queens (Es 1:11; 2:17; 8:15). Made of gold (Ps 21:3; Zec 6:11). An ornament (Eze 16:12; 23:42). Set with gems (2Sa 12:30; 1Ch 20:2: Zec 9:16; Isa 62:3). Given victor in games (1Co 9:25; 2Ti 2:5). Of thorns (M't 27:29; M'k 15:17; Joh 19:5).
Figurative: Of gracious visitation (Isa 28:5). Of heavenly reward (1Co 9:25; 2Ti 4:8; Jas 1:12; 1Pe 5:4; Re 2:10; 3:11).
Symbolical: Re 4:4, 10; 6:2; 9:7; 12:1, 3; 13:1; 14:14; 19:12.
CRUCIFIXION. The reproach of (Ga 3:13; 5:11). Of Jesus, see Jesus, History of. Of two malefactors (M't 27:38). Of disciples, foretold (M't 23:34).
See Cross.
Figurative: Of old nature (Ro 6:6; Ga 5:24). Of self-life (Ga 2:20; 6:14).
See Cross, Figurative.
CRUELTY. *Instances of:* Of Sarah to Hagar (Ge 16:6; 21:9-14). Egyptians to the Israelites (Ex 5:6-18). Peninnah to Hannah (1Sa 1:4-7; 2:3). Of Jews to Jesus (M't 26:67; 27:28-31); soldiers to Jesus (Lu 22:64; Joh 19:3). In war (Isa 13:16, 18).
See Animals, Cruelty to; Kindness; Love; Malice; Prisoners of War.
CRUSE, a vessel for liquids (1Sa 26:11; 1Ki 14:3; 2Ki 2:20).
CRYSTAL, a precious stone (Job 28:17; Eze 1:22; Re 4:6; 21:11; 22:1).
CUBIT. A measure of distance (Ge 6:16; De 3:11; Eze 40:5; 43:13; Re 21:17). Who can add to his height (M't 6:27; Lu 12:25).
CUCKOO, a bird. Forbidden as food (Le 11:16; De 14:15).
CUCUMBER (Nu 11:5; Isa 1:8).
CUD, chewing of, was one of the facts by which clean and unclean animals

were distinguished (Le 11:3-8; De 14:3-8).

CUMMIN, a plant bearing a small aromatic seed (Isa 28:25, 27; M't 23:23).

CUNEIFORM, a system of writing by symbolic wedge-shaped characters upon clay tablets used chiefly in the Mesopotamian area in ancient times. More than half a million such clay tablets have been found.

CUP (Ge 40:11; 2Sa 12:3; 1Ki 7:26; M't 23:25). Made of silver (Ge 44:2); gold (1Ch 28:17; Jer 52:19). Used in the institution of the Lord's Supper (M't 26:27; M'k 14:23; Lu 22:20; 1Co 10:21). Of the table of devils (1Co 10:21).

Figurative: Of sorrow (Ps 11:6; 73:10; 75:8; Isa 51:17, 22; Jer 25:15-28; Eze 23:31-34; M't 20:22, 23; 26:39; M'k 14:36; Lu 22:42; Joh 18:11; Re 14:10). Of consolation (Jer 16:7). Of joy (Ps 23:5). Of salvation (Ps 116:13).

CUPBEARER, palace official who served wine at a king's table (Ge 40:11; 1Ki 10:5; 2Ch 9:4; Ne 1:11).

CUPIDITY (See Avarice; Covetousness; Lust.)

CURES, miraculous. (See Miracles; Diseases; Physician.)

CURIOSITY. Insatiable (Pr 27:20). Advised against (Ec 7:21).

Instances of: Of Eve (Ge 3:6). Of Abraham, to know whether God would destroy the righteous in Sodom (Ge 18:23-32). Of Jacob, to know the name of the angel (Ge 32:29). Of the Israelites, to see God (Ex 19:21, 24); to witness the offering in the holy of holies (Nu 4:19, 20). Of Manoah, to know the name of an angel (J'g 13:17, 18). Of the people of Beth-shemish, to see inside the ark (1Sa 6:19). Of the Babylonians, to see Hezekiah's treasures (2Ki 20:13). Of Daniel, to know a vision (Da 12:8, 9). Of Peter, to know what was being done with Jesus (M't 26:58); to know what John would be appointed to do (Joh 21:21, 22). A disciple, to know if there be few that be saved (Lu 13:23). Of Herod, to see Jesus (Lu 9:9; 23:8). Of the Jews, to see Lazarus, after he was raised from the dead (Joh 12:9); and to see Jesus (Joh 12:20, 21). Of the disciples, to know whether Jesus would restore the kingdom of the Jews (Ac 1:6, 7). Of the Athenians, to hear some new thing (Ac 17:19-21). Of angels, to look into the mysteries of salvation (1Pe 1:12).

CURSE. Denounced against, the serpent (Ge 3:14, 15); Adam and Eve (Ge 3:15-19); the ground (Ge 3:17, 18); Cain (Ge 4:11-16); Canaan, Ham's son (Ge 9:24-27); the disobedient (De 28:15-68; Jer 11:31); Meroz (J'g 5:23); Gehazi (2Ki 5:27). Barak commands Balaam to curse Israel (Nu 22:6; 23:11).

See Benedictions.

Paternal (Ge 27:12, 13; 49:5-7). Of the Mosaic law (De 27:15-26; Jos 8:30-34). Assumed for others (M't 27:25). Paul wishes he could assume for Israel (Ro 9:3). See Blessings.

Christ assumed curse of Mosaic law for us (Ga 3:13). See Jesus, Vicarious death.

CURSING. Of parents (Ex 21:17; M't 15:4; M'k 7:10). Shimei curses David (2Sa 16:5-8). The precepts of Jesus concerning (M't 5:44; Lu 6:28). Apostolic (Ro 12:14).

See Anathema Maran-atha; Blasphemy; God, Name of, Not to Be Profaned; Oath.

CURTAINS. For tabernacle (Ex 26; 27:9-18; 36:8-18). In the palace of Ahasuerus (Es 1:6).

See Tabernacle; Tapestry.

Figurative: Isa 40:22; 54:2; Jer 4:20; 10:20; 49:29.

CUSH. 1. Son of Ham (Ge 10:6-8; 1Ch 1:8-10).

2. A Benjamite, title of (Ps 7).

3. Land of (Ge 2:13; Ps 68:31; Isa 18:1). See Ethiopia.

CUSHAN, poetic form of Cush (Hab 3:7). See Ethiopia.

CUSHI. 1. A messenger, who brought tidings to David (2Sa 18:21-32).

2. Father of Shelemiah (Jer 36:14).

3. Father of Zephaniah (Zep 1:1).

CUSTOM, when not referring to a tax, usually means "manner," "way," or "statute" (Ge 31:35; J'g 11:39; Jer 32:11). In NT it means "manner," "usage" (Lu 1:9; Ac 6:14), and "religious practices."

CUSTOM, RECEIPT OF. The Romans imposed tribute or taxes upon the Jews as upon all their subjects for the maintenance of their provincial government. Matthew was a tax collector or publican, and left his work to follow Jesus (M't 9:9).

CUTH, called also Cuthah. A district of Asia, from which colonists were transported to Samaria (2Ki 17:24-30; Ezr 4:10).

CUTTINGS (cuttings in the flesh), a heathen practice, including tattooings, gashes, castrations, etc., usually done in mourning for the dead and to propitiate deities, but forbidden to the Israelites (Le 19:28; 21:5; De 14:1; Jer 16:6).

CYLINDER SEALS, a cylinder, measuring from 1-½ to 3 inches long and usually made of clay, on which inscriptions were made.

CYMBAL, a musical instrument. Of brass (1Ch 15:19, 28; 1Co 13:1). Used in the tabernacle service (2Sa 6:5; 1Ch 13:8; 15:16, 19, 28); in the temple service (2Ch 5:12, 13; 1Ch 16:5, 42; 25:1, 6; Ps 150:5). Used on special occasions: Day of atonement (2Ch 29:25); laying of the foundation of the second temple (Ezr 3:10, 11); dedication of the wall (Ne 12:27, 36).

CYPRESS (Isa 44:14; Song 1:14 (marg.); Song 4:13 (marg.). R.V. Henna).

CYPRUS (copper). An island (Ac 21:3; 27:4). Barnabas born in (Ac 4:36). Persecuted Jews preached the gospel at (Ac 11:19, 20). Visited by Barnabas and Saul (Ac 13:4-12). Barnabas and Mark visit (Ac 15:39). Mnason, a disciple of (Ac 21:16).

CYRENE, CYRENIAN (wall), city in N Africa, W of Egypt, c. 10 miles from the coast. Originally a Greek city, it passed into the hands of the Romans. Simon, who helped Jesus carry His cross, came from there (Lu 23:26). People from Cyrene were in Jerusalem on the day of Pentecost (Ac 2:10). Jews from the synagogue of the Cyrenians disputed with Stephen (Ac 6:9).

CYRENIUS, governor of Syria (Lu 2:2).

CYRUS, king of Persia. Issues a decree for the emancipation of the Jews and rebuilding the temple (2Ch 36:22, 23; Ezr 1; 3:7; 4:3; 5:13, 14; 6:3). Prophecies concerning (Isa 13:17-22; 21:2; 41:2; 44:28; 45:1-4, 13; 46:11; 48:14, 15).

D

DABAREH (See Daberath.)

DABBASHETH, a place on the boundary line of Zebulun (Jos 19:11).

DABERATH, called also Dabareh. A town of Issachar (Jos 19:12; 21:28). Assigned to the Levites (1Ch 6:72).

DAGGER, a short sword (J'g 3:16-22).

DAGON (fish?), pagan deity with body of fish, head and hands of man. Probably god of agriculture. Worshiped in Mesopotamia and Canaan; temples in Ashdod (1Sa 5:1-7). Gaza (J'g 16:21-30), and in Israel (1Ch 10:10). Samson destroyed the temple in Gaza (J'g 16:30).

DAILY SACRIFICE, THE. Ordained in Mount Sinai (Nu 28:6). A lamb as a burnt offering morning and evening (Ex 29:38, 39; Nu 28:3, 4). Doubled on the sabbath (Nu 28:9, 10).

Required to be: With a meat and drink offering (Ex 29:40, 41; Nu 28:5-8). Slowly and entirely consumed (Le 6:9-12). Perpetually observed (Ex 29:42; Nu 28:3, 6). Peculiarly acceptable (Nu 28:8; Ps 141:2). Secured God's presence and favor (Ex 29:43, 44). Times of offering, were seasons of prayer (Ezr 9:5; Da 9:20, 21; w Ac 3:1). Restored after the captivity (Ezr 3:3). The abolition of, foretold (Da 9:26, 27; 11:31).

Illustrative of: Christ (Joh 1:29, 36; 1Pe 1:19). Acceptable prayer (Ps 141:2).

DALAIAH (See Delaiah.)

DALE, THE KING'S. 1. Place near Jerusalem where Abram met Melchizedek (Ge 14:17).

2. Absalom's memorial (2Sa 18:18).

DALMANUTHA, a town on the W coast of the Sea of Galilee (M'k 8:10).

DALMATIA (deceitful), province on NE shore of Adriatic Sea called also Illyricum (Ro 15:19; 2Ti 4:10).

DALPHON, son of Haman (Es 9:7).

DAMAGES AND COMPENSATIONS. Enumerated (Nu 5:5-8). For assault (Ex 21:18, 19, 22). For personal injury (Ex 21:28-34). For deception (Le 6:1-5). For slander (De 22:13-19). For seduction (De 22:28, 29).

See Fine.

DAMARIS, a female convert of Athens (Ac 17:34).

DAMASCUS. An ancient city (Ge 14:15; 15:2). Capital of Syria (1Ki 20:34; Isa 7:8; Jer 49:23-29; Eze 47:16, 17). Laid under tribute to David (2Sa 8:5, 6). Besieged by Rezon (1Ki 11:23, 24). Recovered by Jeroboam (2Ki 14:28). Taken by king of Assyria (2Ki 16:9). Walled (Jer 49:27; 2Co 11:33). Garrisoned (2Co 11:32). Luxury in (Am 3:12). Paul's experiences in (Ac 9; 22:5-16; 26:12-20; 2Co 11:32; Ga 1:17).

Prophecies concerning (Isa 8:4; 17:1, 2; Jer 49:23-29; Am 1:3, 5; Zec 9:1).

Wilderness of (1Ki 19:15).

See Syria.

DAMNATION, when referring to the future it means primarily eternal separation from God with accompanying awful punishments (M't 5:29; 10:28; 23:33; 24:51). The severity of the punishment is determined by the degree of sin (Lu 12:36-48), and is eternal (Isa 66:24; M'k 3:29; 2Th 1:9; Jude 6, 7).

DAN. 1. Fifth son of Jacob and Bilhah (Ge 30:6; 35:25). Descendants of (Ge 46:23; Nu 26:42, 43). See Tribe of, below. Blessed of Jacob (Ge 49:16, 17).

2. Tribe of: Census of (Nu 1:39; 26:42, 43). Inheritance of, according to the allotment of Joshua (Jos 19:40-47); of Ezekiel (Eze 48:1). Position of, in journey and camp, during the exodus (Nu 2:25, 31; 10:25). Blessed by Moses (De 33:22). Fail to conquer the Amorites (J'g 1:34, 35). Conquests by (Jos 19:47; J'g 18:27-29). Deborah upbraids, for cowardice (J'g 5:17). Idolatry of (J'g 18). Commerce of (J'g 5:17; Eze 27:19).

See Israel, Tribes of.

3. A city of the tribe of Dan. Called also Laish, and Leshem (Ge 14:14; De 34:1; J'g 20:1; Jer 8:16). Captured by the people of Dan (Jos 19:47). Idolatry established at (J'g 18; 1Ki 12:28, 29; Am 8:14). Captured by Ben-hadad (1Ki 15:20; 2Ch 16:4).

DANCING. Of children (Job 21:11). Of women (Ex 15:20; J'g 11:34; 21:19-21; 1Sa 18:6; 21:11). Of David (2Sa 6:14-16; 1Ch 15:29).

In the market-place (M't 11:16, 17). At feasts (J'g 21:19-21; M't 14:6; M'k 6:22; Lu 15:23-25). As a religious ceremony (Ps 149:3; 150:4). Idolatrous (Ex 32:19, 25).

Figurative: Of joy (Ps 30:11; Ec 3:4; Jer 31:4 13; La 5:15).

DANIEL (God is my judge). 1. A Jewish captive, called also Belteshazzar. Educated at king's court (Da 1). Interprets visions (Da 2; 4; 5). Promotion and executive authority of (Da 2:48, 49; 5:11, 29; 6:2). Conspiracy against, cast into the lions' den (Da 6).

Prophecies of (Da 4:8, 9; 7-12; M't 24:15).

Abstinence of (Da 1:8-16). Wisdom of (Da 1:17; Eze 28:3). Devoutness of (Da 2:18; 6; 9; 10; 12; Eze 14:14). Courage and fidelity of (Da 4:27; 5:17-23; 6:10-23). Worshiped by Nebuchadnezzar (Da 2:6).

2. David's son. Called also Chileab (2Sa 3:3; 1Ch 3:1).

3. A descendant of Ithamar, and a companion of Ezra (Ezr 8:2; Ne 10:6).

DANIEL, BOOK OF, a prophetic book which stands among the "writings" in the Hebrew OT (which consists of "the law, prophets, and writings") because while he had the gift of a prophet (M't 24:15), his position was that of a governmental official. The book is apocalyptic in character and abounds in symbolic and figurative language, and as a result it has been subject to many different interpretations. The first half of the book (chs. 1-6) consists of six narratives on the life of Daniel and his friends; their education, his revelation of Nebuchadnezzar's dream-image, the trial by a fiery furnace, his prediction of Nebuchadnezzar's madness, his interpretation of the handwriting on the wall, and his ordeal in the lion's den. The second half (7-12) consists of four apocalyptic visions, predicting the course of world history. There are references to the book in the NT (M't 24:15; Lu 1:19, 26; Heb 11:33, 34). Chs. 2:4b-7:28 are composed in Aramaic; the rest is in Hebrew. His book was designed to inspire Jewish exiles with confidence in Jehovah (4:34-37).

DAN-JAAN, place, probably in Dan, covered by David's census (2Sa 24:6).

DANNAH, a city in the mountains of Judah (Jos 15:49).

DARA (See Darda.)

DARDA, called also Dara. A famous wise man (1Ki 4:31; 1Ch 2:6).

DARIC, Persian gold coin used in Palestine after the return from the captivity (Ezr 2:69; Ne 7:70-72 ASV, RSV). Worth c. $5.00.

DARIUS, a common name for Medo-Persian rulers. 1. Darius the Mede (Gubaru), son of Ahasuerus (Da 5:31; 9:1); made governor of Babylon by Cyrus, but he seems to have ruled for only a brief time (Da 10:1; 11:1); prominent in the Book of Daniel (6:1, 6, 9, 25, 28; 11:1).

2. Darius Hystaspes, 4th and greatest of the Persian rulers (521-486 B.C.); reorganized government into satrapies and extended boundaries of empire; great builder; defeated by Greeks at Marathon 490 B.C.; renewed edict of Cyrus and helped rebuild the temple (Ezr 4:5, 24; 5:5-7; 6:1-12; Hag 1:1; 2:1, 10, 18; Zec 1:1, 7; 7:1). Died in 486 B.C. and was succeeded by Xerxes, grandson of Cyrus the Great.

3. Darius, the Persian, last king of Persia (336-330 B.C.); defeated by Alexander the Great in 330 B.C. (Ne 12:22). Some scholars identify him with Darius II (Nothus), who ruled Persia and Babylon (423-408 B.C.).

DARKNESS. Over the face of the earth (Ge 1:2; Job 38:9; Jer 4:23). Called Night (Ge 1:5). God creates (Isa 45:7). Miraculous: In Egypt (Ex 10:21, 22; Ps 105:28); at Sinai (Ex 20:21; Heb 12:18); at the crucifixion (M't 27:45; M'k 15:33).

Figurative: Of judgments (Pr 20:20; Isa 8:22; 13:10; Jer 4:28; 13:16; La 3:2; Eze 32:7, 8; Joe 2:2, 10; Am 4:13; 5:18, 20; 8:9; Mic 7:8; M't 24:29; M'k 13:24; Lu 23:45; Re 8:12; 9:2; 22:13; 25:30). Of powers of evil (Lu 22:53; Eph 6:12; Col 1:13; 1Th 5:5; Re 16:10).

Of the abode of the lost (M't 8:12; 22:13; 25:30).

Of spiritual blindness (Isa 9:2; 42:16; 50:10; M't 4:16; 6:22, 23; Lu 1:79; 11:34; Joh 1:5; 3:19-21; 8:12; 11:9, 10; Ac 26:18; Ro 1:21; 13:12, 13; 1Co 4:5; 2Co 4:6; 6:14; Eph 5:8, 11; 1Th 5:4, 5; 1Pe 2:9; 1Jo 1:5-7; 2:8-11). See Blindness, Spiritual.

Symbolic: Of divine inscrutability (2Sa 22:10-12; Ps 18:11; 97:2). On Mt.

Sinai (Ex 19:16; 20:21; De 4:11; 5:22; Heb 12:18). In the Sanctuary (1Ki 8:12; 2Ch 6:1). See Tabernacle, Most Holy Place.

DARKON, descendant of Solomon's servant, Jaala, who returned with Zerubbabel from exile (Ezr 2:56; Ne 7:58).

DART, a light javelin (Nu 25:7; 1Sa 18:10; 2Sa 18:14; Job 41:29).

Figurative: Eph 6:16.

DATE, a fruit (2Ch 31:5 [marg.])

DATHAN, a conspirator against Moses (Nu 16:1-35; 26:9; De 11:6; Ps 106:17).

DAUGHTER, a word of various uses in the Bible, it refers to both persons and things, often without regard to kinship or sex. 1. Daughter (Ge 11:29) or female descendant (Ge 24:48).

2. Women in general (Ge 28:6; Nu 25:1).

3. Worshipers of the true God (Ps 45:10; Isa 62:11; M't 21:5; Joh 12:15).

4. City (Isa 37:22).

5. Citizens (Zec 2:10).

DAUGHTER-IN-LAW. *Filial:* Instance of, Ruth (Ru 1:11-18; 4:15).

Unfilial: Prophecy of (Mic 7:6; M't 10:35).

DAVID (beloved, Chieftain). 1. King of Israel. Genealogy of (Ru 4:18-22; 1Sa 16:11; 17:12; 1Ch 2:3-15; M't 1:1-6; Lu 3:31-38). A shepherd (1Sa 16:11). Kills a lion and a bear (1Sa 17:34-36). Anointed king, while a youth, by the prophet Samuel, and inspired (1Sa 16:1, 13; Ps 89:19-37). Chosen of God (Ps 78:70).

Described to Saul (1Sa 16:18). Detailed as armorbearer and musician at Saul's court (1Sa 16:21-23). Slays Goliath (1Sa 17). Love of Jonathan for (1Sa 18:1-4). Popularity and discreetness of (1Sa 18). Saul's jealousy of (1Sa 18:8-30). Is defrauded of Merab, and given Michal to wife (1Sa 18:17-27). Jonathan intercedes for (1Sa 19:1-7). Probably writes Psalm 11 at this period of his life.

Conducts a campaign against, and defeats, the Philistines (1Sa 19:8). Saul attempts to slay him; he escapes to Ramah, and dwells at Naioth, whither Saul pursues him (1Sa 19:9-24). About this time writes Psalm 59. Returns, and Jonathan makes covenant with him (1Sa 20). Escapes by way of Nob, where he obtains shewbread and Goliath's sword from Abimelech (1Sa 21:1-6; M't 12:3, 4); to Gath (1Sa 21:10-15). At this time probably writes Psalms 34, 35, 52, 56, 120. Recruits an army of insurgents, goes to Moab, returns to Hareth (1Sa 22). Probably writes Psalms 17, 58, 64, 109, 142. Saves Keilah (1Sa 23:1-13). Makes second covenant with Jonathan (1Sa 23:16-18). Goes to the wilderness of Ziph, is betrayed to Saul (1Sa 23:13-26). Writes a psalm on the betrayal (Ps 54), and probably Psalms 22, 31, 140. Saul is diverted from pursuit of (1Sa 23:27, 28). At this time probably writes Psalm 12. Goes to En-gedi (1Sa 23:29). Refrains from slaying Saul (1Sa 24). Writes Psalm 57. Covenants with Saul (1Sa 26). Marries Nabal's widow, Abigail, and Ahinoam (1Sa 25). Dwells in the wilderness of Ziph, has opportunity to slay Saul, but takes his spear only, Saul is contrite (1Sa 26). Flees to Achish and dwells in Ziklag (1Sa 27). List of men who join him (1Ch 12:1-22). Conducts an expedition against Amalekites, misstates the facts to Achish (1Sa 27:8-12). At this time probably writes Psalm 141. Is refused permission to accompany the Philistines to battle against the Israelites (1Sa 28:1, 2; 29). Rescues the people of Ziklag, who had been captured by the Amalekites (1Sa 30). Probably writes Psalm 13. Death and burial of Saul and his sons (1Sa 31; 2Sa 21:1-14). Slays the murderer of Saul (2Sa 1:1-16). Lamentation over Saul (2Sa 1:17-27).

After dwelling one year and four months at Ziklag (1Sa 27:7), goes to Hebron, and is anointed king by Judah (2Sa 2:1-4, 11; 5:5; 1Ki 2:11; 1Ch 3:4; 11:1-3). List of those who join him at Hebron (1Ch 12:23-40). Ish-bosheth, son of Saul, crowned (2Sa 2-4). David wages war against, and defeats, Ish-bosheth (2Sa 2:13-32; 3:4). Demands the restoration of Michal, his wife (2Sa 3:14-16). Abner revolts from Ish-bosheth, and joins David, but is slain by Joab (2Sa 3). Punishes Ish-bosheth's murderers (2Sa 4).

Anointed king over all Israel, after reigning over Judah at Hebron seven years and six months, and reigns thirty-three years (2Sa 2:11; 5:5; 1Ch 3:4;

11:1-3; 12:23-40; 29:27). Makes conquest of Jerusalem (2Sa 5:6; 1Ch 11:4-8; Isa 29:1). Builds a palace (2Sa 5:11; 2Ch 2:3). Friendship of, with Hiram, king of Tyre (2Sa 5:11; 1Ki 5:1). Prospered of God (2Sa 5:10, 12; 1Ch 11:9). Fame of (1Ch 14:17). Philistines make war against, and are defeated by him (2Sa 5:17, 25).

Assembles thirty thousand men to escort the ark to Jerusalem with music and thanksgiving (2Sa 6:1-5). Uzzah is stricken when he attempts to steady the ark (2Sa 6:6-11). David is terrified, and leaves the ark at the house of Obed-edom (2Sa 6:9-11). After three months brings the ark to Jerusalem with dancing and great joy (2Sa 6:12-16; 1Ch 13). Organized the tabernacle service (1Ch 9:22; 15:16-24; 16:4-6, 37-43). Offers sacrifice, distributes gifts, and blesses the people (2Sa 6:17-19). Michal upbraids him for his religious enthusiasm (2Sa 6:20-23). Desires to build a temple, is forbidden, but receives promise that his seed should reign forever (2Sa 7:12-16; 23:5; 1Ch 17:11-14; 2Ch 6:16; Ps 89:3, 4; 132:11, 12; Ac 15:16; Ro 15:12). Interpretation and fulfillment of this prophecy (Ac 13:22, 23). At this time, probably, writes Psalms 15, 16, 24, 101, 138. Conquers the Philistines, Moabites, and Syria (2Sa 8).

Treats Mephibosheth, the lame son of Jonathan, with great kindness (2Sa 9:6; 19:24-30). Sends commissioners with a message of sympathy to Hanun, son of the king of Ammon; the message misinterpreted, and commissioners treated with indignity; David retaliates by invading his kingdom, and defeating the combined armies of the Ammonites and Syrians (2Sa 10; 1Ch 19). Probably writes Psalms 18, 20, 21.

Commits adultery with Bath-sheba (2Sa 11:2-5). Wickedly causes the death of Uriah (2Sa 11:6-25). Takes Bath-sheba to be his wife (2Sa 11:26, 27). Is rebuked by the prophet Nathan (2Sa 12:1-14). Repents of his crime and confesses his guilt (Ps 6; 32; 38; 39; 40; 51). Is chastised with grievous affliction on account of his crime (Ps 38; 41; 69). Death of his infant son by Bath-sheba (2Sa 12:15-23). Solomon is born to (2Sa 12:24, 25).

Ammonites defeated and tortured (2Sa 12:26-31). Amnon's crime, his murder by Absalom, and Absalom's flight (2Sa 13). Absalom's return (2Sa 14:1-24). Absalom's usurpation (2Sa 14; 15). David's flight from Jerusalem (2Sa 15:13-37). He probably writes, at this time Pss 5, 7, 26, 61, 69, 70, 86, 143. Shimei curses him (2Sa 16). Crosses the Jordan (2Sa 17:21-29). Absalom's defeat and death (2Sa 18). Laments the death of Absalom (2Sa 18:33; 19:1-4). Upbraided by Joab (2Sa 19:5-7). David upbraids the priests for not showing loyalty amid the murmurings of the people against him (2Sa 19:9-15). Shimei sues for clemency (2Sa 19:16-23). Mephibosheth sues for the king's favor (2Sa 19:24-30). Barzillai rewarded (2Sa 19:31-40). Judah accused by the ten tribes of stealing him away (2Sa 19:41-43). Returns to Jerusalem (2Sa 20:1-3). At this time, probably, composes Psalms 27, 66, 122, 144.

Sheba's conspiracy against David, and his death (2Sa 20). Makes Amasa general (2Sa 19:13). Amasa is slain (2Sa 20:4-10). Consigns seven sons of Saul to the Gibeonites to be slain to atone for Saul's persecution of the Gibeonites (2Sa 21:1-14). Buries Saul's bones, and his sons' (2Sa 21:12-14).

Defeats the Philistines (2Sa 21:15-22; 1Ch 20:4-8). Takes the military strength of Israel without divine authority, and is reproved (2Sa 24; 1Ch 21; 27:24). Probably composes Psalms 30, 131. Marries Abishag (1Ki 1:1-4). Probably composes Psalms 19, 111.

Reorganizes the tabernacle service (1Ch 22-26; 2Ch 7:6; 8:14; 23:18; 29:27-30; 35:15; Ezr 3:10; 8:20).

Adonijah usurps the scepter, Solomon appointed to the throne (1Ki 1; 1Ch 23:1). Delivers his charge to Solomon (1Ki 2:1-11; 1Ch 22:6-19; 28; 29). Probably composes Psalms 23, 145.

Last words of (2Sa 23:1-7). Death of (1Ki 2:10; 1Ch 29:28; Ac 2:29, 30). Sepulchre of (Ac 2:29). Age of, at death (2Sa 5:4, 5; 1Ch 29:28). Length of reign, forty years (1Ki 2:11; 1Ch 29:27, 28).

Wives of (2Sa 3:2-5; 11:3, 27; 1Ch 3:5). Children born at Hebron (2Sa 3:2-5; 1Ch 3:4); at Jerusalem (2Sa 5:14-16; 1Ch 3:5-8; 14:4-7). Descendants of (1Ch 3).

Civil and military officers of (2Sa 8:16-18). See Cabinet.

Lists of his heroes, and of their exploits (2Sa 23; 1Ch 11; 12:23-40).

Devoutness of (1Sa 13:14; 2Sa 6:5, 14-18; 7:18-29; 8:11; 24:25; 1Ki 3:14; 1Ch 17:16-27; 29:10; 2Ch 7:17; Zec 12:8; Pss 6; 7; 11; 13; 17; 22; 26; 27:7-14; 28; 31; 35; 37; 38; 39; 40:11-17; 42; 43; 51; 54; 55; 56; 57; 59; 60; 61; 62; 64:1-6; 66; 69; 70; 71; 86; 101; 108; 120:1, 2; 140; 141; 142; 143; 144; Ac 13:22).

Justice in the administration of (2Sa 8:15; 1Ch 18:14). Discreetness of (1Sa 18:14, 30). Meekness of (1Sa 24:7; 26:11; 2Sa 16:11; 19:22, 23). Merciful (2Sa 19:23).

David as musician (1Sa 16:21-23; 1Ch 15:16; 23:5; 2Ch 7:6; 29:26; Ne 12:36; Am 6:5); poet (2Sa 22); See Psalms of David; prophet (2Sa 23:2-7; 1Ch 28:19; M't 22:41-46; Ac 2:25-38; 4:25).

Type of Christ (Pss 2; 16; 18:43; 69:7-9, 20, 21, 26, 29; 89:19-37). Jesus called son of (M't 9:27; 12:23; 15:22; 20:30, 31; 21:9; 22:42; M'k 10:47, 48; Lu 18:37, 39).

Prophecies concerning him and his kingdom (Nu 24:17, 19; 2Sa 7:11-16; 1Ch 17:9-14; 22; 2Ch 6:5-17; 13:5; 21:7; Ps 89:19-37; Isa 9:7; 16:5; 22:20-25; Jer 23:5; 33:15-26; Lu 1:32, 33).

Chronicles of, written by Samuel, Nathan, and Gad (1Ch 29:29, 30).

2. A prophetic name for Christ (Jer 30:9; Eze 34:23, 24; 37:24, 25; Ho 3:5).

DAVID, CITY OF. 1. Portion of Jerusalem occupied by David in 1003 B.C.; 2500 feet above sea-level. Originally a Canaanite city (Eze 16:3), it dates back to the 3rd millennium. Solomon enlarged the City of David for the temple and other buildings, and later kings enlarged the city still more (2Ch 32:4, 5, 30; 2Ki 20:20; Isa 22:9-11).

2. Bethlehem (Lu 2:11).

DAY. A creative period (Ge 1:5, 8, 13, 19, 23, 31; 2:2). Divided into twelve hours (Joh 11:9). Prophetic (Da 8:14, 26; 12:11, 12; Re 9:15; 11:3; 12:6). Six working days ordained (Ex 20:9; Eze 46:1). Sixth day of the week called preparation day (M'k 15:42; Joh 19:14, 31, 42). First day of the week called the Lord's day (Re 1:10). With the Lord as a thousand years (2Pe 3:8).

Day's journey, eighteen or twenty miles (Ex.3:18; 1Ki 19:4; Jon 3:4). Sabbath day's journey, about two thousand paces (Ac 1:12). The seventh of the week ordained as a day of rest; See Sabbath.

DAY OF ATONEMENT, an annual Hebrew feast when the high priest offered sacrifices for the sins of the nation (Le 23:27; 25:9). It was the only fast period required by Mosaic law (Le 16:29; 23:31). It was observed on the 10th day of the 7th month; a day of great solemnity and strictest conformity to the law.

DAY OF CHRIST. The period connected with reward and blessing at the coming of Christ for believers (1Co 1:8; 5:5; 2Co 1:14; Ph'p 1:6, 10; 2:16). Note: 2Th 2:2 is correctly translated "The day of the Lord," signifying a time of judgment. See below.

DAY OF THE LORD. The period commencing with the second advent of Christ and terminating with the making of a new heaven and a new earth (Isa 65:17-19; 66:22; 2Th 2:2; 2Pe 2:13; Re 21:1). Preceded and introduced by apocalyptic judgments (Re 4:1-19:6).

DAY'S JOURNEY. Eighteen or twenty miles (Ex 3:18; 1Ki 19:4; Jon 3:4). Sabbath day's journey, about two thousand paces (Ac 1:12).

DAYSMAN (to act as umpire), a mediator or arbitrator (Job 9:33). In Job it means that no human being is worthy of acting as a judge of God.

DAYSPRING (to break forth), poetic name for dawn (Job 38:12).

DAYSTAR (light-giving), the planet Venus; seen as a morning star, heralding the dawn (Isa 14:12; 2Pe 1:19; Re 22:16).

DEACON, an ecclesiastic charged with the temporal affairs of the church. Ordained by the apostles (Ac 6:1-6). Qualifications of (1Ti 3:8-13). The Greek word translated deacon signifies servant, and is so translated in M't 23:11; Joh 12:26. Also translated minister (M'k 10:43; 1Co 3:5; 1Th 3:2).

DEACONESS (Ro 16:1 [*R. V.* marg.]).

DEAD. Raised to life, instances of: Son of the widow of Zarephath (1Ki 17:17-23); Shunammite's son (2Ki 4:32-37); young man laid in Elisha's sepulchre (2Ki 13:21); widow's son (Lu 7:12-15); Jairus' daughter (Lu 8:49-55); Lazarus (Joh 11:43, 44); Dorcas (Ac 9:37-40); Eutychus (Ac 20:9-12; see Heb 11:35). Prepared for burial by washing (Ac 9:37); anointing (M't 26:12); wrapping in linen (M't 27:59). Burned. See Cremation.

Burnings of incense made for (2Ch 16:14; 21:19; Jer 34:5).

See Burial; Cremation; Embalming.

Preparation for burial: by washing (Ac 9:37); by anointing (M't 26:12); by wrapping in linen (M't 27:59). Incense burnt for (2Ch 16:14; 21:19; Jer 34:5).

Pictured as, rest (Job 3:13-19); sleep (Job 14:11-15, 21; Da 12:12); hopelessness (Job 17:13-15; Ec 9:5, 6; Eze 32:27, 30); separation from God (Ps 6:5; 30:9; 88:10-12; 115:17).

Life after (Job 14:12-15; Ps 49:15; Da 12:2; Lu 20:35, 36; Joh 11:25). Cognizance after (Eze 32:31; Lu 16:19-31).

Abode of: the pit (Job 17:13-15); Abraham's bosom (Lu 16:22); hell (Lu 16:23); paradise (Lu 23:43).

Figurative of lack of understanding (Pr 21:16).

See Burial; Death; Mourning; Resurrection; Righteous, Promises to; Wicked, Punishment of.

DEAD SEA, lies southeast of Jerusalem. Called Salt Sea (Ge 14:3; Nu 34:12); Sea of the Plain (De 3:17; 4:49; Jos 3:16); East Sea (Joe 2:20); Former Sea (Zec 14:8).

Prophecy concerning (Eze 47:7-10, 18).

DEAD SEA SCROLLS, discovered, in 1947, by Arabic Bedouin, in caves a mile or so W of the NW corner of the Dead Sea, at Qumran. So far MSS have been found in 11 caves, and they are mostly dated as coming from the last century B.C. and the first century A.D. At least 382 MSS are represented by the fragments of Cave Four alone, c. 100 of which are Biblical MSS. These include fragments of every book of the Hebrew Bible except Esther. Some of the books are represented in many copies. Not all the MSS are in fragments; some are complete or nearly complete. In addition to Biblical books, fragments of apocryphal and apocalyptic books, commentaries, Thanksgiving Psalms, and sectarian literature have been found. Near the caves are the remains of a monastery of huge size, the headquarters of a monastic sect of Jews called the Essenes. The discoveries at Qumran are important for Biblical studies in general. They are of great importance for a study of the OT text, both Hebrew and the LXX. They are also of importance in relation to the NT, as they furnish the background to the preaching of John the Baptist and Jesus. There is no evidence that either John the Baptist or Jesus was a member of the group.

DEAFNESS. Law concerning (Le 19:14). Inflicted by God (Ex 4:11). Miraculous cure of (M't 11:5; M'k 7:32; 9:25).

Figurative: Of moral insensibility (Isa 6:10; 29:18; 35:5; Eze 12:2; M't 13:15; Joh 12:40; Ac 28:26, 27).

See Blindness, Spiritual; Conscience, Dead; Impenitence; Obduracy.

DEATH, PHYSICAL. Universal to mankind (Ec 3:2, 19-21; Ro 5:12, 14; 1Pe 1:24). Time of, unknown (Ge 27:2; Ps 39:4, 13). Nearness to (Jos 23:14; 1Sa 20:3). Separates spirit and body (Ec 12:5, 7).

Does not end conscious existence (Lu 20:34-38; 23:39-43; Re 20:12, 13); exemplified in the appearance of Moses and Elijah at the transfiguration of Jesus (M't 17:2, 3; M'k 9:4, 5; Lu 9:30-33).

Not to be feared by the righteous (M't 10:28). Brings rest to the righteous (Job 3:13, 17-19). Dispossesses of earthly goods (Job 1:21; Ps 49:17; Lu 12:16-20; 1Ti 6:7).

A judgment (Ge 2:17; 3:19; 6:7, 11-13; 19:12, 13, 24, 25; Jos 5:4-6; 1Ch 10:13, 14). God's power over (De 32:39; 1Sa 2:6; Ps 68:20; 2Ti 1:10). Christ's power over (Heb 2:14, 15; Re 1:18). To be destroyed (Isa 25:8; Ho 13:14; 1Co 15:21, 22, 26, 55-57; Re 20:14; 21:4).

Preparation for (2Ki 20:1; Lu 12:35-37); by Moses (Nu 27:12-23); by David (1Ki 2:1-10); by Ahithophel (2Sa 17:23). Apostrophe to (Ho 13:14; 1Co 15:55).

Called Sleep (De 31:16; 1Ki 14:31; 15:8, 24; 16:6, 28; Job 7:21; 14:12; Ps 76:5, 6; Jer 51:39; Da 12:2; Joh 11:11; Ac 7:60; 13:36; 1Co 15:6, 18, 51; 1Th 4:13-15).

Described as: Giving up the ghost (Ge 25:8; 35:29; La 1:19; Ac 5:10). King of terrors (Job 18:14). A change (Job 14:14). Going to thy fathers (Ge 15:15; 25:8; 35:29). Putting off this tabernacle (2Pe 1:14). Requiring the soul (Lu 12:20). Going the way whence there is no return (Job 16:22). Being gathered to our people (Ge 49:33). In silence (Ps 94:17; 115:17). Returning to dust (Ge 3:19). Being cut down (Job 14:2). Fleeing as a shadow (Job 14:2). Departing (Ph'p 1:23).

Desired (Jer 8:3; Re 9:6). By Moses (Nu 11:15). By Elijah (1Ki 19:4). By Job (Job 3; 6:8-11; 7:1-3, 15, 16; 10:1). By Jonah (Jon 4:8). By Simeon (Lu 2:29). By Paul (2Co 5:2, 8; Ph'p 1:20-23).

Exemption from: Enoch (Ge 5:24; Heb 11:5). Elijah (2Ki 2). Promised to saints, when Christ returns for believers (1Co 15:51; 1Th 4:15, 17). No death in heaven (Lu 20:36; Re 21:4).

Inevitable (2Sa 14:14; Job 7:1, 8-10, 21; 10:21, 22; 14:2, 5, 7-12, 14, 19-21; 16:22; 21:23, 25, 26, 32, 33; 30:23; 34:15, 19; Ps 49:7-10; 82:7; 89:48; 144:4; Ec 2:14-18; 5:15; 8:8; 9:5, 10; Isa 51:12; Jer 9:21; Zec 1:5; Joh 9:4; Heb 9:27; 13:14; Jas 1:10, 11).

Of the Righteous: A transition (Lu 16:22; 23:43). Balaam extols (Nu 23:10). Peaceful (Ps 37:37). Precious in the sight of the Lord (Ps 116:15). A merciful providence in (Isa 57:1, 2). Anticipated with confidence (Pr 14:32; Lu 2:29; Ac 7:59; Ro 14:7, 8; 1Co 3:21-23; 2Co 5:1, 4, 8; 1Th 5:9, 10; 2Ti 4:6-8; Heb 11:13). Hope in (Da 12:13; 1Co 15:51-57; 2Co 1:9, 10; 1Th 4:13, 14; 2Pe 1:11, 14; Re 14:13).

Of the Wicked (Job 18:14, 18; 20:4, 5, 8, 11; 21:13, 17, 18, 23-26; 24:20, 24; 27:8, 19-23; Ps 37:1, 2, 9, 10, 35, 36; 49:7, 9, 10, 14, 17, 19, 20; Pr 5:22, 23; 11:7, 10; 21:16; Ec 8:10; Isa 14:11, 15). Sudden (Nu 16:32; Pr 10:25, 27; Isa 17:14; Ac 5:3-10). A judgment (Nu 16:29, 30; 1Sa 25:38; Job 36:12, 14, 18, 20; Ps 55:23; 58:9; 78:50; 92:7; Pr 2:22; 14:32; Isa 26:14; Jer 16:3, 4; Eze 28:8, 10; Am 9:10; Lu 12:20).

Scenes of: Of Jacob (Ge 49:1-33; Heb 11:21). Of Moses (De 34:1-7). Of Samson (J'g 16:25-30). Of Eli (1Sa 4:12-18). Of the wife of Phinehas (1Sa 4:19-21). Of Zechariah (2Ch 24:22). Of Jesus (M't 27:34-53; M'k 15:23-38; Lu 23:27-49; Joh 19:16-30). Of Stephen (Ac 7:59, 60).

Penalty: Shall not be remitted (Nu 35:31). In the Mosaic law the death penalty was inflicted for, murder (Ge 9:5, 6; Nu 35:16-21, 30-33; De 17:6); adultery (Le 20:10; De 22:24); incest (Le 20:11, 12, 14); bestiality (Ex 22:19; Le 20:15, 16); sodomy (Le 18:22; 20:13); rape of a betrothed virgin (De 22:25); perjury (Zec 5:4); kidnapping (Ex 21:16; De 24:7); upon a priest's daughter, who committed fornication (Le 21:9); witchcraft (Ex 22:18); offering human sacrifice (Le 20:2-5); striking or cursing father or mother (Ex 21:15, 17; Le 20:9); disobedience to parents (De 21:18-21); theft (Zec 5:3, 4); blasphemy (Le 24:23); Sabbath desecration (Ex 35:2; Nu 15:32-36); prophesying falsely or propagating false doctrines (De 13:1-10); sacrificing to false gods (Ex 22:20); refusing to abide by the decision of court (De 17:12); treason (1Ki 2:25; Es 2:23); sedition (Ac 5:36, 37).

Not inflicted on testimony of less than two witnesses (Nu 35:30; De 17:6; 19:15).

Modes of Execution of Death Penalty: Burning (Ge 38:24; Le 20:14; 21:9; Jer 29:22; Eze 23:25; Da 3:19-23). Stoning (Le 20:2, 27; Nu 14:10; 15:33-36; De 13:10; 17:5; 22:21, 24; Jos 7:25; 1Ki 21:10; Eze 16:40). Hanging (Ge 40:22; De 21:22, 23; Jos 8:29; Es 7:10). Beheading (M't 14:10; M'k 6:16, 27, 28). Crucifixion (M't 27:35, 38; M'k 15:24, 27; Lu 23:33). The sword (Ex 32:27, 28; 1Ki 2:25, 34, 46; Ac 12:2).

Executed, by the witnesses (De 13:9; 17:7; Ac 7:58); by the congregation (Nu 15:35, 36; De 13:9).

Figurative: (Ro 6:2-11; 7:1-11; 8:10, 11; Col 2:20; 2Ti 2:11. Symbolized: By the pale horse (Re 6:8).

See Dead; Regeneration; Spiritual Death; Second Death.

DEBIR. 1. King of Eglon (Jos 10:3-27).

2. A town in the mountains of Judah. Called also Kirjath-sannah, and Kirjath-sepher, which signifies a city of books (Jos 15:15, 16). Anakim expelled from, by Joshua (Jos 11:21). Taken by Othniel (Jos 15:15-17, 49; J'g 1:12, 13). Allotted to the Aaronites (Jos 21:15).

3. A place near the valley of Achor (Jos 15:7).

DEBORAH (bee). 1. Nurse to Rebecca (Ge 24:59). Buried beneath an oak under Beth-el (Ge 35:8).

2. The prophetess, a judge of Israel (J'g 4:4, 5; 5:7). Inspires Barak to defeat Sisera (J'g 4:6-16). Triumphant song of (J'g 5).

DEBT. Injunction against (Ro 13:8).

Security for: Warnings against becoming surety for others (Pr 11:15; 22:26). Raiment taken as, must be returned by sundown (Ex 22:25-27; De 24:10-13; Job 22:6; Am 2:8). Houses and property (Ne 5:3, 4). Children (Job 24:9). Millstones forbidden (De 24:6).

See Debtor; Creditor; Surety.

DEBTOR. Laws concerning (Ex 21:2-6; 22:10-15; Le 25:14-17, 25-41, 47-55; De 24:10-13; Ne 10:31; M't 5:25, 26, 40; 18:25). Sold for debt (2Ki 4:1-7; Ne 5:3-5; M't 18:25). Imprisoned for debt (M't 18:30). Oppressed (2Ki 4:1-7; Ne 5:3-5; Job 20:18, 19; M't 18:28-30). Mercy toward, enjoined (M't 18:23-27). Wicked (Lu 20:9-16).

See Creditor; Debt; Surety.

DECALOGUE (ten words). Written by God (Ex 24:12; 31:18; 32:16; De 5:22; 9:10; Ho 8:12). Divine authority of (Ex 20:1; 34:27, 28; De 5:4-22). Called Words of the Covenant (Ex 34:28; De 4:13). Tables of Testimony (Ex 31:18; 34:29; 40:20).

Enumerated (Ex 20:1-17; De 5:7-21).

Confirmed, by Jesus (M't 19:18, 19; 22:34-40; Lu 10:25-28); by Paul (Ro 13:8-10).

See Commandments.

DECAPOLIS (ten cities). Ten cities situated in one district on the east of the Sea of Galilee (M't 4:25; M'k 5:20; 7:31).

DECEIT. Is falsehood (Ps 119:118). The tongue an instrument of (Ro 3:13). Comes from the heart (M'k 7:22). Characteristic of the heart (Jer 17:9). God abhors (Ps 5:6). Forbidden (Pr 24:28; 1Pe 3:10). Christ was perfectly free from (Isa 53:9, w 1Pe 2:22).

Saints free from (Ps 24:4; Zep 3:13; Re 14:5); purpose against (Job 27:4); avoid (Job 31:5); shun those addicted to (Ps 101:7); pray for deliverance from those who use (Ps 43:1; 120:2); delivered from those who use (Ps 72:14); should beware of those who teach (Eph 5:6; Col 2:8); should lay aside, in seeking truth (1Pe 2:1). Ministers should lay aside (2Co 4:2; 1Th 2:3).

The wicked are full of (Ro 1:29); devise (Ps 35:20; 38:12; Pr 12:5); utter (Ps 10:7; 36:3); work (Pr 11:18); increase in (2Ti 3:13); use, to each other (Jer 9:5); use, to themselves (Jer 37:9; Ob 3:7); delight in (Pr 20:17).

False teachers are workers of (2Co 11:13); preach (Jer 14:14; 23:26); impose on others by (Ro 16:18; Eph 4:14); sport themselves with (2Pe 2:13). Hypocrites devise (Job 15:35). Hypocrites practice (Ho 11:12). False witnesses use (Pr 12:17). A characteristic of antichrist (2Jo 7). Characteristic of the apostasy (2Th 2:10).

Evil of: hinders knowledge of God (Jer 9:6). Keeps from turning to God (Jer 8:5). Leads to pride and oppression (Jer 5:27, 28), to lying (Pr 14:25). Often accompanied by fraud and injustice (Ps 10:7; 43:1). Hatred often concealed by (Pr 26:24-26). The folly of fools is (Pr 14:8). The kisses of an enemy are (Pr 27:6). Blessedness of being free from (Ps 24:4, 5; 32:2). Punishment of (Ps 55:23; Jer 9:7-9).

See Confidence, False; Deception; Falsehood; Flattery; Hypocrisy.

DECEPTION. *Instances of:* By Satan (Ge 3:4). Abraham, in stating that Sarah was his sister (Ge 12:13; 20:2). Isaac, in stating that his wife was his sister (Ge 26:7). Jacob and Rebekah, in imposing Jacob on his father, and Jacob's impersonating Esau (Ge 27:6-23). Jacob's sons, in entrapping the Shechemites (Ge 34:13-31); in representing to their father that Joseph had been destroyed by wild beasts (Ge 37:29-35). Joseph, in his ruse with his brethren (Ge 42-44). The Gibeonites, in misrepresenting their habitat (Jos 9:3-15). Ehud deceives Eglon, and slays him (J'g 3:15-30). Delilah deceives Samson (J'g 16:4-20). David feigns madness (1Sa 21:10-15). Amnon deceives Tamar by feigning sickness (2Sa 13:6-14). Hushai deceives Absalom (2Sa 16:15-19). Sanballat tries to deceive Nehemiah (Ne 6). By Absalom, when he avenged his sister (2Sa 13:24-28); when he began his conspiracy (2Sa 15:7). The old prophet (1Ki 13:18). Gehazi (2Ki 5:20).

Job's friends (Job 6:15). Doeg (Ps 52:2). Herod (M't 2:8). Pharisees (M't 22:16). Chief priests (M'k 14:1). Lawyer (Lu 10:25). Ananias and Sapphira (Ac 5:1).

See Deceit; Hypocrisy; Falsehood; False Witness.

Self: See Confidence, False; Flattery.

DECISION. *Injunctions concerning:* Choosing life (De 30:19). Cleaving unto the Lord (Jos 23:8; Ac 11:23). Serving the Lord (Jos 24:15; 1Sa 12:20; 1Ki 18:21; Isa 50:7; M't 6:24; 8:21, 22; Lu 9:59-62; 16:13; 1Co 15:58). Walking righteously (Jos 1:7; 2Ch 19:11; Pr 4:25-27; M't 4:17; 2Th 3:13; 1Ti 6:11-14; Heb 12:1; 1Pe 1:13; 2Pe 1:10). Abiding in Christ (Joh 15:4, 5, 7, 9; 1Jo 2:24, 28.

Steadfastness in: obedience (Joh 8:31; 1Co 15:58; Col 2:6, 7; 2Th 2:15, 17; 2Pe 3:17, 18; 2Jo 8); grace (Ac 13:43; 2Ti 2:1, 3); faith (Ac 14:22; 1Co 16:13; Ph'p 1:27; Col 1:23; Heb 3:6-8, 14; 4:14; 10:23, 35; 1Pe 5:8, 9; Jude 20, 21); Christian liberty (Ga 5); the Lord (Ph'p 4:1); holiness (1Th 3:8, 13); sound doctrine (Eph 4:14; 2Ti 1:13, 14; Tit 1:7, 9; Heb 2:1; 13:9, 13).

Instances of: Abel (Heb 11:4). Enoch (Heb 11:5, 6). Noah (Heb 11:7). Abraham (Heb 11:8, 17-19). Jacob (Ge 28:20-22). Joseph (Ge 39:9). Moses (Nu 12:7; Heb 3:5; 11:24-27). Israelites (Ex 19:7, 8; 24:3, 7; De 4:4; 5:27; 26:17; Jos 22:34; 24:21-25; 1Ki 19:18; 2Ki 11:17; 2Ch 11:16; 13:10, 11; 15:12, 15; 23:16; 29:10; Ezr 10:3-44; Ne 9:38; 10:28-31; Jer 34:15; 42:5, 6; 50:5; Ho 11:12). Levites (Ex 32:26). Caleb (Nu 14:6-10, 24; De 1:36; Jos 14:14). Balaam (Nu 22:15-18; 24:13). Phinehas (Nu 25:7-13). Joshua (Jos 24:15). Gideon (J'g 6:25-28). Ruth (Ru 1:16). Saul (1Sa 11:4-7). David (1Sa 17:32-37; 2Sa 22:22-24). Psalmist (Ps 17:3; 26:6, 11; 27:3-8; 40:9, 10; 56:12; 57:7, 8; 71:17; 86:11; 101:2, 3; 108:1; 116:9, 13, 14, 16; 119:8, 30, 31, 38, 44-46, 57, 94, 106, 115, 125, 145, 146). A prophet of Judah (1Ki 13:8-10). Elijah (1Ki 18:22). Jehoshaphat (1Ki 22:7, 8; 2Ch 18:6, 7). Micaiah (1Ki 22:13, 14; 2Ch 18:12, 13). Naaman (2Ki 5:13-17). Hezekiah (2Ki 18:6; 2Ch 15:17). Josiah (2Ki 22:2; 23:3, 25; 2Ch 34:31). Nehemiah (Ne 6:11; w chapters 2, 4, 5, 6). Esther (Es 4:16). Job (Job 2:9, 10). Daniel (Da 1:8). The three Hebrews (Da 3:11, 12, 16-18). Matthew (M't 9:9). Joseph (M'k 15:43). Nathanael (Joh 1:49). Martha (Joh 11:27). Disciples (Lu 18:28; Joh 6:68, 69; Ac 2:42). Paul (Ac 9:29; Ro 1:16; 8:38, 39; Ph'p 1:20, 21; 2Ti 4:7, 8). Church, of Ephesus (Re 2:2, 3); of Sardis (Re 3:4, 8, 10). Saints (Re 14:4).

See Character.

DECISION, VALLEY OF, place where God will some day gather all nations for judgment (Joe 3:2, 12, 14).

DECREE, an official ruling or law (Da 2:9; Es 1:20; Jon 3:7; Ac 16:4; Re 13:8).

DEDAN. 1. Son of Raamah (Ge 10:7; 1Ch 1:9).

2. Son of Jokshan (Ge 25:3; 1Ch 1:32).

3. A country, probably bordering on Edom (Jer 49:8; Eze 25:13; 27:15, 20; 38:13).

DEDANIM, descendants of Dedan (Isa 21:13).

DEDICATION. Law concerning dedicated things (Le 27; Nu 18:14; 1Ch 26:26, 27). Must be without blemish (Le 22:18-23; Mal 1:14). Not redeemable (Le 27:28, 29). Offering must be voluntary (Le 1:3; 22:19). See Offerings; Vows.

Of the tabernacle (Nu 7). Solomon's temple (1Ki 8; 2Ch 7:5). Second temple (Ezr 6:16, 17). Of the wall of Jerusalem (Ne 12:27-43). Of houses (De 20:5). Of Samuel by his mother (1Sa 1:11, 22).

Of Self. See Consecration.

For instances of liberality in dedicated things, see Liberality.

DEDICATION, FEAST OF, annual Jewish feast celebrating the restoration of the temple following its desecration by Antiochus Epiphanes. Jesus delivered a discourse at this feast (Joh 10:22ff).

DEED, to land (Jer 32:12, 14, 44).

See Land.

DEEP, the ocean (Ne 9:11), chaos (Ge 1:2), deepest part of sea (Ge 49:25), abyss (Lu 8:31; Re 9:1; 11:7).

DEER, called also, Fallow Deer, Hart, Hind, Roebuck. Designated among the clean animals, to be eaten (De 12:15; 14:5). Provided for Solomon's household (1Ki 4:23). Fleetness of (2Sa 2:18; 1Ch 12:8; Pr 6:5; Song 8:14; Isa 35:6). Surefootedness of (2Sa 22:34). Gentleness of (Pr 5:19).

DEFENSE, an argument made before a court. Of Jeremiah (Jer 26:12-16); Peter (Ac 4:8-13; 5:23-29); Stephen (Ac 7); Paul (Ac 22; 23:1-6; 24:10-21; 26:1-23).

Military defenses, see Fort; Armies.

DEFILEMENT. Laws relating to (Le 7:18-21; 11:43; 22:2-7). Caused by leprosy (Le 13:3, 44-46; 14; 22:4-7); gonorrhea (Le 15:1-15; 22:4); copulation (Le 15:17); spermatorrhea (Le 15:16, 17); childbirth (Le 12:2-8; Lu 2:22); menses (Le 15:19-33; 2Sa 11:4); touching the dead (Nu 19:11-22; 31:19, 20); touching carcass of any unclean animal (Le 11:39, 40; 17:15, 16; 22:8); touching carcass of an unclean thing (Le 5:2-13; 11:8, 24-28, 31-38; 14:46-57; 15:5-11; De 23:10, 11); slaying in battle (Nu 31:19, 20). Contact with sinners falsely supposed to cause (Joh 18:28).

Of priests (Le 16:26, 28; Nu 19:7-10; Eze 44:25, 26).

Egyptian usage, concerning (Ge 43:32).

See Ablution; Purification; Uncleanness.

DEFORMITY (See Blemish.)

DEGRADATION of God's people (Ex 32:25; Eze 16:6; 20:31; 2Pe 2:22).

DEGREES, or steps in the dial of Ahaz (2Ki 20:9-11). The word *degrees* occurs in the titles of Psalms 120 to 134, but the reason is uncertain. Also used to mean rank or order (1Ch 15:18; 17:17; Ps 62:9; Lu 1:52; Jas 1:9).

DEGREES, SONGS OF, title given Psalms 120-134. Uncertainty exists as to the origin of the title. Various theories are held.

DEHAVITES (Ezr 4:9).

DEKAR, father of one of Solomon's purveyors (1Ki 4:9).

DELAIAH (freed by Jehovah). 1. Descendant of David (1Ch 3:1-24).

2. Head of 23rd course of priests (1Ch 24:18).

3. Prince who tried to save Jeremiah's roll from destruction (Jer 36:12, 25).

4. Ancestor of tribe that returned under Zerubbabel (Ezr 2:60; Ne 7:62).

5. Father of Shemaiah (Ne 6:10).

DELIGHTING IN GOD: Commanded (Ps 37:4). Reconciliation leads to (Job 22:21, 26). Observing the sabbath leads to (Isa 58:13, 14).

Saints' Experience in: Communion with God (Song 2:3). The law of God (Ps 1:2; 119:24, 35). The goodness of God (Ne 9:25). The comforts of God (Ps 94:19).

Hypocrites: Pretend to (Isa 58:2). In heart despise (Job 27:10; Jer 6:10). Promises to (Ps 37:4). Blessedness of (Ps 112:1).

DELILAH (dainty one), Philistine woman who lured Samson to his ruin (J'g 16:4-20).

DELIVERANCE (See Affliction; God, Providence of; Prayer, Answered.)

DELIVERER, appellation of Jesus (Ro 11:26).

DELUGE (See Flood.)

DELUSION, SELF (See Self-delusion.)

DEMAGOGISM. *Instances of:* Absalom (2Sa 15:2-6). Pilate (M't 27:17-26; M'k 15:15; Lu 23:13-24; Joh 18:38-40; 19:6-13). Felix (Ac 24:27). Herod (Ac 12:3).

DEMAS (popular), fellow laborer with Paul (Col 4:14; Ph'm 24) who later deserted him (2Ti 4:10).

DEMETRIUS (belonging to Demeter). 1. Disciple praised by John (3Jo 12).

2. Silversmith at Ephesus who made trouble for Paul (Ac 19:23-27).

DEMONS. Worship of (Le 17:7; De 32:17; 2Ch 11:15; Ps 106:37; M't 4:9; Lu 4:7; 1Co 10:20, 21; 1Ti 4:1; Re 13:4). Worship of, forbidden (Le 17:7; Zec 13:2; Re 9:20).

Possession by, instances of: Saul (1Sa 16:14-23; 18:10, 11; 19:9, 10). Two men of the Gergesenes (M't 8:28-34; M'k 5:2-20). The dumb man (M't 9:32, 33). The blind and dumb man (M't 12:22; Lu 11:14). The daughter of the Syrophenician (M't 15:22-29; M'k 7:25-30). The lunatic child (M't 17:14-18; M'k 9:17-27; Lu 9:37-42). The man in the synagogue (M'k 1:23-26; Lu 4:33-35). Mary Magdalene (M'k 16:9; Lu 8:2, 3). The herd of swine (M't 8:30-32).

Cast out by Jesus (M't 4:24; 8:16; M'k 3:22; Lu 4:41).

Power over, given the disciples (M't 10:1; M'k 6:7; 16:17). Cast out by the disciples (M'k 9:38; Lu 10:17); by Peter (Ac 5:16); by Paul (Ac 16:16-18; 19:12); by Philip (Ac 8:7). Disciples could not expel (M'k 9:18, 28, 29). Sceva's sons exorcise (Ac 19:13-16). Parable of the man repossessed (M't 12:43-45).

Jesus falsely accused of being possessed of (M'k 3:22-30; Joh 7:20; 8:48; 10:20).

Testify to the divinity of Jesus (M't 8:29; M'k 1:23, 24; 3:11; 5:7; Lu 8:28; Ac 19:15).

Adversaries of men (M't 12:45). Sent to foment trouble between Abimelech and the Shechemites (J'g 9:23). Messages given false prophets by (1Ki 22:21-23).

Believe and tremble (Jas 2:19). To be judged at the general judgment (M't 8:29, w 2Pe 2:4; Jude 6).

Punishment of (M't 8:29; 25:41; Lu 8:28; 2Pe 2:4; Jude 6; Re 12:7-9).

See Satan.

DENARIUS (See Money.)

DENS, used as places of refuge (J'g 6:2; Heb 11:38; Re 6:15).

DENYING JESUS (See Jesus, Rejected.)

DEPRAVITY. Inherent in man (Ge 6:5-8; 8:21; Job 4:17-19; 9:2, 3, 20, 29-31; 11:12; 14:4; 15:14-16; 25:4-6; Ps 5:9; 51:5; 58:1-5; 94:11; 130:3; Pr 10:20; 20:6, 9; 21:8; Isa 1:5, 6; 51:1; Jer 13:23; 16:12; 17:9; Ho 6:7; Mic 7:2-4; M't 7:17; 12:34, 35; 15:19; M'k 7:21-23; Joh 3:19; 8:23; 14:17; Ro 1:21-32; 2:1; 6:6, 19, 20; 7:5, 11-15, 18-25; 8:5-8, 13; 1Co 2:14; 3:3; 5:9, 10; 2Co 5:14; Ga 5:17, 19-21; Eph 2:1-3, 12; 4:17-19, 22; Jas 4:5; 1Pe 1:18; 2:25; 1Jo 1:8, 10; 2:16).

Universal (Ge 6:11-13; 2Ch 6:36; Ps 14:1-3; 53:1-3; 143:2; Ec 7:20; Isa 53:6; 64:6; Mic 7:2-4; Ro 3:9-19, 23; 5:6, 12-14; 11:32; Ga 3:10, 11, 22; Jas 3:2; 1Jo 5:19).

See Fall of Man; Sin.

DEPUTY, an officer who administers the functions of a superior in his absence (1Ki 22:47; Ac 13:7, 8; 18:12; 19:38).

DERBE, a city of Lycaonia. Paul flees to (Ac 14:6, 20). Visited by Paul and Silas (Ac 16:1). Gaius born in (Ac 20:4).

DERISION, the wicked held in, by God (Ps 2:4; Pr 1:26).

Instances of: Sarah, when the angels gave her the promise of a child (Ge 18:12). The evil children of Beth-el deride Elisha (2Ki 2:23). The people of Israel scoff at Hezekiah (2Ch 30:1-10).

See Irony; Sarcasm; Scoffing.

DESERTS. Vast barren plains (Ex 5:3; Joh 6:13). Uninhabited places (M't 14:15; M'k 6:31).

Described as: Uninhabited and lonesome (Jer 2:6). Uncultivated (Nu 20:5; Jer 2:2). Desolate (Eze 6:14). Dry and without water (Ex 17:1; De 8:15). Trackless (Isa 43:19). Great and terrible (De 1:19). Waste and howling (De 32:10). Infested with wild beasts (Isa 13:21; M'k 1:13). Infested with serpents (De 8:15). Infested with robbers (Jer 3:2; La 4:19). Danger of travelling in (Ex 14:3; 2Co 11:26). Guides required in (Nu 10:31; De 32:10).

Phenomena of, Alluded to: Mirage or deceptive appearance of water (Jer 15:18 [marg.]). Simoon or deadly wind (2Ki 19:7; Jer 4:11). Tornadoes or whirlwinds (Isa 21:1). Clouds of sand and dust (De 28:24; Jer 4:12, 13).

Mentioned in Scripture: Arabian or great desert (Ex 23:31). Bethaven (Jos 18:12). Beersheba (Ge 21:14; 1Ki 19:3, 4). Damascus (1Ki 19:15). Edom (2Ki 3:8). Engedi (1Sa 24:1). Gibeon (2Sa 2:24). Judea (M't 3:1). Jeruel (2Ch 20:16). Kedemoth (De 2:26). Kadesh (Ps 29:8). Maon (1Sa 23:24, 25): Paran (Ge 21:21; Nu 10:12). Shur (Ge 16:7; Ex 15:22). Sin (Ex 16:1). Sinai (Ex 19:1, 2; Nu 33:16). Ziph (1Sa 23:14, 15). Zin (Nu 20:1; 27:14). Of the Red Sea (Ex 13:18). Near Gaza (Ac 8:26). Heath often found in (Jer 17:6). Parts of, afforded pasture (Ge 36:24; Ex 3:1). Inhabited by wandering tribes (Ge 21:20, 21; Ps 72:9; Jer 25:24). The persecuted fled to (1Sa 23:14; Heb 11:38). The disaffected fled to (1Sa 22:2; Ac 21:38).

Illustrative of: Barrenness (Ps 106:9; 107:33, 35). Those deprived of all blessings (Ho 2:3). The world (Song 3:6; 8:5). The Gentiles (Isa 35:1, 6; 41:19). What affords no support (Jer 2:31). Desolation by armies (Jer 12:10-13; 50:12).

DESIGN, in nature, evidence of (Job 12:7-11; Pr 16:4, *R.V.*).

DESIRE, SPIRITUAL. For divine piety (Ps 17:1; 51:1-4, 7-13; 119:82; Hab 3:2). For divine fellowship (Ps 62:1; 63:1, 8). For divine help (Ps 25:5, 15; 68:28; 119:77, 116, 117).

Exhortations concerning (Ps 70:4; 105:4; Isa 55:1-3, 6; Ho 10:12).

For God (Ps 24:6; 27:8; 33:20; 40:1; 42; 69:3; 73:26; 119:10, 12, 19, 20, 25,

40, 81, 88, 123, 131, 132, 135, 136, 149, 156, 174; 123:1, 2; 130:5, 6; 143:6-12; Isa 8:17, 19; 26:8, 9; M't 13:17; Lu 10:42; Ph'p 3:12-14; 1Pe 1:10). For his holy courts (Ps 84:2).

Reward of (De 4:29; Ps 34:10; 37:4, 9, 34; 107:9; 119:2; Pr 2:3-5; Isa 40:31; Jer 29:13; M't 5:6; Lu 1:53; 6:21; Joh 6:35; Heb 11:6).

See Hunger, Spiritual; Thirst, Figurative.

Evil: See Imagination; Lust.

DESIRE OF ALL NATIONS, some expositors refer the prophecy to Christ's first advent; others, to the second advent; still others deny a Messianic application altogether and hold it means the precious gifts of all nations (Hag 2:7).

DESOLATION, ABOMINATION OF. Phrase found in Daniel (11:31 & 12:11) considered referring to 1) the idolatrous image to be set up in the restored temple at Jerusalem in the last days, and/or 2) the idolatrous desecration of the temple by Antiochus Epiphanes in 168 B.C., and/or 3) the Roman destruction of the temple under Titus in 70 A.D. Christ refers to (Lu 21:20).

DESPAIR (See Despondency.)

DESPISERS, general references to (Pr 1:30; 9:8; M't 7:6; Ac 13:41; Ro 2:4; 2Ti 3:3; Heb 10:28; 2Pe 2:10).

DESPONDENCY. (Ec 2:20; Isa 35:3, 4; Heb 12:12, 13). Caused, by corrective judgments (Nu 17:12, 13; De 28:65-67; Isa 2:19; Ho 10:8; M't 24:30; Lu 23:29, 30; Re 6:14-17; 9:5, 6); by deferred hope (Pr 13:12); by adversity (Job 4:5; 9:16-35; 17:7-16).

Lament in (Job 3:1-26; 17:13-16; Ps 6:6; 22:1, 2; 55:4-7; 77:7-9; 88:3-17; Jer 8:20; La 3:1-20; 5:15-22; Mic 7:1-7).

Instances of: Cain, when God pronounced judgment upon him (Ge 4:13, 14). Hagar, when cast out of the household of Abraham (Ge 21:15, 16). Moses, when sent on his mission to the Israelites (Ex 4:1, 10, 13; 6:12); at the Red Sea (Ex 14:15); when the people lusted for flesh (Nu 11:15). The Israelites, on account of the cruel oppressions of the Egyptians (Ex 6:9). Joshua, over the defeat at Ai (Jos 7:7-9). Elijah when he fled from Jezebel to the wilderness and sat under the juniper tree, and wished to die (1Ki 19:4). Jonah, after he had preached to the Ninevites (Jon 4:3, 8). The mariners with Paul (Ac 27:20).

See Affliction, Consolation in; Righteous, Promises to.

DESPOTISM (See Government, Monarchical, Tyranny in.)

DETECTIVES (Lu 20:20).

See Spies.

DEUEL, called also Reuel. Captain of the tribe of Dan (Nu 1:14; 2:14; 7:42; 10:20).

DEUTERONOMY (second law), the Jewish name for it is "words," from the opening expression, "These are the words which Moses spake." Mosaic authorship is claimed in 31:9, 24, 26. The book contains three farewell addresses of Moses, given by him in sight of Canaan, which he was forbidden to enter, and a renewal of Israel's covenant with God.

1. First discourse (1-4).
2. Second discourse (5-26).
3. Third discourse (27-30).
4. Last counsels; parting blessings (31-34).

DEVIL (slanderer), one of the principal titles of Satan, the arch-enemy of God and of man. It is not known how he originated, unless Isa 14:12-20 and Eze 28:12-19 give us a clue, but it is certain that he was not created evil. He rebelled against God when in a state of holiness and apparently led other angels into rebellion with him (Jude 6; 2Pe 2:4). He is a being of superhuman power and wisdom, but not omnipotent or omniscient. He tries to frustrate God's plans and purposes for human beings. His principal method of attack is by temptation. His power is limited and he can go only as far as God permits. On the Judgment Day he will be cast into hell to remain there forever.

DEVOTED THING, that which is set apart unto the Lord, and therefore no longer belongs to the former owner (Jos 6:17-19).

DEVOTION, *To God.* See Religion. For conspicuous instances of, let the student study Enoch, Noah, Abraham, Moses, David's later history, Solomon's earlier life, Josiah, Asa, Isaiah, Elijah, Jeremiah, Daniel, Shadrach, Meshach and Abednego.

To Jesus. See Peter; John; Paul; Mary Magdalene.

For elaborated topics covering the subject, see Love of Man for God; Consecration; Zeal.

DEW. A merciful providence (De 33:13). Forms imperceptibly (2Sa 17:12); in the night (Job 29:19). From the clouds (Pr 3:20). Called the dew of heaven (Da 4:15). Absence of (1Ki 17:1). Miraculous profusion and absence of (J'g 6:36-40).

See Meteorology.

Figurative: Ps 110:3; Isa 26:19; Ho 6:4; 13:3; 14:5.

DIADEM, the Hebrew word is usually rendered "mitre" or "turban," and was a headdress worn by men (Job 29:14), women ("hoods," Isa 3:23), priests (Eze 21:26), and kings (Isa 28:5; 62:3). Very different from the crown (Gr. *stephanos*), which was given to victorious athletes. Diadems were made of silk cloth and were covered with gems.

DIAL, a sundial, used to tell time during the day (2Ki 20:11; Isa 38:8).

DIAMOND, one of the jewels in the breastplate (Ex 28:18; 39:11; Jer 17:1; Eze 28:13).

DIANA, goddess of the Ephesians (Ac 19:24, 27, 28, 35).

DIASPORA (that which is sown), the name applied to the Jews living outside of Palestine and maintaining their religious faith among the Gentiles. By the time of Christ the diaspora must have been several times the population of Palestine.

DIBLAIM, father of Hosea's wife (Ho 1:3).

DIBLATH, probably an early copyist's error for Riblah, a town c. 50 miles S of Hamath (Eze 6:14).

DIBON. 1. Called also Dibon-gad and Dimon. A city on the northern banks of the Arnon (Nu 21:30). Israelites encamp at (Nu 33:45). Allotted to Gad and Reuben (Nu 32:3, 34; Jos 13:9, 17). Taken by Moab (Isa 15:2,9; Jer 48:18, 22).

2. A city in the tribe of Judah (Ne 11:25); probably identical with Dimonah (Jos 15:22).

DIBRI, father of Shelomith (Le 24:11).

DIDRACHMA (See Money.)

DIDYMUS (twin), surname of Thomas (Joh 11:16; 20:24; 21:2).

DIKLAH, son of Joktan, and name of a district inhabited by his descendants (Ge 10:27; 1Ch 1:21).

DILEAN, a city of Judah (Jos 15:38).

DILIGENCE. Jesus an example of (M'k 1:35; Lu 2:49).

Required by God in seeking him (1Ch 22:19; Heb 11:6); obeying him (De 6:17; 11:13); hearkening to him (Isa 55:2); striving after perfection (Ph'p 3:13, 14); cultivating Christian graces (2Pe 1:5); keeping the soul (De 4:9); keeping the heart (Pr 4:23); labors of love (Heb 6:10-12); following every good work (1Ti 3:10); guarding against defilement (Heb 12:15); seeking to be found spotless (2Pe 3:14); making our calling sure (2Pe 1:10); self-examination (Ps 77:6); lawful business (Pr 27:23; Ec 9:10); teaching religion (2Ti 4:2; Jude 3); instructing children (De 6:7; 11:19); discharging official duties (De 19:18); saints should abound in (2Co 8:7).

Required in the service of God (Joh 9:4; Ga 6:9). Is not in vain (1Co 15:58). Preserves from evil (Ex 15:26). Leads to assured hope (Heb 6:11). God rewards (De 11:14; Heb 11:6).

In temporal matters leads to favor (Pr 11:27); prosperity (Pr 10:4; 13:4); honor (Pr 12:24; 22:29).

Figurative: Pr 6:6-8.

Exemplified: Ruth (Ru 2:17). Hezekiah (2Ch 31:21). Nehemiah and his helpers (Ne 4:6). Psalmist (Ps 119:60). Apostles (Ac 5:42). Apollos (Ac 18:25). Titus (2Co 8:22). Paul (1Th 2:9). Onesiphorus (2Ti 1:17).

See Industry; Zeal; Idleness; Slothfulness.

DIMNAH, Levite town in Zebulun (Jos 21:35). May be same as Rimmon (1Ch 6:77).

DIMON, town in Moab, generally called "Dibon" (q.v.), but in Isa 15:9 twice written Dimon, c. 4 miles N of Aroer.

DIMONAH, town in S of Judah (Jos 15:22), probably the same as the "Dibon" of Ne 11:25.

DINAH. Daughter of Jacob and Leah (Ge 30:21). Ravishment of (Ge 34).

DINAITE, a people brought from Assyria to colonize Samaria (2Ki 17:24; Ezr 4:7-10).

DINHABAH, a city of Edom (Ge 36:32; 1Ch 1:43).

DINNER, eaten at noon (Ge 43:16).
See Feasts.

DIONYSIUS, THE AREOPAGITE, member of the Areopagus, Athenian supreme court; converted by Paul (Ac 17:34).

DIOSCURI (sons of Zeus), twin sons of Zeus named Castor and Pollux; regarded by sailors as guardian deities (Ac 28:11).

DIOTREPHES (nurtured by Zeus), domineering Christian leader condemned by John (3Jo 9, 10).

DIPLOMACY. Ecclesiastical: Paul, in winning souls to Christ (1Co 9:20-23); in circumcising Timothy (Ac 16:3); in performing certain temple services to placate the Jews (Ac 21:20-25, w Ga 6:12).

Corrupt practices in: The officers of Nebuchadnezzar's court to secure the destruction of Daniel (Da 6:4-15).

Instances of: Abimelech (Ge 21:22, 23; 26:26-31). The Gibeonites, in securing a league with the Israelites through deception (Jos 9:3-16). Of Jephthah, with the king of Moab, unsuccessful (J'g 11:12-28). Of Abigail (1Sa 25:23-31). Of Hiram, to secure the good will of David (2Sa 5:11). Of Toi, to promote the friendship of David (2Sa 8:10). David, in sending Hushai to Absalom's court (2Sa 15:32-37; 16:15-19; 17:1-14). The wise woman of Abel (2Sa 20:16-22). Absalom winning the people (2Sa 15:2-6). Solomon, in his alliance with Hiram (1Ki 5:1-12; 9:10-14, 26, 27; 10:11); by intermarriage with other nations (1Ki 1:1-5). Ambassadors from Ben-hadad to Ahab (1Ki 20:31-34). Jehoash purchases peace from Hazael (2Ki 12:18). Ahaz purchases aid from the king of Assyria (2Ki 16:7-9). Rab-shakeh, in trying to induce Jerusalem to capitulate by bombastic harangue (2Ki 18:17-37; 19:1-13; Isa 36:11-22). Sanballat, in an attempt to prevent the rebuilding of Jerusalem by Nehemiah (Ne 6).

The people of Tyre and Sidon, in securing the favor of Herod (Ac 12:20-22). Paul, in arraying the Pharisees and Sadducees against each other at his trial (Ac 23:6-10).

See Prudence; Tact.

DISBELIEF (See Unbelief.)

DISCERNING OF SPIRITS, the ability to discern between those who spoke by the Spirit of God and those who were moved by false spirits (1Co 12:10).

DISCIPLE, a name given to the followers of any teacher. Of John the Baptist (M't 9:14). Of Jesus (M't 10:1; 20:17; Ac 9:26; 14:20; 21:4). The seventy sent forth (Lu 10:1). First called Christians at Antioch (Ac 11:26).

See Apostles; Righteous.

DISCIPLESHIP, tests of (M't 10:32-39; Lu 14:26, 27, 33; Joh 21:15-19).

See Commandments.

DISCIPLINE, of armies, for disobedience of orders (Jos 7:10-26; J'g 21:5-12).

See Armies.

Church Discipline (See Church, Discipline in.)

DISCONTENTMENT (See Murmuring; Contentment.)

DISCOURAGEMENT (See Despondency.)

DISEASE. Sent from God (Le 14:34). As judgments (Ps 107:17; Isa 3:17). Instances of: Upon the Egyptians, see Plagues; upon Nabal (1Sa 25:38); David's child (2Sa 12:15); Gehazi (2Ki 5:27); Jeroboam (2Ch 13:20); Jehoram (2Ch 21:12-19); Uzziah (2Ch 26:17-20).

Threatened as judgments (Le 26:16; De 7:15; 28:22, 27, 28, 35; 29:22).

Healing of, from God (Ex 15:26; 23:25; De 7:15; 2Ch 16:12; Ps 103:3; 107:20). In answer to prayer: Of Hezekiah (2Ki 20:1-11; Isa 38:1-8); David (Ps 21:4; 116:3-8).

Miraculous healing of, a sign to accompany the preaching of the word (M'k 16:18). See Miracles.

Physicians employed for (2Ch 16:12; Jer 8:22; M't 9:12; M'k 5:26; Lu 4:23). Remedies used (Pr 17:22; 20:30; Isa 38:21; Jer 30:13; 46:11); poultices (2Ki 20:7); ointments (Isa 1:6; Jer 8:22); emulsions (Lu 10:34).

Of the sexual organs (Le 15; 22:4; Nu 5:2; De 23:10). See Circumcision; Menstruation; Gonorrhea. Treatment of fractures (Eze 30:21).

See Affliction.

Figurative: Ps 38:7; Isa 1:6; Jer 30:12.

Various kinds of: See Abortion; Ague; Atrophy; Blain; Blemish; Blindness; Boil; Congestion; Consumption; Deafness; Demons; Dropsy; Dysentery; Dyspepsia; Epilepsy; Fever; Gonorrhea;

Gout; Hemorrhage; Hemorrhoids; Insanity; Itch; Lameness; Leprosy; Murrain; Paralysis; Pestilence; Scab; Scall; Scurvy; Spermatorrhea; Stammering; Sunstroke; Tumor; Worm.

Of the bowels. See Bowels.

DISFELLOWSHIP. *From God and Man:* Of the uncircumcised (Ge 17:14). Of violators of the law, of unleavened bread (Ex 12:15); of sacrifices (Le 17:9; 19:5-7); of purification (Nu 19:20). Of those defiled, by eating prohibited food (Le 7:25, 27; 17:10; 19:8); by touching the dead (Nu 19:13); by committing abominations (Le 18:29; 20:3-6).

Enjoined: For blasphemy (Nu 15:31). For schism (Ro 16:17). For heresy (1Ti 6:3-5; Tit 3:10, 11; 2Jo 10, 11). For immorality (M't 18:17, 18; 1Co 5:1-7, 11, 13; 2Th 3:6).

DISGUISES, examples of (Ge 38:14; 1Sa 28:8; 1Ki 14:2; 20:38; 22:30; 2Ch 35:22).

DISH, usually made either of baked clay or of metal. Orientals ate from a central platter or dish (M't 26:23).

DISHAN, son of Seir (Ge 36:21, 30; 1Ch 1:38).

DISHON. 1. Son of Seir (Ge 36:21, 30; 1Ch 1:38).

2. Grandson of Seir (Ge 36:25; 1Ch 1:41).

DISHONESTY. In not paying debts (Ps 37:12, 21; Jas 5:4). In collusion with thieves (Ps 50:18). In wicked devices for gain (Job 24:2-11; Pr 1:10-14; 20:14; Isa 32:7; Jer 22:13; Eze 22:29; Ho 12:7; Am 3:10; 8:5; Mic 6:10, 11).

Denounced (Jer 7:8-10; 9:4-6, 8; Ho 4:1, 2; Na 3:1). Forbidden (Le 19:13, 35, 36; De 25:13-16; Ps 62:10; Pr 3:27, 28; 11:1; 20:10, 23; 1Th 4:6). Penalties for (Le 6:2-7; Pr 20:17; Zep 1:9; Zec 5:3, 4). Parable concerning (Lu 16:1-8).

Instances of: Abimelech's servants usurp a well of water (Ge 21:25; 26:15-22). Jacob obtains his brother's birthright by unjust advantage (Ge 25:29-33); steals his father's blessing (Ge 27:6-29); Laban's flocks by skillful manipulation (Ge 30:31-43). Rebekah's guile in Jacob's behalf (Ge 27:6-17). Laban's treatment of Jacob (Ge 29:21-30; 31:36-42). Rachel steals the household gods (Ge 31:19). Simeon and Levi deceive the Shechemites (Ge 34:15-31). Achan hides the wedge of gold and the Babylonish garment (Jos 7:11-26). Micah steals eleven hundred pieces of silver (J'g 17:2). Micah's priest steals his images (J'g 18:14-21). Joab's guile in securing Absalom's return (2Sa 14:2-20). Ahab usurps Naboth's vineyard (1Ki 21:2-16). Judas' hypocritical sympathy for the poor (Joh 12:6).

See Diplomacy; Hypocrisy; Injustice; Treason.

DISOBEDIENCE TO GOD. Originated in Adam (Ro 5:19). Characteristic of all (Ro 1:32; Eph 2:2; 5:6; Col 3:6; Tit 1:16; 3:3; Heb 2:2; 1Pe 2:8). Temptation to (Ge 3:1-5).

Denunciations against (Nu 14:11, 12, 22, 23; 32:8-13; De 18:19; 28:15-68).

Punishment for (Le 26:14-46; De 28:15-68). See Wicked.

Punishment of: Of the Egyptians by plagues, see Plagues. See also Sin, Punishment of.

Instances of: Of Adam and Eve, eating the forbidden fruit (Ge 3:6-11). Of Lot, in refusing to go to the mountain, as commanded by the angels (Ge 19:19, 20). Of Lot's wife, in looking back upon Sodom (Ge 19:26). Of Moses, in making excuses when commissioned to deliver Israel (Ex 4:13, 14); when he smote the rock (Nu 20:11, 23, 24). Of Aaron, at the smiting of the rock by Moses (Nu 20:23, 24). Of Pharaoh, in refusing to let the children of Israel go (Ex 5:2; 7:13, 22, 23; 8:15, 19, 32; 9:12, 34; 10:20, 27; 11:10; 14:8). Of the children of Israel, in gathering excessive quantities of manna (Ex 16:19, 20); in refusing to enter the promised land (De 1:26, w Nu 14:1-10; Jos 5:6; Ps 106:24, 25). Of Nadab and Abihu, in offering strange fire (Le 10:1, 2). Of Balaam, in accompanying the messengers from Balak (Nu 22:22). Of Achan, in secreting the wedge of gold and the Babylonian garment (Jos 7:15-26). Of Saul, in offering a sacrifice (1Sa 13:13); in sparing Agag and the spoils of the Amalekites (1Sa 15; 28:18). Of David, in his adultery, and in the slaying of Uriah (2Sa 12:9). Of Solomon, in building places for idolatrous worship (1Ki 11:7-10). Of the prophet of Judah, in not keeping the commandment to deliver his message to Jeroboam without delay (1Ki 13). Of a man of

Israel, who refused to smite the prophet (1Ki 20:35, 36). Of Ahab, in suffering the king of Assyria to escape out of his hands (1Ki 20:42). Of priests, in not performing their functions after the due order (1Ch 15:13). Of the people of Judah (Jer 43:7); in going to dwell in Egypt contrary to divine command (Jer 44:12-14). Of Jonah, in refusing to deliver the message to the Ninevites (Jon 1). Of the blind men Jesus healed, and commanded not to publish their healing (M't 9:30, 31). Of the leper whom Jesus healed, and commanded not to publish the fact (M'k 1:45). Of Paul, in going to Jerusalem contrary to repeated admonitions (Ac 21:4, 10-14).

Of the Righteous, see Commandments.

Of Children, see Children, Commandments to.

DISPENSATION (law or arrangement of a house), in 1Co 9:17; Eph 3:2 and Col 1:25 it means "stewardship," "office," "commission"—words involving the idea of administration. In Eph 1:10 the word dispensation refers to God's plan of salvation. The NT used the word in a twofold sense: with respect to one in authority, it means an arrangement or plan; with respect to one under authority, it means a stewardship or administration.

DISPENSATIONS. An era of time during which man's obedience to God is tested according to the revelation of God available to him. From two dispensations (or covenants) to seven (innocence, conscience, human government, promise, law, grace, the kingdom) are held by various schools of interpretation.

DISPERSION. Of the descendants of Noah (Ge 10). After building the tower of Babel (Ge 11:1-9; De 32:8). Of the Jews, foretold (Jer 16:15; 24:9; Joh 7:35).

DISPLAY. General References to (Es 1:4; 5:11; Isa 39:2; Lu 20:46; Ac 25:23). In Religious Service (2Ki 10:16; M't 6:2, 5, 16; 23:5).

DISPUTE, about property (See Property.)

DISSEMBLING. *Instances of:* Joseph (Ge 42:7-20; 43:26-34). David (1Sa 21:13-15).

See Deception; Hypocrisy.

DISSENSION, in churches (1Co 1:10-13; 3:3, 4; 11:18, 19).

DISSIPATION, dangers of (Job 1:5).

See Drunkenness.

DISTAFF (Pr 31:19).

DITCH, *Figurative:* Pr 23:27.

DIVES (rich), name applied to the rich man in the parable of the rich man and Lazarus (Lu 16:19-31) in the Vulgate

DIVINATION, the practice of foreseeing or foretelling future events or discovering hidden knowledge; forbidden to Jews (Le 19:26; De 18:10; Isa 19:3; Ac 16:16). Various means were used: reading omens, dreams, the use of the lot, astrology, necromancy, and others.

DIVINITY OF CHRIST (See Jesus, Divinity of.)

DIVISIONS: Forbidden in the church (1Co 1:10). Condemned in the church (1Co 1:11-13; 11:18). Unbecoming in the church (1Co 12:24, 25).

Are Contrary to the: Unity of Christ (1Co 1:13; 12:13). Desire of Christ (Joh 17:21-23). Purpose of Christ (Joh 10:16). Spirit of the primitive church (1Co 11:16). Are a proof of a carnal spirit (1Co 3:3). Avoid those who cause (Ro 16:17). Evil of, illustrated (M't 12:25).

DIVORCE. Mosaic laws concerning (Ex 21:7-11; De 21:10-14; 24:1-4). Authorized for fornication (M't 5:31, 32; 19:3-11). Unjust reproved (Mal 2:14-16). From heathen wives, required by Ezra (Ezr 10:1-16). Disobedience, a cause for, among the Persians (Es 1:10-22). Final, after remarriage of either party (Jer 3:1). Christ's injunctions concerning (M'k 10:2-12; Lu 16:18). Paul's injunctions concerning (1Co 7:10-17).

Figurative (Isa 50:1; 54:4; Jer 3:8).

See Marriage.

DIZAHAB, place in region of Sinai where Moses gave farewell address (De 1:1).

DOCTOR, a teacher, or master (M't 8:19; Lu 2:46; 5:17; Ac 5:34; 1Ti 1:7).

See Physician; Disease.

DOCTRINES. Origin in God (Joh 7:16, 17). Set forth by church councils (Ac 15:6-29).

False: Jesus accuses scribes and Pharisees of teaching (M't 5:19, 20; 15:9).

Teachers, to be avoided (Ro 16:17,

18; 1Co 3:11, 21; 1Ti 1:3-7; 6:3-5, 20, 21); accursed (Ga 1:6-8; Jude 4, 11); rejected (Tit 1:10, 11, 14; 3:10, 11; 2Jo 9-11). Admonitions against (Ro 16:17, 18; Eph 4:14; Col 2:4, 8, 18-23; 1Ti 1:3-7; 4:7; 6:20, 21; 2Ti 2:16; Tit 3:10, 11; Heb 13:9).

Called: heresies (1Co 11:18, 19; 2Pe 2:1, 2); corruption (2Co 2:17; 11:3, 4; Ga 1:6-8; 2Ti 2:14-18; 3:6-9; 2Pe 2:14-19).

Origin: man (M't 15:9; Ro 16:17, 18; 1Co 3:11, 21; 2Co 2:17; Eph 4:14; Col 2:4, 8, 18-23; 2Ti 3:6-9, 13; Tit 1:10, 11, 14; 2Pe 2:1-3); Satan (2Co 11:3, 4; 1Ti 4:1-3); Antichrist (1Jo 4:3; 2Jo 7, 9-11).

See Ministers, False; Schism; Teachers, False.

DODAI, officer in David's army (1Ch 27:4).

DODANIM, son of Javan (Ge 10:4).

DODAVAH, Eliezer's father (2Ch 20:37).

DODO. 1. Grandfather of Tola (J'g 10:1).

2. Son of Ahohi (2Sa 23:9).

3. Father of one of David's mighty men (2Sa 23:24).

DOEG. An Edomite, present when Ahimelech helped David (1Sa 21:7; 22:9, 22; Ps 52 [title]). Slew eighty-five priests (1Sa 22:18, 19).

DOER, OF THE WORD. Exemplification of belief (M't 7:21; 12:50; Lu 11:28; Ro 2:13-15; 2Co 8:11; Jas 1:22-27; 4:11).

See Hearers.

DOG. Price of, not to be brought into the sanctuary (De 23:18). Shepherd dogs (Job 30:1). Habits of: Licking blood (1Ki 21:19; 22:38); licking sores (Lu 16:21); returns to his vomit (Pr 26:11; 2Pe 2:22); lapping of (J'g 7:5). Dumb and sleeping (Isa 56:10, 11).

Greyhound (Pr 30:31). Epithet of contempt (1Sa 17:43; 24:14; 2Sa 3:8; 9:8; 16:9; 2Ki 8:13; Isa 56:10, 11; M't 15:26).

Figurative: Ph'p 3:2; Re 22:15.

DOGMATISM (See Commandments, of Men.)

DOMICILE. *Rights of* (De 24:10, 11).

DOMINION, OF MAN (See Man, Dominion of.)

DONATIONS (See Liberality.)

DOOR. Posts of, sprinkled with the blood of the paschal lamb (Ex 12:22); the law to be written on (De 11:20). Hinges for (Pr 26:14); made of gold (1Ki 7:5). Doors of the temple made of two leaves, cherubim and flowers carved upon, covered with gold (1Ki 6:31-35).

Figurative: Door of hope (Ho 2:15); of opportunity (1Co 16:9; Re 3:8); closed (M't 25:10; Lu 13:25; Re 3:7).

DOORKEEPER, keeper of doors and gates in public buildings, temples, walled cities, etc., often called "porter" (2Ki 7:10; 1Ch 23:5; Ps 84:10; Ezr 7:24; M'k 13:34).

DOPHKAH, station of Israelites between Red Sea and Sinai (Nu 33:12).

DOR. A town and district of Palestine (Jos 11:2). Conquered by Joshua (Jos 12:23; 1Ki 4:11). Allotted to Manasseh, although situated in the territory of Asher (Jos 17:11; J'g 1:27).

DORCAS (gazelle), Christian woman living at Joppa whom Peter raised from the dead (Ac 9:36-43).

DOTHAN (two wells), place c. 13 miles N of Shechem where Joseph was sold (Ge 37:17) and Elisha saw vision of angels (2Ki 6:13-23).

DOUBTING. In prayer (M't 21:21; Jas 1:6-8). Admonishings against (Pr 24:10; M't 8:26; 14:31; 17:17; M'k 4:49; 9:19; Lu 8:25; 9:40).

Instances of: Job (Job 3; 4:3-6; 9:16-23; 30:20, 21). Abraham (Ge 12:12, 13; 15:8). Sarah (Ge 18:12-14). Lot (Ge 19:30). Moses (Ex 3:11; 4:1, 10, 13; 5:22, 23; 6:12; Nu 11:21, 22). Israelites (Ex 14:10-12, 15; 1Sa 17:11, 24; Isa 40:27, 28; 49:14, 15). Gideon (J'g 6:13, 15). Samuel (1Sa 16:1, 2). Psalmists (Ps 22:2; 31:22; 42:5, 6; 49:5; 73:13-17; 77:3, 7-9). Obadiah (1Ki 18:7-14). Elijah (1Ki 19:13-18). Jeremiah (Jer 1:6; 8:18; 32:24, 25; 45:3; La 3:8, 17, 18; 5:20).

Christ's disciples (M't 8:23-27; 14:29-31; 17:14-21; 28:17; M'k 4:38, 40; 9:14-29; 16:10, 11; Lu 8:25; 9:40, 41; Joh 14:8-11; 20:24-27). John the Baptist (M't 11:2, 3). Ananias (Ac 9:13, 14). Peter (M't 14:30, 31). Thomas (Joh 20:25). Early believers (1Pe 1:6).

See Cowardice; Murmuring.

DOUGH. First of, offered to God (Nu 15:19-21; Ne 10:37). Kneaded (Jer 7:18; Ho 7:4). Part of, for priest (Eze 44:30).

See Bread; Oven.

DOVE, TURTLE. Sent out from the ark by Noah (Ge 8:8-11). Mourning of (Isa

38:14; 59:11; Na 2:7). Domesticated (Isa 60:8). Nests of (Jer 48:28). Harmlessness of, typical of Christ's gentleness (M't 10:16). Sacrificial uses of (Ge 15:9). Prescribed for purification: Of women (Le 12:6, 8; Lu 2:24); of Nazarites (Nu 6:10); of lepers (Le 14:22). Burnt offering of (Le 1:14-17). Trespass offering of, for the impecunious (Le 5:7-10; 12:8). Sin offering, for those who touched any dead body (Nu 6:10). Market for, in the temple (M't 21:12; Joh 2:14).

Symbolical: Of the Holy Spirit (M't 3:16; Lu 3:22; Joh 1:32).

See Pigeon.

DOVE COTE, opening of pigeon-house (Isa 60:8).

DOVE'S DUNG, used as food in famine (2Ki 6:25). See Plants.

DOWRY. Sum paid to parents for a daughter taken as wife (Ex 22:16, 17); by Shechem for Dinah (Ge 34:12); by Boaz for Ruth (Ru 4:3-9); by David to Saul for Michal (1Sa 18:25).

DOXOLOGY (See Praise.)

DRACHMA (See Money.)

DRAGON. Any terrible creature, as a venomous serpent (De 32:33; Ps 91:13); a sea serpent (Ps 74:13; 148:7; Isa 27:1); a jackal (Isa 13:22; 34:13; 35:7; 43:20; Jer 9:11; 10:22; 14:6; 49:33; 51:37; Mic 1:8; Mal 1:3).

A term applied to Pharaoh (Isa 51:9); to Satan (Re 20:2).

Symbolical: Eze 29:3; 32:2; Re 12; 13; 16:13.

DRAM. Called also Drachm. A Persian coin of differently estimated value (1Ch 29:7; Ezr 2:69; 8:27; Ne 7:70-72).

DRAMA (See Pantomime.)

DRAUGHT HOUSE, privy or water-closet (2Ki 10:27).

DRAWER OF WATER, one who brought water from a well or a spring to a house (De 29:11; Jos 9:23-27).

DRAWING, of pictures on tile (Eze 4:1).

DREAM. Evanescent (Job 20:8). Vanity of (Ec 5:3, 7).

Revelations by (Nu 12:6; Job 33:15-17; Jer 23:28; Joel 2:28; Ac 2:17). The dreams of the butler and baker (Ge 40:8-23); Pharaoh (Ge 41:1-36).

Interpreted by Joseph (Ge 40:12, 13, 18, 19; 41:25-32); Daniel (Da 2:16-23, 28-30; 4). Delusive (Isa 29:7, 8).

False prophets pretended to receive revelations through (De 13:1-5; Jer 23:25-32; 27:9; 29:8; Zec 10:2).

See Vision.

Instances of: Of Abimelech, concerning Sarah (Ge 20:3). Of Jacob, concerning the ladder (Ge 28:12); the ring-straked cattle (Ge 31:10-13); concerning his going down into Egypt (Ge 46:2). Of Laban, concerning Jacob (Ge 31:24). Of Joseph, concerning the sheaves (Ge 37:5-10). Of the Midianite concerning the cake of barley (J'g 7:13). Of Solomon, concerning his choice of wisdom (1Ki 3:3-15). Of Eliphaz, of a spirit speaking to him (Job 4:12-21). Of Daniel, concerning the four beasts (Da 7). Of Joseph, concerning Mary's innocence (M't 1:20, 21); concerning the flight into Egypt (M't 2:13); concerning the return into Palestine (M't 2:19-22). Of Pilate's wife, concerning Jesus (M't 27:19). Cornelius' vision, concerning Peter (Ac 10:3-6). Peter's vision of the unclean beasts (Ac 10:10-16). Paul's vision of the man in Macedonia, crying, "Come over into Macedonia" (Ac 16:9); relating to his going to Rome (Ac 23:11); concerning the shipwreck, and the safety of all on board (Ac 27:23, 24).

DRESS. Of fig leaves (Ge 3:7). Of skins (Ge 3:21). Of other materials, see Hair; Goats' Hair; Leather; Linen; Sackcloth; Silk; Wool. Mixed materials in, forbidden (De 22:11). Men forbidden to wear women's, and women forbidden to wear men's (De 22:5). Rules with respect to women's (1Ti 2:9, 10; 1Pe 3:3). Not to be held over night as a pledge for debt (Ex 22:26). Ceremonial purification of (Le 11:32; 13:47-59; Nu 31:20). Rending of, see Mourning.

Of the head: Bonnets [*R. V.*, head-tires], prescribed by Moses, for the priests (Ex 28:40; 29:9; 39:28); by Ezekiel (Eze 44:18). Hats [turbans, *R. V. margin*] worn by men (Da 3:21). Bonnets [*R. V.* head-tires], worn by women (Isa 3:20; Eze 24:17, 23). Hoods [turban, *R. V.*] (Isa 3:23). Kerchiefs (Eze 13:18, 21).

Various articles of: Mantle (Ezr 9:3; 1Ki 19:13; 1Ch 15:27; Job 1:20); many colored (2Sa 13:18); purple (Joh 19:2, 5). Robe (Ex 28:4; 1Sa 18:4). Shawls (Isa 3:22. Embroidered coat (Ex 28:4, 40;

1Sa 2:19; Da 3:21). Sleeveless shirt, called coat (M't 5:40; Lu 6:29; Joh 19:23; Ac 9:39). Cloak (2Ti 4:13; Joh 19:2, 5). Hosen (Da 3:21). Skirts (Eze 5:3). Mufflers (Isa 3:19). Wimples [satchels, *R. V.*] (Isa 3:22). Sashes (Isa 3:20). See Veil.

Changes of raiment, the folly of excessive (Job 27:16). Uniform vestments kept in store for worshipers of Baal (2Ki 10:22, 23; Zep 1:8); for wedding feast (M't 22:11). Presents made of changes of raiment (Ge 45:22; 1Sa 18:4; 2Ki 5:5; Es 6:8; Da 5:7). Vestments of priests, see Priest; of mourning, see Mourning.

Figurative: Filthy, of unrighteousness (Isa 64:6). Of righteousness and of iniquity, see Color, Symbolism of.

Symbolical: Filthy, of iniquity (Zec 3:3, 4).

DRINK. Beverages of the Jews were water (Ge 24:11-18), wine (Ge 14:18; Joh 2:3), and milk (J'g 4:19).

DRINK OFFERING, offering of oil and wine to God accompanying many sacrifices (Ex 29:40, 41).

DRIVING, rapid, by Jehu (2Ki 9:20).

DROMEDARY (1Ki 4:28; Es 8:10 [*R. V.*, swift steeds]; Isa 60:6).

DROPSY (Lu 14:2).

DROSS, refuse separated from molten ore or metal.

Figurative: Ps 119:119; Pr 25:4; 26:23; Isa 1:22; Eze 22:18, 19.

DROUGHT: Ge 31:40; 1Ki 17, 18; Jer 14:1-6. Sent by God as a judgment (De 28:23, 24; 1Ki 8:35; 2Ch 6:26; 7:13; Ho 13:15).

See Famine; Meteorology; Rain.

Figurative: Ps 32:4; Isa 44:3.

DRUNKARD. Described (Pr 23:29-35). End result: poverty (Pr 23:21; Isa 28:1, 3); cut off (Joe 1:5); destroyed (Na 1:10); trodden under feet (Isa 28:1, 3); shame (Hab 2:16); death (De 21:20, 21). Insatiable appetite of (Hab 2:5, 6). Excluded from kingdom (1Co 6:9, 10).

The psalmist mocked by (Ps 69:12). Fellowship with, forbidden (1Co 5:11). Punishment of (De 21:20, 21).

See Drunkenness; Wine; Temperance; Total Abstinence.

DRUNKENNESS. Repugnancy of (Isa 28:7, 8; 56:12; Ho 7:5, 14; Joe 1:5; 3:3; Am 2:8, 12; M't 24:49; Lu 12:45). Mockery of (Ps 69:12; Pr 20:1).

Consequences of (Pr 21:17; 23:21, 29-35; Isa 19:14; 24:9-11; 28:7; Ho 4:11). Death penalty for (De 21:20, 21; 29:19-20; Jer 25:27). Excludes from kingdom of God (1Co 6:9, 10; Ga 5:19-21).

Forbidden (1Sa 1:14; Pr 23:20, 31, 32; 31:4-7; Lu 21:34; Ro 13:13; 1Co 11:21-30; Eph 5:18; 1Th 5:7, 8; 1Pe 4:3). Woes denounced against (Isa 5:11, 12, 22; 28:1, 3, 7, 8; Am 6:1, 6; Na 1:10; Hab 2:15, 16).

Figurative: Isa 28:8; 51:17, 21-23; 63:6; Jer 25:15, 16, 27, 28; 51:7-9; La 3:15; Eze 23:31-34; Hab 2:15, 16.

See Abstinence; Drunkard; Sobriety; Wine.

Instances of: Noah (Ge 9:21). Lot (Ge 19:33). Nabal (1Sa 25:36). Uriah (2Sa 11:13). Amnon (2Sa 13:28). Elah (1Ki 16:9). Ben-hadad and his thirty-two confederate kings (1Ki 20:16). Ahasuerus (Es 1:10, 11). Belshazzar (Da 5:1-6). Believers (1Co 11:21).

Falsely Accused of: Hannah (1Sa 1:12-16). Jesus (M't 11:19). The Apostles (Ac 2:13-15).

DRUSILLA, daughter of Herod Agrippa I; married first to Azizus, king of Emesa; later to Felix, procurator of Judea (Ac 24:24, 25).

DRY PLACES: Nu 20:2; 2Ki 3:9; Ps 68:6; Isa 1:30; Jer 14:3; 17:6.

DUKE, Title of the princes of Edom (Ge 36:15-43; Ex 15:15, 1Ch 1:51-54). Of the Midianites (Jos 13:21).

DULCIMER, [*R. V.*, marg., bagpipe] (Da 3:5, 10, 15).

See Music, Instruments of.

DUMAH (silence). 1. Son of Ishmael (Ge 25:14; 1Ch 1:30; Isa 21:11, 12).

2. A city of Canaan assigned to Judah (Jos 15:52).

DUMB, stricken of God (Ex 4:11; Lu 1:20, 64); miraculous healing of, by Jesus (M't 9:32, 33; 12:22; 15:30, 31; M'k 7:37; 9:17, 25, 26).

See Deafness.

DUNG, laws were made regarding excrement of human beings and animals used in sacrifice (De 23:12-14; Ex 29:14; Le 8:17). Dry dung was often used as fuel (Eze 4:12-15); also fertilizer (Isa 25:10; Lu 13:8).

DUNGEON, in prisons (Jer 38:6; La 3:53).

See Prisons.

DUNG GATE, gate in Jerusalem wall that led out to the valley of Hinnom where rubbish was dumped (Ne 3:14).

DURA, plain of Babylon where Nebuchadnezzar set up his image (Da 3:1).

DUST. Man made from (Ge 2:7; 3:19, 23; Ec 3:20). Casting of, in anger (2Sa 16:13). Shaking from feet (M't 10:14; Ac 13:51). Put on the head in mourning (Jos 7:6; 1Sa 4:12; 2Sa 1:2; 15:30; Job 2:12; 42:6).

DUTY, tribute levied on foreign commerce by Solomon (1Ki 10:15).

DUTY. Escape from, sought by Moses (Ex 3:11; 4:1, 10, 13; 6:12, 30); by Jonah (Jon 1:1-15); by Ananias (Ac 9:13, 14).

Of Man to God: To love (De 6:5; 11:1; 30:15-20; Jos 23:11; Ps 31:23; M't 22:37; Lu 12:27). To obey (De 10:12, 13; 30:15-20; Jos 22:5; Pr 23:26; M't 12:50; 22:21; 23:23; Lu 17:10; Joh 14:15, 21; 15:14; Ac 4:19, 20; 5:29).

Of Man to Man: To love (Le 19:18; M't 19:19; 22:39; M'k 12:31; Joh 13:34; Ro 13:8-10; Ga 5:14; Jas 2:8). To help (Isa 58:6, 7; M't 25:34-46; Lu 10:23-36). To forgive (M't 18:21-35; Lu 17:3, 4; Eph 4:32; Col 3:13). To practice "the golden rule" toward (M't 7:12). To respect a brother's conscience (Ro 14:1-23; 1Co 8:1-13). To restore a sinning brother (Ga 6:1, 2).

See Commandments; Children; Husband; Minister, Duties of; Parents; Wife.

DWARF (thin, small, withered), could not officiate at the altar (Le 21:20).

DYEING (Ex 25:5; 26:14; Isa 63:1; Eze 23:15).

DYING (See Death.)

DYSENTERY (Ac 28:8).

DYSPEPSIA, of Timothy (1Ti 5:23).

E

EAGLE. Forbidden as food (Le 11:13; De 14:12). Swift flight of (De 28:49; Job 9:26; Pr 30:19; Jer 4:13; 49:22; La 4:19). Nest of (De 32:11; Job 39:27-30; Jer 49:16). Bears her young on her wings (Ex 19:4; De 32:11). Long life of (Ps 103:5). Bald (Mic 1:16). Gier-eagle (Le 11:18).

Figurative: Ex 19:4; De 32:11; Jer 48:40; Ho 8:1.

Symbolical: Eze 1:10; 10:14; 17:3; Da 7:4; Re 4:7; 12:14.

EAR. Blood put upon, in consecration of priests (Ex 29:20; Le 8:23); in cleansing lepers (Le 14:14, 25). Anointed with oil in purifications (Le 14:17, 28). Bored as a sign of servitude (Ex 21:5, 6).

See Deafness.

Figurative: Anthropomorphic uses of: Thou wilt hear me, O God: incline thine ear unto me *and hear* (Ps 17:6).

Give ear unto my cry (Ps 39:12).

I cried unto God . . . and he gave ear unto me (Ps 77:1).

Give ear, O Shepherd (Ps 80:1).

Give ear, O God (Ps 84:8).

EARLY RISING, General References to (Ge 19:27; 26:31; Ex 8:20; 34:4; Jos 3:1; 6:15; J'g 6:38; 1Sa 5:4; 9:26; 15:12; 17:20; 2Ch 20:20; Pr 31:15; Da 6:19; M'k 16:2). To Do Evil (Ex 32:6; Nu 14:40; Job 24:14; Isa 5:11; Zep 3:7).

EARNEST, a pledge or token (Ps 86:17; 2Co 1:22; 5:5; Eph 1:14).

See Token.

EARNESTNESS (See Zeal.)

EAR-RING. Of gold (Pr 25:12). Offering of, for the golden calf (Ex 32:2, 3); for the tabernacle (Ex 35:22). Worn for idolatrous purposes (Ge 35:4; Isa 3:20).

EARTH. Primitive condition of (Ge 1:2, 6, 7; Job 26:7; Ps 104:5-9; Jer 4:23). Design of (Isa 45:18). Ancient notions concerning (1Sa 2:8; Job 9:6; Re 7:1). Cursed of God (Ge 3:17, 18; Ro 8:19-22). Circle of (Isa 40:22). God's footstool (Isa 66:1; La 2:1). Given to man (Ps 115:16). Early divisions of (Ge 10; 11; De 32:8). Perpetuity of (Ge 49:26; De 33:15; Ps 78:69; 104:5; Ec 1:4; Hab 3:6).

Created, by God (Ge 1:1; Ex 20:11; 2Ki 19:15; 2Ch 2:12; Ne 9:6; Job 38:4; Ps 90:2; 102:25; 115:15; 124:8; 146:6; Pr 8:22-26; Isa 37:16; 45:18; Jer 10:12; 27:5; 32:17; 51:15; Joh 17:24; 2Pe 3:5; Re 10:6; 14:7); by Christ (Joh 1:3, 10; Heb 1:10). See Creation; God, Creator.

Is the Lord's (Ex 9:29; 19:5; De 10:14; Ps 24:1; 50:12; 1Co 10:26). Created for habitation (Isa 45:18).

Destruction of, foretold (Ps 102:25-27; Isa 24:19, 20; 51:6; M't 5:18; 24:3, 6, 14, 29-31, 35-39; M'k 13:24-37; Lu 21:26-36; 2Pe 3:10-13; Re 20:11; 21:1). A new earth (Isa 65:17; 66:22; 2Pe 3:13; Re 21:1).

EARTHENWARE (See Pottery.)

EARTHQUAKES (Job 9:6; Ps 18:7; 46:2, 3; 104:32; Jer 4:24). As judgments (Ps 18:15; 60:2; Isa 13:13, 14; 24:19, 20; 29:6; Na 1:5). Prophecies of (Eze 38:19; Zec 14:4; M't 24:7; M'k 13:8; Lu 21:11; Re 11:19).

Instances of: At Sinai (Ex 19:18; Ps 68:8; 77:18; 114:4-7; Heb 12:26). When Korah, Dathan, and Abiram were swallowed up (Nu 16:31, 32). When Jonathan and his armorbearer attacked the garrison at Gibeah (1Sa 14:15). When the Lord revealed himself to Elijah in the still small voice (1Ki 19:11). In Canaan, in the days of Uzziah, king of Judah (Am 1:1; Zec 14:5). At the crucifixion of Jesus (M't 27:51). At the resurrection of Jesus (M't 28:2). When Paul and Silas were in prison at Philippi (Ac 16:26).

Figurative: Ps 60:2.

Symbolical: Re 6:12-14; 11:13; 16:18, 20.

EAST (place of the sunrise, east), a significant direction for the Hebrews (Ex 38:13; Nu 3:38; 10:14; Eze 10:19; 11:23; 43:2, 4). "Children of the east" means people of lands E of Palestine (Job 1:3).

EAST SEA (See Dead Sea.)

EAST WIND, hot, dry wind coming from the E (Jer 4:11); destructive (Ge 41:6; Eze 17:10); used as a means of judgment by God (Isa 27:8; Jer 18:17).

EASTER (passover), rendered *Easter* in Ac 12:4 KJV, but should be *Passover,* as in ASV. The day on which the church celebrates the resurrection of Jesus Christ.

EATING. The host acting as waiter (Ge 18:8). Favored guests served an extra portion (Ge 43:34). Table used in (J'g 1:7). Sitting at table (Ex 32:6). Reclining on couches (Am 4, 6, 7; Lu 7:37, 38; Joh 13:25). Ablutions before (M't 15:2).

See Feasts; Food; Gluttony.

EBAL. 1. Son of Joktan (1Ch 1:22).

2. A Horite (Ge 36:23; 1Ch 1:40).

3. A mountain of Ephraim. Half of the tribes of Israel stand on, to respond Amen to the curses of the law (De 11:29; 27:12, 13; Jos 8:33). Altar built on (Jos 8:30).

See Gerizim.

EBED (servant). 1. Father of Gaal (J'g 9:26-45).

2. Son of Jonathan (Ezr 8:6).

EBED-MELECH (servant of the king), Ethiopian eunuch who pulled Jeremiah out of a miry dungeon (Jer 39:15-18). Prophecy concerning (Jer 39:16-18).

EBEN-EZER (stone of help), town of Ephraim where Israelites were defeated by Philistines (1Sa 5:1). Later, after defeating Philistines, the Israelites erected a memorial stone, calling it Eben-ezer (1Sa 7:12).

EBER (beyond), called also Heber. 1. The probable founder of the Hebrew race (Ge 10:21-25; 11:14; 1Ch 1:19, 25; Lu 3:35). Prophecy concerning (Nu 24:24).

2. A Gadite, called Heber (1Ch 5:13).

3. A Benjamite (1Ch 8:12).

4. A Benjamite of Jerusalem (1Ch 8:22).

5. A priest (Ne 12:20).

EBIASAPH, called also Asaph. A son of Korah (1Ch 6:23; 9:19; 26:1).

EBONY, a fossil. Merchandise in (Eze 27:15).

EBRONAH, the thirtieth camping place of the Israelites (Nu 33:34, 35).

ECBATANA, capital of Media, where Cyrus issued decree authorizing rebuilding of temple called Achmetha (Ezr 6:2).

ECCLESIASTES (preacher). Heb title **qoheleth, an official speaker in an assembly—the Preacher;** Gr. **Ekklesiastes.** Traditionally ascribed to Solomon. Author seems to speak from standpoint of general rather than special revelation; examines life from every angle to see where satisfaction can be found, and finds it only in God. In the meantime we are to enjoy the good things of life as gifts of God, but in everything we must remember the Creator. Two divisions of thought in the book: the futility of life; the answer of practical faith.

ECCLESIASTICISM. The Jewish, rebuked by Jesus (M't 9:10-13; 23:2-4, 8-10, 13-35; M'k 9:49, 50); to be overthrown (M't 21:19, 20, 28-44). Traditional rules of the Jewish (M't 15:1-20; M'k 7:2-23). See Commandments of Men, Arrogance of (M't 12:2-7; 23:4).

See Ministers, False; Church; Usurpation, in Ecclesiastical Affairs.

ECLIPSE. Of the sun and moon (Isa 13:10; Eze 32:7, 8; Joel 2:10, 31; 3:15; Am 8:9; Mic 3:6; M't 24:29; M'k 13:24; Ac 2:20; Re 6:12, 13; 8:12).

See Sun; Moon.

Figurative: Isa 60:19.

ECONOMY, POLITICAL (See Economics; Government.)

ECONOMICS. Political (Ge 41:33-57). Household (Pr 24:27; 31:10-31; Ec 11:4-6; Joh 6:12, 13).

See Family; Frugality; Industry.

ECUMENICISM (derived from Gr. oikoumene, the whole inhabited world), a movement among Christian religous groups—Protestant, Eastern Orthodox, Roman Catholic—to bring about a closer unity in work and organization. The word is not found in the Bible, but Biblical backing for the movement is found in John 17 where Jesus prays for the unity of His church.

ED, name of the altar, erected by the tribes, Reuben, Gad, and Manasseh at the fords of the Jordan (Jos 22:34).

EDAR, tower near which Jacob encamped on way back to Canaan (Ge 35:21).

EDEN (delight). 1. The garden of Eden (Ge 2:8-17; 3:23, 24; 4:16; Isa 51:3; Eze 28:13; 31:9, 16, 18; 36:35; Joe 2:3).

2. A mart of costly merchandise (2Ki 19:12; Isa 37:12; Eze 27:23; Am 1:5).

3. A Gershonite (2Ch 29:12).

4. A Levite (2Ch 31:15).

EDER (floods), called also Edar.

1. A place near Ephrath (Ge 35:21).

2. A City of Judah (Jos 15:21).

3. A grandson of Merari (1Ch 23:23; 24:30).

EDOM (red). 1. A name of Esau, possibly on account of his being covered with red hair (Ge 25:25, 30; 36:1, 8, 19).

2. A name of the land occupied by the descendants of Esau. It extended from the Elanitic Gulf to the Red Sea, and was called also Idumea (Ge 32:3; 36:16, 17, 21; Jer 40:11).

Noted for its wise men (Ob 8). Sins of (Ob 10-14). Prophecies concerning (Jer 25:21-23; 27:1-11; Da 11:41).

See Edomites.

Figurative: Of the foes of Zion (Isa 63:1).

Wilderness of (2Ki 3:8).

EDOMITES, called also Edom. Descendants of Esau (Ge 36). Kings of (Ge 36:31-39; Nu 20:14; 1Ch 1:43-50; Eze 32:29; Am 2:1). Dukes of (Ge 36:9-43; Ex 15:15; 1Ch 1:51-54). Land of (Ge 32:3; De 2:4, 5, 12).

Protected by divine command from desolation by the Israelites (De 2:4-6); from being held in abhorrence by the Israelites (De 23:7). Refuse to the Israelites passage through their country (Nu 20:18-21). Saul makes war against (1Sa 14:47). David makes conquest of (1Ki 11:14-16; 1Ch 18:11-13); garrisons (2Sa 8:14); writes battle songs concerning his conquest of (Ps 60:8, 9; 108:9, 10). Become confederates of Jehoshaphat (2Ki 3:9, 26). Ruled by a deputy king (1Ki 22:47). The Lord delivers the army of, into the hands of Jehoshaphat (2Ch 20:20, 23). Revolt in the days of Joram (2Ki 8:20-22; 2Ch 21:8-10). Amaziah, king of Judah, invades the territory of (2Ki 14:5-7, 10; 2Ch 25:11, 12; 28:17). Join Babylon in war against the Israelites (Eze 35:5; Am 1:9-11; Ob 11-16). A Jewish prophet in Babylon denounces (Ps 137:7; Eze 25:12-14; 35:3-10). Children of the third generation might be received into the congregation of Israel (De 23:8). Prophecies concerning (Ge 25:23; 27:29, 37-40; Nu 24:18; Isa 11:14; 21:11, 12; 34; 63:1-4; Jer 9:25, 26; 27:1-11; 49:7-22; La 4:21, 22; Eze 25:12-14; 32:29, 30, 35; 36:5; Joe 3:19; Am 1:11, 12; 9:12; Ob 1-21; Mal 1:2-5).

EDREI (strong). 1. A chief city of Og, king of Bashan (De 1:4; Jos 12:4). Assigned to Manasseh (Jos 13:12, 31). Located c. 10 miles NE of Ramoth-Gilead.

2. City of Naphtali, location unknown (Jos 19:37).

EDUCATION (See Instruction; Teachers; Schools; Mathematics.)

EGG (whiteness) Job 6:6; Lu 11:12, appears also in the plural form (De 22:6; Job 39:14; Isa 10:14).

EGLAH (heifer), wife of David (2Sa 3:5; 1Ch 3:3).

EGLAIM, city of Moab (Isa 15:8).

EGLON. 1. City of Canaan located between Gaza and Lachish (Jos 10:3, 5, 23); captured by Joshua (Jos 10:36, 37; 12:12); assigned to Judah (Jos 15:39).

2. King of Moab who captured Jericho from Israelites (J'g 3:12, 13, 14, 21).

EGOTISM (See Conceit.)

EGYPT. *The Country of.* Called Rahab (Ps 87:4; 89:10); Land of Ham (Ps 105:23; 106:22). Limits of (Eze 29:10). Fertility of (Ge 13:10). Productions of (Nu 11:5; Ps 78:47; Pr 7:16; Isa 19:5-9). Irrigation employed in (De 11:10). Imports of (Ge 37:25, 36). Exports of (Pr 7:16; Eze 27:7); of horses (1Ki 10:28, 29).

Famine in (Ge 41; Ac 7:11). Armies of (Ex 14:7; Isa 31:1). Army of destroyed in the Red Sea (Ex 14:5-31; Isa 43:17). Magi of (Ge 41:8; Ex 7:11; 1Ki 4:30; Ac 7:22). Priests of (Ge 41:45; 47:22). Idols of (Eze 20:7, 8).

Overflowed by the Nile (Am 8:8; 9:5). Plagues in, see Plagues. Joseph's captivity in, and subsequent rule over, see Joseph. Civil war in (Isa 19:2). The king acquires title to land of (Ge 47:18-26). Abraham dwells in (Ge 12:10-20; 13:1). Israelites in bondage in, see Israelites. Joseph takes Jesus to (M't 2:13-20).

Prophecies against (Ge 15:13, 14; Isa 19; 20:2-6; 45:14; Jer 9:25, 26; 43:8-13; 44:30; 46; Eze 29-32; Ho 8:13; Joe 3:11; Zec 10:11).

See Egyptians.

Symbolical: Re 11:8.

River, or Brook of: Perhaps identical with Sihor, which see. A small stream flowing into the Mediterranean Sea, the western boundary of the land promised to the children of Israel (Ge 15:18; Nu 34:5; Jos 13:3; 15:4, 47; 1Ki 8:65; 2Ki 24:7; Isa 27:12; Eze 47:19; 48:28).

EGYPTIANS. Descendants of the Mizraim (Ge 10:6, 13, 14). Wisdom of (1Ki 4:30). The art of embalming the dead practiced by (Ge 50:2, 3, 26). Hospitality of, to Abraham (Ge 12:10-20). Slaves bought by (Ge 37:36). Oppress the Israelites (Ex 1, 2). Refuse to release the Israelites (Ex 5-10). Visited by plagues (Ex 7-12; Ps 78:43-51); firstborn of, destroyed (Ex 12:29; Ps 78:51; 105:36; 136:10). Send the Israelites away (Ex 12:29-36). Pursue Israelites, and the army of, destroyed (Ex 14:5-30; Ps 106:11; Heb 11:29).

Abhorred shepherds (Ge 46:34). Refused to eat with Hebrews (Ge 43:32). Alliances with, forbidden to the Israelites (Isa 30:2; 31:1; 36:6; Eze 17:15; 29:6). Eligible to membership in Israelitish congregation in the third generation (De 23:7, 8).

Invade the land of Israel: Under Shishak (1Ki 14:25, 26; 2Ch 12:2-9); Pharaoh-nechoh (2Ki 23:29-35; 2Ch 35:20-24; 36:3, 4). Aid the Israelites against the Chaldeans (Jer 37:5-11). Intermarry with the Jews (1Ki 3:1).

An enthusiastic Egyptian instigated rebellion against Roman government (Ac 21:38).

Prophecies of dispersion and restoration of (Eze 29:12-15; 30:23, 26). Conversion of, foretold (Isa 19:18).

See Egypt.

EHI (See Ehud.)

EHUD (union). 1. A descendant of Benjamin (1Ch 8:6). Called Ehi (Ge 46:21). Probably identical with Ahiram, mentioned in Nu 26:38, and Aharah (1Ch 8:1), and Ahoah (verse 4), and Ahiah (verse 7), and Aher (1Ch 7:12).

2. Son of Bilhan (1Ch 7:10).

3. A Benjamite, the assassin of Eglon (J'g 3:16).

EKER, son of Ram (1Ch 2:27).

EKRON (eradication). One of the five chief cities of the Philistines (Jos 13:3). Conquered and allotted to Judah (Jos 15:11, 45; J'g 1:18). Allotted to Dan (Jos 19:43). The Ark of God taken to (1Sa 5:10). Temple of Baalzebub at (2Ki 1:2).

Prophecies against (Jer 25:20; Am 1:8; Zep 2:4, Zec 9:5).

EL (God), generic word for God in the Semitic languages; Canaanite chief god was El; name borrowed by Hebrews from Canaanites, although they usually used plural form **Elohim.** Often used in compounds.

ELA, father of commissary officer of Solomon (1Ki 4:18, RSV).

ELADAH, son of Ephraim (1Ch 7:20).

ELAH (terebinth). 1. Chief of Edom (Ge 36:41).

2. Valley in which David killed Goliath (1Sa 17:2, 19; 21:9).

3. King of Israel, son of Baasha; killed by Zimri (1Ki 16:8-10).

4. Father of Hoshea, the last king of Israel (2Ki 15:30; 17:1; 18:1, 9).

5. Son of Caleb (1Ch 4:15).

6. Benjamite (1Ch 9:8).

ELAM. 1. Son of Shem (Ge 10:22; 1Ch 1:17).

2. Son of Shashach (1Ch 8:24).

3. Son of Meshelemiah (1Ch 26:3).

4. Ancestor of family which returned from exile (Ezr 2:31; Ne 7:34).

5. Another ancestor of a returned family (Ezr 2:31; Ne 7:34).

6. Father of two sons returned from exile (Ezr 8:7).

7. Ancestor of man who married a foreign woman (Ezr 10:2, 26).

8. Chief who sealed covenant with Nehemiah (Ne 10:14).

9. Priest who took part in dedication of the wall (Ne 12:42).

ELAM, country situated on the E side of the Tigris opposite Babylonia; was one of the earliest civilizations; figures prominently in Babylonian and Assyrian history. Some of its people were brought to Samaria by the Assyrians (Ezr 4:9, 10). Elamites at Jerusalem on day of Pentecost (Ac 2:9).

ELAMITES. Descendants of Elam, whose name was given to the district of Elam (Ge 10:22). Present at Pentecost (Ac 2:9).

ELASAH. 1. Man who married foreign woman (Ezr 10:22).

2. Son of Shaphan; took letter to exiles in Babylon for Jeremiah (Jer 29:3).

ELATH (lofty trees), called also Eloth. A city of Idumea (De 2:8; 1Ki 9:26; 2Ch 8:17).

Conquest of, by Uzziah (2Ch 26:2); by the Syrians (2Ki 16:6).

EL-BETHEL (the God of the House of God), name given by Jacob to Luz because God there revealed Himself to him (Ge 35:7).

ELDAAH (God has called), a descendant of Abraham (Ge 25:4; 1Ch 1:33).

ELDAD (God has loved), one of Moses' 70 elders (Nu 11:24-29).

ELDERS. *In the Mosaic system* (De 1:13, 15; Heb 11:12). See Government, Mosaic; Senate.

In the church: Ordained (Ac 14:23; Tit 1:5-9). Received gifts on behalf of church (Ac 11:29, 30).

Overseers of the church (Ac 15:2-29; 16:4, 5; 20:17, 28-32; 21:18; 1Ti 5:17-19; 1Pe 5:1-5). Performed ecclesiastical duties (1Ti 4:14; Jas 5:14, 15).

Apocalyptic Vision of: Re 4:4, 10; 5:5, 6, 8, 11, 14; 7:11, 13; 11:16; 14:3; 19:4.

See Deacon. Also see Church, Government of.

ELEAD (God has testified), a descendant of Ephraim (1Ch 7:21).

ELEADAH (See Eladah.)

ELEALEH (God doth ascend), a city of Moab. Taken by the Israelites (Nu 32:3, 37). Repossessed by the Moabites (Isa 15:4; 16:9).

ELEASAH (God has made). Name of two men, or of one man, uncertain which, called also Elasah. (Compare 1Ch 2:39; 8:37; 9:43, w Jer 29:3 & Ezr 10:22).

ELEAZER (God has helped). 1. Son of Aaron (Ex 6:23; 28:1). Married a daughter of Putiel, who bore him Phinehas (Ex 6:25). After the death of Nadab and Abihu is made chief of the tribe of Levi (Nu 3:32). Duties of (Nu 4:16).

Succeeds Aaron as high priest (Nu 20:26, 28; De 10:6). Assists Moses in the census (Nu 26:63). With Joshua, divides Palestine (Nu 34:17). Death and burial of (Jos 24:33). Descendants of (1Ch 24:1-19).

2. An inhabitant of Kirjath-jearim who attended the ark (1Sa 7:1, 2).

3. A Merarite Levite (1Ch 23:21, 22; 24:28).

4. Son of Dodo, and one of David's distinguished heroes (2Sa 23:9, 10, 13; 1Ch 11:12).

5. Son of Phinehas (Ezr 8:33; Ne 12:42).

6. A returned Israelitish exile (Ezr 10:25).

7. Ancestor of Joseph, the husband of Mary (M't 1:15).

ELECT (chosen), those chosen by God for some special purpose (Ps 106:23; Isa 43:20; 45:4). Among the elect mentioned in Scripture are Moses, Israelites, Christ, angels, Christ's disciples.

ELECTION. Of grace (M't 22:14; Joh 15:16; 17:6; Ro 11:5; Eph 1:4; 2:10; 2Th 2:13; 1Pe 2:9). See Foreordination.

Of Christ as Messiah (Isa 42:1; 1Pe 2:6). Of good angels (1Ti 5:21). Of Israel (De 7:6; Isa 45:4). Of ministers (Lu 6:13; Ac 9:15). Of churches (1Pe 5:13). Of rulers (Ne 11:1).

See Predestination.

ELECTIONEERING. By Absalom (2Sa 15:1-6). Adonijah (1Ki 1:7).

ELEGY. A song of sorrow. By David, on Saul and Jonathan (2Sa 1:17, 19-27); on Abner (2Sa 3:33, 34).

See the Book of Lamentations. See also Poetry; Rhetoric.

EL-ELOHE-ISRAEL, name of an altar erected by Jacob near Shechem (Ge 33:20).

ELEMENTS (rows, series, alphabet, first principles of a science, physical elements, primary constituents of the universe, heavenly bodies, planets, personal cosmic powers). In Heb 5:12, first principles; Ga 4:3, 9, heathen deities and practices; Col 2:8, 20, rudiments.

ELEPH, town of Benjamin, near Jerusalem (Jos 18:28).

ELEPHANT (Job 40:15 [marg. *A. V.*]). See Ivory.

ELEUSIS, place in Attica where worshipers of Demeter were initiated into religious mysteries involving rebirth.

ELEVEN, THE, the 11 apostles who remained after the defection of Judas (M'k 16:14; Lu 24:9, 33; Ac 2:14).

ELHANAN. 1. A distinguished warrior in the time of David, who slew Lahmi, the brother of Goliath, the Gittite (2Sa 21:19. Compare 1Ch 20:5).

2. Son of Dodo, one of David's heroes (2Sa 23:24; 1Ch 11:26).

ELI. High priest (1Sa 1:25; 2:11; 1Ki 2:27). Judge of Israel (1Sa 4:18). Misjudges and rebukes Hannah (1Sa 1:14). His benediction upon Hannah (1Sa 1:17, 18; 2:20). Officiates when Samuel is presented at the tabernacle (1Sa 1:24-28). Indulgent to his corrupt sons (1Sa 2:22-25, 29; 3:11-14). His solicitude for the ark (1Sa 4:11-18). Death of (1Sa 4:18).

Prophecies of judgments upon his house (1Sa 2:27-36; 3, w 1Ki 2:27).

ELI, ELI, LAMA SABACHTHANI (my God, my God, why hast Thou forsaken me), one of the seven cries of Jesus from the cross (M't 27:46; M'k 15:34).

ELIAB. 1. A Reubenite, progenitor of Dathan and Abiram (Nu 26:8, 9; 16:1, 12; De 11:6).

2. Son of Helon (Nu 1:9; 2:7; 7:24, 29; 10:16).

3. Ancestor of Samuel (1Ch 6:27). Called also Elihu (1Sa 1:1); and Eliel (1Ch 6:34).

4. Son of Jesse, and eldest brother of David (1Sa 16:6; 17:13, 28; 1Ch 2:13). A prince in the tribe of Judah (1Ch 27:18).

5. A hero of the tribe of Gad (1Ch 12:9).

6. A Levite, a porter and musician (1Ch 15:18, 20; 16:5).

ELIADA. 1. Son of David (2Sa 5:16; 1Ch 3:8).

2. Benjamite general (2Ch 17:17).

3. Father of Rezon (1Ki 11:23). KJV had Eliadah.

ELIADAH, an Aramite (1Ki 11:23).

ELIAH. 1. Son of Jeroham (1Ch 8:27).

2. Israelite who divorced foreign wife (Ezra 10:26).

ELIAHBA, one of David's heroes (2Sa 23:32; 1Ch 11:33).

ELIAKIM (God sets up). 1. Master of Hezekiah's household; sent by the king to negotiate with invading Assyrians (2Ki 18:17-37; Isa 36:1-22) and then to seek help of Isaiah the prophet (2Ki 19:2; Isa 37:2).

2. Original name of king Jehoiakim (2Ki 23:34; 2Ch 36:4).

3. Priest (Ne 12:41).

4. Ancestor of Jesus (M't 1:13).

5. Another and earlier ancestor of Jesus (Lu 3:30).

ELIAM. 1. Father of Bath-sheba (2Sa 11:3). Called Ammiel (1Ch 3:5).

2. One of David's valiant men (2Sa 23:34). Called Ahijah (1Ch 11:36).

ELIAS, Greek form of the name Elijah, used in KJV in all occurrences in the NT.

ELIASAPH. 1. A chief of the tribe of Dan (Nu 1:14; 2:14; 7:42, 47; 10:20).

2. Son of Lael (Nu 3:24).

ELIASHIB (God restores). 1. Head of 11th priestly course (1Ch 24:12).

2. Judahite (1Ch 3:24).

3. High priest (Ne 3:1, 20, 21; 13:4, 7, 28).

4. Levite who put away his foreign wife (Ezr 10:24).

5. Man who married a foreign wife (Ezr 10:27).

6. Another man who married a foreign wife (Ezr 10:36).

7. Ancestor of man who helped Ezra (Ezr 10:6; Ne 12:10, 22, 23).

ELIATHAH, a musician (1Ch 25:4, 27).

ELIDAD, a prince of Benjamin (Nu 34:21).

ELIEL (God is God). 1. Ancestor of Samuel (1Ch 6:34). Called Eliab in 1Ch 6:27.

2. Chief of Manasseh (1Ch 5:24).

3. Son of Shimhi (1Ch 8:20).

4. Son of Shashak (1Ch 8:22).

5. Captain in David's army (1Ch 11:46).

6. One of David's heroes (1Ch 11:47).

7. Gadite; perhaps same as 5 or 6 (1Ch 12:11).

8. Chief of Judah; perhaps same as 5 (1Ch 15:9).

9. Chief Levite (1Ch 15:11).

10. Levite overseer (2Ch 31:13).

ELIENAI, a Benjamite citizen of Jerusalem (1Ch 8:20).

ELIEZER (God is help). 1. Steward of Abraham (Ge 15:2). Perhaps same as servant mentioned in Ge 24.

2. Son of Moses and Zipporah (Ex 18:4; 1Ch 23:15, 17; 26:25).

3. Grandson of Benjamin (1Ch 7:8).

4. Priest (1Ch 15:24).

5. Reubenite chief (1Ch 27:16).

6. Prophet who rebuked Jehoshaphat (2Ch 20:37).

7. Chieftain sent to induce Israelites to return to Jerusalem (Ezr 8:16).

8. Priest who put away foreign wife (Ezr 10:18).

9. Levite who did the same (Ezr 10:23).

10. Son of Harim who did the same (Ezr 10:31).

11. Ancestor of Jesus (Lu 3:29).

ELIHOENAI (to Jehovah are my eyes). See also Elioenai. 1. Man who returned with Ezra (Ezr 8:4).

2. Korahite doorkeeper of tabernacle

(1Ch 26:3). In KJV, Elioenai; ASV, RSV, Eliehoenai.

ELIHOREPH, son of Shisha (1Ki 4:3).

ELIHU (He is my God). 1. Son of Barachel the Buzite (Job 32-37).

2. Son of Tohu (1Sa 1:1). Probably identical with Eliel (1Ch 6:34), and Eliab (1Ch 6:27).

3. A Manassite warrior, who joined David at Ziklag (1Ch 12:20).

4. A porter of the temple (1Ch 26:7).

5. A chief of the tribe of Judah (1Ch 27:18). Possibly Eliab, the oldest of David (1Sa 16:6).

ELIJAH (Jehovah is God). 1. The Tishbite, a Gileadite and prophet, called Elias in the authorized version of the NT. Persecuted by Ahab (1Ki 17:2-7; 18:7-10). Escapes to the wilderness, where he is miraculously fed by ravens (1Ki 17:1-7). By divine direction goes to Zarephath, where he is sustained in the household of a widow, whose meal and oil are miraculously increased (1Ki 17:8-16). Returns, and sends a message to Ahab (1Ki 18:1-16). Meets Ahab and directs him to assemble the prophets of Baal (1Ki 18:17-20). Derisively challenges the priests of Baal to offer sacrifices (1Ki 18:25-29). Slays the prophets of Baal (1Ki 18:40). Escapes to the wilderness from the fierceness of Jezebel (1Ki 19:1-18). Fasts forty days (1Ki 19:8). Despondency and murmuring of (1Ki 19:10, 14). Consolation given to (1Ki 19:11-18). Flees to the wilderness of Damascus; directed to anoint Hazael king over Syria, Jehu king over Israel, and Elisha to be a prophet in his own stead (1Ki 19:9-21). Personal aspect of (2Ki 1:8).

Piety of (1Ki 19:10, 14; Lu 1:17; Ro 11:2; Jas 5:17). His translation (2Ki 2:11). Appears to Jesus at his transfiguration (M't 17:3, 4; M'k 9:4; Lu 9:30). Antitype of John the Baptist (M't 11:14; 16:14; 17:10-12; M'k 9:12, 13; Lu 1:17; Joh 1:21-25).

Miracles of: Increases the oil of the widow of Zarephath (1Ki 17:14-16). Raises from the dead the son of the woman of Zarephath (1Ki 17:17-24). Causes rain after a drought of three and a half years (1Ki 18:41-45; Jas 5:17, 18). Causes fire to consume the sacrifice (1Ki 18:24, 36-38). Calls fire down upon the soldiers of Ahaziah (2Ki 1:10-12; Lu 9:54).

Prophecies of: Foretells a drought (1Ki 17:3); the destruction of Ahab and his house (1Ki 21:17-29; 2Ki 9:25-37); the death of Ahaziah (2Ki 1:2-17); the plague sent as a judgment upon the people in the time of Jehoram, king of Israel (2Ch 21:12-15).

2. Called also Eliah. A Benjamite chief (1Ch 8:27).

3. A post-exile Jew (Ezr 10:21).

ELIKA, one of David's chiefs (2Sa 23:25).

ELIM (terebinths), 2nd stopping-place of Israelites in the wilderness (Ex 15:27; 16:1; Nu 33:9, 10).

ELIMELECH (my God is king), husband of Naomi (Ru 1:2, 3; 2:1, 3; 4:3, 9).

ELIOENAI (to Jehovah are my eyes). 1. Son of Neariah (1Ch 3:23, 24).

2. Simeonite prince (1Ch 4:36).

3. Benjamite (1Ch 7:8).

4. Man who put away his foreign wife (Ezr 10:22).

5. Man who divorced foreign wife (Ezr 10:27).

6. Priest, perhaps same as 4 (Ne 12:41).

ELIPHAL (God has judged), one of David's mighty men (1Ch 11:35). Perhaps same as Eliphelet in 2Sa 23:34.

ELIPHALET, son of David (2Sa 5:16; 1Ch 14:7).

ELIPHAZ (God is gold). 1. Son of Esau by Adah (Ge 36:4-16; 1Ch 1:35, 36).

2. Chief of Job's three friends (Job 2:11); in his speeches he traces all affliction to sin.

ELIPHELEH, Levite musician (1Ch 15:18, 21).

ELIPHELET. 1. A distinguished warrior (2Sa 23:34).

2. A son of David (1Ch 3:6). Called Elpalet (1Ch 14:5).

3. A son of David, probably identical with 2, above (2Sa 5:16; 1Ch 3:8; 14:7). Called Eliphalet in 2Sa 5:16; 1Ch 14:7.

4. A descendant of Saul (1Ch 8:39).

5. A companion of Ezra (Ezr 8:13).

6. An Israelite, probably identical with No. 5, above (Ezr 10:33).

ELISABETH, wife of Zacharias and mother of John the Baptist (Lu 1:5-60).

ELISEUS (Lu 4:27). See Elisha.

ELISHA, successor to the prophet Elijah. Elijah instructed to anoint (1Ki 19:16). Called by Elijah (1Ki 19:19). Ministers unto Elijah (1Ki 19:21). Witnesses Elijah's translation, receives a double portion of his spirit (2Ki 2:1-15; 3:11). Mocked by the children of Beth-el (2Ki 2:23, 24). Causes the king to restore the property of the hospitable Shunammite (2Ki 8:1-6). Instructs that Jehu be anointed king of Israel (2Ki 9:1-3). Life of, sought by Jehoram (2Ki 6:31-33). Death of (2Ki 13:14-20). Bones of, restore a dead man to life (2Ki 13:21).

Miracles of: Divides the Jordan (2Ki 2:14). Purifies the waters of Jericho by casting salt into the fountain (2Ki 2:19-22). Increases the oil of the woman whose sons were to be sold for debt (2Ki 4:1-7). Raises from the dead the son of the Shunammite (2Ki 4:18-37). Neutralizes the poison of the pottage (2Ki 4:38-41). Increases the bread to feed one hundred men (2Ki 4:42-44). Heals Naaman the leper (2Ki 5:1-19; Lu 4:27). Sends leprosy as a judgment upon Gehazi (2Ki 5:26, 27). Recovers the ax that had fallen into a stream by causing it to float (2Ki 6:6). Reveals the counsel of the king of Syria (2Ki 6:12). Opens the eyes of his servant to see the hosts of the Lord (2Ki 6:17). Brings blindness upon the army of Syria (2Ki 6:18).

Prophecies of: Foretells a son to the Shunammite woman (2Ki 4:16); plenty to the starving in Samaria (2Ki 7:1), death of the unbelieving prince (2Ki 7:2); seven years' famine in the land of Canaan (2Ki 8:1-3); death of Ben-hadad, king of Syria (2Ki 8:7-10); elevation of Hazael to the throne (2Ki 8:11-15); the victory of Jehoash over Syria (2Ki 13:14-19).

ELISHAH (God saves), son of Javan, whose name was given to an ancient land and its people, not identified (Ge 10:4; 1Ch 1:7; Eze 27:7).

ELISHAMA. (God has heard). 1. Grandfather of Joshua (Nu 1:10; 2:18; 7:48, 53; 10:22; 1Ch 7:26).

2. A son of David (2Sa 5:16; 1Ch 3:8; 14:7).

3. Another son of David, elsewhere called Elishua, which see (1Ch 3:6).

4. A descendant of Judah (1Ch 2:41).

5. Probably identical with No. 4 (2Ki 25:25; Jer 41:1).

6. A secretary to Jehoiakim (Jer 36:12, 20, 21).

7. A priest sent by Jehoshaphat to teach the law (2Ch 17:8).

ELISHAPHAT, a Jewish captain (2Ch 23:1).

ELISHEBA, wife of Aaron (Ex 6:23).

ELISHUA, son of David (2Sa 5:15; 1Ch 14:5). Called Elishama in 1Ch 3:6.

ELIUD, ancestor of Christ (M't 1:14, 15).

ELIZABETH (God is my oath), wife of Zacharias (Lu 1:5-57); mother of John the Baptist; kinswoman to Mary, RSV.

ELIZAPHAN (God has concealed). 1. A Levite (Ex 6:22; Le 10:4; Nu 3:50; 1Ch 15:8).

2. A prince of Zebulun (Nu 34:25).

3. Probably identical with 1, above (2Ch 29:13).

ELIZUR, a chief of Reuben (Nu 1:5; 2:10; 7:30, 35; 10:18).

ELKANAH (God has possessed). 1. Grandson of Korah (Ex 6:24; 1Ch 6:23).

2. Father of Samuel; a descendant of preceding (1Sa 1:1, 4, 8, 19, 21, 23; 2:11, 20; 1Ch 6:27, 34).

3. A Levite (1Ch 6:25, 36).

4. Possibly identical with 3, above (1Ch 6:26, 35).

5. A Levite (1Ch 9:16).

6. A Levite who joined David at Ziklag (1Ch 12:6).

7. A doorkeeper for the ark, perhaps identical with 6, above (1Ch 15:23).

8. A prince of Ahaz (2Ch 28:7).

ELKOSH, birthplace of Nahum the prophet (Na 1:1).

ELLASAR, city-state in Babylonia in time of Abraham (Ge 14:1, 9).

ELM (Ho 4:13).

ELMODAM, an ancestor of Jesus (Lu 3:28).

ELNAAM, father of two distinguished warriors (1Ch 11:46).

ELNATHAN (God has given). 1. Grandfather of Jehoiachin (2Ki 24:8).

2. Son of Achbor (Jer 26:22). May be same as 1.

3. Levites who helped Ezra (Ezr 8:16).

ELOHIM, the most frequent Hebrew word for God; plural "Elohim" (Ge 1:1). Used of heathen gods (Ex 18:11), angels (Ps 8:5), judges (Ex 21:6), and Jehovah.

ELON. 1. Father-in-law of Esau (Ge 26:34; 36:2).
2. A son of Zebulun (Ge 46:14; Nu 26:26).
3. A town of Dan (Jos 19:43).
4. A Hebrew judge (J'g 12:11, 12).

ELON-BETH-HANAN. A town of Dan (1Ki 4:9). Perhaps identical with Elon in Jos 19:43.

ELONITES, descendants of Elon, son of Zebulun (Nu 26:26).

ELOTH (See Elath.)

ELPAAL, a Benjamite (1Ch 8:11, 12, 18).

ELPALET. A son of David (1Ch 14:5). Called Eliphalet in 1Ch 3:6.

ELPARAN, a place in the wilderness of Paran (Ge 14:6).

EL SHADDAI, probably "Almighty God," the name by which God appeared to Abraham, Isaac, and Jacob (Ex 6:3).

ELTEKEH, a city of Dan (Jos 19:44; 21:23).

ELTEKON, a city of Judah (Jos 15:59).

ELTOLAD. A city of Judah (Jos 15:30; 19:4). Called Tolad in 1Ch 4:29.

ELUL. Sixth month [September]. The Jews finish the wall of Jerusalem in (Ne 6:15). Zerubbabel builds the temple in (Hag 1:14, 15).

ELUZAI, a Benjamite (1Ch 12:5).

ELYMAS, a false prophet, punished with blindness (Ac 13:8, 10).

ELZABAD. 1. A Gadite (1Ch 12:12).
2. A Korhite (1Ch 26:7).

ELZAPHAN (See Elizaphan.)

EMANCIPATION, of all Jewish servants (Ex 21:2; Le 25:8-17, 39-41; De 15:12).

Proclamation of: By Zedekiah (Jer 34:8-11); by Cyrus (2Ch 36:23; Ezr 1:1-4).

See Exodus; Jubilee.

EMBALMING. Of Jacob (Ge 50:2, 3); of Joseph (Ge 50:26); of Asa (2Ch 16:14); of Jesus (M'k 15:46; 16:1; Joh 19:39, 40).

EMBEZZLEMENT (Lu 16:1-7).

See Dishonesty; Fraud.

EMBLEMS OF THE HOLY GHOST, THE.

Water: (Joh 3:5; 7:38, 39). Cleansing (Eze 16:9; 36:25; Eph 5:26; Heb 10:22). Fertilizing (Ps 1:3; Isa 27:3, 6; 44:3, 4; 58:11). Refreshing (Ps 46:4; Isa 41:17, 18). Abundant (Joh 7:37, 38). Freely given (Isa 55:1; Joh 4:14; Re 22:17).

Fire: (M't 3:11). Purifying (Isa 4:4; Mal 3:2, 3). Illuminating (Ex 13:21; Ps 78:14). Searching (Zep 1:12, w 1Co 2:10).

Wind: Independent (Joh 3:8; 1Co 12:11). Powerful (1Ki 19:11, w Ac 2:2). Sensible in its effects (Joh 3:8). Reviving (Eze 37:9, 10, 14).

Oil: (Ps 45:7). Healing (Lu 10:34; Jas 5:14; Re 3:18). Comforting (Isa 61:3; Heb 1:9). Illuminating (M't 25:3, 4; 1Jo 2:20, 27). Consecrating (Ex 29:7; 30:30; Isa 61:1).

Rain and Dew: (Ps 72:6). Fertilizing (Eze 34:26, 27; Ho 6:3; 10:12; 14:5). Refreshing (Ps 68:9; Isa 18:4). Abundant (Ps 133.3). Imperceptible (2Sa 17:12, w M'k 4:26-28).

A Dove: (M't 3:16). Gentle (M't 10:16, w Ga 5:22).

A Voice: (Isa 6:8). Speaking (M't 10:20). Guiding (Isa 30:21, w Joh 16:13). Warning (Heb 3:7-11).

A Seal: (Re 7:2). Securing (Eph 1:13, 14; 4:30). Authenticating (Joh 6:27; 2Co 1:22).

Cloven Tongues: (Ac 2:3, 6-11).

EMBROIDERY. In blue and purple and scarlet on the curtains of the tabernacle (Ex 26:1, 36; 27:16); on the girdle and coat of the high priest, mingled with gold (Ex 28:4, 39). On the garments of Sisera (J'g 5:30). On the garments of princes (Eze 26:16). On the garments of women (Ps 45:14; Eze 16:10, 13, 18). Bezaleel and Aholiab divinely inspired for in the work of the tabernacle (Ex 35:30-35; 38:22, 23).

See Tapestry.

EMERALD, a precious stone. Color of the rainbow (Re 4:3). Merchandise of, in Tyre (Eze 27:16; 28:13). Set in the breastplate (Ex 28:18).

Symbolical: In the foundation of the holy city (Re 21:19).

EMERGENCY. (See Decision).

EMERODS (See Hemorrhoids.)

EMIMS, a race of giants (Ge 14:5; De 2:10, 11).

EMMANUEL (God with us), name of child which virgin would bear (Isa 7:14) and at whose birth salvation would be near. Micah 5:2 takes Him to be the Messiah.

EMMAUS, village seven miles from Jerusalem (Lu 24:7-35).

EMMOR, father of Sychem (Ac 7:16). Same as Hamor.

EMPLOYEE. Character of unrighteous (Job 7:1-3; 14:1, 6; M't 20:1-15; 21:33-41; Joh 10:12, 13).

Rights of: Just compensation (M't 10:10; Lu 10:7; Ro 4:4; Col 4:1; 1Ti 5:8); prompt payment (Le 19:13); participation of produce (Le 25:6).

Kindness to exemplified (Ru 2:4; Lu 15:17, 19). Oppression of (De 24:14, 15; Pr 22:16; Mal 3:5; Lu 15:15-17; Jas 5:4).

See Employer; Master; Servants.

EMPLOYER. Required: To be kind (Le 25:40-43; Job 31:13-15; Eph 6:9; Ph'm 15, 16). To grant Sabbath rest (Ex 20:10; De 5:14). To accord just compensation (Jer 22:13; M't 10:10; 20:1-15; Lu 10:7; Ro 4:4; Col 4:1; 1Ti 5:18). To make prompt payment (Le 19:13; De 24:15; Jas 5:4, 5). Not to oppress (De 24:14; Pr 22:16; Mal 3:5).

See Employee; Labor; Master; Servant.

EMULATION. Unto salvation (Ro 11:11, 14); liberality (2Co 8:1-8); giving (2Co 9:1-5); love and good works (Heb 10:24).

Illustrated: In Esau's marriages (Ge 28:6-9). In Jacob's household (Ge 30:1-24).

ENAM (place of a fountain), city in lowland of Judah, possibly translated "open place" (Ge 38:14, 21). Not identified.

ENAN, a man of Naphtali (Nu 1:15; 2:29; 7:78, 83; 10:27).

ENCAMPMENT, places where Israelites encamped on way from Egypt to Canaan (Nu 33). Also headquarters of armies (1Sa 13:16; 2Ch 32:1).

ENCHANTMENT, the use of any form of magic, including divination: forbidden to God's people (De 18:10; Ac 8:9, 11; 13:8, 10; 19:19).

END OF THE WORLD, or consummation of the age (M't 13:39, 49; 24:3; 28:20; Heb 9:26).

EN-DOR (spring of habitation), a city of Manasseh (Jos 17:11). The witch of, consulted by Saul (1Sa 28:7-25). Deborah triumphs at, over Sisera (J'g 4; Ps 83:10).

ENDURANCE (See Perseverance.)

ENEAS (See Aeneas.)

ENEGLAIM, a place near the Dead Sea (Eze 47:10).

ENEMY. Kindness to, enjoined (Ex 23:4, 5; Pr 25:21, 22; M't 5:43-48; Lu 6:27-36; Ro 12:14, 20). Rejoicing at destruction of, forbidden (Pr 24:17, 18); not practiced by Job (Job 31:29, 30). Destruction of, enjoined (Ps 35:1-7). See Prayer, Imprecatory.

Forgiveness of: Enjoined (M't 6:12-15; 18:21-35; M'k 11:25; Lu 17:3, 4; Eph 4:31, 32; Col 3:13; 1Pe 3:9). *Instances of:* Esau, of Jacob (Ge 33:4, 11). Joseph, of brethren (Ge 45:5-15; 50:19-21). Moses, of Miriam and Aaron (Nu 12:1-13). David, of Saul (1Sa 24:10-12; 26:9, 23; 2Sa 1:14-17); of Shimei (2Sa 16:9-13; 19:23; 1Ki 2:8, 9); of Absalom and his co-conspirators (2Sa 18:5, 12, 32, 33; 19:6, 12, 13). The prophet of Judah by Jeroboam (1Ki 13:3-6). Jesus, of his persecutors (Lu 23:34). Stephen, of his murderers (Ac 7:60).

The wickedness of David's (Ps 56:2, 5, 6; 57:4, 6; 62:4; 69:4; 71:10; 102:8; 109:2-5; 129:1-3).

Figurative: Of the devil (M't 13:25, 28, 39).

EN-GANNIM (fountain). 1. A city of Judah (Jos 15:34).

2. A city of Issachar (Jos 19:21; 21:29).

EN-GEDI (fountain of wild goat), called Hazazon-tamar. A city allotted to Judah (Jos 15:62). Built by the Amorites (Ge 14:7; 2Ch 20:2). Famous for its vineyards (Song 1:14).

Wilderness of, in the vicinity of the Dead Sea. David uses as a stronghold (1Sa 23:29; 24). Cave of (1Sa 24:3).

ENGINE, of war (2Ch 26:15; Eze 26:9).

See Armies; Fort.

ENGRAFTING (See Grafting.)

ENGRAVING. In making idols (Ex 32:4). On the stones set in the priest's breastplate (Ex 28:9-11, 21, 36; 39:8-14); in the priest's girdle (Ex 39:6); in the priest's crown (Ex 39:30).

EN-HADDAH (swift fountain), a city of Issachar (Jos 19:21).

EN-HAKKORE (fountain of him who cried), a spring, miraculously supplied to Samson (J'g 15:19).

EN-HAZOR (fountain of the village), fortified city in Naphtali (Jos 19:37).

EN-MISHPAT (fountain of judgment), ancient name of Kadesh (Ge 14:7).
See Kadesh.

ENOCH (consecrated). 1. Cain's eldest son (Ge 4:17).
2. City built by Cain (Ge 4:17).
3. Father of Methuselah (Ge 5:21, 22); walked with God (Ge 5:24); translated to heaven (Ge 5:18-24; Heb 11:5).

ENOCH, BOOKS OF, apocalyptic literature written by various authors and circulated under the name of Enoch; written c. 150 B.C. to A.D. 50.

ENON (mortal), a place E of the Jordan. John baptized near (Joh 3:23).

ENOS, son of Seth (Ge 4:26; 5:6-11; Lu 3:38). Called Enosh (1Ch 1:1).

ENQUIRING OF GOD (See Affliction, Prayer in; Prayer.)

EN-RIMMON (fountain of a pomegranate), a city of Judah, probably identical with Ain and Rimmon (Ne 11:29).

EN-ROGEL (fountain of feet), a spring near Jerusalem (Jos 15:7; 18:16; 2Sa 17:17). A rebellious feast at (1Ki 1:9).

EN-SHEMESH, a spring between Judah and Benjamin (Jos 15:7; 18:17).

ENSIGN (Ps 74:4; Isa 5:26; 11:10, 12; 18:3; 30:17; 31:9; Zec 9:16).
See Banner; Standard.

EN-TAPPUAH (spring of apple), a spring near Tappuah (Jos 17:7).

ENTERTAINMENTS. Often great (Ge 21:8; Da 5:1; Lu 5:29).

Given on Occasions of: Marriage (M't 22:2). Birth days (M'k 6:21). Weaning children (Ge 21:8). Taking leave of friends (1Ki 19:21). Return of friends (2Sa 12:4; Lu 15:23). Ratifying covenants (Ge 26:30; 31:54). Sheep-shearing (1Sa 25:2, 36; 2Sa 13:23). Harvest home (Ru 3:2-7; Isa 9:3). Vintage (J'g 9:27). Coronation of Kings (1Ki 1:9, 18, 19; 1Ch 12:39, 40; Hos 7:5). Offering voluntary sacrifice (Ge 31:54; De 12:6, 7; 1Sa 1:4, 5, 9). Festivals (1Sa 20:5, 24-26). National deliverance (Es 8:17; 9:17-19). Preparations made for (Ge 18:6, 7; Pr 9:2; M't 22:4; Lu 15:23).

Kinds of, Mentioned in Scripture: Dinner (Ge 43:16; M't 22:4; Lu 14:12). Supper (Lu 14:12; Joh 12:2). Banquet of wine (Es 5:6). Under the direction of a symposiarch or master of the feast (Joh 2:8, 9). Served often by hired servants (M't 22:3; Joh 2:5). Served often by members of the family (Ge 18:8; Lu 10:40; Joh 12:2).

Invitations to: Often addressed to many (Lu 14:16). Often only to relatives and friends (1Ki 1:9; Lu 14:12). Often by the master in person (2Sa 13:24; Es 5:4; Zep 1:7; Lu 7:36). Repeated through servants when all things were ready (Pr 9:1-5; Lu 14:17). Should be sent to the poor (De 14:29, w Lu 14:13).

Often Given in: The house (Lu 5:29). The air, beside fountains (1Ki 1:9). The court of the house (Es 1:5, 6; Lu 7:36, 37). The upper room or guest chamber (M'k 14:14, 15).

Guests at: Saluted by the master (Lu 7:45). Usually anointed (Ps 23:5; Lu 7:46). Had their feet washed when they came a distance (Ge 18:4; 43:24; Lu 7:38, 44). Arranged according to rank (Ge 43:33; 1Sa 9:22; Lu 14:10). Often had separate dishes (Ge 43:34; 1Sa 1:4). Often ate from the same dish (M't 26:23). Forwardness to take chief seats at, condemned (M't 23:6; Lu 14:7, 8). A choice portion reserved in, for principal guests (Ge 43:34; 1Sa 1:5; 1Sa 9:23, 24). Custom of presenting the sop at, to one of the guests, alluded to (Joh 13:26). Portions of, often sent to the absent (2Sa 11:8; Ne 8:10; Es 9:19). Offence given by refusing to go to (Lu 14:18, 24). Anxiety to have many guests at, alluded to (Lu 14:22, 23). Men and women did not usually meet at (Es 1:8, 9; M'k 6:21, w M't 14:11). None admitted to, after the master had risen and shut the door (Lu 13:24, 25). Began with thanksgiving (1Sa 9:13; M'k 8:6). Concluded with a hymn (M'k 14:26). None asked to eat more than he liked at (Es 1:8). Music and dancing often introduced at (Am 6:5; M'k 6:22; Lu 15:25). Often scenes of great intemperance (1Sa 25:36; Da 5:3, 4; Hos 7:5). Given by the guests in return (Job 1:4; Lu 14:12).

ENTHUSIASM. Instances of: Gideon (J'g 6, 7); Jehu (2Ki 9:1-14; 10:1-28).
See Zeal.

ENUMERATION (See Census.)

ENVY. Characteristic of, depravity (Ro 1:29; Tit 3:3); carnality (Ro 13:13; 1Co 3:3; 2Co 12:20; Ga 5:19-21; 1Ti 6:4; Jas 3:14, 16); lust (Jas 4:5). Not characteristic of love (1Co 13:4).

Described as: Destroying (Job 5:2); rotting (Pr 14:30); consuming (Pr 27:4; Song 8:6); vanity (Ec 4:4); cruel (Song 8:6); evil (Jas 3:16).

Forbidden (Ps 37:1, 7; 49:16; Pr 3:31; 23:17; 24:1, 19; Ro 13:13; Ga 5:26; Jas 5:9; 1Pe 2:1). Punishment for (Eze 35:11).

Instances of: Cain, of Abel (Ge 4:4-8). Sarah, of Hagar (Ge 16:5, 6; 21:9, 10). Philistines, of Isaac (Ge 26:14). Rachel, of Leah (Ge 30:1). Leah, of Rachel (Ge 30:15). Laban's sons, of Jacob (Ge 31:1). Joseph's brothers, of Joseph (Ge 37:4-11, 18-20; Ac 7:9). Joshua, of Eldad and Melad (Nu 11:28-30). Miriam and Aaron, of Moses (Nu 12:1-10). Korah, Dathan and Abiram, of Moses (Nu 16:3; Ps 106:16-18). Saul, of David (1Sa 18:8, 9, 29; 1Sa 20:31). Haman, of Mordecai (Es 5:13). Asaph, at prosperity of wicked (Ps 73:3). The wicked, at exaltation or prosperity of the righteous (Ps 112:10; Isa 26:11). The princes of Babylon, of Daniel (Da 6:4). Priests, of Jesus (M't 27:18; M'k 15:10; Joh 11:47). Jews, of Paul and Barnabas (Ac 13:45; 17:5).

EPAENETUS (praised), convert of Paul (Ro 16:5).

EPAPHRAS, a co-laborer with Paul (Col 1:7; 4:12; Ph'm 23).

EPAPHRODITUS (lovely). A messenger of Paul (Ph'p 2:25; 4:18). Sick at Rome (Ph'p 2:26, 27, 30).

EPHAH. 1. A son of Midian (Ge 25:4; 1Ch 1:33; Isa 60:6).

2. Caleb's concubine (1Ch 2:46).

3. Son of Jahdai (1Ch 2:47).

4. A measure of about three pecks. See Measure, Dry.

EPHAI (gloomy), Netophathite; sons warned Gedaliah (Jer 40:8-16; 41:3).

EPHER. 1. A son of Midian (Ge 25:4; 1Ch 1:33).

2. Son of Ezra (1Ch 4:17).

3. A chief of Manasseh (1Ch 5:24).

EPHESDAMMIM (boundary of blood), place between Shocoh and Azekah in Judah, where David killed Goliath (1Sa 17:1). Called Pas-dammim in 1Ch 11:13.

EPHESIANS, EPISTLE TO THE, written by Paul (1:1; 3:1) while a prisoner (3:1; 4:1; 6:20), probably at Rome (Ac 28:30, 31). Written to a number of churches, including Ephesus (1:1). Sets forth the blessings the believer has in Christ. Outline: Doctrine (Redemptive blessings, Jew and Gentile one body in Christ, Paul the messenger of this mystery), 1-3. Practical exhortations (Christians to walk as God's saints; their duties as God's family; the Christian warfare), 4-6.

EPHESUS. Paul visits and preaches in (Ac 18:19-21; 19; 20:16-38). Apollos visits and preaches in (Ac 18:18-28). Sceva's sons attempt to expel a demon in (Ac 19:13-16). Timothy directed by Paul to remain at (1Ti 1:3). Paul sends Tychicus to (2Ti 4:12). Onesiphorus lives at (2Ti 1:18). Church at (Re 1:11). See the Epistle to the Ephesians. Apocalyptic message to (Re 2:1-7).

See Paul's Epistle to the Ephesians.

EPHLAL (judge), a descendant of Pharez (1Ch 2:37).

EPHOD. 1. A sacred vestment worn by the high priest. Described (Ex 28:6-14, 31-35; 25:7). Making of (Ex 39:2-26). Breastplate attached to (Ex 28:22-29). Worn by Aaron (Ex 39:5).

Used as an oracle (1Sa 23:9, 12; 30:7, 8).

An inferior, was worn by the common priests (1Sa 22:18); by Samuel (1Sa 2:18); David (2Sa 6:14). It was called Coat (Ex 28:40; 29:8; 39:27; 40:14; Le 8:13; 10:5).

Made by Gideon, became an idolatrous snare to Israel (J'g 8:27; 17:5; 18:14).

Prophecy concerning the absence of the Ephod from Israel (Ho 3:4).

2. A man of Manasseh (Nu 34:23).

EPHPHATHA. Aramaic word meaning "be opened" (M'k 7:34).

EPHRAIM (double fruit). 1. Second son of Joseph (Ge 41:52). Adopted by Jacob (Ge 48:5). Blessed before Manasseh; prophecies concerning (Ge 48:14-20). Descendants of (Nu 26:35-37; 1Ch 7:20-27). Mourns for his sons (1Ch 7:21, 22).

2. A tribe of Israel. Prophecy concerning (Ge 49:25, 26; Isa 7; 9:18-21; 11:13; 28:1; Jer 31; Ho 5:14; Zec 9:10; 10:7). Numbered at Sinai and in plains of Moab (Nu 1:33; 26:37). Place in camp and march (Nu 2:18, 24; 10:22). Blessed by Moses (De 33:13-17).

Territory allotted to, after the conquest of Canaan (Jos 16:5-9; 17:9, 10,

15-18; 1Ch 7:28, 29). Fail to expel the Canaanites (Jos 16:10). Take Beth-el in battle (J'g 1:22-25). Upbraid Gideon for not summoning them to join the war against the Midianites (J'g 8:1). Join Gideon against the Midianites (J'g 7:24, 25). Their jealousy of Jephthah (J'g 12:1). Defeated by him (J'g 12:4-6). Receive Ish-bosheth as king (2Sa 2:9). Jeroboam set up a golden calf in Beth-el (1Ki 12:29). Revolt from house of David (1Ki 12:25; 2Ch 10:16). Some of tribe join Judah under Asa (2Ch 15:9). Chastise Ahaz and Judah (2Ch 28:7). Join Hezekiah in reinstituting the passover (2Ch 30:18). Join in the destruction of idolatrous forms in Jerusalem (2Ch 31:1). Submit to the scepter of Josiah (2Ch 34:1-6). Envied by other tribes (Isa 11:13; Jer 7:15; Eze 37:16, 19; Ho 13:1). Worshiped Baal (Ho 13:1). Sin of, remembered by God (Ho 13:12). Reallotment of territory to, by Ezekiel (Eze 48:5).

Name of, applied to the ten tribes (2Ch 17:2; 25:6, 7; Isa 7:8, 9; 11:12, 13; 17:3; Jer 31:18, 20; Ho 4:17; 5:3, 5; 6:4, 10; 8:11; 12:14). Tribe of, called Joseph (Re 7:8).

3. Mount of. A range of low mountains (Jos 17:15-18). Joshua has his inheritance in (J'g 2:9). Residence of Micah (J'g 17:8). A place of hiding for Israelites (1Sa 14:22). Sheba resides in (2Sa 20:21). Noted for rich pastures (Jer 50:19). Prophecy concerning its conversion (Jer 31:6).

4. A wood E of the Jordan. Absalom slain in (2Sa 18:6-17).

5. A gate of Jerusalem (2Ki 14:13; 2Ch 25:23; Ne 8:16; 12:39).

6. A city in the territory of Ephraim (2Ch 13:19). Jesus escapes to, from the persecution of Caiaphas (Joh 11:54).

EPHRAIMITE, member of tribe of Ephraim (Jos 16:10; J'g 12).

EPHRAIN (fawn), town taken from Jeroboam by Abijah (2Ch 13:19).

EPHRATAH (fruitful land). 1. Called also Ephrath. The ancient name of Bethlehem-judah (Ge 35:16, 19; 48:7; Ru 4:11; Ps 132:6; Mic 5:2).

2. Second wife of Caleb, mother of Hur (1Ch 2:19, 50; 4:4).

EPHRATH (See Ephratah.)

EPHRON (fawn). 1. Hittite who sold field of Machpelah to Abraham (Ge 23:8, 9).

2. Mt. c. 6 miles NW of Jerusalem (Jos 15:9).

3. City taken from Jeroboam by Abijah (2Ch 13:19).

EPIC, heroic poetry. Miriam's song (Ex 15:1-19, 21). Deborah's song (J'g 5). David's war song (2Sa 22).

See Poetry.

EPICUREANS. Reject John the Baptist (M't 11:18; Lu 7:33). Doctrines propagated by, familiar to Solomon (Ec 2:1-10); to Paul (1Co 15:32). Dispute with Paul (Ac 17:18).

See Sensualism.

EPILEPSY (M'k 9:17-22).

EPISTLE (letter), formal letters containing Christian doctrine and exhortation, referring particularly to the 21 epistles of the NT, divided into Pauline and General epistles. Not all the epistles of the apostles have survived (1Co 5:9).

EQUALITY, of men. (See Man, Equality of All Men.)

EQUITY (See Justice.)

ER (watchful). 1. Son of Judah (Ge 38:3, 6, 7; 46:12; Nu 26:19; 1Ch 2:3).

2. A son of Shelah (1Ch 4:21).

3. An ancestor of Jesus (Lu 3:28).

ERAN (watcher), a grandson of Ephraim (Nu 26:36).

ERASTUS (beloved). 1. Convert of Paul (Ac 19:22).

2. Corinthian Christian (Ro 16:23).

ERECH, Babylonian city founded by Nimrod (Ge 10:10); located 40 miles NW of Ur.

ERI (my watcher), a son of Gad (Ge 46:16; Nu 26:16).

ERRORS, in teachers and doctrines.

See Teachers, False.

ESAIAS (See Isaiah.)

ESAR-HADDON (Ashur has given a brother), son and successor of Sennacherib; ruled 681-669 B. C. (2Ki 19:37; Isa 37:38); restored city of Babylon; conquered Egypt; brought deportees into Samaria (Ezr 4:2); took Manasseh captive (2Ch 33:11).

ESAU (hairy). Eldest of twin sons born to Isaac and Rebekah. Birth of (Ge 25:19-26; 1Ch 1:34). Called Edom (Ge 36:1, 8). A hunter (Ge 25:27, 28). Beloved by Isaac (Ge 25:27, 28). Sells his birthright for a mess of pottage (Ge

25:29-34; Mal 1:2; Ro 9:13; Heb 12:16). Marries a Hittite (Ge 26:34). His marriage to, a grief to Isaac and Rebekah (Ge 26:35). Polygamy of (Ge 26:34; 28:9; 36:2, 3). Is defrauded of his father's blessing by Jacob (Ge 27; Heb 11:20). Meets Jacob on the return of the latter from Haran (Ge 33:1). With Jacob, buries his father (Ge 35:29). Descendants of (Ge 36; 1Ch 1:35-57). Enmity of descendants of, toward descendants of Jacob (Ob 10-14). Ancestor of Edomites (Jer 49:8). Mount of Edom, called Mount of Esau (Ob 8, 9, 18, 19, 21). His name used to denote his descendants and their country (De 2:5; Jer 49:8, 10; Ob 6). Prophecies concerning (Ob 18).

ESCAPE. *None, from judgment of God:* Adam and Eve (Ge 3:7-11). Cain (Ge 4:9-11). Man (Job 34:21, 22; Isa 10:3; M't 23:33; Ro 2:3; 1Th 5:2, 3; Heb 2:2, 3; 12:25, 26; Re 6:15-17).

See Sin, Fruits of, Punishment of; Judgments, No Escape From.

ESCHATOLOGY (doctrine of last things), division of systematic theology dealing with the doctrine of last things such as death, resurrection, second coming of Christ, end of the age, divine judgment, and the future state. The OT teaches a future resurrection and judgment day (Job 19:25, 26; Isa 25:6-9; 26:19; Da 12:2, 3). The NT interprets, enlarges, and completes the OT eschatology. It stresses the 2nd coming of Christ (1Co 15:51, 52), the resurrection (Ro 8:11; 1Co 15), and the final judgment when the unsaved are cast into hell (Re 20) and the righteous enter into heaven (M't 25:31-46). Christians differ on how the millennium in Re 20:1-6 is to be interpreted, dividing themselves into amillennialists, postmillennialists, and premillennialists.

ESCHEAT (See Confiscation.)

ESDRAELON, valley of Jezreel which lies between Galilee on the N and Samaria on the S; assigned to Issachar and Zebulun; scene of important battles in Bible history (J'g 4; 1Sa 31; 2Ki 23:29).

ESDRAS, BOOKS OF (See Apocrypha.)

ESEK (contention), well dug by Isaac's servants in valley of Gerar (Ge 26:20).

ESH-BAAL (man of Baal), or Ishbosheth, son of Saul; ruled two years, and then murdered by David's men (2Sa 2:8-10; 4:5-12). Originally called Eshbaal (1Ch 8:33; 9:39).

ESHBAN (man of understanding), a son of Dishan or Dishon (Ge 36:26; 1Ch 1:41).

ESHCOL (cluster). 1. An Amorite, and ally of Abraham (Ge 14:13, 24).

2. A valley or brook near Hebron (Nu 13:23, 24; 32:9; De 1:24).

ESHEAN, a city in Judah (Jos 15:52).

ESHEK (oppression), descendant of Jonathan (1Ch 8:38-40).

ESHTAOL. A town of Judah (Jos 15:33). Allotted to Dan (Jos 19:41; J'g 18:2, 8, 11). Samson moved by the spirit of the Lord near (J'g 13:25). Samson buried near (J'g 16:31).

ESHTEMOA. 1. Called also Eshtemoh. A town of Canaan assigned to Judah (Jos 15:50). Allotted to the Aaronites (Jos 21:14; 1Ch 6:57). David shared spoil with (1Sa 30:28).

2. A descendant of Ezra (1Ch 4:17, 19).

ESHTON, son of Mehir (1Ch 4:11, 12).

ESLI, an ancestor of Jesus (Lu 3:25).

ESROM, an ancestor of Jesus (M't 1:3; Lu 3:33).

ESSENES, Jewish religious sect not mentioned in the Bible, but described in Josephus, Philo, and Dead Sea Scrolls; most lived communal, celibate lives; observed Law strictly; practiced ceremonial baptisms; apocalyptic; opposed Temple priesthood.

ESTATE, vast landed (Isa 5:8).

See Land.

ESTHER (star), called also Hadassah. Niece of Mordecai (Es 2:7, 15). Chosen queen (Es 2:17). Tells the king of the plot against his life (Es 2:22). Fasts on account of the decree to destroy the Israelites; accuses Haman to the king; intercedes for her people (Es 4-9).

ESTHER, BOOK OF, last of historical books of the OT; author unknown; probably written c. 400 B. C. Peculiar features of book: no mention of the name of God; no mention of prayer. Tells of Jewish girl Esther who became queen of Persia and saved her people from destruction. Outline 1. Esther becomes queen (1-2:17)

2. Jewish danger (2:18-3:15).

3. Jews saved (4-10). In the LXX there

are several interpolations scattered through the story.

ETAM. 1. A village of Simeon (1Ch 4:32).

2. A city in Judah (2Ch 11:6).

3. A name in list of Judah's descendants, but probably referring to No. 2 (1Ch 4:3).

4. A rock where Samson was bound and delivered to the Philistines (J'g 15:8, 11-13).

ETERNAL LIFE, participation in the life of Jesus Christ, the eternal Son of God (Joh 1:4; 10:10; 17:3; Ro 6:23), which reaches its fruition in the life to come (M't 25:46; Joh 6:54; Ro 2:7; Tit 3:7). It is endless in its duration and divine in quality.

See Life, Everlasting.

ETERNAL PUNISHMENT (See Punishment, Eternal.)

ETERNITY. God inhabits (Isa 57:15; Mic 5:2); rules (Jer 10:10).

God, adoration for (Ps 30:12; 41:13); steadfastness of (Ps 72:17; 90:2; M't 6:13); righteousness of (Ps 119:142; 2Co 9:9). See God, Eternity of.

Priestly order of Melchizedek (Ps 110:4). See Christ, Eternity of.

Existence of man (M't 18:18); angels (Jude 6). See Life, Everlasting; Punishment, Eternal.

ETHAM, second camping place of Israel (Ex 13:20; Nu 33:6, 7).

ETHAN. 1. Wise man in Solomon's time (1Ki 4:31; Ps 89 title).

2. Son of Zerah (1Ch 2:6, 8).

3. Descendant of Gershon (1Ch 6:42, 43).

4. Levite singer (1Ch 6:44; 15:17, 19).

ETHANIM. Seventh month [October]. Feast of Trumpets in (Le 23:23-25). Day of Atonement, on the tenth day of (Le 23:26-32). Feast of Tabernacles in (Le 23:33-43). Jubilee proclaimed on the tenth day of (Le 25:9). Temple dedicated in (1Ki 8:2). Altar restored in, after the captivity (Ezr 3:1, 6).

ETHBAAL, king of Sidon; father of Jezebel (1Ki 16:31).

ETHER, a city of Canaan. Assigned to Judah (Jos 15:42). Subsequently allotted to Simeon (Jos 19:7). Called Tochen in 1Ch 4:32.

ETHIOPIA, a region in Africa, inhabited by the descendants of Ham. The inhabitants of, black (Jer 13:23). Within the Babylonian empire (Es 1:1). Rivers of (Ge 10:6; Isa 18:1). Bordered Egypt on the S (Eze 29:10). Was called the land of Cush (mentioned in Ge 10:6; 1Ch 1:9; Isa 11:11). Warriors of (Jer 46:9; 2Ch 1:9; Isa 11:11). Warriors of (Jer 46:9; 2Ch 12:3; Eze 38:5). Defeated by Asa (2Ch 14:9-15; 16:8). Invaded Syria (2Ki 19:9). Merchandise of (Isa 45:14). Moses marries a woman of (Nu 12:1). Ebelmelech, at the court of Babylon, native of; kindly treats Jeremiah (Jer 38:7-13; 39:15-38). Candace, queen of (Ac 8:27) A eunuch from, becomes a disciple under the preaching of Philip (Ac 8:27-39). Prophecies concerning the conversion of (Ps 68:31; 87:4; Isa 45:14; Da 11:43). Desolation of (Isa 18:1-6; 20:2-6; 43:3; Eze 30:4-9; Hab 3:7; Zep 2:12).

ETHIOPIAN EUNUCH, treasurer of Candace, queen of the Ethiopians (Ac 8:26-39); became Christian through Philip.

ETHNAN, grandson of Ashur (1Ch 4:7).

ETHNI, an ancestor of Asaph (1Ch 6:41).

ETIQUETTE (See Manners.)

EUBULUS. Roman Christian who sent greeting with Paul (2Ti 4:21).

EUCHARIST. One name for the Lord's Supper, meaning "giving of thanks."

Instituted (M't 26:17-29; M'k 14:22-25; Lu 22:19, 20; Joh 13:1-4).

Celebrated by early Church (Ac 2:42, 46; 20:7; 1Co 11:26). Bread and cup of, symbols of body and blood of Christ (M't 26:26-28; 1Co 10:16, 17, 21, 22; 11:23-25). Self-examination before taking enjoined (1Co 11:27-32). Profanation of, forbidden (1Co 11:20-22, 33, 34).

EUERGETES, "benefactors," a title of honor (Lu 22:25).

EUNICE, Timothy's mother (2Ti 1:5. See Ac 16:1).

EUNUCH, castrated male, used as custodians of royal harems and court officials (Da 1:3; Ac 8:27; 2Ki 20:18; Jer 41:16; Es 1:10-15; 2:21). Not practiced by Jews; eunuchs not allowed to enter congregation (De 23:1).

EUODIAS (fragrant), Christian woman at Philippi (Ph'p 4:2).

EUPHRATES (to break forth). A river in the garden of Eden (Ge 2:14). The eastern limit of the kingdom of Israel (Ge 15:18; Ex 23:31; De 1:7; 11:24; Jos

1:4; 2Sa 8:3; 1Ki 4:21; 1Ch 5:9; 18:3). Pharaoh-nechoh, king of Egypt, made conquest to (2Ki 24:7; Jer 46:2-10). On the banks of, Jeremiah symbolically buries his girdle (Jer 13:1-7). Casts the roll containing the prophecies against Babylon into (Jer 51:59-64).

Symbolical: The inundations of, of the extension of the empire of Assyria (Isa 8:6-8). In the symbolisms of the Apocalypse (Re 9:14; 16:12).

EUROCLYDON (an east wind raising mighty waves). E wind raising mighty waves on Mediterranean; shipwrecked Paul (Ac 27:14).

EUTYCHUS (fortunate), youth who fell asleep while Paul preached and fell out of window to his death; was restored to life by Paul (Ac 20:9, 10).

EVANGELISM (See Ministers, Duties of; Zeal.)

EVANGELIST (one who announces good news), 1. One who preached the good news of Jesus Christ from place to place (Ac 8:25; 14:7; 1Co 1:17).

2. Writer of one of the four gospels.

EVAPORATION (Ps 135:7; Jer 10:13; 51:16; Am 5:8; 9:6).

EVE (life, living). Creation of (Ge 1:26-28; 2:21-24; 1Ti 2:13). Named by Adam (Ge 2:23; 3:20). Beguiled by Satan (Ge 3; 2Co 11:3; 1Ti 2:14). Clothed with fig leaves (Ge 3:7); with skins (Ge 3:21). Curse denounced against (Ge 3:16). Messiah promised to (Ge 3:15). Children of (Ge 4:1, 2, 25; 5:3, 4).

EVENING, The. The day originally began with (Ge 1:5). Divided into two, commencing at 3 o'clock, and sunset (Ex 12:6, [*marg.*] Nu 9:3, [*marg.*]).

Called: Even (Ge 19:1; De 28:67). Eventide (Jos 8:29; Ac 4:3). Cool of the day (Ge 3:8). Stretches out its shadows (Jer 6:4). The outgoings of, praise God (Ps 65:8). Man ceases from labor in (Ru 2:17; Ps 104:23). Wild beasts come forth in (Ps 59:6, 14; Jer 5:6).

A Season For: Meditation (Ge 24:63). Prayer (Ps 55:17; M't 14:15, 23). Exercise (2Sa 11:2). Taking food (M'k 14:17, 18; Lu 24:29, 30). Humiliation often continued until (Jos 7:6; 20:23, 26; 21:2; Ezr 9:4, 5). Custom of sitting at the gates in (Ge 19:1). All defiled persons unclean until (Le 11:24-28; 15:5-7; 17:15; Nu 19:19). Part of the daily sacrifice offered in (Ex 29:41; Ps 141:2; Da 9:21). Paschal lamb killed in (Ex 12:6, 18). The golden candlestick lighted in (Ex 27:21, w Ex 30:8). The sky red in, a token of fair weather (M't 16:2).

EVENING SACRIFICE, one of two daily offerings prescribed in Mosaic ritual (Ex 29:38-42; Nu 28:3-8).

EVERLASTING ARMS (De 33:27; Isa 46:4; M'k 10:16).

EVERLASTING FIRE (See Fire, Everlasting.)

EVERLASTING LIFE (See Life, Everlasting.)

EVERLASTING PUNISHMENT (See Punishment, Eternal.)

EVI, prince of Midian, slain (Nu 31:8; Jos 13:21).

EVICTION, of Tenants (M't 21:41; M'k 12:9).

EVIDENCE. Concealment of, punished (Le 5:1). Two or more witnesses required in to sustain an allegation (Nu 35:30; De 17:6, 7; 19:15; M't 18:16; Heb 10:28). Entire community involved in (Le 24:14). False forbidden (Ex 20:16; 23:1, 7; Pr 24:28; M't 19:18). Punishment for falsehood in (De 19:16-21). Self-incriminating, extorted (Jos 7:19-21).

See Witness; False Witness; Accusation, False; Self-Crimination.

EVIL. Tree of good and (Ge 2:9, 17). Knowledge of (Ge 3:5, 22). In the heart (Ge 6:5; 8:21; Lu 6:45).

To be abhorred (Ps 97:10; Am 5:15; Ro 12:9). To be forsaken (Ps 34:14; 37:27; Pr 3:7; 1Pe 3:11). Not to be recompensed (Ro 12:17; 1Th 5:15; 1Pe 3:9).

Appearance of to be avoided (Ro 14:1-23; 1Co 8:7-13; 10:28-33; 1Th 4:11, 12; 5:22); exemplified by Paul, refusing to eat that which was offered to idols (1Co 8:13); in supporting himself (1Co 9:7-23).

See Company, Evil; Imagination, Evil; Nonresistance.

EVIL FOR EVIL (See Retaliation.)

EVIL FOR GOOD. If I have rewarded evil unto him that was at peace with me; (yea, I have delivered him that without cause is mine enemy:) Let the enemy persecute my soul, and take *it;* yea, let him tread down my life upon the earth, and lay mine honour in the dust (Ps 7:4, 5).

They rewarded me evil for good *to* the spoiling of my soul (Ps 35:12).

And they have rewarded me evil for good, and hatred for my love (Ps 109:5).

Whoso rewardeth evil for good, evil shall not depart from his house (Pr 17:13).

Instances of: Joseph accuses his brethren of rendering (Ge 44:4). Israelites, to Moses (Ex 5:21; 14:11; 15:24; 16:2, 3; 17:3, 4). Nabal returns, to David (1Sa 25:21); Saul returns, to David (1Sa 19:1, 4, 5, 10). David, to Uriah (2Sa 11); to Joab (1Ki 2:4, 5, 6).

See Enemies; Good for Evil.

EVILDOERS, Warnings to (Ps 34:16; 37:9; 94:16; 119:115; Isa 9:17; 14:20; 31:2). Examples of (J'g 2:11; 3:7; 4:1; 6:1; 10:6; 13:1; 1Ki 14:22; 15:26; 16:7; 2Ki 8:27; 13:2; 14:24; 15:9, 28; 17:2; 21:2; 23:32; 24:9; Ne 9:28; Isa 65:12; 2Ti 4:14).

EVIL-MERODACH, son and successor of Nebuchadnezzar. Released Jehoiachin from prison (2Ki 25:27-30; Jer 52:31-34).

EVIL PUT AWAY (De 13:5; 17:7; 19:19; 21:21; 22:21; 24:7; Job 22:23; 1Co 5:13).

EVIL SPEAKING (See Speaking, Evil.)

EVIL SPIRITS (See Demons.)

EWE, female sheep.

EXALTATION. *Of Christ:* See Jesus, Exaltation of.

Of Self: See Self-Exaltation.

EXAMPLE. *Bad:* Admonitions against (Le 18:2, 3; 20:23; De 18:9; 2Ch 30:7; Isa 8:11; Ho 4:9, 15; Zec 1:4; M't 23:1-3; 1Co 8:9-13; 10:6; Eph 4:17; 3Jo 11). Corrupting (Pr 22:24, 25; Jer 16:12; 17:1, 2; Eze 20:18; Ho 4:9; 5:5).

Good: Enjoined (1Ti 4:12; Tit 2:7, 8; 1Pe 5:3). Inspiring (Ne 5:8-19; 1Th 1:6-8; 1Pe 2:11-25). To be imitated (Heb 13:7; Jas 5:10, 11). Illustrated (Ps 101:2; 1Pe 3:5, 6).

God, our: In holiness (Le 11:44; 19:2). In perfection (M't 5:48). In mercy (Lu 6:36). In not discriminating (Eph 6:9).

Christ, our: In service (M't 20:28; M'k 10:43-45; Lu 22:27; Joh 13:13-17, 34; Ph'p 2:5-8). In meekness (2Co 10:1; 1Pe 2:20-25). In self-renunciation (Ro 15:2-7; 2Co 8:7; Eph 5:1, 2; 1Jo 3:16). In enduring persecution (1Pe 3:17, 18; 4:1). In forgiving (Col 3:13). In obedience (1Jo 2:6). In steadfastness (Heb 12:2, 3). In perseverance (Re 3:21). See Jesus, Our Example.

Paul, our: Enjoined (1Co 4:16; 11:1; Ph'p 3:17; 4:9; 1Ti 1:16; 2Ti 1:13). In self-control (1Co 7:7, 8). In self-maintenance (1Th 3:7-10). In beneficence (Ac 20:35).

See Influence.

EXCHANGERS (See Money Changers.)

EXCOMMUNICATION, disciplinary exclusion from church fellowship. Jews had temporary and permanent excommunication. Early church practiced it (1Co 5:5; 1Ti 1:20).

EXCUSES. For disobedience (Ge 3:12, 13; Ex 32:22-24; De 30:11-14). For rejecting salvation (Lu 14:18-20; Joh 15:22; Ac 24:25; Ro 1:20, 21; 3:19). Inexcusable (Ro 2:1).

Examples: For release from duty: By Moses, when commissioned to deliver Israel (Ex 3:11; 4:1, 10-14); by Gideon (J'g 6:12-17); by Jesus' disciples (M't 8:21; Lu 9:59-62). When called to be a prophet: Elisha (1Ki 19:19-21); Isaiah (Isa 6:5-8); Jeremiah (Jer 1:5-10). For physical healing: Naaman, the leper (2Ki 5:10-14).

EXECUTIONER (Ge 37:36; Pr 16:14; Jer 39:9 [marg.]; Da 2:14 [marg.]; M't 14:10).

See Punishment.

EXHORTATIONS, SPECIAL, To Avoid Various Forms (Pr 4:15; Ro 16:17; 1Ti 6:20; 2Ti 2:16, 23; Tit 3:9). To Choose Between Good and Evil (Ex 32:26; De 30:19; Jos 24:15; 1Ki 18:21).

EXILE, usually refers to the period of time during which the Southern Kingdom (Judah) was forcibly detained in Babylon. Began in reign of Jehoiakim (609-598 B. C.) and ended with decree of Cyrus permitting Jews to return to Palestine (536 B. C.).

EXODUS (a going out), departure of Israel from Egypt under Moses (Exodus).

EXODUS, BOOK OF, 2nd book of the Bible. "Exodus" means "a going out," referring to departure of Israel from Egypt. Date is not altogether certain—from 1280 to 1447 B. C. Outline 1. Israel in Egypt (1:1-12:36).

2. The Journey to Sinai (12:37-19:2).
3. Israel at Sinai (19:3-40:38).

EXORCISM (to adjure), the expelling of demons by means of magical formulas and ceremonies (M't 12:27; M'k 9:38; Ac 19:13).

EXPIATION, the act or means of making amends or reparation for sin.

EXPECTATION. Of the Righteous (Ps 62:5; Pr 24:14; Ph'p 1:20). Of the Wicked (Pr 10:28; 11:7, 23; Zec 9:5; Ac 12:11).

EXPECTATION OF THE MESSIAH. See Messianic Hope.

EXPEDIENCY. To avoid offending others weaker (Ro 14:1, 2, 14-22; 1Co 6:12; 8:8-13; 9:22, 23; 10:23-29, 32, 33). To save men (1Co 9:19-23). Rule governing (1Co 10:30, 31).

Exemplified by Paul, in circumcising Timothy (Ac 16:3); in purifying himself at the temple (Ac 21:23-27).

See Evil, Appearance of, To Be Avoided; Prudence.

EXPERIENCE, Solomon's (Ec 1:2). Religious, relating of (See Testimony, Religious.)

EXPERIMENT, in worldly pleasure, Solomon's (Ec 1; 2).

EXPIATION (See Atonement.)

EXPORTS. From Egypt: Of horses and chariots, and linen yarn (1Ki 10:28, 29; 2Ch 1:16, 17); of corn (Ge 42; 43). From Gilead: of spices (Ge 37:25). From Ophir: of gold (1Ki 10:11; 22:48; 1Ch 29:4). From Tarshish: of gold (1Ki 10:22); ivory, apes, and peacocks (1Ki 10:22); silver, iron, tin, lead, brass, slaves (Eze 27:12, 13). From Arabia: of sheep and goats (Eze 27:21). Palestine: honey (Eze 27:17).

See Imports; Commerce.

EXPOSTULATION (See Reproof.)

EXTERMINATION (See War of.)

EXTORTION. Prayed upon the wicked, by David (Ps 109:11). Warning against (Pr 22:16). Purged out of the land (Isa 16:4); judged by God (Eze 22:12). Cruel (Mic 2:3).

Scribes and Pharisees accused of, by Christ (M't 23:25): Pharisee judges himself not guilty of (Lu 18:11).

Forbidden (Lu 3:13, 14). Cause for disfellowship (1Co 5:10, 11). Excludes from the kingdom of God (1Co 6:10).

Instances of: Jacob, in demanding Esau's birthright for a mess of pottage (Ge 25:31). Pharaoh, in exacting of the Egyptians, lands and persons for corn (Ge 47:13-26). The Jews, after the captivity (Ne 5:1-13).

See Usury.

EXTRADITION. *Instances of:* Elijah from hiding, to Ahab by Obadiah (1Ki 18:7, 10). Urijah from Egypt, to Jehoiakim by Elnathan and company (Jer 26:21-23). Early believers from Damascus, chief priests in Jerusalem by Paul (Ac 9:2, 14; 22:5).

EXTRAVAGANCE. Not to be pursued (Pr 21:17, 20; Lu 16:19). See Gluttony.

EYE. Anthropomorphisms, figurative of God's omniscience (Ps 11:4; Pr 15:3); justice (Am 9:8); holiness (Hab 1:13); care (Ps 33:18, 19; 34:15; 121:3-5; Isa 1:15; 1Pe 3:12); glory (Isa 3:8). See also, Anthropomorphisms.

Figurative: Of the moral state (M't 7:3-5; 13:15, 16; M'k 7:22). Of moral perception (M't 6:22, 23; M'k 8:18; Lu 10:23; Ac 26:18).

Of insatiable desire (Pr 27:20; Ec 1:18; 2Pe 2:14; Ho 2:16). Of evil pleasure (M't 5:29; 18:9; M'k 9:27).

EYE FOR EYE (See Retaliation.)

EYES, OPENED (Ge 21:19; Nu 22:31; 2Ki 6:17; Lu 24:31).

EYES, PAINTING OF, ancients painted eyelids to enhance the beauty of the feminine face (Jer 4:30; Eze 23:40).

EYESALVE, a preparation for the eyes: also used figuratively for restoration of spiritual vision.

EZBAI, father of Naarai (1Ch 11:37). Possibly identical with Paarai in 2Sa 22:35.

EZBON. 1. A son of Gad (Ge 46:16). Called Ozni in Nu 26:16.

2. Son of Bela (1Ch 7:7).

EZEKIAS (See Hezekiah.)

EZEKIEL (God strengthens), a priest. Time of his prophecy (Eze 1:1-3). Persecution of (Eze 3:25).

Visions of: of God's glory (Eze 1; 8; 10; 11:22); of Jews' abominations (Eze 8:5, 6); of their punishment (Eze 9:10); of the valley of dry bones (Eze 37:1-14); of a man with measuring line (Eze 40-48); of the river (Eze 47:1-5).

Teaches by pantomime: Feigns dumbness (Eze 3:26; 24:27; 33:22); symbolizes the siege of Jerusalem by drawings on a tile (Eze 4); shaves himself (Eze 5:1-4); removes his stuff to illustrate the approaching Jewish captivity (Eze 12:3-7); sighs (Eze 21:6, 7); employs a boiling pot to symbolize the destruction of Jerusalem (Eze 24:1-14); omits mourning at the death of his wife (Eze 24:16-27); prophesies by parable of an eagle (Eze 17:2-10). Other parables (Eze 15; 16; 19; 23).

Prophecies of, concerning various nations (Eze 25-29). His popularity (Eze 33:31, 32).

EZION-GEBER (the giant backbone). Last encampment of Israel before coming to the wilderness of Zin (Nu 33:35, 36; De 2:8). Solomon, built a navy at (1Ki 9:26); visited (2Ch 8:17). Jehoshaphat's ships, built at (2Ch 20:36); wrecked at (1Ki 22:48).

EZRA. A famous scribe and priest (Ezr 7:1-6, 10-12, 21; Ne 12:36). Appoints a fast (Ezr 8:21). Commissioned by Artaxerxes to rebuild the temple in Jerusalem, which he directs (Ezr 7:8). Persecuted by Tatnai, the governor (Ezr 6:3-17). Darius renews the decree of Cyrus for rebuilding the temple, which he directs to completion (Ezr 6:1-15). His charge to the priests (Ezr 8:29). Exhorts people to put away heathen wives (Ezr 10:1-17). Reads the law (Ne 8). Reforms corruption (Ezr 10; Ne 13). Participates in the dedication of the wall of Jerusalem (Ne 12:27-43).

F

FABLE, a narrative in which animals and inanimate objects speak as if they were human beings. There are two fables in the OT (J'g 9:7-15 & 2Ki 14:9), though the word "fable" does not appear. In the NT it has the meaning of fiction, a story that is improbable or untrue (1Ti 1:4; 4:7; 2Ti 4:4; Tit 1:14; 2Pe 1:16).

FACE. Character revealed in (Isa 3:9). Transfigured: of Moses (Ex 34:29-35); Jesus (M't 17:2; Lu 9:29). Covering of (Isa 6:2). Disfiguring of, in fasting (M't 6:16).

FAINTING (La 2:12; Da 8:27).

FAIR has the meaning of beautiful (Ac 7:20), clean (Zec 3:5), persuasive (Pr 7:21). It is not used to describe complexion.

FAIR HAVENS, a small bay on the S coast of Crete, about 5 miles E of Cape Matala, where Paul stayed for a short time on his way to Rome (Ac 27:8-12).

FAIRS occurs only in the KJV; the ASV translates it "wares" (Eze 27:12, 14, 16, 19, 27).

FAITH has both an active and a passive sense in the Bible. The former meaning relates to one's loyalty to a person or fidelity to a promise; the latter, confidence in the word or assurance of another. In the OT (KJV) the word faith occurs only twice (De 32:20; Hab 2:4), and the word believe appears less than thirty times. Faith is taught by the examples of the servants of God who committed their lives to Him in unwavering trust and obedience. OT faith is never mere assent to a set of doctrines or outward acceptance of the Law, but utter confidence in the faithfulness of God and a loving obedience to His will.

In the NT *faith* and *believe* occur almost 500 times. The NT makes the claim that the promised Messiah had come, and that Jesus of Nazareth was the promised Messiah. To believe on Him meant to become a Christian, and was pivotal in the experience of the individual. Jesus offered Himself as the object of faith, and made plain that faith in Him was necessary for eternal life.

The first Christians called themselves believers (Ac 2:44), and endeavored to persuade others to believe in Jesus (Ac 6:7; 28:24). In the epistles of Paul faith is contrasted with works as a means of salvation (Ro 3:20-22). Faith is trust in the person of Jesus, the truth of His teaching, and the redemptive work which He accomplished at Calvary.

Faith may also refer to the body of truth which constitutes the whole of the Christian message (Jude 3).

Explained (Ps 118:8, 9; Lu 17:6; 18:8; 1Ti 4:12; Heb 11:1-3, 6). The gift of God (Ro 12:3). Weak (M't 6:25-34; 14:31; Lu 9:40; 17:5). Prayer for increase of (M'k 9:24; Lu 17:5).

The just live by (Hab 2:4; Ro 1:17; Ga 3:11; Heb 10:38).

Secures salvation (Col 2:12; 2Th 2:13; Heb 4:1-11; 6:1, 12, 18).

Inspired, by God's goodness (Ps 36:7, 9); by the Holy Spirit (1Co 12:8, 9).

Miracles wrought by (M't 17:18-20; 21:21, 22; M'k 9:23; 11:23, 24).

Reckoned for righteousness (Ro 4:3; Ga 3:6; Jas 2:23).

Strengthened by miracles: Of Abraham (Ge 15:8-18); of Gideon (J'g 6:17, 36-40); of Hezekiah (2Ki 20:8-11); of Zacharias (Lu 1:18-20, 64).

In affliction, exemplified by Job (Job 13:15, 16; 14:15; 16:19; 19:25-27).

In adversity: Exemplified, by Hagar (Ge 16:15); by Moses (Nu 14:8, 9); by Asa (2Ch 14:11); by Jehoshaphat (2Ch 20:12); by Hezekiah (2Ch 32:7, 8); by Nehemiah (Ne 1:10; 2:20); by the psalmist (Ps 3:3, 5, 6; 4:3, 8; 6:8, 9; 7:1, 10; 9:3, 4; 11:1; 13:5; 17:6; 20:5-7; 31:1, 3-6, 14, 15; 32:7; 33:20-22; 35:10; 38:9, 15; 42:5, 6, 8; 43:5; 44:5, 8; 46:1-3, 5, 7; 54:4; 55:16, 17, 23; 56:3, 4, 8, 9; 57:1-3; 59:9, 17; 60: 9, 10, 12; 61:2, 4, 6, 7; 62:1, 5, 6, 7; 63:6, 7; 69:19, 35, 36; 70:5; 71:1, 3, 5-7, 14, 16, 20, 21; 73:23, 24, 26, 28; 86:2, 7; 89:18, 26; 91:1, 2, 9, 10; 92:10, 15; 94:14, 15, 17, 18, 22; 102:13; 108:10-13; 118:6, 7, 10, 14, 17; 119:42, 57, 74, 81, 114, 166; 121:2; 138:7, 8; 140:6, 7, 12; 142:3, 5; 143:8, 9); by Jeremiah (La 3:24); by Daniel (Da 3:16, 17); by Jonah (Jon 2:2); by Micah (Mi 7:7-9, 20); by Paul (Ac 27:25; 2Co 1:10;

4:8, 9, 13, 16-18; Ph'p 1:19-21; 1Ti 4:10; 2Ti 1:12, 13; 4:7, 8, 18); by the author of Epistle to the Hebrews (Heb 10:34).

Enjoined: (Ps 4:5; 115:9, 11; Ec 11:1; Isa 26:4; M't 6:25-34; M'k 1:15; 11:22; Lu 12:32; 1Ti 6:11, 12, 17; Jas 1:6). In time of public danger (Ex 14:13; Nu 21:34; De 1:21, 29, 30; 3:2, 22; 7:17-21; 20:1; 31:8, 23; Jos 10:25; J'g 6:14-16; 2Ki 19:6, 7; 2Ch 20:15, 17, 20; 32:7, 8; Ne 4:14; Isa 37:6; Jer 42:11). In time of adversity (Ps 37:3, 5, 7; 55:22; 62:8; Isa 43:1, 2, 5, 10; 44:2, 8).

Upon public leaders (Jos 1:9 [w vs 5-9]; 2Ch 15:7). Upon the young (Pr 3:5, 6, 24-26). Upon the discouraged (Isa 35:3, 4; 41:10, 13, 14; 50:10). Upon widows (Jer 49:11).

Exemplified: By Asa (2Ch 14:11). By Jehoshaphat (2Ch 20:12). By Hezekiah (2Ch 32:8). By Job (Job 1:21, 22; 2:10; 5:8, 9; 19:25-27). By the psalmists, in the great hymns prepared for public worship and private meditation setting forth supreme confidence in God (Ps 4:3, 8; 11:1; 13:5, 6; 16:1, 2, 5, 8-11; 18:1-3, 30-50; 20:5-8; 23; 25:1-15; 27:1-14; 31:1-5, 22-24; 40:1-11; 46:1-11; 56:10-13; 57:1-11; 60:6-12; 61:1-8; 62:5-12; 63:1-8); and the following psalms in their entirety (91; 95; 105-108; 115-118; 121; 123-126; 130; 135; 136; 138; 139; 140; 145-150). By Isaiah (Isa 8:10, 17; 12:2; 17:13, 14; 25:9; 26:1, 8; 33:1, 22; 50:7-9; 63:16; 64:8). By Jeremiah (Jer 14:9, 22; 16:19; 17:17; 20:11).

Instances of: Abel (Heb 11:4). Noah, in building the ark (Ge 6:14-22; Heb 11:7). Abraham, in forsaking the land of his nativity at the command of God (Ge 12:1-4; Heb 11:8); in believing the promise of many descendants (Ge 12:7; 15:4-6; Ro 4:18-21; Heb 11:11, 12); in the offering up of Isaac (Ge 22:1-10; Heb 11:17-19). Jacob, in blessing Joseph's sons (Ge 48:8-21; Heb 11:21). Joseph, concerning God's providence in his being sold into Egypt, and the final deliverance of Israel (Ge 50:20, 24; Heb 11:22). Jochebed, in caring for Moses (Ex 2:2, 3; Heb 11:23). Pharaoh's servants, who obeyed the Lord (Ex 9:20). Moses, in espousing the cause of his people (Heb 11:24-28); at the death of Korah (Nu 16:28, 29).

Israelites (Ps 22:4, 5); for forty years wanderings (De 8:2); by the waters of Meribah (Ps 81:7); when Aaron declared the mission of himself and Moses (Ex 4:31); in the battle with the Canaanites (1Ch 5:20); and other conquests (2Ch 13:8-18). Caleb, in advising to take the land of promise (Nu 13:30; 14:6-9); when he asked for Hebron (Jos 14:12). Rahab, in hospitality to the spies (Jos 2:9, 11; Heb 11:31). The spies sent to reconnoiter Jericho (Jos 2:24). Conquest of Jericho (Jos 6: Heb 11:30). Manoah's wife (J'g 13:23). Hannah (1Sa 1). Jonathan, in smiting the Philistines (1Sa 14:6).

David, in smiting Goliath (1Sa 17:37, 45-47); in choosing to fall into the hands of the Almighty in his punishment for numbering Israel (2Sa 24:14); in believing God's promise that his kingdom would be a perpetual kingdom (Ac 2:30).

Job (Job 1:21, 22; 2:10). Eliphaz, in the overruling providence of God, that afflictions are for the good of the righteous (Job 5:6-27). Mordecai, in deliverance of the Jews (Es 4:14).

Elijah, in his controversy with the priests of Baal (1Ki 18:32-38). Widow of Zarephath in feeding Elijah (1Ki 17:13-15). Amaziah, in dismissing the Ephraimites in obedience to the command of God, and going alone to battle against the Edomites (2Ch 25:7-10). Hezekiah (2Ki 18:5; 19).

Daniel, in the lion's den (Da 6). The three Hebrews who refused to worship Nebuchadnezzar's idol (Da 3:13-27). Nebuchadnezzar (Da 6:16).

Ninevites, in obeying Jonah (Jon 3:5). Ezra, in making the journey from Babylon to Jerusalem without a military escort (Ezr 8:22). Habakkuk (Hab 3:17-19).

Mary (Lu 1:38). Joseph, in obeying the vision about Mary and to flee into Egypt (M't 1:18-24; 2:13, 14). Simeon, when he saw Jesus in the temple (Lu 2:25-35). The ancient worthies (Heb 11:32-34). Paul (Ro 8:18, 28, 38, 39; 1Co 9:26; 2Co 5:7; Ga 5:5).

Trial of (De 8:2). Is precious (1Pe 1:7). By tribulations (M't 24:21-25; 2Th 1:3-5). By deferred hope (Heb 6:13-15). By temptations (Jas 1:3, 12). To prove depth of faith (1Ch 29:17; Ps 26:2). To test spirituality (M't 13:9-22; Lu 8:13, 14).

Instances of trial of: Noah (Ge 6:14-22; Heb 11:7). Abraham, when commanded to leave his native land (Ge 12:1-4; Heb 11:8); when commanded to offer Isaac (Ge 22:1-19; Heb 11:17-19). Moses, when sent to Pharaoh (Ex 3:11, 12; 4:10-17; Heb 11:25-29); at the Red Sea, by the murmurings of the people (Ex 14:15; Heb 11:9). Joshua and the children of Israel, in the method of taking Jericho (Jos 6; Heb 11:30). Gideon, when commanded to deliver Israel (J'g 6:36-40; 7; Heb 11:32). Job, by affliction and adversity (Job 1; 2). Ezra, in leaving Babylon without a military escort (Ezr 8:22). Daniel, when forbidden by decree to pray to Jehovah (Da 6:4-23; Heb 11:32, 33). The three Hebrews, when commanded to worship Nebuchadnezzar's image (Da 3:8-30; Heb 11:32-34).

The Syrophenician woman (M't 15:21-28; M'k 7:24-30). The two blind men who appealed to Jesus for sight (M't 9:28).

The disciples: By the question of Jesus, as to who he was (M't 16:15-20; Lu 9:20, 21); by their inability to cast out the evil spirit from the epileptic (M't 17:14-21; M'k 9:14-29; Lu 9:37-42); in the tempest at sea (M't 8:23-27; M'k 4:36-41; Lu 8:22-26). Of Philip, when questioned by Jesus as to how the multitude would be fed (Joh 6:5, 6). Of Peter, when asked whether he loved Jesus (Joh 21:15-17).

See Tribulation.

Rewards of: Protection (2Sa 22:31; Ps 5:11; 9:9, 10; 18:30; 33:18-20; Pr 29:25; 30:5; Jer 39:18; Na 1:7; Heb 13:5, 6). Prosperity (Pr 28:25; Isa 57:13; Jer 17:7, 8). Spiritual peace (Ps 2:12; 32:10; 40:4; 84:5, 12; Isa 26:3; Ro 15:13). Eternal life (2Ti 1:1, 8).

See Faith in Christ.

FAITH IN CHRIST. All things possible by (M'k 9:23; Lu 17:6). Enjoined (M't 17:7; Joh 6:20; 20:27, 29; 1Jo 3:23). Prayer for increase of (M'k 9:24). Salvation by (M'k 16:16; Lu 7:50; Joh 1:12; 3:14-18, 36; 5:24; 6:40, 47; 7:38; 12:36, 46; 20:31; Ac 10:43; 6:29, 35, 45; 11:25, 26, 40; 13:48; 15:9, 11; 16:31; 20:21; 26:18; Ro 1:16, 17; 3:22-28; 4:1-25; 5:1, 2; 9:31-33; 10:4-10; 11:20; 1Co 1:21; 2:5; Ga 2:16; 3:1-29; 5:5, 6; Eph 1:12-14; 2:8; 3:12, 17; 1Ti 1:16; 2Ti 1:13; 3:15; 1Pe 1:9; 2:6, 7; 2Pe 1:1; Re 3:20).

Christ, the focus of faith (Ps 2:12; Heb 12:2).

The Christian triumphs by (Ro 8:35, 37; 2Co 1:24; Eph 4:13; 6:16; Ph'p 3:9; Col 1:23; 2:7; Heb 10:22, 38, 39; 13:7; 1Pe 1:5, 7-9, 21; 1Jo 5:4, 5, 10, 14).

Fruitful of good works (Joh 14:12; Jas 2:1-26).

Exemplified by: Abraham (Joh 8:56). The wise men of the East (M't 2:1, 2, 11). The disciples (M't 4:18-22; M'k 1:16-20; Lu 5:4-11; Joh 1:35-49; 6:68, 69; 16:27, 30, 33). The disciples, through the miracle at Cana of Galilee (Joh 2:11). Philip (Joh 1:45, 46). Nathanael (Joh 1:49). Jews at Jerusalem (Joh 2:23; 8:30; 11:45; 12:11). Peter (M't 4:18-22; 16:16; M'k 1:16-20; Lu 5:4, 5; Joh 6:68, 69). Andrew (M't 4:18-22; M'k 1:16-20; Joh 1:41). James and John (M't 4:21, 22; M'k 1:19, 20). The Samaritans, who believed through the preaching of Jesus (Joh 4:39-42); of Philip (Ac 8:9-12).

The nobleman, for the healing of his son (Joh 4:46, 47, 50). The leper (M't 8:2; M'k 1:40; Lu 5:12, 13). Those who brought the paralytic to Jesus (M't 9:1, 2; M'k 2:1-5; Lu 5:18-20). The centurion, for the healing of his servant (M't 8:5-10, 13; Lu 7:3-9). The woman who was a sinner (Lu 7:38, 44-48, 50). The sick of Gennesaret (M't 14:36; M'k 3:10; 6:54-56). The disciples in the storm (M't 14:33).

The woman with the issue of blood (M't 9:21, 22; M'k 5:28; Lu 8:44, 48). Jairus, for the healing of his daughter (M't 9:18, 23-25; M'k 5:22, 23; Lu 8:41, 42). Two blind men (M't 9:27-30). The people who saw the feeding of the five thousand (Joh 6:14). The Syrophenician woman (M't 15:22-28; M'k 7:25-30). Those who brought the deaf and dumb man to Jesus (M'k 7:32). The people of Decapolis (M't 15:30). The father of the demoniac child (M't 17:14, 15; M'k 9:24; Lu 9:38, 42).

The blind man whom Jesus healed on the Sabbath (Joh 9:13-38). Mary, the sister of Martha (Lu 10:38-42; Joh 11:32). The people in Bethany beyond the Jordan (Joh 10:41, 42). The Samaritan leper (Lu 17:11-19). Blind Bartimaeus, and a fellow blind man (M't 20:30-34; M'k 10:46-52; Lu 18:35-42). Zacchaeus (Lu 19:1-6).

The thief, on the cross (Lu 23:42). John, the disciple, after the resurrection (Joh 20:8). Thomas, after the resurrection (Joh 20:28).

By three thousand, at Pentecost (Ac 2:41). By five thousand (Ac 4:4). By multitudes (Ac 5:14). By the Ethiopian eunuch (Ac 8:36, 38). By the cripple at Lystra (Ac 14:8-10). By Stephen (Ac 6:8, 55-56). By Paul (2Co 12:9, 10; Ga 2:20; Ph'p 4:13; 2Ti 1:12; 4:18; Ro 7:24, 25).

People, of Lydda and Sharon (Ac 9:35); of Joppa (Ac 9:42); of Antioch (Ac 11:21-24). Barnabas (Ac 11:24). Eunice, Lois, and Timothy (Ac 16:1; 2Ti 1:5). Lydia (Ac 16:14). Philippian jailer (Ac 16:31-34). Crispus (Ac 18:8). The Corinthians (Ac 18:8; 1Co 15:11). Jews at Rome (Ac 28:24). Ephesians (Eph 1:13, 15). Colossians (Col 1:2, 4). Thessalonians (1Th 1:6; 3:6-8; 2Th 1:3, 4). Philemon (Ph'm 5). Church at Thyatira (Re 2:19).

FAITH, DOCTRINES OF JESUS. The belief(s) held, in common, by apostles and early believers (Ac 6:7; 16:5; 1Co 16:13; Ga 1:23; 3:23, 25; 6:10; Ph'p 1:27; 1Ti 3:9; 4:1; 5:8; 6:10, 21; 2Ti 3:8; 4:7; Tit 1:1, 4, 13; 3:15; Jude 3; Re 2:13).

FAITHFUL SAYINGS: 1Ti 1:15; 4:9; 2Ti 2:11; Tit 3:8.

FAITHFULNESS. Required (M't 24:45-51 w Lu 12:36-48; M't 25:14-30 w Lu 19:12-27); of stewards (1Co 4:2); of servants (Eph 6:5-9; Col 3:22).

A fruit of the Spirit (Ga 5:22). Scarce (Ps 12:1; Pr 20:6). Tested (Lu 16:10-12).

Rewards of (Ps 31:23; Pr 28:20; M't 10:22; 13:12; 25:29; M'k 13:13; Heb 10:34; Re 2:10).

Instances and Exemplifications of: Abraham (Ga 3:9). Abraham's servant (Ge 24:33). Moses (Nu 12:7; Heb 3:5). David (2Sa 22:22-25). Elijah (1Ki 19:10, 14). Josiah (2Ki 22:2). Abijah (2Ch 13:10-12). Jehoshaphat (2Ch 20:1-30). Workmen in temple repairs (2Ki 12:15; 2Ch 34:12). Hanani and Hananiah (Ne 7:1, 2). Nehemiah's treasurer (Ne 13:13). Job (Job 1:21, 22; 2:9, 10). The three Hebrew captives (Da 3:16-18). Daniel (Da 6:10). Jesus (Joh 4:34; Heb 3:2). Paul (1Ti 1:12; 2Ti 4:7).

See Reward, A Motive to Faithfulness.

See also, God, Faithfulness of; Jesus, Faithfulness; Minister, Faithfulness of.

FALCON, a carnivorous bird (Le 11:14; De 14:13).

FALL OF MAN, THE. The fall of man as related in Genesis 3 is the historical choice by which man sinned voluntarily, and consequently involved all the human race in evil (Ro 5:12; 1Co 15:22). By the fall, man was alienated from God. Man was created in God's own image, with a rational and moral nature like God's, with no inner impulse to sin and with a will free to choose the will of God. Yielding to the outward temptation turned him from God and created an environment in which sin became a potent factor. Redemption from the fall is accomplished through the second Adam, Jesus Christ (Ro 5:12-21; 1Co 15:21, 22, 45-49).

Means of: By transgression of commandments (Ge 2:16, 17; 3:1-3, 6, 11, 12; Job 31:33; Isa 43:27; Hos 6:7). Through deception of Satan (Ge 3:4, 5, 13; 2Co 11:3; 1Ti 2:14). Through evil desire (Ge 3:6; Ec 7:29).

Consequences of: Knowledge of nakedness (Ge 3:7); of guilt (Ge 3:8-10). Cursing of serpent (Ge 3:14, 15); of the ground (Ge 3:17, 18). Multiplying of sorrows (Ge 3:16-19). Death, physical (Ge 3:19; Ro 5:12, 14; 1Co 15:21, 22); spiritual (Ro 5:12, 14, 18, 19, 21).

See Depravity of Man.

FALLOW DEER (See Animals.)

FALLOW GROUND is untilled ground (Jer 4:3; Ho 10:12).

FALSE ACCUSATION (See Accusation, False.)

FALSE CHRISTS. Jesus warned His disciples that imitators and pretenders would follow Him who would try to deceive His followers (M't 24:5-11, 23-25; M'k 13:6, 21, 23; Lu 21:8).

FALSE CONFIDENCE. In self (De 29:19; 1Ki 20:11; Pr 3:5; 23:4; 26:12; 28:26; Isa 5:21; Ro 12:16; 2Co 1:9). In outward resources (Ps 20:7; 33:17; 44:6; 49:6; Pr 11:28; Isa 22:11; 31:1-3; Jer 48:7; Zep 4:6; M'k 10:24). In man (Ps

33:16; 62:9; 118:8; 146:3, 4; Isa 2:22; Jer 17:5; Ho 5:13; 7:11).

Instances of: At Babel (Ge 11:4). Sennacherib, in the siege of Jerusalem (2Ki 19:23). Asa, in relying on Syria rather than on God (2Ch 16:7-9). Hezekiah, in the defenses of Jerusalem (Isa 22:11). Peter, in asserting his devotion to Jesus (M't 26:35; Lu 22:33, 34; Joh 13:37, 38).

See Confidence, False.

FALSEHOOD. Forbidden (Ex 20:16; 23:1; Le 19:11, 12, 16; Pr 34:13 w 1Pe 3:10; Pr 3:3; 17:7; Ec 5:6; Zep 3:13; Eph 4:25, 29; Col 3:9; 1Ti 1:9, 10). Destructive (Pr 11:9; 26:18, 19, 24-26, 28; Isa 32:7).

An abomination to the Lord (Ps 5:6, 9; Pr 6:12, 13, 16-19; 12:22; 27:14). Abhorred by the righteous (Ps 31:18; 59:12; 101:5, 7; 119:29, 69, 163; 120:2-4; 144:8, 11; Pr 10:18; 13:5; 20:17).

Refrained from by the righteous (Job 27:4; 31:5, 6, 33; 36:4; Pr 14:5, 25; Isa 63:8). Practiced by the wicked (Ps 10:7; 28:3; 36:3; 50:19, 20; 52:2-4; 58:3; 62:4; 109:2; Pr 2:12-15; 12:17, 20; 19:28; 21:6; Isa 28:15; 57:11; 59:3, 4, 12, 13; Jer 7:8, 28; 9:3, 5, 6, 8; 12:6; Ho 4:1, 2; Ob 7; Mic 6:12; Na 3:1; Joh 8:44, 45; 1Ti 4:2; 1Pe 3:16). Wicked easily misled by (Pr 14:8; 17:4). All guilty of (Job 13:4; Ps 116:11).

Atonement for (Le 6:2-7). Punishment for (Ps 12:2, 3; 52:5; 55:23; 63:11; Pr 10:10, 31; 12:19; 14:5, 25; 19:5, 9; Jer 50:38; Re 21:8, 27; 22:15). Exposure of (Pr 10:9).

See Accusation, False; Conspiracy; Deceit; Deception; False Witness; Flattery; Hypocrisy; Perjury; Teachers, False.

Instances of: Satan, in deceiving Eve (Ge 3:4, 5); in impugning Job's motives for being righteous (Job 1:9, 10; 2:4, 5); in his false pretensions to Jesus (M't 4:8, 9; Lu 4:6, 7). Adam and Eve, in attempting to evade responsibility (Ge 3:12, 13). Cain, in denying knowledge of his brother (Ge 4:9). In the answers of Job's friends (Job 21:34). Abraham, in denying that Sarah was his wife (Ge 12:11-19; 20:2). Sarah, to the angels, denying her derisive laugh of unbelief (Ge 18:15); in denying to the king of Gerar, that she was Abraham's wife (Ge 20:5, 16). Isaac, denying that Rebekah was his wife (Ge 26:7-10). Rebekah and Isaac, in the conspiracy against Esau (Ge 27:6-24, 46). Jacob's sons, in the scheme to destroy the Shechemites by first having them circumcised (Ge 34).

Joseph's brethren in deceiving their father into a belief that Joseph was killed by wild beasts (Ge 37:29-35). Potiphar's wife, in falsely accusing Joseph (Ge 39:14-17). Joseph, in the deception he carried on with his brethren (Ge 42-44). Pharaoh, in dealing deceitfully with the Israelites (Ex 7-12).

Aaron, in attempting to shift responsibility for the making of the golden calf (Ex 32:1-24). Rahab, in denying that the spies were in her house (Jos 2:4-6). The Gibeonites, ambassadors, in the deception they perpetrated upon Joshua and the elders of Israel in leading them to believe that they came from a distant region, when in fact they dwelt in the immediate vicinity (Jos 9). Ehud, in pretending to bear secret messages to Eglon, king of Moab, while his object was to assassinate him (J'g 3:16-22). Sisera, who instructed Jael to mislead his pursuers (J'g 4:20). Saul, in professing to Samuel to have obeyed the commandment to destroy all spoils of the Amalekites, when in fact he had not obeyed (1Sa 15:1-20); in accusing Ahimelech of conspiring with David against himself (1Sa 22:11-16). David lied to Ahimelech, professing to have a mission from the king, in order that he might obtain provisions and armor (1Sa 21); in feigning madness (1Sa 21:13-15); and other deceits with the Philistines (1Sa 27:8-12); the falsehood he put in the mouth of Hushai, of friendship to Absalom (2Sa 15:34-37).

Michal, in the false statement that David was sick, in order to save him from Saul's violence (1Sa 19:12-17). The Amalekite who claimed to have slain Saul (2Sa 1:10-12). Hushai, in false professions to Absalom (2Sa 16:16-19); in his deceitful counsel to Absalom (2Sa 17:7-14).

The wife of the Bahurimite who saved the lives of Hushai's messengers, sent to apprise David of the movements of Absalom's army (2Sa 17:15-22). The murder, under false pretense: Of Adonijah (1Ki 2:23); of Shimei (1Ki 2:42,

43); of Jeroboam's wife (1Ki 14:2). The old prophet of Bethel who misguided the prophet of Judah (1Ki 13:11-22); Jeroboam's wife, feigning herself another woman (1Ki 14:5-7).

The conspirators against Naboth (1Ki 21:7-13). Gehazi, when he ran after Naaman, and misrepresented that Elisha wanted a talent of silver and two changes of raiment (2Ki 5:20-24). Hazael, servant of the king of Syria, lied to the king in misstating the prophet Elisha's message in regard to the king's recovery (2Ki 8:7-15). Jehu lied to the worshipers of Baal in order to gain advantage over them, and destroy them (2Ki 10:18-28). Zedekiah, in violating his oath of allegiance to Nebuchadnezzer (2Ch 36:13, Eze 16:59; 17:15-20). Samaritans, in their efforts to hinder the rebuilding of the temple at Jerusalem (Ezr 4). Sanballat, in trying to obstruct the rebuilding of Jerusalem (Ne 6). Haman, in his conspiracy against the Jews (Es 3:8). Jeremiah's adversaries in accusing him of joining the Chaldeans (Jer 37:13-15). Princes of Israel, when they went to Jeremiah for a vision from the Lord (Jer 42:20).

Herod, to the wise men, in professing to desire to worship Jesus (M't 2:8).

Jews, in falsely accusing Jesus of being gluttonous and a winebibber (M't 11:19); in refusing to bear truthful testimony concerning John the Baptist (M't 21:24-27); falsely accusing Jesus of blasphemy, when he remitted sin (M't 9:2-6; M'k 2:7; Lu 5:21); and announced that he was the Son of God (M't 26:65; M'k 14:64; Joh 10:33-38).

Peter, in denying Jesus (M't 26:69-75; M'k 14:68-71; Lu 22:56-62; Joh 18:25-27). The Roman soldiers, who said the disciples stole the body of Jesus (M't 28:13, 15).

The disobedient son, who promised to work in the vineyard, but did not (M't 21:30). Ananias and Sapphira falsely state that they had sold their land for a given sum (Ac 5:1-10).

Stephen's accusers, who falsely accused him of blaspheming Moses and God (Ac 6:11-14). Paul's traducers, falsely accusing him of treason to Caesar (Ac 16:20, 21; 17:5-7; 24:5; 25:7, 8). The Cretians *are* always liars, evil beasts, slow bellies (Tit 1:12).

See Accusation, False; Conspiracy; False Witness; Hypocrisy; Perjury; Teachers, False.

FALSE PROPHET. Any person pretending to possess a message from God, but not possessing a divine commission (Jer 29:9). The false prophet is mentioned in the Book of Revelation (Re 19:20) and is usually identified with the two-horned beast of Revelation 13:11-18.

FALSE TEACHERS (See Teachers, False.)

FALSE WITNESS. Forbidden (Ex 20:16; 23:1-3; Le 6:1-5; 19:11, 12, 16; De 5:20; Pr 24:28; M't 19:18; Lu 3:14; 18:20; 1Ti 1:9, 10). Proverbs concerning (Pr 6:16-19; 12:17; 14:5, 8, 25; 19:5, 9; 21:28; 24:28; 25:18).

Proceeds from corrupt heart (M't 15:19). Innocent suffer from (Ps 27:12; 35:11). God hates (Pr 6:16-19). Punishment for (De 19:16-20; Pr 19:5, 9; 21:28; Zec 5:3, 4).

See Perjury; Falsehood; Evidence, Laws Concerning; Witness.

Instances of: Witnesses against Naboth (1Ki 21:13); against Jesus (M't 26:59-61; M'k 14:54-59); against Stephen (Ac 6:11, 13); against Paul (Ac 16:20, 21; 17:5-7; 24:5; 25:7, 8).

FAME OF JESUS (M't 4:24, 25; 9:31; 14:1; M'k 1:28; Lu 4:14, 37; 5:15).

FAMILIAR SPIRITS. Consulting of, forbidden (Le 19:31; 20:6, 27; De 18:10, 11); vain (Isa 8:19; 19:3). Those who consulted, to be cut off (Le 20:6, 27).

Instances of Those Who Consulted: Saul (1Sa 28:3-25; 1Ch 10:13).

See Demons; Necromancy; Witchcraft.

FAMILY. The concept of the family in the Bible differs from the modern institution. The Hebrew family was larger than families today, including the father of the household, his parents, if living, his wife or wives and children, his daughters and sons-in-law, slaves, guests and foreigners under his protection. Marriage was arranged by the father of the groom and the family of the bride, for whom a dowry, or purchase money was paid to her father (Ge 24). Polygamy and concubinage were practiced, though not favored bv God. The husband could divorce the wife, but she could not divorce him.

The father of a family had the power

of life and death over his children. To dishonor a parent was punishable by death (Ex 21:15, 17). The NT concept followed that of the OT. Parents and children, husbands and wives, masters and slaves were enjoined to live together in harmony and love (Eph 5:22-6:9).

Of Saints: Blessed (Ps 128:3, 6). Should be taught God's Word (De 4:9, 10). Worship God together (1Co 16:19). Be duly regulated (Pr 31:27; 1Ti 3:4, 5, 12). Live in unity (Ge 45:24; Ps 133:1). Live in mutual forbearance (Ge 50:17-21; M't 18:21, 22). Rejoice together before God (De 14:26). Deceivers and liars should be removed from (Ps 101:7). Warned against departing from God (De 29:18). Punishment of irreligious (Jer 10:25).

Good, Exemplified: Abraham (Ge 18:19). Jacob (Ge 35:2). Joshua (Jos 24:15). David (2Sa 6:20). Job (Job 1:5). Lazarus of Bethany (Joh 11:1-5). Cornelius (Ac 10:2, 33). Lydia (Ac 16:15). Jailer of Philippi (Ac 16:31-34). Crispus (Ac 18:8). Lois (2Ti 1:5).

Instituted (Ge 2:23, 24). Government of (Ge 3:16; 18:19; Es 1:20, 22; 1Co 7:10; 11:3, 7-9; Eph 5:22-24; Col 3:18; 1Ti 3:2, 4, 5, 12; 1Pe 3:1, 6). Duty to (Isa 58:7). Husband should provide for (Ge 30:30; 1Ti 5:8).

Persian customs in (Es 1:10-22); see Harem. Idolatrous (Jer 7:18).

See Children; Husband; Wife; Orphan; Widow.

Infelicity in: Caused, by indiscreetness (Pr 11:22; 12:4; 14:1; 30:21, 23; 38:21, 23); by hatred (Pr 15:17); by contention (Pr 18:19; 19:13; 21:9, 19; 25:24; 27:15, 16).

Instances of Infelicity in: Of Abraham, on account of Hagar (Ge 16:5; 21:10, 11). Of Isaac, on account of disagreement between Jacob and Esau (Ge 27:4-46). Of Jacob, bigamic jealousy between Leah and Rachel (Ge 29:30-34; 30:1-25). Moses and Zipporah (Ex 4:25, 26). Elkanah, on account of bigamic feuds (1Sa 1:4-7). David and Michal (2Sa 6:16, 20-23). Ahasuerus, on account of Vashti's refusing to appear before his drunken courtiers (Es 1:10-22).

Religion in: Purpose: to keep the way of the Lord (Ge 18:19); to keep children from sinning (Job 1:5); to be an example to the household (Ps 101:2).

Manifested, in observance of religious rites (Ge 17:12-14; 35:2-4, 7; Lu 2:21; Ac 10:2, 47, 48; 16:15, 25-34; 1Co 1:16); in religious instruction of children (De 4:9, 10; 11:19, 20); in household consecration (De 12:5-12; Jos 24:15; Ac 10:1, 2; 18:8).

Observed by: Job (Job 1:5); Abraham (Ge 12:7, 8; 13:3, 4; 18:19); Joshua (Jos 24:15); David (Ps 101:2).

FAMINE. Pharaoh forewarned of, in dreams (Ge 41). Described (De 28:53-57; Isa 5:13; 9:18-21; 17:11; Jer 5:17; 14:1-6; 48:33; La 1:11, 19; 2:11-22; 4:4-10; Joe 1:17-20). Sent as a judgment (Le 26:19-29; De 28:23, 24, 38-42; 1Ki 17:1; 2Ki 8:1; 1Ch 21:12; Ps 105:16; 107:33, 34; Isa 3:1-8; 14:30; Jer 14:15-22; 19:9; 29:17, 19; La 5:4, 5, 10, Eze 4:16, 17; 5:16, 17; 14:13; Joe 1:15, 16; Am 4:6-9; 5:16, 17; Hag 1:10, 11; M't 24:7; Lu 21:11; Re 6:5-8).

Cannibalism in (De 28:53; 2Ki 6:28). Righteous delivered from (Job 5:20; Ps 33:19; 37:19).

Figurative: Am 8:11.

Instance of: In Canaan (Ge 12:10; 26:1; 2Sa 21:1; 1Ki 17; 18:1; 2Ki 6:25-29; 7:4). In Jerusalem, from siege (2Ki 25:3; Jer 52:6). In Egypt (Ge 41:53-57). Universal (Ac 11:28).

FAN, used for winnowing grain (Isa 30:24; Jer 15:7; 51:2; M't 3:12).

FANATICISM. The prophets of Baal (1Ki 18:28). The Jews against Christ (Joh 19:15). The Jews in stoning Stephen (Ac 7:57). Saul in persecuting the church (Ac 9:1). The Jews in their rage against Paul (Ac 21:36; 22:23).

FAREWELLS, allusions to (Ru 1:14; Lu 9:61; Ac 18:21; 20:38; 21:6; 2Co 13:11).

FARMING was the chief occupation of the people of Israel after the conquest of Canaan. Each family received a piece of ground marked by boundaries that could not be removed (De 19:14). Plowing took place in the autumn, when the ground was softened by the rains. Grain was sown during the month of February; harvest began in the spring, and usually lasted from Passover to Pentecost. The grain was cut with a sickle, and gleanings were left for the poor (Ru 2:2). The grain was threshed out on the threshing-floor, a saucer-shaped area of beaten clay 25 or more feet in diameter, on which animals dragged a sledge over the sheaves to beat out the grain. The grain was winnowed by tossing it into the air to let the chaff blow away, and was then sifted to remove impurities (Ps 1:4). Wheat and barley were the most important crops, but other grains and vegetables were cultivated as well.

FARTHING. This word is used to translate two different words in the Greek text: *assarion* (M't 10:29; Lu 12:6), a Roman coin worth, in American money, about 1½ cents; in old English money, about 3 farthings; and *kodrantes* (M't 5:26; M'k 12:42), worth in American money, about two-fifths of a cent; in old English money, less than a farthing.

FASTING. Enjoined (Joe 1:14; 2:12, 13). Precepts concerning (M't 6:16-18). Accompanied by, prayer (Da 9:3; M't 17:21; 1Co 7:5); confession of sin (1Sa 7:6; Ne 9:1, 2); humiliation (De 9:18; Ne 9:1); reading of the Scriptures (Jer 36:6).

Observed on occasions of, public calamities (2Sa 1:12; Ac 27:33); afflictions (Ps 35:13; Da 6:18); private afflictions (2Sa 12:16); approaching danger (Es 4:16; Ac 27:9, 33, 34); religious observances (Zec 8:19); ordination of ministers (Ac 13:3; 14:23).

In times of bereavement: of the people of Jabesh-gilead, for Saul and his sons (1Sa 31:13; 1Ch 10:12); of David, at the time of Saul's death (2Sa 1:12); of his child's sickness (2Sa 12:16, 21-23); of Abner's death (2Sa 3:35).

Habitual: of the Israelites (Zec 8:19); by John's disciples (M't 9:14); by Anna (Lu 2:37); by Pharisees (M't 9:14; M'k 2:18; Lu 18:12); by Cornelius (Ac 10:30); by Paul (2Co 6:5; 11:27).

Prolonged: for three weeks, by Daniel (Da 10:2, 3); forty days, by Moses (Ex 24:18; 34:28; De 9:9, 18); Elijah (1Ki 19:8); Jesus (M't 4:2; M'k 1:12, 13; Lu 4:1, 2).

Of the disobedient, unacceptable (Isa 58:3-7; Jer 14:12; Zec 7:5; M't 6:16).

See Humiliation; Humility.

Instances of: Of the Israelites, in the conflict between the other tribes with the tribe of Benjamin, on account of the wrong suffered by a Levite's concubine (J'g 20:26); when they went to Mizpeh for the ark (1Sa 7:6). Of David, at the death of Saul (2Sa 1:12); during the sickness of the child born to him by Bath-sheba (2Sa 12:16-22); while interceding in prayer for his friends (Ps 35:13); in his zeal for Zion (Ps 69:10); in prayer for himself and his adversaries (Ps 109:4, 24). Of Ahab, when Elijah prophesied the destruction of himself and his house (1Ki 21:27; w verses 20-29). Of Jehoshaphat, at the time of the invasion of the confederated armies of the Canaanites and Syrians (2Ch 20:3). Of Ezra, on account of the idolatrous marriages of the Jews (Ezr 10:6). Of Nehemiah, on account of the desolation of Jerusalem and the temple (Ne 1:4). Of the Jews, when Jeremiah prophesied against Judea and Jerusalem (Jer 36:9), in Babylon, with prayer for divine deliverance and guidance (Ezr 8:21, 23). Of Darius, when he put Daniel in the lions' den (Da 6:18). Of Daniel, on account of the captivity of the people, with prayer for their deliverance (Da 9:3); at the time of his vision (Da 10:1-3). Ninevites, when Jonah preached to them (Jon 3:5-10). By Paul, at the time of his conversion (Ac 9:9). Of the disciples, at the time of the consecration of Barnabas and Saul (Ac 13:2, 3). Of the consecration of the elders (Ac 14:23).

FAT. The layer of fat around the kidneys and other viscera of sacrificial animals which was forbidden for food, but which was burned as an offering to Jehovah (Le 4:31). Sometimes the word is used in the KJV as equivalent to "vat," a receptacle into which the grape juice flowed when pressed from the fruit (Joe 2:24; Isa 63:2).

Offered in sacrifice (Ex 23:18; 29:13, 22; Le 1:8; 3:3-5, 9-11, 14-16; 4:8-10; 7:3-5; 8:16, 25, 26; 10:15; 17:6; 1Sa 2:15, 16; Isa 43:24). Belonged to the Lord (Le 3:16). Forbidden as food (Le 3:16, 17; 7:23). Idolatrous sacrifices of (De 32:38).

Figurative: Ge 45:18; 49:20; Ps 37:20; 81:16; Isa 25:6.

FATHER has various meanings in the Bible. It may denote 1. An immediate male progenitor (Ge 42:13).

2. A male ancestor, immediate or remote (Ge 17:4; Ro 9:5).

3. A spiritual ancestor (Ro 4:11; Joh 8:44).

4. The originator of a mode of life (Ge 4:20).

5. An advisor (J'g 17:10), or a source

(Job 38:28). God is called the Father of the universe (Jas 1:17) and the Creator of the human race (Mal 2:10).

FATHERHOOD, OF GOD (See God, Fatherhood of.)

FATHER-IN-LAW. Hospitable to son-in-law, a man of Bethlehem-judah (J'g 19:3-9). Unjust, Laban to Jacob (Ge 29:21-23; 31:7, 39-42).

FATHERLESS (See Orphan.)

FATHERS' GOD (Ex 3:13; De 1:11; 4:1; Jos 18:3; 2Ch 28:9; 29:5).

FATHOM (Ac 27:28).

FATLING. A clean animal fattened for offering to God (Ps 66:15; 2Sa 6:13).

FATTED CALF (Lu 15:23).

FAULT FINDING (See Murmuring; Uncharitableness.)

FAVOR (See God, Grace of.)

FAVORITISM. *Instances of:* Jacob, for Rachel (Ge 29:30, 34). Elkanah, for Hannah (1Sa 1:4, 5). Rebekah, for Jacob (Ge 27:6-17). Jacob, for Joseph (Ge 37:3, 4). Joseph, for Benjamin (Ge 43:34). Forbidden in parents (De 21:15-17).

See Partiality.

FEAR (See Cowardice. Also Fear of God, below.)

FEAR OF GOD. *Reverence:* Expressed in the Old Testament (Ge 35:5; Ex 18:21; 20:18-30; Le 22:32; De 4:10; 5:29; 6:2; 10:12, 20, 21; 14:23; 17:13; 28:49, 58; Jos 24:14; 1Sa 12:14, 24; 2Sa 23:3; 1Ki 8:40; 2Ki 17:36, 39; 1Ch 16:30; 2Ch 19:7, 9; Ezr 10:3; Job 28:28; 37:24; Ps 2:11; 4:4; 15:4; 19:9; 22:23, 25; 31:19; 33:8, 18; 34:11; 37:7, 9, 11; 46:10; 52:6; 60:4; 64:9; 67:7; 72:5; 76:7, 11; 85:9; 86:11; 89:7; 90:11; 96:4, 9; 99:1; 102:15; 103:11, 13, 17; 111:5, 10; 112:1; 115:11, 13; 118:4; 119:63, 74, 79; 128:1, 4; 130:4; 135:20; 145:19; 147:11; Pr 1:7; 2:5, 6; 3:7; 8:13; 9:10; 10:27; 13:13; 14:2, 16, 26, 27; 15:16, 33; 16:6; 19:23; 22:4; 23:17; 24:21; 28:14; 31:30; Ec 3:14; 7:18; 8:12; 12:13; Isa 2:10, 19-21; 25:3; 29:13, 23; 33:6, 13; 50:10; 59:19; 60:5; Jer 5:22; 10:7; 32:39, 40; 33:9; Ho 3:5; Mic 7:16, 17; Zep 1:7; 3:7; Zec 2:13; Mal 1:6; 3:16; 4:2). Expressed in the New Testament (M't 10:28; Lu 1:50; 12:5; 23:40; Ac 10:35; 13:16, 26; Ro 11:20; 2Co 5:11; 7:1; Eph 5:21; 6:5; Ph'p 2:12; Col 3:22; Heb 5:5, 7; 12:28, 29; Jas 2:19; 1Pe 1:17; 3:2, 15; 1Jo 4:16-18; Re 11:18; 14:7; 19:5).

Described: As clean (Ps 19:9); as hating evil (Pr 8:13); as prolonging life (Pr 10:27); as a fountain of life (Pr 14:27); as wisdom (Job 28:28; Pr 15:33); as the beginning of wisdom (Ps 111:10; Pr 1:7; 9:10; 15:33).

Cultivated (Ex 3:5; 19:12, 13; Heb 12:18-24). Secures divine blessing (De 5:29; Ps 25:12, 13; 31:19; 33:18; 34:7, 9; 85:9; 103:11, 13, 17; 111:5; 112:1; 115:11, 13; 128:1-4; 145:19; Pr 22:4; Ec 7:18; 8:12; Mal 4:2; Lu 1:50; Ac 10:35). A bond of fellowship among righteous (Mal 3:16). Universality of, foretold (Ps 6:11; 9; 102:15).

Enjoined (Le 19:14, 32; 25:19, 36, 43; De 6:13; 10:20; 13:4; Jos 24:14; 1Sa 12:24; 2Ki 17:36; 1Ch 16:30; 2Ch 19:7, 9; Ne 5:9; Ps 2:11; 4:4; 22:23; 34:9; 96:4; Pr 3:7; 23:17; 24:21; Ec 5:7; 12:13; Isa 8:13; 29:23; Ro 11:20; Col 3:22; 1Pe 2:17; Re 14:7).

Deters from sin (Ex 20:18-20; Pr 16:6; Jer 32:39, 40). Averts temporal calamity (De 28:49, 58; 2Ki 17:36, 39; Pr 19:23).

A motive: To obedience (Nu 32:15; De 6:13-15; 7:4; De 8:5, 6; 10:12, 13, 20; 13:4, 6-11; 14:23; 17:11-13; 21:18-21; 28:14-68; 31:11-13; 1Sa 12:24, 25; Job 13:21; 31:1-4, 13-15, 23; Isa 1:20; Jer 4:4; 22:5; M't 10:28; Lu 12:4, 5; 2Co 5:10, 11; 2Ti 4:1, 2; 2Pe 3:10-12; Re 14:9, 10). To filial obedience (De 21:21). To respect of others (Le 19:14, 30; 25:17, 36, 43). To truthfulness (De 15:9; 19:16-20).

Motives to: God's majesty (Jer 10:7); power (Jos 4:24; Ps 99:1; Jer 5:22; M't 10:28; Lu 12:5); power and justice (Job 37:23, 24); wrath (Ps 90:11); judgments (Isa 1:20); providence (1Sa 12:2-4); forgiveness (Ps 130:4).

See Conviction of Sin; Faith.

Guilty, experienced (Job 15:20-25; 18:11; Pr 1:24-27; 10:24; Isa 2:19-21; 33:14; Da 5:6; Mic 7:17; Ro 8:15; 2Ti 1:7; Jas 2:19; Re 6:16). Instances of guilty fear: Adam and Eve (Ge 3:8-13). The guards at Jesus' tomb (M't 28:4). Judas (M't 27:3-5). Devils (Jas 2:19).

Instances of Those Who Feared: Noah, in preparing the ark (Heb 11:7). Abraham, tested in the offering of his son Isaac (Ge 22:12). Jacob, in the vision of the ladder, and the covenant of God (Ge 28:16, 17; 42:18). The midwives of Egypt, in refusing to take the lives of the Hebrew children (Ex 1:17,

21). The Egyptians, at the time of the plague of thunder and hail and fire (Ex 9:20). The nine and one-half tribes of Israel west of Jordan (Jos 22:15-20). Phinehas, in turning away the anger of God at the time of the plague (Nu 25:11, w verses 6-15). Obadiah, in sheltering one hundred prophets against the wrath of Jezebel (1Ki 18:3, 4). Jehoshaphat, in proclaiming a feast, when the land was about to be invaded by the armies of the Ammonites and Moabites (2Ch 20:3). Nehemiah, in his reform of the public administration (Ne 5:15). Hanani, which qualified him to be ruler over Jerusalem (Ne 7:2). Job, according to the testimony of Satan (Job 1:8). David (Ps 5:7; 119:38). Hezekiah, in his treatment of the prophet Micah, who prophesied evil against Jerusalem (Jer 26:19). Jonah, in the tempest (Jon 1:9). The Jews, in obeying the voice of the Lord (Hag 1:12). Levi, in receiving the covenant of life and peace (Hag 1:5). The women at the sepulcher (M't 28:8). Cornelius, who feared God with all his house (Ac 10:2).

See Punishment, Design of, to Secure Obedience; Reward, A Motive for Faithfulness.

FEASTS. Ancient customs at: Men alone present at (Ge 40:20; 43:32, 34; 1Sa 9:22; Es 1:8; M'k 6:21; Lu 14:24); women alone (Es 1:9). Men and women attend (Ex 32:6, w verses 2, 3; Da 5:1-3). Riddles propounded at (J'g 14:12). Marriage feasts provided by the bridegroom (J'g 14:10, 17). Guests arranged according to age (Ge 43:33); rank (1Sa 9:22; Lu 14:8-10). Reclined on couches (Am 6:4, 7; Lu 7:38; Joh 13:25). Served in one dish (M't 26:23). Were presided over by a governor (Joh 2:8, 9). Host served (Ge 18:8). Wine served at (Es 5:6; 7:7). Music at (Isa 5:12; Am 6:4, 5; Lu 15:25). Dancing at (M't 14:6; Lu 15:25). Given by kings (1Sa 20:5; 25:36; 2Sa 9:10; 1Ki 2:7; 4:22; 18:19; Es 1:3-8; Da 5:1-4). Drunkenness at (1Sa 25:36; Es 1:10; Da 5:1-4).

Covenants ratified by (Ge 26:28-30). Celebrations by: Birthdays (Ge 40:20; M'k 6:21); coronations (1Ki 1:25; 1Ch 12:38-40); national deliverances (Es 8:17; 9:17-19).

Figurative: M't 22:1-14; Lu 14:16-24; Re 19:9, 17.

Annual Festivals: Instituted by Moses. Designated as Solemn Feasts (Nu 15:3; 2Ch 8:13; La 2:6; Eze 46:9); Set Feasts (Nu 29:39; Ezr 3:5). Appointed Feasts (Isa 1:14); Holy Convocations (Le 23:4). First and last days were Sabbatic (Le 23:39, 40; Nu 28:18-25; 29:12, 35; Ne 8:1-18). Kept with rejoicing (Le 23:40; De 16:11-14; 2Ch 30:21-26; Ezr 6:22; Ne 8:9-12, 17; Ps 42:4; 122:4; Isa 30:29; Zec 8:19). Divine protection given during (Ex 34:24).

The three principal, were Passover, Pentecost, Tabernacles. All males were required to attend (Ex 23:17; 34:23; De 16:16; Ps 42:4; 122:4; Eze 36:38; Lu 2:41; Joh 4:45; 7). Aliens permitted to attend (Joh 12:20; Ac 2:1-11). Attended by women (1Sa 1:3, 9; Lu 2:41). Observed: by Jesus (M't 26:17-20; Lu 2:41, 42; 22:15; Joh 2:13, 23; 5:1; 7:10; 10:22); by Paul (Ac 18:21; 19:21; 20:6, 16; 24:11, 17).

See for full treatment of annual feasts, Passover; Pentecost; Purim; Tabernacles; Trumpets.

FEET. Bells worn on (Isa 3:16, 18). Washing of, as an example, by Jesus (Joh 13:4-14). Sitting at (De 33:3; Lu 10:39; Ac 22:3).

See Ablution.

FELIX (HAPPY) governor of Judaea. Paul tried before (Ac 23:24-35; 24). Trembles under Paul's preaching (Ac 24:25). Leaves Paul in bonds (Ac 24:26, 27; 25:14).

FELLOES, the exterior parts of the rim of a wheel (1Ki 7:33).

FELLOW, a term of reproach (Ge 19:9; 1Sa 21:15; 2Ki 9:11; M't 12:24; 26:61; Lu 23:2; Ac 17:18; 22:22; 24:5).

FELLOWSHIP. Defined (Ec 4:9, 12; Am 3:3).

With God (Ex 33:11, 14-17; Le 26:12; Am 3:3; 2Co 13:11; 1Jo 1:3, 5-7). Signified, in men walking with God (Ge 5:22, 24; 6:9); in God dwelling with men (Ex 29:45; Ps 101:6; Isa 57:15; Zec 2:10; Joh 14:23; 2Co 6:16; 1Jo 3:24; 4:13; Re 21:3, 4). Through Christ (M'k 9:37; Joh 17:21, 23). See Communion, with God.

With Christ (M't 18:20; Lu 24:32; 1Co 1:9; 10:16; 1Jo 1:3, 5-7; Re 3:20). Signified, in Christ dwelling with men (Joh 6:56; 14:23; Eph 3:17; Col 1:27; 1Jo 3:24; 4:13); in our union with Christ

(Joh 15:1-8; 17:21-23, 26; Ro 7:4; 8:1, 10, 17; 11:17; 12:5; 1Co 6:13-15, 17; 12:12, 27; 2Co 11:2; 13:5; Eph 5:30; Col 3:3; 1Th 5:9, 10; Heb 2:11; 1Jo 5:12, 20). Attained, by doing God's will (M't 12:48-50; Lu 8:21); by keeping God's commandments (1Jo 3:6, 25); by walking in the light (1Jo 1:3, 5-7); by receiving Christ (M'k 9:37; Re 3:20); by abiding, in Christ (1Jo 2:6, 24, 28; 3:6, 24); in his doctrine (2Jo 9); through a gathering of believers (M't 18:20); commemorating Christ's death (1Co 10:16). Through the Spirit (Joh 14:16; 1Jo 3:6, 24; 4:13). See Communion, of Christ.

With the Holy Spirit (Joh 14:16, 17; Ro 8:9; 1Co 3:16; 2Co 13:14; Ga 4:6; Ph'p 2:1). See Communion, Holy Spirit.

Of the righteous: In unity of purpose (Ps 119:63; 133:1-3; Am 3:3; Mal 3:16; Joh 17:11, 21-23; Ac 1:14; 2:1, 42, 44-47; 17:4; Ro 15:6, 7; 1Co 1:10; Ph'p 1:3, 5, 27; 2:1, 2; Col 2:2; 1Pe 3:8, 9). In worship (Ps 55:14; 1Co 10:16, 17; Eph 5:19; Col 3:16). In ministry (M't 20:25-28; M'k 10:42-45; Lu 22:32; Ac 20:35; Ro 1:12; 15:1-7; Ga 6:2, 10; 1Th 4:18; 5:11, 14; Heb 3:13; 10:24, 25; 1Pe 2:17; 1Jo 3:14; 4:7, 8, 11-13). In brotherhood (1Sa 23:16; M't 23:8; Joh 13:34; 15:17; Ro 14:1-4, 10, 13-21; 1Co 1:10; 12:13; 16:19, 20; Ga 6:10; Eph 2:14-21; 5:30; Heb 13:1). Exemplified (Lu 24:13-15; Ga 2:9).

With the wicked. Impoverishing (Pr 28:19). Implicating (Ps 50:18). Debauching (Ps 50:18; Pr 12:11; 29:24; 1Co 15:33; 2Pe 2:18, 19). Abhorred by the righteous (Ge 49:6; Ex 33:15, 16; Ezr 6:21, 22; 9:14; Ps 6:8; 26:4, 5).

Punishment on account of (Nu 25:1-8; 33:55, 56; De 31:16, 17; Jos 23:12, 13; J'g 3:5-8; Ezr 9:7, 14; Ps 106:34, 35, 41, 42; Re 2:16, 22, 23).

Forbidden (Ex 23:32, 33; 34:12-16; Nu 16:26; De 7:2, 3; 12:30; 13:6-11; Jos 23:6, 7, 13; Ezr 9:12; 10:11; Ps 1:1; Pr 1:10-15; 4:14, 15; 9:6; 14:7; Isa 52:11; M't 18:17; Ro 16:17; 1Co 5:9-11; 2Co 6:14-17; Eph 5:11; 2Th 3:6, 14, 15; 1Ti 6:3-5; 2Ti 3:2-7; 2Pe 3:17; 2Jo 9:11; Re 18:1-4.

The evil of fellowship with the wicked exemplified: By Solomon (1Ki 11:1-8); Rehoboam (1Ki 12:8, 9); Jehoshaphat (2Ch 18:3; 19:2; 20:35-37); Jehoram (2Ch 21:6); Ahaziah (2Ch 22:3-5); Israelites (Ezr 9:1, 2); Israel (Eze 44:7); Judas Iscariot (M't 26:14-16).

Instances of Those Who Avoided Fellowship With the Wicked: Man of God (1Ki 13:7-10). Nehemiah (Ne 6:2-4; 10:29-31). David (Ps 101:4-7; 119:115). Jeremiah (Jer 15:17). Joseph of Arimathaea (Lu 23:51). Church of Ephesus (Re 2:6).

See Company, Evil; Influence, Evil.

FENCE (Song 4:12). Made of stone walls (Nu 22:24; Ps 62:3; Pr 24:30, 31; Isa 5:2; Mic 7:11). Hedge (Ec 10:8; Isa 5:5; Na 3:17; M't 21:33; Pr 15:19; Ho 2:6).

Figurative: Eze 22:30.

FENCED CITY. An allusion to the custom of enclosing settlements with walls for protection against invasion (De 3:5).

FERRET (Le 11:30).

FERRYBOAT (2Sa 19:18).

FERTILE CRESCENT. A modern description of the territory from the Persian Gulf to Egypt, which is watered by the Euphrates, Tigris, Orontes, Jordan, and Nile rivers.

FESTIVALS (See Feasts.)

FESTUS, PORCIUS (festal, joyful). Was the Roman governor who succeeded Felix in the province of Judea (Ac 24:27). He presided at the hearing of the apostle Paul when he made his defense before Herod Agrippa II (Ac 24:27; 26:32). When Paul appealed to Caesar, Festus sent him to Rome. The date of Festus' accession is uncertain, probably A.D. 59/60. He died in office in A.D. 62.

FETTERS. Used for securing prisoners (2Ch 33:11; 36:6; M'k 5:4). Made of brass (J'g 16:21; 2Ki 25:7). Made of iron. See Chains.

FEVER (Le 26:16; De 28:22; Job 30:30; Ps 22:15; M't 8:14; Ac 28:8).

FEW SAVED, the number saved spoken of as few (M't 7:14; 22:14; Lu 13:24; 1Pe 3:20; Re 3:4).

FICKLENESS (See Instability.)

FIELD. The Biblical field was generally not enclosed, but was marked off from its neighbors by boundary markers. "Field of Moab" (Ge 36:35) means any plot in the territory of Moab.

FIG. Common to Palestine (Nu 13:23; De 8:8); to Egypt (Ps 105:33). Employed as a remedy (2Ki 20:7; Isa 38:21). Traffic in (Ne 13:15). Dried and preserved

(1Sa 30:12). Cakes of, sent by Abigail to David (1Sa 25:18-35). Aprons made of fig leaves, by Adam and Eve (Ge 3:7).

FIG TREE. In an allegory (J'g 9:11). Jeremiah's parable of (Jer 24:2, 3). Barren, parable of (Lu 13:6-9; 21:29-31).

Figurative: M't 24:32; Re 6:13.

FIGHT OF FAITH (1Ti 6:12; 2Ti 4:7; Heb 10:32; 11:34. See 2Ch 20:17).

FIGURE. See Figurative under principal topics throughout the work. See also Allegory; Pantomime; Parables; Symbols; Types.

FILE, used for sharpening edged tools (1Sa 13:21).

FILLET. "Fillets" (Ex 27:10, 11; 38:10-19) were the rods between the columns that supported the hangings of the Tabernacle.

FINANCES. Methods of raising money. (See Tribute; Temple; Money.)

FINE. For theft (Ex 22:4, 7-9; Pr 6:30, 31). For personal injury (Ex 21:22, 30). For sin of ignorance (Nu 5:5-8; Le 5:15, 16; 22:14). For deception (Le 6:5, 6).

See Damages.

FINGER, six on one hand (2Sa 21:20).

FINGER OF GOD (Ex 8:19; 31:18; Ps 8:3; Da 5:5; Lu 11:20).

FINGERBREADTH, a unit of measurement (Jer 52:21).

FINING-POT is the crucible in which ore is melted to be purified from dross (Pr 17:3; 27:21).

FIR TREE. Wood of, used for building (1Ki 6:15, 34; Song 1:17). Ships made of (Eze 27:5). Instruments of music made of (2Sa 6:5).

FIRE. Used as a signal in war (Jer 6:1). Furnaces of (Da 3:6). Children caused to pass through (2Ki 16:3; 17:17).

Miracles connected with: Miraculously descends upon, and consumes, Abraham's sacrifice (Ge 15:17); David's (1Ch 21:26); Elijah's (1Ki 18:38); Solomon's, at dedication of the temple (2Ch 7:1). Display of, in the plagues of Egypt (Ex 9:24); at Elijah's translation (2Ki 2:11). Consumes the conspirators with Korah, Dathan, and Abiram (Nu 16:35); the captains and their fifties (2Ki 1:9-12).

Torture by (Le 2:19; Jer 29:22; Eze 23:25, 47; Da 3).

Pillar of fire (Ex 13:21, 22; 14:19, 24; 40:38; Nu 9:15-23).

See Cloud, Pillar of.

Figurative: Of cleansing (Isa 6:6, 7); spiritual power (Ps 104:4; Jer 20:9; M't 3:11; Lu 3:16); judgments (De 4:24; 32:22; Isa 33:14; Jer 23:29; Am 1:4, 7, 10, 12, 14; 2:2; Mal 3:2; Lu 12:49; Re 20:9); of the destruction of the wicked (M't 13:42, 50; 25:41; M'k 9:48; Re 9:2; 21:8).

Everlasting Fire (Isa 33:14; M't 18:8; 25:41; M'k 9:48).

A Symbol: Of God's presence (Ge 15:17); in the burning bush (Ex 3:2); on Sinai (Ex 19:18). Tongues of, on the apostles (Ac 2:3).

See Arson.

FIREBRAND, a remnant of a burnt stick (Am 4:11), torches used as weapons (Pr 26:18), and burning wood used for light (J'g 7:16).

FIREPAN, a vessel for carrying live coals (Ex 27:3; 38:3; 2Ki 25:15).

FIRKIN, about nine gallons (Joh 2:6).

FIRMAMENT, the expanse above the earth (Ge 1:6-8, 14-17, 20; Ps 19:1; Da 12:3).

FIRST BEGOTTEN, a term applied to the Lord Jesus Christ in Hebrews 1:6 and Revelation 1:5.

FIRSTBORN, of man and beast, reserved to himself by God (Ex 13:2, 12-16; 22:29, 30; 34:19, 20; Le 27:26; Nu 3:13; 8:17, 18; De 15:19-23; Ne 10:36).

Redemption of (Ex 13:13; 34:20; Le 27:27; Nu 3:40-51; 18:15-17). Levites taken instead of firstborn of the families of Israel (Nu 3:12, 40-45; 8:16-18).

Birthright of the: Had precedence over other sons of the family (Ge 4:7); a double portion of inheritance (De 21:15-17); royal succession (2Ch 21:3). Honorable distinction of (Ex 4:22; Ps 89:27; Jer 31:9; Ro 8:29; Col 1:15; Heb 1:6; 12:23; Re 1:5). Sold by Esau (Ge 25:29-34; 27:36; Ro 9:12, 13; Heb 12:16). Forfeited by Reuben (Ge 49:3, 4; 1Ch 5:1, 2). Set aside: that of Manasseh (Ge 48:15-20; 1Ch 5:1); Adonijah (1Ki 2:15); Hosah's son (1Ch 26:10).

See Birthright.

FIRST DAY OF THE WEEK (See Sunday.)

FIRST FRUITS. First ripe of fruits, grain, oil, wine, and first of fleece, required as an offering (Ex 22:29; Le 2:12-16; Nu 18:12; De 18:4; 2Ch 31:5; Ne 10:35, 37, 39; Pr 3:9; Jer 2:3; Ro

11:16). Offerings of, must be free from blemish (Nu 18:12); presented at the tabernacle (Ex 22:29; 23:19; 34:26; De 26:3-10); belonged to the priests (Le 23:20; Nu 18:12, 13; De 18:3-5). Freewill offerings of, given to the prophets (2Ki 4:42).

Wave offering of (Le 23:10-14, 17). As a heave offering (Nu 15:20; Ne 10:37; Eze 44:30). To be offered as a thank offering upon entrance into the Land of Promise (De 26:3-10).

Figurative: Ro 8:23; 11:16; 1Co 15:20, 23; Jas 1:18.

FIRSTLING (See Firstborn.)

FISH. Creation of (Ge 1:20-22). Appointed for food (Ge 9:2, 3). Clean and unclean (Le 11:9-12; De 14:9, 10). Taken with nets (Ec 9:12; Hab 1:14-17; M't 4:21; Lu 5:2-6; Joh 21:6-8); hooks (Isa 19:8; Am 4:2; M't 17:27); spears (Job 41:7).

Ponds for: in Heshbon (Song 7:4); in Egypt (Isa 19:10). Traffic in (Ne 13:16; Joh 21:13). Broiled (Joh 21:9-13; Lu 24:42). Miracles connected with: Jonah swallowed by (Jon 1:17; 2; M't 12:40); of the loaves and fishes (M't 14:19; 15:36; Lu 5:6; 9:13-17); coin obtained from mouth of (M't 17:27); great draught of (Lu 5:4-7; Joh 21:6); furnished to the disciples by Jesus after his resurrection (Lu 24:42; Joh 21:9-13).

Figurative: Eze 47:9, 10.

FISH GATE, an ancient gate on the E side of Jerusalem near Gihon where Tyrians held a fish market (2Ch 33:14; Ne 13:16).

FISH POOL (See Song 7:4).

FISH SPEAR (Job 41:7.)

FISHERMEN, certain apostles (M't 4:18-21; M'k 1:16-19; Joh 21:2, 3).

Figurative: Jer 16:16; M't 4:19.

FISHHOOK, a metal hook used both to catch fish (M't 17:27) and to keep them captive (Am 4:2).

FITCH (Isa 28:25-27; Eze 4:9).

FLAG. 1. [*R.V.*, Bulrush.] (Ex 2:3, 5; Job 8:11; Isa 18:6; Jon 2:5).

2. An ensign.

See Ensign.

FLAGON, a large container for wine (Isa 22:24). In 2Samuel 6:19 the Hebrew means "raisins."

FLATTERY. Condemned and rebuked (Job 17:5; 32:21, 22; Ps 12:2, 3; Pr 20:19; 22:16; 24:24; 27:14, 21; 28:23; Lu 6:26). Deceive, the simple (Ro 16:18); self (Ps 36:2).

Practiced, by enemy (Ps 5:8, 9; 12:2; Pr 26:28; 29:5; Da 11:21, 34; Jude 16); by seducing women (Pr 2:16; 5:3; 6:24; 7:5, 21); against God (Ps 78:36); against the rich (Pr 14:20; 19:4, 6; 22:16). Not practiced by Paul (Ga 1:10; 1Th 2:4-6).

Instances of: By Jacob (Ge 33:10). By Gideon (J'g 8:1-3). By Mephibosheth (2Sa 9:8). By woman of Tekoah (2Sa 14:17-20). By Absalom (2Sa 15:2-6). By Israel and Judah (2Sa 19:41-43). By Adonijah (1Ki 1:42). By Ahab (1Ki 20:4). By false prophets (1Ki 22:13). By Darius's courtiers (Da 6:7). By Herodians (Lu 20:21). By Tyrians (Ac 12:22). Tertullus flatters Felix (Ac 24:2-4). Paul flatters Felix (Ac 24:10). By Agrippa (Ac 26:2, 3).

FLAX. In Egypt (Ex 9:31). In Palestine (Jos 2:6). Linen made from (Pr 31:13; Isa 19:6; Ho 2:5, 9). Robes made of (Es 1:16; Eze 40:3).

See Linen.

Figurative: Smoking flax not quenched (Isa 42:3; M't 12:20).

FLEA (1Sa 24:14; 26:20).

FLEECE is the shorn wool of a sheep (De 18:4).

FLESH. 1. The soft part of the body of men or animals.

2. All living creatures (Ge 6:18).

3. Humanity in general (Nu 16:22).

4. Intellect and volition contrasted with emotional desire (M't 26:41).

5. Human nature deprived of the Holy Spirit and dominated by sin (Ro 7:14; Col 1:18; 1Jo 2:16).

FLESHHOOK. Used in the tabernacle, (Ex 27:3; 38:3; Nu 4:14; 1Sa 2:13, 14). Made of gold (1Ch 28:17); of brass (2Ch 4:16).

FLIES (Ec 10:1). Plague of (Ex 8:21-31; Ps 78:45; 105:31).

Figurative: Isa 7:18.

FLINT (De 8:15; 32:13; Ps 114:8; Isa 50:7; Eze 3:9).

FLOCK, a collection of sheep under the care of a shepherd, sometimes including goats as well (Ge 27:9; 30:32). Used figuratively of Christ's disciples (Lu 12:32; 1Pe 5:2, 3).

FLOOD, the deluge. Foretold (Ge 6:13, 17). History of (Ge 6-8). References to

(Job 22:16; Ps 90:5; M't 24:38; Lu 17:26, 27; Heb 11:7; 1Pe 3:20; 2Pe 2:5). The promise that it should not recur (Ge 8:20, 21; Isa 54:9).

See Meteorology.

FLOUR, fine-crushed and sifted grain, generally wheat, rye, or barley (J'g 6:19).

FLOWER (See Plants.)

FLUTE (Da 3:5, 7, 10, 15).

See Music, Instruments of.

FOAL (See Animals.)

FODDER, the mixed food of cattle (Job 6:5).

FOOD. *Articles of:* Milk (Ge 49:12; Pr 27:27; butter (De 32:14; 2Sa 17:29); cheese (1Sa 17:18; Job 10:10); bread (Ge 18:5; 1Sa 17:17); parched corn (Ru 2:14; 1Sa 17:17); flesh (2Sa 6:19; Pr 9:2); fish (M't 7:10; Lu 24:42); herbs (Pr 15:17; Ro 14:2; Heb 6:7); fruit (2Sa 16:2); dried fruit (1Sa 25:18; 30:12); honey (Song 5:1; Isa 7:15); oil (De 12:17; Pr 21:17; Eze 16:13); vinegar (Nu 6:3; Ru 2:14); wine (2Sa 6:19; Joh 2:3, 10).

Prepared by females (Ge 27:9; 1Sa 8:13; Pr 31:15). Thanks given before (M'k 8:6; Ac 27:35). A hymn sung after (M't 26:30). Men and women did not partake together (Ge 18:8, 9; Es 1:3, 9).

From God (Ge 1:29, 30; 9:3; 48:15; Job 36:31; Ps 23:5; 103:5; 104:14, 15; 111:5; 136:25; 145:15; 147:9; Pr 30:8; Isa 3:1; M't 6:11; Ac 14:17; Ro 14:14, 21; 1Ti 4:3-5).

Things prohibited as (Ex 22:31; Le 11:4-8, 10-20, 41, 42; 17:13-15). Peter's vision concerning (Ac 10:10-16). Flesh unwarrantedly forbidden as (1Ti 4:3. 4). Paul's teaching concerning the eating of food offered to idols (Ro 14:2-23; 1Co 8:4-13; 10:18-32).

See Bread; Eating; Oven.

FOOL in Scripture connotes conceit and pride, or deficiency in judgment rather than mental inferiority.

Lacking in understanding (Pr 3:35; 9:13, 21; 10:13; 15:21; 26:1, 3-12; Ec 7:4-6). Of an uncontrolled temper (Ec 7:9). Deficient in conscience (Pr 10:23). Willful (Pr 1:7; 27:22). Unperceptive (M't 7:26, 27). Gullible (Pr 14:8, 15). Unknowledgeable (Pr 15:7).

Described as: Idle (Ec 4:5). Wasteful (Pr 21:20). Loquacious (Pr 10:8, 10; 29:11; Ec 10:12-14). Meddlesome (Pr 20:3). Contentious (Pr 1:18; 18:6, 7; 29:9). Unfilial (Pr 10:1; 15:20; 17:25; 19:13). Despising wisdom (Pr 1:7, 22; 18:2). Atheistic (Ps 14:1; 53:1). Iniquitous (Ps 5:5; 107:17; Tit 3:3). Clamorous (Pr 9:13). A reproach (Ps 74:18, 22). A dreamer (Pr 17:24). Deceitful (Pr 1:14, 18). Mocker (Pr 14:9).

Causes sorrow (Pr 10:1; 14:13; 17:25; 19:13). To be avoided (Pr 14:8); forsaken (Pr 9:6). Afflicted (Ps 107:17).

Parables of: Of the foolish virgins (M't 25:1-13); of the rich fool (Lu 12:16-20).

FOOT. Washing the feet of the disciples by Jesus (Joh 13:4-16); by disciples (1Ti 5:10).

See Ablutions; Purifications.

For footwear, see Shoe.

Figurative: M't 18:8.

FOOTMAN, a runner before kings and princes (1Sa 8:11; 2Sa 15:1; 1Ki 1:5).

FOOTSTOOL, a literal support for the feet (2Ch 9:18), a figure of subjection (Ps 110:1; Isa 66:1; M't 5:35).

FORD, a shallow place in a stream where men and animals could cross on foot (Ge 32:22; Isa 16:2).

FOREHEAD, the part of the face above the eyes, often revealing the character of the person: shamelessness (Jer 3:3), courage (Eze 3:9), or godliness (Re 7:3).

FOREIGNER. Among the Jewish people, anyone outside the nation was regarded as inferior (Ge 31:15), and possessed restricted rights. He could not eat the Passover (Ex 12:43), enter the sanctuary (Eze 44:9), become king (De 17:15, or intermarry on equal terms (Ex 34:12-16). They could be included in the nation by accepting the Law and its requirements. In the NT the word is applied to those who are not members of God's kingdom (Eph 2:19).

FOREKNOWLEDGE OF GOD (See God, Foreknowledge of, Wisdom of.)

FOREMAN (See Master Workman.)

FOREORDINATION (See Predestination.)

FORERUNNER. Figurative of Christ (Heb 6:20).

FORESKIN, the fold of skin cut off in the process of circumcision (Ge 17:11, 14).

FORESTS. Tracts of land covered with trees (Isa 44:14). Underwood often in (Isa 9:18). Infested by wild beasts (Ps

50:10; 104:20; Isa 56:9; Jer 5:6; Mic 5:8). Abounded with wild honey (1Sa 14:25, 26). Often afforded pasture (Mic 7:14).

Mentioned in Scripture: Bashan (Isa 2:13; Eze 27:6; Zec 11:2). Hareth (1Sa 22:5). Ephraim (2Sa 18:6, 8). Lebanon (1Ki 7:2; 10:17). Carmel (2Ki 19:23; Isa 37:24). Arabia (Isa 21:13). The south (Eze 20:46, 47). The king's (Ne 2:8). Supplied timber for building (1Ki 5:6-8). Were places of refuge (1Sa 22:5; 23:16). Jotham built towers in (2Ch 27:4). The power of God extends over (Ps 29:9). Called on to rejoice at God's mercy (Isa 44:23). Often destroyed by enemies (2Ki 19:23; Isa 37:24; Jer 46:23).

Illustrative: Of the unfruitful world (Isa 32:19). (A fruitful field turned into,) of the Jews rejected by God (Isa 29:17; 32:15).

(Destroyed by fire,) of destruction of the wicked (Isa 9:18; 10:17, 18; Jer 21:14).

FORGERY, by Jezebel (1Ki 21:8).

FORGETTING GOD. A characteristic of the wicked (Pr 2:17; Isa 65:11). Backsliders guilty of (Jer 2:32; 3:21).

Is forgetting his covenant (De 4:23; 2Ki 17:38); works (Ps 78:7, 11; 106:13); benefits (Ps 103:2; 106:7); word (Heb 12:5; Jas 1:25); law (Ps 119:153, 176; Ho 4:6); church (Ps 137:5); past deliverances (J'g 8:34; Ps 78:42); power to deliver (Isa 51:13-15).

Encouraged by false teachers (Jer 23:27). Prosperity leads to (De 8:12-14; Ho 13:6). Trials should not lead to (Ps 44:17-20). Resolve against (Ps 119:16, 93). Cautions against (De 6:12; 8:11). Exhortation to those guilty of (Ps 50:22).

Punishment of (Job 8:12, 13; Ps 9:17; Isa 17:10, 11; Eze 23:35; Hos 8:14); threatened (Job 8:13; Ps 9:17; 50:22; Isa 17:10; Jer 2:32; Ho 8:14).

See Backsliders; Forsaking God.

FORGIVENESS, Of Enemies. Enjoined (Pr 24:17; M't 5:43-48; 18:21-35; M'k 11:25; Lu 6:27-37; 17:3, 4; Eph 4:32; Col 3:13; Ph'm 10, 18); by giving (Pr 25:21, 22; M't 5:39-41; Ro 12:20); by showing kindness to enemy's beast (Ex 23:4, 5).

A condition of divine forgiveness (M't 6:12-15; 18:21-35; M'k 11:25; Lu 11:4).

Spirit of, blesses (Ro 12:14; 1Co 4:12, 13; 1Pe 3:9); disallows retaliation (Pr 24:29; Ro 12:17, 19); disallows rejoicing (Pr 24:17).

FORM. In religious service (1Ch 15:13, 14; 2Ch 29:34). Irregularity in (2Ch 30:2-5, 17, 20; M't 12:3, 4). See Church and State.

FORMALISM. Despised by God (Ps 50:8-15; Isa 1:11-15; 29:13-16; Jer 6:20; 14:12; Am 5:21-23; Mal 1:6-14; Lu 13:24-27; 2Ti 3:1-5). Empty (M't 15:8, 9; Ro 2:17-29; 1Co 7:19; Ph'p 3:4-7).

Rejected by God for, obedience (1Sa 15:22; Ec 5:1; 1Co 7:19); thanksgiving (Ps 50:8-15; 69:30, 31); contrition (Ps 51:16, 17; Mic 6:6, 7); mercy (Ho 6:6; M't 9:13; 12:7); a pure heart (M't 15:8, 9; Ro 2:17-29); repentance (M't 9:13).

FORNICATION. Illicit sexual intercourse in general—*i.e.* adultery (Ac 15:20, 29; 21:25; Ro 1:29; 1Co 5:1; 6:13, 18; 7:2). More specifically and primarily unlawful sexual intercourse of an unwed person (M't 15:19; M'k 7:21; 1Co 6:9, 18; Ga 5:19). It was commonly associated with heathen worship (Jer 2:20; 3:6), and was used as a figure of disloyalty to God (Eze 16:3-22).

See Adultery.

FORSAKING GOD. Idolaters guilty of (1Sa 8:8; 1Ki 11:33). The wicked guilty of (De 28:20). Backsliders guilty of (Jer 15:6).

Is Forsaking: His house (2Ch 29:6). His covenant (De 29:25; 1Ki 19:10; Jer 22:9; Da 11:30). His commandments (Ezr 9:10). The right way (2Pe 2:15). Trusting in man is (Jer 17:5). Leads men to follow their own devices (Jer 2:13). Prosperity tempts to (De 31:20; 32:15). Wickedness of (Jer 2:13; 5:7). Unreasonableness and ingratitude of (Jer 2:5, 6). Brings confusion (Jer 17:13). Followed by remorse (Eze 6:9). Brings down His wrath (Ezr 3:22). Provokes God to forsake men (J'g 10:13; 2Ch 15:2; 24:20, 24). Resolve against (Jos 24:16; Ne 10:29-39). Curse pronounced upon (Jer 17:5). Sin of, to be confessed (Ezr 9:10). Warnings against (Jos 24:20, 1Ch 28:9). Exemplified. Children of Israel (1Sa 12:10). Saul (1Sa 15:11). Ahab (1Ki 18:18). Amon (2Ki 21:22). Kingdom of Judah (2Ch 12:1, 5; 2Ch 21:10; Isa 1:4; Jer 15:6). Kingdom of Israel (2Ch 13:11, w 2Ki 17:7-18). Many disciples (Joh 6:66). Phygellus (2Ti 1:15). Balaam (2Pe 2:15).

FORT, a military defense. Field fortifications (De 20:19, 20; 2Ki 25:1; Eze 4:2; 17:17; 26:8). Defenses of cities (2Ch 26:15; Isa 25:12). See Castles; Towers; Walls. Erected in vineyards and herding grounds (2Ch 26:10; Isa 5:2; M't 21:33; M'k 12:1; Lu 20:9). Caves used for (J'g 6:2; 1Sa 23:29; Isa 33:16).

Figurative: Of God's care (2Sa 22:2, 3, 47; Ps 18:2; 31:3; 71:3; 91:2; 144:2; Pr 18:10; Na 1:7).

FORTIFICATION (a military defense). Field made during military operations (De 20:19, 20; 2Ki 25:1; Jer 6:6; 32:24; 33:4; Eze 4:2; 17:17; 26:8; Da 11:15). Defenses of cities (2Sa 5:9; 2Ch 11:10, 11; 26:9, 15; Ne 3:8; 4:2; Isa 22:10; 25:12; 29:3; Jer 51:53; Na 3:14). Erected in vineyards and herding grounds (2Ch 26:10; Isa 5:2; M't 21:33; M'k 12:1). Caves used for (J'g 6:2; 1Sa 23:26).

Figurative: Of God's care (2Sa 22:2, 3, 47; Ps 18:2; 31:3; 71:3; 91:2; 144:2; Pr 18:10; Na 1:7).

FORTITUDE (See Courage.)

FORTUNATUS (blessed, fortunate) a Corinthian Christian, a friend of Paul (1Co 16:17).

FORTUNE, changes of. See illustrated in lives of, Joseph, from slave to prime minister; Pharaoh's butler and baker (Ge 40); David, from shepherd boy to king, noting the vicissitudes. See also Jeroboam; Haman; Mordecai; Esther; Job; Daniel.

FORTUNE TELLING (See Sorcery.)

FORTY. Remarkable coincidences in the number.

Days: Of rain, at the time of the flood (Ge 7:17); of flood, before sending forth the raven (Ge 8:6). For embalming (Ge 50:3). Of fasting: By Moses (Ex 24:18; 34:28; De 9:9, 25); Elijah (1Ki 19:8); Jesus (M't 4:2). Spies in the land of promise (Nu 13:25). Of probation, given to the Ninevites (Jon 3:4). Christ's stay after the resurrection (Ac 1:3). Symbolical (Eze 4:6).

Years: Wanderings of the Israelites in the Wilderness (Ex 16:35; Nu 14:34). Peace in Israel (J'g 3:11; 5:31; 8:28). Egypt to be desolated (Eze 29:11); to be restored after (Eze 29:13).

Stripes: Administered in punishing criminals (De 25:3; 2Co 11:24).

FORUM APPII, "the market of Appius," a place 43 miles SE of Rome, where Paul was met by friends (Ac 28:15).

FOUNDATION, the lowest part of a building, and on which it rests (Lu 14:29; Ac 16:26).

Figuratively Applied to: The heavens (2Sa 22:8). The earth (Job 38:4; Ps 104:5). The world (Ps 18:15; M't 13:35). The mountains (De 32:22). The ocean (Ps 104:8). Kingdoms (Ex 9:18).

Laid for: Cities (Jos 6:26; 1Ki 16:34). Walls (Ezr 4:12; Re 21:14). Houses (Lu 6:48). Temples (1Ki 6:37; Ezr 3:10). Towers (Lu 14:28, 29).

Described as: Of stone (1Ki 5:17). Deep laid (Lu 6:48). Strongly laid (Ezr 6:3). Joined together by corner stones (Ezr 4:12 w 1Pe 2:6, and Eph 2:20). Security afforded by (M't 7:25; Lu 6:48).

Illustrative of: Christ (Isa 28:16; 1Co 3:11). Doctrines of the apostles (Eph 2:20). First principles of the Gospel (Heb 6:1, 2). Decrees and purposes of God (2Ti 2:19). Magistrates (Ps 82:5). The righteous (Pr 10:25). Hope of saints (Ps 87:1). Security of saints' inheritance (Heb 11:10).

FOUNDING (See Molding.)

FOUNTAIN, *Figurative:* Of divine grace (Ps 36:9; Jer 2:13); of the salvation of the gospel (Joe 3:18; Zec 13:1; Re 7:17). The turbid, of the debasement of character (Pr 25:26).

FOUNTAIN GATE, a gate in the walls of Jerusalem (Ne 2:14; 3:15; 12:37).

FOUNTAIN OF LIFE (Ps 36:9; Pr 13:14; 14:27; Jer 2:13; Zec 13:1; Re 7:17).

FOWLER, a bird-catcher (Ps 91:3; 124:7; Ho 9:8).

FOX. Dens of (M't 8:20; Lu 9:58). Samson uses, to burn the field of the Philistines (J'g 15:4). Depredations of (Ps 63:10; Song 2:15).

Figurative: Of unfaithful prophets (Eze 13:4). Of craftiness (Lu 13:32). Of heretics (Song 2:15).

FRACTURES, treatment of (Eze 30:21).

FRANKINCENSE. An ingredient of the sacred oil (Ex 30:34). Used with showbread (Le 24:7); with meat offerings (Le 2:1, 2, 15, 16; 6:15). Prohibited, in sin offerings when they consist of turtle-doves or pigeons (Le 5:11); in making an offering of memorial (Nu 5:15). A perfume (Song 3:6). Commerce in (Re 18:11-13). Used as an incense (Isa 43:23; 60:6; 66:3; Jer 6:20). Gift of (M't 2:11).

FRATERNITY. Enjoined, by Moses upon the Israelites (De 15:7-15; Jos 1:14, 15); by David (Ps 22:22; 133:1-3); by God (Mal 2:10); by Jesus (Ps 22:22; M't 5:22-24; 18:15-18, 21, 22, 35; 23:8; 25:40; Joh 13:34; 15:12; 21:17); by Paul (Ro 12:10; 1Co 6:1-8; Ga 6:1, 2; 1Th 4:9; 2Th 3:14, 15); in Hebrews (Heb 13:1); by Peter (1Pe 1:12; 2:17; 3:8; 2Pe 1:5, 7); by John (1Jo 2:9-11).

Unity (Ps 133:1-3); broken (Zec 11:14).

Incompatible, with selfishness (1Jo 3:17); with pride of title (M't 23:8); with indifference to another's conscience (1Co 8:1-13; 10:28, 29).

Nazarites, vows of (Nu 6:1-21; La 4:7; Am 2:11, 12; Ac 21:24-31). See Nazarites.

Exemplified: By Abraham and Lot (Ge 13:8). By Jonathan and David (1Sa 18:1; 19:2-7; 20:17, 41, 42; 23:16-18). By early Christians (Ac 2:42-47). By Paul (Ro 9:2, 3; 10:1; 1Co 9:20-22). By James, Cephas, and John (Ga 2:9). By Epaphroditus (Ph'p 2:25, 26). By the Thessalonian church (2Th 1:3).

See Brother; Church; Fellowship; Friendship; Love.

FRATRICIDE. *Instances of:* Cain (Gen 4:8). Abimelech (J'g 9:5). Absalom (2Sa 13:28, 29). Solomon (1Ki 2:23-25); Jehoram (2Ch 21:4).

See Homicide.

FRAUD (See Dishonesty.)

FREEDMEN, synagogue of (Ac 6:9).

See Emancipation.

FREEDOM, from servitude.

(See Emancipation; Jubilee.)

FREEMAN, a slave who has been granted his freedom (1Ch 7:22), or a free man as contrasted with a slave (Gal 4:22, 23).

FREE-WILL (See Blessings, Contingent Upon Obedience.)

FREE-WILL OFFERINGS (Le 22:21, 23; 23:38; Nu 29:39; De 12:6, 17; 2 Ch 31:14; Ezr 3:5; 7:16; 8:28; Ps 119:108).

See Beneficence; Gifts; Giving; Liberality; Offerings.

FRET. The verb means to be irritated, angry, or nervous (Ps 37:1, 7, 8); the noun refers to a painful type of leprosy (Le 13:51, 52).

FRIENDS. Affectionate (De 13:6; 1Sa 18:1; 20:17; Joh 15:33). Sympathetic (Job 2:11; 6:14; Ps 35:14). Of mutual help (Pr 27:9, 19). Faithful (Pr 17:17; 18:24; 27:6). Mercenary (Pr 14:20; 19:4, 6). Cause rejoicing (Pr 27:9). Not to forsake (Pr 27:10). Forsaken (Pr 17:9; 27:14). See Friendship.

Jesus calls his disciples (Lu 12:4; Joh 15:14, 15).

False (Zec 13:6; Ps 41:9; 88:18). Instances of: Pharaoh's butler to Joseph (Ge 40:23). Delilah to Samson (J'g 16:4-20). The Ephraimite's wife (J'g 19:1, 2). Job's friends (Job 6:15-30; 16:20; 19:13-22). David to Joab (1Ki 2:5, 6); to Uriah (2Sa 11). Ahithophel to David (2Sa 15:12). David's friends to David (Ps 31:11, 12; 35:11-16; 41:9; 55:12-14, 20, 21; 88:8, 18; Ac 1:16). Judas (M't 26:48, 49). Jesus' disciples (M't 26:56, 58). Paul's friends (2Ti 4:16).

See Hypocrisy.

FRIENDSHIP. Value of (Ec 4:9-12). Faithfulness in (Ps 35:13, 14; Pr 17:9, 17; 27:6, 9, 10, 14, 17, 19). Temptations growing out of (De 13:6-9; Pr 22:24-27).

Promoted, by fidelity (Pr 11:13); by sympathy (Job 6:14, 15); by mutual understanding (Am 3:3); by not wearing out one's welcome (Pr 25:17, 19).

See Friend.

Instances of: Abraham and Lot (Ge 14:14-16). Ruth and Naomi (Ru 1:16, 17). Samuel and Saul (1Sa 18:1-4; 20; 23:16-18; 2Sa 1:17-27; 9:1-13). David and Abiathar (1Sa 22:23). David and Nahash (2Sa 10:2). David and Hiram (1Ki 5:1). David and Mephibosheth (2Sa 9). David and Hushai (2Sa 15:32-37; 16; 17:1-22). David and Ittai (2Sa 15:19-21). Joram and Ahaziah (2Ki 8:28, 29; 9:16). Jehu and Jehonadab (2Ki 10:15-27). Job and his three friends (Job 2:11-13). Daniel and his three companions (Da 2:49).

Mary, Martha, and Lazarus, and Jesus (Lu 10:38-42; Joh 11:1-46). The Marys, and Joseph of Arimathaea, for Jesus (M't 27:55-61; 28:1-8; Lu 24:10; Joh 20:11-18); Luke and Theophilus (Ac 1:1). Paul and his nephew (Ac 23:16). Paul, Priscilla, and Aquila (Ro 16:3, 4). Paul, Timothy, and Epaphroditus (Ph'p

2:19, 20, 22, 25).

FRINGES. Prescribed for vesture worn by the Israelites (Nu 15:38-41; De 22:12). Made broad by the Pharisees (M't 23:5).

FROGS, plague of (Ex 8:2-14; Ps 78:45; 105:30).

Symbolical: Re 16:13.

FRONTLETS. A leather band worn on the forehead (Ex 13:6-16; De 6:1-8; 11:18).

See Phylactery.

FROST appeared in winter on the high elevations in Bible lands (Job 37:10; 38:29).

FROWARDNESS (Ps 101:4; Pr 3:32; 4:24; 8:13; 10:31; 11:20; 22:5).

FRUGALITY. The mark of a man that is strong (Pr 11:16); diligent (Pr 12:27); good (Pr 13:22); wise (Pr 21:17, 20); prudent (Pr 22:3); industrious (Eph 4:28). The mark of a virtuous woman (Pr 31:27).

Admonition regarding (Pr 23:20, 21). Enjoined by Jesus (Joh 6:12).

Cloak of covetousness (M'k 14:4, 5).

Instances of: The provisions made by the Egyptians against famine (Ge 41:48-54); the gathering of manna (Ex 16:17, 18, 22-24); the gathering of bread and fish after the feeding of the multitudes (M't 14:20; 15:37).

See Extravagance; Industry.

FRUITS. *Natural:* Created (Ge 1:11, 12, 27-29). See under respective headings of various fruit-producing trees.

Spiritual: See Righteousness, Fruits of; Sin, Fruits of; Spirit, Fruit of.

FRUIT TREES, care for (De 20:19, 20).

FRYING PAN, properly a saucepan for boiling or baking (Le 2:7; 7:9).

FUEL. Wood, charcoal, dried grass, and even the dung of animals was used for fuel (Eze 4:12, 15; M't 6:30; Joh 18:18).

FUGITIVES, from servitude, not to be returned (De 23:15, 16).

Instances of: From slavery, Shimei's servants (1Ki 2:39); Onesimus (Ph'm 1).

See Exodus.

From Justice: Moses (Ex 2:15); Absalom (2Sa 13:34-38).

From the wrath of the king: David (1Sa 21:10); Jeroboam (1Ki 11:40); Joseph, to Egypt (M't 2:13-15).

FULLER (Mal 3:2; M'k 9:3).

FULLER'S FIELD, a field outside Jerusalem where fullers washed the cloth that they were processing (2Ki 18:17; Isa 7:3; 36:2).

FULLNESS OF TIME (Da 6:24; M'k 1:15; Ga 4:4; Eph 1:10; 1Ti 2:6; Tit 1:3; Heb 9:26).

FUNERAL, the ceremonies used in disposing of a dead human body. In Palestine the body was buried within a few hours after death in a tomb or cave. The body was washed, anointed with spices, and wrapped in cloths (Joh 12:7; 19:39, 40). Refusal of proper burial was utter disgrace (Jer 22:19).

FURLONG, one eighth of a mile (Lu 24:13; Joh 11:18; Re 21:16).

FURNACE. Uses of: For refining silver (Eze 22:22; Mal 3:3); gold (Pr 17:3). For melting lead and tin (Eze 22:20). For capital punishment, Shadrach, Meshach, and Abed-nego cast into, by Nebuchadnezzar (Da 3:6-26).

Figurative: Of affliction (De 4:20; 1Ki 8:51; Ps 12:6; Isa 48:10; Jer 11:4). Of lust (Ho 7:4). Of hell (Mal 4:1; M't 13:42, 50; Re 9:2).

FURNITURE. The principle reference to furniture in the Bible concerns the articles in the Tabernacle and Temple. Common people had little furniture; kings had bedsteads (De 3:11) and tables (J'g 1:7).

FUTURE LIFE (See Immortality; Eschatology.)

FUTURE PUNISHMENT (See Punishment, Eternal.)

G

GAAL (loathing), son of Ebed, who led the men of Shechem in a revolt against Abimelech, the son of Gideon (J'g 9:26-41).

GAASH (quaking), a foothill of Mount Ephraim. Joshua's inheritance embraced (Jos 24:30). Joshua buried on the north side of (Jos 24:30; J'g 2:9). Brooks of (2Sa 23:30).

GABA, called also Geba. A city of Canaan allotted to Benjamin (Jos 18:24; Ezr 2:26; Ne 7:30).

GABBAI (collector), a chief of Benjamin (Ne 11:8).

GABBATHA (height, ridge), the place called "the Pavement" (Joh 19:13) where Jesus was tried before Pilate.

GABRIEL (man of God), a messenger of God. Appeared to Daniel (Da 8:16; 9:21); to Zacharias (Lu 1:11-19); to Mary (Lu 1:26-29).

GAD (fortune). 1. Jacob's seventh son (Ge 30:11; 35:26; Ex 1:4). Children of (Ge 46:16; Nu 26:15-18; 1Ch 5:11). Prophecy concerning (Ge 49:19).

2. A tribe of Israel. Blessed by Moses (De 33:20). Enumeration of, at Sinai (Nu 1:14, 24, 25); in the plains of Moab (Nu 26:15-18); in the reign of Jotham (1Ch 5:11-17). Place of, in camp and march (Nu 2:10, 14, 16). Wealth of, in cattle, and spoils (Jos 22:8; Nu 32:1). Petition for their portion of land E of the Jordan (Nu 32:1-5; De 3:12, 16, 17; 29:8). Boundaries of territory (Jos 13:24-28; 1Ch 5:11). Aid in the conquest of the region W of the Jordan (Nu 32:16-32; Jos 4:12, 13; 22:1-8). Erect a monument to signify the unity of the tribes E of the Jordan with the tribes W of the river (Jos 22:10-14).

Disaffected toward Saul as king, and joined the faction under David in the wilderness of Hebron (1Ch 12:8-15, 37, 38). Join the Reubenites in the war against the Hagarites (1Ch 5:10, 18-22). Smitten by the king of Syria (2Ki 10:32, 33). Carried into captivity to Assyria (1Ch 5:26). Land of, occupied by the Ammonites, after the tribe is carried into captivity (Jer 49:1). Reallotment of territory to, by Ezekiel (Eze 48:27, 29).

3. A prophet of David (2Sa 24:11). Bids David leave Adullam (1Sa 22:5). Bears the divine message to David offering choice between three evils, for his presumption in numbering Israel (2Sa 24:11-14; 1Ch 21:9-13). Bids David build an altar on threshing floor of Ornan (2Sa 24:18, 19; 1Ch 21:18, 19). Assists David in arranging temple service (2Ch 29:25). Writings of (1Ch 29:29).

GADARA, GADARENES, one of the cities of the Decapolis near the SE end of the Sea of Galilee, near which the demoniacs lived whom Jesus healed (M'k 5:1; Lu 8:26, 37; M't 8:28, Gr. text).

GADDI, a chief of Manasseh. One of the twelve spies who explored Canaan (Nu 13:11).

GADDIEL, a chief of Zebulun. One of the twelve spies (Nu 13:10).

GADI, father of Menahem, a king of Israel (2Ki 15:14-20).

GAHAM, a son of Nahor by his concubine Reumah (Ge 22:24).

GAHAR, one of the Nethinim (Ezr 2:47; Ne 7:49).

GAIUS. 1. A Macedonian, and a companion of Paul. Seized at Ephesus (Ac 19:29).

2. A man of Derbe; accompanied Paul from Macedonia (Ac 20:4).

3. A Corinthian, whom Paul baptized (Ro 16:23; 1Co 1:14).

4. Man to whom John's third epistle was addressed (3Jo).

GALAL. 1. A Levite (1Ch 9:15).

2. Son of Jeduthun (1Ch 9:16; Ne 11:17).

GALATIA, a province of Asia Minor. Its churches visited by Paul (Ac 16:6; 18:23). Collection taken in, for Christians at Jerusalem (1Co 16:1). Peter's address to (1Pe 1:1). Churches in (Ga 1:1, 2). See Paul's epistle to Galatians.

GALATIANS, EPISTLE TO THE, is a short but important letter of Paul, containing a protest against legalism and a clear statement of the gospel of God's grace. It was written shortly after the close of the first missionary journey to the churches of Galatia (Ga 1:1) to counteract the propaganda of certain Jewish teachers who insisted that to faith in Christ must be added circumcision and obedience to the Mosaic Law (2:16; 3:2, 3; 4:10, 21; 5:2-4; 6:12). After the introduction to the epistle (1:1-10) Paul attempted to vindicate his apostolic authority (1:11-2:21), and then proceeded to explain the meaning of justification by faith (3:1-4:31), concluding with a discussion on the nature of the Christian life of liberty (5:1-6:10). The conclusion (6:11-17) and benediction (6:18) constituted a personal appeal to the Galatians to return to their initial faith.

GALBANUM, a fragrant gum used in the sacred oil (Ex 30:34).

GALEED (a heap of witnesses), the name given by Jacob to the heap of stones which he and Laban raised as a memorial of their compact (Ge 31:47, 48).

GALILEAN, a native of Galilee (M't 26:69; Joh 4:45; Ac 1:11; 5:37).

GALILEE (the ring, circuit). The northern district of Palestine. A city of refuge in (Jos 20:7; 21:32; 1Ch 6:76). Cities in, given to Hiram (1Ki 9:11, 12). Taken by king of Assyria (2Ki 15:29). Prophecy concerning (Isa 9:1; M't 4:15). Called Galilee of the Nations (Isa 9:1). Herod, tetrarch of (M'k 6:21; Lu 3:1; 23:6, 7). Jesus resides in (M't 17:22; 19:1; Joh 7:1, 9). Teaching and miracles of Jesus in (M't 4:23, 25; 15:29-31; M'k 1:14, 28, 39; 3:7; Lu 4:14, 44; 5:17; 23:5; Joh 1:43; 4:3, 43-45; Ac 10:37). People of, receive Jesus (Joh 4:45, 53). Disciples were chiefly from (Ac 1:11; 2:7). Women from, ministered to Jesus (M't 27:55, 56; M'k 15:41; Lu 23:49, 55). Jesus appeared to his disciples in, after his resurrection (M't 26:32; 28:7, 10, 16, 17; M'k 14:28; 16:7; Joh 21).

Routes from, to Judaea (J'g 21:19; Joh 4:3-5). Dialect of (M'k 14:70). Called Gennesaret (M't 14:34; M'k 6:53). Churches in (Ac 9:31).

GALILEE, SEA OF, called also "the lake of Gennesaret" (Lu 5:1), or "the Sea of Chinnereth" (Nu 34:11; De 3:17) from the Hebrew meaning "harp-shaped," the shape of the sea, or "the Sea of Tiberias" because Herod's capital was on its shores (Joh 6:1; 21:1). The lake is 13 miles long and 8 miles wide, filled with sweet and clear water, and full of fish. Because it was located in a pocket in the hills, it was subject to sudden violent storms.

GALL. 1. The secretion of the human gall bladder (Job 16:13).

2. The poison of serpents (20:14).

3. A bitter and poisonous herb (Jer 9:15), perhaps used as an anodyne to deaden pain (M't 27:34).

Figurative: Gall of bitterness (Ac 8:23).

GALLERY, a balcony of the temple in Ezekiel's vision (Eze 41:16; 42:3, 5, 6).

GALLEY (See Ship.)

GALLIM (heaps), a town of Benjamin (Isa 10:30; 1Sa 25:44).

GALLIO, proconsul of Achaia. Dismisses complaint of Jews against Paul (Ac 18:12-17).

GALLOWS. Used for execution of criminals (Es 2:23; 5:14; 6:4; 7:9, 10; 9:13, 25). Reproach of being hanged upon (Ga 3:13).

See Punishment.

GAMALIEL (reward of God). 1. Chief of tribe of Manasseh (Nu 1:10; 2:20; 10:23).

2. An eminent Pharisee and teacher of the Law, the teacher of Paul (Ac 22:3). He was broadminded and tolerant toward early Christians (5:34-39).

GAMES. Foot races (1Co 9:24, 26; Ga 2:2; Ph'p 2:16; Heb 12:1). Gladiatorial (1Co 4:9; 9:26; 15:32; 2Ti 4:7).

Figurative: Of the Christian life (1Co 9:24, 26; Ga 5:7; Ph'p 2:16; 3:14; Heb 12:1). Of a successful ministry (Ga 2:2; Ph'p 2:16). Fighting wild beasts, of spiritual conflict (1Co 4:9; 9:26; 15:32; 2Ti 4:7).

GAMMADIM (probably **valiant men),** the garrison in the watchtowers of Tyre (Eze 27:11).

GAMUL, the head of the twenty-second course of priests (1Ch 24:17).

GARDEN, a cultivated piece of ground planted with flowers, vegetables, shrubs, or trees, fenced with a mud or stone wall (Pr 24:31) or with thorny hedges (Isa 5:5). Gardens were sometimes used for burial places (Ge 23:17; 2Ki 21:18, 26; Joh 19:41). The future state of the saved is figuratively represented by a garden (Re 22:1-5).

GARDENER (See Occupations and Professions.)

GAREB (scabby). 1. One of David's

warriors (2Sa 23:38; 1Ch 11:40).

2. A hill near Jerusalem (Jer 31:39).

GARLANDS (Ac 14:13).

GARLIC (Nu 11:5).

GARMENT, of righteousness (Isa 61:10; M't 22:11; 2Co 5:3; Re 3:18; 7:14; 16:15; 19:8).

See Dress; Robe.

GARMITE, a name applied to Keilah (1Ch 4:19).

GARNER, a barn or storehouse (Ps 144:13; Joe 1:17; M't 3:12).

GARRISON, a fortress manned by soldiers, used chiefly for the occupation of a conquered country (1Sa 10:5; 13:3; 14:1, 6; 2Sa 8:6, 14).

GASHMU, sometimes called Geshem, an Arabian who opposed Nehemiah's restoration of Jerusalem (Ne 2:19; 6:1, 2, 6).

GATAM, grandson of Esau (Ge 36:11, 16; 1Ch 1:36).

GATES. Of cities (De 3:5; Jos 6:26; 1Sa 23:7; 2Sa 18:24; 2Ch 8:5). Made of iron (Ac 12:10); wood (Ne 1:3); brass (Ps 107:16; Isa 45:2). Double doors (Isa 45:1; Eze 41:24).

The open square of, a place for idlers (Ge 19:1; 1Sa 4:18; Ps 69:12; Pr 1:21; Jer 17:19, 20). Religious services held at (Ac 14:13). The law read at (Ne 8). Place for the transaction of public business, announcement of legal transactions (Ge 23:10, 16); conferences on public affairs (Ge 34:20); holding courts of justice (De 16:18; 21:19; 22:15; Jos 20:4; Ru 4:1; 2Sa 15:2; Pr 22:22; Zec 8:16). Place for public concourse (Ge 23:10; Pr 1:21; 8:3; Jer 14:2; 22:2). Thrones of kings at (1Ki 22:10; 2Ch 18:9; Jer 38:7; 39:3). Punishment of criminals outside of (De 17:5; Jer 20:2; Ac 7:58; Heb 13:12). Closed at night (Jos 2:5, 7); on the Sabbath (Ne 13:19). Guards at (2Ki 7:17; Ne 13:19, 22). Jails made in the towers of (Jer 20:2). Bodies of criminals exposed to view at (2Ki 10:8).

Figurative: Of the people of a city (Isa 3:26). Of the gospel (Isa 60:11). Of the powers of hell (M't 16:18); of death (Job 38:17; Ps 9:13); of the grave (Isa 38:10). Of righteousness (Ps 118:19). Of salvation (Ge 28:17; Ps 24:7; 118:19, 20; Isa 26:2; M't 7:13). Of death (Isa 38:10).

Symbolical: Re 21:12, 13, 21, 25.

GATH (winepress). One of the five chief cities of the Philistines (Jos 13:3; 1Sa 6:17; Am 6:2; Mic 1:10). Anakim, a race of giants, inhabitants of (Jos 11:22). Goliath dwelt in (1Sa 17:4; 1Ch 20:5-8). Obed-edom belonged to (2Sa 6:10). The ark taken to (1Sa 5:8). Inhabitants of, called Gittites (Jos 13:3). David takes refuge at (1Sa 21:10-15; 27:2-7). Band of Gittites, attached to David (2Sa 15:18-22). Taken by David (1Ch 18:1). Shimei's servants escape to (1Ki 2:39-41). Fortified by Rehoboam (2Ch 11:8). Taken by Hazael (2Ki 12:17). Recovered by Jehoash (2Ki 13:25). Besieged by Uzziah (2Ch 26:6). Called Methegammah, in 2Sa 8:1.

GATH-HEPHER (winepress of the well), a town on the border of Zebulun (Jos 19:12, 13, ASV) and birthplace of Jonah the prophet (2Ki 14:25).

GATH-RIMMON (winepress of Rimmon). 1. A city of Dan on the Philistine plain (Jos 19:45).

2. A town of Manasseh, W of Jordan, assigned to Levites (Jos 14:25).

GAULANITIS, a province NE of the Sea of Galilee, ruled by Herod Antipas.

GAZA (strong). 1. Called also Azzah. A city of the Philistines (Jos 13:3; Jer 25:20). One of the border cities of the Canaanites (Ge 10:19). A city of the Avim and Anakim (De 2:23; Jos 11:22). Allotted to Judah (Jos 15:47; J'g 1:18). A temple of Dagon, situated at (J'g 16:23). Samson dies at (J'g 16:21-31). On the western boundary of the kingdom of Israel in the time of Solomon (1Ki 4:24). Smitten by Pharaoh (Jer 47:1). Prophecies relating to (Am 1:6, 7; Zep 2:4; Zec 9:5). Desert of (Ac 8:26-39).

2. A city of Ephraim (J'g 6:4; 1Ch 7:28).

GAZATHITES, inhabitants of Gaza (Jos 13:3). Called Gazites in J'g 16:2.

GAZELLE (See Animals.)

GAZER, called also Gezer (2Sa 5:25; 1Ch 14:16).

GAZEZ, the name of the son and of the grandson of Ephah (1Ch 2:46).

GAZZAM, one of the Nethinim (Ezr 2:48; Ne 7:51).

GEBA (hill), a town in the territory of Benjamin (Jos 18:24 ASV, RSV), assigned to the Levites (Jos 21:17). Jonathan defeated the Philistines at Geba (1Sa 13:3). Asa fortified the city (1Ki

15:22), and in Hezekiah's time it was the northernmost city of Judah (2Ki 23:8). Men from Geba returned after the exile (Ezr 2:26).

GEBAL (border). 1. A seaport of Phoenicia N of Sidon, the modern Jebeil, 25 miles N of Beirut. The land of the Gebalites is mentioned in Joshua 13:5, 6. The town was renowned for its expert stonemasons (1Ki 5:17, 18 ASV) and for shipbuilding (Eze 27:9).

2. A land between the Dead Sea and Petra (Ps 83:6-8).

GEBER. 1. One of Solomon's purveyors in Ramoth-Gilead (1Ki 4:13).

2. The son of Uri (1Ki 4:19).

GEBIM, a place near Anathoth (Isa 10:31).

GECKO (See Animals.)

GEDALIAH. 1. Governor appointed by Nebuchadnezzar after carrying the Jews into captivity (2Ki 25:22-24). Jeremiah committed to the care of (Jer 39:14; 40:5, 6). Warned of the conspiracy of Ishmael by Johanan, and the captains of his army (Jer 40:13-16). Slain by Ishmael (2Ki 25:25, 26; Jer 41:1-10).

2. A musician (1Ch 25:3, 9).

3. A priest, who divorced his Gentile wife after the exile (Ezr 10:18).

4. Ancestor of Zephaniah (Zep 1:1).

5. A prince who caused imprisonment of Jeremiah (Jer 38:1).

GEDEON (See Gideon.)

GEDER. An ancient city of Canaan (Jos 12:13). Possibly identical with Gedor, 2 or 3.

GEDERAH (wall), the modern Jedireh, located between the valleys of Sorek and Aijalon in the hills of Judah (Jos 15:36).

GEDEROTH, a city in plain of Judah (Jos 15:41; 2Ch 28:18).

GEDEROTHAIM, a city in plain of Judah (Jos 15:36).

GEDOR (wall). 1. A city in mountains of Judah (Jos 15:58).

2. The town of Jeroham (1Ch 12:7). Possibly identical with Geder, which see.

3. Valley of, taken by Simeonites (1Ch 4:39).

See Geder.

4. An ancestor of Saul (1Ch 8:31; 9:37).

5. Either a place or a person, authorities disagree (1Ch 4:4, 18).

GEHAZI (valley of vision), the servant of Elisha (2Ki 4:8-37; 5:1-27; 8:4-6). He was punished for avarice by becoming a leper.

GEHENNA (valley of Hinnom), a valley on the W and SW of Jerusalem which formed part of the border between Judah and Benjamin (Jos 15:8; 18:16; Ne 11:30, 31). It later became the place of pagan sacrifice (2Ch 28:3; 33:6; Jer 32:35). Josiah defiled it by making it the city dump, where fires were kept constantly burning to consume the refuse (2Ki 23:10). Jewish apocalyptic writers called it the entrance to hell, and it became a figure of hell itself. Jesus used the term in this sense (M't 5:22 ASV; 18:9; 23:15). See Hades, Hell.

GELILOTH. A place mentioned (Jos 18:17), as marking the boundary of Benjamin. In Jos 15:7, Gilgal is substituted.

GEMALLI (camel rider), father of Ammiel, and one of the twelve spies (Nu 13:12).

GEMARIAH (accomplishment of the Lord). 1. Son of Shaphan the scribe and friend of Jeremiah (Jer 36:10-25).

2. A son of Hilkiah, sent as ambassador to Nebuchadnezzar (Jer 29:3).

GENEALOGY (Nu 1:18; 2Ch 12:15; Ezr 2:59; Ne 7:5; Heb 7:3). Of no spiritual significance (M't 3:9; 1Ti 1:4; Tit 3:9).

From Adam to Noah (Ge 4:16-22; 5; 1Ch 1:1-4; Lu 3:36-38); to Abraham (Ge 11:10-32; 1Ch 1:4-27; Lu 3:34-38); to Jesus (M't 1:1-16; Lu 3:23-38). Of the descendants of Noah (Ge 10); of Nahor (Ge 22:20-24); of Abraham, by his wife Keturah (Ge 25:1-4; 1Ch 1:32, 33); of Ishmael (Ge 25:12-16; 1Ch 1:28-31); of Esau (Ge 36; 1Ch 1:35-54); of Jacob (Ge 35:23-26; Ex 1:5; 6:14-27; Nu 26; 1Ch 2-9); of Pharez to David (Ru 4:18-22). Of the Jews who returned from the captivity (Ezr 7:1-5; 8:1-15; Ne 7; 11:12). Of Joseph (M't 1; Lu 3:23-38).

GENEALOGY OF JESUS CHRIST. Two genealogies are given in the NT: in Matthew 1:1-17 and in Luke 3:23-28. Matthew traces the descent of Jesus from Abraham and David, and divides it into three sets of fourteen generations. He omits three generations after Joram, namely Ahaziah, Joash, and Amaziah (1Ch 3:11, 12). Contrary to Hebrew practice, he names five women: Tamar, Rahab, Ruth, Bathsheba, and Mary. The sense of "begat" in Hebrew genealogies is not exact: it indicated immediate or remote descent, an adoptive relation, or legal heirship. Luke's genealogy moves from Jesus to Adam, agreeing with I Chronicles 1:1-7. 24-28 between Abraham and Adam. From David to Abraham he agrees with Matthew; from Jesus to David he differs from Matthew. Perhaps Matthew gives the line of legal heirship, while Luke gives the line of physical descent.

GENERALS. Distinguished. (See Abraham; Joshua; Saul; David; Joab; Amasa; Gideon; Benaiah; Naaman; Jephthah; Ben-hadad; Sennacherib). See Captains.

GENERATION, in the OT the translation of two Hebrew words, (1) *toledhoth,* referring to lines of descent from an ancestor (Ge 2:4; 5:1; 6:9; Ru 4:18), and (2) *dor,* meaning a period of time (De 32:7; Ex 3:15; Ps 102:24), or all the men living in a given period (J'g 3:2), or a class of men having a certain quality (Ps 14:5), or a company gathered together (Ps 49:19).

In the NT *generation* translates four Greek words, all having reference to descent: (1) *genea,* for lines of descent from an ancestor (M't 1:17); or all the men living in a given period (M't 11:16); or a class of men having a certain quality (M't 12:39); or a period of time (Ac 13:36); (2) *genesis,* meaning genealogy (M't 2:17); (3) *gennema,* meaning brood or offspring (M't 3:7; 12:34; 23:33); (4) *genes,* clan, race, kind, nation (1Pe 2:9).

GENERATION, EVIL (De 32:5; Pr 30:12; M't 3:7; 12:39, 45; Lu 9:41; Ac 2:40).

GENEROSITY (See Liberality.)

GENESIS, the first book of the Bible. The name is derived from a Greek word meaning "origin" or "beginning" which is the title of the book in the Greek Septuagint. It contains the beginnings of physical life (1-2), the growth of civilization to the Flood (3-8), and the descendants of Noah to Abraham (9-11:26). Genesis 11:27 through 50:26 traces the history of Abraham and Lot; Ishmael and Isaac; Jacob and Esau; and Joseph and his brethren in Egypt.

GENIUS, mechanical, a divine inspiration (Ex 28:3; 31:2-11; 35:30-35; 36:1).

GENNESARET. 1. "The land of Gennesaret" is a plain on the NW shore of the Sea of Galilee (M't 14:34; M'k 6:53).

2. "The Lake of Gennesaret" is the same as the Sea of Galilee (Lu 5:1). See Galilee, Sea of.

GENTILES (nation, people). Usually meaning non-Israelite people.

Ways of, condemned (Jer 10:2, 3; Eph 4:17-19). God's forbearance toward (Ac 14:16); impartiality toward (Ro 2:9-11). Ignorant worship practices of (M't 6:7, 8, 31, 32; Ac 17:4, 16, 22-27; 1Co 10:20; 12:2). Wicked practices of (Ro 1:18-32; Ga 2:15; Eph 5:12; 1Th 4:5; 1Pe 4:3, 4). Moral responsibility of (Ro 2:14, 15).

See Idolatry; Missions.

Prophecies of the conversion of (Ge 12:3; 22:18; 49:10; De 32:21; Ps 2:8; 22:27-31; 46:4, 10; 65:2, 5; 66:4; 68:31, 32; 72:8-11, 16, 19; 86:9; 102:15, 18-22; 145:10, 11; Isa 2:2-4; 9:2, 6, 7; 11:6-10; 18:7; 24:16; 35:1, 2, 5-7; 40:5; 42:1-12; 45:6, 8, 22-24; 49:1, 5, 6, 18-23; 54:1-3; 55:5; 56:3, 6-8; 60:1-14; 65:1; 66:12, 19, 23; Jer 3:17; 4:2; 16:19-21; Da 2:35, 44, 45; 7:13, 14; Ho 2:23; Joe 2:28-32; Am 9:11, 12; Mic 4:3, 4; Hag 2:7; Zec 2:10, 11; 6:15; 8:20-23; 9:1, 10; 14:8, 9, 16; Mal 1:11; M't 3:9; 8:11; 12:17-21; 19:30; M'k 10:31; Lu 13:29, 30; 21:24; Joh 10:16; Ac 9:15).

See Church, Prophecies Concerning.

Conversion of (Ac 10:45; 11:1-18; 13:2, 46-48; 14:27; 15:7-31; 18:4-6; 26:16-18; 28:28; Ro 1:5-7; 9:22-30; 10:19, 20; 11:11-13, 17-21; 15:9-12; Ga 1:15, 16; 2:2; 3:14; Eph 3:1-8; Col 3:11; 1Th 2:16; 1Ti 3:16; 2Ti 1:11; Re 11:15; 15:4).

See Kingdom of Jesus, Prophecies Concerning.

GENTILES, COURT OF THE, the part of the Temple, which the Gentiles might enter.

GENTLENESS. Of Christ (Isa 40:11; M't 11:29; 2Co 10:1). See Jesus, Compassion of, Humility of, Meekness of.

Of God (2Sa 22:36; Ps 18:35; Isa 40:11). See God, Compassion of, Long-suffering of.

Of Paul (1Th 2:7).

A fruit of the Spirit (Ga 5:22; Jas 3:17). Required, in the Lord's servants (2Ti 2:24-26); in all Christians (Tit 3:1, 2).

See Humility; Kindness; Meekness; Patience.

GENUBATH (theft). A son of Hadad the Edomite (1Ki 11:20).

GEOLOGY. Origin, in God (Ge 1:9, 10; 1Sa 2:8; 2Sa 22:16; Job 12:8, 9; Ps 18:15; 24:1, 2; 104:5; 136:6; Pr 30:4; 2Pe 3:5-7). Control, by God (Job 28:9-11; Ps 104:5-13; Pr 30:4; Hab 3:9). Infinity of (Jer 31:37). Destruction of (2Pe 3:5-7).

See Astronomy; Creation; Earth; Hot Springs; Meteorology.

GERA (grain), a name common to tribe of Benjamin. 1. A son of Benjamin (Ge 46:21).

2. A grandson of Benjamin (1Ch 8:3, 5).

3. The father of Ehud (J'g 3:15).

4. A son of Ehud (1Ch 8:7).

5. Father of Shimei (2Sa 16:5).

GERAH. A weight equal to thirteen and seven tenths grains, Paris. Also a coin equivalent to about three cents American money, and three half-pence English money (Ex 30:13; Le 27:25; Nu 3:47).

GERAR (circle, region) 1. A city of the Philistines (Ge 10:19). Abimelech, king of (Ge 20:1; 26:6). Visited by Abraham (Ge 20:1); by Isaac (Ge 26:1; 2Ch 14:13, 14).

2. A valley (Ge 26:17-22).

GERASA, a city E of the Jordan midway between the Sea of Galilee and the Dead Sea, the modern Jerash. The city is not mentioned in the NT, but the adjective Gerasene is mentioned in Mark 5:1.

GERGESA, a place probably midway of the Sea of Galilee, where the bank is steep (M't 8:28 KJV, and RSV margin; M'k 5:1 RSV margin; Lu 8:26, 37 ASV, RSV margins).

GERGESENES (See Gadarenes.)

GERIZIM. Mount of blessing (De 11:29; 27:12; Jos 8:33). Jotham addresses the Shechemites from, against the conspiracy of Abimelech (J'g 9:7). Samaritans worship at (Joh 4:20).

GERSHOM (to cast out, stranger). 1. Son of Moses (Ex 2:22; 18:3; 1Ch 23:15, 16; 26:24).

2. See Gershon.

3. A descendant of Phinehas (Ezr 8:2).

4. A Levite (J'g 18:30).

GERSHON, called also Gershom. Son of Levi (Gen 46:11; Ex 6:16, 17; Nu 3:17-26; 4:22-28, 38; 7:7; 10:17; 26:57; Jos 21:6; 1Ch 6:1, 16, 17, 20, 43, 62, 71; 15:7; 23:6).

GERSHONITES, descendants of Gershon (Nu 3:25; 4:24, 38; 7:7).

GERZITES, GIZRITES, or GERIZZITES, a tribe named with the Geshurites and the Amalekites (1Sa 27:8).

GESHAM, a descendant of Caleb (1Ch 2:47).

GESHEM, an Arabian who opposed the work of Nehemiah (Ne 2:19; 6:1, 2), identical with Gashmu (6:6).

GESHUR (bridge). 1. District E of the sources of the Jordan. The inhabitants of, not subdued by the Israelites (De 3:14; Jos 13:2-13; 1Ch 2:23). Inhabitants of one of the villages of, exterminated, and the spoils taken by David (1Sa 27:8). David marries a princess of (2Sa 3:3; 1Ch 3:2). Absalom takes refuge in, after the murder of Amnon (2Sa 13:37, 38; 15:8).

GETHER, the third son of Aram (Ge 10:23; 1Ch 1:17).

GETHSEMANE, a garden near Jerusalem. Jesus betrayed in (M't 26:36-50; M'k 14:32-46; Lu 22:39-49; Joh 18:1, 2).

GEUEL, a representative from the tribe of Gad sent to spy out Canaan (Nu 13:15).

GEZER (portion) called also Gazer, Gazara, Gazera, and Gob. A Canaanitish royal city; king of, defeated by Joshua (Jos 10:33; 12:12). Canaanites not all expelled from, but made to pay tribute (Jos 16:10; J'g 1:29). Allotted to Ephraim (Jos 16:10; 1Ch 7:28). Assigned to Levites (Jos 2:21). Battle with Philistines at (1Ch 20:4; 2Sa 21:18). Smitten by David (1Sa 27:8). Fortified by Solomon (1Ki 9:15-17).

GHOR, THE, the upper level of the Jordan valley, about 150 feet above the river channel.

GHOST, the human spirit as distinguished from the body. To "give up the ghost" means to breathe one's last, to die (Ge 25:8; 35:29; 49:33; Job 11:20; M't 27:50; Joh 19:30). "Holy Ghost" in KJV is translated "Holy Spirit" in ASV, RSV. Unlike modern usage, it does not refer to an apparition.

GIAH, a place on the way to the wilderness of Gibeon (2Sa 2:24).

GIANTS, men of exceptional height and strength, called *nephilim* (Ge 6:4 ASV, RSV, Nu 13:33), and *rephaim* (De 2:11, 20, ASV, RSV). Representatives of the giants were Og, king of Bashan (Jos 12:4; 13:12), and Goliath, whom David slew (1Sa 17).

GIBBAR, a man whose children returned from captivity with Zerubbabel (Ezr 2:20).

GIBBETHON. A city of Dan (Jos 19:44). Allotted to the Levites (Jos 21:23). Besieged by Israel, while in possession of Philistines (1Ki 15:27; 16:15, 17).

GIBEA, a descendant of Judah (1Ch 2:49).

GIBEAH. 1. Of Judah (Jos 15:57).

2. Of Saul. Called also Gibeah of Benjamin. The people's wickedness (J'g 19:12-30; Ho 9:9; 10:9). Destroyed by the Israelites (J'g 20). The city of Saul (1Sa 10:26; 15:34; 22:6). The ark of the covenant conveyed to, by the Philistines (1Sa 7:1; 2Sa 6:3). Deserted (Isa 10:29).

3. Another town in Benjamin, called also Gibeath (Jos 18:28).

4. Gibeah in the field (J'g 20:31). Probably identical with Geba, which see.

GIBEON (pertaining to a hill) 1. A city of the Hivites (Jos 9:3, 17; 2Sa 21:2). The people of, adroitly draw Joshua into a treaty (Jos 9). Made servants by the Israelites, when their sharp practice was discovered (Jos 9:27). The sun stands still over, during Joshua's battle with the five confederated kings (Jos 10:12-14). Allotted to Benjamin (Jos 18:25). Assigned to the Aaronites (Jos 21:17). The tabernacle located at (1Ki 3:4; 1Ch 16:39; 21:29; 2Ch 1:2, 3, 13). Smitten by David (1Ch 14:16). Seven sons of Saul slain at, to avenge the inhabitants of (2Sa 21:1-9). Solomon worships at, and offers sacrifices (1Ki 3:4); God appears to him in dreams (1Ki 3:5; 9:2). Abner slays Asahel at (2Sa 3:30). Ishmael, the son of Nethaniah, defeated at, by Johanan (Jer 41:11-16).

2. Pool of (2Sa 2:13; Jer 41:12).

GIBEONITES. Descended from the Hivites and Amorites (Jos 9:3, 7, w 2Sa 21:2). A mighty and warlike people (Jos 10:2). Cities of (Jos 9:17).

Israel: Deceived by (Jos 9:4-13). Made a league with (Jos 9:15). Spared on account of their oath (Jos 9:18, 19). Appointed, hewers of wood (Jos 9:20-27). Attacked by the kings of Canaan (Jos 10:1-5). Delivered by Israel (Jos 10:6-10). Saul sought to destroy (2Sa 21:2). Israel plagued for Saul's cruelty to (2Sa 21:1). Effected the destruction of the remnant of Saul's house (2Sa 21:4-9). The office of the Nethinim probably originated in (1Ch 9:2). Part of, returned from the captivity (Ne 7:25).

GIBLITES, the inhabitants of Gebal or Byblos (Jos 13:5). See Gebal.

GIDDALTI, a son of Heman (1Ch 25:4, 29).

GIDDEL. 1. One of the Nethinim (Ezr 2:47; Ne 7:49).

2. One of Solomon's servants (Ezr 2:56; Ne 7:58).

GIDEON (feeler, hewer). Call of, by an angel (J'g 6:11, 14). His excuses (J'g 6:15). Promises of the Lord to (J'g 6:16). Angel attests the call to, by miracle (J'g 6:21-24). He destroys the altar of Baal, and builds one to the Lord (J'g 6:25-27). His prayer tests (J'g 6:36-40). Leads an army against, and defeats the Midianites (J'g 6:33-35; 7; 8:4-12). Ephraimites chide, for not inviting them to join in the campaign against the Midianites (J'g 8:1-3). Avenges himself upon the people of Succoth (J'g 8:14-17). Israel desires to make him king, he refuses (J'g 8:22, 23). Makes an ephod which becomes a snare to the Israelites (J'g 8:24-27). Had seventy sons (J'g 8:30). Death of (J'g 8:32). Faith of (Heb 11:32).

GIDEONI (cutter down), father of Abidan (Nu 1:11; 2:22; 7:60, 65; 10:24).

GIDOM (desolation), limit of pursuit after battle of Gibeah (J'g 20:45).

GIER EAGLE (See Birds.)

GIFT, GIVING. At least eleven words are used in the Bible to mean giving: *eshkar*, a reward (Ps 72:10); *minhah*, an offering to a superior (J'g 3:15); *mattan*, that given to gain a favor (Ge 34:12), or as an act of submission (Ps 68:29); *mattena* and *mattanah*, an offering (Ge 25:6; Da 2:6); *shohadh*, a bribe (De 16:19); in the NT, *dosis* and *doron*, anything given (Lu 21:1; Jas 1:17); *doma*, a present (M't 7:11); *charis* and *charisma*, special endowment (Ro 1:11; 1Ti 4:14).

GIFTS FROM GOD. Himself: In Christ, the Saviour (Isa 42:6; 55:4; Joh 3:16; 4:10; 6:32, 33); in the Holy Spirit, the Comforter: See Holy Spirit.

Temporal: Food and raiment (M't 6:25, 33). Rain and fruitful seasons (Ge 8:22; 27:28; Le 26:4, 5; Isa 30:23). Wisdom (2Ch 1:12). Peace (Le 26:6; 1Ch 22:9). Gladness (Ps 4:7). Strength and power (Ps 29:11; 68:18). Wisdom and knowledge (Ec 2:26; Da 2:21-23; 1Co 1:5-7). Talents (M't 25:14, 15).

All good things (Ps 21:2; 34:10; 84:11; Isa 42:5; Eze 11:19; Joh 16:23, 24; Ro 8:32; 1Ti 6:17; Jas 1:17; 2Pe 1:3).

To be used and enjoyed (Ec 3:13; 5:19, 20; 1Ti 4:4, 5). Should cause us to remember God (De 8:18). All creatures partake of (Ps 136:25; 145:15, 16). Prayer for (Zec 10:1; M't 6:11).

See Presents.

Spiritual: Of the Spirit (Ro 11:29; 12:6-8; 1Co 7:7; 12:4-11; 13:2; Eph 4:7; 1Pe 4:10). Life, eternal (Isa 42:5; Eze 11:19; Joh 3:16, 17, 36; 6:27; Ro 5:16-18; 6:23). Grace (Jas 4:6). Wisdom (Pr 2:6; Jas 1:5). Repentance (Ac 11:28). Faith (Eph 2:8; Ph'p 1:29). Rest (M't 11:28). Glory (Joh 17:22).

See Blessings from God; Charisma; Tongues.

GIHON (burst forth). 1. A river in Egypt (Ge 2:13).

2. Pools near Jerusalem (1Ki 1:33, 38, 45). Hezekiah brings the waters of the upper pool by an aqueduct into the city of Jerusalem (2Ch 32:4, 30; 33:14; Ne 2:13-15; 3:13-16; Isa 7:3; 22:9-11; 36:2).

GILALAI, a priest and musician (Ne 12:36).

GILBOA (bubbling), a hill S of Jezreel, where Saul was defeated by the Philistines, and died (1Sa 28:4; 31:1-8; 1Ch 10:1-8).

GILEAD (rugged). 1. A region E of the Jordan allotted to the tribes of Reuben and Gad and half tribe of Manasseh (Nu 32:1-30; De 3:13; 34:1; 2Ki 10:33). Reubenites expel the Hagarites from (1Ch 5:9, 10, 18-22). Ammonites make war against; defeated by Jephthah (J'g 11; Am 1:13). The prophet Elijah a native of (1Ki 17:1). David retreats to, at the time of Absalom's rebellion (2Sa 17:16, 22, 24). Pursued into, by Absalom (2Sa 17:26). Absalom defeated and slain in the forests of (2Sa 18:9).

Hazael, king of Syria, smites the land of (2Ki 10:32, 33; Am 1:3). Invaded by Tiglath-pileser, king of Syria (2Ki 15:29). A grazing country (Nu 32:1; 1Ch 5:9). Exported spices, balm, and myrrh (Ge 37:25; Jer 8:22; 46:11).

Figurative: Of prosperity (Jer 22:6; 50:19).

2. A mountain (J'g 7:3; Song 4:1; 6:5).

3. A city (Ho 6:8; 12:11).

4. Grandson of Manasseh (Nu 26:29, 30; 27:1; 36:1; Jos 17:1, 3; 1Ch 2:21, 23; 7:14, 17).

5. Father of Jephthah (J'g 11:1, 2).

6. A chief of Gad (1Ch 5:14).

GILGAL (circle of stones). 1. Place of the first encampment of the Israelites W of the Jordan (Jos 4:19; 9:6; 10:6, 43; 14:6). Monument erected in, to commemorate the passage of the Jordan by the children of Israel (Jos 4:19-24). Circumcision renewed at (Jos 5:2-9). Passover kept at (Jos 5:10, 11). Manna ceased at, after the passover (Jos 5:12). Quarries at (J'g 3:19). Eglon, king of Moab, resides and is slain at (J'g 3:14-26). A judgment seat, where Israel, in that district, came to be judged by Samuel (1Sa 7:16). Saul proclaimed king over all Israel at (1Sa 11:15), an altar built at, and sacrifice offered (1Sa 11:15; 13:4-15; 15:6-23). Agag, king of the Amalekites, slain at, by Samuel (1Sa 15:33). Tribe of Judah assembles at, to proceed to the E side of the Jordan to conduct king David back after the defeat of Absalom (2Sa 19:14, 15, 40-43). A school of the prophets at (2Ki 4:38-40).

Prophecies concerning (Ho 4:15; 9:15; 12:11; Am 4:4; 5:5).

2. A royal city in Canaan. Conquered by Joshua (Jos 12:23).

GILOH, home of Ahithophel, one of David's counsellors (2Sa 15:12; Jos 15:51).

GIMZO (place of lush sycamores), a town off the Jerusalem Highway, 3 miles SW of Lydda (2Ch 28:18).

GIN, a trap to catch game (Amos 3:5); or a plot to deceive and destroy (Ps 140:5; 141:9; Job 18:9; Isa 8:14).

GINATH (protector), the father of Tibni (1Ki 16:21).

GINNETHO (See Ginnethon.)

GINNETHON, a priest who returned to Jerusalem with Zerubbabel (Ne 10:6; 12:4).

GIRDLE. Worn by the high priest (Ex 28:4, 39; 39:29; Le 8:7; 16:4); other priests (Ex 28:40; 29:9; Le 8:13); women (Isa 3:24). Embroidered (Ex 28:8, 27, 28; 29:5; Le 8:7). Made of linen (Pr 31:24); of leather (2Ki 1:8; M't 3:4). Traffic in (Pr 31:24). Used to bear arms (1Sa 18:4; 2Sa 20:8; 2Ki 3:21).

Figurative: Isa 11:5; 22:21; Eph 6:14.

Symbolical: Jer 13:1-11; Ac 21:11; Re 15:6.

GIRGASHITES. Land of, given to Abraham and his descendants (Ge 15:21· De 7:1; Jos 3:10; Ne 9:8). Delivered to the children of Israel (Jos 24:11).

GISPA (listener), an overseer of the Nethinim (Ne 11:21).

GITTAH-HEPHER, a prolonged form of Gath-Hepher, which see (Jos 19:13).

GITTAIM (two wine presses), a town of Benjamin to which the Beerothites fled (Ne 11:31, 33; 2Sa 4:3). The site is unknown.

GITTITES (of Gath), natives of Gath (Jos 13:1-3; 2Sa 6:8-11; 15:18; 21:19).

GITTITH, a word found in the titles of Psalms 8, 81, 84. It may denote a musical instrument imported from Gath, or may be the title of a tune.

GIVING. Rules for: Without ostentation (M't 6:1-4). Regularly (1Co 16:2). Liberally (2Co 9:6-15). Cheerfully (2Co 8:11, 12; 9:7).

See Alms; Beneficence; Liberality.

GIZONITE, the title of one of David's bodyguards (1Ch 1:34).

GLADIATOR, one who contends with wild beasts (1Co 5:32).

GLADNESS (See Joy.)

GLASS was manufactured as early as 2500 B. C. by the Egyptians, and later by the Phoenicians, who promoted its commercial use, especially in jewelry. The Hebrews seem to have been unacquainted with it, for it is mentioned only once in the OT (Job 28:17). The glass mentioned by Paul (2Co 3:18) and by James (Jas 1:23, 24) was properly not glass at all, but the mirror of polished bronze. The allusions in Revelation 21:18, 21, refer to crystal glass.

GLEAN, the Hebrew custom of allowing the poor to follow the reapers, and to gather the grain or grapes that remained after the harvest (J'g 8:2; Ru 2:2, 16; Isa 17:6).

GLEANING. Laws concerning (Le 19:9, 10; 23:22; De 24:19, 20).

See Orphan; Stranger; Widow.

Figurative: J'g 8:2; Isa 17:6; Jer 49:9; Mic 7:1.

Instances of: Ruth in the field of Boaz (Ru 2:2, 3).

GLEDE, a carnivorous bird (De 14:13).

GLORIFIED SAINTS. Great cloud of witnesses (Heb 12:1); just men made perfect (Heb 12:23; Re 6:11). 144,000 (Re 14:1-5).

Under the altar (Re 6:9); before the throne (Re 14:3). Sing song, of redemption (Re 14:3); of worship (Re 15:2-4).

GLORIFYING GOD. Commanded (1Ch 16:28; Ps 22:23; Isa 42:12). Due to him (1Ch 16:29); for his holiness (Ps 99:9; Re 15:4); mercy and truth (Ps 115:1; Ro 15:9); faithfulness and truth (Isa 25:1); wondrous works (M't 15:31; Ac 4:21); judgments (Isa 25:3; Eze 28:22; Re 14:7); deliverances (Ps 50:15); grace to others (Ac 11:18; 2Co 9:13; Ga 1:24).

Accomplished by: Relying on his promises (Ro 4:20); praising him (Ps 50:23); doing all to glorify him (1Co 10:31); dying for him (Joh 21:19); suffering for Christ (1Pe 4:14, 16); glorifying Christ (Ac 19:17; 2Th 1:12); bringing forth fruits of righteousness (Joh 15:8; Ph'p 1:11); patience in affliction (Isa 24:15); faithfulness (1Pe 4:11). Required in body and spirit (1Co 6:20). Shall be universal (Ps 86:9; Re 5:13).

Saints: Should resolve on (Ps 69:30; 118:28); unite in (Ps 34:3; Ro 15:6); persevere in (Ps 86:12). All the blessings of God are designed to lead to (Isa 60:21; 61:3). The holy example of the saints may lead others to (M't 5:16; 1Pe 2:12).

All, by nature, fail in (Ro 3:23). The wicked averse to (Da 5:23; Ro 1:21). Punishment for not (Da 5:23, 30; Mal 2:2; Ac 12:23; Ro 1:21). Heavenly hosts engaged in (Re 4:11).

Exemplified: By David (Ps 57:5); the multitude (M't 9:8; 15:31); the virgin Mary (Lu 1:46); the angels (Lu 2:14); the shepherds (Lu 2:20); by Jesus (Joh 17:4); the man sick of the palsy (Lu 5:25); the woman with infirmity (Lu 13:13); the leper whom Jesus healed (Lu 17:15); the blind man (Lu 18:43), the centurion (Lu 23:47); the church at Jerusalem (Ac 11:18); the Gentiles at Antioch (Ac 13:48); Abraham (Ro 4:20); Paul (Ro 11:36).

GLORY, concerning God, the exhibition of His divine attributes and perfections (Ps 19:1) or the radiance of His presence (Lu 2:9); concerning man, the manifestation of his commendable qualities, such as wisdom, righteousness, self-control, ability, etc. Glory is the destiny of believers (Ph'p 3:21; Ro 8:21; 1Co 15:43).

Spiritual: Is given by God (Ps 84:11); is given by Christ (Joh 17:22); is the work of the Holy Ghost (2Co 3:18).

Eternal: Procured by the death of Christ (Heb 2:10); accompanies salvation by Christ (2Ti 2:10); inherited by saints (1Sa 2:8; Ps 73:24; Pr 3:35; Col 3:4; 1Pe 5:10); saints called to (2Th 2:14; 1Pe 5:10); saints prepared unto (Ro 9:23); enhanced by afflictions (2Co 4:17); present afflictions not worthy to be compared with (Ro 8:18); of the church shall be rich and abundant (Isa 60:11-13); the bodies of saints, shall be raised in (1Co 15:43; Ph'p 3:21); saints shall be, of their ministers (1Th 2:19, 20); afflictions of ministers are, to saints (Eph 3:13).

Temporal: Is given by God (Da 2:37); passeth away (1Pe 1:24). The devil tries to seduce by (M't 4:8). Of hypocrites turned to shame (Ho 4:7). Seek not, from man (M't 6:2; 1Th 2:6). Of the wicked is in their shame (Ph'p 3:19). Ends in destruction (Isa 5:14).

Of God: Exhibited in Christ (Joh 1:14; 2Co 4:6; Heb 1:3). Ascribed to God (Ga 1:5).

Exhibited in his name (De 28:58; Ne 9:5); his majesty (Job 37:22; Ps 93:1; 104:1; 145:5, 12; Isa 2:10); his power (Ex 15:1, 6; Ro 6:4); his works (Ps 19:1; 111:3); his holiness (Ex 15:11).

Described as great (Ps 138:5); eternal (Ps 104:31); rich (Eph 3:16); highly exalted (Ps 8:1; 113:4).

Exhibited to Moses (Ex 34:5-7; w Ex 33:18-23); Stephen (Ac 7:55); his church (De 5:24; Ps 102:16).

Enlightens the church (Isa 60:1, 2; Re 21:11, 23). Saints desire to behold (Ps 63:2; 90:16). God is jealous of (Isa 42:8). The earth is full of (Isa 6:3). The knowledge of, shall fill the earth (Hab 2:14).

GLUTTONY. Impoverishes (Pr 23:21). Deadens moral sensibilities (Am 6:4-7; Lu 12:19, 20, 45, 46; Ph'p 3:19). Loathsome (Pr 30:21, 22).

Punished, by death (De 21:20, 21); plagues (Nu 11:32, 33).

Associated with drunkenness (De 21:20, 21; Pr 23:21; Ec 10:17; Lu 12:45, 46; Ro 13:13; 1Pe 4:3). Proverb relating to (Isa 22:13; 1Co 15:32).

Jesus falsely accused of (M't 11:19; Lu 7:34). Warnings against (Pr 30:21, 22; Lu 21:34; Ro 13:13, 14; 1Pe 4:2, 3).

Instances of: Esau (Ge 25:30-34; Heb 12:16, 17). Israelites (Ex 16:20, 21; Nu 11:4, 32-35; Ps 78:18). Sons of Eli (1Sa 2:12-17). Belshazzar (Da 5:1).

GNASH. To grind the teeth together as an expression of rage (Job 16:19); hatred (Ps 37:12); frustration (Ps 112:10). In the NT it expresses anguish and failure rather than anger (M't 8:12; 13:42, 50; 25:30).

GNASHING OF TEETH. Of the enemy, in maliciousness (Job 16:9; Ps 35:16; 37:12; 112:10; La 2:16). Of the lost, from anguish of spirit (M't 8:12; 13:42; 22:13; 24:51; 25:30; Lu 13:28).

GNAT (See Insects.)

GOAD, an instrument of torture (1Sa 13:21). Six hundred men slain with, by Shamgar, a judge of Israel (J'g 3:31).

Figurative: Of mental incentive (Ec 12:11).

GOAT. Designated as one of the clean animals to be eaten (De 14:4, with Le 11:1-8). Used for food (Ge 27:9; 1Sa 16:20); for the paschal feast (Ex 12:5; 2Ch 35:7); as a sacrifice by Abraham (Ge 15:9); by Gideon (J'g 6:19); Manoah (J'g 13:19). Milk of, used for food (Pr 27:27). Hair of, used for clothing (Nu 31:20); pillows (1Sa 19:13); curtains of the tabernacle (Ex 26:7; 35:23; 36:14). Used for tents, see Tabernacles. Regulations of Mosaic law required that a kid should not be killed for food before it was eight days old (Le 22:27), nor seethed in its mother's milk (Ex 23:19). Numerous (De 32:14; Song 4:1; 6:5; 1Sa 25:2; 2Ch 17:11). Wild, in Palestine (1Sa 24:2; Ps 104:18).

GOATH, a place near Jerusalem (Jer 31:39).

GOATS' HAIR (Ex 25:4; 26:7; 35:6; 36:14; Nu 31:20).

GOB (pit, cistern), the site of two of David's battles with the Philistines (2Sa 21:18).

GOBLET (See Cup.)

GOD. *Access to:* Israel (De 4:7); the pure of heart (Ps 24:3, 4); the thirsty (Isa 55:3); Gentiles (Ac 14:27); enemies of God (Col 1:21, 22); believers (Heb 4:16; 1Pe 1:17); the cleansed (Jas 4:8). Through hope (Ps 27:4; 43:2); fear (Ps 145:18, 19; 1Pe 1:17); prayer (M't 6:6; Heb 4:10); faith (Heb 11:6); love (1Jo 4:16). Through Christ (Joh 10:7, 9; 14:6; Ro 5:2; Eph 2:13, 18; 3:12; Col 1:21, 22; Heb 7:19, 25; 10:19, 22; 1Pe 1:17). Satisfying (Ps 65:4).

Anger of: See Anger of God.

Appearance of: To Adam (Ge 3:8-21). To Abraham (Ge 17:1; 18:2-33). To Jacob, at Peniel (Ge 32:30); at Bethel (Ge 35:7, 9). To Moses, in the burning bush (Ex 3:2; De 33:16; M'k 12:26; Lu 20:37; Ac 7:30); at Sinai (Ex 19:16-24; 24:10; 33:18-23). To Moses and Joshua (De 31:14, 15). To princes of Israel, at Sinai (Ex 24:9-11). To Gideon (J'g 6:11-24). To Solomon (1Ki 3:5; 9:2; 11:9; 2Ch 1:7-12; 7:12-22). To Isaiah (Isa 6:1-5). To Ezekiel (Eze 1:26-28).

Compassion of: See Longsuffering of; Mercy of; below.

Condescension of (Ps 113:5, 6). Manifested: In reasoning with Noah (Ge 6:11-13); with Moses (Ex 4:2-17); with sinners (Isa 1:18-20). In entering into covenant with Abraham (Ge 15:1-21; 18:1-22). In indulging Abraham's intercession for Sodom (Ge 18:2-33). In indulging Moses' prayer to behold his glory (Ex 33:18-23). In indulging Gideon's tests (J'g 6:36-40). In his care of man (Ps 8:4-6; 144:3). In redemption (Joh 3:16; Ro 5:8; Heb 6:17, 18).

Creator (Ps 148:3-5; Pr 16:4; Isa 45:7; 66:2; Jer 51:19; Am 4:13; M'k 13:19; Ac 7:50; Ro 1:20; 1Co 11:12; Heb 2:10; 3:4; Re 4:11). Of the earth (Ge 1:1, 2, 9, 10; 2:1-4; Ex 20:11; 1Sa 2:8; 2Ki 19:15; Ne 9:6; Job 38:4, 7-10; Ps 24:1, 2; 89:11; 90:2; 95:5; 102:25; 104:2, 3, 5, 6, 24, 30; 119:90; 121:2; 124:8; 136:5-9; 146:5, 6; Pr 3:19; 8:26-29; Isa 37:16; 40:28; 42:5; 44:24; 45:12, 18; 48:13; 51:13, 16; Jer 10:12; 27:5; 32:17; 51:15; Jon 1:9; Ac 4:24; 14:15; 17:24, 25; Re 10:6; 14:7). Of the heavens (Ge 1:1, 6-8; 2:1-4; Ex 20:11; 2Ki 19:15; 1Ch 16:26; Ne 9:6; Job 9:8, 9; 37:16, 18; Ps 8:3; 19:1, 4; 96:5; 102:25; 104:2, 3, 5, 6, 24, 30; 121:2; 124:8; 136:5; 146:5, 6; Pr 3:19; 8:26-28; Isa 37:16; 42:5; 44:24; 45:18; Jer 32:17; Am 5:8; Ac 4:24; 14:15; Re 10:6; 14:7). Of the sun, moon and stars (Ge 1:14-19; Ps 136:7-9). Of the seas (Ge 1:9, 10; Ex 20:11; Ne 9:6; Ps 95:5; 146:5, 6; Pr 8:26-29; Jon 1:9; Ac 4:24; 14:15; Re 10:6; 14:7). Of vegetation (Ge 1:11, 12). Of animals (Ge 1:20-25; Job 12:7-9; Jer 27:5). Of man (Ge 1:26-28; 2:7; 5:1, 2; 9:6; Ex 4:11; De 4:32; 32:6, 15, 18; Job 10:3, 8, 9, 11, 12; 31:15; 33:4; 34:19; Ps 94:9; 95:6; 100:3; 119:73; 149:2; Pr 20:12; 22:2; Ec 7:29; 12:1; Isa 17:7; 42:5; 43:1, 7, 15; 44:2, 24; 45:12; 51:13; 64:8; Jer 27:5; Zec 12:1; Mal 2:10; M'k 10:6; Ac 17:24-29; 1Co 12:18, 24, 25; Heb 12:9; 1Pe 4:19).

Through Christ (Ro 11:36; 1Co 8:6; Eph 3:9; Heb 1:1, 2). See Jesus, Creator. By his word (Ps 33:6, 7, 9; 2Co 4:6; Heb 11:3; 2Pe 3:5). By his will (Re 4:11).

Dissertations on: His works and providence (Job 5:8-20). The administration of his government (Job 9:2-35; 10:1-22). His sovereignty (Job 12:7-20; 26:1-14). His providence and grace (Job 33:4-30; Ps 107). His righteousness (Job 34:10-30; 35:1-16; Na 1:2-9). His majesty and justice (Job 36:37). His majesty and works (Ps 104:105).

Dwells with the righteous (Ex 25:8; 29:45; Le 26:11, 12; 1Ki 6:13; Eze 37:26, 27; 2Co 6:16; Re 21:3).

Eternity of (Ge 21:33; Ex 3:15; 15:18; De 32:40; 33:27; 1Ch 16:36; 29:10; Ne 9:5; Job 36:26; Ps 9:7; 41:13; 90:1, 2, 4; 92:8; 93:2; 102:12, 24-27; 145:13; 146:10; Isa 40:28; 44:6; 57:15; 63:16; Jer 10:10; La 5:19; Da 4:3, 34; Hab 1:12; Ro 1:20; 16:26; Eph 3:21; 1Ti 1:17; 6:15, 16; 2Pe 3:8; Re 4:8-10; 11:17).

Faithfulness of (Ge 9:16; 28:15; Le 26:44, 45; De 4:31; J'g 2:1; 1Sa 12:22; Isa 42:16; 44:21; 49:7, 14-16; Jer 29:10; 31:36, 37; 32:40; 33:14, 20, 21, 25, 26; Eze 16:60; Ho 2:19, 20; Ro 3:3, 4; Heb 6:10, 13-19). Confidence in (Nu 23:19; De 32:4; 2Sa 7:28; 1Ch 28:20; Ne 1:5; Ps

36:5; 40:10; 89:1, 2, 5, 8, 14, 24, 28, 33, 34; 92:1, 2, 15; 94:14; 105:8, 42; 111:5, 7-9; 119:90, 91; 132:11; Isa 25:1; La 3:23; Da 9:4; Mic 7:20; 1Co 1:9; 10:13; 2Co 1:18-20; 1Th 5:24; 2Th 3:3; 2Ti 2:13, 19; Tit 1:2; Heb 10:23; 11:11; 1Pe 4:19; 2Pe 3:9; 1Jo 1:9).

Exemplified (Ge 21:1; 24:27; Ex 2:24; 6:4, 5; De 7:8, 9; 9:5; Jos 21:45; 23:14; 1Ki 8:15, 20, 23, 24, 56; 2Ki 8:19; 13:23; 2Ch 6:4-15; 21:7; Ne 1:5; 9:7, 8; Ps 98:3; Hag 2:5; Lu 1:54, 55, 68-70, 72, 73; Ac 13:32, 33; Heb 6:10, 13-19).

Fatherhood of: Taught in the Old Testament (Ex 4:22; De 14:1; 32:5, 6; 2Sa 7:14; 1Ch 28:6; 29:10; Ps 68:5; 89:26; Isa 1:2; 9:6; 63:16; 64:8; Jer 3:19; Ho 1:10; 11:1). Taught by Jesus (M't 5:45; 6:4, 8, 9; 7:11; 10:20, 29, 32, 33; 11:25-27; 12:50; 13:43; 15:13; 16:17, 27; 18:10, 14, 19; 20:23; 26:29, 39; M'k 8:38; 11:25; 13:32; Lu 2:49; 10:21, 22; 11:2, 13; 22:29; 23:46; 24:49; Joh 1:14, 18; 2:16; 4:21, 23; 5:17-23, 36, 37, 43; 6:27, 32, 44-46; 8:19, 27, 38, 41, 42, 49; 10:15, 29, 30, 32, 33, 36-38; 12:26-28, 50; 13:1, 3; 14:2, 6-13, 16, 20, 21, 23, 24, 26, 31; 15:8-10, 16, 23, 24, 26; 16:3, 10, 15, 23, 25-28; 17:1, 5, 11, 21, 24; 20:17, 21). Taught by the apostles (Ac 1:4; 2:33; Ro 1:3, 4, 7; 8:14-16; 1Co 1:3; 8:6; 15:24; 2Co 1:3; 6:18; Ga 1:1, 3, 4; 4:4-7; Eph 1:2, 3, 17; 2:18; 3:14; 4:6; 5:20; 6:23; Ph'p 1:2; Col 1:2, 3, 12; 3:17; 1Th 1:1, 3; 3:11, 13; 2Th 1:1, 2; 2:16; 1Ti 1:2; 2Ti 1:2; Tit 1:4; Heb 1:5, 6; 12:9; Jas 1:17, 27; 3:9; 1Pe 1:2, 3, 17; 1Jo 1:2; 2:1, 13, 15, 22-24; 3:1; 4:14; 2Jo 3, 4, 9; Jude 1; Re 1:5, 6; 3:5; 14:1). See Spiritual Adoption.

Favor of: See Grace of, below.

Foreknowledge of (Ac 15:18). Of contingencies (1Sa 23:10-12). Of future events (Isa 42:9; 44:7; 45:11; 46:9, 10; 48:5, 6; Jer 1:5; Da 2:28, 29; Ac 2:23). Of human needs (M't 6:8). Of the day of judgment (M't 24:36; M'k 13:32). Of the redeemed (Ro 8:29; 11:2; 1Pe 1:2).

Glory of (Ps 24:8-10; 57:5, 11; 72:18, 19; Isa 40:5; Ph'p 1:11). Described (Eze 1:26-28; Hab 3:3-6). Transcendent (Ps 113:4). Shall endure forever (Ps 104:31). Ascribed by angels (Lu 2:14). To be ascribed by men (Ps 29:2; Ro 11:36).

Manifested: In the burning bush (Ex 3:2). In Mount Sinai (Ex 19:18 w Ex 20:18, 19; De 4:11, 12, 33, 36; 5:5, 24, 25; Ex 24:10, 17; 33:18-23; 34:5, 29-35; Heb 12:18-21). In the tabernacle (Ex 40:34, 35). In the heavens (2Sa 22:10-15; Ps 18:9-14; 19:1). In his sovereignty (Ps 97:2-6; 145:5, 11, 12; Isa 6:1-5; 24:23; Jude 24, 25). In the church (Isa 35:2; 60:1, 2, 19-21; 61:3; 62:3; Eph 3:21). In Christ (Joh 13:31, 32; 14:13; 17:1). To Ezekiel (Eze 3:12, 23; 8:4). To Stephen (Ac 7:35).

Goodness of (Ex 33:19; De 30:9; Ps 25:8-10; 31:19; 33:5; 36:7; 86:5; 100:5; 106:1; 119:68; Na 1:7; M't 5:45; Ac 14:17; Jas 1:17).

Enduring (Ps 52:1). Leads to repentance (Ro 2:4).

Gratefully acknowledged (1Ch 16:34; 2Ch 5:13; 7:3; Ps 68:19; 107:8, 9, 43; 118:29; 135:3; 136;1; 145:7, 9; Isa 63:7).

Manifested: In gracious providences (M't 7:11). To the righteous (Ps 31:19; La 3:25; Ro 11:22). To the wicked (Lu 6:35).

Grace of: Unmerited favor (De 7:7,8; 2Ch 30:9; Eph 1:6; Tit 2:11; Heb 4:16). Divine help (Ps 84:11; 1Co 10:13; 2Co 1:12; 12:9; 1Pe 1:5). No warrant for sinful indulgence (Ro 6:1, 15). Intercessory prayer for (Joh 17:11, 12, 15; 1Th 1:1; 5:28; 2Pe 1:2). Exhortation against rejecting (2Co 6:1, 2). Exemplified with respect to Jacob and Esau (Ro 9:10-16).

Manifested: In drawing men to Christ (Joh 6:44, 45); in redemption (Eph 1:5-9, 11, 12); in justification (Ge 15:6; Ro 3:22-24; 4:4, 5, 16; 5:2, 6-8, 15-21; Tit 3:7); in passing over transgression (Nu 23:20, 21; Ne 9:17; Ro 3:25); in salvation (Ro 11:5, 6; Eph 2:8, 9; 2Ti 1:9); in calling to service (Ga 1:15, 16); in spiritual growth (Eph 3:16); in spiritual gifts (1Co 1:4-8; Eph 4:7, 11).

Manifested: In character and conduct (2Co 1:12; Ph'p 2:13); in the character and conduct of the righteous (1Co 15:10; 2Co 1:12; Ph'p 2:13); in sustaining the righteous (1Ch 17:8; 2Co 12:9; 1Pe 1:5; Jude 24); in sustaining in temptation (1Co 10:13; Re 3:10).

Manifestation of: To Enoch (Ge 5:24). To Noah (Ge 6:8, 17, 18). To Abraham (Ge 12:2; 21:22). To Ishmael (Ge 21:20). To Isaac (Ge 26:24). To Jacob (Ge 46:3, 4; 48:16). To Joseph (Ge 39:2, 3, 23). To

Moses (Ex 3:12; 33:12-17). To Israel (De 4:7). To Naphtali (De 33:23). To Joshua (Jos 1:5, 9). To Job (Job 10:12). To David (1Sa 25:26, 34; 2Sa 7:8-16). To Jeremiah (Jer 15:20). To the righteous (Ps 5:12; Ac 4:33).

Guidance of (Ge 12:1; 24:27; Ps 23:2, 3; 48:14; 73:24; Pr 3:6; Jer 3:4; 32:19; Lu 1:79; Joh 10:3, 4). By pillars of cloud and fire (Ex 13:21; Ne 9:19). By his presence (Ex 15:13; 33:13-15; De 32:10, 12; Ps 78:52; 80:1; 107:7). By the ark of the covenant (Nu 10:33). By his counsel (2Sa 22:29; Ps 5:8; 25:9; Isa 48:17). By his Spirit (Joh 16:13). Prayed for (Ps 25:5; 27:11; 31:3; 61:2). Promised (Ps 32:8; Isa 40:11; 42:16; 58:11).

Holiness of (Jos 24:19; 1Sa 6:20; 1Ch 16:10; Job 6:10; 15:15; 25:5; Ps 11:7; 22:3; 36:6; 47:8; 60:6; 89:35; 98:1; 105:3; 111:9; 119:142; 145:17; Pr 9:10; Isa 5:16; 6:3; 29:19, 23; 41:14; 43:14, 15; 45:19; 47:4; 49:7; 52:10; 57:15; Eze 36:21, 22; 39:7, 25; Da 4:8; Ho 11:9; Hab 1:12, 13; Lu 1:49; Joh 17:11; Ro 1:23; 1Jo 2:20; Re 4:8; 6:10; 15:4).

Incomparable (Ex 15:11; 1Sa 2:2; Job 4:17-19). Without iniquity (De 32:4; 2Ch 19:7; Job 34:10; 36:23; Ps 92:15; Jer 2:5; La 3:38; M't 19:17; M'k 10:18; Lu 18:19; Jas 1:13).

A reason for man's holiness (Le 11:44; 19:2; 20:26; 21:8; 2Ch 19:7; M't 5:48; 1Pe 1:15, 16). A reason for thanksgiving (Ps 30:4; 99:3, 5, 9; Isa 12:6). A reason for reverent approach to God (Ex 3:5; Jos 5:15).

Light, figurative of (1Jo 1:5).

See Sin, Separates from God; God, Perfections of, Righteousness of, below.

Human forms and Appearances of: See Anthropomorphisms.

Immanence of (Ac 17:27, 28).

Immutable (Nu 23:19, 20; 1Sa 15:29; Ps 102:27; Isa 40:28; Jas 1:17). In purpose (Job 23:13; Ps 33:11; Pr 19:21; Ec 3:14; 7:13; Isa 31:2; Heb 6:17, 18). In faithfulness (Ps 119:89-91). In mercy (Isa 59:1; Ho 13:14; Mal 3:6; Ro 11:29).

Impartial (De 10:17). Despises none (Job 36:5). No respecter of persons (2Ch 19:7; Job 34:19; 37:24; Ac 10:34, 35; Ro 2:6, 11; Eph 6:8, 9; Col 3:25; 1Pe 1:17).

Incomprehensible (Job 15:8; 37:1-24; Isa 40:12-31; 55:8, 9; M't 11:27; 1Co 2:16).

Infinite (1Ki 8:27; 2Ch 2:6; 6:1, 18; Ps 147:5; Jer 23:24).

Invisible (Ex 20:21; 33:20; De 4:11, 12, 15; 5:22; 1Ki 8:12 w 2Ch 6:1; Job 9:11; 23:8, 9; Ps 18:11; 97:2; Joh 1:18; 5:37; 6:46; Ro 1:20; Col 1:13-15; 1Ti 1:17; 6:16; Heb 11:27; 1Jo 4:12).

Jealous (Ex 20:5, 7; 34:14; De 4:24; 5:9, 11; 6:15; 29:20; 32:16, 21; Jos 24:19; 2Ch 16:7-10; Isa 30:1, 2; Eze 23:25; 36:5; 39:25; Joe 2:18; Na 1:2; Zec 1:14; 1Co 10:22).

Judge (Ge 16:5; J'g 11:27; 1Sa 2:3, 10; 24:12, 15; 1Ch 16:33; Job 21:22; Ps 11:4, 5; 26:1, 2; 35:24; 43:1; 50:4, 6; 58:11; 75:7; 76:8, 9; 82:8; 94:1, 2; 135:14; Pr 16:2; 29:26; Ec 3:17; 11:9; 12:14; Isa 3:13, 14; 28:17, 21; 30:18, 27; 33:22; Jer 32:19; Da 7:9, 10; Na 1:3; Mal 3:5; Ac 17:31; 1Co 5:13; Heb 10:30, 31; 12:22, 23; Re 6:16, 17; 11:18; 16:5; 18:8).

Just (Ge 18:21, 25; Nu 16:22; De 32:4; Ne 9:33; Job 4:17; 8:3; 34:10-12; Ps 7:9, 11; 9:4, 7, 8; 67:4; 96:10, 13; 98:9; Isa 26:7; 45:21; Jer 32:19; Ro 2:2, 5-16; 3:4-6, 26; 11:22, 23; Eph 6:8, 9; 1Pe 1:17; Re 19:2).

Incorruptible (De 10:17; 2Ch 19:7; Job 8:3; 34:19).

Justice of (De 32:4; 2Sa 22:25; 1Ki 8:32; Job 31:13-15; Ps 51:4; 62:12; 89:14; 97:2; 145:17; Pr 21:2, 3; 24:12; Isa 61:8; Jer 9:24; 11:20; 20:12; 32:19; 50:7; Eze 14:23; 18:25, 29, 30; 33:7-19; Da 9:7, 14; Na 1:3, 6; Zep 3:5; Ac 17:31; Ro 2:2, 5-16; Heb 6:10; 1Pe 1:17; 2Pe 2:9; 1Jo 1:9; Jude 6; Re 11:18; 15:3).

Knowledge of (Ge 6:5; 1Sa 2:3; Job 12:13, 22; 21:22; 22:13, 14; 26:6; 28:23, 24; 36:4, 5; 37:16; Ps 147:4, 5; Pr 3:19, 20; Isa 40:13, 14, 26-28; 46:9, 10; M't 24:36; M'k 13:32; Ro 11:33, 34; 1Co 1:25; 1Jo 1:5).

Of man's state and condition (Ge 16:13; Ex 3:7; De 2:7; 2Ki 19:27; 2Ch 16:9; Job 23:10; 31:4; 34:21, 25; Ps 1:6; 11:4; 33:13-15; 37:18; 38:9; 66:7; 69:19; 103:14; 119:168; 139:1-4, 6, 12, 14-16; 142:3; Pr 5:21; 15:3, 11; Isa 29:15, 16; 37:28; 66:18; Jer 23:24; 32:19; Am 9:2-4; M't 10:29, 30; 1Co 8:3).

Of man's heart (Ge 20:6; De 31:21; 1Sa 16:7; 2Sa 7:20; 1Ki 8:39; 1Ch 28:9; 29:17; 2Ch 6:30; Job 11:11; Ps 7:9; 44:21; 94:9-11; Pr 15:11; 16:2; 17:3;

21:2; 24:12; Jer 11:20; 16:17; 17:10; 20:12; Eze 11:5; Am 4:13; M't 6:4, 8, 18, 32; Lu 16:15; Ac 1:24; 15:8; 1Co 3:20; 1Th 2:4; Heb 4:13; 1Jo 3:20). See Foreknowledge of, above; Wisdom of, below.

Light (Da 2:22; Jas 1:17; 1Jo 1:5).

Longsuffering of (Ge 6:3; 15:16; Ex 34:6; Nu 14:18; Ps 86:15; 103:8-10; Isa 5:1-4; 30:18; 48:9, 11; 57:16; Jer 7:13, 23-25; 9:24; Eze 20:17; Joe 2:13; Hab 1:2-4; M't 21:33-41; M'k 12:1-9; Lu 20:9-16; Ac 14:16; Ro 3:25; 15:5; 1Pe 3:20).

Abused (Ne 9:28-31; Pr 1:24-27; 29:1; Ec 8:11; Isa 5:1-4; Jer 7:13, 23-25; M't 24:48-51; Lu 13:6-9). See Mercy of, below.

Manifested: In deferring judgments (Mic 7:18; Lu 13:6-9; Ac 17:20; Ro 9:22, 23; 2Pe 3:9, 15). In giving time for repentance (Jer 11:7; M't 23:37; Lu 13:34; Ro 2:4).

Love of (De 4:37; 7:7, 8, 13; 10:15, 18; 23:5; 33:3, 12; 2Sa 12:24; Job 7:17; Ps 42:8; 47:4; 69:16; Ho 11:1; Mal 1:2; 2Co 13:11, 14; 1Jo 3:1; 4:12, 16, 19; Jude 21).

Everlasting (2Ch 20:21; Jer 31:3). Better than life (Ps 63:3).

For the wicked (M't 18:12-14; Lu 15:4-7, 11-27; Ro 5:8; Eph 2:4, 5). For the righteous (Ps 103:13; 146:8; Pr 15:9; Joh 14:21, 23; 16:27; 17:10, 23, 26; Ro 1:7; 9:13; 11:28; 2Th 2:16). For the cheerful giver (2Co 9:7).

Exemplified (Ex 19:4-6; Le 20:24, 26; De 32:9-12; 2Sa 7:23, 24; Ps 48:9, 14; Isa 43:1-4; 49:13-16; 54:5, 6, 10; 62:4, 5; 63:7-9; 66:13; Jer 3:14, 15; Eze 16:8; Ho 2:19, 20, 23; Zec 2:8).

In forgiveness of sins (Isa 38:17; Tit 3:4, 5). In the gift of his Son (Joh 3:16; 1Jo 4:8-10). In chastisements (Heb 12:6).

Mercy of (Ex 20:2, 6 w De 5:10; Ex 33:19; De 4:31; 7:9; 1Ki 8:23; 2Ch 30:9; Ezr 9:9; Ps 18:50; 25:6, 8; 31:7; 32:10; 36:5; 57:10; 62:12; 69:16; 98:3; 108:4; 111:4; 116:5; 117:2; 119:64, 156; 138:2; 146:7, 8; Isa 60:10; Jer 9:24; 31:20; 32:18; Da 9:4; Ho 2:23; Zec 10:6; Lu 6:36; Ac 17:30; Ro 9:15; 11:32; 15:9; 2Co 1:3; Heb 4:16; 1Pe 1:3; 2Pe 3:9).

Everlasting (1Ch 16:34, 41; 2Ch 5:13; 7:3, 6, 14; Ezr 3:11; Ps 89:1, 2, 28; 100:5; 103:17; 106:1; 107:1; 117:1-4, 29; 136:1-26).

Manifested: In withholding punishment (Ge 8:21; 18:26, 30-32; Ex 32:14; Nu 16:48; 2Sa 24:14, 16; 2Ki 13:23; Ezr 9:13; Job 11:6; Isa 12:1; 54:9; Eze 16:6, 42, 63; 20:17; Ho 11:8, 9; Joe 2:13, 18; Jon 4:2, 10, 11; Mal 3:6). In rescuing from destruction (Ge 19:16; Nu 21:8; J'g 2:18; 2Ki 14:26, 27; Ne 1:10; 9:17-20, 27-31). In leading his people (Ex 15:13). In comforting the afflicted (2Co 12:9). In hearing prayer (Ex 22:27; Heb 4:16). In solicitude for sinners (De 5:29; 32:29; J'g 10:16; 2Ch 36:15; Isa 65:2, 8; Jer 2:9; 7:25; Eze 18:23, 31, 32; 33:11; M't 18:12-14; Lu 15:4-7; 1Ti 2:4, 6). In forbearance toward sinners (2Ch 24:18, 19; Ps 145:8, 9; La 3:22, 23, 31-33; Da 4:22-27; Na 1:3). In granting forgiveness (Ex 34:6, 7; Nu 14:18-20; 2Sa 12:13; 2Ch 7:14; Job 33:14-30; Ps 32:1, 2, 5; 65:3; 78:38, 39; 85:2, 3; 86:5, 13, 15; 99:8; 103:3, 8-14; 130:3, 4, 7, 8; Pr 16:6; 28:13; Isa 55:7-9; Jer 3:12, 22; 31:20, 34; 33:8, 11; 36:3; 50:20; Eze 36:25; Da 9:9; Ho 14:4; Mic 7:18, 19; M't 6:14; 18:23-27; Lu 1:50, 77, 78; Ac 3:19; 26:18; Ro 10:12, 13; 2Co 5:19; Eph 1:6-8; 2:4-7; 1Ti 1:13; Tit 3:5; Heb 8:12; 1Jo 1:9).

Symbolized: In the mercy-seat (Ex 25:17).

Name of: Proclaimed (Ex 6:3; 15:3; 34:5, 14; Ps 83:18). To be reverenced (Ex 20:7; De 5:11; 28:58; Ps 111:9; Mic 4:5; 1Ti 6:1). To be praised (Ps 34:3; 72:17). Not to be profaned (Ex 20:7; Le 18:21; 19:12; 20:3; 21:6; 22:2, 32; De 5:11; Ps 139:9; Isa 52:5; Ro 2:24; Re 16:9). Profaned (Ps 139:20).

Omnipotent (Ge 17:1; 18:14; Job 42:2; Ac 26:8; Re 19:6; 21:22). See Power of, below.

Omnipresent (Ge 28:16; 1Ki 8:27; 2Ch 2:6; Ac 7:48, 49; Ps 139:3, 5, 7-10; Jer 23:23, 24; Ac 17:24, 27, 28). See Presence of, below.

Omniscient. See Knowledge of, above; Wisdom of, below.

Perfection of (De 32:4; 2Sa 22:31; Ps 18:30; M't 5:48; Ro 12:2; Jas 1:17; 1Jo 1:5; Re 15:3). See Holiness of, above; Righteousness of, below.

Personality of: See Unity of, below.

Power of (Ex 9:16; 15:6, 7, 11, 12; Nu 11:23; De 7:21; 11:2; Job 37:23 w vs 1-22; Ps 21:13; 29:3-9; 62:11; 68:34, 35; 74:13, 15; 77:14, 16, 18; 78:12-51; 79:11;

89:8, 13; 93:1, 4; 105:26-41; 106:8; 111:6; 135:6, 8-12; 147:5, 16-18; Isa 26:4; 40:12, 22, 24, 26, 28; 51:10, 15; 63:12; Jer 5:22; 27:5; 32:17, 27; Da 2:20; M't 19:26 w M'k 10:27 & Lu 18:27; 22:29; M'k 14:36; Lu 1:49, 51; 1Co 6:14; Re 19:1).

Supreme (De 32:39; Jos 4:24; 1Sa 2:6, 7; 14:6; 1Ch 29:11, 12; 2Ch 14:11; 25:8, 9; Job 5:9; 23:13, 14; 26:7-14; 36:5, 22, 27-33; 38:8, 11; 40:9; 42:2; Ps 104:7, 9, 29, 30, 32; Da 4:35).

Irresistible (De 32:39 w Job 10:7; 1Sa 2:10; 2Ch 20:6; Job 9:4-7, 10, 12, 13, 19; 11:10; 12:14-16; 14:20; 41:10, 11; Ps 66:3, 7; 76:7; Isa 14:24, 27; 31:3; 43:13, 16, 17; 46:10, 11; 50:2, 3; Na 1:3-6). Incomparable (De 3:24; Job 40:9; Ps 89:8). Omnipotent (Ge 18:14; Jer 32:27; M't 19:26). Everlasting (Ro 1:20).

Creation by (Jer 10:12). The resurrection of Christ by (1Co 6:14; 2Co 13:4); of saints by (1Co 6:14).

Manifested in behalf of saints (De 33:26, 27; 2Ch 16:9; Ezr 8:22; Ne 1:10; Jer 20:11; Da 3:17).

Manifested in his works (De 3:24; Ps 33:9; 107:25, 29; 114:7, 8; Pr 30:4; Isa 48:13; Jer 10:12, 13; 51:15; Ro 1:20). See Omnipotent, above.

Presence of (Ge 16:13; 28:16; Ex 20:24; 29:42, 43; 30:6; 33:14; De 4:34-36, 39; 1Ki 8:27; Ps 139:3, 5, 7-10; Isa 57:15; 66:1; Jer 23:23, 24; 32:18, 19; Jon 1:3, 4; Ac 17:24, 27, 28; 1Co 12:6).

Manifested on the mercy-seat, see Shekinah.

Preserver (Ne 9:6; Job 33:18; Ps 3:3; 12:7; 17:7; 68:6; 73:23; Isa 27:3; 49:8; Jer 2:6; Da 5;23; M't 10:29-31; Lu 12:6, 7; 21:18; Joh 17:11, 15; 1Pe 3:12, 13; 2Pe 2:9).

Of the righteous (Ge 15:1; 28:15; 49:24, 25; Ex 8:22, 23; 9:26; 11:7; 12:13, 17, 23; 15:2, 13, 16, 17; 19:4; 23:20-31; De 1:30, 31; 32:10; 33:12, 25-28; Jos 23:10; 1Sa 2:9; 2Sa 22:1-51; 2Ch 16:9; Job 1:10; 5:11, 18-24; 10:12; Ps 9:9; 18:14; 23:1-6; 31:20, 23; 32:6, 8; 34:7, 15, 17, 19-22; 37:17, 23, 24, 28, 32, 33; 41:1-3; 46:1, 7; 50:15; 84:11; 91:1, 3, 4, 7, 9, 10, 14, 15; 102:19, 20; 103:2-5; 107:9, 10, 13; 116:6; 118:13; 121:3, 4, 7, 8; 125:1-3; 145:14, 19, 20; 146:7, 8; Pr 2:7, 8; 10:3, 30; Isa 25:4; 30:21, 26; 33:16; 40:11, 29, 31; 42:16; 43:2; 46:3, 4; 52:12; 58:11; 63:9; Jer 31:9, 10, 28; Eze 11:16; 34:11-16, 22, 31; Da 3:27, 28; Joe 2:18; Zec 2:5, 8; M't 4:6; 1Co 10:13; 2Ti 4:18; 2Th 3:3; Jas 4:15).

His preserving care exemplified: To Noah and his family, at the time of the flood (Ge 6:8, 13-21; 7; 8:1, 15, 16). To Abraham and Sarah, in Egypt (Ge 12:17); in Gerar (Ge 20:3). To Lot, when Sodom was destroyed (Ge 19). To Hagar, when Abraham cast her out (Ge 21:17, 19). To Jacob, when he fled from home (Ge 35:3); when he fled from Laban, his father-in-law (Ge 31:24, 29); when he met Esau (Ge 33:3-10); as he journeyed in the land of Canaan (Ge 35:3). To Joseph, in Egypt (Ge 39:2, 21). To Moses, in his infancy (Ex 2:1-10).

To the Israelites: In bringing about their deliverance from bondage (Ex 1:9-12; 2:23-25; 3:7-9). In exempting the land of Goshen from the plague of flies (Ex 8:22). In preserving their cattle from the plague of murrain (Ex 9:4-7). In exempting the land of Goshen from the plague of darkness (Ex 10:21-23). In saving the firstborn, when the plague of death destroyed the firstborn of Egypt (Ex 12:13, 23). In deliverance from Egypt (Ex 13:3, 17-22; 14; 19:4; Le 26:13); in the wilderness (Ex 40:36-38; Nu 9:17-23; 10:33; 22:12; 23:8; De 1:31; 23:5; 26:7-9). In victories under Joshua, over the Canaanites (Jos chaps 6-11; 24:11-13); under Othniel (J'g 3:9-11); under Ehud (J'g 3:15-30); under Shamgar (J'g 3:31); under Deborah (J'g 4:5); under Gideon (J'g 7; 8:1-23); under Jephthah (J'g 11:29-40); under David (1Sa 17:45-49); under Ahab (1Ki 20). In delivering the kingdom of Israel from Syria (2Sa 8). In delivering Israel by Jeroboam II (2Ki 14:26, 27); by Abijah (2Ch 13:4-18). In delivering from the oppressions of the king of Syria (2Ki 13:2-5).

To the kingdom of Judah: In delivering from Egypt (2Ch 12:2-12); from the Ethiopian host (2Ch 14:11-14). In giving peace with other nations (2Ch 17). In delivering them from the army of the Assyrians (2Ki 19).

To David (1Sa 17:32, 45-47; 2Sa 7; 1Ch 11:13, 14). To Hezekiah (2Ki 19). To Job (1:9-12; 2:6). To Jeremiah and Baruch (Jer 36:26). To Daniel and the three Hebrew captives (Da 2:18-23; 3:27, 28; 6). To Jonah (Jon 1:17). To the wise men of the east (M't 2:12). To Jesus and his parents (M't 2:13, 19-22). To Peter (Ac 12:3-17). To Paul and Silas (Ac 16:26-39). To Paul (Ac 27:24; 28:5, 6 w M'k 16:18). See Providence of, below. See Poor, God's care of.

Providence of (Ge 24:7, 40-50, 56; 26:24; Le 26:4-6, 10; De 8:18; 11:12-15; 15:4-6; 32:11-14; 1Sa 2:6-9; 1Ki 11:14-40; 1Ch 29:14, 16; Ps 23:1-6; 34:7, 9, 10; 71:6, 7, 15; 107:1-43; 127:1-5; 136:5-25; 144:12-15; 147:8, 9, 13, 14; Pr 16:33; Ec 2:24; 3:13; 5:19; Isa 46:4; 51:2; 55:10; Eze 36:28-38; Joe 2:18-26; M't 5:45; Ro 8:28; Jas 4:15).

In providing for temporal necessities (Ge 1:29, 30; 2:16; 8:22; 9:1-3; 28:20, 21; 48:15, 16; 49:24, 25; Ex 16:15; Le 25:20-22; De 2:7; 7:13-15; 8:4; 10:18; 28:2-13; 29:5; Ru 1:6; Ne 9:24, 25; Job 5:8-11; 22:18, 25; Ps 36:6, 7; 37:3, 19, 22, 25, 34; 65:9-13; 67:6; 85:12; 104:10-15; 111:5; 136:25; 145:15, 16; Isa 43:20; 48:21; Jer 5:24; 27:6; Ho 2:8; Jon 4:6; Zec 10:1; M't 6:26, 30-33; 10:29-31; Lu 12:6, 7, 24-28; 22:35; Joh 6:31; Ac 14:17; 2Co 9:10).

In sending prosperity (Ps 75:7; 127:1, 2; Isa 48:14, 15; 54:16, 17; Eze 29:19, 20). In sending adversity (1Sa 2:6-9; 2Sa 17:14; Ps 75:7; Ec 3:10). In saving from adversity (Ge 7:1; Ex 9:26; 15:26; 23:25, 26; Ps 103:3-5; 116:1-15; 118:5, 6, 13, 14; 146:7-9; Da 6:20-22).

In delivering from enemies (Ge 14:20; Ex 3:17; 6:7; 14:29, 30; 23:22; 34:24; De 20:4; 23:14; 30:4, 20; 31:3, 8; 2Ki 20:6; 2Ch 20:3-30; 32:8; Ezr 8:22, 23; Ps 18:17, 27; 44:1-3; 61:3; 78:52-55; 97:10; 105:14-45 w Ac 7:34-36; 124:1-8; Pr 16:7). In thwarting evil purpose (Ge 5:20 w 45:5-7 & Ps 105:17 & Ac 7:9, 10; Ex 14:4; Nu 23:7, 8, 23 w 22:12-18 & 24:10-13; Ezr 5:5; Ne 6:16; Es 7:10 w 6:1-12 & 9:25; Job 5:12, 13 w Isa 8:9, 10; Ps 33:10; Ac 5:38, 39). In turning curse into blessing (De 23:4, 6; Ph'p 1:12, 19). In exalting the lowly (2Sa 7:8, 9; 1Ch 17:7, 8; Ps 68:6; 113:7, 8). In leading men to repentance (Am 4:7-12). In punishing evil-doers (De 2:30; Jos 10:10, 11, 19; 11:20; J'g 9:23, 24; 1Ch 5:26; Isa 41:2, 4).

In punishing rulers (Da 5:18, 22). In punishing nations (De 9:4, 5; Job 12:23; Eze 29:19, 20). In ordaining instruments of chastisement (Isa 13:3-5). In using the heathen to execute his purpose (Ezr 6:22; Isa 44:28; 45:1-6, 13).

In fulfilling prophecy (1Ki 12:15; 2Ch 10:15; 36:22, 23; Ezr 1:1; Ac 3:17, 18).

In nature (Job 12:7-20; 37:6-24; 38:25-27, 41; 39:5, 6; Ps 104:16-19, 24-30; 135:7; Jer 10:13; 51:16; 14:22; 31:35).

Instances of: Saving Noah (Ge 7:1; 2Pe 2:5). The call of Abraham (Ge 12:1). Protecting Abraham, Sarah, and Abimelech (Ge 20:3-6). Deliverance of Lot (Ge 19). Care of Isaac (Ge 26:2, 3); of Jacob (Ge 31:7). The mission of Joseph (Ge 37:5-10; 39:2, 3, 21, 23; 45:7, 8; 50:20; Ps 105:17-22). Warning Pharaoh of famine (Ge 41). Delivering the Israelites (Ex 3:8; 11:3; 13:18; Ac 7:34-36). The pillar of cloud (Ex 13:21; 14:19, 20). Dividing the Red Sea (Ex 14:21). Delaying and destroying Pharaoh (Ex 14:25-30). Purifying the waters of Marah (Ex 15:25). Supplying manna and quail (Ex 16:13-15; Nu 11:31, 32). Supplying water at Meribah (Nu 20:7-11; Ne 9:10-25). Protection of homes while at feasts (Ex 34:24). In the conquest of Canaan (Ps 44:2, 3). Saving David's army (2Sa 5:23-25). The revolt of the ten tribes (1Ki 12:15, 24; 2Ch 10:15). Fighting the battles of Israel (2Ch 13:12, 18; 14:9-14; 16:7-9; 20:15, 17; 22; 23; 32:21, 22). Restoring Manasseh after his conversion (2Ch 33:12, 13). Feeding Elijah and the widow (1Ki 17; 19:1-8). In prospering Hezekiah (2Ki 18:6, 7; 2Ch 32:29); and Asa (2Ch 14:6, 7); and Jehoshaphat (2Ch 17:3, 5; 20:30); and Uzziah (2Ch 26:5-15); and Jotham (2Ch 27:6); and Job (Job 1:10; 42:10, 12); and Daniel (Da 1:9). In turning the heart of the king of Assyria to favor the Jews (Ezr 6:22). In rescuing Jeremiah (La 3:52-58 w Jer 38:6-13). Restoration of the Jews (2Ch 36:22, 23; Ezr 1:1). Rescuing the Jews from Haman's plot (the book of Esther). Rebuilding the walls of Jerusalem (Ne 6:16). Warning Joseph in dreams (M't 1:20; 2:13, 19, 20); and the wise men of the east (M't 2:12, 13). Deliverance of Paul (2Co 1:10). Restoring Epaphroditus (Ph'p 2:27). Banishment of John to Patmos (Re 1:9).

Mysterious and Misinterpreted: The silence of God (Job 33:13). The adversity of the righteous (Ec 7:15; 8:14). The prosperity of the wicked (Job 12:6; 21:7; 24:1; Ps 73:2-5, 12-17; Ec 7:15; 8:14; Jer 12:1, 2; Mal 3:14, 15). Likeness in the lot of the righteous and the wicked (Ec 9:2, 11). Permitting the violence of the wicked toward the righteous (Job 24:1-12; Hab 1:2, 3, 11, 13, 14).

Rejected: By Israel (1Sa 8:7, 8; Isa 65:12; 66:4). By Saul (1Sa 15:26). See Jesus, Rejected.

Repentance Attributed to (Ge 6:6, 7; Ex 32:14; J'g 2:18; 1Sa 15:35; 2Sa 24:16; 1Ch 21:15; Ps 106:45; Jer 26:19; Am 7:3; Jon 3:10). See Anthropomorphisms.

Righteousness of (Ge 18:25; J'g 5:11; Ps 7:9; 72:1; 88:12; 89:16; 119:40; 143:1; Isa 41:10; 56:1; Jer 4:2; 9:24; Mic 7:9; Ac 17:31).

Ascribed by men (Ex 9:27; Ezr 9:15; Job 36:3; Ps 5:8; 48:10; 71:15, 19; 89:14; 97:2; 116:5; 145:7, 17; Jer 12:1; Da 9:7, 14; 2Ti 4:8). Ascribed by Jesus (Joh 17:25). Ascribed by the angel (Re 16:5). Revealed in the heavens (Ps 50:6). Revealed in the gospel (Ro 1:17; 3:4-6, 21, 22; 10:3, 4; 2Pe 1:1).

Endures forever (Ps 119:142, 144; Isa 51:8). See Holiness of, Perfection of, above.

Saviour (Ex 6:6, 7; Ps 3:8; 18:30; 28:8; 31:5; 33:18, 19; 34:22; 37:39, 40; 74:12; 76:8, 9; 85:9; 96:2; 98:2, 3; 111:9; 118:14; 121:7; 149:4; Isa 26:1; 33:22; 35:4; 43:3, 11, 12, 14; 45:15, 17, 21, 22; 46:12, 13; 49:25; 50:2; 59:1; 60:16; 63:8, 16; Jer 3:23; 14:8; 33:6; Eze 37:23; Ho 1:7; 13:4; Joe 3:16; Jon 2:9; Lu 1:68; Joh 3:16, 17; Ro 8:30-32; 1Ti 2:3, 4; 4:10; Tit 1:2, 3; 2:10, 11; 3:4, 5; 1Jo 4:9, 10).

Called Redeemer (Ps 19:14; Isa 41:14; 47:4; 48:17; Jer 50:34); salvation (Ps 27:1; 62:1, 2, 6, 7; Isa 12:2); God of salvation (Ps 25:5; 65:5; 68:19, 20; 88:1); rock of salvation (De 32:15, 31); shield (De 33:29).

From national adversity (Ex 15:2; Isa 25:4, 9; 52:3, 9, 10).

From sin (Job 33:24, 27-30; Isa 44:22-24; Ro 1:16); through Christ (2Ti 1:9).

Self-Existent: Hath life in himself (Joh 5:26). Is the I am that I am (Ex 3:14). Is the first and the last (Isa 44:6). Is the living God (Jer 10:10). Lives forever (De 32:40). Needs nothing (Ac 17:24, 25).

Sovereign (Ex 20:3; Job 25:2; 33:13; 41:11; Ps 44:4; 47:8; 59:13; 74:12; 82:1, 8; 83:18; 93:1, 2; 95:3-5; 96:10; 97:1, 5, 9; 98:6; 99:1; 103:19; 105:7; 113:4; 115:3, 16; 136:2, 3; Isa 24:23; 33:22; 40:22, 23; 43:15; 44:6; 52:7; 66:1; La 3:37; Mic 4:7, 13; Mal 1:14; Joh 10:29; 19:11; Ac 7:49; Ro 9:19; 11:36; Eph 4:6; 1Ti 6:15, 16; Heb 1:3; Jas 4:12; Re 4:11; 19:6).

Of heaven (2Ch 20:6). Of earth (Ex 9:29; Jos 3:11; Ps 24:1, 10; 47:2, 7, 8; 50:10-12; Isa 54:5; Jer 10:10; 1Co 10:26). Of heaven and earth (Ge 14:18-20, 22; 24:3; Ex 19:5; De 4:39; 10:14, 17; Jos 2:11; 2Ki 19:15; 1Ch 29:11, 12; Ne 9:6; Ps 89:11; 135:5, 6; M't 6:10; 11:25; Lu 10:21; Ac 17:24-26; Re 11:4, 13, 17).

Of the spirits of all flesh (Nu 27:16; De 32:39; Job 12:9, 10, 16, 17; Ps 22:28, 29; Ec 9:1; Isa 45:23; Jer 18:1-23; Eze 18:4; Ro 14:11).

In human affairs (Ps 75:6, 7; Jer 27:5-7; 32:27, 28; Eze 16:50; 17:24; Da 2:20, 21, 47; 4:3, 17, 25, 34, 35, 37; 5:18, 26-28).

Everlasting (Ex 15:18; Ps 10:16; 29:10; 66:7; 145:11-13; 146:10; La 5:19; Da 6:26).

Spirit (Joh 4:24; Ac 17:29). See Holy Spirit.

Teacher (Job 36:22; Ps 94:10, 12; 119:135, 171; Isa 28:26; 54:13; Joh 6:45; 1Th 4:9).

Truth (Ge 24:27; Ex 34:6; Nu 23:19; 1Sa 15:29; Ps 25:10; 31:5; 33:4; 43:3; 57:3, 10; 71:22; 86:11, 15; 89:14; 108:4; 132:11; 138:2; Isa 25:1; 65:16; Da 4:37; Joh 8:26; Ro 3:4, 7; Tit 1:2; Rev 6:10; 15:3).

Endures to all generations (Ps 117:2; 146:6).

Ubiquitous: See Omnipresent, above.

Unchangeable: See Immutable, above.

Unity of (De 6:4; Isa 42:8). Taught by Jesus (M'k 12:29, 32; Joh 17:3); by Paul (1Co 8:4, 6; Ga 3:20; Eph 4:6; 1Ti 2:5). Disbelieved in by Syrians (1Ki 20:28). Believed in by devils (Jas 2:19).

Unsearchable (De 29:29; Job 5:8, 9; 9:10; 11:7-9; 26:9, 14; 36:26; 37:5, 23; Ps 77:19; 139:6; 145:3; Pr 30:4; Ec 3:11; 11:5; Isa 40:28; 45:15; 55:8, 9; Ro 11:33, 34; 1Co 2:10, 11, 16).

Symbolized: By Darkness (Ex 20:21;

De 4:11; 5:22; 1Ki 8:12; Ps 18:11; 97:2). By the cloud upon the mercy-seat (Le 16:2).

Name of, secret (J'g 13:18). Dwells in thick darkness (1Ki 8:12; Ps 97:2). Known only to Christ, and to those to whom Christ reveals him (M't 11:27).

See Mysteries.

Voice of: See Anthropomorphisms.

Wisdom of (Ezr 7:25; Job 9:4; 12:13, 16; Isa 31:2; Da 2:20-22, 28; Ro 11:33; 16:27; 1Co 1:24, 25).

Infinite (Ps 147:5). Manifold (Eph 3:10). Ascribed by angels (Re 7:12).

Works made in (Ps 104:24; 136:5; Pr 3:19, 20; Jer 10:12). See Knowledge of, above.

Works of: In creation (Job 9:8, 9; Ps 8:3-5; 89:11; 136:5-9; 139:13, 14; 148:4, 5; Ec 3:11; Jer 10:12); good (Ge 1:10, 18, 21, 25). Faithful (Ps 33:4). Wonderful (Ps 26:7; 40:5). Incomparable (Ps 86:8). In his overruling providence in the affairs of men (Ps 26:7; 40:5; 66:3; 75:1; 111:2, 4, 6; 118:17; 145:4-17). See Creation.

GODLESSNESS. *Described as:* Destitute of the love of God (Joh 5:42, 44); forgetting God (Job 8:11-13; Ps 9:17; 50:22; Isa 17:10; Jer 2:32); ignoring God (Job 35:10; Ps 28:5; 52:7; 53:2, 3; 54:3; 55:19; 86:14; Isa 5:12; 22:11; 30:1; 31:1; Ho 7:2-4); forsaking God (De 32:15); despising God (1Sa 2:30; Ps 36:1; Pr 14:2; Joh 15:23-25); loving deceits (Isa 30:9-11); devoid of understanding (Ps 14:2, 3; 53:4; Isa 1:3; Ro 1:21, 22; 3:11; Eph 4:18); rebellious (Ps 2:2; Isa 30:2; Da 5:23); hate God (De 7:10); enemies to God (Col 1:21; Jas 4:4); carnality (Ro 8:6-8); impugning God's justice (Eze 33:17-20; Mal 2:17); atheistical (Ps 10:4); wilfully sinning (Heb 10:26, 27).

See Impenitence; Obduracy; Prayerlessness; Reprobacy; Unbelief; Wicked.

GODLINESS (See Holiness; Righteousness.)

GODLY (See Righteous.)

GODS (See Idol; Idolatry; Image.)

GOG. 1. A Reubenite (1Ch 5:4).

2. A Scythian prince. Prophecy against (Eze 38; 39; Re 20:8).

GOLAN, a town in Bashan. Given to Manasseh as a city of refuge (De 4:43; Jos 20:8). A Levitical city (Jos 21:27; 1Ch 6:71).

GOLD. Exported from Havilah (Ge 2:11, 12). From Ophir (1Ki 9:28; 10:11; 1Ch 29:4; 2Ch 8:18; Job 22:24); Tarshish (1Ki 22:48); Parvaim (2Ch 3:6); Sheba (1Ki 10:10; 2Ch 9:9; Ps 72:15); Uphaz (Jer 10:9).

Refined (Job 28:19; 31:24; Pr 8:19; 17:3; 27:21; Zec 13:9; Mal 3:3). Used in the arts: Beaten work (2Ch 9:15); made into wire threads and wrought into embroidered tapestry (Ex 39:3); apparel (Ps 45:9, 13); in ornamenting the priests' garments (Ex 39); modeled into forms of fruits (Pr 25:11); into ornaments (Ge 24:22; Ex 3:22; 11:2; 28:11; Nu 31:50, 51; Song 1:10; 5:14; Eze 16:17); crowns made of (Ex 25:25; 37:2-11; 39:30; Es 8:15; Ps 21:3; Zec 6:11); candlesticks made of, for the tabernacle (Ex 25:31-38; 37:17-24); shields of (1Ki 10:16, 17); overlaying with (Ex 25:11, 13, 24, 28, w 1-40; 26:27, 29; 30:5; 36:34, 36, 38; 37:2, 4, 11, 15; 1Ki 6:20-22, 28, 30, 32, 35); bedsteads made of (Es 1:6). Wedge of (Jos 7:21; Isa 13:12).

Used as money (Ge 44:8, w verse 1; 1Ch 21:25; Ezr 8:25-28; Isa 13:17; 60:9; Eze 7:19; 28:4; M't 2:11; 10:9; Ac 3:6; 20:33; 1Pe 1:18). Solomon rich in (1Ki 10:2, 14, 21).

Vessels and utensils made of, for the tabernacle (Ex 25:26, 29, 38, 39; 37:16); for the temple (1Ch 18:11; 22:14, 16; 29:2-7). Altar, lamps, and other articles made of (1Ki 7:48, 49-51; 2Ki 25:15; Jer 52:19; Ezr 8:27; Da 5:3); see Overlaying with, above.

Belongs to God (Eze 16:17).

Figurative: Ec 12:6; Jer 51:7; La 4:1; 1Co 3:12.

Symbolical: Da 2:32-45; Re 21:18, 21.

See Goldsmith.

GOLDEN CANDLESTICK (See Candlestick.)

GOLDEN RULE: "Do unto others . . ." (M't 7:12; Lu 6:31). See also "Thou shalt love thy neighbor . . ." (Le 19:18; Ro 13:9; Ga 5:14).

GOLDSMITH (2Ch 2:7, 14; Ne 3:8, 31, 32; Isa 40:19; 41:7; 46:6).

See Gold.

GOLGOTHA (skull), the place of the crucifixion of Christ, located outside of Jerusalem (M't 27:33; M'k 15:22) on the public road (Joh 19:20).

GOLIATH (exile), a giant champion of

Gath. Defied armies of Israel and is slain by David (1Sa 17; 21:9; 22:10). His sons (2Sa 21:15-22; 1Ch 20:4-8).

GOMER. 1. Son of Japheth (Ge 10:2, 3; 1Ch 1:5, 6).

2. A people descended from Gomer (Eze 38:6).

3. Wife, or concubine, of Hosea (Ho 1:3).

GOMORRAH. One of the "cities of the plain" (Ge 10:19; 13:10). Its king defeated by Chedorlaomer (Ge 14:2, 8-11). Wickedness of (Ge 18:20). Destroyed (Ge 19:24-28; De 29:23; 32:32; Isa 1:9, 10; 13:19; Jer 23:14; 49:18; 50:40; Am 4:11; Zep 2:9; M't 10:15; M'k 6:11; Ro 9:29; 2Pe 2:6; Jude 7).

GONORRHEA (Le 15).

GOOD AND EVIL. Choice between, by Adam and Eve (Ge 3). Exhortation to choose between (Jos 24:15). Conflict between (Re 16:13-21). Subjective conflict between (Ro 7:9-25).

GOOD FOR EVIL. Injunctions by Christ concerning (M't 5:44-48; Lu 6: 27-36).

Returning: Instances of: Abraham, to Abimelech (Ge 20:14-18). David, to Saul (1Sa 24:17; 26). Elisha, to the Syrians (2Ki 6:22, 23). David, to his enemies (Ps 35:12-14). Jesus, to his crucifiers (Lu 23:34). Stephen (Ac 7:60).

See Golden Rule; Evil for Good; Nonresistance.

GOOD NEWS (Pr 15:30; 25:25). See Gospel.

GOPHER WOOD, the wood from which Noah's ark was made (Ge 6:14), most probably cypress.

GOSHEN (mound of earth). 1. A district in Egypt especially adapted to herds and flocks. Israelites dwelt in (Ge 45:10; 46:28; 47). Exempted from plagues (Ex 8:22; 9:26).

2. A town and district of Judah (Jos 10:41; 11:16; 15:51).

GOSPEL. From God (Joh 17:7, 8, 14; 2Th 2:14). Contrasted with the law (Lu 16:16; Joh 1:16, 17; Ac 12:24; 19:20; 2Co 3:6-11). Called the New Covenant (Jer 31:31-34; Heb 7:22; 8:6-13; 9:8-15; 10:9; 12:22-24).

Described as: Dispensation of grace (Eph 3:2). Doctrine according to godliness (1Ti 6:3). Everlasting gospel or eternal good tidings (Re 14:6). The faith (Jude 3). Form of sound words (2Ti 1:13). Glorious gospel (1Th 1:11). Glorious gospel of Christ (2Co 4:1). Good tidings (Isa 40:9; 41:27; 52:7; 61:1; M't 11:5; Lu 7:22; Ac 13:32, 33; 1Pe 1:25). Gospel, of Christ (Ro 1:16; 1Co 9:12, 18; Ga 1:7; Ph'p 1:27; 1Th 3:2); of God (Ro 1:1; 15:16; 1Th 2:8; 1Pe 4:17); of grace of God (Ac 20:24); of Jesus Christ (M'k 1:1); of the kingdom (M't 4:23; 24:14); of peace (Eph 6:15); of salvation (Eph 1:13). The kingdom of God (Lu 16:16). The law of liberty (Jas 1:25). Ministration of the Spirit (2Co 3:8). Mystery, of Christ (Eph 3:4); of the gospel (Eph 6:19). Power of God (Ro 1:16; 1Co 1:18). Preaching of Jesus Christ (Ro 16:25). Word, of Christ (Col 3:16); of faith (Ro 10:8); of God (1Th 2:13; 1Pe 1:23); of life (Ph'p 2:16); of the Lord (1Pe 1:25); of reconciliation (2Co 5:19); of salvation (Ac 13:26); of truth (2Co 2:16; Eph 1:13). Words, of this life (Ac 5:20).

Likened to: a mustard seed (M't 13:31, 32; M'k 4:30-33; Lu 13:18, 19); good seed (M't 13:24-30, 36-43); leaven (M't 13:33); a pearl of great price (M't 13:45, 46; Lu 13:20, 21); a treasure hidden in a field (M't 13:44); a householder (M't 20:1-16); a feast (Lu 14:16-24).

Dissemination of (Ac 14:3; 16:17; 20: 24); enjoined (M't 24:14; 28:18-20; M'k 13:10; 16:15; Ac 5:20; Ro 10:15-18; 16: 25, 26; 1Co 1:18, 21, 24, 25; 9:16-18; Eph 3:8-11). Desired by prophets, righteous, kings (M't 13:17; Lu 23:34). Hid from the lost (2Co 4:3, 4). Comes in power, word, assurance (1Th 1:5).

Proclaimed, to Abraham (Ga 3:8); by angels (Lu 2:10, 11; Re 14:6). Preached, by Jesus (M't 4:23; M'k 1:14, 15); by Peter (Ac 10:36); by Paul (Ac 13:32, 33; 20:24; Ro 15:29; 1Co 9:16-18; Ga 2:2; Col 1:5, 6, 23); to the Gentiles (Ga 2:2; Eph 3:8; Col 1:23, 26-29); to both Jews and Gentiles (Ro 1:16; 1Co 1:24); to the poor M't 11:4-6; Lu 7:22); to the dead (1Pe 3:19; 4:6); to every (all) nation (Lu 2:10, 11; Ro 16:26; Re 14:6).

Life and immortality brought to light in (2Ti 1:10). Salvation through (Ro 1: 16, 17; 1Co 15:1, 2; Eph 1:13, 14; Jas 1:21; 1Pe 1:23).

Prophecies concerning (Isa 2:3-5; 4:2-6; 9:2, 6, 7; 25:7-9; 29:18, 24; 32:3, 4; 35:5-10; 40:9; 41:27; 42:6, 7; 46:13;

49:13; 51:4-6; 52:7; 55:1-5; 60:1-22; 61:1-3; Jer 31:31-34; Eze 34:23-31; 47:1-12; Joe 2:28-32; Mic 4:1-7; M't 24:14; Lu 1:67-79; 2:12-14, 34). Fulfilled by Christ (Lu 4:18, 19).

See Church, Prophecies Concerning; Jesus, Kingdom of, Mission of; Kingdom of Heaven.

GOSSIP. Proverbs concerning (Pr 16: 28; 26:20). Forbidden (Le 9:16; Ps 50: 20; Pr 11:3; 20:19; Eze 22:9).

See Slander; Speaking, Evil.

GOURD. Jonah's believed to be a vine resembling the American squash, used in Assyria to cover booths (Jon 4:6-10). The wild gourd mentioned in 2Ki 4:30 is supposed to be a plant in appearance like the cucumber.

GOUT (?) (2Ch 16:12).

GOVERNMENT. Paternal functions of (Ge 41:25-57). Civil service school provided by (Da 1:3-20). Maintains a system of public instruction (2Ch 17:7-9).

Constitutional: It was provided in the law of Moses that in the event of the establishment of a monarchy a copy of the law of Moses should be made and that the king should be enjoined to study this law all the days of his life and conform his administration thereto (De 17:18-20). This constituted the fundamental law and had its likeness to the constitution of modern governments. When David was crowned king of all Israel he made a league in the nature of a constitution which was a basis of good understanding between himself and the people (2Sa 5:3). When Joash was enthroned a covenant, which must have been in the nature of a limitation of monarchical power, was made between him and the people (2Ch 23:3, 11). In v. 11 this covenant is called a "testimony" and no doubt, refers to the law of Moses (De 17:18-20), which, it is quite probable, had been preserved sacredly by Jehoiada, the priest. Zedekiah made a covenant with the people proclaiming liberty (Jer 34:8-11). That the king of the Medes and Persians was restricted by a constitution which "altereth not," is evident from Da 6:12-15. See Constitution; Israel, History of; Judges; Kings.

Corruption in (1Ki 21:5-13; Pr 25:5; Mic 3:1-4, 9-11).

Instances of Corruption in: Pilate, in delivering Jesus to death to please the clamorous multitude (M't 27:24; Joh 19:12-16). Felix, who hoped for money from Paul (Ac 24:26). See Court, Corrupt; Church, Corrupt; Rulers, Wicked.

Duty of Citizens to: To pay taxes (M't 22:17-21; Lu 20:22-25). To render obedience to civil authority (Ro 13:1-7; Tit 3:1; 1Pe 2:13-17).

God in (2Ch 22:7; Jer 18:6; Eze 21:25-27; 29:19, 20). In appointment of Saul as king (1Sa 9:15-17; 10:1). In Saul's rejection (1Sa 15:26-28; Ac 13:22). In appointment, of David (1Sa 16:1, 7, 13; 2Sa 7:13-16; Ps 89:19-37; Ac 13:22); of Solomon (1Ki 2:13-15). In counseling Solomon (1Ki 9:2-9). In magnifying Solomon (1Ch 29:25). In reproving Solomon's wickedness (1Ki 11:9-13). In raising adversaries against Solomon (1Ki 11:14, 23). In rending the nation of Israel in two (1Ki 11:13; 12:1-24; 2Ch 10:15; 11:4). In blotting out the house of Jeroboam (1Ki 14:7-16; 15:27-30). In appointment of kings (1Ki 14:14; 16:1, 2; 1Ch 28:4, 5; Da 2:20, 21, 37; 4:17; 5:18-23). In destruction of nations (Jer 25:12-17; Am 9:8; Hag 2:22).

Relation of God to (Ps 22:28; Pr 8:15, 16; Isa 9:6, 7; Jer 1:9, 10; 18:6-10; 25:12-17; Eze 21:25-27; 29:19, 20; Da 2:20, 21, 37; 4:17; 5:18-28; 10:13; Ho 8:4; Am 9:8; Hag 2:21, 22; Joh 19:10, 11).

See God, Sovereign; Jesus, Kingdom of.

Mosaic: Administrative and judicial system (Ex 18:13-26; Nu 11:16, 17, 24, 25; De 1:9-17).

Popular Government, by a National Assembly, or its Representatives: Accepted the law given by Moses (Ex 19:7, 8; 24:3, 7; De 29:10-15). Refused to make conquest of Canaan (Nu 14:1-10). Chose, or ratified, the chief ruler (1Sa 10:24 w 8:4-22; 11:14, 15; 2Sa 3:17-21; 5:1-3; 1Ch 29:22; 2Ch 23:3). Possessed veto power over king's purposes (1Sa 14:44, 45). Constituted the court in certain capital cases (Nu 35:12, 24, 25).

Delegated, Senatorial Council: Closely associated with Moses and subsequent leaders (Ex 3:16, 18; 4:29-31; 12:21; 17:5, 6; 18:12; 19:7, 8; 24:1, 14; Le 4:15; 9:1; Nu 11:16, 17, 30; 16:25; De 1:13-15;

5:23; 27:1; 29:10-15; 31:9, 28; Jos 7:6; 8:10, 32, 33; 23:2, 3, 6; 24:1, 24, 25; J'g 21:16-25; Ac 5:17, 18, 21-41).

Miscellany of Facts Relating to the Senate: Demands a king (1Sa 8:4-10, 19-22). Saul pleads to be honored before (1Sa 15:30). Chooses David as king (2Sa 5:3; 1Ch 11:3). Closely associated with David (2Sa 12:17; 1Ch 15:25; 21:16). Joins Absalom in his usurpation (2Sa 17:4). David upbraids (2Sa 19:11). Assists Solomon at the dedication of the temple (1Ki 8:1-3; 2Ch 5:2-4). Counsels king Rehoboam (1Ki 12:6-8, 13). Counsels king Ahab (1Ki 20:7, 8). Josiah assembles, to hear the law of the Lord (2Ki 23:1; 2Ch 34:29, 30).

Legislates with Ezra in reforming certain marriages with the heathen (Ezr 9:1; 10:8-14). Legislates in later times (M't 15:2, 7-9; M'k 7:1-13). Sits as a court (Jer 26:10-24). Constitutes, with priests and scribes, a court for the trial of both civil and ecclesiastical causes (M't 21:23; 26:3-5, 57-68; 27:1, 2; M'k 8:31; 14:43, 53-65; 15:1; Lu 22:52-54, 66-71; Ac 4:1-21; 6:9-15). Unfaithful to the city (La 1:19). Seeks counsel from prophets (Eze 8:1; 14:1; 20:1, 3). Corrupt (1Ki 21:8-14; Eze 8:11, 12; M't 26:14, 15 w 27:3, 4).

A similar senate existed among the Egyptians (Ge 50:7); and among the Midianites and Moabites (Nu 22:4, 7); and Gibeonites (Jos 9:11).

Executive Officers of Tribes and Cities, called Princes or Nobles, Members of the National Assembly (Nu 1:4-16, 44; 7:2, 3, 10, 11, 18, 24, 54, 84; 10:4; 16:2; 17:2, 6; 27:2; 31:13, 14; 32:2; 34:18-29; 36:1; Jos 9:15-21; 17:4; 22:13-32; 1Ki 21:11-14; Ne 3:9, 12, 16, 18, 19).

The Mosiac Judicial System, see Court; Judge; Levites; Priests; Ruler; Sanhedrin; Synagogue.

Ecclesiastical: See Church, Government of; Church and State; Priests.

Imperial (Ge 14:1; Jos 11:10; 1Ki 4:21; Es 1:1; Da 4:1; 6:1-3; Lu 2:1).

Monarchical: Tyranny in: By Pharaoh (Ex 1:8-22; 2:23, 24; 3:7; 5:1-10). By Saul (1Sa 22:6, 12-19). By David (2Sa 11:14-17). By Solomon (1Ki 2:23-25, 28-34, 36-46). By Rehoboam (1Ki 12:1-16). By Ahab and Jezebel (1Ki 21:7-16). By Jehu (2Ki 10:1-14). By Ahasuerus (Es 1:11, 12, 19-22; 3:6-15; 8:8-13). By Nebuchadnezzar (Da 1:10; 2:5-13; 5:19). By Herod (M'k 6:27, 28).

Municipal: Devolving on a local senate and executive officers (De 19:12; 21:2-8, 18-21; 22:13-21; 25:7-9; Jos 20:4; J'g 8:14-16; 11:5-11; Ru 4:2-11; 1Sa 11:3; 16:4; 30:26; 1Ki 21:8-14; 2Ki 10:1-7; Ezr 10:8, 14; Ne 3:9, 12, 16, 18, 19; La 5:14).

Patriarchal (Ge 27:29, 37).

Provincial (Ezr 4:8, 9; 5:3, 6; 6:6; 8:36; Ne 2:7, 9; 5:14; Da 6:1-3; M't 27:2; 28:14; Lu 2:2; 3:1; Ac 24:1).

Representative (De 1:13-15; Jos 9:11). See Delegated, Senatorial Council, above.

Theocratic (Ex 19:3-8; De 26:16-19; 29:1-13; J'g 8:23; 1Sa 8:6, 7; 10:19; 12:12; Isa 33:22).

See God, Sovereign; Jesus, Kingdom of.

GOZAN. A city located in NE Mesopotamia on the Habor River, to which the Israelites were deported by the Assyrians (2Ki 17:6; 18:11; 19:12; 1Ch 5:26).

GRACE, a term employed by the Biblical writers with a wide variety of meaning: charm, sweetness, loveliness (Ps 45:2); the attitude of God toward men (Tit 2:11); the method of salvation (Eph 2:5); the opposite of legalism (Ga 5:4); the impartation of spiritual power or gifts (1Co 12:6; 2Ti 2:1); the liberty which God gives to men (Jude 4).

Before meals, see Prayer, Before Food; Thanksgiving, Before Food.

GRACE OF GOD. Unmerited favor (De 7:7, 8; 2Ch 30:9; Eph 1:6; Tit 2:11; Heb 4:16). Abundant (1Ti 1:14). No warrant for sinful indulgence (Ro 6:1, 15).

Divine help (Ge 20:6; Job 10:12; Ps 84:11; 94:17-19; 138:3; 1Co 10:13; 2Co 1:12; 12:9; 1Pe 1:5).

Growth in (Ps 84:7; Pr 4:18; Ph'p 1:6, 9-11; 3:12-15; Col 1:10, 11; 2:19; 1Th 3:10, 12, 13; 2Th 1:3; Heb 6:1, 3; 1Pe 2:1-3; 2Pe 3:18). Believers to be stewards of (1Pe 4:10).

Intercessory prayer for (Ps 143:11; Da 9:18; Joh 17:11, 12, 15; 1Th 1:1; 5:28; 2Pe 1:2). Exhortation against rejecting (2Co 6:1, 2). With respect to Jacob and Esau (Ro 9:10-16).

Manifested: In drawing men to Christ (Joh 6:44, 45); redemption (Eph 1:5-9,

11, 12); justification (Ge 15:6; Ro 3:22-24; 4:4, 5, 16; 5:2, 6-8, 15-21; Tit 3:7); passing over transgressions (Nu 23:20, 21; Ne 9:17; Ro 3:25); salvation (Ro 11:5, 6; Eph 2:8, 9; 2Ti 1:9); calling to service (Ga 1:15, 16); spiritual growth (Eph 3:16); spiritual gifts (1Co 1:4-8; Eph 4:7, 11).

Manifested: In character and conduct (2Co 1:12; Ph'p 2:13); the character and conduct of the righteous (1Co 15:10; 2Co 1:12; Ph'p 2:13); sustaining the righteous (1Ch 17:8; Da 10:18, 19; 2Co 12:9; 1Pe 1:5; 5:10; Jude 24); sustaining in temptation (Ge 20:6; 1Co 10:13; Re 3:10).

Manifestations of: To Enoch (Ge 5:24). To Noah (Ge 6:8, 17, 18). To Abraham (Ge 12:2; 21:22). To Ishmael (Ge 21:20). To Isaac (Ge 26:24). To Jacob (Ge 46:3, 4; 48:16). To Joseph (Ge 39:2, 3, 23). To Moses (Ex 3:12; 33:12-17). To Israel (De 4:7). To Naphtali (De 33:23). To Joshua (Jos 1:5, 9). To Job (Job 10:12). To David (1Sa 25:26, 34; 2Sa 7:8-16). To Daniel (Da 10:18, 19). To Jeremiah (Jer 15:20). To the righteous (Ps 5:12; Ac 4:33).

See God, Grace of.

GRACES. Christian (M't 5:3-11; Ro 5:3-5; 1Co 13:1-8, 13; Ga 5:22, 23; 1Pe 1:5-9).

See Character; Charitableness; Courage; Gentleness; Hope; Kindness; Knowledge; Longsuffering; Love; Meekness; Mercy; Patience; Peace; Perseverance; Purity; Righteousness, Fruits of; Stability; Temperance; Wisdom.

GRAFF, GRAFT, a horticultural process by which the branches of a cultivated tree may be inserted into the trunk of a wild tree (Ro 11:17ff.).

GRAIN (See Plants.)

GRANARY, a storehouse for grain and other dry crops (M't 3:12; Lu 3:17). See Garner.

GRANDFATHER, called Father (Ge 10:21).

GRAPE. Cultivated in vineyards, by Noah (Ge 9:20); the Canaanites (Nu 13:24; De 6:11; Jos 24:13); Edomites (Nu 20:17); Amorites (Nu 21:22; Isa 16:8, 9); Philistines (J'g 15:5). Grown, at Abel (J'g 11:33 [marg.]); Baal-hamon (Song 8:11); Carmel (2Ch 26:10); Engedi (Song 1:14); Jezreel (1Ki 21:1); Lebanon (Ho 14:7); Samaria (Jer 31:5); Shechem (J'g 9:27); Shiloh (J'g 21:20, 21); Timnath (J'g 14:5).

Culture of (Le 25:3, 11; De 28:39; 2Ch 26:10; Song 6:11; Isa 5:1; Jer 31:5).

Wine made of (Jer 25:30). Wine of, forbidden to Nazarites (Nu 6:4). See Nazarites.

See Vine; Vineyards; Wine.

Figurative: De 32:32; Ps 128:3; Jer 2:21; Eze 15; Ho 10:1; Re 14:18-20.

Fable of (J'g 9:12, 13).

Parables of the Vine (Ps 80:8-14; Eze 17:6-10; 9:10-14; Joh 15:1-5).

Proverb of (Eze 18:2).

See Vine; Vineyards; Wine.

GRASS. Created on the third creative day (Ge 1:11). Mown (Ps 72:6). God's care of (M't 6:30; Lu 12:28). On roofs of houses (Ps 129:6).

Figurative: Ps 90:5, 6; Isa 40:6; 1Pe 1:24; Jas 1:10, 11.

GRASSHOPPER (Nu 13:33; Ec 12:5; Isa 40:22; Na 3:17).

See Locust.

GRATE, a copper network, placed under the top of the great altar, to hold the sacrifice while burning (Ex 27:4; 35:16; 38:4, 5).

GRATITUDE (See Thankfulness.)

GRAVE. Prepared by Jacob (Ge 50:5). Defilement from touching (Nu 19:16, 18). Weeping at (2Sa 3:32; Joh 11:31; 20:11). Of parents, honored (2Sa 19:37). Welcomed (Job 3:20-22). Resurrection from: Of Lazarus (Joh 11:43, 44; 12:17); of Jesus (M't 28:5, 6; 1Co 15:12-20); of saints after Jesus' resurrection (M't 27:52, 53); of all the dead foretold (Joh 5:28; 1Co 15:22-54).

See Burial.

GRAVE CLOTHES. Preparatory to burial, the body was washed and anointed with spices, then wrapped in a winding sheet, bound with gravebands, and the head wrapped in a square cloth (Joh 11:44; 19:40).

GRAVEL. *Figurative:* Pr 20:17.

GRAVEN IMAGE, a carved image of wood, stone, or metal, generally used as an idol (Isa 44:9-17; 45:20; De 7:5).

GRAVING (See Engraving.)

GREAT OWL (See Birds.)

GREAT SEA (See Mediterranean Sea.)

GREATNESS, Of God (De 3:24; Ps 77:13; 95:3; 104:1; 135:5; 145:3; Isa

12:6; Jer 32:18; Mal 1:11). Of Christ (Isa 53:12; 63:1; M't 12:6; Lu 11:31; Ph'p 2:9, 10).

GREAVES (1Sa 17:6).

GREECE. Inhabitants of, called Gentiles (M'k 7:26; Joh 7:35; Ro 2:10; 3:9; 1Co 10:32; 12:13); desire to see Jesus (Joh 12:20-23); marry among the Jews (Ac 16:1); accept the Messiah (Ac 17:2-4, 12, 34); persecute the early Christians (Ac 6:9-14; 9:29; 18:17). Gentiles called Greeks (Ro 10:12; Ga 3:28; Col 3:11).

Schools of philosophy in Athens (Ac 19:9). Philosophy of (1Co 1:22, 23). Poets of (Ac 17:28).

See Athens; Epicureans; Stoicism.

GREED (See Covetousness.)

GREEK LANGUAGE was a branch of the Indo-European family from which most of the languages of Europe are descended. The Attic dialect spoken in Athens and its colonies on the Ionian coast was combined with other dialects in the army of Alexander the Great, and was spread by his conquests through the East. Greek was widely spoken in Palestine, and became the chief language of the early church (Ac 21:37).

GREEK VERSIONS. There are four translations of the Hebrew OT into Greek: (1) the Septuagint, originating in Alexandria about 275 B. C.; (2) the version of Aquila (c. A. D. 125), produced by the Jews when Christians took over the Septuagint; (3) the version of Theodotion, a second century revision of the Septuagint; and (4) the version of Symmachus, an idiomatic translation, probably of the second century.

GREYHOUND (Pr 30:31).

GRIEF, attributed to the Holy Spirit (Eph 4:30; Heb 3:10, 17). See Affliction; Sorrow.

GRIND, to pulverize grain between two millstones (M't 24:41; Lu 17:35).

GROUND. Man made from (Ge 2:7; 3:19, 23; Job 4:19; 33:6). Animals from (Ge 2:19). Vegetables from (Ge 2:9).

Cursed (Ge 3:17; 5:29).

GROVES [*R. V.* Asheroth, Asherah, Asherine, and in Ge 21:33 tamarisk tree], probably an image or images of the Canaanitish goddess Asherah.

See Ashtoreth.

Forbidden to be established (De 16:21; Isa 1:29; 17:8; 27:9; Mic 5:14). Worshiped by Israelites (J'g 3:7; 1Ki 14:15, 23; 15:13; 18:19; 2Ki 13:6; 17:10, 16; 21:3-7; 2Ch 24:18; Jer 17:2).

Destroyed by Gideon (J'g 6:28); Hezekiah (2Ki 18:4); Josiah (2Ki 23:14; 2Ch 34:3, 4); Asa (2Ch 14:3); Jehoshaphat (2Ch 17:6; 19:3).

See Idolatry.

GUARD, the translation of a number of Hebrew and Greek words:
(1) *tabbah*, slaughterer (Ge 37:36; 2Ki 25:8; Da 2:14);
(2) *ruts*, runner, trusted messengers of a king (1Ki 14:27, 28);
(3) *mishmar*, watch (Ne 4:22);
(4) *mishma'ath*, guard (2Sa 23:23);
(5) *spekoulator*, "executioner," a guard, a spy (M'k 6:27);
(6) *koustodia*, watch (M't 27:65).

GUDGODAH (cleft). A station of the Israelites in the wilderness (De 10:7); probably identical with Hor-Hagidgad in Nu 33:32, 33.

GUEST. Salutations to (Ge 18:2). Abraham's hospitality to (see Hospitality). Rules for the conduct of (Pr 23:1-3, 6-8; 25:6, 7, 17; Lu 10:5-7; 14:7-11; 1Co 10:27).

See Hospitality.

GUEST CHAMBER, a room in which to eat (1Sa 9:22; M'k 14:14; Lu 22:11).

GUIDANCE (See God, Guidance of.)

GUILE (See Conspiracy; Deceit; Fraud; Hypocrisy.)

GUILELESSNESS. Enjoined (Ps 34:13; 1Pe 2:1; 3:10). Of Jesus (1Pe 2:22). Of Nathanael (Joh 1:47). A grace of the righteous (Ps 32:2).

GUILT, the deserving of punishment because of infraction of a law. Guilt could be the result of unconscious sin (Le 5:17), or could be incurred by the group for the sin of an individual (Jos 7:10-15). There are degrees of guilt (Lu 12:47, 48; Ac 17:30), but in the sight of God all men are guilty of sin (Ro 3:19).

See Conviction of Sin.

GUNI. 1. Son of Naphtali (Ge 46:24; Nu 26:48; 1Ch 7:13).

2. Father of Abdiel (1Ch 5:15).

GUNITE, of the family of Guni (Nu 26:48).

GUR, place where Jehu slew Ahaziah (2Ki 9:27).

GUR-BAAL (sojourn of Baal), a town

probably located S of Beersheba (2Ch 26:7).

GUTTER, the channel or tunnel through which David's soldiers obtained access to the Jebusite fortress of Jerusalem (2Sa 5:8).

H

HAAHASHTARI, son of Naarah (1Ch 4:6).

HABAIAH (Jehovah has hidden), priest whose descendants were excluded from priesthood (Ezr 2:61).

HABAKKUK (embrace), prophet of the book which bears his name; wrote when the temple was still standing (2:20; 3:19), between c. 605-587 B. C., probably during the reign of the Judean king Jehoiakim. Outline. 1. Perplexity of the prophet as to why the sinful Jews are not punished, and why God should use a heathen nation to punish the Jews (1).

2. God's answer that the proud Chaldeans will themselves be punished (2).

3. Prayer of Habakkuk (3).

HABAZINIAH, head of the family of Rechabites (Jer 35:3).

HABERGEON, a part of the defensive armor of a soldier (Ex 28:32; 39:23).

See Breastplate.

HABIRU, a people mentioned in Mari, Nuzi, and Amarna tablets; fundamental meaning seems to be "wanderers"; of mixed racial origin, including both Semites and non-Semites. Connection with Hebrews is obscure.

HABIT (Jer 13:23; 22:21; Mic 2:1).

HABOR, a river of Mesopotamia (2Ki 17:6; 18:11; 1Ch 5:26).

HACHALIAH, father of Nehemiah (Ne 1:1; 10:1).

HACHILAH, a hill in Judah where David and his followers hid from Saul (1Sa 23:19; 26:3).

HACHMON (wise), father of Jehiel and Jashobeam (1Ch 27:32; 11:11).

HADAD (fierceness). 1. Grandson of Abraham (Ge 25:15; KJV has Hadar).

2. Early king of Edom (1Ch 1:50).

3. Earlier king of Edom (Ge 36:35; 1Ch 1:46).

4. Edomite prince (1Ki 11:14-25).

5. Supreme god of Syria—deity of storm and thunder.

HADADEZER, called also Hadarezer. King of Zobah, vanquished by David (2Sa 8:3-13; 10:15-19; 1Ki 11:23; 1Ch 18:3-10; 19:6-19).

HADADRIMMON, a place in the valley of Megiddon (Zec 12:11).

HADAR. 1. Son of Ishmael (Ge 25:15).

2. King of Edom (Ge 36:39).

See Hadad.

HADAREZER (See Hadadezer.)

HADASHAH, a town in Judah (Jos 15:37).

HADASSAH (a myrtle), Jewish name of Esther (Es 2:7).

See Esther.

HADATTAH, probably an adjective qualifying Hazor, making it equivalent to New Hazor (Jos 15:25).

HADES. The unseen world, translated hell in KJV, but in the *R.V.* the word Hades is retained (M't 11:23; 16:18; Lu 10:15; 16:23; Ac 2:27, 31; Re 1:18; 6:8; 20:13, 14).

Realm (or State) of the Dead. Usually expressed in Hebrew by Sheol and in Greek by Hades (2Sa 22:6; Job 26:5; Ps 6:5; 17:15; 30:9; 49:15; 86:13; 88:10-12; 115:17; 116:3; Pr 15:24; 21:16; 27:20; Ec 9:4-6; Isa 5:14; Jon 2:2; Lu 23:42, 43; Joh 8:22; 2Co 12:4).

See Hell; Immortality; Paradise; Righteous, Future State of; Sheol; Spirit; Wicked, Punishment of.

HADID (sharp), a city of Benjamin. Captives of, returned from Babylon (Ezr 2:33; Ne 7:37; 11:34).

HADLAI (ceasing, forbearing), father of Amasa (2Ch 28:12).

HADORAM. 1. Descendant of Shem (Ge 10:27; 1Ch 1:21).

2. Son of Ton, or Toi (1Ch 18:10). Called Joram (2Sa 8:10).

3. Chief officer of the tribute under Rehoboam (2Ch 10:18). Probably identical with Adoniram of 1Ki 4:6; 5:14; and Adoram of 2Sa 20:24.

HADRACH, a district of Syria (Zec 9:1).

HAGAB (locust), ancestor of Nethinim who returned with Zerubbabel (Ezr 2:46).

HAGABA, called also Hagabah. One of the Nethinim (Ezr 2:45; Ne 7:48).

HAGAR (emigration, flight), a servant of Abraham and handmaid of Sarah. Given by Sarah to Abraham to be his wife (Ge 16). Descendants of (Ge 25:12-15; 1Ch 5:10, 19-22; Ps 83:6). Called Agar (Ga 4:24, 25).

HAGARENES, HAGARITES, descendants of Ishmael with whom Saul made war (1Ch 5:10; 18:22; 27:31).

HAGGAI (festal), prophet to the Jews in 520 B. C., little known of his personal history; contemporary with Zechariah and Darius Hystaspes. Outline. 1. Call and encouragement to build (1).

2. The Messianic hope (2).

HAGGERI (wanderer), father of Mibhar (1Ch 11:38).

HAGGI (festal), son of Gad (Ge 46:16; Nu 26:15).

HAGGIAH (a festival of Jehovah), a Levite (1Ch 6:30).

HAGGITH (festal), wife of David. Mother of Adonijah (2Sa 3:4; 1Ki 1:5, 11; 2:13; 1Ch 3:2).

HAGIOGRAPHA (holy writings), 3rd division of Heb OT: Psalms, Proverbs, Job, Song of Solomon, Ruth, Lamentations, Ecclesiastes, Esther, Daniel, Ezra, Nehemiah, 1 and 2 Chronicles.

HAI (the heap). 1. Town E of Bethel and near Bethaven (Ge 12:8; 13:3; Jos 7, 8). Spelled Ai in KJV.

2. City of the Ammonites (Jer 49:3).

HAIL (Job 38:22; Hag 2:17). Plague of, in Egypt (Ex 9:18-29; Ps 78:48; 105:32). Destroys army of the Amorites (Jos 10:11).

Figurative: Isa 28:2; Re 8:7; 11:19; 16:21.

HAIR. Numbered (M't 10:30; Lu 12:7). Worn long by women (Isa 3:24; Lu 7:38; 1Co 11:5, 6, 15; 1Ti 2:9; 1Pe 3:3; Re 9:8); by Absalom (2Sa 14:26). Worn short by men (1Co 11:14). Symbolical dividing of (Eze 5:1, 2).

See Baldness; Caul; Leprosy; Mourning; Nazarite.

HAKKATAN (the little one), father of Johanan (Ezr 8:12).

HAKKOZ (the nimble), KJV sometimes has Koz, once Coz. 1. Descendant of Aaron (1Ch 24:10; Ezr 2:61; Ne 3:4, 21).

2. Judahite (1Ch 4:8).

HAKUPHA (bent, bowed), one of the Nethinim (Ezr 2:51; Ne 7:53).

HALAH, a place to which Israelite captives were transported (2Ki 17:6; 18:11; 1Ch 5:26).

HALAK, (smooth), a mountain, the southern limit of Joshua's conquests (Jos 11:17; 12:7).

HALF-HOMER, a measure of about seven or eight gallons.

See Measure, Dry.

HALHUL, a city in Judah (Jos 15:58).

HALI (ornament), a border town of Asher (Jos 19:25).

HALL. 1. Court of the high priest's palace (Lu 22:55).

2. Official residence of a Roman governor (M't 27:27; M'k 15:16).

HALLEL (praise). Pss 113-118 called the "Egyptian Hallel"; Ps 136, "the Hallel." Pss 120-136 often called the "Great Hallel."

HALLELUJAH (praise ye Jehovah), liturgical ejaculation urging all to praise Jehovah. Occurs at the beginning of Psalms 106, 111-113, 117, 135, 146-150 and at the close of 104-106, 113, 115-117, 135, 146-150.

HALOHESH (the whisperer), called also Hallohesh. Father of Shallum (Ne 3:12). Sealed the covenant with Nehemiah (Ne 10:24).

HALLOW (to render or **treat as holy),** to set apart for sacred use; to hold sacred; to reverence as holy (Ex 20:11; M't 6:9).

HAM. 1. Son of Noah (Ge 5:32; 9:18, 24; 1Ch 1:4). Provokes his father's wrath and is cursed by him (Ge 9:18-27). His children (Ge 10:6-20; 1Ch 1:8-16).

2. Patronymic of the descendants of Ham (1Ch 4:40; Ps 78:51; 105:23, 27; 106:22).

3. Place where Chedorlaomer smote the Zuzims (Ge 14:5).

HAMAN, prime minister of Ahasuerus, king of Persia (Es 3:1, 10; 7:7-10).

HAMATH (fortification), called also Hemath. A city of upper Syria (Nu 13:21; 34:8; Jos 13:5; 1Ki 8:65; Eze 47:16). Inhabited by Canaanites (Ge 10:18). Prosperity of (Am 6:2). David receives gifts of gold and silver from Toi, king of (2Sa 8:9, 10; 1Ch 18:3, 9, 10). Conquest of, by Jeroboam (2Ki 14:25, 28); by the Chaldeans (2Ki 25:20, 21). Israelites taken captive to (Isa 11:11). Prophecy concerning (Jer 49:23). Solomon builds store cities in (2Ch 8:4).

HAMATH-ZOBAH, a town on the border of Palestine. Subdued by Solomon (2Ch 8:3).

HAMATH (hot spring). 1. Fortified city of Naphtali, c. 1 mile S of Tiberias (Jos 19:35).

2. Founder of Rechabites (RSV 1Ch 2:55).

HAMMEDATHA, father of Haman (Es 3:1, 10; 8:5; 9:10, 24).

HAMMELECH, name of a man, or possibly only an appellation, meaning "the king" (Jer 36:26; 38:6).

HAMMER, a tool used for a variety of purposes: smoothing metals (Isa 41:7), driving tent pins (J'g 4:21), forging (Isa 44:12), etc. Sometimes used figuratively for any crushing power (Jer 23:29; 50:23).

HAMMOLEKETH (the queen), daughter of Machir (1Ch 7:17, 18).

HAMMON (hot spring). 1. A city of Asher (Jos 19:28).

2. A Levitical city of Naphtali (1Ch 6:76). Possibly identical with Hammath and Hammothdor, which see.

HAMMOTH-DOR (warm springs of Dor), Naphtali (Jos 21:32). Possibly identical with Hammath (Jos 19:35). Called Hammon (1Ch 6:76).

HAMMURABI, king of Babylon (1728-1686 B.C.); not the same as Amraphel of Ge 14:1-12; great builder and lawgiver (Code of Hammurabi).

HAMONAH (multitude), prophetic name of city near which Gog is defeated (Eze 39:16).

HAMON-GOG, VALLEY OF (multitude of God), prophetic name for place E of Dead Sea where "multitude of Gog" will be buried (Eze 39:11-15).

HAMOR (ass), father of Shechem. Jacob buys ground from (Ge 33:19; Jos 24:32; J'g 9:28). Murdered by the sons of Jacob (Ge 34:26; 49:6). Called Emmor (Ac 7:16).

HAMUEL (warmth of God), a Simeonite (1Ch 4:26).

HAMUL (pitied, spared), son of Pharez (Ge 46:12; Nu 26:21; 1Ch 2:5).

HAMUTAL (father-in-law is dew), wife of Josiah; mother of Jehoahaz and Zedekiah (2Ki 23:31; 24:18; Jer 52:1).

HANAMEEL, cousin of Jeremiah, to whom he sold a field in Anathoth (Jer 32:7-12).

HANAN (gracious). 1. Son of Shashak (1Ch 8:23).

2. Son of Azel (1Ch 8:38; 9:44).

3. One of David's mighty men (1Ch 11:43).

4. One of the Nethinim (Ezr 2:46; Ne 7:49).

5. A Levite (Ne 8:7; 10:10). Probably identical with the one mentioned in Ne 13:13.

6. A chief who sealed the covenant with Nehemiah (Ne 10:22, 26).

7. An officer in the temple (Jer 35:2-10).

HANANEEL (God is gracious), name of a tower forming part of the wall of Jerusalem (Ne 3:1; 12:39; Jer 31:38; Zec 14:10).

HANANI (gracious). 1. Son of Heman (1Ch 25:4, 25).

2. A prophet who rebuked Asa, king of Judah (2Ch 16:7).

3. Father of Jehu the prophet (1Ki 16:1, 7; 2Ch 19:2; 20:34). Possibly identical with 2.

4. A priest (Ezr 10:20).

5. A brother of Nehemiah and keeper of the gates of Jerusalem (Ne 1:2; 7:2).

6. A priest and musician (Ne 12:36).

HANANIAH (Jehovah is gracious). 1. Son of Heman (1Ch 25:4, 23).

2. A captain of Uzziah's army (2Ch 26:11).

3. Father of Zedekiah (Jer 36:12).

4. A prophet of Gibeon who uttered false prophecies in the temple during the reign of Zedekiah (Jer 28).

5. Grandfather of Irijah (Jer 37:13).

6. Son of Shashak (1Ch 8:24).

7. Hebrew name of Shadrach, which see.

8. Son of Zerubbabel (1Ch 3:19, 21).

9. Son of Bebai (Ezr 10:28).

10. An apothecary and priest (Ne 3:8).

11. Son of Shelemiah (Ne 3:30).

12. A keeper of the gates of Jerusalem (Ne 7:2).

13. One who sealed the covenant (Ne 10:23).

14. A priest in time of Jehoiakim (Ne 12:12, 41).

HAND. Imposition of hands (Heb 6:2); in consecration (Ge 48:14; Ex 29:10, 15, 19; Le 1:4; 3:2, 8, 13; 4:15, 24, 33; 16:21); in ordaining the Levites (Nu 8:10, 11); Joshua (Nu 27:18-23; De 34:9); Timothy (1Ti 4:14; 2Ti 1:6); in healing (M'k 6:5; 7:32; 16:18; Lu 4:40; Ac 28:8); in blessing children (M't 19:13; M'k 10:16); in solemnizing testimony (Le 24:14). Lifted up in benediction (Le 9:22; Lu 24:50); in prayer, see Prayer, Attitudes in.

Ceremonial washing of (M't 15:2; M'k 7:2-5). See Ablutions; Clean.

Symbolical of righteousness (Job 17:9). Washing of, a symbol of innocency (De 21:6; M't 27:24).

Clasping of, in token of contract (Ezr 10:19; Pr 6:1; 17:18; La 5:6; Eze 17:18); of friendship (2Ki 10:15; Job 17:3). Right hand lifted up in swearing (Ge 14:22; Ps 106:26; Isa 62:8); symbol of power (Isa 23:11; 41:10); place of honor (Ps 45:9; 80:17).

Figurative: (M't 5:30; 18:8; M'k 9:43). Anthropomorphic use of: Hand of the Lord waxed short (Nu 11:23); is mighty (Jos 4:24); was heavy (1Sa 5:6); against the Philistines (1Sa 7:13); on Elijah (1Ki 18:46); not shortened (Isa 59:1); was with the early Christians (Ac 11:21). For extended anthropomorphisms consult concordances under the word hand.

See Anthropomorphisms.

HANDBREADTH, a measure, about four inches (Ex 25:25; 1Ki 7:26; 2Ch 4:5; Ps 39:5; Isa 48:13; Eze 40:5, 43; Jer 52:21).

See Span, Fingerbreadth.

HANDICRAFT, trade requiring manual skill.

HANDKERCHIEF, sometimes translated "napkin," used for a variety of purposes (Lu 19:20-23; Joh 11:44; 20:7; Ac 19:12).

HANDLE, door knob (Song 5:5).

HANDMAID or **HANDMAIDEN,** female slave or servant.

HANDS, IMPOSITION OF, a ceremony having the idea of transference, identification, and devotion to God (Ex 29:10, 15, 19; Le 16:21; Ac 8:14-17; 2Ti 1:6).

HANDSTAFF, rod carried in hand (Eze 39:9).

HANES, a place in Egypt (Isa 30:4).

HANGING, not a form of capital punishment in Bible times. Where used, except in 2Sa 17:23; M't 27:5, it refers to the suspension of a body from a tree or post after the criminal had been put to death (Ge 40:19, 22; De 21:22).

HANGINGS, material hung in the tabernacle so as to preserve the privacy and sacredness of that which was within (Ex 27:9-19; M't 27:51).

HANIEL (grace of God). An Asherite (1Ch 7:39).

HANNAH (grace), mother of Samuel. Her trials and prayer, and promise (1Sa 1:1-18). Samuel born to, dedicates him to God, leaves him at the temple (1Sa 1:19-28). Her hymn of praise (1Sa 2:1-10). Visits Samuel at the temple from year to year (1Sa 2:18, 19). Children of (1Sa 2:20, 21).

HANNATHON, a city of Zebulun (Jos 19:14).

HANNIEL (the favor of God). 1. A son of Ephod, appointed by Moses to divide the land among the several tribes (Nu 34:23).

2. A son of Ulla (called Haniel in 1Ch 7:39).

HANOCH (initiation). 1. Grandson of Abraham by Keturah (Ge 25:4; 1Ch 1:33).

2. Son of Reuben (Ge 46:9; Ex 6:14; 1Ch 5:3).

HANUN (favored). 1. King of Ammon who provoked David to war (2Sa 10:1-5; 1Ch 19:1-5).

2. Two men who helped repair wall of Jerusalem (Ne 3:13, 30).

HAPHRAIM (two pits), a city of Issachar (Jos 19:19).

HAPPINESS. *Of the Wicked:* Limited to this life (Ps 17:14; Lu 16:25); short (Job 20:5); uncertain (Lu 12:20); vain (Ec 2:1; 7:6).

Is derived from their wealth (Job 21:13; Ps 52:7); their power (Job 21:7; Ps 37:35); their worldly prosperity (Ps 17:14; 73:3, 4, 7); gluttony (Isa 22:13; Hab 1:16); drunkenness (Isa 5:11; 56:12); vain pleasure (Job 21:12; Isa 5:12); successful oppression (Hab 1:15). Marred by jealousy (Es 5:13); often interrupted by judgments (Nu 11:33; Job 15:21; Ps 73:18-20; Jer 25:10, 11). Leads to sorrow (Pr 14:13). Leads to recklessness (Isa 22:12). Sometimes a stumbling-block to saints (Ps 73:3, 16; Jer 12:1; Hab 1:13). Saints often permitted to see the end of (Ps 73:17-20); envy not (Ps 37:1). Woe against (Am 6:1; Lu 6:25).

Illustrated (Ps 37:35, 36; Lu 12:16-20; 16:19-25).

Exemplified: Israel (Nu 11:33). Haman (Es 5:9-11). Belshazzar (Da 5:1). Herod (Ac 12:21-23).

Of the righteous: In the Lord, through abundance (Ps 36:8; Ec 2:24-26; 3:12, 13, 22); chastisement (Job 5:17-27); fellowship (Ps 133:1); good works (Pr 14:21; Ec 3:12; M't 5:3-9); hope (Ro

5:2); obedience (Ps 40:8; 128:1, 2; 144:15; 146:5; Pr 16:20; 28:14; 29:18); peace (Ph'p 4:7); persecution (M't 3:10, 11; 2Co 12:10; 1Pe 3:14; 4:12); protection (De 33:29; Isa 12:2, 3); satisfaction (Ps 63:5); trust (Pr 16:20); wisdom (Pr 3:13-18).

Beatitudes (M't 5:3-12).

See Joy; Peace; Praise.

HARA, place in Assyria to which Israelites were exiled by Assyrians (1Ch 5:26).

HARADAH (terror), one of the camps of Israel (Nu 33:24, 25).

HARAN (mountaineer). 1. Father of Lot and brother of Abraham (Ge 11:26-31).

2. Son of Caleb (1Ch 2:46).

3. A Levite (1Ch 23:9).

4. Called also Charran. A place in Mesopotamia to which Terah and Abraham migrated (Ge 11:31; 12:4, 5; Ac 7:4). Death of Terah at (Ge 11:32). Abraham leaves, by divine command (Ge 12:1-5). Jacob flees to (Ge 27:43; 28:7; 29); returns from, with Rachel and Leah (Ge 31:17-21). Conquest of, by king of Assyria (2Ki 19:12). Merchants of (Eze 27:23). Idolatry in (Jos 24:2, 14; Isa 37:12).

HARARITE (mountain dweller), area in hill country of either Judah or Ephraim (2Sa 23:11, 33; 1Ch 11:34).

HARBONA, HARBONAH (ass driver), chamberlain of Ahasuerus (Es 1:10; 7:9).

HARE, forbidden as food (Le 11:6; De 14:7).

HAREM, Persian household (Es 2:3, 13, 14).

HAREPH (scornful), son of Caleb (1Ch 2:51).

HARETH, a forest in which David found refuge from Saul (1Sa 22:5).

HARHAIAH, father of Uzziel (Ne 3:8).

HARHAS, grandfather of the husband of Huldah, the prophetess (2Ki 22:14). Called Hasrah (2Ch 34:22).

HARHUR (fever), head of family that returned with Zerubbabel (Ezr 2:51; Ne 7:53).

HARIM (consecrated). 1. Priest (1Ch 24:8).

2. Family that returned with Zerubbabel (Ezr 2:39; Ne 7:35).

3. Family of priests (Ezr 2:39; 10:21; Ne 7:42; 12:15).

4. Family that married foreign wives (Ezr 10:31).

5. Father of worker on the wall (Ne 4:11).

6. Man who sealed covenant (Ne 10:27).

HARIPH (autumn). 1. One of the exiles (Ne 7:24). Probably the same as Jorah (Ezr 2:18).

2. One who sealed the covenant (Ne 10:19).

HARLOT. Shamelessness of (Pr 2:16; 7:11-27; 9:13-18). Machinations of (Pr 7:10; 9:14-17; Isa 23:15, 16; Ho 2:13). To be shunned (Pr 5:3-20; 7:25-27). Hire of, not to be received at the temple (De 23:18).

Rahab (Jos 2:3-6; 6:17, 23, 25; Heb 11:31).

See Adultery; Harlotry.

HARLOTRY, forbidden (Le 19:29; De 23:17).

Punishment of (Le 21:9).

See Adultery; Whoredom.

HARNEPHER, Asherite (1Ch 7:36).

HAROD (trembling), spring beside which Gideon encamped (J'g 7:1).

HARODITE, patronymic of Shammah and Elika (2Sa 23:25).

HAROEH (the seer), grandson of Caleb (1Ch 2:52).

HAROSHETH OF THE GENTILES, town in N Palestine c. 16 miles NW of Megiddo; home of Sisera (J'g 4:2, 13, 16).

HARP, a stringed instrument of music (Isa 38:20; Eze 33:32; Hab 3:19). With three strings (1Sa 18:6 [marg.]); ten strings (Ps 33:2; 92:3; 144:9; 150:4). Originated with Jubal (Ge 4:21). Made of almug wood (1Ki 10:12). David skilful in manipulating (1Sa 16:16, 23). Used in worship (1Sa 10:5; 1Ch 16:5; 25:1-7; 2Ch 5:12, 13; 29:25; Ps 33:2; 43:4; 49:4; 57:8; 71:22; 81:2; 93:3; 98:5; 108:2; 147:7; 149:3; 150:3). Used, in national jubilees, after the triumph over Goliath (1Sa 18:6 [marg.]); over the armies of Ammon and Moab (2Ch 20:28, w verses 20-29); when the new walls of Jerusalem were dedicated (Ne 12:27, 36). Used in festivities (Ge 31:27; Job 21:11, 12; Isa 5:12; 23:16; 24:8; 30:32; Eze 26:13; Re 18:22); in mourning (Job 30:31). Discordant (1Co 14:7). Hung on the willows by the captive Jews (Ps 137:2). Heard in heaven, in John's apocalyptic vision (Re 5:8; 14:2; 15:2). The symbol used in the psalmody to indicate when the harp was to be introduced in the music was Neginoth (see titles of Pss 4; 6; 54; 55; 61; 67; 76).

See Music, Instruments of.

HARROW, instrument for dragging or leveling off a field (Job 39:10; "breaking clods," Isa 28:24; Ho 10:11).

HARROWS, instrument of iron to cut conquered peoples (2Sa 12:31; 1Ch 20:3).

HARSHA (dumb, silent), one of the Nethinim (Ezr 2:52; Ne 7:54).

HART (See Deer.)

HARUM (made high), a descendant of Judah (1Ch 4:8).

HARUMAPH, father of Jedaiah (Ne 3:10).

HARUPHITE, designation of Shephatiah (1Ch 12:5).

HARUZ (diligent), father-in-law of King Manasseh (2Ki 21:19).

HARVEST. Sabbath to be observed in (Ex 34:21). Sabbath desecrated in (Ne 13:15-22).

Of wheat at Pentecost, in Palestine (Ex 34:22; Le 23:15-17); and before vintage (Le 26:5). Of barley, before wheat (Ex 9:31, 32).

Celebrated with joy (J'g 9:27; Isa 9:3; 16:10; Jer 48:33). Promises of plentiful (Ge 8:22; Jer 5:24; Joe 2:23, 24).

Figurative: Job 24:6; Ps 10:5; Jer 8:20; Joe 3:13; M't 9:37; 13:39; Lu 10:2; Re 14:15.

See Pentecost, Feast of; Tabernacles, Feast of; First Fruits; Reaping; Gleaning.

HASADIAH (whom Jehovah esteems), son of Zerubbabel (1Ch 3:20).

HASENUAH. 1. Benjamite (1Ch 9:7).

2. Father of assistant overseer of Jerusalem (Ne 11:9).

HASHABIAH (whom Jehovah esteems).
1. Ancestor of Ethan (1Ch 6:45).
2. Ancestor of Shemaiah (1Ch 9:14; Ne 11:15).
3. Son of Jeduthun (1Ch 25:3).
4. Civil official in David's time (1Ch 26:30).
5. Overseer of tribe of Levi (1Ch 27:17).
6. Chief of Levites (2Ch 35:9).
7. Levite teacher (Ezr 8:19).
8. Chief priest (Ezr 8:24).
9. Worker on the wall (Ne 3:17).
10. Priest (Ne 12:21).
11. Ancestor of Uzzi (Ne 11:22).
12. Chief of Levites (Ne 3:17; 12:24).

HASHABNAH, man who sealed covenant with Nehemiah (Ne 10:25).

HASHABNIAH. 1. Father of Hattush (Ne 3:10).

2. A Levite (Ne 9:5).

HASHBADANA, a man who stood by Ezra as he read the law (Ne 8:4).

HASHEM, father of several members of David's guard (1Ch 11:34).

HASHMANNIM, translated "heaven of heavens," meaning unknown (Ps 68:33).

HASHMONAH, a camp of the Israelites (Nu 33:29, 30).

HASHUB (considerate), 1. Son of Pahath-moab (Ne 3:11).

2. One of the captivity who assisted in repairing the wall of Jerusalem (Ne 3:23).

3. Head of a family (Ne 10:22).

4. Called also Hasshub. A Levite (1Ch 9:14; Ne 11:15).

HASHUBAH (consideration), a descendant of King Jehoiakim (1Ch 3:20).

HASHUM. 1. Family which returned from exile (Ezr 2:19; 10:33; Ne 7:22).

2. Priest who stood at side of Ezra when he read law (Ne 8:4).

3. Chief of people who sealed the covenant (Ne 10:18). May be same as 2.

HASHUPHA, family which returned from exile with Zerubbabel (Ezr 2:43; Ne 7:46).

HASMONAEANS (See Maccabees.)

HASRAH, grandfather of Shallum (2Ch 34:22); "Harhas" in 2Ki 22:14.

HASSENAAH, father of sons who built fish gate in Jerusalem (Ne 3:3).

HASTE, in judgment, by Moses and the Israelites (Nu 32:1-19; Jos 22:10-34).

See Rashness.

HASUPHA (See Hashupha.)

HAT (See Dress.)

HATACH, a chamberlain in the court of Ahasuerus (Es 4:5, 6, 9, 10).

HATHATH (terror), a son of Othniel (1Ch 4:13).

HATIPHA, one of the Nethinim (Ezr 2:54; Ne 7:56).

HATITA, a porter of the temple (Ezr 2:42; Ne 7:45).

HATRED. Is blinding (1Jo 2:9, 11); carnal (Ga 5:19, 20); murderous (1Jo 3:15); unforgiving (M't 6:15). Leads to deceit (Pr 26:24-26). Opposite of love (Pr 15:17). Prevents from loving God (1Jo 4:20). Produces strife (Pr 10:12).

Toward the righteous (Ps 25:19; 35:19; M't 10:22; Joh 15:18, 19, 23-25; 17:14).

Forbidden (Eph 4:31; Col 3:8); toward, a brother (Le 19:17); an enemy (M't 5:43, 44).

Justified against iniquity (Ps 97:10; 101:3; 119:104, 128, 163; 139:21, 22); of God (Ps 5:5; 45:7; Isa 61:8; Mal 2:16).

See Envy; Jealousy; Malice; Revenge.

HATSIHAM MENUCHOTH, marginal reading on 1Ch 2:54 in KJV which is eliminated in ASV.

HATTIL (waving), a returned exile (Ezr 2:57; Ne 7:59).

HATTIN, HORNS OF (hollows), hill near village of Hattin on which, tradition says, Christ delivered the Sermon on the Mount.

HATTUSH. 1. Descendant of Zerubbabel (1Ch 3:22).

2. Man who returned from Babylon (Ezr 8:2).

3. Worker on the wall (Ne 3:10). May be same as 2.

4. Man who sealed covenant (Ne 10:4). May be same as 2 or 3.

5. Priest who returned with Zerubbabel (Ne 12:2).

HAUGHTINESS (See Pride.)

HAURAN (black), plateau E of Jordan and N of Gilead (Eze 47:16, 18). Called Bashan in ancient times; in time of Romans, Auranitis.

HAVILAH (sand land). 1. Son of Cush (Ge 10:7; 1Ch 1:9).

2. Son of Joktan (Ge 10:29; 1Ch 1:23).

3. Land encompassed by Pishon river (Ge 2:11, 12).

4. One of the boundaries of the Ishmaelites (Ge 25:18; 1Sa 15:7).

HAVOTH-JAIR, called also Bashan-Havoth-Jair in De 3:14. Certain villages E of the Jordan (Nu 32:41; J'g 10:4).

HAWK, a carnivorous and unclean bird (Le 11:16; De 14:15; Job 39:26).

HAY (Pr 27:25; Isa 15:6; 1Co 3:12).

HAZAEL (God sees), king of Syria. Anointed king by Elijah (1Ki 19:15). Conquests by (2Ki 8:28, 29; 9:14; 10:32, 33; 12:17, 18; 13:3, 22; 2Ch 22:5, 6). Conspires against, murders, and succeeds to the throne of Ben-hadad (2Ki 8:8-15). Death of (2Ki 13:24).

HAZAIAH (Jehovah sees), a man of Judah (Ne 11:5).

HAZAR (a settlement), often prefixed to descriptive place names; also used for encampments of nomads.

HAZAR-ADDAR, called also Adar, a place on the southern boundary of Canaan (Nu 34:4; Jos 15:3).

HAZAR-ENAN (village of fountains), the NE boundary point of the promised land (Nu 34:9, 10; Eze 47:17; 48:1).

HAZAR-GADDAH (village of good fortune), a town in the southern district of Judah (Jos 15:27).

HAZAR-HATTICON (middle-village), a place on the boundary of Hauran, probably E of Damascus (Eze 47:16).

HAZARMAVETH (village of death), son and descendants of Joktan (Ge 10:26; 1Ch 1:20).

HAZAR-SHUAL (village of the jackal), town in S Judah (Jos 15:28; 19:3; 1Ch 4:28; Ne 11:27).

HAZAR-SUSAH (village of a mane), called also Hazar-susim, a city of Judah (Jos 19:5; 1Ch 4:31).

HAZAZON-TAMAR, town on W coast of Dead Sea (Ge 14:7), KJV has "Hazezon-tamar."

HAZEL, KJV has "almond tree," which is better (Ge 30:37).

HAZELELPONI, daughter of Etam (1Ch 4:3).

HAZERIM (villages), a district in the S of Canaan (De 2:23).

HAZEROTH, a station in the journeyings of the children of Israel (Nu 11:35; 12:16; 33:17, 18; De 1:1).

HAZEZON-TAMAR, called also Hazazon-tamar, ancient name of En-gedi (Ge 14:7; 2Ch 20:2).

HAZIEL (God sees), a Levite (1Ch 23:9).

HAZO, a son of Nahor (Ge 22:22).

HAZOR (enclosed place). 1. City c. 5 miles W of waters of Merom, ruled by Jabin (Jos 11:1, 10); conquered by Joshua and, later, by Deborah and Barak (J'g 4; 1Sa 12:9); fortified by Solomon (1Ki 9:15); its inhabitants taken into exile by Assyria (2Ki 15:29).

2. Town in S of Judah (Jos 15:23).

3. Another town in S Judah (Jos 15:25).

4. Town N of Jerusalem (Ne 11:33).

5. Region in S Arabia (Jer 49:28-33).

HAZOR-HADATTAH, a city of Judah (Jos 15:25).

HEAD. Shaven when vows were taken (Ac 21:24). Diseases of (Isa 3:17). Anointed (Le 14:18, 29).

HEADBANDS (Isa 3:20).

HEAD OF THE CHURCH. Christ, who gives the church life, direction, strength (Eph 1:22; 5:23; Col 1:18).

HEADSTONE (See Cornerstone.)

HEALING. The Lord the healer (Ge 20:17; Ex 15:26; Ps 6:2; 30:2; 103:3; Ac 4:30).

In answer to prayer (Jas 5:14-16); of Miriam (Nu 12:10-15); of Jeroboam (1Ki 13:1-6); of Hezekiah (2Ki 20:1-7).

By Elisha, of Naaman (2Ki 5:1-14).

By Jesus: The nobleman's son (Joh 4:46-53). The impotent man (Joh 5:2-9). A leper (M't 8:2-4; M'k 1:40-45; Lu 5:12-13). Peter's mother-in-law (M't 8:14, 15). Man with palsy (M't 9:2-8; M'k 2:1-12; Lu 5:17-26). The man with the withered hand (M't 12:9-13; M'k 3:1-5; Lu 6:6-10). The centurion's servant (M't 8:5-13; Lu 2:1-10). Demoniacs (M't 8:28-34 w M'k 5:1-20 & Lu 8:26-36; M't 12:22; 17:14-18; M'k 9:14-27; Lu 9:38-42; 11:14). Blind and dumb (M't 9:27-33; 12:22; 20:30-34; M'k 8:22-25; 10:46-52; Lu 18:35-43). Woman with issue of blood (M't 9:20-22; M'k 5:25-34; Lu 8:43-48). Many sick (M't 8:16; 9:35; 14:14, 35, 36; 15:30, 31; 19:2; M'k 6:5, 53-56; Lu 4:40; 9:11). Daughter of the Syrophenician woman (M't 15:22-28; M'k 7:25-30). Woman with an infirmity (Lu 13:10-13). Ten lepers (Lu 17:12-14). See Miracles, of Jesus.

Power of, given, to the apostles (M't 10:1, 8; M'k 3:13-15; 6:7, 13; Lu 9:1, 2, 6); to the seventy (Lu 10:9, 17); to all believers (M'k 16:18). Special gifts of (1Co 12:9, 28, 30).

By the apostles: The lame man, in Jerusalem (Ac 3:2-10); in Lystra (Ac 14:8-10). Sick, in Jerusalem (Ac 5:15, 16); on the island of Melita (Ac 28:8, 9). Aeneas (Ac 9:34).

Figurative (Ps 41:4; 147:3).

See Miracles.

HEARERS. Heedless (Eze 33:30-32; M't 7:26, 27; 13:14, 15, 19-22; Lu 6:49; 8:11-14; Ro 2:13; Jas 1:22-24). Obedient (M't 7:24, 25; 13:23; Lu 6:47, 48; 8:15; Jas 1:25).

HEART. Seat of affection and source of action (De 5:29; 6:5, 6; 2Ch 12:14; Ps 57:7; 112:7; Pr 4:23; 14:30; 15:13-15; 16:1; M't 9:4; 12:33, 35; 15:18-20; 23:26; M'k 7:21-23). Lives forever (Ps 22:26). Of the heathen, taught of God (Ro 2:14-16).

Changed (Ps 51:10). Instances of: Saul (1Sa 10:9); Solomon (1Ki 3:11, 12); Paul (Ac 9:1-18).

Hardening of: Forbidden (Heb 3:8, 15; 4:7). Instances of: Pharaoh (Ex 4:21; 7:3, 13, 22; 8:15, 32; 9:12, 35; 10:1; 14:8); Sihon (De 2:30); King of Canaan (Jos 11:20); others (1Sa 6:6).

Known to God (De 31:21; 1Sa 16:7; 2Sa 7:20; 1Ki 8:39; 1Ch 28:9; 2Ch 6:30; Job 11:11; 16:19; 31:4; Ps 1:6; 44:21; 51:10; 94:11; 139:1-12; Pr 5:21; 16:2; 21:2; Isa 66:18; Jer 12:13; 17:10; Eze 11:5, 19-21; 36:25, 26; Lu 16:15; Ac 1:24; 15:8; Ro 8:27; 1Co 3:20; Heb 4:12; Re 2:23). To Christ (Ro 8:27; Re 2:23).

Regenerate: Is penitent (Ps 34:18; 51:10, 17; 147:3; Pr 15:3). Renewed (De 30:6; Ps 51:10; Eze 11:19; 18:31; 36:26; Joh 3:3, 7; Ro 2:29; Eph 4:22-24; Col 3:9, 10; Heb 10:22; Jas 4:8). Pure (Ps 24:4; 66:18; Pr 20:9; M't 5:8; 2Ti 2:22; 1Pe 3:15). Enlightened (2Co 4:6). Established (Ps 57:7; 108:1; 112:7, 8; 1Th 3:13). Refined by affliction (Pr 17:3). Tried or tested (1Ch 29:17; Ps 7:9; 26:2; Pr 17:3; Jer 11:20; 12:3; 20:12; 1Th 2:4; Heb 11:17; Re 2:2, 10). Strengthened (Ps 27:14; 112:8; 1Th 3:13). Graciously affected of God (1Sa 10:26; 1Ch 29:18; Ezr 6:22; 7:27; Pr 16:1; 21:1; Jer 20:9; Ac 16:14).

Should, Render to God: Obedience (De 10:12; 11:13; 26:16; 1Ki 2:4; Ps 119:1, 12; Eph 6:6). Faith (Ps 27:3; 112:7; Ac 8:37; Ro 6:17; 10:10). Trust (Pr 3:5). Love (De 6:5, 6; M't 22:37). Fear (Ps 119:161; Jer 32:40). Fidelity (Ne 9:8). Zeal (2Ch 17:16; Jer 20:9). Seek God (2Ch 19:3; 30:19; Ezr 7:10; Ps 10:17; 84:2). Be, Joyful (1Sa 2:1; Ps 4:7; 97:11; Isa 65:14; Zec 10:7). Perfect (1Ki 8:61; Ps 101:2). Upright (Ps 97:11; 125:4). Clean (Ps 51:10; 73:1). Pure (Ps 24:4; Pr 22:11; M't 5:8; 1Ti 1:5; 2Ti

2:22; Jas 4:8; 1Pe 1:22). Sincere (Lu 8:15; Ac 2:46; Eph 6:5; Col 3:22; Heb 10:22). Repentant (De 30:2; Ps 34:18; 51:17). Devout (1Sa 1:13; Ps 4:4; 9:1; 27:8; 77:6; 119:10, 69, 145). Wise (1Ki 3:9, 12; 4:29; Job 9:4; Pr 8:10; 10:8; 11:29; 14:33; 23:15). Tender (1Sa 24:5; 2Ki 22:19; Job 23:16; Ps 22:14; Eph 4:32). Holy (Ps 66:18; 1Pe 3:15). Compassionate (Jer 4:19; La 3:51). Lowly (M't 11:29).

The Unregenerate: Is full of iniquity (Ge 6:5; 8:21; 1Sa 17:28; Pr 6:14, 18; 11:20; Pr 20:9; Ec 8:11; 9:3; Jer 4:14, 18; 17:9; Ac 8:21-23; Ro 1:21). Loves evil (De 19:18; Ps 95:10; Jer 17:5). A fountain of evil (M't 12:34, 35; M'k 7:21). See Depravity. Wayward (2Ch 12:14; Ps 101:4; Pr 6:14; 11:20; 12:8; 17:20; Jer 5:23; Heb 3:10). Blind (Ro 1:21; Eph 4:18). See Blindness, Spiritual. Is double (1Ch 12:33; Ps 12:2; Pr 28:14; Isa 9:9; 10:12; 46:12; Ho 10:2; Jas 1:6, 8). See Instability. Is hard (Ps 76:5; Eze 2:4; 3:7; 11:19; 36:26; M'k 6:52; 10:5; 16:14; Joh 12:40; Ro 1:21; 2:5). See Impenitence; Obduracy. Is deceitful (Jer 17:9). Proud (2Ki 14:10; 2Ch 25:19; Ps 101:5; Pr 18:12; 28:25; Jer 48:29; 49:16). See Pride. Is subtle (Pr 7:10). See Hypocrisy. Is sensual (Eze 6:9; Ho 13:6; Ro 8:7). See Lasciviousness. Is worldly (2Ch 26:16; Da 5:20; Ac 8:21, 22). Judicially hardened (Ex 4:21; Jos 11:20; Isa 6:10; Ac 28:26, 27). Malicious (Ps 28:3; 140:2; Pr 24:2; Ec 7:26; Eze 25:15). See Malice. Is impenitent (Ro 2:5). See Impenitence. Is diabolical (Joh 13:2; Ac 5:3). Covetous (Jer 22:17; 2Pe 2:14). See Covetousness. Is foolish (Pr 12:23; 22:15; Ec 9:3). Under the wrath of God (Ro 1:18, 19, 31; 2:5, 6).

See Regeneration; Sanctification.

HEARTH (Ge 18:6; Isa 30:14; Jer 36:22, 23).

See Brazier.

HEAT, Jonah overcome with (Jon 4:8). See Sunstroke.

HEATH, shrub growing on W slopes of Lebanon (Jer 17:6; 48:6).

HEATHEN. Under this head are grouped all who are not embraced under the Abrahamic covenant. Cast out of Canaan (Le 18:24, 25; Ps 44:2); and their land given to Israel (Ps 78:55; 105:44; 135:12; 136:21, 22; Isa 54:1-3). Excluded from the temple (La 1:10).

Wicked Practices of (See Idolatry).

Divine revelations given to: Abimelech (Ge 20:3-7); Pharaoh (Ge 41:1-28); Balaam (Nu 22); Nebuchadnezzar (Da 4:1-18); Belshazzar (Da 5:5, 24-29); Cyrus (2Ch 36:23; Ezr 1:1-4); the Magi (M't 2:1-11); the centurion (M't 8:5-13; Luke 7:2-9); Cornelius (Ac 10:1-7).

Pious people among (Isa 65:5; Ac 10:35). Instances of: Melchizedek (Ge 14:18-20). Abimelech (Ge 20). Balaam (Nu 22). Jethro (Ex 18). Cyrus (Ezr 1:1-3). Eliphaz (Job 4). Bildad (Job 8). Zophar (Job 11). Elihu (Job 32). Nebuchadnezzar, after his restoration (Da 4). The Ninevites (Jon 3:5-10). The Magi (M't 2:1-12). The centurion of Capernaum (M't 8:5-13; Lu 7:2-9); of Caesarea (Ac 10).

Believed in Christ (M't 8:5-13; Lu 7:2-9).

See Gentiles.

HEAVE OFFERING (See Offerings).

HEAVE SHOULDER (See Offerings).

HEAVEN. *God's Dwelling Place* (De 26:15; 1Ki 8:30, 39, 43, 49; 1Ch 16:31; 21:26; 2Ch 2:6; 6:21, 27, 30, 33, 35, 39; 7:14; 30:27; Ne 9:27; Job 22:12, 14; Ps 2:4; 11:4; 20:6; 33:13; 102:19; 103:19; 113:5, 6; 123:1; 135:6; Ec 5:2; Isa 57:15; 63:15; 66:1; Jer 23:24; La 3:41, 50; Da 5:23; Zec 2:13; M't 5:34, 45; 6:9; 10:32, 33; 11:25; 12:50; 16:17; 18:10, 14; M'k 11:25, 26; 16:19; Ac 7:49, 55, 56; Ro 1:18; Heb 8:1; Re 8:1; 12:7-9; 21:22-27; 22:1-5).

Figurative: Of divine government (M't 16:19; 18:18; 23:22). Of God (M't 21:25).

The Future Home of the Righteous (2Ki 2:11; M't 5:12; 13:30, 43; Lu 16:22; Joh 12:8, 26; 13:36; 17:24; 2Co 5:1; Ph'p 3:20; Col 1:5, 6, 12; 3:9; 1Th 4:17; Heb 10:34; 11:10, 16; 12:22; 1Pe 1:4; Re 2:7; 3:21.

Called: A city (Heb 11:10, 16); a garden (M't 3:21); a house (Joh 14:2, 3; 2Co 5:1); a kingdom (M't 25:34; Lu 12:32; 22:29, 30); the kingdom of Christ and of God (Eph 5:5); a heavenly country (Heb 11:16); a rest (Heb 4:9; Re 14:13); glory (Col 3:4); paradise (Lu 23:43; 2Co 12:2, 4; Re 2:7).

Everlasting (2Co 5:1; Heb 10:34; 13:14; 1Pe 1:4; 2Pe 1:11). Allegorical representatives of (Re 4:1-11; 5:1-14; 7:9-17; 14:1-3; 15:1-8; 21; 22:1-5). No marriage in (M't 22:30; Lu 20:34-36). Names of the righteous written in (Lu 10:20; Heb 12:22-24). Treasures in (M't 6:20; 19:21; Lu 12:33). Joy in (Ps 16:11; Lu 15:6, 7, 10). Righteousness dwells in (2Pe 3:13). No sorrow in (Re 7:16, 17; 21:4). The wicked excluded from (Ga 5:21; Eph 5:5; Re 22:15).

See Righteous, Promises to.

HEAVEN OPENED (M't 3:16; Ac 7:56; 10:11; Re 19:11).

HEAVENLY PLACES (Eph 1:3, 20; 2:6; 3:10).

HEAVENS, PHYSICAL (Ge 1:1; 2Ch 2:6; 6:18; Job 38:31-33; Ps 19:1; 50:6; 68:33; 89:29; 103:11; 113:4; 115:16; 136:5; Jer 31:37; Eze 1:1; M't 24:29, 30; Ac 2:19, 20).

Created (Ge 1:1; 2:1; Ex 20:11; 1Ch 16:26; 2Ch 2:12; Ne 9:6; Job 9:8; Ps 8:3; 19:1; 33:6, 9; 102:25; 148:4-6; Pr 8:27; Isa 37:16; 40:22; 142:5; 45:12, 18; Jer 10:12; 32:17; 51:15; Ac 4:24; 14:15; Heb 1:10; Re 10:6; 14:7). See Creation; God, Creator; Heavens, New.

Destruction of (Job 14:12; Ps 102:25, 26; Isa 51:6; M't 5:18; 24:35; Heb 1:10-12; 2Pe 3:10, 12; Re 6:12-14; 20:11; 21:1, 4).

Figurative: Of divine judgments (Isa 34:4).

HEAVENS, NEW. To be created (Isa 65:17; 66:22; 2Pe 3:13; Re 21:1-4).

HEAVING AND WAVING (See Offerings).

HEBER (associate). 1. Great-grandson of Jacob (Ge 46:17).

2. Kenite whose wife Jael killed Sisera (J'g 4:11-21).

3. Son of Ezrah (KJV "Ezra") (1Ch 4:18).

4. Benjamite (1Ch 8:17).

5. Gadite (1Ch 5:13).

6. Benjamite (1Ch 8:22).

7. Father of Peleg and Joktan (Lu 3:35).

HEBREW. A word supposed to be a corruption of the name of Eber, who was an ancestor of Abraham (Ge 10:24; 11:14-26). See Genealogy. Applied to Abraham (Ge 14:13); and his descendants (Ge 39:14; 40:15; 43:32; Ex 2:6; De 15:12; 1Sa 4:9; 29:3; Jon 1:9; Ac 6:1; 2Co 11:22; Ph'p 3:5). Used to denote the language of the Jews (Joh 5:2; 19:20; Ac 21:40; 22:2; 26:14; Re 9:11).

See Israelites; Jews.

HEBREW LANGUAGE. The NW branch of the Semitic language family; has close affinity to Ugaritic, Phoenician, Moabitic, and the Canaanite dialects; sister languages include Arabic, Akkadian, and Aramaic. Except for a few passages in Ezra, Daniel, and Jeremiah, it is the language of the OT.

HEBREW OF THE HEBREWS, pure-blooded, very strict Jew (Ph'p 3:4-6).

HEBREWS, EPISTLE TO THE. Authorship uncertain; authors suggested: Paul, Timothy, Barnabas, Apollos; place of writing also uncertain; probably written before A. D. 70; written to Christians in danger of lapsing from faith. Outline. 1. Pre-eminence of Christ (1:1-4:13). Christ superior to angels and to Moses.

2. Priesthood of Christ (4:14-10:18). Christ a priest like Melchizedek.

3. Perseverance of Christians (10:19-12:29).

4. Postscript: Exhortations, personal concerns, benediction (13:1-25).

HEBRON (league). 1. A city of Asher (Jos 19:28).

2. A city of Judah, S. of Jerusalem. When built (Nu 13:22). Fortified (2Ch 11:10). Called Kirjath-arba (Ge 23:2); Arb (Ge 35:27; Jos 15:13). Abraham dwells and Sarah dies at (Ge 23:2). Hoham, king of, confederated with other kings of the Canaanites against Joshua (Jos 10:3-39). Children of Anakim dwell at (Nu 13:22; Jos 11:21). Conquest of, by Caleb (Jos 14:6-15; J'g 1:10, 20). A city of refuge (Jos 20:7; 21:11, 13). David crowned king of Judah at (2Sa 2:1-11; 3); of Israel (2Sa 5:1-5). The burial place of Sarah (Ge 23:2); Abner (2Sa 3:32); Ish-bosheth (2Sa 4:12). The conspirators against Ish-bosheth hanged at (2Sa 4:12). Absalom made king at (2Sa 15:9, 10). Jews of the Babylonian captivity dwell at (Ne 11:25). Pool of (2Sa 4:12).

3. Son of Kohath (Ex 6:18; Nu 3:19; 1Ch 6:2, 18; 23:12, 19).

4. The patronymic of Mareshah (1Ch 2:42, 43; 15:9).

HEDGE. A fence (Job 1:10; Isa 5:5; Jer 49:3; La 3:7; Eze 13:5; 22:30; Ho 2:6;

Mic 7:4; M'k 12:1); of thorns (Pr 15:19).
People sheltered in (Lu 14:23).
See Fence.

HEEDFULNESS. Commanded (Ex 23:13; Pr 4:25-27).

Necessary. In the care of the soul (De 4:9). In the house and worship of God (Ec 5:1). In what we hear (M'k 4:24). In how we hear (Lu 3:18). In keeping God's commandments (Jos 22:5). In conduct (Eph 5:15). In speech (Pr 13:3; Jas 1:19). In worldly company (Ps 39:1; Col 4:5). In giving judgment (1Ch 19:6, 7). Against sin (Heb 12:15, 16). Against unbelief (Heb 3:12). Against idolatry (De 4:15, 16). Against false Christs, and false prophets (M't 24:4, 5, 23, 24). Against false teachers (Ph'p 3:2; Col 2:8; 2Pe 3:16, 17). Against presumption (1Co 10:12).

Promises to (1Ki 2:4; 1Ch 22:13).

HEGAI or **HEGE,** eunuch in charge of Ahasuerus' harem (Es 2:3, 8, 15).

HEGIRA (See Exodus.)

HEIFER. When used as sacrifice, must be without blemish and must not have come under the yoke (Nu 19:2; De 21:3). An atonement for murder (De 21:1-9). The red heifer used for the water of separation (Nu 19; Heb 9:13).

Used for draught (J'g 14:18); for treading out wheat (Ho 10:11). Tractable (Ho 10:11). Intractable (Ho 4:16).

See Kine; Offering.

Figurative: Of backsliders (Ho 4:16). Of the obedient (Ho 10:11).

HEIFER, RED (See Animals.)

HEIR. Mosaic law relating to inheritance of (Nu 27:8-11; 36:1-8; Jos 17:3-6); prescribing right of, to redeem alienated land (Le 25:25; Ru 4:1-12); to inherit slaves (Le 25:45, 46); firstborn son to have double portion (De 21:15-17).

Children of wives and concubines are (Ge 15:3; 21:10; 25:5, 6; Ga 4:30). All possessions left to (Ec 2:18, 19). Minor, under guardians (Ga 4:1, 2).

See Birthright; Firstborn; Inheritance; Orphan; Will.

Figurative: Of spiritual adoption (Ro 8:14-17; Ga 3:29; 4:6, 7; Tit 3:7; Jas 2:5). See Adoption.

HELAH, a wife of Asher (1Ch 4:5).

HELAM, place in Syrian desert E of Jordan where David defeated forces of Hadarezer (2Sa 10:16, 17).

HELBAH (a fertile region), a town of Asher (J'g 1:31).

HELBON (fertile), a village near Damascus, noted for fine wines (Eze 27:18).

HELDAI. 1. The Netophathite. One of David's heroes (1Ch 27:15). Called Heled (1Ch 11:30); and Heleb (2Sa 23:29).

2. An Israelite (Zec 6:10).

HELEB, one of David's valiant men of war (2Sa 23:29).

HELED, brave soldier (1Ch 11:30).

HELEK, son of Gilead (Nu 26:30; Jos 17:2).

HELEM (health). 1. A descendant of Asher (1Ch 7:35).

2. Probably same as Heldai (Zec 6:10, 14).

HELEPH (change), town of Naphtali (Jos 19:33).

HELEZ. 1. One of David's mighty men (2Sa 23:26; 1Ch 11:27; 27:10).

2. A man of Judah (1Ch 2:39).

HELI, father of Joseph, the husband of Mary (Lu 3:23); or perhaps the father of Mary, the mother of Jesus.

HELIOPOLIS (city of the sun), city near S end of Nile Delta called "On" in the Bible (Ge 41:45; 46:20).

HELKAI, a priest (Ne 12:15).

HELKATH, called also Hukok. A Levitical town (1Ch 6:75; Jos 19:25; 21:31).

HELKATH HAZZURIM (the field of the sharp knives), plain near pool of Gibeon where soldiers of Joab and Abner fought (2Sa 2:12-16).

HELL. The word used in the King James Version of the OT to translate the Hebrew word sheol, signifying the unseen state (De 32:22; 2Sa 22:6; Job 11:8; 26:6; Ps 9:17; 16:10; 18:5; 55:15; 86:13; 116:3; 139:8; Pr 5:5; 7:27; 9:18; 15:11, 24; 23:14; 27:20; Isa 5:14; 14:9, 15; 28:15, 18; 57:9; Eze 31:16, 17; 32:21, 27; Am 9:2; Jon 2:2; Hab 2:5).

Translation of the Greek word hades in NT of King James Version, the unseen world (M't 11:23; 16:18; Lu 10:15; 16:23; Ac 2:27, 31; Re 1:18; 6:8; 20:13, 14); of the Greek word gehenna, signifying the place of torment (M't 5:22, 29, 30; 10:28; 18:9; 23:15, 33; M'k 9:43, 45, 47; Lu 12:5; Jas 3:6); of the Greek word tartarus, signifying the infernal region (2Pe 2:4).

Sheol is also translated grave in King James Version (Ge 37:35; 42:38; 44:29, 31; 1Sa 2:6; 1Ki 2:6, 9; Job 7:9; 14:13; 17:13; 21:13; 24:19; Ps 6:5; 30:3; 31:17; 49:14, 15; 88:3; 89:48; 141:7; Pr 1:12; 30:16; Ec 9:10; Song 8:6; Isa 14:11; 38:10, 18; Eze 31:15; Ho 13:14); pit (Nu 16:30, 33; Job 17:16).

The English revisers insert the Hebrew word sheol in places where hell, grave, and pit were used in the AV as translations of the word sheol, except in De 32:22; Ps 55:15; 86:13; and in the prophetical books. The American revisers invariably use Sheol in the American text, where it occurs in the original.

Figurative: Of divine judgments (De 32:22; Eze 31:15-17).

The future state, or abode, of the wicked (Ps 9:17; Pr 5:5; 9:18; 15:24; 23:14; Isa 30:33; 33:14; M't 3:12; 5:22, 29, 30; 7:13; 8:11, 12; 10:28; 13:30, 38-42, 49, 50; 16:18; 18:8, 9, 34, 35; 22:13; 25:30, 41, 46; M'k 9:43-48; Lu 3:17; 16:23-28; Ac 1:25; 2Th 1:9; 2Pe 2:4; Jude 6, 23; Re 2:11; 9:1, 2; 11:7; 14:10, 11; 19:20; 20:10, 15; 21:8).

See Wicked, Punishment of.

HELLENISTS, Jews who made Greek their tongue (Ac 6:1; 9:29). See RSV.

HELM (Ac 27:40; Jas 3:4).

HELMET, a defensive headgear worn by soldiers (1Sa 17:5, 38; 2Ch 26:14; Jer 46:4; Eze 23:24).

Figurative: Isa 59:17; Eph 6:17; 1Th 5:8.

HELON (valorous), father of Eliab (Nu 1:9; 2:7; 7:24, 29; 10:16).

HELPMEET, helper (Ge 2:18).

HELPS, one of the gifts of the Spirit, probably the ability to perform helpful works in a gracious manner (1Co 12:7-11, 28-31).

HEM OF A GARMENT, fringes or tassels on the borders of the Jewish outer garment (Nu 15:38, 39).

HEMAM, a son of Lotan (Ge 36:22). Called Homam (1Ch 1:39).

HEMAN (faithful). 1. A man noted for wisdom, to whom Solomon is compared (1Ki 4:31; 1Ch 2:6).

2. "The singer," a chief Levite, and musician (1Ch 6:33; 15:17, 19; 16:41). The king's seer (1Ch 25:5). His sons and daughters temple musicians (1Ch 6:33; 25:1-6). "Maschil of," title of Psalm 88.

HEMATH 1. Another form for Hamath (Am 6:14).

2. An unknown person or place (1Ch 2:55).

HEMDAN (pleasant), son of Dishon (Ge 36:26).

HEMLOCK, a poisonous and bitter plant (Ho 10:4; Am 6:12).

See Gall.

HEMORRHAGE. Menstruation (Le 15:19; M't 9:20; Lu 8:43). A woman suffers twelve years (M'k 5:25-29).

See Menstruation.

HEMORRHOIDS, a disease with which the Philistines were afflicted (1Sa 5:6, 12; 6:4; 5:11; De 28:27).

See Disease; Tumor.

HEN, son of Zephaniah (Zec 6:14).

Figurative: M't 23:37; Lu 13:34.

HENA, a city on the Euphrates (2Ki 18:34; 19:13; Isa 37:13).

HENADAD, a Levite (Ezr 3:9; Ne 3:18, 24; 10:9).

HENOCH (See Enoch.)

HEPHER (pit, well). 1. Son of Gilead, and ancestor of Zelophehad (Nu 26:32, 33; 27:1; Jos 17:2, 3).

2. Son of Naarah (1Ch 4:6).

3. One of David's heroes (1Ch 11:36).

4. A city west of the Jordan (Jos 12:17; 1Ki 4:10).

HEPHZIBAH (my delight is in her). 1. Wife of Ḥezekiah (2Ki 21:1).

2. Symbolical name given to Zion (Isa 62:4).

HERALD (Isa 40:3; Da 3:4). Signified by the word preacher (1Ti 2:7; 2Ti 1:11; 2Pe 2:5). See *R. V.* [marg.]

HERBS, given for food (Ge 1:29, 30; Pr 15:17).

See Vegetation.

HERD. Herds of cattle were used in plowing, threshing, sacrifice (Ge 18:17; Job 1:3; 42:12).

HERDMAN, person in charge of cattle (Ge 13:7) or pigs (M't 8:33); despised in Egypt (Ge 46:34), but honored in Israel (Ge 47:6; 1Ch 27:29).

HEREDITY. Like begets like (Ge 5:3; Job 14:4; Joh 3:6, 7).

Results of: Natural, depravity (Job 21:19; Ps 51:5; 58:3; Isa 48:8; Joh 9:2; Ro 5:12; Eph 2:3). Judicial, ordained consequences of parental conduct (Ex 20:5, 6; 34:7; Nu 14:18, 33; De 5:9; Ps 37:28; Isa 14:20, 21; 65:6, 7; Jer 32:18;

Ro 5:12; 1Co 15:22). Does not fix moral status (Jer 31:29, 30; Eze 18:1-32; M't 3:9).

HERES (sun). 1. District around Aijalon (J'g 1:35).

2. Place E of the Jordan (J'g 8:13 ASV, RSV).

3. Egyptian city, translated "city of destruction" (Isa 19:18), undoubtedly Heliopolis.

HERESH, a Levite (1Ch 9:15).

HERESY. Propagandism of, forbidden under severe penalties (De 13; Tit 3:10, 11; 2Jo 10, 11). Teachers of, among early Christians (Ac 15:24; 2Co 11:4; Ga 1:7; 2:4; 2Pe 2; Jude 3-16; Re 2:2). Paul and Silas accused of (Ac 16:20, 21, 23). Paul accused of (Ac 18:13). Disavowed by Paul (Ac 24:13-17).

See Teachers, False.

HERMAS, a Christian at Rome (Ro 16:14).

HERMES, 1. Greek god (messenger), same as Mercury in Latin (Ac 14:12).

2. Friend of Paul at Rome, called Hermas (Ro 16:14).

HERMOGENES, a Christian, who deserted Paul (2Ti 1:15).

HERMON (sacred mountain), mt. marking S terminus of Anti-Lebanon range; 30 miles SW of Damascus; 9,000 ft. above sea level; marks N boundary of Palestine; has three peaks. Has borne several names: "Shenir" or "Senir" (De 3:9), "Sirion" (De 3:9), "Sion" (De 4:48). Probably mt. of Transfiguration (M't 17:1). Seat of Baal worship (J'g 3:3). Modern Jebel esh Sheikh.

HEROD. Idumean rulers of Palestine (47 B. C.-A. D. 79). Line started with Antipater, whom Julius Caesar made procurator of Judaea in 47 B. C. 1. Herod the Great, first procurator of Galilee, then king of the Jews (37-4 B. C.); built Caesarea, temple at Jerusalem; slaughtered children at Bethlehem (M't 2:1-18). At his death his kingdom was divided among his three sons: Archelaus, Herod Antipas, and Philip.

2. Archelaus ruled over Judaea, Samaria, and Idumea (4 B. C.-A. D. 6), and was removed from office by the Romans (M't 2:22).

3. Herod Antipas ruled over Galilee and Perea (4 B. C.-A. D. 39); killed John the Baptist (M't 14:1-12); called "fox" by Jesus (Lu 13:32).

4. Philip, tetrarch of Batanaea, Trachonitis, Gaulanitis, and parts of Jamnia (4 B. C.-A. D. 34). Best of the Herods.

5. Herod Agrippa I; grandson of Herod the Great; tetrarch of Galilee; king of Palestine (A. D. 41-44); killed James the apostle (Ac 12:1-23).

6. Herod Agrippa II. King of territory E of Galilee (c. A. D. 53-70); Paul appeared before him (Ac 25:13-26; 32).

HERODIANS, a Jewish faction. Seek to entangle Jesus (M't 22:16; M'k 12:13). Conspire to slay Jesus (M'k 3:6; 12:13).

HERODIAS, granddaughter of Herod the Great who had John the Baptist put to death (M't 14:3-6; M'k 6:17; Lu 3:19).

HERODION. A Roman Christian (Ro 16:11).

HERON, large aquatic bird Jews could not eat (Le 11:19; De 14:18).

HESED (mercy), father of one of Solomon's officers (1Ki 4:10).

HESHBON (reckoning). A city of the Amorites (Nu 21:25-35; De 1:4). Built by Reuben (Nu 32:37). Allotted to Gad (Jos 21:38, 39). Fish-pools at (Song 7:4). Prophecy concerning (Isa 16:8; Jer 48:2, 34, 35; 49:1-3).

HESHMON, a town in the S of Judah (Jos 15:27).

HETH, son of Canaan, and ancestor of the Hittites (Ge 10:15; 23:3, 5, 7, 10, 16, 18; 27:46; 49:32; 1Ch 1:13).

See Hittites.

HETHLON, a place on the northern frontier of Palestine (Eze 47:15; 48:1).

HEXATEUCH, a term referring to the Pentateuch and Joshua as though it were a literary unit.

HEZEKI, a Benjamite (1Ch 8:17).

HEZEKIAH (Jehovah has strengthened). 1. King of Judah (2Ki 16:20; 18:1, 2; 1Ch 3:13; 2Ch 29:1; M't 1:9). Religious zeal of (2Ch 29; 30; 31). Purges the nation of idolatry (2Ki 18:4; 2Ch 31:1; 33:3). Restores the true forms of worship (2Ch 31:2-21). His piety (2Ki 18:3, 5, 6; 2Ch 29:2; 31:20, 21; 32:32; Jer 26:19). Military operations of (2Ki 18:19; 1Ch 4:39-43; 2Ch 32; Isa 36; 37). Sickness and restoration of (2Ki 20:1-11; 2Ch 32:24; Isa 38:1-8). His psalm of thanksgiving (Isa 38:9-22). His lack of wisdom in showing his resources to commissioners of Babylon (2Ki 20:12-19; 2Ch 32:25, 26, 31; Isa 39). Prospered of God (2Ki 18:7; 2Ch 32:27-30). Conducts the brook Gihon into Jerusalem (2Ki 18:17; 20:20; 2Ch 32:4, 30; 33:14; Ne 2:13-15; 3:13, 16; Isa 7:3; 22:9-11; 36:2). Scribes of (Pr 25:1). Death and burial of (2Ki 20:21; 2Ch 32:33). Prophecies concerning (2Ki 19:20-34; 20:5, 6, 16-18; Isa 38:5-8; 39:5-7; Jer 26:18, 19).

2. Son of Neariah (1Ch 3:23).

3. One of the exiles (Ezr 2:16; Ne 7:21); called Hizkijah (Ne 10:17).

HEZION (vision), grandfather of Benhadad (1Ki 15:18).

HEZIR (swine). 1. A Levite (1Ch 24:15).

2. A prince of Judah (Ne 10:20).

HEZRAI, called also Hezro. A Carmelite (2Sa 23:35; 1Ch 11:37).

HEZRO (See Hezrai.)

HEZRON (enclosure). 1. Son of Pharez (Ge 46:12). Ancestor of the Hezronites (Nu 26:6, 21; 1Ch 2:5, 9, 18, 21, 24).

2. A son of Reuben (Ge 46:9; Ex 6:14; 1Ch 4:1; 5:3). Descendants of, called Hezronites (Nu 26:6).

HIDDAI. One of David's heroes (2Sa 23:30). Called Hurai (1Ch 11:32).

HIDDEKEL, ancient name of the river Tigris (Ge 2:14; Da 10:4).

HIEL (God liveth). Rebuilder of Jericho (1Ki 16:34). In him was fulfilled the curse pronounced by Joshua (Jos 6:26).

HIERAPOLIS (sacred city), ancient Phrygian city near Colossae (Col 4:13).

HIEROGLYPHICS (See Writing.)

HIGGAION, musical term probably meaning "solemn sound" (Ps 9:16; 92:3).

HIGH PLACES. A term used to describe places of worship (Ge 12:8; 22:2, 14; 31:54; 1Sa 9:12; 2Sa 24:25; 1Ki 3:2, 4; 18:30, 38; 1Ch 16:39; 2Ch 1:3; 33:17). Signify a place of idolatrous worship (Nu 22:41; 1Ki 11:7; 12:31; 14:23; 15:14; 22:43; 2Ki 17:9, 29; Jer 7:31). Licentious practices at (Eze 16:24-43). The idolatrous, to be destroyed (Le 26:30; Nu 33:52). Asa destroys (2Ch 14:3); Jehoshaphat (2Ch 17:6); Hezekiah (2Ki 18:4); Josiah (2Ki 23:8).

See Groves; Idolatry.

HIGH PRIEST (See Priest.)

HIGHWAYS. From, Gibeon to Bethhoron (Jos 10:10); Bethel to Shechem (J'g 21:19); Judea to Galilee, by way of Samaria (Joh 4:3-5, 43). To Bethel (J'g 20:31); to Gibeah (J'g 20:31); to cities of refuge (De 19:3). Built by rulers (Nu 20:17; 21:22).

Figurative: Pr 16:17; Isa 11:16; 35: 8-10; 40:3, 4; M't 3:3; 7:13, 14.

HILEN, a city of Judah. Assigned to the priests (1Ch 6:58). Called Holon (Jos 15:51; 21:15).

HILKIAH (portion of Jehovah). 1. Father of Eliakim (2Ki 18:18).

2. Merarite Levite (1Ch 6:45).

3. Merarite Levite (1Ch 26:11).

4. High priest who found book of the Law and sent it to Josiah (2Ki 22, 23; 2Ch 34:14).

5. Priest who returned with Zerubbabel (Ne 12:7).

6. Father of Jeremiah (Jer 1:1).

7. Father of Gemariah who stood by Ezra at Bible reading (Ne 8:4).

HILL COUNTRY, any region of hills and valleys, but in Scripture generally the higher part of Judaea (Lu 1:39, 65).

HILLEL (he has praised). Father of Abdon (J'g 12:13, 15).

HILLS, perpetual (Ge 49:26; Hab 3:6).

HIN. A measure for liquids, and containing one-sixth or one-seventh of a bath. Jewish authorities disagree as to the exact capacity. Probably equivalent to about one gallon one quart, or one gallon one and one-half quarts (Ex 29:40; Le 19:36; 23:13).

HIND (See Deer.)

HINGE, contrivance enabling a door or window to swing in its place (1Ki 7:50); often used figuratively for something of great importance.

HINNON. A valley W and SW of Jerusalem (Jos 15:8; 18:16; 2Ki 23:10; Ne 11:30). Children offered in sacrifice in (2Ch 28:3; 33:6; Jer 7:31, 32; 19:2, 4, 6; 32:35). Possibly valley of vision identical with (Isa 22:1, 5).

See Tophet.

HIP AND THIGH, expression denoting thoroughness with which Samson slew Philistines (J'g 15:8).

HIPPOPOTAMUS (Job 40:15 [marg. *R. V.*]).

HIRAH, an Adullamite (Ge 38:1, 12).

HIRAM. 1. Called Huram, king of Tyre. Builds a house for David (2Sa 5:11; 1Ch 14:1; 2Ch 2:3). Aids Solomon in building the temple (1Ki 5; 2Ch 2:3-16). Dissatisfied with cities given by Solomon (1Ki 9:11-13). Makes presents of gold and seamen to Solomon (1Ki 9:14, 26-28; 10:11).

2. Called also Huram. An artificer sent by King Hiram to execute the artistic work of the interior of the temple (1Ki 7:13-45; 2Ch 2:13; 4:11-16).

HIRE, law concerning hired property (Ex 22:14, 15).

See Employer; Master; Servant; Wages.

HIRED SERVANT. Jacob (Ge 29:15; 30:26); re-employed (Ge 30:27-34; 31:6, 7, 41). Laborers for a vineyard (M't 20:1-15). The prodigal (Lu 15:15-19).

Kindness to (Ru 2:4). Treatment of, more considerate than that accorded slaves (Le 25:53).

Rights of: To receive wages (M't 10:10; Lu 10:7; Ro 4:4; 1Ti 5:18; Jas 5:4); daily (Le 19:13; De 24:15). To share in spontaneous products of land in Sabbatic year (Le 25:6). Wages of, paid in portion of flocks or products (Ge 30:31, 32; 2Ch 2:10); or in money (M't 20:2, 9, 10). Oppression of, forbidden (De 24:14; Col 4:1). Oppressors of, punished (Mal 3:5).

Mercenary (Job 7:2). Unfaithful (Joh 10:12, 13).

See Master; Servant; Wages.

HIRELING, laborer who works for his wages (De 24:15; M't 20:1-6).

HISTORY (Job 8:8-10).

See Books; books of Genesis, Joshua, Judges, Ruth, Samuel, Kings, Chronicles, Ezra, Nehemiah, Esther; Israel, History of; Jesus, Life of.

HITTITES. A tribe of Canaanites. Children of Heth (Ge 10:15; 23:10). Sell a burying-ground to Abraham (Ge 23). Esau intermarries with (Ge 26:34; 36:2). Dwelling place of (Ge 23:17-20; Nu 13:29; Jos 1:4; J'g 1:26). Their land given to the Israelites (Ex 3:8; De 7:1; Jos 1:4). Conquered by Joshua (Jos 9:1, 2; chapters 10-12; 24:11). Intermarry with Israelites (J'g 3:5-7; Ezr 9:1). Solomon intermarries with (1Ki 11:1; Ne 13:26). Pay tribute to Solomon (1Ki 9:20, 21). Retain their own kings (1Ki 10:29; 2Ki 7:6; 2Ch 1:17). Officers from, in David's army (1Sa 26:6; 2Sa 11:3; 23:39).

HIVITES. A tribe of Canaanites (Ge 10:17; 1Ch 1:15). Shechemites and Gibeonites were families of (Ge 34:2; Jos 9:7; 11:19). Esau intermarries with (Ge 26:34; 36:2). Dwelling place of (Jos 11.3; J'g 3:3; 2Sa 24:7). Their land given to the Israelites (Ex 23:23, 28; De 20:17; J'g 3:5). Conquered by Joshua (Jos 9:1; 12:8; 24:11). Pay tribute to Solomon (1Ki 9:21; 2Ch 8:8).

HIZKIAH, an ancestor of Zephaniah (Zep 1:1).

HIZKIJAH, probably identical with Hezekiah, the exile, which see.

HOBAB (beloved), brother-in-law of Moses (Nu 10:29; J'g 4:11 KJV has "father-in-law").

HOBAH, a place N of Damascus (Ge 14:15).

HOD (majesty), a son of Zophah (1Ch 7:37).

HODAIAH, son of Elioenai (1Ch 3:24).

HODAVIAH. 1. Chief in Manasseh (1Ch 5:24).

2. Benjamite (1Ch 9:7).

3. Levite whose descendants returned with Zerubbabel (Ezr 2:40). Also called Hodevah (Ne 7:43) and Judah (Ezr 3:9).

HODESH, wife of Shaharaim (1Ch 8:9).

HODEVAH, a Levite (Ne 7:43).

HODIAH, called also Hodijah. 1. Wife of Ezra (1Ch 4:19).

2. A Levite (Ne 8:7; 9:5; 10:10, 13).

3. An Israelitish chief (Ne 10:18).

HOGLAH, a daughter of Zelophehad (Nu 26:33; 27:1; 36:11; Jos 17:3).

HOHAM, Amorite king who entered into a league against Joshua (Jos 10:3).

HOLIDAY. For rest. See Sabbath. One year in seven (Le 25:2-7).

See Jubilee.

HOLINESS. Sin and holiness, sinful man and the holy Jehovah, were the dominant ideas in the Mosaic law. The supreme purpose of the system of Mosaic ordinances was to impress Israel as a separated people and through Israel to impress all people for all time that a holy God can be pleased by none but holy people. This is a central truth of the true religion. The student must, therefore, seek for this spiritual purpose through all the ordinances of the law. Defilement and uncleanness, exclusion of the unclean from the congregation atonements and atoning sacrifices, washings and purifications, whole burnt offerings, unblemished priests and unblemished offerings, typifying unblemished and uncorrupted motives in worship and service—all these were ordained as object lessons to teach that there is a difference between unholiness and holiness and thus to exalt holiness as the supreme lesson of life.

As in the books of the Mosaic law, so throughout the Holy Scriptures, the attainment of holiness is a dominant theme.

Attribute of God (Jos 24:19; 1Sa 6:20; Job 6:10; Ps 22:3; 47:8; 60:6; 89:35; 111:9; 145:17; Isa 5:16; 6:3; 29:19, 23; 41:14; 43:14, 15; 47:4; 49:7; 57:15; Eze 36:21, 22; 39:7, 25; Ho 11:9; Hab 1:12, 13; Lu 1:49; Joh 17:11; Ro 1:23; Re 4:8; 6:10; 15:4).

Described (Ro 14:17); as walking in uprightness (Isa 57:2); as a highway (Isa 35:8); as departing from evil (Ps 34:14; 37:27); as satisfying (Joh 6:35); as crucifying the flesh (Ga 5:24); as a new creature (Ga 6:15); as a new man (Eph 4:24; Col 3:10); as a rest (Heb 4:3, 9); as pure, peaceable, gentle (Jas 3:17).

Enjoined (Ge 17:1; Ex 22:31; Le 10:8-10; 11:44, 45; 19:2; 20:7, 26; Nu 15:40; De 13:17; 18:13; Jos 7:13; 2Ch 20:21; Job 5:24; Ps 4:4; 97:10; Isa 52:1, 11; Mic 6:8; Zep 2:3; M't 5:29, 30, 48; 12:33; Joh 5:14; Ro 6:1-23; 1Co 3:16; 5:7; 15:34; 2Co 6:14-17; 7:1; Eph 1:4; 5:1, 3, 8-11; 1Th 4:3, 4, 7; 5:22, 23; 2Th 2:13; 1Ti 4:12; 5:22; 6:11, 12; 2Ti 2:19, 21, 22; 1Pe 1:5; 2Pe 1:5-8; 1Jo 2:1, 5, 29; 2Jo 4; Re 18:4).

Upon Israel (Ex 19:6; 22:31; De 7:6; 26:19; 28:9; Isa 4:3; 52:1, 11; 60:1, 21; Zec 8:3; 14:20, 21); the church (2Co 11:2; 1Pe 2:5, 9; Re 19:8).

Exhortations to (M't 5:30; Joh 5:14; Ro 6:13, 19; 12:1, 2; 13:12-14; 1Co 6:13, 19, 20; 10:31; 2Co 13:7, 8; Eph 4:22-24; Col 3:5, 12-15; 1Th 2:12; 3:13; 1Ti 4:12; Tit 2:9, 10, 12; 1Pe 4:1; 2Pe 3:11, 12, 14; 3Jo 11.

Motives to: God's holiness (Ge 17:1; Le 11:44, 45; 19:2; 20:26; Isa 6:1-8; M't 5:48; 1Pe 1:15, 16); God's mercies (Ro 12:1).

A condition of eternal salvation (Heb 12:14).

Taught: By figures (Isa 61:9-11; M't 12:33; 1Co 3:17; Eph 2:21). By mottoes (Ex 28:36; Zec 14:20).

By disfellowship: Of the uncircumcised (Ge 17:14). Of those who violated the law, of unleavened bread (Ex 12:15); of sacrifices (Le 17:9; 19:5-7); of purification (Nu 19:20). Of those who were defiled (Le 7:25, 27; 13:5, 21, 26; 17:10; 18:29; 19:8; 20:3-6; Nu 5:2, 3; 19:13). Of those who were guilty of blasphemy (Nu 15:31).

Typified: In unblemished offerings (Ex 12:5; Le 1:3, 10; 3:1, 6; 4:3, 23; 5:15; 6:6; 9:2, 3; 22:19, 21; Nu 28:3, 9, 11, 19, 31; 29:2, 8, 13, 17, 20, 23, 26, 29, 32, 36). In washing of offerings (Le 1:9, 13). In washing of priests (Ex 29:4; Le 8:6; 1Ch 15:14). In washing of garments (Le 11:28, 40; 13:6, 34; 14:8, 9, 47; 15:5-13; Nu 19:7, 8, 10, 19, 21). In purifications (Le 12:4, 6-8; 15:16-18, 21, 22, 27; 16:4, 24, 26, 28; 17:15, 16). By differentiating between clean and unclean animals (Le 11:1-47; 20:25; De 14:3-20).

See God, Holiness of; Sanctification.

HOLM, a tree (Isa 44:14).

HOLON. 1. Levitical city in hill country of Judah (Jos 15:51); called Hilen in 1Ch 6:58.

2. Moabite town (Jer 48:21).

HOLY (See Sanctification.)

HOLY DAY (See Holiday.)

HOLY GHOST (See Holy Spirit.)

HOLY OF HOLIES. Most holy place, in the tabernacle (Le 4:6); in the temple (1Ki 6:16).

Separated from the holy place by the veil (Ex 26:33; Heb 9:3). Contained mercy seat and ark of the testimony (Ex 26:34; 40:20, 21; 1Ki 8:6); the cherubim (Ex 25:18-20; 26:34; 37:7-9; Heb 9:3-5).

Divine dwelling place (Ex 25:8, 21, 22; Ex 26:34; Le 16:2; Nu 7:39). Entered by the high priest on the day of atonement (Ex 26:34; Le 16:12, 13; Heb 9:6, 7). Atonement made for (Ex 26:34; Le 16:15-17, 33).

See Holy Place; Tabernacle.

HOLY PLACE. In the tabernacle and the temple. Separated from the most holy place by the veil (Ex 26:33).

Contents of: Altar of incense (Ex

30:1-6; 40:5, 26); the table of shewbread (Ex 40:4, 24; Heb 9:2); the candlestick (Ex 26:35; 40:4, 24; Heb 9:2). See various articles by name.

Priests, ministered in (Ex 29:30; 39:1, 41; Heb 9:6); required to eat sin offering in (Le 6:25, 26; 10:17).

See Sanctuary; Tabernacle; Temple.

HOLY SPIRIT (Ge 1:2; Ps 51:11; M't 1:18, 20; Ga 3:2, 3, 14; 6:8; Col 1:8; Heb 6:4). Convinces of sin (Ge 6:3; Joh 16:8-11). Comforts (Joh 14:16, 17, 26; 15:26; 16:7-14; Ac 9:31). Guides (Joh 16:13; Ac 13:2-4; 15:8, 28; 16:6, 7; Ro 8:4, 14; Ga 5:16, 18, 25). Helps our infirmities (Ro 8:26). Regenerates (Joh 3:5, 6; 2Co 3:3, 18; Tit 3:5, 6). Sanctifies (Ro 15:16; 1Co 6:11; 2Th 2:13; 1Pe 1:2). Dwells in believers (Ro 8:11). Invites to salvation (Re 22:17).

Communion with (2Co 13:14; Ph'p 2:1). Given to every man (1Co 12:7). Given, in answer to prayer (Lu 11:13; Ac 8:15); through imposition of hands (Ac 8:17-19; 19:6).

Access to the Father by (Eph 2:18). Prayer in (Eph 6:18; Jude 20). Wisdom and strength from (Ne 9:20; Zec 4:6; Eph 3:16). Liberty from (2Co 3:17). Love of God given by (Ro 5:5).

Ministers commissioned by (Ac 20:28). Christian baptism in the name of, with the name of Father and Son (M't 28:19). Gospel preached in power of (1Co 2:4, 10; 1Th 1:5; 1Pe 1:12). Word of God, sword of (Eph 6:17). Water, a symbol of (Joh 7:38, 39).

Demons cast out by (M't 12:28). Power to bestow, not purchasable (Ac 8:18-20).

Poured upon: Israel (Isa 32:15; Eze 39:29); the Gentiles (Ac 10:19, 20, 44-47; 11:15, 16); all flesh (Joe 2:28, 29; Ac 2:17).

Christians, are temples of (1Co 3:16; 6:19); are filled with (Ac 2:4, 33; 4:8, 31; 6:5; 8:17; 11:24; 13:9, 52; Eph 5:18; 2Ti 1:14); have fellowship with (Ro 8:9, 11; 1Co 3:16; 6:19; 2Co 13:14; Ph'p 2:1); receive earnest of (2Co 1:22; 5:5; Eph 1:13, 14); are sealed with (2Co 1:22; Eph 1:13; 4:30); have righteousness, peace, and joy in (Ro 14:17; 15:13; 1Th 1:6); are unified by (1Co 12:13).

Immaculate conception of Jesus by (M't 1:20; Lu 1:35).

Jesus anointed and led by (Isa 61:1; M't 3:16; 4:1; M'k 1:10; Lu 3:22; 4:18; Joh 1:32, 33; Ac 10:38; Heb 9:14).

Testifies that Jesus is Lord (Joh 15:26; 16:14; 1Co 12:3).

Baptism of (M't 3:11; M'k 1:8; Lu 3:16; Joh 1:33; 20:22; Ac 1:5; Ac 11:16; 19:2-6; 1Jo 2:20, 27).

Fruits of (Ro 8:23; Ga 5:22, 23).

Gifts of: Foretold (Isa 44:3; Joe 2:28, 29). Of different kinds (1Co 12:4-6, 8-10, 28). Bestowed for the confirmation of the gospel (Ro 15:19; Heb 2:4).

Inspiration of (M't 10:20; M'k 13:11; Lu 12:12; 1Co 2:4, 10-14; 1Ti 4:1).

Instances of Inspiration of: Joseph (Ge 41:38). Bezaleel (Ex 31:3; 35:31). The seventy elders (Nu 11:17). Balaam (Nu 24:2).

The Judges: Othniel (J'g 3:10); Gideon (J'g 6:34); Jephthah (J'g 11:29).

King Saul (1Sa 11:6). King David (1Ch 28:11, 12).

The prophets (2Pe 1:21). Azariah (2Ch 15:1). Zechariah (2Ch 24:20). Zacharias (Lu 1:67). Elizabeth (Lu 1:41). Simeon (Lu 2:25, 26). John the Baptist (Lu 1:15).

The disciples (Ac 6:3; 7:55; 8:29; 9:17; 10:45).

Intercession of (Ro 8:26, 27).

Power of: Promised (Lu 24:49; Ac 1:8; 2:38). On Christ (M't 12:28; Lu 4:14). On ministers (Ac 2:4; Ro 15:19). On the righteous (Ro 15:13; Eph 3:16).

Revelations from (M'k 12:36; Lu 2:26, 27; Joh 16:13; 1Co 2:10, 11; Eph 3:5; 1Ti 4:1; Heb 3:7; 2Pe 1:21; Re 2:7, 11, 29; 14:13).

Sin against (Ac 8:18-22; 1Jo 5:16). By grieving (Isa 63:10, 11, 14; Eph 4:30). By resisting (Ac 5:9; 7:51; Eph 4:30; 1Th 5:19; Heb 10:29). By blaspheming (M't 12:31, 32; M'k 3:29; Lu 12:10). By lying to (Ac 5:3).

Withdrawn from incorrigible sinners (Ge 6:3; De 32:30; Jer 7:29; Hos 4:17, 18; 9:12; Ro 1:24, 26, 28).

Instances of Withdrawal from Incorrigible Sinners: Antediluvians (Ge 6:3-7). Israelites (De 1:42; 28:15-68; 31:17, 18). Saul (1Sa 16:14; 18:12; 28:15, 16; 2Sa 7:15).

Witness of (Ac 5:32; Ro 8:15, 16; 9:1; 2Co 1:22; 5:5; Ga 4:6; Eph 1:13, 14; Heb 10:15; 1Jo 3:24; 4:13; 5:6-8).

HOLY TRINITY (M't 3:16; 28:19; Lu 3:22; Joh 1:32, 33; 14:16, 17, 26; 16:7, 13-15; Ac 1:2, 4, 5; 2:33; 10:38; Ro 8:9, 11; 1Co 12:3; 2Co 1:21, 22; 13:14; Ga 4:4, 6; 2Th 2:13, 14, 16; Tit 3:4-6; Heb 9:14; 1Pe 1:12).

See God; Jesus; Holy Spirit.

HOMAGE. Rendered, to Joseph (Ge 41:43); to kings (1Ki 1:16, 23, 31); to princes (Es 3:2, 5); to Mordecai (Es 6:11); to Daniel (Da 2:46).

Refused, by Peter (Ac 10:25, 26); by Paul and Barnabas (Ac 14:11-18); by the angel seen by John in his vision (Re 10:10; 22:8, 9).

See Worship.

HOMAN, called also Heman. An Edomite (Ge 36:22; 1Ch 1:39).

HOME (See Family.)

HOMELESS (Job 24:8; La 4:5; Lu 9:58; 1Co 4:11).

HOMER, a measure. (See Measure.)

HOMESTEAD. Mortgaged (Ne 5:3). When alienable, and when inalienable (Le 25:25-34).

See Lands.

HOMICIDE. Accidental (Ex 21:13; Nu 35:11-15, 22-28, 32; De 4:41-43; 19:1-10; Jos 20:1-9.

Felonious, or murder (Job 24:14; Ps 10:8; 38:12; 94:3, 6; Pr 12:6; 28:17; Isa 59:3; Jer 2:34; 7:9, 10; 19:4; Eze 22:9; Hos 4:1-3; Hab 2:10, 12). God's abhorrence of (Ps 5:6; 9:12; Pr 6:16, 17).

Forbidden (Ex 20:13; De 5:17; Pr 1:15, 16; Jer 22:3; M't 5:21; 19:18; M'k 10:19; Lu 18:20; Ro 13:9; 1Ti 1:9; Jas 2:11; 1Pe 4:15; 1Jo 3:12, 15).

Through conspiracy (Ps 37:32; Pr 1:11, 12). In hearts of wicked (M't 15:19; M'k 7:21). Impenitence for (Re 9:21). Penitence for (Ps 51:1-17). Inquest over suspected (De 21:1-9).

Instances of: By Cain (Ge 4:8). Lamech (Ge 4:23, 24). Simeon and Levi (Ge 34:25-31). Pharaoh (Ex 1:16, 22). Moses (Ex 2:12). Ehud (J'g 3:16-23). Abimelech (J'g 9:5, 18, 56). Joab (2Sa 3:24-27; 20:9, 10; 1Ki 2:5). Solomon (1Ki 2:23-46). Rechab and Baanah (2Sa 4:5-8). David (2Sa 11:14-17; 12:9). Absalom (2Sa 13:22-29). Baasha (1Ki 15:27-29). Zimri (1Ki 16:9-11). Ahab and Jezebel (1Ki 21:10-24). Hazael (2Ki 8:15). Jehu (2Ki 9:24-37). Athaliah (2Ki 11:1). Of Joash by his servants (2Ki 12:20, 21). Menahem (2Ki 15:16). Of Sennacherib, by his sons (2Ki 19:37; Isa 37:38). Manasseh (2Ki 21:16; 24:4). Of Amon, by his servants (2Ki 21:23). Jehoram (2Ch 21:4). Joash (2Ch 24:21). Amaziah's soldiers (2Ch 25:12). Nebuchadnezzar (Jer 39:6). Ishmael (Jer 41:1-7). Herod I (M't 2:16). Herod (M't 14:10; M'k 6:27). Barabbas (M'k 15:7; Ac 3:14).

Punishment for (Le 24:17; De 19:11-13; Ps 55:23). By a curse (Ge 4:9-12; 49:7; De 27:24, 25). By death (Ge 9:5, 6; Ex 21:12, 14; Nu 35:16-21, 30-33; De 17:6; 1Ki 21:19; Eze 35:6; Ho 1:4). By everlasting punishment (Re 21:8; 22:15).

Instances of punishment for: Cain (Ge 4:11-15). The murderer of Saul (2Sa 1:15, 16). David (2Sa 12:9-18). Joab (1Ki 2:31-34). Haman (Es 7:10). The murderers of Ishbosheth (2Sa 4:11, 12); of Joash (2Ki 14:5).

HONEY (Ex 16:31; 2Sa 17:29; Pr 25:27; Song 4:11; Isa 7:15; M't 3:4; Lu 24:42). Not to be offered with sacrifices (Le 2:11). Found in rocks (De 32:13; Ps 81:16); upon the ground (1Sa 14:25). Samson's riddle concerning (J'g 14:14). Sent as a present by Jacob to Egypt (Ge 43:11). Plentiful in Palestine (Ex 3:8; Le 20:24; De 8:8; Eze 20:6); in Assyria 2Ki 18:32). An article of merchandise from Palestine (Eze 27:17).

HOOD (Isa 3:23). See Dress.

HOOF, parting of, one of the physical marks used for distinguishing clean and unclean animals (Le 11:3-8; De 14:3-8).

HOOKS. For tabernacle, made of gold (Ex 26:32, 37; 36:36); silver (Ex 27:10; 38:10-12, 17, 19). In the temple, seen in Ezekiel's vision (Eze 40:43). Used for catching fish (Eze 29:4). For pruning (Isa 2:4; 18:5; Joe 3:10).

See Fleshhooks.

Figurative: Eze 38:4.

HOOPOE (See Birds.)

HONESTY. Prayer of (Ps 7:3, 4). Promises for (Ps 15:5; 24:4). Pleases God (Pr 11:1; 12:22). Proceeds from God (Pr 16:11; 20:10). Golden rule of (M't 7:12; Lu 6:31).

Enjoined (Le 19:35, 36; De 16:20; 25:13-16; Pr 4:25; Eze 45:10; M'k 10:19; Lu 3:12, 13; Ro 13:13; Ph'p 4:8; Col 3:22; 1Th 4:11, 12; 1Ti 2:2; 1Pe 2:11, 12).

Instances of: Jacob, returning money placed in sacks (Ge 43:12). Samuel, incorruptible in his judicial duties (1Sa 12:3-5). Overseers of temple repairs, with whom no reckoning was kept (2Ki 12:15; 22:4-7). Treasurers of the temple (Ne 13:13). Paul, in all his actions (Ac 24:16; 2Co 4:1, 2; 7:2; 8:21). The writer of Hebrews (13:18).

See Integrity; Righteousness; Dishonesty.

HOPE. In God (Ps 31:24; 33:22; 38:15; 39:7; 43:5; 71:5, 14; 78:7; 130:7; 146:5; Jer 17:7; La 3:21, 24, 26; 1Pe 1:21). A helmet (1Th 5:8). An anchor (Heb 6:18, 19).

Joy in (Pr 10:28; Ro 5:2; 12:12; Heb 3:6).

Of God's calling (Eph 1:18; 4:4). Of eternal life (Col 1:5, 6, 23, 27; Tit 1:2; 2:13; 3:7; 1Pe 1:3, 13; 1Jo 3:3). Of the resurrection (Ac 23:6; 24:14, 15; 26:6, 7; 28:20).

Deferred (Pr 13:12). Of wicked shall perish (Job 8:13; 11:20; 27:8; Pr 10:28: 11:7, 23).

Grounds of: God's word (Ps 119:74, 81; Ro 15:4); God's mercy (Ps 33:18); Jesus Christ (1Th 1:3; 1Ti 1:1).

Instances of (Job 31:24, 28; Ps 9:18; 16:9; 119:116; Pr 14:32; 23:18, 22; 24:14; Ho 2:15; Zec 9:12; Ro 4:18; 5:3-5; 15:13; 1Co 13:13; 2Co 3:12; Ga 5:5; Eph 2:12; Ph'p 1:20; 2Th 2:16; Heb 6:11; 1Pe 3:15).

HOPHNI. Son of Eli (1Sa 1:3). Sin of (1Sa 2:12-36; 3:11-14). Death of (1Sa 4:4, 11, 17).

HOR, mountain on which Aaron died (Nu 20:22-29; 21:4; 33:38, 39; 34:7, 8; De 32:50).

HORAM, king of Gezer (Jos 10:33).

HOREB (drought, desert), a range of mountains of which Sinai is chief (Ex 3:1; 17:6; 33:6; De 1:2, 6, 19; 4:10, 15; 5:2; 9:8; 29:1; 1Ki 8:9; 19:8; 2Ch 5:10; Ps 106:19; Mal 4:4).

See Sinai.

HOREM, a fortification in Naphtali (Jos 19:38).

HOR-HAGIDGAD (hollow), Israelite encampment (Nu 33:32, 33), called Gudgodah in De 10:7.

HORI (cave-dweller). 1. Son of Lotan (Ge 36:22, 30; 1Ch 1:39).

2. A Simeonite (Nu 13:5).

HORITE, HORIM, people conquered by Chedorlaomer (Ge 14:6); may be same as Hivites (Ge 34:2; Jos 9:7); thought to be Hurrians, from highlands of Media.

HORMAH (a devoted place). A city SW of the Dead Sea (Nu 14:45; 21:1-3; De 1:44). Taken by Judah and Simeon (J'g 1:17; Jos 12:14). Allotted to Simeon (Jos 19:4; 1Ch 4:30). Within the territory allotted to Judah (Jos 15:30; 1Sa 30:30).

HORN, used to hold the anointing oil (1Sa 16:1; 1Ki 1:39). Used for a trumpet, see Trumpet.

Figurative: Of divine protection (2Sa 22:3). Of power (1Ki 22:11; Ps 89:24; 92:10; 132:17).

Symbolical: Da 7:7-24; 8:3-9, 20; Am 6:13; Mic 4:13; Hab 3:4; Zec 1:18-21; Re 5:6; 12:3; 13:1, 11; 17:3-16.

HORNET, or wasp (Ex 23:28; De 7:20; Jos 24:12).

HORONAIM (two hollows), a town of Moab (Isa 15:5; Jer 48:3, 5, 34).

HORONITE, Sanballat, the (Ne 2:10, 19; 13:28).

HORSE. Description of: Great strength (Job 39:19-25); swifter than eagles (Jer 4:13); snorting and neighing of (Isa 5:28; Jer 8:16); a vain thing for safety (Ps 33:17; Pr 21:31). Used by the Egyptians in war (Ex 14:9; 15:19), the Israelites (1Ki 22:4). Used for cavalry (2Ki 18:23; Jer 47:3; 51:21). Egypt famous for (Isa 31:1). Forbidden to kings of Israel (De 17:16). Hamstrung by Joshua (Jos 11:6, 9); David (2Sa 8:4). Israel reproved for keeping (Isa 2:7; 3:1; Eze 17:15; Ho 14:3). Exported from Egypt (1Ki 10:28, 29; 2Ch 9:25, 28); from Babylon (Ezr 2:66; Ne 7:68). Bits for (Jas 3:3); bells for (Zec 14:20); harness for (Jer 46:4). Color of (Zec 1:8). Commerce in (Re 18:13; see Exported, above). Dedicated to religious uses (2Ki 23:11).

Symbolical: Zec 1:8; Re 6:2-8; 9:17; 19:11-21.

HORSE GATE, one of the gates of Jerusalem (Ne 3:28-32; Jer 31:38-40).

HORSE LEECH, bloodsucking worm which clings to the flesh (Pr 30:15).

HORTICULTURE, encouraged (Le 19:23-25; De 20:19, 20).

See Agriculture; Grafting; Pruning.

HOSAH (refuge). 1. A city of Asher (Jos 19:29).

2. A Levite (1Ch 16:38; 26:10, 11).

HOSANNA (save now), originally a prayer, "Save, now, pray" (Ps 118:25) chanted when Jesus entered Jerusalem (M't 21:9-15; M'k 11:9, 10; Joh 12:13).

HOSEA (salvation), 8th cent. B. C. prophet during reigns of Uzziah, Jotham, Ahaz of Judah, and Hezekiah and Jeroboam II of Israel (Ho 1:1), contemporary with the prophets Isaiah, Amos, and Micah. Outline. 1. Hosea's unhappy marriage and its results (1-3).

2. Priests condone immorality (4).

3. Israel's sin will be punished unless she repents (5).

4. Israel's sin is thoroughgoing; her repentance half hearted (6).

5. Inner depravity and outward decay (7).

6. Nearness of judgment (8).

7. Impending calamity (9).

8. Israel's guilt and punishment (10).

9. God pursues Israel with love (11).

10. Exhortation to repentance, with promised restoration (12-14).

HOSHAIAH (Jehovah has saved). 1. One of the returned exiles (Ne 12:32).

2. A distinguished Jewish captive (Jer 42:1; 43:2).

HOSHAMA, son of Jeconiah, king of Judah (1Ch 3:18).

HOSHEA (salvation) 1. Called also Oshea. The original name of Joshua (Nu 13:8, 16; De 32:44).

2. A chief of Ephraim (1Ch 27:20).

3. King of Israel. Assassinates Pekah and usurps the throne (2Ki 15:30). Evil reign of (2Ki 17:1, 2). Becomes subject to Assyria (2Ki 17:3). Conspires against Assyria and is imprisoned (2Ki 17:4). Last king of Israel (2Ki 17:6; 18:9-12; Ho 10:3, 7).

4. A Jewish exile (Ne 10:23).

HOSPITALITY. Unselfish (Lu 14:12-14). Deceitful guise of (Pr 9:1-5; 23:6-8). Parable of (M't 22:2-10).

Enjoined (Isa 58:6, 7; M't 25:34-39; Ro 12:13; 1Ti 3:2; 5:10; Tit 1:7, 8; Heb 13:2; 1Pe 4:9-11; 3Jo 5-8). Toward strangers, enjoined (Ex 22:11; 23:9; Le 19:10, 33, 34; 24:22; De 10:18, 19; 26:12, 13; 27:19).

Instances of: Pharaoh to Abraham (Ge 12:16). Melchizedek to Abraham (Ge 14:18). Abraham to angels (Ge 18:1-8). Lot to an angel (Ge 19:1-11). Abimelech to Abraham (Ge 20:14, 15). Sons of Heth to Abraham (Ge 23:6, 11). Laban, to Abraham's servant (Ge 24:31-33); to Jacob (Ge 29:13, 14). Isaac to Abimelech (Ge 26:30). Joseph to his brethren (Ge 43:31-34). Pharaoh to Jacob (Ge 45:16-20; 47:7-12). Jethro to Moses (Ex 2:20). Rahab to the spies (Jos 2:1-16). Man of Gibeah to the Levite (J'g 19:16-21). Pharaoh to Hadad (1Ki 11:17, 22). Jeroboam to the prophet of Judah (1Ki 13:7). The widow of Zarephath to Elijah (1Ki 17:10-24). The Shunammite to Elisha (2Ki 4:8). Elisha to the Syrian spies (2Ki 6:22). Job to strangers (Job 31:32). David to Mephibosheth (2Sa 9:7-13). King of Babylon to Jehoiachin (2Ki 25:29, 30). Nehemiah to rulers and Jews (Ne 5:17-19).

Martha to Jesus (Lu 10:38; Joh 12:1, 2). Pharisees to Jesus (Lu 11:37, 38). Zacchaeus to Jesus (Lu 19:1-10). Disciples to Jesus (Lu 24:29). The tanner to Peter (Ac 10:6, 23). Lydia to Paul and Silas (Ac 16:15). Barbarians to Paul (Ac 28:2). Publius to Paul (Ac 28:7). Phoebe to Paul (Ro 16:2). Onesiphorus to Paul (2Ti 1:16). Gaius (3Jo 5:8).

Rewarded, Instances of: Rahab (Jos 6:17, 22-25). Widow of Zarephath (1Ki 17:10-24).

See Feasts; Guests; Strangers.

HOST. Army (Ge 21:22); angels (Ps 103:21; Jos 5:14); heavenly bodies (De 4:19); creation (Ge 2:1); God of hosts (1Sa 17:45); one who shows hospitality (Ro 16:23; Lu 10:35).

HOSTAGE (2Ki 14:14; 2Ch 15:24).

HOSTILITY. To the Righteous (Mic 7:6; M't 10:21, 35, 36; M'k 13:12; Lu 12:53).

HOTHAM, son of Heber (1Ch 7:32).

HOTHAN, an Aroerite (1Ch 11:44).

HOTHIR, son of Heman (1Ch 25:4, 28).

HOT SPRINGS (Ge 36:24).

HOUGHING (to hamstring an animal), of horses (Jos 11:6, 9; 2Sa 8:4; 1Ch 18:4).

HOURS. A division of time. Twelve, in the day (Joh 11:9; M't 20:3-12; 27:45, 46); in the night (Ac 23:23).

Symbolical: Re 8:1; 9:15.

HOUSE. Built of stone (Le 14:40-45; Isa 9:10; Am 5:11); brick (Ge 11:3; Ex 1:11-14; Isa 9:10); wood (Song 1:17; Isa 9:10). Built into city walls (Jos 2:15).

Used for worship (Ac 1:13, 14; 12:12;

Ro 16:5; 1Co 16:19; Col 4:15; Ph'm 2).

"A man's castle" (De 24:10, 11).

Architecture of: Foundations of stone (1Ki 5:17; 7:9; Ezr 6:3; Jer 51:26). Figurative (Ps 87:1; Isa 28:16; 48:13; Ro 15:20; 1Co 3:11; Eph 2:20; 1Ti 6:19; Heb 6:1; Re 21:14). Corner stone (Job 38:6; Ps 144:12). Figurative (Ps 118:22; Isa 28:16; Eph 2:20; 1Pe 2:6).

Porches (J'g 3:23; 1Ki 7:6, 7); courts (Es 1:5); summer apartment (J'g 3:20, w Am 3:15; 1Ki 17:19); inner chamber (1Ki 22:25); chambers (Ge 43:30; 2Sa 18:33; 2Ki 1:2; 4:10; Ac 1:13; 9:37; 20:8); guest chamber (M'k 14:14); pillars (Pr 9:1); with courts (Ne 8:16); lattice (J'g 5:28); windows (J'g 5:28; Pr 7:6); ceiled and plastered (De 5:5); hinges (Pr 26:14).

Roofs, flat (Jos 2:6; J'g 16:27; 1Sa 9:25; 2Sa 11:2; 16:22; Isa 15:3; 22:1; M't 24:17; Lu 12:3); battlements required in Mosaic law (De 22:8). Prayer on (Ac 10:9). Altars on (2Ki 23:12; Jer 19:13; 32:29; Zep 1:5). Booths on (Ne 8:16); Used as place to sleep (Jos 2:8; Ac 10:9); as dwelling place (Pr 21:9; 25:24).

Painted (Jer 22:14; Eze 8:10, 12). Chimneys of (Ho 13:3). Texts of scripture on doorposts of (De 6:9). Laws regarding sale of (Le 25:29-33; Ne 5:3). Dedicated (De 20:5; Ps 30 [title]).

Figurative: 2Sa 7:18; Ps 23:6; 36:8; Joh 14:2; 2Co 5:1; 1Ti 3:15; Heb 3:2).

HOUSE OF GOD. A place of prayer (M't 21:13; M'k 11:17; Lu 19:46). Holy (Ec 5:1; Isa 62:9; Eze 43:12; 1Co 3:17).

See Synagogue; Tabernacle; Temple.

HOUSETOPS, as places of resort (Jos 2:6; 1Sa 9:25; Ne 8:16; Pr 21:9; M't 10:27; 24:17; Lu 5:19; Ac 10:9).

HUKKOK, a place on the boundary line of Naphtali (Jos 19:34).

HUKOK (See Helkath.)

HUL, son of Aram (Ge 10:23; 1Ch 1:17).

HULDAH (weasel) a prophetess. Foretells the destruction of Jerusalem (2Ki 22:14-20: 2Ch 34:22-28).

HUMAN SACRIFICE (See Offering, Human.)

HUMILIATION AND SELF-AFFLICTION. Enjoined (Le 16:29-31; 23:26-32; Ezr 8:21-23; 2Ch 7:14).

See Fasting; Humility.

HUMILITY (Ps 51:17; 69:32; 138:6; Pr 3:34; 11:2; 12:15; 16:19; Isa 57:15; 66:2; Lu 10:21; 2Co 7:6; Ga 6:14; Jas 4:6).

Enjoined (De 15:15; Pr 25:6, 7; 27:2; 30:32; Ec 5:2; Jer 45:5; Mic 6:8; M't 18:2-4; 20:26, 27; M'k 9:33-37; 10:43, 44; Lu 9:46-48; 14:10; 17:10; 22:24-27; Joh 13:14-16; Ro 11:18-20, 25; 12:3, 10, 16; 1Co 3:18; 4:6; 10:12; Ga 5:26; Eph 4:1, 2; 5:21; Ph'p 2:3-11; Col 3:12; Jas 1:9, 10; 4:10; 1Pe 5:3, 5, 6).

Feigned, forbidden (Col 2:18-23).

Rewards of (Job 5:11; 22:29; Ps 138:6; Pr 15:33; 18:12; 22:4; 29:23; M't 5:3; 23:12; Lu 1:52; 14:11; 18:13, 14).

Exemplified in: Abraham (Ge 18:27, 32); Jacob (Ge 32:10); Joseph (Ge 41:16); Moses (Ex 3:11; 4:10); David (1Sa 18:18-23; 23:14; 26:20; 2Sa 7:18-20; 1Ch 17:16-18; 29:14); the psalmist (Ps 8:3, 4; 73:22; 131:1-2; 141:5; 144:3); Solomon (1Ki 3:7; 2Ch 1:10; 2:6); Mephibosheth (2Sa 9:8); Ahab (1Ki 21:29); kings and princes of Israel (2Ch 12:6, 7, 12); Josiah (2Ki 22:18, 19; 2Ch 34:26, 27); Job (Job 7:17, 18; 9:14, 15; 40:4, 5; 42:2-6); Elihu (Job 32:4-7; 33:6); Ezra (Ezr 9:13, 15); Agur (Pr 30:2, 3); Isaiah (Isa 6:5); Hezekiah (Isa 38:15); Jeremiah (Jer 1:6; 10:23, 24); Daniel (Da 2:30); Ezra and the Jews (Ezr 8:21, 23); Elisabeth (Lu 1:43); John the Baptist (M't 3:14; M'k 1:7; Lu 3:16; Joh 1:27; 3:29, 30); Jesus (M't 11:29; 13:4-16); woman of Canaan (M't 15:27); the righteous (M't 25:37-40); the publican (Lu 18:13); centurion (M't 8:8; Lu 7:6, 7); Peter (Ac 2:12); Paul (Ac 20:19; Ro 7:18; 1Co 2:1-3; 15:9, 10; 2Co 3:5; 11:30; 12:5-12; Eph 3:8; Ph'p 3:12, 13; 4:12; 1Ti 1:15).

HUMTAH. A city of Judah (Jos 15:54).

HUNGER. Man does not live by bread alone (De 8:3; M't 4:4; Lu 4:3). Labor excites (Pr 16:26). Source of temptation (Ge 25:29-34; Ex 16:2, 3; Heb 12:16). An occasion of the temptation of Jesus (M't 4:3, 4; Lu 4:2, 3). Of an enemy, an opportunity for good works (Pr 25:21, 22; Ro 12:20).

Experienced by Jesus (M't 21:18; M'k 11:12). Endured, by Jesus during his temptation (M't 4:2-4; Lu 4:2-4); by Paul for Christ's sake (1Co 4:11). Foretold as a judgment upon the Israelites (Isa 8:21; 9:20).

Figurative: Of spiritual desire (Ps 107:9; Pr 2:3-5; Isa 55:1, 2; Am 8:11-13;

M't 5:6; Lu 1:53; 6:21; Joh 6:35; 1Pe 2:2).

See Appetite; Famine; Desire, Spiritual; Thirst.

HUNTING. Authorized in the Mosaic law (Le 17:13). By Nimrod (Ge 10:9). By Esau (Ge 27:3, 5, 30, 33). By Ishmael (Ge 21:20). Of lion (Job 10:16). Fowling (1Sa 26:20; Ps 140:5; 141:9, 10; Pr 1:17; Ec 9:12; La 3:52; Am 3:5).

Figurative: Jer 16:16.

HUPHAM, son of Benjamin; founder of Huphamites (Nu 26:39).

HUPHAMITES (See Hupham.)

HUPPAH, priest in David's time (1Ch 24:13).

HUPPIM (coast people), a Benjamite (Ge 46:21; 1Ch 7:12, 15).

HUR. 1. An Israelite who assisted in supporting Moses' hands during battle (Ex 17:10, 12; 24:14).

2. A son of Caleb (Ex 31:2; 35:30; 38:22; 1Ch 2:19, 20; 2Ch 1:5).

3. A king of Midian (Nu 31:8; Jos 13:21).

4. Called Ben Hur, an officer of Solomon's commissary (1Ki 4:8 [marg.]).

5. Father of Caleb (1Ch 2:50; 4:4).

6. A son of Judah (1Ch 4:1).

7. A ruler (Ne 3:9).

HURAI, one of David's heroes (1Ch 11:32). Called Hiddai in 2Sa 23:30.

HURAM (noble-born). 1. Benjamite (1Ch 8:5).

2. King of Tyre (2Ch 2:3, 11, 12). Usually called Hiram.

3. Tyrian artificer (2Ch 2:13; 4:11, 16).

HURI, father of Abihail (1Ch 5:14).

HURRIANS (See Horites.)

HUSBAND. Relation of, to wife (Ge 2:23, 24; M't 19:5, 6; M'k 10:7; 1Co 7:3-5; Eph 5:22-33). May give wife bill of divorcement (De 24:1-4). Law relating to, in cases where wife's virtue is questioned (Nu 5:11-31; De 22:13-21). Exemptions for (De 24:5). Chastity of (Pr 5:15-20; Mal 2:14-16). Duties of (Ec 9:9; Col 3:19; 1Pe 3:7); to provide for family (Ge 30:30; 1Ti 5:8). Rights of (1Co 7:3, 5). Sanctified in the wife (1Co 7:14, 16). Headship of (1Co 11:3).

Faithful: Isaac (Ge 24:67); Joseph (M't 1:19, 20). Unreasonable and oppressive (Es 1:10-22).

Figurative: Isa 54:5, 6; Jer 3:14; 31:32; Ho 2:19, 20.

HUSBANDMAN. An agriculturalist (M't 21:33-46; M'k 12:1-9; Joh 15:1; 1Co 3:9).

Parable of, describing the unfaithful Jews, given over to corruption and hypocrisy (M't 21:33-46; M'k 12:1-12; Lu 20:9-19).

Figurative: Joh 15:1; 1Co 3:9.

See Agriculture.

HUSBANDRY (See Husbandman; Agriculture; Animals.)

HUSHAH. Son of Ezer (1Ch 4:4). Probably called Shuah (1Ch 4:11).

HUSHAI, Archite; counselor of David who overthrew counsels of Ahithophel (2Sa 15:32, 37; 16:16-18; 17:5-15; 1Ch 27:33).

HUSHAM, a Temanite (Ge 36:34, 35; 1Ch 1:45, 46).

HUSHATHITE, THE, patronymic of Sibbecai, one of David's heroes (2Sa 21:18; 1Ch 11:29; 20:4; 27:11).

HUSHIM. 1. Son of Dan (Ge 46:23). Called Shuham (Nu 26:42).

2. A Benjamite (1Ch 7:12).

3. Wife of Shaharaim (1Ch 8:8, 11).

HUSK, a pod (Nu 6:4; 2Ki 4:42). Eaten by the prodigal son (Lu 15:16).

HUZ, son of Nahor (Ge 22:21).

HUZZAB, probably a region E of the Tigris (Na 2:7).

HYACINTH. 1. Deep purple (Re 9:17). KJV has "jacinth."

2. A precious stone (Re 21:20. RV has "sapphire."

HYBRIDIZING, forbidden (Le 19:19).

HYENA (See Animals.)

HYGIENE (1Co 6:18; 9:25).

See Sanitation.

HYKSOS, a W Semitic people who ruled an empire embracing Syria and Palestine; conquered Egypt c. 1700 B. C.

HYMENAEUS, apostate Christian excommunicated by Paul (1Ti 1:19, 20; 2Ti 2:16-18).

HYMN (See Psalms; Song.)

HYPOCRISY. Described (Job 31:33, 34; Ps 5:6, 9; 52:4; 78:34-37; Isa 29:13; 32:5, 6; 48:1, 2; 58:2-5; Jer 12:2; 17:9; Eze 33:30-32; Ho 6:4; 10:1, 4; Zec 7:5, 6; M't 15:3-9; 21:28-32; M'k 7:5-13; 9:50; Lu 14:34, 35; 18:11, 12; Ro 9:6, 7; 1Co 5:8; 13:1; 2Co 4:2; 1Jo 1:6, 10; 2:4, 9, 19; 4:20; Re 3:1).

Abhorred by God (Job 13:16; Ps 50:16, 17; Pr 15:8; 21:27; Isa 1:9-15; 9:17; 10:6; 58:2-5; 61:8; 65:2-5; 66:3-5;

Jer 5:2; 6:20; 7:4, 8-10; Eze 5:11; 20:39; Ho 8:13; 9:4; 11:12; Am 5:21-27; Zec 7:5, 6; Mal 1:6-14; 2:13). Rebuked by Jesus (M't 3:7, 8; 7:7, 8; 9:13; 15:7-9; 16:3; 23:2-33; Lu 6:46; 11:39, 42, 44; 12:54-56; 13:13-17; Joh 6:26, 70; 7:19; 15:2, 6; Re 2:9; 3:9). Exposed by Paul (Ro 2:1, 3, 17-29; 2Co 5:12; Ga 6:3; Ph'p 3:2, 18, 19; 1Ti 4:2; 2Ti 3:5, 13; Tit 1:16).

Betrays friends (Ps 55:12-14, 20-23; Pr 11:9; 25:19; Ob 7: Zec 13:6).

Of harlots (Pr 7:10-21). Of false teachers (Mic 3:11; Ro 16:17, 18; 2Pe 2:1-3, 17, 19). Of dishonest buyers (Pr 20:14).

Warning to (Job 15:31, 33, 34; 17:8; 20:4, 5; 27:8-10; 34:30). Warning against (Pr 23:6-8; 26:18, 19, 23-26; Jer 9:8; Mic 7:5; M't 6:1, 2, 5, 16, 24; 7:5, 15, 21-23; 16:6; 23:14; M'k 8:15; 12:38-40; Lu 12:1, 2; 13:26, 27; 16:13, 15; 20:46, 47; Jas 1:8, 22-24, 26; 3:17; 4:8; 1Pe 2:1, 16; Jude 12, 13).

Punishment for (Job 8:13-15; 36:13, 14; Ps 55:23; 101:7; Isa 29:15, 16; 33:14; Jer 42:20-22; Eze 5:11; 14:3, 4, 7, 8; Ho 8:13; 9:4; M't 22:12, 13; 24:50, 51; 25:41-45; Ro 1:18).

See Deceit; Deception.

Instances of: Jacob, in impersonating Esau and deceiving his father (Ge 27). Jacob's sons, in deception of their father concerning Joseph (Ge 37:29-35). Joseph's deception of his brethren (Ge 42-44). Pharaoh (Ex 8:15, 28, 29, 32; 9:27-35; 10:8-29). Balaam (Jude 11, w Nu 22-24). Delilah, the wife of Samson (J'g 16). Jael (J'g 4:8-21). Ehud (J'g 3:15-25). Rabshakeh (2Ki 18:17-37). Ahaz (Isa 7:12 w verses 17-25). Johanan (Jer 42:1-12, 20, 22). Ishmael (Jer 41:6, 7). The false prophets (Eze 13:1-23). Herod (M't 2:8). Judas (M't 26:25, 48; Joh 12:5, 6). Pilate (M't 27:24). Pharisees (M't 15:1-9; 22:18; M'k 12:13, 14; Joh 8:4-9; 9:24; 19:15). The ruler (Lu 13:14-17). Spies sent to entrap Jesus (Lu 20:21). Priests and Levites (Lu 10:31, 32). Chief priests (Joh 18:28). Ananias and Sapphira (Ac 5:1-10). Simon Magus (Ac 8:18-23). Peter and other Christians at Antioch (Ga 2:11-14). Judaizing Christians in Galatia (Ga 6:13). False teachers at Ephesus (Re 2:2).

See Conspiracy; Treachery.

HYSSOP. A plant indigenous to western Asia and northern Africa (1Ki 4:33). The Israelites used, in sprinkling the blood of the paschal lamb upon the lintels of their doors (Ex 12:22); in sprinkling blood in purifications (Le 14:4, 6, 51, 52; Heb 9:19). Used in the sacrifices of separation (Nu 19:6). Used in giving Jesus vinegar on the cross (Joh 19:29).

Figurative: Of spiritual cleansing (Ps 51:7).

I

I AM THAT I AM, a name of deity (Ex 3:14; Re 1:4, 11, 17).

IBHAR (he chooses), son of David (2Sa 5:15; 1Ch 3:6; 14:5).

IBLEAM, town given to the tribe of Manasseh (Jos 17:11). Ahaziah slain there (2Ki 9:27). Generally identified with Bileam (1Ch 6:70).

IBNEIAH (Jehovah builds), a Benjamite (1Ch 9:8).

IBNIJAH (Jehovah builds), a Benjamite (1Ch 9:8).

IBRI (a Hebrew), a Levite (1Ch 24:27).

IBZAN, 10th judge of Israel (J'g 12:8-10); had 30 sons and 30 daughters.

ICE (Job 6:16; 38:29; Ps 147:17; Pr 25:13).

ICHABOD (inglorious), son of Phinehas, Eli's son (1Sa 4:19ff).

ICONIUM. A city of Asia Minor. Paul preaches in (Ac 13:51; 14:21, 22; 16:2); is persecuted by the people of (Ac 14:1-6; 2Ti 3:11).

ICONOCLASM. Idols to be destroyed (Ex 23:24; 34:13; Nu 33:52; De 7:5, 25, 26; 12:1-4; J'g 2:2; Jer 50:2). Destroyed by Jacob (Ge 35:2-4); Moses (Ex 32:19, 20); Gideon (J'g 6:28-32); David (2Sa 5:21; 1Ch 14:12); Jehu (2Ki 10:26-28); Jehoiada (2Ki 11:18); Hezekiah (2Ki 18:3-6); Josiah (2Ki 23:4-20); Asa (2Ch 14:3-5; 15:8-16); Jehoshaphat (2Ch 17:6; 19:3); Jews (2Ch 30:14); Manasseh (2Ch 33:15).

See Idolatry.

IDALAH, a town of Zebulun (Jos 19:15).

IDBASH (honey-sweet), a descendant of Judah (1Ch 4:3).

IDDO. 1. Father of Ahinadab (1Ki 4:14).

2. A descendant of Gershom (1Ch 6:21).

3. A son of Zechariah (1Ch 27:21).

4. A prophet (2Ch 9:29; 12:15; 13:22).

5. Ancestor of Zechariah (Ezr 5:1; 6:14; Zec 1:1, 7).

6. A priest (Ne 12:4, 16).

7. The chief of the Jews established at Casiphia (Ezr 8:17).

IDENTIFICATION. With Jesus, price of (M't 4:19; 8:22; 9:9; 16:24; 19:21; M'k 2:14; 8:34; 10:21; Lu 5:27; 9:23; 18:22; Joh 15:14, 18, 19; 16:2); indication of (Joh 10:27; 12:26; Ac 11:26).

IDLENESS. Comparisons regarding (Pr 15:19; 18:9; 22:13; 26:13-16; Ec 4:5). Poverty from (Pr 6:6-11; 10:4, 5; 12:9, 24, 27; 13:4; 14:23; 19:15; 20:4, 13; 23:21; 24:30-34; Ec 10:18). Denounced (Pr 21:25, 26; Isa 56:10; Lu 19:20-24; 2Th 3:10, 11; 1Ti 5:13).

A sin of Sodom (Eze 16:49). Other instances of (M't 20:6, 7; Ac 17:21).

See Laziness; Slothfulness; Industry.

IDOL. Manufacture of (Ex 20:4; 32:4, 20; De 4:23; Isa 40:19, 20; 44:9-12, 17; Hab 2:18; Ac 19:24, 25). Manufacture of, forbidden (Ex 20:4; 34:17). Made of gold (Ex 32:3, 4; Ps 115:4-7; 135:15-17; Isa 2:20; 30:22; 31:7; Ho 8:4), silver (Isa 2:20; 30:22; 31:7; Ho 8:4); wood and stone (Le 26:1; De 4:28; 2Ki 19:18; Isa 37:19; 41:6; 44:13-19; Eze 20:32). Coverings of (Isa 30:22).

Prayer to, unanswered (1Ki 18:25-29). Falls down before the ark of Jehovah (1Sa 5:1-5). Used by Michal to save the life of David (1Sa 19:13-17). Derided (Ps 115:4-8; 135:15-18; Isa 44:9-17). To be abandoned (Isa 2:20). To be destroyed (De 12:3). Things offered to, not to be eaten (Ex 34:15). Paul's instructions concerning eating things offered to (1Co 8; 10:25-33).

See Iconoclasm; Idolatry.

IDOLATRY. *Wicked Practices of:* Human sacrifices (Le 18:21; 20:2-5; De 12:31; 18:10; 2Ki 3:26, 27; 16:3; 17:17, 18; 21:6; 23:10; 2Ch 28:3; 33:6; Ps 106:37, 38; Isa 57:5; Jer 7:31; 19:4-7; 32:35; Eze 16:20, 21; 20:26, 31; 23:37, 39; Mic 6:7); practices of, relating to the dead (De 14:1); licentiousness of (Ex 32:6, 25; Nu 25:1-3; 1Ki 14:24; 15:12; 2Ki 17:30; 23:7; Eze 16:17; 23:1-44; Ho 4:12-14; Am 2:8; Mic 1:7; Ro 1:24, 26, 27; 1Co 10:7, 8; 1Pe 4:3, 4; Re 2:14, 20-22; 9:20, 21; 14:8; 17:1-6).

Other Customs of: Offered burnt offerings (Ex 32:6; 1Ki 18:26; Ac 14:13); libations (Isa 57:6; 65:11; Jer 7:18; 19:13; 32:29; 44:17, 19, 25; Eze 20:28); of wine (De 32:38); of blood (Ps 16:4; Zec 9:7); meat offerings (Isa 57:6; Jer

7:18; 44:17; Eze 16:19); peace offerings (Ex 32:6).

Incense burned on altars (1Ki 12:33; 2Ch 30:14; 34:25; Isa 65:3; Jer 1:16; 11:12, 17; 44:3; 48:35; Eze 16:18; 23:41; Ho 11:2). Prayers to idols (J'g 10:14; Isa 44:17; 45:20; 46:7; Jon 1:5). Praise (J'g 16:24; Da 5:4).

Singing and dancing (Ex 32:18, 19). Music (Da 3:5-7). Cutting the flesh (1Ki 18:28; Jer 41:5). Kissing (1Ki 19:18; Ho 13:2; Job 31:27). Bowing (1Ki 19:18; 2Ki 5:18). Tithes and gifts (2Ki 23:11; Da 11:38; Am 4:4, 5).

Annual Feasts: 1Ki 12:32; Eze 18:6, 11, 12, 15; 22:9; Da 3:2, 3.

Objects of: Sun, moon, and stars (De 4:19; 2Ki 17:16; 21:3, 5; 2Ch 33:3, 5; Job 31:26-28; Jer 7:17-20; 8:2; Eze 8:15, 16; Zep 1:4, 5; Ac 7:42). Images of angels (Col 2:18); animals (Ro 1:23). Gods of Egypt (Ex 12:12). Golden calf (Ex 32:4). Brazen serpent (2Ki 18:4). Net and drag (Hab 1:16). Pictures (Nu 33:52; Isa 2:16). Pictures on walls (Eze 8:10). Earrings (Ge 35:4).

See Shrine.

Folly of (De 4:28; 32:37, 38; J'g 6:31; 10:14; 1Sa 5:3, 4; 12:21; 1Ki 18:25-29; 2Ki 19:18; 2Ch 25:15; Ps 106:19, 20; 115:4, 5, 8; 135:15-18; Isa 37:19; 44:9-20; 45:20; 46:1, 2, 6, 7; Jer 2:28; 11:12; 16:19, 20; 48:13; 51:17; Ho 8:5, 6; Zec 10:2; Ac 14:13, 15; 17:22, 23, 29; Ro 1:22, 23; 1Co 8:4; 10:5; 12:2; Ga 4:8; Re 9:20).

Folly of, illustrated by contrast of idols with the true God (Ps 96:5; Isa 40:12-26; 41:23-29; Jer 10:5; 14:22; Da 5:23; Hab 2:18, 19, 20).

Folly of, exemplified in the ruin of Israel (2Ch 28:22, 23).

Denounced (De 12:31; 27:15; Job 31:26-28; Ps 44:20, 21; 97:7; Isa 42:17; 45:16; Jer 3:1-11; 32:34, 35; Eze 16:16-63; 43:7-9; Ho 1:2; 2:2-5; 4:12-19; 5:1-3; 9:10; 13:2, 3; Jon 2:8; Am 4:4, 5; Hab 1:16; Ac 17:16-29; Ro 1:25; 1Co 6:9, 10).

Forbidden (Ge 35:2; Ex 20:3-6, 23; 23:13, 24, 32, 33; 34:14, 17; Le 19:4; 26:1, 30; De 4:15-28; 5:7-9; 7:2-5, 16; 11:16, 17; 16:21, 22; Ps 81:9; Eze 8:8-18; 14:1-8; 16:15-63; 20:7, 8, 16, 18, 24, 27-32, 39; 23:7-49; Ac 15:20-29; 1Co 10:14, 20-22; 1Jo 5:21).

Prophecies relating to (Isa 46:1, 2). Its punishments (Nu 33:4; De 31:16-21, 29; Isa 21:9; Jer 51:44, 47, 52). Its end (Isa 2:8, 18, 20; 17:7, 8; 27:9; 31:7; Jer 10:11, 15; Ho 10:2; 14:8; Mic 5:13, 14; Zep 2:11; Zec 13:2).

Punishment of (De 8:19; 11:28; 13:6-9; 17:2-5; 28:14-18; 30:17, 18; 32:15-26; J'g 2:3; 1Ki 9:6-9; Ne 9:27-37; Ps 16:4; 59:8; 78:58-64; 106:34-42; Isa 1:29-31; 2:6-22; 30:22; 65:3-7; Jer 1:15, 16; 5:1-17; 7; 8:1, 2, 19; 13:9-27; 16; 17:1-6; 18:13-17; 19; 22:5-9; 44; Eze 6; 8:8-18; 9; 14:1-8; 16:15-63; 20:7, 8, 24-39; 22:4; 23:9, 10, 22-49; 44:10-12; Ho 8:5-14; 10; 13:1-4; Am 3:14; 5:5; Mic 1:1-9; 5:12-14; 6:16; Zep 1; Mal 2:11-13; Re 21:8; 22:15).

See Idol; Iconoclasm.

IDUMAEA, (pertaining to Edom), Greek and Roman name for Edom (M'k 3:8).

IFS, OF THE BIBLE (See Blessings, Contingent.)

IGAL (God redeems) 1. Spy of Issachar (Nu 13:7).

2. One of David's heroes (2Sa 23:36).

3. Descendant of Jeconiah (1Ch 3:22).

IGDALIAH (Jehovah is great), father of Hanan (Jer 35:4).

IGEAL (God redeems), son of Shemaiah (1Ch 3:22).

IGNORANCE. Characteristic of man (Job 8:9; 28:12, 13, 20, 21; Pr 8:5; 19:2; Ec 7:23, 24; Jer 10:23; Ho 4:14; Joh 13:7).

Concerning God (1Sa 3:7; Job 11:7, 8, 12; 36:26, 29; 37:5, 15, 16, 19, 23; Ps 139:6; Pr 30:3, 4; Ac 17:23, 30); his works (Ec 3:11; 8:17; 11:5); his wisdom (1Co 2:7-10).

Concerning the future (Pr 27:1; Ec 8:6, 7; Ac 1:7; 1Co 13:9, 12). Concerning the Holy Spirit (Ac 19:2). Concerning the Scripture (M't 22:29; M'k 12:24; Joh 20:9; 1Ti 1:7).

Concerning snares of the wicked (Pr 7:6-23; 9:14-18; 22:3; 27:12).

Remedy for (Jas 1:5, 6).

Sins of: Sacrifices for (Le 4:1-35; 5:4-19; Nu 15:22-29; Eze 45:20). Forgiven (1Ti 1:12, 13; Heb 5:2). Forgiven on account of reparation (Ge 20:1-7).

Evil consequences of (Isa 5:13; Ho 4:6). Alienates from God (Eph 4:18, 19). Darkens understanding (Lu 23:34; Joh

16:2, 3; Ac 3:17; 1Co 2:8).

Punishment of (Eze 3:18; 33:6, 8; Lu 12:48). By fines (Le 22:14).

Instances of Punishment of Sins of: Pharaoh (Ge 12:11-17). Abimelech (Ge 20:1-18).

See Knowledge, Wisdom.

IIM (heaps, ruins). 1. An encampment of the Israelites (Nu 33:45).

2. A town in the extreme S of Judah (Jos 15:29).

IJE-ABARIM (ruins of Abarim), one of the later halting places of Israel (Nu 21:11; 33:44).

IJON (a ruin), a town of Naphtali (1Ki 15:20; 2Ki 15:29; 2Ch 16:4).

IKKESH (crooked), father of Ira (2Sa 23:26; 1Ch 11:28; 27:9).

ILAI, one of David's heroes (1Ch 11:29); called Zalmon in 2Sa 23:28.

ILLYRICUM, called also Dalmatia. Visisted by Paul (Ro 15:19); by Titus (2Ti 4:10). Now part of Yugoslavia.

IMAGE. For idols.

See Idolatry.

Figurative: Man created in, of God (Ge 1:26, 27; 5:1; 9:6; Jas 3:9). Regenerated into (Ps 17:15; Ro 8:29; 2Co 3:18; Eph 4:24; Col 3:10; 1Jo 3:1-3). Christ, of God (Col 1:15; Heb 1:3). Of jealousy (Eze 8:3, 5).

See Idol; Idolatry.

IMAGE, NEBUCHADNEZZAR'S. Symbolic figure seen by Nebuchadnezzar in a dream the meaning of which was interpreted by Daniel (Da 2).

IMAGE OF GOD. Man is created by God in His own image (Ge 1:26, 27; 5:1, 3; 9:6; 1Co 11:7; Eph 4:24; Col 3:10; Jas 3:9). The image is not corporeal but rational, spiritual, and social. The fall of man destroyed, but did not obliterate the image. Restoration of the image begins with regeneration.

IMAGE WORSHIP (See Idol.)

IMAGINATION. Of man, evil (Ge 6:5; 8:21; De 29:19, 20; Pr 6:16-18); vain (Ro 1:21). An abomination to God (Pr 6:16-18). Condemned, as equal to act (M't 5:28).

Known of God (1Ch 28:9). To be subjected by control (2Co 10:3, 5).

IMLA (fulness), called also Imlah. Father of Michaiah the prophet (1Ki 22:8, 9; 2Ch 18:7, 8).

IMMANUEL (God is with us), a child borne by a maiden whose birth was foretold by Isaiah, and who was to be a sign to Ahaz (Isa 7:14); at his birth salvation would be near. Many prophecies cluster around this child (Isa 8:9, 10; 9:6, 7; 11:1; Mic 5:2, 3; M't 1:22, 23).

IMMER. 1. A family of priests (1Ch 9:12; Ezr 2:37; 10:20; Ne 7:40; 11:13).

2. Head of a division of priests (1Ch 24:14).

3. Name of a man or town (Ezr 2:59; Ne 7:61).

4. Father of Zadok (Ne 3:29).

5. Father of Pashur (Jer 20:1, 2).

IMMORTALITY. The Biblical concept of immortality is not simply the survival of the soul after bodily death, but the self-conscious continuance of the whole person, body and soul together, in a state of blessedness, due to the redemption of Christ and the possession of "eternal life." The Bible nowhere attempts to prove this doctrine, but everywhere assumes it as an undisputed postulate. The condition of believers in their state of immortality is not a bare endless existence, but a communion with God in eternal satisfaction and blessedness.

Exemption from death and annihilation.

Apparently understood by David (2Sa 12:23; Ps 21:4; 22:26; 23:6; 37:18, 27; 86:12; 133:3; 145:1, 2); Nehemiah (Ne 9:5); Job (Job 14:13); the psalmists (Ps 49:7-9; 73:26; 121:8).

Moses at the bush assured of (Ex 3:6; M't 22:32; M'k 12:26, 27; Lu 20:36-38; Ac 7:32). Hope of, sustained Abraham (Heb 11:10); comforted David (2Sa 12:23).

Implied: In the translation of Enoch (Ge 5:24; Heb 11:5); of Elijah (2Ki 2:11); in redemption from Sheol (Ps 16:10, 11); in the spirit returning to God (Ec 3:21; 12:7); in the soul surviving the death of the body (M't 10:28); in the appearance of Moses and Elijah at the transfiguration of Jesus (M't 17:2-9; M'k 9:2-10; Lu 9:29-36); in the abolition of death (Isa 25:8); in the Savior's promise to his disciples (Joh 14:2, 3); in the resurrection (Isa 26:19; Da 12:2, 3; Joh 6:40; 1Co 15:12-25; 1Th 4:13-18; 5:10); in eternal inheritance (Ac 20:32; 26:18; Heb 9:15; 1Pe 1:3-5); in the everlasting punishment of the wicked (2Th 1:7-9); in the judgment (2Pe 3:7).

Taught: by Christ (M't 16:26; 19:16, 17; 25:46; M'k 10:30; Lu 9:25; 10:25-28; Joh 3:14-16, 36; 5:39, 40; 6:39, 40, 44, 47, 50-58; 10:28; 11:25, 26; 14:19; 17:2-3; Re 3:4); by Paul (Ro 2:7; 6:22, 23; 1Co 15:12-25; 2Co 5:1; Ga 6:8; Col 1:5, 6; 2Th 2:16; 1Ti 4:8; 6:12, 19; 2Ti 1:9, 10; Tit 1:2; 3:7); by John (1Jo 2:17, 25; 5:13; Re 1:7; 22:5); by Jude (Jude 21); in Hebrews (Heb 9:15; 10:34; 11:5, 10, 13-16; 13:14).

See Resurrection; Righteous, Promises to; Judgment; Wicked, Punishment of.

IMMUTABILITY (unchangeableness), the perfection of God by which He is devoid of all change in essence, attributes, consciousness, will, and promises (Mal 3:6; Ps 33:11; 102:26).

IMNA (God defends), son of Helem (1Ch 7:35).

IMNAH (right hand). 1. Firstborn of Asher (1Ch 7:30).

2. A Levite (2Ch 31:14).

IMPENITENCE. Admonitions against (Ps 95:8; Jer 6:16-19; Ps 95:8; 2Co 12:21; Heb 3:8; Re 2:5, 16, 21, 22; 3:3). Leads to destruction (M't 24:38, 39, 48-51; Lu 13:3, 5; Re 16:9-21).

Judgments: Denounced against (Le 23:29; 26:21-43; De 29:19-21; 1Sa 15:23; Ps 7:11-13; 50:17, 21; 68:21; 81:11, 12; 107:11, 12; Pr 1:24-31; 11:3; 15:10, 32; 19:16; 28:13, 14; 29:1; Eze 3:19, 26; 33:4, 5, 9; Ho 7:13, 14; M't 11:16-21; 12:41, 42; 13:15; 23:37, 38; Lu 7:35; 10:13; 13:34; Ro 2:4, 5); denounced against Israel's (Isa 65:12, 15; 66:4; Jer 12:11; 13:17, 27; 14:10; 15:6, 7; 19:15; 26:4-6; Eze 3:19, 26; 20:8, 13, 21; Da 9:13; Zec 7:11-13; Mal 2:2).

Reason given: Evil company (Jer 2:25). Hypocrisy (Jer 3:10). Idolatry (Isa 46:12, 13; Jer 44:17; Eze 20:8; Ho 4:17, 11:2, 7; Re 9:20, 21). Lack of understanding or spiritual blindness (Job 33:14; Ps 32:9; 82:5; Pr 26:11; Ho 5:4). Leniency (Ec 8:11; Isa 26:10). Material abundance (Ps 52:1; Isa 32:9-11). Obstinacy (Isa 48:4, 8; Jer 8:5-7; Eze 2:4; Ac 7:51). Rebellion (Job 9:2, 4; 24:13; Ps 10:3; 50:17; 78:8; Pr 21:29; Isa 57:11; Jer 5:21-24; 6:10, 16-19; 44:10; Eze 2:4, 5; 12:2; 22:8, 13, 21). Refusal to listen (Ps 58:3-5; 106:24, 25; Isa 28:12; 42:22-25; Jer 6:16-19; 7:13, 14, 24, 28; 11:8; 16:12; 17:33; 22:21; 25:4; 26:4-6; 29:19; 32:33; 35:14-17; 44:16, 17; Eze 3:5-7; 20:8; Zec 1:4; 7:11-13; M't 13:15; Lu 16:31). Seeming lack of hope (Jer 2:25; 18:12).

Instances of: Pharaoh (Ex 9:30, 34; 10:27; 14:5-9). Israelites (Nu 14:22, 23; 2Ki 17:14; 2Ch 24:19; 36:16, 17; Ne 9:16, 17, 29, 30; Jer 36:31). Eli's sons (1Sa 2:25). Amaziah (2Ch 25:16). Manasseh (2Ch 33:10). Amon (2Ch 33:23). Zedekiah (2Ch 36:12, 13; Jer 37:2). Jehoiakim and his servants (Jer 36:22-24). Belshazzar (Da 5:22, 23). The rich young man (M't 19:22). Jews (M't 27:4, 25; M'k 3:5).

See Affliction, Obduracy in; Backsliders; Blindness, Spiritual; Infidelity; Obduracy; Unbelief; Reprobates.

IMPORTS. Of Israel. From Egypt: horses, chariots and linen (1Ki 10:28, 29; 2Ch 1:16). From Gilead: spices, balm and myrrh (Ge 37:25). From Ophir: gold (1Ki 10:11; 22:48; 1Co 29:4). From Tarshish: gold, ivory, apes and peacocks (1Ki 10:22; 2Ch 9:21); silver, iron, lead, brass and slaves (Eze 27:12, 13). From Arabia: sheep and goats (Eze 27:21).

Of Egypt: From Gilead: spices, balm and myrrh (Ge 37:25).

Of Tyre: All commodities from and of the trade world (Eze 27:12-25).

IMPORTUNITY (See Prayer.)

IMPOSITION OF HANDS (See Hands, Imposition of.)

IMPRECATION. *Instances of:* Ruth (Ru 1:17). Samuel (1Sa 3:17). David (2Sa 1:21; 3:28, 29). Shimei (2Sa 16:5, 13).

IMPRECATORY PSALMS. Psalms—especially Nos. 2, 37, 69, 109, 139, 143—which contain expressions of an apparent vengeful attitude towards enemies. For some people these Psalms constitute one of the "moral difficulties" of the OT.

IMPRISONMENT. Of Joseph (Ge 39:20). Jeremiah (Jer 38:6). John the Baptist (M't 11:2; 14:3). Apostles (Ac 5:18). Paul and Silas (Ac 16:24). Peter (Ac 12:4).

Of debtors (M't 5:26; 18:30).

See Prison; Prisoners; Punishments.

IMPUTATION (See Impute.)

IMPUTE, to attribute something to a

person, or reckon something to the account of another. Aspects of the doctrine found in the NT: the imputation of Adam's sin to his posterity; the imputation of the sin of man to Christ; the imputation of Christ's righteousness to the believer (Ge 2:3; Ro 3:24; 5:15; Ga 5:4; Tit 3:7; 1Pe 2:24).

IMRAH (God resists), a chief of the tribe of Asher (1Ch 7:36).

IMRI. 1. A man of Judah (1Ch 9:4).

2. Father of Zaccur (Ne 3:2).

INCARNATION (becoming flesh), the doctrine that the eternal Son of God became human, and that He did so without in any manner or degree diminishing His divine nature (Joh 1:4; Ro 8:3; 1Ti 3:16).

INCENDIARISM (See Arson.)

INCENSE. Formula for compounding (Ex 30:34, 35). Uses of (Ex 30:36-38; Le 16:12; Nu 16:17, 40, 46; De 33:10). Compounded by Bezaleel (Ex 37:29); by priests (1Ch 9:30). Offered morning and evening (Ex 30:7, 8; 2Ch 13:11); on the golden altar (Ex 30:1-7; 40:5, 27; 2Ch 2:4; 32:12); in making atonement (Le 16:12, 13; Nu 16:46, 47; Lu 1:10). Unlawfully offered by Nadab and Abihu (Le 10:1, 2); Korah, Dathan, and Abiram (Nu 16:16-35); by Uzziah (2Ch 26:16-21). Offered in idolatrous worship (1Ki 12:33; Jer 41:5; Eze 8:11). Presented by the wise men to Jesus (M't 2:11).

See Altar of Incense.

Figurative: Of prayer (Ps 141:2). Of praise (Mal 1:11). Of an acceptable sacrifice (Eph 5:2).

Symbolical: Of the prayers of saints (Re 5:8; 8:3, 4).

INCEST. Defined and forbidden (Le 18:6-18; 20:11, 12, 17-21; De 22:30; 27:20-23; Eze 22:11; 1Co 5:1).

Instances of: Lot with his daughters (Ge 9:31-36). Abraham (Ge 20:12, 13). Nahor (Ge 11:29). Reuben (Ge 35:22; 49:4). Amram (Ex 6:20). Judah (Ge 38:16-18; 1Ch 2:4). Amnon (2Sa 13:14). Absalom (2Sa 16:21, 22). Israel (Am 2:7). Herod (M't 14:3, 4; M'k 6:17, 18; Lu 3:19).

Instances of marriage of near of kin: Isaac with Rebekah (Ge 24:15, 67). Jacob with Leah and Rachel (Ge 29:23, 30). Rehoboam (2Ch 11:18).

INCINERATION (See Cremation.)

INCONSISTENCY. Hypocritical (M't 7:3-5; 23:3, 4). Inexcusable (Ro 2:1, 21-23).

Instances of: Jehu (2Ki 10:16-31). The Jews, in oppressing the poor (Ne 5:8, 9); in accusing Jesus of violating the Sabbath (Joh 7:22, 23). Peter and the other disciples, in requiring of the Gentiles that which they did not require of themselves (Ga 2:11-14).

See Deceit; Deception; Hypocrisy.

INDECISION. About God (1Ki 18:21; Ho 10:2; M't 6:24). About ethics (M't 26:11; Jas 1:8; 4:17; Re 3:15).

See Decision; Instability; Lukewarmness.

Instances of: Moses at the Red Sea (Ex 14:15). Joshua at Ai (Jos 7:10). Esther (Es 5:8). Rulers, who believed in Jesus (Joh 12:42). Felix (Ac 24:25).

INDIA, probably the eastern limit of the kingdom of Ahasuerus (Es 1:1; 8:9).

INDICTMENTS. *Instances of:* Naboth on charge of blasphemy (1Ki 21:13, w *vs.* 1-16). Jeremiah of treasonable prophecy, but of which he was acquitted (Jer 26:1-24); a second indictment (Jer 37:13-15). Three Hebrew captives on the charge of contumacy (Da 3:12, w *vs.* 1-28). Daniel of contumacy (Da 6:13, w *vs.* 1-24). Jesus, under two charges, first, of blasphemy (M't 26:61; M'k 14:58; M't 26:63-65; M'k 14:61-64; Lu 22:67-71; Joh 19:7); the second, of treason (M't 27:11, 37; M'k 15:2, 26; Lu 23:2, 3, 38; Joh 18:30, 33; 19:12, 19-22).

Stephen for blasphemy (Ac 6:11, 13). Paul (Ac 17:7; 18:13; 24:5; 25:18, 19, 26, 27). Paul and Silas (Ac 16:20, 21).

Indictment quashed (Ac 18:14-16).

INDUSTRY. Brings prosperity (Pr 10:4, 5; 12:11, 24, 27; 13:4, 11; 21:5; 22:29; 28:19). Enjoined (Ge 2:15; Ex 23:12; 35:2; De 5:13; Pr 20:13; 27:23-27; Ec 9:10; 11:4, 6; Ro 12:11; Eph 4:28; 1Th 4:11, 12; 2Th 3:10-12; 1Ti 5:8). Instigation (Pr 16:26). Profitable (Pr 14:4, 23). Reflections concerning (Ec 1:3; 2:10, 11, 17-22).

Exemplified: By ants and conies (Pr 30:25, 26). By prudent wife (Pr 31:27 w 13-26).

Instances of: Jeroboam (1Ki 11:28). Paul (Ac 18:3; 20:33, 34; 1Co 4:12; 1Th 2:9; 2Th 3:8).

See Frugality; Idleness; Slothfulness.

INFANTICIDE. (Ex 1:15, 16; Nu 31:17; M't 2:16-18; Ac 7:19).

INFANTS. See Children.

INFIDELITY. Disbelief in God (Nu 15:30, 31; 2Ch 32:14-19; Isa 29:16).

Prosperity tempts to (De 32:15). Arguments against (Job 12:7-25; Ps 94:8, 9; Isa 10:15; 19:16; 45:9, 18; Ro 1:20; 9:20, 21).

Exemplified: In mocking God (Ps 14:1, 6; 50:21; Isa 57:4-11; Eze 36:2; Da 3:15; Ac 17:18; 2Pe 3:3, 4; Jude 18, 19). In mocking God's servants (1Ki 22:24; 2Ki 2:23; 2Ch 30:6, 10; 36:16; Jer 17:15; 43:2; Eze 20:49; Ac 2:13). In rejecting God (Ex 5:2; Job 15:25, 26; 21:14, 15; Ps 14:1; 53:1; 106:24, 25; Jer 2:31). In rejecting Christ (M't 12:24; 27:39-44; M'k 3:22; Lu 11:15; 19:14, 27); by anti-Christ (Da 7:25; 8:25; 11:36, 37). In doubting God's help (Ex 17:7; Ps 3:2; 78:19, 20-22; 107:11, 12). In impugning God's holiness (Job 35:3; Ps 10:11, 13; Eze 18:2, 29; Mal 1:7; 3:14); God's knowledge (Job 22:13, 14, 17; Ps 59:7; 64:5; 73:11; Isa 29:15; Eze 8:12); God's mercy (Ps 42:3); God's righteousness (Eze 18:2, 29).

Punishment for (Nu 15:30, 31; De 29:19-21; Ps 12:3, 4; Pr 3:34; 9:12; 19:29; 24:9; Isa 3:8; 5:18, 19, 24, 25; 28:9, 10, 14-22; 47:10, 11; Jer 5:12, 14; 48:42; 50:24, 29; Eze 9:9, 10; 32:20; Ho 7:5, 13, 15; Am 5:18; 7:16, 17; Mic 7:10; Zep 1:12; Lu 19:14, 27; Heb 10:28, 29; 2Pe 2:1).

Of friends (Ps 41:9; M't 26:14-16, 47-50; M'k 14:10, 11, 43-46; Lu 22:3-6, 47, 48; Joh 13:18; 18:2-5).

See Presumption; Skepticism; Unbelief.

INFINITY. See God, Infinite.

INFIRMITY. Physical (Ec 12:3). Of Isaac (Ge 27:1). Of Jacob (Ge 48:10). Moses exempt from (De 34:7). Caleb exempt from (Jos 14:11). Of Eli (1Sa 3:2). Of Barzillai (2Sa 19:32).

See Affliction; Blindness; Deafness; Lameness; Old Age; Taste.

INFLAMMATION. See Diseases.

INFLUENCE. Solicited, Bath-sheba for Adonijah (1Ki 2:13-18).

Profferred, Elisha for Shunammite woman (2Ki 4:12, 13).

Intercession in behalf of friends: Of Jonathan for David (1Sa 19:1-6, 20:4-9); of nobles of Judah in behalf of Tobiah (Ne 6:17-19); of mother of Zebedee's children for sons (M't 20:20-24); of Blastus for Tyre and Sidon (Ac 12:20).

Good. Injunctions concerning (M't 5:13-16; M'k 4:21, 22; Lu 8:16; 11:33-36; Joh 7:38; 1Co 7:14, 16; Ph'p 2:15; 1Th 1:7, 8; 1Ti 6:1; Heb 11:4; 1Pe 2:11, 12; 3:1, 2, 15, 16).

Instances of: David over his successors (1Ki 3:3; 2Ki 18:3; 22:2; 2Ch 29:2; 34:2). Asa over Jehoshaphat (1Ki 22:42, 43). Joash over Amaziah (2Ki 14:3). Amaziah over Azariah (2Ki 15:1-3). Uzziah over Jotham (2Ki 15:34). Josiah, in religious zeal (2Ki 22; 23:1-25; 2Ch 34:35). Hezekiah, for religious reform (2Ch 29; 30; 31). Ezra, against marriage with idolaters (Ezr 10:1, 9). Nehemiah, during the rebuilding of the walls of Jerusalem (Ne 4:7-23; 5).

Evil. Of ruler over servants (Pr 22:12). Of wicked parents over children (Jer 17:1, 2). Of wicked priest and people (Ho 4:9). Warnings against (Pr 22:24, 25; Lu 12:1; 1Co 5:6-8; Ga 5:7-9; 2Ti 2:14, 17, 18; Heb 12:15). Parable of (M't 13:24, 25).

Instances of: Eve over Adam (Ge 3:6). Solomon's wives (1Ki 11:3, 4). The young men over Rehoboam (1Ki 12:8-14; 2Ch 10:8-14). Rehoboam over Abijam (1Ki 15:3). Jeroboam over Nadab (1Ki 15:25, 26). Jezebel over Ahab (1Ki 21:4-16, 25). Ahab over Ahaziah (1Ki 22:52, 53; 2Ki 8:25-27). Ahab over Jehoram (2Ki 8:16, 18; 2Ch 21:5, 6; 22:3-5). Jeroboam over Israel (2Ki 17:21, 22). Manasseh over Judah (2Ki 21:9; 2Ch 33:9). Manasseh over Amon (2Ki 21:20, 21). Jehoiakim over Jehoiachin (2Ki 24:9).

Political (1Ki 2:13-18; 2Ki 4:12, 13; Ne 6:17-19; Pr 19:6; 29:26; Da 5:10-12; M't 20:20-24; Ac 12:20). See Politics.

See Example.

INGATHERING, FEAST OF (See Tabernacles, Feast of.)

INGRAFTING (See Grafting.)

INGRATITUDE. *To God* (Ro 1:21; 2Ti 3:2). Prosperity tempts (De 6:10-12; 8:12-14; 32:6, 13, 15, 18; 2Ch 26:15, 16; Jer 5:7-9, 24; Ho 13:6). Punishment for (De 28:47, 48; 1Ki 16:1-3; 2Ch 32:25; Ps 78:16, 17, 27-32, 42-68; Da 5:18, 20, 21).

Instances of: Levites (Nu 16:9, 10). Israel (De 31:16; J'g 2:10-12; 8:34, 35; 10:11, 13, 14; 1Sa 8:7, 8; 10:19; Ne 9:25, 26, 35; Ps 106:7, 21; Isa 1:2; Jer 2:6-9, 17, 31; 4:7; 7:13, 19; 11:1, 3; Am 3:1, 2; Mic 6:3, 4). Saul (1Sa 15:17, 19). David (2Sa 12:7-9). Baasha (1Ki 16:1, 2). Jerusalem (Eze 16:17). Man (Ro 1:21; 2Ti 3:2).

To Jesus: The nine lepers (Lu 17:12-18). His own people (Joh 1:11).

Of Man to Man (Pr 17:13; 2Ti 3:2). Instances of: Laban to Jacob (Ge 31). Pharaoh's butler to Joseph (Ge 40:23). Israelites to Moses (Ex 16:3; 17:2-4; Nu 16:12-14); to Gideon (J'g 8:35). Shechemites (J'g 9:17, 18). Men of Keilah to David (1Sa 23:5-12). Saul to David (1Sa 24). Nabal (1Sa 25:21). David to Joab (1Ki 2:5, 6); with the history of Joab's services to David (See Joab). David to Uriah (2Sa 11:6-17). David's companions to David (Ps 35:11-16; 38:20; 41:9; 109:4, 5). Citizens (Ec 9:14-16). Joash (2Ch 24:22). Jeremiah's enemies (Jer 18:20).

INHERITANCE. Of children (Ge 24:36; 25:5; 2Ch 21:3). Of children of concubines (Ge 15:3; 21:9-11; 25:6). Of children of polygamous marriages (De 21:15). Of daughters (Nu 27:8; Job 42:15). Of all mankind (Ec 2:18, 19). Of servants (Pr 17:2). Of real estate inalienable (1Ki 21:3; Jer 32:6-8; Eze 46:16-18).

Law concerning (Nu 27:6-11). Lesson concerning, of prodigal (Lu 15:12, 25-31). Proverbs concerning (Pr 17:2; 20:21).

Instance of: Israel to Joseph (Ge 48:21, 22).

Figurative. Spiritual (M't 25:34; Ac 20:32; 26:18; Ro 8:16, 17; Ga 4:7; Eph 1:11-14; Col 3:24; Tit 3:7; Heb 1:14; 9:15-17).

See Firstborn; Heir; Testament; Will.

INHOSPITABLENESS. *Instances of:* Toward the Israelites: Edom (Nu 20: 18-21); Sihon (Nu 21:22, 23); Ammonites and Moabites (De 23:3-6). Men of Gibeah toward a Levite (J'g 19:15). Nabal toward David (1Sa 25:10-17). Samaritans toward Jesus (Lu 9:53).

See Hospitality.

INIQUITIES, OUR (Job 14:17; Ps 40:12; 90:8; 130:3; Isa 59:2; 64:6; Jer 2:22; Mic 7:19). See Sin.

INIQUITY, general references to (Job 15:16; Ps 41:6; 53:1; Isa 5:18; Jer 30:14; Eze 9:9; Ho 14:1; Mic 2:1; M't 23:28; 24:12; Ro 6:19). See Sin.

INJUSTICE. An abomination, to God (Pr 17:15); to the just (Pr 29:27). In civil administration (Ps 82:2; Ec 5:8; La 3:34-36). In gains, unstable (Pr 28:8; Am 5:11, 12). Job innocent of (Job 16:16, 17; 31:13-15). Judged (Pr 11:7; Ec 3:16; Lu 16:10; 1Th 4:7; Re 22:11). Practiced by the wicked (Isa 26:10); without shame (Zep 3:5). Protection from, given (Ps 12:5); interceded (Ps 43:1).

INK. Any liquid used with pen or brush to form written characters (Jer 36:18; 2Co 3:3; 2Jo 12; 3Jo 13).

INKHORN (Eze 9:2, 3, 11).

INN, a lodging place for travelers. Inns in the modern sense were not very necessary in ancient times, since travelers found hospitality the rule (Ex 2:20; J'g 19:15-21; 2Ki 4:8; Ac 28:7; Heb 13:2). Ancient inns were usually mere shelters for man and beast, although often strongly fortified.

INNOCENCY. Signified by washing the hands (De 21:6; Ps 26:6; M't 27:24). Found in Daniel (Da 6:22); Jeremiah (Jer 2:35). Professed by Pilate (M't 27:24).

Contrasted with guilt (compare Ge 2:25; 3:7-11).

INNOCENT. Not to suffer for guilty (De 24:16; 2Ki 14:6; 2Ch 25:4; Jer 31:29, 30; Eze 18:20).

INNOCENTS, SLAUGHTER OF, the slaughter, by Herod the Great, of children in Bethlehem (M't 2:16-18).

INNUENDO (Ps 35:19; Pr 6:13; 10:10). See Accusation, False.

INQUEST (De 21:1-9).

I.N.R.I., the initials of the Latin superscription on the cross of Jesus, standing for IESUS NAZARENUS, REX IUDAEORUM, Jesus of Nazareth, King of the Jews (M't 27:37; M'k 15:26; Lu 23:38; Joh 19:19).

INSANITY (Pr 26:18). Feigned by David (1Sa 21:13-15). Sent as a judgment from God (De 28:28; Zec 12:4). Nebuchadnezzar's (Da 4:32-34). Jesus accused of (M'k 3:21; Joh 10:20). Paul (Ac 26:24, 25). Cured by Jesus (M't 4: 24; 17:15). Demoniacal: Saul (1Sa 16: 14; 18:10).

False accusation of: Against Jesus

(M'k 3:21; Joh 10:20); against Paul (Ac 26:24, 25; 2Co 5:13).

See Demons, Possession by.

INSCRIPTIONS. On gravestones (2Ki 23:17). On the miter of the high priest (Ex 28:36). On the holy crown (Ex 39:30). On the bells of horses (Zec 14:20).

Over Jesus at the crucifixion (M't 27:37; M'k 15:26; Lu 23:38; Joh 19:19).

INSECTS. Created by God (Ge 1:24, 25).

Divided Into: Clean and fit for food (Le 11:21, 22). Unclean and abominable (Le 11:23, 24).

Mentioned in Scripture: Ant (Pr 6:6; 30:25). Bee (J'g 14:8; Ps 118:12; Isa 7:18). Beetle (Le 11:22). Caterpillar (Ps 78:46; Isa 33:4). Cankerworm (Joe 1:4; Na 3:15, 16). Earthworm (Job 25:6; Mic 7:17). Flea (1Sa 24:14). Fly (Ex 8:22; Ec 10:1; Isa 7:18). Gnat (M't 23:24). Grasshopper (Le 11:22; J'g 6:5; Job 39:20). Hornet (De 7:20). Locust (Ex 10:12, 13). Bald locust (Le 11:22). Lice (Ex 8:16; Ps 105:31). Maggot (Ex 16:20). Moth (Job 4:19; Job 27:18; Isa 50:9). Palmer-worm (Joe 1:4; Am 4:9). Spider (Job 8:14; Pr 30:28). Fed by God (Ps 104:25, 27; Ps 145:9, 15).

INSINCERITY (See Hypocrisy.)

INSINUATION (See Innuendo.)

INSOMNIA. *Instances of:* Ahasuerus (Es 6:1). Nebuchadnezzar (Da 6:18).

INSPIRATION (breathed into). Claims that the Scriptures are or were (1Ki 13:20; 2Ch 33:18; 36:15; Ne 9:30; Job 33:14-16; Isa 51:16; Jer 7:25; 17:16; Da 9:6, 10; Ho 12:10; Joe 2:28; Am 3:7, 8; Zec 7:12; Lu 1:70; Ac 3:18; Ro 1:1, 2; 1Co 12:7-11; 2Ti 3:16; Heb 1:1; 2Pe 1:21; Re 10:7; 22:6, 8). Instances: Of Enoch (Jude 14). Joseph (Ge 40:8; 41:16, 38, 39). Moses (Ex 3:14, 15; 4:12, 15, 27; 6:13, 29; 7:2; 19:9-19; 24:16; 25:22; 33:9, 11; Le 1:1; Nu 1:1; 7:8, 9; 9:8-10; 11:17, 25; 12:6-8; 16:28, 29; De 1:5, 6; 5:4, 5, 31; 34:10, 11; Ps 103:7). Aaron (Ex 6:13; 12:1). The tabernacle workmen (Ex 28:3; 31:3, 6; 35:31; 36:1). The seventy elders (Nu 11:16, 17, 24, 25). Eldad and Medad (Nu 11:26-29). Balaam (Nu 23:5, 16, 20, 26; 24:2-4, 15, 16). Joshua (De 34:9; Jos 4:15). Samuel (1Sa 3:1, 4-10, 19-21; 9:6, 15-20; 15:16). Saul (1Sa 10:6, 7, 10-13; 19:23, 24). Messengers of Saul (1Sa 19:20, 23). David (2Sa 23:2, 3; 1Ch 28:19; M'k 12:36). Nathan (2Sa 7:3, 4, 8). Gad (2Sa 24:11). Ahijah (1Ki 14:5). Elijah (1Ki 17:1, 24; 19:15; 2Ki 10:10). Micaiah (1Ki 22:14, 28; 2Ch 18:27). Elisha (2Ki 2:9; 3:11, 12, 15; 6:8-12, 32; 15:8). Jahaziel (2Ch 20:14). Azariah (2Ch 15:1, 2). Zechariah, the son of Jehoiada (2Ch 24:20; 26:5). Isaiah (2Ki 20:4; Isa 6:1-9; 8:11; 44:26; Ac 28:25). Jeremiah (2Ch 26:12; Jer 1:9; 2:1; 7:1; 11:1, 18; 13:1-3; 16:1; 18:1; 20:9; 23:9; 24:4; 25:3; 26:1, 2, 12; 27:1, 2; 29:30; 33:1; 34:1; 42:4, 7; Da 9:2). Ezekiel (Eze 1:1, 3; 2:1, 2, 4, 5; 3:10-12, 14, 16, 17, 22, 24, 27; 8:1; 11:1, 4, 5, 24; 33:22; 37:1; 40:1; 43:5, 6). Daniel (Da 2:19; 7:16; 8:16; 9:22; 10:7-9). Hosea (Ho 1:1, 2). Joel (Joe 1:1). Amos (Am 3:7, 8; 7:14, 15). Obadiah (Ob 1). Jonah (Jon 1:1; 3:1, 2). Micah (Mic 1:1; 3:8). Habakkuk (Hab 1:1). Haggai (Hag 1:13). Zechariah (Zec 2:9; 7:8). Elisabeth (Lu 1:41). Zacharias (Lu 1:67). Simeon (Lu 2:26, 27). Disciples (M't 10:19; M'k 13:11; Lu 12:11, 12; 21:14, 15; Ac 21:4). The apostles (Ac 2:4). Philip (Ac 8:29). Agabus (Ac 11:28; 21:10, 11). John the apostle (Re 1:10, 11).

See Prophecy; Prophet; Revelation; Word of God, Inspiration of.

INSTABILITY. Warnings against (Pr 24:21, 22; 27:8; M't 6:24; 8:19-22; 12:25; 13:20, 21; M'k 4:16, 17; Lu 8:13; 9:57-62; Eph 4:14; Heb 13:9; Jas 1:6-8; 4:8; 2Pe 2:14; Re 2:4; 3:2).

Instances of: Reuben (Ge 49:4). Pharaoh (Ex 8:15,32; 9:34; 10:8-11, 16-20; 14:5). Israel (Ex 19:8; 24:3, 7; 32:8-10; J'g 2:17; 1Ki 18:21; Ps 106:12, 13; Jer 2:36). Saul in his feelings toward David (1Sa 18:19). David, in yielding to lust (2Sa 11:2-4). Solomon, in yielding to his idolatrous wives (1Ki 11:1-8). Ephraim and Judah (Ho 6:4). Jews (Ho 6:4, 5; Joh 5:35). Lot's wife (Lu 17:32). Disciples (Joh 6:66). Mark (Ac 15:38). Galatians (Ga 1:6; 4:9-11).

See Backsliding; Hypocrisy; Indecision.

INSTINCT. Of animals (Pr 1:17; Isa 1:3). Of birds (Jer 8:7).

See Animals; Birds.

INSTRUCTION. By Jesus (M't 5:2-48; Lu 4:16-21; 24:27; Joh 7:14; 8:2).

Provision for, made by the state (2Ch 17:7-9; Da 1:3-5, 17-20). Precept upon precept, line upon line (Isa 28:10). Sought (Ps 90:12; 119:12; 143:8, 10). Giving heed to, enjoined (Pr 4:1, 2, 10, 13, 20; 5:1, 2; 22:17; 23:12, 23). Lack of (2Ch 15:3; Pr 24:30-34). Hated (Ps 50:17; Pr 1:29, 30; 5:12, 13; Jer 32:33; Lu 20:1, 2).

From nature (Pr 24:30-34; Ec 1:13-18; 3; 4:1; M't 6:25-30). From the study of human nature (Ec chaps. 3-12).

In religion (Ex 24:12; Le 10:11; De 24:8; 27:14-26; 31:9-13; 33:10; 2Ch 17:8, 9; 35:3; Ne 8:7-13; Mal 2:6, 7). By means of, the law (De 27:1-26; Ro 2:18; Ga 3:24, 25); proverbs (Pr 1:1-6, 20-30); songs (De 31:19; 32:1-44). By priests (Ezr 7:10; Mal 2:7). Jesus (M't 5:1, 2; M'k 6:2; 12:35; Lu 4:16; 19:47; 20:1-8; 21:37, 38; 24:27; Joh 7:14; 8:2). Preachers (Ro 10:14; 1Co 12:28, 29; Eph 4:11; Col 1:2, 8). Teachers (2Ki 23:2; Ne 8:7, 8; 1Co 12:28, 29; Eph 4:11). Symbols (see Symbols). Parables (see Parables). Inscriptions on doors and gates (De 11:20, 21); on monuments (Jos 8:30-35). The public reading of the law (De 31:9-13; Jos 8:25; Ne 8:2, 3).

By object lessons: Passover feast (Ex 12:26, 27). Dedication of firstlings (Ex 13:14-16). Phylacteries (Ex 13:9, 16). Legends (Ex 28:36; 39:30; De 6:6-9; 11:18-20; Zec 14:20; M't 27:37). The pot of manna, a reminder of God's care (Ex 16:32). The sacred oil, a symbol of holiness (Ex 30:31). The pillar of twelve stones at the fords of the Jordan (Jos 4:7, 19-24). Fringes on the borders of garments (Nu 15:38, 39). The garment rent in pieces (1Ki 11:30-32). The symbolical wearing of sackcloth and going barefoot (Isa 20:2, 3). The linen girdle (Jer 13:1-11). Potter's vessel (Jer 19:1-12). Basket of figs (Jer 24). Bonds and yokes (Jer 27:2-11; 28). By stones being put in a brick kiln (Jer 3:8-10). Illustrations on a tile (Eze 4:1-3). Lying on one side in public view for a long period (Eze 4:4-8). Eating bread baked with dung (Eze 4:9-17). Shaving the head (Eze 5). Moving household goods (Eze 12:3-16). Eating and drinking sparingly (Eze 12:18-20). Sighing (Eze 21:6, 7). The boiling pot (Eze 24:1-14). Widowhood (Eze 24:16-27). Two sticks joined together (Eze 37:16-22).

Of children: By parents, enjoined (Ex 10:2; 12:26, 27; 13:8-10, 14-16; De 4:9, 10; 6:6-9; 11:18, 19; Ps 78:5-8; Pr 22:6; Isa 38:19; Eph 6:4). Law concerning (De 31:9-13; Jos 8:35). Exemplified (Ps 34:11; Pr 20:7; Ac 22:3; 2Ti 3:15). See Children.

By types: See Ablution; Blemish; Defilement; Disfellowship; Types.

See Beasts, Clean and Unclean; Firstborn; Holiness; Passover; Pillar; Purifications.

INSTRUMENTALITY (See Agency.)

INSTRUMENTS, MUSICAL (See Music.)

INSURGENTS, army of, David's (1Sa 22:1, 2.)

INSURRECTION (Ps 6:42). Described by David in Ps 55. Led by Bichri (2Sa 20); Absalom (see Absalom); Barabbas (M'k 15:7).

INTEGRITY. Essential (Ex 18:21; Lu 16:10; 2Co 8:21).

Enjoined (De 16:19, 20; Pr 4:25-27; Isa 56:1; Mic 6:8; Zec 7:9; Lu 3:13, 14; 6:31; 11:42; Ro 13:5; 14:5, 14, 22; Eph 6:6; Ph'p 4:8; Col 3:22, 23; 1Ti 1:5; 3:9; Tit 1:7, 8; 1Pe 2:12; 3:16). Rewards of (2Sa 22:21; Ps 15:1-5; 18:20; 24:3-5; Pr 10:9; 20:7; 28:20; Isa 26:7; 33:15, 16; Jer 7:5, 7; Eze 18:5, 7-9). Proverbs concerning (Pr 2:2, 5, 9; 3:3, 4; 4:25-27; 10:9; 11:3, 5; 12:22; 14:30; 15:21; 16:11; 19:1; 20:7; 21:3, 15; 22:11; 28:6, 20).

Instances of: Pharaoh, when he learned that Sarah was Abraham's wife (Ge 12:18-20). Abraham, in instructing his family (Ge 18:19). Abimelech, when warned of God that the woman he had taken into his household was Isaac's wife (Ge 26:9-11). Jacob, in the care of Laban's property (Ge 31:39). Joseph, in resisting Potiphar's wife (Ge 39:8-12); in his innocence of the charge on which he was cast into the dungeon (Ge 40:15). Moses, in taking nothing from the Israelites in consideration of his services (Nu 16:15). Samuel, in exacting nothing from the people on account of services (1Sa 12:4, 5). Workmen, who repaired the temple (1Ki 12:15; 22:7). Priests who received the offerings of gold and other gifts for the renewing of the temple under Ezra (Ezr 2:24-30, 33, 34). Nehemiah, reforming the civil service, and receiving no compensation for his own services (Ne 5:14-19). Job (Job 1:

8; 2:3; 10:7; 13:15; 16:17; 27:4-6; 29:14; 31:1-40). The psalmist (Ps 7:3-5, 8; 17:3; 26:1-3; 69:4; 73:15; 119:121). The Rechabites, in keeping the Nazirite vows (Jer 35:12-19). Daniel, in maintaining uprightness of character (Da 6:4). The three Hebrews, who refused to worship Nebuchadnezzar's idol (Da 3:16-21, 28). Levi, in his life and service (Mal 2:6). Joseph, the husband of Mary, in not jealously accusing her of immorality (M't 1:19). Zacchaeus, in the administration of his wealth (Lu 19:8). Nathanael, in whom was no guile (Joh 1:47). Joseph, a counselor (Lu 23:50, 51). Peter, when offered money by Simon Magus (Ac 8:18-23). Paul and Barnabas (Ac 14:12-15). Paul (Ac 23:1; 24:16; Ro 9:1; 2Co 4:2; 5:11; 7:2; 1Th 2:4). The author of Hebrews (Heb 13:18).

See Character; Dishonesty; Fraud; Honesty; Justice; Righteousness.

INTEMPERANCE. See Abstinence; Drunkards; Drunkenness; Temperance; Wine.

INTERCESSION. *Of man with God* (Jer 27:18). Priestly (Ex 28:12, 29, 30, 38; Le 10:17). For spiritual blessing (Nu 6:23-26; 1Sa 12:23; Job 1:5; 42:8-10). To avert judgment (Ge 20:7; Ex 32:9-14; Nu 14:11-21; 16:45-50; De 9:18-20, 25-29; Isa 65:8). For deliverance from enemies (1Sa 7:5-9; Isa 37:4). For healing of disease (Jas 5:14-16). For the obdurate, unavailing (Jer 7:16; 11:14; 14:11).

Enjoined (Jer 29:7; Joel 2:17; M't 5:44; Eph 6:18; 1Ti 2:1, 2; 1Jo 5:16).

Exemplified (Ge 48:16; Ex 32:31, 32; 34:9; Nu 10:35, 36; 27:16, 17; Jos 7:8, 9; J'g 5:31; Ru 2:12; 1Sa 1:17; 12:23; 2Sa 24:17; 1Ki 8:29, 38, 39, 44, 45; 1Ch 29:18, 19; 2Ch 6:40, 41; 30:18, 19; Ps 7:9; 12:1; 20:1-4; 25:22; 28:9; 36:10; 51:18; 80:1, 2, 14-19; 122:7, 8; 125:4; 132:9, 10; 134:3; 141:5; Isa 62:1; 63:17-19; 64:8-12; Jer 18:20; Eze 9:8; 11:13; Da 9:3-19; Joe 2:17; Mic 7:14; M't 5:44; 6:10; Ac 7:60; 8:15; Ro 1:9; 10:1; 1Co 1:3; 2Co 9:10, 14; 13:7; Ga 1:3; 6:16; Eph 1:15-19; 3:14-19; Ph'p 1:3-5, 9; Col 1:3, 4, 9; 2:1, 2; 4:12; 1Th 1:2; 3:10, 12, 13; 5:23; 2Th 1:11; 2:16, 17; 3:5, 16; 2Ti 1:3; 4:16; Ph'm 4, 6; Heb 13:20, 21; 1Pe 5:10).

Instances of: Abraham, in behalf of Sodom (Ge 18:23-32); in behalf of Abimelech (Ge 20:17, 18). Abraham's servant, in behalf of his master (Ge 24:12). Jacob, in behalf of his children (Ge 49). Moses, in behalf of Pharaoh (Ex 8:12, 13, 30, 31; 9:33; 10:18, 19). Moses for Israel (Nu 16:20-22; 21:7; De 33:6-17; Ps 106:23), for Miriam (Nu 12:13-15). David, for Israel (2Sa 24:17). Solomon, for Israel (1Ki 8:29-53). Ezra, for Israel (Ezr 9:5-15). Nehemiah, in behalf of Judah and Jerusalem (Ne 1:4-9). Asaph, for the church (Ps 80:83). Korah, for the church (Ps 85:1-7). Jeremiah, for Israel (Jer 14:7-22). Amos, for Israel (Am 7:2-6). Syro-Phoenician woman, for her daughter (M't 15:22). Disciples, in behalf of Peter's wife's mother (Lu 4:38, 39). Parents, for lunatic son (M't 17:15; M'k 9:17-27). Others, who sought Jesus in behalf of the afflicted (M't 12:22; 15:22, 30; 17:14-18; M'k 1:32; 2:3; Lu 5:18-20; Joh 4:47, 49). Paul for the church (Ac 20:32). Onesiphorus (2Ti 1:16, 18). For Paul, by the churches (Ac 14:26; 15:40).

Solicited: Instances of: By Pharaoh, of Moses (Ex 8:8, 28; 9:28; 10:17; 12:32); and by the Israelites (Nu 21:7). By Israel, of Samuel (1Sa 12:19). By Jeroboam, of a prophet (1Ki 13:6). By Hezekiah, of Isaiah (2Ki 19:1-4). By Zedekiah, of Jeremiah (Jer 37:3); and by Johanan (Jer 42:1-6). By Daniel, of Shadrach, Meshach and Abed-nego (Da 2:17, 18). By Darius, of the Jews (Ezr 6:10). By Simon Magus, of Peter (Ac 8:24). By Paul, of the churches (Ro 15:30-32; 2Co 1:11; Eph 6:19, 20; 1Th 5:25; 2Th 3:1; Heb 13:18).

Answered: Instances of: Of Moses, in behalf of Pharaoh, for the plague of frogs to be abated (Ex 8:12, 15); the plague of flies (Ex 8:30-32); the plague of rain, thunder, and hail (Ex 9:27-35); plague of locusts (Ex 10:16-20); plague of darkness (Ex 10:21-23). Of Moses, for the Israelites, during the battle with the Amalekites (Ex 17:11-14); after the Israelites had made the golden calf (Ex 32:11-14, 31-34; De 9:18-29; 10:10; Ps 106:23); after the murmuring of the people (Ex 33:15-17); when the fire of the Lord consumed the people (Nu 11:1, 2); when the people murmured on account of the report of the spies (Nu 14:11-20); that the fiery serpents might be abated (Nu 21:4-9); that Miriam's leprosy might be healed (Nu 12:13); in behalf of Aaron, on account of his sin in making the golden calf (De 9:20). Of Samuel, for deliverance from the oppressions of the Philistines (1Sa 7:5-14). The prophet of Israel, for the restoration of Jeroboam's withered hand (1Ki 13:1-6). Of Elijah, for the raising from the dead the son of the hospitable widow (1Ki 17:20-23). Of Elisha, for the raising from the dead the son of the Shunammite woman (2Ki 4:33-36). Of Isaiah, in behalf of Hezekiah and the people, to be delivered from Sennacherib (2Ki 19).

Intercessional influence of the righteous (Ge 18:26-32; 19:22; 26:4, 5, 24; 1Ki 11:12, 13, 34; 15:4; 2Ki 8:19; 2Ch 21:7; Ps 103:17, 18; Isa 37:35; Jer 5:1; Eze 14:14, 16, 18, 20; M't 24:22; Ro 11:27, 28; Re 5:8; 8:3, 4).

Of man with Jesus: see Mediation.

Of man with man: Instances of: Reuben for Joseph (Ge 37:21,22). Judah for Joseph (Ge 37:26, 27). Judah with Joseph (Ge 44:18-34). Pharaoh's chief baker for Joseph (Ge 41:9-13 w 40:14). Rahab for her people (Jos 2:12, 13). Aaron for Miriam (Nu 12:12). Jonathan for David (1Sa 19:1-7). Abigail for Nabal (1Sa 25:23-35). Joab for Absalom (2Sa 14:1-24). Bath-sheba, for Solomon (1Ki 1:11-22, 28-31); for Adonijah (1Ki 2:13-25). Esther for her people (Es 7:2-6). Ebed-melech for Jeremiah (Jer 38:7-13). Elisha offers to see the king for the Shunammite (2Ki 4:13). The king of Syria for Naaman (2Ki 5:6-8). Paul for Onesimus (Ph'm 10-21).

Of Jesus (Lu 22:31, 32; 23:33, 34; Joh 14:16; 17:9, 11, 15-17, 20-22; Ro 8:34; Heb 7:25; 9:24; 1Jo 2:1, 2). See Jesus, Mediator.

See Children, Of the Righteous, Blessed of God; Prayer, Intercession.

INTEREST. Income from loaning money, usually called usury in the Scriptures, but not generally signifying unlawful or unjust rates.

Exaction of: From poor Hebrew, forbidden (Ex 22:25; Le 25:36, 37; De 23:19). From stranger, authorized (De 23:20). Unprofitable (Pr 28:8). Rebuked (Ne 5:1-13; Eze 22:12).

Non-exaction of, rewarded (Ps 15:5; Eze 18:8, 9, 17). Lender and borrower equal before God (Isa 24:2).

See Borrowing; Debt; Debtors; Lending; Money; Usury.

INTERMEDIATE STATE. Period of time which elapses between death and the resurrection. For the righteous it is one of blessedness (2Co 5:8); for the wicked it is one of conscious suffering (Lu 16:19-31).

INTERPRETATION. Of dreams (see Dreams). Of foreign tongues (1Co 14:9-19), see Tongues.

INTERPRETER. Of dreams (Ge 40:8; 41:16; Da 2:18-30). Of languages (Ge 42:23; 2Ch 32:31; Ne 8:8; Job 33:23). In Christian churches (1Co 12:10, 30; 14:5, 13, 26-28).

Figurative: Job 33:23.

INTOLERANCE, religious. Exemplified by Cain (Ge 4:8); Joshua (Nu 11:24-28); James and John (M'k 9:38, 39; Lu 9:49); the Jews, in persecuting Jesus (see Jesus). History of, in persecuting the disciples (Ac 4:1-3, 15-21; 17:13); and Stephen (Ac 6:9-15; 7:57-59; 8:1-3); and Paul (Ac 13:50; 17:5; 18:13; 21:28-31; 22:22, 23; 23:2).

Of idolatrous religions, taught by Moses (Ex 22:20; De 13; 17:1-7). Exemplified by Elijah (1Ki 18:40); Jehu (2Ki 10:18-31), by the Jews, at the time of the religious revival under the leadership of Azariah (2Ch 15:12, 13).

See Persecution.

INTOXICANTS (See Wine.)

INTOXICATION (See Drunkenness; Abstinence.)

INTRIGUE (See Conspiracy.)

INVECTIVE (See Satire.)

INVENTION (Pr 8:12). Of musical instruments: By Jubal (Ge 4:21); by David (1Ch 23:5; 2Ch 7:6; 29:26; Am 6:5). The use of metals (Ge 4:22). Engines of war (2Ch 26:15).

INVESTIGATION. By Solomon, into nature and design of things (Ec 1:13-18; 2:1-12; 7:25; 8:17; 12:9-14).

INVITATIONS. The "Comes" of God's word (Ge 7:1; Nu 10:29; Isa 1:18; 55:1; M't 11:28; 22:4; Lu 14:17; Re 22:17). Divine pleadings (Pr 1:24; Isa 1:18; 55:1; Eze 18:31; Mic 6:3; M't 23:37; Ro 10:21; 2Co 5:20). Divine Call. To repentance (Jer 35:15; Eze 33:11; Ho 6:1; M't 22:3; 2Co 5:20; Re 3:20). To leadership (Ge 12:1; Ex 3:10; J'g 6:14; 1Ki 19:19; Isa 6:8; Ac 26:16). Universality of (Isa 45:22; 55:1; M't 22:9; Joh 7:37; Ro 10:12; 1Ti 2:4; Re 22:17). Refused by men (Ps 81:11; Isa 65:12; Jer 7:13; Ho 9:17; M't 22:3; Joh 5:40; Ro 10:21). Warnings (Ge 19:17; De 29:20; Jos 24:20; 1Sa 12:15; Isa 28:14; Jer 13:16; Jon 3:4; Heb 12:25; 2Pe 3:17).

IPHEDEIAH (Jehovah redeems), a Benjamite (1Ch 8:25).

IR (watcher), a Benjamite (1Ch 7:12).

IRA. 1. A priest (2Sa 20:26).

2. The Ithrite, one of David's heroes (2Sa 23:38; 1Ch 11:40).

3. A Tekoite, one of David's heroes (2Sa 23:26; 1Ch 11:28; 27:9).

IRAD, son of Enoch (Ge 4:18).

IRAM, a duke of Edom (Ge 36:43; 1Ch 1:54).

IR-HA-HERES, city of Egypt, translated "city of destruction" (Isa 19:18). Site unknown.

IRI, a son of Bela (1Ch 7:7).

IRIJAH (Jehovah sees), a captain of the guard who imprisoned the prophet Jeremiah (Jer 37:13, 14).

IR-NAHASH, whether a man or a town is not clear (1Ch 4:12).

IRON. 1. First recorded use of (Ge 4:22). Ore of (De 8:9; Job 28:2). Melted (Eze 22:20). Used in the temple (1Ch 22:3; 29:2, 7). Articles made of: Ax (2Ki 6:6; 2Ch 18:10; Ec 10:10; Isa 10:34); bedstead (De 3:11); breastplate (Re 9:9); chariot (Jos 17:16, 18; J'g 1:19; 4:3); fetters (Ps 105:18; 107:10, 16; 149:8); file (Pr 27:17); furnace (De 4:20; 1Ki 8:51; Jer 11:4); gate (Ac 12:10); harrow (2Sa 12:31); horn (1Ki 22:11; 2Ch 18:10; Mic 4:13); idols (Da 2:33; 5:4, 23); pans (Eze 4:3; 27:19); pen (Job 19:24; Jer 17:1); pillars (Jer 1:18); rods for scourging (Ps 2:9; Re 2:27; 12:5; 19:15); threshing instruments (Am 1:3); tools (1Ki 6:7); vessels (Jos 6:24); weapons (Nu 35:16; 1Sa 17:7; Job 20:24; 41:7); yokes (De 28:48; Jer 28:13, 14).

Stones of (De 8:9; Job 28:2; Isa 60:17).

See Steel.

Figurative: 2Sa 23:7; Jer 15:12; 1Ti 4:2.

2. A city of Naphtali (Jos 19:38).

IRONY. *Instances of:* Michal to David (2Sa 6:20). Elijah to the priests of Baal (1Ki 18:27). Job to his accusers (Job 12:2). Ezekiel to the prince of Tyre (Eze 28:3-5). Micaiah (1Ki 22:15). Amos to the Samaritans (Am 4:4). Jesus to Pharisees (M'k 2:17). Pharisees and Herodians to Jesus (M't 22:16). Roman soldiers to Jesus (M't 27:29; M'k 15:17-19; Lu 23:11; Joh 19:2, 3). Pilate, calling Jesus king (M'k 15:19; Joh 19:15). Superscription of Pilate over Jesus (M't 27:37; M'k 15:26; Lu 23:38; Joh 19:19). Agrippa to Paul (Ac 26:28).

See Sarcasm; Satire.

IRPEEL (God heals), a city of Benjamin (Jos 18:27).

IRRIGATION (De 11:10; Pr 21:1; Ec 2:6; Isa 58:11).

Figurative: 1Co 3:6, 8.

IR-SHEMESH (city of the sun), a city of Dan (Jos 19:41).

IRU, eldest son of Caleb (1Ch 4:15).

ISAAC (one laughs). 1. Miraculous son of Abraham (Ge 17:15-19; 18:1-15; 21:1-8; Jos 24:3; 1Ch 1:28; Ga 4:28; Heb 11:11). Ancestor of Jesus (M't 1:2). Offered in sacrifice by his father (Ge 22:1-19; Heb 11:17; Jas 2:21). Is provided a wife from among his kindred (Ge 24; 25:20). Abrahamic covenant confirmed in (Ge 26:2-5; 1Ch 16:15-19). Dwells in the south country at the well Lahai-roi (Ge 24:62; 25:11). With Ishmael, buries his father in the cave of Machpelah (Ge 25:9). Esau and Jacob born to (Ge 25:19-26; 1Ch 1:34; Jos 24:4). Dwells in Gerar (Ge 26:7-11). Prospers (Ge 26:12-14). Possesses large flocks and herds (Ge 26:14). Digs wells, and is defrauded of them by the herdsmen of Abimelech (Ge 26:15, 21). Removes to the valley of Gerar, afterward called Beer-sheba (Ge 26:22-33). His old age, last blessing upon his sons (Ge 27:18-40). Death and burial of (Ge 35:27-29; 49:31). His filial obedience (Ge 22:9). His peaceableness (Ge 26:14-22). Was a prophet (Ge 27:28, 29, 39, 40; Heb 11:20). His devoutness (Ge 24:63; 25:21; 26:25; M't 8:11; Lu 13:28). Prophecies concerning (Ge 17:16-21; 18:10-14; 21:12; 26:2-5, 24; Ex 32:13; 1Ch 16:16; Ro 9:7).

2. A designation of the ten tribes (Am 7:9).

ISAIAH (salvation of Jehovah) called also Esaias. Son of Amos (Isa 1:1). Prophesies in the days of Uzziah, Jotham, Ahaz, and Hezekiah, kings of Judah (Isa 1:1; 6:1; 7:1, 3; 14:27; 20:1; 36:1; 38:1; 39:1); at the time of the invasion by Tartan, of Assyria (Isa 20:1). Symbolically wears sackcloth, and walks barefoot, as a sign to Israel (Isa 20:2, 3). Comforts and encourages Hezekiah and the people in the siege of Jerusalem by Rab-shakeh (2Ki 18; 19; Isa 37:6, 7). Comforts Hezekiah in his affliction (2Ki 20:1-11; Isa 38). Performs the miracle of the returning shadow to confirm Hezekiah's faith (2Ki 20:8-11). Reproves Hezekiah's folly in exhibiting his resources to the commissioners from Babylon (2Ki 20:12-19; Isa 39). Is chronicler of the times of Uzziah and Hezekiah (2Ch 26:22; 32:32).

Prophecies, Reproofs, and Exhortations of: Foretells punishment of the Jews for idolatry, and reproves self-confidence and distrust of God (Isa 2:6-20). Foretells the destruction of the Jews (Isa 3). Promises to the remnant restoration of divine favour (Isa 4:2-6; 6). Delineates in the parable of the vineyard the ingratitude of the Jews, and reproves it (Isa 5:1-10). Denounces existing corruptions (Isa 5:8-30). Foretells the ill success of the plot of the Israelites and Syrians against Judah (Isa 7:1-16). Pronounces calamities against Israel and Judah (Isa 7:16-25; 9:2-6). Foretells prosperity under Hezekiah, and the manifestation of the Messiah (Isa 9:1-7). Pronounces vengeance upon the enemies of Israel (Isa 9:8-12). Denounces the wickedness of Israel, and foretells the judgments of God (Isa 9:13-21). Pronounces judgments against false prophets (Isa 10:1-4). Foretells the destruction of Sennacherib's armies (Isa 10:5-34); the restoration of Israel and the triumph of the Messiah's kingdom (Isa 11). The burden of Babylon (Isa 13; 14:1-28). Denunciation against the Philistines (Isa 14:9-32). Burden of Moab (Isa 15; 16). Burden of Damascus (Isa 17). Obscure prophecy, supposed by some authorities to be directed against the Assyrians, by others against the Egyptians, and by others against the Ethiopians (Isa 18). The burden of Egypt (Isa 19; 20). Denunciations against Babylon (Isa 21:1-10). Prophecy concerning Seir (Isa 21:11, 12); Arabia (Isa 21:13-17); concerning the conquest of Jerusalem, the captivity of Shebna, and the promotion of Eliakim (Isa 22:1-22); the overthrow of Tyre (Isa 23); the judgments upon the land, but that a remnant of the Jews would be saved (Isa 25; 26; 27). Reproves Ephraim for his wickedness, and foretells the destruction by Shalmaneser (Isa 28:1-5). Declares the glory of God upon the remnant who are saved (Isa 28:5, 6). Exposes the corruptions in Jerusalem and exhorts to repentance (Isa 28:7-29). Foretells the invasion of Sennacherib, the distress of the Jews and the destruction of the Assyrian army (Isa 29:1-8). Denounces the hypocrisy of the Jews (Isa 29:9-17). Promises a reformation (Isa 29:18-24). Reproves the people for their confidence in Egypt, and their contempt of God (Isa 30:1-17; 31:1-6). Declares the goodness and longsuffering of God toward them (Isa 30:18-26; chapters 32-35). Reproves the Jews for their spiritual blindness and infidelity (Isa 42:18-25). Promises ultimate restoration of the Jews (Isa 43:1-13). Foretells the ultimate destruction of Babylon (Isa 43:14-17; 47). Exhorts the people to repent (Isa 43:22-28). Comforts the church with promises, exposes the folly of idolatry, and their future deliverance from captivity by Cyrus (Isa 44; 45:1-5; 48:20). Foretells the conversion of the Gentiles, and triumph of the gospel (Isa 45:5-25). Denounces the evils of idolatry (Isa 46). Reproves the Jews for their idolatries and other wickedness (Isa 48). Exhorts to sanctification (Isa 56:1-8). Foretells calamities to Judah (Isa 59:9-12, w chapters 57-59).

Foreshadows the person and the kingdom of the Messiah (chapters 32-35; 42; 45; 49-56; 59; verses 15-21, and chapters 60-66).

ISCAH, daughter of Haran and sister of Lot (Ge 11:29).

ISCARIOT (See Judas.)

ISHBAH, father of Eshtemoa (1Ch 4:17).

ISHBAK, son of Abraham and Keturah (Ge 25:2; 1Ch 1:32).

ISHBI-BENOB, a giant warrior slain by Abishai (2Sa 21:16).

ISH-BOSHETH (man of shame). Son of Saul. Called Esh-baal in 1Ch 8:33; 9:39. Made king by Abner (2Sa 2:8-10). Deserted by Abner (2Sa 3:6-12). Restores Michal, David's wife, to David

(2Sa 3:14-16). Assassinated (2Sa 4:5-8). Avenged by David (2Sa 4:9-12).

ISHI (my husband). 1. A name of Deity (Hos 2:16).

2. A son of Appaim (1Ch 2:31).

3. A descendant of Judah (1Ch 4:20).

4. A Simeonite (1Ch 4:42).

5. One of the heads of Manasseh (1Ch 5:24).

ISHIAH (Jehovah forgets). 1. Man of Issachar (1Ch 7:3).

2. Levite (1Ch 24:21).

3. Another Levite (1Ch 23:20, Jesiah in KJV).

4. One of David's heroes (Jesaiah, 1Ch 12:6).

ISHIJAH, one of the sons of Harim (Ezr 10:31).

ISHMA, a descendant of Judah (1Ch 4:3).

ISHMAEL (God hears). 1. Son of Abraham (Ge 16:11, 15, 16; 1Ch 1:28). Prayer of Abraham for (Ge 17:18, 20). Circumcised (Ge 17:23-26). Promised to be the father of a nation (Ge 16:11, 12; 17:20; 21:12, 13, 18). Sent away by Abraham (Ge 21:6-21). With Isaac buries his father (Ge 25:9). Children of (Ge 25:12-18; 1Ch 1:29-31). Daughter of, marries Esau (Ge 28:9; 36:2, 3). Death of (Ge 25:17, 18).

2. Father of Zebadiah (2Ch 19:11).

3. A son of Azel (1Ch 8:38; 9:44).

4. One of the captains of hundreds (2Ch 23:1).

5. A priest of the exile (Ezr 10:22).

6. A son of Nethaniah. Assassinated Gedaliah, governor of Judah under king of Babylon, and takes captive many Jews (Jer 40:8-16; 41:1-11; 2Ki 25:23-25). Defeated by Johanan, and put to flight (Jer 41:12-15).

ISHMAELITES, THE. Descended from Abraham's son, Ishmael (Ge 16:15, 16; 1Ch 1:28). Divided into twelve tribes (Ge 25:16). Heads of tribes of (Ge 25:13-15; 1Ch 1:29-31).

Called: Hagarites (1Ch 5:10). Hagarenes (Ps 83:6). Arabians (Isa 13:20). Original possessions of (Ge 25:18). Governed by kings (Jer 25:24). Dwelt in tents (Isa 13:20). Rich in cattle (1Ch 5:21). Wore ornaments of gold (J'g 8:24). Were the merchants of the east (Ge 37:25; Eze 27:20, 21). Traveled in large companies or caravans (Ge 37:25; Job 6:19). Waylaid and plundered travelers (Jer 3:2). Often confederate against Israel (Ps 83:6).

Overcome by: Gideon (J'g 8:10-24). Reubenites and Gadites (2Ch 5:10, 18-20). Uzziah (2Ch 26:7). Sent presents to Solomon (1Ki 10:15; 2Ch 9:14). Sent flocks to Jehoshaphat (2Ch 17:11).

Predictions Respecting: To be numerous (Ge 16:10; 17:20). To be wild and savage (Ge 16:12). To be warlike and predatory (Ge 16:12). To be divided into twelve tribes (Ge 17:20). To continue independent (Ge 16:12). To be a great nation (Ge 21:13, 18). To be judged with the nations (Jer 25:23-25). Their glory to be diminished (Isa 21:13-17). Their submission to Christ (Ps 72:10, 15). Probably preached to by St. Paul (Ga 1:17).

ISHMAIAH (Jehovah hears). 1. Gibeonite (1Ch 12:4).

2. Chief of Zebulunites (1Ch 27:19).

ISHMEELITE (See Ishmaelite.)

ISHMERAI (Jehovah keeps), a chief Benjamite (1Ch 8:18).

ISHOD (man of majesty), one of the tribe of Manasseh (1Ch 7:18).

ISHPAN (he will hide), son of Shashak (1Ch 8:22).

ISHTAR, Semitic goddess worshipped in Phoenicia, Canaan, Assyria, and Babylonia, and sometimes even by the Israelites, called Ashtoreth or Ashtaroth (J'g 2:13; 10:6; 1Ki 11:5; 2Ki 23:13); worship usually accompanied by lascivious rites.

ISHTOB (the men of Tob), place in Palestine which supplied Ammonites with soldiers against David (2Sa 10:6, 8).

ISHUAH (he will level), called also Isuah. Son of Asher (Ge 46:17; 1Ch 7:30).

ISHUI, called also Ishuai, Isui, and Jesui. Son of Asher (Ge 46:17; Nu 26:44; 1Ch 7:30).

2. Son of Saul (1Sa 14:49).

ISLAND, ISLE. 1. Dry land, as opposed to water (Isa 42:15).

2. Body of land surrounded by water (Jer 2:10).

3. Coastland (Ge 10:5; Isa 20:6).

4. The farthest regions of the earth (Isa 41:5; Zep 2:11).

ISHMACHIAH (Jehovah sustains), overseer of the temple (2Ch 31:13).

ISMAIAH (Jehovah hears). 1. Gibeonite (1Ch 12:4).

2. Zebulunite chief (1Ch 27:19).

ISPAH, a chief Benjamite (1Ch 8:16).

ISRAEL. 1. A name given to Jacob (Ge 32:24-32; 2Ki 17:34; Ho 12:3, 4).

2. A name of the Christ in prophecy (Isa 49:3).

3. A name given to the descendants of Jacob, a nation. Called also Israelites and Hebrews (Ge 43:32; Ex 1:15; 9:7; 10:3; 21:2; Le 23:42; Jos 13:6, etc.; 1Sa 4:6; 13:3, 19; 14:11, 21; Ph'p 3:5).

Tribes of Israel were named after the sons of Jacob. In lists usually the names Levi and Joseph, two sons of Jacob, do not appear. The descendants of Levi were consecrated to the rites of religion, and the two sons of Joseph, Ephraim and Manasseh, were adopted by Jacob in Joseph's stead (Ge 48:5; Jos 14:4), and their names appear in the catalogues of tribes instead of those of Levi and Joseph, as follows: Asher, Benjamin, Dan, Ephraim, Gad, Issachar, Judah, Manasseh, Naphtali, Reuben, Simeon, Zebulun.

Names of, seen in John's vision, on the gates of the New Jerusalem (Re 21:12).

Prophecies concerning (Ge 15:5, 13; 25:23; 26:4; 27:28, 29, 40; 48:19; 49; De 33); of the multitude of (Ge 13:16; 15:5; 22:17; 26:4; 28:14); of their captivity in Egypt (Ge 15:13, 14; Ac 7:6, 7).

Divided into families, each of which had a chief (Nu 25:14; 26; 36:1; Jos 7:14; 1Ch 4-8).

Number of, who went into Egypt (Ge 46:8-27; Ex 1:5; De 10:22; Ac 7:14). Number of, at the time of the exodus (Ex 12:37, 38, w Ge 47:27; Ex 1:7-20; Ps 105:24; Ac 7:17). Number of, fit for military service when they left Egypt (Ex 12:37); at Sinai, by tribes (Nu 1:1-50) after the plague (Nu 26); when David numbered (2Sa 24:1-9; 1Ch 21:5, 6; 27:23, 24); after the captivity (Ezr 2:64; Ne 7:66, 67); in John's apocalyptic vision (Re 7:1-8).

Dwelt in Goshen (Ge 46:28-34; 47:4-10, 27, 28). Dwelt in Egypt four hundred and thirty years (Ex 12:40, 41, w Ge 15:13; Ac 7:6; Ga 3:17). Were enslaved and oppressed by the Egyptians (Ex 1; 2; 5; Ac 7:18-36). Their groaning heard of God (Ex 2:23-25). Moses commissioned as deliverer (Ex 3:2-22; 4:1-17). The land of Egypt plagued on their account (see Egypt). Exempt from the plagues (Ex 8:22, 23; 9:4-6, 26; 10:23; 11:7; 12:13). Children were spared when the firstborn of the Egyptians were slain (Ex 12:13, 23). Instituted the passover (Ex 12:1-28). Borrowed jewels from the Egyptians (Ex 11:2, 3; 12:35, 36; Ps 105:37). Urged by the Egyptians to depart (Ex 12:31-39). Journey from Rameses to Succoth (Ex 12:37-39). Made the journey by night (Ex 12:42). The day of their deliverance to be a memorial (Ex 12:42; 13:3-16). Led of God (Ex 13:18, 21, 22). Providentially cared for (De 8:3, 4; 29:5, 6; 34:7; Ne 9:21; Ps 105:37). See Manna; Cloud, Pillar of.

Journey from Succoth to Etham (Ex 13:20); to Pi-hahiroth (Ex 14:2; Nu 33:5-7). Pursued by the Egyptians (Ex 14:5-31). Pass through the Red Sea (Ex 14:19-22; De 11:4; Ps 78; 105; 106; 107; 136). Order of march (Nu 2). Journey to Marah (Ex 15:23; Nu 33:8). Murmur on account of the bitter water (Ex 15:23-25); water of, sweetened (Ex 15:25). Journey to Elim (Ex 15:27; Nu 33:9). For the itinerary, see Nu 33.

Murmured for food (Ex 16:2, 3). Provided with manna and quails (Ex 16:4-36). Murmured for want of water at Rephidim (Ex 17:2-7); water miraculously supplied from the rock at Meribah (Ex 17:5-7). Defeat the Amalekites (Ex 17:13; De 25:17, 18). Arrive at Sinai (Ex 19:1; Nu 33:15). At the suggestion of Jethro, Moses' father-in-law, they organize a system of government (Ex 18:25; De 1:9-18). The message of God to them, requiring that they shall be obedient to his commandments, and as a reward they would be to him a holy nation, and their reply (Ex 19:3-8). Sanctify themselves for receiving the law (Ex 19:10-15). The law delivered to (Ex 20; 21; 22; 23; 24:1-4; 25; 26; 27; 28; 29; 30; 31; Le 1-25; 27; De 5; 15:16). The people receive it and covenant obedience to it (Ex 24:3, 7). Idolatry of (Ex 32; De 9:17-21). The anger of the Lord in consequence (Ex 32:9-14). Moses' indignation; breaks the tables of stone; enters the camp; commands the Levites; three thousand slain (Ex 32:19-35). Visited by a plague (Ex 32:35). Obduracy of (Ex 33:3; 34:9; De 9:12-29). God withdraws his presence (Ex 33:1-3). The mourning of, when God refused to lead them (Ex 33:4-10). Tables renewed (Ex 34). Pattern for the tabernacle and the appurtenances, and forms of worship to be observed (Ex 25-31). Gifts consecrated for the creation of the tabernacle (Ex 35; 36:1-7; Nu 7). The erection of the tabernacle; the manufacture of the appurtenances, including the garments of the priests; and their sanctification (Ex 36:8-38; chapters 37-40). First sacrifice offered by, under the law (Le 8:14-36; 9:8-24). Second passover observed (Nu 9:1-5).

March out of the wilderness (Nu 10:11-36. For itinerary, see Nu 33). Order of camp and march (Nu 2). Arrive at the border of Canaan (Nu 12:16). Send twelve spies to view the land (Nu 13; 32:8; De 1:22, 25; Jos 14:7). Return with a majority and minority report (Nu 13:26-33; 14:6-10). Murmuring over the report (Nu 14:1-5). The judgment of God upon them in consequence of their unbelief and murmuring (Nu 14:13-39). Reaction, and their purpose to enter the land; are defeated by the Amalekites (Nu 14:40-45; De 1:41-45). Abide at Kadesh (De 1:46). Return to the wilderness, where they remain thirty-eight years, and all die except Joshua and Caleb (Nu 14:20-39). Rebellion of Korah, Dathan, and Abiram (Nu 16:1-40; De 11:6). Murmur against Moses and Aaron; are plagued; fourteen thousand seven hundred die; plague stayed (Nu 16:41-50). Murmur for want of water in Meribah; the rock is smitten (Nu 20:1-13). Are refused passage through the country of Edom (Nu 20:14-21). The death of Aaron (Nu 20:22, 29; 33:38, 39; De 10:6). Defeat the Canaanites (Nu 21:1-3). Are scourged with serpents (Nu 21:4-9). Defeat the Amorites (Nu 21:21-32; De 2:24-35), and the king of Baasha (Nu 21:33-35; De 3:1-17). Arrive in the plains of Moab, at the fords of the Jordan (Nu 22:1; 33:48, 49). Commit idolatry with the people of Moab (Nu 25:1-5). Visited by a plague in consequence; twenty-four thousand die (Nu 25:6-15; 26:1). The people numbered for the allotment of the land (Nu 26). The daughters of Zelophehad sue for an inheritance (Nu 27:1-11; Jos 17:3-6). Conquest of the Midianites (Nu 31). Nations dread (De 2:25). Renew the covenant (De 29). Moses dies, and people mourn (De 34). Joshua appointed leader (Nu 27:18-23; De 31:23). See Joshua.

All who were numbered at Sinai perished in the wilderness except Caleb and Joshua (Nu 26:63, 65; De 2:14-16). Piety of those who entered Canaan (Jos 23:8; J'g 2:7-10; Jer 2:2, 3). Men chosen to allot the lands of Canaan among the tribes and families (Nu 34:17-29). Remove from Shittim to Jordan (Jos 3:1). Cross Jordan (Jos 4). Circumcision observed and passover celebrated (Jos 5). Jericho taken (Jos 6). Ai taken (Jos 7 and 8). Make a league with the Gibeonites (Jos 9). Defeat the five Amoritish kings (Jos 10). Conquest of the land (Jos 21:43-45, w J'g 1). The land allotted (Jos 15-21).

Two and one-half tribes return from the west side of the Jordan; erect a memorial to signify the unity of the tribes; the memorial misunderstood; the controversy which followed; its amicable adjustment (Jos 22). Joshua's exhortation immediately before his death (Jos 23). Covenant renewed, death of Joshua (Jos 24; J'g 2:8, 9). Religious fidelity during the life of Joshua (Jos 24:31; J'g 2:7).

Under the Judges: Public affairs administered four hundred and fifty years by the judges (J'g 2:16-19; Ac 13:20). The original inhabitants not fully expelled (J'g 1:27-36; 3:1-7). Reproved by an angel for not casting out the original inhabitants (J'g 2:1-5). People turn to idolatry (J'g 2:10-23). Delivered for their idolatry to the king of Mesopotamia during eight years; their repentance and deliverance (J'g 3:8-11). Renew their idolatry, and are put under tribute to the king of Moab during eighteen years; repent and are delivered by Ehud; eighty years of peace follow (J'g 3:12-30). Shamgar resists a foray of the Philistines and delivers Israel (J'g 3:31). People again do evil and are put under bonds for twenty years to the king of Syria (J'g 4:1-3). Delivered by Deborah, a prophetess, and judged (J'g 4; 5). Seven years of bondage to the Midianites; delivered by Gideon (J'g 6; 7; 8:1-28; see Gideon) Return to idolatry (J'g 8:33, 34). Abimelech foments an inter-tribal war (J'g 9). Judged by Tola twenty-three years (J'g 10:1, 2); by Jair twenty-two years (J'g 10:3, 4). People backslide, and are given over to the Philistines for chastisement eighteen years; repent and turn to the Lord; delivered by Jephthah (J'g 10:6-18; 11). Ephraimites go to war against other tribes; defeated by Jephthah (J'g 12:1-7). Judged by Ibzan seven years (J'g 12:8-10); by Elon ten years (J'g 12:11, 12); by Abdon eight years (J'g 12:13-15). Backslide again and are chastised by the Philistines forty years (J'g 13:1). Judged by Samson twenty years (J'g 15:20, w chapters 13-16). Scandal of the Bethlehemite's concubine, and the consequent war between the Benjamites and the other tribes (J'g 19-21). Judged by Eli forty years (1Sa 4:18, w chapters 1-4). Smitten by the Philistines at Eben-ezer (1Sa 4:1, 2, 10, 11). Demand a king (1Sa 8:5-20; Ho 13:10).

Under the Kings Before the Separation Into Two Kingdoms: Saul anointed king (1Sa 10; 11:12-15; 12:13). Ammonites invade Israel, are defeated (1Sa 11). Philistines smitten (1Sa 14). Amalekites defeated (1Sa 15). David anointed king (1Sa 16:11-13). Goliath slain (1Sa 17). Israel defeated by the Philistines, and Saul and his sons slain (1Sa 31. See Saul). David defeats the Amalekites (1Sa 30; 2Sa 1:1); made king (2Sa 2:4, 11). Ishbosheth made king (2Sa 2:8-10).

The conflict between the two political factions (2Sa 2:12-32; 3:1).

David made king over all Israel (2Sa 5:1-5). Conquests of David (2Sa 8); Absalom's rebellion (2Sa 15-18. See David).

Solomon anointed king (1Ki 1:32-40). Temple built (1Ki 6). Solomon's palace built (1Ki 7). Solomon's death (1Ki 11:41-43. See Solomon).

The Revolt of the Ten Tribes: Foreshadowing circumstances indicating the separation: Disagreement after Saul's death (2Sa 2; 1Ch 12:23-40; 13). Lukewarmness of the ten tribes, and zeal of Judah for David in Absalom's rebellion (2Sa 19:41-43). The rebellion of Sheba (2Sa 20). The two factions are distinguished as Israel and Judah during David's reign (2Sa 21:2). Providential (Zec 11:14).

Revolt consummated under Rehoboam, son and successor of Solomon (1Ki 12).

The name of the ten tribes that revolted from the house of David. Called also Jacob (Ho 12:2).

List of the kings of Israel, and the period of time in which they reigned. For the facts of their reigns see under each name:

1. Jeroboam, twenty-two years.
2. Nadab, about two years.
3. Baasha, twenty-four years.
4. Elah, two years.
5. Zimri, seven days.
6. Omri, twelve years.
7. Ahab, twenty-two years.
8. Ahaziah, two years.
9. Jehoram, twelve years.
10. Jehu, twenty-eight years.
11. Jehoahaz, seventeen years.
12. Jehoash, sixteen years.
13. Jeroboam II, forty-one years.
14. Zachariah, six months.
15. Shallum, one month.
16. Menahem, ten years.
17. Pekahiah, two years.
18. Pekah, twenty years.
19. Hoshea, nine years.

The ten tribes carried captive to Assyria.

History of: War continued between the two kingdoms all the days of Rehoboam and Jeroboam (1Ki 14:30); and between Jeroboam and Abijam (1Ki 15:7); and between Baasha and Asa (1Ki 15:16, 32). Famine prevails in the reign of Ahab (1Ki 18:1-6). Israel, called also Samaria, invaded by, but defeats, Benhadad, king of Syria (1Ki 20). Moab rebels (2Ki 1:1; 3). Army of Syria invades Israel, but peacefully withdraws through the tact of the prophet Elisha (2Ki 6:8-23). Samaria besieged (2Ki 6:24-33; 7); city of, taken, and the people carried to Assyria (2Ki 17). The land repeopled (2Ki 17:24).

The remnant that remained after the able-bodied were carried into captivity affiliated with the kingdom of Judah (2Ch 30:18-26; 34:6; 35:18).

Prophecies Concerning: Of captivity, famine, and judgments (1Ki 14:15, 16;

17:1; 20:13-28; 2Ki 7:1, 2, 17; 8:1; Isa 7:8; 8:4-7; 9:8-21; 17:3-11; 28:1-8; Ho 1:1-9; 2:1-13; chapters 4; 8; 9; 10; 11:5, 6; 12:7-14; 13; Am 2:6-16; chapters 3-9).

Of restoration (Ho 2:14-23; 11:9-11; 13:13, 14; 14:8).

Of the reunion of the ten tribes and Judah (Jer 3:18; Eze 37:16-22).

See the following:

Judah. The nation composed of the tribes of Judah and Benjamin, called Judah (Isa 11:12, 13; Jer 4:3), and Jews (See Jews) ruled by the descendants of David.

In the historical books of the Kings and the Chronicles the nation is called Judah, but in the prophecies it is frequently referred to as Israel, as in Isa 8:14; 49:7.

List of rulers and the periods of time over which they reigned:

1. Rehoboam, seventeen years.
2. Abijah, or Abijam, three years.
3. Asa, forty-one years.
4. Jehoshaphat, twenty-five years.
5. Jehoram, eight years.
6. Ahaziah, one year.

Athaliah's usurpation, six years.

7. Joash, or Jehoash, forty years.
8. Amaziah, twenty-nine years.
9. Uzziah, or Azariah, fifty-two years.
10. Jotham, sixteen years.
11. Ahaz, sixteen years.
12. Hezekiah, twenty-nine years.
13. Manasseh, fifty-five years.
14. Amon, two years.
15. Josiah, thirty-one years.
16. Jehoahaz, Josiah's son, three months.
17. Jehoiakim, Josiah's son, eleven years.
18. Jehoiachin, or Jeconiah, Jehoiakim's son, three months.
19. Zedekiah, or Mattaniah, Josiah's son, eleven years.

For the history of the above kings see under each name.

Rehoboam succeeds Solomon. In consequence of his arbitrary policy ten tribes rebel (1Ki 12). Other circumstances of his reign (1Ki 14:21-31; 2Ch 10; 11; 12). Death of Rehoboam (1Ki 14:31). Abijam's wicked reign (1Ki 15:1-8; 2Ch 13); Asa's good reign (1Ki 15:9-24; 2Ch 14; 15; 16). Asa makes a league with Ben-hadad, king of Syria, to make war against Israel (1Ki 15:16-24). Jehoshaphat succeeds Asa (1Ki 15:24; 2Ch 17; 18; 19; 20; 21:1); joins Ahab against the king of Syria (1Ki 22. See Jehoshaphat). Jehoram, called also Joram, reigns in the stead of his father, Jehoshaphat (2Ki 8:16-24; 2Ch 21). Edom revolts (2Ki 8:20-22). Ahaziah, called also Azariah (2Ch 22:6), and Jehoahaz (2Ch 21:17; 25:23) succeeds Jehoram (2Ki 8:24-29; 2Ch 22); slain by Jehu (2Ki 9:27-29; 2Ch 22:8, 9), Athaliah, his mother, succeeds him (2Ki 11:1-16; 2Ch 22:10-12; 23:1-15). Jehoash, called also Joash, succeeds Athaliah (2Ki 11:21; 12:1-21; 2Ch 24). The temple repaired (2Ki 12). Amaziah reigns, and Judah is invaded by the king of Israel; Jerusalem is taken and the sacred things of the temple carried away (2Ki 14:1-20; 2Ch 25). Azariah, called also Uzziah, succeeds him (2Ki 14:21, 22; 15:1-7; 2Ch 26). Jotham succeeds Uzziah (2Ki 15:7, 32-38; 2Ch 27). Rezin, king of Syria, invades Judah (2Ki 15:37). Jotham is succeeded by Ahaz (2Ki 16:1; 2Ch 28). Judah is invaded by kings of Samaria and Syria; Ahaz hires the king of Assyria to make war on the king of Syria (2Ki 16:5-9). Ahaz changes the fashion of the altar in the temple (2Ki 16:10-18). Hezekiah succeeds Ahaz (2Ki 16:19, 20; 2Ch 29-32). His good reign (2Ki 18:1-8). He revolts from the sovereignty of the king of Assyria (2Ki 18:7). King of Assyria invades Judah, and blasphemes the God of Judah; his army overthrown (2Ki 18:9-37; 19). Hezekiah's sickness and miraculous restoration (2Ki 20). Succeeded by Manasseh (2Ki 20:21; 2Ch 33:1-20). Manasseh's wicked reign (2Ki 21:1-18). Amon succeeds Manasseh on the throne (2Ki 21:18-26; 2Ch 33:20-25). Josiah succeeds Amon; the temple is repaired; the book of the law recovered; religious revival follows; and the king dies (2Ki 22; 23:1-30; 2Ch 34; 35). Josiah is succeeded by Jehoahaz, who reigned three months, was dethroned by the king of Egypt, and the land put under tribute (2Ki 23:30-35; 2Ch 36:1-3). Jehoiakim is elevated to the throne; becomes tributary to Nebuchadnezzar for three years; rebels; is conquered and carried to Babylon (2Ki 24:1-6; 2Ch 36:4-8). Jehoiachin is made king; suffers invasion and is carried to Babylon (2Ki 24:8-16; 2Ch 36:9, 10). Zedekiah is made king by Nebuchadnezzar; rebels; Nebuchadnezzar invades Judah, takes Jerusalem, and carries the people to Babylon, despoiling the temple (2Ki 24:17-20; 25; 2Ch 36:11-21). The poorest of the people were left to occupy the country, and were joined by fragments of the army of Judah, the dispersed Israelites in other lands, and the king's daughters (2Ki 25:12, 22, 23; Jer 39:10; 40:7-12; 52:16). Gedaliah appointed governor over (2Ki 25:22). His administration favorable to the people (2Ki 25:23, 24; Jer 40:7-12). Conspired against and slain by Ishmael (2Ki 25:25; Jer 40:13-16; 41:1-3). Ishmael seeks to betray the people to the Ammonites (Jer 41:1-18). The people, in fear, take refuge in Egypt (2Ki 25:26; Jer 41:14-18; 42:13-18).

Captivity of: Great wickedness the cause of their adversity (Eze 5; 6; 7; 16; 23:22-44). Dwell in Babylon (Da 5:13; 6:13; Jer 52:28-30); by the river Chebor (Eze 1:1; 10:15). Patriotism of (Ps 137). Plotted against, by Haman (Es 3). Are saved by Esther (Es 4-9). Cyrus decrees their restoration (2Ch 36:22, 23; Ezr 1:14). Cyrus directs the rebuilding of the temple, and the restoration of the vessels which had been carried to Babylon (2Ch 36:23; Ezr 1:3-11). Proclamation renewed by Darius and Artaxerxes (Ezr 6: 1-14). Ezra returns with seventeen hundred and fifty-four of the captivity to Jerusalem (Ezr 2). Temple rebuilt and dedicated (Ezr 3-6). Artaxerxes issues proclamation to restore the temple service (Ezr 7). Priests and Levites authorized to return (Ezr 8). Corruptions among the returned captives; their reform (Ezr 9; 10).

Nehemiah is commissioned to lead the remainder of the captivity, forty-nine thousand nine hundred and forty-two, back to Canaan (Ne 2; 7:5-67; Ps 85; 87; 107; 126). Wall of Jerusalem rebuilt and dedicated (Ne 2-6; 12). The law read and expounded (Ne 8). Solemn feast is kept; priests are purified; and the covenant sealed (Ne 8-10). One-tenth of the people, to be determined by lot, volunteer to dwell in Jerusalem, and the remaining nine parts dwell in other cities (Ne 11). Catalogue of the priests and Levites who came up with Zerubbabel (Ne 12). Nehemiah reforms various abuses (Ne 13). Expect a Messiah (Lu 3:15). Many accept Jesus as the Christ (Joh 2:23; 10:42; 11:45; 12:11; Ac 21:20). Reject Jesus (see Jesus, Rejected).

Rejected of God (M't 21:43; Lu 20:16).

Prophecies Concerning: Of their rejection of the Messiah (Isa 8:14, 15; 49:5, 7; 52:14; 53:1-3; Zec 11; 13; M't 21:33; 22:1).

Of war and other judgments (De 28:49-57; 2Ki 20:17, 18; 21:12-15; 22:16, 17; 23:26, 27; Isa 1:1-24; 3; 4:1; 5; 6:9-13; 7:17-25; 8:14-22; 9; 10:12; 22:1-14; 28:14-22; 29:1-10; 30:1-17; 31:1-3; 32:9-14; Jer 1:11-16; 4:5-31; 6; 7:8-34; 8; 9:9-26; 10:17-22; 11:9-23; 13:9-27; 14:14-18; 15:1-14; 16; 17:1-4; 18:15-17; 19; 20:5; 21:4-7; 22:24-30; 25:8-38; chapters 28; 34; 37; 38:1-3; 42:13-22; chapters 43; 44; 45; La 5:6; Eze 4; 5; 11:7-12; chapters 12; 15; 16; 17; 19; 22:13-22; 23:22-35; 24; 33:21-29; Da 9:26-27; Joe 2:1-17; Am 2:4, 5; Mic 2:10; 3; 4:8-10; Hab 1:6-11; Zep 1; Zec 11; 14:1-3; Mal 4:1; M't 21:33, 34; 23:35-38; 24:2, 14-42; M'k 13:1-13; Lu 13:34, 35; 19:43, 44; 21:5-25; 23:28-31; Re 1:7).

Dispersion of (Isa 24:1; Jer 9:16; Ho 9:17; Joe 3:6, 20; Am 9:9; Eze 4:13; 5:10, 12; 20:23; 36:19; Da 9:7; Joh 7:35; Ac 2:5).

Of blessing and restoration (Isa 1:25-27; 2:1-5; 4:2-6; 11:11-13; 25; 26:1, 2, 12-19; 27:13; 29:18-24; 30:18-26; 32:15-20; 33:13-24; 35; 37:31, 32; 40:2, 9; 41:27; 44; 49:13-23; 51; 52:1-12; 60; 61:4-9; 62; 66:5-22; Jer 3:14-18; 4:3-18; 12:14-16; 23:3; 24:1-7; 29:1-14; 30:3-22; 32:36-44; 33; 44:28; Eze 14:22, 23; 16:60-63; 20:40, 41; 36:1-38; 37:12, 21; Da 11:30-45; 12:1; Joe 3; Am 9:9-15; Ob 17-21; Mic 2:12, 13; 5:3; Zep 2:7; Zec 1:14-21; 2:8; 10:5-12; 12:1-14; 13; 14:3-21; Mal 3:4; Ro 11; 2Co 3:16; Re 7:5).

ISRAELITES (See Israel.)

ISSACHAR. Son of Jacob (Ge 30:18; Ex 1:3; 1Ch 2:1). Jacob's prophetic benedictions upon (Ge 49:14, 15). In the time of David (1Ch 7:1-5).

ISSACHAR, THE TRIBE OF. Descended from Jacob's fifth son (Ge 30:17, 18). Predictions respecting (Ge 49:14, 15; De 33:18, 19).

Persons Selected From: To number the people (Nu 1:8). To spy out the land (Nu 13:7). To divide the land (Nu 34:26). Strength of, on leaving Egypt (Nu 1:28, 29; 2:6). Encamped under the standard of Judah east of the tabernacle (Nu 2:5). Next to and under standard of Judah in the journeys of Israel (Nu 10:14, 15). Offering of, at the dedication (Nu 7:18-23). Families of (Nu 26:23, 24). Strength of, on entering Canaan (Nu 26:25). On Gerizim said amen to the blessings (De 27:12). Bounds of their inheritance (Jos 19:17-23). Assisted Deborah against Sisera (J'g 5:15). Officers of, appointed by David (1Ch 27:18). Officers of, appointed by Solomon (1Ki 4:17). Some of, at David's coronation (1Ch 12:32). Number of warriors belonging to, in David's time (1Ch 7:2, 5). Many of, at Hezekiah's passover (2Ch 30:18). Remarkable persons of (J'g 10:1; 1Ki 15:27).

ISUAH (See Ishuah.)

ISSUE OF BLOOD (M't 9:20; M'k 5:25; Lu 8:43).

See Hemorrhage.

ISUI (See Ishul.)

ITALIAN BAND, cohort of Italian soldiers stationed in Caesarea when Peter preached to Cornelius (Ac 10:1).

ITALY (Ac 27:1; Heb 13:24). Aquila and Priscilla expelled from (Ac 18:2).

ITCH (De 28:27).

ITHAI, called also Ittai. One of David's valiant men (2Sa 23:29; 1Ch 11:31).

ITHAMAR. Son of Aaron (Ex 6:23; 28:1; 1Ch 6:3). Intrusted with moneys of the tabernacle (Ex 38:21). Charged with duties of the tabernacle (Nu 4:28; 7:8). Forbidden to lament the death of his brothers, Nadab and Abihu (Le 10:6, 7). Descendants of (1Ch 24:1-19).

ITHIEL (God is). 1. A Benjamite (Ne 11:7).

2. An unidentified person mentioned in Pr 30:1.

ITHMAH (purity), a Moabite (1Ch 11:46).

ITHNAN, a town in the extreme S of Judah (Jos 15:23).

ITHRA (abundance), called also Jether. Father of Amasa (2Sa 17:25; 1Ch 2:17).

ITHRAN (excellent). 1. Son of Dishon (Ge 36:26; 1Ch 1:41).

2. Son of Zophah (1Ch 7:37).

ITHREAM, son of David (2Sa 3:5; 1Ch 3:3).

ITHRITE (excellence), family from which two of David's heroes came (2Sa 23:38; 1Ch 11:40).

ITINERARY, of the Israelites (Nu 33; De 10:6, 7).

See Israel.

ITTAH-KAZIN, a landmark in the boundary line of Zebulun (Jos 19:13).

ITTAI. 1. One of David's heroes (2Sa 23:29; 1Ch 11:31).

2. Gathite who became a loyal follower of David (2Sa 15:18-22; 18:2, 5).

ITURAEA (pertaining to Jetur), region NE of Palestine; its people descended from Jetur, son of Ishmael, and from whom the name Iturea is derived (Ge 25:15); ruled by Philip (Lu 3:1).

IVAH. A district in Babylon conquered by the Assyrians (2Ki 18:34; 19:13; Isa 37:13).

IVORY (Song 5:14; 7:4; Eze 27:15). Exported from Tarshish (1Ki 10:22; 2Ch 9:21); Chittim (Eze 27:6). Ahab's palace made of (1Ki 22:39). Other houses made of (Ps 45:8; Am 3:15). Other articles made of: Stringed instruments (Ps 45:8; thrones (1Ki 10:18; 2Ch 9:17); benches (Eze 27:6); beds (Am 6:4); vessels (Re 18:12).

IZHAR (the shining one), son of Kohath (Ex 6:18, 21; 1Ch 6:2, 18, 38; 23:12, 18).

IZRAHIAH (Jehovah shines), grandson of Tola (1Ch 7:3).

IZRAHITE, patronymic of Shamhuth (1Ch 27:8).

IZRI (Creator, former), perhaps the same as Zeri. Leader of the fourth division of Levitical singers (1Ch 25:11).

J

JAAKAN, called also Akan and Jakan. Son of Ezer (Ge 36:27; De 10:6; 1Ch 1:42).

JAAKOBAH, descendant of Simeon (1Ch 4:36).

JAALA, called also Jaalah. One of the servants of Solomon returned from exile (Ezr 2:56; Ne 7:58).

JAALAM, son of Esau (Ge 36:5, 14, 18; 1Ch 1:35).

JAANAI, a Gadite chief (1Ch 5:12).

JAARE-OREGIM, father of Elhanan, who slew the giant brother of Goliath (2Sa 21:19). Spelled Jair in 1Ch 20:5.

JAASAU, of the family of Bani (Ezr 10:37).

JAASIEL, son of Abner (1Ch 27:21).

JAAZANIAH (Jehovah hears). 1. Called also Jezaniah. A captain who joined Gedaliah at Mizpah (2Ki 25:23; Jer 40:8; 42:1).

2. A Rechabite (Jer 35:3).

3. An idolatrous zealot (Eze 8:11).

4. A wicked prince of Judah (Eze 11:1-13).

JAAZER, JAZER (helpful), Ammonite stronghold E of the Jordan, probably c. 14 miles N of Heshbon; assigned to Gad (Jos 13:24, 25); later given to Levites (Jos 21:39).

JAAZIAH (Jehovah strengthens), a descendant of Merari (1Ch 24:26, 27).

JAAZIEL (God strengthens), a Levite musician (1Ch 15:18).

JABAL, son of Lamech. A shepherd (Ge 4:20).

JABBOK (flowing). A stream on the E of the Jordan, the northern boundary of the possessions of the Ammonites (Nu 21:24; J'g 11:13); of the Reubenites and the Gadites (Jos 12:2; De 3:16). The northern boundary of the Amorites (J'g 11:22).

JABESH (dry). 1. Father of King Shallum (2Ki 15:8-13).

2. Short term for Jabesh-Gilead (1Ch 10:12).

JABESH-GILEAD (dry). A city E of the Jordan (J'g 21:8-15). Besieged by the Ammonites (1Sa 11:1-11). Saul and his sons buried at (1Sa 31:11-13; 2Sa 2:4; 1Ch 10:11, 12). Bones of Saul and his son removed from, by David, and buried at Zelah (2Sa 21:12-14).

JABEZ (to grieve). 1. A city of Judah (1Ch 2:55).

2. The head of a family (1Ch 4:9, 10).

JABIN (able to discern). 1. King of Hazor; defeated and slain by Joshua (Jos 11).

2. Another king of Hazor; defeated by Barak (J'g 4; 1Sa 12:9; Ps 83:9).

JABNEEL (God causes to build). 1. Town in N border of Judah, just S of Joppa (Jos 15:11), modern Jabna. Called Jabneh in 2Ch 26:6. Later called Jamnia.

2. Frontier town of Naphtali (Jos 19:33).

JABNEH, a Philistine city (2Ch 26:6).

JACHAN, a Gadite (1Ch 5:13).

JACHIN (he will set up). 1. Son of Simeon (Ge 46:10; Ex 6:15; Nu 26:12). Called Jarib (1Ch 4:24).

2. Name of a pillar (1Ki 7:21; 2Ch 3:17).

See Boaz.

3. A priest, who returned from exile to Jerusalem (1Ch 9:10; Ne 11:10).

4. A priest, head of one of the courses (1Ch 24:17).

JACINTH (hyacinth), precious stone, probably blue sapphire, in foundation of New Jerusalem (Re 21:20).

JACKAL, a carnivorous animal (Mal 1:3).

JACOB (supplanter). Son of Isaac, and twin brother of Esau (Ge 25:24-26; Jos 24:4; 1Ch 1:34; Ac 7:8). Ancestor of Jesus (M't 1:2). Given in answer to prayer (Ge 25:21). Obtains Esau's birthright for a mess of pottage (Ge 25:29-34; Heb 12:16). Fraudulently obtains his father's blessing (Ge 27:1-29; Heb 11:20). Esau seeks to slay, escapes to Padan-aram (Ge 27:41-46; 28:1-5; Ho 12:12). His vision of the ladder (Ge 28:10-22). God confirms the covenant of Abraham to (Ge 28:13-22; 35:9-15; 1Ch 16:13-18).

Sojourns in Haran with his uncle, Laban (Ge 29; 30; Ho 12:12). Serves fourteen years for Leah and Rachel (Ge 29:15-30; Ho 12:12). Sharp practice of, with the flocks and herds of Laban (Ge 30:32-43). Dissatisfied with Laban's treatment and returns to the land of Canaan (Ge 31). Meets angels of God on the journey, and calls the place Mahanaim (Ge 32:1, 2). Dreads to meet Esau; sends him presents; wrestles with an angel (Ge 32). Name of, changed to Israel (Ge 32:28; 35:10). Reconciliation of, with Esau (Ge 33:4). Journeys to Succoth (Ge 33:17); to Shalem, where he purchases a parcel of ground from Hamor, and erects an altar (Ge 33:18-20). His daughter, Dinah, humbled (Ge 34). Returns to Beth-el, where he builds an altar, and erects and dedicates a pillar (Ge 35:1-7. Deborah, Rebekah's nurse, dies, and is buried at Beth-el (Ge 35:8). Journeys to Ephrath; Benjamin is born to; Rachel dies, and is "buried in the way to Ephrath, which is Bethlehem" (Ge 35:16-19; 48:7). Erects a monument at Rachel's grave (Ge 35:20). The incest of his son, Reuben, and his concubine, Bilhah (Ge 35:22). List of the names of his twelve sons (Ge 35:23-26). Returns to Arbah, the city of his father (Ge 35:27). Dwells in the land of Canaan (Ge 37:1). His partiality for his son, Joseph, and the consequent jealousy of his other sons (Ge 37:3, 4). Joseph's prophetic dream concerning (Ge 37:9-11). His grief over the loss of Joseph (Ge 37:34, 35). Sends into Egypt to buy corn (Ge 42:1, 2; 43:1-14). His grief over the detention of Simeon, and the demand for Benjamin to be taken into Egypt (Ge 42:36). His love for Benjamin (Ge 43:14; 44:29). Hears that Joseph still lives (Ge 45:26-28).

Removes to Egypt (Ge 46:1-7; 1Sa 12:8; Ps 105:23; Ac 7:14, 15). List of his children and grandchildren who went down into Egypt (Ge 46:8-27). Meets Joseph (Ge 46:28-34). Pharaoh receives him, and is blessed by Jacob (Ge 47:1-10). The land of Goshen assigned to (Ge 47:11, 12, 27). Dwells in Egypt seventeen years (Ge 47:28). Exacts a promise from Joseph to bury him with his fathers (Ge 47:29-31). His benediction upon Joseph and his two sons (Ge 48:15-22). Gives the land of the two Amorites to Joseph (Ge 48:22; Joh 4:5). His final prophetic benedictions upon his sons: Upon Reuben (Ge 49:3, 4); Simeon and Levi (Ge 49:5-7); Judah (Ge 49:8-12); Zebulun (Ge 49:13); Issachar (Ge 49:14, 15); Dan (Ge 49:16-18); Gad (Ge 49:19); Asher (Ge 49:20); Naphtali (Ge 49:21); Joseph (Ge 49:22-26); Benjamin (Ge 49:27). Charges his sons to bury him in the field of Machpelah (Ge 49:29, 30). Death of (Ge 49:33). Body of, embalmed (Ge 50:2). Forty days mourning for (Ge 50:3). Burial of (Ge 50:4-13). Descendants of (Ge 29:31-35; 30:1-24; 35:18, 22-26; 46:8-27; Ex 1:1-5; 1Ch 2-9).

Prophecies concerning himself and descendants (Ge 25:23; 27:28, 29; 28:10-15; Ge 31:3; 35:9-13; 46:3; De 1:8; Ps 105:10, 11). His wealth (Ge 36:6, 7). Well of (Joh 4:5-30).

JACOB'S WELL, well near base of Mt. Gerizim where Jesus talked with a Samaritan woman (Joh 4).

JADA (a wise one), Judahite; son of Onam (1Ch 2:26, 28).

JADAU, Israelite who married foreign woman during captivity (Ezr 10:43).

JADDUA (known). 1. Prince who sealed covenant (Ne 10:21).

2. Son of Jonathan; priest who returned from Babylon (Ne 12:11).

JADON (he will plead), one who helped in rebuilding of Jerusalem wall (Ne 3:7).

JAEL (wild goat), wife of Heber, and slayer of Sisera (J'g 4:17-22; 5:6, 24).

JAGUR, a town of Judah (Jos 15:21).

JAH, contraction of Jahweh, occuring in poetry (Ps 68:4) and in compounds of proper names.

JAHATH (God will snatch up). 1. Grandson of Judah (1Ch 4:1, 2).

2. Great-grandson of Levi (1Ch 6:16-20).

3. Levite (1Ch 23:10, 11).

4. Levite (1Ch 24:22).

5. Merarite Levite (2Ch 34:8-12).

JAHAZ, called also Jahaza, Jahazah, and Jahzah. A Levitical city in Reuben, taken from the Moabites (Jos 13:18; 21:36; Isa 15:4; Jer 48:21). Sihon defeated at (Nu 21:23; De 2:32; J'g 11:20).

JAHAZIAH (God sees). Israelite who opposed Ezra in matter of divorcing foreign wives (Ezr 10:15).

JAHAZIEL (God sees). 1. A disaffected Israelite who joined David at Ziklag (1Ch 12:4).

2. A priest (1Ch 16:6).

3. Son of Hebron (1Ch 23:19; 24:23).

4. A Levite, and prophet (2Ch 20:14).

5. A chief, or the father of a chief, among the exiles, who returned from Babylon (Ezr 8:5).

JAHDAI, a descendant of Caleb (1Ch 2:47).

JAHDIEL, head of a family of Manasseh (1Ch 5:24).

JAHDO, son of Buz (1Ch 5:14).

JAHLEEL, son of Zebulun (Ge 46:14; Nu 26:26).

JAHMAI, son of Tola (1Ch 7:2).

JAHWEH (See God.)

JAHZAH, a city of Reuben (1Ch 6:78. See Jahaz).

JAHZEEL, called also Jahziel. A son of Naphtali (Ge 46:24; Nu 26:48; 1Ch 7:13).

JAHZERAH, a priest (1Ch 9:12).

JAHZIEL (1Ch 7:13).

See Jahzeel.

JAILER, of Philippi, converted (Ac 16:27-34).

JAIR (he enlightens). 1. Son of Manasseh. Founder of twenty-three cities in Gilead (Nu 32:41; De 3:14; Jos 13:30; 1Ki 4:13; 1Ch 2:22, 23).

2. A judge of Israel (J'g 10:3-5).

3. A Benjamite (Es 2:5).

4. Father of Elhanan (1Ch 20:5).

JAIRUS. A ruler of the synagogue in Capernaum (M't 9:18). Daughter of, restored to life (M't 9:18, 23-26; M'k 5:22-43; Lu 8:41-56).

JAKAN, Horite (1Ch 1:42). Same as Akan in Ge 36:27 and Jaakan in Ge 36:20, 21, 27.

JAKEH (very religious), father of Agur, a writer of proverbs (Pr 30:1).

JAKIM (God lights). 1. A Benjamite (1Ch 8:19).

2. Head of a sacerdotal division in the tabernacle service (1Ch 24:12).

JALON, son of Ezra (1Ch 4:17).

JAMBRES, an Egyptian magician (Ex 7:11; 2Ti 3:8).

JAMES. 1. An apostle. Son of Zebedee and Salome (M't 4:21; 27:56. See Salome). Brother of John, and a fisherman (Lu 5:10). Called to be an apostle (M't 4:21, 22; 10:2; M'k 1:19, 20; Lu 6:14; Ac 1:13). Surnamed Boanerges by Jesus (M'k 3:17). An intimate companion of Jesus, and present with him: At the great draught of fishes (Lu 5:10); the healing of Peter's mother-in-law (M'k 1:29); the raising of the daughter of Jairus (M'k 5:37; Lu 8:51); the transfiguration of Jesus (M't 17:1; M'k 9:2; Lu 9:28); in Gethsemane (M't 26:37; M'k 14:33). Asks Jesus concerning his second coming (M'k 13:3). Bigotry of (Lu 9:54). Civil ambitions of (M't 20:20-23; M'k 10:35-41). Present at the sea of Tiberias when Jesus revealed himself to the disciples after his resurrection (Joh 21:2; [1Co 15:7?]). Martyred (Ac 12:2).

2. An apostle. Son of Alphaeus (M't 10:3; M'k 3:18; Lu 12:17).

3. Brother of Jesus (M't 13:55; 27:56; M'k 6:3; Lu 24:10; Ga 1:19; 2:9, 12). The brother of Judas (Lu 6:16; Jude 1), and Joses (M'k 15:40. [Witness of Christ's resurrection, 1Co 15:7?] Addresses the council at Jerusalem in favor of liberty for the Gentile converts (Ac 15:13-21). Disciples sent by, to Antioch (Ga 2:12). Hears of the success attending Paul's ministry (Ac 21:18, 19). Epistle of (Jas 1:1).

4. Father of Apostle Judas (not Iscariot) (Lu 6:16; Ac 1:13).

JAMES THE LESS (See James 2.)

JAMES, EPISTLE OF. Written by James (1:1), most likely the brother of the Lord, to Jewish Christians, to comfort them in trials and warn and rebuke them regarding errors and sins into which they had fallen. Outline: 1. Comfort (1).

2. Warnings against specific sins of which they are guilty, such as pride, favoring the rich, misuse of the tongue, believing in faith without works (2-4).

3. Exhortation to patience in suffering and prayer (5).

JAMIN (right hand). 1. Son of Simeon (Ge 46:10; Ex 6:15; Nu 26:12; 1Ch 4:24).

2. Descendant of Hezron (1Ch 2:27).

3. A priest who expounded the law to the exiles who returned to Jerusalem (Ne 8:7).

JAMLECH, descendant of Simeon (1Ch 4:34).

JANNA, ancestor of Joseph (Lu 3:24).

JANNES, an Egyptian magician (Ex 7:11; 2Ti 3:8).

JANOAH, JANOHAH, in KJV of Joshua. 1. Town of Naphtali (2Ki 15:29).

2. Town on boundary of Ephraim (Jos 16:6, 7).

JANUM, a city of Judah (Jos 15:53).

JAPHETH (God will enlarge), son of Noah (Ge 5:32; 6:10; 7:13; 10:21); had seven sons (Ge 10:2); descendants occupied "isles of Gentiles" (Ge 10:5); blessed by Noah (Ge 9:20-27).

JAPHIA (tall). 1. King of Lachish killed by Joshua (Jos 10:3).

2. Son of David (2Sa 5:15; 1Ch 3:7).

3. City in E border of Zebulun (Jos 19:12).

JAPHLET, grandson of Beriah (1Ch 7:33).

JAPHLETI, clan on W border of Ephraim (Jos 16:1-3).

JAPHO, Hebrew form of Joppa, border town in Dan (Jos 19:46).

JARAH (honeycomb), descendant of Gibeon (1Ch 9:42), Jehoaddah in 1Ch 8:36.

JAREB (contender), Assyrian king to whom Ephraim went for help (Ho 5:13).

JARED. 1. Called also Jered. A descendant of Seth (Ge 5:15, 16, 18, 19, 20; 1Ch 1:2).

2. An ancestor of Jesus (Lu 3:37).

JARESIAH, son of Jeroham (1Ch 8:27).

JARHA, Egyptian slave of Sheshan (1Ch 2:34, 35).

JARIB (he strives). 1. Son of Simeon (1Ch 4:24).

2. A chief among the captivity (Ezr 8:16).

3. A priest who married an idolatrous wife (Ezr 10:18).

JARMUTH (height). 1. City of Judah 16 miles W by S of Jerusalem (Jos 15:35); identified with Yarmuk.

2. Levite city of Issachar (Jos 21:28, 29). Ramoth in 1Ch 6:73; Remeth in Jos 19:21).

JAROAH, a descendant of Gad (1Ch 5:14).

JASHEN (brilliant), father of some of David's heroes (2Sa 23:32); Hashem in 1Ch 11:34.

JASHER, BOOK OF, author of book quoted in Jos 10:13; 2Sa 1:18; LXX of 1Ki 8:53.

JASHOBEAM (the people return). 1. Hero who joined David at Ziklag 1Ch 12:6).

2. One of David's chieftains (1Ch 11:11); Adino in 2Sa 23:8, Jashebassebet in margin of ASV.

3. Hachmonite; may be same as 2 (1Ch 27:2, 3).

JASHUB (he returns). 1. Son of Issachar (Nu 26:24). Ge 46:13 has Job in KJV.

2. Shear-Jashub, a son of Isaiah (Isa 7:3).

3. Man who married foreign wife (Ezr 10:29).

JASHUBI-LEHEM, a descendant of Shelah (1Ch 4:22).

JASIEL, one of David's warriors (1Ch 11:47).

JASON (to heal), a Christian at Thessalonica (Ac 17:5, 6, 7, 9); and probably Paul's kinsman, mentioned in Ro 16:21.

JASPER, a precious stone set in the high priest's breastplate (Ex 28:20; 39:13; Eze 28:13; Re 4:3; 21:11, 18, 19).

JATHNIEL, son of Meshelemiah (1Ch 26:2).

JATTIR, a Levitical city (Jos 15:48; 21:14; 1Sa 30:27; 1Ch 6:57).

JAVAN, a son of Japheth; father of Elishah, Tarshish, Kittim, and Dodanim (Ge 10:2; 1Ch 1:5, 7). Javan is same as Greek Ionia, with whom the Hebrews traded (Joe 3:4-6).

2. A city in Arabia in which the Phoenicians traded (Eze 27:13, 19).

JAVELIN, a heavy lance (Eze 39:9); used by Goliath (1Sa 17:6); by Saul (1Sa 18:11; 19:9, 10).

JAZER. 1. A city of refuge E of the Jordan (Jos 21:39). Taken from the Amorites (Nu 21:32; 32:1, 3, 35; Jos 13:25).

2. Sea of (Jer 48:32).

JAZIZ, overseer of David's flocks (1Ch 27:31).

JEALOUSY (Pr 6:34; 27:4; Ec 4:4; Song 8:6). Law concerning, when husband is jealous of his wife (Nu 5:12-31). Image of (Eze 8:3, 4). Forbidden (Ro 13:13).

Attributed to God (Ex 20:5; 34:13, 14; Nu 25:11; De 29:20; 32:16, 21; 1Ki 14:22; Ps 78:58; 79:5; Isa 30:1, 2; 31:1, 3; Eze 16:42; 23:25; 36:5, 6; 38:19; Zep 1:18; 3:8; Zec 1:14; 8:2; 1Co 10:22).

See Anthropomorphisms.

A spirit of emulation (Ro 10:19; 11:11).

See Emulation; Envy.

Figurative: 2 Co 11:2.

Instances of: Cain, of Abel (Ge 4:5, 6, 8). Sarah, of Hagar (Ge 16:5). Joseph's brethren, of Joseph (Ge 37:4-11, 18-28). Saul, of David (1Sa 18:8-30; 19:8-24; 20:24-34). Joab, of Abner (2Sa 3:24-27). Nathan, of Adonijah (1Ki 1:24-26). Ephraimites, of Gideon (J'g 8:1); of Jephthah (J'g 12:1). The brother of the prodigal son (Lu 15:25-32). Sectional, between Israel and the tribe of Judah (2Sa 19:41-43).

JEALOUSY, WATER OF, holy water mixed with dust given by priest to woman accused of infidelity; it brought curse if she was found guilty (Nu 5:11-31).

JEARIM, hill on N border of Judah (Jos 15:10).

JEATERAI, descendant of Gershom (1Ch 6:21).

JEBERECHIAH, father of Zechariah (Isa 8:2).

JEBUS, name of Jerusalem when in possession of Jebusites (Jos 15:63; J'g 19:10); taken by Israelites (J'g 1:8), but stronghold not captured until David's time (2Sa 5:7, 8).

JEBUSITES. One of the tribes of Canaan (De 7:1). Land of, given to Abraham and his descendants (Ge 15:21; Ex 3:8, 17; 23:23, 24; De 20:17; Ex 33:2; 34:10, 11). Conquered by Joshua (Jos 10-12; and 24:11); by David (2Sa 5:6-9). Jerusalem within the territory of (Jos 18:28). Not exterminated, but intermarry with the Israelites (J'g 3:5, 6; Ezr 9:1, 2; 10:18-44). Pay tribute to Solomon (1Ki 9:20, 21).

JECAMIAH, JEKAMIAH. 1. Judahite (1Ch 2:41).

2. Son of King Jeconiah (1Ch 3:17, 18).

JECOLIAH, JECHOLIAH, mother of King Uzziah (2Ch 26:3; 2Ki 15:2).

JECONIAH, variant of Jehoiachin; king of Judah, captured by Nebuchadnezzar (2Ki 24:1-12). Contracted to Coniah in Jer 22:24, 28; 37:1.

JEDAIAH (Jehovah knows). 1. Descendant of Simeon (1Ch 4:37).

2. A returned exile (Ne 3:10).

3. A priest of the captivity (1Ch 9:10; 24:7; Ezr 2:36; Ne 7:39).

4. A priest who dwelt at Jerusalem after the return of the captivity (Ne 11:10; 12:6, 19; Zec 6:10, 14).

5. Another priest, who returned from Babylon with Nehemiah (Ne 12:7, 21).

JEDIAEL. 1. Son of Benjamin (1Ch 7:6, 10, 11).

2. Son of Shimri (1Ch 11:45).

3. A Manassite chief, who joined David at Ziklag (1Ch 12:20).

4. Son of Meshelemiah (1Ch 26:2).

JEDIDAH (beloved), mother of King Josiah (2Ki 22:1).

JEDIDIAH (beloved of Jehovah), name that Nathan gave to Solomon (2Sa 12:24, 25).

JEDUTHUN. A musician of the temple (1Ch 16:41; 25:1). Called Ethan (1Ch 6:44; 15:17). See titles of Psalms 39; 62; 77.

JEEZER, chief in tribe of Manasseh (Nu 26:30; Abiezer in Jos 17:2).

JEGAR-SAHADUTHA (heap of witness), name given by Laban to heap of stones set up as memorial of covenant between him and Jacob; called Galeed by Jacob (Ge 31:47, 48).

JEHALELEEL, JEHALELEL. 1. Descendant of Judah (1Ch 4:16).

2. Merarite Levite (2Ch 29:12).

JEHDEIAH (Jehovah will be glad). 1. Descendant of Moses (1Ch 24:20).

2. Man in charge of David's asses (1Ch 27:30).

JEHEZEKEL (God will strengthen), priest in David's time (1Ch 24:16).

JEHIAH (Jehovah lives), a Levite, and doorkeeper of the ark (1Ch 15:24).

JEHIEL (God lives). 1. A Levite porter (1Ch 15:18). Probably identical with Jehiah, above.

2. A Gershonite Levite (1Ch 23:8; 29:8).

3. A companion of David's sons (1Ch 27:32).

4. Son of Jehoshaphat (2Ch 21:2).

5. Son of Heman (2Ch 29:14).

6. A Levite overseer in the temple (2Ch 31:13).

7. A priest who gave extraordinary offerings for the passover (2Ch 35:8).

8. Father of Obadiah (Ezr 8:9).

9. Father of Shechamah (Ezr 10:2).

10. Name of two priests who married idolatrous wives (Ezr 10:21, 26).

JEHIELI, son of Laadan (1Ch 26:21, 22).

JEHIZKIAH (Jehovah strengthens), Israelite chief in days of Ahaz, king of Judah (2Ch 28:12).

JEHOADAH, descendant of King Saul (1Ch 8:36); Jarah in 1Ch 9:42.

JEHOADDAN, wife of King Joash of Judah (2Ch 25:1); Jehoaddin in 2Ki 14:2 ASV.

JEHOAHAZ (Jehovah has grasped). 1. Son of Jehu, and king of Israel (2Ki 10:35; 13:1-9).

2. Son of Jehoram, king of Judah (2Ch 21:17). See Ahaziah.

3. Called also Shallum. King of Judah, and successor of Josiah (2Ki 23:30, 31; 1Ch 3:15; 2Ch 36:1; Jer 22:11). Wicked reign of (2Ki 23:32). Pharaoh-nechoh, king of Egypt, invades the kingdom of, defeats him, and takes him captive to Egypt (2Ki 23:33-35; 2Ch 36:3, 4). Prophecies concerning (Jer 22:10, 11, 12).

JEHOASH, JOASH. 1. Grandson of Benjamin (1Ch 7:8).

2. Descendant of Judah (1Ch 4:22).

3. Father of Gideon (J'g 6:12).

4. Keeper of David's cellars of oil (1Ch 27:28).

5. Israelite who joined David at Ziklag (1Ch 12:3).

6. Son of King Ahab (1Ki 22:26).

7. King of Judah from 884-848 B. C. (2Ki 11-13; 2Ch 24, 25).

8. King of Israel from 848-832 B. C. (2Ki 13:10-13; 14:8-16; 2Ch 25:17-24).

JEHOHANAN (Jehovah is gracious). 1. A porter of the tabernacle (1Ch 26:3).

2. A military chief under Jehoshaphat, whose corps consisted of two hundred and eighty thousand men (2Ch 17:15). Probably identical with a captain of a hundred, in 2Ch 23:1.

3. Son of Bebai (Ezr 10:28).

4. A priest among the exiles who returned from Babylon (Ne 12:13).

5. A chorister in the temple (Ne 12:42).

JEHOIACHIN (Jehovah establishes). King of Judah and successor to Jehoiakim (2Ki 24:6-8; 2Ch 36:8, 9). Called Jeconiah (1Ch 3:16; Jer 24:1). Called Coniah (Jer 22:24; 37:1). Wicked reign of (2Ki 24:9; 2Ch 36:9). Nebuchadnezzar invades his kingdom, takes him captive to Babylon (2Ki 24:10-16; 2Ch 36:10; Es 2:6; Jer 27:20; 29:1, 2; Eze 1:2). Confined in prison thirty-seven years (2Ki 25:27). Released from prison by Evil-merodach, and promoted above other kings, and honored until death (2Ki 25:27-30; Jer 52:31-34). Prophecies concerning (Jer 22:24-30; 28:4). Sons of (1Ch 3:17, 18). Ancestor of Jesus (M't 1:12).

JEHOIADA (Jehovah knows). 1. Father of Benaiah, one of David's officers (2Sa 8:18).

2. A high priest. Overthrows Athaliah, the usurping queen of Judah, and establishes Jehoash upon the throne (2Ki 11; 2Ch 23). Salutary influence of, over Jehoash (2Ki 12:2; 2Ch 24:2, 22). Directs the repairs of the temple (2Ki 12:4-16; 2Ch 24:4-14). Death of (2Ch 24:15, 16).

3. A priest who led three thousand seven hundred priests armed for war (1Ch 12:27).

4. Son of Benaiah (1Ch 27:34).

5. A returned exile (Ne 3:6).

6. A priest mentioned in Jeremiah's letter to the captive Jews (Jer 29:26).

JEHOIAKIM (Jehovah sets up), called also Eliakim. King of Judah (1Ch 3:15). Ancestor of Jesus (M't 1:11). Wicked reign and final overthrow of (2Ki 23:34-37; 24:1-6; 2Ch 36:4-8; Jer 22:13-19; 26:22, 23; 36; Da 1:1, 2). Dies, and is succeeded by his son, Jehoiachin (2Ki 24:6).

JEHOIARIB, JOIARIB (Jehovah will contend).

1. Priest in days of David (1Ch 24:7).

2. Priest who returned from exile (1Ch 9:10).

3. Man who helped Ezra (Ezr 8:16, 17).

4. Judahite (Ne 11:5).

5. Priest (Ne 11:10; 12:6).

JEHONADAB (Jehovah is liberal). 1. Son of David's brother Shimeah (2Sa 13:3).

2. Kenite who helped Jehu abolish Baal-worship in Samaria (2Ki 10:15f). See also Jonadab.

JEHONATHAN (Jehovah gave). 1. Overseer of David's property (1Ch 27:25).

2. Levite (2Ch 17:8).

3. Priest (Ne 12:18).

JEHORAM (Jehovah is exalted). 1. King of Judah (1Ki 22:50; 2Ki 8:16; 1Ch 3:11; 2Ch 21:5). Ancestor of Jesus (M't 1:8). Marries Athaliah, whose wicked counsels influence his reign for evil (2Ki

8:18, 19; 2Ch 21:6-13).

Slays his brothers to strengthen himself in his sovereignty (2Ch 21:4, 13). Edom revolts from (2Ki 8:20-22; 2Ch 21:8-10). Philistines and Arabians invade his territory (2Ch 21:16, 17). Death of (2Ch 21:18-20; 2Ki 8:24). Prophecy concerning (2Ch 21:12-15).

2. A son of Ahab. See Joram.

3. A priest commissioned to go through Israel and instruct the people in the law (2Ch 17:8).

JEHOSHABEATH (the oath of Jehovah), name of Jehosheba (q.v.) as found in 2Ch 22:11.

JEHOSHAPHAT (Jehovah is judge). 1. David's recorder (2Sa 8:16; 20:24; 1Ki 4:3; 1Ch 18:15).

2. One of Solomon's commissariat officers (1Ki 4:17).

3. King of Judah. Succeeds Asa (1Ki 15:24; 22:41; 1Ch 3:10; 2Ch 17:1; M't 1:8). Strengthens himself against Israel (2Ch 17:2). Inaugurates a system of public instruction in the law (2Ch 17:7-9). His wise reign (1Ki 22:43; 2Ch 17:7-9; 19:3-11). His system of tribute (2Ch 17:11). His military forces and armament (2Ch 17:12-19). Joins Ahab in an invasion of Ramoth-gilead (1Ki 22; 2Ch 18). Rebuked by the prophet Jehu (2Ch 19:2). The allied forces of the Amorites, Moabites, and other tribes invade his territory, and are defeated by (2Ch 20). Builds ships for commerce with Tarshish, ships are destroyed (1Ki 22:48, 49; 2Ch 20:35-37). Joins Jehoram, king of Israel, in an invasion of the land of Moab, defeats the Moabites (2Ki 3). Makes valuable gifts to the temple (2Ki 12:18). Death of (1Ki 22:50; 2Ch 21:1). Religious zeal of (1Ki 22:43, 46; 2Ch 17:1-9; 19; 20:1-32; 22:9). Prosperity of (1Ki 22:45, 48; 2Ch 17-20). Bequests of, to his children (2Ch 21:2, 3).

4. Father of Jehu (2Ki 9:2, 14).

5. A priest who assisted in bringing the ark from Obed-edom (1Ch 15:24).

JEHOSHAPHAT, VALLEY OF (Jehovah judges), valley where all nations shall be gathered by Jehovah for judgment (Joe 3:2, 12); may be symbolical.

JEHOSHEBA (Jehovah is an oath), daughter of King Jehoram; wife of high priest Jehoiada; hid Joash from Athaliah (2Ki 11:2).

JEHOSHUA, JEHOSHUAH (Jehovah saves), variant spelling for Joshua (Nu 13:16; 1Ch 7:27).

JEHOVAH, English rendering of Hebrew tetragram *YHWH,* name of God of Israel; original pronunciation unknown, because out of reverence for God's name it was never pronounced. When the vowel points were added to the Hebrew consonantal text, the Jewish scribes inserted into *YHWH* the vowels for Adonai, and read Adonai (Lord) instead. The name is derived from the verb "to be," and so implies eternity of God. There are 10 combinations of the word "Jehovah" in the OT.

JEHOVAH-JIREH (Jehovah will provide), name given by Abraham to place where he was ready to sacrifice Isaac (Ge 22:14).

JEHOVAH-NISSI (Jehovah is my banner), name given by Moses to altar he built as memorial of victory over Amalekites (Ex 17:15).

JEHOVAH-RA-AH (Jehovah is my shepherd), name given by David in the twenty-third Psalm (Ps 23:1).

JEHOVAH-RAPAH (Jehovah heals), name of God as a token of his promise to protect from diseases (Ex 15:26).

JEHOVAH-SHALOM (Jehovah is peace), name Gideon gave to altar at Ophra (J'g 6:24).

JEHOVAH-SHAMMAH (Jehovah is there), name given to heavenly Jerusalem in Ezekiel's vision (Eze 48:35 marg.).

JEHOVAH-TSIDKENU (Jehovah is our righteousness), name given king who is to rule over Israel (Jer 23:6) and His city (Jer 33:16).

JEHOZABAD (Jehovah has bestowed). 1. Son of Shomer, and one of the assassins of King Jehoash (2Ki 12:21; 2Ch 24:26).

2. Son of Obed-edom (1Ch 26:4).

3. A Benjamite chief who commanded one hundred and eighty thousand men (2Ch 17:18).

JEHOZADAK (Jehovah is righteous), called also Josedech and Jozadak. A priest of the exile (1Ch 6:14, 15; Ezr 3:2, 8; 5:2; 10:18; Ne 12:26; Hag 1:1, 12, 14; 2:2, 4; Zec 6:11).

JEHU (Jehovah is he). 1. The prophet who announced the wrath of Jehovah against Baasha, king of Israel (1Ki 16:1, 7, 12; 2Ch 19:2; 20:34).

2. Son of Nimshi, king of Israel (1Ki 19:16; 2Ki 9:1-14). Religious zeal of, in slaying idolaters (2Ki 9:14-37; 10:1-28; 2Ch 22:8, 9). His territory invaded by Hazael, king of Syria (2Ki 10:32, 33). Prophecies concerning (1Ki 19:17; 2Ki 10:30; 15:12; Ho 1:4). Death of (2Ki 10:35).

3. Son of Obed (1Ch 2:38).

4. Son of Josibiah (1Ch 4:35).

5. A Benjamite (1Ch 12:3).

JEHUBBAH, an Asherite (1Ch 7:34).

JEHUCAL (Jehovah is able), man sent by King Zedekiah to Jeremiah for prayers (Jer 37:3); in Jer 38:1, Jucal.

JEHUD, town in Dan, c. 7 miles E of Joppa (Jos 19:45).

JEHUDI (a Jew), prince in Jehoiakim's court (Jer 36:14, 21).

JEHUDIJAH (Jewess), not a proper noun as in KJV, but adjective: Jewess (1Ch 4:18).

JEHUSH, a Benjamite (1Ch 8:39).

JEIEL (God has gathered). 1. Called also Jehiel. A Reubenite (1Ch 5:7).

2. A Benjamite (1Ch 9:35).

3. One of David's heroes (1Ch 11:44).

4. A Levite, and chorister in the tabernacle service (1Ch 15:18, 21; 16:5).

5. A Levite, ancestor of Jehaziel, who encouraged Judah against their enemies (2Ch 20:14).

6. A scribe during the reign of Uzziah (2Ch 26:11).

7. A Levite who cleansed the temple (2Ch 29:13).

8. A chief of the Levites who gave, with other chiefs, five thousand five hundred "small cattle" for sacrifice (2Ch 35:9).

9. A son of Adonikam, an exile who returned to Jerusalem with Ezra (Ezr 8:13).

10. A priest who was defiled by marriage to an idolatrous woman (Ezr 10:43).

JEKABZEEL (God gathers), a city in the S of Judah (Ne 11:25).

JEKAMEAM (the kinsman will raise up), son of Hebron (1Ch 23:19; 24:23).

JEKAMIAH (may Jehovah establish). 1. Judahite (1Ch 2:41).

2. Son of King Jeconiah (Jehoiachin); in AV Jecamiah (1Ch 3:18).

JEKUTHIEL (God will nourish), son of Ezra (1Ch 4:18).

JEMIMA (a dove), daughter of Job born after restoration from affliction (Job 42:14).

JEMUEL, son of Simeon (Ge 46:10; Ex 6:15). Called Nemuel in Nu 26:12 & 1Ch 4:24).

JEPHTHAH (he opens). A judge of Israel. Illegitimate, and therefore not entitled to inherit his father's property (J'g 11:1, 2). Escapes the violence of his half-brothers, dwells in the land of Tob (J'g 11:3). Recalled from the land of Tob by the elders of Gilead (J'g 11:5). Made captain of the host (J'g 11:5-11); and made head of the land of Gilead (J'g 11:7-11). His message to the king of the Ammonites (J'g 11:12-28). Leads the host of Israel against the Ammonites (J'g 11:29-33). His rash vow concerning his daughter (J'g 11:31, 34-40). Falsely accused by the Ephraimites (J'g 12:1). Leads the army of the Gileadites against the Ephraimites (J'g 12:4). Judges Israel six years, dies, and is buried in Gilead (J'g 12:7). Faith of (Heb 11:32).

JEPHUNNEH (it will be prepared). 1. Father of Caleb (Nu 13:6).

2. Son of Jether (1Ch 7:38).

JERAH (moon), son of Joktan (Ge 10:26; 1Ch 1:20).

JERAHMEEL (God pities). 1. Son of Hezron (1Ch 2:9).

2. Son of Kish (1Ch 24:29).

3. An officer of Jehoiakim, king of Judah (Jer 36:26).

JERASH (See Gerasa.)

JERED (descent). 1. Son of Mahalaleel (1Ch 1:2).

2. Judahite (1Ch 4:18).

JEREMAI, of the family of Hashum (Ezr 10:33).

JEREMIAH (Jehovah founds, or **exalts).** in KJV of NT "Jeremy" and "Jeremias" (M't 2:17; 16:14). One of greatest Hebrew prophets (c. 640-587 B. C.); born into priestly family of Anathoth, 2½ miles NE of Jerusalem; called to prophetic office by a vision (Jer 1:4-10), and prophesied during last five kings of Judah (Josiah, Jehoahaz II, Jehoiakim, Jehoiachin, Zedekiah); probably helped Josiah in his reforms (2Ki 23); warned Jehoiakim against Egyptian alliance; prophetic roll destroyed by king (Jer 36); persecuted by nobility in days of last king (Jer 36, 37); Nebuchadnezzar kind to him after the destruction of Jerusalem (Jer 39:11, 12); compelled to go to Egypt with Jews who slew Gedaliah, and there he died (Jer 43:6, 7).

Six other Jeremiahs are briefly mentioned in the OT: 1. Benjamite who came to David at Ziklag (1Ch 12:4).

2, 3. Gadites (1Ch 12:10, 12).

4. Manassite (1Ch 5:24).

5. Father of wife of King Josiah (2Ki 23:30, 31).

6. Rechabite (Jer 35:3).

JEREMIAH, BOOK OF. Written by the prophet Jeremiah; dictated to his secretary Baruch (ch 36); LXX about 1/8 shorter than the Hebrew book; material not arranged in chronological order. Outline: I. Jeremiah's oracles against the theocracy (1:1-25; 38).

A. Prophet's call (1:1-19).

B. Reproofs and admonitions (2:1-20; 18).

C. Later prophecies (21:1-25: 38).

II. Events in the life of Jeremiah (26:1-45:5).

A. Temple sermon and Jeremiah's arrest (26:1-24).

B. Yoke of Babylon (27:1-29: 32).

C. Book of Consolation (30:1-33: 26).

D. Experiences of Jeremiah before Jerusalem fell (34:1-36:32).

E. Jeremiah during siege and destruction of Jerusalem (37:1-39:18).

F. Last years of Jeremiah (40:1-45:5).

III. Jeremiah's oracles against foreign nations (46:1-51:64): Egypt, Philistines, Moab, Ammonites, Edom, Damascus, Kedar and Hazor, Elam, Babylon.

IV. Appendix: The fall of Jerusalem and related events (52:1-34).

JEREMOTH (swollen, thick). 1. Benjamite (1Ch 7:8).

2. Another Benjamite (1Ch 8:14).

3. Merarite Levite (1Ch 23:23; 24:30).

4. Chief of musicians (1Ch 25:4, 22).

5. Prince of Naphtali (1Ch 27:19).

6. Three men who put away foreign wives (Ezr 10:26, 27, 29).

JERIAH (Jehovah sees), called also Jerijah. A descendant of Hebron (1Ch 23:19; 24:23; 26:31).

JERIBAI (Jehovah pleads), a valiant man of David's guard (1Ch 11:46).

JERICHO (moon city). 1. A city E of Jerusalem and near the Jordan (Nu 22:1; 26:3; De 34:1). Called the City of Palm Trees (De 34:3). Situation of, pleasant (2Ki 2:19). Rahab the harlot lived in (Jos 2; Heb 11:31). Joshua sees the "captain of the host" of the Lord near (Jos 5:13-15). Besieged by Joshua seven days; fall and destruction of (Jos 6; 24:11). Situated within the territory allotted to Benjamin (Jos 18:12, 21). The Kenites dwelt at (J'g 1:16). King of Moab makes conquest of, and establishes his capital at (J'g 3:13). Rebuilt by Hiel (1Ki 16:34). Company of "the sons of the prophets," dwelt at (2Ki 2:4, 5, 15, 18). Captives of Judah, taken by the king of Israel, released at, on account of the denunciation of the prophet Oded (2Ch 28:7-15). Inhabitants of, taken captive to Babylon, return to, with Ezra and Nehemiah (Ezr 2:34; Ne 7:36); assist in repairing the walls of Jerusalem (Ne 3:2). Blind men healed at, by Jesus (M't 20:29-34; M'k 10:46; Lu 18:35). Zacchaeus dwelt at (Lu 19:1-10).

2. Plain of (2Ki 25:5; Jer 52:8).

3. Waters of (Jos 16:1). Purified by Elisha (2Ki 2:18-22).

JERIEL, son of Tola (1Ch 7:2).

JERIMOTH (thick). Called also Jeremoth.

1. Son of Bela (1Ch 7:7).

2. Son of Becher (1Ch 7:8).

3. A disaffected Israelite, who denounced Saul and joined David at Ziklag (1Ch 12:5).

4. Son of Mushi (1Ch 23:23; 24:30).

5. Son of Heman (1Ch 25:4).

6. A ruler of the tribe of Naphtali (1Ch 27:19).

7. A son of David (2Ch 11:18).

JERIOTH (tent curtains). Wife of Caleb. Probably identical with Azubah (1Ch 2:18).

JEROBOAM (the people contend). 1. First king of Israel after the revolt. Promoted by Solomon (1Ki 11:28). Ahijah's prophecy concerning (1Ki 11:29-39; 14:5-16). Flees to Egypt to escape from Solomon (1Ki 11:26-40). Recalled from Egypt by the ten tribes on account of disaffection toward Rehoboam, and made king (1Ki 12:1-20; 2Ch 10:12-19). Subverts the religion of Moses (1Ki 12:25-33; 13:33, 34; 14:9, 16; 16:2, 26, 31; 2Ch 11:14; 13:8, 9). Hand of, paralyzed (1Ki 13:1-10). His wife sent to consult the prophet Ahijah concerning her child (1Ki 14:1-18). His wars with Rehoboam (1Ki 14:19, 30; 15:6; 2Ch 11:1-4). His war with Abijah (1Ki 15:7; 2Ch 13). Death of (1Ki 14:20; 2Ch 13:20).

2. King of Israel. Successor to Jehoash (2Ki 14:16, 23). Makes conquest of Hamath and Damascus (2Ki 14:25-28). Wicked reign of (2Ki 14:24). Prophecies concerning (Am 7:7-13). Death of (2Ki 14:29). Genealogies written during his reign (1Ch 5:17).

JEROHAM (may he be compassionate). 1. A Levite, and grandfather of Samuel (1Sa 1:1; 1Ch 6:27, 34).

2. A chief of the tribe of Benjamin (1Ch 8:27).

3. A descendant of Benjamin (1Ch 9:8).

4. A priest, and father of Adaiah, who dwelt in Jerusalem after the exile (1Ch 9:12; Ne 11:12).

5. Father of two Israelites who joined David at Ziklag (1Ch 12:7).

6. The father of Azareel (1Ch 27:22).

7. Father of Azariah (2Ch 23:1).

JERUBBAAL (See Gideon.)

JERUBBESHETH (See Gideon.)

JERUEL (founded by God), a wilderness in the S of Judah (2Ch 20:16).

JERUSALEM (peace). Called Jebus (Jos 18:28; J'g 19:10); Zion (1Ki 8:1; Zec 9:13); City of David (2Sa 5:7; Isa 22:9); Salem (Ge 14:18; Ps 76:2); Ariel (Isa 29:1); City of God (Ps 46:4); City of the Great King (Ps 48:2); City of Judah (2Ch 25:28); The Perfection of Beauty, The Joy of the Whole Earth (La 2:15); The Throne of the Lord (Jer 3:17); Holy Mountain (Da 9:16, 20); Holy City (Ne 11:1, 18; M't 4:5); City of Solemnities (Isa 33:20); City of Truth (Zec 8:3); to be called "The Lord our Righteousness" (Jer 33:16); Jehovah-Shammah (Eze 48:35; [marg.]); New Jerusalem (Re 21:2, 10-27).

Situation and appearance of (Ps 122:3; 125:2; Song 6:4; Mic 4:8). Walls of (Jer 39:4).

Gates of: Old gate, fish gate, sheep gate, prison gate (Ne 3:1, 3, 32; 12:39). Gate of Ephraim (2Ch 25:23; Ne 12:39). Gate of Benjamin (Jer 37:13; Zec 14:10; of Joshua (2Ki 23:8). Old gate (Ne 3:6; 12:39). Corner gate (Zec 14:10). Valley gate (Ne 2:13; 3:13). Dung gate (Ne 2:13; 3:13; 12:31). Gate of the fountain (Ne 2:14; 3:15; 12:37). Water gate (Ne 3:26; 8:1; 12:37). Horse gate (Ne 3:28). King's gate (1Ch 9:18). Shallecheth (1Ch 26:16). High gate (2Ch 23:20). East gate (Ne 3:29). Miphkad (Ne 3:31). Middle gate (Jer 39:3). First gate (Zec 14:10).

Buildings: High priest's palace (Joh 18:15). Castle (Ac 21:34). Stairs (Ne 3:15).

Streets: East street (2Ch 29:4). Street of the house of God (Ezr 10:9). Street of the Water gate, of Ephraim's gate (Ne 8:16). Baker's street (Jer 37:21).

Towers. See Hananeel; Meah; Millo; Ophel; Siloam.

Places in and around: Moriah (2Ch 3:1). The sepulcher of Jesus (Joh 19:41). See Calvary; Gethsemane; Olives, Mount of; Jehoshaphat, Valley of; Tophet.

Measurement of, in Ezekiel's vision (Eze 45:6). Names of the gates of, in Ezekiel's vision (Eze 48:31-34).

The capital of David's kingdom by divine appointment (1Ki 15:4; 2Ki 19:34; 2Ch 6:6; 12:13). To be called God's throne (Jer 3:17). The chief Levites dwelt in (1Ch 9:34). The high priest dwelt at (Joh 18:15). Annual feasts kept at (Eze 36:38, w De 16:16, & Ps 122:3-5; Lu 2:41; Joh 4:20; 5:1; 7:1-14; 12:20; Ac 18:21). Prayers of the Israelites made toward (1Ki 8:38; Da 6:10). Beloved (Ps 122:6; 137:1-7; Isa 62:1-7). See Country, Love of; Patriotism.

Oaths taken in the name of (M't 5:35).

Melchizedek ancient king and priest of (Ge 14:18). King of, confederated with the four other kings of the Amorites, against Joshua and the hosts of Israel (Jos 10:1-5). Confederated kings defeated, and the king of Jerusalem slain by Joshua (Jos 10:15-26). Falls to Benjamin in the allotment of the land of Canaan (Jos 18:28). Conquest of, made by David (2Sa 5:7). The inhabitants of, not expelled (Jos 15:63; J'g 1:21). Conquest of Mount Zion in, made by David (1Ch 11:4-6). The citadel of Mount Zion, occupied by David, and called the City of David (2Sa 5:5-9; 1Ch 11:7). Ark brought to, by David (2Sa 6:12-19). The threshing floor of Araunah within the citadel of (2Sa 24:16). David purchases and erects an altar upon it (2Sa 24:16-25). The city built around the citadel (1Ch 11:8).

Fortified by Solomon (1Ki 3:1; 9:15). The temple built within the citadel (see Temple).

Captured and pillaged by: Shishak, king of Egypt (1Ki 14:25, 26; 2Ch 12:9); by Jehoash, king of Israel (2Ki 14:13, 14; 2Ch 25:23, 24); Nebuchadnezzar, king of Babylon (2Ki 24:8-16; 25:1-17; 2Ch 36:17-21; Jer 1:3; 32:2; 39; 52:4-7, 12-24; La 1:5-8). Walls of, restored and fortified: By Uzziah (2Ch 26:9, 10); by Jotham (2Ch 27:3); Manasseh (2Ch 33:14). Water supply brought in from the Gihon by Hezekiah (2Ki 18:17; 20:20; 2Ch 32:3, 4, 30; Ne 2:13-15; Isa 7:3; 22:9-11; 36:2). Besieged: By Pekah (2Ki 16:5); by the Philistines (2Ch 21:16, 17); by Sennacherib (2Ki 18:13-37; 19:20-37; 2Ch 32). Rebuilding of, ordered by proclamation of Cyrus (2Ch 36:23; Ezr 1:1-4). Rebuilt by Nehemiah under the direction of Artaxerxes (Ne 2-6). Wall of, dedicated (Ne 12:27-43). Temple restored (see Temple).

Roman rulers resided at: Herod I (M't 2:3); Pontius Pilate (M't 27:2; M'k 15:1; Lu 23:1-7; Joh 18:28, 29); Herod III (Ac 12:1-23).

Life and miracles of Jesus connected with (see Jesus, History of).

Gospel first preached at (Mic 4:2; Lu 24:47; Ac 1:4; 2:14). Pentecostal revival occurs at (Ac 2). Stephen martyred at (Ac 6:8-15:7). Disciples persecuted and dispersed from (Ac 8:1-4; 11:19-21).

For personal incidents occurring therein, see biographies of individuals; see also Israelites.

Wickedness of (Lu 13:33, 34). Catalogue of abominations in (Eze 22:3-12, 25-30; 23; 33:25, 26). Led Judah to sin (Mic 1:5).

Prophecies against (Isa 3:1-8; Jer 9:11; 19:6, 15; 21:10; 26:9, 11; Da 9:2, 27; Mic 1:1; 3:12); of pestilence, famine, and war in (Jer 34:2; Eze 5:12; Joe 3:2, 3; Am 2:5); of the destruction of (Jer 7:32-34; 26:18; 32:29, 31, 32; Da 9:24-27). Destruction of, foretold by Jesus (M't 23:37, 38; 24:15; M'k 13:14-23; Lu 13:35; 17:26-37; 19:41-44; 21:20-24).

Prophecies of the rebuilding of (Isa 44:28; Jer 31:38-40; Eze 48:15-22; Da 9:25; Zec 14:8-11). Of final restoration of (Joe 3:20, 21; Zec 2:2-5; 8).

Historical Notices of: Melchizedek was ancient king of (Ge 14:18).

JERUSALEM, NEW, city of God referred to in Re 3:12 and Re 21:2 as coming down out of heaven from God. Ga 4:26 describes the New Jerusalem as the mother of believers.

JERUSHA, JERUSHAH (possessed), wife of King Uzziah and mother of King Jotham (2Ki 15:33; 2Ch 27:1).

JESAIAH (Jehovah saves). 1. Called also Jeshaiah. Grandson of Zerubbabel (1Ch 3:21).

2. Son of Jeduthun (1Ch 25:3, 15).

3. Grandson of Eliezer (1Ch 26:25).

4. A Jew of the family of Elam, who returned from exile (Ezr 8:7).

5. A Levite who joined Ezra to return to Jerusalem (Ezr 8:19).

6. A Benjamite, detailed by lot to dwell in Jerusalem after the exile (Ne 11:7).

JESHANAH (old), a city on the N of Benjamin (2Ch 13:19).

JESHARELAH, ancestral head of course of musicians (1Ch 25:14), called Asarelah in verse 2.

JESHEBEAB, a priest, and head of the fourteenth course (1Ch 24:13).

JESHER (uprightness), son of Caleb (1Ch 2:18).

JESHIMON (a waste, a desert). 1. A place in the Sinaitic peninsula, E of the Jordan (Nu 21:20; 23:28).

2. A place in the desert of Judah (1Sa 23:24; 26:1).

JESHISHAI (aged), a Gadite (1Ch 5:14).

JESHOHAIAH, a descendant of Simeon (1Ch 4:36).

JESHUA (Jehovah is salvation). 1. Called also Jeshuah. A priest, head of the ninth course (1Ch 24:11). Nine hundred and seventy-three of his descendants returned from Babylon (Ezr 2:36; Ne 7:39).

2. A Levite, had charge of the tithes (2Ch 31:15). His descendants returned with Ezra from Babylon (Ezr 2:40; Ne 7:43).

3. Called also Joshua. A priest who accompanied Zerubbabel from Babylon (Ezr 2:2; Ne 7:7; 12:1). Descendants of (Ne 12:10). He rebuilt the altar (Ezr 3:2). Rebuilt the temple (Ezr 3:8-13). Contends with those who sought to defeat the rebuilding (Ezr 4:1-3; 5:1, 2).

4. Father of Jozabad (Ezr 8:33).

5. Son of Pahath-moab (Ezr 2:6; Ne 7:11).

6. Father of Ezer (Ne 3:19).

7. A Levite who explained the law to the people when Ezra read it (Ne 8:7; 12:8).

8. A Levite who sealed Nehemiah's covenant (Ne 10:9).

9. A city of Judah (Ne 11:26).

10. Joshua called (Ne 8:17).

Symbolical: Prophecies concerning (Zec 3; 6:9-15).

See Joshua.

JESHURUN (upright one), a name used poetically for Israel (De 32:15; 33:5, 26; Isa 44:2).

JESIAH. 1. A disaffected Israelite who joined David at Ziklag (1Ch 12:6).

2. A Kohathite Levite (1Ch 23:20).

JESIMIEL (God establishes), a descendant of Simeon (1Ch 4:36).

JESSE. Father of David (Ru 4:17; 1Sa 17:12). Ancestor of Jesus (M't 1:5, 6). Samuel visits, under divine command, to select from his sons a successor to Saul (1Sa 16:1-13). Saul asks, to send David to become a member of his court (1Sa 16:19-23). Sons in Saul's army (1Sa 17:13-28). Dwells with David in Moab (1Sa 22:3, 4). Descendants of (1Ch 2:13-17).

JESTING. Foolish, forbidden (Eph 5:4; See M't 12:36).

JESUI, or sometimes Isui, or Ishuai. 1. Asherite (Ge 46:17; Nu 26:44; 1Ch 7:30).

2. Son of Saul (1Sa 14:49).

JESUS THE CHRIST.

History of: Genealogy of (M't 1:1-17; Lu 3:23-38).

Facts before the birth of: The angel Gabriel appears to Mary (Lu 1:26-38). Mary visits Elisabeth (Lu 1:39-56). Mary's *magnificat* (Lu 1:46-55). An angel appears to Joseph concerning Mary (M't 1:18-25).

Birth of (Lu 2:1-7).

Angels appear to the shepherds (Lu 2:8-20).

Magi visit (M't 2:1-12).

Circumcision of (Lu 2:21). Is presented in the temple (Lu 2:21-38).

Flight into, and return from, Egypt (M't 2:13-23).

Disputes with the doctors in the temple (Lu 2:41-52).

Is baptized by John (M't 3:13-17; M'k 1:9-11; Lu 3:21-23).

Temptation of (M't 4:1-11; M'k 1:12, 13; Lu 4:1-13).

John's testimony concerning him (Joh 1:1-18).

Testimony of John the Baptist concerning (Joh 1:19-34).

Disciples adhere to (Joh 1:35-51).

Miracle at Cana of Galilee (Joh 2:1-12).

Drives the money changers from the temple (Joh 2:13-25). Nicodemus comes to (Joh 3:1-21).

Baptizes (Joh 3:22, w 4:2).

Returns to Galilee (M't 4:12; M'k 1:14; Lu 4:14; Joh 4:1-3).

Visits Sychar, and teaches the Samaritan woman (Joh 4:4-42).

Teaches in Galilee (M't 4:17; M'k 1:14, 15; Lu 4:14, 15; Joh 4:43-45).

Heals a nobleman's son of Capernaum (Joh 4:46-54).

Is rejected by the people of Nazareth, dwells at Capernaum (M't 4:13-16; Lu 4:16-31).

Chooses Peter, Andrew, James, and John as disciples, miracle of the draught of fishes (M't 4:18-22; M'k 1:16-20; Lu 5:1-11).

Preaches throughout Galilee (M't 4:23-25; M'k 1:35-39; Lu 4:42-44).

Heals a demoniac (M'k 1:21-28; Lu 4:31-37).

Heals Peter's mother-in-law (M't 8:14-17; M'k 1:29-34; Lu 4:38-41).

Heals a leper in Galilee (M't 8:2-4; M'k 1:40-45; Lu 5:12-16).

Heals a paralytic (M't 9:2-8; M'k 2:1-12; Lu 5:17-26).

Calls Matthew (M't 9:9; M'k 2:13, 14; Lu 5:27, 28).

Heals an impotent man at the pool of Bethesda on the Sabbath day, is persecuted, and makes his defense (Joh 5).

Defines the law of the Sabbath on the occasion of his disciples plucking the ears of corn (M't 12:9-14; M'k 3:1-6; Lu 6:6-11).

Withdraws from Capernaum to the Sea of Galilee, where he heals many (M't 12:15-21; M'k 3:7-12).

Goes up into a mountain, and calls and ordains twelve disciples (M't 10:2-4; M'k 3:13-19; Lu 6:12-19).

Delivers the "Sermon on the Mount" (M't 5; 6; 7; Lu 6:20-49).

Heals the servant of the centurion (M't 8:5-13; Lu 7:1-10).

Raises from the dead the son of the widow of Nain (Lu 7:11-17).

Receives the message from John the Baptist (M't 11:2-19; Lu 7:18-35).

Upbraids the unbelieving cities about Capernaum (M't 11:20-30).

Anointed by a sinful woman (Lu 7:36-50).

Preaches in the cities of Galilee (Lu 8:1-3).

Heals a demoniac, and denounces the scribes and Pharisees (M't 12:22-37; M'k 3:19-30; Lu 11:14-20).

Replies to the scribes and Pharisees who seek a sign from him (M't 12:38-45; Lu 11:16-36).

Denounces the Pharisees and other hypocrites (Lu 11:37-54).

Discourses to his disciples (Lu 12:1-59).

Parable of the barren fig tree (Lu 13:6-9).

Parable of the sower (M't 13:1-23; M'k 4:1-25; Lu 8:4-18).

Parable of the tares, and other teachings (M't 13:24-53; M'k 4:26-34).

Crosses the Sea of Galilee, and stills the tempest (M't 8:18-27; M'k 4:35-41; Lu 8:22-25).

Miracle of the swine (M't 8:28-33; M'k 5:1-21; Lu 8:26-40).

Returns to Capernaum (M't 9:1; M'k 5:21; Lu 8:40).

Eats with publicans and sinners, and discourses on fasting (M't 9:10-17; M'k 2:15-22; Lu 5:29-39).

Raises to life the daughter of Jairus, and heals the woman who has the issue of blood (M't 9:18-26; M'k 5:22-43; Lu 8:41-56).

Heals two blind men, and casts out a dumb spirit (M't 9:27-34).

Returns to Nazareth (M't 13:53-58; M'k 6:1-6).

Teaches in various cities in Galilee (M't 9:35-38).

Instructs his disciples, and empowers them to heal diseases and cast out unclean spirits (M't 10; M'k 6:6-13; Lu 9:1-6).

Herod falsely supposes him to be John, whom he had beheaded (M't 14:1, 2, 6-12; M'k 6:14-16, 21-29; Lu 9:7-9).

The twelve return; he goes to the desert: multitudes follow him; he feeds five thousand (M't 14:13-21; M'k 6:30-44; Lu 9:10-17; Joh 6:1-14).

Walks on the sea (M't 14:22-36; M'k 6:45-56; Joh 6:15-21).

Teaches in the synagogue in Capernaum (Joh 6:22-65).

Disciples forsake him (Joh 6:66-71).

He justifies his disciples in eating without washing their hands (M't 15:1-20; M'k 7:1-23).

Heals the daughter of the Syrophoenician woman (M't 15:21-28; M'k 7:24-30).

Heals a dumb man (M't 15:29-31; M'k 7:31-37).

Feeds four thousand (M't 15:32-39; M'k 8:1-9).

Refuses to give a sign to the Pharisees (M't 16:1-4; M'k 8:10-12).

Cautions his disciples against the leaven of hypocrisy (M't 16:4-12; M'k 8:13-21).

Heals a blind man (M'k 8:22-26).

Foretells his death and resurrection (M't 16:21-28; M'k 8:31-38; 9:1; Lu 9:21-27).

Is transfigured (M't 17:1-13; M'k 9:2-13; Lu 9:28-36).

Heals a demoniac (M't 17:14-21; M'k 9:14-29; Lu 9:37-43).

Fortells his death and resurrection (M't 17:22, 23; M'k 9:30-32; Lu 9: 43-45).

Miracle of tribute money in the fish's mouth (M't 17:24-27).

Reproves the ambition of his disciples (M't 18:1-35; M'k 9:33-50; Lu 9:46-50).

Reproves the intolerance of his disciples (M'k 9:38, 39; Lu 9:49, 50).

Journeys to Jerusalem to attend the Feast of Tabernacles, passing through Samaria (Lu 9:51-62; Joh 7:2-11).

Commissions the seventy (Lu 10:1-16).

Heals ten lepers (Lu 17:11-19).

Teaches in Jerusalem at the Feast of Tabernacles (Joh 7:14-53; 8).

Answers a lawyer, who tests his wisdom with the question, "What shall I do to inherit eternal life?" by the parable of the good Samaritan (Lu 10:25-37).

Hears the report of the seventy (Lu 10:17-24).

Teaches in the house of Mary, Martha, and Lazarus, in Bethany (Lu 10:38-42).

Teaches his disciples to pray (Lu 11:1-13).

Heals a blind man, who, because of his faith in Jesus, was excommunicated (Joh 9).

Teaches in Jerusalem (Joh 9:39-41; 10:1-21).

Teaches in the temple at Jerusalem, at the Feast of Dedication (Joh 10:22-39).

Goes to Bethabara to escape violence from the rulers (Joh 10:40-42; 11:3-16).

Returns to Bethany, and raises Lazarus from the dead (Joh 11:1-46).

Escapes to the city of Ephraim from the conspiracy led by Caiaphas, the high priest (Joh 11:47-54).

Journeys toward Jerusalem to attend the passover; heals many who are diseased, and teaches the people (M't 19:1, 2; M'k 10:1; Lu 13:10-35).

Dines with a Pharisee on the Sabbath (Lu 14:1-24).

Teaches the multitude the conditions of discipleship (Lu 14:25-35).

Enunciates the parables of the lost sheep, the lost piece of silver, prodigal son, unjust steward (Lu 15:1-32; 16:1-13).

Reproves the hypocrisy of the Pharisees (Lu 16).

Enunciates the parable of the rich man and Lazarus (Lu 16:19-31).

Teaches his disciples concerning offenses, meekness, and humility (Lu 17:1-10).

Teaches the Pharisees concerning the coming of his kingdom (Lu 17:20-37).

Enunciates the parables of the unjust judge, and the Pharisee and publican praying in the temple (Lu 18:1-14).

Interprets the law concerning marriage and divorce (M't 19:3-12; M'k 10:2-12).

Blesses little children (M't 19:13-15; M'k 10:13-16; Lu 18:15-17).

Receives the rich young ruler, who asks what he shall do to inherit eternal life (M't 19:16-22; M'k 10:17-22; Lu 18:18-24).

Enunciates the parable of the vineyard (M't 20:1-16).

Foretells his death and resurrection (M't 20:17-19; M'k 10:32-34; Lu 18:31-34).

Listens to the mother of James and John in behalf of her sons (M't 20:20-28; M'k 10:35-45).

Heals two blind men at Jericho (M't 20:29-34; M'k 10:46-50; Lu 18:35-43).

Visits Zacchaeus (Lu 19:1-10).

Enunciates the parable of the pounds (Lu 19:11-28).

Goes to Bethany six days before the passover (Joh 12:1-9).

Triumphal entry into Jerusalem, while the people throw palm branches in the way (M't 21:1-11; M'k 11:1-11; Lu 19:29-44; Joh 12:12-19).

Enters the temple (M't 21:12; M'k 11:11; Lu 19:45).

Drives the money changers out of the temple (M't 21:12, 13; Lu 19:45, 46).

Heals the infirm in the temple (M't 21:14).

Teaches daily in the temple (Lu 19:47, 48).

Performs the miracle of causing the barren fig tree to wither (M't 21:17-22; M'k 11:12-14, 20-22).

Enunciates the parable of the two sons (M't 21:28-31); the parable of the wicked husbandmen (M't 21:33-46; M'k 12:1-12; Lu 20:9-19); of the marriage (M't 22:1-14; Lu 14:16-24).

Tested by the Pharisees and Herodians, and enunciates the duty of the citizen to his government (M't 22:15-22; M'k 12:13-17; Lu 20:20-26).

Tried by the Sadducees concerning the resurrection of the dead (M't 22:23-33; M'k 12:18-27; Lu 20:27-40); and by a lawyer (M't 22:34-40; M'k 12:28-34).

Exposes the hypocrisies of the scribes and Pharisees (M't 23; M'k 12:38-40; Lu 20:45-47).

Extols the widow who casts two mites into the treasury (M'k 12:41-44; Lu 21:1-4).

Verifies the prophecy of Isaiah concerning the unbelieving Jews (Joh 12:37-50).

Foretells the destruction of the temple, and of Jerusalem (M't 24; M'k 13; Lu 21:5-36).

Laments over Jerusalem (M't 23:37; Lu 19:41-44).

Enunciates the parables of the ten virgins and of the talents (M't 25:1-30).

Foretells the scenes of the day of judgment (M't 25:31-46).

Anointed with the box of precious

ointment (M't 26:6-13; M'k 14:3-9; Joh 12:1-8).

Last passover, and institution of the sacrament of the holy eucharist (M't 26:17-30; M'k 14:12-25; Lu 22:7-20).

Washes the disciples' feet (Joh 13:1-17).

Foretells his betrayal (M't 26:23; M'k 14:18-21; Lu 22:21; Joh 13:18).

Accuses Judas of his betrayal (M't 26:21-25; M'k 14:18-21; Lu 22:21-23; Joh 13:21-30).

Teacnes his disciples, and comforts them with promises, and promises the gift of the Holy Spirit (Joh 14; 15; 16).

Last prayer (Joh 17).

Repairs to Gethsemane (M't 26:30, 36-46; M'k 14:26, 32-42; Lu 22:39-46; Joh 18:1).

Is betrayed and apprehended (M't 26:47-56; M'k 14:43-54; 66-72; Lu 22:47-53; Joh 18:2-12).

Trial of, before Caiaphas (M't 26:57, 58, 69-75; M'k 14:53, 54, 66-72; Lu 22:54-62; Joh 18:13-18, 25-27).

Led by the council to Pilate (M't 27:1, 2, 11-14; M'k 15:1-5; Lu 23:1-5; Joh 18:28-38).

Arraigned before Herod (Lu 23:6-12).

Tried before Pilate (M't 27:15-26; M'k 15:6-15; Lu 23:13-25; Joh 18:39, 40; 19:1-16).

Mocked by the soldiers (M't 27:27-31; M'k 15:16-20).

Is led away to be crucified (M't 27:31-34; M'k 15:20-23; Lu 23:26-32; Joh 19:16, 17).

Crucified (M't 27:35-56; M'k 15:24-41; Lu 23:33-49; Joh 19:18-30).

Taken from the cross and buried (M't 27:57-66; M'k 15:42-47; Lu 23:50-56; Joh 19:31-42).

Arises from the dead (M't 28:2-15; M'k 16:1-11; Lu 24:1-12; Joh 20:1-18).

Is seen by Mary Magdalene (M't 28:1-10; M'k 16:9; Joh 20:11-17); by Peter (Lu 24:34; 1Co 15:5).

Appears to two disciples who journey to Emmaus (M'k 16:12, 13; Lu 24:13-35).

Appears in the midst of the disciples, when Thomas is absent (M'k 16:14-18; Lu 24:36-49; Joh 20:19-23); when Thomas was present (Joh 20:26-29); at the Sea of Galilee (M't 28:16; Joh 21:1-14); to the apostles and upwards of five hundred brethren on a mountain in Galilee (M't 28:16-20, w Ac 10:40-42; See also Ac 13:31; 1Co 15:6, 7).

Appears to James, and also to all the apostles (Ac 1:3-8; 1Co 15:7).

Ascends to heaven (M'k 16:19, 20; Lu 24:50-53; Ac 1:9-12).

Appears to Paul (Ac 9:3-17; 18:9; 22:14, 18; 23:11; 26:16; 1Co 9:1; 15:8).

Stephen's vision of (Ac 7:55, 56).

Appears to John on Patmos (Re 1:10-18).

Miscellaneous Facts Concerning: Brethren of (M't 13:55; M'k 6:3; 1Co 9:5; Ga 1:19). Sisters of (M't 13:56; M'k 6:3).

Was with the Israelites in the wilderness (1Co 10:4, 9; Heb 11:26; Jude 5).

Appearances of, after his resurrection: To Mary Magdalene, and other women (M't 28:1-10; M'k 16:9; Lu 24:1-10; Joh 20:11-17). To Peter (Lu 24:34; 1Co 15:5). To two disciples who journey to Emmaus (M'k 16:12, 13; Lu 24:13-31). In the midst of the disciples, when Thomas is absent, Jerusalem (Joh 20:19-23); when Thomas is present (M'k 16:14-18; Lu 24:36-49; Joh 20:26-29; 1Co 15:5). To certain disciples, Sea of Galilee (Joh 21:1-14). To the eleven disciples, mountain in Galilee (M't 28:16). To upwards of five hundred, Galilee (1Co 15:6). To James, and also all the apostles, Jerusalem (Ac 1:3-8; 1Co 15:7). To Paul (Ac 9:3-6; 23:11; 26:13-18; 1Co 9:1; 15:8).

In Stephen's vision (Ac 7:55, 56). To John, in a vision, on Patmos (Re 1:10-18).

Ascension of (M'k 16:19; Lu 24:50, 51; Joh 14:2-4; Ac 1:9; 3:21; Eph 1:20; 4:8-10; 1Ti 3:16; Heb 1:3; 4:14; 9:24). Foretold (Ps 47:5; 68:18; Lu 24:26, 50; Joh 1:51; 6:62; 7:33; 14:2, 3, 12, 28; 16:5, 7, 10, 16, 28; 17:13; 20:17).

Atonement by (Ro 3:24-26; 5:11, 15; 1Th 1:10; Heb 13:12; 1Jo 2:2; 3:5; 4:10; Re 5:6, 9; 13:8).

Made once for all (Heb 7:27; 9:24-28; 10:10, 12, 14; 1Pe 3:18).

Vicarious (Isa 53:4-12; M't 20:28; Joh 6:51; 11:49-51; Ga 1:4; 3:13; Eph 5:2; 1Th 5:9, 10; Heb 2:9; 1Pe 2:24).

Through his blood (Lu 22:20; 1Co 1:23; Eph 2:13-15; Heb 9:12-15, 25, 26;

12:24; 13:12, 20, 21; 1Jo 5:6; Re 1:5; 5:9; 7:14; 12:11).

For reconciliation (Ro 5:1-21; 2Co 5:18, 19, 21; Eph 2:16, 17; Col 1:20-22; Heb 2:17).

For remission of sins (Zec 13:1; M't 26:28; Lu 24:46, 47; Joh 1:29; Ro 4:25; 1Co 15:3; Ga 1:3, 4; Eph 1:7; Col 1:14; Heb 1:3; 10:1-20; 1Jo 1:7; 3:5).

Atonement by, typified (Ex 29:36, 37; 30:10, 15, 16; Le 1:4; 5:6, 16, 18; 6:7; 8:34; 9:2, 3, 7; 10:17; 12:7, 8; 14:18-20, 31, 53; 15:14, 15, 29, 30; 16:6, 10, 11, 16-18, 24, 27, 30, 32-34; 17:11; 23:27, 28; 25:9; Nu 8:19, 21; 16:46; 25:13; 28:22, 30; 29:5; 31:50).

Atoning blood of (M't 26:28; M'k 14:24; Lu 22:20; Eph 1:7; 2:13; Heb 9:14; 10:19; 1Jo 1:7).

Atoning blood of, typified (Ex 12:7, 13, 22, 23; 24:6, 8; 29:12, 15, 20, 21; 30:10; Le 1:5, 10, 11; 3:2, 8, 13; 4:5-7, 17, 18, 25, 30, 34; 5:8, 9; 6:30; 7:2; 8:2, 15, 19, 23, 24, 30; 9:9, 18; 14:6, 14, 15, 25; 16:14, 15, 18, 19, 27; 17:6, 11; Nu 18:17; 19:2-4; De 12:27; 2Ki 16:13, 15; 2Ch 29:22; 30:16; 35:11; Eze 43:20; 45:19, 20; 1Pe 1:19).

Benevolence of: Manifested in his companionship with sinners (M't 9:10-12; M'k 2:14-17; Lu 5:30; 15:2; 19:5-10). See Compassion of, and Love of, below.

Compassion of: For those who were in spiritual distress (Isa 42:3; M't 9:36; 12:20; 18:12, 13; 23:37; M'k 1:41; 6:34; Lu 7:13; 13:34; 15:4-9, 20-24; 19:41, 42; Joh 11:33-38; 18:8, 9; 2Co 8:9; Heb 4:15; 5:2). For those who were in temporal adversity (Isa 53:4; 63:9; M't 8:3, 16, 17; 14:14; 15:32; 20:34; M'k 8:2, 3). For his sheep (Isa 40:11; M'k 6:34).

Condescension of (Lu 22:27; Joh 13:5, 14; 2Co 8:9; Ph'p 2:7, 8; Heb 2:11).

Confessing: See Confession of Christ; Testimony, Religious.

Creator (Joh 1:3, 10; 1Co 8:6; Eph 3:9; Col 1:16, 17; Heb 1:2, 10; Re 3:14).

Death of (Joh 12:32, 33; Ac 5:30; 7:52; Heb 2:14; 12:2, 24; Re 5:12; 13:8). Foretold (Ge 3:15 w Heb 2:14); by the psalmist (Ps 22:1 w M't 27:46 & M'k 15:34; Ps 22:17 w M't 27:36 & Lu 23:35; Ps 22:18 w M't 27:35 & M'k 15:24 & Lu 23:34 & Joh 19:23, 24; Ps 34:20 w Joh 19:36; Ps 69:21 w M't 27:34, 48 & M'k 15:36 & Lu 23:36 & Joh 19:28-30); by Isaiah (Isa 52:14; 53:7-12); by Zechariah (Zec 12:9, 10 w M't 26:31); by Jesus, himself (M't 12:40 w Lu 11:30; M't 16:4, 21; 17:12, 13, 22, 23; 20:17-19; 21:33-39; 26:2, 12, 18; M'k 8:31; 9:31; 10:32-34; 14:8, 9; Lu 9:22, 44; 12:50; 17:25; 18:31-33; 22:15, 21, 37; Joh 2:19, 21; 10:11, 15, 17, 18; 12:7, 24, 32-34; 14:19; 18:11).

Paul's testimony concerning (Ac 17:3; 26:22, 23; 1Co 1:17, 18, 23, 24; 2:2; 15:3, 4; 2Co 4:10, 11; 13:4; Ga 3:1; 1Th 2:15; 4:14).

For Circumstances of the death of, see History of, above.

Design of his death: To make reconciliation (Ro 5:6-11; Eph 2:13-16).

To redeem (Isa 53:4-6, 8, 10-12 w vs 1-12; M't 20:28; 26:28; M'k 10:45; 14:24; Joh 6:51; 10:11, 17; 11:49-52; Ac 20:28; 26:23; Ro 3:24, 25; 8:3, 32; 1Co 5:7; 6:20; 8:11; 15:3; Ga 1:4; 3:13; 4:4, 5; Eph 1:6, 7; 5:2, 25-27; Col 1:14, 20, 22; 2:14, 15; 1Th 1:10; 1Ti 2:6; Tit 2:14; Heb 2:9, 10, 14, 15, 18; 7:27; 9:12-17, 25, 26, 28; 10:10, 12, 14, 17-20; 1Pe 1:18, 19; 2:21, 24; 3:18; 1Jo 2:2; 3:16; 4:10; Re 1:5, 6; 5:9, 10; 13:8).

To purge sins (Zec 13:1; Lu 24:46, 47; Joh 1:29; Heb 1:3; 13:11, 12; 1Jo 1:7; Re 7:14, 15.

To secure forgiveness (Ac 5:30, 31; Ro 4:25).

To save (Joh 3:14-17; Ro 6:3-5, 9, 10; 14:9, 15; 2Co 5:14, 15, 19, 21; 8:9; Ga 2:20; 1Th 5:9, 10).

Vicarious death of (Isa 53:4-12; M't 20:28; Joh 6:51; 11:49, 51; Ga 3:13; Eph 5:2; 1Th 5:9, 10; Heb 2:9; 1Pe 2:24).

Vicarious death of, typified (Ex 29:11, 15, 16, 20, 38-42; Le 1:5, 11, 15; 3:2, 8, 13; 4:4, 15, 24, 29; 6:25; 7:2; 8:15, 19; 9:8, 15, 18, 19, 23, 24; 14:13, 19, 25; 2Ch 29:22, 24; 30:15; 35:1).

See Atonement; Redemption.

Voluntary death of (Isa 50:6; 53:12; Lu 9:51; 12:50; 22:15, 42; Joh 10:17, 18; 18:5, 8, 11; Ph'p 2:8; Heb 7:27; 9:26; 1Jo 3:16).

Divine Sonship of: Testified to: By God, at his baptism (M't 3:17; M'k 1:11; Lu 3:22); at the transfiguration (M't 17:5; M'k 9:7; Lu 9:35; 2Pe 1:17); in his commandment to believe in (1Jo 3:23).

Testified to: By himself (M't 11:27 w

Lu 10:22; M't 26:63, 64; 27:43; M'k 14:61, 62; Lu 22:70; Joh 3:16-18, 34-36; 6:27, 40, 46, 57; 9:35-37; 11:4; 19:7).

Testified to: By the disciples (M't 14:33; 1Jo 4:14); unclean spirits (M't 8:29; M'k 3:11; 5:7 w Lu 8:28; Lu 4:41); Mark (M'k 1:1); John the Baptist (Joh 1:34); John, the apostle (Joh 1:14, 18; 1Jo 1:7; 2:22-24; 3:8, 23; 4:9, 10, 14; 5:5, 9, 10, 13, 20; 2Jo 3; Re 2:18); Nathanael (Joh 1:49); Martha (Joh 11:27); the centurion (M't 27:54; M'k 15:39); Peter (Ac 3:13; 13:33); Paul (Ro 1:3, 4, 9; 8:3, 29, 32; 1Co 1:9; 15:24, 27, 28; 2Co 1:3, 19; Ga 1:16; 4:4; Eph 1:3; Col 1:3; 1Th 1:10); author of the Epistle to the Hebrews (Heb 1:1-3, 5; 4:14; 5:5, 8; 6:6; 7:3; 10:29).

Declared God to be his Father (M't 15:13; 18:10, 19; 20:23; 26:53, 63, 64; Lu 10:22; 22:29; Joh 5:19-21, 23, 26, 27, 30, 36, 37; 8:16, 19, 26-29, 38, 49, 54; 10:15, 17, 18, 29, 30, 36-38; 11:41; 12:49, 50; 13:3; 14:7, 9-11, 13, 16, 20, 21, 23, 24, 28, 31; 15:1, 8-10, 15, 23, 24; 16:15, 27, 28, 32; 17:1-26; 20:17, 21).

Peter's confession of (M't 16:15-17).

Prophecies concerning (Ps 2:7; Lu 1:32, 35).

Worshipped by the disciples as the Son of God (M't 14:33).

See Divinity of, below; Relation of, to the Father, below; Son of God and Son of Man, below.

Divinity of: Indicated by the titles ascribed to him, as: Immanuel (Isa 7:14 w M't 1:23); first and last (Re 1:17; 22:13); God (Ps 102:24-27 w Heb 1:10-13; Joh 1:1; 20:28; Ro 9:5; 1Jo 5:20, 21); God and Saviour Jesus Christ (2Pe 1:1); God our Saviour (Tit 2:13); Holy One (Ac 3:14); King of kings and Lord of lords (Re 17:14); Lord (Ps 110:1 w M't 22:42-45; Isa 40:3 w M't 3:3; Ac 20:28); Lord of hosts (Isa 8:13, 14, w 1Pe 2:8); My Lord and My God (Joh 20:28); Lord of all (Ac 10:36; Ro 10:12); mighty God (Isa 9:6); only begotten of the Father (Joh 1:14, 18; 3:16, 18; 1Jo 4:9); Son of God (M't 26:63-67; M'k 1:1; 15:39; 1Co 1:9; 2Co 1:19; Ga 2:20; Eph 4:13; Heb 1:2; 2Pe 1:17; 1Jo 1:2, 3; 3:23; 5:10, 12, 13, 20); Son of Man (Da 7:13, 14; M't 11:19; 12:8). See Divine Sonship of, above; Son of God, Son of Man, below.

Divinity of, As Jehovah (Isa 40:3, w M't 3:3); Jehovah of glory (Ps 24:7, 10, w 1Co 2:8, Jas 2:1); Jehovah our righteousness (Jer 23:5, 6, w 1Co 1:30); Jehovah above all (Ps 97:9, w John 3:31); Jehovah the first and the last (Isa 44:6, w Re 1:17; Isa 48:12-16, w Re 22:13); Jehovah's fellow and equal (Zec 13:7; Ph'p 2:6); Jehovah of hosts (Isa 6:1-3 w Joh 12:41; Isa 8:13, 14, w 1Pe 2:8); Jehovah (Ps 110:1, w M't 22:42-45); Jehovah the shepherd (Isa 40:10, 11; Heb 13:20); Jehovah, for whose glory all things were created (Pr 16:4, w Col 1:16); Jehovah the messenger of the covenant (Mal 3:1, w Lu 7:27). Invoked as Jehovah (Joe 2:32, w 1Co 1:2); as the eternal God and Creator (Ps 102:24-27, w Heb 1:8, 10-12); the mighty God (Isa 9:6); the great God and Saviour (Ho 1:7, w Tit 2:13); God over all (Ro 9:5); God the Judge (Ec 12:14, w 1Co 4:5; 2Co 5:10; 2Ti 4:1), Emmanuel (Isa 7:14, w M't 1:23); King of kings and Lord of lords (Da 10:17, w Re 1:5; 17:14); the Holy One (1Sa 2:2, w Ac 3:14); the Lord from heaven (1Co 15:47); Lord of the sabbath (Ge 2:3, w M't 12:8); Lord of all (Ac 10:36; Ro 10:11-13). Son of God (M't 26:63-67); the only begotten Son of the Father (Joh 1:14, 18; 3:16, 18; 1Jo 4:9). His blood is called the blood of God (Ac 20:28). One with the Father (Joh 10:30, 38; 12:45; 14:7-10; 17:10). As sending the Spirit equally with the Father (Joh 14:16, w Joh 15:26). As unsearchable equally with the Father (Pr 30:4; M't 11:27). As Creator of all things (Isa 40:28; Joh 1:3; Col 1:16); supporter and preserver of all things (Ne 9:6, w Col 1:17; Heb 1:3). Acknowledged by Old Testament saints (Ge 17:1, w Ge 48:15, 16; 32:24-30, w Ho 12:3-5; J'g 6:22-24; 13:21, 22; Job 19:25-27).

Is one with the Father (Joh 5:17, 18, 23; 10:30, 33, 38; 12:45; 14:7-10, 11; 17:11, 21, 22).

Sends the Holy Spirit equally with the Father (Joh 14:16).

Identical with the Adonai, Almighty, of the Old Testament (Joh 12:40, 41 w Isa 6:8-11); and the Jehovah of the Old Testament (Joh 19:37 w Zec 12:16).

Testimony concerning: By the Father (Joh 5:32, 34, 37; 6:27; 8:18; Ac 3:33; 1Jo 5:9); at his baptism (M't 3:16, 17;

M'k 1:11; Lu 3:22); at his transfiguration (M't 17:5; M'k 9:7; Lu 9:35; 2Pe 1:17).

By Jesus concerning himself (Joh 5:18, 31, 36; 8:18, 42; 10:33, 36, 38; 12:45; 14:11-13; 16:27, 28; 17:5, 8, 24, 25; 19:7); to Peter and other disciples (M't 16:16, 17; M'k 8:29, 30; Lu 9:20, 21); to the Jews (M't 22:43, 44; Joh 5:23; 10:30, 33, 36, 38; 12:45); to his disciples (Joh 16:27, 28); to the woman of Samaria (Joh 4:25, 26); to the restored blind man (Joh 9:35-37); to Philip (Joh 14:7-11, 20); to Caiaphas (M't 26:63, 64; M'k 34:61, 62; Lu 22:67-70); to Pilate (Joh 18:36, 37; 1Ti 6:13).

By the angel, to Joseph (M't 1:23); to Mary (Lu 1:32, 35). John the Baptist (Joh 1:29-34; 5:33). John, the apostle (Joh 1:14, 18; 13:3; 1Jo 2:22-24). The disciples (Joh 16:30). Paul (Ac 9:20). The author of the Epistle to the Hebrews (Heb 11:26). The Scriptures (Joh 5:39). Thomas (Joh 20:28). Demons (M't 8:29; M'k 1:23, 24; 3:11; 5:6, 7; Lu 4:34, 41).

Is creator of all things (Joh 1:3; Col 1:16, 17).

Has power to forgive sins (M't 1:21; 9:6; M'k 2:5; Lu 5:20; Col 3:13).

Paul's apostleship from (Ga 1:1).

Invoked with the Father and the Holy Spirit in benedictions (Ro 1:7; 1Co 1:3; 2Co 1:2; Ga 1:3; Eph 1:2; 6:23, 24; 1Th 1:1; 3:11; 2Th 1:1, 2; 2:16, 17; 2Ti 1:2).

All power given to (M't 28:17, 18).

Eternity ascribed to (Joh 1:1, 2; 1Jo 1:1). See Eternity of, below.

Is judge (2Co 5:10). See Judge, below.

Eternity of: Called everlasting Father (Isa 9:6). Was before creation (Joh 1:1, 2, 15; 17:5, 24; Col 1:17; 2Ti 1:9). Was from the beginning (1Jo 2:13). Was from everlasting (Mic 5:2). Continueth forever (Ps 102:24-27 w Heb 1:10-13; Ps 110:4; Eph 3:21; Heb 7:16, 24, 25; Re 5:13, 14). The same yesterday, today and forever (Heb 13:8).

Exaltation of (Ps 2:8, 9; 68:18; Eph 4:8). In glory (M't 26:64; M'k 16:19; Lu 22:69; 24:26; Joh 7:39; Ac 2:33, 34; 3:20, 21; 7:55, 56; Ro 8:17, 34; Eph 1:20-22; 4:10; Col 3:1; 1Ti 3:16; Heb 1:3; 10:12, 13; 12:2; 1Pe 3:22; Re 3:21). As Lord of heaven and earth (Ph'p 2:9-11; Col 2:15). To be Saviour (Ac 5:31). To be priestly mediator (Heb 4:10, 14; 6:20; 7:26; 8:1; 9:24).

Example, An. Claimed himself (M't 11:29; 20:28; M'k 10:43-45; Lu 22:26, 27; Joh 10:4; 13:13-15, 34; 17:14, 18, 21, 22; Re 3:21). Referred to by Paul (Ro 8:29; 13:14; 15:2-7; 2Co 4:10; 8:9; 10:1; Ga 3:27; 6:2; Eph 4:13, 15, 24; 5:2; 6:9; Ph'p 2:5-8; Col 3:10, 11, 13; 1Th 1:6); by other apostles (Heb 3:1; 12:2-4; 1Pe 1:15; 2:21-24; 3:17, 18; 1Jo 2:6; 3:1-3, 16; 4:17).

Faith in. See Faith in Christ; Salvation, Conditions of.

Faithfulness of (Isa 11:5; Lu 4:43; Joh 7:18; 8:29; 9:4; 14:3; 17:8; Heb 3:2; Re 1:5; 3:14). In mediation (Heb 2:17).

Genealogy of. See Jesus, History of, above.

Glorification of (Joh 7:39; 12:16; 17:1; Ac 7:55, 56; Heb 8:1).

Head of the Church (Ps 118:22, 23 w M't 21:42, 43 & M'k 12:10; Isa 28:16 w Eph 2:2-22 & 1Pe 2:6; Lu 20:17, 18 w 1Pe 2:7; Joh 15:1-8; 1Co 3:11; Eph 1:22, 23; 4:15; 5:23-32; Col 1:18; 2:10, 19; 3:11; Re 2:2-28; 3:1, 7; 22:16).

Holiness of: Foretold (Ps 45:7; Isa 11:4, 5; Jer 23:5; Zec 9:9). Professed by himself (Joh 5:30; 7:18; 8:46; 14:30; Re 3:7).

Testified to: By the angel to his mother (Lu 1:35). Demons (M'k 1:24; Lu 4:34). The centurion at his crucifixion (Lu 23:47). By Stephen (Ac 7:52). Peter (Joh 6:69; Ac 3:14; 4:27-30; 1Pe 1:19; 2:22). John (1Jo 2:1, 29; 3:5). Paul (Ac 13:35; 2Co 5:21). The author of the Epistle to the Hebrews (Heb 1:9; 4:15; 7:26-28; 9:14).

Humanity of (Ps 22:22; Joh 1:14). Took on himself the nature of man (Ph'p 2:7, 8; Heb 2:9, 10, 14-18). Was born of flesh (Isa 9:6; M't 1:18-25; Lu 2:11-14; 1Jo 4:2; 2Jo 7).

Called: Seed of the woman (Ge 3:15; Ga 4:4); son of David (M't 20:30, 31; 21:9; 22:42; M'k 12:35; Lu 18:38); a prophet like unto Moses (De 18:15-19; Ac 3:22, 23; 7:37).

Humility of (2Co 8:9; Ph'p 2:7, 8). Became a servant (Lu 22:27; Joh 13:5, 14). See Meekness of, below.

Impeccability of, see Holiness of, above; Temptation of, below.

Incarnation of (Joh 16:28; 1Ti 3:16). Foretold (Ge 3:15; De 18:15-18; Ps 2:7 w Ac 13:33 and Heb 1:5; Isa 7:14-16;

9:6; 11:1; Joh 7:42). Through the generation of the Holy Spirit (M't 1:1, 16-18, 23; Lu 1:26-56). Made a little lower than the angels (Heb 2:9, 14). Made flesh (Lu 24:39; Joh 1:14; 20:27; Ro 8:3; 1Co 15:47; 2Co 5:16; Ga 4:4; Ph'p 2:7, 8; Heb 1:3, 6; 2:17, 18 w vs 9-17; 10:5; 1Jo 1:1-3; 4:2; 2Jo 7). In the lineage of Judah (Heb 7:14). Made of the seed of David (M't 22:45; Ro 1:3; 9:5; Re 22:16). Was the son of Mary (M't 13:55; Lu 2:1-21).

See Humanity of, above; Relation of, to the Father, below.

Intercession of, see Mediation of, below.

Judge (M't 3:12 w Lu 3:17; M't 25:31-34; Ac 10:42; Ro 2:16; 1Co 4:4, 5; 2Co 5:10; 2Ti 4:1, 8; Re 2:23). Prophecy concerning (Isa 2:4 w Mic 4:3; Isa 11:3, 4; Mic 5:1).

Ordained of God (Joh 5:22; Ac 17:31). Righteous (2Ti 4:8).

Justice of (2Sa 23:3; Zec 9:9; M't 27:19; Joh 5:30; Ac 3:14; 22:14).

King: Prophecies concerning (Ge 49:10; 1Sa 2:10; 2Sa 7:12 w Ac 2:30; Ps 2:6; 18:43, 44; 45:3-7; 72:5, 8, 11; 89:3, 4, 19-21, 23, 27, 29, 36, 37; 110:1, 2 w M't 22:42-45; Ps 132:11, 17, 18; Isa 9:6, 7; 22:22; 32:1; 52:7, 13; Jer 23:5; 30:9; 33:17; Eze 37:24, 25; Da 2:35, 44; 7:13, 14; Ho 3:5; Mic 5:2, 4; Zec 6:12, 13; 9:9, 10; M't 2:2, 6; 21:5; Lu 1:32, 33). Appointed by the Father (Lu 22:29, 30; Ac 2:30, 36 w 2Sa 7:12; Ac 5:31; Eph 1:20-22; Heb 2:7, 8).

Authority of (M'k 2:28; Joh 5:27); universal (M't 11:27 w Lu 10:22; M't 28:18; Lu 19:27; Joh 3:31, 33; 13:3; 17:2; Ro 9:5; 10:12; 14:9; Col 2:10; Heb 1:2-15; 2:7, 8; 1Pe 3:22; Re 3:7, 14, 21).

Dominion of, universal (Ac 10:36; 1Co 15:23-28; Eph 1:20-22; Ph'p 2:9-11; Re 1:5-7, 18; 11:15). Future glory of (M't 19:28; 25:31-34; 26:64; M'k 14:62; Lu 22:69; Heb 10:12, 13; Re 5:13).

Kingship of: Avowed by himself (M't 21:5; 27:11; Lu 23:2; Joh 18:36, 37). Ascribed, by disciples (Lu 19:38; Joh 1:49; 12:13, 15; Ac 17:7); in superscription on the cross (Joh 19:12, 19).

Symbolical statements concerning (Re 5:5, 12; 6:2, 15-17; 14:14; 17:14; 19:11, 12, 15, 16).

See Lordship of, below.

Kingdom of: Brings joy and gladness (Ps 46:4; Isa 25:6; 35; 52:9; 55:12). Brings peace (Ps 46:9; Isa 11:6-9). Is within us (Lu 17:21). Truth (Joh 18:37). Not of this world (Joh 18:36).

Keys of (M't 16:19). Glad tidings of (Lu 8:1). Mysteries of (Lu 8:10). Is not meat and drink (Ro 14:17).

Likened: To a man who sowed good seed (M't 13:24-30, 38-43; M'k 4:26-29); a grain of mustard seed (M't 13:31, 32; M'k 4:30, 31; Lu 13:18, 19); leaven (M't 13:33; Lu 13:21); a treasure (M't 13:44); a pearl (M't 13:45); a net (M't 13:47-50); a king who called his servants to a reckoning (M't 18:23-35); a householder (M't 20:1-16); a king who made a marriage feast for his son (M't 22:2-14; Lu 14:16-24); ten virgins (M't 25:1-13); a man traveling into a far country, who called his servants and delivered to them his goods (M't 25:14-30; Lu 19:12-27).

Prophecies concerning the kingdom of: Its character: To enlighten (Jer 31:34; Heb 8:11); bring peace (Ps 46:9; Isa 65:25; Mic 4:3-7); bring salvation (Isa 62:11); bring joy (Isa 25:6; 35:1-10; 42:1-7, 18-21; Lu 2:10). Shall be a river of salvation (Eze 47:1-12; Zec 14:8, 9, 16, 20, 21).

Its perpetuity (Isa 51:6, 8; Lu 1:33; Heb 1:8; 2Pe 1:11).

Its transforming power (Isa 35:1-10; 55:12, 13; 65:17-25).

Its future glory and greatness (Isa 49:22, 23; Hag 2:7-9; Re 21:9-27).

Its universality (Ge 12:3; 22:18; 49:10; Ps 72:5, 8-11, 16, 17, 19; 89:1-37; 113:3; Isa 9:6, 7; 40:4-11; 42:1-7; 49:1-26; 52:10; 54:1-3; 59:19-21; Jer 3:14-19); (according to many learned interpreters Da 2:35, 44; 7:13, 14, 18, 22, 27; Hab 2:14; Zec 9:1, 10; M't 8:11; Lu 13:29, 30; Re 14:6).

Its unity (Joh 10:16).

Its growth (M't 13:31-33; Lu 13:21). Ends of earth shall turn unto Him (Ps 66:4; 86:9; Isa 2:2-4; 45:14; 60:1-9; Jer 3:17; 16:19-21; 33:16; Eze 17:22, 23; Mic 4:1-4; Zep 2:11; Zec 2:10, 11; 6:15; 8:20-23). Shall embrace the heathen (Ps 2:8; 68:31, 32; 110:4-6; Ho 2:23; Am 9:11, 12; Mal 1:11).

Its final triumph (Ge 3:15; Ps 2:9; Isa 11:1-13; Da 2:44; 7:9-14, 27; M't 16:18; Ac 2:34, 35; 1Co 15:24-28; Eph 1:10;

Ph'p 2:10, 11; Heb 10:13; 12:23, 24, 27, 28; Re 5:9, 10, 13, 14; 6:2; 11:15; 12:10; 19:11-21; 20:1-3).

Secular notions concerning: To restore the kingdom of Israel (M'k 11:9, 10; Joh 6:15; Ac 1:6, 7). Rank of princes in the kingdom of (M't 20:20-23; M'k 10:35-40; Lu 9:46-48).

Love of (Ps 69:9; Re 3:9, 19). Constraining (2Co 5:13, 14). Passeth knowledge (Eph 3:17-19).

For his disciples (Joh 10:3, 4, 11, 14-16; 13:1, 23; 14:1-3, 18, 21, 27; 15:9-13, 15; 17:6-26; Ro 8:35, 37-39; 2Th 2:13). Children (M't 19:13-15; M'k 10:13, 14, 16; Lu 18:15, 16). His mother (Joh 19:26, 27). The lost (Isa 40:11; M't 18:12, 13; M'k 8:12; Lu 13:34).

Exemplified: In renunciation (2Co 8:9; Ph'p 2:6-8). Compassion (Isa 42:3; M't 9:36; 14:14; 15:32; Lu 7:13; 22:31, 32; Joh 11:5, 33-36; Ac 10:38; Heb 4:15). Solicitude for others (M't 23:37; Lu 23:28, 34; Joh 18:8, 9). His sacrifice (Ga 2:20; Eph 5:2, 25, 29, 30; 1Jo 3:16; Re 1:5). His vicarious suffering (Isa 53:4; M't 8:17; Ro 15:3). Redemption (Ps 72:14; Isa 63:9).

Lordship of. The sovereignty of the Messiah, as conceived by Old Testament writers, seems best described by the word King (see King above); but New Testament writers use the word Lord. Jesus said of himself, The son of man is Lord even of the Sabbath (M't 12:8; M'k 2:28). The student will find suggestions for profitable reflection in a study of the various forms of expression used by the authors of the epistles in which they attribute Lordship to our Savior (M't 12:8; Ac 2:36; Ro 1:7; 5:1, 11, 21; 6:23; 7:25; 8:39; 10:9; 13:14; 14:14; 15:6, 30; 16:20; 1Co 1:2, 3, 7-10; 5:4; 6:11; 8:6; 9:1; 11:25; 12:3; 15:31, 57; 16:23; 2Co 1:2, 3, 14; 4:5, 14; 8:9; 11:31; 13:14; Ga 1:3; 6:14, 18; Eph 1:2, 3, 17; 3:11; 5:20; 6:23, 24; Ph'p 1:2, 11; 2:19; 3:20; 4:23; Col 1:3; 2:6; 3:17, 24; 1Th 1:1, 3, 11, 13; 4:1; 5:10, 24, 28; 2Th 1:1, 2, 7, 12; 2:1, 8, 15, 16; 3:6, 12, 18; 1Ti 1:2, 12; 6:3, 14; 2Ti 1:2; Ph'm 1, 3, 5, 25; Jas 1:1; 2:1; 1Pe 1:3; 3:15; 2Pe 1:2, 8, 14, 16; 2:20; 3:18; Jude 4, 18, 21, 25).

Mediation of (Joh 14:6, 14; 16:23, 24, 26; 20:31; Ro 1:8; 5:1, 2; 6:23; 1Co 6:11; 15:57; 2Co 1:20; Eph 3:12; 4:32; 5:20; Col 3:17; 1Ti 2:1, 3, 5; Heb 9:11-28; 13:15; 1Pe 2:5; 1Jo 2:1, 2, 12). As a priest (Ps 110:4; Zec 6:13; Heb 2:17; 3:1, 2; 4:14, 15; 5:5, 6, 10; 6:19, 20; 7:1, 3, 19, 21, 24-28; 8:1, 2, 6; 9:11; 10:19-21).

Through his sacrifice (Eph 2:13-18; Heb 10:11, 12; 12:24).

Exemplified in his intercession (Isa 53:12; Lu 13:8, 9; 22:31, 32; 23:33, 34; Joh 14:16; 17:9, 11, 15-17, 19-22; Ro 8:34).

See Priesthood of, below.

Meekness of (M't 11:29; M'k 14:60, 61; 15:3-5; 2Co 10:1; Ph'p 2:8). Prophecies concerning (Ps 45:4; Isa 42:1-3; 50:5, 6; 52:1, 14; 53:7; M't 12:19, 20; 21:5; Ac 8:32).

Exemplified: In not resenting false accusation (M'k 2:6-11). In submitting to enemies (M't 26:47-63; 27:12-14; Joh 8:48-50; Heb 12:2, 3; 1Pe 2:23). In praying for enemies (Lu 23:34). In becoming a servant (Ph'p 2:7).

See Humility of, above; Meekness.

Messiah: Messianic Psalms (Pss 2; 67:1-7; 68; 69; 72; 96; 98:1-9; 110:1-7).

Prophecies concerning (Da 9:25, 26; Ac 3:18, 20).

Simeon's testimony to (Lu 2:28-32).

Andrew's belief in (Joh 1:41, 45). Peter's confession of (M't 16:15, 16; M'k 8:29; Lu 9:20; Joh 6:69).

His own testimony to his messiahship (M't 11:3-6; 26:63, 64; Lu 24:27; Joh 4:25, 26, 29, 42; 5:33, 36, 37, 39, 46; 6:27; 8:14, 17, 18, 25, 28, 56; 13:19).

Called David's son (M't 22:42-45; M'k 12:35-37; Lu 20:41-44).

Anointed of God (Ps 2:2; Ac 4:26, 27).

Proclaimed, by apostles (Ac 9:22; 13:27; 17:2, 3; 26:6, 7, 22, 23; 28:23; Ro 1:1-3; 1Co 15:3; 1Pe 1:10, 11; 2Pe 1:16-18; 1Jo 5:6-9).

See King, and Lordship, above. See Son of Man, below. See also Messianic Hope.

Miracles of: Water made wine (Joh 2:1-11).

First miraculous draught of fishes (Lu 5:1-11).

Demoniac in the synagogue healed (M'k 1:23-26; Lu 4:33-36).

Heals Simon's wife's mother (M't 8:14, 15; M'k 1:29-31; Lu 4:38, 39).

Heals diseases in Galilee (M't 4:23, 24; M'k 1:34).

Miracles at Jerusalem (Joh 2:23).

Cleanses the leper (M't 8:1-4; M'k 1:40-45; Lu 5:12-16).

Heals the paralytic (M't 9:1-8; M'k 2:1-12; Lu 5:17-26).

Heals the impotent man (Joh 5:1-16).

Restores the withered hand (M't 12:9-13; M'k 3:1-5; Lu 6:6-11).

Heals multitudes from Judah, Jerusalem, and coasts of Tyre and Sidon (Lu 6:17-19).

Heals the centurion's servant (M't 8:5-13; Lu 7:1-10).

Heals demoniacs (M't 8:16, 17; Lu 4:40, 41).

Raises the widow's son (Lu 7:11-16).

Heals in Galilee (Lu 7:21, 22).

Heals a demoniac (M't 12:22-37; M'k 3:19-30; Lu 11:14, 15, 17-23).

Stills the tempest (M't 8:23-27; M'k 4:35-41; Lu 8:22-25; M't 14:32).

Healing of the diseased in the land of Gennesaret (M't 14:34-36).

The demoniacs in Gadara healed (M't 8:28-34; M'k 5:1-20; Lu 8:26-39).

Raises Jairus' daughter (M't 9:18, 19, 23-26; M'k 5:22-24, 35-43; Lu 8:41, 42, 49-56).

Heals the woman with the issue of blood (M't 9:20-22; M'k 5:25-34; Lu 8:43-48).

Opens the eyes of two blind men in the house (M't 9:27-31).

A devil cast out and a dumb man cured (M't 9:32, 33).

Five thousand fed (M't 14:15-21; M'k 6:35-44; Lu 9:12-17; Joh 6:5-14).

Heals sick in Galilee (M't 14:14).

Walking on the sea (M't 14:22-33; M'k 6:45-52; Joh 6:14-21).

The daughter of the Syrophenician healed (M't 15:21-28; M'k 7:24-30).

Healing of lame, blind, dumb, and maimed, near the Sea of Galilee (M't 15:30).

Four thousand fed (M't 15:32-39; M'k 8:1-9).

One deaf and dumb cured (M'k 7:31-37).

One blind cured (M'k 8:22-36).

Lunatic child healed (M't 17:14-21; M'k 9:14-29; Lu 9:37-43).

Piece of money in the fish's mouth (M't 17:24-27).

The ten lepers cured (Lu 17:11-19).

Opening the eyes of one born blind (Joh 9).

Raising of Lazarus (Joh 11:1-54).

Woman with the spirit of infirmity cured (Lu 13:10-17).

The dropsy cured (Lu 14:1-6).

Two blind men cured near Jericho (M't 20:29-34; M'k 10:46-52; Lu 18:35-43).

The fig tree blighted (M't 21:17-22; M'k 11:12-14, 20-24).

Healing of Malchus' ear (Lu 22:49-51).

Second draught of fishes (Joh 21:6).

Not particularly described (M't 4:23, 24; 14:14; 15:30; M'k 1:34; Lu 6:17-19; 7:21, 22; Joh 2:23; 3:2). Resurrection (M't 28:6; M'k 16:6; Lu 24:6; Joh 20:1-18). Holds the vision of his disciples, that they should not recognize him (Lu 24:16, 31, 35). His appearances and disappearances (Lu 24:15, 31, 36-45; Joh 20:19, 26). Opening the understanding of his disciples (Lu 24:45). His ascension (Lu 24:51; Ac 1:9).

See Miracles.

Mission of (Isa 42:7; M't 18:12-14; Lu 12:49-53; Joh 4:25, 34; 18:37).

To fulfill the law and the prophets (Mic 5:2; M't 5:17; Ro 10:4). To be Lord of all (Ro 14:9; 15:8, 9; 2Co 5:15; Eph 4:10). To glorify the Father (Joh 17:4).

To preach the gospel (Isa 61:1; M't 4:23; 9:13; M'k 1:38; Lu 4:18, 19, 43; 5:31, 32; 8:1). Preach repentance (Lu 5:30-32; 24:47; Ac 3:26; 5:31). Bring life (Joh 6:51; 10:10; 2Co 5:14, 21). Give light (Isa 9:2; 42:6; Lu 1:78, 79; 2:30-32, 34; Joh 1:1-9; 9:39; 12:46, 47).

To condemn sin (Ro 8:3, 4). Die for sinners (Ro 5:6-8). Be propitiation for sin (M't 20:28; M'k 10:45; Lu 24:26, 46; Joh 6:51; Ac 26:23; Ro 4:24, 25; 5:6-8; 2Co 5:18; Ga 1:3, 4; 4:4, 5; Heb 2:9, 14; 9:26; 1Jo 3:5, 8; 4:8, 10). Purge sins (Zec 13:1; Mal 3:2, 3). Give remission of sins (Ac 10:43; Ro 4:25). Destroy the works of the devil (Ge 3:15; Joh 3:8).

To bring salvation (M't 1:21; 15:24; 18:12-14; Lu 19:10; Joh 3:13-17; Ro 14:15; 1Ti 1:15). Deliver from fear of death (Heb 2:15). Deliver from temptation (Heb 2:18). Comfort the contrite (Isa 61:1-3). Baptize with the Holy Spirit, and with fire (M't 3:11, 12; Lu 3:16).

Preaches to spirits in prison (1Pe 3:19; 4:9); compare (Eph 4:9).

Names, Appellations, and Titles of: Adam (1Co 15:45). Advocate (1Jo 2:1). Almighty (Re 1:8). Alpha and Omega (Re 1:8). Amen (Re 3:14). Angel (Ge 48:16; Ex 23:20, 21). Angel of his presence (Isa 63:9). Anointed (Ps 2:2). Apostle (Heb 3:1). Arm of the Lord (Isa 51:9, 10). Author and finisher of our faith (Heb 12:2).

Beginning and end of the creation of God (Re 3:14; 22:13). Beloved (Eph 1:6). Bishop (1Pe 2:25). Blessed and only Potentate (1Ti 6:15). Branch (Jer 23:5; Zec 3:8). Bread of life (Joh 6:48). Bridegroom (M't 9:15). Bright and morning star (Re 22:16). Brightness of the Father's glory (Heb 1:3).

Captain of the Lord's host (Jos 5:14). Captain of salvation (Heb 2:10). Carpenter (M'k 6:3). Carpenter's son (M't 13:55). Chief Shepherd (1Pe 5:4). Chief corner stone (1Pe 2:6). Chiefest among ten thousand (Song 5:10). Child (Isa 9:6; Lu 2:27, 43). Chosen of God (1Pe 2:4). Christ (M't 1:16; Lu 9:20). The Christ (M't 16:20; M'k 14:61). Christ, a King (Lu 23:2). Christ Jesus (Ac 19:4; Ro 3:24; 8:1; 1Co 1:2; 1Co 1:30; Heb 3:1; 1Pe 5:10, 14). Christ Jesus our Lord (1Ti 1:12; Ro 8:39). Christ of God (Lu 9:20). Christ, the chosen of God (Lu 23:35). Christ the Lord (Lu 2:11). Christ the power of God (1Co 1:24). Christ the wisdom of God (1Co 1:24). Christ, the Son of God (Ac 9:20). Christ, Son of the Blessed (M'k 14:61). Commander (Isa 55:4). Consolation of Israel (Lu 2:25). Corner stone (Eph 2:20). Counsellor (Isa 9:6). Covenant of the people (Isa 42:6).

David (Jer 30:9). Daysman (Job 9:33). Dayspring (Lu 1:78). Day star (2Pe 1:19). Deliverer (Ro 11:26). Desire of all nations (Hag 2:7). Door (Joh 10:7).

Elect (Isa 42:1). Emmanuel (Isa 7:14). Ensign (Isa 11:10). Eternal life (1Jo 5:20). Everlasting Father (Isa 9:6).

Faithful and True (Re 19:11). Faithful witness (Re 1:5). Faithful and true witness (Re 3:14). Finisher of faith (Heb 12:2). First and last (Re 1:17; 2:8; 22:13). First begotten (Heb 1:6). First begotten of the dead (Re 1:5). Firstborn (Ps 89:27). Foundation (Isa 28:16). Fountain (Zec 13:1). Forerunner (Heb 6:20). Friend of sinners (M't 11:19).

Gift of God (Joh 4:10). Glory of Israel (Lu 2:32). God (Joh 1:1). God blessed for ever (Ro 9:5). God manifest in the flesh (1Ti 3:16). God of Israel, the Saviour (Isa 45:15). God of the whole earth (Isa 54:5). God our Saviour (1Ti 2:3). God's dear Son (Col 1:13). God with us (M't 1:23). Good Master (M't 19:16). Governor (M't 2:6). Great shepherd of the sheep (Heb 13:20).

Head of the church (Eph 5:23). Heir of all things (Heb 1:2). High priest (Heb 4:14). Head of every man (1Co 11:3). Head of the church (Col 1:18). Head of the corner (M't 21:42). Holy child Jesus (Ac 4:30). Holy one (Ps 16:10; Ac 3:14). Holy one of God (M'k 1:24). Holy one of Israel (Isa 41:14; 54:5). Holy thing (Lu 1:35). Hope [our] (1Ti 1:1). Horn of salvation (Lu 1:69).

I am (Joh 8:58). Image of God (Heb 1:3). Israel (Isa 49:3).

Jehovah (Isa 40:3). Jehovah's fellow (Zec 13:7). Jesus (M't 1:21). Jesus Christ (M't 1:1; Joh 1:17; 17:3; Ac 2:38; 4:10; 9:34; 10:36; 16:18; Ro 1:1, 3, 6; 2:16; 5:15, 17; 6:3; 1Co 1:1, 4; 2:2; 2Co 1:19; 4:6; 13:5; Ga 2:16; Ph'p 1:8; 2:11; 1Ti 1:15; Heb 13:8; 1Jo 1:7; 2:1). Jesus Christ our Lord (Ro 1:3; 6:11, 23; 1Co 1:9; 7:25). Jesus Christ our Saviour (Tit 3:6). Jesus of Nazareth (M'k 1:24; Lu 24:19). Jesus of Nazareth, King of the Jews (Joh 19:19). Jesus, the King of the Jews (M't 27:37). Jesus, the Son of God (Heb 4:14). Jesus, the Son of Joseph (Joh 6:42). Judge (Ac 10:42). Just man (M't 27:19). Just one (Ac 3:14; 7:52; 22:14). Just person (M't 27:24).

King (M't 21:5). King of Israel (Joh 1:49). King of the Jews (M't 2:2). King of saints (Re 15:3). King of kings (1Ti 6:15; Re 17:14). King of glory (Ps 24:7-10). King of Zion (M't 21:5). King over all the earth (Zec 14:9).

Lamb (Re 5:6, 8; 6:16; 7:9, 10, 17; 12:11; 13:8, 11; 14:1, 4; 15:3; 17:14; 19:7, 9; 21:9, 14, 22, 23, 27). Lamb of God (Joh 1:29). Lawgiver (Isa 33:22). Leader (Isa 55:4). Life (Joh 14:6). Light (Joh 8:12). Light, everlasting (Isa 60:20). Light of the world (Joh 8:12). Light to the Gentiles (Isa 42:6). Light, true (Joh 1:9). Living bread (Joh 6:51). Living stone (1Pe 2:4). Lion of the tribe of

Judah (Re 5:5). Lord (Ro 1:3). Lord of lords (Re 17:14; 19:16). Lord of all (Ac 10:36). Lord our righteousness (Jer 23:6). Lord God Almighty (Re 15:3). Lord from heaven (1Co 15:47). Lord and Saviour Jesus Christ (2Pe 1:11; 3:18). Lord Christ (Col 3:24). Lord Jesus (Ac 7:59; Col 3:17; 1Th 4:2). Lord Jesus Christ (Ac 11:17; 16:31; 20:21; Ro 5:1, 11; 13:14). Lord Jesus Christ our Saviour (Tit 1:4). Lord of glory (Jas 2:1). Lord of Hosts (Isa 44:6). Lord, mighty in battle (Ps 24:8). Lord of the dead and living (Ro 14:9). Lord of the sabbath (M'k 2:28). Lord over all (Ro 10:12). Lord's Christ (Lu 2:26). Lord, strong and mighty (Ps 24:8). Lord, the, our righteousness (Jer 23:6). Lord, your holy one (Isa 43:15). Lord, your redeemer (Isa 43:14).

Man Christ Jesus (1Ti 2:5). Man of sorrows (Isa 53:3). Master (M't 23:8). Mediator (1Ti 2:5). Messenger of the covenant (Mal 3:1). Messiah (Joh 1:41). Messiah the Prince (Da 9:25). Mighty God (Isa 9:6). Mighty one of Israel (Isa 30:29). Mighty one of Jacob (Isa 49:26). Mighty to save (Isa 63:1). Minister of the sanctuary (Heb 8:2). Morning star (Re 22:16). Most holy (Da 9:24). Most mighty (Ps 45:3).

Nazarene (M't 2:23).

Offspring of David (Re 22:16). Only begotten (Joh 1:14). Only begotten of the Father (Joh 1:14). Only begotten Son (Joh 1:18). Only wise God, our Saviour (Jude 25).

Passover (1Co 5:7). Plant of renown (Eze 34:29). Potentate (1Ti 6:15). Power of God (1Co 1:24). Physician (M't 9:12). Precious corner stone (Isa 28:16). Priest (Heb 7:17). Prince (Ac 5:31). Prince of life (Ac 3:15). Prince of Peace (Isa 9:6). Prince of the kings of the earth (Re 1:5). Prophet (De 18:15, 18; M't 21:11; Lu 24:19). Propitiation (1Jo 2:2).

Rabbi (Joh 1:49). Rabboni (Joh 20:16). Ransom (1Ti 2:6). Redeemer (Isa 59:20). Resurrection and life (Joh 11:25). Redemption (1Co 1:30). Righteous branch (Jer 23:5). Righteous judge (2Ti 4:8). Righteous servant (Isa 53:11). Righteousness (1Co 1:30). Rock (1Co 10:4). Rock of offence (1Pe 2:8). Root of David (Re 5:5; 22:16). Root of Jesse (Isa 11:10). Rose of Sharon (Song 2:1). Ruler in Israel (Mic 5:2).

Salvation (Lu 2:30). Sanctification (1Co 1:30). Sanctuary (Isa 8:14). Saviour (Lu 2:11). Saviour, Jesus Christ (2Ti 1:10; Tit 2:13; 2Pe 1:1). Saviour of the body (Eph 5:23). Saviour of the world (1Jo 4:14). Sceptre (Nu 24:17). Second man (1Co 15:47). Seed of David (2Ti 2:8). Seed of the woman (Ge 3:15). Servant (Isa 42:1). Servant of rulers (Isa 49:7). Shepherd (M'k 14:27). Shepherd and bishop of souls (1Pe 2:25). Shepherd, chief (1Pe 5:4). Shepherd, good (Joh 10:11). Shepherd, great (Heb 13:20). Shepherd of Israel (Ps 80:1). Shiloh (Ge 49:10). Son of the Father (2Jo 3). Son of God (see Jesus, Son of God). Son of Man (see Jesus, Son of Man). Son of the blessed (M'k 14:61). Son of the highest (Lu 1:32). Son of David (M't 9:27). Star (Nu 24:17). Son of righteousness (Mal 4:2). Surety (Heb 7:22). Stone (M't 21:42). Stone of stumbling (1Pe 2:8). Sure foundation (Isa 28:16).

Teacher (Joh 3:2). True God (1Jo 5:20). True vine (Joh 15:1). Truth (Joh 14:6).

Unspeakable gift (2Co 9:15).

Very Christ (Ac 9:22). Vine (Joh 15:1).

Way (Joh 14:6). Which is, which was, which is to come (Re 1:4). Wisdom (Pr 8:12). Wisdom of God (1Co 1:24). Witness (Isa 55:4; Re 1:5). Wonderful (Isa 9:6). Word (Joh 1:1). Word of God (Re 19:13). Word of life (1Jo 1:1).

Those who use his name must depart from evil (2Ti 2:19).

In His Name: 1Co 6:11; Ph'p 2:9; Col 3:17; Re 19:16. Prayer (Joh 14:13; 16:23, 24, 26; Eph 5:20; Col 3:17; Heb 13:15). Miracles performed (Ac 3:6; 4:10; 19:13); baptism (M't 28:19; Ac 2:38). Preaching (Lu 24:47). Faith (M't 12:21; Joh 1:12; 2:23). Remission of sins (Lu 24:47; Ac 10:43; 1Jo 2:12). Life (Joh 20:31). Salvation (Ac 4:12; 10:43).

See Intercession of, above; and Priesthood of, below.

Obedience of: Foretold (Ps 40:8; Isa 11:5, 6; Heb 10:7-9). To his parents (Lu 2:51). To God (Lu 2:49; Joh 4:34; 5:30, 36; 6:38; 8:29, 46, 55; 9:4; 14:31; 15:10; 17:4).

Exemplified: In his baptism (M't 3:15). Sufferings (M't 26:39, 42; M'k 14:36; Lu 22:42; Heb 5:8). Death (Joh 19:30; Ph'p 2:8).

Omnipotence of (Ps 45:3-5; 110:3; Isa 9:6; 40:10; 50:2, 3; Isa 63:1; M't 6:7; 28:18; 12:13, 28, 29; M'k 3:27; Lu 5:17; 9:1; 11:20-22; Joh 2:10; 5:21, 28, 29; 10:17, 18, 28; Ph'p 3:20, 21; Col 1:17; 2Th 1:9; 1Ti 6:16; Heb 1:3; 7:25; 2Pe 1:16; Re 1:8; 3:7; 5:12).

Omnipresence of (M't 18:20; 28:20; Joh 3:13; Eph 1:23).

Omniscience of (Re 2:18,23; 5:5, 12; Col 2:3). Manifested in his knowledge, of the Father (M't 11:27; Joh 7:29); men's hearts (M't 9:4; 12:25; 17:27; 22:18; M'k 2:8; Lu 5:22; 6:8; 9:46-48; 11:17; 22:10-12 w M'k 14:13-15; Joh 1:48; 2:24, 25; 4:16-19, 28, 29; 5:42; 6:64; 13:11; 21:17); future events (M't 24:25; Joh 13:1, 3, 10; 16:30, 32; 18:4; 21:6); the coin in the fish's mouth (M't 17:27); the presence of schools of fishes (Lu 5:4-7; Joh 21:6).

Our example (Joh 10:4; Heb 3:1, 2; 1Jo 2:6; Re 14:4). In meekness (M't 11:29; Heb 12:2-4; 1Pe 2:21-24). Humility (Lu 22:26, 27; Joh 13:13-15, 34; 2Co 10:1; Ph'p 2:5-8). Ministering (M't 20:28; M'k 10:43-45; 2Co 8:9 with context; Ga 6:2). Loving others (Joh 13:34; Eph 5:2). Character (Ro 8:29; 15:2, 3, 5, 7; 1Pe 1:15, 16; 1Jo 3:1-3, 16; 4:17). Enduring suffering (1Pe 3:17, 18).

Parables of: The wise and foolish builders (M't 7:24-27; Lu 6:47, 49).

Two debtors (Lu 7:41-47).

The rich fool (Lu 12:16-21).

The servants waiting for their lord (Lu 12:35-40).

Barren fig tree (Lu 13:6-9).

The sower (M't 13:3-9, 18-23; M'k 4:1-9, 14-20; Lu 8:5-8, 11-15).

The tares (M't 13:24-30, 36-43).

Seed growing secretly (M'k 4:26-29).

Mustard seed (M't 13:31, 32; M'k 4:30-32; Lu 13:18, 19).

Leaven (M't 13:33; Lu 13:20, 21).

Hid treasure (M't 13:44).

Pearl of great price (M't 13:45, 46).

Drawnet (M't 13:47-50).

Unmerciful servant (M't 18:23-35).

Good samaritan (Lu 10:30-37).

Friend at midnight (Lu 11:5-8).

Good shepherd (Joh 10:1-16).

Great supper (Lu 14:15-24).

Lost sheep (M't 18:12-14; Lu 15:3-7).

Lost piece of money (Lu 15:8-10).

The prodigal and his brother (Lu 15:11-32).

The unjust steward (Lu 16:1-9).

Rich man and Lazarus (Lu 16:19-31).

Importunate widow (Lu 18:1-8).

Pharisee and publican (Lu 18:9-14).

Laborers in the vineyard (M't 20:1-16).

The pounds (Lu 19:11-27).

The two sons (M't 21:28-32).

Wicked husbandmen (M't 21:33-44; M'k 12:1-12; Lu 20:9-18).

Marriage of the king's son (M't 22:1-14).

Fig tree leafing (M't 24:32; M'k 13:28, 29).

Man taking a far journey (M'k 13:34-37).

Ten virgins (M't 25:1-13).

Talents (M't 25:14-30).

The vine (Joh 15:1-5).

Passion of: See Sufferings of.

Peccability of: See Temptation of.

Perfections of (Col 2:3). Was the image of God (2Co 4:4; Col 1:15). All the fullness of the Father dwelt in him (Col 1:19; 2:9). Was righteous (Isa 11:5; Joh 7:18; 2Co 1:19). Guileless (Isa 53:9). Sinless (M't 27:3, 4; Ac 13:28; 2Co 5:21). Faithful (2Th 3:3; 2Ti 2:13; Heb 3:2). Full of grace and truth (Joh 1:14, 18; Col 2:3). Just in judgment (Joh 5:30).

Perfected through sufferings (Heb 2:10).

Perfections of typified (Le 21:17-21).

Persecutions of, see Persecution.

Popularity of (M't 4:24; 8:1; 13:2; 14:13, 35; 19:1, 2; 21:8-11; M'k 1:33; 2:2; 3:7, 20; 5:21; 6:33, 55, 56; 10:1; 11:8-10; 12:37; Lu 4:14, 15, 42; 5:1; 9:11; 12:1; 19:35-38; Joh 6:15; 12:12, 13, 19).

Power of (Ps 110:3; 1Co 1:24).

Called Mighty God (Isa 9:6). Has all power (M't 28:18; Joh 10:17, 18, 28; 17:2; Ph'p 3:20, 21; 2Th 1:9; 1Ti 6:16; 2Pe 1:16; Re 3:7; 5:12).

Manifested: In creation (Joh 1:3, 10; Col 1:16). Salvation of men (Heb 7:25). Upholding all things (Col 1:17; Heb

1:3). Forgiving sins (M't 9:2, 6; M'k 2:5, 10; Lu 5:20, 24; Col 3:13). Healing diseases (M't 8:3, 16; 9:6, 7; 12:13; M'k 5:27-34; Lu 5:17; 6:19; Ac 10:38). Casting out demons (M't 8:16; 12:28, 29; M'k 3:27; Lu 11:20-22). Stilling the tempest (M't 8:27). Giving apostles power to heal (M't 10:1; M'k 6:7; Lu 9:11). Resurrection (Joh 2:19; 10:17, 18).

Prayers of (M't 11:25, 26; Lu 3:21; 11:1). In secret (M't 14:23; M'k 1:35; 6:46; Lu 5:16; 6:12; 9:18, 28, 29). At the grave of Lazarus (Joh 11:41, 42). For Peter (Lu 22:32). For believers (Joh 17:1-26). In Gethsemane (M't 26:36-39; M'k 14:32-35; Lu 22:41-44; Heb 5:7). On the cross (M't 27:46; Lu 23:34, 46).

Preexistence of: Was in the beginning (Joh 1:1-3; 1Jo 2:13, 14; Re 3:14). Came from heaven (Joh 3:13; 6:62; Ph'p 2:5-7). Came from the Father (Joh 13:3; 16:28). Was before creation (Joh 17:5, 24; 2Ti 1:9; 1Jo 1:1, 2; 1Pe 1:20). Maker of all things (Joh 1:3; 1Co 8:6; Col 1:15-17; Heb 1:1, 2, 8-12; Re 4:11). Before Abraham (Joh 8:56-58). With the Israelites in the wilderness (1Co 10:4, 9; Jude 5).

Prescience of: See Omniscience of.

Priesthood of: Appointed and called by God (Heb 3:1, 2; 5:4, 5), after the order of Melchizedek (Ps 110:4, w Heb 5:6; 6:20; 7:15-17); superior to Aaron and the Levitical priests (Heb 7:11, 16, 22; 8:1, 2, 6). Consecrated with an oath (Heb 7:20, 21). Has an unchangeable priesthood (Heb 7:23, 28). Is of unblemished purity (Heb 7:26, 28), faithful (Heb 3:2). Needed no sacrifice for himself (Heb 7:27).

Offered himself a sacrifice (Heb 9:14, 26). His sacrifice superior to all others (Heb 9:13, 14, 23). Offered sacrifice but once (Heb 7:27). Made reconciliation (Heb 2:17). Obtained redemption for us (Heb 9:12). Entered into heaven (Heb 4:14; 10:12). Sympathizes with saints (Heb 2:18; 4:15). Intercedes (Heb 7:25; 9:24). Blesses (Nu 6:23-26, w Ac 3:26). On his throne (Zec 6:13). Appointment of, an encouragement to steadfastness (Heb 4:14).

Typified: Melchizedek (Ge 14:18-20). Aaron and his sons (Ex 40:12-15).

Promises of, to his disciples: Of everlasting life (M't 19:28; M'k 10:29, 30; Lu 18:29, 30; 23:43; Joh 5:25-29; 6:54, 57, 58; 12:25, 26). Of power (Lu 24:49; Joh 7:38, 39; Ac 1:4-8). Of the comforter (Joh 14:16, 26; 15:26, 27; 16:7-14). Of his mediatorship (Joh 16:23, 24, 26).

Prophecies concerning (Ge 18:18; 22:18; 26:4; 28:14; Isa 53:2-12; M't 8:17; Ga 3:8, 16).

Described in prophecy as: The branch (Isa 11:1 w Ro 15:12; Jer 23:5, 6; 33:15; Zec 3:8); corner stone (Ps 118:22; Isa 28:16); ensign to the people (Isa 11:10); fountain for sin (Zec 13:1); king (Zec 9:9); leader and commander (Isa 55:4, 5); light to Gentiles (Isa 42:6, 7; 49:6; 52:10, 15; Lu 2:31, 32); Lord (Isa 40:3, 5; 35:2; Jer 31:34; Mal 3:1-3; Lu 3:4); God's elect, RV chosen (Isa 42:1); priest (Ps 110:4); prophet (De 18:15, 18; Ac 3:22-24); redeemer (Isa 59:20); ruler in Israel (Mic 5:2); savior (Isa 62:10, 11; M't 1:21; Lu 1:31); seed of woman (Ge 3:15); shepherd (Isa 40:11; Eze 34:23); son of man (Da 7:13, 14).

Future Glory and Power of (Re 19:11, 12, 15). To have universal dominion (Ps 72:5, 8-11, 17, 19; Isa 2:2-4; 9:6, 7; 60:1-9; Mic 4:1-4; according to many learned interpreters Da 2:35, 44; 7:18, 22, 27). To be King of kings (Ps 72:5, 8-11, 17, 19; Re 1:5-7; 11:15; 12:10; 17:14; 19:16; 20:4, 6). To sit at right hand of God (M'k 14:62; 1Pe 3:22). To be judge (Jude 14, 15; Re 2:23; 6:16, 17; 14:14-16).

Prophet (De 18:15, 18; M't 21:11, 46; Lu 7:16; 13:33; 24:19; Joh 4:19; 6:14; 7:40; 9:17; Ac 3:22, 23; 7:37). Foretold (Isa 52:7; Na 1:15). Anointed with the Holy Ghost (Isa 42:1; 61:1, w Lu 4:18; Joh 3:34). Reveals God (M't 11:27; Joh 3:2, 13, 34; 17:6, 14, 26; Heb 1:1, 2). Declared his doctrine to be that of the Father (Joh 8:26, 28; 12:49, 50; 14:10, 24; 15:15; 17:8, 26). Foretold things to come (M't 24:3-35; Lu 19:41-44). Faithful (Lu 4:43; Joh 17:8; Heb 3:2; Re 1:5; 3:14). Abounded in wisdom (Lu 2:40, 47, 52; Col 2:3). Mighty in deed and word (M't 13:54; M'k 1:27; Lu 4:32; Joh 7:46). Unostentatious in his teaching (Isa 42:2; M't 12:17-20). God commands us to hear (De 18:15; Ac 3:22). God will severely visit neglect of (De 18:10; Ac 3:23; Heb 2:3).

Received: Multitudes attend his ministry (M't 8:1; 13:2; 14:13, 35; 19:1, 2; M'k 1:37, 45; 2:2, 15; 3:7, 20, 21; 4:1; 5:21; 10:1; 11:18; 12:37; Lu 9:11; 12:1; 19:48; 21:38; M'k 11:18; Joh 6:2; 8:2).

Many believe on him (M't 4:24; 21:8-11, 15; M'k 2:12; 6:55, 56; 11:8-10; Lu 6:17-19; 7:16, 17; 19:36-38, 47, 48; 23:27; Joh 2:11, 23; 4:45; 8:30; 10:41, 42; 11:45-48; 12:9, 11-13, 18-21, 42).

Authority of his teaching confessed (M'k 1:22; Lu 4:32; Joh 3:2; 7:46).

With astonishment and gladness (M't 9:8, 27, 28, 33; 13:54; 15:31; M'k 1:27; 2:12; 5:42; 7:37; Lu 4:36, 37, 42; 5:26; 13:17; 18:43; Joh 7:31, 40-44; 9:17, 24, 25, 29, 30, 33; 11:37).

Instances of his being received: By Matthew (M't 9:9); by Peter and other fishermen (M'k 1:16-20; Lu 5:3-11); by Philip (Joh 1:43, 45); by Nathanael (Joh 1:45-50); by Zacchaeus (Lu 19:1-10); by thief on the cross (Lu 23:40-42); by three thousand at Pentecost (Ac 2:41; 4:4).

Redeemer, see Savior, below. See also Redemption.

Rejected (Lu 9:26; 10:16; 11:23; Heb 6:4, 5, 6; 1Pe 2:4, 7, 8; 1Jo 2:22, 23; 4:3; 2Jo 7).

By Jews (M't 13:54-58 w Isa 6:9, 10; M't 23:37; M'k 6:3-6; Lu 7:34; 13:34; 19:27, 42; 22:67; Joh 1:11; 5:38, 40, 43; 7:3-5, 12, 13, 15, 25-27; 8:13, 21, 22, 24, 45-47, 53; 9:16, 17, 24; 10:20, 21, 24, 33; 11:46-48; 12:37, 48; Ac 13:46; 18:5, 6; 22:18; 28:24, 25, 27; Ro 3:3; 9:31, 32; 10:16, 21; 1Co 1:8). By Gadarenes (M't 8:34; M'k 5:17; Lu 8:37). By Greeks (1Co 1:23). By followers (Joh 6:36, 60-66).

Prophecies concerning his rejection (Ps 2:1-3; 118:22; Isa 53:1-4; Lu 9:44).

Foretold by himself (M't 11:16-19; M'k 9:12; Lu 4:23-29; 7:31-35; 17:25; Joh 15:18, 20, 24); in the parable of the feast (Lu 14:16-24 w M't 22:2-14); in the parable of the house built on the sand (M't 7:26, 27; Lu 6:46-49).

Punishment for rejection of, foretold (M't 8:12; 10:14, 15, 33; 12:38-45; M'k 12:1-12; 16:16; Lu 20:9-18; 2Ti 2:12; Heb 6:6; 10:29; 2Pe 2:1).

Relation of, to the Father (Ps 110:1; M't 11:27; 1Th 5:18; Heb 2:9).

Called God his Father (M't 20:23; 26:39; M'k 13:32; Re 2:27).

In the beginning with God (Joh 1:1, 2, 14). Sent of God (Joh 3:34, 35; 4:34; 6:27, 32, 33, 38-40, 44-46; 7:16, 28, 29, 33; 8:16, 19, 28, 29, 38, 40, 42, 49, 54, 55; 9:4; 11:41, 42; 12:44, 49, 50; 17:1-10, 24-26; 1Co 1:30; Heb 3:2; 1Pe 2:4, 23; 1Jo 4:9, 10, 14). Endued with the Holy Spirit (Isa 42:1; 61:1; Mic 5:4; Ac 10:38). Son of God (Joh 5:19-26, 37, 45; Ro 8:32; 15:6; Heb 1:2, 3; 5:5-10; 2Pe 1:17). One with the Father (Joh 10:18, 25, 30, 32, 33, 36-38; 14:7, 9-14, 20, 24; 15:23-26). Subject unto the Father (Ps 110:1; M'k 10:40; Joh 20:17; Ac 2:22, 33, 36; 3:13, 26; 4:27; 1Co 15:24, 27, 28). Image of God (2Co 4:4, 6; Ph'p 2:6; Col 1:15, 19). God raised him from the dead (Ac 13:37; Ro 1:4; Eph 1:17, 20-22; 1Pe 1:21).

Ascended unto the Father (Lu 24:51; Joh 16:5, 10, 28; Ac 1:9-11; Re 3:12, 21).

See Divinity of, Humanity of, and Divine Sonship of, above.

Resurrection of: Prophecies concerning (Ps 2:7; 16:9, 10; Isa 55:3; Ac 13:33, 34).

Foretold by himself (M't 12:40; 16:4, 21; 17:23; 20:19; 26:32; 27:52, 53, 63; M'k 8:31; 9:9, 10; 10:34; 14:58; Lu 9:22; 18:33; 24:7, 46; Joh 2:19, 21, 22).

Certified: By angels (M't 28:6, 7; M'k 16:6, 7; Lu 24:5-7); by Mary Magdalene (M't 28:1-8; M'k 16:10; Lu 24:10; Joh 20:18); by Cleopas and his fellow disciple (M'k 16:12, 13; Lu 24:13-35); by Luke (Ac 1:3, 22); by Peter (Ac 2:24, 31, 32 w Ps 16:9, 10; Ac 3:15; 4:10, 33; 5:30-32; 10:40, 41; 1Pe 1:3, 21; 3:18, 21); by Paul (Ac 13:30-34 w Ps 2:7; Ac 17:2, 3, 31; 26:23, 26; Ro 1:4; 4:24, 25; 5:10; 6:4, 5, 9, 10; 8:11, 34; 1Co 6:14; 15:3, 4, 20-23 w vs 5-8, 12-20; 2Co 4:10, 11, 14; 5:15; 13:4; Ga 1:1; Eph 1:20; Ph'p 3:10; Col 1:18; 2:12; 1Th 1:10; 4:14; 2Ti 2:8); by the author of the epistle to the Hebrews (Heb 13:20); by John (Re 1:5, 18).

Appears to the eleven apostles after his resurrection (M'k 16:14; Lu 24:36-51; Joh 20:19-29).

For our justification (Ro 4:25). For our salvation (Ro 5:10; 10:9).

An earnest of the general resurrection (Ro 6:5; 1Co 6:14; 15:21-23; 2Co 4:14; 1Th 4:14; 1Pe 1:3).

The theme of apostolic preaching (Ac

2:24, 31, 32; 3:15; 4:10, 33; 5:30-32; 10:40, 41; 17:2, 3).

See Resurrection.

Reticence of (Isa 53:7; M't 26:63; 27:12, 14; M'k 14:61; 15:4, 5; Joh 19:9; 1Pe 2:23).

Revelations by: Concerning his kingdom (M't 8:11, 12; 10:23, 34; 13:24-50; 16:18, 28; 21:43, 44; 24:14; M'k 9:1; 16:17, 18; Lu 9:27; 12:40-53; 13:24-35; 17:20-37; Joh 4:21, 23; 5:25-29; 6:39, 54; 12:35; 13:19; 14:29; 16:4). His rejection by the Jews (M't 21:33-44; Lu 17:25). His betrayal (M't 26:21, 23-25). His crucifixion (Joh 3:14; 8:28; 12:32 w Lu 24:6, 7). Judgments upon the Jews (M't 23:37-39). The destruction of the temple, and Jerusalem (M't 24; M'k 13; Lu 19:41-44). The destruction of Capernaum (M't 11:23; Lu 10:15).

Concerning persecutions of Christians (M't 23:34-36). His being forsaken by his disciples (Joh 16:32). Lazarus (Joh 11:4, 11, 23, 40). Peter (Joh 21:18-23). Fame of the woman who anointed his head (M't 26:13; M'k 14:8, 9). False christs (M't 24:4, 5, 23-26; M'k 13:5, 6, 21-23; Lu 17:23, 24; 21:8). Things to come (Re 1:1).

Concerning his death and resurrection (M't 12:39, 40; 16:21; 17:12, 22, 23; 20:18, 19; 21:33-39; 26:2, 18, 21, 23, 24, 45, 46; 27:63; M'k 8:31; 9:31; 10:32-34; Lu 9:22-24; 17:25; 18:31-33; 22:15, 37; Joh 2:19; 10:15, 17; 12:7, 23, 32; 13:18-27; 14:19; 16:20, 32). His ascension (Joh 7:33, 34; 8:21; 13:33; 16:10, 16).

Righteousness of, see Holiness of, above.

Salvation by, see Salvation.

Saviour (M't 1:21; Ac 5:31; 13:23, 38, 39, 47; 15:11; 16:31; 1Co 1:30; 15:57; Eph 5:23; Ph'p 3:20; 1Ti 1:1, 15; 2Ti 1:9, 10, 12; 2:10; 3:15; Tit 1:4; Heb 2:3; 5:9; 2Pe 1:11; 2:20; 1Jo 3:5; 4:9, 14; 5:11-13).

Through his death (Ro 3:25; 4:25; 5:1, 6, 8-10; Ga 1:4; 2:20; Eph 2:13-18, 20; 5:2, 25, 26; Col 1:12-14; 1Th 1:10; 5:9, 10; Tit 2:13, 14; 1Pe 1:18, 19; 3:18; 1Jo 4:10).

Through his resurrection (Ac 3:26; Ro 10:9; 1Co 15:17; 1Pe 3:21); his intercession (Heb 7:22, 25).

By redemption (Ro 3:24). By reconciliation (Ro 5:15, 17-19, 21; 2Co 5:18, 19, 21; Eph 2:7, 13-18, 20; Heb 2:17).

The only (Ac 4:12; 1Co 3:11).

Prophecies concerning Him as Saviour (Ps 72:4, 12-14, 17; Isa 42:6, 7; 49:6, 8, 9; 59:16, 17, 20; 61:1-3; Zec 9:9; Mal 4:2; Lu 1:68-77; 4:18, 19).

Illustrated: By parables of lost sheep, and lost coin (M't 18:12, 13; Lu 15:1-10).

Testified to: By angels (Lu 2:11). Simeon (Lu 2:30-32). Himself (Lu 5:31, 32 w M't 9:12, 13; Lu 19:10; Joh 5:33, 34, 40; 6:27, 32, 33, 35, 37, 39, 51, 53-58; 7:37-39; 8:12; 9:5, 39; 10:7, 9-11, 14-16, 27, 28; 11:25, 26; 12:47; 14:6; 17:2, 3, 12). John (Joh 1:29). The people of Sychar (Joh 4:42). The heavenly host (Re 5:5-14).

See Death of, Design of, above.

Second coming of (M't 26:64; Joh 14:28, 29; 21:22; Ac 1:11; 3:20, 21; 1Co 11:26; Ph'p 3:20, 21; 1Th 1:10; 2:19; 3:13; 4:15-17; 2Th 2:1-5, 8; 1Ti 6:14, 15; Tit 2:13; 2Pe 3:3, 4).

At an unexpected time (M't 24:3, 27, 30, 31, 37-39, 42-44; 24:36; 25:6, 10, 13, 19; M'k 13:1-37; Lu 12:37-40; 17:22-30; 21:5-35; 1Th 5:2, 3, 23; 2Pe 3:8-14; Re 16:15; 22:20).

In heavenly glory (M't 16:27; 25:31; M'k 8:38; 13:26, 27; 14:62; Lu 9:26; 21:27).

To judge the world (M't 16:27; 25:31-46; Lu 19:12, 13, 15; 1Co 1:7, 8; 4:5; 2Th 1:7-10; 2Ti 4:1; Re 22:12).

To receive his saints (Joh 14:3, 18; 1Co 15:23; Col 3:4; 2Th 1:10; 2Ti 4:8; Heb 9:28; 1Pe 5:4; 1Jo 3:2).

Exhortations in view of (Jas 5:7-9; 1Pe 1:7, 13; 4:13; 1Jo 2:28; Re 3:11).

Shepherd: Jesus the True: Foretold (Ge 49:24; Isa 40:11; Eze 34:23; 37:24). The chief (1Pe 5:4). The good (Joh 10:11, 14). The great (Mic 5:4; Heb 13:20).

His sheep he knows (Joh 10:14, 27). He calls (Joh 10:3). He gathers (Isa 40:11; Joh 10:16). He guides (Ps 23:3; Joh 10:3, 4). He feeds (Ps 23:1, 2; Joh 10:9). He cherishes tenderly (Isa 40:11). He protects and preserves (Jer 31:10; Eze 34:10; Zec 9:16; Joh 10:28). He laid down his life for (Zec 13:7; M't 26:31; Joh 10:11, 15; Ac 20:28). He gives eternal life to (Joh 10:28).

Typified: David (1Sa 16:11).

Son of God. Acclaimed by God (Ps 2:4 w Ac 13:13; Ps 89:26, 27; M't 3:17; 17:5; M'k 1:11; 9:7; Lu 3:22; 9:35; 2Pe 1:17). Proclaimed by angels (Lu 1:32, 35; Re 2:18). Claimed by Christ (M't 10:40; 11:27; 15:13; 18:10, 19; 20:23; 21:37; 26:53, 63, 64; 27:43; M'k 14:61, 62; Lu 10:22; 20:13; 22:29, 70; Joh 5:17, 19-37; 6:27, 38, 40, 46, 57, 69; 7:17, 28, 29; 8:16, 19, 26-29, 38-42, 49, 54; 9:35-37; 10:15-18, 29, 30, 36-38; 11:4, 27, 41; 12:49, 50; 14:7-13, 16, 20, 24, 28, 31; 15:1, 8-10, 23, 24; 16:5, 15, 27, 28, 32; 17:1; 20:17, 21, 31); as equality with the Father (M't 10:40; 11:27; Lu 10:22; Joh 1:1, 2; 8:16, 19; 10:15-18, 29, 30, 36-38; 14:7-13, 16, 20, 24, 28, 31; 15:23, 24; 16:15).

Recognized, by the disciples (M't 14:33; 16:15-17); Peter (M't 16:15-17); the centurion (M't 27:54; M'k 15:39); Nathanael (Joh 1:49, 50); Martha (Joh 11:27); Satan, who tempted him (M't 4:3, 6; Lu 4:3, 9); unclean spirits or devils (M'k 3:11; 5:7; Lu 4:41; 8:28).

Claim to, recognized by the Jews (M't 27:43; Joh 19:7); high priest (M'k 14:61, 62).

Testified to, by Mark (M'k 1:1); Luke (Ac 3:13); John (Joh 1:1, 2, 14, 18, 34; 3:16-18, 34-36; 13:3; 1Jo 1:7; 2:22-24; 3:8, 23; 4:9, 10, 14; 5:5, 9, 10, 13, 20; 2Jo 3); Paul (Ro 1:3, 4, 9; 8:3, 29, 32; 1Co 1:9; 15:24, 27, 28; 2Co 1:3, 19; Ga 1:16; 4:4; Eph 1:3; 3:14; Col 1:3, 15, 19; 3:17; 1Th 1:10); in epistle to the Hebrews (Heb 1:1-3, 5; 4:14; 5:5, 8; 6:6; 7:3; 10:29).

Belief in, basis of eternal life (Joh 1:1, 2, 12; 3:16-18, 34-36; 6:40; 20:31; 1Jo 2:22-24; 3:23; 5:5, 9, 10, 13, 20); basis for growth and purity (Joh 15:1, 8-10; 1Jo 1:7). Denial of, basis of antichrist (1Jo 2:22-24).

See Deity of, above; Relation of, to the Father, above. See Son of God.

Son of Man. Used in a Messianic sense (Da 7:13, 14).

Used by Jesus: Of Himself (M't 11:19 w 27; 16:13; M'k 14:21, 41; Lu 6:22; 7:34; 18:31; Joh 1:51; 3:13). In a Messianic sense, of His coming (M't 10:23; 16:27, 28; 24:27, 30, 37, 44; 25:13, 31; M'k 13:26; Lu 9:26; 12:40; 17:22, 24, 26, 30; 18:8; 21:27); of His kingdom (M't 16:28; 19:28; M'k 8:38; 14:62); of His judgment (M't 24:29, 30; M'k 8:38; Lu 9:26; 12:8, 10; 21:36); of His Lordship or deity (M't 12:8; 13:37, 41; 16:13 w 16, 27, 28; 19:28; 24:27; M'k 2:28; Lu 6:5; 12:8, 10; 17:22, 24; 21:36; 22:69; 3:13; 6:27, 53, 62; Joh 12:23; 13:31); His suffering and death (M't 12:40; 17:9, 12, 22; 20:18, 28; 26:2, 24, 25; M'k 8:31; 9:9, 12, 31; 10:33, 34, 45; 14:21, 41; Lu 9:22, 44; 11:30; 17:22-26; 18:31; 22:22, 48; 24:7; Joh 3:14; 8:28; 12:23; 13:31); His resurrection (M't 12:40; 17:9, 22, 23; 20:18, 19; M'k 8:31; 9:9, 31; 10:33, 34; Joh 6:62; 12:23; 13:31).

Of Himself, as the supreme man (M't 8:20; 12:32); a servant of man (M't 20:28; M'k 10:45; Lu 9:56, 58); the forgiver of sins (M't 9:6; M'k 2:10; Lu 5:24; 12:10); the Redeemer (M't 18:11; 20:28; Lu 12:8; 19:10; 6:27, 53).

Used by, the angel at the empty tomb, in quoting Christ (Lu 24:7); Stephen, in his vision of Jesus (Ac 7:56); John, in his vision of Jesus Christ (Re 1:13; 14:14).

Synonymous with *Christ,* as used by, Caiaphas the high priest (M't 26:63 w 65; M'k 14:61, 62); the religious leaders (Lu 22:70 w 66-71 & 23:35); the people in questioning Him (Joh 12:34).

The title is a reference to the humanity or human nature of Jesus, designating him as the God-Man (M't 8:20 & 12:32).

See Son of Man.

Sovereignty of, see King, above; Lordship of, above.

Sufferings of. Foretold: By the psalmist (Ps 22:6-8, 11-13, 17-21 w M't 27:35 & M'k 15:24 & Lu 23:34 & Joh 19:23, 24; Ps 69:7-9, 20); by prophets (Isa 50:6; 52:13, 14; 53:1-12 w M't 26:67 & 27:26 & Lu 22:37 & Joh 12:38); Mic 5:1; Zec 11:12, 13; Lu 24:26, 46; 1Pe 1:11); by himself (M't 16:21; 17:12, 22, 23; 20:17-19; M'k 8:31; 9:12; 10:32-34; Lu 9:22; 18:31-33; Joh 3:14; 13:21).

In Gethsemane (M't 26:38-45; M'k 14:34-39; Lu 22:42-44; Joh 18:11).

In Pilate's judgment hall (M't 27:24-30; M'k 15:15-20; Joh 19:16-18).

At his crucifixion (M't 27:31-50; M'k 15:34, 36; Lu 23:33-46; Joh 19:28).

Apostolic teaching concerning (Ac

3:18; 17:3; 2Co 1:5; Ph'p 2:8; 3:10; Heb 2:9; 4:15; 5:7, 8; 12:2, 3; 1Pe 1:11; 2:21-23; 3:18; 4:1, 13; Re 5:6; 19:13).

See Death of, above; Persecution of, above.

Sympathy of, see Compassion of, above; Love of, above.

Teacher (M't 5:1, 2; Joh 7:46; Ac 1:1). From God (Joh 3:2).

Taught with authority (M't 7:29; 23:8; M'k 1:22); without respect of persons (M't 22:16; M'k 12:14; Lu 20:21); by the sea-side (M'k 4:1); in cities and villages (M't 11:1; M'k 6:6; Lu 23:5); in synagogues (M't 4:23; M'k 1:21; Lu 4:15; 6:6); in the temple (M't 21:23; 26:55; M'k 12:35; Lu 21:37; Joh 8:2); in the wilderness (M'k 6:34).

Temptation of (Lu 22:28). In all points as we are (Heb 4:15).

By the devil (M't 4:1-11; M'k 1:12, 13; Lu 4:1-13).

Typified: In offerings (Ge 4:4; 8:20; 22:13; Ex 12:5-7; 24:5; 29:36, 37; Le 1:4, 10-12; 3:6, 12; 4:3-7, 14-18, 20, 23-25, 28-30, 32-34; 5:6-11, 16, 18; 6:6, 7; 7:2; 8:14, 15, 18, 19, 22-24; 9:2, 7-9, 18; 12:6-8; 14:12-14, 25, 30, 31; 15:15, 29, 30; 16:3, 5, 9, 11, 14-16, 21, 22; 19:21, 22; 22:18, 19; 23:12, 18, 19, 27, 28; Nu 6:10, 11, 14, 16, 17; 7; 8:8, 12; 15:24, 25, 27; 28:3, 4, 9, 11, 15, 19, 22, 23, 27, 30; 29:5, 8, 11, 13, 16-34, 38; 1Ch 29:21; 2Ch 7:5; 29:21-24; Ezr 6:17, 20; 8:35; Eze 43:18-27; 45:15, 18-23).

In the passover (Ex 12:3, 5; Nu 28:16). In the corner stone (Ps 48:21-23; Isa 28:16; M'k 12:10, 11).

In David (Eze 34:23, 24; 37:24, 25; Ho 3:5). Solomon (Ps 72). Hezekiah (Isa 32:1).

Unchangeable (Heb 13:8).

Union of, with the righteous. See Righteous, Union of, with Christ.

Wisdom of (M'k 6:2; Lu 2:40, 46, 47, 52; Joh 7:15). See Omniscience, above.

Worship of (1Co 1:2; 2Co 12:8, 9; Ph'p 2:10, 11). John's vision of (Re 5:8, 9, 12-14; 7:10).

Enjoined (Joh 5:23; Heb 1:6).

Instances of: By the wise men (M't 2:2). A certain ruler (M't 9:18). The disciples (M't 14:33). Canaanitish woman (M't 15:25). A leper (M't 8:2). Women after his resurrection (M't 28:9). The eleven disciples after his resurrection (M't 28:17; Lu 24:52). The multitudes (M'k 11:9, 10 w M't 21:9). Simon Peter (Lu 5:8). Blind man whom Jesus healed (Joh 9:38). Unclean spirits (M'k 3:11). A man with unclean spirit (M'k 5:6, 7). Stephen (Ac 7:59, 60). Paul (1Ti 1:12; 2Pe 3:18).

Zeal of: For God's house (Lu 2:49; Joh 2:17 w Ps 69:9). In obedience to God (Joh 4:32, 34; 9:4; Ro 15:3). In doing good (Ac 10:38). In preaching the gospel (M't 4:23; 9:35; M'k 6:6; Lu 4:43 w M'k 1:38; 8:1). In giving himself as a sacrifice (Lu 9:51; 12:50; 13:32, 33; 1Ti 6:13).

JETHER (abundance). 1. In Ex 4:18 KJVmarg., for Jethro, father-in-law of Moses.

2. Gideon's eldest son (J'g 8:20, 21).

3. Father of Amasa (1Ch 2:17).

4. Judahite (1Ch 2:32).

5. Judahite (1Ch 4:17).

6. Asherite, same as Ithran (?) (cf. 1Ch 7:37, w vs 38).

JETHETH, Edomite chieftain (Ge 36:40; 1Ch 1:51).

JETHLAH (lofty place), a city of Dan (Jos 19:42).

JETHRO (excellence), priest of Midian and father-in-law of Moses (Ex 3:1); personal name probably Reuel (Ex 2:18; 3:1); father of Zipporah, whom Moses married (Ex 3:1, 2); advised Moses (Ex 18:14-24).

JETUR, son of Ishmael and descendants (Ge 25:15; 1Ch 1:31); Itureans of NT times.

JEUEL. 1. Judahite (1Ch 9:6).

2. Levite (2Ch 29:13, Jeiel).

3. Leader in Ezra's company (Ezr 8:13), Jeiel in KJV.

JEUSH (he comes to help). 1. Son of Esau (Ge 36:5).

2. Benjamite (1Ch 7:10).

3. Gershonite Levite (1Ch 23:10, 11).

4. Descendant of Jonathan (1Ch 8:39), Jehush in KJV.

5. Son of Rehoboam (2Ch 11:19).

JEUZ (he counsels), head of a Benjamite family (1Ch 8:10).

JEWEL, JEWELRY. Articles of jewelry in OT times: diadems, bracelets, necklaces, anklets, rings for fingers, gold nets for hair, pendants, head-tire gems, amulets and pendants with magical meanings, jeweled perfume and ointment boxes, crescents for camels; used for personal adornment and utility and for religious festivals. Not much said about jewelry in NT; most condemnatory (1Ti 2:9; Jas 2:2). The New Jerusalem is adorned with jewels (Re 21:19).

JEWS. A corrupted form, doubtless, of Judah, and applied to the people of the kingdom of Judah and Benjamin (2Ki 16:6; 25:25; 2Ch 32:18). After the dissolution of the kingdom of Israel, the name was applied to all Israelites as well as to those of the two tribes (M't 27:11; Ac 2:5).

Wickedness of (Isa 1:4-25; 2:6-10; 3:9; 59:2-15; 65:2-7; Jer 5:1; 6:21-28; 44:1-3; Eze 5:6; 12:2; 16:2, 15-47, 57-63). See the book of Jeremiah which deals chiefly with the wickedness of, and prophecies of the corrective judgments of God to be inflicted upon.

Captive in Babylon (2Ki 24:1-20; 25:1, 21). Haman's plot against (Es 3:6-15). Feast of Purim instituted to commemorate their deliverance from Haman's plot (Es 9:26-32).

The proclamation of Cyrus authorizing their return to the land of Canaan (2Ch 36:22, 23; Ezr 1:2-4); and of Artaxerxes (Ezr 7:11-26).

After the captivity: Return from Babylon (Ezr 7:1-9; 8:31, 32). Lists of those who returned from Babylon (Ezr 2:1-67; 8:1-20; Ne 7:6-69; 12:1-21). Rebuild the temple (Ezr 3:8-13). Rebuilding suspended during the reign of Artaxerxes (Ezr 4:1-24). Resumption of the rebuilding interfered with by Tatnai, governor of the province, by protest followed by a letter to Darius (Ezr 5). Darius' reply to Tatnai authorizing the rebuilding of the temple; temple completed (Ezr 6:1-15).

Vessels of the temple, that were taken to Babylon by Nebuchadnezzar, returned by command of Cyrus (Ezr 1:7-11, 13, 14; 6:5). Liberality of Artaxerxes toward the temple (Ezr 7:14-23).

Make marriages among the Canaanites: Ezra institutes reforms (Ezr 10). Rebuild the walls of Jerusalem under proclamation of Artaxerxes (Ne chps 2-4, 6). Walls dedicated (Ne 12:27-43).

Mission of Jesus to (M't 10:5, 6; 15:24; M'k 7:27). Disbelieve in Jesus (M't 13:5-8; Joh 5:38, 40, 43; 6:36; 12:37). Reject Jesus (Lu 13:34; 17:25; Joh 1:11). Crucify Jesus, see Crucifixion. Some accept Jesus (Joh 2:23; 10:42; 11:45; 12:11; Ac 21:20). Devout, among them (Ac 2:5). Spurned Paul's preaching (Ac 13:46; 18:5, 6; 28:24-27). Persecuted Paul (Ac 9:22, 23; 13:50; 20:3, 19; 23:12-30; 2Co 11:24). Entrusted with the oracles of God (Ac 7:38; Ro 3:1, 2).

Prophecies concerning: Their rejection of the Messiah (Isa 49:5, 7; 52:14; 53:1-3; Zec 13; M't 21:33-39; 22:1-5).

War and other judgments (Isa 3; 4:1; 5; 6:9-13; 7:17-25; 8:14-22; 10:12; 22:1-14; 28:14-22; 29:1-10; 30:1-17; 31:1-3; 32:9-14; Jer 1:11-16; 4:5-31; 6; 7:8-34; 8; 9:9-26; 10:17-22; 11:9-23; 13:9-27; 14:14-18; 15:1-14; 16; 17:1-4; 18:15-17; 19; 20:5; 21:4-7; 22:24-30; 25:8-38; chps 28, 34, 37; 38:1-3; 42:13-22; chps 43-45; La 5:6; Eze 4; 5; 11:7-12; chps 12, 15-17, 19; 22:13-22; 23:22-35; 24; 33:21-29; Da 9:26, 27; Joe 2:1-17; Am 2:4, 5; Mic 3; 4:8-10; Hab 1:6-11; Zep 1; Zec 14:1-3; Mal 4:1; M't 21:33-45; 23:35-38; 24:2, 14-42; M'k 13:1-13; Lu 13:34, 35; 19:43, 44; 21:5-25; 23:28-31; Re 1:7).

Dispersion of (Isa 24:1; Jer 9:16; Ho 9:17; Joe 3:6, 20; Am 9:9; Eze 4:13; 5:10, 12; 20:23; 36:19; Da 9:7).

Blessing and restoration of (Isa 1:25-27; 2:1-5; 4:2-6; 11:11-13; 25; 26:1, 2, 12-19; 27:13; 29:18-24; 30:18-26; 32:15-20; 33:13-24; 35; 37:31, 32; 40:2, 9; 41:27; 44; 49:13-23; 51; 52:1-12; 60; 61:4-9; 62; 66:5-22; Jer 3:14-18; 4:3-18; 12:14-16; 23:3; 24:1-7; 30:3-22; 32:36-44; 33; 44:28; Eze 14:22, 23; 16:60-63; 20:40, 41; 36:1-38; 37:12, 21; Da 11:30-45; 12:1; Joe 3; Am 9:9-15; Ob 17-21; Mic 2:12, 13; 5:3; Zep 2:7; Zec 1:14-21; 2; 8; 10:5-12; 12:1-14; 13; 14:3-21; Mal 3:4; Ro 11).

See Judah, Kingdom of.

JEZANIAH (Jehovah hears), Maacathite captain when Jerusalem fell (2Ki 25:23; Jer 40:7, 8).

JEZEBEL (unexalted). Daughter of Ethbaal, a Zidonian, and wife of Ahab (1Ki 16:31). Was an idolatress and persecuted the prophets of God (1Ki 18:4, 13, 19; 2Ki 3:2, 13; 9:7, 22). Vowed to kill Elijah (1Ki 19:1-3). Wickedly accomplishes the death of Naboth (1Ki 21:5-16). Death of, foretold (1Ki 21:23;

2Ki 9:10). Death of, at the hand of Jehu (2Ki 9:30-37).

Figurative: Re 2:20.

JEZER (form, purpose), son of Naphtali (Ge 46:24; Nu 26:49; 1Ch 7:13).

JEZIAH (Jehovah unites), an Israelite who married an idolatrous wife (Ezr 10:25).

JEZIEL, a disaffected Israelite who joined David at Ziklag (1Ch 12:3).

JEZLIAH (Jehovah delivers), a Benjamite (1Ch 8:18).

JEZOAR (the shining one), son of Helah (1Ch 4:7).

JEZRAHIAH (Jehovah appears). 1. Descendant of Issachar called Izrahiah (1Ch 7:3).

2. Musician (Ne 12:42).

JEZREEL (God sows). 1. A city in the S of Judah (Jos 15:56; 1Sa 25:43; 27:3; 29:1, 11).

2. A city of Issachar (Jos 19:18; 2Sa 2:9). Ahab's residence in (1Ki 18:45, 46; 21:1). Naboth's vineyard in (1Ki 21:1). Joram's residence in (2Ki 8:29). Jehu kills King Ahab, his wife, and friends at (2Ki 9:15-37; 10:11). Prophecies concerning (Ho 1:4, 5, 11).

3. A valley (Jos 17:16). Place of Gideon's battle with the Midianites (J'g 6:33). Place of the defeat of the Israelites under Saul and Jonathan (1Sa 29:1, 11; 31:1-6; 2Sa 4:4).

4. A descendant of Etam (1Ch 4:3).

5. Figurative of Israel (Ho 1:4, 5, 11).

JIBSAM (fragrant), son of Tola (1Ch 7:2).

JIDLAPH (he weeps), son of Nahor (Ge 22:22).

JIMNAH (good fortune), called also Jimna. Son of Asher (Ge 46:17; Nu 26:44).

JIPHTAH, a city of Judah (Jos 15:43).

JIPHTHAH-EL, a valley in Zebulun (Jos 19:14, 27).

JOAB (Jehovah is father). 1. Son of David's sister (1Ch 2:16). Commander of David's army (2Sa 8:16; 20:23; 1Ch 11:6; 18:15; 27:34). Dedicated spoils of his battles (1Ch 26:28). Defeated the Jebusites (1Ch 11:6). Defeats and slays Abner (2Sa 2:13-32; 3:27; 1Ki 2:5). Destroys all the males in Edom (1Ki 11:16; See Ps 60, title). Defeats the Ammonites (2Sa 10:7-14; 1Ch 19:6-15). Captures Rabbah (2Sa 11:1, 15-25; 12:26-29; 1Ch 20:1, 2).

Procures the return of Absalom to Jerusalem (2Sa 14:1-24). Barley field of, burned by Absalom (2Sa 14:29-33). Pursues and kills Absalom (2Sa 18). Censures David for lamenting the death of Absalom (2Sa 19:1-8). Replaced by Amasa as commander of David's army (2Sa 17:25; 19:13). Kills Amasa (2Sa 20:8-13; 1Ki 2:5). Causes Sheba to be put to death (2Sa 20:16-22). Opposes the numbering of the people (2Sa 24:3; 1Ch 21:3). Numbers the people (2Sa 24:4-9; 1Ch 21:4, 5; 27:23, 24). Supports Adonijah as successor to David (1Ki 1:7; 2:28). Slain by Benaiah, under Solomon's order (1Ki 2:29-34).

2. A grandson of Kenaz (1Ch 4:14).

3. An Israelite (or the name of two Israelites) whose descendants returned from Babylon to Jerusalem (Ezr 2:6; 8:9; Ne 7:11).

4. "House of Joab" (1Ch 2:54). Probably identical with 1.

JOAH (Jehovah is brother). 1. Son of Asaph (2Ki 18:18, 26; Isa 36:3, 11, 22).

2. A descendant of Gershom (1Ch 6:21; 2Ch 29:12).

3. A son of Obed-edom (1Ch 26:4).

4. A Levite, who repaired the temple (2Ch 34:8).

JOAHAZ (Jehovah has grasped), father of Joah, recorder of King Josiah (2Ch 34:8).

JOANNA. 1. Wife of Chuza, the steward of Herod Agrippa, and a disciple of Jesus (Lu 8:3; 24:10).

2. An ancestor of Jesus (Lu 3:27).

JOASH (Jehovah has given). 1. Son of Becher (1Ch 7:8).

2. Keeper of the stores of oil (1Ch 27:28).

3. Father of Gideon (J'g 6:11, 29, 31; 7:14; 8:13, 29-32).

4. Son of Ahab, king of Israel (1Ki 22:26; 2Ch 18:25).

5. Called also Jehoash. Son of Ahaziah and king of Judah. Saved from his grandmother by Jehosheba, his aunt, and hidden for six years (2Ki 11:1-3; 2Ch 22:11, 12). Anointed king by the priest, Jehoiada (2Ki 11:12-21; 2Ch 23). Righteousness of, under influence of Jehoiada (2Ki 12:2; 2Ch 24:2). Repaired the temple (2Ki 12:4-16; 2Ch 24:4-14, 27). Wickedness of, after Jehoiada's death (2Ch 24:17-22), Procured peace

from Hazael, king of Syria, by gift of dedicated treasures from the temple (2Ki 12:17, 18; 2Ch 24:23, 24). Prophecy against (2Ch 24:19, 20). Put Jehoiada's son to death (2Ch 24:20-22; M't 23:35). Diseases of (2Ch 24:25). Conspired against and slain (2Ki 12:20, 21; 2Ch 24:25, 26).

6. A king of Israel (See Jehoahaz).

7. A descendant of Shelah (1Ch 4:22).

8. One of David's officers (1Ch 12:3).

JOATHAM, son of Uzziah; king of Judah (M't 1:9).

JOB. 1. A man who dwelt in Uz (Job 1:1). Righteousness of (Job 1:1, 5, 8; 2:3; Eze 14:14, 20). Riches of (Job 1:3). Trial of, by affliction of Satan (Job 1:13-19; 2:7-10). Fortitude of (Job 1:20-22; 2:10; Jas 5:11). Visited by Eliphaz, Bildad, and Zophar as comforters (Job 2:11-13). Complaints of, and replies by his three friends to Job chapters 3-37. Replied to by God (Job 38-41). Submission of, to God (Job 40:3-5; 42:1-6). Later blessings and riches of (Job 42:10-16). Death of (Job 42:16, 17).

2. See Jashub.

JOBAB (howl). 1. Son of Joktan (Ge 10:29; 1Ch 1:23).

2. 2nd king of Edom (Ge 36:33; 1Ch 1:44, 45).

3. King of Madon (Jos 11:1; 12:19).

4. Benjamite (1Ch 8:9).

5. Benjamite (1Ch 8:18).

JOCHEBED (Jehovah is glory). Mother of Miriam, Aaron, and Moses (Ex 6:20; Nu 26:59). Nurses Moses when he is adopted by Pharaoh's daughter (Ex 2:1-9).

JOED (Jehovah is witness), a Benjamite (Ne 11:7).

JOEL (Jehovah is God). 1. Son of Samuel (1Sa 8:2; 1Ch 6:33; 15:17). Called Vashni (1Ch 6:28).

2. A Simeonite (1Ch 4:35).

3. A Reubenite (1Ch 5:4, 8).

4. A Gadite (1Ch 5:12).

5. A Kohathite Levite (1Ch 6:36).

6. Descendant of Issachar (1Ch 7:3).

7. One of David's valiant men (1Ch 11:38). Called "Igal, son of Nathan" (2Sa 23:36).

8. Name of two Gershonites (1Ch 15:7, 11; 23:8; 26:22).

9. Prince of Manasseh (1Ch 27:20).

10. A Kohathite who assisted in the cleansing of the temple (2Ch 29:12).

11. One of Nebo's family (Ezr 10:43).

12. Son of Zichri (Ne 11:9).

13. One of the twelve minor prophets, probably lived in the days of Uzziah (Joe 1:1; Ac 2:16).

JOEL, BOOK OF. Dates suggested range from c. 830 to 350 B.C.; no clear indication in book of time of writing; background of book a locust plague, regarded by prophet as punishment for sin, causes him to urge nation to repent of its sins and predict a worse visitation, the future Day of the Lord. Outline. 1. Locust plague and its removal (1:1-2:27).

2. Future day of the Lord (2:28-3:21).

a. Spirit of God to be poured out (2:28-32);

b. judgment of the nations (3:1-17);

c. blessing upon Israel following judgment (3:18-21).

JOELAH (let him help), one of David's recruits at Ziklag (1Ch 12:7).

JOEZER (Jehovah is help), a Korhite, who joined David at Ziklag (1Ch 12:6).

JOGBEHAH (lofty), city in Gilead assigned to Gad (Nu 32:35; J'g 8:11).

JOGLI (led into exile), a prince of Dan (Nu 34:22).

JOHA. 1. A Benjamite (1Ch 8:16).

2. One of David's valiant men (1Ch 11:45).

JOHANAN (Jehovah has been gracious). 1. Jewish leader who tried to save Gedaliah from plot to murder him (Jer 40:13, 14); took Jews, including Jeremiah, to Egypt (Jer 40-43).

2. Son of King Josiah (1Ch 3:15).

3. Son of Elioenai (1Ch 3:24).

4. Father of Azariah, high priest in Solomon's time (1Ch 6:9, 10).

5. Benjamite; joined David at Ziklag (1Ch 12:4).

6. Gadite; captain in David's army (1Ch 28:12, 14).

7. Ephraimite chief (2Ch 28:12).

8. One of those who left Babylon with Ezra (Ezr 8:12).

9. Son of Tobiah, who married a Jewess in days of Nehemiah (Ne 6:18).

10. Son of Eliashib (Ezr 10:6).

11. High priest, grandson of Eliashib (Ne 12:22).

JOHN (Jehovah has been gracious). 1. John the Baptist (q.v.).

2. The apostle, the son of Zebedee, and brother of James. (See John, the Apostle).

3. John Mark (see Mark).

4. Father of Simon Peter (Joh 1:42; 21:15, 17, called Jonas in KJV).

5. Jewish religious dignitary who called Peter and John to account for their preaching about Jesus (Ac 4:6).

6. Father of Mattathias (1Macc 2:1).

7. Eldest son of Mattathias (1Macc 9:36).

8. Father of Eupolemus (1Macc 4:11).

9. John Hyrcanus, son of Simon (1Macc 13:53; 16:1).

10. Jewish envoy (2Macc 11:17).

JOHN, THE APOSTLE. Son of Zebedee and Salome, and brother of James (M't 4:21; 27:56; M'k 15:40; Ac 12:1, 2); lived in Galilee, probably in Bethsaida (Lu 5:10; Joh 1:44); fisherman (M'k 1:19, 20); became disciple of Jesus through John the Baptist (Joh 1:35); called as apostle (M'k 1:19, 20; Lu 5:10); one of three apostles closest to Jesus (others, Peter and James); at raising of Jairus' daughter (M'k 5:37; Lu 8:51); transfiguration (M't 17:1; M'k 9:2; Lu 9:28); Gethsemane (M't 26:37; M'k 14:33); asked Jesus to call fire down on Samaritans, and given name Boanerges (sons of thunder) (M'k 3:17; Lu 9:54); mother requested that John and James be given places of special honor in coming kingdom (M'k 10:35); helped Peter prepare Passover (Lu 22:8); lay close to Jesus' breast at Last Supper (Joh 13:25); present at trial of Jesus (Joh 18:15, 16); witnessed crucifixion of Jesus (Joh 19:26, 27); recognized Jesus at Sea of Galilee (Joh 21:1-7); active with Peter in apostolic church (Ac 3:1-4:22; 8:14-17). Lived to old age; 4th Gospel, three epistles, and Revelation attributed to him.

JOHN THE BAPTIST, forerunner of Jesus; son of Zacharias and Elizabeth, both of priestly descent (Lu 1:5-25, 56-58); lived as Nazirite in desert (Lu 1:15; M't 11:12-14, 18); began ministry beyond Jordan in 15th year of Tiberias Caesar (Lu 3:1-3); preached baptism of repentance in preparation of coming of Messiah (Lu 3:4-14); baptized Jesus (M't 3:13-17; M'k 1:9, 10; Lu 3:21; Joh 1:32); bore witness to Jesus as Messiah (Joh 1:24-42); imprisoned and put to death by Herod Antipas (M't 14:6-12; M'k 6:17-28); praised by Jesus (M't 11:7-14; Lu 7:24-28); disciples loyal to him long after his death (Ac 18:25).

JOHN, EPISTLES OF. The First Epistle of John. Evidently written by author of 4th Gospel; date uncertain, but apparently late in 1st century; purpose: to warn readers against false teachers (Gnostic) and exhort them to hold fast to Christian faith and fulfill Christian duties, especially love; false teachers called anti-Christs (2:18, 22; 4:3); plan of Epistle is difficult to follow, but thoughts repeated often are the necessity of doing righteousness as an evidence of divine sonship, the necessity of love for the brethren, and believing that Jesus is the Christ come in the flesh.

The Second Epistle of John. Written to exhort readers to hold fast to the commandments which they had received, to warn against false teachers who deny that Christ is come in the flesh, and to tell them that he will soon visit them. "Elect lady" may be woman or church.

The Third Epistle of John. Addressed to Gaius to commend him for his Christian life and hospitality to evangelists sent by John and to censure Diotrephes for his bad conduct.

JOHN, THE GOSPEL OF. Early tradition and internal evidence of the Gospel show that this book was written by the apostle John. Early tradition also places the writing of the book sometime toward the close of the 1st century A.D., in Asia Minor. The author states his purpose in 20:30, 31: to show that Jesus is the Christ, the Son of God, and that those believing this might have life in His name. Some of the characteristics which distinguish the Gospel from the others are: an emphasis on the deity of Christ; stress upon the King rather than upon the kingdom; non-parabolic teaching; emphasis upon the coming and work of the Holy Spirit.

Outline: 1. Incarnate Word (1:1-18).

2. Testimony to Jesus' Messiahship (1:19-2:11).

3. Christ's self-revelation through words and deeds (2:12-12:50).

4. Christ's self-revelation in His crucifixion and resurrection (13-21).

JOHN MARK (See Mark.)

JOIADA (Jehovah knows). 1. Repaired walls of Jerusalem (Ne 3:6; in KJV Jehoiada).

2. Son of Eliashib (Ne 12:10; 13:28).

JOIAKIM (Jehovah raises up), father of Eliashib (Ne 12:10, 12, 26).

JOIARIB (Jehovah pleads). 1. A returned exile (Ezr 8:16).

2. A descendant of Judah (Ne 11:5).

3. A priest who returned from Babylon (Ne 12:6, 19).

4. See Jehoiarib.

JOKDEAM, a city of Judah (Jos 15:56).

JOKIM (Jehovah raises up), a descendant of Shelah (1Ch 4:22).

JOKMEAM (let the people arise), a Levitical city of Ephraim (1Ch 6:68).

JOKNEAM, a Levitical city of Zebulun (Jos 12:22; 19:11; 21:34).

See Jokmeam.

JOKSHAN, son of Abraham, by Keturah (Ge 25:2, 3, 6; 1Ch 1:32).

JOKTAN, son of Elur (Ge 10:25, 26, 29; 1Ch 1:19, 20, 23).

JOKTHEEL. 1. A city of Judah (Jos 15:38).

2. A name given by Amaziah to Shelah, a stronghold of Edom (2Ki 14:7; 2Ch 25:11, 12). Called rock in J'g 1:36.

JONA (See Jonah, Jonas.)

JONADAB (Jehovah is bounteous). 1. Nephew of David. His complicity with Amnon in his rape of Tamar (2Sa 13:3-5). Comforts David on death of Amnon (2Sa 13:32-35).

2. Called also Jehonadab. A Rechabite and companion of Jehu (2Ki 10:15-23). His sons refuse to drink wine in obedience to his command (Jer 35:5-10, 16-19).

See Rechabites.

JONAH (dove). Prophet of Israel; son of Amittai; predicted victory over Syria through Jeroboam II, who reigned 790-750 B. C.; author of Book of Jonah (2Ki 14:25; Jon 1:1).

JONAH, BOOK OF, written to show that God's gracious purposes are not limited to Israel, but extend to the Gentile world; a great work on foreign missions (4:11); while found among the Minor Prophets, there is little prophecy in it. Outline: 1. Jonah's commission, disobedience, and punishment (1:1-16).

2. Jonah's deliverance (1:17-2:10).

3. Jonah preaches; Nineveh repents and is spared (3).

4. God's mercy defended (4).

JONAN (Jehovah is gracious), an ancestor of Christ (Lu 3:30).

JONAS. 1. See Jonah.

2. Father of Peter (Joh 21:15-17). Called Jona (Joh 1:42).

JONATH-ELEM-RECHOKIM,UPON, probably the melody to which Ps 56 was written.

JONATHAN (Jehovah has given). 1. A Levite of Bethlehem, who becomes a priest for Micah; accepts idolatry; joins the Danites (J'g 17:7-13; 18:1-30).

2. Son of Saul (1Sa 14:49). Victory of, over the Philistine garrison of Geba (1Sa 13:3, 4, 16); over Philistines at Michmash (1Sa 14:1-18). Under Saul's curse pronounced against any who might take food before he was avenged of his enemies (1Sa 14:24-30, 43). Rescued by the people (1Sa 14:43-45). Love of, for David (1Sa 18:1-4; 19:1-7; 20; 23:16-18). Killed in battle with Philistines (1Sa 31:2, 6; 2Sa 21:12-14; 1Ch 10:2). Buried by inhabitants of Jabesh-gilead (1Sa 31:11-13). Mourned by David (2Sa 1:12, 17-27). Son of, cared for by David (2Sa 4:4; 9; 1Ch 8:34).

3. Son of Abiathar (2Sa 15:27). Acts as spy for David (2Sa 15:27, 28; 17:17-22). Informs Adonijah of Solomon's succession to David (1Ki 1:42-48).

4. Nephew of David, slays a giant, and becomes one of David's chief warriors (2Sa 21:21; 1Ch 20:7).

5. One of David's heroes (2Sa 23:32; 1Ch 11:34).

6. A son of Jada (1Ch 2:32, 33).

7. Secretary of the cabinet of David (1Ch 27:32).

8. Father of Ebed (Ezr 8:6).

9. Son of Asahel (Ezr 10:15).

10. Called also Johanan. A descendant of Jeshua (Ne 12:11, 22).

11. Name of two priests (Ne 12:14, 35).

12. A scribe (Jer 37:15, 20; 38:26).

13. Son of Kareah (Jer 40:8).

JOPPA, once in KJV Japho (Jos 19:46); ancient walled town on coast of Palestine, c. 35 miles NW of Jerusalem; assigned to Dan; mentioned in Amarna letters; seaport for Jerusalem. In NT times Peter there raised Dorcas to life (Ac 9:36f) and received vision of sheet filled with animals (Ac 10:1ff; 11:5ff). Now called Jaffa.

JORAH, family which returned with Zerubbabel (Ezr 2:18). Called Hariph in Ne 7:24.

JORAI (whom Jehovah teaches), a Gadite (1Ch 5:13).

JORAM (Jehovah is exalted), same as longer form Jehoram. 1. Son of king of Hamath (2Sa 8:10).

2. Levite (1Ch 26:25).

3. Son of Ahab, king of Israel (2Ki 8:29).

4. King of Judah (2Ki 8:21-24; 11:2; 1Ch 3:11; M't 1:8).

5. Priest (2Ch 17:8).

JORDAN (descender). A river in Palestine. Empties into the Dead Sea (Jos 15:5). Fords of (Ge 32:10; Jos 2:7; J'g 3:28; 7:24; 8:4; 10:9; 12:5, 6; 2Sa 2:29; 17:22, 24; 19:15, 31; 1Ch 19:17). Swelling of, at harvest time (Jos 3:15; Jer 12:5); and in the early spring (1Ch 12:15). The waters of, miraculously separated for the passage of the Israelites (Jos 3; 4; 5:1; Ps 114:3); of Elijah (2Ki 2:6-8); of Elisha (2Ki 2:14). Crossed by a ferryboat (2Sa 19:18). Naaman washes in, for the healing of his leprosy (2Ki 5:10-14). John the Baptist baptizes in (M't 3:6; M'k 1:5); baptizes Jesus in (M't 3:13; M'k 1:9).

Plain of: (Ge 13:10-12). Israelites camped in (Nu 22:1; 26:3, 63). Solomon's foundry in (1Ki 7:46; 2Ch 4:17).

JORIM, an ancestor of Jesus (Lu 3:29).

JORKOAM, descendant of Caleb (1Ch 2:44).

JOSABAD (Jehovah has bestowed), a famous archer who joined David at Ziklag (1Ch 12:4).

JOSAPHAT (See Jehoshaphat.)

JOSE, an ancestor of Jesus (Lu 3:29).

JOSEDECH (Jehovah is righteous), father of Jeshua the high priest (Ezr 3:2, 8) who went into captivity under Nebuchadnezzar.

JOSEPH (may God add). 1. Son of Jacob (Ge 30:24). Personal appearance of (Ge 39:6). His father's favorite child (Ge 33:2; 37:3, 4, 35; 48:22; 1Ch 5:2; Joh 4:5). His father's partiality for, excites the jealousy of his brethren (Ge 37:4, 11, 18-28; Ps 105:17; Ac 7:9). His prophetic dreams of his fortunes in Egypt (Ge 37:5-11). Sold into Egypt (Ge 37:27, 28). Is falsely reported to his father as killed by wild beasts (Ge 37:29-35). Is bought by Potiphar, an officer of Pharaoh (Ge 37:36). Is prospered of God (Ge 39:2-5, 21, 23). Is falsely accused, and cast into prison; is delivered by the friendship of another prisoner (Ge 39; 40; Ps 105:18). Is an interpreter of dreams: of the two prisoners (Ge 40:5-23); of Pharaoh (Ge 41:1-37). His name is changed to Zaphnath-paaneah (Ge 41:45). Is promoted to authority next to Pharaoh at thirty years of age (Ge 41:37-46; Ps 105:19-22). Takes to wife the daughter of the priest of On (Ge 41:45). Provides against the years of famine (Ge 41:46-57). Exports the produce of Egypt to other countries (Ge 41:57). Sells the stores of food to the people of Egypt, exacting of them all their money, flocks and herds, lands and lives (Ge 47:13-26). Exempts the priests from the exactions (Ge 47:22, 26).

His father sends down into Egypt to buy corn (Ge 42; 43; 44). Reveals himself to his brethren; sends for his father; provides the land of Goshen for his people; and sustains them during the famine (Ge 45; 46; 47:1-12). His two sons (Ge 41:50, 52). See Ephraim; Manasseh. Mourns the death of his father (Ge 50:1-14). Exacts a pledge from his brethren to convey his remains to Canaan (Ge 50:24, 25; Heb 11:22, w Ex 13:19; Jos 24:32; Ac 7:16). Death of (Ge 50:22-26).

Kindness of heart (Ge 40:7, 8). His integrity (Ge 39:7-12); humility (Ge 41:16; 45:7-9); wisdom (Ge 41:33-57); piety (Ge 41:51, 52); faith (Ge 45:5-8). Was a prophet (Ge 41:38, 39; 50:25; Ex 13:19). God's providence with (Ge 39: 2-5; Ps 105:17-22). His sons conjointly called Joseph (De 33:13-17). Descendants of (Ge 46:20; Nu 26:28-37).

2. Father of Igal the spy (Nu 13:7).

3. Of the sons of Asaph (1Ch 25:2, 9).

4. A returned exile (Ezr 10:42).

5. A priest (Ne 12:14).

6. Husband of Mary (M't 13:55; M'k 6:3; M't 1:18-25; Lu 1:27). His genealogy (M't 1:1-16; Lu 3:23-38). An angel appears and testifies to the innocency of

his betrothed (M't 1:19-24). Dwells at Nazareth (Lu 2:4). Belongs to the city of Bethlehem (Lu 2:4). Goes to Bethlehem to be enrolled (Lu 2:1-4). Jesus born to (M't 1:25; Lu 2:7). Presents Jesus in the temple (Lu 2:22-39). Returns to Nazareth (Lu 2:39). Warned in a dream to escape to Egypt in order to save the child's life (M't 2:13-15). Warned in a dream to return to Nazareth (M't 2:19-23). Attends the annual feast at Jerusalem with his family (Lu 2:42-51).

7. Of Arimathaea. Begs the body of Jesus for burial in his own tomb (M't 27:57-60; M'k 15:42-47; Lu 23:50-56; Joh 19:38-42).

8. Three ancestors of Joseph (Lu 3:24, 26, 30).

9. Called also Barsabas, surnamed Justus. One of the two persons nominated in place of Judas (Ac 1:21, 22, 23).

10. A designation of the ten tribes of Israel (Am 5:6).

JOSES. 1. One of the brethren of Jesus (M't 13:55; 27:56; M'k 6:3; 15:40, 47).

2. A Levite, surnamed Barnabas by the apostles (Ac 4:36).

JOSHAH (Jehovah's gift), a descendant of Simeon (1Ch 4:34).

JOSHAPHAT (Jehovah has judged). 1. One of David's mighty men (1Ch 11:43).

2. Priest (1Ch 15:24), Jehoshaphat in KJV.

JOSHAVIAH, one of David's bodyguards (1Ch 11:46).

JOSHBEKASHAH, leader of the 17th course of musicians (1Ch 25:4, 24).

JOSHEB-BASSEBET (he that sitteth in the seat), one of David's mighty men (2Sa 23:8 ASV). probably corruption of Jashobeam, as in 1Ch 11:11.

JOSHUA (Lord is salvation). 1. Called also Jehoshua, and Jehoshuah, and Oshea. Son of Nun (Nu 13:8; 1Ch 7:27). Intimately associated with Moses (Ex 24:13; 32:17; 33:11). A religious zealot (Nu 11:28). Sent with others to view the promised land (Nu 13:8). Makes favorable report (Nu 14:6-10). Rewarded for his courage and fidelity (Nu 14:30, 38; 32:12). Commissioned, ordained, and charged with the responsibilities of Moses' office (Nu 27:18-23; De 1:38; 3:28; 31:3, 7, 23; 34:9). Divinely inspired (Nu 27:18; De 34:9; Jos 1:5, 9; 3:7; 8:8). His life miraculously preserved when he made a favorable report of the land (Nu 14:10). Promises to (Jos 1:5-9). Leads the people into the land of Canaan (Jos 1-4; Ac 7:45; Heb 4:8). Renews circumcision of the children of Israel; reestablishes the passover; has a vision of the angel of God (Jos 5). Besieges and takes Jericho (Jos 6). Takes Ai (Jos 7; 8). Makes a league with the Gibeonites (Jos 9:3-27). The kings of the six nations of the Canaanites confederate against him (Jos 9:1, 2); make war upon the Gibeonites; are defeated and slain (Jos 10). Defeats seven other kings (Jos 10:28-43). Makes conquest of Hazor (Jos 11). Completes the conquest of the whole land (Jos 11:23). List of the kings whom Joshua smote (Jos 12). Allots the land (Jos 13-19). Sets the tabernacle up in Shiloh (Jos 18:1). Sets apart cities of refuge (Jos 20); forty-eight cities for the Levites (Jos 21). Exhortation of, before his death (Jos 23; 24). Survives the Israelites who refused to enter Canaan (Nu 26:63-65). His portion of the land (Jos 19:49, 50). Death and burial of (Jos 24:29, 30). Esteem in which he was held (Jos 1:16-18). Faith of (Jos 6:16). Military genius of, as exhibited at the defeat of the Amalekites (Ex 17:13); at Ai (Jos 8); in Gibeon (Jos 10); at Hazor (Jos 11). Age of, at death (J'g 2:8).

2. An Israelite (1Sa 6:14, 18).

3. A governor of Jerusalem (2Ki 23:8).

4. Called also Jeshua. The high priest of the captivity (Ezr 2:2). Assists Zerubbabel in restoring the temple (Ezr 3; 4:1-6; 5; Hag 1:1, 12-14; 2:2).

Symbolical: Of the restoration of the church (Zec 3; 6:9-15).

JOSHUA, BOOK OF, 6th book of Bible; first of "historical books" in English, but first of prophets in Heb. OT. Tells how Joshua, Moses' successor, conquered Canaan, as promised by God (Jos 1:1; 24:31). Author not named; date uncertain, but probably prior to 1200 B.C. Outline: 1. Conquest of Canaan (1-12).

2. Apportionment of territory to tribes (13-22).

3. Joshua's farewell address (22-24).

JOSIAH (Jehovah supports him). 1. King of Judah (2Ki 21:24-26; 22:1; 1Ch 3:14; 2Ch 33:25). Ancestor of Jesus (M't

1:10, 11). Slain in battle with Pharaoh-nechoh (2Ki 23:29, 30; 2Ch 35:20-24). Lamentations for (2Ch 35:25). Piety of: exemplified in his repairing the temple (2Ki 22:3-7; 2Ch 34:1-4). Solicitude when the copy of the law was discovered and read to him (2Ki 22:8-20; 2Ch 34:14-33); in keeping a solemn passover (2Ki 23:21-23; 2Ch 35:1-19). Called Josias (M't 1:10, 11). Prophecies concerning (1Ki 13:1-3). Destroys the altar and high places of idolatry (2Ki 23:3-20, 24, 25).

2. Son of Zephaniah (Zec 6:10).

JOSIAS (See Josiah.)

JOSIBIAH, a Simeonite (1Ch 4:35).

JOSIPHIAH (Jehovah will increase), ancestor of family which returned with Ezra (Ezr 8:10).

JOT, smallest letter of Heb. alphabet, similar to our apostrophe sign, . Used figuratively for something of apparently small moment (M't 5:17, 18).

JOTBAH (pleasantness). A place in Judah (2Ki 21:19). Called Jotbath in De 10:7.

JOTBATH, encampment of Israel (De 10:7).

JOTBATHAH, the twentieth encampment of Israel (Nu 33:33, 34).

JOTHAM (Jehovah is perfect). 1. Son of Gideon; speaker of the 1st Bible parable (J'g 9:5-57).

2. Judahite (1Ch 2:47).

3. Eleventh king of Judah; son of Uzziah, whose regent he was for a time; successful, righteous king (2Ki 15:5-38; 2Ch 27); contemporary of Isaiah (Isa 1:1), Hosea (Ho 1:1), Micah (Mic 1:1); ancestor of Jesus (M't 1:9, KJV has Joatham).

JOURNEY, SABBATH DAY'S, 3000 feet (Ac 1:12).

JOY (Ps 30:5, 11; 33:21; 97:11; 132:16; Pr 29:6). From God (Ec 2:26; Ro 15:13). In the Lord (Ps 9:2; 104:34; Isa 9:3; 29:19; 41:16; 61:10; Lu 1:47; Ro 5:11). In Christ (Ph'p 3:3; 4:4; 1Pe 1:8). In the word of God (Ps 19:8; 119:14, 16, 111, 162; Jer 15:16). In worship (2Ch 7:10; Ezr 6:22; Ne 12:43; Ps 42:4; 43:4; 71:23; Isa 56:7; Zep 3:14; Zec 2:10; 9:9). A fruit of the Spirit (Ga 5:22; Eph 5:18, 19). For salvation (Ps 13:5; 20:5; 21:1, 6; 35:9; Isa 12:2, 3; 25:9; 35:1, 2, 10; 55:12; Ro 5:2; 14:17). On account of a good conscience (2Co 1:12). Over a sinner's repentance (Lu 15:6-10, 22-32).

Under adversity (Ps 126:5, 6; Isa 61:3; M't 5:12; Ac 5:41; 2Co 6:10; 7:4; 8:2; 12:10; Col 1:11; 1Th 1:6; Heb 10:34; Jas 1:2; 1Pe 4:13).

Fullness of (Ps 16:11; 36:8; 63:5; Jo 15:11; 16:24; Ac 2:28; 1Jo 1:4). Everlasting (Isa 51:11; 61:7). In heaven (M't 25:21; Lu 15:7, 10).

Attributed to God (De 28:63; 30:9; Jer 32:41).

Enjoined (De 12:18; Ne 8:10; Ps 2:11; 5:11; 32:11; 68:3; 97:12; 100:1, 2; 105:3, 43; 149:2, 5; Joe 2:23; Lu 2:10; 6:23; 10:20; Ro 12:12; 1Th 5:16).

Instances of: Of Moses and the Israelites, when Pharaoh and his army were destroyed (Ex 15:1-22). Of Deborah and the Israelites, when Sisera was overthrown (J'g 5). Of Jephthah's daughter, when he returned from his victory over the Ammonites (J'g 11:34). Of Hannah, when Samuel was born (1Sa 2:1-11). Of Naomi, when Boaz showed kindness to Ruth (Ru 2:20; 4:14). Of the Israelites: When Saul was presented as their king (1Sa 10:24); when David slew Goliath (1Sa 18:6, 7); when they repaired to David to Hebron to make him king (1Ch 12:40); when they took the ark from Kirjath-jearim (1Ch 13:8); when they brought the ark from the house of Obed-edom to Jerusalem (1Ch 15:16, 25, 28); when they made gifts to the house of God (1Ch 29:9); when they kept the dedication of the temple, and the feast of tabernacles under Ezra (Ezr 6:16, 22). Of the Jews, after hearing, anew, the word of God (Ne 8:9-18); when they turned away from idolatry (2Ch 15:14, 15; 23:18, 21; 29:30, 36; 30:21, 23, 26); when the wall of Jerusalem was dedicated (Ne 12:43); when the foundation of the second temple was laid (Ezr 3:11-13).

Of David, over the offerings of the princes and people for the house of God (1Ch 29:10-19). Jews, over the hanging of Haman (Es 8:15, 16, w 7:10).

Of Elisabeth, when Mary visited her (Lu 1:5-44). Of Mary, when she visited Elisabeth (Lu 1:46-56). Of Zacharias, when John was born (Lu 1:67-79). Of angels, when Jesus was born (Lu 2:13, 14). Of the shepherds when they saw the infant Jesus (Lu 2:20). Of the Magi (M't 2:10). Of Simeon, when Jesus was presented in the temple (Lu 2:28-32). Of the disciples, because the devils were subject to them (Lu 10:17). Of the father, when his prodigal son returns (Lu 15:20-32). Of angels, when sinners repent (Lu 15:7, 10). Of the disciples, when Jesus triumphantly entered Jerusalem (M't 21: 8, 9; M'k 11:8-10). Of the women who returned from the Lord's sepulcher (M't 28:8). The disciples, after the resurrection of Jesus (Lu 24:41). Of the disciples in the temple after the ascension of Jesus (Lu 24:53). Of the disciples in the temple because they had received the gift of the Holy Ghost (Ac 2:46, 47). Of the impotent man, healed by Peter (Ac 3:8). Of Paul, when he went up to Jerusalem (Ac 20:22-24). Of Paul and Silas, in the jail at Philippi (Ac 16:25). Of Rhoda, when she heard Peter at the gate (Ac 12:14). Of the disciple at Jerusalem, when Peter told them about the conversion of Cornelius and other Gentiles (Ac 11:18). Of Barnabas, when he saw the success of the gospel at Antioch (Ac 11:22, 23). Of Paul and the Corinthians, because the excommunicated member repented (2Co 1:24; 2:3). Of Paul and Titus, because of the hospitality of the Corinthians (2Co 7:13, w 8:6; Ro 15:32; 1Co 16:18). Of the Macedonians, when they made a contribution for the Christians at Jerusalem (2Co 8:2). Of Paul, when he prayed for the Philippians (Ph'p 1:4). Of Thessalonians, when they believed Paul's gospel (1Th 1:6). Of Paul, rejoicing over his converts (1Th 2:19, 20; 3:9; Ph'm 7). Of early Christians, when they believed in Jesus (1Pe 1:8, 9).

See Happiness; Praise; Thanksgiving.

Of the Wicked. Short (Job 20:5). Vanity (Ec 2:10; 7:6; 11:8, 9). Shallow (Pr 14:13; 15:21). Overshadowed by impending judgment and sorrow (Pr 14: 13; Ec 11:8, 9; Isa 16:10; Jas 4:10).

JOZABAD (Jehovah endows). 1. Gederathite; joined David at Ziklag (1Ch 12:4, Josabad in KJV).

2. Two Manassites who also joined David (1Ch 12:20).

3. Levites (2Ch 31:13).

4. Chief Levite (2Ch 35:9).

5. Levite who assisted Ezra (Ezr 8:33).

6. Man who put foreign wife away (Ezr 10:22).

7. Another such man (Ezr 10:23).

8. Levite who helped Nehemiah (Ne 8:7).

9. Chief Levite in Nehemiah's time (Ne 11:16).

JOZACHAR, (whom Jehovah has remembered). One of the two servants of Joash, king of Judah, who slew him in Millo (2Ki 12:21). Called Zabad (2Ch 24:26).

JOZADAK (Jehovah is righteous), father of priest who returned with Zerubbabel (Ezr 3:2, etc). Called Josedech in Haggai and Zechariah.

JUBAL, son of Lamech; inventor of harp and pipe (Ge 4:21).

JUBILEE. Called: Acceptable Year of the Lord (Isa 61:2). The Year of Liberty (Eze 46:17).

Laws concerning (Le 25:8-55; 27:17-24; Nu 36:4).

See Sabbatic Year.

JUBILEES, BOOK OF, Jewish apocalyptic book written in intertestamental period.

JUCAL (Jehovah is able), prince who put Jeremiah in prison (Jer 38:1).

JUDA (See Judah.)

JUDAEA (See Judea.)

JUDAH (praised). 1. Son of Jacob (Ge 35:23). Intercedes for Joseph's life when his brethren were about to slay him, and proposes that they sell him to the Ishmaelites (Ge 37:26, 27). Takes two wives (Ge 38:1-6). Dwells at Chezib (Ge 38:5). His incest with his daughter-in-law (Ge 38:12-26). Goes down into Egypt for corn (Ge 43:1-10; 44:14-34; 46:28). Prophetic benediction of his father upon (Ge 49:8-12). The ancestor of Jesus (M't 1:2, 3; Re 5:5).

2. Tribe of: Prophecies concerning (Ge 49:10). Enrollment of the military forces of, at Sinai (Nu 1:26, 27; 2:4); at Bezek (1Sa 11:8; 2Sa 24:9); in the plain of Moab (Nu 26:22). Place of, in camp and march (Nu 2:3, 9; 10:14). By whom commanded (Nu 2:3). Moses' benediction upon (De 33:7). Commissioned of God to lead in the conquest of the promised land (J'g 1:1-3, w verses 4-21). Make David king (2Sa 2:1-11; 5:4, 5). Upbraided by David for lukewarmness toward him after Absalom's defeat (2Sa

19:11-15). Accused by the other tribes of stealing the heart of David (2Sa 19:41-43). Loyal to David at the time of the insurrection led by Sheba (2Sa 20:1, 2). Is accorded the birthright forfeited by Reuben (1Ch 5:1, 2; 28:4; Ps 60:7). Loyal to the house of David at the time of the revolt of the ten tribes (1Ki 12:20). Inheritance of (Jos 15; 18:5; 19:1, 9).

3. Name of two exiled priests (Ezr 10:23; Ne 12:8).

4. A Benjamite (Ne 11:9).

5. A prince or priest who assisted in the dedication of the walls of Jerusalem (Ne 12:34, 36).

JUDAISM. 1. The religion of the Jews. To yield place to the Gospel (M't 3:8, 9; 5:17-19, 21-44; 9:16, 17).

2. A corrupt form of Christianity (Ac 15:1; 21:20-25; Ga 3-6).

See Teachers, False.

JUDAS (praised). 1. Surnamed Iscariot. Chosen as an apostle (M't 10:4; M'k 3:19; Lu 6:16; Ac 1:17). Treasurer of the disciples (Joh 12:6; 13:29). His covetousness exemplified by his protest against the breaking of the box of ointment (Joh 12:4-6); by his bargain to betray Jesus for a sum of money (M't 26:14-16; M'k 14:10, 11; Lu 22:3-6; Joh 13:2). His apostasy (Joh 17:12). Betrays the Lord (M't 26:47-50; M'k 14:43-45; Lu 22:47-49; Joh 18:2-5; Ac 1:16-25). Returns the money to the rulers of the Jews (M't 27:3-10). Hangs himself (M't 27:5; Ac 1:18). Prophecies concerning (M't 26:21-25; M'k 14:18-21; Lu 22:21-23; Joh 13:18-26; 17:12; Ac 1:16, 20, w Ps 41:9; 109:8; Zec 11:12, 13).

2. One of the brethren of Jesus (M't 13:55; M'k 6:3); and writer of the epistle of Jude (Jude 1).

3. Brother of James (Lu 6:16; Ac 1:13).

4. An apostle, probably identical with Lebbaeus, or Thaddaeus (Joh 14:22).

5. Of Galilee, who stirred up a sedition among the Jews soon after the birth of Jesus (Ac 5:37).

6. A disciple who entertained Paul (Ac 9:11).

7. Surnamed Barsabas. A Christian sent to Antioch with Paul and Barnabas (Ac 15:22-32).

JUDE, writer of last of NT epistles; brother of James (1:1); probably brother of Jesus (M'k 6:3).

JUDE, EPISTLE OF, author calls himself brother of James; both probably brothers of Jesus, and did not accept His claims until after the resurrection. Date: prior to A. D. 81. Occasion for writing: appearance of an alarming heresy with immoral tendencies, perhaps Gnosticism. Outline: 1. Introduction (1-4).

2. Condemnation of false teachers (5-16).

3. Admonitions (17-23).

4. Doxology (24, 25).

JUDEA. 1. Called also Judah and Judaea. The southern division of Palestine. It extended from the Jordan and Dead Sea to the Mediterranean, and from Shiloh on the N to the wilderness on the S (M't 4:25; Lu 5:17; Joh 4:47, 54). In Lu 1:5 the term applies to all Palestine. In M't 19:1, M'k 10:1, and Lu 23:5 it applies to the territory E of Jordan.

2. Wilderness of. Called Beth-arabah (Jos 15:6, 61). Assigned to Benjamin (Jos 18:22). John the Baptist preaches in (M't 3:1; Lu 3:3).

JUDGE. Must be, righteous (Ex 18:21, 22; Le 19:15; De 16:18-20; 1Ki 3:9; Ps 58:1, 2; 72:1, 2, 4); intelligent (De 1:12, 13; Isa 28:6). Must judge righteously (De 1:16, 17). Jurisdiction of (1Sa 2:25). Inferior and superior (De 17:8-11). Held circuit courts (1Sa 7:16). Rules for guidance of (Ex 18:22; De 19:16-19; 25:1-3; 2Ch 19:5-10; Pr 24:23; Eze 44:24; Joh 7:24).

Kings and other rulers as (2Sa 8:15; 15:2; 1Ki 3:16-28; 10:9; 2Ki 8:1-6; Ps 72:1-4; M't 27:11-26; Ac 23:34, 35; 24; 25:11, 12). Priests and Levites as (De 17:9; 1Ch 23:4; 2Ch 19:8; Eze 44:23, 24; M't 26:57-62). Women as, Deborah (J'g 4:4).

Persian government provided (Ezr 7:25).

Corrupt (1Sa 8:3; Ps 82:2-4; Isa 5:22, 23; Da 9:12; Mic 7:3; Zep 3:3).

Instances of Corrupt: Eli's sons (1Sa 2:12-17, 22-25). Samuel's sons (1Sa 8:1-5). The judges of Jezreel (1Ki 21:8-13). Pilate (M't 27:24, 26; M'k 15:15, 19-24). Felix (Ac 24:26, 27).

Of Israel, executives and leaders of the nation. During the time when the land was ruled by judges (J'g 2:16-19; Ac 13:20).

Othniel (J'g 3:9-11). Ehud (J'g 3:15, 30). Shamgar (J'g 3:31). Deborah (J'g 4:4, 5). Gideon (J'g 6:11-40; 7:8). Abimelech (J'g 9:1-54). Tola (J'g 10:1, 2). Jair (J'g 10:3-5). Jephthah (J'g 12:7). Ibzan (J'g 12:8-10). Elon (J'g 12:11, 12). Abdon (J'g 12:13, 14). Samson (J'g 15:20; 16:31).

Eli (1Sa 4:18). Samuel (1Sa 7:6, 15-17). The sons of Samuel (1Sa 8:1-5).

See Courts; Justice; Witness. See also God, Judge.

JUDGES, BOOK OF. Seventh book of the OT; takes its title from the men who ruled Israel from death of Joshua to Samuel, their principal function being that of military deliverers to the oppressed Hebrews; no claim to authorship in book, and no clear indication of date of writing of book; covers period of c. 300 years. Outline: 1. Introduction (1:1-2:10).

2. Main body of book, describing cycles of failure, oppression, and relief by judges. Activities of 13 judges described (2:11-16:31).

3. Appendix (17-21).

JUDGING (See Uncharitableness.)

JUDGMENT. *General:* Forewarned (Ec 11:9; 12:14; M't 8:29 w 2Pe 2:4 & Jude 6; M't 13:30, 40-43, 49, 50; 25; M'k 8:38; Ac 24:25; 2Th 1:7, 8; Heb 6:2). Fierce and fiery (M't 3:12; 10:15; 11:22; 12:36-42; Lu 3:17; 10:10-14; 11:31, 32; 13:24-29; Ac 2:19, 20).

According to opportunity and works (Ge 4:7; 1Sa 26:23; Job 34:11, 12; Ps 62:12; Pr 12:14; 24:11, 12; Isa 3:10, 11; 59:18; Jer 17:10; 32:19; Eze 7:3, 4, 27; 18:4-9, 19-32; 33:18-20; Ho 4:9; 12:2; Zec 1:6; Lu 12:47, 48; 13:6-9; 19:12-27; Joh 3:19, 20; Ro 2:5-12; 1Co 3:8, 12-15; 2Co 11:15; Ga 6:7, 8; Eph 6:7, 8; Col 3:25; Heb 10:26-30; 12:25; Jas 2:13; 1Pe 1:17; 2Pe 2:20, 21; Re 2:23; 20:12, 13).

Design of: To exhibit a basis for rewards and punishments (2Co 5:10; 2Ti 4:8; Re 11:18; 22:12). Revealing secrets (Ec 12:14; Lu 12:2, 3; Ro 2:16; 1Co 3:13).

Who will be the Judge: God (1Ch 16:33; Ps 9:7; 50:4, 6; 96:13; 98:9; Ec 12:14; Da 7:9. 10; Ro 2:5, 16; 3:6; 2Ti 4:8; Heb 10:30; 12:23; 13:4; 1Pe 4:5; Re 20:11-15).

Jesus Christ (M't 7:22, 23; 13:30, 40-43, 49, 50; 16:25, 27, 31; 25:31-46; M'k 8:38; Joh 5:22; 12:28; Ac 10:42; 17:31; Ro 2:16; 14:10; 1Co 4:5; 2Co 5:10; 2Th 1:7, 8; 2Ti 4:1; 2Pe 2:9; 3:10; Re 1:7; 6:15-17).

The saints (M't 19:28; 1Co 6:2; Jude 14).

Time of: Appointed (M't 13:30; Ac 17:31; Heb 9:27; 2Pe 3:7, 10-12). Known to God only (M'k 13:32).

Who shall be judged: The righteous and wicked (Ec 3:17; M't 25:31-46; Jude 14, 15; Re 11:18). The wicked (Job 21:30; Eze 18:20-28; 2Pe 2:9; 3:7). The living and the dead (Ac 10:42; 2Ti 4:1; 1Pe 4:5). All must be made manifest (M'k 4:22; Ac 17:31; 2Co 5:10). Kings and princes, bondmen and freemen (Re 6:15, 16). Fallen angels (2Pe 2:4; Jude 6).

See God, Judge; Jesus; Punishment, According to Deeds.

JUDGMENT-HALL (See Pretorium.)

JUDGMENT-SEAT (M't 27:19; Ac 18:12; 25:10). Of Christ (Ro 14:10).

JUDGMENTS. Denounced against Solomon (1Ki 11:9-14, 23); Jeroboam (1Ki 14:7-15); Ahab and Jezebel (1Ki 21:19-24); Ahaziah (2Ch 22:7-9); Manasseh (2Ch 33:11).

Denounced against disobedience (Le 26:14-39; De 28:15-68; 29; 32 19-43).

Design of: To correct (De 30:1, 2; 1Ki 8:33, 34; 2Ch 7:13; Job 5:17; 23:10; 34:31, 32; Ps 94:12, 13; 107:10-14, 17; Pr 3:11; Isa 9:13, 14; 26:9; Jer 24:5; 30:11; La 1:5, 12; Eze 20:37, 43; Ho 2:6, 7; 5:15; 1Co 11:32; Heb 12:5-11). To humble (2Co 12:7).

Misunderstood (Jer 16:10; Joe 2:17). No escape from (Ex 20:7; 34:7; Isa 2:10, 12-19, 21; Eze 14:13, 14; Am 5:16-20; 9:1-4; M't 23:33; Heb 2:1-3; 10:28, 29; 12:25; Re 6:16, 17). See Escape. Executed by human instrumentality (Jer 51:2). Delayed (Ps 10:6; 50:21; 55:19). See Punishment, Delayed.

Instances of: On the serpent (Ge 3:14, 15); Eve (Ge 3:16); Adam (Ge 3:17-19); Cain (Ge 4:11-15); the Antediluvians (Ge 6, 7); Sodomites (Ge 19:23-25); Egyptians, the plagues and overthrow (Ex 7-14); Nadab and Abihu (Le 10:1-3);

Miriam (Nu 12:1-15).

Upon the Israelites: For worshiping Aaron's calf (Ex 32:35); for murmuring (Nu 11:1, 33, 34; 14:22, 23, 32, 35-37; 21:6; 25:4, 5, 9). The forty years' wandering, a judgment (Nu 14:26-39; 26:63-65; De 2:14-17); delivered into the hands of the Assyrians (2Ki 17:6-41); Chaldeans (2Ch 36:14-21).

Upon the Canaanites (Le 18:25; De 7; 12:29-32); with the conquest of, by Joshua. See Canaanites.

Upon Abimelech (J'g 9:52-57); Uzzah (2Sa 6:7); Eli's house (1Sa 2:27-36 w 4:10-22); the prophet of Judah, for disobedience (1Ki 13:1-24); Zimri (1Ki 16:18, 19); Gehazi (2Ki 5:27); Sennacherib (2Ki 19:35-37); Hananiah, the false prophet (Jer 28:15, 17).

See Chastisement; Punishment; Sin, Punishment of.

JUDITH. 1. Wife of Esau (Ge 26:34).

2. Heroine of apocryphal book of Judith.

JULIA, a Christian woman in Rome (Ro 16:15).

JULIUS, Roman centurion to whom Paul was entrusted (Ac 27:1, 3).

JUNIA, a kinsman of Paul (Ro 16:7).

JUNIPER, a tree (1Ki 19:4, 5; Job 30:4; Ps 120:4).

JUPITER, a Greek and Roman deity (Ac 14:12, 13; 19:35).

JURISDICTION (See Church and State.)

JURY. Of ten men (Ru 4:2). Of seventy men, elders (senators) (Nu 11:16, 17, 24, 25).

JUSHAB-HESED (mercy has returned), son of Zerubbabel (1Ch 3:20).

JUST SHALL LIVE BY FAITH. (Hab 2:4; Ro 1:17; Ga 3:11; Heb 10:38).

JUSTICE. From God (Ps 72:1, 2; Pr 29:26). Enjoined (Ex 23:1-3, 6-8; Le 19:13-15; De 16:18-20; 25:1-4; Ps 82:3, 4; 106:3; Pr 18:5; Isa 1:17; Jer 7:5, 7; La 3:35, 36; Mic 6:8; Zec 7:9; 8:16; Joh 7:24, 51). Without respect of persons (Pr 24:23; 28:21).

Perverted (Ec 3:16; 5:8; Isa 59:14, 15; Jer 22:3; Am 5:7, 11, 12; Mic 7:3; Hab ' M't 12:7). Rewarded (Jer 22:4, 15, 1t, Eze 18:5-9).

Of God, see God, Justice of.

See Court; Injustice; Judge.

JUSTIFICATION, the act of divine grace which restores the sinner to the relationship with God that he would have had if he had not sinned; pardon of sin. The word is used also to denote the state of the sinner after he is restored to divine favor.

Not imputing guilt to the sinner (Ps 32:2; Isa 53:11; Zec 3:4; Joh 5:24; Ro 4:6; 8:1).

From God (Isa 45:24, 25; 50:8; 54:17; 61:10; Ro 3:25; 8:30, 33; 2Co 5:19, 21; Tit 3:7); based on his righteousness (Ps 71:16; 89:16; Isa 42:21; 46:12, 13; 51:5, 6; 56:1; Ro 1:16, 17; Ga 5:4-6).

Not by the law (Ro 3:20; Ga 2:16; 3:11; 5:4-6). By faith (Ge 15:6; Hab 2:4; Ro 1:16, 17; 3:20-22, 24-26, 28, 30; 4:2-25; 5:1; 9:30-32; 10:4, 6, 8-11; Ga 2:14-21; 3:6, 8, 9, 21, 22, 24; 5:4-6; Ph'p 3:8, 9; Heb 11:4, 7; Jas 2:20-23, 26). Through Christ (Isa 53:11; Jer 23:6; Ac 13:39; Ro 3:20-25; 5:9, 11, 16-18, 21; 1Co 1:30; 6:11; Col 2:13, 14).

Fruits of: Peace (Ro 5:1). Holiness (Ro 6:22).

Example of: Abraham (Ge 15:6; Ro 4:3).

See Adoption; Forgiveness; Regeneration; Sanctification; Sin, Confession of, Forgiveness of.

JUSTUS (just). 1. A disciple nominated with Matthias to succeed Judas Iscariot (Ac 1:23).

2. A believer in Corinth (Ac 18:7).

3. Called also Jesus. A disciple in Rome (Col 4:11).

JUTTAH (extended), a Levitical city in Judah (Jos 15:55; 21:16).

K

KAB (See Cab, also Weights and Measures.)

KABZEEL (whom God gathers), a city of Judah (Jos 15:21; 2Sa 23:20; 1Ch 11:22).

KADESH (be holy), also known as En-mishpat (Ge 14:7), place c. 70 miles S of Hebron, in vicinity of which Israel wandered for 37 years (De 1:46; Nu 33:37, 38; De 2:14); Miriam died there (Nu 20:1); Moses sent spies to Palestine from there (Nu 13:21-26; De 1:19-25); Moses displeased God there by striking instead of speaking to rock (Nu 20:2-13). Often called Kadesh-barnea (Nu 32:8; De 2:14).

KADESH-BARNEA (See Kadesh.)

KADMIEL (God is in front). 1. A Levite (Ezr 2:40; 3:9; Ne 7:43; 12:8, 24).

2. A Levite who assisted in leading the devotions of the people (Ne 9:4, 5; 10:9).

KADMONITES (children of the East), ancient Arab tribe between Egypt and Euphrates (Ge 15:18-21).

KAIN (smith). 1. Town in Judah (Jos 15:57), Cain in KJV.

2. Tribal name; KJV has "Kenite" (Nu 24:22; J'g 4:11).

KALLAI (swift), a priest (Ne 12:20).

KAMON (See Camon.)

KANAH (reeds). 1. Brook flowing between Ephraim and Manasseh into Mediterranean (Jos 16:8; 17:9).

2. City c. 8 miles SE of Tyre, near boundary of Manasseh (Jos 19:28).

KAREAH (bald), called also Careah. Father of Johanan (2Ki 25:23; Jer 40:8, 13; 41:11, 13, 14, 16).

KARKAA (ground), a city of Judah (Jos 15:3).

KARKOR, place E of Jordan where Gideon defeated Midianites (J'g 8:10). Exact location unknown.

KARTAH (city), a city of Zebulun (Jos 21:34).

KARTAN, a Levitical city in Naphtali (Jos 21:32).

KATTATH, a city in Zebulun (Jos 19:15).

KEDAR (mighty, dark). 1. Son of Ishmael (Ge 25:13; 1Ch 1:29).

2. A nomadic clan of the Ishmaelites (Ps 120:5; Song 1:5; Isa 21:16; 42:11; 60:7; Jer 49:28). Flocks of (Isa 60:7; Jer 49:28). Princes and commerce of (Eze 27:21).

KEDEMAH (eastward), son of Ishmael (Ge 25:15; 1Ch 1:31).

KEDEMOTH (eastern parts). A city of Moab, allotted to Reuben and the Merarite Levites (Jos 13:18; 1Ch 6:79). Encircled by a wilderness of same name (De 2:26).

KEDESH (sacred place). 1. A city of Judah (Jos 15:23). Possibly identical with Kadesh-barnea.

2. Called also Kishion and Kishon. A Canaanite city taken by Joshua (Jos 12:22; 19:20; 21:28; 1Ch 6:72).

3. Called also Kedesh-naphtali. A city of refuge (Jos 20:7; 21:32). Home of Barak and Heber (J'g 4:6, 9, 11). Captured by Tiglath-pileser (2Ki 15:29).

KEDESH NAPHTALI (See Kedesh.)

KEDRON (See Kidron.)

KEEPERS, of the prison (Ge 39:22; Ac 5:23; 12:6; 16:27, 36).

KEHELATHAH (gathering), an encampment of Israel (Nu 33:22, 23).

KEILAH. 1. One of a group of nine cities in the southern part of Palestine allotted to Judah (Jos 15:44). Philistines make a predatory excursion against, after harvest (1Sa 23:1). David rescues (1Sa 23:2-13). Rulers of, aid in restoring the wall of Jerusalem after the captivity (Ne 3:17, 18).

2. A descendant of Caleb (1Ch 4:19).

KELAIAH, called also Kelita. A Levite who divorced his Gentile wife after the captivity and assisted Ezra in expounding the law (Ezr 10:23; Ne 8:7; 10:10).

KEMUEL. 1. Son of Nahor; uncle of Laban and Rebekah (Ge 22:21).

2. Prince of Ephraim (Nu 34:24).

3. Father of Hashabiah, leading Levite (1Ch 27:17).

KENAN, great-grandson of Adam (1Ch 1:2). In KJV of Ge 5:9-14 Cainan.

KENATH (possession), Amorite city in region of Bashan in kingdom of Og (Nu 32:42; 1Ch 2:22, 23).

KENAZ (hunting). 1. Grandson of Esau (Ge 36:11, 15; 1Ch 1:36).

2. A duke of Edom (Ge 36:42; 1Ch 1:53).

3. Brother of Caleb (Jos 15:17; J'g 1:13; 3:9, 11; 1Ch 4:13).

4. Grandson of Caleb (1Ch 4:15).

KENEZITE, KENIZZITE, descendants of Kenaz (Ge 15:19). Caleb (Nu 32:12) and Othniel (Jos 15:17) were Kenizzites.

KENITES (smith). 1. A Canaanitish tribe whose country was given to Abraham (Ge 15:19; Nu 24:21-23).

2. The descendants of Jethro, a Midianite, father-in-law of Moses. Join the Israelites and dwell at Jericho (J'g 1:16; 4:11; 1Ch 2:55); later in the wilderness of Judah (J'g 1:16, 17). Jael, one of the, betrays and slays Sisera (J'g 4:17-21).

KENOSIS (emptying), a term applied to Christ's taking the form of a servant in the incarnation (Ph'p 2:7).

KERCHIEF (See Handkerchief.)

KEREN-HAPPUCH (beautifier), youngest daughter of Job (Job 42:14).

KERIOTH (cities). 1. A city of Judah (Jos 15:25).

2. Called also Kirioth. A city of Moab (Jer 48:24, 41; Am 2:2).

KEROS, ancestor of Nethinim who returned with Zerubbabel (Ezr 2:44; Ne 7:47).

KETTLE, cooking vessel or basket (1Sa 2:14).

KETURAH, Abraham's 2nd wife; mother of six sons, ancestors of Arabian tribes (Ge 25:1-6; 1Ch 1:33).

KEY (J'g 3:25). A symbol of authority (Isa 22:22; M't 16:19; Re 1:18; 3:7; 9:1; 20:1).

Figurative: Lu 11:52.

KEZIA, second daughter of Job (Job 42:14).

KEZIZ, a valley and city of Benjamin (Jos 18:21).

KIBROTH-HATTAAVAH (the graves of lust or greed), a station where the Israelites were miraculously fed with quails (Nu 11:31-35; 33:16, 17; De 9:22).

KIBZAIM, a Levitical city in Ephraim (Jos 21:22).

KID (See Animals: Goats).

KIDNAPPING, forbidden (Ex 21:16; De 24:7).

Instance of: J'g 21:20-23.

KIDNEY, used with surrounding fat as burnt offering (Ex 29:13, 22; Le 3:4, 10, 15; 4:9); regarded as seat of the emotions translated "reins" (Job 19:27; Ps 7:9).

KIDRON, called also Cedron. A valley and stream between Jerusalem and the Mount of Olives (1Ki 2:37; Ne 2:15; Jer 31:40). David flees from Absalom across (2Sa 15:23). Destruction of idols at, by Asa, Josiah, and the Levites (1Ki 15:13; 2Ki 23:6, 12; 2Ch 29:16). Source of, closed by Hezekiah (2Ch 32:4). Jesus crossed, on the night of his agony (Joh 18:1).

KILLING (See Homicide.)

KINAH, a city of Judah (Jos 15:22).

KINDNESS. Enjoined (Zec 7:9, 10; M't 5:42; Lu 6:30, 34, 35; Ac 20:35; Ro 12:15; 15:1, 2; Ga 6:1, 2, 10; Eph 4:32; Col 3:12; 1Pe 3:8, 9; 1Jo 3:17, 18). Enjoined, to enemies (Ex 23:4, 5; Lu 6:34, 35); to strangers (Le 19:34); to a brother (De 22:1).

Inspired by love (1Co 13:4-7). Commends ministers (2Co 6:6). Rewards of (Pr 14:21; M't 5:7; 25:34, 35).

Of God (Lu 6:35). Good women (Pr 31:26; 1Ti 5:9, 10). Good men (Ps 112:5; Heb 5:2).

Of Jesus, see Jesus, Compassion of.

Instances of: Sons of Heth to Abraham (Ge 23:6, 11). Keeper of the prison to Joseph (Ge 39:21-23). Pharaoh to Jacob (Ge 45:16-20; 47:5, 6). Pharaoh's daughter to Moses (Ex 2:6-10). Moses to Jethro's daughters (Ex 2:17, 19). Jethro to Moses (Ex 2:20). Rahab to the spies (Jos 2:4-16). Boaz to Ruth (Ru 2:8-16; 3:15). David to Nabal (1Sa 25:15, 16). Abigail to David (1Sa 25:14-35). David to Mephibosheth (2Sa 9:1-13). Joab to Absalom (2Sa 14:1-24). Obadiah to the prophets of the Lord (1Ki 18:4). Ahab to Benhadad (1Ki 20:32-34). The Shunammite woman to Elisha (2Ki 4:8-10). Elisha to the Shunammite woman (2Ki 4:13-17, 28-37; 8:1). Evil-merodach to Jehoiachin (2Ki 25:28-30). Jehoshabeath to Joash (2Ch 22:11). Nehemiah and the nobles to the people (Ne 5:8-19). Mordecai to Esther (Es 2:7). Ebed-melech to Jeremiah (Jer 38:7-13). Nebuchadnezzar to Jeremiah (Jer 39:11, 12).

Joseph to Mary (M't 1:19, 24). Centurion to his servant (Lu 7:2-6). Jews to Mary and Martha (Joh 11:19, 33). John to Mary (Joh 19:27). Felix to Paul (Ac

24:23). Julius to Paul (Ac 27:3, 43). Barbarians to Paul (Ac 28:2, 7). Onesiphorus to Paul (2Ti 1:16-18).

KINE, Pharaoh's dream of (Ge 41:2-7, 26-30).

See Cattle.

Figurative: Am 4:1.

KINGDOM OF GOD, the sovereign rule of God manifested in Christ to defeat His enemies, creating a people over whom He reigns, and issuing in a realm or realms in which the power of His reign is experienced. All they are members of the kingdom of God who voluntarily submit to the rule of God in their lives. Entrance into the kingdom is by the new birth (Joh 3:3-5); two stages in the kingdom of God; present and future in an eschatological sense; Jesus said that his ability to cast out demons was evidence that the kingdom of God had come among men (M't 12:28); the term "kingdom of heaven" is often used synonymously with "kingdom of God" in the Bible.

The "kingdom of God" is a more comprehensive term, embracing all created intelligences both in heaven and on earth who are willingly subject to God and thus in fellowship with Him. The "kingdom of heaven" generally describes any type of rulership God may assert on the earth at a given period. See below.

KINGDOM OF HEAVEN. Likened to a man who sowed good seed (M't 13:24-30, 38-43; M'k 4:26-29), to a grain of mustard seed (M't 13:31, 32; M'k 4:30, 31; Lu 13:18, 19); to leaven (M't 13:33; Lu 13:21); to a treasure (M't 13:44); to a pearl (M't 13:45); to a net (M't 13:47-50); to a king who called his servants to a reckoning (M't 18:23-35); to a householder (M't 20:1-16); to a king who made a marriage feast for his son (M't 22:2-14; Lu 14:16-24); to ten virgins (M't 25:1-13); to a man traveling into a far country, who called his servants, and delivered to them his goods (M't 25:14-30; Lu 19:12-27).

"My kingdom is not of this world" (Joh 18:36).

Children of the (M't 18:3; 19:14; M'k 10:14; Lu 18:16). Rich cannot enter (M't 19:23, 24; M'k 10:23-25; Lu 18:24, 25, 29, 30). Keys of (M't 16:19). Glad tidings of (Lu 8:1). Mysteries of (Lu 8:10). Is not meat and drink (Ro 14:17).

See Church: Jesus, Kingdom of.

KINGDOM OF ISRAEL (See Israel.)

KINGDOM OF JUDAH (See Judah.)

KINGDOM OF SATAN (M't 12:26).

KINGS. Israel warned against seeking (1Sa 8:9-18). Sin of Israel in seeking (1Sa 12:17-20). Israel in seeking, rejected God as their king (1Sa 8:7; 10:19). Israel asked for, that they might be like the nations (1Sa 8:5, 19, 20). First given to Israel in anger (Ho 13:11). God reserved to Himself the choice of (De 17:14, 15; 1Sa 9:16, 17; 16:12). When first established in Israel, not hereditary (De 17:20, w 1Sa 13:13, 14; 15:28, 29). Rendered hereditary in the family of David (2Sa 7:12-16; Ps 89:35-37). Of Israel not to be foreigners (De 17:15). Laws for the government of the kingdom by, written by Samuel (1Sa 10:25).

Forbidden to Multiply: Horses (De 17:16). Wives (De 17:17). Treasure (De 17:17). Required to write and keep by them, a copy of the divine law (De 17:18-20). Had power to make war and peace (1Sa 11:5-7). Often exercised power arbitrarily (1Sa 22:17, 18; 2Sa 1:15; 4:9-12; 1Ki 2:23, 25, 31).

Ceremonies at Inauguration of: Anointing (1Sa 10:1; 16:13; Ps 89:20). Crowning (2Ki 11:12; 2Ch 23:11; Ps 21:3). Proclaiming with trumpets (2Sa 15:10; 1Ki 1:34; 2Ki 9:13; 11:14). Enthroning (1Ki 1:35, 46; 2Ki 11:19). Girding on the sword (Ps 45:3). Putting into their hands the books of the law (2Ki 11:12; 2Ch 23:11). Covenanting to govern lawfully (2Sa 5:3). Receiving homage (1Sa 10:1; 1Ch 29:24). Shouting "God save the king" (1Sa 10:24; 2Sa 16:16; 2Ki 11:12). Offering sacrifice (1Sa 11:15). Feasting (1Ch 12:38, 39; 29:22). Attended by a bodyguard (1Sa 13:2; 2Sa 8:18; 1Ch 11:25; 2Ch 12:10). Dwelt in royal palaces (2Ch 9:11; Ps 45:15). Arrayed in royal apparel (1Ki 22:30; M't 6:29). Names of, often changed at their accession (2Ki 23:34; 24:17).

Officers of: Prime minister (2Ch 19:11, w 2Ch 28:7). First Counsellor (1Ch 27:33). Confidant or king's special friend (1Ki 4:5; 1Ch 27:33). Comptroller of the household (1Ki 4:6; 2Ch 28:7). Scribe or secretary (2Sa 8:17; 1Ki 4:3).

Captain of the host (2Sa 8:16; 1Ki 4:4). Captain of the guard (2Sa 8:18; 20:23). Recorder (2Sa 8:16; 1Ki 4:3). Providers for the king's table (1Ki 4:7-19). Master of the wardrobe (2Ki 22:14; 2Ch 34:22). Treasurer (1Ch 27:25). Storekeeper (1Ch 27:25). Overseer of the tribute (1Ki 4:6; 12:18). Overseer of royal farms (1Ch 27:26). Overseer of royal vineyards (1Ch 27:27). Overseer of royal plantations (1Ch 27:28). Overseer of royal herds (1Sa 21:7; 1Ch 27:29). Overseer of royal camels (1Ch 27:30). Overseer of royal flocks (1Ch 27:31). Armor-bearer (1Sa 16:21). Cup-bearer (1Ki 10:5; 2Ch 9:4). Approached with greatest reverence (1Sa 24:8; 2Sa 9:8; 14:22; 1Ki 1:23). Presented with gifts by strangers (1Ki 10:2, 10, 25; 2Ki 5:5; M't 2:11). Right hand of, the place of honor (1Ki 2:19; Ps 45:9; 110:1). Attendants of, stood in their presence (1Ki 10:8; 2Ki 25:19). Exercised great hospitality (1Sa 20:25-27; 2Sa 9:7-13; 19:33; 1Ki 4:22, 23, 28).

Their Revenues Derived From: Voluntary contributions (1Sa 10:27, w 1Sa 16:20; 1Ch 12:39, 40). Tribute from foreign nations (1Ki 4:21, 24, 25; 2Ch 8:8; 17:11). Tax on produce of the land (1Ki 4:7-19). Tax on foreign merchandise (1Ki 10:15). Their own flocks and herds (2Ch 32:29). Produce of their own lands (2Ch 26:10). Sometimes nominated their successors (1Ki 1:33, 34; 2Ch 11:22, 23). Punished for transgressing the divine law (2Sa 12:7-12; 1Ki 21:18-24).

Who Reigned Over all Israel: Saul (1Sa 11:15, 31; 1Ch 10). David (2Sa 2:4; 1Ki 2:11; 1Ch 11-29). Solomon (1Ki 1:39; 11:43; 2Ch 1-9). Rehoboam (first part of his reign) (1Ki 12:1-20; 2Ch 10:1-16).

Who Reigned Over Judah: Rehoboam (latter part of his reign) (1Ki 12:21-24; 14:21-31; 2Ch 10:17, chapter 12). Abijam or Abijah (1Ki 15:1-8; 2Ch 13). Asa (1Ki 15:9-24; 2Ch 14; 16:14). Jehoshaphat (1Ki 22:41-50; 2Ch 17; 21:1). Jehoram or Joram (2Ki 8:16-24; 21). Ahaziah (2Ki 8:25-29; 9:16-29; 2Ch 22:1-9). Athaliah, mother of Ahaziah (usurper) (2Ki 11:1-3; 2Ch 22:10-12). Joash or Jehoash (2Ki 11:4; 12; 2Ch 23, 24). Amaziah (2Ki 14:1-20; 2Ch 25). Azariah or Uzziah (2Ki 14:21, 22; 15:1-7; 2Ch 26). Jotham (2Ki 15:32-38; 2Ch 27). Ahaz (2Ki 16; 2Ch 28). Hezekiah (2Ki 18-20, 2Ch 29-32). Manasseh (2Ki 21:1-18; 2Ch 33:1-20). Amon (2Ki 21:19-26; 2Ch 33:21-25). Josiah (2Ki 22; 23:1-30; 2Ch 34; 35). Jehoahaz (2Ki 23:31-33; 2Ch 36:1-4). Jehoiakim (2Ki 23:34-37; 24:1-6; 2Ch 36:5-8). Jehoiachin (2Ki 24:8-16; 2Ch 36:9, 10). Zedekiah (2Ki 24:17-20; 25:1-7; 2Ch 36:11-21).

Who Reigned Over Israel: Jeroboam (1Ki 12:20, 25; 14:20). Nadab (1Ki 15:25-27, 31). Baasha (1Ki 15:28-34; 16:1-7). Elah (1Ki 16:8-14). Zimri (1Ki 16:11, 12, 15-20). Omri (1Ki 16:23-28). Ahab (1Ki 16:29-22:40). Ahaziah (1Ki 22:51-53; 2Ki 1). Jehoram or Joram (2Ki 3-9:26). Jehu (2Ki 9:3-10; 36). Jehoahaz (2Ki 13:1-9). Jehoash or Joash (2Ki 13:10-25; 14:8-16). Jeroboam the Second (2Ki 14:23-29). Zachariah (2Ki 15:8-12). Shallum (2Ki 15:13-15). Menahem (2Ki 15:16-22). Pekahiah (2Ki 15:23-26). Pekah (2Ki 15:27-31; 16:5). Hoshea (2Ki 17:1-6). Called the Lord's anointed (1Sa 16:6; 24:6; 2Sa 19:21).

Conspiracies Against: Absalom against David (2Sa 15:10). Adonijah against Solomon (1Ki 1:5-7). Jeroboam against Rehoboam (1Ki 12:12, 16). Baasha against Nadab (1Ki 15:27). Zimri against Elah (1Ki 16:9, 10). Omri against Zimri (1Ki 16:17). Jehu against Joram (2Ki 9:14). Shallum against Zachariah (2Ki 15:10). Menahem against Shallum (2Ki 15:14). Pekah against Menahem (1Ki 15:25). God chooses (De 17:15; 1Ch 28:4-6). God ordains (Ro 13:1). God anoints (1Sa 16:12; 2Sa 12:7). Set up by God (1Sa 12:13; Da 2:21). Removed by God (1Ki 11:11; Da 2:21). Christ is the Prince of (Re 1:5). Christ is the King of (Re 17:14). Reign by direction of Christ (Pr 8:15). Supreme judges of nations (1Sa 8:5). Resistance to, is resistance to the ordinance of God (Ro 13:2). Able to enforce their commands (Ec 8:4). Numerous subjects the honor of (Pr 14:28). Not saved by their armies (Ps 33:16). Dependent on the earth (Ec 5:9).

Should: Fear God (De 17:19). Serve Christ (Ps 2:10-12). Keep the law of God (1Ki 2:3). Study the Scriptures (De

17:19). Promote the interests of the Church (Ezr 1:2-4; 6:1-12). Nourish the Church (Isa 49:23). Rule in the fear of God (2Sa 23:3). Maintain the cause of the poor and oppressed (Pr 31:8, 9). Investigate all matters (Pr 25:2). Not pervert judgment (Pr 31:5). Prolong their reign by hating covetousness (Pr 28:16). Throne of, established by righteousness and justice (Pr 16:12; 29:14).

Specially Warned Against: Impurity (Pr 31:3). Lying (Pr 17:7). Hearkening to lies (Pr 29:12). Intemperance (Pr 31:4, 5). The gospel to be preached to (Ac 9:15; 26:27, 28). Without understanding, are oppressors (Pr 28:16). Often reproved by God (1Ch 16:21). Judgments upon, when opposed to Christ (Ps 2:2, 5, 9).

When Good: Regard God as their strength (Ps 99:4). Speak righteously (Pr 16:10). Love righteous lips (Pr 16:13). Abhor wickedness (Pr 16:12). Discountenance evil (Pr 20:8). Punish the wicked (Pr 20:26). Favor the wise (Pr 14:35). Honor the diligent (Pr 22:29). Befriend the good (Pr 22:14). Are pacified by submission (Pr 16:14; 25:15). Evil counsellors should be removed from (2Ch 22:3, 4; Pr 25:5). Curse not, even in thought (Ex 22:28; Ec 10:20). Speak no evil of (Job 34:18; 2Pe 2:10). Pay tribute to (M't 22:21; Ro 13:6, 7). Be not presumptuous before (Pr 25:6).

Should Be: Honored (Ro 13:7; 1Pe 2:17). Feared (Pr 24:21). Reverenced (1Sa 24:8; 1Ki 1:23, 31). Obeyed (Ro 13:1, 5; 1Pe 2:13). Prayed for (1Ti 2:1, 2). Folly of resisting (Pr 19:12; 20:2). Punishment for resisting the lawful authority of (Ro 13:2). Guilt and danger of stretching out the hand against (1Sa 26:9; 2Sa 1:14). They that walk after the flesh despise (2Pe 2:10; Jude 8). Good—Exemplified: David (2Sa 8:15). Asa (1Ki 15:11). Jehoshaphat (1Ki 22:43). Amaziah (2Ki 15:3). Uzziah (2Ki 15:34). Hezekiah (2Ki 18:3). Josiah (2Ki 22:2).

KINGS, I AND II, BOOKS OF. These are named in English by subject-matter: four centuries of kings of Israel, from David (his death in 930 B. C.) to Jehoiachin (in Babylon, after 561); provide a sequel to books of Samuel, which embrace the reigns of Saul and David; the two books were originally written as a unit, which was divided in two at the time of the LXX translation; shows how God rewards the good and punishes the wicked. Outline: 1. Solomon's reign (1Ki 1-11).

2. Kings of Israel and Judah (1Ki 12-2Ki 18).

3. Kings of Judah to exile (2Ki 18-25).

KING'S GARDEN, near Pool of Siloam (2Ki 25:4; Jer 39:4; 52:7; Ne 3:15).

KING'S HIGHWAY, ancient N and S road E of the Jordan through Edom and Moab (Nu 20:17; 21:22). The road is still in use.

KING'S VALE, OR DALE, Valley of Shaveh E of Jerusalem (Ge 14:17; 2Sa 18:18).

KINSMAN (near relative), in OT: one who has a right to redeem or avenge; one too closely related for marriage; a neighbor, friend, or acquaintance; in the NT, one of the same race (Lu 14:12; Joh 18:26; Ro 9:3).

KIR (inclosure, wall). The inhabitants of Damascus carried into captivity to, by the king of Assyria (2Ki 16:9). Prophecies concerning (Isa 22:6; Am 1:5; 9:7).

KIR OF MOAB (See Kir.)

KIR-HARASETH, called also Kir-haresh; Kir-hareseth, and Kir-heres. A city of Moab (2Ki 3:25; Isa 16:7, 11; Jer 48:31, 36). Called Kir of Moab (Isa 15:1).

KIRIATH, KIRJATH (city), city of Benjamin (Jos 18:28).

KIRIATHAIM, KIRJATHAIM (double city). 1. Town in Moab N of Arnon; assigned to Reuben (Nu 32:37; Jos 13:19).

2. City of Gershonite Levites in Naphtali (1Ch 6:76). Kartan in Jos 21:32.

KIRIOTH, town of Moab (Jer 48:24, 41; Am 2:2).

KIRJATH-ARBA (city of Arba), ancient name for Hebron (Ge 23:2; Jos 14:15; 15:54; 20:7).

KIRJATH-ARIM (See Kirjath-Jearim.)

KIRJATH-HUZOTH, a residence of Balak (Nu 22:39).

KIRJATH-JEARIM (city of woods), called also Baalah, one of the four cities of the Gibeonites. Inhabitants of, not smitten, on account of the covenant made by the Israelites with the Gibeonites, but put under servitude (Jos 9:17, with verses 3-27).

In the territory allotted to Judah (Jos 15:9, 60; 18:14). The Philistines bring the ark to (1Sa 6:21, w verses 1-21); ark remains twenty years at (1Sa 7:1, 2; 1Ch 13:5, 6). David brings the ark from (2Sa 6:1-11; 1Ch 13:5-8; 2Ch 1:4). Inhabitants of, who were taken into captivity to Babylon, returned (Ezr 2:25; Ne 7:29). Urijah, the prophet, an inhabitant of (Jer 26:20).

KIRJATH-SANNAH, a city of Judah (Jos 15:49).

See Debir.

KIRJATH-SEPHER (Jos 15:15, 16).

See Debir.

KISH (bow, power). 1. Father of Saul (1Sa 9:1-3; 10:21; 2Sa 21:14, Called Cis in Ac 13:21).

2. A Benjamite (1Ch 8:30; 9:36).

3. A Levite (1Ch 23:21, 22; 24:29).

4. A Levite (2Ch 29:12).

5. Great grandfather of Mordecai (Es 2:5).

KISHI, called also Kushaiah. Father of Ethan, a chief assistant in the temple music (1Ch 6:44; 15:17).

KISHION, city of Issachar (Jos 19:20; 21:28 KJV Kishon; in 1Ch 6:72 called Kedesh).

KISHON (cunning), called also Kison. A noted river of Palestine emptying into the Mediterranean near the northern base of Mount Carmel; Sisera defeated at, and his army destroyed in (J'g 4:7, 13; 5:21; Ps 83:9). Prophets of Baal destroyed by Elijah at (1Ki 18:40).

KISS. Of affection (Ge 27:26, 27; 31:55; 33:4; 48:10; 50:1; Ex 18:7; Ru 1:14; 2Sa 14:33; 19:39; Lu 15:20; Ac 20:37). The feet of Jesus kissed by the penitent woman (Lu 7:38). Deceitful (Pr 27:6); of Joab, when he slew Amasa (2Sa 20:9, 10); of Judas, when he betrayed Jesus (M't 26:48; Lu 22:48). Holy (Ro 16:16; 2Co 13:12; 1Th 5:26; 1Pe 5:14).

KITE, a bird forbidden as food (Le 11:14; De 14:13).

KITHLISH, town in lowlands of Judah (Jos 15:40); site unknown.

KITRON, a city of Zebulun (J'g 1:30).

KITTIM. 1. Descendants of Javan (Ge 10:4; 1Ch 1:7).

2. KJV Chittin; Cyprus (Isa 23:1, 12; Jer 2:10; Eze 27:6).

KNEADING TROUGH, shallow vessel for kneading dough with hands (Ex 8:3; 12:34).

KNEE, bowing the knee or kneeling regarded as act of reverence (Ge 41:43; 2Ki 1:13) and subjection (Isa 45:23; Ph'p 2:10).

KNIFE. An edged tool used by Abraham in offering Isaac (Ge 22:6). Of the temple, returned from Babylon (Ezr 1:9). Used for sharpening pens (Jer 36:23). Self-flagellation with, in idolatrous worship (1Ki 18:28).

KNOP (capital). 1. Knob ornamenting candlestick in tabernacle (Ex 25:31-36; 37:17-22).

2. Ornaments carved on walls of Solomon's Temple (1Ki 6:18).

KNOWLEDGE. Of good and evil (Ge 2:9, 17; 3:22). Is power (Pr 3:20; 24:5). Desire for (1Ki 3:9; Ps 119:66; Pr 2; 3; 12:1; 15:14; 18:15). Rejected (Ho 4:6). Those who reject are destroyed (Ho 4:6). Fools hate (Pr 1:22, 29). A divine gift (1Co 12:8). Is pleasant (Pr 2:10). Shall be increased (Da 12:4).

The earth shall be full of (Isa 11:9). Fear of the Lord is the beginning of (Pr 1:7). Of more value than gold (Pr 8:10). The priest's lips should keep (Mal 2:7).

Of salvation (Lu 1:77). Key of (Lu 11:52). Now we know in part (1Co 13:9-12). Of God more than burnt offering (Ho 6:6). Of Christ (Ph'p 3:8).

See God, Knowledge of; Jesus, Omniscience of; Wisdom.

KOA, people E of Tigris, between Elam and Media (Eze 23:23).

KOHATH. Son of Levi (Ge 46:11; Ex 6:16). Grandfather of Moses, Aaron, and Miriam (Nu 26:58, 59). Father of the Kohathites, one of the divisions of the Levites (Ex 6:18; Nu 3:19, 27).

See Levites.

KOLAIAH (voice of Jerusalem). 1. A Benjamite and ancestor of Sallu (Ne 11:7).

2. Father of the false prophet Ahab (Jer 29:21).

KORAH, KORAHITE. 1. Son of Esau (Ge 36:5, 14, 18; 1Ch 1:35).

2. Grandson of Esau (Ge 36:16).

3. Descendant of Caleb (1Ch 2:43).

4. Levite from whom the Korahites

were descended (Ex 6:24; 1Ch 6:22). In KJV also Korhites, Korathites.

5. Son of Izhar and grandson of Kohath (Ex 6:21, 24; 1Ch 6:37; 9:19).

KORE. 1. A Korahite (1Ch 9:19; 26:1).

2. A Levite, keeper of the east gate (2Ch 31:14).

KORHITES, a division of the Levites. (See Levites.)

KOZ. 1. Priest whose descendants returned from exile (Ezr 2:61; Ne 7:63).

2. Ancestor of Meremoth, who helped repair wall (Ne 3:4, 21).

KUSHAIAH, Merarite Levite (1Ch 15:17); called Kishi in 1Ch 6:44.

L

LAADAH, son of Shelah (1Ch 4:21).

LAADAN. 1. A descendant of Ephraim (1Ch 7:26).

2. A Levite, called also Libni (1Ch 6:17; 23:7-9; 26:21).

LABAN (white). 1. Son of Bethuel (Ge 28:5). Brother of Rebekah (Ge 22:23; 24:15, 29). Receives the servant of Abraham (Ge 24:29-33). Receives Jacob, and gives him his daughters in marriage (Ge 29:12-30). Jacob becomes his servant (Ge 29:15-20, 27; 30:27-43). Outwitted by Jacob (Ge 30:37-43; 31:1-21). Pursues Jacob, overtakes him at Mount Gilead, and covenants with him (Ge 31:22-55).

2. Place in Plains of Moab (De 1:1).

LABOR. Honorable (Ps 128:2; Pr 21:25; 1Th 4:11). Laborers protected by laws (De 24:14). Creative work of God described as labor (Ge 2:2). Onerous labor the result of the curse (Ge 3:17-19).

Sleep of labor sweet (Ec 5:12). Enjoined (Ge 3:19; Ex 20:9-11; 23:12; 34:21; Le 23:3; Lu 13:14; Ac 20:35; Eph 4:28; 1Th 4:11; 2Th 3:10-12).

Compensation for (Le 19:13; De 25:4; 1Co 9:9; 1Ti 5:18; Jer 22:13; Mal 3:5; M't 20:1-15; Lu 10:7; Jas 5:4); of servants must not be oppressive (De 24:14, 15).

Paul, an example in (2Th 3:8-13).

See Capital and Labor; Employee; Employer; Idleness; Industry; Master; Servant.

LACE, cord used to bind high priest's breastplace to the ephod (Ex 28:28, 37; 39:21, 31).

LACHISH, Canaanite royal city and Judean border fortress, occupying strategic valley 25 miles SW of Jerusalem; identified with Tell ed-Duweir, a mound excavated by J. K. Starkey from 1932 to 1938. Joshua captured it (Jos 10:31-33; De 7:2); burned c. 1230 B. C.; fortified by Rehoboam (2Ch 11:9); besieged by Sennacherib in 701 B. C. (2Ch 32:9); destroyed by Nebuchadnezzar together with Jerusalem (2Ki 24; 25; Jer 34:7); resettled after exile (Ne 11:30). Lachish Letters (ostraca) from time of Jeremiah reveal much about city.

LACHRYMATORY (Ps 56:8).

LADDER, mentioned only in Ge 28:12 in English Bible, where it means "staircase."

LAEL, father of Eliasaph (Nu 3:24).

LAHAD, a descendant of Judah (1Ch 4:2).

LAHAI-ROI, called also Beer-lahairoi. A well near Kadesh. Hagar fled to (Ge 16:7-14). Isaac dwells at (Ge 24:62; 25:11).

LAHMAM, town in Judean Shephelah (Jos 15:40), perhaps same as modern el-Lahm.

LAHMI. Brother of Goliath. Slain by Elhanan (2Sa 21:19; 1Ch 20:5).

LAISH. 1. Called also Leshem (See Dan).

2. A native of Gallim (1Sa 25:44; 2Sa 3:15).

3. A town near Jerusalem (Isa 10:30).

LAKE, of fire (Re 19:20; 20:10, 14, 15; 21:8).

LAKUM, LAKKUM, town of Naphtali (Jos 19:33), location unknown.

LAMA SABACHTHANI, the dying wail of Jesus (M't 27:46; M'k 15:34. See Ps 22:1).

LAMB, used for food (De 32:14; Am 6:4) and for sacrifices (Ge 4:4; 22:7), especially at Passover (Ex 12:3-5). Sacrificial lambs typical of Christ (Joh 1:29; Re 5:6, 8).

Offering of (Le 3:7; 5:6; 22:23; 23:12; Nu 7:15, 21; 28:3-8); at the daily morning and evening sacrifices (Ex 29:38-42). Offering of, at the feast, of the passover (Ex 12:15); Pentecost (Le 23:18-20); tabernacles (Nu 29:13-40); the new moon (Nu 28:11); trumpets (Nu 29:2). Offering of, on the Sabbath day (Nu 28:9); at purifications (Le 12:6; 14:10-25); by the Nazarite (Nu 6:12); for sin of ignorance (Le 4:32).

Figurative: The wolf dwelling with, a figure of Messiah's reign (Isa 11:6; 65:25). A type of young believers (Joh 21:15).

A name given to Christ (Joh 1:29, 36; Re 5:6, 8, 12, 13; 6:1, 16; 7:9, 10, 14; 12:11; 13:8; 14:4, 10; 17:14; 19:7, 9; 21:9, 14, 22, 23, 27; 22:1, 3). Jesus compared to (Isa 53:7; Ac 8:32; 1Pe 1:19).

LAMB OF GOD, an appellation of

Jesus (Joh 1:29; Re 6:16; 7:9, 10, 14, 17; 12:11; 13:8; 14:1, 4; 15:3; 17:14; 19:7; 21:9, 14, 22, 23, 27; 22:1, 3).

LAME (See Diseases.)

LAMECH. 1. Father of Jabal, Jubal, and Tubalcain (Ge 4:18-24).

2. Son of Methuselah, and father of Noah, lived 777 years (Ge 5:25-31; 1Ch 1:3). Ancestor of Jesus (Lu 3:36).

LAMENESS. Disqualified priests from exercising the priestly office (Le 21:18). Disqualified animals for sacrificial uses (De 15:21). Hated by David (2Sa 5:8). Healed by Jesus (M't 11:5; 15:31; 21:14; Lu 7:22); by Peter (Ac 3:2-11).

Figurative: Heb 12:13.

LAMENTATIONS. Of David (Ps 60:1-3). Of Jeremiah (See the Book of Lamentations). Of Ezekiel (Eze 19; 28:12-19).

See Elegy.

LAMENTATIONS, BOOK OF. Author not stated, but ancient authorities ascribe it to Jeremiah. LXX, Vulgate, and English Bible place it after Jeremiah, but in Hebrew Bible it appears between Ruth and Ecclesiastes. Title accurately designates contents; the book bewails the siege and destruction of Jerusalem, and sorrows over the sufferings of the inhabitants during this time; makes poignant confession of sin on behalf of the people and their leaders, acknowledges complete submission to the Divine will, and prays that God will once again favor and restore His people. Five poems (the first four consisting of acrostics based on Hebrew alphabet) make up the five chapters.

LAMP. For the tabernacle (Ex 25:31-40; 35:14; 37:17-23; 39:37). Kept burning at night in the tabernacle, and cared for by priests (Ex 27:20, 21; 30:7, 8; Le 24:2-4; 1Sa 3:3).

In the temple (1Ki 7:49; 2Ch 4:20, 21; 13:11). Carried in procession (M't 25:1-8). Made of gold (Ex 25:31-40; 37:17-24); burned olive oil (Ex 27:20).

Figurative: Of joy (Jer 25:10). Life (Job 18:5, 6; 21:17; Pr 13:9; 20:20). The word of God (Ps 119:105; Pr 6:23; 2Pe 1:19). Spiritual illumination (M't 6:22). Religious influence (M't 5:15; M'k 4:21; Lu 8:16; 11:33). Christ (Re 21:23).

Symbolical (Re 4:5; 8:10). See Candlestick.

LANCE (See Javelin; Spear.)

LAND. Appeared on third creative day (Ge 1:9). Original title to, from God (Ge 13:14-17; 15:7; Ex 23:31; Le 25:33). Bought and sold (Ge 23:3-18; 33:19; Ac 4:34; 5:1-8).

Sale and redemption of, laws concerning (Le 25:15, 16, 23-33; 27:17-24; Nu 36:4; Jer 32:7-16, 25, 44; Eze 46:18). Conveyance of, by written deeds and other forms (Ge 23:3-20; Ru 4:3-8, 11; Jer 32:9-14); witnessed (Ge 23:10, 11; Ru 4:9-11; Jer 32:9-14).

Sold for debt (Ne 5:3-5). Rights in, alienated (2Ki 8:1-6). Leased (Lu 20:9-16; M't 21:33-41).

Priests' part in (Ge 47:22; Eze 48:10). King's part in (Eze 48:21). Widow's dower in (Ru 4:3-9). Unmarried woman's rights in (Nu 27:1-11; 36:1-11).

To rest every seventh year for the benefit of the poor (Ex 23:11). Products of, for all (Ec 5:9). Monopoly of (Ge 47:20-26; Isa 5:8; Mic 2:1, 2). See Mortgage.

Rules for apportioning Canaan among the tribes. (See Canaan; also Eze 47:22.)

LANDMARKS, protected from fraudulent removal (De 19:14; 27:17; Job 24:2; Pr 22:28; 23:10; Ho 5:10).

LANE, alley of a city (Lu 14:21).

LANGUAGE. Unity of (Ge 11:1, 6). Confusion of (Ge 11:1-9; 10:5, 20, 31). Dialects of the Jews (J'g 12:6; M't 26:73). Many spoken at Jerusalem (Joh 19:20; Ac 2:8-11). Speaking in unknown, in religious assemblies, forbidden (1Co 14:2-28).

Gift of (M'k 16:17; Ac 2:7, 8; 10:46; 19:6; 1Co 12:10; 14).

Mentioned in Scripture: Of Ashdod (Ne 13:24); Chaldee (Da 1:4); Egyptian (Ac 2:10; Ps 114:1); Greek (Lu 23:38; Ac 21:37); Latin (Lu 23:38; Joh 19:20); Lycaonia (Ac 14:11); Parthia and other lands (Ac 2:9-11); Syria (2Ki 18:26; Ezr 4:7; Da 2:4).

LANTERN (Joh 18:3).

LAODICEA. A Phrygian city. Paul's concern for (Col 2:1). Epaphras' zeal for (Col 4:13). Epistle to the Colossians to be read in (Col 4:15, 16). Message to, through John (Re 1:11; 3:14-22).

LAODICEA, CHURCH AT (See Laodicea.)

LAODICEANS, EPISTLE TO, letter

mentioned by Paul in Col 4:16; could be a lost letter of Paul's or the Epistle to the Ephesians. An apocryphal Epistle to the Laodiceans consisting of 20 verses exists.

LAPIDARY, one who cuts precious stones (Ex 31:5; 35:33).

LAPIDOTH, husband of Deborah (J'g 4:4).

LAPPED, LAPPETH. Hebrew verb used to indicate alertness (J'g 7:5-7) and disgust (1Ki 21:19; 22:38).

LAPWING, a bird forbidden as food (Le 11:19; De 14:18).

LARCENY (See Theft.)

LASCIVIOUSNESS. Unbridled lust, licentiousness, wantonness. Forbidden (Col 3:5; 1Th 4:3-6).

Warnings against (Pr 2:16-18; 5:3-5, 8-13; 7:6-27; 9:13-18; 30:18-20; 31:3; Ro 13:13; 1Co 6:13, 15-18; 1Pe 4:2, 3; Jude 4, 7).

Iniquitous practices in (Joe 3:3; Ro 1:22-29). Proceeds from unregenerate heart (M'k 7:21-23; Ga 5:19; Eph 4:17-19). Impenitence in (2Co 12:21).

Excludes from the kingdom of God (1Co 6:9, 10, 13, 15-18; 9:27; Ga 5:19, 21; Eph 5:5).

Lascivious practices in idolatrous worship, see Idolatry, Wicked practices of.

See Adultery; Incest; Lust; Rape; Sensuality; Sodomy; Whore; Whoredom.

Figurative: Eze 16:15-59. (See Whoredoms.)

Instances of: Sodomites (Ge 19:5). Lot's daughters (Ge 19:30-38). Judah (Ge 38:15, 16). The Gibeahites (J'g 19:22-25). Eli's sons (1Sa 2:22). David (2Sa 5:13; 11:2-27). Amnon (2Sa 13:1-14). Solomon (1Ki 11:1-3). Rehoboam (2Ch 11:21-23). Persian kings (Es 2:3, 13, 14, 19).

LASEA, seaport town on S coast of Crete; visited by Paul (Ac 27:8).

LASHA, place near Sodom and Gomorrah (Ge 10:19). Site not identified.

LASHARON (to Sharon), king of, killed by Joshua (Jos 12:18).

LATCHET (sandal-thong), strap to fasten sandal to foot. Often used figuratively (Ge 14:23; Isa 5:27; M'k 1:7).

LATIN (Lu 23:38; Joh 19:20).

LATTICE, latticework used for privacy, ventilation, decoration (J'g 5:28; 2Ki 1:2; translated "casement," Pr 7:6).

LAUGHTER, used to express joy (Ge 21:6; Lu 6:21), derision (Ps 2:4), disbelief (Ge 18:13).

LAVER. Directions for making (Ex 30:18-20). Situation of, in the tabernacle, tent of the congregation, and the altar (Ex 40:7). Sanctified (Ex 30:28; 40:11; Le 8:11). Used for washing (Ex 40:30-32).

Brazen, made by Solomon for the temple (1Ki 7:23-26, 30, 38, 39; 2Ch 4:2-14). Altered by Ahaz (2Ki 16:17). Broken and carried to Babylon by the Chaldeans (2Ki 25:13, 16; Jer 52:17, 20).

Figurative: Re 4:6; 15:2, in connection with Ex 38:8; 1Ki 7:23.

LAW. 1. Ten commandments given to Moses (Ex 20:3-17; De 5:6-21), summarized God's requirements of man.

2. Torah, first five books of OT (M't 5:17; Lu 16:16).

3. OT (Joh 10:34; 12:34).

4. God's will in words, acts, precepts (Ex 20:1-17; Ps 19). OT Jews manifested their faith in Jehovah by observing the law. Christ fulfilled the law; respected, loved it, and showed its deeper significance (M't 5:17-48). Purpose of OT law to prepare way for coming of Christ (Ga 3:24). Law shows man's sinfulness, but cannot bring victory over sin (Ro 3-8; Ga). Jesus' summary of the law: it demands perfect love for God and love for one's neighbor comparable to that which one has for himself (M't 22:35-40).

Made for the lawless (1Ti 1:8-10). To be obeyed (M't 22:21; Lu 20:22-25).

Of God (Ps 119:1-8). Holy (Ro 7:12). Perfect (Ps 19:7-9; Jas 1:25). Spiritual (Ro 7:14). To be obeyed (1Jo 5:3). Love, the fulfilling of (Ro 13:10; 1Ti 1:5).

See Litigation; Commandments; Duty to God.

Of Moses: Contained in the books, Exodus, Leviticus, Numbers and Deuteronomy. Divine authority for (Ex 19:16-24; 20:1, 2; 24:12-18; 31:18; 32:15, 16; 34:1-4, 27, 28; Le 26:46; De 4:10-13, 36; 5:1-22; 9:10; 10:1-5; 33:2-4; 1Ki 8:9; Ezr 7:6; Ne 1:7; 8:1; 9:14; Ps 78:5; 103:7; Isa 33:22; Mal 4:4; Ac 7:38, 53; Ga 3:19; Heb 9:18-21).

Given at Sinai (Ex 19; De 1:1; 4:10-13, 44-46; 32:2; Hab 3:3). Received by the disposition of angels (De 32:2; Ps

68:17; Ac 7:53; Ga 3:19; Heb 2:2). Was given because of transgression until the Messiah came (Ga 3:19). Engraved on stone (Ex 20:3-17; 24:12; 31:18; 32:16; 34:29; 40:20; De 4:13; 5:4-22; 9:10); on monuments (De 27:2-8; Jos 8:30-35). See Tables; Commandments.

Preserved in the ark of the covenant (Ex 25:16; De 31:9, 26). To be written, on door posts (De 6:9; 11:20); on frontlets for the forehead, and on parchment for the hand (Ex 13:9, 16; Re 6:4-9; 11:18-21). Children instructed in, (See Children; Instruction).

Expounded, by priests and Levites (Le 10:11; De 33:10; 2Ch 35:3); by princes, priests, and Levites (Ezr 7:10; Ne 8:1-18); from city to city (2Ch 17:7-10); in synagogues (Lu 11:16; Ac 13:14-52; 15:21 w 9:20 & 14:1; 17:1-3; 18:4, 26). Expounded to the assembled nation at the feast of tabernacles in the sabbatic year (De 31:10-13). Rehearsed by Moses, with many admonitions (De 4:44-46; chps 5-34).

Obedience to, enjoined (De 4:40; 5:32; 6:17; 7:11; 8:1, 6; 10:12, 13; 11:1, 8, 32; 13:4; 16:12; 27:1; 30:16; 32:46; Jos 1:7; 22:5; 1Ki 2:3; 8:61; 2Ki 17:37). Found by Hilkiah in the house of the Lord (2Ki 22:8; 2Ch 34:14).

Blessings and curses of, responsively read by Levites and people at Ebal and Gerizim (De 27:12-26; Jos 8:33-35).

Formed a constitution on which the civil government of the Israelites was founded, and according to which rulers were required to rule (De 17:18-20; 2Ki 11:12; 2Ch 23:11). See Government; Constitution.

Was given because of transgressions until the coming of the Messiah (Ga 3:19). Was committed to the Jews (Ro 3:1, 2). Brings the knowledge of sin (Ro 3:20; 7:7).

Prophecies in, of the Messiah (Lu 24:44; Joh 1:45; 5:46; 12:34; Ac 26:22, 23; 28:23; Ro 3:21, 22). See Jesus, Prophecies Concerning.

Epitomized by Jesus (M't 22:40; M'k 12:29-33; Lu 10:27).

Temporary (Jer 3:16; Da 9:27; Heb 10:1-18). Weakness of (Ro 8:3, 6).

Fulfilled by Christ (M't 5:17-45; Ac 6:14; 13:39; Ro 10:3, 4; Eph 2:15; Heb 8:4-13; 9:8-24; 10:3-9).

Superceded by the gospel (Lu 16:16, 17; Joh 1:17; 4:20-24; 8:35 w Ga 4:30, 31; Ac 10:28; 15:1-20; 21:20-25; Ro 7:1-6; 2Co 3:7-14; Ga 2:3-9, 19; 4:4-31; 5:1-18; Col 2:14-23; Heb 7:5-9).

LAW OF MOSES (See Law.)

LAWGIVER. God is the only absolute lawgiver (Jas 4:12); instrumentally, Moses bears this description (Joh 1:17; 7:19).

LAWSUITS, to be avoided (Pr 25:8-10; M't 5:25, 26; 1Co 6:1-8).

See Actions at Law; Adjudication; Arbitration; Compromise; Courts; Justice.

LAWYER, One versed in the Mosaic law. Test Jesus with questions (M't 22:35; Lu 10:25-37). Jesus' satire against (Lu 11:45-52). Zenas, a (Tit 3:13).

See Litigation.

LAYING ON OF HANDS, symbolic act signifying impartation of inheritance rights (Ge 48:14-20), gifts and rights of an office (Nu 27:18, 23); dedication of animals (Le 1:4), priests (Nu 8:10), people for special service (Ac 6:6; 13:3).

LAZARUS (God has helped). 1. Brother of Martha and Mary; raised from dead by Jesus (Joh 11:1-12:19).

2. Beggar who died and went to Abraham's bosom (Lu 16:19-31).

LAZINESS (Pr 12:27; 18:9; 19:24; 21:25; 22:13; 26:13, 14-16).

Brings, adversity (Pr 12:24; Ec 10:18); destruction (Pr 13:4; 19:15; 20:4; 23:21; 24:30-34).

Admonitions against (Pr 6:6-11; 10:4, 5, 26; 15:19). Denounced (M't 25:26, 27). Of ministers, denounced (Isa 56:10). Forbidden (Ro 12:11; Heb 6:12).

See Idleness; Slothfulness.

LEAD. A mineral (Ex 15:10). Purified by fire (Nu 31:22; Jer 6:29; Eze 22:18, 20). Used in making inscriptions on stone (Job 19:24). Lead-founder (Jer 6:29; Eze 22:18, 20). Trade in (Eze 27:12). Used for weighing (Zec 5:7, 8).

LEADERSHIP. *Instances of:* Abraham, Moses, Joshua, Gideon, Deborah. See each respectively.

LEAF, leaf of a tree, page of a book, leaf of a door. Metaphorically, green leaves symbolize prosperity, and dry leaves ruin and decay (Ps 1:3; Pr 11:28; Job 13:25; Isa 1:30).

LEAGUE (See Alliances; Treaty.)

LEAH. Daughter of Laban (Ge 29:16).

Married to Jacob (Ge 29:23-26). Children of (Ge 29:31-35; 30:9-13, 17-21). Flees with Jacob (Ge 31:4, 14, 17; 33:2-7). "Builder of the house of Israel" (Ru 4:11).

LEARNING (See Instruction; Knowledge.)

LEASE, of real estate (M't 21:33-41; M'k 12:1-9; Lu 20:9-16). See Land.

LEASING, obsolete KJV word for falsehood (Ps 4:2; 5:6).

LEATHER, designates the tanned hide of animals. Skins were used for rough clothing, as well as for armor, bags, sandals, and writing materials (Le 13:48; Eze 18:10; M't 3:14; Heb 11:37).

LEAVEN. For bread (Ex 12:34, 39; Ho 7:4; M't 13:33). Leavened bread used with peace offering (Le 7:13; Am 4:5); with wave offering (Le 23:15-17). Leavened bread forbidden with meat offerings (Le 2:11; 6:17; 10:12; Ex 23:18; 34:25); at the passover (Ex 12:19, 20; 13:3, 4, 7; 23:18); with blood (Ex 23:18; 34:25).

A type of sin (1Co 5:6-8).

Figurative: Of the hypocrisy of the Pharisees (M't 16:6-12; M'k 8:15; Lu 12:1). Of other evils (1Co 5:6-8; Ga 5:9). Parable of (M't 13:33; Lu 13:21).

LEBANA, LEBANAH (white), ancestor of family which returned from exile (Ezr 2:45; Ne 7:48).

LEBANON. A mountain range. Northern boundary of the land of Canaan (De 1:7; 3:25; 11:24; Jos 1:4; 9:1). Early inhabitants of (J'g 3:3). Snow of (Jer 18:14). Streams of (Song 4:15). Cedars of (J'g 9:15; 2Ki 19:23; 2Ch 2:8; Ps 29:5; 104:16; Isa 2:13; 14:8; Eze 27:5). Other trees of (2Ki 19:23; 2Ch 2:8). Flower of (Na 1:4). Beasts of (Isa 40:16). Fertility and productiveness of (Ho 14:5-7). "House of the forest of" (1Ki 7:2-5). Valley of (Jos 11:17; 12:7). Tower of (Song 7:4). Solomon had cities of store in (1Ki 9:19).

Figurative: Isa 29:17; Jer 22:6.

LEBAOTH (lionesses), town in S Judah (Jos 15:32); also called Beth-lebaoth (Jos 19:6) and probably, Beth-birei (1Ch 4:31).

LEBBAEUS (hearty), one of Christ's apostles, also called Thaddaeus (M't 10:3) and Judas (Lu 6:16; Ac 1:13).

LEBONAH (frankincense), a city on the highway from Beth-el to Shechem (J'g 21:19).

LECAH (walking), a town or person in Judah (1Ch 4:21).

LEEK (Nu 11:5).

LEES (something preserved), sediment of wine (Isa 25:6). Also used figuratively to describe blessings of Messianic times, spiritual lethargy, inevitability of God's judgment (Jer 48:11; Ps 75:8).

LEFT, used with a variety of meanings; simple direction; North (Ge 14:15); lesser blessing (Ge 48:13-19), weakness (J'g 3:15, 21, etc.)

LEFT-HANDED (J'g 3:15; 20:16).

LEGENDS. "Holiness to the LORD," engraved on the high priest's mitre (Ex 28:36; 39:30); on bells of horses, on pots and bowls (Zec 14:20). "This is Jesus, the King of the Jews" (M't 27:37). Precepts written on door posts and gates, and worn on the hand and forehead (De 6:6-9; 11:18-20; Isa 57:8).

LEGION. 1. Largest single unit in Roman army, including infantry and cavalry.

2. Vast number (M't 26:53; M'k 5:9).

LEGISLATION, class, forbidden (Ex 12:49; Le 24:22; Nu 9:14; 15:15, 29; Ga 3:28).

Supplemental, concerning Sabbath-breaking (Nu 15:32-35); inheritance (Nu 27:1-11). See Government; Law.

LEGS, of the crucified broken (Joh 19:31, 32).

LEHABIM, third son of Mizraim (Ge 10:13) and descendants, the Libyans (Eze 30:5; 38:5).

LEHI (jawbone), place where Samson killed 1000 Philistines with a jawbone of ass (J'g 15:9, 14).

LEMUEL (devoted to God), king, otherwise unknown, to whom his mother taught the maxims in Pr 31:2-9; probably Solomon (Pr 31:1).

LENDING. To the poor, enjoined (Le 25:35; De 15:7, 11); enjoined by Christ (M't 5:42; Lu 6:34, 35). Encouraged (Ps 112:5; Pr 19:17). God, the merciful Lender (Ps 37:25, 26). Borrower to be released in the year of release (De 15:1-6).

Things forbidden as security of loans: Millstones (De 24:6). Widow's raiment (De 24:17).

Lender: Forbidden, to take interest from poor Hebrews (Ex 22:25-27; Le

25:36, 37; De 23:19, 20); to enter debtor's house for security (De 24:10, 11); to keep pawned raiment overnight (De 24:12, 13). Oppression of (Ne 5:1-13). Is master of borrower (Pr 22:7). Lender and borrower will be equal (Isa 24:1, 2). Wicked, punished (Pr 28:9; Eze 18:13).

See Borrowing; Interest; Money.

LENTILES (Ge 25:34; 2Sa 17:28; 23:11; Eze 4:9).

LEOPARD. A carnivorous animal (Song 4:8). Fierceness of (Jer 5:6; 13:23; Ho 13:7; Hab 1:8).

Figurative: Da 7:6. Taming of, the triumph of the gospel (Isa 11:6).

LEPROSY, Law concerning (Le 13; 14; 22:4; Nu 5:1-3; 12:14; De 24:8; M't 8:4; Lu 5:14; 17:14). Sent as a judgment. On Miriam (Nu 12:1-10); Gehazi (2Ki 5:27); Uzziah (2Ch 26:20, 21). Entailed (2Ki 5:27). Isolation of lepers (Le 13:46; Nu 5:2; 12:14; 2Ki 15:5; 2Ch 26:21). Separate burial of (2Ch 26:23).

Instances of leprosy not mentioned above: Four lepers outside Samaria (2Ki 7:3); Azariah (2Ki 15:5); Simon (M'k 14:3).

Healed: Miriam (Nu 12:13, 14); Naaman (2Ki 5:8-14); by Jesus (M't 8:3; M'k 1:40-42; Lu 5:13; 17:12-14).

Disciples empowered to heal (M't 10:8).

LESHEM (gem), city renamed Dan, at extreme N of Palestine (1Sa 3:20); variant of Laish.

LETTER, designates an alphabetical symbol, rudimentary education (Joh 7:15), written communication, the external (Ro 2:27, 29), Jewish legalism (Ro 7:6; 2Co 3:6). In ancient times correspondence was privately delivered. Archaeology has uncovered many different kinds of letters.

LETTERS. Written by David to Joab (2Sa 11:14); king of Syria to king of Israel (2Ki 5:5, 6); Rabshakeh to Hezekiah (Isa 37:9-14); King of Babylon to Hezekiah (Isa 39:1); Sennacherib to Hezekiah (2Ki 19:14). Of Artaxerxes to Nehemiah (Ne 2:7-9). Open letter from Sanballat to Nehemiah (Ne 6:5). Luke to Theophilus, the books of Luke and Acts (Ac 1:1). Claudius Lysias to Felix (Ac 23:25-30). Letter of intercession by Paul to Philemon in behalf of Onesimus (Ph'm 1); of recommendation (2Co 3:1).

LETTUSHIM, LETUSHIM (sharpened), second son of Dedan, grandson of Abraham (Ge 25:3).

LEUMMIM (peoples, nations), third son of Dedan (Ge 25:3).

LEVI (joined). Son of Jacob (Ge 29:34; 35:23; 1Ch 2:1). Avenges the seduction of Dinah (Ge 34; 49:5-7). Jacob's prophecy regarding (Ge 49:5-7). His age at death (Ex 6:16). Descendants of, made ministers of religion (See Levites.)

LEVIATHAN. Possibly a crocodile (Job 41; Ps 104:26). The crooked serpent (Isa 27:1).

Figurative: Ps 74:14.

LEVIRATE MARRIAGE, Jewish custom according to which when an Israelite without male heirs died the nearest relative married the widow, and the first born son became the heir of the 1st husband (De 25:5-10).

LEVITES. The descendants of Levi. Set apart as ministers of religion (Nu 1:47-54; 3:6-16; 16:9; 26:57-62; De 10:8; 1Ch 15:2). Substituted in the place of the firstborn (Nu 3:12, 41-45; 8:14, 16-18; 18:6). Religious zeal of (Ex 32:26-28; De 33:9, 10; Mal 2:4, 5). Consecration of (Nu 8:6-21). Sedition among, led by Korah, Dathan, Abiram, and On, on account of jealousy toward Moses and Aaron (Nu 16, w 4:19, 20).

Three divisions of: Each having the name of one of its progenitors, Gershon, Kohath, and Merari (Nu 3:17). Gershonites and their duties (Nu 3:18-26; 4:23-26; 10:17). Ruling chief over the Gershonites was the second son of the ruling high priest (Nu 4:28). Kohathites, consisting of the families of the Amramites, Izeharites, Hebronites, Uzzielites (Nu 3:27; 4:18-20). Of the Amramites, Aaron and his family were set apart as priests (Ex 28:1; 29:9; Nu 3:38; 8:1-14; 17; 18:1); the remaining families appointed to take charge of the ark, table, candlestick, altars, and vessels of the sanctuary, the hangings, and all the service (Nu 3:27-32; 4:2-15). The chief over the Kohathites was the oldest son of the ruling high priest (Nu 3:32; 1Ch 9:20). Merarites (Nu 3:20, 33-37; 4:31-33; 7:8; 10:17; 1Ch 6:19, 29, 30; 23:21-23). The chief over the Merarites was the second son of the ruling high priest (Nu 4:33).

Place of, in camp and march (Nu 1:50-53; 2:17; 3:23-35). Cities assigned to, in the land of Canaan (Jos 21). Lodged in the chambers of the temple (1Ch 9:27, 33; Eze 40:44). Resided also in villages outside of Jerusalem (Ne 12:29).

Age of, when inducted into office (Nu 4:3, 30, 47; 8:23-26; 1Ch 23:3, 24, 27; Ezr 3:8); when retired from office (Nu 4:3, 47; 8:25, 26).

Functions of: Had charge of the tabernacle in camp and on the march (Nu 1:50-53; 3:6-9, 21-37; 4:1-15, 17-49; 8:19, 22; 18:3-6); and of the temple (1Ch 9:27-29; 23:2-32; Ezr 8:24-34).

Bore the ark of the covenant (De 10:8; 1Ch 15:2, 26, 27). Ministered before the ark (1Ch 16:4). Custodians and administrators of the tithes and other offerings (1Ch 9:26-29; 26:28; 29:8; 2Ch 24:5, 11; 31:11-19; 34:9; Ezr 8:29, 30, 33; Ne 12:44). Prepared the shewbread (1Ch 23:28, 29). Assisted the priests in preparing the sacrifice (2Ch 29:12-36; 2Ch 35:1-18). Killed the passover for the children of the captivity (Ezr 6:20, 21). Teachers of the law (De 33:10; 2Ch 17:8, 9; 30:22; 35:3; Ne 8:7-13; Mal 2:6, 7). Were judges (De 17:9; 1Ch 23:4; 26:29; 2Ch 19:8-11; Ne 11:16). See Judges.

Were scribes of the sacred books (See Scribes.) Pronounced the blessings of the law in the responsive service at Mount Gerizim (De 27:12; Jos 8:33). Were porters of the doors. (See Porters.) Were overseers in building and the repairs of the temple (1Ch 23:2-4; Ezr 3:8, 9). Were musicians of the temple service. (See Music.) Supervised weights and measures (1Ch 23:29).

List of those who returned from captivity (Ezr 2:40-63; 7:7; 8:16-20; Ne 7:43-73; 12). Sealed the covenant with Nehemiah (Ne 10:9-28).

Emoluments of: In lieu of landed inheritance, forty-eight cities with suburbs were assigned to them (Nu 35:2-8, w 18:24 & 26:62; De 10:9; 12:12, 18, 19; 14:27-29; 18:1-8; Jos 13:14; 14:3; 18:7; 1Ch 6:54-81; 13:2; 2Ch 23:2; Eze 34:1-5). Assigned to, by families (Jos 21:4-40). Suburbs of their cities were inalienable for debt (Le 25:32-34). Tithes and other offerings (Nu 18:24, 26-32; De 18:1-8; 26:11-13; Jos 13:14; Ne 10:38, 39; 12:44, 47). First fruits (Ne 12:44, 47). Spoils of war, including captives (Nu 31:30, 42-47). See Tithes. Tithes withheld from (Ne 13:10-13; Mal 3:10). Pensioned (2Ch 31:16-18). Owned lands (De 18:8, w 1Ki 2:26). Land allotted to, by Ezekiel (Eze 48:13, 14).

Enrollment of, at Sinai (Nu 1:47-49; 2:33; 3:14-39; 4:2, 3; 26:57-62; 1Ch 23:3-5). Degraded from the Levitical office by Jeroboam (2Ch 11:13-17; 13:9-11). Loyal to the ruler (2Ki 11:7-11; 2Ch 23:7).

Intermarry with Canaanites (Ezr 9:1, 2; 10:23, 24). Exempt from enrollment for military duty (Nu 1:47-54, w 1Ch 12:26). Subordinate to the sons of Aaron (Nu 3:9; 8:19; 18:6).

Prophecies concerning (Jer 33:18; Eze 44:10-14; Mal 3:3); of their repentance of the crucifixion of the Messiah (Zec 12:10-13). John's vision concerning (Re 7:7).

LEVITICUS (relating to the Levites), third book of the Pentateuch; authorship ascribed to Moses by tradition; describes duties of priests and Levites; emphasizes holiness of God and the need to approach Him through proper channels. Outline: 1. Sacrifices and offerings (1-7).

2. Duties of priests (8-10).
3. Cleanliness and holiness (11-22).
4. Feasts (23).
5. Promises and warnings (25-27).

LEVY (tribute), people conscripted to perform forced labor for another (1Ki 5:13, 14; 9:21).

LEX TALIONIS (See Retaliation.)

LIARS. All men liars (Ps 116:11). Satan a (Joh 8:44, 55). Prohibited the Kingdom of Heaven (Re 21:8).

See Deceit; Deception; Falsehood; Hypocrisy.

LIBATION, pouring out of wine or some other liquid as an offering to a deity as an act of worship (Ex 29:40, 41; Jer 44:17-25).

LIBERALITY. Enjoined (Ex 22:29, 30; 23:15; 34:20; Le 23:22; 25:35-43; De 12:11, 12, 17-19; Pr 3:27, 28; M't 5:42; Ac 20:35; Ro 12:8; 2Co 8:7, 9, 11-14, 24; 1Ti 6:18; Heb 13:16).

In offerings, for tabernacle (Ex 25:1-8; 35:4-29; 36:3-6; 38:8); for the temple

(Hag 1:8); with the Levites (De 12:11, 12, 17-19; 18:1-8). For the temple enjoined by Cyrus (Ezr 1:2-4).

In offerings for sacrifice (2Sa 24:24). In paying tithes (De 14:27-29). In gifts to God (Ps 76:11).

Toward the poor (De 15:7-11; 24:19-22; Ne 8:10; Ps 41:1-3; Isa 58:6, 7; M't 19:21, 22; M'k 10:21; Lu 3:10, 11; Ro 12:13; 15:27; 2Co 9:6-15; Ga 2:10; Eph 4:28; 1Ti 5:16; 6:17-19; Jas 2:15, 16; 1Jo 3:17, 18); by the ideal woman (Pr 31:20).

Toward liberated Hebrew slaves (De 15:12-18).

According to ability (Nu 35:8; De 16:10, 17; 1Co 16:1-3; 2Co 8:12). Without ostentation (M't 6:1-4). At own will (Le 19:5; 22:9). With a willing heart (1Ch 29:5; Pr 21:26; 2Co 8:12; 9:1-6; Ph'm 14). With love (1Co 13:3).

Rewards for (Ps 112:5, 9; Pr 3:9, 10; 11:24, 25; 13:7; 14:21; 19:6, 17; 22:9; 28:27; Ec 11:1, 2; Isa 32:8; 58:10-12; Eze 18:7-16; Mal 3:10-12; M't 5:42; 25:34-40, 46; Lu 6:30-38; 12:33, 34; Heb 6:10).

See Alms; Beneficence; Charitableness; Emoluments of; Giving; Ministers; Poor, Duty to; Rich; Riches; Tithe.

Instances of: King of Sodom to Abraham (Ge 14:21). Jacob, consecrating the tenth of his income (Ge 28:22). Pharaoh to Joseph's people (Ge 45:18-20). Israelites at the erection of the tabernacle (Ex 35:21-29; 36:3-7; 38:8; Nu 7; 31:48-54; Jos 18:1). Reubenites (Jos 22:24-29). David (2Sa 7:2; 1Ch 17:1; 2Sa 8:11; 1Ki 7:51; 8:17, 18; 1Ch 21:24; 22; 26:26; 28:2; 29:2-5, 17; Ps 132:1-5). Barzillai and others to David (2Sa 17:27-29; 19:32). Araunah for sacrifice (2Sa 24:22, 23). Joab to David (2Sa 12:26-28).

Israelites' offerings for the temple (1Ch 29:6-9, 16, 17). Samuel (1Ch 26:27, 28). Solomon (1Ki 4:29; 5:4, 5; 2Ch 2:1-6; 1Ki 6; 7:51; 8:13). Queen of Sheba to Solomon (1Ki 10:10). Asa and Abijam (1Ki 15:15). Elisha toward Elijah (1Ki 19:21). Jehoshaphat (2Ki 12:18). Joash and his people (2Ki 12:4-14; 2Ch 24:4-14). David (1Ch 16:3). Hezekiah (2Ch 29; 30:1-12; 31:1-10, 21). Manasseh (2Ch 33:16). Josiah (2Ki 22:3-6; 2Ch 34:8-13; 35:1-19).

Jews after the captivity (Ezr 1:5, 6; 2:68, 69; 3:2-9; 5:2-6; 6:14-22; 8:25-35; Ne 3; 4:6; 6:3; 7:70-72; 10:32-39; 13:12, 31; Hag 1:12-14; 2:18, 19). Cyrus (Ezr 1:2-4, 7-11; 3:7; 5:13-15; 6:3). Darius (Ezr 6:7-12). Artaxerxes (Ezr 7:13-27; 8:24-36). The Magi (M't 2:11). Centurion (Lu 7:4, 5). Mary Magdalene (Lu 8:2, 3). The good Samaritan (Lu 10:33-35). Poor widow (Lu 21:2-4). Christians in Jerusalem (Ac 2:44, 45; 4:32-37); in Antioch (Ac 11:29); at Philippi (Ph'p 4:18); Corinth (2Co 8:19; 9:1-13); Macedonia (2Co 8:1-4). People of Melita to Paul (Ac 28:10).

LIBERTINES, freedmen (Ac 6:9).

LIBERTY, freedom, whether physical, moral, or spiritual. Israelites who had become slaves were freed in year of jubilee (Le 25:8-17). Through Christ's death and resurrection the believer is free from sin's dominion (Joh 1:29; 8:36; Ro 6, 7), Satan's control (Ac 26:18), the law (Ga 3), fear, the second death, future judgment.

Of Hebrew bondservants, in Sabbatic year (Ex 21:2; De 15:12; Jer 34:14); in year of Jubilee (Le 25:10, 40).

Political (Ac 22:28).

Religious: In Rome (Ac 28:31).

Spiritual (Ps 119:45; Isa 61:1; Lu 4:18; Joh 8:32, 33, 36; Ro 6:6, 22; 8:1, 2; 1Co 7:22; 2Co 3:17; Ga 2:4; 1Pe 2:16).

Figurative: Of the gospel (Jas 1:25; 2:12).

LIBNAH (whiteness). 1. A station of the Israelites in the desert (Nu 33:20).

2. A city of Judah, captured by Joshua (Jos 10:29-32, 39; 12:15). Allotted to the priests (Jos 21:13; 1Ch 6:57). Sennacherib besieged; his army defeated near (2Ki 19:8, 35; Isa 37:8-36).

LIBNI (white). 1. Son of Gershon (Ex 6:17; Nu 3:18; 1Ch 6:17, 20). Descendants called Libnites (Nu 3:21; 26:58).

2. Grandson of Merari (1Ch 6:29).

LIBRARIES. Libraries, both public and private, were not uncommon in ancient times in the Oriental, Greek, and Roman worlds. The Dead Sea Scrolls is one example of an ancient library that has survived to modern times.

LIBYA. Region N of Egypt (Eze 30:5; 38:5; Ac 2:10). Called also Lubim and Phut, which see.

LIBYANS, the inhabitants of Libya (Jer 46:9; Da 11:43).

LICE, plague of (Ex 8:16-19; Ps 105:31).

LICENTIOUSNESS (See Adultery; Lasciviousness.)

LIEUTENANTS, official title of satraps governing large provinces of the Persian empire (Ezr 8:36; Es 3:12; 8:9; 9:3).

LIFE. Breath of (Ge 2:7). Called spirit of God (Job 27:3). Tree of (Ge 2:9; 3:22, 24; Pr 3:18; 13:12; Re 2:7). Sacredness of, an inference from what is taught in the law concerning murder, see Homicide. Vanity of (Ec 1-7).

Weary of: Job (Job 3; 7:1-3; 10:18, 19). Jeremiah (Jer 20:14-18); Elijah (1Ki 19:1-4); Jonah (Jon 4:8); Paul (Ph'p 1:21-24). See Suicide.

Hated (Ec 2:17). To be hated for Christ's sake (Lu 14:26). What shall a man give in exchange for (M't 16:26; M'k 8:37). He that loses it for Christ's sake shall save it (M't 10:39; 16:25, 26; Lu 9:24; Joh 12:25).

Long, promised (Ge 6:3; Ps 91:16); to Solomon (1Ki 3:11-14); to the wise (Pr 3:16; 9:11); to the obedient (De 4:40; 22:7; Pr 3:1, 2); to those who honor parents (Ex 20:12; De 5:16); to those who show kindness to animals (De 22:7); given to those who fear God (Pr 10:27; Isa 65:20). See Longevity.

Brevity of (Ge 47:9; Job 10:9, 20, 21; 13:12, 25, 28; Ps 89:47, 48; 90:10; 146:4; Isa 2:22). Compared, to a shadow (1Ch 29:15; Job 8:9; 14:1, 2; Ps 102:11; 144:3, 4; Ec 6:12); to a weaver's shuttle (Job 7:6-10); to a courier (Job 9:25, 26); to a handbreadth (Ps 39:4, 5, 11); to a wind (Ps 78:39); to grass (Ps 90:3, 5, 6, 9, 10; 102:11; 103:14-16; Isa 40:6-8, 24; 51:12; Jas 1:10, 11; 1Pe 1:24); to a leaf (Isa 64:6); to a vapor (Jas 4:14).

Uncertainty of (1Sa 20:3; Job 4:19-21; 17:1; Pr 27:1; Lu 12:20). End of, certain (2Sa 14:14; Ps 22:29; Ec 1:4; Isa 38:12). See Death.

From God (Ge 2:7; De 8:3; 30:20; 32:39; 1Sa 2:6; Job 27:3; Ps 30:3; 104:30; Ec 12:7; Isa 38:16; Ac 17:25, 28; Ro 4:17; 1Ti 6:13; Jas 4:15).

Spiritual (De 8:3). From Christ (Joh 1:4; 6:27, 33, 35; 10:10; 17:2, 3; Ro 6:11; 8:10; Col 3:4). Through faith (Joh 3:14-16; 5:24-26, 40; 6:40, 47; 11:25, 26; 20:31; Ga 2:19, 20). Signified, in figure of new birth (Joh 3:3-8; Tit 3:5); in figure of death, burial, and resurrection (Ro 6:4-8).

Everlasting (Ps 21:4; 121:8; 133:3; Isa 25:8; Da 12:2; M't 19:16-21, 29; 25:46; M'k 10:17-21, 29, 30; Lu 18:18-22, 29, 30; 20:36; Joh 3:14-16, 36; 4:14; 5:24, 25, 29, 39; 6:27, 40, 47, 50-58, 68; 10:10, 27, 28; 12:25, 50; 17:2, 3; Ac 13:46, 48; Ro 2:7; 5:21; 6:22, 23; 1Co 15:53, 54; 2Co 5:1; Ga 6:8; 1Ti 1:16; 4:8; 6:12, 19; 2Ti 1:10; Tit 1:2; 3:7; 1Jo 2:25; 3:15; 5:11-13, 20; Jude 21; Re 1:18). See Immortality.

LIFE, THE BOOK OF, figurative expression denoting God's record of those who inherit eternal life (Ph'p 4:3; Re 3:5; 21:27).

LIGHT. *Physical:* Created (Ge 1:3-5; Ps 74:16; Isa 45:7; 2Co 4:6). Miraculous (Ex 13:21; De 1:33; M't 17:2; M'k 9:3; Lu 9:29; Ac 9:3; 12:7; 26:13).

Figurative: (1Ki 11:36). Of the Lord (Ps 27:1; Isa 60:19, 20; Jas 1:17; 1Jo 1:5, 7; 2:8-10). The Lord's word (Ps 119:105; Pr 6:23). Personal influence for righteousness (M't 5:14-16; M'k 4:21; Lu 8:16). The righteous (Lu 16:8; Eph 5:8, 14; Ph'p 2:15; 1Th 5:5). John the Baptist (Joh 5:35). Spiritual understanding (Isa 8:20; Lu 11:33-36; 2Co 4:6). Of the gospel (2Co 4:4, 6). Spiritual wisdom (Ps 119:130; Isa 2:5; 2Pe 1:19). Righteousness (M't 5:16; Ac 26:18; 1Pe 2:9). Heavenly glory (Re 21:23). Christ's heavenly glory (1Ti 6:16). Christ's kingdom (Isa 58:8). The Savior (Isa 49:6; Mal 4:2; M't 4:16; Lu 2:32; Joh 1:4, 5, 7-9; 3:19-21; 8:12; 9:5; 12:35, 36, 46; Re 21:23).

LIGHTNING (Job 28:26; 37:3; 38:25, 35; Ps 18:14; 77:18; 78:48; 97:4; 135:7; 144:6; Jer 10:13; 51:16; Eze 1:13, 14; Da 10:6; Na 2:4; Zec 9:14; 10:1; M't 24:27; 28:3; Lu 10:18; Re 4:5; 8:5; 11:19; 16:18).

Plague of, sent upon Egypt (Ex 9:23; Ps 77:18; 78:48; 105:32).

LIGN-ALOE, a tree, not identified by naturalists (Nu 24:6).

LIGURE, a precious stone (Ex 28:19; 39:12).

LIKHI, Manassite (1Ch 7:19).

LILY. The principal chapiters of the temple ornamented with carvings of (1Ki 7:19, 22, 26). Molded on the rim of the molten laver in the temple (1Ki 7:26;

2Ch 4:5). Lessons of trust gathered from (M't 6:28-30; Lu 12:27).

Figurative: Of the lips of the beloved (Song 5:13).

LIME (Isa 33:12; Am 2:1).

LINE, usually a measuring line (2Sa 8:2; Ps 78:55); a portion (Ps 16:6); sound made by a musical chord (Ps 19:4).

LINE OF JUDGMENT, the divine (2Ki 21:13; Isa 28:17; 34:11; La 2:8; Am 7:8).

LINEN. Exported from Egypt (1Ki 10:38; Eze 27:7); from Syria (Eze 27:16). Curtains of the tabernacle made of (Ex 26:1; 27:9). Vestments of priests made of (Ex 28:5-8, 15, 39-42). Livery of royal households made of (Ge 41:42; Es 8:15). Garments for men made of (Ge 41:42; Eze 9:2; Lu 16:19); for women (Isa 3:23; Eze 16:10-13). Bedding made of (Pr 7:16). Mosaic law forbade its being mingled with wool (Le 19:19; De 22:11). The body of Jesus wrapped in (M'k 15:46; Joh 20:5).

Figurative: Pure and white, of righteousness (Re 15:6; 19:8, 14).

LINTEL, horizontal beam forming the upper part of doorway (Ex 12:22, 23).

LINUS, a Christian at Rome (2Ti 4:21).

LION. King of beasts (Mic 5:8). Fierceness of (Job 4:10; 28:8; Ps 7:2; Pr 22:13; Jer 2:15; 49:19; 50:44; Ho 13:8). The roaring of (Ps 22:13; Pr 20:2). Strength of (Pr 30:30; Isa 38:13; Joe 1:6). Instincts of, in taking prey (Ps 10:9; 17:12; La 3:10; Am 3:4; Na 2:12). Lair of, in the jungles (Jer 4:7; 25:38). The bases in the temple ornamented by mouldings of (1Ki 7:29, 36). Twelve statues of, on the stairs leading to Solomon's throne (1Ki 10:19, 20). Samson's riddle concerning (J'g 14:14, 18). Proverb of (Ec 9:4). Parable of (Eze 19:1-9). Kept in captivity (Da 6). Sent as judgment upon the Samaritans (2Ki 17:25, 26). Slain by Samson (J'g 14:5-9); David (1Sa 17:34, 36); Benaiah (2Sa 23:20); saints (Heb 11:33). Disobedient prophet slain by (1Ki 13:24-28); an unnamed person slain by (1Ki 20:36). Used for the torture of criminals (Da 6:16-24; 7:12; 2Ti 4:17).

Figurative: Of a ruler's wrath (Pr 19:12; Jer 5:6; 50:17; Ho 5:14); of Satan (1Pe 5:8); of divine judgments (Isa 15:9).

Symbolical: Ge 49:9; Isa 29:1 [marg.]; Eze 1:10; 10:14; Da 7:4; Re 4:7; 5:5; 9:8, 17; 13:2.

LITIGATION, to be avoided (M't 5:25; Lu 12:58; 1Co 6:1-8).

See Actions at Law; Adjudication; Arbitration; Compromise.

LITTER, portable couch or sedan borne by men or animals (Isa 66:20).

LITTLE EVILS, so called (Pr 6:10; Ec 10:1; Song 2:15; 1Co 5:6).

LITTLE OWL (See Birds.)

LIVER, considered center of life and feeling (Pr 7:23); used especially for sacrifice (Ex 29:13) and divination (Eze 21:21).

LIVERY, of seizin. See Land, Conveyance of.

LIVING CREATURES, apparently identical with cherubim (Eze 1:5-22; 3:13; Re 4:6-9).

LIVING GOD (Jos 3:10; 1Sa 17:26; Ps 42:2; 84:2; Isa 37:17; Jer 23:36; Da 6:26; M't 26:63; Ac 14:15; 1Th 1:19; Heb 10:31; Re 7:2).

LIZARD (Le 11:30; Pr 30:28).

LO-AMMI (not my people), symbolic name for Hosea's third child (Ho 1:9, 10; 2:23).

LOAVES. Miracle of the five (M't 14:15-21; 16:9; M'k 6:37-44; Lu 9:12-17; Joh 6:5-13); of the seven (M't 15:34-38; 16:10; M'k 8:1-10).

See Bread.

LOBBYING (Ezr 4:4, 5).

See Diplomacy; Influence, Political.

LOCK, LOCKS. 1. Beams of wood or iron used for fastening gates or doors (Ne 3:3; Song 5:5).

2. Hair of the head (J'g 16:13, 19).

LOCUST. Authorized as food (Le 11:22); used as (M't 3:4; M'k 1:6). Plague of (Ex 10:1-19; Ps 105:34, 35). Devastation by (De 28:38; 1Ki 8:37; 2Ch 7:13; Isa 33:4; Joe 1:4-7; Re 9:7-10). Sun obscured by (Joe 2:2, 10). Instincts of (Pr 30:27).

In AV often inaccurately translated grasshopper, as in J'g 6:5; 7:12; Job 39:20; Jer 46:23.

See Grasshopper.

Figurative: Jer 46:23.

Symbolical: Re 9:3-10.

LOD. A city in Benjamin (1Ch 8:12; Ezr 2:33; Ne 7:37; 11:35). Called Lydda (Ac 9:38).

LO-DEBAR (without pasture). A city in

Manasseh (2Sa 9:4, 5; 17:27). Home of Mephibosheth, the lame son of Jonathan (2Sa 9:3-5).

LODGE, temporary shelter erected in a garden for a watchman guarding ripening fruit (Isa 1:8).

LOFT, upper chamber or story of a building (1Ki 17:19; Ac 20:9).

LOG, a measure for liquids, holding about a pint (Le 14:10, 12, 15, 24).

LOGIA, Greek word for non-Biblical sayings of Christ, such as those in the so-called Gospel of Thomas discovered in 1945.

LOGOS, philosophical and theological term translated "Word" referring to the dynamic principle of reason operating in the world, and forming a medium of communion between God and man. In the NT the concept is found principally in Johannine contexts (Joh 1:1ff; 1Jo 1:1; Re 19:13).

LOIN, part of body between ribs and hip bones. It is the place where the girdle was worn (Ex 12:11; 2Ki 1:8) and the sword fastened (2Sa 20:8).

LOIS, grandmother of Timothy, commended by Paul for her faith (2Ti 1:5).

LONGEVITY (Ge 6:3; Ps 90:10). Promised, to the obedient (Ex 20:12; De 4:40; 22:7); to the righteous (Job 5:26; Ps 21:4; 34:11-13; 91:16; Pr 3:2, 16; 9:11; 10:27; Isa 65:20; 1Pe 3:10, 11); to Solomon (1Ki 3:11-14).

Instances of: Adam, 930 years (Ge 5:5). Seth, 912 years (Ge 5:8). Enos, 905 years (Ge 5:11). Cainan, 910 years (Ge 5:14). Mahalaleel, 895 years (Ge 5:17). Jared, 962 years (Ge 5:20). Enoch, 365 years (Ge 5:23). Methuselah, 969 years (Ge 5:27). Lamech, 777 years (Ge 5:31). Noah, 950 years (Ge 9:29). Shem (Ge 11:11). Arphaxad (Ge 11:13). Salah (Ge 11:15). Eber (Ge 11:17). Peleg (Ge 11:19). Reu (Ge 11:21). Serug (Ge 11:23). Nahor (Ge 11:25). Terah, 205 years (Ge 11:32). Sarah, 127 years (Ge 23:1). Abraham, 175 years (Ge 25:7). Isaac, 180 years (Ge 35:28). Jacob, 147 years (Ge 47:28). Joseph, 110 years (Ge 50:26). Amram, 173 years (Ex 6:20). Aaron, 123 years (Nu 33:39). Moses, 120 years (De 31:2; 34:7). Joshua, 110 years (Jos 24:29). Eli, 98 years (1Sa 4:15). Barzillai, 80 years (2Sa 19:32). Job (Job 42:16). Jehoiada, 130 years (2Ch 24:15). Anna (Lu 2:36, 37). Paul (Ph'm 9).

See Old Age.

LONGSUFFERING (1Ti 1:16). A Christian grace (1Co 13:4, 7; 2Co 6:4-6; Ga 5:22; Col 1:11; 2Ti 3:10; 4:2). Enjoined (Eph 4:2; Col 3:12, 13).

See Charitableness; God, Longsuffering of; Patience.

LOOKING BACKWARD, toward the old life (Ge 19:17, 26; Nu 11:5; 14:4; Lu 9:62).

LOOKING-GLASS (See Mirror.)

LORD, a term applied to both men and God, expressing varied degrees of honor, dignity, and majesty; applied also to idols (Ex 22:8; J'g 2:11, 13); used of Jesus as Messiah (Ac 2:36; Ph'p 2:9-11; Ro 1:4; 14:8).

LORD'S DAY, the day especially associated with the Lord Jesus Christ; a day consecrated to the Lord; the 1st day of the week, commemorating the resurrection of Jesus (Joh 20:1-25) and the pouring out of the Spirit (Ac 2:1-41); set aside for worship (Ac 20:7).

LORD'S PRAYER, THE, prayer taught by Jesus as a model of how His disciples should pray (M't 6:9-13; Lu 11:2-4).

LORD'S SUPPER, instituted by Christ on the night of His betrayal immediately after Passover feast to be a memorial of His death and a visible sign of the blessings of salvation that accrue from His death. Goes by various names: body and blood of Christ (M't 26:26, 28), communion of the body and blood of Christ (1Co 10:16), bread and cup of the Lord (1Co 11:27), breaking of bread (Ac 2:42; 20:7), Lord's Supper (1Co 11:20). Not to be observed unworthily (1Co 11:27-32).

LO-RUHAMAH (not pitied), symbolic name given to Hosea's daughter (Ho 1:6, 8; 2:4, 23).

LOST SHEEP, parable of (M't 18:12, 13; Lu 15:4-7).

LOST, THE (See Wicked, Punishment of.)

LOT, THE (Pr 16:33; 18:18; Isa 34:17; Joe 3:3). The scapegoat chosen by (Le 16:8-10).

The land of Canaan divided among the tribes by (Nu 26:55; Jos 15; 18:10; 19:51; 21; 1Ch 6:61, 65; Eze 45:1; 47:22; 48:29; Mic 2:5; Ac 13:19). Saul chosen king by (1Sa 10:20, 21). Priests and

Levites designated by, for sanctuary service (1Ch 24:5-31; 26:13; Ne 10:34; Lu 1:9). Used after the captivity (Ne 11:1). An apostle chosen by (Ac 1:26). Achan's guilt ascertained by (Jos 7:14-18); Jonathan's (1Sa 14:41, 42); Jonah's (Jon 1:7). Used to fix the time for the execution of condemned persons (Es 3:7; 9:24). The garments of Jesus divided by (Ps 22:18; M't 27:35; M'k 15:24; Joh 19:23, 24).

LOT. 1. Feast of (See Purim.)

2. The son of Haran. Accompanies Terah from Ur of the Chaldees to Haran (Ge 11:31). Migrates with Abraham to the land of Canaan (Ge 12:4). Accompanies Abraham to Egypt; returns with him to Beth-el (Ge 13:1-3). Rich in flocks, and herds, and servants; separates from Abraham, and locates in Sodom (Ge 13:5-14). Taken captive by Chedorlaomer; rescued by Abraham (Ge 14:1-16). Providentially saved from destruction in Sodom (Ge 19; Lu 17:28, 29). Righteous (2Pe 2:7, 8). Disobediently protests against going to the mountains, and chooses Zoar (Ge 19:17-22). His wife disobediently longs after Sodom, and becomes a pillar of salt (Ge 19:26; Lu 17:32). Commits incest with his daughters (Ge 19:30-38). Descendants of (see Ammonites; Moabites.)

LOTAN (a wrapping up), son of Seir (Ge 36:20, 22, 29).

LOTS, CASTING (Le 16:8; Nu 26:55; Jos 18:10; 1Sa 14:41; Es 3:7; Pr 16:33; 18:18; Jon 1:7; M't 27:35; Ac 1:26).

LOVE (1Co 13; 14:1; Col 1:8; 2:2; 1Th 1:3; 5:8; 1Ti 6:11; 2Ti 1:7; Ph'm 5; Heb 10:24; 1Jo 4:7, 16-18).

The theme of the Song of Solomon, and usually interpreted as an allegory representing the love of the Messiah for the church and of his church for the Messiah (Song chps 1-8). See Church, Love For.

Of man for man (Ro 5:7; Jas 1:27). Defined (Lu 10:25-37; 1Co 13:1-13). Is edifying (1Co 8:1). Precious (Pr 15:17). Unquenchable (Pr 17:17; Song 8:6, 7). A fruit of the Spirit (Ga 5:22). Promotes peace (Pr 10:12; 17:9). A proof, of discipleship of Jesus (Joh 13:34, 35): of regeneration (1Jo 3:14, 19).

Enjoined (Le 19:18; M't 5:40-42; 7:12; 19:19; 22:39, 40; M'k 12:30-33; Lu 6:30-38; Ro 12:9, 15; 13:8-10; 1Co 10:24; 16:14; Ga 6:1, 2, 10; Eph 4:2, 32; 5:2; Ph'p 1:9; Col 3:14; 1Th 3:12; 1Ti 1:5; 4:12; 6:11; 2Ti 2:22; Jas 2:8; 2Pe 1:7; 1Jo 4:20, 21).

Enjoined, toward strangers (Le 19:34; De 10:19); toward enemies (Pr 24:17; M't 5:43-48; Lu 6:35; Ro 12:14, 20); toward fellow Christians (Joh 13:14, 15, 34, 35; 15:12, 13, 17; Ro 12:9, 10, 15, 16; 14:19, 21; 15:1, 2, 5, 7; 16:1, 2; 1Co 14:1; 2Co 8:7, 8; Ga 5:13, 14; 6:1, 2, 10; Eph 4:2, 32; Ph'p 2:2; Col 2:2; 3:12-14; 1Th 3:12; 5:8, 11, 14; 1Ti 6:2; Ph'm 16; Heb 10:24; 13:13; 1Pe 1:22; 2:17; 3:8, 9; 4:8; 2Pe 1:7; 1Jo 3:11, 14, 16-19, 23; 4:7, 11, 12, 20, 21; 2Jo 5). Demonstrated by obedience (1Jo 5:1, 2).

Rewards of (M't 10:41, 42; 25:34-40, 46; M'k 9:41; 1Jo 2:10).

Exemplified: By Paul (Ac 26:29; Ro 1:11, 12; 9:1-3; 1Co 4:9-16; 8:13; 2Co 1:3-6, 14, 23, 24; 2:4; 3:2; 4:5; 6:4-6, 11-13; 7:1-4; 11:2; 12:14-16, 19-21; 13:9; Ga 4:19, 20; Eph 3:13; Ph'p 1:3-5, 7, 8, 23-26; 2:19; 4:1; Col 1:3, 4, 24, 28, 29; 2:1, 5; 4:7; 1Th 2:7, 8, 11, 12, 17-20; 3:5, 7-10, 12; 2Th 1:4; 2Ti 1:3, 4, 8; 2:10; Tit 3:15; Ph'm 9, 12, 16).

Instances of: Abraham for Lot (Ge 14:14-16). Moses for Israel (Ex 32:31, 32). David and Jonathan (1Sa 18:1; 20:17). Israel and Judah for David (1Sa 18:16). David's subjects for David (2Sa 15:30; 17:27-29). Hiram for David (1Ki 5:1). Obadiah for the prophets (1Ki 18:4). Nehemiah for Israelites (Ne 5:10-18). Job's friends (Job 42:11). Centurion for his servant (Lu 7:2-6). Good Samaritan (Lu 10:29-37). Stephen (Ac 7:60). Roman Christians for Paul (Ac 28:15). Priscilla and Aquila for Paul (Ro 16:3, 4).

See Brother; Fraternity; Friendship.

Of man for woman: Isaac for Rebekah (Ge 24:67). Jacob for Rachel (Ge 29:20, 30). Shechem for Dinah (Ge 34:3, 12). Boaz for Ruth (Ru chps 2-4).

Of man for God: Defined (1Jo 5:3; 2Jo 6). Incompatible, with love of the world (1Jo 2:15); with hatred of brother (1Jo 4:20, 21); with guilty fear (2Ti 1:7; 1Jo 4:18). Reasons for (Ps 116:1; 1Jo 4:19).

The gift of God (De 30:6; 2Ti 1:7); through the Holy Spirit (Ro 5:5).

Enjoined (De 6:5; 10:12; 11:1, 13, 22;

19:9; 30:16, 19, 20; Jos 22:5; 23:11; Ps 31:23; Pr 23:26; M't 22:37, 38; M'k 12:29, 30, 32, 33; Lu 11:42; 2Th 3:5; Jude 21). Tested (De 13:3). Obedience proof of (1Jo 2:5; 5:1, 2; 2Jo 6).

Leads to liberality (1Jo 3:17, 18); hate of evil (Ps 97:10); love from God (Ps 8:17). Rewards of (Ex 20:6; De 5:10; 7:9; Ps 37:4; 69:35, 36; 91:14; 145:20; Isa 56:6, 7; Jer 2:2, 3; Ro 8:28; 1Co 8:3).

Exemplified (Ps 18:1; 63:5, 6; 73:25, 26; 103).

For Jesus: Enjoined (M't 10:37, 38; Joh 15:9; 1Co 16:22). Love of God produces (Joh 8:42). Obedience results from (Joh 14:15, 21, 23; 2Co 5:6, 8, 14, 15).

Rewards of (M't 25:34-40, 46; M'k 9:41; Lu 7:37-50; Joh 16:27; Eph 6:24; 2Ti 4:8; Heb 6:10; Jas 1:12; 2:5).

Instances of love for Jesus: Mary (M't 26:6-13; Lu 10:39; Joh 12:3-8). Peter (M't 17:4; Joh 13:37; 18:10; 20:3-6; 21:15-17). The healed demoniac (M'k 5:18; Lu 8:38). Thomas (Joh 11:16). The disciples (M'k 16:10; Lu 24:17-41; Joh 16:27; 20:20). Mary Magdalene and other disciples (M't 27:55, 56, 61; 28:1-9; Lu 8:2, 3; 23:27, 55, 56; 24:1-10; Joh 20:1, 2, 11-18). Joseph of Arimathea (M't 27:57-60). Nicodemus (Joh 19:39, 40). Women of Jerusalem (Lu 23:27). Paul (Ac 21:13; Ph'p 1:20, 21, 23; 3:7, 8; 2Ti 4:8). Philemon (Ph'm 5). Early Christians (1Pe 1:8; 2:7); lost that love (Re 2:4).

See also Jesus, Love of.

Of Children for Parents: See Children.

Of God: See God, Love of.

Of Money: The root of evil (1Ti 6:10). See Riches.

Of Parents for Children: See Parents.

LOVE FEAST, a common meal eaten by early Christians in connection with the Lord's Supper to express and deepen brotherly love (1Co 11:18-22, 33, 34; Jude 12).

LOVERS. *Instances of:* Isaac for Rebekah (Ge 24:67). Jacob for Rachel (Ge 29:20, 30). Shechem for Dinah (Ge 34:3, 12). Boaz for Ruth (Ru 2-4).

LOVING-KINDNESS, the kindness and mercy of God toward man (Ps 17:7; 26:3).

LOYALTY. Enjoined (Ex 22:28; Nu 27:20; Ezr 6:10; 7:26; Job 34:18; Pr 24:21; Ec 8:2; 10:4; Ro 13:1; Tit 3:1). Enforced (Ezr 10:8; Pr 17:11). Disloyalty (2Pe 2:10).

See Patriotism.

Instances of: Israelites (Jos 1:16-18; 2Sa 3:36, 37; 15:23, 30; 18:3; 21:17; 1Ch 12:38). David (1Sa 24:6-10; 26:6-16; 2Sa 1:14). Uriah (2Sa 11:9). Ittai (2Sa 15:21). Hushai (2Sa 17:15, 16). David's soldiers (2Sa 18:12, 13; 23:15, 16). Joab (2Sa 19:5, 6). Barzillai (2Sa 19:32). Jehoiada (2Ki 11:4-12). Mordecai (Ex 2:21-23).

LUBIM, probably the Libyans; always mentioned in conjunction with Egyptians or Ethiopians (2Ch 12:3; 16:8; Na 3:9).

LUCAS, fellow-laborer of Paul (Ph'm 24).

See Luke.

LUCIFER (See Satan, Devil.)

LUCIUS. 1. A Christian at Antioch (Ac 13:1).

2. A kinsman of Paul (Ro 16:21).

LUD, a son of Shem (Ge 10:22; 1Ch 1:17).

LUDIM. 1. Son of Mizraim (Ge 10:13; 1Ch 1:11).

2. Descendants of Ludim (Ge 10:13). Warriors (Isa 66:19; Jer 46:9; Eze 27:10; 30:5).

LUHITH, a city of Moab (Isa 15:5; Jer 48:5).

LUKE. A disciple. A physician (Col 4:14). Wrote to Theophilus (Lu 1:1-4; Ac 1:1, 2). Accompanies Paul in his tour of Asia and Macedonia (Ac 16:10-13; 20:5, 6); to Jerusalem (Ac 21:1-18); to Rome (Ac 27; 28; 2Ti 4:1; Ph'm 24).

LUKE, GOSPEL OF. Third book of NT, written, according to tradition, by Luke the beloved physician and coworker of Paul. Preface to Acts shows that the Gospel was written before it, somewhere c. A. D. 58-60; both books were done by the same person, as tradition and internal evidence show. The author states in the preface (1:2) that he collected his material from eyewitnesses. Outline: 1. Thirty years of private life (1-4:13).

2. Galilean ministry of Jesus (4:14-9:50).

3. Journey from Galilee to Jerusalem (9:51-19:44).

4. Last days of Jesus in Jerusalem. His crucifixion and burial (19:45-23:56).

5. Resurrection and appearances of the risen Lord and His ascension (24:1-53).

LUKEWARMNESS (Re 3:2, 5, 16).

Instances of: The Reubenites and other tribes, when Deborah called on them to assist Sisera (J'g 5:16, 17). Israel (Ho 10:2). The Jews (Ne 3:5; 13:11; Hag 1:2-11). The church, at Pergamos (Re 2:14-16); Thyatira (Re 2:20-24); Sardis (Re 3:1-3); Laodicea (Re 3:14-16).

See Backsliding; Blindness, Spiritual.

LUNACY (See Insanity; Demons.)

LUST (evil desires). Sinful (Job 31:9-12; M't 5:28). Worldly (1Jo 2:16, 17). Chokes the word (M'k 4:19). Tempts to sin (Ge 3:6; Jas 1:14, 15; 2Pe 2:18).

Forbidden (Ex 20:17; Pr 6:24, 25; Ro 13:14; Eph 4:22; Col 3:5; 1Th 4:5; Tit 2:12; 1Pe 2:11). The righteous restrain (1Co 9:27). Wicked under power of (Joh 8:44; Ro 1:24, 26, 27; 1Ti 6:9; Jas 4:1-3; 1Pe 4:3; 2Pe 3:3; Jude 16, 18).

Warnings against (1Co 10:6, 7; 2Ti 2:22).

Of Israelites (Ps 106:13, 14).

See Adultery; Covetousness; Incest; Lasciviousness; Sensuality; Sodomy.

LUTE (See Musical Instruments.)

LUZ (turning aside). 1. Town on N boundary of Benjamin (Jos 16:2; 18:13).

2. Hittite town (J'g 1:26).

LYCAONIA. A province of Asia Minor. Paul visits towns of (Ac 14:6-21; 16:1, 2).

LYCIA. A province of Asia Minor. Paul visits (Ac 27:5).

LYDDA, called also Lod. A city of Benjamin (1Ch 8:12; Ezr 2:33; Ne 11:35). Peter heals Aeneas in (Ac 9:32-35).

LYDIA. 1. A woman of Thyatira, who with her household was converted through the preaching of Paul (Ac 16:14, 15). Entertains Paul and Silas (Ac 16:15, 40).

2. Incorrectly put for Lud (Eze 30:5).

LYING, lying spirit from God (1Ki 22:21-23; 2Ch 18:20-22).

See Falsehood; Hypocrisy.

LYRE (See Musical Instruments.)

LYSANIAS, a tetrarch (Lu 3:1).

LYSIAS, chief captain of Roman troops in Jerusalem (Ac 24:7, 22).

See Claudias Lysias.

LYSTRA. One of two cities of Lycaonia, to which Paul and Barnabas fled from persecutions in Iconium (Ac 14:6-23; 2Ti 3:11). Church of, elders ordained for, by Paul and Barnabas (Ac 14:23). Timothy a resident of (Ac 16:1-4).

M

MAACHAH (oppression). 1. Son of Nahor (Ge 22:24).

2. Called also Maacah. Mother of Absalom (2Sa 3:3; 1Ch 3:2).

3. Called also Maoch. Father of Achish (1Sa 27:2; 1Ki 2:39).

4. Called also Michaiah. Mother of Abijam and grandmother of Asa (1Ki 15:2, 10-13; 2Ch 11:20-23; 13:2; 15:16).

5. Wife of Machir (1Ch 7:15, 16).

6. Concubine of Caleb (1Ch 2:48).

7. Wife of Jehiel (1Ch 8:29; 9:35).

8. Father of Hanan (1Ch 11:43).

9. Father of Shephatiah (1Ch 27:16).

10. Called also Maacah and Maachathi. A small kingdom E of Bashan (De 3:14; Jos 12:5; 2Sa 10:6, 8; 1Ch 19:6, 7).

MAACHATHI, MAACHATHITES, people of the nation of Maachah, in the region of Bashan (De 3:14; Jos 12:5; 13:11; 2Sa 23:34; 1Ch 4:19).

MAADAI (ornaments), Israelite who married a foreign woman (Ezr 10:34).

MAADIAH (Jehovah is ornament), chief priest who returned from exile with Zerubbabel (Ne 12:5).

MAAI (to be compassionate), priest who blew trumpet at dedication of wall (Ne 12:36).

MAALEH-ACRABBIM (ascent of Akrabbim), area assigned to tribe of Judah (Jos 15:3).

MAARAH (a place naked of trees), a city of Judah (Jos 15:59).

MAASEIAH (work of Jehovah). 1. Levite musician (1Ch 15:18, 20).

2. Army captain who assisted Jehoiada in overthrowing Athaliah (2Ch 23:1).

3. Officer of Uzziah (2Ch 26:11).

4. Son of Ahaz, king of Judah (2Ch 28:7).

5. Governor of Jerusalem in Josiah's reign (2Ch 34:8).

6. Priest who married foreign woman (Ezr 10:18).

7. Another priest who married foreign woman (Ezr 10:21).

8. Another priest who married foreign woman (Ezr 10:22).

9. Israelite who married foreign woman (Ezr 10:30).

10. Father of Azariah (Ne 2:23).

11. Priest; assistant of Ezra (Ne 8:4).

12. Man who explained law to people (Ne 8:7).

13. Chief who sealed covenant with Nehemiah (Ne 10:25).

14. Descendant of son of Baruch (Ne 11:5).

15. Benjamite (Ne 11:7).

16. Priest who blew trumpet at dedication of temple (Ne 12:26).

MAASIAI (work of Jehovah), priestly family after exile (1Ch 9:12).

MAATH (to be small), an ancestor of Jesus (Lu 3:26).

MAAZ (wrath), a son of Ram (1Ch 2:27).

MAAZIAH (consolation of Jehovah). 1. A priest (1Ch 24:18).

2. A priest who sealed the covenant with Nehemiah (Ne 10:8).

MACCABEES (hammer?), Hasmonean Jewish family of Modin that led revolt against Antiochus Epiphanes, king of Syria, and won freedom for the Jews. The family consisted of the father, Mattathias, an aged priest, and his five sons: Johanan, Simon, Judas, Eleazar, Jonathan. The name Maccabee was first given to Judas, perhaps because he inflicted sledgehammer blows against the Syrian armies, and later was also used for his brothers. The revolt began in 168 B.C. The temple was recaptured and sacrifices were resumed in 165 B.C. The cleansing of the temple and resumption of sacrifices have been celebrated annually ever since in the Feast of Dedication. The Maccabees served as both high priests and kings. The story of Maccabees is told in two books of the Apocrypha, I and II Maccabees. The following were the most prominent of the Maccabees: Judas (166-160 B.C.), Jonathan (160-142 B.C.), Simon (142-134 B.C.), John Hyrcanus (134-104 B.C.), Aristobulus (104-103 B.C.), Alexander Jannaeus (103-76 B.C.), Alexandra (76-67 B.C.), Aristobulus II (66-63). In 63 B.C. the Romans took over when Pompey conquered the Israelites.

MACEDONIA. A country in southeastern Europe. Paul has a vision concerning (Ac 16:9); preaches in, at Philippi (Ac 16:12); revisits (Ac 20:1-6;

2Co 2:13; 7:5). Church at, sends contributions to the poor in Jerusalem (Ro 15:26; 2Co 8:1-5). Timothy visits (Ac 19:22). Disciples in (Ac 19:23; 27:2).

MACEDONIAN EMPIRE, THE. Called the kingdom of Grecia (Da 11:2).

Illustrated by the: Brazen part of the image in Nebuchadnezzar's dream (Da 2:32, 39). Leopard with four wings and four heads (Da 7:6, 17). Rough goat with notable horn (Da 8:5, 21). Philippi the chief city of (Ac 16:12).

Predictions Respecting: Conquest of the Medo-Persian kingdom (Da 8:6, 7; 11:2, 3). Power and greatness of Alexander its last king (Da 8:8; 11:3). Division of it into four kingdoms (Da 8:8, 22). Divisions of it ruled by strangers (Da 11:4). History of its four divisions (Da 11:4-29). The little horn to arise out of one of its divisions (Da 8:8-12). Gospel preached in, by God's desire (Ac 16:9, 10). Liberality of the churches of (2Co 8:1-5).

MACHAERUS, fortress stronghold built by Alexander Janneus (90 B.C. ?) and used as a citadel by Herod Antipas; located on E of Dead Sea; John the Baptist was put to death there (M't 14:3ff).

MACHBANAI (clad with a cloak), a Gadite warrior (1Ch 12:13).

MACHBENAH (bond), place in Judah (1Ch 2:49). "Father" may mean "founder."

MACHI, Gadite; father of Geuel, one of 12 spies (Nu 13:15).

MACHIR (sold). 1. One of the sons of Manasseh (Ge 50:23). Father of the Machirites (Nu 26:29; 36:1). The land of Gilead allotted to (Nu 32:39, 40; De 3:15; Jos 13:31). Certain cities of Bashan given to (Jos 13:31; 17:1).

2. A man of Lo-debar who took care of Jonathan's lame son, Mephibosheth (2Sa 9:4, 5; 17:27).

MACHNADEBAI, Israelite who divorced foreign wife (Ezr 10:40).

MACHPELAH (a doubling), the burying place of Sarah, Abraham, Isaac, Rebekah, Leah, and Jacob (Ge 23:9, 17-20; 25:9; 49:30, 31; 50:13; Ac 7:16).

MADAI, people descended from Japheth (Ge 10:2; 1Ch 1:5).

MADMANNAH (dunghill). 1. Town in S Judah 8 miles S of Kirjath-sepher (Jos 15:31).

2. Grandson of Caleb (1Ch 2:48, 49).

MADMENAH (dunghill), a city of Benjamin (Isa 10:31).

MADNESS (See Insanity.)

MADON (contention), Canaanite city near modern Hattin (Jos 11:1; 12:19).

MAGBISH (congregating), name of man or place (Ezr 2:30).

MAGDALA, town on NW shore of Sea of Galilee, 3 miles N of Tiberias (M't 15:39). Dalmanutha in M'k 8:10. Home of Mary Magdalene.

MAGDALEN, MAGDALENE (See Mary.)

MAGDIEL (God is noble), chief of Edom (Ge 36:43; 1Ch 1:54).

MAGI, originally a religious caste among the Persians; devoted to astrology, divination, and interpretation of dreams. Later the word came to be applied generally to fortune tellers and exponents of esoteric religious cults throughout the Mediterranean world (Ac 8:9; 13:6, 8). Nothing is known of the magi of the Nativity story (M't 2); they may have come from S Arabia.

MAGIC, the art or science of influencing or controlling the course of nature, events, and supernatural powers through occult science of mysterious arts (Ge 41:8; Ex 7:11, 22; 8:7, 18; Ac 19:19). Includes necromancy, exorcism, dreams, shaking arrows, inspecting entrails of animals, divination, sorcery, astrology, soothsaying, divining by rods, witchcraft (1Sa 28:8; Eze 21:21; Ac 16:16).

MAGICIAN. A person who claims to understand and explain mysteries by magic (Da 1:20). Failed to interpret Pharaoh's dreams (Ge 41:8, 24); Nebuchadnezzar's (Da 2:2-13; 4:7). Wrought apparent miracles (Ex 7:11, 12, 22; 8:7, 18).

MAGISTRATE. An officer of civil law (J'g 18:7; Ezr 7:25; Lu 12:11, 58; Ac 16:20, 22, 35, 38). Obedience to, enjoined (Tit 3:1).

See Government; Rulers.

MAGNA CHARTA, of the Israelites. (See Constitution.)

MAGNANIMITY. *Instances of:* Joshua and the elders of Israel to the Gibeonites who had deceived the Israelites (Jos 9:3-27). Of Moses (see Moses). David to

Saul (1Sa 24:3-11). Ahab to Benhadad (1Ki 20:32-34).

See Charitableness.

MAGNIFICAT, song of praise by Mary recorded in Lu 1:46-55.

MAGOG (land of Gog?). 1. Son of Japheth (Ge 10:2; 1Ch 1:5).

2. Land of Gog; various identifications: Scythians, Lydians, Tartars of Russia. Used symbolically for forces of evil (Re 20:7-9).

MAGOR-MISSABIB (terror on every side), a symbolical name given by Jeremiah to Pashur (Jer 20:3-6).

MAGPIASH (moth killer), Israelite who sealed covenant with Nehemiah (Ne 10:20).

MAGUS, SIMON (See Simon.)

MAHALAH (disease), grandson of Manasseh (1Ch 7:18).

MAHALALEEL (praise of God). 1. Called also Maleleel. Son of Cainan (Ge 5:12-17; 1Ch 1:2; Lu 3:37).

2. A man of Judah (Ne 11:4).

MAHALATH (sickness). 1. Daughter of Ishmael (Ge 28:9).

2. Wife of Rehoboam (2Ch 11:18).

3. Musical term in heading of Ps 53 and 88.

MAHALI (sick), son of Merari (Ex 6:19).

MAHANAIM (two hosts). The place where Jacob had the vision of angels (Ge 32:2). The town of, allotted to Gad (Jos 13:26, 30). One of the Levitical cities (Jos 21:38). Ishbosheth establishes himself at, when made king over Israel (2Sa 2:8-12). David lodges at, at the time of Absalom's rebellion (2Sa 17:27-29; 1Ki 2:8).

MAHANEH-DAN (camp of Dan). 1. Place between Zorah and Eshtaol (J'g 13:25).

2. Place W of Kirjath-jearim (J'g 18:12).

MAHARAI (impetuous), one of David's warriors (2Sa 23:28; 1Ch 11:30; 27:13).

MAHATH (seizing). 1. Kohathite; ancestor of Heman the singer (1Ch 6:35).

2. Levite who helped Hezekiah (2Ch 29:12; 31:13).

MAHAVITE, family name of Eliel, one of David's warriors (1Ch 11:46).

MAHAZIOTH (visions), son of Heman (1Ch 25:4, 30).

MAHER-SHALAL-HASH-BAZ (the spoil speeds, the prey hastens), symbolic name Isaiah gave his son (Isa 8:1, 3).

MAHLAH (disease). 1. Daughter of Zelophehad (Nu 26:33; 27:1ff; 36; Jos 17:3ff).

2. Daughter of Hammoleketh (1Ch 7:18).

MAHLI (sick). 1. Son of Merari (Ex 6:19; 1Ch 6:19; Ezr 8:18).

2. Son of Mushi (1Ch 6:47; 23:23; 24:30).

MAHLITE, descendant of Mahli, son of Merari (Nu 3:33; 26:58; 1Ch 23:22).

MAHLON (sick), son of Naomi, and first husband of Ruth (Ru 1:2, 5; 4:9, 10).

MAHOL (dance), father of Heman, Chalcol, and Darda (1Ki 4:31).

MAID, MAIDEN. 1. Female slave (Ex 2:5; 21:20, 26).

2. Virgin (Ex 22:16; J'g 19:24).

3. Girl (Ex 2:5; Ru 2:8, 22, 23).

4. Girl of marriageable age (Ge 24:43; Ex 2:8; Ps 68:25; Song 1:3; 6:8; Pr 30:19; Isa 7:14).

5. Maid servant (Ge 16:2, 3, 5, 6, 8).

MAIL. 1. Information, public or private. Carried by post (Es 3:13; 8:10).

2. Armor (1Sa 17:5). See Armor.

MAIMED (See Diseases.)

MAJESTY, name of God (Heb 1:3; 8:1). See God.

MAJORITY AND MINORITY REPORTS, of the spies (Nu 13:26-33; 14:6-10).

MAKAZ, a place in Judah (1Ki 4:9).

MAKHELOTH, an encampment of Israel (Nu 33:25, 26).

MAKKEDAH (a place of shepherds). A city in Judah, conquered by Joshua (Jos 10:28; 12:16). Five kings of the Amorites hide in a cave of, and are slain by Joshua (Jos 10:5, 16-27).

MAKTESH (mortar), a district where merchants traded (Zep 1:11).

MALACHI (messenger of Jehovah or my messenger), prophet of Judah who lived c. 450-400 B. C.; author of OT book which bears his name; nothing known of him beyond what is said in his book; contemporary of Nehemiah (Mal 2:11-17; Ne 13:23-31). Principal themes of book: sin and apostasy of Israel; judgment that will fall upon the faithless and blessing upon the faithful. Outline: 1. Sins of the priests (1:1-2:9).

2. Sins of the people (2:10-4:1).

3. Coming of the Sun of Righteousness (4:2-6).

MALCHAM, MALCAM, either Milcom, an idol of the Moabites and Ammonites (Zep 1:5; Jer 49:3) or their king (Am 1:15; Jer 49:1); maybe both.

MALCHIAH, MALCHIJAH (my king is Jehovah). 1. Gershonite (1Ch 6:40).

2. Ancestor of Adaiah (1Ch 9:12; Ne 11:12).

3. Priest (1Ch 24:9).

4. Israelite who married foreign woman (Ezr 10:25).

5. Another who did same thing (Ezr 10:25).

6. Another who did same thing (Ezr 10:31).

7. Son of Harim (Ne 3:11).

8. Son of Rechab (Ne 3:14).

9. Goldsmith (Ne 3:31).

10. Man who assisted Ezra (Ne 8:4).

11. Israelite who sealed covenant with Nehemiah (Ne 10:3).

12. Priest (Ne 12:42). May be same as No. 11.

13. Father of Pashur who helped arrest Jeremiah (Jer 21:1; 38:1).

MALCHIEL (God is my king), son of Beriah (Ge 46:17; Nu 26:45; 1Ch 7:31).

MALCHIJAH (See Malchiah.)

MALCHIRAM (my king is high), son of Jeconiah (1Ch 3:18).

MALCHI-SHUA (king of aid), son of King Saul (1Sa 14:49; 31:2; KJV Melchishua; 1Ch 8:33; 9:39).

MALCHUS, servant of the high priest; Peter assaults in Gethsemane; healed by Jesus (M't 26:51; M'k 14:47; Lu 22:50, 51; Joh 18:10).

MALEFACTOR, crucified with Jesus (M't 27:38-44; Lu 23:32-39).

MALELEEL (See Mahaleel.)

MALFEASANCE IN OFFICE. *Instances of:* The lessees of the vineyard, in one of the parables of Jesus (M'k 12:1-8; Lu 20:9-15). The steward mentioned in one of the parables of Jesus (Lu 16:1-7).

MALICE. Outgrowth of original sin (Ge 3:15). Hated by God (Pr 6:16-19). Reacts (Job 15:35; Ps 7:15, 16; 26:2, 27; Jer 20:10). Blinds those possessed of (1Jo 2:9-11; 4:20). Is murderous (1Jo 3:13-15). Precludes divine forgiveness (M't 6:15; 18:28-35).

Forbidden (Le 19:14, 17, 18; 2Ki 6:21, 22; Pr 20:22; 24:17, 18, 29; Zec 7:10; 8:17; M't 5:38-41; Lu 6:29; Ro 12:19; 1Co 5:8; 14:20; Eph 4:31; Col 3:8; 1Th 5:15; 1Pe 2:1; 3:9).

The wicked filled with (De 32:32, 33; Ps 10:7-10, 14; Pr 4:16, 17; 6:14; 21:10; 30:14; Isa 59:4-6; M't 13:25, 28; Joh 8:44; Ro 1:29-32; Ga 5:19-21; Tit 3:3; 3Jo 10). Punishment for (De 27:17, 18; Pr 6:14, 15; 17:5; 28:10; Isa 29:20, 21; 36:2; Eze 18:18; 28:3, 6, 7, 12-17; 26:2, 3; Am 1:11; Mic 2:1; M't 26:52; Jas 2:13).

Not practiced by Job (Job 31:29, 30). Psalmist demands retribution (Ps 10:7-10, 14; 70:2, 3; 71:10-13, 24). Proverbs concerning (Pr 4:16, 17; 6:14, 15, 18, 19; 10:6, 12; 11:17; 12:10; 14:17, 22; 15:17; 16:30; 17:5; 20:22; 21:10; 24:8, 17, 18, 29; 26:2, 27; 28:10; 30:14).

Instances of: Cain toward Abel (Ge 4:8; 1Jo 3:12). Ishmael toward Sarah (Ge 21:9). Sarah toward Hagar (Ge 21:10). Philistines toward Isaac (Ge 26:12-15, 18-21). Esau toward Jacob (Ge 27:41, 42). Joseph's brethren toward Joseph (Ge 37:2-28; 42:21; Ac 7:9, 10). Potiphar's wife toward Joseph (Ge 39:14-20). Ammonites toward the Israelites (De 23:3, 4). Saul toward David (1Sa 18:8-29; 19; 20:30-33; 22:6-23; 23:7-28; 26:1, 2, 18). David toward Michael (2Sa 6:21-23); toward Joab (1Ki 2:5, 6); toward Shimei (1Ki 2:8, 9). Shimei toward David (2Sa 16:5-8). Ahithophel toward David (2Sa 17:1-3). Jezebel toward Elijah (1Ki 19:1, 2). Ahaziah toward Elijah (2Ki 1:7-15). Jehoram toward Elisha (2Ki 6:31). Samaritans toward the Jews (Ezr 4; Ne 2:10; 4:6). Haman toward Mordecai (Es 3:5-15; 5:9-14). The psalmist's enemies (Ps 22:7, 8; 35:15, 16, 19-21; 38:16, 19; 41:5-8; 55:3; 56:5, 6; 57:4, 6; 59:3, 4, 7; 62:3, 4; 64:2-6; 69:4, 10-12, 26; 86:14; 102:8; 109:2-5, 16-18; 140:1-4). Jeremiah's enemies (Jer 26:8-11; 38:1-6). Nebuchadnezzar toward Zedekiah (Jer 52:10, 11). Daniel's enemies (Da 6:4-15). Herodias toward John (M't 14:3-11; M'k 6:24-28). James and John toward the Samaritans (Lu 9:54). Enemies of Jesus (Ps 22:11; M't 27:18, 27-30, 39-43; M'k 12:13;

15:10, 11, 16-19, 29-32; Lu 11:53, 54; 23:10, 11, 39; Joh 18:22, 23). Paul's enemies (Ac 14:5, 19; 16:19-24; 17:5; 19:24-35; 21:27-31, 36; 22:22, 23; 23:12-15; 25:3; Ph'p 1:15-17).

See Conspiracy; Hatred; Homicide; Jealousy; Persecution; Retaliation; Revenge.

MALINGERING. *Instance of:* David feigning madness (1Sa 21:13-15).

MALLOTHI (I have uttered), son of Heman, a singer (1Ch 25:4, 26).

MALLOWS, a plant (Job 30:4).

MALLUCH (counselor). 1. Levite; ancestor of Ethan (1Ch 6:44).

2. Man who married foreign woman (Ezr 10:29).

3. Another such man (Ezr 10:32).

4. Priest who came with Zerubbabel (Ne 12:2).

5. Chief of people who sealed covenant (Ne 10:27).

MALTA (See Melita.)

MAMMON (riches), Aramaic word for riches (M't 6:24; Lu 16:11, 13).

MAMRE (strength). 1. A plain near Hebron. Abraham resides in (Ge 13:18; 14:13). Entertains three angels, and is promised a son (Ge 18:1-15). Isaac dwells in (Ge 35:27).

2. An Amorite and confederate of Abraham (Ge 14:13, 24).

MAN. Created (Ge 1:26, 27; 2:7; 5:1, 2; De 4:32; Job 4:17; 10:2, 3, 8, 9; 31:15; 33:4; 34:19; 35:10; 36:3; Ps 8:5; 100:3; 119:73; 138:8; 139:14, 15; Ec 7:29; Isa 17:7; 42:5; 43:7; 45:12; 64:8; Jer 27:5; Zec 12:1; Mal 2:10; M't 19:4; M'k 10:6; Heb 2:7); in the image of God (Ge 1:26, 27; 9:6; Ec 7:29; 1Co 11:7; 15:48, 49; Jas 3:9); a little lower than the angels (Job 4:18-21; Ps 8:5; Heb 2:7, 8); than God (Ps 8:5); above other creatures (M't 10:31; 12:12).

Design of: to have dominion over all creation (Ge 1:26, 28; 2:19, 20; 9:2, 3; Ps 8:6-8; Jer 27:6; 28:14; Da 2:38; Heb 2:7, 8; Jas 3:7); for the glory and pleasure of God (Pr 16:4; Isa 43:7).

Equality of all men (Job 21:26; 31:13-15; Ps 33:13-15; Pr 22:2; M't 20:25-28; 23:8-11; M'k 10:42-44; Ac 10:28, 34, 35; 17:26); under the gospel (Ga 3:28). See Race, Unity of.

Mortal (Job 4:17; Ec 2:14, 15; 3:20; 1Co 15:21, 22; Heb 9:27). See Immortality. Insignificance of (Ge 6:3; 18:27; Job 4:18, 19; 7:17; 15:14; 22:2-5; 25:4-6; 35:2-8; 38:4, 12, 13; Ps 8:3, 4; 78:39; 144:3, 4).

A spirit (Job 4:19; 14:10; 32:8; Ps 31:5; Pr 20:27; Ec 1:8; 3:21; 12:7; Isa 26:9; Zec 12:1; M't 4:4; 10:28; 26:41; M'k 14:38; Lu 22:40; 23:46; 24:39; Joh 3:3-8; 4:24; Ac 7:59; Ro 1:9; 2:29; 7:14-25; 1Co 2:11; 6:20; 7:34; 14:14; 2Co 4:6, 7, 16; 5:1-9; Eph 3:16; 4:4; 1Th 5:23; Heb 4:12; Jas 2:26).

See Duty; Ignorance; Neighbor; Young Men.

MAN OF SIN (See Antichrist.)

MAN, SON OF, a phrase used by God in addressing Daniel (Da 8:17) and Ezekiel (over 80 times); by Daniel in describing a personage he saw in a night vision (Da 7:13, 14); and many times by Jesus when referring to Himself, undoubtedly identifying Himself with the Son of Man of Daniel's prophecy and emphasizing His union with mankind (Lu 9:56; 19:10; 22:48; Joh 6:62). See Son of Man.

MANAEN (comforter), an associate of Herod in his youth, and a Christian teacher (Ac 13:1).

MANAHATH (resting place). 1. Son of Shobal (Ge 36:23; 1Ch 1:40).

2. A city in Benjamin (1Ch 8:6).

MANAHETHITES. 1. Descendants of Shobal, son of Caleb (1Ch 2:52).

2. Descendants of Salma, son of Caleb (1Ch 2:54).

MANASSEH (one who forgets). 1. Son of Joseph and Asenath (Ge 41:50, 51; 46:20); adopted by Jacob on his deathbed (Ge 48:1, 5-20). Called Manasses (Re 7:6).

2. Tribe of. Descendants of Joseph. The two sons of Joseph, Ephraim and Manasseh, were reckoned among the primogenitors of the twelve tribes, taking the places of Joseph and Levi.

Adopted by Jacob (Ge 48:5). Prophecy concerning (Ge 49:25, 26). Enumeration of (Nu 1:34, 35; 26:29-34). Place of in camp and march (Nu 2:18, 20; 10:22, 23). Blessing of Moses on (De 33:13-17). Inheritance of one-half of tribe E of Jordan (Nu 32:33, 39-42). One-half of tribe W of Jordan (Jos 16:9; 17:5-11). The eastern half assist in the conquest of the country W of the Jordan

(De 3:18-20; Jos 1:12-15; 4:12, 13). Join the other eastern tribes in erecting a monument to testify to the unity of all Israel; misunderstood; make satisfactory explanation (Jos 22). Join Gideon in war with the Midianites (J'g 6; 7). Malcontents of, join David (1Ch 12:19, 31). Smitten by Hazael (2Ki 10:33). Return from captivity (1Ch 9:3). Reallotment of territory to, by Ezekiel (Eze 48:4). Affiliate with the Jews in the reign of Hezekiah (2Ch 30). Incorporated into kingdom of Judah (2Ch 15:9; 34:6, 7).

See Israel, Tribes of.

3. [Moses, *R. V.*] Father of Gershom (J'g 18:30).

4. King of Judah. History of (2Ki 21:1-18; 2Ch 33:1-20).

5. Two Jews who put away their Gentile wives after the captivity (Ezr 10:30, 33).

MANASSES, name used in NT for "Manasseh" (M't 1:10; Re 7:6).

MANASSITES (forgetting), descendants of Joseph's son Manasseh (Ge 41:51).

MANDRAKE (Ge 30:14-16; Song 7:13).

MANEH. A weight. Rendered pound (1Ki 10:17; Ezr 2:69; Ne 7:71, 72). Equal to one hundred shekels (1Ki 10:17, w 2Ch 9:16).

See Weights.

MANGER, stall or trough for cattle (Lu 2:7-16; 13:15).

MANNA. Miraculously given to Israel for food in the wilderness (Ex 16:4, 15; Ne 9:15).

Called: God's manna (Ne 9:20). Bread of heaven (Ps 105:40). Bread from heaven (Ex 16:4; Joh 6:31). Corn of heaven (Ps 78:24). Angel's food (Ps 78:25). Spiritual meat (1Co 10:3). Previously unknown (De 8:3, 16).

Described as: Like coriander seed (Ex 16:31; Nu 11:7). White (Ex 16:31). Like in color to bdellium (Nu 11:7). Like in taste to wafers made with honey (Ex 16:31). Like in taste to oil (Nu 11:8). Like hoar frost (Ex 16:14). Fell after the evening dew (Nu 11:9). None fell on the Sabbath day (Ex 16:26, 27). Gathered every morning (Ex 16:21). An omer of, gathered for each person (Ex 16:16). Two portions of, gathered the sixth day on account of the Sabbath (Ex 16:5, 22-26). He that gathered much or little had sufficient and nothing over (Ex 16:18). Melted away by the sun (Ex 16:21).

Given: When Israel murmured for bread (Ex 16:2, 3). In answer to prayer (Ps 105:40). Through Moses (Joh 6:31, 32). To exhibit God's glory (Ex 16:7). As a sign of Moses' divine mission (Joh 6:30, 31). For forty years (Ne 9:21). As a test of obedience (Ex 16:4). To teach that man does not live by bread only (De 8:3, w M't 4:4). To humble and prove Israel (De 8:16). Kept longer than a day (except on the Sabbath) became corrupt (Ex 16:19, 20).

The Israelites: At first covetous of (Ex 16:17). Ground, made into cakes and baked in pans (Nu 11:8). Counted, inferior to food of Egypt (Nu 11:4-6). Loathed (Nu 21:5). Punished for despising (Nu 11:10-20). Punished for loathing (Nu 21:6). Ceased when Israel entered Canaan (Ex 16:35; Jos 5:12).

Illustrative of: Christ (Joh 6:32-35). Blessedness given to saints (Re 2:17). A golden pot of, laid up in the holiest for a memorial (Ex 16:32-34; Heb 9:4).

MANNERS. Social customs. Obeisance to strangers (Ge 18:2; 19:1). Standing while guests eat (Ge 18:8); in presence of superiors (Ge 31:35; Job 29:8); of the aged (Le 19:32). Courteousness enjoined (1Pe 3:8). Rules for guests (Pr 23:1, 2; 1Co 10:27).

See Salutations.

MANOAH (rest), a Danite of Zorah and father of Samson (J'g 13:2-24).

MANSERVANT (See Servant.)

MANSIONS, abiding places (Joh 14:2).

MANSLAUGHTER (See Fratricide; Homicide; Regicide.)

MANSLAYER, person who has killed another human being accidentally; could find asylum in cities of refuge (Nu 35; De 4:42; 19:3-10; Jos 20:3).

MANTLE. Rent in token of grief (Ezr 9:3; Job 1:20; 2:12). Of Elijah (1Ki 19:19; 2Ki 2:8, 13, 14).

See Dress.

MANURE. Used as fertilizer (Isa 25:10; Lu 13:8; 14:34, 35).

MANUSCRIPTS, DEAD SEA (See Dead Sea Scrolls.)

MAOCH (a poor one), father of Achish who protected David (1Sa 27:2; 29:1-11).

MAON (habitation). 1. Descendant of Caleb (1Ch 2:42-45).

2. Town S of Hebron (1Sa 23:24-28; 25:1-3).

MAONITES, enemies of Israel, called Menuhim, probably from Arabian peninsula (J'g 10:11, 12; Ezr 2:5).

MARA (bitter), name Naomi called herself (Ru 1:20).

MARAH (bitterness), the first station of the Israelites, where Moses made the bitter waters sweet (Ex 15:22-25; Nu 33:8, 9).

MARALAH, a landmark on the boundary of Zebulun (Jos 19:11).

MARANATHA (our Lord comes!), expression of greeting and encouragement after a solemn warning (1Co 16:22, RSV).

MARBLE. In the temple (1Ch 29:2). Pillars of (Es 1:6; Song 5:15). Merchandise of (Re 18:12). Mosaics of (Es 1:6).

MARCUS, Roman name of John Mark, kinsman of Barnabas (Ac 13:13; 15:39).

MARESHAH (possession). 1. A city of Judah (Jos 15:44; 2Ch 11:8; 14:9, 10). Birthplace of Eliezer the prophet (2Ch 20:37). Prophecy concerning (Mic 1:15).

2. Father of Hebron (1Ch 2:42).

3. A son of, or possibly a city founded by, Laadah (1Ch 4:21).

MARI, ancient city of Euphrates Valley, discovered in 1933 and subsequently excavated. 20,000 cuneiform tablets have been found, throwing much light upon ancient Syrian civilization. Mari kingdom was contemporary with Hammurabi of Babylon and the Amorite tribes of Canaan, ancestors of the Hebrews.

MARINER (1Ki 9:27; 2Ch 8:18; Isa 42:10; Eze 27:27). Perils of (Ps 107:23-30; Jon 1:5; Ac 27:17-44). Cowardice of (Ac 27:30).

See Ship; Commerce.

MARK, a word with various meanings: a special sign or brand (Ge 4:15; Ga 6:17), a sign of ownership (Eze 9:4, 6; Re 7:2-8), signature (Job 31:35 RSV), a target (1Sa 20:20), a form of tattooing banned by the Lord (Le 19:28), a goal to be attained (Ph'p 3:14), a particular brand denoting the nature or rank of men (Re 13:16).

MARK, JOHN (a large hammer), author of second Gospel. John was his Jewish name, Mark (Marcus) his Roman; called John (Ac 13:5, 13), Mark (Ac 15:39), "John, whose surname was Mark" (Ac 12:12); relative of Barnabas (Col 4:10); accompanied and then deserted Paul on 1st missionary journey (Ac 12:25; 13:13); went with Barnabas to Cyprus after Paul refused to take him on second missionary journey (Ac 15:36-39); fellow-worker with Paul (Ph'm 24); recommended by Paul to church at Colosse (Col 4:10); may have been young man of Mark 14:51, 52. Early tradition makes him the "interpreter" of Peter in Rome and founder of the church in Alexandria.

MARK, GOSPEL OF, second of the four Gospels, and the shortest. Both early tradition and internal evidence of the Gospel make John Mark the author; probably written between c. 64-69 in Rome at the request of Roman Christians who wanted a record of Peter's preaching about Jesus. Characteristics of the Gospel: rapidity of action, vividness of detail, and picturesqueness of description. Outline: 1. Baptism and temptation of Jesus (1:1-13).

2. Galilean ministry (1:14-9:50).

3. Ministry in Perea (10).

4. Passion Week and resurrection (11-16).

MARKET. A place for general merchandise. Held at gates (See Gates.) Judgment seat at (Ac 16:19). Traffic of, in Tyre, consisted of horses, horsemen, mules, horns, ivory, and ebony, emeralds, purple, broidered wares, linen, coral, agate, honey, balm, wine, wool, oil, cassia, calamus, charioteers' clothing, lambs, rams, goats, precious stones, and gold, spices, and costly apparel (Eze 27: 13-25).

MAROTH, a city of Judah (Mic 1:12).

MARRIAGE. Divine institution of (Ge 2:18, 20-24; M't 19:4-6; M'k 10:7, 8; 1Co 6:16; Eph 5:31). Based on law of nature (1Co 11:11, 12 w Ge 2:18). Unity of husband and wife in (Ge 2:23, 24; M't 19:5, 6; M'k 10:2-10; 1Co 6:16; Eph 5:31, 33). Commended (Pr 18:22; Heb 13:4). Obligations under, inferior to duty to God (De 13:6-10; M't 19:29; Lu 14:26). Indissoluble except for adultery (Mal 2:13-16; M't 5:31, 32; M'k 10:11, 12; Lu 16:18; Ro 7:1-3; 1Co 7:39, 40). Dissolved by death (M't 22:29, 30; M'k

12:24, 25; Ro 7:1-3). Enjoined on exiled Jews (Jer 29:6). Enjoined for sake of chastity (1Co 7:1-7). None in the resurrection state (M't 22:29, 30; M'k 12:24, 25). Levirate (the brother required to marry a brother's widow) (Ge 38:8, 11; De 25:5-10; Ru 4:5; M't 22:24-27; M'k 12:19-23; Lu 20:28-33).

Mosaic laws concerning: Of priests (Le 21:1, 7, 13-15). Captives (De 21:10-14). Divorced persons (De 24:1-5). An unbetrothed maid who has been seduced (Ex 22:16, 17). Within tribes (Nu 36:8). Incestuous, forbidden (Le 18:6-18 w De 22:30; Le 20:14, 17, 19-21; M'k 6:17, 18).

Among antediluvians (Ge 6:2). Among relatives, Abraham and Sarah (Ge 11:29; 12:13; 20:2, 9-16); Isaac and Rebekah (Ge 24:3, 4, 67); Jacob and his wives (Ge 28:2; 29:15-30).

Parents contract for their children: Hagar selects a wife for Ishmael (Ge 21:21). Abraham for Isaac (Ge 24). Laban arranges for his daughters' marriage (Ge 29). Samson asks his parents to procure him a wife (J'g 14:2). Parents' consent required in the Mosaic law (Ex 22:17). Presents given to parents to secure their favor (Ge 24:53; 34:12; 1Sa 18:25). Nuptial feasts (Ge 29:22; J'g 14:12; Es 2:18; M't 22:11, 12). Jesus present at (Joh 2:1-5). Ceremony attested by witnesses (Ru 4:1-11; Isa 8:1-3). Bridegroom exempt one year from military duty (De 24:5). Bridal ornaments (Isa 49:18; Jer 2:32). Bridal presents (Ge 24:53). Herald preceded the bridegroom (M't 25:6). Wedding robes adorned with jewels (Isa 61:10). Festivities attending (Jer 7:34; 16:9; 25:10; Re 18:23).

Wives obtained by purchase (Ge 29:20, 27-29; 31:41; Ru 4:10; 2Sa 3:14; Ho 3:2; 12:12); by kidnapping (J'g 21:21-23). Given by kings (1Sa 17:25; 18:17, 27). Daughters given in, as rewards of valor (J'g 1:12; 1Sa 17:25; 18:27).

Wives taken by edict (Es 2:2-4, 8-14). David gave 100 Philistine foreskins for a wife (2Sa 3:14).

Wives among the Israelites must be Israelites (Ex 34:16; De 7:3, 4; Ezr 9:1, 2, 12; Ne 10:30; 13:26, 27; Mal 2:11). Betrothal a quasi-marriage (M't 1:18; Lu 1:27). Discouraged among the Corinthians (1Co 7:8, 9, 25-40 w v 1). Celibacy deplored (J'g 11:38; Isa 4:1). Unhappiness in (Pr 21:9, 19).

Of widows (Ro 7:1-3; 1Co 7:39, 40; 1Ti 5:14). Of ministers (Le 21:7, 8, 13, 14; Eze 44:22; 1Co 9:5; 1Ti 3:2, 12). Prophecies concerning the forbidding of (1Ti 4:1, 3).

Figurative: Isa 54:5; 62:4, 5: Jer 3:14; 31:32; Eze 16:8; Ho 2:19, 20; Eph 5:23-32; Re 19:7-9). Parables of (M't 22:2-10; 25:1-10; M'k 2:19, 20; Joh 3:29; 2Co 11:2.

See Bride; Bridegroom; Divorce; Husband; Wife.

MARROW, heart of the bone (Job 21:24), used figuratively of good things (Ps 63:5; Isa 25:6).

MARS HILL (Hill of Ares), hill in Athens dedicated to Ares, god of war (Ac 17:16-34).

MARSENA, counselor of King Ahasuerus (Es 1:10-14).

MARSH, swamp lands (Eze 47:11).

MARTHA (lady). Sister of Mary and Lazarus (Joh 11:1). Ministers to Jesus (Lu 10:38-42; Joh 12:2). Beloved by Jesus (Joh 11:5).

See Lazarus; Mary.

MARTYR (witness), one who dies to bear witness to a cause (Ac 22:20; Re 17:6).

MARTYRDOM. Of prophets (M't 23:34; Lu 11:50; Re 16:6). Followers of Jesus exposed to (M't 10:21, 22, 39; 23:34; 24:9; M'k 13:12; Lu 21:16, 17). Must be incited by love (1Co 13:3).

Allegorical reference to (Re 6:9-11; 11:7-12; 17:6).

Spirit of, required by Jesus (M't 16:25; Lu 9:24; Joh 12:25); possessed by the righteous (Ps 44:22; Ro 8:36; Re 12:11).

See Persecution.

Instances of: Abel (Ge 4:3-8). Prophets slain by Jezebel (1Ki 18:4, 13). Zechariah (2Ch 24:21, 22). John the Baptist (M'k 6:18-28). Jesus (See Jesus). Stephen (Ac 7:58-60). James the apostle (Ac 12:2). The prophets (M't 22:6; 23:35; Ro 11:3; 1Th 2:15; Heb 11:32-37).

MARY. Miriam in OT. 1. See Mary, The Virgin.

2. Mother of James and Joses (M't 27:56; M'k 15:40; Lu 24:10), probably the wife of Clopas (Joh 19:25); wit-

nessed crucifixion and visited grave on Easter morning (M't 27:56; 28:1).

3. Mary Magdalene; Jesus cast seven demons out of her (M'k 16:9; Lu 8:2); followed body of Jesus to grave (M't 27:61) and was first to learn of the resurrection (M't 28:1-8; M'k 16:9).

4. Mary of Bethany; sister of Lazarus and Martha; lived in Bethany (Joh 11:1); commended by Jesus (Lu 10:42); anointed feet of Jesus (Joh 12:3).

5. Mother of John Mark; sister of Barnabas (Col 4:10); home in Jerusalem meeting place of Christians (Ac 12:12).

6. Christian at Rome (Ro 16:6).

MARY THE VIRGIN, wife of Joseph (M't 1:18-25); kinswoman of Elizabeth, the mother of John the Baptist (Lu 1:36); of the seed of David (Ac 2:30; Ro 1:3; 2Ti 2:8); mother of Jesus (M't 1:18, 20; Lu 2:1-20); attended to ceremonial purification (Lu 2:22-38); fled to Egypt with Joseph and Jesus (M't 2:13-15); lived in Nazareth (M't 2:19-23); took twelve-year-old Jesus to temple (Lu 2:41-50); at wedding in Cana of Galilee (Joh 2:1-11); concerned for Jesus' safety (M't 12:46; M'k 3:21, 31ff; Lu 8:19-21); at the cross of Jesus (Joh 19:25ff), where she was entrusted by Jesus to care of John (Joh 19:25-27); in the Upper Room (Ac 1:14). Distinctive Roman Catholic doctrines about Mary: Immaculate Conception (1854) and Assumption of Mary (1950).

MASCHIL, word of uncertain meaning found in titles of Psalms 32, 42, 44, 45, 52, 54, 55, 74, 78, 88, 89, 142.

MASH, son of Aram (Ge 10:22, 23); called "Meshech" in 1Ch 1:17.

MASHAL, called also Mishal and Misheal. A Levitical city in Asher (Jos 19:26; 21:30; 1Ch 6:74).

MASKING, by Tamar (Ge 38:14).

MASON. A trade in the time of David (2Sa 5:11); of later times (2Ki 12:12; 22:6; 1Ch 14:1; Ezr 3:7).

MASREKAH (vineyard), royal city of King Samlah, in Edom (Ge 36:31, 36; 1Ch 1:47).

MASSA (burden), tribe descended from Ishmael near Persian Gulf (Ge 25:14; 1Ch 1:30).

MASSACRE. Authorized by Moses (De 20:13, 16). Decree to destroy the Jews (Es 3).

Instances of: Inhabitants of Heshbon (De 2:34); of Bashan (De 3:6); of Ai (Jos 8:24-26); of Hazor (Jos 11:11, 12); of the cities of the seven kings (Jos 10:28-40). Midianites (Nu 31:7, 8). Prophets of Baal (1Ki 18:40). Worshipers of Baal (2Ki 10:18-28). Sons of Ahab (2Ki 10:1-8). Seed royal of Athaliah (2Ki 11:1). Inhabitants of Tiphsah (2Ki 15:16). Edomites (2Ki 14:7).

See Captive.

MASSAH (strife), site of rock in Horeb from which Moses drew water (Ex 17:1-7; De 6:16; 9:22); connected with Meribah (De 33:8).

MASTER. Jesus called (M't 8:19; 10:25; 23:8; 26:18, 25, 49; M'k 14:45; Lu 8:24; Joh 13:13, 14). Jesus prohibited the appellation (M't 23:8).

MASTER, OF SERVANTS. Violent, to be punished (Ex 21:20, 21, 26, 27).

Duties of, to servants: Must, allow Sabbath rest (De 5:14); compensate (Jer 22:13; Ro 4:4; Col 4:1; 1Ti 5:18); pay promptly (Le 19:13; De 24:15; Jas 5:4). Forbidden, to oppress (Le 19:13; 25:43; De 24:14; Job 31:13, 14; Pr 22:16; Mal 3:5); to threaten (Eph 6:9). Exhorted, to show kindness (Ph'm 10-16); to show wisdom (Pr 29:12, 21).

See Employer; Employee; Hired Servant; Servant.

Good: Instances of: Abraham (Ge 18:19); Job (Job 31:13-15); the centurion (Lu 7:2).

Unjust: Instances of: Sarah to Hagar (Ge 16:6). Laban to Jacob (Ge 31:7); Potiphar's wife to Joseph (Ge 39:7-20).

MASTER WORKMAN (Pr 8:30; 1Co 3:10).

Instances of: Tubal-cain (Ge 4:22); Bezaleel (Ex 31:2-11; 35:30-35); Hiram (1Ki 7:13-50; 2Ch 2:13, 14; 4:11-18).

See Art.

MATERIALISM (Ac 23:8).

See Infidelity.

MATHUSALA (See Methuselah.)

MATRED (expulsion), mother of Mehetabel, wife of Hadar (Ge 36:39), who is called "Hadad" in 1Ch 1:50.

MATRI (rainy), head of Benjamite family (1Sa 10:21).

MATTAN (a gift). 1. A priest of Baal slain in the idol temple at Jerusalem (2Ki 11:18; 2Ch 23:17).

2. Father of Shephatiah (Jer 38:1).

MATTANAH (a gift), encampment of Israel in wilderness (Nu 21:18).

MATTANIAH (gift from Jehovah). 1. Original name of King Zedekiah (2Ki 24:17).

2. Chief choir leader and watchman (Ne 11:17; 12:8, 25).

3. Levite (2Ch 20:14).

4. Son of Elam (Ezr 10:26).

5. Son of Zattu (10:27).

6. Son of Pahath-Moah (10:30).

7. Son of Bani (Ezr 10:37).

8. Grandfather of Hanan (Ne 13:13).

9. Son of Heman; head musician (1Ch 25:4, 5, 7, 16).

10. Levite who assisted Hezekiah (2Ch 29:13).

MATTATHA, an ancestor of Jesus (Lu 3:31).

MATTATHAH (gift of Jehovah), one of the family of Hashum (Ezr 10:33).

MATTATHIAS (gift of Jehovah). 1. Assistant of Ezra, spelled Mattathiah (Ne 8:4).

2. Name borne by two ancestors of Christ (Lu 3:25, 26).

3. Priest; founder of Maccabee family (1Macc 2). See also 1Macc 11:70; 16:14-16; 2Macc 14:19.

MATTENAI (a gift from Jehovah). 1. Two Israelites who put away their Gentile wives after the captivity (Ezr 10:33, 37).

2. A priest in the time of Joiakim (Ne 12:19).

MATTHAN (gift of God), grandfather of Joseph, Mary's husband (M't 1:15).

MATTHAT (gift of God). 1. Father of Heli, ancestor of Joseph (Lu 3:24).

2. Father of Jorim, and ancestor of Joseph (Lu 3:29).

MATTHEW, son of Alphaeus (M'k 2:14); tax collector, also called Levi (M'k 2:14; Lu 5:27); called by Jesus to become disciple (M't 9:9; M'k 2:14; Lu 5:27) and gave feast for Jesus; appointed apostle (M't 10:3; M'k 3:18; Lu 6:15; Ac 1:13).

MATTHEW, GOSPEL OF, unanimously ascribed to Matthew the Apostle by early church fathers; date and place of origin are unknown, although there is good reason to believe it was written before A. D. 70. Outline: 1. Birth and early years of the Messiah (1:1-4:16).

2. Galilean ministry of Jesus (4:17-18:35).

3. Perean ministry (19, 20).

4. Passion Week and resurrection (21-28). Characteristics: a didactic Gospel; shows fulfilment of OT prophecies in Christ; stresses Christ as King; structure of Gospel woven around five great discourses.

MATTHIAS (gift of Jehovah), apostle chosen by lot to take place of Judas (Ac 1:15-26); had been follower of Christ (Ac 1:21, 22).

MATTITHIAH (gift of Jehovah). 1. A Levite who had charge of the baked offerings (1Ch 9:31).

2. A Levite musician (1Ch 15:18, 21; 16:5).

3. A chief of the fourteenth division of temple musicians (1Ch 25:3, 21).

4. An Israelite who divorced his Gentile wife after the captivity (Ezr 10:43).

5. A prince who stood by Ezra when he read the law to the people (Ne 8:4).

MATTOCK, single-headed pickaxe with point on one side and broad edge on other side (1Sa 13:20, 21; Isa 7:25).

MAUL (a breaker), war club or club used by shepherds (Pr 25:18).

MAW, one of the stomachs of a ruminating animal (De 18:3).

MAZZAROTH, probably signs of the zodiac (see Job 38:32).

See Music.

MEADOW. 1. Place where reeds grow (Ge 41:2, 18).

2. Pasture land (J'g 20:33).

MEAH (hundred), a tower in Jerusalem (Ne 3:1; 12:39).

MEAL, ground grain used for both food and sacrificial offerings (Ge 18:6; Le 2:1).

MEAL OFFERING (See Offerings.)

MEARAH (cave), town in NE Palestine belonging to Zidonians (Jos 13:4).

MEASURE. The following modern equivalents of ancient measurements are based upon the latest researches, and are probably as nearly correct as is possible at this time:

Dry: 1. Bushel, about a peck (M't 5:15; M'k 4:21; Lu 11:33).

2. Cab, or kab, about two quarts (2Ki 6:25).

3. Cor, equal to one homer or ten ephahs, equal to about eleven and one-

ninth bushels (1Ki 4:22; 5:11; 2Ch 2:10; 27:5; Ezr 7:22).

4. Ephah, equal to three seah, and in liquid, to a bath, containing about a bushel and a half (Ex 16:36; Lev 5:11; 6:20; 19:36; Nu 5:15; 28:5; J'g 6:19; Ru 2:17; 1Sa 1:24; 17:17; Isa 5:10; Eze 45:10, 11, 13, 24; 46:5, 7, 11, 14; Am 8:5; Zec 5:6-10).

5. Half-homer, about five and a half bushels (Ho 3:2).

7. Omer, about one bushel (Ex 16:16, 18, 22, 32, 33, 36).

8. Seah, about a peck and a half (Ge 18:6; 1Sa 25:18; 1Ki 18:32; 2Ki 7:1, 16, 18).

9. Tenth deal, about a gallon, equal to one-tenth of an ephah (Ex 29:40; Le 14:10, 21; 23:13, 17; 24:5; Nu 15:4, 6, 9; 28:9, 12, 13, 20, 21, 28, 29; 29:3, 4, 9, 10, 14, 15).

Liquid: 1. Bath, about eight gallons and a half (1Ki 7:26, 38; 2Ch 2:10; 4:5; Ezr 7:22; Isa 5:10; Eze 45:10, 11, 14; Lu 16:6).

2. Firkin, nearly nine gallons (Joh 2:6).

3. Hin, about a gallon and a half (Ex 29:40; 30:24; Le 19:36; 23:13; Nu 15:4-10; 28:5, 7, 14; Eze 4:11; 45:24; 46:5, 7, 11, 14).

4. Log, about a pint, one-twelfth of a hin (Le 14:10, 12, 15, 21, 24).

See Weights.

Linear: 1. Finger (Jer 52:21).

2. Handbreadth (Ex 25:25; 37:12; 1Ki 7:26; 2Ch 4:5; Ps 39:5; Eze 40:5, 43; 43:13).

3. Span (Ex 28:16; 1Sa 17:4; Isa 40:12; 48:13; La 2:20; Eze 43:13).

4. Cubit, the length of the forearm (See Cubit.)

5. Reed, probably six cubits (Eze 40:5).

6. Fathom (Ac 27:28).

7. Pace (2Sa 6:13).

8. Furlong (Lu 24:13).

9. Mile, probably nine-tenths of an English mile (M't 5:41).

10. Sabbath day's journey, two thousand paces (Ac 1:12).

False and Just: Just required (Le 19:35, 36; De 25:13-16; Pr 16:11). False (Ho 12:7-9); an abomination (Pr 11:1: 20:10, 23; Mic 6:10-12).

See Dishonesty; Integrity.

MEAT (See Food.)

MEAT OFFERING (See Offerings, Meat.)

MEBUNNAI (well-built), one of David's bodyguards (2Sa 23:27), called Sibbechai in 2Sa 21:18.

MECHANIC (Pr 8:30; 1Co 3:10).

Instances of: Tubal-cain (Ge 4:22). Bezaleel (Ex 31:2-11; 35:30-35). Hiram (1Ki 7:13-50; 2Ch 2:13, 14; 4:11-18).

See Art.

MECHERATHITE, description of Hepher (1Ch 11:36).

MEDAD (affectionate), one of the seventy elders who did not go to the tabernacle with Moses, but prophesied in the camp (Nu 11:26-29).

MEDAN (strife), son of Abraham and Keturah (Ge 25:2; 1Ch 1:32).

MEDDLING (See Busybody; Talebearer.)

MEDEBA. A city of Moab (Nu 21:30). An idolatrous high place (Isa 15:2). Allotted to Reuben (Jos 13:9, 16). David defeats army and the Ammonites at (1Ch 19:7-15).

MEDES. Inhabitants of Media. Israelites distributed among, when carried to Assyria (2Ki 17:6; 18:11). Palace in the Babylonian province of (Ezr 6:2). An essential part of the Medo-Persian empire (Es 1:1-19). Supremacy of, in the Chaldean empire (Da 5:28, 31; 9:1; 11:1).

MEDIA (See Medes.)

MEDIATION. *Between men and God* (Ex 18:19; Job 9:33; Ga 3:19). Solicited by Israel (Ex 20:19, 20; De 5:27).

Instances of: By Moses (Ex 32:11-13; 34:9; Nu 14:13-19; 27:5; De 5:5; 9:18-20, 25-29). Aaron (Nu 16:47, 48). Joshua, (Jos 7:6-9). Samuel (1Sa 8:10, 21). David (2Sa 24:17).

Between men and Jesus: In behalf of the afflicted (M't 12:22; 15:30; M'k 1:32). The four friends for the paralytic (M't 2:3; Lu 5:18-20). Jairus (M't 9:18; M'k 5:23; Lu 8:41). The nobleman for his son (Joh 4:47, 49). The father of the epileptic for his son (M't 17:15; M'k 9:17, 18). The Syrophenician woman for her daughter (M't 15:22; M'k 7:24-26). The disciples for Peter's wife's mother (M'k 1:30; Lu 4:38, 39).

Between men and men: Reuben for Joseph (Ge 37:21, 22). Judah for Joseph

(Ge 37:26, 27). Pharaoh's chief baker for Joseph (Ge 41:9-13 w 40:14). Jonathan for David (1Sa 19:1-7). Abigail for Nabal (1Sa 25:23-35). Joab for Absalom (2Sa 14:1-24). Bath-sheba for Solomon (1Ki 1:15-31); for Adonijah (1Ki 2:13-25). Ebed-melech for Jeremiah (Jer 38:7-13). Elisha offers to see the king for the Shunammite (2Ki 4:13). The king of Syria for Naaman (2Ki 5:6-8). Paul for Onesimus (Ph'm 10-21).

See Intercession; Jesus, Mediator.

MEDICINE. Used (1Sa 38:21; Lu 10:34). See Diseases; Physician.

Figurative (Pr 17:22; Isa 1:6; Jer 8:22; 30:13; 46:11; 51:8, 9). Allegorical (Eze 47:12; Re 22:2).

MEDITATION. On the Lord (Ps 63:5, 6; 104:34; 139:17, 18). On the law of the Lord (Ps 1:2; 19:14; 49:3; 119:11, 15, 16, 23, 48, 55, 59, 78, 97-99, 148); enjoined (Jos 1:18). On the works of the Lord (Ps 77:10-12; 143:5).

Instances of: Isaac (Ge 24:63). The Psalmist (Ps 4:4; 39:3); concerning the wicked (Ps 73:12-22).

MEDITERRANEAN SEA. Mentioned in Scripture as: The sea (Ezr 3:7). The Great Sea (Nu 34:6, 7; Jos 1:4; 9:1; 15:12, 47; 23:4; Eze 47:10, 15, 20; 48:28). Sea of the Philistines (Ex 23:31). Sea of Joppa (Ezr 3:7). The hinder sea (De 11:24; Zec 14:8). The uttermost sea (De 11:24). The utmost sea (Joe 2:20). The western sea (Joe 2:20; Zec 14:8).

MEEKNESS. Advantageous (Ps 25:9; Pr 14:29; 17:1; 19:11; Ec 7:8; 10:4; Am 3:3; 1Co 13:4, 5, 7). Honorable (Pr 20:3). Potent (Pr 15:1, 18; 16:32; 25:15; 29:8).

Enjoined (Zep 2:3; M't 5:38-41 w Lu 6:29; M't 11:29; M'k 9:50; Ro 12:14, 18; 14:19; 1Co 6:7; 7:15; 10:32; 2Co 13:11; Ga 6:1; Eph 4:1, 2; Ph'p 2:14, 15; Col 3:12, 13; 1Th 5:14, 15; 1Ti 3:3; 6:11; 2Ti 2:24, 25; Tit 2:2, 9; 3:2; Heb 10:36; 12:14; Jas 1:4, 19, 21; 3:13; 1Pe 2:18-23; 3:4, 11, 15; 2Pe 1:5-7).

A fruit of the Spirit (Ga 5:22, 23, 26).

Rewards of (Ps 22:26; 37:11; 76:8, 9; 147:6; 149:4; Isa 29:19; M't 5:5; 11:29).

Instances of: Abraham (Ge 13:8, 9). Isaac (Ge 26:20-22). Moses (Ex 16:7, 8; 17:2-7; Nu 12:3; 16:4-11). Gideon (J'g 8:2, 3). Hannah (1Sa 1:13-16). Saul (1Sa 10:27). David (1Sa 17:29; 2Sa 16:9-14; Ps 38:13, 14). The Psalmist (Ps 120:5-7). Jesus (Isa 11:4; 42:1-4; 53:7; La 3:28-30; M't 11:29; 12:19, 20; 26:47-54; 27:13, 14; M'k 15:4, 5; Lu 23:34; 2Co 10:1; 1Pe 2:21-23). See Jesus, Humility of; Meekness of. Stephen (Ac 7:60). Paul (Ac 21:20-26; 1Co 4:12, 13; 2Co 12:10; 1Th 2:7; 2Ti 4:16). The Thessalonians (2Th 1:4). Job (Jas 5:11). The angel (Jude 9). Of God (La 3:22, 28-30). See God, Meekness of. See Humility; Kindness; Patience.

MEGIDDO (place of troops), city on the Great Road linking Gaza and Damascus, connecting the coastal plain and the Plain of Esdraelon (Jos 12:21; 17:11; J'g 1:27; 5:19); fortified by Solomon (1Ki 9:15); wounded Ahaziah died there (2Ki 9:27); Josiah lost life there in battle with Pharaoh Necho (2Ki 23:29, 30; 2Ch 35:20-27). Large-scale excavations have revealed a great deal of material of great archaeological value.

MEGIDDON (See Megiddo.)

MEHETABEEL, a person whose grandson tried to intimidate Nehemiah (Ne 6:10).

MEHETABEL (God benefits), wife of Hadar (Ge 36:39; 1Ch 1:50).

MEHIDA (renowned), a person whose descendants returned from Babylon (Ezr 2:52; Ne 7:54).

MEHIR (price, hire), son of Chelub (1Ch 4:11).

MEHOLATHITE, an inhabitant of a city in Issachar (1Sa 18:19; 2Sa 21:8).

MEHUJAEL, descendant of Cain; father of Methusael (Ge 4:18).

MEHUMAN, eunuch of Ahasuerus, king of Persia (Es 1:10).

MEHUNIM, called also Meunim. A person whose descendants returned from exile (Ezr 2:50; Ne 7:52).

ME-JARKON, a city in Dan (Jos 19:46).

MEKONAH, a city in Judah (Ne 11:28).

MELATIAH, a Gibeonite who assisted in repairing the wall of Jerusalem (Ne 3:7).

MELCHI. 1. Ancestor of Jesus (Lu 3:24).

2. Remote ancestor of Jesus (Lu 3:28).

MELCHIAH (See Malchiah.)

MELCHESEDEC (See Melchizedek.)

MELCHISHUA, called also Malchishua. Son of King Saul (1Sa 14:49; 31:2; 1Ch 8:33; 9:39; 10:2).

MELCHIZEDEK, MELCHISEDEK (king of righteousness), priest and king of Salem (Jerusalem); blessed Abram in the name of Most High God and received tithes from him (Ge 14:18-20); type of Christ, the Priest-King (Ps 110:4; Heb 5:6-10; 6:20; 7).

MELEA, ancestor of Jesus (Lu 3:31).

MELECH (king), son of Micah (1Ch 8:35; 9:41).

MELICU, a priest (Ne 12:14).

MELITA, an island in the Mediterranean. Paul shipwrecked on the coast of (Ac 28:1-10).

MELODY (See Music.)

MELON (Nu 11:5).

MELZAR (overseer), the steward whom the prince of the eunuchs set over Daniel and the three Hebrew children (Da 1:11-16).

MEMBER, any feature or part of the body (Job 17:7; Jas 3:5).

MEMORIAL. Passover (Ex 12:14). See Passover.

Firstborn set apart as a (Ex 13:12-16). Pot of manna (Ex 16:32-34). Feast of tabernacles (Le 23:43). Shoulder stones of the ephod (Ex 28:12). Atonement money (Ex 30:16). The twelve stones of Jordan (Jos 4:1-9).

The Lord's supper (Lu 22:19; 1Co 11:24-26).

See Pillar.

MEMPHIS, capital city of Egypt, on W bank of Nile c. 20 miles S of modern Cairo; its destruction foretold by prophets (Isa 19:13; Jer 2:16; 44:1; 46:14, 19; Eze 30:13, 16; all RSV). See also Noph.

MEMUCAN, one of the seven princes of Ahasuerus who counsels the king to divorce Queen Vashti (Es 1:14-21).

MENAHEM (comforted), 16th king of Israel; evil; slew his predecessor, Shallum (2Ki 15:13-22).

MENAN, an ancestor of Jesus (Lu 3:31).

MENE, MENE, TEKEL, UPHARSIN, four Aramaic words of uncertain interpretation, but probably meaning "numbered, numbered, weighed, and found wanting," which suddenly appeared on the walls of Belshazzar's banquet hall (Da 5).

MENI (fate, destiny), probably Canaanite god of good luck or destiny (Isa 65:11). Translated "number" in KJV.

MENSES (See Menstruation.)

MENSTRUATION. Law relating to (Le 15:19-30; 20:18; Eze 18:6). Cessation of, in old age (Ge 18:11). Immunities of women during (Ge 31:35). Uncleanness of (Isa 30:22).

Figurative: Isa 30:22; La 1:17; Eze 36:17.

MEONENIM, plain near Shechem named for a diviner's tree (J'g 9:37), exact site unknown.

MEONOTHAI (my dwelling), father of Ophrah (1Ch 4:14).

MEPHAATH (splendor), a Levitical city in Reuben (Jos 13:18; 21:37; 1Ch 6:79; Jer 48:21).

MEPHIBOSHETH. 1. Son of Saul by Rizpah, whom David surrendered to the Gibeonites to be slain (2Sa 21:8, 9).

2. Son of Jonathan (2Sa 4:4). Called Merib-baal (1Ch 8:34; 9:40). Was lame (2Sa 4:4). David entertains him at his table (2Sa 9:1-7; 21:7). Property restored to (2Sa 9:9, 10). His ingratitude to David at the time of Absalom's usurpation (2Sa 16:1-4; 19:24-30). Property of, confiscated (2Sa 16:4; 19:29, 30).

MERAB (increase). Daughter of King Saul (1Sa 14:49). Betrothed to David by Saul (1Sa 18:17, 18); but given to Adriel to wife (1Sa 18:19).

MERAIAH (rebellious), a priest (Ne 12:12).

MERAIOTH (rebellious). 1. High priest (1Ch 6:6, 7).

2. Priest; ancestor of Hilkiah (1Ch 9:11).

3. Another priestly ancestor of Helkai (Ne 12:15). May be same as "Meremoth" in Ne 12:3.

MERARI (bitter), youngest son of Levi; progenitor of Merarites (Nu 3:17, 33-37; Jos 21:7, 34-40).

MERATHAIM (rebellion), symbolic name for Babylon (Jer 50:21).

MERCENARIES (See Soldiers.)

MERCHANDISE (See Commerce.)

MERCHANT (Ge 23:16; 37:28; 1Ki 10:15, 28; 2Ch 9:14; Ne 3:32; 13:20; Job 41:6; Song 3:6; Isa 23:2; 47:15; Eze 17:4; 27:13, 17, 21-36; 38:13; Ho 12:7; Na 3:16; M't 13:45; Re 18:3, 11, 23).

See Commerce.

MERCURIUS (Hermes), son of Zeus; messenger of the Greek gods. People of

Lystra called Paul "Mercury" (Ac 14:12).

MERCURY (See Mercurius.)

MERCY (Ps 85:10; Pr 20:28; Ho 4:1; Jas 2:13). A grace of the godly (Ps 37:25, 26; Pr 11:17; 12:10; 14:22, 31; Ro 12:8). Of the wicked, cruel (Pr 12:10). Iniquity atoned by (Pr 16:6).

Enjoined (Pr 3:3; Ho 12:6; Mic 6:8; M't 9:13; 12:7; 23:23; Lu 6:36; Col 3:12, 13). To be shown with cheerfulness (Ro 12:8). Rewards of (2Sa 22:26; Ps 18:25; 37:25, 26; Pr 14:21; 21:21; M't 5:7).

See God, Mercy of; Kindness.

Instances of: The prison keeper, to Joseph (Ge 39:21-23). Joshua to Rahab (Jos 6:25). The Israelites to the man of Beth-el (J'g 1:23-26). David to Saul (1Sa 24:10-13, 17).

MERCY SEAT. Description of (Ex 25:17-22). Placed on the ark of the testimony (Ex 26:34; 30:6; 31:7; 40:20; Heb 9:5). Materials of, to be a freewill offering (Ex 35:4-12). Made by Bezaleel (Ex 37:1, 6-9).

Sprinkled with blood (Le 16:14, 15). The shekinah upon (Ex 25:22; 30:6, 36; Le 16:2; Nu 7:89; 17:4; 1Sa 4:4; 2Sa 6:2; 2Ki 19:15; 1Ch 13:6; Ps 80:1; Ps 99:1; Isa 37:16; Heb 4:16).

In Solomon's temple (1Ch 28:11).

See Tabernacle.

MERED (rebellion), son of Ezra (1Ch 4:17, 18).

MEREMOTH (elevations). 1. Priest who returned from exile (Ne 12:3).

2. Another priest who returned from exile (Ezr 8:33; Ne 3:4, 21).

3. Man who divorced foreign wife (Ezr 10:36).

4. Priest who signed covenant with Nehemiah (Ne 10:5).

MERES (worthy), one of the princes of Persia (Es 1:14).

MERIBAH (contention). 1. Place NW of Sinai where God gave Israelites water from rock (Ex 17:1-7).

2. Place near Kadesh-barnea where God also gave Israelites water from a rock. Because of Moses' loss of temper God did not permit him to enter the Promised Land (Nu 20:1-13).

MERIB-BAAL (Baal contends), son of Jonathan (1Ch 8:34; 9:40). May be same as Mephibosheth.

MERIBAH-KADESH (See Meribah.)

MERIT, personal. (See Grace.)

MERODACH, Marduk, the chief god of the Babylonians (Jer 50:2).

MERODACH BALADAN (Marduk has given a son), twice king of Babylon (722-710; 703-702 B. C.); invited Hezekiah to join conspiracy against Assyria (2Ki 20:12-19; Isa 39:1-8).

MEROM (high place), place near headwaters of Jordan river where Joshua defeated N coalition (Jos 11:5, 7). Identified with Lake Huleh.

MERONOTHITE, inhabitant of Meronoth, a region in Galilee, given to Naphtali (1Ch 27:30).

MEROZ. A place N of Mount Tabor. Deborah and Barak curse the inhabitants of, in their song of triumph (J'g 5:23).

MESECH (See Meshech.)

MESHA. 1. Place in S Arabia (Ge 10:30).

2. Benjamite (1Ch 8:9).

3. Descendant of Judah (1Ch 2:42).

4. King of Moab in days of Ahab, Ahaziah, and Jehoram (2Ki 3:4).

MESHACH, a name given by the chief eunuch to Mishael, one of the three Hebrew children (Da 1:7; 2:49; 3:12-30).

MESHECH (tall). 1. Called also Mesech. Son of Japheth (Ge 10:2; 1Ch 1:5).

2. Son of Shem (1Ch 1:17).

3. A tribe (Ps 120:5).

4. The Moschi (Eze 27:13; 32:26; 38:2, 3).

MESHELEMIAH, father of Zechariah (1Ch 9:21; 26:1, 2, 9); "Shelemiah" in 1Ch 26:14.

MESHEZABEEL (God delivers). 1. Ancestor of Meshullam (Ne 3:4).

2. Covenanter with Nehemiah (Ne 10:21).

3. Judahite (Ne 11:24).

MESHILLEMITH, a priest (1Ch 9:12).

MESHILLEMOTH (recompense). 1. Father of an Ephraimite who protested against the attempt of the Israelites to enslave their captive brethren (2Ch 28:12, 13).

2. A priest (Ne 11:13).

MESHOBAB, a Simeonite (1Ch 4:34).

MESHULLAM (reconciled). 1. Grandfather of Shaphan (2Ki 22:3).

2. Son of Zerubbabel (1Ch 3:19).

3. Leading Gadite (1Ch 5:13).

4. Chief Benjamite (1Ch 8:17).

5. Father of Sallu (1Ch 9:7).

6. Benjamite of Jerusalem (1Ch 9:8).
7. Priest (1Ch 9:11; Ne 11:11).
8. Ancestor of priest (1Ch 9:12).
9. Kohathite (2Ch 34:12).
10. Israelite who returned with Ezra (Ezr 8:16).
11. Man active in matter of putting away foreign wives (Ezr 10:15).
12. Divorced foreign wife (Ezr 10:29).
13. Son of Berechiah; helped rebuild Jerusalem wall (Ne 3:4, 30; 6:18).
14. Another repairer of wall (Ne 3:6).
15. Helper of Ezra (Ne 8:4).
16. Priest (Ne 10:7).
17. Priest who sealed covenant (Ne 10:20).
18. Benjamite (Ne 11:7).
19. Priest (Ne 12:13).
20. Possibly the same man (Ne 12:33).
21. Another priest (Ne 12:16).
22. Levite (Ne 12:25).

MESHULLEMETH, wife of Manasseh and mother of Amon (2Ki 21:19).

MESOBAITE, name of place otherwise unknown (1Ch 11:47).

MESOPOTAMIA (middle river). The country between the Tigris and the Euphrates. Abraham a native of (Ac 7:2). Nahor dwelt in (Ge 24:10). People who dwelt in, called Syrians (Ge 25:20). Balaam from (De 23:4). The children of Israel subjected to, eight years under the judgments of God (J'g 3:8); delivered from, by Othniel (J'g 3:9, 10). Chariots hired from, by the Ammonites (1Ch 19:6, 7). People of, present at Pentecost (Ac 2:9).

See Babylon; Chaldea.

MESS, any dish of food sent to the table (Ge 43:34; 2Sa 11:8; Heb 12:16).

MESSENGER. *Figurative:* Hag 1:13; Mal 2:7; 3:1; 4:5, 6; M't 11:10; M'k 1:2; Lu 7:27. Of Satan (2Co 12:7).

MESSIAH (anointed one); the basic meaning of the Heb. *mashiah* and the Gr. *Christos* is "anointed one." In the OT the word is used of prophets, priests, and kings who were consecrated to their office with oil. The expression "the Lord's anointed" and its equivalent is not used as a technical designation of the Messiah, but refers to the king of the line of David, ruling in Jerusalem, and anointed by the Lord through the priest. With the possible exception of Da 9:25, 26 the title "Messiah" as a reference to Israel's eschatological king does not occur in the OT. It appears in this sense later in the NT, where He is almost always called "the Christ." The OT pictures the Messiah as one who will put an end to sin and war and usher in universal righteousness and through His death will make vicarious atonement for the salvation of sinful men. The NT concept of the Messiah is developed directly from the teaching of the OT. Jesus of Nazareth is the Messiah; He claimed to be and the claim was acknowledged by His disciples (Lu 4:18, 19; Ac 4:27; 10:38).

See Jesus.

MESSIANIC HOPE (M't 13:17; Joh 8:56; Ac 9:22; Heb 11:13; 1Pe 1:10-12). Created by prophecy (Ge 49:10; Nu 24:17; 1Sa 1:10; 2Sa 7:12, 13; Isa 9:6, 7; 11:1-9; 33:17; 40:3-5; 55:3-5; 62:10, 11; Jer 23:5, 6; 33:15-17; Da 2:44; 7:13, 14; 9:24-27; Mic 5:2; Zec 9:9; Mal 3:1-3; Ac 13:27); by the covenant with David to establish his throne forever (2Sa 7:12-16; 1Ch 17:11-14; 22:10; 28:7 w the Messianic Psalms); by the Messianic Psalms (Ps 2; 21; 22; 45; 72; 87; 89; 96; 110; 132:11, 17, 18). Confirmed in the vision of Mary (Lu 1:30-33).

Exemplified, by the priest, Zacharias (Lu 1:68-79); by the prophet, Simeon (Lu 2:25, 29-32); by the prophetess, Anna (Lu 2:36-38); by the wise men of the East (M't 2:1-12); by John the baptist (M't 11:3); by the people (Joh 7:31, 40-42; 12:34); by Caiaphas (M't 26:63; M'k 14:61); by Joseph of Arimathea (M'k 15:43; Lu 23:51); by the disciples on the way to Emmaus (Lu 24:21); by Paul (Ac 26:6, 7).

See Jesus, Prophecies Concerning.

MESSIAS (See Messiah.)

METAL (See Brass [copper]; Gold; Iron; Lead; Silver; Tin.)

METAPHOR, Jesus spoke in (M'k 4:11). See Parables.

METEOROLOGY. Controlled by God (Ge 2:5, 6; 27:39; Job 9:7; 26:7, 8, 11; Ps 19:2-6; 104:2, 3, 7, 13, 19, 20; 107:25; Ec 11:3; Isa 13:13; 24:18; 50:3; Jer 4:11, 12; 10:13; 51:16; Da 2:21; Ho 8:7; Joe 2:30, 31; Am 9:6; Na 1:3; M't 24:27, 29; Lu 21:25; Joh 3:8; Ac 2:19, 20; 2Pe 2:17; Jude 12). Tempest stilled by Jesus (M't 8:24-27; Lu 8:22-25).

Weather, affected by good men's prayers (1Sa 12:16-18; 1Ki 18:41-45; Isa 5:5, 6; Jas 5:17, 18); forecast of (M't 16:2, 3; Lu 12:54-56).

In the land of Uz (Job 27:20, 21; 28:24-27; 29:19; 36:27-33; 37:6-22; 38:8-11, 22, 24-37). In Palestine (Ps 18:10-15; 29:3-10; 48:7; 65:8-12; 133:3; 135:6, 7; 147:7, 8; 148:7, 8; Pr 25:23; 26:1; 30:4; Ec 1:6, 7; Ho 6:4; 13:15). The autumnal storms of the Mediterranean (Ac 27:9-20, 27).

Phenomena of: The deluge (Ge 7:8). Fire from heaven on the cities of the plain (Ge 19:24, 25). Plagues of hail, thunder, and lightning in Egypt (Ex 9:22-29; Ps 78:17-23); of darkness (Ex 10:22, 23). East wind that divided the Red Sea (Ex 14:21); that brought the quails (Nu 11:31, 32; Ps 78:26-28). Pillar of cloud and fire (See Pillar). Sun stood still (Jos 10:12, 13). Dew on Gideon's fleece (J'g 6:36-40). Stars in their courses fought against Sisera (J'g 5:20). Stones from heaven (Jos 10:11). Fire from heaven at Elijah's command (2Ki 1:10-14). The whirlwind which carried Elijah to heaven (2Ki 2:1, 11).

Wind under God's control (Ps 107:25). East wind (Ps 48:7). Rain, formation of (Ps 135:6, 7). Dew, copious (Ps 133:3). Rain in answer to Samuel's prayer (1Sa 12:16-18); Elijah's prayer (1Ki 18:41-45). Rain discomfits the Philistine army (1Sa 7:10). Wind destroyed Job's children (Job 1:18, 19). Darkness at the crucifixion (M't 27:45; Lu 23:44, 45).

See Astronomy; Celestial Phenomena; Dew; Hail; Rain.

Symbolical: Used in the Revelation of John (Re 6:12-14; 7:1; 8:3-12; 9:1, 2, 17-19; 10:1-6; 11:6; 12:1-4, 7-9; 14; 15:1-4; 16:8, 17-21; 19:11-18; 20:11; 21:1).

METEYARD, archaic word for "measures of length" (Le 19:35).

METHEG-AMMAH (the bridle of metropolis), town David took from Philistines (2Sa 8:1).

METHUSAEL, father of Lamech (Ge 4:18).

METHUSELAH (man of the javelin), son of Enoch and grandfather of Noah (Ge 5:21-27; 1Ch 1:3).

MEUNIM (the people of Maon), people who lived in Arab city near Petra (1Ch 4:41, translated "habitations"). "Mehunims" in 2Ch 26:7 KJV; "Mehunim" in Ezra 2:50, where they are counted among the "Nethinim" at the return.

MEZAHAB, grandfather of Mehetabel (Ge 36:39; 1Ch 1:50).

MIAMIN (from the right hand). 1. Israelite who divorced foreign wife (Ezr 10:25).

2. Priest who returned with Zerubbabel (Ne 12:5).

3. "Mijamin" in 1Ch 24:9 and Ne 10:7 is the same word in Hebrew.

MIBHAR (choice), one of David's valiant men (1Ch 11:38).

MIBSAM (sweet odor). 1. Son of Ishmael (Ge 25:13; 1Ch 1:29).

2. Son of Shallum (1Ch 4:25).

MIBZAR (a fortress), chief of Edom (Ge 36:42; 1Ch 1:53).

MICAH (who is like Jehovah?). 1. Ephraimite whose mother made an image for which he secured a priest; both image and priest were later stolen by the tribe of Dan (J'g 17, 18).

2. Reubenite (1Ch 5:5).

3. Grandson of Jonathan (1Ch 8:34; 9:40).

4. Levite (1Ch 23:20).

5. Father of one of Josiah's officers, called "Achbor" in 2Ki 22:12 and "Abdon" in 2Ch 34:20.

6. Prophet Micah, the Morasthite; prophesied in reigns of Jotham, Ahaz, and Hezekiah (Mic 1:1; Jer 26:18).

7. Son of Imlah (2Ch 18:14), usually called Micaiah.

8. Simeonite (Judith 6:15).

MICAH, BOOK OF, 6th of the Minor Prophets; comes from late 700's; predicts fall of Samaria which occurred in 722, but has much to say of the sins of Jerusalem in days of Hezekiah c. 700 B. C. Outline: 1. Desolation of Samaria and Jerusalem foretold (1:1-3:12).

2. Eventual blessings for Zion (4:1-8).

3. Invasions and deliverance by the Davidic ruler (4:9-5:15).

4. Condemnation for sins (6:1-7:6).

5. Eventual help from God (7:7-20).

MICAIAH (who is like Jehovah?), prophet living in Samaria c. 900 B. C. who predicted the death of King Ahab (1Ki 22; 2Ch 18).

MICE (See Mouse.)

MICHA (who is like Jehovah?). 1. Grandson of Jonathan (2Sa 9:12).

2. Levite covenanter (Ne 10:11).

3. Another Levite (Ne 11:17).

4. Another (Ne 11:22; "Micah" in 1Ch 9:15).

MICHAEL. 1. An Asherite (Nu 13:13).

2. Two Gadites (1Ch 5:13, 14).

3. A Gershonite Levite (1Ch 6:40).

4. A descendant of Issachar (1Ch 7:3).

5. A Benjamite (1Ch 8:16).

6. A captain of the thousands of Manasseh who joined David at Ziklag (1Ch 12:20).

7. Father of Omri (1Ch 27:18).

8. Son of Jehoshaphat. Slain by his brother, Jehoram (2Ch 21:2-4).

9. Father of Zebadiah (Ezr 8:8).

10. The Archangel. His message to Daniel (Da 10:13, 21; 12:1). Contention with the devil (Jude 9). Fights with the dragon (Re 12:7).

MICHAH (See Micah, Micha.)

MICHAIAH (who is like Jehovah?). 1. Father of Achbor (2Ki 22:12-14).

2. Daughter of Uriel of Gibeah (2Ch 13:2).

3. Prince of Judah (2Ch 17:7).

4. Ancestor of priest in Nehemiah's time (Ne 12:35).

5. Priest (Ne 12:41).

6. Grandson of Shaphan the Scribe (Jer 36:11-13).

MICHAL, daughter of Saul. Given to David as a reward for slaying Goliath (1Sa 18:22-28). Rescues David from death (1Sa 19:9-17). Saul forcibly separates them and she is given in marriage to Phalti (1Sa 25:44). David recovers, to himself (2Sa 3:13-16). Ridicules David on account of his religious zeal (2Sa 6:16, 20-23).

MICHMAS, MICHMASH (hidden place), place in Benjamin c. 8 miles NE of Jerusalem; Jonathan led Israelites to victory over Philistines there (1Sa 13:14; Ne 11:31).

MICHMETHAH, a city between Ephraim and Manasseh (Jos 16:6; 17:7).

MICHRI, a Benjamite (1Ch 9:8).

MICHTAM, word of uncertain meaning found in the titles of six psalms (16, 56-60).

MIDDIN, city in Judah in wilderness just W of Dead Sea (Jos 15:61).

MIDDLE WALL, barrier between Court of the Gentiles and the Court of the Jews in the temple in Jerusalem (Eph 2:14).

MIDIAN, son of Abraham by Keturah (Ge 25:2, 4; 1Ch 1:32, 33).

MIDIANITES. Descendants of Midian, son of Abraham by Keturah (Ge 25:1, 2, 4; 1Ch 1:32, 33). Called Ishmaelites (Ge 37:25, 28; J'g 8:24). Were merchantmen (Ge 37:28). Buy Joseph and sell him to Potiphar (Ge 37:28, 36). Defeated by the Israelites under Phinehas; five of their kings slain; the women taken captives: cities burned; and rich spoils taken (Nu 31). Defeated by Gideon (J'g 6-8). Owned multitudes of camels, and dromedaries, and large quantities of gold (Isa 60:6). A snare to the Israelites (Nu 25:16-18). Prophecies concerning (Isa 60:6; Hab 3:7).

MIDNIGHT, scenes at (Ex 11:4; M't 25:6; Ac 16:5; 20:7).

MIDWIFERY (Ge 35:17; Ex 1:15-21; Eze 16:4).

MIGDAL-EL (tower of God), a city of Naphtali (Jos 19:38).

MIGDAL-GAD (tower of Gad), a city of Judah (Jos 15:37).

MIGDOL. 1. A place near the Red Sea where the Israelites encamped (Ex 14:2; Nu 33:7, 8).

2. A city on the northeastern border of lower Egypt (Jer 44:1; 46:14).

MIGRON (precipice). A city in Benjamin. Saul encamps near, under a pomegranate tree (1Sa 14:2). Prophecy concerning (Isa 10:28).

MIJAMIN (from the right hand). 1. Priest in David's time (1Ch 24:9).

2. Covenanter priest (Ne 10:7).

3. Priest who returned from exile (Ne 12:5).

4. Man who divorced foreign wife (Ezr 10:25).

MIKLOTH (rods). 1. A Benjamite of Jerusalem (1Ch 8:32; 9:37, 38).

2. A ruler in the reign of David (1Ch 27:4).

MIKNEIAH, a doorkeeper of the temple, and musician (1Ch 15:18, 21).

MILALAI, a priest who took part in the dedication of the walls of Jerusalem (Ne 12:36).

MILCAH. 1. Wife of Nahor and mother of Bethuel (Ge 11:29; 22:20-23; 24: 15, 24, 47).

2. Daughter of Zelophehad. Special legislation in regard to the inheritance of (Nu 26:33; 27:1-7; 36:1-12; Jos 17:3, 4).

MILCOM (See Moloch.)

MILDEW, fungus growth destructive of grains and fruits (De 28:22; 1Ki 8:37; Am 4:9; Hag 2:17).

MILE (M't 5:41).

MILETUS, called also Miletum. A seaport in Asia Minor. Paul visits (Ac 20:15); and sends to Ephesus for the elders of the church, and addresses them at (Ac 20:17-38). Trophimus left sick at (2Ti 4:20).

MILITARY INSTRUCTION, of children (2Sa 1:18).

See Armies.

MILK. Used for food (Ge 18:8; J'g 4:19; Song 5:1; Eze 25:4; 1Co 9:7). Of goats (Pr 27:27); sheep (De 32:14; Isa 7:21, 22); camels (Ge 32:15); cows (De 32:14; 1Sa 6:7, 10). Churned (Pr 30:33). Kid not to be seethed in its mother's (Ex 23:19; De 14:21).

Figurative: Ex 3:8, 17; 13:5; 33:3; Nu 13:27; De 26:9, 15; Isa 55:1; 60:16; Jer 11:5; 32:22; Eze 20:6; Joe 3:18; 1Co 3:2; Heb 5:12, 13; 1Pe 2:2.

MILL (Jer 25:10). Upper and nether stones of (De 24:6; Job 41:24; Isa 47:2). Used in Egypt (Ex 11:5). Operated by women (M't 24:41); and captives (J'g 16:21; La 5:13). Manna ground in (Nu 11:8). Sound of, to cease (Re 18:22).

See Millstone.

MILLENNIUM, the Latin word for "1000 years." It comes from Re 20:1-15 where the expression appears six times. It refers to a period when Christ rules upon earth and Satan is bound. When Jesus shall have triumphed over all forms of evil (1Co 15:24-28; 2Th 2:8; Rev 14:6-18; 19:11-16); at the restoration of all things (Ac 3:21). When the creation shall be delivered from the corruption of evil (Ro 8:19-21). When the Son of Man shall sit on the throne of his glory (M't 19:28; Lu 22:28-30); and the righteous shall be clothed with authority (Da 7:22; M't 19:28; Lu 22:28-30; 1Co 6:2; Re 2:5); and possess the kingdom (M't 25:34; Lu 12:32; 22:29).

Christ rules from his throne in Zion or Jerusalem (Isa 65:17-25; Zep 3:11-13; Zec 9:9, 10; 14:16-21); and fulfills the promise of the kingdom of God on earth (M't 16:18, 19; 26:29; M'k 14:25; Heb 8:11).

See Church, Prophecies Concerning; Jesus, Kingdom of; Second Coming of.

MILLET (Eze 4:9).

MILLO (fulness). 1. The house of Millo, possibly a clan at Shechem (J'g 9:6, 20).

2. A name given to part of the citadel of Jerusalem (2Sa 5:9; 1Ch 11:8). King Solomon raises a levy to repair (1Ki 9:15, 24; 11:27). Repaired by King Hezekiah (2Ch 32:5). King Joash murdered at (2Ki 12:20).

MILLSTONE. Not to be taken in pledge (De 24:6). Probably used in executions by drowning (M't 18:6; M'k 9:42; Lu 17:2). Abimelech killed by one being hurled upon him (J'g 9:53). Figurative of the hard heart (Job 41:24).

MINA (See Weights and Measures.)

MINCING (Isa 3:16).

MIND, in Scripture often meaning "heart," "soul," in the NT often used in ethical sense (Ro 7:25; Col 2:18).

MINERALS OF THE BIBLE. The science of mineralogy is a recent one, and did not exist in ancient times. It is often impossible to be certain that when a mineral name is used in the Bible, it is used with the same meaning as that attached in modern mineralogy. The following minerals are mentioned in the Bible. 1. Precious stones: adamant (Eze 3:9; Zec 7:12), agate (Ex 28:19), amber (Eze 1:4, 27; 8:2), amethyst (Ex 28:19; Re 21:20), bdellium (Nu 11:7), beryl (Da 10:6), carbuncle (Isa 54:12), carnelian (same as sardius), chalcedony (Re 21:19), chrysolyte (Re 21:20), coral (Job 28:18), chrysoprasus (Re 21:20), crystal (Job 28:17), diamond (Ex 28:18), emerald (Ex 28:18), jacinth (Re 9:17), jasper (Eze 28:13), ligure (Ex 28:19), onyx (Ge 2:12), pearl (Job 28:18), ruby (Job 28:18), sapphire (Ex 24:10), sardius (Ex 28:17), sardonyx (Re 21:20), topaz (Ex 28:17).

2. Metals: gold (Ge 2:11, 12), silver (M't 10:9), iron (Nu 31:22), copper or "brass" (Ge 4:22), lead (Ex 15:10), tin (Nu 31:22), mercury (quicksilver), translated "dross" (Ps 119:119).

3. The common minerals: alabaster (M't 26:7), brimstone (sulfur) (Ge 19:24), marble (1Ch 29:2), nitre (Pr 25:20; Jer 2:22), water.

MINES, MINING, ancient occupation

of man; described in Job 28:1-11; De 8:9; 1Ki 7:13-50.

MINGLED PEOPLE, in Ex 12:38 the reference is to non-Israelite people who left Egypt with the Israelites. In Jer 25:20 and 50:37 the term is used for the mixed blood of certain of Israel's enemies.

MINIAMIN. 1. Levite (2Ch 31:15).

2. Head of family of priests (Ne 12:17).

3. Priest in Nehemiah's time (Ne 12:41).

MINISTER. An officer in civil government. Joseph (Ge 41:40-44); Ira (2Sa 20:26); Zabud (1Ki 4:5); Ahithophel (1Ch 27:33); Zebadiah (2Ch 19:11); Elkanah (2Ch 28:7); Haman (Es 3:1); Mordecai (Es 10:3, with chapters 8; 9); Daniel (Da 2:48; 6:1-3).

See Cabinet.

MINISTER, a sacred teacher. Likened to sowers (Ps 126:6; M't 13:3-8; M'k 4:3-8; Lu 8:5-8). Teachers of schools (1Sa 19:20; 2Ki 2:3, 5, 15; 4:38; 2Ch 15:3; 17:7-9; Ac 13:1).

Hired (J'g 17:10; 18:4). Exempt from taxation (Ezr 7:24). In politics (2Sa 15:24-27). In war (2Ch 13:12, 14).

Influential in public affairs (1Sa 12:6-10); designate kings (1Sa 9:15, 16; 10:1; 16:1-13); recommend civil and military appointments (2Ki 4:13). Expostulate with rulers: Samuel with Saul (1Sa 13:11-14; 15:10-31); Nathan with David (2Sa 12:1-4); Elijah with Ahab (1Ki 18:17, 18).

Recreation for (M'k 6:31, 32). Take leave of congregations (Ac 20:17-38). Personal bearing of (Tit 2:7, 8). Preach without ecclesiastical authority (Ga 1:15-24; 2:1-9). Work of, will be tried (1Co 3:12-15). Responsibility of (Eze 3:17-21; 33:8; M't 10:14-40; Ac 18:6; 20:26, 27; 1Co 1:23; 2Co 2:15-17; 5:11, 18, 19; 1Ti 6:20). Speaking evil of, forbidden (Jude 8:10). Clothed with authority (1Th 5:12; Tit 1:13, 14; 2:15; 3:1, 2, 8, 9; Heb 13:6, 7, 17; see Epistles to Timothy and Titus in full). Clothed with salvation (2Ch 6:41). Exhorted to grow in grace (1Ti 6:11; 2Ti 2:22).

Marriage of (Le 21:7-15; M't 8:14; M'k 1:30; 1Co 9:5; 1Ti 3:2, 12; Tit 1:5-7).

Incorruptible: Balaam (Nu 22:18, 37, 38; 23:8, 12; 24:12-14 w 2Pe 2:15, 16); Micaiah (1Ki 22:13, 14); Peter (Ac 8:18-23). Patience of (Jas 5:10). Inconsistent (M't 27:3-7).

Love of, for the church, exemplified by Paul (Ph'p 1:7; 1Th 1:2-4; 2:8, 11). Kindness to, Ebed-melech to Jeremiah (Jer 38:7-13). Fear of (1Sa 16:4). Example to the flock (Ph'p 3:17; 2Th 3:9; 1Ti 4:12; Tit 2:1, 7, 8; 1Pe 5:3). Intolerance of (M't 15:23; 19:13; M'k 10:13; Lu 18:15). Message of, rejected (Jer 7:27; Eze 33:30-33). God's care of (1Ki 17:1-16; 19:1-8; M't 10:29-31; Lu 12:6, 7). Their calling, glorious (2Co 3:7-11). Discouragements of (Isa 30:10, 11; 53:1; Eze 3:8, 9, 14; Hab 1:2, 3; M't 13:57; M'k 6:3, 4; Lu 4:24; Joh 4:44).

Defended (Jer 26:16-24; Ac 23:9). Beloved (Ac 20:37, 38; 21:5, 6).

Sent forth two and two: Disciples (M'k 6:7); Paul and Barnabas (Ac 13:2, 3); Judas and Silas (Ac 15:27); Barnabas and Mark (Ac 15:37, 39); Paul and Silas (Ac 15:40); Paul and Timothy (Ac 16:1-4); Paul and Titus (2Co 8:19, 23); Timothy and Erastus (Ac 19:22); Titus and a companion (2Co 12:18).

Call of (Am 2:11; M't 9:38; Ro 10:14, 15; Eph 4:11, 12; Heb 5:4). Aaron and his sons (Ex 28:1; 1Ch 23:13; Heb 5:4). Levites (Nu 3:5-13; 16:5, 9). Samuel (1Sa 3:4-10). Elisha (1Ki 19:16, 19). Isaiah (Isa 6:8-10). Jeremiah (Jer 1:5). Jonah (Jon 1:1, 2; 3:1, 2). The twelve apostles (M't 4:18-22 w M'k 1:17-20; M't 9:9 w M'k 2:14 & Lu 5:27; M't 10:1-5; Joh 1:43). The seventy disciples (Lu 10:1, 2). Paul (Ac 13:2, 3; 20:24; 22:12-15; 26:14-18; Ro 1:1; 1Co 1:1, 27, 28 w 2Co 1:1 and Col 1:1; 1Co 9:16-19; 2Co 5:18-20; Ga 1:15, 16; Eph 3:7, 8; Col 1:25-29; 1Ti 1:12-14; 2:7; 2Ti 1:11; Tit 1:5). Barnabas (Ac 13:2, 3). Archippus (Col 4:17). See Call, Personal; Excuses.

Character and qualifications of: (Le 10:3-11). Blameless (1Ti 3:2-4, 7-13; Tit 1:5-9). Compassionate (Heb 5:2). Consecrated (Nu 16:9, 10). Consistent (Ro 2:21-23). Courageous (Jer 1:7, 8, 17-19; Ac 20:22, 24; 2Ti 1:7). Diligent (2Ch 29:11; 1Co 15:10). Eager to serve (Isa 6:8). Endued with power (Lu 24:49; Ac 1:8; 4:8, 31; Ga 2:8). Gentle (2Ti 2:24, 25). A good example (Tit 2:1, 7, 8, 15; Jas 3:1, 13, 16-18). Holy (Le 21:6; Isa 6:7; 52:11; Mal 2:6; Joh 17:17; 1Co 9:27; 2Ti 2:21; Tit 1:5-9). Humble (M't

20:25-28; 23:8, 10, 11; Lu 22:27; Joh 13:13-17; 15:20; 2Co 4:5). Meek (1Co 4:12, 13; 2Co 10:1). Patient (Jas 5:10). Preserving (M't 10:22-24; 2Co 4:1, 8-10). Prepared (Ezr 7:10). Responsible (1Pe 4:10, 11). Saved (2Ch 6:41). Sincere (2Co 4:1, 2). Strong (2Ti 2:1). Tactful (1Co 9:18-23; 10:23, 28-33; 2Co 6:3; 12:16). Willing to suffer hardship (2Ti 2:3; 4:5). Wise (Mal 2:7; Pr 11:30; M't 10:16; Lu 6:39; 2Co 4:6; 2Ti 2:7; 3:14, 16, 17).

Not contentious (2Ti 2:14, 23, 24; Tit 3:9). Not of the world (Joh 15:19; 17:16). Not entangled with the world (2Ti 2:4, 5).

Zealous (Jer 20:9; Eze 34:1-31; 2Ti 1:6-8; 4:2). See Zeal. Instances of zealous: Titus (2Co 8:16, 17); Epaphroditus (Ph'p 2:25-30); Epaphras (Col 4:12, 13); John, in his vision (Re 5:4, 5).

Faithful (1Sa 2:35; M't 24:45; Lu 12:42-44; Ac 20:22, 24; 1Co 2:2; 2Co 6:4-7). Instances of faithful: Moses (De 4:26; 30:19; Heb 3:2, 5); Micaiah (2Ch 18:12, 13); Azariah (2Ch 26:16-20); Balaam (Nu 22:18, 38; 23:8, 12; 24:12-14); Nathan (2Sa 12:1-14); Isaiah (Isa 22:4, 5; 39:3-7); Jeremiah (Jer 17:16; 26:1-15; 28; 37:9, 10, 16-18); John the Baptist (M't 3:2-12; M'k 6:18; Lu 3:7-19); the apostles (Ac 4:19, 20, 31; 5:21, 29-32); Peter (Ac 2:14-40; 3:12-26; 4:8-12; 8:18-23); Paul (Ac 15:25, 26; 17:16, 17; 19:8; 20:26, 27); Tychicus (Col 4:7).

See all of 1, 2Timothy; Titus.

Described as: Ambassadors for Christ (2Co 5:20; Eph 6:20). Angels of the Church (Re 1:20; 2:1, 8, 12, 18; 3:1, 7, 14). Apostles (Lu 6:13; Re 18:20). Apostles of Jesus Christ (Tit 1:1). Defenders of the Faith (Ph'p 1:7). Elders (1Ti 5:17; 1Pe 5:1). Evangelists (Eph 4:11; 2Ti 4:5). Fishers of men (M't 4:19; M'k 1:17). Laborers (M't 9:38 w Ph'm 1). Laborers in the Gospel of Christ (1Th 3:2). Lights (Joh 5:35). Men of God (De 33:1; 1Ti 6:11). Messengers of the Church (2Co 8:23); of the Lord of Hosts (Mal 2:7).

Ministers of God (Isa 61:6; 2Co 6:4); of the Lord (Joe 2:17); of Christ (Ro 15:16; 1Co 4:1); of the Sanctuary (Eze 45:4); of the Gospel (Eph 3:7; Col 1:23); of the Word (Lu 1:2); of the New Testament (2Co 3:6); of the Church (Col 1:24, 25); of Righteousness (2Co 11:15).

Overseers (Ac 20:28). Pastors (Jer 3:15; Joh 21:16-18; Eph 4:11). Preachers (Ro 10:14; 1Ti 2:7). Preachers of righteousness (2Pe 2:5). Servants of God (Tit 1:1; Jas 1:1); of the Lord (2Ti 2:24); of Jesus Christ (Ph'p 1:1; Jude 1); of the Church (2Co 4:5). Shepherds (Jer 23:4). Soldiers of Christ (Ph'p 2:25; 2Ti 2:3, 4). Stars (Re 1:20; 2:1). Stewards of God (Tit 1:7); of the grace of God (1Pe 4:10); of the Mysteries of God (1Co 4:1). Teachers (Isa 30:20; Eph 4:11). Watchmen (Isa 62:6; Eze 33:7). Witnesses (Ac 1:8; 5:32; 26:16). Workers together with God (2Co 6:1).

Duties of (Eph 4:11, 12). To preach (M't 10:7; Ro 1:14, 15). To preach the unsearchable riches of Christ (Eph 3:8-12). To admonish (Isa 58:1; 62:6, 7). To exhort (2Co 5:20; 1Ti 4:13; 6:17, 18; 2Pe 1:12-16). To warn (Jer 7:25; Eze 33:1-9). To reprove (Eze 6:11; 34:2-31; Jon 1:2; 2Co 7:8); see Reproof. To teach (Le 10:11; 2Ki 17:27, 28; 2Ch 15:3; Ezr 7:10; Jer 26:2; Eze 44:23; M't 10:7, 27; 28:19, 20; M'k 10:43-45; Ac 5:20; 6:4; 16:4; 18:9, 10; 26:16-18; Ro 1:15; 12:6, 7; 2Co 10:8; Eph 3:8-10; 4:11, 12; 1Ti 2:7; 4:13-16; 2Ti 2:2, 14, 15, 24, 25; 4:1, 2, 5). To teach the lordship of Jesus (2Co 4:5). To serve (M't 20:25-28; M'k 10:43-45; 2Co 4:5). To make converts to Christ (M't 28:19, 20). To win souls (Pr 11:30; Joh 4:35-38; 2Co 5:18, 20). To witness for Christ (Lu 24:48; Joh 15:27; Ac 1:22; 10:42; 22:15). To do the work of an evangelist (2Ti 4:5). To give himself continually to prayer (Ac 6:4). To lament over the worldliness and sins of the church (Joe 1:13-15; 2:17). To speak boldly (Eph 6:20). To minister to all without respect of persons or races (Ro 1;14, 15). To exercise authority in the church (M't 16:19; 18:18; 1Co 4:19-21; 2Co 7:8, 9, 12, 15; 13:2, 3, 10; 2Th 3:4; 1Ti 1:3, 4, 11, 18; 5:19-22; 1Pe 5:1-3). To feed the flock (Jer 3:15; 23:4, 22, 28; Joh 21:15-17; Ac 20:28; 1Co 14:1-33; 1Pe 5:2-4). To strengthen the discouraged (Lu 22:32). To comfort the people (Isa 40:1, 2, 9, 11; 1Th 3:2).

Charges delivered to (Nu 18:1-7; 27:18-23; De 31:7, 8, 14-23; Jos 1:1-9; Jer 1:17-19; Eze 3:4; M't 10:5-42; Lu

10:1-16; 1Ti 1:18-20; 2:1-15; 3:1-16; 4:1-16; 5:1-22; 6:1-21; 2Ti 1:6-13; 2:1-26; 3:1-17; 4:1-8).

Duty of the church to: To esteem (1Th 5:13). To pray for (2Ch 6:41; Ps 132:9; M't 9:37, 38; Ac 4:29; 12:5; Ro 15:30-32; 2Co 1:11; Eph 6:18-20; Ph'p 1:19; Col 4:2-4; 1Th 5:25; 2Th 3:1, 2; Ph'm 22; Heb 13:18, 19). To imitate the example of (1Co 11:1; Ph'p 3:17; 2Th 3:7; Heb 13:7). To submit to the authority of (1Co 11:2; 16:16; 1Th 5:12, 13; 2Th 3:4; Heb 13:7, 17).

To provide for the support, of priest and Levite (Nu 18:20, 21; De 10:9; 14:27; 18:1-4; Jos 13:14; 18:7; Jer 31:14; Eze 44:28); of the twelve apostles (M't 10:9, 10; M'k 6:8; Lu 22:35); of the seventy disciples (Lu 10:7, 8); of Christian preachers (1Co 9:3, 4, 7-14; Ga 6:6; Ph'p 4:10-18; 1Ti 5:18).

Right of support, waived by Paul (Ac 20:33-35; 1Co 9:15-18; 2Co 11:7-10; 12:13-18; 1Th 2:5, 6, 9; 2Th 3:7-9).

See Church, Duties of to Ministers.

False and corrupt (1Ki 12:31; Ne 13:29; Jer 2:8; 6:13, 14; 8:10, 11; 12:10; La 2:14; Eze 22:25, 28; 44:8, 10; Ho 9:7, 8; Zep 3:4; Mal 1:6-10; 2Ti 4:3). Mercenary (1Sa 8:3; Isa 56:11; Mic 3:11). Presumptuous (De 18:20-22; Joh 5:43). Insincere (Ph'p 1:15, 16). Brutish (Jer 10:21). Adulterous (1Sa 2:22; Jer 23:14; Ho 6:9). Murderous (Ho 6:9).

Pervert the truth (2Co 2:17; 11:3, 4, 13-15; Ga 1:6-8; 1Ti 4:1-3, 7). Cause the people to err (Isa 3:12; Jer 50:6). Addicted to strong drink (Isa 28:7; 56:12). Indifferent to good and evil (Isa 56:10; Eze 22:26).

Desired by the wicked (Isa 30:10, 11; Jer 5:13, 14, 30, 31; Am 2:11, 12; Mic 2:11).

Denunciations against (Isa 5:20; Jer 23:11-40; La 4:13, 14; Eze 13:1-23; 34:1-10, 16-22; M't 23:4-7, 13-36; 2Pe 2:1-22).

Warnings against (De 13:1-4; Isa 8:19, 20; Jer 14:13-16; 27:9-18; M't 5:19; 7:15-23; 15:9, 13, 14 w Lu 6:39; M't 23:3, 4, 13; 24:4, 5, 11, 24, 26, 48-51; M'k 13:21, 22; Lu 21:8; Joh 10:1, 5, 8, 10, 12, 13; Ac 20:20, 30; Eph 4:14; Ph'p 3:2; Col 2:4, 8, 18, 19; 1Ti 1:3-7; 6:3-5; 2Ti 2:17, 18; Tit 1:10-14; 1Jo 2:18, 19, 22, 23, 26; 4:1-3, 5; 2Jo 7, 10, 11; Re 2:12, 14, 15, 18, 20-23).

Judgments upon (Isa 29:10, 11; Ho 5:1; Ga 5:10).

Punishment of (De 13:1, 5; 18:20; Isa 43:27, 28; Jer 14:15; 23:1, 2, 11, 15, 21; 27:9-18; La 4:13, 14; Eze 14:9, 10; Ho 4:5, 6, 8-13; Mic 3:5-7; Zec 10:3; 13:2-5; Mal 2:1-3, 8, 9; Lu 12:45, 46; 2Pe 2:3; Jude 4, 11).

Instances of false and corrupt: Nadab and Abihu (Le 10:1, 2). Korah, Dathan, and Abiram (Nu 16:1-40). Eli's sons (1Sa 2:12-17, 22, 25, 29, 34; 3:13; 4:11). Samuel's sons (1Sa 8:1-3). The old prophet of Bethel (1Ki 13:11-32). Jonathan (J'g 17:7-13; 18). Noadiah (Ne 6:14). Priests under, Jehoash (2Ki 12:7; 2Ch 24:5, 6); Hezekiah (2Ch 30:3, 5). Priests and Levites (Ezr 2:61, 62; 9:1, 2; 10:18-24; Ne 13:4-9, 28, 29; Zec 7:5, 6). Hananiah (Jer 28). Jonah (Jon 1:1-6). Scribes and Pharisees (M't 23:15, 16); Caiaphas (M't 26:2, 3, 57, 63-65; Joh 11:49-51; 18:14). Judas (M't 26:14-16, 21-25, 47-50; 27:3-5; Joh 12:4-6; Ac 1:18). Judaizing Christians (Ga 3:1, 2; 4:17; 6:12, 13). Hymenaeus (1Ti 1:20; 2Ti 2:17, 18). Alexander (1Ti 1:20). Philetus (2Ti 2:17, 18).

Hospitality to: Woman of Zarephath to Elijah (1Ki 17:10-16). The Shunammite to Elisha (2Ki 4:8-10). The barbarians to Paul (Ac 28:1-10). Simon the tanner to Peter (Ac 9:43). The Philippian jailer (Ac 16:33, 34). Aquila and Priscilla to Paul (Ac 18:3); to Apollos (Ac 18:26). Justus to Paul (Ac 18:7). Philip the evangelist to Paul (Ac 21:8-10).

Joys of (Joh 4:36-38; 2Co 2:14; 7:6, 7; Ph'p 2:16; 1Th 2:13, 19, 20; 3:8, 9; 2Jo 4; 3Jo 4).

Ordination of: Matthias (Ac 1:26); seven deacons (Ac 6:5, 6); Paul and Barnabas (Ac 13:3); Timothy (1Ti 4:14).

See Priests; Levites.

Prayer for: Enjoined (M't 9:37, 38; Lu 10:2; Ro 15:30-32; 2Co 1:11; Eph 6:18-20; Ph'p 1:19; Col 4:2-4; 1Th 5:25; 2Th 3:1, 2; Ph'm 22; Heb 13:18, 19). Exemplified (2Ch 6:41; Ps 132:9; Ac 1:24, 25; 4:29; 6:6; 12:5; 14:23).

Precepts for guidance of (Jer 1:7, 8, 17-19; Eze 2:6-8; M't 7:6; 10:7, 8, 11-13, 16, 25-28; Lu 10:1-11; Col 4:17; 1Ti 1:3, 4, 11, 18, 19; 4:6, 7, 12-16; 5:1-3, 7-11, 19-22; 6:3, 4, 10-14, 17-21; 2Ti 1:6-8;

2:2-7, 14-16, 23-25; 4:1, 2, 5; 1Pe 5:1-4; 2Pe 1:12-16).

Promises to (2Sa 23:6, 7; Ps 126:5, 6; Jer 1:7-10, 17-19; 15:20, 21; 20:11; Da 12:3; M't 10:28-31; 28:20; Lu 10:19; 12:11, 12; 24:49; Joh 4:36-38; Ac 1:4, 5, 8; 18:9, 10; 1Co 3:8; 9:9, 10; 2Co 2:14-16; 7:6, 7; Ph'p 2:16; 1Th 2:13, 19, 20; 3:8, 9; 1Pe 5:4; 3Jo 4). See Righteous, Promises to.

Success Attending: Jonah (Jon 1:5, 6, 9, 14, 16; 3:4-9). Apostles (Ac 2:1-4, 41). Philip (Ac 8:6, 8, 12). Peter (Ac 9:32-35). Paul (Ac 13:16-43; 1Co 4:15; 9:2; 15:11; 2Co 3:2, 3; 12:12; 13:4; Ph'p 2:16; 1Th 1:5). Apollos (Ac 18:24-28). See Revivals.

Trials and Persecutions of: Foretold (M't 10:16-27 w Joh 13:16; M't 23:34). Rehearsed (M't 23:34).

Instances of Trials and Persecutions of: Elijah (1Ki 17:2-7; 18:7-10; 19:1-10). Micaiah (1Ki 22:24-27; 2Ch 18:23-26). Hanani (2Ch 16:10). Zechariah (2Ch 24:20-22, 25; M't 23:35; Lu 11:51). Isaiah (Isa 20:2, 3). Jeremiah (Jer 11:19-21; 15:10, 15; 17:15-18; 18:18-23; 20:1-3, 7-18; 32:2, 3; 33:1; 37:15-21; 38:6-13; 39:15; 43:1-7; La 3:53-55). Ezekiel (Eze 3:24, 25; 24:15-18). Hosea (Ho 1:2). Amos (Am 5:10; 7:10-17). The apostles (Ac 5:17-42). Peter (Ac 12:3-19). Paul (Ac 9:23-25, 29, 30; 14:4-6, 11-20; 16:16-24; 17:5-10, 13, 14; 18:12, 13; 20:3; 21:27-40; 22:22-30; 23:10-35; 24:26, 27; 27:9-44; 1Co 2:1-4; 4:9-13; 2Co 6:4-10; 7:5; 11:23-33; 12:7-10; Eph 3:1, 13; 2Ti 1:8, 16; 2:9; 4:16, 17); see Paul, Persecutions of. See also Accusation, False; Persecution.

Zealous: Titus (2Co 8:16, 17). Epaphroditus (Ph'p 2:25-30). Epaphras (Col 4:12, 13). Tychicus (Col 4:7). John, in his vision (Re 5:4, 5). See Zeal.

MINNI, a district of Armenia (Jer 51:27).

MINNITH, a place E of the Jordan (J'g 11:33; Eze 27:17).

MINORS, legal status of (Ga 4:1, 2). See Orphan; Young Men.

MINORITY REPORT (See Reports.)

MINSTREL, in the OT a player upon a stringed instrument; in the NT a piper (1Sa 16:23; M't 9:23).

MINT (M't 23:23; Lu 11:42).

MIPHKAD, name of one of the gates of Jerusalem (Ne 3:31).

MIRACLES. Called Marvelous Things (Ps 78:12); Marvelous Works (Isa 29:14; Ps 105:5); Signs and Wonders (Jer 32:21; Joh 4:48; 2Co 12:12).

Performed through the power of God (Joh 3:2; Ac 14:3; 15:12; 19:11); of the Holy Ghost (M't 12:28; Ro 15:19; 1Co 12:9, 10, 28, 30); in the name of Christ (M'k 16:17; Ac 3:16; 4:30). Faith required in those who perform (M't 17:20; 21:21; Joh 14:12; Ac 3:16; 6:8). Faith required in those for whom they were performed (M't 9:28; M'k 9:22-24; Ac 14:9). Power to work, given the disciples (M'k 3:14, 15; 16:17, 18, 20). Demanded by unbelievers (M't 12:38, 39; 16:1; Lu 11:16, 29; 23:8). Alleged miracles performed by magicians (Ex 7:10-12, 22; 8:7); by other impostors (M't 7:22). Performed through the powers of evil (2Th 2:9; Re 16:14). Wrought in support of false religions (De 13:1, 2); by false christs (M't 24:24); by false prophets (M't 24:24; Re 19:20); by the Witch of En-dor (1Sa 28:7-14); Simon Magus (Ac 8:9-11). Not to be regarded (De 13:3). Deceive the ungodly (2Th 2:10-12; Re 13:14; 19:20). A mark of apostasy (2Th 2:3, 9; Re 13:13).

Catalogue of, and Supernatural Events: Creation (Ge 1). Flood (Ge 7; 8). Confusion of tongues (Ge 11:1-9). Fire on Abraham's sacrifice (Ge 15:17). Conception of Isaac (Ge 17:17; 18:12; 21:2). Destruction of Sodom (Ge 19). Lot's wife turned to salt (Ge 19:26). Closing of the wombs of Abimelech's household (Ge 20:17, 18). Opening of Hagar's eyes (Ge 21:19). Conception of Jacob and Esau (Ge 25:21). Opening of Rachel's womb (Ge 30:22). Flaming bush (Ex 3:2). Transformation of Moses' rod into a serpent (Ex 4:3, 4, 30; 7:10, 12). Moses' leprosy (Ex 4:6, 7, 30). Plagues in Egypt (see Plagues). Pillar of cloud and fire (Ex 13:21, 22; 14:19, 20). Passage of the Red Sea (Ex 14:22). Destruction of Pharaoh and his army (Ex 4:23-30). Sweetening the waters of Marah (Ex 15:25). Manna (Ex 16:4-31). Quails (Ex 16:13). Defeat of Amalek (Ex 17:9-13). Transfiguration of the face of Moses (Ex 34:29-35). Water from the rock (Ex 17:5, 7). Thundering and lightning on Sinai (Ex 19:16-20; 24:10, 15-17; De 4:33). Miriam's leprosy (Nu 12:10-15). Judgments by fire (Nu 11:1-3).

Destruction of Korah (Nu 16:31-35; De 11:6, 7). Plague (Nu 16:46-50). Aaron's rod buds (Nu 17:1-9). Waters from the rock in Kadesh (Nu 20:8-11). Scourge of serpents (Nu 21:6-9). Destruction of Nadab and Abihu (Le 10:1, 2). Balaam's ass speaks (Nu 22:23-30). Preservation of Moses (De 34:7). Jordan divided (Jos 3:14-17: 4:16-18). Fall of Jericho (Jos 6:20). Midianites destroyed (J'g 7:16-22). Hail on the confederated kings (Jos 10:11). Sun and moon stand still (Jos 10:12-14). Dew on Gideon's fleece (J'g 6:37-40). Samson's strength (J'g 14:6; 16:3, 29, 30). Samson supplied with water (J'g 15:19). Fall of Dagon (1Sa 5:1-4). Cows return the ark (1Sa 6:7-14). Hemorrhoids (1Sa 5:9-12; 6:1-18). Destruction of the people of Beth-shemesh (1Sa 6:19, 20). Thunder (1Sa 12:16-18). Destruction of Uzzah (2Sa 6:1-8). Plague in Israel (1Ch 21:14-26). Fire on the sacrifices of Aaron (Le 9:24); of Gideon (J'g 6:21); of Manoah (J'g 13:19, 20); of Solomon (2Ch 7:1); of Elijah (1Ki 18:38). Jeroboam's hand withered (1Ki 13:3-6). Appearance of blood (2Ki 3:20-22). Panic of the Syrians (2Ki 7:6, 7). Elijah is fed by ravens (1Ki 17:6); by an angel (1Ki 19:1-8); increases the widow's meal and oil (1Ki 17:9-16; Lu 4:26); raises the widow's son (1Ki 17:17-24). Rain in answer to Elijah's prayer (1Ki 18:41-45). Elijah brings fire on Ahaziah's army (2Ki 1:10-12); divides Jordan (2Ki 2:8). Elijah's translation (2Ki 2:11).

Elisha divides Jordan (2Ki 2:14); sweetens the waters of Jericho (2Ki 2:19-22); increases a widow's oil (2Ki 4:1-7); raises the Shunammite's child (2Ki 4:18-37); renders harmless the poisoned pottage (2Ki 4:38-41); feeds one hundred men (2Ki 4:42-44); cures Naaman (2Ki 5:1-19); smites Gehazi with leprosy (2Ki 5:26, 27); causes the ax to float (2Ki 6:6); reveals the counsel of the king of Syria (2Ki 6:12); causes the eyes of his servant to be opened (2Ki 6:17); smites with blindness the army of the king of Syria (2Ki 6:18); the dead man restored to life (2Ki 13:21).

Destruction of Sennacherib's army (2Ki 19:35; Isa 37:36); return of the shadow on the sun dial (2Ki 20:9-11); Hezekiah's cure (Isa 38:21); deliverance of Shadrach, Meshach, and Abed-nego (Da 3:23-27); of Daniel (Da 6:22); the sea calmed on Jonah being cast into it (Jon 1:15); Jonah in the fish's belly (Jon 1:17; 2:10); his gourd (Jon 4:6, 7). Conception by Elisabeth (Lu 1:18, 24, 25); The incarnation of Jesus (M't 1:18-25; Lu 1:26-80). The appearance of the star of Bethlehem (M't 2:1-9). The deliverance of Jesus (M't 2:13-23).

Of Jesus, in Chronological Order: Water made wine (Joh 2:1-11). Heals the nobleman's son (Joh 4:46-54). Draught of fishes (Lu 5:1-11). Heals the demoniac (M'k 1:23-26; Lu 4:33-36). Heals Peter's mother-in-law (M't 8:14-17; M'k 1:29-31; Lu 4:38, 39). Cleanses the leper (M't 8:1-4; M'k 1:40-45; Lu 5:12-16). Heals the paralytic (M't 9:1-8; M'k 2:1-12; Lu 5:17-26). Healing of the impotent man (Joh 5:1-16). Restoring the withered hand (M't 12:9-13; M'k 3:1-5; Lu 6:6-11). Restores the centurion's servant (M't 8:5-13; Lu 7:1-10). Raises the widow's son to life (Lu 7:11-16). Heals a demoniac (M't 12:22-37; M'k 3:11; Lu 11:14, 15). Stills the tempest (M't 8:23-27; 14:32; M'k 4:35-41; Lu 8:22-25). Casts devils out of two men of Gadara (M't 8:28-34; M'k 5:1-20; Lu 8:26-39). Raises from the dead the daughter of Jairus (M't 9:18, 19, 23-26; M'k 5:22-24, 35-43; Lu 8:41, 42, 49-56). Cures the woman with the issue of blood (M't 9:20-22; M'k 5:25-34; Lu 8:43-48). Restores two blind men to sight (M't 9:27-31). Heals a demoniac (M't 9:32, 33). Feeds five thousand people (M't 14:15-21; M'k 6:35-44; Lu 9:12-17; Joh 6:5-14). Walks on the sea (M't 14:22-33; M'k 6:45-52; Joh 6:16-21). Heals the daughter of the Syrophenician woman (M't 15:21-28; M'k 7:24-30). Feeds four thousand people (M't 15:32-39; M'k 8:1-9). Restores one deaf and dumb (M'k 7:31-37). Restores a blind man (M'k 8:22-26). Restores lunatic child (M't 17:14-21; M'k 9:14-29; Lu 9:37-43). Tribute money obtained from a fish's mouth (M't 17:24-27). Restores ten lepers (Lu 17:11-19). Opens the eyes of a man born blind (Joh 9). Raises Lazarus from the dead (Joh 11:1-46). Heals the woman with the spirit of infirmity (Lu 13:10-17). Cures a man with dropsy (Lu 14:1-6). Restores two blind men near Jericho (M't 20:29-34; M'k 10:46-52; Lu 18:35-43). Curses a fig tree (M't

21:17-22; M'k 11:12-14, 20-24). Heals the ear of Malchus (Lu 22:49-51). Second draught of fishes (Joh 21:6).

Of the Disciples of Jesus: By the seventy (Lu 10:17-20); by other disciples (M'k 9:39; Joh 14:12); by the apostles (Ac 3:6, 12, 13, 16; 4:10, 30; 9:34, 35; 16:18). Peter cures the sick (Ac 5:15, 16); Aeneas (Ac 9:34); raises Dorcas (Ac 9:40); causes the death of Ananias and Sapphira (Ac 5:5, 10). Peter and John cure a lame man (Ac 3:2-11). Peter and other apostles delivered from prison (Ac 5:19-23; 12:6-11; 16:26). Philip carried away by the Spirit (Ac 8:39). Paul strikes Elymas with blindness (Ac 13:11); heals a cripple (Ac 14:10); casts out evil spirits, and cures sick (Ac 16:18; 19:11, 12; 28:8, 9); raises Eutychus to life (Ac 20:9-12); shakes a viper off his hand (Ac 28:5). Paul cured of blindness (Ac 9:3-6, 17, 18).

Convincing effect of, on: Children of Israel (Ex 4:28-31; 14:31; Nu 17:1-13). Pharaoh's servants (Ex 10:7). Pharaoh (Ex 10:16, 17; 12:31, 32). Egyptians (Ex 12:33; 1Sa 6:6). The Canaanites (Jos 2:9-11; 5:1). Gideon (J'g 6:17-22, 36-40; 7:1). People who witnessed Elijah's (1Ki 18:24, 37-39). Naaman (2Ki 5:14, 15). Nebuchadnezzar (Da 2:47; 3:28, 29; 4:2, 3). Darius (Da 6:20-27). Simon Peter (Lu 5:4-11). Disciples of Jesus (Joh 2:11, 22, 23; 20:30, 31). The nobleman whose child Jesus healed (Joh 4:48-53). People who witnessed Christ's (Joh 7:31; 11:43-45; 12:10, 11). People who witnessed Philip's (Ac 8:6). People who witnessed Peter's (Ac 9:32-42). Sergius Paulus, the deputy (Ac 13:8-12). Gentiles (Ro 15:18, 19).

Resisted by the obdurate (Ne 9:17; Ps 78:10-32; Joh 9:24-28; 15:24, 25).

Design of, to: Reveal God (Ex 7:5, 17; 8:8-10, 22; 9:4-16, 29; 10:1, 2; 14:4, 18; De 4:33-39; Jos 4:23, 24; 1Ki 18:24, 37-39; Jer 32:20). Produce faith in God (Ex 14:31; Nu 14:11; Jos 3:7-17; 2Ch 7:1-3; Ps 106:9-12). Produce the fear of God (1Sa 12:17, 18; Da 6:20-27; Jon 1:14-16). Constrain to obedience (Ex 16:4-6; 19:4, 5; De 11:1-8; 29:1-9; J'g 2:7; Ps 78:10-32). Glorify God (Lu 5:26; Joh 11:4; Ac 4:21, 22). Attest the messiahship of Jesus (M't 11:2-5 w Lu 7:19-22; M'k 2:9-12 w Lu 5:24-26; Lu 18:42, 43; Joh 2:11; 4:48; 5:36; 11:4, 40-42; 14:11; 15:24). Glorify Jesus (Ac 3:1-13). Attest God's servants (Ex 4:2-9; 19:9; Nu 16:28-35; 1Sa 12:17, 18; Zec 2:9; Ac 2:22; Heb 2:4). Preserve the righteous (Da 3:28, 29; 6:20-27). Change wicked purposes (Ex 3:19, 20; 9:16, 17; 10:16, 17; 11:1-10; 12:29-33; 14:24, 25).

Miraculous Gifts of the Holy Ghost: Foretold (Isa 35:4-6; Joe 2:28, 29). Of different kinds (1Co 12:4-6). Enumerated (1Co 12:8-10, 28). Christ was endued with (M't 12:28). Poured out on Pentecost (Ac 2:1-4). Communicated on preaching the gospel (Ac 10:44-46); by laying on of the apostles' hands (Ac 8:17, 18; 19:6); for the confirmation of the gospel (M'k 16:20; Ac 14:3; Ro 15:19; Heb 2:4); for the edification of the church (1Co 12:7; 14:12, 13). To be sought after (1Co 12:31; 14:1). Temporary nature of (1Co 13:8). Not to be neglected (1Ti 4:14; 2Ti 1:6); or despised (1Th 5:20); or purchased (Ac 8:20).

MIRE. *Figurative:* Ps 40:2; 69:2.

MIRIAM. 1. Sister of Aaron and Moses; saved life of the baby Moses (Ex 2:4, 7, 8); prophetess (Ex 15:20); criticized Moses for his marriage (Nu 12); buried at Kadesh (Nu 20:1).

2. Judahite (1Ch 4:17).

MIRMA (fraud) a Benjamite (1Ch 8:10).

MIRROR, ancient mirrors were made of polished metal (Ex 38:8; Job 37:18; 1Co 13:12; Jas 1:23).

MISCEGENATION. Forbidden by Abraham (Ge 24:3); Jacob (Ge 28:1); Moses (Ex 34:12-16; De 7:3, 4); Joshua (Jos 23:12). Reasons for prohibition (Ex 34:16; De 7:4; Jos 23:12, 13).

Results of (J'g 3:6, 7).

Instances of: Moses (Nu 12:1); Esau (Ge 26:34, 35); Israel (Nu 25:1, 6-8; J'g 3:5-8).

MISER (Ec 4:7, 8).

MISGAB (a lofty place), an unknown place mentioned in Jer 48:1.

MISHAEL (who is like God?). 1. A son of Uzziel, helps carry the bodies of Nadab and Abihu out of the camp (Ex 6:22; Le 10:4).

2. A Jew who stood by Ezra when he read the law to the people (Ne 8:4).

3. Called also Meshach. One of three Hebrew children trained with Daniel at the court of Babylon (Da 1:6, 7, 11-20).

Assists Daniel in interpreting Nebuchadnezzar's dream (Da 2:17-23). Cast into the fiery furnace (Da 3:13-30).

MISHAL, Levitical city in Asher (Jos 21:30); "Misheal" in Jos 19:26 and "Mashal" in 1Ch 6:74.

MISHAM, son of Elpaal (1Ch 8:12).

MISHEAL, called also Mishal. A Levitical city (Jos 19:26; 21:30).

MISHMA. 1. Son of Ishmael (Ge 25:14; 1Ch 1:30).

2. Of the tribe of Simeon (1Ch 4:25, 26).

MISHMANNAH (fatness), a Gadite who joined David at Ziklag (1Ch 12:10).

MISHRAITES, family of Kirjath-jearim in Judah (1Ch 2:53).

MISJUDGMENT. *Instances of:* Of the Reubenites and Gadites (Nu 32:1-33; Jos 22:11-31). Of Hannah (1Sa 1:14-17).

See Accusations, False; Uncharitableness.

MISPERETH, called also Mizpar. A Jew who returned with Zerubbabel from Babylon (Ezr 2:2; Ne 7:7).

MISREPHOTH-MAIM (hot springs), place near Sidon and Tyre (Jos 11:8; 13:6).

MISSIONS. Religious propagandism (2Ki 17:27, 28; 1Ch 16:23, 24). Enjoined (Ps 96:3, 10; M't 28:19; M'k 16:15; Lu 24:47, 48). Prophecy concerning (M't 24:14; M'k 13:10). Peter's vision concerning (Ac 10:9-20).

Ordained by Jesus (M't 24:14; 28:19; M't 16:15, 16; Lu 24:47-49). Saul and Barnabas ordained for (Ac 13:2-4, 47). Paul appointed to (Ac 26:14-18; 1Co 16:9). Practiced by the Psalmist (Ps 18:49); Jonah (Jon 3:1-9).

Symbolized by the flying angel (Re 14:6, 7).

Missionary Hymn (Ps 96).

The first to do homage to the Messiah were heathen (M't 2:11).

See Gentiles, Call of; Heathen; Jesus, King; Jesus, Kingdom of, Prophecies Concerning.

Missionaries, All Christians Should Be As: After the example of Christ (Ac 10:38). Women and children as well as men (Ps 8:2; Pr 31:26; M't 21:15, 16; Ph'p 4:3; 1Ti 5:10; Tit 2:3-5; 1Pe 3:1). The zeal of idolaters should provoke to (Jer 7:18). The zeal of hypocrites should provoke to (M't 23:15). An imperative duty (J'g 5:23; Lu 19:40). The principle on which (2Co 5:14, 15). However weak they may be (1Co 1:27). From their calling as saints (Ex 19:6; 1Pe 2:9). As faithful stewards (1Pe 4:10, 11). In youth (Ps 71:17; 148:12, 13). In old age (De 32:7; Ps 71:18). In the family (De 6:7; Ps 78:5-8; Isa 38:19; 1Co 7:16; 1Pe 2:12). In first giving their own selves to the Lord (2Co 8:5). In declaring what God has done for them (Ps 66:16; 116:16-19). In hating life for Christ (Lu 14:26). In openly confessing Christ (M't 10:32). In following Christ (Lu 14:27; 18:22). In preferring Christ above all relations (Lu 14:26; 1Co 2:2). In joyfully suffering for Christ (Heb 10:34). In forsaking all for Christ (Lu 5:11). In a holy example (M't 5:16; Ph'p 2:15; 1Th 1:7). In holy conduct (1Pe 2:12). In holy boldness (Ps 119:46). In dedicating themselves to the service of God (Jos 24:15; Ps 27:4). In devoting all property to God (1Ch 29:2, 3, 14, 16; Ec 11:1; M't 6:19, 20; M'k 12:44; Lu 12:33; 18:22, 28; Ac 2:45; 4:32-34). In holy conversation (Ps 37:30, w Pr 10:31; Pr 15:7; Eph 4:29; Col 4:6). In talking of God and His works (Ps 71:24; 77:12; 119:27; 145:11, 12). In showing forth God's praises (Isa 43:21). In inviting others to embrace the gospel (Ps 34:8; Isa 2:3; Joh 1:46; 4:29). In seeking the edification of others (Ro 14:19; 15:2; 1Th 5:11). In admonishing others (1Th 5:14; 2Th 3:15). In reproving others (Le 19:17; Eph 5:11). In teaching and exhorting (Ps 34:11; 51:13; Col 3:16; Heb 3:13; 10:25). In interceding for others (Col 4:3; Heb 13:18; Jas 5:16). In aiding ministers in their labors (Ro 16:3, 9; 2Co 11:9; Ph'p 4:14-16; 3Jo 6). In giving a reason for their faith (Ex 12:26, 27; De 6:20, 21; 1Pe 3:15). In encouraging the weak (Isa 35:3, 4; Ro 14:1; 15:1; 1Th 5:14). In visiting and relieving the poor and sick (Le 25:35; Ps 112:9, w 2Co 9:9; M't 25:36; Ac 20:35; Jas 1:27). With a willing heart (Ex 35:29; 1Ch 29:9, 14). With a superabundant liberality (Ex 36:5-7; 2Co 8:3). Encouragement to (Pr 11:25, 30; 1Co 1:27; Jas 5:19, 20). Blessedness of (Da 12:3). Illustrated (M't 25:14; Lu 19:13).

See Ministers.

MIST. 1. Steamy vapor rising from ground (Ge 2:6).

2. Dimness of vision (Ac 13:11).

3. Description of false teachers (2Pe 2:17).

MITE. About one-fifth of a cent (M'k 12:42). Widow's (Lu 21:2).

MITER (Ex 28:4, 36-39; 39:28-31; Eze 21:26).

MITHCAH (sweetness), an encampment of the Israelites (Nu 33:28, 29).

MITHNITE, patronymic designation of Joshaphat (1Ch 11:43).

MITHRAISM, cult of Mithras, Persian sun-god, widely disseminated in the Roman Empire in the 1st cent. A. D.

MITHREDATH (given by Mithras). 1. Treasurer of Cyrus (Ezr 1:8).

2. A Persian officer who joined in writing a letter inimical to the Jews (Ezr 4:7).

MITYLENE. Capital of Lesbos. Paul visits (Ac 20:14, 15).

MIXED MULTITUDE, non-Israelites who travelled and associated with children of Israel (Nu 11:4-6; Ne 13:3).

MIZAR (small), hill near Mt. Hermon (Ps 42:6).

MIZPAH (watchtower). 1. A city allotted to Benjamin (Jos 18:26). The Israelites assemble at (J'g 20:1-3); and decree the penalty to be visited upon the Benjamites for their maltreatment of the Levite's concubine (J'g 20:10). Assembled by Samuel that he might reprove them for their idolatry (1Sa 7:5). Crown Saul king of Israel at (1Sa 10:17-25). A judgment seat of Samuel (1Sa 7:16). Walled by Asa (1Ki 15:22; 2Ch 16:6). Temporarily the capital of the country after the children of Israel had been carried away captive (2Ki 25:23, 25; Jer 40:6-15; 41:1-14) Captivity returned to (Ne 3:7, 15, 19).

2. A valley near Lebanon (Jos 11:3, 8).

3. A city in Moab. David gives his parents to the care of the king of (1Sa 22:3, 4).

4. A city in the lowland of Judah (Jos 15:38).

5. A town in Gilead (Jos 10:17; J'g 11:34). May be location of treaty between Jacob and Laban (Ge 31:48, 49).

MIZPAR, co-worker of Zerubbabel (Ezr 2:2). "Mispereth" in Ne 7:7.

MIZPEH (See Mizpah.)

MIZRAIM. 1. Son of Ham (Ge 10:6, 13; 1Ch 1:8, 11); progenitor of Egyptians, people of N Africa, Hamitic people of Canaan.

2. Usual Hebrew word for "Egypt," always so translated in RSV.

MIZZAH (terror), son of Reuel (Ge 36:13, 17; 1Ch 1:37).

MNASON, a native and Christian of Cyprus who entertained Paul (Ac 21:16).

MOAB (seed). 1. Son of Lot (Ge 19:37).

2. Plains of. Israelites come in (De 2:17, 18). Military forces numbered in (Nu 26:3, 63). The law rehearsed in, by Moses (Nu 35:36; De 29-33). The Israelites renew their covenant in (De 29:1). The land of promise allotted in (Jos 13:32).

MOABITES. Descendants of Lot through his son Moab (Ge 19:37). Called the people of Chemosh (Nu 21:29). The territory E of Jordan, bounded on the N by the river Arnon (Nu 21:13; J'g 11:18). Children of Israel commanded not to distress the Moabites (De 2:9). Refuse passage of Jephthah's army through their territory (J'g 11:17, 18). Balak was king of (Nu 22:4); calls for Baalam to curse Israel (Nu 22-24; Jos 24:9; Mic 6:5). Are a snare to the Israelites (Nu 25:1-3; Ru 1:4; 1Ki 11:1; 1Ch 8:8; Ezr 9:1, 2; Ne 13:23). Land of, not given to the Israelites as a possession (De 2:9, 29). David takes refuge among, from Saul (1Sa 22:3, 4). David conquers (2Sa 8:2; 23:20; 1Ch 11:22; 18:2-11). Israelites had war with (2Ki 3:5-27; 13:20; 24:2; 2Ch 20). Prophecies concerning judgments upon (Jer 48).

MOABITE STONE, THE, black basalt stele, 2 by 4 ft., inscribed by Mesha, king of Moab, with 34 lines in the Moabite language (practically a dialect of Hebrew), giving his side of the story recorded in 2Ki 3.

MOADIAH, a priest (Ne 12:17).

MOB, at Thessalonica (Ac 17:5); Jerusalem (Ac 21:28, 30); Ephesus (Ac 19:29-40).

MOCKING. Ishmael mocks Sarah (Ge 21:9). Elijah mocks the priests of Baal (1Ki 18:27). Zedekiah mocks Micaiah (1Ki 22:24). Children mock Elisha (2Ki 2:23). The tormentors of Job mock (Job 15:12; 30:1). The persecutors of Jesus mock him (M't 26:67, 68; 27:28-31, 39-44; M'k 10:34; 14:65; 15:17-20,

29-32; Lu 23:11; Joh 19:2, 3, 5; 1Pe 2:23). The Ammonites mock God (Eze 25:3). Tyre mocks Jerusalem (Eze 26:2). The obdurately wicked mock (Isa 28:15, 22; 2Pe 3:3).

See Scoffing.

Figurative: Ec 7:16; 1Co 7:31.

MODESTY, of women (1Ti 2:9).

Instances of: Saul (1Sa 9:21). Vashti (Es 1:11, 12). Elihu (Job 32:4-7).

See Humility.

MOLADAH (birth), town c. 10 miles E of Beersheba (Ne 11:26).

MOLDING (Job 28:2; Eze 24:11). Of images (Ex 32:4, 8; 34:17; Le 19:4; De 9:12); pillars (1Ki 7:15); laver (1Ki 7:23); done in the plain of Jordan (1Ki 7:46; 2Ch 4:17); mirrors (Job 37:18).

MOLE (Le 11:30; Isa 2:20).

MOLECH, called also Moloch and Milcom. An idol of the Ammonites (Ac 7:43). Worshiped by the wives of Solomon, and by Solomon (1Ki 11:1-8). Children sacrificed to (2Ki 23:10; Jer 32:35; 2Ki 16:3; 21:6; 2Ch 28:3; Isa 57:5; Jer 7:31; Eze 16:20, 21; 20:26, 31; 23:37, 39; see Le 18:21; 20:2-5).

MOLID (begetter), Judahite (1Ch 2:29).

MOLTEN SEA (See Tabernacle.)

MONARCHY. Described by Samuel (1Sa 8:11-18).

See Government; King.

MONEY. Silver used as (Ge 17:12, 13, 23, 27; 20:16; 23:9, 13; 31:15; 37:28; 42:25-35; 43:12-23; 44:1-8; 47:14-18; Ex 12:44; 21:11, 21, 34, 35; 22:7, 17, 25; 30:16; Le 22:11; 25:37, 51; 27:15, 18; Nu 3:48-51; 18:16; De 2:6, 28; 14:25, 26; 21:14; 23:19; J'g 5:19; 16:18; 17:4; 1Ki 21:2, 6, 15; 2Ki 5:26; 12:4, 7-16; 15:20; 22:7, 9; 23:35; 2Ch 24:5, 11, 14; 34:9, 14, 17; Ezr 3:7; 7:7; Ne 5:4, 10, 11; Es 4:7; Job 31:39; Ps 15:5; Pr 7:20; Ec 7:12; 10:19; Isa 43:24; 52:3; 55:1, 2; Jer 32:9, 10, 25, 44; La 5:4; Mic 3:11; M't 25:18, 27 (Argurion, Greek); 28:12, 15; M'k 14:11; Lu 9:3; 19:15, 23; 22:5; Ac 7:16; 8:20).

Gold used as (Ge 13:2; 24:35; 44:8; w verse 1; 1Ch 21:25; Ezr 8:25-27; Isa 13:17; 46:6; 60:9; Eze 7:19; 28:4; M't 2:11; 10:9; Ac 3:6; 20:33; 1Pe 1:18).

Copper used as (M'k 6:8; 12:41).

Weighed (Ge 23:16; 43:21; Job 28:15; Jer 32:9, 10; Zec 11:12). Image on (M't 22:20, 21). Conscience (J'g 17:2; M't 27:3, 5). Atonement (Ex 30:12-16; Le 5:15, 16). Sin (2Ki 12:16). Value of, varied corruptly (Am 8:5). Love of, the root of evil (1Ti 6:10).

See Farthing; Gerah; Mite; Penny; Pound; Shekel; Silver; Talent.

MONEY CHANGER, one who changed foreign currency into sanctuary money at a profit (M't 21:12).

MONOPOLY. Of lands (Isa 5:8; Mic 2:2); by Pharaoh (Ge 47:19-26); of food (Pr 11:26).

MONOTHEISM (one god), belief that there is but one God.

MONSTERS (See Animals.)

MONTH. Ancient use of (Ge 7:11; 8:4). Twelve months reckoned to a year (1Ch 27:1-15).

1. Abib (April). The Jewish calendar began with (Ex 12:2; 13:4; De 16:1). Passover instituted and celebrated in (Ex 12:1-28; 23:15). Israelites left Egypt in (Ex 13:4). Tabernacle set up in (Ex 40:2, 17). Israelites arrive at Zin, in (Nu 20:1). Cross Jordan in (Jos 4:19). Jordan overflows in (1Ch 12:15). Decree to put the Jews to death in (Es 3:12). The death of Jesus in (M't 26:27). After the captivity called Nisan (Ne 2:1; Es 3:7).

2. Zif (May) (1Ki 6:1, 37). Israel numbered in (Nu 1:1, 18). Passover to be observed in, by the unclean and others who could not observe it in the first month (Nu 9:10, 11). Israel departed from the wilderness of Zin in (Nu 10:11). Temple begun in (1Ki 6:1, 2Ch 3:2). An irregular passover celebrated in (2Ch 30:1-27). Rebuilding of the temple begun in (Ezr 3:8).

3. Sivan (June) (Es 8:9). Asa renews the covenant of himself and people in (2Ch 15:10).

4. Tammuz (July). The number only appears in the Bible. Jerusalem taken by Nebuchadnezzar in (Jer 39:2; 52:6, 7).

5. Ab (August). Number only mentioned. Aaron died on the first day of (Nu 33:38). Temple destroyed in (2Ki 25:8-10; Jer 1:3; 52:12-30). Ezra arrived at Jerusalem in (Ezr 7:8, 9).

6. Elul (September). Wall of Jerusalem finished in (Ne 6:15). Temple built in (Hag 1:14, 15).

7. Ethanim (October) (1Ki 8:2). Feasts held in (Le 23:24, 27; Ne

8:13-15). Jubilee proclaimed in (Le 25:9). Solomon's temple dedicated in (1Ki 8:2). Altar rebuilt and offerings renewed in (Ezr 3:1, 6).

8. Bul (November). The temple finished in (1Ki 6:38). Jeroboam's idolatrous feast in (1Ki 12:32, 33; 1Ch 27:11).

9. Chisleu (December) (Ezr 10:9; Jer 36:9, 22; Zec 7:1).

10. Tebeth (January) (Ezr 2:16). Nebuchadnezzar besieges Jerusalem in (2Ki 25:1; Jer 52:4).

11. Sebat (February) (Zec 1:7). Moses probably died in (De 1:3).

12. Adar (March) (Es 3:7). Second temple finished in (Ezr 6:15). Feast of Purim in (Es 9:1-26).

Months in prophecy (Re 11:2).

MONUMENT (See Pillar.)

MOON. Created by God (Ge 1:16; Ps 8:3; 136:7-9). Its light (Job 31:26; Ec 12:2; Song 6:10; Jer 31:35; 1Ch 15:41). Its influences (De 33:14; Ps 121:6). Seasons of (months) (Ps 104:19). Joseph's dream concerning (Ge 37:9). Stands still (Jos 10:12, 13; Hab 3:11). Worship of, forbidden (De 4:19; 17:3). Worshiped (2Ki 23:5; Job 31:26, 27; Jer 7:18; 8:2; 44:17-19, 25). No light of, in heaven (Re 21:23). Darkening of (Job 25:5; Isa 13:10; 24:23; Eze 32:7; Joe 2:10, 31; 3:15; M't 24:29; M'k 13:24; Lu 21:25; Ac 2:20; Re 6:12; 8:12).

Figurative: Shining of (Isa 30:26; 60:19; Re 21:23).

Symbolical: Re 12:1.

Feast of the New Moon: Nu 10:10; 28:11-15; 1Ch 23:31; 2Ch 31:3; Ezr 3:5. Traffic at time of, prohibited (Am 8:5).

MORAL AGENCY (See Contingencies.)

MORAL LAW (See Law.)

MORALITY (See Duty of man to man; Integrity; Neighbor.)

MORASTHITE, inhabitant of Moresheth (Jer 26:18; Mic 1:1).

MORDECAI. A Jewish captive in Persia (Es 2:5, 6). Foster father of Esther (Es 2:7). Informs Ahasuerus of a conspiracy against his life, and is rewarded (Es 2:21-23; 6:1-11). Promoted in Haman's place (Es 8:1, 2, 15; 10:1-3). Intercedes with Ahasuerus for the Jews; establishes the festival of Purim in commemoration of their deliverance (Es 8; 9).

MOREH (teacher). 1. A plain near Shechem and Gilgal (Ge 12.6; De 11:30).

2. A hill in the plain of Jezreel where the Midianites encamped (J'g 7:1, 12).

MORESHETH-GATH (possession of Gath), town c. 5 miles W of Gath in the Shephelah (Mic 1:1; Jer 26:18).

MORIAH, place to which Abraham went to offer up Isaac (Ge 22:2). Solomon built temple on Mt. Moriah (2Ch 3:1), but it is not certain whether it is the same place.

MORNING. The second part of the day at the creation (Ge 1:5, 8, 13, 19, 23, 31). The first part of the natural day (M'k 16:2). Ordained by God (Job 38:12). Began with first dawn (Jos 6:15; Ps 119:147). Continued until noon (1Ki 18:26; Ne 8:3). First dawning of, called the eyelids of the morning (Job 3:9 [marg.]; 41:18). The outgoings of, made to rejoice (Ps 65:8).

The Jews: Generally rose early in (Ge 28:18; J'g 6:28). Eat but little in (Ec 10:16). Went to the temple in (Lu 21:38; Joh 8:2). Offered a part of the daily sacrifice in (Ex 29:38, 39; Nu 28:4-7). Devoted a part of, to prayer and praise (Ps 5:3; 59:16; 88:13). Gathered the manna in (Ex 16:21). Began their journeys in (Ge 22:3). Held courts of justice in (Jer 21:12; M't 27:1). Contracted covenants in (Ge 26:31). Transacted business in (Ec 11:6; M't 20:1). Was frequently cloudless (2Sa 23:4). A red sky in, a sign of bad weather (M't 16:3). Ushered in by the morning star (Job 38:7).

Illustrative: Of the resurrection day (Ps 49:14). (Breaking forth,) of the glory of the church (Song 6:10; Isa 58:8). (Star of,) of the glory of Christ (Re 22:16). (Star of,) of reward of saints (Re 2:28). (Clouds in,) of the shortlived profession of hypocrites (Ho 6:4). (Wings of,) of rapid movements (Ps 139:9). (Spread upon the mountains,) of heavy calamities (Joe 2:2).

MORNING SACRIFICE (See Offerings.)

MORSEL, a meal (Heb 12:16).

MORTAL, MORTALITY. A mortal is a being subject to death (Ro 8:11; 1Co 15:53, 54).

MORTAR. 1. An instrument for pulverizing grains (Nu 11:8; Pr 27:22).

See Grinding; Mill.

2. A cement (Ex 1:14). Slime used as, in building tower of Babel (Ge 11:3). Used to plaster houses (Le 14:42-45). Untempered, not enduring (Eze 13:10-15; 22:28). To be trodden to make firm (Na 3:14).

Figurative: Isa 41:25.

MORTGAGE, on land (Ne 5:3).

See Land.

MORTIFICATION, *Instances of:* David's ambassadors, sent to Hanun (2Sa 10:1-5). Judas (M't 27:3-5).

See Humility.

MOSAIC, picture or design made by setting tiny squares or cones of varicolored marble, limestone, or semiprecious stones in some medium such as plaster to tell a story or to form a decoration.

MOSERA. An encampment of the Israelites where Aaron died (De 10:6). Probably identical with Moseroth, below.

MOSEROTH (bond), an encampment of the Israelites (Nu 33:30, 31).

MOSES (drawn out, born). A Levite and son of Amram (Ex 2:1-4; 6:20; Ac 7:20; Heb 11:23). Hidden in an ark (Ex 2:3). Discovered and adopted by the daughter of Pharaoh (Ex 2:5-10). Learned in all the wisdom of Egypt (Ac 7:22). His loyalty to his race (Heb 11:24-26). Takes the life of an Egyptian; flees from Egypt; finds refuge among the Midianites (Ex 2:11-22; Ac 7:24-29). Joins himself to Jethro, priest of Midian; marries his daughter Zipporah; has two sons (Ex 2:15-22; 18:3, 4). Is herdman for Jethro in the desert of Horeb (Ex 3:1). Has the vision of the burning bush (Ex 3:2-6). God reveals to him his purpose to deliver the Israelites and bring them into the land of Canaan (Ex 3:7-10). Commissioned as leader of the Israelites (Ex 3:10-22; 6:13). His rod miraculously turned into a serpent, and his hand made leprous, and each restored (Ex 4:1-9, 28). With his wife and sons leaves Jethro to perform his mission (Ex 4:18-20). His controversy with his wife on account of circumcision (Ex 4:20-26). Meets Aaron in the wilderness (Ex 4:27, 28).

With Aaron assembles the leaders of Israel (Ex 4:29-31). With Aaron goes before Pharaoh, in the name of Jehovah demands the liberties of his people (Ex 5:1). Rejected by Pharaoh; hardships of the Israelites increased (Ex 5). People murmur against Moses and Aaron (Ex 5:20, 21; 15:24; 16:2, 3; 17:2, 3; Nu 14:2-4; 16:41; 20:2-5; 21:4-6; De 1:12, 26-28). See Israel. Receives comfort and assurance from the Lord (Ex 6:1-8). Unbelief of the people (Ex 6:9). Renews his appeal to Pharaoh (Ex 6:11). Under divine direction brings plagues upon the land of Egypt (Ex 7-12). Secures the deliverance of the people and leads them out of Egypt (Ex 13). Crosses the Red Sea; Pharaoh and his army are destroyed (Ex 14). Composes a song for the children of Israel on their deliverance from Pharaoh (Ex 15). Joined by his family in the wilderness (Ex 18:1-12).

Institutes a system of government (Ex 18:13-26; Nu 11:16-30; De 1:9-18). Receives the law and ordains divers statutes. (See Law of Moses.) Face of, transfigured (Ex 34:29-35; 2Co 3:13). Sets up the tabernacle. (See Tabernacle.) Reproves Aaron for making the golden calf (Ex 32:22, 23); for irregularity in the offerings (Le 10:16-20). Jealousy of Aaron and Miriam toward (Nu 12). Rebellion of Korah, Dathan, and Abiram against (Nu 16). Appoints Joshua as his successor (Nu 27:22, 23; De 31:7, 8, 14, 23; 34:9).

Not permitted to enter Canaan, but views the land from Mount Pisgah (Nu 27:12-14; De 1:37; 3:23-29; 32:48-52; 34:1-8). Death and burial of (Nu 31:2; De 32:50; 34:1-6). Body of, disputed over (Jude 9). One hundred and twenty years old at death (De 31:2). Mourning for, thirty days in the plains of Moab (De 34:8). His virility (De 31:2; 34:7).

Present with Jesus on the mount of transfiguration (M't 17:3, 4; M'k 9:4; Lu 9:30).

Type of Christ (De 18:15-18; Ac 3:22; 7:37).

Benedictions of: Upon the people (Le 9:23; Nu 10:35, 36; De 1:11). Last benediction upon the twelve tribes (De 33).

Character of: Murmurings of (Ex 5:22, 23; Nu 11:10-15). Impatience of (Ex 5:22, 23; 6:12; 32:19; Nu 11:10-15; 16:15; 20:10; 31:14). Respected and feared (Ex 33:8). Faith of (Nu 10:29; De 9:1-3; Heb 11:23-28). Called the man of God (De 33:1). God spake to, as a man to his friend (Ex 33:11). Magnified of

God (Ex 19:9; Nu 14:12-20; De 9:13-29, w Ex 32:30). Magnanimity of, toward Eldad and Medad (Nu 11:29). Meekness of (Ex 14:13, 14; 15:24, 25; 16:2, 3, 7, 8; Nu 12:3; 16:4-11). Obedience of (Ex 7:6; 40:16, 19, 21). Unaspiring (Nu 14:12-20; De 9:13-29, w Ex 32:30).

Intercessory Prayers of: See Intercession, Instances of; Solicited, Instances of; Answered, Instances of.

Miracles of: See Miracles.

Prophecies of: Ex 3:10; 4:5, 11, 12; 6:13; 7:2; 17:16; 19:3-9; 33:11; Nu 11:17; 12:7, 8; 36:13; De 1:3; 5:31; 18:15, 18; 34:10, 12; Ho 12:13; M'k 7:9, 10; Ac 7:37, 38.

MOSES, ASSUMPTION OF, anonymous Jewish apocalyptic book, probably written early in 1st century A. D.; gives prophecy of future of Israel.

MOSES, LAW OF (See Law.)

MOST HIGH, name applied to God (Ge 14:18, 19, 20, 22; Ps 7:17).

MOTE, particle of dust or splinter of wood that might enter the eye (M't 7:3-5; Lu 6:41, 42).

MOTH. An insect (Job 4:19; 27:18; Ps 39:11). Destructive of garments (Job 13:28; Isa 50:9; 51:8; Ho 5:12).

Figurative: M't 6:19, 20; Jas 5:2.

MOTHER. Reverence for, enjoined (Ex 20:12; Le 19:3; De 5:16; Pr 23:22; M't 15:4; 19:19; M'k 7:10; 10:19; Lu 18:20; Eph 6:2). To be obeyed (De 21:18; Pr 1:8; 6:20). Love for (1Ki 19:20); must be subordinate to love for Christ (M't 10:37).

Sanctifying influence of (2Ti 1:5). Dishonoring of, to be punished (Ex 21:15; Le 20:9; Pr 20:20; 28:24; 30:11, 17; M't 15:4-6; M'k 7:10-12).

Love of (Isa 49:15; 66:13). Exemplified by: Hagar (Ge 21:14-16). The mother of Moses (Ex 2:1-3). Hannah (1Sa 1:20-28). Rizpah (2Sa 21:8-11). Bathsheba (1Ki 1:16-21). The mother whose child was brought to Solomon (1Ki 3:16-26). The woman whose sons were to be taken for debt (2Ki 4:1-7). The Shunammite (2Ki 4:18-37). Mary the mother of Jesus (Lu 2:41-50). The bereaved mothers of Bethlehem (M't 2:16-18). The Syrophenician woman (M't 15:21-28; M'k 7:24-30).

Grieves over wayward children (Pr 10:1; 19:26; 29:15). Rejoices over good children (Pr 23:23-35).

Incest with, forbidden (Le 18:7). Wicked (Ge 27:6-17).

MOTHER-IN-LAW (M't 10:35). Not to be defiled (Le 18:17; 20:14; De 27:23). Beloved by Ruth (Ru 1:14-17). Peter's, healed by Jesus (M'k 1:30, 31).

MOTIVE. Ascribed to God (Ps 106:8; Eze 36:21, 22, 32). Right, required (M't 6:1-18). Sinful, illustrated by Cain (Ge 4:7; 1Jo 3:12).

Misunderstood: The tribes of Reuben and Gad, in asking inheritance E of Jordan (Nu 32:1-33); when they built the memorial (Jos 22:9-34). David's, by King Hanun (2Sa 10:2, 3; 1Ch 19:3, 4). The king of Syria's, in sending presents to the king of Israel by Naaman (2Ki 5:5-7). Job's in his righteousness (Job 1:9-11; 2:4, 5).

MOTTO (See Legend.)

MOUNTAIN. Melted (Ps 97:5; De 4:11; 5:23; J'g 5:5; Isa 64:1-3; Mic 1:4; Na 1:5). Overturning and removing of (Job 9:5; 14:18; 28:9; Eze 38:20). Abraham offers Isaac upon Mount Moriah, afterward called Mount Zion, the site of the temple (Ge 22:2; see Zion). Horeb appointed as a place for the Israelites to worship (Ex 3:12). Used for idolatrous worship (De 12:2; 1Sa 10:5; 1Ki 14:23; Jer 3:6; Ho 4:13). Jesus tempted upon (M't 4:8; Lu 4:5). Jesus preaches from (M't 5:1). Jesus goes up into, for prayer (M't 14:23; Lu 6:12; 9:28); is transfigured upon (M't 17:1-9; M'k 9:2-10; Lu 9:28-36); meets his disciples on, after his resurrection (M't 28:16, 17). Signals from (Isa 13:2; 18:3; 30:17). Removed by faith (M't 17:20; 21:21; M'k 11:23). Burning mountains (see Volcano).

MOUNT OF BEATITUDES, site of the Sermon on the Mount (M't 5-7); exact location unknown.

MOUNT EPHRAIM (See Ephraim.)

MOURNING. For the dead: Head uncovered (Le 10:6; 21:10); lying on ground (2Sa 12:16); personal appearance neglected (2Sa 14:2); cutting the flesh (Le 19:28; 21:1-5; De 14:1; Jer 16:6, 7; 41:5); lamentations (Ge 50:10; Ex 12:30; 1Sa 30:4; Jer 22:18; M't 2:17, 18); fasting (1Sa 31:13; 2Sa 1:12; 3:35). Priests prohibited, except for nearest of kin (Le 21:1-11). For Nadab and Abihu forbidden (Le 10:6). Sexes separated in (Zec 12:12, 14).

Hired mourners (2Ch 35:25; Ec 12:5;

Jer 9:17; M't 9:23).

Abraham mourned for Sarah (Ge 23:2); Egyptians, for Jacob seventy days (Ge 50:1-3); Israelites, for Aaron thirty days (Nu 20:29).

David's lamentations over the death of Saul and his sons (2Sa 1:17-27); the death of Abner (2Sa 3:33, 34); the death of Absalom (2Sa 18:33).

Jeremiah and the singing men and singing women lament for Josiah (2Ch 35:25).

For calamities and other sorrows: Rending the garments (Ge 37:29, 34; 44:13; Nu 14:6; J'g 11:35; 2Sa 1:2, 11; 3:31; 13:19, 31; 15:32; 2Ki 2:12; 5:8; 6:30; 11:14; 19:1; 22:11, 19; Ezr 9:3, 5; Job 1:20; 2:12; Isa 37:1; Jer 41:5; M't 26:65; Ac 14:14). Wearing mourning dress (Ge 38:14; 2Sa 14:2). See Sackcloth. Cutting or plucking off the hair and beard (Ezr 9:3; Jer 7:29). See Baldness. Covering the head and face (2Sa 15:30; 19:4; Es 6:12; Jer 14:3, 4); and the upper lip (Le 13:45; Eze 24:17, 22; Mic 3:7 [marg.]). Laying aside ornaments (Ex 33:4, 6). Walking barefoot (2Sa 15:30; Isa 20:2). Laying the hand on the head (2Sa 13:19; Jer 2:37). Ashes put on the head (Eze 27:30). Dust on the head (Jos 7:6). Dressing in black (Jer 14:2). Sitting on the ground (Isa 3:26).

Caused ceremonial defilement (Nu 19:11-16; 31:19; Le 21:1). Prevented offerings from being accepted (De 26:14; Ho 9:4).

See Elegy.

MOUSE. Forbidden as food (Le 11:29); used as food (Isa 66:17). Images of (1Sa 6:4, 5, 11, 18).

MOUTH, has various connotations: literal mouth, language, opening; sometimes personified (Ps 119:108; Pr 15:14; Re 19:15).

MOWING. This was done by hand with a short sickle—originally of flint, later of metal. The king's mowings were the portion of the harvest taken by the king as taxes (Ps 76:6; 90:6; 129:7; Am 7:1).

MOZA (sunrise). 1. A son of Caleb (1Ch 2:46).

2. A Benjamite (1Ch 8:36, 37; 9:42, 43).

MOZAH, a city of Benjamin (Jos 18:26).

MUFFLER (Isa 3:19).

MULBERRY TREE (2Sa 5:23, 24; Ps 84:6 [marg.]).

MULE. Uses of: For royal riders (2Sa 13:29; 18:9; 1Ki 1:33, 38); ridden by posts (Es 8:10, 11); by saints in Isaiah's prophetic vision of the kingdom of Christ (Isa 66:20); as pack animals (2Ki 5:17; 1Ch 12:40). Tribute paid in (1Ki 10:25). Used in barter (Eze 27:14); by the captivity in returning from Babylon (Ezr 2:66; Neh 7:68); in war (Zec 14:15).

MULTITUDE FED, miraculously (Ex 16:13; Nu 11:31; 2Ki 4:43; M't 14:21; 15:38).

MUMMIFICATION (See Embalm.)

MUNITIONS, fortifications (Na 2:1).

MUPPIM, son or descendant of Benjamin (Ge 46:21). Called Shupham (Nu 26:39) and Shuppim (1Ch 7:12, 15). Shephuphan of 1Ch 8:5 may be same person.

MURDER, forbidden on penalty of death (Ge 9:4-6; Ex 21:14; Le 24:17; De 19:11-13); a murdered man's nearest relative had the duty to pursue the slayer and kill him (Nu 35:19), but the slayer could flee to a city of refuge, where he would be tried and then either turned over to the avenger or be protected (Nu 35:9-34; De 19:1-10).

MURMURING. Forbidden (1Co 10:10; Ph'p 2:14; Jas 5:9). Rebuked (Job 15:11-13; Ec 7:10; La 3:39; Ro 9:19, 20). Punishment for (Nu 14:26-37; 17:10, 11). Foolish (Pr 19:3).

Against God: Cain (Ge 4:13, 14). Moses (Ex 5:22, 23; Nu 11:11-15). Israelites (Ex 16:8, 12; 17:2, 3; Nu 11:1-10; 14; 16:41; 20:2-5; 21:5, 6; De 1:26-28; Ps 44:9-26; 106:24-26; Mal 3:14). Korah (Nu 16:8-11). Job (Job 3; 6; 7; 9; 10; 13; 16:6-14; 19:7-20; 30; 33:12, 13). David (2Sa 6:8; Ps 116:10, 11). The Psalmist (Ps 73:13-22). Elijah (1Ki 19:4, 10). Jonah (Jon 4). Jews, against Jesus (Joh 6:41-43, 52).

Against Moses: By the Israelites (Ex 5:21; 14:11, 12; 15:24; 16:2, 3; 17:2, 3; Nu 14; 16:2, 3, 14, 41; 20:2-5).

Instances of: Rachel (Ge 30:1). Asaph (Ps 73:3). Solomon (Ec 2:17, 18). Hezekiah (Isa 38:10-18). Jeremiah (Jer 20:14-18; La 3). Martha (Lu 10:40). Prodigal's brother (Lu 15:29, 30).

See Doubt; Envy; Ingratitude. See also Contentment; Resignation.

MURRAIN, a plague of Egypt (Ex. 9:3, 6; Ps 78:50 [marg.]).

MUSHI, MUSHITES, Merarite Levite;

progenitor of Mushites (Ex 6:19; Nu 3:20; 26:58; 1Ch 6:19, 47; 23:21, 23).

MUSIC. Used, at the crowning of kings (1Ki 1:39, 40; 2Ch 23:13, 18); in national triumphs (Ex 15:1-21; Nu 21:17-21; J'g 5:1-31; 11:34; 1Sa 18:6, 7); in worship (1Ch 6:31, 32; 15:16-22, 24, 27, 28; 16:4-36, 42; 23:5; 25:1-7; 2Ch 5:12, 13; 20:19, 21, 22, 28; 29:25-30; 35:15; Ezr 2:64, 65; 3:10, 11; Ne 12:27-47; Ps 33:1-3; 68:4, 25, 26, 32; 81:1-3; 87:7; 92:1-3; 95:1, 2; 98:1-8; 104:33; 105:2; 135:1-3; 144:9; 149:1-3, 6; 150:1-6; M'k 14:26; 1Co 14:15; Eph 5:19; Col 3:16; Heb 2:12); at the offering of sacrifices (2Ch 29:27, 28); in idolatrous worship (Da 3:4-7, 10, 15); for dancing (M't 11:17); in mirth (Ge 31:27; 2Sa 19:35; Job 21:12; Ec 2:8; Isa 5:12); in revelry (Am 5:12; 6:5); in mourning (2Ch 35:25); in preparing for funerals (M't 9:23).

Refrained from in sorrow (Job 30:31; Pr 25:20; Isa 16:10; 24:8, 9; Eze 26:13; Re 18:22). Captive Jews refrained from (Ps 137:1-4).

Teachers of (1Ch 15:22; 25:7, 8; 2Ch 23:13). Physical effect of, on man (1Sa 16:15, 16, 23; Eze 33:32). Precentor (Ne 12:42). Chief musician (Ne 12:42; Hab 3:19). Chambers for musicians in the temple (Eze 40:44). In heaven (Re 5:8, 9; 14:2, 3; 15:2, 3).

Allegorical (Re 5:8, 9; 14:2, 3; 15:2, 3; 18:22). Symbolic, of judgment (Isa 23:16); of God's emotions (Isa 30:29, 32; Jer 31:4).

Instruments of: Invented by, Jubal (Ge 4:21); David (1Ch 23:5; 2Ch 7:6; 29:26; Am 6:5). Made by, Solomon (1Ki 10:12; 2Ch 9:11; Ec 2:8); Tyrians (Eze 28:13).

Kinds: Cornet (Da 3:5, 7, 10. See Trumpet). Cymba or Cymbal (1Ch 15:19, 28; 1Co 13:1. See Cymbal). Dulcimer, a double pipe (Da 3:5, 10, 15). Flute (Da 3:5, 7, 10, 15). Gittith, a stringed instrument (Ps 8; 81; 84, titles). Harp (1Sa 10:5; 16:16, 23; 1Ch 16:5. See Harp). Organ, probably composed of pipes furnishing a number of notes (Ge 4:21; Job 21:12; 30:31; Ps 150:4). Pipe (1Sa 10:5; Isa 30:20. See Pipe). Psaltery (1Ch 16:5. See Psaltery). Sackbut, a harp (Da 3:5, 7, 10, 15). Tabret or Timbrel or Tambourine (Ex 15:20. See Timbrel). Trumpet (Jos 6:4. See Trumpet). Viol, a lyre (Isa 5:12; 14:11; Am 5:23; 6:5).

Symbols Used in: Alamoth. Literally *virgins.* A musical term which appears in 1Ch 15:20 and in the title of Psalm 46. It seems to indicate the rendering of the song by female voices, possibly soprano.

Al-taschith. It appears in the titles of Psalms 57, 58, 59, 75, and seems to have been used to indicate the kind of ode, or the kind of melody in which the ode should be sung.

Higgaion. In Ps 92:3, according to Gesenius, it signifies the murmuring tone of a harp, and hence that the music should be rendered in a plaintive manner. In Ps 9:16, combined with "Selah," it may have been intended to indicate a pause in the vocal music while the instruments rendered an interlude. In Ps 19:14, Mendelssohn translates it "meditation, thought." Hence that the music was to be rendered in a mode to promote devout meditation.

Mahalath, Maschil, Leannoth. These terms are found in the titles of Psalm 53 and 88. Authorities grope in darkness as to their signification. They may indicate the instruments to be played or the melody to be sung.

Maschil. This musical sign occurs in the titles of Psalms 32, 42, 44, 45, 52, 53, 54, 55, 74, 79, 88, 89, 142. The meaning is obscure. But its signification where it occurs elsewhere than in the titles of Psalms is equivalent to the English word "instruction," or to become wise by instruction; hence Ps 47:7, "Sing ye praises with understanding."

Michtam. A musical term in the titles of Psalms 16, 56, 57, 58-60. Luther interprets as "golden," that is, precious. Ewald interprets it as signifying a plaintive manner.

Muth-Labben, in the title of Psalm 9. Authorities, ancient and modern, differ as to the probable signification. Gesenius and De Wette interpret it, "with the voice of virgins, by boys." Others derive the word from a different Hebrew root, and interpret it as indicating that the Psalm was a funeral ode.

Neginah and Neginoth appear in the titles of Psalms 4, 54, 55, 61, 67, and Hab. 3:19. Its use seems to have been to indicate that the song should be accompanied by stringed instruments.

Nehiloth, in the title of Psalm 5. It seems to indicate, according to Gesenius, that when this Psalm was sung it was to be accompanied by wind instruments.

Selah. This term appears frequently in the Psalms. Its use is not known. Possibly it signified a pause in the vocal music while an instrumental interlude or finale was rendered.

Sheminith, in the titles of Psalms 5 and 12, translated "eighth," probably indicates the measure, movement, or pitch.

Shiggaion, in the title of Psalm 7, and its plural, Shigionoth, in the title of Hab 3, are supposed to have been musical terms to guide in rendering the song. At the close of the chapter the author refers the ode "to the chief musician, on my stringed instruments." The term may suggest the movement in interpreting the music set to it.

Shoshannim and Shushan-eduth, in the titles to Psalms 45, 60, 69, 80, seem to indicate the manner in which these Psalms were to be rendered. Kimchi, Tremellius, and Eichhorn render it "hexachorda," that is, that in singing these Psalms instruments of six strings were to accompany.

MUSTARD SEED. Kingdom of heaven compared to (M't 13:31, 32; M'k 4:31, 32; Lu 13:19). Faith compared to (M't 17:20).

MUSTER, of troops (1Sa 14:17; 2Sa 20:4; 1Ki 20:26; 2Ki 25:29; Isa 13:4).

See Armies.

MUTHLABBEN, expression of doubtful meaning; probably name of the tune to which Ps 9 was sung (Ps 9 title).

MUTINY, Israelites against Moses (Nu 14:4).

See Conspiracy.

MUZZLE. Mosaic law forbade muzzling of oxen when they were treading out the grain (De 25:4).

MYRA. A city of Lycia. Paul visits (Ac 27:5, 6).

MYRRH, a fragrant gum. A product of the land of Canaan (Song 4:6, 14; 5:1). One of the compounds in the sacred anointing oil (Ex 30:23). Used as a perfume (Es 2:12; Ps 45:8; Pr 7:17; Song 3:6; 5:13). Brought by wise men as a present to Jesus (M't 2:11). Offered to Jesus on the cross (M'k 15:23). Used for embalming (Joh 19:39). Traffic in (Ge 37:25; 43:11).

MYRTLE (Ne 8:15; Isa 41:19; 55:13; Zec 1:8).

MYSIA, district occupying NW end of Asia Minor bounded by the Aegean, the Hellespont, the Propontis, Bithynia, Phrygia, and Lydia. In 133 B. C. it fell to the Romans and they made it a part of the province of Asia. Traversed by Paul (Ac 16:7, 8).

MYSTERIES. Of God (De 29:29; Job 15:8; Ps 25:14; Pr 3:32; Am 3:5; Heb 5:11). Of iniquity (2Th 2:7). Of redemption (M't 11:25; 13:11, 35; M'k 4:11; Lu 8:10; Ro 16:25, 26; 1Co 2:7-10; 2Co 3:12-18; Eph 1:9, 10; 3:3-5, 9, 18, 19; 6:19; Col 1:25-27; 2:2; 4:3; 1Ti 3:9, 16; 1Pe 1:10-12; Re 10:7). Of regeneration (Joh 3:8-12).

MYSTERY RELIGIONS, a cult of certain deities which involved a private ceremonial of initiation, and a secret ritual; little is known about the rites of worship and initiation, for the initiates made vows of secrecy, but it is quite certain that the worship had to do with sin, ritual uncleanness, purification, regeneration, and spiritual preparation for another life.

N

NAAM (pleasant), son of Caleb (1Ch 4:15).

NAAMAH (pleasant). 1. Daughter of Lamech and Zillah (Ge 4:22).

2. Wife of Solomon; mother of Rehoboam (1Ki 14:21, 31).

3. Town in Judah (Jos 15:41), site unknown.

NAAMAN (pleasant). 1. Son of Benjamin (Ge 46:21).

2. Son of Bela (Nu 26:40; 1Ch 8:4).

3. Son of Ehud (1Ch 8:7).

4. A Syrian general, healed of leprosy by Elisha (2Ki 5:1-23; Lu 4:27).

NAAMATHITE, inhabitant of Naamah (Job 2:11, 11:1; 20:1; 42:9).

NAAMITES, descendants of Naaman, grandson of Benjamin (Nu 26:40).

NAARAH (a girl) 1. Wife of Ashur (1Ch 4:5f).

2. Place on border of Ephraim (Jos 16:7).

NAARAI, called also Paarai. One of David's heroes (1Ch 11:37).

NAARAN, a city in the eastern limits of Ephraim (1Ch 7:28).

NAARATH, a city on the southern boundary of Ephraim (Jos 16:7).

NAASHON, called also Naasson and Nahshon. A captain of Judah's host (Ex 6:23; Nu 1:7; 2:3; 7:12, 17; 10:14). In the lineage of Christ (M't 1:4; Lu 3:32).

NABAL (fool), rich sheepmaster of Maon in Judah who insulted David and was saved from vengeance by his wife Abigail, who after Nabal's death became David's wife (1Sa 25:1-42).

NABATEA, NABATEANS, Arabian tribe named in Apocrypha but not in Bible. Their king Aretas IV controlled Damascus when Paul was there (2Co 11:32). Capital was Petra.

NABONIDAS, NABONIDUS, last ruler of Neo-Babylonian Empire (556-539 B.C.); his son Belshazzar (Da 5; 7:1; 8:1) was co-regent with him from the 3rd year of his reign.

NABOPOLASSAR, first ruler of the Neo-Babylonian Empire (626-605 B.C.). Allied with Medes and Scythians, he overthrew the Assyrian Empire, destroying Nineveh in 612 B. C., as prophesied by Zep 2:13-15.

NABOTH, a Jezreelite. His vineyard forcibly taken by Ahab; stoned at the instigation of Jezebel (1Ki 21:1-19). His murder avenged (2Ki 9:21-36).

NACHON, NACON, Benjamite at whose threshing floor Uzzah was smitten for touching the ark (2Sa 6:6). Called "Chidon" in 1Ch 13:9.

NACHOR, grandfather of Abraham; in genealogy of Jesus (Lu 3:34).

NADAB. 1. Son of Aaron (Ex 6:23). Called to Mount Sinai with Moses and Aaron to worship (Ex 24:1, 9, 10). Set apart to priesthood (Ex 28:1, 4, 40-43). Offers strange fire to God; and is destroyed (Le 10:1, 2; Nu 3:4; 26:61). Is buried (Le 10:4, 5). His father and brothers forbidden to mourn (Le 10:6, 7).

2. Son and successor of Jeroboam (1Ki 14:20). His wicked reign: murdered by Baasha (1Ki 15:25-31).

3. Great-grandson of Jerahmeel (1Ch 2:28, 30).

4. A Benjamite (1Ch 8:30; 9:36).

NAGGAI, NAGGE, ancestor of Christ (Lu 3:25).

NAHALIEL, a station of the Israelites (Nu 21:19).

NAHALLAL, called also Nahalal and Nahalol. A Levitical city (Jos 19:15; 21:35; J'g 1:30).

NAHAM (comfort), descendant of Judah through Caleb (1Ch 4:19).

NAHAMANI, a Jewish exile (Ne 7:7).

NAHARAI, NAHARI, Beerothite, Joab's armor-bearer (2Sa 23:37).

NAHASH. 1. Ammonite king defeated by Saul (1Sa 11:1, 2; 12:12).

2. Ammonite king whose son insulted David's messengers, and David avenged the insult (2Sa 10; 1Ch 19).

3. Father of Abigail and Zeruiah (2Sa 17:25).

NAHATH. 1. Son of Reuel (Ge 36:13, 17; 1Ch 1:37).

2. Called also Toah and Tohu. A Levite (1Ch 6:26, 34; 1Sa 1:1).

3. A Levite and overseer of the sacred offerings (2Ch 31:13).

NAHBI, a prince of Naphtali, and one of the twelve spies (Nu 13:14).

NAHOR. 1. Grandfather of Abraham

(Ge 11:22-26; 1Ch 1:26). In the lineage of Christ (Lu 3:34).

2. Brother of Abraham (Ge 11:26; Jos 24:2). Marriage and descendants of (Ge 11:27, 29; 22:20-24; 24:15, 24).

NAHSHON, leader of tribe of Judah (Nu 1:7; 2:3; 10:14); sister Elisheba married Aaron (Ex 6:23, KJV "Naashon"). In genealogies of Jesus the KJV has "Naasson" (M't 1:4; Lu 3:32).

NAHUM, THE ELKOSHITE (compassionate); name is a shortened form of Nehemiah. Author of Book of Nahum; native of Elkosh; prophesied between 663 and 606 B. C. (Na 1:1; 3:8-11).

NAHUM, BOOK OF, a book predicting the downfall of Nineveh, the capital of Assyria. Written between 663 and 612 B.C. Outline: 1. Poem concerning the greatness of God (1:1-15).

2. Poem detailing the overthrow of Nineveh (2:1-3:19).

NAIL. 1. Finger-nail (De 21:12; Da 4:33; 7:19).

2. Tent-pin (J'g 4:21, 22; 5:26); peg driven in wall to hang things on (Ezr 9:8; Isa 22:23-25).

3. Nails of metal—iron, bronze, gold (1Ch 22:3; 2Ch 3:9).

NAIN, a city in Galilee. Jesus restores to life a widow's son in (Lu 7:11).

NAIOTH, place in or near Ramah of Benjamin where Samuel lived with a band of prophets (1Sa 19:18-20:1).

NAKED. 1. Without any clothing (Ge 2:25; 3:7-11).

2. Poorly clad (Job 22:6).

3. Without an outer garment (Joh 21:7). Often used figuratively for spiritual poverty (Re 3:17) and lack of power (Ge 42:9).

NAME. Value of a good (Pr 22:1; Ec 7:1). A new name given, to persons who have spiritual adoption (Isa 62:2); to Abraham (Ge 17:5); Sarah (Ge 17:15); Jacob (Ge 32:28); Peter (M't 16:18); Paul (Ac 13:9). Intercessional influence of the name of Jesus (see Jesus, In His Name).

Symbolical (Ho 1:3, 4, 6, 9; 2:1); of prestige (1Ki 1:47).

NAMES OF JESUS (See Jesus, Names of.)

NANNAR, name given at Ur to Babylonian moon-god Sin.

NAOMI. Wife of Elimelech; mother-in-law of Ruth; dwelt in Moab; returns to Bethlehem; kinswoman of Boaz (Ru 1-4).

NAPHISH, son of Ishmael; progenitor of tribe, probably the Nephushesim (Ge 25:15; 1Ch 1:31; 5:19).

NAPHTALI. 1. Son of Jacob and Bilhah (Ge 30:7, 8; 35:25). Jacob blesses (Ge 49:21). Sons of (Ge 46:24; 1Ch 7:13).

2. Tribe of. Census of (Nu 1:42, 43; 26:48-50). Position assigned to, in camp and march (Nu 2:25-31; 10:25-27). Moses' benediction on (De 33:23). Inheritance of (Jos 19:32-39; J'g 1:33; Eze 48:3).

Defeat Sisera (J'g 4:6, 10; 5:18). Follow Gideon (J'g 6:35; 7:23). Aid in conveying the ark to Jerusalem (Ps 68:27). Military operations of (1Ch 12:34, 40); against (1Ki 15:20; 2Ki 15:29; 2Ch 16:4).

Prophecies concerning (Isa 9:1, 2; Re 7:6).

NAPHTUHIM, the inhabitants of central Egypt (Ge 10:13; 1Ch 1:11).

NAPKIN, cloth for wiping off perspiration (Lu 19:20; Joh 11:44; 20:7).

NARCISSUS, a believer at Rome (Ro 16:11).

NARD (See Plants, Spikenard.)

NATHAN (God has given). 1. Prophet during reigns of David and Solomon; told David that not he but Solomon was to build the temple (2Sa 7; 1Ch 17); rebuked David for sin with Bathsheba (2Sa 12:1-25); helped get throne for Solomon (1Ki 1:8-53); wrote chronicles of reign of David (1Ch 29:29) and Solomon (2Ch 9:29); associated with David in arranging musical services for house of God (2Ch 29:25).

2. Son of David (2Sa 5:14; 1Ch 14:4).

3. Father of Igal (2Sa 23:36).

4. Judahite (1Ch 2:36).

5. Israelite who returned from exile (Ezr 8:16).

6. Man who put away foreign wife (Ezr 10:39).

NATHANAEL (God has given), disciple of Jesus (Joh 1:45-51); identified commonly with Bartholomew. Church Fathers use the two names interchangeably.

NATHAN-MELECH (king's gift), officer of Josiah (2Ki 23:11).

NATION. People divided into nations

after the flood (Ge 10:1-32). Ordained of God (Ac 17:26). Righteousness exalts (Pr 14:34).

Peace of (Job 34:29; Ps 33:12; 89:15-18). Promises of peace to (Le 26:6; 1Ki 2:33; 2Ki 20:19; 1Ch 22:9; Ps 29:11; 46:9; 72:3, 7; 128:6; Isa 2:4; 14:4-7; 60:17, 18; 65:25; Jer 30:10; 50:34; Eze 34:25-28; Ho 2:18; Mic 4:3, 4; Zec 1:11; 3:10; 8:4, 5; 9:10; 14:11). Prayer for peace (Jer 29:7; 1Ti 2:1, 2). Peace given by God (Jos 21:44; 1Ch 22:18; 23:25; Ps 147:13, 14; Ec 3:8; Isa 45:7). Instances of national peace (Jos 14:15; J'g 3:11, 30; 1Ki 4:24, 25). See War.

See Government; King; Rulers.

Involved in sins, of rulers (Ge 20:4, 9; 2Sa 24:10-17; 1Ki 15:26, 30, 34; 2Ki 24:3; 1Ch 21:7-17; Jer 15:4); of other individuals, as Achan (Jos 7:1, 11-26).

Atonement made for (2Ch 29:21). Penitent, promises to (Le 26:40-42; De 4:29-31; 5:29; 30:1-10; 2Ch 7:13, 14; Jer 3:22).

In adversity, prayer of (J'g 6:7; 10:10; 21:2-4; 2Ch 7:13, 14; Ps 74; Jer 3:21; 31:18; Joe 2:12); prayer for (Ezr 9:6-15; Ne 1:4-11; Ps 74; 84:1-7; Isa 63:7-19; Jer 6:14; 8:11, 20, 21; 9:1, 2; 14:7, 20; La 2:20-22; Da 9:3-21). See Sin, National.

Sins of (Isa 30:1, 2); chastised (Isa 14:26, 27; Jer 5:29; 18:6-10; 25:12-33; Eze 2:3-5; 39:23, 24; Da 7:9-12; 9:3-16; Ho 7:12; Joe 1:1-20; Am 9:9; Zep 3:6, 8). Perish (Ps 9:17; Isa 60:12).

Chastisement of (Le 18:24-30; 26:28; De 11:2; 2Ch 6:24, 26, 28; 7:13, 14; Ps 106:43; Jer 2:30; 30:14; 31:18-20; 46:28; La 1:5; Ho 7:12; 10:10; Hag 2:17).

Judgments denounced against, on account of its unrighteousness (De 9:5; Ps 9:17; Isa 3:4-8; 14:24-27; 19:4; 59:1-15; 60:12; Jer 2:19, 35-37; 5:6-29; 6; 9:7-26; 12:14, 17; 18:6-10; 25:12-33; 50:45, 46; 51; Eze 2:9, 10; 7; 22:12-31; 24:6-24; 33:25-29; Ho 4:1-10; 7:12, 13, 16; 13; Am 2; 3; 5; 9:8-10; Mic 6:13-16; Zep 3:8).

Instances of punishment of: The Canaanites (De 9:5). The Sodomites (Ge 19:24, 25, 28, 29; La 4:6). The Egyptians (Ex chps 7-11; 12:1-36; 14). The Israelites (2Sa 21:1; 24:14-16; 2Ki 24:2-4, 20; 2Ch 28:1, 5-8, 16-19; 29:8, 9; 30:7; 36:16-20; Ezr 9:7; Ne 9:36, 37; Jer 2:15, 16; 5:3; 30:11-15; La 1:3, 8, 14; Eze 36:16-20; 39:17-24; Joe 1:1-20; Am 4:6-11).

See Government; Kings; Ruler.

NATIONAL RELIGION. Supported by taxes (Ex 30:11-16; 38:26). Ministers of, supported by state (1Ki 18:19; 2Ch 11:13-15). Subverted by Jeroboam (1Ki 12:26-33; 2Ch 11:13-15). Idolatrous, established by Jeroboam (1Ki 12:26-33).

NATIONS BLESSED IN ABRAHAM (Ge 12:23; 18:18; 22:18; 26:4; Ac 3:25; Ga 3:8).

NATURAL RELIGION (See Religion, Natural).

NATURAL. 1. Full of sap (De 34:7).

2. Man: Sensuous (1Co 15:44). Unconverted (1Co 2:14). Birth (Jas 1:23).

NATURALIZATION. Giving rights of citizenship to aliens (Ac 22:28).

Figurative: Eph 2:12, 13, 19).

NATURE. The entire compass of one's life (Jas 3:6). The inherent character of a person or thing (Ro 1:26; 2:14; 11:21-24). Disposition (2Pe 1:4).

Laws of, uniform in operation: In the vegetable kingdom (Ge 1:11, 12; M't 7:16-18; Lu 6:43, 44; 1Co 15:36-38; Ga 6:7; Jas 3:12); animal kingdom (Ge 1:21, 24, 25; Jer 13:23); succession of seasons (Ge 8:22); succession of day and night (Ge 8:22; Jer 33:20).

NAUGHTINESS (See Sin.)

NAUM, an ancestor of Jesus (Lu 3:25).

NAVE, hub of a wheel (1Ki 7:33).

NAVEL; muscle, body (Pr 3:8); umbilical cord not cut (Eze 16:4).

NAVIGATION, sounding in (Ac 27:28). See Commerce; Mariner; Navy.

NAVY. Solomon's (1Ki 9:26); Hiram's (1Ki 10:11); of Chittim (Da 11:30, 40).

See Commerce; Mariner; Navigation.

NAZARENE, 1. Inhabitant of Nazareth (M't 2:23).

2. A Christian (Ac 24:5).

NAZARETH, a village in Galilee. Joseph and Mary dwell at (M't 2:23; Lu 1:26, 27, 56; 2:4, 39, 51). Jesus from (M't 21:11; M'k 1:24; 10:47; Lu 4:34; 18:37; 24:19). People of, reject Jesus (Lu 4:16-30). Its name opprobrious (Joh 1:46).

NAZARETH DECREE, an inscription on a slab of white marble, dating c. A.D. 40 to 50, by Claudius Caesar, found in Nazareth, decreeing capital punishment for anyone disturbing graves and tombs.

NAZIRITE, NAZARITE (consecrated), an Israelite who consecrated himself or herself and took a vow of separation and self-imposed abstinence for the purpose of some special service. The Nazirite vow included a renunciation of wine, prohibition of the use of the razor, and avoidance of contact with a dead body. The period of time for the vow was anywhere from 30 days to a lifetime (Nu 6:1-21; J'g 13:5-7; Am 2:11, 12).

Instances of: Samson (J'g 13:5, 7; 16:17). Samuel (1Sa 1:11). Rechabites (Jer 35). John the Baptist (M't 11:18; Lu 1:15; 7:33).

NEAH, a city in Zebulun (Jos 19:13).

NEAPOLIS, a seaport of Macedonia. Paul visits (Ac 16:11).

NEARIAH. 1. Son of Shemaiah (1Ch 3:22, 23).

2. A Simeonite captain (1Ch 4:42).

NEBAI, signer of the covenant with Nehemiah (Ne 10:19).

NEBAIOTH, called also Nebajoth. Son of Ishmael (Ge 25:13; 28:9; 36:3; 1Ch 1:29). Prophecies concerning (Isa 60:7).

NEBALLAT, a town occupied by the Benjamites after the captivity (Ne 11:34).

NEBAT, father of Jeroboam (1Ki 11:26; 12:2).

NEBO. 1. A city allotted to Reuben (Nu 32:3, 38; 1Ch 5:8). Prophecies concerning (Isa 15:2; Jer 48:1, 22).

2. A mountain range E of the Jordan. Moses views Canaan from (De 32:49, 50); dies on (De 34:1).

3. A city in Judah (Ezr 2:29; Ne 7:33).

4. The ancestor of certain Jews (Ezr 10:43).

5. A Babylonian idol (Isa 46:1).

NEBUCHADNEZZAR, NEBUCHADREZZAR. 1. 4th Dynasty ruler of Old Babylonian Empire (c. 1140 B. C.).

2. Ruler of Neo-Babylonian empire (605-562 B.C.); son of Nabopolassar; conquered Pharaoh Necho at Carchemish (605 B.C.); destroyed Jerusalem and carried Jews into captivity (587 B. C.) (2Ki 25:1-21); succeeded by son Evil-Merodach. Often mentioned in OT (1Ch 6:15; 2Ch 36; Ezr 1:7; 2:1; 5:12, 14; 6:5; Ne 7:6; Es 2:6; Jer 21:2; 52:4; Da 1-5).

NEBUSHASBAN (Nebo, save me), chief officer of Nebuchadnezzar (Jer 39:11-14).

NEBUZARADAN (Nebo has given seed), Nebuchadnezzar's general when the Babylonians besieged Jerusalem (2Ki 25:1, 11, 12, 20; Jer 52:12ff); conducted captives to Babylon.

NECHO, NECHOH, NECCO, pharaoh of Egypt (609-595 B. C.); defeated Josiah at battle of Megiddo (2Ki 23:29; 2Ch 35:20ff); defeated by Nebuchadnezzar at battle of Carchemish (2Ki 24:7).

NECK, term often used in Bible with literal and figurative meanings (Ex 32:9; De 9:13; Ps 75:5; Ac 7:51).

NECKLACE, ornamental chain worn around the neck (Isa 3:19).

NECROMANCER, NECROMANCY, consulting with the dead; forbidden by Mosaic law (De 18:10, 11); King Saul consulted with Witch of Endor (1Sa 28:7-25).

Judgment upon (Isa 8:19; 29:4). See Sorcery; Witchcraft.

NEDABIAH, sons of Jeconiah (1Ch 3:18).

NEEDLE (M't 19:24; M'k 10:25; Lu 18:25).

NEEDLE'S EYE, expression used by Jesus in M't 19:24. He meant that it is absurd for a man bound up in his riches to expect to enter the kingdom of God.

NEEDLEWORK, art of working in with the needle various kinds of colored threads in cloth (J'g 5:30; Ps 45:14).

NEESING. Elizabethan English for "sneezing" or "snoring" (Job 41:18).

NEGEB (dry), the desert region lying to the S of Judea, sometimes translated "the south" (Ge 12:9; 13:1; 20:1; Nu 13:29; 1Sa 27:5f).

NEGINOTH (See Music.)

NEHELAMITE, designation of Shaiah, a false prophet (Jer 29:24, 31, 32).

NEHEMIAH (Jehovah has comforted). 1. Leader of Jews who returned with Zerubbabel (Ezr 2:2; Ne 7:7).

2. Son of Azbuk; helped rebuild walls of Jerusalem (Ne 3:16).

3. Son of Hachaliah; governor of Persian province of Udah after 444 B. C.; cupbearer to King Artaxerxes of Persia (Ne 1:11; 2:1); rebuilt walls of Jerusalem

(Ne 1:4-6); cooperated with Ezra in numerous reforms (Ne 8); nothing known of the end of his life.

NEHEMIAH, BOOK OF. Closes history of the Biblical period. Closely allied to the Book of Ezra, it was attached to it in the old Jewish reckoning. Gives the history and reforms of Nehemiah the governor from 444 to c. 420 B. C. Outline:

1. Nehemiah returns to Jerusalem (1; 2).
2. Building despite opposition (3: 1-7:4).
3. Genealogy of the first returning exiles (7:5-73).
4. Revival and covenant sealing (8:1-10:39).
5. Dwellers at Jerusalem and genealogies (11:1-12:26).
6. Dedication of the walls (12:27-47).
7. Final reforms (13:1-31).

NEHILOTH, musical term found in title to Ps 5. May mean "wind instrument."

NEHUM, chief of Judah who returned with Zerubbabel; also called "Rehum" (Ezr 2:2; Ne 7:7).

NEHUSHTA, wife of Jehoiakim, king of Judah, and mother of Jehoiachin (2Ki 24:6, 8).

NEHUSHTAN, the brazen serpent (2Ki 18:4).

NEIEL, a landmark on the boundary of Asher (Jos 19:27).

NEIGHBOR. Defined (Lu 10:25-37). Duty to, defined in Golden Rule (M't 7:12). Love worketh no ill to (Ro 13:10). Love for, enjoined (Le 19:18; M't 19:19; 22:39; M'k 12:31-33; Lu 10:25-37; Ro 13:9, 10; Ga 5:14; Jas 2:8, 9). Kindness to, enjoined (Ex 23:4, 5; De 22:1-4; Isa 58:6, 7; Ga 6:10). Charitableness toward, enjoined (Ro 15:2). Benevolence toward, enjoined (Pr 3:28, 29). Righteous treatment of, enjoined (Zec 8:16, 17). Honesty toward, enjoined (Le 19:13).

Kindness to, rewarded (Isa 58:8-14; M't 25:34-46). Righteous treatment of, rewarded (Ps 15:1-3). False witness against, forbidden (Ex 20:16; Le 19:16). Hatred of, forbidden (Le 19:17). Oppression of, denounced (Jer 22:13). Penalty for violation of the rights of (Le 6:2-5).

See Duty; Man.

NEKEB, a city in Naphtali (Jos 19:33).

NEKODA, head of a family of Nethinim who could not prove Israelitish descent (Ne 7:50, 62; Ezr 2:60).

NEMUEL. 1. Brother of Dathan and Abiram (Nu 26:9).

2. Son of Simeon (Ge 46:10; Nu 26:12; 1Ch 4:24). "Jemuel" is a variant.

NEOPHYTES (M'k 4:33; Joh 16:4, 12; 1Ch 3:1, 2; 8:9).

NEPHEG (sprout, shoot). 1. Brother of Korah, Dathan, and Abiram (Ex 6:21).

2. Son of David (2Sa 5:15; 1Ch 3:7; 14:6).

NEPHEW, grandson (J'g 12:14), descendant (Job 18:19; Isa 14:22), grandchild (1Ti 5:4).

NEPHILIM, antediluvians (Ge 6:4); aboriginal dwellers in Canaan (Nu 13:32, 33); not angelic fallen beings (De 1:28).

NEPHISH (See Naphish.)

NEPHISHESIM, a family of the Nephinim (Ne 7:52).

NEPHTHALIM (See Naphtali.)

NEPHTOAH (an opening), spring and town on border of Judah and Benjamin (Jos 15:9; 18:15); two miles NW of Jerusalem; modern Lifta.

NEPHUSIM, variant reading of Nephishesim (Ezr 2:50).

NEPOTISM. Of Joseph (Ge 47:11, 12). Of Saul (1Sa 14:50). Of David (2Sa 8:16; 19:13). Of Nehemiah (Ne 7:2).

NER (lamp). 1. Father of Abner (1Sa 14:50; 26:14).

2. Grandfather of King Saul (1Ch 8:33).

NEREUS, a Christian at Rome (Ro 16:15).

NERGAL, Babylonian deity of destruction (2Ki 17:30).

NERGAL-SHAREZER, the name of princes of Babylon (Jer 39:3, 13).

NERI, an ancestor of Jesus (Lu 3:27).

NERIAH (whose lamp is Jehovah), father of Baruch (Jer 32:12).

NERIGLISSAR (See Nergal-Sharezer.)

NERO, 5th Roman emperor (A. D. 54-68); killed many Christians when Rome burned in A. D. 64; called "Caesar" in Ac 25:11; Ph'p 4:22.

NEST. Bird's (Nu 24:21; M't 8:20). Birds stir (De 32:11).

NET. Of checker work (1Ki 7:17). Hidden in a pit (Ps 35:7, 8). Set for birds (Pr 1:17); wild animals (Isa 51:20). Fish caught in (M't 4:18-21; 13:47; Lu 5:4; Joh 21:6-11).

See Snare.

Figurative: Job 18:8; 19:6; Ps 9:15; 10:9; 25:15; 31:4; 35:7, 8; 57:6; 66:11; 140:5, 141:10; Pr 12:12; 29:5; Ec 7:26; 9:12; Isa 19:8; Eze 26:5, 14; 47:10; Ho 7:12.

NETHANEEL (God has given). 1. The prince of Issachar. Numbers the tribe (Nu 1:8). Captain of the host of Issachar (Nu 2:5; 10:15). Liberality of, for the tabernacle (Nu 7:18-23).

2. A priest and doorkeeper for the ark (1Ch 15:24).

3. A Levite (1Ch 24:6).

4. Son of Obed-edom, and porter of the temple (1Ch 26:4).

5. A prince sent by Jehoshaphat to teach the law in the cities of Judah (2Ch 17:7).

6. A Levite (2Ch 35:9).

7. A priest who divorced his Gentile wife (Ezr 10:22).

8. A priest (Ne 12:21).

9. A Levite and musician (Ne 12:36).

NETHANIAH (whom Jehovah gave). 1. Father of Ishmael (2Ki 25:23, 25; Jer 40:8, 14, 15; 41:1, 2, 6, 7, 9-12).

2. A singer, and chief of the temple musicians (1Ch 25:2, 12).

3. A Levite appointed by Jehoshaphat to accompany the princes who were to teach the law in Judah (2Ch 17:8).

4. Father of Jehudi (Jer 36:14).

NETHINIM (given ones), large group of servants who performed menial tasks in the temple (1Ch 9:2; Ezr 2:43-58; 8:17-20; Ne 7:46-56); probably descended from Midianites (Nu 31:47), Gibeonites (Jos 9:23), and other captives. They are usually listed with priests, Levites, singers, and porters (Ezr 2:70).

NETOPHAH, NETOPHATHITES, village of Judah and its inhabitants; c. three miles S of Jerusalem (2Sa 23:28, 29; 1Ch 2:54; 9:16; Ne 12:28).

NETTLES, an obnoxious plant (Pr 24:31; Isa 34:13).

Figurative: Job 30:7; Ho 9:6; Zep 2:9.

NETWORK, white cloth (Isa 19:9), ornamental carving upon pillars of Solomon's temple (1Ki 7:18, 42), a grate for the great altar of burnt-offerings at the tabernacle (Ex 27:4; 38:4).

NEW BIRTH, THE. The corruption of human nature requires (Joh 3:6; Ro 8:7, 8). None can enter heaven without (Joh 3:3).

Effected by: God (Joh 1:13; 1Pe 1:3). Christ (1Joh 2:29). The Holy Ghost (Joh 3:6; Tit 3:5).

Through the Instrumentality of: The word of God (Jas 8:18; 1Pe 1:23). The resurrection of Christ (1Pe 1:3). The ministry of the gospel (1Co 4:15). Is of the will of God (Jas 1:18). Is of the mercy of God (Tit 3:5). Is for the glory of God (Isa 43:7).

Described As: A new creation (2Co 5:17; Ga 6:15; Eph 2:10). Newness of life (Ro 6:4). A spiritual resurrection (Ro 6:4-6; Eph 2:1, 5; Col 2:12; 3:1). A new heart (Eze 36:26). A new spirit (Eze 11:19; Ro 7:6). Putting on the new man (Eph 4:24). The inward man (Ro 7:22; 2Co 4:16). Circumcision of the heart (De 30:6, w Ro 2:29; Col 2:11). Partaking of the divine nature (2Pe 1:4). The washing of regeneration (Tit 3:5). All saints partake of (Ro 8:16, 17; 1Pe 2:2; 1Jo 5:1).

Produces: Likeness to God (Eph 4:24; Col 3:10). Likeness to Christ (Ro 8:29; 2Co 3:18; 1Jo 3:2). Knowledge of God (Jer 24:7; Col 3:10). Hatred of sin (1Jo 3:9; 5:18). Victory over the world (1Jo 5:4). Delight in God's law (Ro 7:22).

Evidenced by: Faith in Christ (1Jo 5:1). Righteousness (1Jo 2:29). Brotherly love (1Jo 4:7). Connected with adoption (Isa 43:6, 7; Joh 1:12, 13). The ignorant cavil at (Joh 3:4). Manner of effecting—Illustrated (Joh 3:8). Preserves from Satan's devices (1Jo 5:18).

NEW CREATURE (See Regeneration.)

NEW MOON. Feast of (Nu 10:10; 28:11-15; 1Ch 23:31; 2Ch 31:3). Traffic at time of, suspended (Am 8:5).

NEW TESTAMENT, a collection of 27 documents regarded by the church as inspired and authoritative, consisting of four Gospels, the Acts of the Apostles, 21 epistles, and the Book of Revelation. All were written during the apostolic period, either by apostles or by men closely associated with apostles. The Gospels tell the story of the coming of the Messiah, the 2nd person of the Trinity, to become the Saviour of the world; the Acts of the Apostles, describe the beginnings and growth of the church;

the epistles set forth the significance of the person and work of Christ; while the Book of Revelation tells of the consummation of all things in Jesus Christ. The formation of the NT canon was a gradual process, the Holy Spirit working in the church and guiding it to recognize and choose those Christian books God wanted brought together to form the Christian counterpart of the Jewish OT. By the end of the 4th century the NT canon was practically complete.

NEW THINGS (Isa 42:9; 43:19; 48:6; 65:17; 2Co 5:17; Re 21:5).

NEW YEAR (See Feasts, Feast of Trumpets.)

NEZIAH (sincere), one of the Nethinim (Ezr 2:54; Ne 7:56).

NEZIB, a city in Judah (Jos 15:43).

NIBHAZ, an idol (2Ki 17:31).

NIBSHAN, a city of Judah (Jos 15:62).

NICANOR, a deacon of the church at Jerusalem (Ac 6:5).

NICODEMUS (victor over the people), Pharisee; member of the Sanhedrin; came to Jesus at night for conversation (Joh 3); spoke up for Jesus before Sanhedrin (Joh 7:25-44); brought spices for burial of Jesus (Joh 19:39-42).

NICOLAITANS (Re 2:6, 15).

NICOLAS (conqueror of the people), a proselyte of Antioch, and deacon of the church at Jerusalem (Ac 6:5, 6).

NICOPOLIS (city of victory), city of Epirus situated on Gulf of Actium, founded by Augustus Caesar (Tit 3:12).

NIGER (black), surname of Symeon, leader of the church at Antioch (Ac 13:1-3).

NIGHT (Ge 1:5, 16, 18). Meditations in (Ps 19:2; 77:6; 119:148; 139:11). Worship in (Ps 134:1). Jesus prays all night (Lu 6:12). No night in heaven (Re 21:25; 22:5).

Divided into watches (Ex 14:24; J'g 7:19; 1Sa 11:11; Ne 12:9; Ps 63:6; 119:148; La 2:19; M't 14:25; Lu 12:38). Divided into hours (Ac 23:23). Used figuratively (Isa 15:1; 21:11, 12; Joh 9:4; Ro 13:12; 1Th 5:5).

NIGHT HAWK, forbidden as food (Le 11:16; De 14:15).

NILE (meaning not certainly known), main river of Egypt and of Africa, 4,050 miles long; in the KJV usually called "The River," but never the "Nile"; begins at Lake Victoria and flows northward to the Mediterranean; annual overflow deposits rich sediment which makes N Egypt one of the most fertile regions in the world. Moses was placed on the Nile in a basket of bulrushes; turning of the Nile into blood was one of the 10 plagues (Ex 7:20, 21); on its bank grows the papyrus reed from which the famous papyrus writing material is made. Also called "Sihor" in KJV (Isa 23:3).

NIMRAH (limpid, flowing water), a city in Gad (Nu 32:3).

NIMRIM, waters on the borders of Gad and Moab (Isa 15:6; Jer 48:34).

NIMROD, son of Cush. "A mighty hunter before the Lord" (Ge 10:8, 9; 1Ch 1:10). Founder of Babylon. (See Babylon.)

NIMRUD, ancient Calah in Assyria, founded by Nimrod.

NIMSHI, father of Jehu (2Ki 9:2, 20).

NINEVEH. Capital of the Assyrian empire (Ge 10:11, 12). Contained a population of upwards of one hundred and twenty thousand when Jonah preached (Jon 4:11). Extent of (Jon 3:4). Sennacherib in (2Ki 19:36, 37; Isa 37:37, 38). Jonah preaches to (Jon 1:1, 2; 3). Nahum prophesies against (Na 1-3); Zephaniah foretells the desolation of (Zep 2:13-15).

NISAN, the first month in the Jewish calendar.

(See Month.)

NISROCH, an idol (2Ki 19:36, 37; Isa 37:37, 38).

NITER, mixture of washing and baking sodas found in deposits around alkali lakes of Egypt. Used to make soap (Jer 2:22; Mal 3:2).

NO (city of the god Amon), capital of Upper Egypt, c 400 miles S of Cairo; fuller name, "No-amon," (Jer 46:25); classical writers called it Thebes.

NOADIAH (with whom Jehovah meets). 1. Levite who returned to Jerusalem after exile (Ezr 8:33).

2. False prophetess who tried to terrorize Nehemiah (Ne 6:14).

NOAH (rest) 1. Son of Lamech (Ge 5:28; 29); righteous in a corrupt age (Ge 6:8, 9; 7:1; Eze 14:14); warned people of Flood 120 years (Ge 6:3); built ark (Ge 6:12-22); saved from flood with wife and family, together with beasts and fowl of every kind (Ge 7:8); repeopled earth (Ge 9:10); lived 950 years. "Noe" in M't 24:37; Lu 3:36.

2. Daughter of Zelophehad (Nu 26:33; 27:1; 36:11; Jos 17:3).

NOB. A city of Benjamin (Ne 11:31, 32). Called "the city of the priests" (1Sa 22:19). Abode of Ahimelech, the priest (1Sa 21:1; 22:11). Probable seat of the tabernacle in Saul's time (1Sa 21:4, 6, 9). David flees to, and is aided by Ahimelech (1Sa 21:1-9; 22:9, 10). Destroyed by Saul (2Sa 22:19). Prophecy concerning (Isa 10:32).

NOBAH (barking). 1. Manassite; took Kenath from Amorites (Nu 32:42).

2. Town near which Gideon defeated Midianites (J'g 8:11).

NOBAI (See Nebai.)

NOBLEMAN, one belonging to a king (Joh 4:46-53); or one well born (Lu 19:12-27).

NOD (wandering), region E of Eden to which Cain went (Ge 4:16).

NODAB, tribe of Arabs, probably Ishmaelites E of the Jordan (1Ch 5:19).

NOE (See Noah.)

NOGAH (brilliance), son of David (1Ch 3:7; 14:6).

NOHAH (rest), son of Benjamin (1Ch 8:2).

NOLLE PROSEQUI, of the complaint against Paul (Ac 18:12-17).

NON (See Nun.)

NONCONFORMITY. See Church and State; Form; Formalism.

NONE LIKE GOD (Ex 8:10; 15:11; De 33:26; 2Sa 7:22; 1Ki 8:23; 1Ch 17:20; Ps 89:6; Isa 40:18; M'k 12:32).

NONRESISTANCE. Enjoined (M't 5:38-41; Ro 12:17-21; 1Th 5:15; 1Pe 2:19-23). Forgive those who wrong you (M't 18:15, 21-35; Lu 6:36, 37; Eph 4:32; Jas 2:13; 1Pe 3:9). Love your enemies (Ex 23:4, 5; Job 31:29, 30; Pr 25:21, 22; M't 5:43-48; M't 6:14, 15; Lu 6:27-36; 10:30-37; Ro 12:17-21; 13:10; 1Jo 3:10, 11). Return good for evil (Pr 15:1; 25:21, 22; M't 5:38-41; 6:14, 15; Ro 12:17-21; 1Th 5:15; 1Pe 3:9). Seek peace (Ps 34:14; 133:1-3; M't 5:9; 18:15; 2Co 13:11; Ga 5:22; Col 3:12, 13; Heb 12:14; Jas 3:17, 18; 1Pe 3:11). Suffer gladly for Christ (M't 5:10-12; Lu 6:22, 23; Joh 15:20; Ac 5:41; Ro 12:14; 1Co 4:12, 13; 13:7; Ga 5:22; Col 3:12, 13; 1Pe 2:19-23; 3:14).

Christ our example (Lu 23:34; 1Pe 2:19-23; 1Jo 2:6). Exemplified by Stephen (Ac 7:60).

See Revenge; Good for Evil; Evil for Good.

NOON (De 28:29; Job 11:17; Ps 55:17; 91:6; Isa 58:10; Ac 22:6).

NOPH. A city of Egypt (Jer 2:16). Prophecy against Jews in (Jer 44). Prophecies against (Isa 19:13; Jer 46:13-19; Eze 30:13-16).

NOPHAH, a city of Sihon (Nu 21:30).

NORTH, often merely as a point of the compass; but sometimes a particular country, usually Assyria or Babylonia (Jer 3:18; 46:6; Eze 26:7; Zep 2:13).

NOSE. Jewels for (Pr 11:22; Isa 3:21; Eze 16:12). Mutilated (Eze 23:25).

NUMBERS. Hebrews did not use figures to denote numbers. They spelled numbers out in full; from second century B.C. they used Hebrew letters of the alphabet for numbers. Numbers were often used symbolically; some had special religious significance (De 6:4; Ge 2:2; Ex 20:3-17, especially 1, 3, 7, 10, 12, 40, 70, 666, 1,000).

NUMBERS, BOOK OF, 4th book of the Pentateuch; called Numbers because Israelite fighting force was twice numbered (1:2-46; 26:2-51). Hebrew title is *In the Wilderness* because the book describes the 40-year wilderness wandering of the Israelites after the arrival at Sinai (Ex 19). Outline: 1. Additional legislation; organization of the host (1-10:11).

2. March from Sinai to Kadesh-Barnea (10:12-12:16).

3. Debacle at Kadesh (13; 14).

4. Wanderings in wilderness (15-21:11).

5. Conquest of Trans-Jordan and preparations to enter Canaan (21:12-36:13).

NUN, father of Joshua (Ex 33:11).

NURSE (Ge 24:59; 35:8; Ex 2:7; Ru 4:16; 2Ki 11:2; Isa 60:4; 1Th 2:7). Careless (2Sa 4:4).

NUT (Ge 43:11; Song 6:11).

NYMPHAS. A Christian of Laodicea. House of, used as a place of worship (Col 4:15).

O

OAK, a tree. Grew in Palestine (Ge 35:4). Absalom hung in the boughs of (2Sa 18:9, 14). Deborah buried under (Ge 35:8). Oars made of (Eze 27:6).

Figurative: Am 2:9.

OAR (Isa 33:21; Eze 27:6, 29).

OATH, a solemn qualification. Used in solemnizing covenants: Between Abraham and the king of Sodom (Ge 14:22, 23); and Abimelech (Ge 21:22, 23); between Isaac and Abimelech (Ge 26:26-29, 31). Abraham requires oath of his servant Eliezer (Ge 24:2, 3, 9). Esau confirms the sale of his birthright by (Ge 25:33). Jacob confirms the covenant between him and Laban by (Ge 31:53); requires Joseph to swear that he would bury him with his fathers (Ge 47:28-31). Joseph requires a like oath (Ge 50:25). Rahab requires an oath from the spies (Jos 2:12-14; 6:22). The Israelites confirm the covenant with the Hivites (Jos 9:3-20). Moses covenants with Caleb by (Jos 14:9). The elders of Gilead confirm their pledge to Jephthah by (J'g 11:10). The Israelites swear in Mizpeh (J'g 21:5). Ruth swears to Naomi (Ru 1:17). Boaz swears to Ruth (Ru 3:13). Saul swears to Jonathan (1Sa 19:6). Jonathan and David confirm a covenant by (1Sa 20:3, 13-17). David swears to Saul (1Sa 24:21, 22; 2Sa 21:7). Saul swears to the witch of En-dor (1Sa 28:10). David swears not to eat until the sun goes down (2Sa 3:35). Joab confirms his word by (2Sa 19:7). David swears to Bathsheba that Solomon shall be king (1Ki 1:28, 29). Solomon confirms his word by (1Ki 2:23); so also does Shimei (1Ki 2:42). Elisha seals his vow to follow Elijah by (2Ki 2:2). King of Samaria confirms his word with an (2Ki 6:31). Gehazi confirms his lie by (2Ki 5:20). Jehoiada requires an oath from the rulers (2Ki 11:4). Zedekiah violates (2Ch 36:13). Ezra requires, of the priests and Levites (Ezr 10:5, 19); so also does Nehemiah (Ne 5:12, 13). Zedekiah swears to Jeremiah (Jer 38:16). Gedaliah confirms his word by (Jer 40:9). Peter confirms his denial of Jesus by (M'k 14:71).

Attributed to God: Ge 22:16; Ps 89:35; 95:11; 105:9; 132:11; Isa 14:24; 45:23; Jer 11:5; 22:5; 49:13; 51:14; Lu 1:73; Heb 3:11, 18; 4:3; 6:13, 14, 17; 7:21, 28; Re 10:6.

Required of Christ (M't 26:63). Christ's teachings concerning (M't 23:18-22). Paul confirms certain statements by (2Co 1:23; Ga 1:20). Samuel affirms his honesty of administration by (1Sa 12:5). Written in the law of Moses (Da 9:11). Mosaic law concerning (Ex 23:1).

Used, in solemnizing testimony (Ex 22:10, 11; Nu 5:19-24; De 6:13; 10:20; 1Ki 8:31, 32; Ps 15:1-4; Heb 6:16); in confirming allegiance to sovereigns (Ec 8:2); as a result of returning to God (Jer 4:2).

Heard, in Daniel's vision (Da 12:7); in John's vision (Re 10:5, 6).

Profane: Forbidden (Ex 20:7; Le 19:12; De 5:11; M't 5:33-37; Jas 5:12). Unrighteous, forbidden (Le 19:12; Ho 4:15); punishment for (Le 6:2-5). Wicked, made by Israelites (Isa 48:1; Jer 5:2, 7; 7:8, 9); made by Herod (M't 14:7, 9; M'k 6:23, 26); made by enemies of Paul (Ac 23:12-14).

Idolatrous: (Jer 12:16).

See Covenant; False Witness; God, Profaning His Name; Perjury.

OBADIAH (servant of Jehovah). 1. Governor of Ahab's household (1Ki 18:3-16).

2. Judahite (1Ch 3:21).

3. Chief of Issachar (1Ch 7:3).

4. Son of Azel (1Ch 8:38).

5. Levite who returned from captivity (1Ch 9:16) called "Abda" in Ne 11:17.

6. Gadite soldier (1Ch 12:9).

7. Father of Ishmaiah, prince of Zebulun (1Ch 27:19).

8. Prince of Judah (2Ch 17:7).

9. Merarite Levite (2Ch 34:12).

10. Jew who returned from captivity (Ezr 8:9).

11. Priestly covenanter with Nehemiah (Ne 10:5).

12. Gate-keeper in Jerusalem (Ne 12:25).

13. Prophet who wrote Book of Obadiah.

OBADIAH, BOOK OF. 4th of the minor prophets. Subject—the destruction of Edom, which from time immemorial had been hostile to Israel. The book is undated, but a probable date is late in the 8th century B. C., during the reign of Ahaz of Judah, when Edom and the Philistines were associated in warfare against Judah (verse 19). Outline: 1. Judgment pronounced upon Edom (1-14).

2. Israel's restoration in the day of Jehovah (15-21).

OBAL, called also Ebal. A son of Joktan (Ge 10:28; 1Ch 1:22).

OBDURACY. Angers God (Ps 78:31; Isa 57:17). Warnings against (Ps 95:8-11; Heb 3:8, 15; 4:7). Punishment for (Le 26:23-25; Ps 78:31, 32; Pr 1:24-31; 29:1; Jer 3:2; Am 4:6-11).

Instances of: The antediluvians (Ge 6:3, 5, 7). Sodomites (Ge 19:14). Pharaoh (Ex 7:14, 22, 23; 8:15, 19, 32; 9:7, 12, 35; 10:20, 28; 11:10; 14:5-8). Israelites (Nu 14:22; Ne 9:28, 29; Ps 78:32; Isa 9:13, 14; Jer 2:20; 5:3; Am 4:6-12; Zec 7:11, 12). Sons of Eli (1Sa 2:22-25). Brothers of rich man (Lu 16:31). Man in the last days (Re 9:20, 21).

See Affliction, Obduracy in; Impenitence; Reprobacy.

OBED (worshiper). 1. Son of Boaz and grandfather of David (Ru 4:17-22; 1Ch 2:12; M't 1:5; Lu 3:32).

2. Son of Ephlal and grandson of Zabad (1Ch 2:37, 38).

3. One of David's heroes (1Ch 11:47).

4. Son of Shemaiah. A gatekeeper of the temple (1Ch 26:7).

5. Father of Azariah (2Ch 23:1).

OBED-EDOM (one who serves Edom). 1. A Korhite Levite. Doorkeeper of the ark (1Ch 15:18, 24; 26:4-8). David leaves ark with (2Sa 6:10; 1Ch 13:13, 14). Ark removed from (2Sa 6:12; 1Ch 15:25). Appointed to sound with harps (1Ch 15:21). Appointed to minister before the ark (1Ch 16:4, 5, 37, 38).

2. A doorkeeper of the temple (1Ch 16:38).

3. A conservator of the vessels of the temple in time of Amaziah (2Ch 25:24).

OBEDIENCE. Better than sacrifice (1Sa 15:22; Ps 40:6-9; Pr 21:3; Jer 7:22, 23; Hos 6:6; Mic 6:6-8; M't 9:13; 12:7; M'k 12:33; Heb 10:8, 9).

Enjoined (Ge 17:9; Ex 23:22; Le 19:19, 36, 37; 20:8, 22; 22:31; Nu 15:38-40; 30:2; De 4:1-40; 5:1-33; 6:1-25; 8:1-6, 11-20; 10:12, 13; 11:1-3, 8, 9, 13-28, 32; 13:4; 26:16-18; 27:1-10; 32:46; Jos 22:5; 23:6, 7; 24:14, 15; 1Sa 12:14, 20, 24; 15:22; 2Ki 17:37, 38; 1Ch 16:15; 28:9, 10, 20; Ezr 7:23; Ps 76:11; Pr 7:1; Ec 12:13; Jer 26:13; 38:20; Da 7:27; Mal 4:4; Eph 6:6-8; Ph'p 2:12; 1Ti 6:14, 18; Jas 1:22-25; 2:10-12; 1Pe 1:2, 14).

Proof of love (Joh 14:15, 21; 1Jo 2:5, 6; 5:2, 3; 2Jo 6, 9). Proof that we know God (1Jo 2:3, 4).

Vows of (Ex 24:7; Jos 24:24; Ps 119:15, 106, 109).

Justification by, under Mosaic law (Le 18:5; Eze 20:11, 13, 21; Lu 10:28; Ro 10:5; Ga 3:10, 12).

Prayer for guidance in (Ps 143:10). Cannot be rendered to two masters (M't 6:24).

Rewarded (Ge 18:19; Le 26:3-13; Nu 14:24; De 7:12-15; 28:1-15; Jos 14:6-14; 2Ki 21:8; Isa 1:19).

Rewarded, by: Prosperity (De 7:9, 12-15; 15:4; Jos 1:8; 1Ki 2:3, 4; 9:3-5; 1Ch 22:13; 28:7, 8; 2Ch 26:5; 27:6; Job 36:11; Pr 28:7; Jer 7:3-7; 11:1-5; 22:16; Mal 3:10-12; 1Jo 3:22); long life (De 4:1, 40; 32:47; 1Ki 3:14; Pr 3:1, 2; 19:16); victory over enemies (Ex 23:22; Pr 16:7); triumph over adversities (M't 7:24, 25; Lu 6:46-48); divine favor (Ex 19:5; 20:6; De 5:10; 11:26, 27; 12:28; 1Ki 8:23; Ne 1:5; Ps 25:10; 103:17, 18, 20; 112:1; 119:2; Pr 1:33; Jer 7:23; 11:4; M't 5:19; 25:20-23; Lu 11:28; 12:37, 38; Joh 12:26; 13:17; Jas 1:25; Re 22:7); fellowship with Christ (M't 12:50; M'k 3:35; Lu 8:21; Joh 14:23; 15:10, 14; 1Jo 3:24); everlasting life (M't 19:17, 29; Joh 8:51; 1Jo 2:17; Re 2:10).

Exemplified (De 33:9; Ps 1:2; 103; 1Th 1:9; Re 2:19).

By, Noah (Ge 6:9, 22; 7:5; Heb 11:7); Abraham (Ge 12:1-4; 17:23; 18:19; 21:4; 22:12, 18; 26:3-5; Ne 9:8; Ac 7:3-8; Heb 11:8-17; Jas 2:21). Bethuel and Laban (Ge 24:50); Jacob (Ge 35:1, 7); Laban (Ge 31:29); Moses (Nu 27:12-22; Heb 3:2, 3); Moses and Aaron (Ex 7:6; 40:16, 21, 23, 32); Israelites (Ex 12:28; 32:25-29; 39:42, 43; Nu 9:20, 21, 23; De 33:9; Jos 22:2; J'g 2:7; Ps 99:7); Israelites under the preaching of Haggai (Hag 1:12).

By, Caleb (Nu 14:24; De 1:36; Jos

14:6-14); Joshua (Jos 10:40; 11:15); Reubenites (Jos 22:2, 3); Gideon (J'g 6:25-28); David (1Ki 11:6, 34; 15:5; 2Ch 29:2; Ac 13:22); Elijah (1Ki 17:5).

By, the psalmist (Ps 17:3; 26:3-6; 119:30, 31, 40, 44, 45, 47, 48, 51, 54-56, 59, 60, 67, 69, 100-102, 105, 106, 110, 112, 119, 166-168); Elisha (1Ki 19:19-21); Hezekiah (2Ki 18:6; 20:3; 2Ch 31:20, 21; Isa 38:3); Josiah (2Ki 22:2; 23:24, 25); Asa (2Ch 14:2); Jehoshaphat (2Ch 17:3-6; 20:32; 22:9); Uzziah (2Ch 26:4, 5); Jotham (2Ch 27:2); Levites (2Ch 29:34); Cyrus (Ezr 1:1-4); Ezra (Ezr 7:10); Hanani (Ne 7:2); Job (Job 1:8).

By, the three Hebrews (Da 3); Jonah (Jon 3:3); Ninevites (Jon 3:5-10); Zacharias (Lu 1:6); Simeon (Lu 2:25); Joseph (M't 1:24; 2:14); Mary (Lu 1:38).

By Jesus (M't 3:15; 26:39, 42; Lu 22:42; Joh 4:32, 34; 5:30; 6:38; 8:28, 29; 9:4; 12:49, 50; 14:31; 17:4; Ph'p 2:8; Heb 3:2).

By, John the Baptist (M't 3:15); John and James (M'k 1:19, 20); Matthew (M't 9:9); Simon and Andrew (M'k 1:16-18); Levi (M'k 2:14); the rich young man (M't 19:20; M'k 10:20; Lu 18:21); the disciples (Joh 17:6; Ac 4:19, 20; 5:29); Cornelius (Ac 10:2); Paul (Ac 23:1; 24:17; 26:4, 5; Ph'p 3:7-14; 2Ti 1:3). By Paul and Timothy (2Co 1:12; 6:3). By Paul, Timothy, and Sylvanus (1Th 2:10). By the Christians at Rome (Ro 6:17).

To Civil Law: See Citizen.

Filial: See Children.

See Blessing, Contingent upon Obedience; Commandments; Duty; Faithfulness; Law.

OBEISANCE, the act of bowing low or of prostrating one's self in token of respect or submission (Ge 43:28; Ex 18:7; 2Sa 1:2).

OBIL (camel driver), an Ishmaelite. Camel keeper for David (1Ch 27:30).

OBJECT TEACHING (See Instruction.)

OBLATION (See Offering.)

OBLIGATION. A motive of obedience (De 4:32-40; chapters 6-11; 26:16; 32:6; 1Sa 12:24; 1Ch 16:12; Ro 2:4; 2Co 5:15). Acknowledgment of (Ps 116:12-14, 17).

See Duty.

OBLIQUITY, moral.

See Depravity.

OBOTH (water bags), a camping place of Israel in the forty years' wandering (Nu 21:10, 11; 33:43, 44).

OBSEQUIOUSNESS. *Instances of:* Abigail (1Sa 25:23-31, 41). Mephibosheth (2Sa 9:8). The woman of Tekoah (2Sa 14:4-20).

OBSTETRICS (Eze 16:4).

See Midwife.

OCCULT SCIENCE (See Sorcery.)

OCCUPATIONS AND PROFESSIONS: apothecary; artificer—a worker with any materials, as carpenter, smith, engraver, etc. (Ge 4:22; Isa 3:3); author; baker; barber; beggar; butler; carpenter; chamberlain, an officer to look after the personal affairs of a sovereign; clerk; confectioner, a female perfumer or apothecary (1Sa 8:13); coppersmith; counselor; doctor of the law (Ac 5:34, 40); diviner, one who obtains or seems to obtain secret knowledge, particularly of the future; dyer; farmer; fisherman; fuller, one who washed or bleached clothing (2Ki 18:17; Isa 7:3); herdsman; hunter; judge; lawyer (M't 22:35; Lu 7:30); magician; mason; musician; nurse; physician; plowman; porter—a gatekeeper; potter; preacher; priest; prophet (-ess); publican—collector of Roman revenue; rabbi—teacher of Jewish law; recorder; robber; ruler; sailor; saleswoman (Ac 16:14); schoolmaster; scribe; seer; senators—elders of Israel (Ps 105:22); sergeant—Roman lictors who attended the chief magistrates when they appeared in public (Ac 16:35, 38); servant; servitor; sheepmaster; sheep-shearer; shepherd; silversmith; singer; slave; smith; soldier; sorcerer; spinner; steward; tanner; taskmaster; tax collector; teacher; tentmaker; tetrarch; tiller; town clerk; treasurer; watchman; weaver; wizard; writer.

OCRAN, an Asherite and the father of Pagiel who numbered Israel (Nu 1:13; 2:27; 10:26).

ODED (he has restored). 1. A prophet in Samaria (2Ch 28:9).

2. Father of the prophet Azariah (2Ch 15:1).

ODOR, pleasant or unpleasant smell (Ge 8:21; Le 1:9-17; Joh 11:39). Also used figuratively (Re 5:8).

OFFENSE, used in a variety of ways: injury, hurt, damage, occasion of sin, stumbling block, infraction of law, sin, transgression, state of being offended.

OFFERINGS. Holy (Le 2:3; 6:17, 25, 27, 29; 7:1, 6; 10:12; Nu 18:9, 10). Offered at door of the tabernacle (Le 1:3; 3:2; 17:4, 8, 9); of the temple (1Ki 8:62; 12:27; 2Ch 7:12).

All animal sacrifices, must be eight days old or over (Le 22:27); must be without blemish (Ex 12:5; 29:1; Le 1:3, 10; 22:18-22; De 15:21; 17:1; Eze 43:23; Mal 1:8, 14; Heb 9:14; 1Pe 1:19); must be salted (Le 2:13; Eze 43:24; M'k 9:49); accompanied with leaven (Le 7:13; Am 4:5); without leaven (Ex 23:18; 34:25); eaten (1Sa 9:13). Ordinance relating to scapegoat (Le 16:7-26). Atonement for sin made by (See Atonement).

Figurative: Ps 51:17; Jer 33:11; Ro 12:1; Ph'p 4:18; Heb 13:15.

Animal Sacrifices: A type of Christ (Ps 40:6-8, w Heb 10:1-14; Isa 53:11, 12, w Le 16:21; Joh 1:29; 1Co 5:7; 2Co 5:21; Eph 5:2; Heb 9:19-28; 10:1, 11, 12; 13:11-13; Re 5:6).

Burnt: (Le 9:2). Its purpose was to make an atonement for sin (Le 1:4; 7). Ordinances concerning (Ex 29:15-18; Le 1; 5:7-20; 6:9-13; 17:8, 9; 23:18, 26-37; Nu 15:24, 25; 19:9; 28:26-31; 29). Accompanied by other offerings (Nu 15:3-16). Skins of, belonged to priests (Le 7:8). Offered daily, morning and evening (Ge 15:17; Ex 29:38-42; Le 6:20; Nu 28; 29:6; 1Ch 16:40; 2Ch 2:4; 13:11; Ezr 3:3; Eze 46:13-15). Music with (Nu 10:10).

Offered, by Noah (Ge 8:20); in idolatrous worship (Ex 32:6; 1Ki 18:26; 2Ki 10:25; Ac 14:13). For cleansing leprosy (Le 14).

Daily: Sacrificial (Ex 29:38-42; Le 6:20; Nu 28:3-8; 29:6; 1Ki 18:29; 1Ch 16:40; 2Ch 2:4; 13:11; Ezr 3:3-6; 9:4, 5; Ps 141:2; Eze 46:13-15; Da 9:21, 27; 11:31).

Drink: Libations of wine offered with the sacrifices (Ge 35:14; Ex 29:40, 41; 30:9; Le 23:13, 18; Nu 6:17; 15:24; 28:5-15, 24-31; 29:6-11, 18-40; 2Ki 16:13; 1Ch 29:21; 2Ch 29:35; Ezr 7:17).

Free Will: (Le 23:38; Nu 29:39; De 12:6; 2Ch 31:14; Ezr 3:5). Must be perfect (Le 22:17-25). To be eaten, at tabernacle (De 12:17, 18); by priests (Le 7:16, 17). With meat and drink offerings (Nu 15:1-16). Obligatory (De 16:10); when signified in a vow (De 23:23).

Heave: Given to the priests' families as part of their emoluments (Le 10:14; Nu 5:9; 18:10-19, 24). Consecrated by being elevated by the priest (Ex 29:27). Consisted of the right thigh or hind quarter (Ex 29:27, 28; Le 7:12-14, 32, 34; 10:15); spoils, including captives and other articles of war (Nu 31:29, 41). When offered (Le 7:12-14; Nu 6:20; 15:19-21). In certain instances this offering was brought to the tabernacle, or temple (De 12:6, 11, 17, 18). To be offered on taking possession of the land of Canaan (Nu 15:18-21).

Human Sacrifices: Forbidden (Le 18:21; 20:2-5; De 12:31). Offered by Abraham (Ge 22:1-19; Heb 11:17-19); by Canaanites (De 12:31); Moabites (2Ki 3:27); Israelites (2Ki 16:3; 2Ch 28:3; 2Ki 23:10; Isa 57:5; Jer 7:31; 19:5; 32:35; Eze 16:20, 21; 20:26, 31; 23:37, 39); by the Sepharvites to idols (2Ki 17:31). To demons (Ps 106:37, 38); and to Baal (Jer 19:5, 6).

Insufficiency of (Heb 8:7-13; 9:1-15; 10:1-12, 18-20). Unavailing, when not accompanied by piety (1Sa 15:22; Ps 40:6; 50:8-14; 51:16, 17; Pr 21:3, 27; Isa 1:11-14; 66:3; Jer 6:20; 7:21-23; 14:12; Hos 6:6; 8:13; Am 5:21-24; Mic 6:6-8; M't 9:13; 12:7; M'k 12:33).

Meat (RV Meal, but better stated food offering, as it provided food for the priests): Ordinances concerning (Ex 29:40, 41; 30:9; 40:29; Le 2; 5:11, 12; 6:14-23; 7:9-13, 37; 9:17; 23:13, 16, 17; Nu 4:16; 5:15, 18, 25, 26; 8:8; 15:3-16, 24; 18:9; 28:5, 9, 12, 13, 20, 21, 26-31; 29:3, 4, 14). To be eaten in the holy place (Le 10:13; Nu 18:9, 10). Offered with animal sacrifices (Nu 15:3-16). Not mixed with leaven (Le 2:4, 11; 6:14-18; 10:12, 13; Nu 6:15, 17). Storerooms for, in the temple (Ne 12:44; 13:5, 6); provided for in the vision of Ezekiel (Eze 42:12).

Peace: Laws concerning (Ex 20:24; 24:5; Le 3:6; 7:11-18; 9:3, 4, 18-22; 19:5; 23:10; Nu 6:14; 10:10). Offered, by the princes (Nu 7:17; 23:29, 35, 41, 47, 53, 59, 65, 71, 77, 83, 88); by Joshua (Jos 8:31); by David (2Sa 6:17; 24:25).

Offered in idolatrous worship (Ex 32:6). Offered by harlots (Pr 7:14).

Sin: Ordinances concerning (Ex

29:10-14 w Heb 13:11-13; Le 4; 5; 6:1-7, 26-30; 9:1-21; 12:6-8; 14:19, 22, 31; 15:30; 23:19; Nu 6:10, 11, 14, 16; 8:8, 12; 15:27; 28:15, 22-24, 30; 29:5, 6, 11, 16-38). Temporary (Da 11:31; Heb 9, 10).

Special Sacrifices: In consecration of the altar (see Altar); of priests (see Priests); of the temple (see Temple, dedication of); for leprosy (see Leprosy); for defilement (see Defilement).

Thank: Ordinances concerning (Le 7:11-15; 22:29; De 12:11, 12).

Trespass: Ordinances concerning (Le 5; 6:1-7; 7:1-7; 14:10-22; 15:15, 29, 30; 19:21, 22; Nu 6:12; Ezr 10:19). To be eaten by the priests (Le 7:6, 7; 14:13; Nu 18:9, 10). Offered by idolaters (1Sa 6: 3, 8, 17, 18). See Sin Offering, above.

Vow: Le 7:16, 17; 22:17-25; De 23:21-23.

Wave: Ordinances concerning (Ex 29:22, 26-28; Le 7:29-34; 8:25-29; 9:19-21; 10:14, 15; 23:10, 11, 17, 20; Nu 5:25; 6:19, 20). Belonged to the priests (Ex 29:26-28; Le 7:31, 34; 8:29; 9:21; 23:20; Nu 18:11, 18). To be eaten (Le 10:14, 15; Nu 18:11, 18, 19, 31).

Wood: Fuel for the temple (Ne 10:34; 13:31).

OFFICER. *Civil:* Chosen by the people (De 1:13-16); appointed by kings (2Sa 8:16-18; 20:23-26; 1Ki 4:1-19; 9:22; Ezr 7:25).

See Government; Judge; Ruler.

Ecclesiastical: See Priest; Levite; Apostle; Elder; Deacon; Minister.

OFFSCOURING, contemptuous word for sweepings, scraps, filth, dung, etc. (La 3:45; 1Co 4:13).

OG, king of Bashan. A man of gigantic stature (Nu 21:33; De 3:11; Jos 12:4; 13:12). Defeated and slain by Moses (Nu 21:33-35; De 1:4; 3:1-7; 29:7; 31:4; Jos 2:10; 9:10; Ps 135:10, 11; 136:18-20). Land of, given to Gad, Reuben, and Manasseh (Nu 32:33; De 3:8-17; 4:47-49; 29:7, 8; Jos 12:4-6; 13:12, 30, 31; 1Ki 4:19; Ne 9:22; Ps 136:20, 21).

OHAD, son of Simeon (Ge 46:10; Ex 6:15).

OHEL (tent), son of Zerubbabel (1Ch 3:20).

OHOLAH, OHOLIBAH, symbolic names for Samaria and Jerusalem (Eze 23 RSV).

OIL. Sacred (Ex 30:23-25; 31:11; 35:8, 15, 28; 37:29; 39:38; Nu 4:16; 1Ch 9:30). Punishment for profaning (Ex 30:31-33). Used for idols (Eze 23:41). Illuminating, for tabernacle (Ex 25:6; 27:20; Le 24:2-4). For domestic use (M't 25:3). Used for food (Le 2:4, 5; 14:10, 21; De 12:17; 1Ki 17:12-16; Pr 21:17; Eze 16:13; Ho 2:5). For the head (Ps 23:5; 105:15; Lu 7:46). For anointing kings (1Sa 10:1; 16:1, 13; 1Ki 1:39).

Tribute paid in (Ho 12:1). Commerce in (2Ki 4:1-7).

Petroleum [?] (Job 29:6).

See Anointing; Ointment.

OIL TREE (See Plants.)

OINTMENT. *Not Sacred:* 2Ki 20:13; Es 2:12; Ec 7:1; 10:1; Song 1:3; 4:10; Am 6:6; M'k 14:3-5; Joh 12:3-5. The alabaster box of (M't 26:7).

Sacred: Formula for (Ex 30:23-25). Uses of (Ex 30:26-33). Compounded by Bezaleel (Ex 37:1, 29).

See Oil, Sacred.

OLD AGE. Wise (1Ki 12:6-8; 2Ch 10:6-8; Job 12:12). Devout (Lu 2:37). Exemplary, enjoined (Tit 2:2, 3). Deference toward (Le 19:32; Job 32:4-9). Righteous, is glorious (Pr 16:31). Wasted, is bitter (Ge 47:9; Ec 6:3, 6; 12:1-7).

Promised to the righteous (Ge 15:15; Job 5:26; Ps 34:12-14; 91:14, 16; Pr 3:1, 2). God's care in (Isa 46:4). Psalmist prays not to be forsaken in (Ps 71:9, 18). David enjoys (1Ch 29:28).

Infirmities in (2Sa 19:34-37; Ps 90:10). Vigor in (De 34:7; Ps 92:12-14). Join in praise to the Lord (Ps 148:12, 13).

Paul, the aged (Ph'm 9). See Longevity; Infirmities.

OLD GATE, gate in NW corner of Jerusalem in Nehemiah's time (Ne 3:6).

OLD TESTAMENT. Bible from Genesis to Malachi; composed of 39 books—five of law, 12 of history, five of poetry, five of major prophets, and 12 of minor prophets. Classification of our present Hebrew Bibles is different—five of law, eight of prophets, and 11 of miscellaneous writings; these 24 contain all our 39 books. All of these books were regarded by Israelites as Scripture, inspired and authoritative, before the first century A.D. They appeared over a period of c.

1000 years. The authors of many of them are unknown.

OLIVE, a fruit tree. Branch of, brought by the dove to Noah's ark (Ge 8:11). Common to the land of Canaan (Ex 23:11; De 6:11; 8:8); Israelites commanded to cultivate in the land of promise (De 28:40). Branches of, used for booths (Ne 8:15). Bears flowers (Job 15:33). Precepts concerning gleaning the fruit of (De 24:20; Isa 17:6). Cherubim made of the wood of (1Ki 6:23, 31-33). Fable of (J'g 9:8).

Figurative: Of prosperity (Ps 128:3). The wild, a figure of the Gentiles; the cultivated, of the Jews (Ro 11:17-21, 24).

Symbolical: Zec 4:2-12; Re 11:4.

Fruit of: Oil extracted from, used as illuminating oil in the tabernacle (Ex 39:37; Le 24:2; Zec 4:12). See Oil.

OLIVES, MOUNT OF, (called Olivet in two KJV contexts: 2Sa 15:30; Ac 1:12). A ridge, c. 1 mile long, with four identifiable summits, E of Jerusalem, beyond the Valley of Jehoshaphat, through which flows the Kidron stream. Gethsemane, Bethphage, and Bethany are on its slopes (2Sa 15:30; Zec 14:4; M't 21:1; 24:3; 26:30; M'k 11:1; 13:3; 14:26; Lu 19:29, 37; 22:39; Joh 8:1; Ac 1:12).

OLIVET (See Olives, Mount of.)

OLYMPAS, a believer at Rome (Ro 16:15).

OMAR, son of Eliphaz, grandson of Esau (Ge 36:11, 15; 1Ch 1:36).

OMEGA, Alpha and Omega, the all-comprehensiveness of Christ (Re 1:8, 11; 21:6; 22:13).

OMER, one-tenth part of an ephah. A dry measure containing, according to the Rabbins, two quarts, but according to Josephus, three and one-half quarts (Ex 16:16-18, 36).

OMNIPOTENCE, the attribute of God which describes His ability to do whatever He wills. He cannot do anything contrary to His nature as God, such as to ignore sin, to sin, or to do something absurd or self-contradictory. God is not controlled by His power, but has complete control over it; otherwise He would not be a free being. Although the word "omnipotence" is not found in the Bible, the Scriptures clearly teach the omnipotence of God (Job 42:2; Jer 32:17; M't 19:26; Lu 1:37; Re 19:6).

See God, Omnipotent; Jesus, Power of.

OMNIPRESENCE, the attribute of God by virtue of which He fills the universe in all its parts and is present everywhere at once. Not a part, but the whole of God is present in every place. The Bible teaches the omnipresence of God (Ps 139:7-12; Jer 23:23, 24; Ac 17:27, 28). This is true of all three members of the Trinity.

See God, Omnipresent.

OMNISCIENCE, the attribute by which God perfectly and eternally knows all things which can be known, past, present, and future. God's omniscience is clearly taught in Scripture (Ps 147:5; Pr 15:11; Isa 46:1).

See God, Omniscience of; Jesus, Omniscience of.

OMRI. 1. King of Israel. Was commander of the army of Israel, and was proclaimed king by the army upon news of assassination of King Elah (1Ki 16:16). Defeats his rival, Tibni, and establishes himself (1Ki 16:17-22). Surrendered cities to king of Syria (1Ki 20:34). Wicked reign and death of (1Ki 16:23-28). Denounced by Micah (Mic 6:16).

2. Son of Becher, grandson of Benjamin (1Ch 7:8).

3. A descendant of Pharez (1Ch 9:4).

4. Son of Michael, and ruler of tribe of Issachar in time of David (1Ch 27:18).

ON. 1. Capital of lower Egypt (Ge 41:45; 46:20).

2. A leader of the Reubenites who rebelled against Moses (Nu 16:1).

ONAM (strong), a son of Shobal (Ge 36:23; 1Ch 1:40).

2. Son of Jerahmeel (1Ch 2:26, 28).

ONAN (strong), son of Judah. Slain for his refusal to raise seed to his brother (Ge 38:4, 8-10; 46:12; Nu 26:19; 1Ch 2:3).

ONE ANOTHER. Responsibilities of fellow believers to (1Pe 4:7-10). All believers members of (Ro 12:5; Eph 4:25).

Enjoined to: Admonish (Ro 15:14; Col 3:16 w 2Th 3:15). Assemble together with (Heb 10:24). Bear burdens of (Ga 6:2). Comfort (1Th 4:18; 5:11 w 14). Confess faults to (Jas 5:16). Consider above self (Heb 10:24). Be courteous (1Pe 3:8). Edify (Ro 14:18; 1Th 5:11).

Encourage (Heb 10:24). Equality with (Ro 12:16; 15:5, 7; 1Co 11:33; 12:25; Ph'p 2:3). Exhort daily (Heb 3:13). Have fellowship with (1Jo 1:7). Forgive (Eph 4:32; Col 3:13). Do good to (1Th 5:15). Be hospitable to (1Pe 4:9); in greeting (Ro 16:16; 1Co 16:20; 2Co 13:12; 1Pe 5:5). Be kind to (Eph 4:32). Love (Joh 13:34, 35; 15:12, 17; Ro 12:10; 13:8; 1Co 12:25; Ga 5:13; Eph 4:2, 32; 1Th 3:12; 4:9; 1Pe 1:22; 2:17; 3:8; 1Jo 3:11, 23; 4:7, 11, 12; 2Jo 5). Minister to (1Pe 4:10). Be patient with (Eph 4:2; Col 3:13). Be at peace with (M't 9:50; 1Th 5:13). Pray for (Jas 5:16). Prefer (Ro 12:10; Ph'p 2:3; 1Ti 5:21). Provoke to love and good works (Heb 10:24). Serve (Ga 5:13; 1Pe 4:10); by washing feet of (Joh 13:14). Be subject to (1Pe 5:5); husband and wife, each to be subject to (Eph 5:21). Teach (Col 3:16). Wait for (1Co 11:33).

Not to: Deceive (1Co 7:5); devour and consume (Ga 5:15); do evil to (1Th 5:5); envy (Ga 5:26); grudge (Jas 5:9); judge (Ro 14:13); lie to (Le 19:11; Col 3:9); owe anything to (Ro 13:8); provoke (Ga 5:26); speak evil of (Jas 4:11).

Love of, exemplified (2Th 1:3).

ONE GOD (De 4:35; 6:4; 32:39; 2Sa 7:22; 1Ch 17:20; Ps 83:18; 86:10; Isa 43:10; 44:6; 45:18; M'k 12:29; 1Co 8:4; Eph 4:6; 1Ti 2:5; 1Jo 5:7).

ONESIMUS (profitable), runaway slave of Philemon of Colossae; converted through Paul, who wrote Epistle to Philemon in his behalf (Col 4:9; Ph'm).

ONESIPHORUS (profit-bringer), a Christian of Ephesus (2Ti 1:16, 17; 4:19).

ONION (Nu 11:5).

ONLY-BEGOTTEN, title applied to our Lord by John (Joh 1:14, 18; 3:16, 18; 1Jo 4:9) and once in Hebrews (11:17) in connection with His uniqueness.

ONO (strong), town in Benjamin, c. 6 miles SE of Joppa (1Ch 8:12; Ne 6:2; 11:35).

ONYCHA, a component of the sacred ointment, made from the shells of a species of mussel, possessing an odor (Ex 30:34).

ONYX. Precious stone (Job 28:16; Eze 28:13). Used in erecting the temple (1Ch 29:2). Seen in the foundations of the city of the New Jerusalem in John's apocalyptic vision (Re 21:20). Exported from Havilah (Ge 2:12). Used in the breastplate (Ex 28:9-12, 20; 39:6, 13). Contributed by Israelites for the priests' garments (Ex 25:7; 35:9).

OPHEL (hill), a gate in the wall of the city and the temple (2Ch 27:3; 33:14; Ne 3:26, 27).

OPHIR. 1. Son of Joktan (Ge 10:29; 1Ch 1:23).

2. A country celebrated for its gold and other valuable merchandise. Products of, used by Solomon and Hiram (1Ki 9:28; 10:11; 2Ch 8:18; 9:10). Jehoshaphat sends ships to, which are wrecked (1Ki 22:48). Gold of, proverbial for its fineness (1Ch 29:4; Job 22:24; 28:16; Ps 45:9; Isa 13:12).

OPHNI, a town of the Benjamites (Jos 18:24).

OPHRAH (hind). 1. A city in Benjamin (Jos 18:23; 1Sa 13:17). Possibly identical with Ephrain (2Ch 13:19); and Ephraim (Joh 11:54).

2. A city in Manasseh, home of Gideon (J'g 6:11, 24; 8:27, 32; 9:5).

3. Son of Meonothai (1Ch 4:14).

OPINION, *Public.* Kings influenced by. (See Kings.) Jesus inquires about (M't 16:13; Lu 9:18). Feared by Nicodemus (Joh 3:2); Joseph of Arimathaea (Joh 19:38); the parents of the man who was born blind (Joh 9:21, 22); rulers, who believed in Jesus, but feared the Pharisees (Joh 12:42, 43); chief priests, who feared to answer the questions of Jesus (M't 21:26; M'k 11:18, 32; 12:12); and to further persecute the disciples (Ac 4:21; 5:26).

Concessions to: By Paul, in circumcising Timothy (Ac 16:3). James and the Christian elders, who required Paul to observe certain rites (Ac 21:18-26). Disciples, who urged circumcision (Ga 6:12). Peter and Barnabas with others (Ga 2:11-14).

See Prudence.

Corrupt Yielding to: By Herod, in the case of John the Baptist (M'k 6:26); of Peter (Ac 12:3); by Peter, concerning Jesus (M't 26:69-75); by Pilate (M't 27:23-27; M'k 15:15; Lu 23:13-25; Joh 18:38, 39; 19:4-16); by Felix and Festus, concerning Paul (Ac 24:27; 25:9).

OPPORTUNITY. Providential (1Co 16:9; 2Co 2:12). Neglected (Lu 12:47).

Spurned (Pr 1:24, 25; M't 23:34-38; Lu 14:16-24). Lost (Nu 14:40-43; Pr 1:28; Jer 8:20; Hos 5:6; M't 24:50, 51; 25:1-10, 24-28 w Lu 19:20-24; Lu 13:25-28).

Terrible consequences, of neglecting (Eze 3:19; M't 25:3-13, 24-30, 41-46); of spurning (Pr 1:24-32; M't 10:14, 15; 11:20-24).

The measure of responsibility (Pr 1:24-30; Jer 8:20; Eze 3:19; 33:1-17; Ho 5:6; M't 10:14, 15; 11:20-24; 23:34-48; 25 w Lu 19:20-24; Lu 12:47; 13:25-28; 14:16-24).

See Judgment, According to Opportunity and Works; Responsibility.

OPPRESSION. God, a refuge from (Ps 9:9; 12:5). Prayer for deliverance from (Ps 17:8, 9; 44:24; 74:21; 119:121, 134; Isa 38:14). Oppressors punished (Job 27:13-23; Ps 72:4; 103:6; Isa 10). Seeming hopelessness under (Ec 4:1). Forbidden (Ex 22:21-24; De 23:15, 16; 24:14, 15; Pr 22:22; Zec 7:10). Warning, against (Ps 62:10; Eze 45:9; Jas 2:6); to relieve (Isa 1:17).

God's aid promised against (Ps 12:5; 72:4, 14; Isa 58:6; Jer 50:34). God will judge (Ps 10:17, 18; 103:6; Ec 5:8; Isa 10; Jer 21:12; 22:17; Eze 22:7; Am 4:1; Mic 2:2; Hab 2:5-11; Mal 3:5; Jas 5:4). God will reward those who fight against (Isa 33:15, 16).

National, God judges (Ac 7:7); relieved (Ex 3:9; 12:30-39; De 26:7, 8; J'g 2:14; 6; 7; 8; 10; 11; 2Ki 13; Isa 52:4).

Proverbs concerning (Pr 3:31; 14:31; 22:16, 22; 28:3; 30:14; Ec 4:1; 5:8; 7:7).

Instances of: Hagar, by Sarah (Ge 16:6). Jacob, by Laban (Ge 31:39). Israelites, by Egyptians (Ex 1:10-22; 5); by Assyrians (Isa 52:4). Rehoboam resolves to oppress the Israelites (1Ki 12:14). Strangers and the poor and needy, by Israelites (Eze 22:29; Am 5:11, 12; 8:4-6). Of people, by the scribes and Pharisees (M't 23:2-4).

ORACLE. 1. An utterance from deity (2Sa 16:23).

2. Utterance of prophecy, translated "burden" (Isa 14:28; 15:1; Eze 12:10; Na 1:1).

3. Holy of Holies in the temple (1Ki 6:5f).

ORACLES. Scriptures called (Ac 7:38; Ro 3:2; Heb 5:12; 1Pe 4:11).

ORATOR. 1. Isa 3:3 (KJV) has "eloquent orator," where ASV correctly reads "skilful enchanter."

2. A public speaker, esp. an advocate (Ac 24:1). *Instances of:* Jonah (Jon 3:4-10). The Apostles (Ac 2:1-41). Tertullus (Ac 24:1). Apollos (Ac 18:24-28).

Instances of: Judah (Ge 44:18-44); Aaron (Ex 4:14-16). Moses (De chps 1-4:40). Jonah (Jon 3:4-10). Peter (Ac 2:14-40; 3:12-26; 4:8-12; 10:34-48; 11:4-17). Stephen (Ac 7:2-60). Paul and Barnabas (Ac 14:14-17). Paul (Ac 13:16-41; 17:22-31; 22:1-21; 24:10-21; 26:1-29; 27:21-25). James (Ac 15:13-21). Apollos (Ac 18:24-28). Herod (Ac 12:21). Tertullus (Ac 24:1). The town-clerk (Ac 19:35-41).

ORDINANCE. A decree (Ex 12:14, 24, 43; 13:10; 15:25; Nu 9:14; 10:8; 15:15; 18:8; Isa 24:5; Mal 4:4; Ro 13:2; 1Pe 2:13).

Insufficiency, in salvation (Isa 1:10-17; Ga 5:6; 6:15; Eph 2:15; Col 2:14, 20-23; Heb 9:1, 8-10).

See Form; Formalism.

ORDAIN, ORDINATION, act of conferring a sacred office upon someone, as: deacons (Ac 6:6); missionaries (Ac 13:3); elders (Ac 14:23). OT priests were ordained to office (Ex 28:41; 29:9).

Instances of: Priests (Ex 29:1-9, 19-35; 40:12-16; Le 8:6-35; Heb 7:21). Apostles (M'k 3:14). Ministers, the seven deacons (Ac 6:5, 6); Paul and Barnabas (Ac 13:2, 3); Timothy (1Ti 4:14).

OREB (raven). 1. A prince of Midian, overcome by Gideon and killed by the Ephraimites (J'g 7:25; 8:3; Ps 83:11).

2. A rock E of the Jordan, where Oreb was slain (J'g 7:25; Isa 10:26).

OREN (cedar), son of Jerahmeel (1Ch 2:25).

ORGAN (See Music, Instruments of.)

ORION, the constellation of (Job 9:9; 38:31; Isa 13:10; Am 5:8).

ORNAMENT (See Dress.)

ORNAN, Jebusite prince (called "Araunah" in 2Sa 24:16ff) whose threshing-floor David purchased (1Ch 21:15-25).

ORONTES, chief river in Syria, almost 400 miles long, rises in Anti-Lebanon range, and flows N for most of its course.

ORPAH (neck), daughter-in-law of Naomi (Ru 1:4, 14).

ORPHAN. To be visited (Jas 1:27). Beneficent provision for (De 14:28, 29; 16:10, 11, 14; 24:19-22; 26:12, 13). Kindness toward (Job 29:12, 13; 31:16-18, 21). God the friend of (Ex 22:22-24; De 10:18; Ps 10:14, 17, 18; 27:10; 68:5; 146:9; Pr 23:10, 11; Jer 49:11; Ho 14:3; Mal 3:5). Justice to, required (De 24:17-22; 27:19; Ps 82:3; Isa 1:17, 23; Jer 7:6, 7; 22:3). Oppressed (Job 6:27; 22:9; 24:3, 9; Isa 10:1, 2; Jer 5:28).

See Adoption; Children; Widow.

Instances of: Lot (Ge 11:27, 28). Daughters of Zelophehad (Nu 27:1-5). Jotham (J'g 9:16-21). Mephibosheth (2Sa 9:3). Joash (2Ki 11:1-12). Esther (Es 2:7). A type of Zion in affliction (La 5:3).

OSEE, Hoshea, so called (Ro 9:25).

OSHEA (See Joshua.)

OSNAPPAR (See Ashurbanipal.)

OSPREY, a carnivorous bird. Forbidden as food (Le 11:13; De 14:12).

OSSIFRAGE, a carnivorous bird. Forbidden as food (Le 11:13; De 14:12).

OSTENTATION, in prayer and almsgiving (M't 6:1; Pr 25:14; 27:2).

OSTIA, the port of Rome, on the Tiber mouth, some 16 miles from the city.

OSTRACA, inscribed fragments of pottery, or potsherds. Some important ancient documents have come down to us in this form (e.g. the Lachish Letters).

OSTRICHES (Job 39:13-18; La 4:3; Isa 13:21; 34:13; 43:20). The cry of (Mic 1:8). In *A. V.* occurs the word owl, but in the *R. V.*, the word ostrich (Le 11:16; De 14:15; Job 30:29; Isa 43:20; Jer 50:39; Mic 1:8).

OTHNI, son of Shemaiah (1Ch 26:7).

OTHNIEL, son of Kenaz and nephew of Caleb. Conquers Kirjath-sepher, and as reward secures Caleb's daughter to wife (Jos 15:16-20; J'g 1:12, 13). Becomes deliverer and judge of Israel (J'g 3:8-11). Death of (J'g 3:11). Descendants of (1Ch 4:13, 14).

OUCHES. 1. Settings for precious stones on high-priest's ephod (Ex 28:11).

2. A rich texture inwrought with gold thread or wire (Ps 45:13).

OUTCASTS, general references to (Isa 11:12; 16:3; 27:13; Jer 30:17).

OVEN; ancient ovens were primitive— often a hole in the ground coated with clay and in which a fire was made. The dough was spread on the inside and baked. Sometimes ovens were made of stone, from which the fire is raked when the oven is very hot, and into which the unbaked loaves are placed (Ex 8:3; Le 2:4; 7:9; 11:35; 26:26; Ho 7:4-7).

Figurative: Ps 21:9; Mal 4:1; M't 6:30; Lu 12:28.

OVERCOMING (See Perseverance.)

OVERSEER; inspector (Ge 39:4, 5), foreman (2Ch 2:18), bishop, overseer (Ac 20:28).

OWL, a carnivorous bird. Unclean (Le 11:16, 17; De 14:16). In *R. V.* ostrich is substituted (Le 11:16; De 14:15; Job 30:29; Isa 13:21; 34:11, 13; 43:20; Jer 50:39; Mic 1:8).

OWNER OF A SHIP, ship-owner or the sailing-master of a ship engaged in state service (Ac 27:11).

OX (See Bullock; Cattle.)

OX GOAD, pointed stick used to urge the ox to further effort (J'g 3:31).

OZEM. 1. Son of Jesse (1Ch 2:15).

2. Son of Jerahmeel (1Ch 2:25).

OZIAS, a form given to the name of King Uzziah (M't 1:8, 9).

See Uzziah.

OZNI, son of God and father of the Oznites (Nu 26:16).

P

PAARAI (devotee of Peor). One of David's valiant men (2Sa 23:35). Called Naarai in 1Ch 11:37.

PACK ANIMALS, used for transporting army supplies (1Ch 12:40).

PADAN-ARAM (plain of Aram), region near head of fertile crescent; sometimes called simply "Mesopotamia"; in Ge 48:7, "Padan" only (Ge 31:18).

PADON (redemption), one of the Nethinim (Ezr 2:44; Ne 7:47).

PAGIEL (a meeting with God), son of Ocran and leader of the tribe of Asher at time of exodus (Nu 1:13; 2:27; 7:72, 77; 10:26).

PAHATH-MOAB (governor of Moab), the ancestor of an influential family of Judah, which returned to Jerusalem from the captivity (Ezr 2:6; 10:30; Ne 3:11; 7:11).

PAI. A city in Edom (1Ch 1:50). Called Pau in Ge 36:39.

PAIN. Experienced on earth (Job 14:22; 30:17, 18; La 3:5; Re 16:10). Chastens (Job 33:19). None in Heaven (Re 21:4).

See Afflictions.

PAINTING. Around the eyes, to enlarge their appearance (2Ki 9:30; Jer 4:30; Eze 23:40). Of rooms (Jer 22:14). Of portraits (Eze 23:14).

See Picture.

PALACE. For kings (1Ki 21:1; 2Ki 15:25; Jer 49:27; Am 1:12; Na 2:6). Of David (2Sa 7:2). Of Solomon (1Ki 7:1-12). At Babylon (Da 4:29; 5:5; 6:18). At Shushan (Ne 1:1; Es 1:2; 7:7; Da 8:2). Archives kept in (Ezr 6:2). Proclamations issued from (Am 3:9).

Figurative: Of a government (Am 1:12; 2:2; Na 2:6).

PALAL (he judges). Son of Uzai. One of the workmen in rebuilding the walls of Jerusalem (Ne 3:25).

PALE HORSE, symbol of death (Re 6:8).

PALESTINE. The name is derived from Philistia, an area along the S seacoast occupied by the Philistines (Ps 60:8); original name was Canaan (Ge 12:5); after the conquest it came to be known as Israel (1Sa 13:19), and in the Greco-Roman period, Judea. The land was c. 70 miles wide and 150 miles long, from the Lebanon mts. in the N to Beersheba in the S. The area W of the Jordan was 6,000 miles; E of the Jordan, 4,000 miles. In the N, from Acco to the Sea of Galilee, the distance is 28 miles. From Gaza to the Dead Sea in the S the distance is 54 miles. The land is divided into five parts: the Plain of Sharon and the Philistine Plain along the coast; adjoining it, the Shepheleh, or foothills region; then the central mt. range; after that the Jordan valley; and E of the Jordan the Transjordan plateau. The varied configuration of Palestine produces a great variety of climate. The Maritime Plain has an annual average temperature of 57 degrees at Joppa; Jerusalem averages 63 degrees; while Jericho and the Dead Sea area have a tropical climate. As a result, plants and animals of varied latitudes may be found. The winter season, from Nov. to April, is mild and rainy; the summer season, from May to October, is hot and dry. Before the conquest the land was inhabited by Canaanites, Amorites, Hittites, Horites, and Amalekites. These were conquered by Joshua, judges, and kings. The kingdom was split in 931 B.C.; the N kingdom was taken into captivity by the Assyrians in 722 B.C.; the S kingdom by the Babylonians in 587 B.C. From 587 B.C. to the time of the Maccabees the land was under foreign rule by the Babylonians, Persians, Alexander the Great, Egyptians, and Syrians. In 63 B. C. the Maccabees lost control of the land to the Romans, who held it until the time of Mohammed. In NT times Palestine W of the Jordan was divided into Galilee, Samaria, and Judea; and E of the Jordan into the Decapolis and Perea.

PALLU (distinguished), called also Phallu. Son of Reuben (Ge 46:9; Ex 6:14; Nu 26:5, 8; 1Ch 5:3).

PALM TREE. Deborah judged Israel under (J'g 4:5). Wood of, used in the temple (1Ki 6:29, 32, 35; 2Ch 3:5). In the temple seen in the vision of Ezekiel (Eze 40:16; 41:18). Branches of, thrown in the way when Jesus made his triumphal entry into Jerusalem (Joh

12:13). Jericho was called the City of Palm Trees (De 34:3).

Figurative: Of the prosperity of the righteous (Ps 92:12). Used as a symbol of victory (Re 7:9).

PALMER WORM, probably a kind of locust (Joe 1:4; 2:25; Am 4:9).

PALSY (See Paralysis.)

PALTI (God delivers). 1. Spy from Benjamin (Nu 13:9); "Phalti" in KJV of 1Sa 25:44.

2. Man to whom Saul gave Michal, David's wife (1Sa 25:44).

PALTIEL (God delivers). 1. Prince of Issachar (Nu 34:26).

2. Once "Phaltiel" in KJV (2Sa 3:15), the same as Palti 2.

PALTITE (delivered), one of David's mighty men (2Sa 23:26); "Pelonite" in 1Ch 11:27; 27:10.

PAMPHYLIA. A province in Asia Minor. Men of, in Jerusalem (Ac 2:10). Paul goes to (Ac 13:13, 14; 14:24). John, surnamed Mark, in (Ac 13:13; 15:38). Sea of (Ac 27:5).

PANIC. In armies (Le 26:17; De 32:30; Jos 23:10; Ps 35:5). From God (Ge 35:5; Ex 15:14-16; J'g 7:22; 1Sa 14:15-20; 2Ki 7:6, 7; 2Ch 20:22, 23).

See Armies.

PANNAG, meaning uncertain; perhaps an article of trade (Eze 27:17).

PANTOMIME. By Isaiah (Isa 20:2, 3). By Ezekiel (Eze 4:1-8; 12:18). Agabus (Ac 21:11).

PAP, breast (Lu 11:27; Re 1:13).

PAPER (2Jo 12).

See Parchment.

PAPHOS. A city of Cyprus. Paul blinds a sorcerer in (Ac 13:6-13).

PAPYRUS, reed which grows in swamps and along rivers or lakes, especially along the Nile; from 8-12 feet tall; used to make baskets, sandals, boats, and especially paper—the most common writing material of antiquity. The NT books were undoubtedly all written on papyrus (Job 8:11; Isa 18:2).

PARABLE (likeness). 1. Proverbial saying (1Sa 10:12; 24:14); prophetic figurative discourse (Nu 23:7, 18, 24); poem (Nu 21:27-30; Ps 49:5; 78:2); riddle (Ps 49:4; Eze 17:2).

2. A story in which things in the spiritual realm are compared with events that could happen in the temporal realm; or, an earthly story with a heavenly meaning (M't 13; Lu 15). Differs from fable, myth, allegory, proverb. Characteristic teaching method of Jesus.

PARABLES. *Listing of:* Of the trees (J'g 9:8-15). Of the lamb (2Sa 12:1-6). Of the woman of Tekoa (2Sa 14:5-12). Of the garment rent in pieces (1Ki 11:30-32). Of the prisoner of war (1Ki 20:39-42). Of the thistle and cedar (2Ki 14:9). Of a vine of Egypt (Ps 80:8-16). Of the vineyard (Isa 5:1-7; 27:2, 3). Of the husbandman (Isa 28:23-29). Of the skins filled with wine (Jer 13:12-14). Of the two eagles (Eze 17). Of lions' whelps (Eze 19:1-9). Of Aholah and Aholibah (Eze 23). The boiling pot (Eze 24:3-5). The gourd (Jon 4:10, 11). The sheet let down from heaven in Peter's vision (Ac 10:10-16). The two covenants (Ga 4:22-31). The mercenary soldier (2Ti 2:3, 4). Husbandman (2Ti 2:6). Furnished house (2Ti 2:20, 21). The athlete (2Ti 2:5). Looking-glass (Jas 1:23-25).

See Jesus, Parables of; Symbols; Types.

PARACLETE (advocate), one who pleads another's cause. Used by Christ of the Holy Spirit in John's Gospel (14:16, 26; 15:26; 16:7) and of Christ in 1Jo 2:1.

PARADISE (park), park (Ec 2:5); forest (Ne 2:8); orchard (Song 4:13); home of those who die in Christ (Lu 23:43). Exact location uncertain.

PARADOX. Of: Wealth (Pr 13:7). Wisdom (1Co 3:18). Life (M't 10:39; 16:25; M'k 8:35; Lu 17:33; Joh 12:25). Christian life (2Co 6:4, 8-10; 12:4, 10, 11; Eph 3:17-19; Ph'p 3:7). New Jerusalem (Rev 21:18, 21).

PARAH (heifer), a city in Benjamin (Jos 18:23).

PARALLELISM, a characteristic of OT Hebrew verse, which has neither rhyme nor meter, but parallelism—the repetition in successive phrases of similar or contrasting ideas.

PARALYSIS. Cured by Jesus (M't 4:24; 8:6, 13; 9:2, 6); by Philip (Ac 8:7); Peter (Ac 9:33, 34).

PARAMOUR, male lover (Eze 23:20).

PARAN (ornamental). Desert or wilderness of (Ge 21:21; Nu 10:12; 12:16; 13:3, 26; De 1:1). Mountains of (De 33:2; Hab 3:3). Israelites encamp in (Nu 12:16).

David takes refuge in (1Sa 25:1). Hadad flees to (1Ki 11:17, 18).

PARBAR (suburb), some building on the W side of the temple area translated "suburbs" (2Ki 23:11; 1Ch 26:18).

PARCHED GROUND, mirage (Isa 35:7).

PARCHMENT (2Ti 4:13).

PARDON, forgiveness. God demands a righteous ground for pardoning the sinner—the atoning work of Christ (Ex 34:9; 1Sa 15:25, 26; Isa 55:7).

PARENTS. To be reverenced (Ex 20:12; Le 19:3; De 5:16; M't 15:4; 19:19; M'k 7:10; 10:19; Lu 18:20). Obeyed (Pr 1:8; 6:20; 23:22; Eph 6:1; Col 3:20). Covenant blessings of, entailed upon children (Ge 6:18; Ex 20:6; Ps 103:17). Curses upon, entailed upon children (Ex 20:5; Le 20:5; Isa 14:20; Jer 9:14; La 5:7). Involved in children's wickedness (1Sa 2:27-36; 4:10-18).

Fathers to rule household (Ge 18:19; Le 20:9; Pr 3:12; 13:24; 19:18; 1Ti 3:4, 5, 12; Tit 1:6; Heb 12:7); to govern with kindness (Eph 6:4; Col 3:21); a prerequisite to church leadership (1Ti 3:4, 5, 12). Mother, beloved (Pr 31:28).

Cursing of, to be punished (Ex 21:17; Le 20:9).

Beloved. By Joseph (Ge 46:29). Rahab (Jos 2:12, 13). Ruth (Ru 1:16, 17) Elisha (1Ki 19:20).

Duties of: To provide for children (2Co 12:14; 1Ti 5:8). To instruct children in righteousness (Ex 10:2; 12:27; 13:8, 14; De 4:9, 10; 6:7, 20-25; 11:18-21; 32:46; Ps 78:5, 6; Pr 22:6, 15; 27:11; Isa 38:19; Joe 1:3; Eph 6:4; 1Th 2:11). To discipline children (Pr 19:8; 22:6, 15; 23:13, 14; 29:15, 17).

Indulgent: Eli (1Sa 2:27-36; 3:13, 14); David (1Ki 1:6).

Influence of: Evil (1Ki 15:26; 22:52, 53; 2Ki 8:27; 21:20; 2Ch 21:6; 22:3). Good (1Ki 22:43; 2Ki 15:3, 34). See Influence.

Love of: Reflection of God's love (Ps 103:13; Pr 3:12; Isa 66:13 w 49:15; M't 7:9-11; Lu 11:11-13). Must be exceeded by love for Christ (M't 10:37). To be taught (Tit 2:4).

Parental affection exemplified: By Hagar (Ge 21:15, 16); Rebekah's mother (Ge 24:55); Isaac and Rebekah (Ge 25:28); Isaac (Ge 27:26, 27); Laban (Ge 31:26-28); Jacob (Ge 37:3, 4; 42:4, 38; 43:13, 14; 45:26-28; 48:10, 11); Moses' mother (Ex 2); Naomi (Ru 1:8, 9); Hannah (1Sa 2:19); David (2Sa 12:18-23; 13:38, 39; 14:1, 33; 18:5, 12, 13, 33; 19:1-6); Rizpah (2Sa 21:10); the mother of the infant brought to Solomon by the harlots (1Ki 3:22-28); Mary (M't 12:46; Lu 2:48; Joh 2:5; 19:25); Jairus (M'k 5:23); father of demoniac (M'k 9:24); nobleman (Joh 4:49).

Paternal blessings: Of Noah (Ge 9:24-27); Abraham (Ge 17:18); Isaac (Ge 27:10-40; 28:3, 4); Laban (Ge 31:55); Jacob (Ge 48:15-20; 49:1-28); reproaches (Ge 9:24, 25; 49:3-7).

Partiality of: Isaac for Esau (Ge 25:28); Rebekah for Jacob (Ge 25:28; 27:6-17); Jacob for Joseph (Ge 33:2; 37:3; 48:22); for Benjamin (Ge 42:4). See Partiality.

Prayers in behalf of children: Of Hannah (1Sa 1:27); David (2Sa 7:25-29; 1Ch 17:16-27; 2Sa 12:16; 1Ch 22:12; 29:19); Job (Job 1:5).

See Children, Instruction of.

PARENTAL BLESSINGS, very important in OT times; often prophetic of a child's future (Ge 27:4, 12, 27-29).

PARLOR (1Sa 9:22).

PARMASHTA (the very first), son of Haman (Es 9:9).

PARMENAS (constant), one of seven men chosen for daily ministration to the poor (Ac 6:5).

PARNACH, father of Elizaphan (Nu 34:25).

PAROSH (a flea), called also Pharosh. The ancestor of one of the families which returned to Jerusalem from captivity in Babylon (Ezr 2:3; 8:3; Ne 7:8; 10:14).

PAROUSIA (presence, coming), a Greek word frequently used in NT of our Lord's return (M't 24:3; 1Co 15:23; 1Th 3:13; 1Th 4:15; 2Pe 1:16); a visit of a person of high rank.

PARRICIDE (2Ki 19:37; 2Ch 32:21; Isa 37:38).

PARSHANDATHA (inquisitive), son of Haman (Es 9:7).

PARSIMONY. Of the Jews toward the temple (Hag 1:2, 4, 6, 9); toward God (Mal 3:8, 9). Punishment of (Hag 1:9-11).

See Liberality.

PARTHIANS, the inhabitants of Parthia, a country northwest of Persia (Ac 2:9).

PARTIALITY. Forbidden, among brethren (1Ti 5:21); by parents (De 21:15-17). Effects upon children (Ge 37:4). See Parents.

Instances of: Of brothers: Joseph for Benjamin (Ge 43:30, 34). Of parents: Isaac for Esau (Ge 25:25); Rebekah for Jacob (Ge 25:28; 27:6-17); Jacob, for Joseph (Ge 33:2; 37:3, 4; 48:22); for Benjamin (Ge 42:4). Of husbands: Jacob for Rachel (Ge 29:30); Elkanah for Hannah (1Sa 1:4, 5).

See Respect of Persons.

PARTICEPS CRIMINIS (2Jo 11).

See Collusion.

PARTITION, MIDDLE WALL OF, probably the wall in the temple area in Jerusalem separating the court of the Gentiles from the courts into which only Jews might enter (Eph 2:14).

PARTNERSHIP, with God (1Co 3:7, 9; 2Co 6:1; Ph'p 2:13).

See Providence.

PARTRIDGE (1Sa 26:20; Jer 17:11).

PARUAH (blooming), father of Jehoshaphat (1Ki 4:17).

PARVAIM, an unknown gold region (2Ch 3:6).

PASACH (to divide), son of Japhlet (1Ch 7:33).

PASCHAL LAMB (See Passover.)

PAS-DAMMIM (place of bloodshed). A battle between David and the Philistines, fought at (1Ch 11:13). Called Ephes-Dammim in 1Sa 17:1.

PASEAH (lame). 1. Called also Phaseah. A son of Eshton (1Ch 4:12).

2. Ancestor of a family which returned to Jerusalem from captivity in Babylon (Ezr 2:49; Ne 7:51).

3. Father of Jehoiada, probably identical with preceding (Ne 3:6).

PASHUR. 1. A priest, son of Malchiah (1Ch 9:12). An influential man, and ancestor of an influential family (Jer 21:1; 38:1; Ezr 2:38; 10:22; Ne 7:41; 10:3; 11:12).

2. Son of Immer and governor of the temple. Beats and imprisons Jeremiah (Jer 20:1-6).

3. Father of Gedaliah, who persecuted Jeremiah (Jer 38:1).

PASSAGE, ford of a river (Ge 32:23), mountain pass (1Sa 13:23), a crossing (Jos 22:11).

PASSENGER (See Commerce.)

PASSION (Ac 1:3).

See Jesus, Sufferings of.

PASSOVER. Institution of (Ex 12:3-49; 23:15-18; 34:18; Le 23:4-8; Nu 9:2-5, 13, 14; 28:16-25; De 16:1-8, 16; Ps 81:3, 5). Design of (Ex 12:21-28).

Special passover, for those who were unclean, or on journey, to be held in second month (Nu 9:6-12; 2Ch 30:2-4). Lamb killed by Levites, for those who were ceremonially unclean (2Ch 30:17; 35:3-11; Ezr 6:20). Strangers authorized to celebrate (Ex 12:48, 49; Nu 9:14).

Observed at place designated by God (De 16:5-7); with unleavened bread (Ex 12:8, 15-20; 13:3, 6; 23:15; Le 23:6; Nu 9:11; 28:17; De 16:3, 4; M'k 14:12; Lu 22:7; Ac 12:3; 1Co 5:8). Penalty for neglecting to observe (Nu 9:13).

Reinstituted by Ezekiel (Eze 49:21-24).

Observation of, renewed by the Israelites on entering Canaan (Jos 5:10, 11); by Hezekiah (2Ch 30:1); by Josiah (2Ki 23:22, 23; 2Ch 35:1, 18); after return from captivity (Ezr 6:19, 20). Observed by Jesus (M't 26:17-20; Lu 22:15; Joh 2:13, 23; 13). Jesus in the temple at time of (Lu 2:41-50). Jesus crucified at time of (M't 26:2; M'k 14:1, 2; Joh 18:28). The lamb of, a type of Christ (1Co 5:7). Lord's supper ordained at (M't 26:26-28; M'k 14:12-25; Lu 22:7-20).

Prisoner released at, by the Romans (M't 27:15; M'k 15:6; Lu 23:16, 17; Joh 18:39). Peter imprisoned at time of (Ac 12:3).

Christ called our passover (1Co 5:7).

See Feasts.

PASSPORTS, given to Nehemiah (Ne 2:7-9).

PASTOR (Jer 22:22).

See Shepherd.

PASTORAL EPISTLES. A common title for 1 and 2 Timothy and Titus, which were written by the apostle Paul to his special envoys sent on specific missions in accordance with the needs of the hour. 1 Timothy was written to Timothy at Ephesus while Paul was still traveling in the coastal regions of the Aegean Sea; Titus was written to Titus in Crete, probably from Nicopolis or some other city in Macedonia; 2 Timothy, from Romè toward the end of the second imprisonment. The epistles concern church organization and discipline, including such matters as the appointment of bishops and deacons, the opposition of heretical or rebellious members, and the provision for maintenance of doctrinal purity.

The authorship of these Epistles has been disputed because of differences in vocabulary and style from the other epistles ascribed to Paul, and because their references to his travels do not accord with the itineraries described in Acts. The differences though real, have been exaggerated, and can be explained on the basis of a change of time, subject-matter, and destination. These are letters written by an old man to his understudies and successors at the close of his career, and for churches that have passed the pioneering stage. The historical references can be fitted into Paul's biography if he were released from the first imprisonment mentioned in Acts, and if he resumed traveling before his final imprisonment and execution. There is no theological discrepancy between the Pastorals and the other epistles, for while these emphasize good works, they emphasize also salvation by faith (Tit 3:5).

Background: Released from the first imprisonment, Paul left Titus on Crete to organize the churches (Tit 1:5) and went to Ephesus, where he stationed Timothy (1Ti 1:3, 4). Proceeding to Macedonia, he wrote to Timothy and Titus. Evidently Paul had visited the Ionian cities just before his last arrest, for he mentions Troas, Corinth, and Miletus (2Ti 4:13, 20). He had been deserted by most of his friends (4:10, 11) and had already stood trial once (4:16).

Outlines: 1 Timothy: 1. Personal Testimony (1:1-20);

2. Official Regulations (2:1-4:5);

3. Administrative Counsel (4:6-6:21).

Titus: 1. Church Administration (1:1-16);

2. Individual Conduct (2:1-3:8);

3. Personal Advice (3:9-15).

2Timothy: 1. Memories of the Past (1:1-18);

2. Mandate for the Future (2:1-26);

3. Menace of Apostasy (3:1-17);

4. Memoranda for Action (4:1-22).

PATARA, a Lycian city in Asia Minor. Visited by Paul (Ac 21:1, 2).

PATHROS, a part of Upper Egypt, Jewish captives in (Isa 11:11; Jer 44:1, 15; Eze 29:14). Prophecy against (Eze 30:14).

PATHRUSIM, a descendant of Mizraim and ancestor of the Philistines (Ge 10:14; 1Ch 1:12).

PATHS, RIGHT (Ps 16:11; 23:3; 25:10; 119:35; Pr 2:9; 4:11, 18; Isa 2:3; 26:7; Heb 12:13).

PATHWAY OF SIN. General References to (Pr 2:15; 12:15; 13:15; 14:12; 15:9; Isa 49:8; M't 7:13). Walking in (De 29:19; Jer 7:24; Eph 2:2; Ph'p 3:18; 1Pe 4:3; 2Pe 2:10; 3:3; Jude 18).

PATIENCE. Commended (Ec 7:8, 9; La 3:26, 27). Enjoined (Ps 37:7-9; Eph 4:2; Col 3:12, 13; 1Th 5:14; 1Ti 6:11; 2Ti 2:24, 25; Tit 2:2; Heb 12:1; Jas 5:7, 8; 2Pe 1:5, 6). A fruit of tribulation (Ro 5:3, 4; Re 1:9). A grace of the righteous (Lu 8:15; 21:19; Ro 2:7; 8:25; 12:12; 15:4, 5; 1Co 13:4, 5; 2Co 6:4-6; 12:12; Col 1:10, 11; 1Th 1:3; 2Th 3:5; Heb 6:12; 10:36; Jas 1:3, 4, 19; 1Pe 2:19-23; Re 14:12). Prerequisite of a bishop (1Ti 3:2). Propagates peace (Pr 15:18). Possible because of God's righteousness (Re 13:10).

Instances of: Isaac toward the people of Gerar (Ge 26:15-22). Moses (Ex 16:7, 8). Job (Job 1:21; Jas 5:11). David (Ps 40:1). Simeon (Lu 2:25). Paul (2Ti 3:10). Prophets (Jas 5:10). The Thessalonians (2Th 1:4). The church at Ephesus (Re 2:2, 3); and Thyatira (Re 2:19). John (Re 1:9).

Of Jesus (1Pe 2:21-23; Re 1:9). See Jesus.

See Longsuffering; Meekness.

PATMOS, an island in the Agean Sea. John an exile on (Re 1:9).

PATRIARCHS, PATRIARCHAL AGE, name given in NT to those who founded the Hebrew race and nation: Abraham (Heb 7:4), sons of Jacob (Ac 7:8, 9), David (Ac 2:29). The term is now commonly used to refer to the persons whose names appear in the genealogies and covenant-histories before the time of Moses (Ge 5, 11).

PATRIARCHAL GOVERNMENT (See Government.)

PATRICIDE, of Sennacherib (2Ki 19:37; Isa 37:38).

PATRIOTISM. Enjoined (Ps 51:18; 122:6, 7). Exhortation concerning (2Sa 10:12). Religious ceremonial for the fostering of, enjoined (De 26:1-11). Appealed to in battle (2Sa 10:12). Song of (J'g 5:1-31; Ps 85:1-13; 137:1-6). Lack of, lamented (La 5:1-22).

Instances of: Moses (Heb 11:24-26). Deborah and Barak (J'g 4; 5). The tribes of Zebulun and Naphtali (J'g 5:18-20). Eli (1Sa 4:17, 18). Phinehas' wife (1Sa 4:19-22). Joab (2Sa 10:12). Uriah (2Sa 11:11). The Psalmist (Ps 51:18; 85:1-13). Hadad (1Ki 11:21, 22). The lepers of Samaria (2Ki 7:9). Jewish exiles (Ne 1:1-11; 2:1-20; Ps 137:1-6). Nehemiah (Ne 1:2, 4-11; 2:3). The Jews in public defense (Ne 2:3; 4:1-23). Isaiah (Isa 62:1). Jeremiah (Jer 8:11, 21, 22; 9:1, 2; La 5:1-22).

Lacking in: The tribes of Reuben, Asher and Dan (J'g 5:15-17). Inhabitants, of Morez (J'g 5:23); of Succoth and Penuel (J'g 8:4-17).

See Country, Love of.

PATROBAS, a believer at Rome (Ro 16:14).

PATTERN, of the tabernacle (Heb 8:5-9:23).

See Tabernacle.

PAU (bleating), called also Pai. A city of Edom (Ge 36:39; 1Ch 1:50).

PAUL. Called also Saul (Ac 8:1; 9:1; 13:9). Of the tribe of Benjamin (Ro 11:1; Ph'p 3:5). Personal appearance of (2Co 10:1, 10; 11:6). Born in Tarsus (Ac 9:11; 21:39; 22:3). Educated at Jerusalem in the school of Gamaliel (Ac 22:3; 26:4). A zealous Pharisee (Ac 22:3; 23:6; 26:5; 2Co 11:22; Ga 1:14; Ph'p 3:5). A Roman (Ac 16:37; 22:25-28). Persecutes the Christians; present at, and gives consent to, the stoning of Stephen (Ac 7:58; 8:1, 3; 9:1; 22:4). Sent to Damascus with letters for the arrest and return to Jerusalem of Christians (Ac 9:1, 2). His vision and conversion (Ac 9:3-22; 22:4-19; 26:9-15; 1Co 9:11; 15:8; Ga 1:13; 1Ti 1:12, 13). Is baptized (Ac 9:18; 22:16). Called to be an apostle (Ac 22:14-21; 26:16-18; Ro 1:1; 1Co 1:1; 9:1, 2; 15:9; Ga 1:1, 15, 16; Eph 1:1; Col 1:1; 1Ti 1:1; 2:7; 2Ti 1:1, 11; Tit 1:1, 3). Preaches in Damascus (Ac 9:20, 22). Is persecuted by the Jews (Ac 9:23, 24). Escapes by being let down from the wall in a basket; goes to Arabia (Ga 1:17); Jerusalem (Ac 9:25, 26; Ga 1:18, 19). Received by the disciples in Jerusalem (Ac 9:26-29). Goes to Caesarea (Ac 9:30; 18:22). Sent unto the Gentiles (Ac 13:2, 3, 47, 48; 22:17-21; Ro 11:13; 15:16; Ga 1:15-24). Has Barnabas as his companion (Ac 11:25, 26). Teaches at Antioch one year (Ac 11:26). Conveys the contributions of the Christians in Antioch to the Christians in Jerusalem (Ac 11:27-30). Returns with John to Antioch (Ac 12:25). Visits Seleucia (Ac 13:4); Cyprus (Ac 13:4). Preaches at Salamis (Ac 13:5); at Paphos (Ac 13:6). Sergius Paulus, deputy of the country, is a convert of (Ac 13:7-12). Contends with Elymas the sorcerer (Ac 13:6-12). Visits Perga in Pamphylia (Ac 13:13). John, a companion of, departs for Jerusalem (Ac 13:13). Visits Antioch in Pisidia, and preaches in the synagogue (Ac 13:14-41). His message received gladly by the Gentiles (Ac 13:42, 49). Persecuted and expelled (Ac 13:50, 51). Visits Iconium, and preaches to the Jews and Greeks; is persecuted; escapes to Lystra; goes to Derbe (Ac 14:1-6). Heals an impotent man (Ac 14:8-10). The people attempt to worship him (Ac 14:11-18). Is persecuted by certain Jews from Antioch and Iconium, and is stoned (Ac 14:19; 2Co 11:25; 2Ti 3:11). Escapes to Derbe, where he preaches the gospel, and returns to Lystra, and to Iconium, and to Antioch, confirms the souls of the disciples, exhorts them to continue in the faith, and ordains elders (Ac 14:19-23). Revisits Pisidia, Pamphylia, Perga, Attalia, and Antioch, in Syria, where he abode (Ac 14:24-28). Contends with the Judaizing Christians against circumcision (Ac 15:1, 2). Refers the question as to circumcision to the apostles and elders at Jerusalem (Ac 15:2, 4). He declares to the apostles at Jerusalem the miracles and wonders God had wrought among the Gentiles by them (Ac 15:12). Returns to Antioch, accompanied by Barnabas, Judas, and Silas, with letters to the Gentiles (Ac 15:22, 25).

Makes his second tour of the churches

(Ac 15:36). Chooses Silas as his companion, and passes through Syria and Cilicia, confirming the churches (Ac 15: 36-41). Visits Lystra; circumcises Timothy (Ac 16:1-5). Goes through Phrygia and Galatia; is forbidden by the Holy Ghost to preach in Asia; visits Mysia; essays to go to Bithynia, but is restrained by the Spirit; goes to Troas, where he has a vision of a man saying, "Come over into Macedonia, and help us;" immediately proceeds to Macedonia (Ac 16:6-10). Visits Samothracia and Neopolis; comes to Philippi, the chief city of Macedonia; visits a place of prayer at the river side; preaches the word; the merchant, Lydia, of Thyatira, is converted and baptized (Ac 16:11-15). Reproves the soothsayer; causes the evil spirit to come out of the damsel who practices divination (Ac 16:16-18). Persecuted, beaten, and cast into prison with Silas; sings songs of praise in the prison; an earthquake shakes the prison; he preaches to the alarmed jailer, who believes, and is baptized with his household (Ac 16:19-34). Is released by the civil authorities on the ground of his being a Roman citizen (Ac 16:35-39; 2Co 6:5; 11:25; 1Th 2:2). Is received at the house of Lydia (Ac 16:40). Visits Amphipolis, and Apollonia, and Thessalonica, preaches in the synagogue (Ac 17:1-4). Is persecuted (Ac 17:5-9; 2Th 1:1-4). Escapes to Berea by night; preaches in the synagogue; many honorable women, and men, not a few, believe (Ac 17:10-12). Persecuted by the Jews who come from Thessalonica; is conducted by the brethren to Athens (Ac 17:13-15). Disputes on Mars' Hill with Grecians (Ac 17:16-34). Visits Corinth; dwells with Aquila and his wife, Priscilla, who were tentmakers; joins in their handicraft; reasons in the synagogue every Sabbath; is rejected of the Jews; turns to the Gentiles; makes his abode with Justus; continues there one year and six months, teaching the word of God (Ac 18:1-11). Persecuted by Jews, drawn before the deputy, charged with wicked lewdness; accusation dismissed; takes his leave after many days, and sails unto Syria, accompanied by Aquila and Priscilla (Ac 18:12-18). Visits Ephesus, where he leaves Aquila and Priscilla; enters into a synagogue, where he reasons with the Jews; starts on his return journey to Jerusalem; visits Caesarea; goes over the country of Galatia and Phrygia, in order, strengthening the disciples (Ac 18:18-23). Returns to Ephesus; baptizes in the name of the Lord Jesus, and lays his hands upon the disciples, who are baptized with the Holy Ghost; preaches in the synagogue, remains in Ephesus for the space of two years; heals the sick (Ac 19:1-12). Reproves the exorcists; casts an evil spirit out of a man, and many believe, bringing their books of sorcery to be burned (Ac 19:13-20; 1Co 16:8, 9). Sends Timothy and Erastus into Macedonia, but remains himself in Asia for a season (Ac 19:21, 22). The spread of the gospel through his preaching interferes with the makers of idols; he is persecuted, and a great uproar of the city is created; the town clerk appeases the people; dismisses the accusation against Paul, and disperses the people (Ac 19:23-41; 2Co 1:8; 2Ti 4:14). Proceeds to Macedonia after confirming the churches in those parts; comes into Greece and abides three months; returns through Macedonia, accompanied by Sopater, Aristarchus, Secundus, Gaius, Timothy, Tychicus, and Trophimus (Ac 20:1-6). Visits Troas; preaches until break of day; restores to life the young man who fell from the window (Ac 20:6-12). Visits Assos, Mitylene, Chios, Samos, Trogyllium, and Miletus, hastening to Jerusalem, to be there at Pentecost (Ac 20:13-16). Sends for the elders of the church of Ephesus; rehearses to them how he had preached in Asia, and his temptations and afflictions testifying repentance toward God; declares he was going bound in spirit to Jerusalem; exhorts them to take heed to themselves and the flock over whom the Holy Ghost had made them overseers; kneels down and prays and takes his departure (Ac 20:17-38). Visits Coos, Rhodes, Patara; takes ship for Tyre; tarries at Tyre seven days; is brought on his way by the disciples to the outskirts of the city; kneels down and prays; takes ship; comes to Ptolemais; salutes the brethren, and abides one day (Ac 21:1-7). Departs for Caesarea; enters the house of Philip, the Evangelist; is admonished by Agabus not to go to Jerusalem; proceeds nevertheless to Jerusalem (Ac 21:8-15). Is received by the brethren gladly; talks of the things that had been wrought among the Gentiles by his ministry; enters the temple; the people are stirred against him by Jews from Asia; an uproar is created; he is thrust out of the temple; the chief captain of the garrison interposes and arrests him (Ac 21:17-33). His defense (Ac 21:33-40; 22:1-21). Is confined in the castle (Ac 22:24-30). Is brought before the council; his defense (Ac 22:30; 23:1-5). Is returned to the castle (Ac 23:10). Is cheered by a vision, promising him that he shall bear witness in Rome (Ac 23:11). Jews conspire against his life (Ac 23:12-15). Thwarted by his nephew (Ac 23:16-22). Is escorted to Caesarea by a military guard (Ac 23:23-33). Is confined in Herod's Judgment Hall in Caesarea (Ac 23:35). His trial before Felix (Ac 24). Remains in custody for two years (Ac 24:27). His trial before Festus (Ac 25:1-12). Appeals to Caesar (Ac 25:10-12). His examination before Agrippa (Ac 25:13-27; 26). Is taken to Rome in custody of Julius, a centurion, and guard of soldiers; takes shipping, accompanied by other prisoners, and sails by way of the coasts of Asia; stops at Sidon, and at Myra (Ac 27:1-5). Transferred to a ship of Alexandria; sails by way of Cnidus, Crete, Salamis, and the Fair Havens (Ac 27:6-8). Predicts misfortune to the ship; his counsel not heeded, and the voyage resumed (Ac 27:9-13). The ship encounters a tempest; Paul encourages and comforts the officers and crew; the soldiers advise putting the prisoners to death; the centurion interferes, and all on board, consisting of two hundred and seventy-six souls, are saved (Ac 27:14-44). The ship is wrecked, and all on board take refuge on the island of Melita (Ac 27:14-44). Kind treatment by the inhabitants of the island (Ac 28:1, 2). Is bitten by a viper and miraculously preserved (Ac 28:3-6). Heals the ruler's father and others (Ac 28:7-10). Is delayed in Melita three months; proceeds on the voyage; delays at Syracuse; sails by Rhegium and Puteoli; meets brethren who accompany him to Rome from Appii forum; arrives at Rome; is delivered to the captain of the guard; is permitted to dwell by himself in custody of a soldier (Ac 28:11-16). Calls the chief Jews together; states his situation; is kindly received; expounds the gospel; testifies to the kingdom of heaven (Ac 28:17-29). Dwells two years in his own hired house, preaching and teaching (Ac 28:30, 31).

Supports himself (Ac 18:3; 20:33-35). Sickness of, in Asia (2Co 1:8-11). His resolute determination to go to Jerusalem against the repeated admonition of the Holy Ghost (Ac 20:22, 23; 21:4, 10-14). Caught up to the third heavens (2Co 12:1-4). Has "a thorn in the flesh" (2Co 12:7-9; Ga 4:13, 14). His independence of character (1Th 2:9; 2Th 3:8). Persecutions of (1Th 2:2; Heb 10:34). Persecutions endured by, see below. Zeal of (See Zeal, of Paul).

Persecutions of (Ac 9:16, 23-25, 29; 14:19; 16:19-24; 20:22, 23; 21:13, 27, 28-33; 22:22-24; 23:10, 12-15; Ro 8:35-37; 1Co 4:9, 11-13; 2Co 1:8-10; 4:8, 9; 6:4, 5, 8-10; 11:23-27, 32, 33; 12:10; Ga 5:11; 6:17; Ph'p 1:30; Col 1:24; 1Th 2:2, 14, 15; 3:4; 2Ti 1:12; 2:9, 10; 3:11, 12; 4:16, 17).

Character of (2Co 10:1, 10; 11:6; Ga 4:13). Cheerful in adversity (Ac 10:25; Ro 8:35-37; 2Co 4:8-10; 12:10; 2Ti 2:10; 3:11, 12; 4:16, 17). Courageous (Ac 9:29; 20:22-24; 21:13; Eph 6:20; 1Th 2:2). Purposeful, even when the Holy Spirit warns him not to go to Jerusalem (Ac 20:22, 23; 21:4, 10-14). Indomitable (Ro 8:35-37; 1Co 4:9-13; 2Co 4:8-12; 6:4-10; 11:23-33; 12:10; 1Th 2:2; 2Ti 1:12; 3:11; 4:17). Joyous in suffering (Ac 16:25; Ph'p 2:17; Col 1:24; 2Ti 2:9). Meek (1Co 4:12, 13; 2Ti 4:16). Self forgetful (1Co 4:9, 11-13). Self-supporting (Ac 18:3; 20:33-35; 2Co 11:7, 9; 1Th 2:9; 2Th 3:8). Tactful (1Co 9:19-22; 10:33; Ph'm 8-21). Zealous (Ro 9:3; 2Co 5:11-14; 6:4-10; 11:22-33; 12:10, 14, 15; Ph'p 3:6-16; Col 1:29). Ready for death (2Ti 4:6-8).

PAULUS, SERGIUS, Roman proconsul of Cyprus; became Christian through Paul (Ac 13:6-12).

PAVEMENT, THE, courtyard outside palace in Jerusalem where Pilate passed public sentence on Jesus (Joh 19:13).

PAVILION (booth, tent), movable tent or canopy (1Ki 20:12; Jer 43:10). Figuratively of God's protection (Ps 27:5) or majesty (Job 36:29 ASV).

PAWN (Ex 22:26; De 24:10-13, 17; Job 24:3; Pr 22:27; Eze 18:5, 7, 12; 33:15; Am 2:8).

See Surety.

PEACE. From God (Isa 45:7; 1Co 14:33).

Social: Beneficence of (Ps 133:1; Pr 15:17; 17:1, 14; Ec 4:6). Honorable (Pr 20:3).

Enjoined (Ge 45:24; Ps 34:14; Jer 29:7; M'k 9:50; Ro 12:18; 14:19; 2Co 13:11; Eph 4:3, 31, 32; 1Th 5:13; 1Ti 2:2; 2Ti 2:22; Heb 12:14; 1Pe 3:10, 11). Love of, enjoined (Zec 8:19).

Promised (Le 26:6; Job 5:23, 24; Isa 2:4; 11:6-9, 13; 60:17, 18; Ho 2:18). The righteous assured of (Pr 16:7). Broken by the gospel (M't 10:21, 22, 34-36; Lu 12:51-53). Moses' efforts in behalf of, resented (Ex 2:13, 14; Ac 7:26-28).

Promoters of, promised joy (Pr 12:20); adoption (M't 5:9); fruit of righteousness (Jas 3:17, 18); good will (Lu 2:14).

Instances of promoters of: Abraham (Ge 13:8, 9); Abimelech (Ge 26:29); Mordecai (Es 10:3); David (Ps 120:7).

See Charitableness; Nation, Peace of.

Spiritual: Through Christ (Isa 2:4; 9:6, 7; 11:6, 13; Mic 4:3, 5; Lu 1:7a; Joh 7:38; 14:27; Ac 10:36; Ro 5:1; 10:15). To the world (Isa 2:4; 11:6-9; Lu 2:14). To God's children (Isa 54:10, 13).

From God (Job 34:29; Ps 29:11; 72:3, 7; 85:8; Jer 33:6; Eze 34:25; Hag 2:9; Mal 2:5; Ro 15:13, 33; 16:20; 1Co 1:3; 14:33; 2Co 1:2; Ga 1:3; Ph'p 4:7, 9; 1Th 1:1; 5:23; 2Th 3:16; 1Ti 1:2; 2Ti 1:2; Tit 1:4; Ph'm 3; Heb 13:20; Re 1:4). From Christ (M't 11:29; Joh 14:27; 16:33; 20:19; Eph 2:14-17; Col 3:15; Re 1:4, 5).

A fruit, of the Spirit (Ro 14:17; Ga 5:22); of righteousness (Ro 2:10). Assured to the righteous (Ps 37:4, 11, 37; 125:1, 5; Pr 3:17, 24; Isa 26:3, 12; 32:2, 17, 18; 55:2, 12; 57:1, 2, 9; Ro 8:6).

Through, the reconciliation of Christ (Isa 53:5; Joh 7:38; Ro 5:1; Col 1:20); acquaintance with God (Job 22:21, 26; Ps 4:8; 17:15; 73:25, 26; Isa 12:1, 2; 25:7, 8; 28:12; Lu 2:29); loving God's law (Ps 1:1, 2; 119:165); obedience (Ps 26:12, 13; Isa 48:18; Jer 6:16).

None, to the wicked (Isa 57:20, 21). To be made with God (Isa 27:5).

See Charitableness; Joy; Praise.

PEACE OFFERINGS (Ex 20:24; 24:5; Le 3:6; 7:11; 19:5). Offered by the princes (Nu 7:17); by Joshua (Jos 8:31); by David (2Sa 6:17; 24:25).

See Offerings.

PEACOCK (1Ki 10:22; 2Ch 9:21; Job 39:13).

PEARL (Job 28:18; Re 17:4; 18:12, 16). "Pearl of great price" (M't 13:46). Ornaments made of (1Ti 2:9).

Figurative: M't 7:6.

Symbolical: Re 21:21.

PECULIAR PEOPLE. People belonging to God (De 26:18; Tit 2:14; 1Pe 2:9).

PEDAHEL (God delivers), chief of Naphtali (Nu 34:28).

PEDAHZUR (the rock), father of Gamaliel (Nu 1:10; 2:20; 7:54, 59; 10:23).

PEDAIAH (Jehovah redeems). 1. Grandfather of Jehoiakim (2Ki 23:36).

2. Father of Zerubbabel (1Ch 3:18).

3. Father of Joel, chief of Manasseh (1Ch 27:20).

4. Man who helped build wall of Jerusalem (Ne 3:25).

5. Benjamite, father of Joed (Ne 11:7).

6. Levite; temple treasurer (Ne 13:13).

PEEP, cry of a bird (Isa 10:14) and noise made by wizards uttering sounds that are supposed to come from the dead (Isa 8:19).

PEKAH (to open), son of Remaliah the 18th king of Israel; murdered Pekahiah; reigned 734-714 B.C. (2Ki 15:27); made league with Damascus against Judah (2Ki 15:37, 38); became subject to Assyria (2Ki 15:29); murdered by Hoshea (2Ki 15:25-31; 2Ch 28:5-15).

PEKAHIAH (Jehovah has opened), Israel's 17th king; son of Menahem; wicked and idolatrous (2Ki 15:24); murdered by Pekah (2Ki 15:22-25).

PEKOD (visitation), Aramaean tribe living to E and near mouth of the Tigris (Jer 50:21; Eze 23:23).

PELAIAH (Jehovah is wonderful). 1. Son of Elioenai (1Ch 3:24).

2. A Levite who assisted Ezra in in-

structing the people in the law (Ne 8:7; 10:10).

PELALIAH (Jehovah has judged), priest; father of Jeroham and Amzi (Ne 11:12).

PELATIAH (Jehovah has delivered). 1. Grandson of Zerubbabel (1Ch 3:21).

2. Simeonite military leader (1Ch 4:42).

3. Man who sealed covenant with Nehemiah (Ne 10:22).

4. Prince of Israel; Ezekiel prophesied against him (Eze 11:2, 13).

PELEG (division), son of Eber (Ge 10:25; 11:16-19; 1Ch 1:19, 25).

PELET (deliverance). 1. Son of Jahdai (1Ch 2:47).

2. Son of Azmaveth (1Ch 12:3).

PELETH (swiftness). 1. A Reubenite (Nu 16:1).

2. Son of Jonathan (1Ch 2:33).

PELETHITES (courier). A part of David's bodyguard (1Ki 1:38; 2Sa 8:18; 20:7, 23; 1Ch 18:17). Absalom's escort (2Sa 15:18).

PELICAN (Le 11:18; De 14:17; Ps 102:6).

PELLA, city E of the Sea of Galilee; one of the cities forming the Decapolis.

PELONITE (separates). 1. An Ephraimite (1Ch 11:27; 27:10).

2. An appellation of Ahijah the prophet (1Ch 11:36).

PEN (J'g 5:14; Ps 45:1; Isa 8:1; Jer 8:8; 3Jo 13). Made of iron (Job 19:24; Jer 17:1).

PENALTY. Vicariously assumed: by Rebekah (Ge 27:13); Abigail (1Sa 25:24); the woman of Tekoa (2Sa 14:9); the persecutors of Jews (M't 27:25); Jesus for the human race (Ga 3:13). Paul desires to assume for Israel (Ro 9:3). See Vicarious Suffering.

See Judgments; Punishments; Sin, Punishment of; Wicked, Punishment of.

See also penalties under various crimes.

PENCE (See Money.)

PENDANT (See Dress.)

PENIEL, PENUEL (face of God). 1. Place where Jacob wrestled with angel of Jehovah (Ge 32:24-32), not far from Succoth.

2. Son of Hur (1Ch 4:4).

3. Son of Shashak (1Ch 8:25).

PENITENCE (See Repentance; Sin, Confession of.)

PENITENT. *Promises to:* Of mercy (Le 26:40-42; De 4:29-31; 30:1-10; 2Ki 22:19; 1Ch 28:9; Job 22:23-29; 33:26-28; Ps 6:8, 9; 9:10; 22:26; 90:14, 15; 145:18, 19; 147:3; Isa 27:5; M't 5:4; 7:7-11 w Lu 11:9-13; M't 12:20, 31; Lu 12:10).

Of forgiveness (Ps 32:5, 6; 34:18; 51:17; 86:5; Isa 55:7; Eze 18:21-23; 33:10-16; M't 6:14, 15; 11:28-30; Lu 6:37; 15:4-32 w M't 18:12-14; Lu 18:10-14; Joh 6:37; Ac 13:38, 39; 1Jo 1:9).

Of salvation (Ps 145:18, 19; M't 18:11; Lu 4:18; 19:10; Ro 10:9-13; Heb 7:25).

Of divine favor (Nu 5:6, 7; Isa 66:2).

See Forgiveness; Repentance; Sin, Confession of. See also Obduracy; Reprobacy.

PENKNIFE (Jer 36:23).

PENINNAH (coral), one of the wives of Elkanah (1Sa 1:2).

PENNY. About seventeen cents, later fifteen cents (M't 18:28; M'k 6:37; 14:5; Lu 7:41; 10:35). Roman, bore Caesar's image (M't 22:19-21). A day's wages (M't 20:2-14). See Money.

PENS for writing (J'g 5:14; Job 19:24; Ps 45:1; Isa 8:1; Jer 8:8; 17:1).

PENSION, of Levites (2Ch 31:16-18).

PENTATEUCH, THE (law or teaching), 1st five books of the Bible; covers period of time from creation to end of the Mosaic era; authorship attributed to Moses in Scripture. Outline: 1. Era of beginnings (Ge 1:1-11:32).

2. Patriarchal period (Ge 12:1-50:26).

3. Emancipation of Israel (Ex 1:1-19:2).

4. Religion of Israel (Ex 19:3-Le 27:34).

5. Organization of Israel (Nu 1:1-10:10).

6. Wilderness wanderings (Nu 10:11-22:1).

7. Preparations for entering Canaan (Nu 22:2-36:13).

8. Retrospect and prospect (De).

PENTECOST (50th day). 1. Jewish Feast of Weeks (Ex 34:22; De 16:9-11), also called the Feast of Harvest (Ex 23:16) and the day of First-Fruits (Nu 28:26), which fell on the 50th day after the Feast of the Passover. The feast originally celebrated the dedication of the first-fruits of the corn harvest, the last Palestinian crop to ripen. The ritual of the feast is described in Le 23:15-21. Institution of (Ex 23:16; 34:22; Le 23:15-21; Nu 26:31; De 16:9-12, 16). Called, in the New Testament, Day of Pentecost (Ac 2:1; 20:16; 1Co 16:8). See Feasts, Annual Feasts.

2. The Christian Pentecost fell on the same day as the Jewish Feast of Weeks. The coming of the Holy Spirit (Ac 2) transformed the Jewish festival into a Christian anniversary, marking the beginning of the Christian church.

PENURIOUSNESS (See Parsimony.)

PENUEL. 1. Called also Peniel. City built where Jacob wrestled with the angel (Ge 32:31; J'g 8:8, 9, 17; 1Ki 12:25).

2. Chief of Gedor (1Ch 4:4).

3. A Benjamite (1Ch 8:25).

PEOPLE, common. Heard Jesus gladly (M't 7:28; 9:8, 33; 13:54; M'k 6:2).

PEOR (opening). 1. Mt. in Moab near town of Beth-Peor (De 3:29).

2. Contraction for Baal-Peor (Nu 25:18; 31:16; Jos 22:17). See Baal-Peor.

PERAEA, name given by Josephus to the region E of the Jordan; known in the Gospels as "beyond Jordan" (M't 4:15, 25; M'k 3:7, 8); the word "Peraea" does not occur in the Bible.

PERAZIM, MOUNT, usually identified with Baal-perazim, where David obtained a victory over the Philistines (2Sa 5:20; 1Ch 14:11).

PERDITION (destruction), in the NT the word refers to the final state of the wicked, one of loss or destruction (Joh 17:12; Ph'p 1:28; 2Th 2:3; 1Ti 6:9).

PERDITION, SON OF, phrase used to designate Judas Iscariot (Joh 17:12) and the "man of sin" who is the Antichrist (2Th 2:3).

PEREA (See Peraea.)

PERES (divided), one of the words written on a wall for Belshazzar and interpreted by Daniel (Da 5:1-29).

PERESH (dung), son of Machir (1Ch 7:16).

PEREZ, son of Judah by Tamar (Ge 38:29); ancestor of Perezites (Nu 26:20, KJV "Pharzites"), David and Jesus (Ru 4:12; M't 1:3). Called "Pharez" in Ge 46:12; Nu 26:20, 21.

PEREZ-UZZA (breach of Uzzah), name of place where Uzzah was struck dead for touching the ark of God (2Sa 6:8).

PERFECTION (completeness). From God (Ps 18:32; 1Pe 5:10). Through Christ (Col 1:21, 22, 28; 2:9-11; Heb 10:14; 13:20, 21; 1Pe 5:10; 1Jo 3:6-10). Through God's love (1Jo 4:12).

Ascribed to: Noah (Ge 6:8, 9); Jacob (Nu 23:21); David (1Ki 11:4, 6); Asa (1Ki 15:14); Job (Job 1:1); Zacharias and Elisabeth (Lu 1:6); Nathanael (Joh 1:47); man of peace (Ps 37:31, 37); man of wisdom (1Co 2:6); man of God (2Ti 3:17); man of self-control (Jas 3:2); man of His Word (1Jo 2:5).

Blessings of (Ps 106:3; 119:1-3, 6; M't 5:6). Desire for (M't 5:6; 2Ti 3:17); in Job (Job 9:20, 21); David (Ps 101:2); Paul (Ph'p 3:12-15).

Enjoined (Ge 17:1; De 5:32; 18:13; Jos 23:6; 1Ki 8:61; 1Ch 28:9; M't 5:48; 2Co 7:1; 13:11; Ph'p 1:10; 2:15; Col 3:14; Jas 1:4).

None without sin (2Ch 6:36; Ec 7:20). Prayer for (1Ch 29:19; 2Co 13:9; Col 4:12; 1Th 3:10, 13; Heb 13:20, 21). Program for (Eph 4:11-13; Heb 6:1; 1Jo 2:5). Requirements for (De 5:32; Jos 23:6; 1Ki 8:61; 1Ch 29:19; M't 19:21; 2Co 7:1). Reward of (Ps 37:31, 37; Pr 2:21; Lu 6:40; 1Jo 5:18).

See God, Perfection of; Holiness; Sanctification.

PERFIDY (See Conspiracy; Hypocrisy; Treachery.)

PERFUME, for personal use (Pr 7:17; 27:9; Song 3:6; Isa 3:20, 24 RSV) and for incense (Ex 30:34-38).

PERGA, the capital of Pamphylia. Paul preaches in (Ac 13:13, 14; 14:25).

PERGAMOS, a city of Mysia. One of the "seven churches" in (Re 1:11; 2:12-17).

PERIDA (divided), one of the servants of Solomon. Descendants of, returned to Jerusalem, from captivity in Babylon (Ne 7:57). Called Peruda in Ezra 2:55.

PERIZZITES. One of the seven nations in the land of Canaan (Ge 13:7). Territory of, given to Abraham (Ge 15:20; Ex 3:8; 23:23). Doomed to destruction (De 20:17). Not all destroyed; Israelites marry among (J'g 3:5-7; Ezr 9:1, 2).

See Canaanites.

PERJURY (Isa 48:1; Jer 5:2; 7:9; 1Ti 1:9, 10). Forbidden (Le 19:12; Zec 8:17;

M't 5:33). Penalty for (Le 6:2-7). Judgments upon perjurers (Ho 10:4; Zec 5:3, 4; Mal 3:5).

Instances of: Zedekiah (2Ch 36:13). Witnesses against Naboth (1Ki 21:8-13); against David (Ps 35:11); against Jesus (M't 26:59-61; M'k 14:56-59); against Stephen (Ac 6:11, 13, 14). Peter, when he denied Jesus with an oath (M't 26:74; M'k 14:71).

See Falsehood; False Witness; Oath.

PERSECUTION. *Of Jesus* (Ac 4:27; Heb 12:2, 3; 1Pe 4:1). Meekly endured (Isa 50:6).

Foretold (Ge 3:15; Isa 49:7; 50:6; 52:14; 53:2-10; Mic 5:1; Zec 12:10; M't 2:13). Typified, in the persecutions of Israel's kings (Ps 2:1-5; 22:1, 2, 6-8, 11-21; 69:1-21 w Ro 15:3; 109:25).

By the Jews (M't 12:14; 22:15; 26:3, 4; M'k 12:13; 15:14; Lu 6:11; 11:53, 54; 20:20; 22:2-5, 52, 53; 23:23; Joh 5:16; 7:1, 7, 19; 11:57; 15:18, 20, 21; 18:22, 23; 19:6, 15; Ac 2:23); in making false imputation (M't 12:24; M'k 3:22; Lu 11:15; Joh 10:20); in bringing false accusation (M't 11:19; Lu 7:34; Joh 8:29, 30); in acts of violence (Lu 4:28, 29; 22:63-65 w M't 26:67 & M'k 14:65); in seeking false testimony (M't 26:59); in seeking his death (M't 26:14-16; M'k 3:6, 21; 14:1, 48; 11:18; Lu 19:47; Joh 7:20, 30, 32; 8:37, 40, 48, 52, 59; 10:31); in crucifying him (Ac 3:13-15; 7:52; 13:27-29; 1Co 2:8).

By Herod (Lu 13:31; 23:11). By the Roman soldiers (M't 27:25-30; M'k 15:15-20; Joh 19:2, 3).

Forsaken by God (M't 15:34).

Of the righteous (Ge 49:23; Ps 11:2; 37:32; 38:20; 74:7, 8; 119:51, 61, 69, 78, 85-87, 95, 110, 157, 161; Pr 29:10, 27; Isa 26:20; 29:20, 21; 59:15; Jer 11:19; 15:10; 18:18; Am 5:10; Ro 8:35; 2Co 12:10; Ga 4:29; 6:17).

By mocking (Ps 42:3, 10; 69:9-12; 119:51; Jer 20:7, 8). By violence (Ps 94:5; Jer 2:30; 50:7; Ac 5:29, 40-42; 7:52; Ga 6:12, 17; 1Th 2:2, 14, 15; Jas 2:6).

By ecclesiastical censure (Joh 9:22, 34; 12:42; 2Ti 4:16, 17).

Divine permissions of, mysterious (Hab 1:13). The mode of divine chastisement (La 1:3).

Extension of church by (Ac 8:1, 4; 11:19-21; Ph'p 1:12-14, 18). Impotent to separate from the love of Christ (Ro 8:17, 35-39).

Exhortations to courage under (Isa 51:12, 16; Heb 12:3, 4; 13:13; 1Pe 3:14, 16, 17; 4:12-14, 16, 19). Courageously endured (Jer 26:11-14; 1Co 4:9-13; 2Co 4:8-12; 6:4, 5, 8-10; 11:23-27; 12:10; 2Th 1:4; 2Ti 1:8, 12; 2:9, 10, 12; Heb 11:25-27, 33-38; Jas 5:6, 10).

Rejoicing under (Ro 5:3; Col 1:24; 1Th 1:6; Heb 10:32-34). Perseverance under (Ps 44:15-18, 22).

Prayer for deliverance from (Ps 70:1-5; 83:1; 140:1, 4; 142:6). Deliverance from (Ps 124; 129:1, 2). John's vision concerning (Re 2:3, 10, 13; 6:9-11; 7:13-17; 12:10, 11; 17:6; 20:4).

Of Christians, foretold (M't 20:22; 23:34, 35; 24:8-10; M'k 13:9, 11-13; Lu 21:12-19; Joh 15:18-21; 16:1, 2; 2Ti 3:2, 3, 12, 13; 1Jo 3:1, 13). Christ offers consolation (M't 8:38; 9:42; Lu 6:22, 23; 17:33; Joh 17:14).

Promises to those who endure (M't 5:10-12; 10:16-18, 21-23, 28-31; Lu 6:22, 23). Should provoke love (1Co 13:3).

Instances of: Abel (Ge 4:8; M't 23:35; 1Jo 3:12). Lot (Ge 19:9). Moses (Ex 2:15; 17:4). David (Ps 31:13; 56:5; 59:1, 2). Prophets martyred by Jezebel (1Ki 18:4). Gideon (J'g 6:28-32). Elijah (1Ki 18:10; 19; 2Ki 1:9; 2:23). Micaiah (1Ki 22:26; 2Ch 18:26). Elisha (2Ki 6:31). Hanani (2Ch 16:10). Zachariah (2Ch 24:21; M't 23:35). Job (Job 1:9; 2:4, 5; 12:4, 5; 13:4-13; 16:1-4; 17:2; 19:1-5; 30:1-10). Jeremiah (Jer 11:19; 15:10, 15; 17:15-18; 18:18-23; 26; 32:2; 33:1; 36:26; 37; 38:1-6). Urijah (Jer 26:23). The prophets (2Ch 36:16; M't 21:35, 36; 1Th 2:15). The three Hebrew children of the captivity (Da 3:8-23). Daniel (Da 6). The Jews (Ezr 4; Ne 4).

John the Baptist (M't 14:3-12). James (Ac 12:2). Simon (M'k 15:21). The disciples (Joh 9:22, 34; 20:19). Lazarus (Joh 9:22, 34; 12:10; 20:19). The apostles (Ac 4:3-18; 5:18-42; 12:1-19; Re 1:9). Stephen (Ac 6:9-15; 7). The church (Ac 8:1; 9:1-14; Ga 1:13). Timothy (Heb 13:23). John (Re 1:9). Antipas (Re 2:13). The church of Smyrna (Re 2:8-10).

Paul (Ac 9:16, 23-25, 29; 16:19-25; 21:2-33; 22:22-24; 23:10, 12-15; 1Co 4:9, 11-13; 2Co 1:8-10; 4:8-12; 6:4, 5, 8-10;

11:23-27, 32, 33; Col 1:24; 1Th 2:2, 14, 15; 2Ti 1:8, 12; 2:9, 10; 3:11, 12; 4:16, 17). See Paul.

PERSEPOLIS, capital of Persia, 30 miles NE of modern Shiraz; founded by Darius I (521-486 B. C.); destroyed by Alexander the Great in 331 B. C.

PERSEVERANCE (Job 17:9; Pr 4:18; Tit 1:9; 1Pe 4:16).

From the Lord (Ps 37:24, 28; Ro 8:30, 33-35; 1Co 1:8, 9; 2Co 1:21, 22); acknowledged (Ps 73:24; 138:8; Ro 8:37-39; Col 2:7; 2Ti 4:18); promised (Jer 32:40; Joh 6:34-40; 10:28, 29).

Enjoined (1Ch 16:11; Ho 12:6; 1Th 5:21; 2Th 2:15-17; 2Ti 2:1, 3, 12; 3:14; Jas 1:4, 25; 1Pe 5:8, 9; Re 22:11). Exhortations to (Ac 11:23; 13:43; 14:21, 22; 1Co 15:58; 16:13; Ga 5:1, 10; Eph 4:14, 15; 6:13, 18; Ph'p 1:27; 3:16; 4:1; Col 1:10, 22, 23; 1Th 3:8; 2Th 3:15; 2Ti 1:13; Heb 2:1; 6:1, 11, 12, 15; 10:23, 35, 36; 12:5-13, 15; 13:9, 13; 2Pe 3:17, 18; Re 16:15).

A proof of discipleship (Joh 8:31, 32). A condition of fruitfulness (Joh 15:4, 5, 7, 9). Intercessory prayer for (Lu 22:31, 32).

Motives to: The example, of Moses (Heb 3:5); of the prophets (Jas 5:10, 11); of Christ (Heb 3:6, 14; 12:2-4); the intercession of Christ (Heb 4:14); the heavenly witnesses (Heb 12:1); acceptance by Christ (2Co 5:9, 15; 1Pe 1:4-7).

Rewards contingent upon (Ga 6:9; Jas 1:12; Re 2:7, 10, 11, 17, 25-28; 3:5, 11, 21; 14:12; 21:7). Eternal life contingent upon (M't 10:22; 24:13; M'k 13:13; Ro 2:6, 7; 2Pe 1:10, 11).

Lacking in: the wayside and other hearers (M'k 4:3-8); churches of Asia (Re 2:5; 3:1-3, 14-18).

Instances of: In prayer, Abraham in interceding for Sodom (Ge 18:23-32); Jacob (Ge 32:24-26); Elijah for rain (1Ki 18:42-45); Paul for the removal of the thorn in his flesh (2Co 12:7-9). Caleb and Joshua, in representing the land of promise (Nu 14:24, 38).

See Character; Instability; Stability.

PERSIA. An empire which extended from India to Ethiopia, comprising one hundred and twenty-seven provinces (Es 1:1; Da 6:1). Government of, restricted by constitutional limitations (Es 8:8; Da 6:8-12). Municipal governments in, provided with dual governors (Ne 3:9, 12, 16-18). The princes advisory in matters of administration (Da 6:1-7). Status of women in, queen sat on the throne with the king (Ne 2:6). Vashti divorced for refusing to appear before the king's courtiers (Es 1:10-22; 2:4).

Israel captive in (2Ch 36:20); captivity foretold (Ho 13:16). Men of, in the Tyrian army (Eze 27:10).

Rulers of: Ahasuerus (Es 1:3). Darius (Da 5:31; 6; 9:1). Artaxerxes I (Ezr 4:7-24). Artaxerxes II (Ezr 7; Ne 2; 5:14). Cyrus (2Ch 36:22, 23; Ezr 1; 3:7; 4:3; 5:13, 14, 17; 6:3; Isa 41:2, 3; 44:28; 45:1-4, 13; 46:11; 48:14, 15). Princes of (Es 1:14).

System of justice (Ezr 7:25). Prophecies concerning (Isa 13:17; 21:1-10; Jer 49:34-39; 51:11-64; Eze 32:24, 25; 38:5; Da 2:31-45; 5:28; 7; 8; 11:1-4).

See Babylon; Chaldea.

PERSIS, a Christian woman in Rome (Ro 16:12).

PERSONAL CALL (See Call, Personal; Ministers, Call of.)

PERSONIFICATION. Of wisdon (Pr 1; 2:1-19; 8; 9). Of the church (Song 1-8).

See Pantomime.

PERUDA, one of the servants of Solomon. Descendants of, return to Jerusalem from captivity in Babylon (Ezr 2:55). Called Perida in Ne 5:57.

PERVERSENESS (Pr 11:3; 12:8; 15:4; 28:6; Eze 9:9; M't 17:17; 1Ti 6:5).

PESHITTA, ancient Syriac translation of the Bible.

PESTILENCE. Sent as a judgment (Le 26:16, 25). Sent upon the Egyptians (see Egypt; Plagues).

PESTLE, an instrument used to grind in a mortar (Pr 27:22).

PETER. Called also Simon Bar-jona and Cephas (M't 16:16-19; M'k 3:16; John 1:42); Simeon (Ac 15:14). A fisherman (M't 4:18; Lu 5:1-7; Joh 21:3). Call of (M't 4:18-20; M'k 1:16-18; Lu 5:1-11). His wife's mother healed (M't 8:14; M'k 1:29, 30; Lu 4:38). An apostle (M't 10:2; 16:18, 19; M'k 3:16; Lu 6:14, Ac 1:13). An evangelist (M'k 1:36, 37). Confesses Jesus as Christ (M't 16:16-19; M'k 8:29; Lu 9:20; Joh 6:68, 69). His presumption in rebuking Jesus (M't 16:22, 23; M'k 8:32, 33); when the throng was pressing Jesus and the woman of infirmity touched him (Lu 8:45); when Jesus foretold his persecution and death (M't 16:21-23; M'k 8:31-33); in refusing to let Jesus wash his feet (Joh 13:6-11). Present at the healing of Jairus' daughter (M'k 5:37; Lu 8:51); at the transfiguration (M't 17:1-4; M'k 9:2-6; Lu 9:28-33; 2Pe 1:16-18); in Gethsemane (M't 26:36-46; M'k 14:33-42; Lu 22:40-46). Seeks the interpretation of the parable of the steward (Lu 12:41); of the law of forgiveness (M't 18:21); of the law of defilement (M't 15:15); of the prophecy of Jesus concerning his second coming (M'k 13:3, 4). Walks upon the water of the sea of Galilee (M't 14:28-31). Sent with John to prepare the Passover (Lu 22:8). Calls attention to the withered fig tree (M'k 11:21). His perfidy foretold by Jesus, and his profession of fidelity (M't 26:33-35; M'k 14:29-31; Lu 22:31-34; Joh 13:36-38). Cuts off the ear of Malchus (M't 26:51; M'k 14:47; Lu 22:50). Follows Jesus to the high priest's palace (M't 26:58; M'k 14:54; Lu 22:54; Joh 18:15). His denial of Jesus, and his repentance (M't 26:69-75; M'k 14:66-72; Lu 22:55-62; Joh 18:17, 18, 25-27). Visits the sepulcher (Lu 24:12; Joh 20:2-6). Jesus sends message to, after the resurrection (M'k 16:7). Jesus appears to (Lu 24:34; 1Co 15:4, 5). Present at the Sea of Tiberias when Jesus appeared to his disciples; leaps into the sea, and comes to land when Jesus is recognized, is commissioned to feed the flock of Christ (Joh 21:1-23). Abides in Jerusalem (Ac 1:13). His statement before the disciples concerning the death of Judas, and his recommendation that the vacancy in the apostleship be filled (Ac 1:15-22). Preaches at Pentecost (Ac 2:14-40). Heals the impotent man in the portico of the temple (Ac 3). Accused by the council; his defense (Ac 4:1-23). Foretells the death of Ananias and Sapphira (Ac 5:1-11). Imprisoned and scourged; his defense before the council (Ac 5:17-42). Goes to Samaria (Ac 8:14). Prays for the baptism of the Holy Ghost (Ac 8:15-18). Rebukes Simon, the sorcerer, who desires to purchase like power (Ac 8:18-24). Returns to Jerusalem (Ac 8:25). Receives Paul (Ga 1:18; 2:9). Visits Lydda; heals Aeneas (Ac 9:32-34). Visits Joppa; dwells with Simon the tanner; raises Dorcas from the dead (Ac 9:36-43). Has a vision of a sheet containing clean and unclean animals (Ac 10:9-16). Receives the servant of the centurion; goes to Caesarea; preaches and baptizes the centurion and his household (Ac 10). Advocates, in the council of the apostles and elders, the preaching of the gospel to the Gentiles (Ac 11:1-18; 15:7-11). Imprisoned and delivered by an angel (Ac 12:3-19). Writes two epistles (1Pe 1:1; 2Pe 1:1). Miracles of (see Miracles).

PETER, FIRST EPISTLE OF; written by Peter the apostle (1:1); written from "Babylon" possibly Rome (5:13); destination—Christians "in Pontus, Galatia, Cappadocia, Asia, and Bithynia" (1:1); date of writing—probably in the middle 60's; purpose—to encourage Christians who had been undergoing persecution. Outline: 1. Salutation (1:1, 2).

2. Nature of salvation (1:3-12).
3. Experience of salvation (1:13-25).
4. Obligations of salvation (2:1-10).
5. Ethics of salvation (2:11-3:12).
6. Confidence of salvation (3:13-4:11).
7. Behavior of the saved under suffering (4:12-5:11).
8. Concluding salutations (5:12-14).

PETER, SECOND EPISTLE OF, written by Peter the apostle (1:1); destination—same as 1 Peter (3:1); place of writing is uncertain, but probably Rome; time of writing was toward the end of Peter's life; occasion—the threat of apostasy. Outline: 1. Salutation (1:1).

2. Character of spiritual knowledge (1:2-21).
3. Nature and perils of apostasy (2:1-22).
4. Doom of the ungodly (3:1-7).
5. Hope of believers (3:8-13).
6. Concluding exhortation (3:14-18).

PETHAHIAH (Jehovah opens up). 1. A priest in the reign of David (1Ch 24:16).

2. A Levite who divorced his Gentile wife (Ezr 10:23). Probably identical with the one mentioned (Ne 9:5).

3. A counselor of Artaxerxes (Ne 11:24).

PETHOR, a city in Mesopotamia. Home of the prophet Balaam (Nu 22:5; De 23:4).

PETHUEL (God's opening), father of the prophet Joel (Joe 1:1).
PETITION. Right of, recognized by Pharaoh (Ex 5:15-18); Israel (Nu 27:1-5; 32:1-5; 36:1-5; Jos 17:4, 14, 16; 21:1, 2); David (1Ki 1:15-21); Rehoboam (1Ki 12:1-17; 2Ch 10); Jehoram (2Ki 8:3, 6).
PETRA (rock, cliff), capital city of the Nabateans mentioned indirectly (J'g 1:36; 2Ki 14:7; Isa 16:1).
PETROLEUM. *Figurative:* Job 29:6.
PEULTHAI (Jehovah is a reward), a porter of the tabernacle (1Ch 26:5).
PHALEC, Greek form of Hebrew Peleg (Lu 3:35).
PHALLU, called also Pallu. Son of Reuben (Ge 46:9; Ex 6:14; Nu 26:5, 8; 1Ch 5:3).
PHALTI (delivered). 1. Spy from Benjamin to search out Canaan (Nu 13:9).
2. Son-in-law of Saul (1Sa 25:44). KJV has "Phaltiel" in 2Sa 3:15.
PHALTIEL (God delivers). 1. Prince of Issachar (Nu 34:26).
2. Son-in-law of Saul (2Sa 3:15). "Phalti" in 1Sa 25:44.
PHANUEL (face of God), father of Anna the prophetess (Lu 2:36).
PHARAOH. 1. King of Egypt at the time of Abraham (Ge 12:14-20; Ps 105:14).
2. Ruler of Egypt at the time of the famine. (See Egypt; Israelites.)
3. Ruler of Egypt at the time of the deliverance and exodus of the children of Israel. (See Israelites.)
4. Father-in-law of Mered (1Ch 4:18).
5. Ruler of Egypt at the time of David (1Ki 11:17-22).
6. Father-in-law of Solomon (1Ki 3:1; 9:16).
7. At the time of Hezekiah (2Ki 18:21).
8. Pharaoh-nechoh. His invasion of Assyria, Josiah's death (1Ki 23:29-35; 24:7; 2Ch 35:20-24; 36:3, 4; Jer 46:2; 47:1).
9. Pharaoh-hophra (Jer 37:4-7; 44; Eze 17:15-17). Prophecies concerning (Jer 44:30; 46:25, 26; Eze 29; 30:21-26).
PHARES (See Pharez.)
PHAREZ (bread), called also Perez and Phares. A twin son of Judah by Tamar (Ge 38:29; 1Ch 2:4). Children of (Ge 46:12; Nu 26:20, 21; 1Ch 2:5; 9:4); return from the captivity (Ne 11:4, 6). In the lineage of Jesus (M't 1:3; Lu 3:33).
PHARISEES. A sect of the Jews (Ac 15:5). Doctrines of (M't 15:9); concerning the resurrection (Ac 23:6, 8); association with publicans and sinners (M't 9:11-13).
Traditions of, in regard to fasting (M't 9:14; Lu 18:12); the washing of hands (M't 15:1-3; M'k 7:1-15); the duties of children to parents (M't 15:4-9); the Sabbath (M't 12:2-8). Denounced by Jesus (M't 23:2-36; Lu 11:39-44). Hypocrisy of, reproved by John (M't 3:7-10); by Jesus (M't 6:2-8, 16-18; 15:1-9; 16:1-12; 21:33-46; 23:2-33; Lu 11:14-54; 12:1; 15:1-9). Reject John (Lu 7:30); Christ (M't 12:38, 39; 15:12; Joh 7:48). Come to Jesus with questions (M't 19:3; 22:15-22).
Minister to Jesus (Lu 7:36; 11:37; 14:1). become disciples of Jesus (Joh 3:1; Ac 15:5; 22:3).
Paul a Pharisee (Ac 23:6; 26:5).
See Herodians; Sadducees.
PHAROSH, called also Parosh. The ancestor of one of the families which returned to Jerusalem from captivity in Babylon (Ezr 2:3; 8:3; 10:25; Ne 7:8; 10:14).
PHARPAR, a river of Damascus. Referred to by Naaman (2Ki 5:12).
PHARZITE, descendant of Pharez, son of Judah (Nu 26:20).
PHASEAH, called also Paseah. Ancestor of a family which returned to Jerusalem from the captivity (Ezr 2:49; Ne 3:6; 7:51).
PHASELIS, Rhodian colony in Lycia (1 Macc. 15:23).
PHASELUS, Latinization of Phasael, alternatively Phasaelus, the son of Antipater the Idumaean, and brother of Herod the Great.
PHEBE (pure), a deaconess of the church at Cenchrea (Ro 16:1).
PHENICE, PHOENIX, town on the S coast of Crete (Ac 27:12). Phenice is also used as a term for Phoenicia.
PHENICIA, called also Phenice. Inhabitants of, descended from Canaan (Ge 10:15, 18, 19). Called Zidonians (J'g 18:7; Eze 32:30). Jews from, hear Jesus (M'k 3:8). Paul visits the churches in (Ac 15:3; 21:2-4; 27:3).
PHI-BESETH (house of the goddess

Bast), a city in Egypt (Eze 30:17). About 40 miles N of Memphis.

PHICHOL, chief captain of the Philistines (Ge 21:22, 32; 26:26).

PHILADELPHIA (brotherly love), a city of Lydia. One of the "Seven churches" at (Re 1:11; 3:7-13).

PHILANTHROPY (Isa 58:6-12). See Alms; Beneficence; Charitableness; Liberality; Neighbor; Poor.

PHILEMON (loving), convert of Paul at Colosse; Epistle to Philemon written to him.

PHILEMON, EPISTLE TO, written by Paul during his first Roman imprisonment, and addressed to "Philemon ... Apphia ... Archippus, and the church in your house." It deals with Philemon's runaway slave, Onesimus, who was converted through Paul, established in the faith by him, and then sent back to Philemon with a plea that Onesimus be forgiven for the wrong done to his master. The slave had apparently absconded with some of his master's money, which he had squandered; and Paul suggests that Philemon not insist on getting his money back, and if he did then Paul would repay it.

PHILETUS (worthy of love), false teacher in the church at Ephesus (2Ti 2:17).

PHILIP (lover of horses). 1. King of Macedonia; father of Alexander the Great; founder of city of Philippi in Macedonia (1Macc 1:1).

2. Philip V, king of Macedonia (1Macc 8:5).

3. Governor of Jerusalem under Antiochus, regent of Syria (2 Macc 5:22).

4. Herod Philip. Married Herodias (M't 14:3; M'k 6:17; Lu 3:19).

5. Herod Philip II, tetrarch of Batanaea, Trachonitis, Gaulanitis, and parts of Jamnia. Best of Herods (Lu 3:1).

PHILIP THE APOSTLE, native of Bethsaida, the same town as Andrew and Peter (Joh 1:44); undoubtedly first a disciple of John the Baptist (Joh 1:43); brought his friend Nathanael to Jesus (Joh 1:45); called to apostleship (M't 10:3; M'k 3:18; Lu 6:14); faith tested by Jesus before feeding of 5,000 (Joh 6:5, 6); brought Greeks to Jesus (Joh 12:20-23); asked to see the Father (Joh 14:8-12); in upper room with 120 (Ac 1:13).

PHILIP THE EVANGELIST, chosen one of the seven deacons (Ac 6:5); a Hellenist, or Greek-speaking Jew; preached in Samaria (Ac 8); Ethiopian eunuch converted through him (Ac 8:26-40); Paul stayed at his home in Caesarea, where he lived with his four unmarried daughters who were prophetesses (Ac 21:8, 9).

PHILIPPI, a city of Macedonia. Paul preaches in (Ac 16:12-40; 20:1-6; 1Th 2:1, 2). Contributes to the maintenance of Paul (Ph'p 4:10-18). Paul sends Epaphroditus to (Ph'p 2:25). Paul writes a letter to the Christians of (Ph'p 1:1).

PHILIPPIANS, EPISTLE TO THE, letter written by Paul in prison, probably from Rome, although this is not stated, to thank the church for the gift of money sent him by the hands of Epaphroditus. There is no word of criticism of the church; the main emphasis is one of joy and triumphant faith. 1. Greetings and thanksgiving (1:1-11).

2. Progress of the gospel (1:12-20).

3. Working and suffering for Christ (1:21-30).

4. Exhortation to humility (2:1-13).

5. Exhortation to the Christian life (2:14-18).

6. Personal remarks involving Timothy and Epaphroditus (2:19-30).

7. Exhortations and warnings (3:1-4:9).

8. Thanksgiving (4:10-20).

9. Final greeting (4:21-22).

PHILISTIA, the sea coast in the W of Dan and Simeon (Ps 60:8; 87:4; 108:9).

PHILISTINES. Descendants of Mizraim (Ge 10:14; 1Ch 1:12; Jer 47:4; Am 9:7). Called Cherethites (1Sa 30:14-16; Eze 25:16; Zep 2:5); Casluhim (Ge 10:14; 1Ch 1:12); Caphtorim (Jer 47:4; Am 9:7). Territory of (Ex 13:17; 23:31; De 2:23; Jos 13:3; 15:47); lords of (Jos 13:3; J'g 3:3; 16:5, 30; 1Sa 5:8, 11; 6:4, 12; 7:7; 29:2, 6, 7).

Kings of: Abimelech I (Ge 20); Abimelech II (Ge26); Achish (1Sa21:10-15; 27:2-12; 28:1, 2; 29). Suffered to remain in Canaan (J'g 3:3, 4). Shamgar slays six hundred with an ox goad (J'g 3:31). (For their history during the leadership of

Samson, see J'g 13-16). Defeat the Israelites; take the ark; suffer plagues, and return the ark (1Sa 4-6). Army of (1Sa 13:5). Defeated by Samuel (1Sa 7), by Saul and Jonathan (1Sa 9:16; 13; 14). Their champion, Goliath, slain by David (1Sa 17). David slays two hundred (1Sa 18:22-30). David finds refuge among (1Sa 27). Defeat the Israelites and slay Saul and his sons (1Sa 31; 1Ch 10:1). Defeated by David (2Sa 5:17-25; 23:9-16; 1Ch 14:8-16). Pay tribute to Jehoshaphat (2Ch 17:11). Defeated by Hezekiah (2Ki 18:8). Prophecies against (Isa 9:11, 12; 14:29-31; Jer 25:17-20; 47; Eze 25:15-17; Am 1:6-8; Zep 2:4-7; Zec 9:5-7).

PHILOLOGUS (fond of learning), Christian in Rome to whom Paul sent a salutation (Ro 16:15).

PHILOSOPHY. The nature of things (Ec 1-7). A philosophical disquisition on wisdom (Job 28). Philosophical inductions and deductions relating to God and His providence (Job 5:8-20; 9; 10:2-21; 12:6-24; 33:12-30; 37). Reveals the mysteries of providence (Pr 25:2; Ro 1:19, 20). Is not sufficient for an adequate knowledge of God (1Co 1:21, 22); or of salvation through the atonement of Jesus Christ (1Co 2:6-10). Employment of, was not Paul's method of preaching the gospel (1Co 1:17, 19, 21; 2:1-5, 13). Greek schools of (Ac 17:18). Rabbinical (Col 2:8, 16-19; 1Ti 6:20).

See Reason; also God, Unclassified Scriptures Relating to.

PHINEHAS (mouth of brass). 1. Son of Eleazar and grandson of Aaron (Ex 6:25; 1Ch 6:4, 50; 9:20; Ezr 7:5; 8:2), who slew Zimri and Cozbi at God's command (Nu 25:6-15; Ps 106:30).

2. Son of Eli; sinful priest (1Sa 1:3; 2:12-17, 22-25, 27-36; 3:11-13). He and his brother were killed by Philistines (1Sa 4).

3. Father of Eleazar who returned from exile (Ezr 8:33).

PHLEGON (burning), a disciple in Rome (Ro 16:14).

PHOENICIA, PHENICIA, country along Mediterranean coast, c. 120 miles long, extending from Arvad or Arados to Dor, just S of Carmel. The Semitic name for the land was Canaan. The term Phoenicia is from a Greek word meaning "dark red," perhaps because the Phoenicians were the discoverers of the crimson-purple dye derived from the murex shellfish. The people were Semites who came in a migration from the Mesopotamian region during the 2nd millennium B. C. They became great seafarers, establishing colonies at Carthage and Spain, and perhaps even reached England. They were famous shipbuilders (Eze 27:9) and carpenters (1Ki 16:31; 18:19). Hiram, one of their kings was friendly with David and Solomon (2Sa 5:11; 1Ki 5:1-12; 2Ch 2:3-16), and another Hiram helped Solomon in the building of the temple in Jerusalem (1Ki 7:13-47; 2Ch 2:13, 14). Jesus healed a Syrophoenician woman's daughter in its regions (M'k 7:24-30). Paul visited Christians there (Ac 15:3; 21:2-7).

PHRYGIA, an inland province of Asia Minor. People from, in Jerusalem (Ac 2:10). Paul in (Ac 16:6; 18:23).

PHURAH (branch), a servant of Gideon (J'g 7:10, 11).

PHUT, called also Put. 1. Son of Ham (Ge 10:6; 1Ch 1:8).

2. The descendants of Phut, or the country inhabited by them (Eze 27:10; Na 3:9; Jer 46:9 [marg.]; Eze 30:5 [marg.]; 38:5 [marg.]).

PHUVAH, PUA, PUAH. 1. Son of Issachar (Ge 46:13; Nu 26:23; 1Ch 7:1).

2. Father of Tola the judge (J'g 10:1).

PHYGELLUS, a Christian in Asia. Turns from Paul (2Ti 1:15).

PHYLACTERY. A small box containing slips of parchment on which were written portions of the law (Ex 13:9, 16; De 6:4-9; 11:18). Worn ostentatiously by the Jews on the head and left arm (M't 23:5).

PHYSICIAN (2Ch 16:12; M't 9:12; M'k 5:26; Lu 8:43). Proverbs about (M'k 2:17; Lu 4:23). Luke a physician (Col 4:14).

Figurative: Job 13:4; Jer 8:22; Lu 5:31.

PHYSIOGNOMY, character revealed in (Isa 3:9).

See Face.

PHYSIOLOGY (Job 10:11; Ps 139:14-16; Pr 14:30).

See Anatomy; Hygiene.

Figurative: Eph 4:16; Col 2:19.

PI-BESETH, a city in lower Egypt.

Prophesied against by Ezekiel (Eze 30:17).

PICTURES, occurs three times in KJV (Nu 33:52), perhaps stone idols are meant (Pr 25:11), inlaid work in gold and silver (Isa 2:16), perhaps the carved figureheads of ships.

PIECE OF SILVER (See Silver.)

PIETY, religious duty.

PIGEON, used as sacrifice (Ge 15:9; Le 1:14; 5:7; 12:8; 14:22; Lu 2:24).

See Dove.

PI-HAHIROTH, the place on the W shore of the Red Sea where Pharaoh overtook the Israelites (Ex 14:2, 9; Nu 33:7, 8).

PILATE, PONTIUS. Roman governor of Judaea (M't 27:2; Lu 3:1). Causes slaughter of certain Galileans (Lu 13:1). Tries Jesus and orders his crucifixion (M't 27; M'k 15; Lu 23; Joh 18:28-40; 19; Ac 3:13; 4:27; 13:28; 1Ti 6:13). Allows Joseph of Arimathaea to take Jesus' body (M't 27:57, 58; M'k 15:43-45; Lu 23:52; Joh 19:38).

PILDASH, son of Nahor (Ge 22:22).

PILEHA, one of those who sealed the covenant with Nehemiah (Ne 10:24).

PILGRIM, sojourner in a strange place (Heb 11:13-16; 1Pe 2:11).

PILGRIMAGE. 1. Jews were expected to make pilgrimages to the temple in Jerusalem for the great feasts (Ps 120-134; Ac 2:5-11).

2. The NT describes Christians as pilgrims (Heb 11:13; 1Pe 2:11).

PILLAR. Of Solomon's temple (1Ki 7:13-22; 2Ki 25:17). Broken and carried to Babylon (2Ki 25:13; Jer 52:17, 20, 21). Of Solomon's palaces (1Ki 7:6).

Used to mark roads (Jer 31:21). Pillar of salt, Lot's wife turned to (Ge 19:26; Lu 17:32). Monuments erected to commemorate events: By Jacob, his vision of angels (Ge 28:18, w 31:13; 35:14); his covenant with Laban (Ge 31:45); by Moses, the covenant between Jehovah and Israel (Ex 24:4); by Joshua, the passing over Jordan (Jos 4:1-9, w De 27:2-6; Jos 8:30); at Shechem (Jos 24:25-27, w J'g 9:6); by Samuel, the discomfiture of the Philistines (1Sa 7:12); by Absalom, to keep his name in remembrance (2Sa 18:18). As a boundary (Jos 15:6, w 18:17); a waymark (1Sa 20:19); a landmark (2Sa 20:8; 1Ki 1:9). Prophecy of one in Egypt (Isa 19:19). Monuments of idolatry, to be destroyed (De 12:3).

Figurative: Re 3:12.

PILLAR OF CLOUD AND FIRE. God guided Israel out of Egypt and through the wilderness by a pillar of cloud by day and fire by night (Ex 13:21, 22). The pillar of cloud rested over the tent of meeting outside the camp whenever the Lord met Moses there (Ex 33:7-11). The cloud and fire were divine manifestations.

PILLOW. 1. A cushion (Ge 28:11, 18; 1Sa 26:7, 11, 16).

2. A support for the head. Stones used for (Ge 28:11, 18). Called bolster (1Sa 26:7, 11, 12, 16). Jesus sleeps on (M'k 4:35).

Figurative: Of false teachers (Eze 13:18, 20).

PILOT, mentioned among the skilled craftsmen of Tyre (Eze 27:8, 27, 28, 29).

PILTAI, a priest who returned to Jerusalem from captivity in Babylon (Ne 12:17).

PIM (See Weights and Measures.)

PIN, tent peg (J'g 4:21; 5:26); stick for beating up woof in the loom (J'g 16:13, 14); crisping pins (Isa 3:22) were probably bags or purses.

PINE, a tree (Ne 8:15; Isa 41:19;60:13).

PINING AWAY (Le 26:39; La 4:9; Eze 4:17; 24:23; 33:10).

PINNACLE, on a building, a turret, battlement, pointed roof or peak. Satan tried to get Jesus to cast Himself down from the pinnacle of the temple (M't 4:5, 6; Lu 4:9).

PINON, chief of Edom of the family of Esau (Ge 36:40, 41; 1Ch 1:52).

PIPE, a wind instrument of music. Used in religious services (1Sa 10:5; Isa 30:29).

See Music, Instruments of.

PIRAM, a king of the Amorites. Overcome and slain by Joshua (Jos 10:3, 16-18, 24-27).

PIRATHON. A place in the land of Ephraim (J'g 12:15). Men of (J'g 12:13; 2Sa 23:30; 1Ch 11:31; 27:14).

PIRATHONITE (See Pirathon.)

PISGAH, a ridge or mountain E of the Jordan, opposite to Jericho. The Israelites come to (Nu 21:20). A boundary of the country assigned to the Reubenites and Gadites (De 3:17; 4:49; Jos 12:3). Balaam prophesies on (Nu 23:14-24). Moses views Palestine from (De 3:27; 34:1-4).

PISIDIA, a province in Asia Minor. Paul visits (Ac 13:14; 14:24).

PISON, one of the rivers of Eden (Ge 2:11).

PISPAH, an Asherite (1Ch 7:38).

PIT, bitumen deposit "slime pits" (Ge 14:10); deep place (M't 12:11; Ge 37:20-29); well or cistern (Jer 14:3; Lu 14:5); earthen vessel (Le 11:33); death, grave, or Sheol (Job 33:18; Isa 14:15; Nu 16:30, 33).

PITCH. 1. Asphalt or bitumen (Ge 14:10; Ex 2:3).

2. To encamp (Ge 12:8; 31:25; Ex 17:1; Nu 1:51; Jos 8:11).

PITCHER, earthenware water jar (Ge 24:14-20; M'k 14:13; Lu 22:10).

PITHOM, Egyptian store city in valley between the Nile and Lake Timsah; dedicated to the sungod Atum (Ex 1:11).

PITHON, son of Micah (1Ch 8:35; 9:41).

PITY, tender, considerate, compassionate feeling for others.

Enjoined (Job 6:14; 1Pe 3:8). For the poor (Pr 19:17; 28:8). Forbidden, to Canaanites (De 7:16); to idolatrous proselytizers (De 13:8); to murderers (De 19:13); to false witnesses (De 19:21); to amazons (De 25:12).

Withholding of, from Jesus, prefigured in David (Ps 69:20). Of God (Ps 103:13; Isa 63:9; Joe 2:18; Jon 4:11; Jas 5:11); withheld from reprobates (Jer 13:14; 21:7; Eze 5:11; 7:4; 8:18; 9:5, 10; Zec 11:6).

Required of believers (Isa 1:17; M't 18:28-35).

See God, Mercy of; Jesus, Compassion of; Mercy.

PLAGUE. As a judgment on the Egyptians (Ps 105; 135:8, 9; Ac 7:36). The plague of blood (Ex 7:14-25); frogs (Ex 8:1, 15); lice (Ex 8:16-19); flies (Ex 8:20). On cattle (Ex 9:1-7). Of boils and blains (Ex 9:8-12); hail (Ex 9:18-34); locusts (Ex 10:1-20); darkness (Ex 10:21-23). Death of the firstborn (Ex 11:4-7; 12:17, 29, 30).

On the Israelites: On account of idolatry (Ex 32:35); after eating quail (Nu 11:33); after refusing to enter the promised land (Nu 14:37); after murmuring on account of the destruction of Korah (Nu 16:41-50); of serpents (Nu 21:6); for the sin of Peor (Jos 22:17), on account of David's sin (2Sa 24:10-25).

On the Philistines (1Sa 6:4, 5).

Denounced as a judgment (Le 26:21; De 28:59). Foretold (Re 11:6; 15:1, 6-8; 16; 22:18, 19).

See Judgments; Pestilence.

PLAIN, broad stretch of level land (Ge 11:2; Eze 3:22).

PLAISTER (See Plaster.)

PLAITING (See Dress.)

PLAN OF SALVATION. (See Jesus, Mission of; Redemption; Salvation.)

PLANE, a tool (Isa 44:13).

PLANET (See Astronomy; Stars.)

PLANTS OF THE BIBLE. The following plants are mentioned in the Bible. Some of them are not identifiable. Algum tree (2Ch 2:8; 11:9); almond (Ex 25:33-36); almug tree probably identical with algum (1Ki 10:11, 12); aloes (Ps 45:8; Joh 19:39); translated "odours"; amomum (Re 18:13); anise (M't 23:23); apple (Song 2:3)—many think that the apricot is meant; aspalathus (Ec 24:15); balm (Eze 27:17); barley (Ho 3:2); bdellium (Nu 11:6, 7); beans (Eze 4:9), box tree (Isa 41:19; 60:13); bramble (J'g 9:14, 15); brier (Eze 28:24); bulrush (Ex 2:3); bush (burning bush) (Ex 3:2, 3); camphire (Song 1:14); cassia (Ex 30:22-25); cedar of Lebanon (Eze 31:3, 5); chestnut (plane tree) (Ge 30:37); cinnamon (Ex 30:23); cockle (Job 31:40); coriander (Ex 16:31); corn (wheat) (De 8:8); cotton (Es 1:5, 6 RSV); cucumber (Nu 11:5); cummin (Isa 28:26, 27); cypress (Isa 44:14); desire (caper) (Ec 12:5); dove's dung (2Ki 6:25); ebony (Eze 27:15); eelgrass (Jon 2:5); elm (Ho 4:13); flag (Ex 2:3, 5); fig (Ge 3:6, 7); fir (Isa 60:13); fitches (Isa 28:25-27); flax, source of linen (Lu 23:52, 53); frankincense (M't 2:11); galbanum (Ex 30:34-36); gall (M't 27:34); garlic (Nu 11:5); gourd (Jon 4:5-7); grape (Ge 40:10, 11); green bay tree (Ps 37:35); hemlock (Ho 10:4); herbs, bitter herbs (Ex 12:8); hyssop (1Ki 4:33); juniper (1Ki 19:3, 4); leeks (Nu 11:5); lentil (Ge 25:29, 30, 34); lilies (of the field) (Lu 12:27); lily (Song 5:13); locusts (M't 3:4); mallows (Job 30:1, 3, 4); mandrake (Ge

30:14-16); melon (Nu 11:5); millet or "pannag" (Eze 4:9; 27:17); mint (Lu 11:42); mulberry tree (2Sa 5:23, 24); mustard (M't 13:31, 32); myrrh (OT) (Ge 37:25, 26, 2.,, (NT) (M't 2:11); myrtle (Zec 1:7, 8); nettle (Job 30:7); nuts (walnut) (Song 6:11); nuts (pistachio) (Ge 43:11); oak (holly oak) (Ge 35:8); oak (valonia oak) (Zec 11:2); oil tree (Isa 41:19); olive (Ex 27:20); onion (Nu 11:5); onycha (Ex 30:34, 35); palm (date) (Nu 33:9); pannag (millet) (Eze 4:9; 27:17); parched corn (wheat, q.v.); pine tree (fir) (Isa 60:13); plane tree (chestnut, q.v.); pomegranate (1Sa 14:2); poplar (Ge 30:37); pulse (2Sa 17:28); reed (Job 40:15. 20-22); rie, rye (spelt) (Ex 9:32); rolling thing (rose of Jericho) (Isa 17:13); rose (narcissus) (Isa 35:1); rose of Sharon (Song 2:1, 2); rue (Lu 11:42); rush (flag) (Ex 2:3); saffron (Song 4:14); shittah tree (Isa 41:18; Ex 25:10); spices (Ge 43:11); spikenard (M'k 14:3); stacte (storax) (Ex 30:34); strange vine (vine, q.v.); sweet cane (sugar cane) (Isa 43:24); sweet cane (calamus, sweet calamus) (Jer 6:20); sycamine (Lu 17:6); sycamore (Am 7:14); tares (M't 13:25); teil (turpentine tree, q.v.); thistles (2Ki 14:9); thorns (crown of thorns) (M'k 15:17); thorns (Isa 7:19); thyine wood (Re 18:12); turpentine tree (teil tree) (Isa 6:13); vine (true) (Ge 40:9-11); vine (wild vine, vine of Sodom, q.v.); vine of Sodom (De 32:23)—it is uncertain what plant is intended; water lily (1Ki 7:19, 22, 26); weeds (eelgrass, q.v.); wheat (Ge 41:22); wild gourd (2Ki 4:39); willow (aspen) (Ps 137:2); willow "withes" (J'g 16:7-9); wormwood (La 3;15, 19).

PLASTER, in Egypt stone buildings, even the finest granite, were plastered, inside and out, to make a smooth surface for decoration (De 27:2, 4). The poor used a mixture of clay and straw. In Palestine an outside clay coating would have to be renewed after the rainy season.

PLASTER, MEDICINAL, in Isa 38:21 a cake of figs applied to a boil.

PLEADING (De 17:8). Of the guilty (Jos 7:19-21). Jesus declined to plead (M't 26:62; M'k 15:2; Lu 23:3; Joh 18:33, 34). Prisoners required to plead (Ac 7:1).

See Defense.

PLEASURE, WORLDLY. Unfulfilling (Job 21:12, 13; Ec 1:17; 2:1-13; 1Ti 5:6). Proverbs and parables concerning (Pr 9:17; 15:21; 21:17; Lu 8:14).

Rejected and judged by God (Job 20:12-16; Isa 5:11, 12; 22:12, 13; 47:8, 9; Am 6:1; Ro 1:32; 2Th 2:12). Rejected, by Moses (Heb 11:25, 26); Paul (2Ti 3:4; Tit 3:3); Peter (2Pe 2:13).

See Happiness; Joy; Worldliness.

PLEDGE, personal property of a debtor held to secure a payment (Ge 38:17, 18). Law of Moses was concerned with protection of the poor. A pledged outer garment had to be restored at sunset for a bed covering (Ex 22:26, 27); a widow's clothing could not be taken (De 24:17); a handmill or its upper millstone could not be taken (De 24:6).

PLEIADES, stars in constellation Taurus (Job 9:9; 38:31).

PLINY, Caius Plinius Caecilius Secundus, called "the Younger," Roman governmental official, famous as the author of literary letters covering all manner of subjects, one of which contains a description of the Christian church in Bithynia, a province which Pliny governed in A. D. 112. The letter, together with the reply of the emperor Trajan are important evidence for the official attitude towards the Christians.

PLOTTING, General References to (Es 3:9; Ps 36:4; 37:12; Pr 6:14; Isa 32:7; Mic 2:1). Against Christ (M't 12:14; 26:4; 27:1; Lu 6:11; 19:47; 22:4; Joh 5:16; 11:47, 53). General Examples of (Ge 37:18; Nu 16:3; J'g 9:1; 2Ki 12:20; 14:19; Da 6:4; M't 12:14; Ac 23:13).

PLOW, PLOUGH. The ancient plow consisted of a forked stick, the trunk hitched to the animals which drew it, the branch braced and terminating in the share, which was at first the sharpened end of the branch, later a metal point. It was ordinarily drawn by a yoke of oxen (Job 1:14; Am 6:12). Such a plow did not turn over the soil; it did little more than scratch the surface.

Figurative: Of afflictions (Ps 129:3).

PLOWSHARE (the blade of a plow), to beat swords into plowshares was symbolic of an age of peace (Isa 2:4); to beat plowshares into swords portended coming war (Joe 3:10).

PLUMB LINE, a cord with a weight,

the plummet, tied to one end; used in testing whether a wall is perpendicular (Am 7:7-9; 2Ki 21:13; Isa 28:17).

PLUMMET (Am 7:7, 8; Zec 4:10).

Figurative: Isa 28:17.

POCHERETH, the ancestor of a family which returned to Jerusalem from captivity in Babylon (Ezr 2:57; Ne 7:59).

POET (a maker); Paul quotes from pagan poets in Ac 17:28; 1Co 15:32; and Tit 1:12. A great deal of the OT is written in the form of poetry.

POETRY. *Acrostic:* Pss 25; 34; 37; 111; 112; 119; 145; Pr 31:10-31; La 1-5.

Didactic: Moses' song (De 32). The Book of Job, the Proverbs, Solomon's Song, the books of prophecy. (See Psalms, Didactic.)

Elegy: On the death of Saul (2Sa 1:19-27). Of Abner (2Sa 3:33, 34). See Elegy.

Epic: Moses' song (Ex 15:1-19). Miriam's song (Ex 15:21). Song of Deborah (J'g 5).

Lyrics, Sacred: Moses' and Miriam's songs (Ex 15). Hannah's song (1Sa 2:1-10). The song of Elizabeth (Lu 1:42-45). Of Mary (Lu 1:46-55). Of Zacharias (Lu 1:68-79). The Psalms, which see.

POETS, PAGAN, QUOTATIONS FROM. NT quotations from pagan poets are confined to Paul. Acts 17:28 contains a quotation from Cleanthes. Titus 1:12 is a quotation from Epimenides. 1Co 15:33 is a quotation from Menander.

POISON, a substance producing a deadly effect, like the venom of reptiles (De 32:24, 33; Job 20:16; Ps 58:4). Vegetable poisons were known in antiquity; hemlock (Ho 10:4 RSV); wild gourd (2Ki 4:39, 40). A poisoned drink is referred to in M'k 16:18.

POLE, standard on which the brazen serpent was displayed (Nu 21:8, 9).

POLICY (See Diplomacy.)

POLITARCH, city magistrate of Thessalonica (Ac 17:6, 8). Sixteen epigraphical inscriptions with the word have been discovered.

POLITICS, statecraft. *Corruption in:* Ps 12:8; in the court of Ahasuerus (Es 3); of Darius (Da 6:4-15).

Instances of: Absalom, electioneering for the throne (2Sa 15:2-6). Pilate, condemning Jesus to gratify popular clamor (M't 27:23-27; M'k 15:15; Lu 23:13-25; Joh 18:38, 39; 19:4-13).

Ministers in: Zadok the priest, a partisan of David (2Sa 15:24-29). Nathan, the prophet, influences the selection of David's successor (1Ki 1:11-40).

Women in: The wise woman of Abel, who saved the city through diplomacy (2Sa 20:16-22). Bath-sheba, in securing the crown for Solomon (1Ki 1:15-21). Herodias, in influencing the administration of Herod (M't 14:3-11; M'k 6:17-28). Mother of Zebedee's children, in seeking favor for her sons (M't 20:20-23).

For Influence in, see Influence, Political.

See Diplomacy; Government.

POLL (skull, head), as a verb, "to shear"; as a noun, "head" (Mic 1:16; Nu 1:2-22).

POLL TAX (See Tax.)

POLLUTION, ceremonial or moral defilement, profanation, and uncleanness (Ex 20:25; 2Pe 2:20).

POLLUX, with Castor, one of the Twin Brothers, sons of Zeus and patrons of sailors (Ac 28:11).

POLYGAMY. Forbidden (De 17:17; Le 18:18; Mal 2:14, 15; M't 19:4, 5; M'k 10:2-8; 1Ti 3:2, 12; Tit 1:6). Authorized (2Sa 12:8).

Tolerated (Ex 21:10; 1Sa 1:2; 2Ch 24:3). Practiced (Job 27:15); by Lamech (Ge 4:19); Abraham (Ge 16); Esau (Ge 26:34; 28:9); Jacob (Ge 29:30); Ashur (1Ch 4:5); Gideon (J'g 8:30); Elkanah (1Sa 1:2); David (1Sa 25:39-44; 2Sa 3:2-5; 5:13; 1Ch 14:3). Solomon (1Ki 11:1-8); Rehoboam (2Ch 11:18-23); Abijah (2Ch 13:21); Jehoram (2Ch 21:14); Joash (2Ch 24:3); Ahab (2Ki 10:1); Jehoiachin (2Ki 24:15); Belshazzar (Da 5:2; see 1Ch 2-8); Hosea (Ho 3:1, 2). Mosaic law respecting the firstborn in (De 21:15-17).

Sought by women (Isa 4:1).

The evil effects of: Husband's favoritism in (De 21:15-17); Jacob's (Ge 29:30; 30:15); Elkanah's (1Sa 1:5); Rehoboam's (2Ch 11:21). Domestic infelicity, in Abraham's family (Ge 16; 21:9-16); Jacob's (Ge 29:30-34; 30:1-23); Elkanah's (1Sa 1:4-7). Upon Solomon (1Ki 11:4-8).

See Concubinage; Marriage.

POLYTHEISM (Ge 31:19; 35:2, 4; Jos 24:2, 23; J'g 2:13; 3:7; 10:16; 17:5; Jer 2:28; 11:13; Da 4:8; 1Co 8:5).

POMEGRANATE, a fruit. Abounded in the land of Canaan (1Sa 14:2). Brought by the spies to show the fruitfulness of the land of Canaan (Nu 13:23). Figures of the fruits of, were embroidered on the ephod (Ex 28:33, 34; 39:24); carved on the pillars of the temple (1Ki 7:18, 20, 42; Jer 52:22, 23). Wine made of (Song 8:2).

POMMEL (basin), bowl-shaped part of the capitals of the temple pillars (2Ch 4:12, 13).

PONTIUS PILATE (See Pilate.)

PONTUS (sea). A province of Asia Minor (Ac 2:9; 1Pe 1:1). Aquila lived in (Ac 18:2).

POOL. Of Gibeon (2Sa 2:13; Jer 41:12). Of Hebron (2Sa 4:12). Of Samaria (1Ki 22:38). Of Heshbon (Song 7:4).

Of Jerusalem: Upper pool (2Ki 18:17; Isa 36:2); lower pool (Isa 22:9); Siloam (Joh 9:7, 11); called Siloah (Neh 3:15); and probably identical with the king's pool (Neh 2:14).

POOR (Job 30:25; 34:19; Ps 37:16; Isa 29:19; M'k 12:43, 44; Joh 12:8; 2Co 6:10). Proverbs concerning (Pr 10:15; 13:7, 8, 23; 24:20, 21, 31; 18:28; 19:1, 4, 7, 17, 22; 20:13; 21:13; 22:2, 9; 23:21; 28:6, 8, 11, 19; 29:14; Ec 4:6, 13; 6:8; 9:15, 16). Always part of society (M't 26:11; M'k 14:7). The lesson, from the poor widow (M'k 12:43, 44); from Lazarus (Lu 16:20, 21); from Judas (Joh 12:6). Attitude toward (Jas 1:9, 10).

Duty to (Ex 22:25-27; 23:11; Le 19:9, 10; 25:25-28, 35-43; De 14:28, 29; 15:2-14; 24:12-21; 26:12, 13; Ne 8:10; Ps 37:21, 26; Ps 41:1-3; 28:27; 29:7; 31:9, 20; 112:4, 5, 9; Isa 1:7; 16:3, 4; 58:7, 10; Eze 18:7; Da 4:27; Zec 7:10; M't 5:42; 19:21; 25:35, 36; M'k 14:7; Lu 3:11; 6:30; 11:41; 12:33; 14:12-14; 18:22; 19:8; Ac 20:35; Ro 12:8, 13, 20; 1Co 13:3; 16:1, 2; 2Co 6:10; 8:9; 9:5-7; Ga 2:10; 6:10; Eph 4:28; 1Ti 5:9, 10, 16; Heb 13:3; Jas 1:27; 2:2-9, 15, 16; 5:4; 1Jo 3:17-19).

God's care of (1Sa 2:7, 8; Job 5:15, 16; 31:15; 34:18, 19, 28; 36:6, 15; Ps 9:8; 10:14; 12:5; 14:6; 34:6; 35:10; 68:10; 69:33; 72:2, 4, 12-14; 74:21; 102:17; 107:9, 36, 41; 109:31; 113:7, 8; 132:15; 140:12; 146:5, 7; Pr 22:2, 22, 23; 29:13; Ec 5:8; Isa 11:4; 14:30, 32; 25:4; 29:19; 41:17; Jer 20:13; Zep 3:12; 11:7; M't 11:5; Lu 4:18; 7:22; 16:22; Jas 2:5). See God, Goodness of, Providence of.

Friendlessness of (Pr 14:20; 19:4, 7). Wisdom of, despised (Ec 9:15, 16).

Warning against neglect of (Pr 20:13; 21:13; 22:16; Eze 16:49). Neglect of, by the disciples (Ac 6:1-6). Neglect of, denounced (M't 25:42-45).

Righteous treatment of, required (Ps 82:3, 4; Pr 22:22; 31:9; Isa 1:17); rewarded (Pr 29:14; Jer 22:16; Eze 18:7, 16, 17; Da 4:27). Compassion toward (Job 30:25; Pr 14:21; 29:7; Heb 13:3; Jas 1:27).

Liberality to (Pr 31:20; Isa 58:7; M't 5:42 w Lu 6:30; Lu 3:11; 19:8; Ro 12:8, 13, 20; 1Co 13:3; 16:1, 2; 2Co 9:1-15; Ga 2:10; Eph 4:28; 1Ti 5:9, 10, 16; Jas 2:15, 16; 1Jo 3:17). Liberality to, rewarded (Pr 19:17; 22:9; 28:27; Ps 112:9; M't 19:21; 25:34-36; Lu 6:35; 12:33; 18:22; Ac 20:35).

Kindness to: Enjoined (Ne 8:10, 12). Rewarded (Ps 41:1-3; Isa 58:10; Lu 14:12-14).

Instances of: By Ruth, to Naomi (Ru 2:2, 11). Boaz, to Ruth (Ru 2:8-16; 3:15). Elijah, to the widow of Zarephath (1Ki 17:12-24). Elisha, to the prophet's widow (2Ki 4:1-7). The Jews. (Es 9:22). Job (Job 29:11-17; 31:16-22, 38-40). The Temanites (Isa 21:14). Nebuzar-adan (Jer 39:10). The good Samaritan (Lu 10:33-35). Zacchaeus (Lu 19:8). Dorcas (Ac 9:36). Cornelius (Ac 10:2, 4). Christian church, at Jerusalem (Ac 6:1); at Antioch (Ac 11:29, 30). Churches of Macedonia and Achaia (Ro 15:25, 26; 2Co 8:1-5). By Paul (Ro 15:25).

Oppression of (Ne 5:1-13; Job 20:19-21; 22:6, 7; 24:4, 7-12; Ps 10:2, 8-10; 37:14; 109:16; Pr 14:31; 17:5; 19:7; 22:7, 16; 28:3, 15; 30:14; Ec 5:8; Isa 3:14, 15; 10:1, 2; 32:6, 7; Eze 18:12; 22:29; Am 2:6; 4:1; 5:11, 12; 8:4-6; Hab 3:14; Jas 2:6; 5:4).

Forbidden (De 24:14; Zec 7:10).

Instances of oppression of (2Ki 4:1; Ne 5:1-5).

Mosaic laws concerning: Atonement money of, must be uniform with that of the rich (Ex 30:15). Inexpensive offerings authorized for (Le 5:7; 12:8; 14:21, 22).

Discrimination, in favor of, forbidden (Ex 23:3; Le 19:15); against, forbidden (Ex 23:6; Jas 2:2-9). Exactions of interest from, forbidden (Ex 22:25; Le 25:35-37). Raiment of, taken in pledge, to be restored (Ex 22:26; De 24:12, 13). To participate triennially in the tithes (De 14:28, 29; 26:12, 13). Gleanings reserved for (Le 19:9, 10; 23:22; De 24:19-21). To share the products of the land in the sabbatic year (Ex 23:11). To be released from debt in sabbatic year (De 15:7-11). To be released from servitude, in sabbatic year (De 15:12); in jubilee (Le 25:39-43). Alienated lands of, to be restored in jubilee (Le 25:25-28).

Figurative: Poor in spirit (Isa 66:2; M't 5:3; Lu 6:20).

See Alms; Beneficence; Creditor; Debtor; Employee; Employer; Liberality; Orphans; Poverty; Rich; Riches; Servants; Wages; Widows.

POPLAR, a tree (Ge 30:37; Ho 4:13).

POPULAR SINS, laws against (Ex 23:2).

See Sin.

POPULARITY. *Instances of:* David (2Sa 3:36). Absalom (2Sa 15:2-6, 13). Job (Job 29).

POPULARITY OF JESUS (M't 4:24; 8:1; 13:2; 14:13, 35; 19:1, 2; 21:8, 9; M'k 1:33; 2:2; 3:7, 20; 5:21; 6:33, 55, 66; 10:1; 11:8-10; 12:37; Lu 4:14, 15, 42; 5:1; 9:11; 12:1; 19:35-38; Joh 6:2, 15; 12:12, 13, 19).

PORATHA, son of Haman (Es 9:8).

PORCH, an area with a roof supported by columns: vestibule (1Ki 7:6ff), colonnade (J'g 3:23), place before a court (M'k 14:68), gateway (M't 26:71).

PORCIUS (See Festus.)

PORPOISE (Ex 25:5; [marg., *R.V.*] 26:14; 36:19; 39:34).

PORTERS. Guards at the city gates, the doors of the king's palace, and doors of the temple (1Ch 9:17-32; 2Ch 34:13; 35:15). Lodged round about the temple in order to be present for opening the doors (1Ch 9:27). One-third were porters of the temple (2Ch 23:4); one-third were porters of the king's house (2Ch 23:5); one-third were porters of the gate of the foundation (2Ch 23:5). They served, also, as porters of the gates of the walls (Ne 12:25). They served in twenty-four courses (1Ch 26:13-19). Their posts were determined by lot (1Ch 24:31; 26:13-19).

PORTION, a part; less than the whole of anything; share (Nu 31:30, 47; Ne 8:10, 12).

POST. 1. Part of a doorway (1Ki 6:33).

2. One who conveys a message speedily (Job 9:25).

POSTERITY PROMISED (Ge 15:5, 18; 17:20; 22:17; 26:14; Le 26:9; De 7:13; Ro 4:18).

POT, utensil of metal or clay for holding liquids or other substances (2Ki 4:38).

POTENTATE (mighty one), person with great power and authority (1Ti 6:15).

POTIPHAR, an officer of Pharaoh. Joseph's master (Ge 37:36; 39:1).

POTI-PHERAH, a priest of On. Joseph's father-in-law (Ge 41:45, 50; 46:20).

POTSHERD, fragment of earthenware (Job 2:8; Isa 45:9).

POTTAGE (boiled), stew of vegetables and meat (Ge 25:29, 30, 34; 2Ki 4:38, 39).

POTTER (See Occupations and Professions.)

POTTER'S FIELD, piece of ground which the priests bought with the money Judas received for betraying our Lord (M't 27:7).

POTTER'S GATE, gate in wall of Jerusalem (Jer 19:2).

POTTERY, one of the oldest of crafts in Bible lands. Place where potter's clay was dug was called "potter's field" (M't 27:7). Pottery was shaped by hand on a potter's wheel, powered by foot or by an apprentice (Jer 18:3-6), then dried and baked in a kiln. Many different items were made: bowls, basins, and cups; cooking pots; jars; decanters, flasks, and juglets; lamps; ovens; braziers; dishes. Thousands of objects have been found by the archaeologists. Careful study has been made of the historical development of pottery styles, so that experts can date and place pottery with considerable accuracy.

POUND. The Hebrew word "maneh" is translated "pound" (1Ki 10:17; Ezr 2:69; Ne 7:71, 72), and is equivalent to about one pound, fourteen ounces. In John

12:3 the weight was equivalent to about twelve ounces. In Luke 19:13-25 the Greek word "mina" is translated "pound," and worth approximately nineteen dollars.

See Measure; Weights.

POVERTY (1Sa 2:7). Destructive (Pr 10:15). A source of temptation (Pr 30:8, 9). To be preferred over wealth, with trouble (Pr 15:16); without right (Pr 16:8; Ec 4:6).

Caused: By laziness (Pr 6:11; 20:13; 24:33, 34); by drunkenness (Pr 23:21); by evil associations (Pr 28:19).

See Poor.

POWER. *Of Christ:* As the Son of God, is the power of God (Joh 5:17-19; 10:28-30); as man, is from the Father (Ac 10:38).

Described as supreme (Eph 1:20, 21: 1Pe 3:22); unlimited (M't 28:18); over all flesh (Joh 17:2); over all things (Joh 3:35; Eph 1:22); glorious (2Th 1:9); everlasting (1Ti 6:16). Is able to subdue all things (Ph'p 3:21).

Exemplified in creation (Joh 1:3, 10; Col 1:16); upholding all things (Col 1:17; Heb 1:3); salvation (Isa 63:1; Heb 7:25); His teaching (M't 7:28, 29; Lu 4:32); working miracles (M't 8:27; Lu 5:17); enabling others to work miracles (M't 10:1; Ac 5:31); giving spiritual life (Joh 5:21, 25, 26); giving eternal life (Joh 17:2), raising the dead (Joh 5:28, 29); rising from the dead (Joh 2:19; 10:18); overcoming the world (Joh 16:33); overcoming Satan (Col 2:15; Heb 2:14); destroying the works of Satan (1Jo 3:8); ministers should make known (2Pe 1:16).

Saints made willing by (Ps 110:3); succored by (Heb 2:18); strengthened by (Ph'p 4:13; 2Ti 4:17); preserved by (2Ti 1:12; 4:18); bodies of, shall be changed by (Ph'p 3:21); rests upon saints (2Co 12:9). Present in the assembly of saints (1Co 5:4). Shall be specially manifested at His second coming (M'k 13:26; 2Pe 1:16). Shall subdue all power (1Co 15:24). The wicked shall be destroyed by (Ps 2:9; Isa 11:4; 63:3; 2Th 1:9).

See Jesus, Omnipotence of, Power of.

Of God: One of His attributes (Ps 62:11).

Expressed by the voice of God (Ps 29:3, 5; 68:33); finger of God (Ex 9:3, 15; Isa 48:13); arm of God (Job 40:9; Isa 52:10); thunder of His power (Job 26:14).

Described as great (Ps 79:11; Na 1:3); strong (Ps 89:13; 136:12); glorious (Ex 15:6; Isa 63:12); mighty (Job 9:4; Ps 89:13); everlasting (Isa 26:4; Ro 1:20); sovereign (Ro 9:21); effectual (Isa 43:13; Eph 3:7); irresistible (De 32:39; Da 4:35); incomparable (Ex 15:11, 12; De 3:24; Job 40:9; Ps 89:8); unsearchable (Job 5:9; 9:10); incomprehensible (Job 26:14; Ec 3:11).

All things possible to (M't 19:26). Nothing too hard for (Ge 18:14; Jer 32:27). Can save by many or by few (1Sa 14:6). Is the source of all strength (1Ch 29:12; Ps 68:35).

Exemplified in the creation (Ps 102:25; Jer 10:12); in establishing and governing all things (Ps 65:6; 66:7); in the miracles of Christ (Lu 11:20); in the resurrection of Christ (2Co 13:4; Col 2:12); in the resurrection of saints (1Co 6:14); in making the gospel effectual (Ro 1:16; 1Co 1:18, 24); in delivering His people (Ps 106:8); in the destruction of the wicked (Ex 9:16; Ro 9:22).

Saints long for exhibitions of (Ps 63:1, 2); have confidence in (Jer 20:11); receive increase of grace by (2Co 9:8); strengthened by (Eph 6:10; Col 1:11); upheld by (Ps 37:17; Isa 41:10); supported in affliction by (2Co 6:7; 2Ti 1:8); delivered by (Nu 1:10; Da 3:17); exalted by (Job 36:22); kept by, unto salvation (1Pe 1:5). Exerted in behalf of saints (1Ch 16:9). Works in and for saints (2Co 13:4; Eph 1:19; 3:20). The faith of saints stands in (1Co 2:5).

Should be acknowledged (1Ch 29:11; Isa 33:13); pleaded in prayer (Ps 79:11; M't 6:13); feared (Jer 5:22; M't 10:28); magnified (Ps 21:13; Jude 25). Efficiency of ministers is through (1Co 3:6-8; Ga 2:8; Eph 3:7). Is a ground of trust (Isa 26:4; Ro 4:21).

The wicked know not (M't 22:29); have against them (Ezr 8:22); shall be destroyed by (Lu 12:5). The heavenly host magnified (Re 4:11; 5:13; 11:17).

See God, Omnipotent, Power of.

Of the Holy Ghost: Is the power of God (M't 12:28, w Lu 11:20). Christ commenced His ministry in (Lu 4:14). Christ wrought His miracles by (M't 12:28).

Exemplified in creation (Ge 1:2; Job 26:13; Ps 104:30); the conception of Christ (Lu 1:35); raising Christ from the dead (1Pe 3:18); giving spiritual life (Eze 37:11-14, w Ro 8:11); working miracles (Ro 15:19); making the gospel efficacious (1Co 2:4; 1Th 1:5); overcoming all difficulties (Zec 4:6, 7). Promised by the Father (Lu 24:49). Promised by Christ (Ac 1:8).

Saints upheld by (Ps 51:12); strengthened by (Eph 3:16); enabled to speak the truth boldly by (Mic 3:8; Ac 6:5, 10; 2Ti 1:7, 8); helped in prayer by (Ro 8:26); abound in hope by (Ro 15:13). Qualifies ministers (Lu 24:49; Ac 1:8, 9). God's word the instrument of (Eph 6:17).

See Holy Spirit.

Spiritual: From God (Isa 40:29-31; Lu 24:49; 1Co 1:24-28; Ph'p 2:13; 2Ti 1:7). From the Holy Spirit (Joh 7:38, 39; Ac 1:8; 2:2-4). On believers (Ac 6:8, 10; 1Co 4:19, 20; Heb 6:5); from Christ (2Co 12:9; Eph 1:19, 20); in the spirit of Elijah (Lu 1:17).

In preaching (Ac 4:33; 6:10; 1Th 1:5); of Christ (Lu 4:32). Through prayer (Ge 32:28; 9:29; Lu 24:49; Ac 1:14; 2:1-4).

PRAETOR, originally the highest Roman magistrate; later, officials elected to administer justice; under the principate the office declined in prestige, power, and functions.

PRAETORIAN GUARD, guard of imperial palace or provincial governor called "Caesar's household" (Ph'p 1:13; 4:22).

PRAETORIUM, in the Gospels it refers to the temporary palace or headquarters of the Roman governor while in Jerusalem (M't 27:27; M'k 15:16; Joh 18:28, 33); in Acts 23:35, the palace of Herod at Caesarea.

PRAISE. Exemplified (Ps 7:17; 22:22, 23; 28:6, 7; 32:11; 34:1-3; 41:1-3; 42:4; 51:15; 65:1; 71:8, 14, 15; 75:1; 79:13; 81:1; 84:4; 86:12; 89:95; 104:33, 34; 109:30; 113:1, 2; 115:18; 118:15; 140:13; 145:1-21; 146:1-10; 148; 149; 150; Isa 24:15, 16; 25:1, 35:10; 38:19; 43:21; 49:13; 51:3; 52:7-10; Jer 31:7; Ro 11:36; 16:27; 1Co 15:57; Eph 3:20, 21; Heb 2:12; Jude 25; Re 1:6; 14:7).

With music (Ps 33:2, 3; 43:3, 4; 47:1, 6, 7; 57:7-9 w 108:1-3; 66:1, 2, 4; 67:4; 68:4, 32-34; 69:30; 71:22; 81:1; 92:1-3; 95:1, 2; 98:4-6; 104:33; 144:9; 149:2, 3; 150:3-5; Jas 5:13).

Daily (1Ch 23:30; Ps 92:1, 2; 145:2). In the night (Ps 42:8; 63:5, 6; 77:6; 92:1-3; 119:62; 134:1; 149:5; Ac 16:25). Seven times a day (Ps 119:164).

Congregational (Ps 22:22; 26:12; 68:26; 111:1; 116:18, 19; 134:1, 2; 135:2; 149:1).

For God's goodness and mercy (Ps 13:6; 63:3-6; 100:5; 101:1; 106:1, 48; 107:8, 9, 15, 21, 31; 117:2; 118:29; 136:1-26; 138:2; 144:1, 2; 145:7-9, 14-21; 146:7-9; Isa 12:1-6; Jer 33:11). For God's greatness (Ps 48:1; 145:3, 10-12; 147:1-20; Isa 24:14). For God's holiness (Ps 99:3, 5, 9). For God's works (Ps 9:1, 2; 107:8, 9, 15, 21, 31, 32; 145:4-6, 10-13; 147:12-18; 150:2).

For deliverance from enemies (Ge 14:20; Ps 44:7, 8; 54:6, 7; 69:16).

For salvation (Isa 61:3).

Enjoined (De 8:10; Ps 9:11; 30:4; 32:11; 33:1-3; 69:34; 70:4; 95:1, 2, 6, 7; 96:1-4, 7-9; 97:12; 100:1-5; 105:1-5; 117:1; 134:1, 2; 135:1-3, 19-21; Isa 42:10-12; Eph 5:19; Heb 13:15; 1Pe 4:11; 5:11). All nations to praise God (Ps 69:34; 103:22; 148:1-14). Angels exhorted to (Ps 103:20, 21; 148:2). In heaven (Ne 9:6; Job 38:7; Ps 103:20, 21; 148:2-4; Isa 6:3; Eze 3:12; Lu 2:13, 14; 15:7, 10; Re 1:6; 4:8-11; 5:9-14; 7:9-12; 11:6, 17; 14:2, 3; 15:3, 4; 19:1-7).

Song of Moses, after the passage of the Red Sea (Ex 15:1-19). Of Miriam (Ex 15:21). Of Deborah, after defeating the Canaanites (J'g 5). Of Hannah (1Sa 2:1-10). Of David, celebrating his deliverance from the hand of Saul (2Sa 22); on bringing the ark to Zion (1Ch 16:8-36); at the close of his reign (1Ch 29:10-19).

The chorus when Solomon brought the ark into the temple (2Ch 5:13).

Psalms of, for God's goodness to Israel (Pss 46; 48; 65; 66; 68; 76; 81; 85; 98; 105; 124; 126; 129; 135; 136). For God's goodness to righteous men (Pss 23; 34; 36; 91; 100; 103; 107; 117; 121). For God's goodness to individuals (Pss 9; 18; 22; 30; 40; 75; 103; 108; 116; 118; 138; 144). For

God's attributes (Pss 8; 19; 22; 24; 29; 33; 47; 50; 65; 66; 76; 77; 92; 93; 95; 96; 97; 98; 99; 104; 111; 113; 114; 115; 134; 139; 147; 148; 150).

Instances of: Israelites (2Ch 7:2, 3; Ne 9:5, 6). The chorus when Solomon brought the ark into the temple (2Ch 5:13). Daniel (Da 2:20, 23). Nebuchadnezzar (Da 4:37). Jonah (Jon 2:9). Mary (Lu 1:46-55). Shepherds (Lu 2:20). The leper (Lu 17:15). Jesus and his disciples (M't 26:30; M'k 14:26). Disciples (Ac 2:46, 47; 4:24). Paul and Silas, in prison (Ac 16:25).

See Prayer, Thankfulness.

PRAYER (Ps 17:1, 6; 22:1, 2, 19; 28:1, 2; 35:22; 55:1, 2, 16, 17; 57:2; 61:1, 2; 70:5; 102:1, 2; 130:1, 2; 141:1, 2; 142:1, 2).

Attitudes in, see Worship.

Boldness in: Enjoined (Heb 4:16). Exemplified by Abraham in his inquiry concerning Sodom (Ge 18:23-32); by Moses, supplicating for assistance in delivering Israel (Ex 33:12, 18). Secret (Ge 24:63; M't 6:6). Silent (Ps 5:1). Weeping in (Ezr 10:1). In loud voice, satirized by Elijah (1Ki 18:27). Long: Of Pharisees (M't 23:14); scribes (M'k 12:40; Lu 20:47). Profuse, to be avoided (Ec 5:2; M't 6:7). Vain repetitions of, to be avoided (M't 6:7).

Daily, in the morning (Ps 5:3; 88:13; 143:8; Isa 32:2). Morning and evening (Ps 92:2). Twice daily (Ps 88:1). Three times a day (Ps 55:17; Da 6:10). In the night (Ps 119:55, 62). All night (Lu 6:12). Without ceasing (1Th 5:17).

Disbelief in (Job 21:15).

Family: By Abraham (Ge 12:7, 8; 13:4, 18). By Jacob (Ge 35:3, 7). Cornelius (Ac 10:2).

Hypocritical, forbidden (M't 6:5). Should be discreet (Ec 5:2).

"Lord's prayer," taught as model to disciples (M't 6:9-13; Lu 11:2-4).

Of the righteous, acceptable (Pr 15:8, 29). Spirit of, from God (Zec 12:10). Divine help in (Ro 8:26).

Postures in: Bowing (Ge 24:26, 48, 52; Ex 4:31; 34:8, 9; 2Ch 29:29). Kneeling (1Ki 8:54; 2Ch 6:13; Ezr 9:5; Ps 95:6; Da 6:10; Lu 22:41; Ac 20:36; 21:5). Hands uplifted (1Ki 8:22; 2Ch 6:12, 13; Ezr 9:5; Isa 1:15; La 3:41; 1Ti 2:8). Standing (Lu 18:11, 13).

Power of (M'k 9:28, 29; Jas 5:16-18). Accompanied by works (Ne 4:9). Kept in divine remembrance (Re 5:8; 8:3, 4).

Prayer Contest: Proposed by Elijah (1Ki 18:24-39).

Private, enjoined (M't 6:6).

Public, should edify (1Co 14:14, 15). Perseverance in (Ro 12:12; Eph 6:18). Evils averted by (Jer 26:19).

Rebuked: Of Moses, at the Red Sea (Ex 14:15); when he prayed to see Canaan (De 3:23-27). Of Joshua (Jos 7:10).

Social (M't 18:19; Ac 1:13, 14; 16:16, 25; 20:36; 21:5). Held in private houses (Ac 1:13, 14; 12:12); in the temple (Ac 2:46; 3:1).

Submissiveness in: Exemplified by Jesus (M't 26:39; M'k 14:36; Lu 22:42); David (2Sa 12:22, 23); Job (Job 1:20, 21). Private, enjoined (M't 6:6). Exemplified: By Lot (Ge 19:20). Eliezer (Ge 24:12). Jacob (Ge 32:9-12). Gideon (J'g 6:22, 36, 39). Hannah (1Sa 1:10). David (2Sa 7:18-29). Hezekiah (2Ki 20:2). Isaiah (2Ki 20:11). Manasseh (2Ch 33:18, 19). Ezra (Ezr 9:5, 6). Nehemiah (Ne 2:4). Jeremiah (Jer 32:16-25). Daniel (Da 9:3, 19). Jonah (Jon 2:1). Habakkuk (Hab 1:2). Anna (Lu 2:37). Jesus (M't 14:23; 26:36, 39; M'k 1:35; Lu 9:18, 29). Paul (Ac 9:11). Peter (Ac 9:40; 10:9). Cornelius (Ac 10:30).

Tokens asked for, as assurance of answer: By Abraham's servant (Ge 24:14, 42-44). By Gideon (J'g 6:36-40).

Answer to: Promised (Ex 33:17-20; 1Ki 8:22-53; 1Ch 28:9; 2Ch 6; Job 8:5, 6; 12:4; 22:27; 33:26; Ps 10:17; 81:10; Pr 10:24; 15:8, 29; 16:1; 58:9; 65:24; Eze 36:37; M't 6:5-9; 18:19, 20; 21:22; M'k 11:24, 25; Lu 11:9-13; 18:6-8; 21:36; 4:10, 23, 24; Joh 16:23-27; Ro 8:26; 10:12, 13; Eph 2:18; 3:20; Heb 4:16; 10:22, 23; Jas 1:5-7; 1Jo 3:22; 5:14, 15); to those in adversity (Ex 6:5, 6 w Ac 7:34; Ex 22:23, 27; Ps 9:10, 12; 18:3; 32:6; 34:15, 17; 37:4, 5; 38:15; 50:15; 55:16, 17; 56:9; 65:2, 5; 69:32, 33; 86:7; 95:15; 102:17-20; Isa 19:20; 30:19; 31:9; Joe 2:18, 19, 32; Zec 10:1, 6; 13:9); to those who diligently seek God (2Ch 7:14; Ps 145:18, 19; Pr 2:3, 5; 3:6; Isa 55:6; Jer 29:12, 13; 33:3; La 3:25; Am 5:4-6; Zep 2:3; Zec 13:9; 7:7-11; Joh 9:31; 15:7, 16; Heb 11:6; Jas 4:8, 10;

5:16); to the meek (M'k 11:25); to the penitent (De 4:30, 31; 2Ch 7:13-15).

Delayed (Ps 22:1, 2; 40:1; 80:4; 88:14; Jer 42:2-7; Hab 1:2; Lu 18:7).

Withheld: Of Balaam (De 23:5; Jos 24:10). Of Job (Job 30:20 w 42:12). Of the Israelites, when attacked by the Amorites (De 1:45). The prayer of Jesus, "Let this cup pass" (M't 26:39, 42, 44 w 45-75 and ch 27).

Exceeds Petition (Eph 3:20). Solomon asked wisdom; the answer included wisdom, riches, honor and long life (1Ki 3:7-14; 2Ch 1:7-12). Disciples prayed for Peter, the answer included Peter's deliverance (Ac 12:15 w *verse* 5).

Different from request: Moses asked to see God's face; God revealed his goodness (Ex 33:18-20). Moses asked to be permitted to cross Jordan; the answer was permission to view the land of promise (De 3:23-27). The Israelites lusted for the fleshpots of Egypt; the answer gave them flesh, but also leanness of soul (Ps 106:14, 15). Martha and Mary asked Jesus to come and heal their brother Lazarus; Jesus delayed, but raised Lazarus from the dead (Joh 11). Paul asked that the thorn in the flesh be removed; the answer was a promise of grace to endure it (2Co 12:8, 9).

Answered (Job 34:28; Ps 3:4; 4:1; 6:8, 9; 18:6; 21:2, 4; 22:4, 5, 24; 28:6; 30:2, 3: 31:22; 34:4-6; 40:1; 66:19, 20; 77:1, 2; 81:7; 99:6-8; 106:44; 107:6, 13; 116:1-8; 118:5, 21; 119:26; 120:1; 138:3; Lam 3:57, 58; Ho 12:4; Jon 2:1, 2, 7; Lu 23:42, 43; Ac 4:31; 2Co 12:8, 9; Jas 5:17, 18).

Instances of Answered: Cain (Ge 4:13-15). Abraham, for a son (Ge 15); entreating for Sodom (Ge 18:23-33); for Ishmael (Ge 17:20); for Abimelech (Ge 20:17). Hagar, for deliverance (Ge 16:7-13). Abraham's servant, for guidance (Ge 24:12-52). Rebecca, concerning her pains in pregnancy (Ge 25:22, 23). Jacob, for deliverance from Esau (Ge 32:9-32; 33:1-17). Moses, for help at the Red Sea (Ex 14:15, 16); at the waters of Marah (Ex 15:25); at Horeb (Ex 17:4-6); in the battle with the Amalekites (Ex 17:8-14); concerning the murmuring of the Israelites for flesh (Nu 11:11-35); in behalf of Miriam's leprosy (Nu 12:13-15). Moses, Aaron, and Samuel (Ps 99:6).

Israelites: for deliverance from bondage (Ex 2:23-25; 3:7-10; Ac 7:34); from Pharaoh's army (Ex 14:10-30); from the king of Mesopotamia (J'g 3:9, 15); Sisera (J'g 4:3, 23, 24; 1Sa 12:9-11); Ammon (J'g 10:6-18; 11:1-33); for God's favor under the reproofs of Azariah (2Ch 15:1-15); from Babylonian bondage (Ne 9:27).

Gideon, asking the token of dew (J'g 6:36-40). Manoah, asking about Samson (J'g 13:8, 9). Samson, asking for strength (J'g 16:28-30). Hannah, asking for a child (1Sa 1:10-17, 19, 20). David, asking whether Keilah would be delivered into his hands (1Sa 23:10-12); and Ziklag (1Sa 30:8); whether he should go into Judah after Saul's death (2Sa 2:1); whether he should go against the Philistines (2Sa 5:19-25). David, in adversity (Ps 118:5; 138:3). Solomon, asking wisdom (1Ki 3:1-13; 9:2, 3). Elijah, raising the widow's son (1Ki 17:22); asking fire on his sacrifice (1Ki 18:36-38); rain (1Ki 17:1; 18:1, 42-45; Jas 5:17). Elisha, leading the Syrian army (2Ki 6:17-20). Jabez, asking for prosperity (1Ch 4:10). Abijah, for victory over Jeroboam (2Ch 13:14-18). Asa, for victory over Zerah (2Ch 14:11-15). The people of Judah (2Ch 15:15). Jehoshaphat, for victory over the Canaanites (2Ch 18:31; 20:6-27). Jehoahaz, for victory over Hazael (2Ki 13:4). Priests and Levites, when blessing the people (2Ch 30:27). Hezekiah and Isaiah, for deliverance from Sennacherib (2Ki 19:14-20; 2Ch 32:20-23); to save Hezekiah's life (2Ki 20:1-7, 11; 2Ch 32:24). Manasseh, for deliverance from the king of Babylon (2Ch 33:13, 19). Reubenites, for deliverance from the Hagarites (1Ch 5:20). The Jews, returning from the captivity (Ezr 8:21, 23). Ezekiel, to have the baking of his bread of affliction changed (Eze 4:12-15). Daniel, for the interpretation of Nebuchadnezzar's dream (Da 2:19-23); interceding for the people (Da 9:20-23); in a vision (Da 10:12). Zacharias, for a son (Lu 1:13). The leper, for healing (M't 8:2, 3; M'k 1:40-43; Lu 5:12, 13). Centurion, for his servant (M't 8:5-13; Lu 7:3-10; Joh 4:50, 51). Peter, asking that Tabitha be restored (Ac 9:40). The disciples, for Peter (Ac

12:5-17). Paul, to be restored to health (2Co 1:9-11).

Confession in (Le 26:40; Ezr 10:1; Lu 15:21; 16:13). Enjoined (Le 5:5; Nu 5:6, 7; Jer 3:13, 25). A condition of forgiveness (1Ki 8:47, 49, 50; Pr 28:13; 1Jo 1:9).

Instances of: (J'g 10:10, 15; 1Sa 12:10; Ne 9:2, 3, 33-35; Ps 31:10; 32:5; 38:4, 18; 40:11, 12; 41:4; 51:2-5; 69:5; 106:6; 119:176; 130:3). Moses for Israel (Ex 32:31, 32; 34:9). Ezra for Judah (Ezr 9:6-15). Nehemiah for Judah (Ne 1:4-11). Isaiah for Judah (Isa 14:20, 21; 59:12-15; 64:5-7). Jeremiah for Judah (Jer 14:7, 20; La 1:18, 20; 3:42). Daniel for Judah (Da 9:5-15).

Enjoined (1Ch 16:11, 35; Ps 105:3, 4; Isa 55:6; La 3:1; Lu 18:1; Eph 1:18; Ph'p 4:6; Col 4:2; 1Th 5:17, 18; 1Ti 2:8; Heb 4:16).

Exemplified: By Eliezer (Ge 24:12). Jacob (Ge 32:9-12). Gideon (J'g 6:22, 36, 39). Hannah (1Sa 1:10, 13). David (2Sa 7:18-29). Solomon at the dedication of the temple (1Ki 8:23-53; 2Ch 6:14-42). Hezekiah (2Ki 20:2). Isaiah (2Ki 20:11). Manasseh (2Ch 33:18, 19). Ezra (Ezr 9:5-15). Nehemiah (Ne 2:4). Jeremiah (Jer 32:16-25). Daniel (Da 9:3-19). Jonah (Jon 2:1-9). Habakkuk (Hab 1:2). Anna (Lu 2:37). Jesus (M't 14:23; 26:36, 39; M'k 1:35; 6:46; Lu 5:16; 6:12; 9:18, 28, 29). Paul (Ac 9:11). Peter (Ac 9:40; 10:9). Cornelius (Ac 10:30).

Importunity in (Ps 17:1-6; 22:1, 2, 19; 28:1, 2; 35:22, 23; 55:1, 2, 16, 17; 57:2; 61:1, 2; 70:5; 86:3, 6; 88:1, 2, 9, 13; 102; 119:145-147; 130:1, 2; 141:1, 2; 142:1, 2; Isa 62:7; Ho 12:4; Lu 11:5-8; 18:1-7).

Instances of Importunity in: Abraham (Ge 18:23-32). Jacob (Ge 32:24-30). Moses (Ex 32:32; 33:12-16; 34:9; De 9:18, 25). Gideon (J'g 6:36-40). Samson (J'g 16:28). Hannah (1Sa 1:10, 11). Elijah (1Ki 18:24-44; Jas 5:17, 18). Hezekiah (2Ki 19:15-19; Isa 38:2, 3). Asa (2Ch 14:11). Ezra (Ezr 9:5). Nehemiah (Ne 1:4-11; 9:32). Isaiah (Isa 64:12). Daniel (Da 9:3, 17-19). Mariners (Jon 1:14). Habakkuk (Hab 1:2).

Two blind men of Jericho (M't 20:30, 31; M'k 10:48; Lu 18:39). The Syrophenician woman (M't 15:22-28; M'k 7:25-30). The centurion (M't 8:5; Lu 7:3, 4). Jesus (M't 26:39, 42; M'k 14:36, 39; Lu 22:42-44; Heb 5:7). Paul (2Co 12:8). Believers (Ro 8:26; Eph 6:18).

Imprecatory (Nu 16:15; 22:6-11; 23:7, 8; 24:9, 10; De 11:29, 30; 27:11-13; 33:11; Jos 8:33, 34; J'g 16:28; 2Sa 16:10-12; Ne 4:4, 5; 5:13; Job 3:1-10; 27:7; Ps 5:10; 6:10; 9:20; 10:2, 15; 25:3; 28:4; 31:17, 18; 35:4, 8, 26; 40:14, 15; 54:5; 55:9, 15; 56:7; 58:7; 59:5, 11, 15; 68:1, 2; 69:23, 24, 27, 28; 70:2, 3; 71:13; 79:10, 12; 83:13-17; 94:2; 109:7, 9-20, 28, 29; 119:78, 84; 129:5; 140:9, 10; 143:12; 144:6; Jer 11:20; 12:3; 15:15; 17:18; 18:21-23; 20:12; La 1:22; 3:64-66; Ga 1:8, 9; 2Ti 4:14, 15).

In Adversity: By Jacob (Ge 43:14). Moses (Ex 32:32). The Israelites (Nu 20:16; De 26:7; J'g 3:9). David (2Sa 22:7). Hezekiah (2Ki 19:16, 19). Jehoshaphat (2Ch 20:4-13). Manasseh (2Ch 33:12, 13). The Psalmist (Ps 5:1-12; 7:1, 2, 6, 7; 13:1-4; 22:1-21; 25:2, 16-19, 22; 27:11, 12; 28:1; 31:1-4, 9, 14-18; 35:1-28; 38:1-22; 43:1-5; 44:4, 23-26; 54:1-3; 55:1-17; 56:1-13; 57:1, 2; 59:1-17; 64:1, 2; 69:1-36; 70:1-5; 71:1-24; 74:1-23; 79:1-13; 94:1-23; 102; 108:6, 12; 109:1, 2, 21, 26-28; 120:2; 140:1-13; 142:1, 2, 5-7; 143:1-12). Jeremiah (Jer 15:15). Jonah (Jon 2:1-9). Stephen (Ac 7:59, 60). Paul and Silas (Ac 16:25).

In Behalf of Nations: See Nations, Prayer for.

Intercessory (Ge 20:7; Jer 27:18; 29:7; M't 5:44; Eph 6:18, 19; 1Ti 2:1; Heb 13:20, 21; Jas 5:14-16). Priestly (Ex 28:12, 29, 30, 38; Le 10:17). For spiritual blessing (Nu 6:23-26; 1Sa 12:23; Job 1:5; 42:8-10). To avert judgments (Ge 20:7; Ex 32:9-14; Nu 14:11-21; 16:45-50; De 9:18-20, 25-29; Isa 65:8). For deliverance from enemies (1Sa 7:5-9; Isa 37:4). For healing disease (Jas 5:14-16).

For the obdurate, unavailing (Jer 7:16; 11:14; 14:11).

Of Moses for Israel (Ex 32:11-14, 31, 32; 34:9; Nu 14:19; 21:7; De 9:18, 20, 24-29). Of Joshua for Israel (Jos 7:6, 7). Of Boaz for Ruth (Ru 2:12). Of Eli for Hannah (1Sa 1:17). Of Samuel for Israel (1Sa 7:9; 12:23). Of David, for Israel (2Sa 24:17; 1Ch 29:18); for Solomon (1Ch 29:19). Of Solomon (1Ki 8:31-53;

2Ch 6:22-42). Of Hezekiah for transgressors (2Ch 30:18, 19). Of Job for his three friends (Job 42:8-10). Of the psalmist for the righteous (Ps 7:9; 28:9; 36:10; 80:14, 15). Of Daniel for Israel (Da 9:3-19). Of Jesus for his murderers (Lu 23:34). Of Stephen for his murderers (Ac 7:60). Of Peter and John for Samaritan believers (Ac 8:15). Of the recipients of bounty for Corinthian donors (2Co 9:14).

Of Paul, for unbelieving Jews (Ro 10:1); for Roman Christians (Ro 1:9); for Ephesian Christians (Eph 1:15-19; 3:14-19); for Philippian Christians (Ph'p 1:3-5, 9); for Colossian Christians (Col 1:3, 9); for Thessalonian Christians (1Th 1:2; 3:10, 12, 13; 5:23; 2Th 1:11, 12; 2:16, 17; 3:5, 16); for Onesiphorus (2Ti 1:16, 18); for Philemon (Ph'm 4). Of Philemon for Paul (Ph'm 22).

See Intercession; Jesus, Mediation of; Mediation.

Solicited (Nu 21:7; Ro 15:30-32; 2Co 1:11; Eph 6:19; Col 4:3; 1Th 5:25; 2Th 3:1; Heb 13:18). See Intercession, Solicited.

Of Jesus (M't 11:25, 26; Lu 3:21; 11:1; Joh 12:27, 28). Before day (M'k 1:35). In secret (M't 14:23; M'k 1:35; 6:46; Lu 5:16; 6:12; 9:18, 28, 29). In a mountain (M't 14:23; M'k 6:46; Lu 6:12; 9:28). In the wilderness (Lu 5:16). Thanksgiving before eating (M't 14:19; 15:36; 26:26, 27; M'k 6:41; 8:6; 1Co 11:24). In distress (Joh 12:27; Heb 5:7). In blessing children (M't 19:13, 15; M'k 10:16). At the grave of Lazarus (Joh 11:41, 42). For Peter (Lu 22:31, 32). For believers (Joh 17:1-26). For the Comforter, the Holy Spirit (Joh 14:16). In Gethsemane (M't 26:36-44; M'k 14:32-35; Lu 22:41-44; Heb 5:7). On the cross (M't 27:46; Lu 23:34, 46). Present ministry, at the right hand of the Father (Heb 7:25). Of his apostles (Ac 1:24, 25).

See Jesus, Prayers of.

Of the Wicked, Not Heard: (De 1:45; 2Sa 22:42; Job 35:12, 13; Ps 18:41; 66:18; Pr 1:24-28; 15:8, 29; 21:13, 27; 28:9; Isa 1:15; 45:19; 59:2; Jer 11:11; 14:12; 15:1; 18:17; La 3:8, 44; Eze 8:18; 20:8, 31; Ho 5:6; Mic 3:4; Zec 7:12, 13; Mal 2:11-13; Joh 9:31; Jas 1:6, 7; 4:3).

To idols (1Ki 18:26-29). See Idolatry. See Wicked, Prayer of.

Penitential: Of David (Ps 51:1-17); the publican (Lu 18:13). See Confession in, above, and Sin, Confession of.

Pleas Offered in (Ex 33:13; Nu 14:13-19; 16:22; De 3:24, 25; 9:26-29; Jos 7:7-9; 2Sa 7:25-29; 2Ki 19:15-19; 2Ch 14:11; Ne 9:32; Ps 9:19, 20; 38:16; 71:18; 74:10, 11, 18, 20-23; 79:10-12; 83:1, 2, 18; 119:42, 73, 146, 149, 153; 143:11, 12; Isa 37:15-20; 63:17-19; La 3:56-63; Joe 2:17).

God's mercy (Ps 69:13, 16; 109:21, 26, 27; 115:1; 119:124). God's providences (Ps 4:1; 27:9). God's promises (Ge 32:9-12; Ex 32:13; 1Ki 8:25, 26, 59, 60; Ne 1:8, 9; Ps 89:49-51; 119:43, 49, 116; Jer 14:21). Personal consecration (Ps 119:94). Personal righteousness (Ps 86:1, 2, 4, 5, 17; 119:38, 145, 173-176; Jer 18:20).

Thanksgiving, and Before Taking Food (Jos 9:14; 1Sa 9:13; Ro 14:6; 1Co 10:30, 31; 1Ti 4:3-5).

See Praise; Thankfulness.

Exemplified: By Jesus (M't 14:19; 15:36; 26:26, 27; M'k 6:41; 8:6, 7; 14:22, 23; Lu 9:16; 22:19; Joh 6:11, 23; 1Co 11:24). By Paul (Ac 27:35).

PRAYERFULNESS. Enjoined (Ro 12:12; Col 4:2; 1Th 5:17). Spirit of, from God (Zec 12:10).

Exemplified by: The Psalmist (Ps 5:1-3; 42:8; 109:4; 116:2). Daniel (Da 6:10). Anna (Lu 2:37). The apostles (Ac 6:4). Cornelius (Ac 10:2). Peter (Ac 10:9). Paul (Ro 1:9; Eph 1:15, 16; Col 1:9; 1Th 3:10; 2Ti 1:3). Widows (1Ti 5:5).

See Prayer; Prayerlessness.

PRAYERLESSNESS (Jos 9:14; Job 15:4; 21:14, 15; Ps 14:4; 53:4; 76:9; Isa 43:22; 67:7; Jer 10:21, 25; Da 9:13; Ho 7:7; Jon 1:6; Zep 1:6).

See Prayer.

PREACHING, the act of exhorting, prophesying, reproving, teaching. Noah called preacher (2Pe 2:5). Solomon called preacher (Ec 1:1, 12). Sitting while (M't 5:1; Lu 4:20; 5:3). Moses slow to (Ex 4:10-12).

Appointed and practiced by Jesus as the method of promulgating the gospel (M't 4:17; 11:1; M'k 16:15, 20; Lu 4:18, 19, 43). Attested to by Paul (Tit 1:3).

Grave responsibility of (2Co 2:14-17).

Repentance, the subject, of John the Baptist's (M't 3:2; M'k 1:4, 15; Lu 3:3); of Christ's (M't 4:17; M'k 1:15); the apostles' (M'k 6:12). The Gospel of the kingdom of God, the subject of Christ's (M'k 1:14, 15; 2:2; Lu 8:1). Christ crucified and risen, the burden of Paul's (Ac 17:3).

Jesus preaches to spirits in prison (1Pe 3:19; 4:9 w Eph 4:9).

Should: Edify (1Co 14:1-25). Be skillful (2Ti 2:15, 16). Be in power (1Th 1:5). Be with boldness (Ac 13:46; 2Co 3:12, 13). Not be, with mere human strategy (M't 11:25, 26 & Lu 10:21 w Ps 8:2; 1Co 1:17-31; 2:1-8, 12, 13); with deceit or flattery (1Th 2:3-6).

Effective: By Azariah (2Ch 15:1-15); Jonah (Jon 3); Haggai (Hag 1:7-12); Peter (Ac 2:14-41); Philip (Ac 8:5-12, 27-38); Paul (Ac 9:20-22; 13:16-43). See Revivals.

Impenitence under: Asa (2Ch 16:7-10); Ahab (2Ch 18:7-26); the Jews (Ac 13:46). See Obduracy.

See Minister; Call, Personal.

PRECEPTS (See Commandments; Laws).

PRECIOUS STONES. In the breastplate of the high priest the stones were set, probably, in the order of the tribes of the children of Israel, reading from the right upper corner to the left. The first stone, sardius was probably the tribal stone for Reuben; topaz for Simeon; carbuncle for Levi; emerald for Judah; sapphire for Issachar; diamond for Zebulun; ligure or jacinth for Dan; agate for Naphtali; amethyst for Asher; beryl for Gad; onyx for Joseph; jasper for Benjamin (Ex 28:9-21; 39:6-14).

Voluntary offerings of, by the Israelites for the breastplate and ephod (Ex 35:27). Exported, from Sheba (1Ki 10:2, 10; 2Ch 9:1, 9; Eze 27:22); from Ophir (1Ki 10:11; 2Ch 9:10).

Partial catalog of (Eze 28:13). Seen in the foundation of the New Jerusalem in John's apocalyptic vision (Re 21:19-21). In kings' crowns (2Sa 12:30; 1Ch 20:2).

Figurative: Isa 54:11, 12.

See Stones; Agate; Amethyst; Beryl; Carbuncle; Crystal; Diamond; Emerald; Jasper; Ruby; Sapphire; Sardius; Topaz.

PREDESTINATION. According to purpose of grace (Ex 33:19; Isa 44:1, 2, 7; Mal 1:2, 3; Ac 13:48; Ro 8:28-30, 33; 9:11-29; 11:5, 7, 8; 1Co 1:26-29; Eph 1:4, 5, 9-11; 3:11; 2Th 2:13; 2Ti 1:9; Tit 1:1, 2; 1Pe 1:2, 20).

Of prosperity to Abraham (Ge 21:12; Ne 9:7, 8). Of Joseph's mission to Egypt (Ge 45:5-7; Ps 105:17-22). Of Israel as a nation (Ge 21:12; De 4:37; 7:7, 8; 10:15; 32:8; 1Sa 12:22; Ps 33:12; 135:4). Of Ishmael as a nation (Ge 21:12, 13; 25:12-18). Of famine in Egypt (Ge 41:30-32). Of judgment to Pharaoh (Ex 9:16). Of David as king (2Ch 6:6; Ps 78:67, 68, 70-72). Of Jehu's dynasty (2Ki 10:30; 15:12). Of the rending of Solomon's kingdom (1Ki 11:11, 12, 31-39; 12:15). Of mercy to the widow at Sidon (Lu 4:25-27).

Of the destruction of the Canaanites (Jos 11:20); of Benhadad (1Ki 20:42); of Ahaziah (2Ch 22:7); of Amaziah and the idolatrous Jews (2Ch 25:20).

Acknowledged by Job (Job 23:13, 14). Of agent to execute divine judgments (2Ki 19:25; 2Ch 22:7; Hab 1:12). Of Jeremiah as prophet (Jer 1:4, 5). Of revelation to a chosen people (M't 11:25, 26; Lu 8:10; 1Co 2:7).

Of the death of Jesus (M't 26:24; M'k 14:21; Lu 22:22; 24:26, 27; Ac 2:23; 3:18; 4:28; Re 13:8). Of Paul to the ministry (Ac 9:15; Ga 1:15, 16; 1Ti 2:7).

Of the times and bounds of nations (Ac 17:26); of times and seasons (Ac 1:7).

Of the standard of righteousness (Eph 2:10). Of the kingdom prepared for the righteous (M't 25:34).

Of salvation and election (M't 20:16, 23; 24:22, 40; M'k 13:20, 22; Lu 10:20; 17:34-36; 18:7; Joh 6:37, 39, 44, 45; 15:16, 19; 17:2, 6, 9; Ac 2:39, 47; 13:48; 22:14; Ro 1:6; 8:28-30, 33; 11:5, 7, 8; 1Co 1:26-29; Eph 1:9-11; Col 3:12; 1Th 1:4; 2:12; 2Th 2:13; 2Ti 1:9; Tit 1:1, 2; Jas 1:18; 1Pe 1:2, 20; 2Pe 1:10).

Of the wicked, to day of evil (Pr 16:4); to condemnation (Jude 4). Of the day of judgment (Ac 17:31).

See Election.

PREPAREDNESS (M't 24:44; 25:1-13; M'k 13:32-37; Lu 12:35-48; 19:41-44).

See Faithfulness.

PRESBYTERY. 1. Organized body of Jewish elders in Jerusalem (Ac 22:5).

2. Christian elders (1Ti 4:14).

PRESCIENCE (See God, Foreknowledge of.)

PRESENTS. To Abraham, by Pharaoh (Ge 12:16); by Abimelech (Ge 20:14). To Rebecca (Ge 24:22). To Esau (Ge 32:13-15). To prophets (1Ki 14:3, 2Ki 4:42). To those in adversity (Job 42:10, 11).

Betrothal (Ge 24:53). Marriage (Es 2:18). Propitiatory (Ge 32:20; 33:8-11; 1Sa 25:27-35; Pr 21:14). To confirm covenants (Ge 21:28-30; 1Sa 18:3, 4). Rewards of service (Da 5:7). Kings to kings (2Sa 8:10; 1Ki 10:10, 13; 15:18, 19).

To corrupt courts, forbidden (Ex 23:8; De 16:19; 27:25; Isa 5:23). See Bribery. See Liberality.

PRESIDENTS, administrative officers in Darius' kingdom (Da 6:2-7).

PRESS, crowd (M'k 2:4; Lu 8:19).

PRESS FAT, the vat or vessel used to collect the liquid from pressed grapes (Hag 2:16).

PRESUMPTION (De 29:19, 20; Ps 10:6; 19:13; 73:8, 9). Admonitions against (Pr 25:6, 7; Lu 14:7-11).

Sins of: the self-righteous (Isa 65:5; Lu 18:11, 12); the selfish rich, in forgetting God (Lu 12:18-20). Temptation to (De 6:16; M't 4:5-7; Lu 4:9-11).

In ignoring God (Isa 10:15; 29:16; 37:23-25; Ro 9:20, 21; Jas 4:13-15). Impeaching God's righteousness (Isa 58:3; Ro 9:20, 21). Defying God (Job 15:25; Ps 94:7; Isa 5:18-25; 14:13, 14; 28:14-18, 22; 29:15, 16, 20; 40:27; 45:9, 10; Ro 1:32; 9:20, 21; 2Th 2:3). Reviling God's prophet (1Ki 22:24). Despising the lordship of Christ, and the authority of the Church (2Pe 2:10, 11).

Warning against (1Co 10:9-12). Excommunication for (Nu 15:30). Proverbs concerning (Pr 18:12, 13; 25:6, 7). Punishment for (Jer 23:34).

Instances of: Satan, when he said to Eve, Ye shall not surely die (Ge 3:1-5). Builders of Babel (Ge 11:4). Abraham, in questioning about Sodom (Ge 18:23-32). Pharaoh (Ex 5:2). Moses, in upbraiding Jehovah (Nu 11:11-15, 22). Nadab and Abihu (Le 10:1, 2). Israelites, in ascending to the top of the hill against the Amalekites (Nu 14:44, 45 w De 1:43); murmuring (Ex 14:11, 12; 17:2, 7; Nu 16:14; 21:5; 1Co 10:9-12); in reviling God (Mal 1:6, 7, 12; 3:7, 8, 13). Korah, Dathan and Abiram (Nu 16:3). Saul, in sacrificing (1Sa 13:8-14); sparing the Amalekites (1Sa 15:3, 9-23). Men of Bethshemesh (1Sa 6:19). Uzzah, in steadying the ark (2Sa 6:6, 7). David's anger at Uzzah's death (2Sa 6:8). David, in numbering Israel (2Sa 24:1-17). Jeroboam (1Ki 13:4). Ben-hadad (1Ki 20:10). The Syrians, in limiting the sovereignty of God (1Ki 20:23, 28). Zedekiah (1Ki 22:24, 25; 2Ch 18:23, 24). Uzziah (2Ch 26:16). Sennacherib (2Ki 19:22; 2Ch 32:13, 14; Isa 37:23-25). Job, in cursing the day of his birth (Job 3); reproved by Eliphaz (Job 4:5). Jonah (Jon 4:1-8).

Peter, in objecting to Jesus' statement that he must be killed (M't 16:21-23; M'k 8:32); in reflecting on his knowledge when he asked, amid a throng, who touched him (Lu 8:45); in objecting to Jesus washing his feet (Joh 13:8); in asking Jesus, "What shall this man do?" (Joh 21:20-22). The disciples, in rebuking those who brought little children to Jesus (M't 19:13; M'k 10:13, 14; Lu 18:15); in their indignation at the anointing of Jesus (M't 26:8, 9; M'k 14:4, 5; Joh 12:5); reproving Jesus (Joh 7:3-5). The brothers of Jesus (Joh 7:3-5). James and John, in desiring to call down fire on the Samaritans (Lu 9:54). Those who reviled Jesus (M't 27:42, 43; M'k 15:29-32). Theudas (Ac 5:36). Sons of Sceva (Ac 19:13, 14). Diotrephes (3Jo 9).

See Blasphemy, which is presumption; Mocking; Pride.

PRETORIUM, called also Common Hall, Hall, and Palace (M't 27:27; M'k 15:16; Joh 18:28, 33; 19:9; Ac 23:35; Ph'p 1:13). See Praetorium.

PRICK (a goad), any slender pointed thing, like a thorn (Nu 33:55); goad of conviction (Ac 9:5).

PRIDE. Admonitions against (De 8:11-14, 17-20; Ps 49:11; 75:4-6; Jer 9:23; M't 23:5-7; Lu 14:8, 9; 20:46, 47; Ro 11:17-21, 25; 12:3, 16; 1Co 4:6-8, 10; 5:2, 6; 8:1, 2; 10:12; 13:4; 14:38; 2Co 10:5, 12, 18; Ga 6:3; Eph 4:17; Ph'p 2:3; 1Ti 2:9; 6:3, 4, 17; 2Ti 3:2, 4; 1Pe 5:3; Re 3:17, 18).

Prayer regarding (Ps 9:20; 10:2-6, 11). Prevented by divine discipline (2Co 12:7). Proceeds from the carnal mind (M'k 7:21, 22; 1Jo 2:16). Leads, to strife (Pr 13:10; 28:25); to destruction (Pr 15:25; 16:18; 17:19; 18:11, 12; Isa 14:12-16; 26:5; 28:3; Da 11:45; Zep 3:11; Mal 4:1; 1Ti 3:6; Re 18:7, 8).

Rebuked (1Sa 2:3-5; 2Ki 14:9, 10; 2Ch 25:18, 19; Job 12:2; Jer 13:9, 15, 17; Hab 2:4, 5, 9). Repugnant to God (Job 37:24; Ps 12:3; 18:27; 31:23; 101:5; 138:6; Pr 6:16, 17; 8:13; 16:5; Jer 50:21, 32; Lu 1:51; Jas 4:6).

Shall be humbled (Le 26:19; Ps 52:6, 7; Pr 11:2; Isa 2:11-17; 3:16-26; 5:13; 13:11; 22:16, 19; 23:7, 9; 24:4, 21; Jer 49:4, 16; Da 4:37; Ob 3, 4; M't 23:12; M'k 10:43; Lu 1:52; 9:46; 18:14; Re 18:7, 8).

Discussed with Job (Job 11:12; 12:2, 3; 13:2, 5; 15:1-13; 18:3, 4; 21:31, 32; 32:9-13; 37:24). Proverbs concerning (Pr 3:34; 6:16, 17; 8:13; 10:17; 11:2, 12; 12:9, 15; 13:10; 14:21; 15:5, 10, 12, 25, 32; 16:5, 18, 19; 17:19; 18:11, 12; 21:4, 24; 25:14, 27; 26:5, 12, 16; 27:2; 28:11, 25; 29:8, 23; 30:12, 13). Cited by the Psalmists (Ps 10:2-6, 11; 49:11; 52:7; 73:6, 8, 9; 119:21, 69, 70, 78).

See The Rich.

Instances of: Pharaoh (Ex 7-11; 12:29-36; 14). Ahithophel (2Sa 17:23). Naaman (2Ki 5:11-13). Hezekiah (2Ki 20:13; 2Ch 32:25, 26, 31; Isa 39:2). Uz-ziah (2Ch 26:16-19). Haman (Es 3:5; 5:11, 13; 6:6; 7:10).

Moab (Isa 16:6, 7; Jer 48:7, 14, 15-29; Zep 2:9). Israel (Isa 9:9, 10; Ho 5:5; 7:10). Assyria (Isa 10:5-16; Eze 31:10, 11). Jerusalem (Eze 16:56). Tyre (Eze 28:2-9, 17). Egypt (Eze 30:6). Nebuchad-nezzar (Da 4:30-34; 5:20). Moab and Ammon (Zep 2:9). Nineveh (Zep 2:15).

The Scribes and the Pharisees (M't 20:6; 23:6-8, 10, 11; M'k 10:43; 12:38, 39; Lu 9:46; 11:43; 18:14; 20:45-47). Herod (Ac 12:21-23).

See Ambition.

PRIEST. *Antemosaic:* Melchizedek (Ge 14:18; Heb 5:6, 10, 11; 6:20; 7:1-21). Jethro (Ex 2:16). Priests in Israel before the giving of the law (Ex 19:22, 24). Called angel (Ec 5:6).

Mosaic: Ex 28:1-4; 29:9, 44; Nu 3:10; 18:7; 1Ch 23:13. Hereditary descent of office (Ex 27:21; 28:43; 29:9). Consecration of (Ex 29:1-9, 19-35; 40:12-16; Le 6:20-23; 8:6-35; Heb 7:21). Is holy (Le 21:6, 7; 22:9, 16). Ablutions of (Ex 40:30-32; Le 16:24); see Consecration of, above. Must be without blemish (Le 21:17-23). Vestments of (Ex 28:2-43; 39:1-29; Le 6:10, 11; 8:13; Eze 44:17-19). Don vestments in temple (Eze 42:14; 44:19). Atonement for (Le 16:6, 24; Eze 44:27). Defilement and purification of (Eze 44:25, 26). Marriage of (Le 21:7-15; Eze 44:22). Chambers for, in temple (Eze 40:45, 46). Exempt from tax (Ezr 7:24). Armed and organized for war at the time of the disaffection toward Saul (1Ch 12:27, 28). Beard and hair of (Eze 44:20).

Twenty-four courses of (1Ch 24:1-19; 28:13, 21; 2Ch 8:14; 31:2; 35:4, 5; Ezr 2:36-39; Ne 13:30). Chosen by lot (Lu 1:8, 9, 23).

Usurpations of office of (Nu 3:10; 16; 18:7; 2Ch 26:18). Priests were appointed by Jeroboam who were not of the sons of Levi (1Ki 12:31; 13:33).

See Levites; Ministers.

Duties of: To offer sacrifices (Le 1:4-17; 2:2, 16; 3:5, 11, 13, 16; 4:5-12, 17, 25, 26, 30-35; 1Ch 16:40; 2Ch 13:11; 29:34; 35:11-14; Ezr 6:20; Heb 10:11; see Offerings). To offer the first fruits (Le 23:10, 11; De 26:3, 4). Pronounce benedictions (Nu 6:22-27; De 21:5; 2Ch 30:27). Teach the law (Le 10:11; De 24:8; 27:14; 31:9-13; 33:10; Jer 2:8; Mal 2:7). Light the lamps in the tabernacle (Ex 27:20, 21; 2Ch 13:11; Le 24:3, 4). Keep the sacred fire always burning (Le 6:12, 13). To furnish a quota of wood for the sanctuary (Ne 10:34). Responsible for the sanctuary (Nu 4:5-15; 18:1, 5, 7). To act as scribes (Ezr 7:1-6; Ne 8:9). Be present at and supervise the tithing (Ne 10:38). Sound the trumpet in calling assemblies and in battle (Nu 10:2-10; 31:6; Jos 6; 2Ch 13:12). Examine lepers (see Leprosy). Purify the unclean (Le 15:31; see Defilement). Value things devoted (Le 27:8, 12). Officiate in the holy place (Heb 9:6). Chiefs of Levites (Nu 3:9, 32; 4:19, 28, 33; 1Ch 9:20). To act as magistrates (Nu 5:14-31; De 17:8-13; 19:17; 21:5; 2Ch 19:8; Eze 44:23, 24). To encourage the army on the eve of battle (De 20:2-4). Bear the ark through the Jordan (Jos 3; 4:15-18); in battle (1Sa 4:3-5).

Emoluments of: No part of the land of Canaan allowed to (Nu 18:20; De 10:9; 14:27; 18:1, 2; Jos 13:14, 33; 14:3; 18:7; Eze 44:28). Provided with cities and suburbs (Le 25:32-34; Nu 35:2-8; Jos 21:1-4, 13-19, 41, 42; 1Ch 6:57-60; Ne 11:3, 20; Eze 45:1-6; 48:8-20). Own lands sanctified to the Lord (Le 27:21). Tithes of the tithes (Nu 18:8-18, 26-32; Ne 10:38). Part of the spoils of war, including captives (Nu 31:25-29). First-fruits (Le 23:20; 24:9; Nu 18:12, 13, 17, 18; De 18:3-5; Ne 10:36). Redemption money (Le 27:23); of firstborn (Nu 3:46-51; 18:15, 16). Things devoted (Le 27:21; Nu 5:9, 10; 18:14). Fines (Le 5:16; 22:14; Nu 5:8). Trespass money and other trespass offerings (Le 5:15, 18; Nu 5:5-10; 18:9; 2Ki 12:16). The shew-bread (Ex 25:30; Le 24:5-9; 2Ch 2:4; 13:11; Ne 10:33; M't 12:4; Heb 9:2). Portions of sacrifices and offerings (Ex 29:27-34; Le 2:2, 3, 9, 10; 5:12, 13, 16; 6:15-18, 26; 7:6-10, 31-34; 10:12-14; 14:12, 13; Nu 6:19, 20; 18:8-19; De 18:3-5; 1Sa 2:13, 14; Eze 44:28-31; 45:1-4; 1Co 9:13; 10:18).

Regulations by Hezekiah concerning emoluments (2Ch 31:4-19). Portion of land allotted to, in redistribution in Ezekiel's vision (Eze 48:8-14). For sustenance of their families (Le 22:11-13; Nu 18:11, 19).

Figurative: Ex 19:6; Isa 61:6; 1Pe 2:9; Re 1:6; 5:10; 20:6.

High Priest: Moses did not denominate Aaron chief or high priest. The function he served was superior to that of other priests. The title appears after the institution of the office (Le 21:10-15; Nu 3:32). For qualifications, consecration, etc., see under the general topic above, Priest, Mosaic Institution of.

Vestments of (Ex 28:2-43; 39:1-31; Le 8:7-9). Respect due to (Ac 23:5).

Duties of: Had charge of the sanctuary and altar (Nu 18:2, 5, 7). To offer sacrifices (Heb 5:1; 8:3). To designate subordinate priests for duty (Nu 4:19; 1Sa 2:36). To officiate in consecrations of Levites (Nu 8:11-21). To have charge of the treasury (2Ki 12:10; 22:4; 2Ch 24:6-14; 34:9). To light the lamps of tabernacle (Ex 27:20, 21; 30:8; Le 24:3, 4; Nu 8:3). To burn incense (Ex 30:7, 8; 1Sa 2:28; 1Ch 23:13). To place shew-bread on the table every Sabbath (Le 24:8). To offer for his own sins of ignorance (Le 4:3-12).

On the Day of Atonement (Ex 30:10; Le 16; Heb 5:3; 9:7, 22, 23).

Judicial (Nu 5:15; De 17:8-13; 1Sa 4:18; Ho 4:4; M't 26:3, 50, 57, 62; Ac 5:21-28; 23:1-5). To number the people (Nu 1:3). Officiate at choice of ruler (Nu 27:18, 19, 21). Distribute spoils of war (Nu 31:26-29).

Emoluments of (See Priest, Emoluments of, above.)

A second priest, under the high priest (Nu 3:32; 4:16; 31:6; 1Ch 9:20; 2Sa 15:24; 2Ki 25:18; Lu 3:2).

Miscellaneous Facts Concerning: Loyal to Rehoboam at the time of the revolt of the ten tribes (2Ch 11:13). Zeal of, in purging the temple (2Ch 29:4-17). Wickedness of (2Ch 36:14). Taken with the captivity to Babylon (Jer 29:1). Return from the captivity (Ezr 1:5; 2:36-39, 61, 70; 3:8; 7:7; 8:24-30; Ne 7:39-42, 63-73; 10:1-8; 12:1-7). Polluted by marrying idolatrous wives (Ezr 9:1, 2; 10:5, 18, 19; Ne 10:28). Restore the altar, and offer sacrifices (Ezr 3:1-7). Supervise the building of the temple (Ezr 3:8-13). Inquire of John the Baptist whether he were the Christ (Joh 1:19). Conspire to destroy Jesus (M't 26:3-5, 14, 15, 47, 51; M'k 14:10, 11, 43-47, 53-66; 15:1; Lu 22:1-6, 50, 54, 66-71; 23:1, 2; Joh 11:47; 19:15, 16, 18). Try and condemn Jesus (M't 26:57-68; 27:1, 2; M'k 14:53-65; Lu 22:54-71; 23:13-24; Joh 18:15-32). Incite the people to ask that Barabbas be released and Jesus destroyed (M't 27:20; M'k 15:11; Lu 23:18). Persecute the disciples (Ac 22:5). Reprove and threaten Peter and John (Ac 4:6-21; 5:17-41). Try, condemn, and stone Stephen (Ac 6:12-15; 7). Paul brought before (Ac 22:30; 23:1-5). Many converts among (Ac 6:7).

Corrupt (Jer 23:11, 12; Eze 22:26; Lu 10:31). Instances of: Eli's sons (1Sa 2:12-17, 22), of the captivity (Ezr 9:1, 2; 10:18-22; Ne 13:4-9, 13, 28, 29).

Idolatrous (1Ki 12:32; 2Ki 10:19; 11:18; 23:5; 2Ch 23:17; 34:4, 5; Jer 48:35; Ho 10:5; Zep 1:4).

Zealous (1Ch 9:10-13). Priestly office

performed by prophets (1Sa 16:5).

PRIMOGENITURE (See Firstborn; Birthright.)

PRINCE, PRINCESS. A prince is a leader, an exalted person clothed with authority. A princess is the daughter or wife of a chief or king. The prince may be the head of a family or tribe, a ruler, governor, magistrate, satrap, or royal descendant (Nu 22:8; 1Sa 18:30). He may also be a spiritual ruler (Isa 9:6) or the ruler of demons (M't 9:34).

PRINCE OF PEACE (See Jesus.)

PRINCIPALITIES. 1. Rule; ruler (Eph 1:21; Tit 3:1).

2. Order of powerful angels and demons (Ro 8:38; Eph 6:12).

PRINT, a mark made by pressure (Le 19:28; Joh 20:25).

PRISCA, PRISCILLA, Priscilla (diminutive of Prisca) was the wife of the Jewish Christian, Aquila, with whom she is always mentioned in the NT; tentmakers; had church in their house; taught Apollos; assisted Paul (Ac 18:2, 26; Ro 16:3; 1Co 16:19, 2Ti 4:19).

PRISON. Prisoners were often put in dry wells or cisterns (Ge 37:24; Jer 38:6-13) or dungeons which were part of a palace (1Ki 22:27). The Herods and the Romans had royal prisons (Lu 3:20; Ac 12:4; 23:10, 35). Jesus foretells imprisonment for His disciples (Lu 21:12). Disobedient spirits are now in prison (1Pe 3:19). Satan will be imprisoned (Re 20:7).

PRISONERS. Joseph (Ge 39:20-23; 40; 41:44). Jeremiah (Jer 38:6-28; 39:14). John the Baptist (M't 11:2; 14:3-12; M'k 6:17; Lu 3:20). Jesus (M't 26:47-75; 27; M'k 14:43-72; 15; Lu 22:47-71; 23; Joh 18:3-40; 19). Apostles (Ac 5:17-42). Peter (Ac 12:3-19). Paul (Ac 16:19-40; 21:27-40; 22-28 inclusive). Silas (Ac 16:19-40).

Required to labor (J'g 16:21). Kept on bread and water of affliction (1Ki 22:27); in chains (Ac 12:6); in stocks (Pr 7:22; Jer 29:26; Ac 16:24).

Confined in court of the palace (Jer 32:2); house of the scribe (Jer 37:15); house of captain of the guard (Ge 40:3). Visited by friends (M't 11:2; Ac 24:23). Bound to soldiers (Ac 12:6, 7).

Severe hardships of, mitigated (Jer 37:20, 21). Cruelty to (Jer 38:6; La 3:53, 54; see Captive). Keepers responsible for (Ac 12:18, 19). Tortured to extort self-incriminating testimony (Ac 22:24). Scourged (M't 27:26; M'k 15:15; Ac 16:23, 33; 2Co 6:5; 11:23, 24). Permitted to make defense (Ac 24:10; 25:8, 16; 26:1; 2Ti 4:16). Kindness to: By the prison keeper to Jeremiah (Jer 38:7-28); by Philippian jailer to Paul (Ac 16:33); by Felix (Ac 24:23); by Julius, the centurion (Ac 27:1, 3; 28:16, 30, 31). To be visited and ministered to (M't 25:35-46). Released at feasts (M't 27:15-17; M'k 15:6; Lu 23:17; Joh 18:39).

Of War: Put to death (Jos 10:16-27; 1Sa 15:33; 27:11; 2Sa 12:31; 2Ki 25:7; 1Ch 20:3; Ho 13:16; Am 1:13; La 3:34); by divine command (Nu 31:9, 17). Thumbs and toes cut off (J'g 1:6, 7). Blinded (2Ki 25:7). See Captive.

Consolations for (Ps 69:33; 79:11; 102:19, 20; 146:7).

See Captive; Imprisonment.

Figurative: Isa 61:1; Lu 4:18.

PRIVILEGE (See Judgment, According to Opportunity; Responsibility.)

PRIZE, a reward of merit (1Co 9:24). *Figurative:* Ph'p 3:14.

PROBATION, (Ro 5:4). Adam on (Ge 2:15-17; 3:3). Amorites (Ge 15:16). Solomon (1Ki 3:14; 9:4-9, w 11:9-12). Taught in parables of the talents and pounds (M't 25:14-30; Lu 19:12-27); the fig tree (Lu 13:6-9); embezzling steward (Lu 16:1-12). Taught by Paul (Heb 6).

None after death (M't 12:32; 25:10-13; 26:24).

See Perseverance.

PROCHORUS, an early Christian deacon (Ac 6:5).

PROCLAMATION. Imperial (2Ch 30:1-10; Es 1:22; 6:9; 8:10-14; Isa 40:3, 9; Da 3:4-7; 4:1; 5:29). Emancipation (2Ch 36:23; Ezr 1:1-4).

PROCONSUL, Roman official who served as deputy consul in a Roman province; term of office usually one year; Sergius Paulus and Gallio were proconsuls (Ac 13:7; 18:12).

PROCURATOR, governor of a Roman province appointed by the emperor; often subject to imperial legate of a larger political area. Pilate, Felix, Festus were procurators (M't 27:2; Ac 23:24; 26:30).

PROCRASTINATION (Eze 11:2, 3; 12:22, 27, 28). Rebuked (M't 8:21, 22;

Lu 9:59, 61). Admonition against (1Th 5:2, 3). Forbidden (Ex 22:29). Warning against (Heb 3:7-19).

Parables of: Evil servant (M't 24:48-51). The five foolish virgins (M't 25:2-13).

See Excuses.

Instances of: Pharaoh (Ex 8:10). Elisha (1Ki 19:20, 21). Esther (Es 5:8). Disciple of Christ whose father died (M't 8:21; Lu 9:59, 61). Felix (Ac 24:25).

PRODIGAL SON (Lu 15:11-32).

PRODIGALITY (See Extravagance; Frugality; Industry.)

PROFANATION. Of God's name (Le 20:3; Pr 30:9), forbidden (Ex 20:7; 18:21; 19:12; 21:6; 22:2, 3; De 5:11). Instances of (Ps 139:20; Isa 52:5; Ro 2:24).

Of the Sabbath (Ne 13:15-22; Eze 20:12, 13, 16; 22:8; 23:38).

Of the house of God (2Ch 33:7; Ne 13:7; Jer 7:11; M't 21:13; M'k 11:17; Lu 19:46).

Of holy things: forbidden (Le 22:15).

See Profane; Profanity.

PROFANE, to desecrate or defile (Ex 31:14; Le 19:8, 12; Eze 22:26; M't 12:5); common as opposed to holy (Eze 28:16; 42:20); godless, unholy (Heb 12:16).

PROFANITY (See Blasphemy; Oath.) Of the name of God, see God, under Miscellaneous Subtopics; of the Sabbath, see Sabbath.

PROFESSION. False (Pr 20:6; Ho 8:2). Of faith in Jesus, see Confession. (See Testimony, Religious.)

PROGNOSTICATION, by astrologers (Isa 47:13).

See Prophecy; Prophets.

PROHIBITION, of the use of intoxicating liquors. To priests on duty (Le 10:9). To Nazarites (Nu 6:3, 4).

See Abstinence, Total; Commandments; Drunkenness.

PROMISE. First promise of the Redeemer (Ge 3:15); promise repeated to Abraham (Ge 12:2, 7); promise made to David that his house would continue forever (2Sa 7:12, 13, 28). Jesus' promise of the Spirit fulfilled at Pentecost. There are hundreds of promises made to believers (Jas 2:5; 1Ti 4:8; 2Pe 3:9).

PROMISES. To the afflicted (see Afflictions, Comfort in; To backsliders (See Backsliders). To children (see Children). To orphans (see Orphans). (See Penitent). To the righteous (see Righteous). To seekers (see Seekers), and other like subjects.

PROMISES, OR GROUND OF ASSURANCE (Heb 6:12; Jas 2:5; 2Pe 1:4; 3:13). Against the recurrence of universal flood (Ge 9:11).

Of answer to prayer (2Ch 7:14; Job 22:27; Ps 2:8; 145:19; Isa 58:9; 65:24; Jer 29:12; 33:3; M't 6:6; 7:7, 8, 11; 17:20; 18:19; 21:22; M'k 11:24; Lu 11:13; Joh 14:13, 14; 15:7, 16; 16:23, 24; Jas 1:5; 5:15, 16; 1Jo 5:14, 15). Of blessings upon worshipers (Ex 20:24; Isa 40:31). Of comfort in sorrow (Ps 46:1; 50:15; 55:22; 146:8; 147:3; Isa 43:2; Lu 6:21; 2Co 1:3, 4; 7:6). Of spiritual enlightenment (Isa 29:18, 24; 35:5, 6; 42:16; M't 10:19; Lu 21:14, 15; Joh 7:17; 8:12, 32; Heb 8:10). Of God's presence (Ex 3:12; De 31:8; 1Sa 10:7). Of Christ's presence with believers (M't 18:20; 28:20). Of forgiveness (Ps 130:4; Isa 1:18; 43:25; 55:7; Jer 31:34; 33:8; M't 6:14; 12:31, 32; M'k 3:28; Lu 12:10; Ac 10:43; 13:38, 39; Jas 5:15, 16; 1Jo 1:9). Of healing (Jas 5:15). Of the Holy Spirit (Joe 2:28; Lu 11:13; 24:49; Joh 7:38, 39; 14:16, 17, 26; 15:26; 16:7; Ac 2:38). Of spiritual adoption (Le 26:12; 2Co 6:17, 18; Heb 8:10). Of victory of the Messiah over Satan (Ge 3:15).

To believers (Jer 17:7, 8; M'k 16:16-18; Joh 3:15, 16; 5:24; 6:35, 40, 47; 7:38; 11:25; 14:12-14; Ro 9:33; 10:9, 11). Backsliders (Le 26:40-42; De 30:1-3; 2Ch 30:9; Jer 3:12-15; Ho 14:4; Mal 3:7). Children (Ex 20:12; De 5:16; M't 19:14; M'k 10:14; Lu 18:15, 16; Eph 6:3).

To the burdened (M't 11:28, 29). The afflicted (Job 33:24-28; 36:15; Ps 9:9; 12:5; 18:27; 41:3; La 3:31). Orphans and widows (De 10:18; Ps 68:5; 146:9; Pr 15:25; Jer 49:11).

To seekers (De 4:29; 1Ch 28:9; 2Ch 15:2; Ezr 8:22; Ps 34:10; 145:18; Jer 29:13; M't 5:6; 6:33; Lu 6:21; Joh 6:37; Ro 10:13; Heb 11:6).

To the faithful (M't 25:21, 23; Lu 12:42-44; 19:16-19; Ro 2:7, 10; Re 2:10). The forgiving, of divine forgiveness (M't 6:14; M'k 11:25; Lu 6:37). The humble (Isa 57:15; M't 5:3; 18:4; 23:12; Lu 6:20; 14:11; 18:14; Jas 4:6; 1Pe 5:5, 6). The liberal (Ps 41:1-3; 112:9; Pr 3:9, 10; 11:25; 22:9; 28:27; Ec 11:1; Isa 58:10, 11; M't 6:4; Lu 6:38; 2Co 9:6, 8). The meek (Ps 10:17; 22:26; 25:9; 37:11; 147:6; 149:4; Pr 29:23; Isa 29:19; M't 5:5). The merciful (2Sa 22:26; Ps 18:25; 41:1-3; M't 5:7). Ministers (Ps 126:5, 6; Jer 1:8; 20:11; Da 12:3; M't 28:20; Joh 4:36, 37; 1Pe 5:4).

To the obedient (Ex 15:26; 19:5, 6; 20:6 w De 5:11; Ex 23:22, 25, 26; De 4:40; 6:2, 3; 12:28; 28:1-6; 30:2-10; 1Ki 3:14; Ne 1:5; Ps 1:1, 3; 25:10; 103:17, 18; 119:1, 2; Pr 1:33; Isa 1:19; Jer 7:23; Eze 18:19; Mal 3:10, 11; M't 5:19; 12:50; M'k 3:35; Lu 8:21; 11:28; Joh 8:51; 12:26; 14:21, 23; 15:10; 1Jo 2:5, 17; 3:24).

To those who fear the Lord (Ps 34:7; 103:11-13, 17; 112:1; 115:13; 128:1-6; 145:19; Pr 10:27; 19:23; Ec 7:18; 8:12). Those who have spiritual desire (Isa 55:1; M't 5:6; Lu 6:21). Those who endure to the end (M't 10:22; 24:13; M'k 13:13; Re 2:7, 11, 17, 26-28; 3:5, 12, 21; 21:7). Those who love their enemies (M't 5:44, 45). Those who rebuke the wicked (Pr 24:25). Those who confess Christ (M't 10:32; Ro 10:9; 1Jo 2:23; 4:15). Peacemakers, of sonship (M't 5:9). Penitents (Le 26:40-42; De 4:20-31; 2Ch 7:14; 30:9; Ps 34:18; 147:3; Isa 1:18; 55:7; M't 5:4). The poor (Ex 22:27; Job 36:15; Ps 12:5; 35:10; 69:33; 72:2, 4, 12-14; 109:31; 132:15; Pr 22:22, 23; Isa 41:17). The pure in heart (M't 5:8). Persecuted saints (M't 5:10, 11; Lu 6:22, 23; 21:12-18; 1Pe 4:14). The wise of heart (Pr 2:10-21).

To the righteous (Job 17:9; 36:11; Ps 1:1-3; 34:7, 22; 37:4, 5; 55:22; 119:1, 105; 138:8; 145:20; 146:8; Pr 25:22; Isa 58:8; Jer 17:7; M't 6:30, 33; 10:22, 42; 24:13; Lu 6:35; 18:6-8; Ro 5:9; 8:30, 31; 1Co 2:9; 3:21, 22; Ga 6:9; Ph'p 4:7; 2Th 3:3; Re 2:17, 26, 28; 3:5; 14:13).

Of answer to prayer (Pr 15:29; M'k 11:23, 24; Joh 14:13, 14; Ac 10:4; 1Pe 3:12; 1Jo 3:22).

Of blessings upon their children (Ps 103:17; 112:2, 3; Isa 59:21).

Of comfort (Isa 25:8; 66:13, 14; M't 5:4; Joh 14:16-18; Re 21:4).

Of deliverance, from temptation (1Co 10:13; Jas 4:7; 2Pe 2:9); from trouble (Job 5:19-24; Ps 33:18, 19; 34:15, 17; 50:15; 97:10, 11; Pr 3:25, 26; Isa 41:10-13; 43:2).

Of divine help (Ps 55:22; Isa 41:10, 11, 13; 2Co 12:9; Ph'p 4:19; Heb 13:5, 6). Of divine guidance (Ps 25:12; 32:8; 37:23, 24; 48:14; 73:24; Pr 3:5, 6). Of divine mercy (Ps 32:10; 103:17, 18; Mal 3:17). Of divine presence (Ge 26:3, 24; 28:15; 31:3; Ex 33:14; De 31:6, 8; Jos 1:5; 1Ki 6:13; Hag 1:13; 2:4, 5; M't 18:20; 28:20; Joh 14:17, 23; 2Co 6:16; 13:11; Ph'p 4:9; Heb 13:5; Jas 4:8; Re 21:3). Of divine likeness (1Jo 3:2).

Of guidance in the church (Isa 4:5, 6). Of peace (Isa 26:3; Joh 16:33; Ro 2:10).

Of refuge in adversity (Ps 33:18, 19; 62:8; 91:1, 3-7, 9-12; Pr 14:26; Na 1:7). Of strength in adversity (Ps 29:11). Of security (Ps 32:6, 7; 84:11; 121:3-8; Isa 33:16).

Of providential care (Ge 15:1; Ex 23:22; Le 26:5, 6, 10; De 33:27; 1Sa 2:9; 2Ch 16:9; Ezr 8:22; Job 5:15; Ps 34:9, 10; 37:23-26; 121:2-8; 125:1-3; 145:19, 20; Pr 1:33; 2:7; 3:6; 10:3; 16:7; Isa 49:9-11; 65:13, 14; Eze 34:11-17, 22-31; Lu 12:7; 21:18; 1Pe 5:7). Of overruling providence (Ro 8:28; 2Co 4:17). Of temporal blessings (Le 25:18, 19; 26:5; De 28:1-13; Ps 37:9; 128:1-6; Pr 2:21; 3:1-4, 7-10; M't 6:26-33; M'k 10:30; Lu 18:29, 30). Of spiritual enlightenment (Isa 2:3; Joh 8:12). Of seeing God (M't 5:8). Of inconceivable spiritual blessings (Isa 64:4; 1Co 2:9).

Of the rest of faith (Heb 4:9). Of wisdom (Jas 1:5). Of ministry of angels (Heb 1:14).

Of dwelling with Christ (Joh 14:2, 3; 17:24; Col 3:4; 1Th 4:17; 5:10). Of everlasting remembrance (Ps 112:6). Of having names written in heaven (Lu 10:20). Of resurrection (Joh 5:29; 1Co 15:48-57; 2Co 4:14; 1Th 4:16). Of heavenly rest (Heb 4:9). Of future glory (M't 13:43; Ro 8:18; Col 3:4; 2Ti 2:10; 1Pe 1:5; 5:4; Re 7:14-17). Of treasure in heaven (M't 10:21; Lu 18:22). Of inheritance (M't 25:34; Ac 20:32; 26:18; Col 1:12; 3:24; Tit 3:7; Heb 9:15; Jas 2:5; 1Pe 1:4). Of heavenly reward (M't 5:12; 13:43; 2Ti 4:8; Heb 11:16; Jas 1:12; 2Pe 1:11; Re 2:7, 10; 22:5, 12, 14).

Of eternal life (Da 12:2, 3; M't 19:29; 25:46; M'k 10:29, 30; Lu 18:29 30; Joh 3:15, 16, 36; 4:14; 5:24, 29; 6:40; 10:28;

12:25; 17:2; Ro 2:7; 6:22, 23; Ga 6:8; 1Th 4:15-17; 1Ti 1:16; 4:8: Tit 1:2; 1Jo 2:25; 5:13; Re 22:5). To reign forever (Re 22:5, compare 1Co 4:8; Re 5:10; 11:15).

See also Blessings, Spiritual; God, Goodness of; Jesus, Compassion of, Love of.

PROMOTION (Ps 75:6, 7; 78:70, 71; 113:7, 8). As a reward of merit (1Ch 11:6).

Instances of: Abraham (Ge 12:2). Joseph, from imprisoned slave to prince (Ge 41:1-45). Moses, from exile to lawgiver (see Moses). Aaron, from slave to high priest (see Aaron). Saul, from obscurity to a scepter (see Saul). David, from shepherd to throne (see David). Jeroboam, from slave to throne (1Ki 11:26-35). Baasha, "out of the dust" to throne (1Ki 16:1, 2). Daniel, from captive to premier (Da 2:48; see Daniel). Shadrach, Meshach, and Abednego (Da 3:30).

PROPAGATION, of species, enjoined (Ge 1:11, 12, 21-25, 28; 9:1, 7).

See Barrenness.

PROPERTY. *In Real Estate* (Ge 23:17, 18; 26:20). Rights in, violated (Ge 21:25-32; 26:18-22). Dedicated (Le 27:16-25). See Land.

Dwellings. Alienated for debt (Le 25:29, 30); by absence (2Ki 8:1-6); in villages, inalienable (Le 25:31-33). Dedicated (Le 27:14, 15).

Confiscation of Naboth's vineyard (1Ki 21:15, 16); Priests exempt from taxes (Ge 47:22). Entail of (Nu 27:1-11; 36:1-9). Inherited (Ec 2:21). Landmarks of, not to be removed (De 19:14; 27:17).

Personal: Rights in, sacred (Ex 20:17; De 5:21). Laws concerning trespass of, and violence to (Ex 21:28-36; 22:9; De 23:25). Strayed, to be returned to owner (Le 6:3, 4; De 22:1-3). Hired (Ex 22:14, 15); or loaned (Ex 22:10-15). Sold for debt (Pr 22:26, 27); rights of redemption of (Jer 32:7). Dedicated to God, redemption of (Le 27:9-13, 26-33). In slaves (Ex 21:4).

PROPHECY. Concerning Jesus (see Jesus). Concerning church (see Church, Prophecies Concerning). Relating to various countries, nations, and cities, see under their respective titles. Respecting individuals, see under their names.

Inspired (Isa 28:22; Lu 1:70; 2Ti 3:16; 2Pe 1:21). "The word of the Lord came unto," etc.: To Elijah (1Ki 17:8; 21:17, 28); Isaiah (Isa 2:1; 8:5; 13:1; 14:28; 38:4); Jeremiah (Jer 1:4; 7:1; 11:1; 13:8; 16:1; 18:1; 25:1, 2; 26:1; 27:1; 29:30; 30:1, 4; 32:1, 6, 26; 33:1, 19, 23; 34:12; 35:12; 36:1; 37:6; 40:1; 43:8; 44:1; 46:1; 49:34; 50:1); Ezekiel (Eze 3:16; 6:1; 7:1; 11:14; 12:1, 8, 17, 21; 13:1; 14:12; 15:1; 16:1; 17:1, 11; 18:1; 20:45; 21:1, 8, 18; 22:1, 17, 23; 23:1; 24:1, 15, 20; 25:1; 26:1; 27:1; 28:1; 11, 20; 29:1, 17; 30:1, 20; 31:1; 32:1, 17; 33:1, 23; 34:1; 35:1; 36:16; 37:15; 38:1). Amos (Am 7:14, 15); Jonah (Jon 3:1); Haggai (Hag 2:1, 10, 20); Zechariah (Zec 1:7; 4:8; 6:9; 7:1, 4, 8; 8:1, 18).

Publicly proclaimed (Jer 11:6). Exemplified in pantomime (Eze 4; 5:1-4; Ac 21:11). Written by an amanuensis (Jer 45:1); in books (Jer 45:1; 51:60).

Proof of God's foreknowledge (Isa 43:9). Sure fulfillment of (Eze 12:22-25, 28; Hab 2:3; M't 5:18; 24:35; Ac 13:27, 29). Cessation of (La 2:9).

Of apostasy (1Jo 2:18; Jude 17, 18); false teachers (2Pe 2:3). Tribulations of the righteous (Re 2:10).

Concerning Jesus, the Messiah, with their Fulfillment. Many of the Messianic prophetic scriptures find their fulfillment in Jesus Christ ("Christ" derived from the Greek rendering of the Hebrew "Messiah"). The first Messianic prophecy (Ge 3:15) concerns the prophetic announcement of the victor over Satan, the victor described as "the seed of the woman." The following offers a summary of those Old Testament Messianic prophecies which the New Testament claims were directly fulfilled in Jesus Christ.

Ge 12:3; 18:18; 22:18 w Ac 3:25; Ga 3:8.

Ge 17:7, 19; 22:16, 17 w Lu 1:55, 72-74.

De 18:15, 18 w Ac 3:22, 23.

Ps 2:1, 2 w Ac 4:25, 26.

Ps 2:7 w Ac 13:33; Heb 1:5; 5:5.

Ps 8:2 w M't 21:16.

Ps 8:4-6 w Heb 2:6-8.

Ps 16:8-11 w Ac 2:25-28, 31.

Ps 16:10 w Ac 13:35.

Ps 22:1 w M't 27:46; M'k 15:34.

Ps 22:18 w M't 27:35; M'k 15:24; Lu

23:34; Joh 19:24.
Ps 22:22 w Heb 2:12.
Ps 31:5 w Lu 23:46.
Ps 41:9 w Joh 13:18; Ac 1:16.
Ps 45:6, 7 w Heb 1:8, 9.
Ps 68:18 w Eph 4:8-10.
Ps 69:21 w M't 27:48; M'k 15:36; Lu 23:36; Joh 19:28, 29.
Ps 69:25; 109:8 w Ac 1:20.
Ps 78:2; w M't 13:35.
Ps 95:7-11 w Heb 3:7-11; 4:3, 5-7.
Ps 102:25-27 w Heb 1:10-12.
Ps 110:1 w M't 22:44; M'k 12:36; Lu 20:42; Ac 2:34, 35; Heb 1:13.
Ps 110:4 w Heb 5:6.
Ps 118:22, 23 w M't 21:42; M'k 12:10, 11; Lu 20:17; Ac 4:11.
Ps 118:25, 26 w M't 21:9; M'k 11:9; Joh 12:13.
Ps 132:11, 17 w Lu 1:69; Ac 2:30.
Isa 7:14 w M't 1:23.
Isa 9:1, 2 w M't 4:15, 16.
Isa 9:7; Da 7:14, 27 w Lu 1:32, 33.
Isa 11:10 w Ro 15:12.
Isa 25:8 w 1Co 15:54.
Isa 28:16 w Ro 9:33; 1Pe 2:6.
Isa 40:3-5 w M't 3:3; M'k 1:3; Lu 3:4-6.
Isa 42:1-4 w M't 12:17-21.
Isa 49:6 w Lu 2:32; Ac 13:47, 48; 26:23.
Isa 53:1 w Joh 12:38; Ro 10:16.
Isa 53:3-6 w Ac 26:22, 23.
Isa 53:4-6, 11 w 1Pe 2:24, 25.
Isa 53:4 w M't 8:17.
Isa 53:9 w 1Pe 2:22.
Isa 53:12 w M'k 15:28; Lu 22:37.
Isa 54:13 w Joh 6:45.
Isa 55:3 w Ac 13:34.
Isa 59:20, 21 w Ro 11:26, 27.
Jer 31:31-34 w Heb 8:8-12; 10:16, 17.
Ho 1:10 w Ro 9:26.
Ho 2:23 w Ro 9:25; 1Pe 2:10.
Joe 2:28-32 w Ac 2:16-21.
Am 9:11, 12 w Ac 15:16, 17.
Mic 5:2 w M't 2:5, 6; Joh 7:42.
Hab 1:5 w Ac 13:40, 41.
Hag 2:6 w Heb 12:26.
Zec 9:9 w M't 21:4, 5; Joh 12:14, 15.
Zec 11:13 w M't 27:9, 10.
Zec 12:10 w Joh 19:37.
Zec 13:7 w M't 26:31, 56; M'k 14:27, 50.
Mal 3:1 w M't 11:10; M'k 1:2; Lu 7:27.
Mal 4:5, 6 w M't 11:13, 14; 17:10-13; M'k 9:11-13; Lu 1:16, 17.

See Jesus, Prophecies Concerning; Kingdom of, prophecies concerning.

See also Prophets; Prophetesses.

Miscellaneous, Fulfilled: The birth and zeal of Josiah (1Ki 13:2; 2Ki 23:1-20). Death of the prophet of Judah (1Ki 13:21, 22, 24-30). Extinction of Jeroboam's house (1Ki 14:5-17); of Baasha's house (1Ki 16:2, 3, 9-13). Concerning the rebuilding of Jericho (Jos 6:26; 1Ki 16:34). The drought, foretold by Elijah (1Ki 17:14). Destruction of Ben-hadad's army (1Ki 20:13-30). The death of a man who refused to smite a prophet (1Ki 20:35, 36). The death of Ahab (1Ki 20:42; 21:18-24; 22:31-38). The death of Ahaziah (2Ki 1:3-17). Elijah's translation (2Ki 2:3-11). Cannibalism among the children of Israel (Le 26:29; De 28:53; 2Ki 6:28, 29; Jer 19:9; La 4:10). The death of the Samaritan lord (2Ki 7:2, 19, 20). The end of the famine in Samaria (2Ki 7:1-18). Jezebel's tragic death (1Ki 21:23; 2Ki 9:10, 33-37). The smiting of Syria by Joash (2Ki 13:16-25). Conquests of Jeroboam (2Ki 14:25-28). Four generations of Jehu to sit upon the throne of Israel (2Ki 10:30, w 2Ki 15:12). Destruction of Sennacherib's army, and his death (2Ki 19:6, 7, 20-37). The captivity of Judah (2Ki 20:17, 18; 24:10-16; 25:11-21). Concerning Christ (see Jesus, Prophecies Concerning). Also see above. Concerning John (M't 3:3). Rachel weeping for her children (Jer 31:15; M't 2:17, 18). Deliverance of Jeremiah (Jer 39:15-18). Invasion of Judah by the Chaldeans (Hab 1:6-11); fulfilled (2Ki 25; 2Ch 36:17-21); Betrayal of Jesus by Judas, prophecy (Ps 41:9); fulfillment (Joh 13:18; 18:1-9); Judas' self-destruction (Ps 69:25; Ac 1:16, 20); fulfilled (M't 27:5; Ac 1:16-20). Outpouring of the Holy Spirit (Joe 2:28, 29); fulfilled (Ac 2:16-21). Spiritual blindness of the Jews (Isa 6:9; 29:13); fulfilled (M'k 7:6, 7; Ac 28:25-27). Mission of Jesus (Ps 68:18); fulfilled (Eph 4:8, 10; see Jesus, Mission of). Captivity of the Jews (Jer 25:11, 12; 29:10, 14; 32:3-5; Da 9:2 w 2Ki 25:1-8; Ezr 1). Of the destruction of the ship in which Paul sailed (Ac 27:10, 18-44).

PROPHETS. Called Seers (1Sa 9:19 2Sa 15:27; 24:11; 2Ki 17:13; 1Ch 9:22; 29:29; 2Ch 9:29; 12:15; 29:30; Isa 30:10; Mic 3:7). Schools of (1Ki 20:35; 2Ki,

2:3-15; 4:1, 38: 9:1). Kept the chronicles (1Ch 29:29: 2Ch 9:29; 12:15). Not honored in their own country (M't 13:57; Lu 4:24-27; Joh 4:44). Officiate at installation of kings (1Ki 1:32-35). Counsellors to kings (1Ki 22:6-28; 2Ki 6:9-12; Isa 37:2, 3; Jer 27:12-15).

Inspired by angels (Zec 1:9, 13, 14, 19; Ac 7:53; Ga 3:19; Heb 2:2). Persecutions of (2Ch 36:16; Am 2:12). Martyrs (Jer 2:30; M't 23:37; M'k 12:5; Lu 13:34; 1Th 2:15; Heb 11:37; Re 16:6).

Emoluments of: Presents (1Sa 9:7, 8; 1Ki 14:3; 2Ki 4:42; 8:8, 9; Eze 13:19). Presents refused by (Nu 22:18; 1Ki 13:7, 8; 2Ki 5:5, 16).

Inspiration of (1Ki 13:20; 2Ch 33:18; 36:15; Ne 9:30; Job 33:14-16; Jer 7:25; Da 9:6, 10; Ho 12:10; Joe 2:28; Am 3:7, 8; Zec 7:12; Lu 1:70; Ac 3:18; Ro 1:1, 2; 1Co 12:7-11; Heb 1:1; 2Pe 1:21; Re 10:7; 22:6, 8). Of, Enoch (Jude 14). Joseph (Ge 40:8; 41:6, 38, 39). Moses (Ex 3:14, 15; 4:12, 15, 27; 6:13, 29; 7:2; 19:9-19; 24:16; 25:22; 33:9, 11; Le 1:1; Nu 1:1; 7:8, 9; 9:8-10; 11:17, 25; 12:6-8; 16:28, 29; De 1:5, 6; 5:4, 5, 31; 34:10, 11; 103:7). Aaron (Ex 6:13; 12:1). Eleazar (Nu 26:1). Balaam (Nu 23:5, 16, 20, 26; 24:2-4, 15, 16). Joshua (Jos 4:15). Samuel (1Sa 3:1, 4-10, 19-21; 9:6, 15-20; 15:16). Saul (1Sa 10:6, 7, 10-13; 19:23, 24). Messengers of Saul (1Sa 19:20, 23). David (2Sa 23:2, 3; M'k 12:36). Nathan (2Sa 7:3, 4, 8). Of Gad (2Sa 24:11). Ahijah (1Ki 14:5). Elijah (1Ki 17:1, 24; 19:15; 2Ki 10:10). Micaiah (1Ki 22:14, 28; 2Ch 18:27). Elisha (2Ki 2:9; 3:11, 12, 15; 15:8; 6:8-12, 32). Jahaziel (2Ch 20:14). Azariah (2Ch 15:1, 2). Zechariah, the son of Jehoiada (2Ch 24:20; 26:5).

Of, Isaiah (2Ki 20:4; Isa 6:1-9; 8:11; 44:26; Ac 28:25). Jeremiah (2Ch 36:12; Jer 1; 2:1; 7:1; 11:1, 18; 13:1-3; 16:1; 18:1; 20:9; 23:9; 24:4; 25:3; 26:1, 2, 12; 27:1, 2; 29:30; 33:1; 34:1; 42:4, 7; Da 9:2). Ezekiel (Eze 1:1, 3; 2:1, 2, 4, 5; 3:10-12, 14, 16, 17, 22, 24, 27; 8:1; 11:1, 4, 5, 24; 33:22; 37:1; 40:1; 43:5, 6). Daniel (Da 2:19; 7:16; 8:16; 9:22; 10:7-9). Hosea (Ho 1:1, 2). Joel (Joe 1:1). Amos (Am 3:7, 8; 7:14, 15). Obadiah (Ob 1:1). Jonah (Jon 1:1; 3:1, 2). Micah (Mic 1:1; 3:8). Habakkuk (Hab 1:1). Haggai (Hag 1:13). Zechariah, the son of Berechiah (Zec 2:9; 7:8). Elisabeth (Lu 1:41). Zacharias (Lu 1:67). Simeon (Lu 2:26, 27). John the Baptist (Lu 3:2). The apostles (Ac 2:4). Philip (Ac 8:29). Agabus (Ac 11:28; 21:10, 11). Disciples at Tyre (Ac 21:4). John, the apostle (Re 1:10, 11).

See Revelation; Word of God, Inspiration of.

False (De 18:21, 22; 1Ki 13:18; Ne 6:12; Jer 23:16-27, 30-32; La 2:14). Warnings against (De 13:1-3; M't 24:5, 23, 24, 26; M'k 13:6, 21, 22; Lu 21:8). Denunciations against (De 18:20; Jer 14:15). Punishment of (De 18:20; Jer 14:13-16; 20:6; 28:16, 17; 29:32; Zec 13:3). Drunken (Isa 28:7).

Instances of false: Noadiah (Ne 6:14); four hundred in Samaria (1Ki 22:6-12; 2Ch 18:5); Pashhur (Jer 20:6); Hanani (Jer 28; Ro 15:16).

Idolatrous (1Ki 18:19, 22, 25-28, 40).

See Ministers, False.

PROPHETESSES (Eze 13:17; Joe 2:28, 29). Miriam (Ex 15:20). Deborah (J'g 4:4). Huldah (2Ki 22:14). Noadiah (Ne 6:14). Isaiah's wife (Isa 8:3). Elisabeth (Lu 1:41-45). Anna (Lu 2:36-38). Daughters of Philip (Ac 21:9). Jezebel (Re 2:20).

See Women.

PROPITIATION (to cover), to appease the wrath of God so that His justice and holiness will be satisfied and He can forgive sin. Propitiation does not make God merciful; it makes divine forgiveness possible. For this, an atonement must be provided; in OT times, animal sacrifices; now, the death of Christ for man's sin. Through Christ's death propitiation is made for man's sin (Ro 3:25; 5:1, 10, 11; 2Co 5:18, 19; Col 1:20-22; 1Jo 2:2; 4:10; Heb 9:5).

PROSELYTE, in OT times a foreign resident (Ex 20:10; De 5:14); in the NT, a person of Gentile origin who had accepted the Jewish religion, whether living in Palestine or elsewhere (M't 23:15; Ac 2:10; 6:5; 13:43). A distinction was apparently made between uncircumcised proselytes, i.e., those who had not fully identified themselves with the Jewish nation and religion; and circumcised proselytes, those who identified themselves fully with Judaism.

PROSPERITY. From God (Ge 33:11; 49:24-26; Ps 127:1; 128:1, 2). Design of (Ec 7:14). Dangers of (De 8:10-18;

31:20; 32:15; Jer 5:7; Ho 13:6). *Evil Effects of* (Ho 4:7). Pride in (2Ch 32:25). Forgetfulness of God in (2Ch 12:1; 26:16). The prosperous despise the unfortunate (Job 12:5). Promised to the righteous (Job 22:23-27). Prudence in. Instances of: Joseph and Daniel as deduced from their general conduct (See Joseph; Daniel.)

See Blessings, Temporal; Rich, The; Riches.

PROSTITUTE, harlot (Le 19:29; De 23:17). The term is often used by the OT prophets to refer to religious unfaithfulness (Isa 1:21; Jer 2:20). In ancient heathen worship a special class of prostitutes was connected with the temples.

"PROTRACTED MEETINGS" (1Ki 8:65; 2Ch 7:8-10; 30:23).

See Revivals.

PROUD (See Pride.)

PROVENDER, feed, as grain or hay fed to cattle, horses, and the like (Ge 24:25, 26; 42:27; J'g 19:19, 21).

PROVERB, pithy saying, comparison or question expressing a familiar or useful truth (Ge 10:9; 1Sa 10:12; Proverbs). Design of (Pr 1:1-4). Written by Solomon (Pr 1:1; 25:1).

Miscellany of: 1Sa 10:12; 24:13, 14; 2Sa 3:8; 20:18; 1Ki 20:11; Pr 1:17; Eze 12:22, 23; 16:44; 18:2-4 w Jer 31:29; Ho 4:9; M't 12:33 w Lu 6:44; Lu 4:23; 14:34; Joh 1:46; 1Co 15:33; Ga 6:7.

PROVERBS, BOOK OF, best representative of Wisdom literature of ancient Israel; claims Solomonic authorship for bulk of book (1:1; 10:1); not a mere collection of ancient maxims for success, but a compendium of moral instruction, dealing with sin and holiness. Author gives instruction on life and holiness in proverbial form. Outline: 1. Introduction (1:1-9).

2. Sin and righteousness personified and contrasted (1:10-9:18).

3. Single-verse contrasts of sin and righteousness (10:1-22:16).

4. Miscellaneous and longer contrasts (22:17-29:27).

5. Righteousness in poems of climax (30:1-31:31).

PROVIDENCE, the universal sovereign reign of God; God's preserving and governing all His creatures, and all their actions (Job 9:5, 6; 28:25; Ps 104:10-25; 145:15; 147:9; M't 4:4; 6:26-28; Lu 12:6, 7; Ac 17:25-28). General providence includes the government of the entire universe, especially the affairs of men. Special providence is God's particular care over the life and activity of the believer (Ro 8:28). See God, Providence of.

PROVINCE, unit of an empire, like those of the Roman empire. In Persia they were called satrapies. Rome's provinces were divided into two categories: imperial, those requiring a frontier army, and ruled by a legate appointed by the emperor; senatorial, those presenting no major problems, and ruled by someone appointed by the Senate—a proconsul (Ac 13:7).

PROVOCATION, any cause of God's anger at sin (1Ki 15:30; 21:22; Eze 20:28; Ne 9:18, 26).

PROXY, in priest's service (2Ch 30:17). See Substitution; Sufferings, Vicarious.

PRUDENCE (Job 34:3, 4; Ps 112:5; Ho 14:9; M't 7:6).

In restraining speech (Ps 39:1; Pr 12:8; 21:23; 23:9; 26:4; 29:11; Am 5:13). In heeding counsel (Pr 15:5; 20:18). In restraining appetite (Pr 23:1, 2). In avoiding strife (Pr 25:8-10; 29:8). In refraining from suretyship (Pr 6:1, 2).

Proverbs concerning (Pr 8:12; 11:13, 15, 29; 12:8, 16, 23; 13:16; 14:8, 15, 16, 18; 15:5, 22; 16:20, 21; 17:2, 18; 18:15, 16; 19:2; 20:5, 16, 18; 21:5, 20, 23; 22:3, 7, 26, 27; 23:1-3, 9; 24:6, 27; 25:8-10; 26:4, 5; 27:12; 29:8, 11; Ec 7:16, 17; 8:2, 3; 10:1, 10).

Illustration of (Lu 14:28-32). Injunctions concerning (Ro 14:16; 1Co 6:12; 8:8-13; 10:25-33; Col 4:5; Jas 1:19).

See Diplomacy; Gentleness; Wisdom.

Instances of: Jacob, in his conduct toward Esau (Ge 32:3-21); toward his sons, after Dinah's defilement (Ge 34:5, 30). Joseph, in the affairs of Egypt (Ge 41:33-57). Jethro's advice to Moses (Ex 18:17-23). The Israelites, in the threatened war with the two and one-half tribes (Jos 22:10-34). Saul, in not slaying the Jabesh-gileadites (1Sa 11:13). David, in his conduct with Saul (1Sa 18:5-30); in overthrowing Ahithophel's counsel (2Sa 15:33-37). Abigail, in averting David's wrath (1Sa 25:18-31). Achish, in dismissing David (1Sa 29). Elijah, in his flight from Jezebel (1Ki 19:3, 4). Rehoboam's counsellors (1Ki 12:7). Jehoram, in suspecting a Syrian stratagem (2Ki 7:12, 13). Nehemiah, in conduct of affairs at Jerusalem (Ne 2:12-16; 4:13-23). Daniel (Da 1:8-14). Certain elders of Israel (Jer 26:17-23). Of Jesus, in charging those who were healed not to advertise his miracles (M't 9:30; 16:20; M'k 3:12; 5:43; 7:36; 8:30; 9:9); going to the feast secretly (Joh 7:10); in walking "no more openly" (Joh 11:54; 12:36); in avoiding his enemies (M't 12:14-16; M'k 3:7; Joh 11:47-54). Joseph, in his conduct toward Mary (M't 1:19). Peter, in escaping Herod (Ac 12:17). Paul, in circumcising Timothy (Ac 16:3); in performing temple rites (Ac 21:20-26); in setting the Jewish sects on each other (Ac 23:6); avoiding suspicion in administering the gifts of the churches (2Co 8:20); his lack of, in his persistence in going to Jerusalem despite the warnings of the Spirit and his friends (Ac 20:22-25, 37, 38; 21:10-14); Paul and Barnabas, in escaping persecution (Ac 14:6); Paul and Silas, in escaping from Berea (Ac 17:10-15). The town clerk of Ephesus, in averting a riot (Ac 19:29-41).

See Diplomacy; Tact.

PRUNING (Le 25:3, 4; Isa 5:6; 18:5; Joh 15:2-6). Pruninghook (Isa 2:4; 18:5; Joe 3:10; Mic 4:3).

PSALMS. Of Moses celebrating the deliverance at the Red Sea (Ex 15:1-19). Didactic songs composed by Moses, celebrating the providence, righteousness, and judgments of God (De 32:1-43; Ps 90). Song of Deborah, celebrating Israel's victory over Sisera (J'g 5). Of Hannah, in thankfulness for a son (1Sa 2:1-10). Of David, celebrating his deliverance (2Sa 22); on the occasion of removing the ark (1Ch 16:7-36); at the close of his reign (2Sa 23:2-7; 1Ch 29:10-19). Of Isaiah (Isa 12; 25; 26). Of Hezekiah, celebrating deliverance from death (Isa 38:9-20). Of Mary (Lu 1:46-55). Elisabeth (Lu 1:42-45). Zacharias (Lu 1:68-79).

Index of Sub-Topics: Psalms of Affliction (3-5, 7, 11, 13, 16, 17, 22, 26-28, 31, 35, 41, 42, 44, 54-57, 59-64, 69-71, 74, 77, 79, 80, 83, 84, 86, 88, 89, 102, 109, 120, 123, 129, 137, 140-143). Didactic Psalms (1, 5, 7, 9-12, 14, 15, 17, 24, 25, 32, 34, 36, 37, 39, 49, 50, 52, 53, 58, 73, 75, 82, 84, 90-92, 94, 101, 112, 119, 121, 125, 127, 128, 131, 133). Historical Psalms (78, 105, 106). Imprecatory Psalms (See Prayer, Imprecatory). Intercessional Psalms (20, 67, 122, 132, 144). Messianic Psalms (See Jesus, Messiah, Messianic Psalms). Penitential Psalms (6, 25, 32, 38, 51, 102, 130, 143). Psalms of Praise (8, 19, 24, 29, 33, 47, 50, 65, 66, 76, 77, 93, 95-97, 99, 104, 111, 113-15, 134, 139, 147, 148, 150). Prophetic Psalms (2, 16, 22, 40, 68, 69, 72, 87, 97, 110, 118). Psalms of Thanksgiving: For God's goodness to Israel (21, 46, 48, 65, 66, 76, 81, 85, 98, 105, 124, 126, 129, 135, 136, 149). For God's goodness to good men (23, 34, 36, 91, 100, 103, 107, 117, 121, 145, 146). For God's mercies to individuals (9, 18, 30, 34, 40, 75, 103, 108, 118, 138, 144).

Author's names are almost always given in the titles: Moses (90), David (3-9, 11-32, 34-41, 51-65, 68-70, 86, 101, 103, 108-110, 122, 124, 131, 133, 138-145). Solomon (72, 127). Asaph (50, 73-83), sons of Korah (42, 44-49, 84, 85, 87, 88), Heman (88), Ethan (89). Many of the psalm titles include musical terms in Hebrew, some designating ancient melodies, others preserving musical instructions. The meaning of some of these terms is uncertain or unknown. Hebrew Psalter is divided into five books: 1. 1-41. 2. 42-72. 3. 73-89. 4. 90-106. 5. 107-150. Each of the psalms exhibits the formal character of Hebrew poetry. This consists, not primarily in rhyme, but in a parallelism of thought. Most of them possess a lyric, singing quality.

PSALMS OF SOLOMON, one of the pseudepigrapha, consisting of 18 psalms in imitation of the canonical psalms, probably written between 64 and 46 B. C.

PSALMODY (See Music.)

PSALTERY, a harp. Used in religious services (2Sa 6:5; 1Ch 13:8; 16:5; 25:1, 5, 6; 2Ch 29:25; Ps 33:2; 57:8; 71:22; 81:2; 92:3; 108:2; 144:9; 150:3; Re 5:8). At the dedication of the new wall when the captivity returned (Ne 12:27). Used in idolatrous worship (Da 3:5, 7, 10, 15).

See Music, Instruments of.

PSEUDEPIGRAPHA, books not in the Hebrew canon or the Apocrypha, ascribed to earlier Jewish authors. They were written chiefly during the intertestamental period.

PTOLEMAIS, a seaport in Asher, formerly called Accho, which see. Paul visits (Ac 21:7).

PTOLEMY, common name of the 15 Macedonian kings of Egypt whose dynasty extended from the death of Alexander the Great in 323 B. C. to the murder of Ptolemy XV, son of Julius Caesar and Cleopatra in 30 B. C.: Ptolemy I, Soter (323-285 B. C.); Ptolemy II, Philadelphus (285-246 B.C.); LXX translated, Golden Age of Ptolemaic Egypt; Ptolemy III (c. 246-222 B. C.); Ptolemy IV, Philopator (222-205 B. C.); Ptolemy V, Epiphanes (205-181 B. C.); Ptolemy VI, Philometor (181-145 B. C.); Ptolemy VII, Physcon (145-117 B. C.); Ptolemy XI was the last of the male line of Ptolemy I, killed by Alexandrians; Ptolemy XII (51-47 B. C.) fled to Rome; Ptolemy XIII had Cleopatra to wife.

PUA, son of Issachar (Nu 26:23); also spelled "Puah" and "Phuvah" (Ge 46:13; 1Ch 7:1).

PUAH. 1. A Hebrew midwife (Ex 1:15).

2. Father of Tola (J'g 10:1).

3. See Phuvah.

PUBLIC OPINION. Kings influenced by: Saul (1Sa 14:45; 15:24); David (2Ch 20:21); Hezekiah (2Ch 30:2); Zedekiah (Jer 38:19, 24-27); Herod (M't 14:5; Ac 12:2, 3); Pilate (Joh 19:6-13).

Jesus inquires about (M't 16:13; M'k 8:27; Lu 9:18). Feared, by Nicodemus (Joh 3:2); by Joseph of Arimathea (Joh 19:38); by the parents of the man who was born blind (Joh 9:21, 22); by rulers who believed in Jesus but feared the Pharisees (Joh 12:42, 43); by Herod (M't 14:5); by chief priests (M't 21:26; M'k 11:18, 32; Lu 12:12; 20:6); by those who feared to further persecute the disciples (Ac 4:21; 5:26).

Concessions to: By Paul, in circumcising Timothy (Ac 16:3). By James and the Christian elders, who required Paul to observe certain rites (Ac 21:18-26). By disciples, who urged circumcision (Ga 6:12). By Peter and Barnabas with others (Ga 2:11-14).

Corrupt yielding to: By Herod, in the case of, John the Baptist (M'k 6:26); Peter (Ac 12:3). By Peter, concerning Jesus (M't 26:69-75; M'k 14:66-72; Lu 22:54-62). By Pilate (M't 27:23-27; M'k 15:15; Lu 23:13-25; Joh 18:38, 39; 19:4-16). By Felix and Festus, concerning Paul (Ac 24:27; 25:9).

PUBLICANS, Roman tax collectors. Disreputable (M't 5:46, 47; 9:11; 11:19; 18:17; 21:31; Lu 18:11). Repent under the preaching of John the Baptist (M't 21:32; Lu 3:12; 7:29). Matthew, the collector of Capernaum, becomes an apostle (M't 9:9; 10:3; M'k 2:14; Lu 5:27). Parable concerning (Lu 18:9-14). Zacchaeus, chief among, receives Jesus into his house (Lu 19:2-10).

PUBLIUS, chief man in the island of Melita. Father of, healed by Paul (Ac 28:7, 8).

PUDENS (modest), a Christian in Rome (2Ti 4:21).

PUHITES (simple), family descended from Caleb (1Ch 2:50, 53).

PUL. 1. King of Assyria. Forced tribute from Manahem, king of Israel (2Ki 15:19; 1Ch 5:26).

2. A place or tribe in Africa (Isa 66:19).

PULPIT, platform used primarily as a position from which to speak (Ne 8:4).

PULSE, a sort of food (Da 1:12, 16).

PUNISHMENT. Assumed for others (Ge 27:13; 1Sa 25:24; 2Sa 14:9; M't 27:25).

See Affliction, Design of; Chastisement; Fine; Judgments; Penalty; Retaliation; Wicked, Punishment of.

Death Penalty: Shall not be remitted (Nu 35:31). In the Mosaic law the death penalty was inflicted for murder (Ge 9:5, 6; Nu 35:16-21, 30-33; De 17:6); adultery (Le 20:10; De 22:24); incest (Le 20:11, 12, 14); bestiality (Ex 22:19; Le 20:15, 16); sodomy (Le 18:22; 20:13); incontinence (De 22:21-24); rape of a betrothed virgin (De 22:25); perjury (Zec 5:4); kidnapping (Ex 21:16; De 24:7); upon a priest's daughter, who committed fornication (Le 21:9); for witchcraft (Ex 22:18); offering human sacrifice (Le 20:2-5); for striking or cursing father or mother (Ex 21:15, 17; Le 20:9); disobedience to parents (De 21:18-21); theft (Zec 5:3, 4); blasphemy (Le 24:11-14, 16, 23); for Sabbath desecration (Ex 35:2; Nu 15:32-36); for prophesying falsely, or propagating false doctrines (De 13:1-10); sacrificing to false gods (Ex 22:20); refusing to abide by the decision of court (De 17:12); for treason (1Ki 2:25; Es 2:23); sedition (Ac 5:36, 37).

Modes of Execution of Death Penalty: Burning (Ge 38:24; Le 20:14; 21:9; Jer 29:22; Eze 23:25; Da 3:19-23); stoning (Le 20:2, 27; 24:14; Nu 14:10; 15:33-36; De 13:10; 17:5; 22:21, 24; Jos 7:25; 1Ki 21:10; Eze 16:40); hanging (Ge 40:22; De 21:22, 23; Jos 8:29); beheading (M't 14:10; M'k 6:16, 27, 28); crucifixion (M't 27:35, 38; M'k 15:24, 27; Lu 23:33); the sword (Ex 32:27, 28; 1Ki 2:25, 34, 46; Ac 12:2).

Executed by the witnesses (De 13:9; 17:7; Ac 7:58); by the congregation (Nu 15:35, 36; De 13:9).

Not inflicted on testimony of less than two witnesses (Nu 35:30; De 17:6; 19:15).

Minor Offenses: Punishable by scourging (Le 19:20; De 22:18; 25:2, 3; Pr 17:10; 19:29; 20:30; M't 27: 26; M'k 15:15; Lu 23:16; Joh 19:1; Ac 22:24, 29); imprisonment (Ge 39:20; 40; see Prison). Confinement within limits (1Ki 2:26, 36-38).

In Divine Government: According to deeds (Job 34:11; Ps 62:12; Pr 12:14; 24:12; Isa 59:13; Jer 17:10; Eze 7:3, 27; 16:59; 39:24; Zec 1:6; M't 5:22; 16:27; 23:14; 25:14-30; Lu 12:47, 48; 2Pe 3:7). See Judgment, According to Opportunity and Deeds.

See Parable of the, Vineyard (Isa 5:1-7); Husbandman (M't 21:33-41); Talents (M't 25:14-30); Servants (Lu 12:47, 48).

Entailed, on children (Ex 34:7; Jer 31:29; La 5:7). Not entailed, on children (De 24:16; 2Ch 25:4).

Delayed (Ps 50:21; 55:19; Pr 1:24-31; Ec 8:11-13; Hab 1:2-4).

Design of, to secure obedience (Ge 2:17; Ex 20:3-5; Le 26:14-39; De 13:10, 11; 17:13; 19:19, 20; 21:21, 22; Pr 19:25; 21:11; 26:3). See Judgments, Design of.

No escape from (Ge 3:7-19; 4:9-11; Job 11:20; 34:21, 22; Pr 1:24-31; 11:21; 16:5; 29:1; Isa 10:3; Jer 11:11; 15:1; 25:28, 29; Eze 7:19; Am 2:14-16; 9:1-4; Zep 1:18; M't 10:28; 23:33; Ro 2:3; 1Th 5:2, 3; Col 3:25; Heb 2:3; 12:25, 26; Re 6:15-17).

Eternal (Isa 34:8-10; Da 12:2; M't 3:12; 10:28; 18:8; 25:41, 46; M'k 3:29; Lu 3:17; Joh 5:29; Heb 6:2; 10:28-31; Re 14:10, 11; 19:3; 20:10).

See Wicked, Punishment of.

PUNISHMENT, EVERLASTING, is taught in Scripture for those who reject God's love revealed in Christ (M't 25:46; Da 12:2). In M't 25:46 the word *aionion* (translated "everlasting" and "eternal") applies to the destiny of both the saved and the lost. Final place of everlasting punishment is called the "lake of fire" (Re 19:20; 20:10, 14, 15); also called "the second death" (Re 14:9-11; 20:6). "Hell" in Scripture translates *Hades,* the unseen realm where the souls of all the dead are. Gehenna is the place of punishment of Hades; paradise is the place of blessing of Hades (Lu 16:19-31). The reason for eternal punishment is the rejection of the love of God in Christ (Joh 3:18, 19).

PUNITES, descendants of Puvah, of the tribe of Issachar (Nu 26:23; 1Ch 7:1).

PUNON, a city of Edom. A camping ground of the Israelites, in their forty years' wandering (Nu 33:42, 43).

PUR (lots), lot cast to destroy Jews in time of Esther (Es 3:7; 9:26). Feast of Purim is a Jewish festival commemorating the deliverance of the Jews from mass murder by Haman.

PURA (See Phurah.)

PURIFICATION. In studying the Mosaic law relating to purifications, it must be kept in mind that sin defiles. To keep this great truth constantly before the mind of the Israelites specific ordinances concerning purifications were given to Moses; the purpose being, by this object lesson, to teach that sin defiles and only the pure in heart can see God. Therefore certain incidents, such as eating that which had died of itself, touching the dead, etc., were signified as defiling, and definite ceremonies were prescribed for persons who were defiled. During the period of defilement, and when performing the ceremonies required of them, the defiled were expected to contemplate the defilement of sin and the need of purification of the heart.

Sanitary and symbolical (Ex 19:10, 14; Heb 9:10). For women after childbirth (Le 12:6-8; Lu 2:22); after menstruation (Le 15:19-33; 2Sa 11:4). After copulation (Le 15:16-18). For spermatorrhea (Le 15:4-18). For those cleansed of leprosy (Le 14:8, 9). For eating that which died of itself (Le 17:15). For those who had slain in battle (Nu 31:19-24). Of priests (Ex 29:4; 30:18-21; 40:12, 30-32; Le 8:6; 16:4, 24, 26, 28; 22:3; Nu 19:7, 8; 2Ch 4:6). Of Levites (Nu 8:6, 7, 21). Of lepers, see Leprosy. Of the Jews before the passover (Joh 11:55). By fire, for things that resist fire (Nu 31:23). By blood (Ex 24:5-8; Le 14:6, 7; Heb 9:12-14, 19-22). By abstaining from sexual intercourse (Ex 19:15). By washing in water parts of animal sacrifices (Le 1:9, 13; 9:14; 2Ch 4:6). Penalty to be imposed upon those who do not observe the ordinances concerning (Le 7:20, 21; 22:3; Nu 19:13, 20).

Water of (Nu 19:17-21; 31:23). Washing hands in water, symbolical of innocence (De 21:6; Ps 26:6). Traditions of the elders concerning (M't 15:2; M'k 7:2-5, 8, 9; Lu 11:38). Of Paul, to show his fidelity to the law (Ac 21:24, 26).

See Ablution; Defilement; Sanitation; Spiritual Purification.

Practiced by: Jacob (Ge 35:2). Moses (Ex 19:10, 14). Aaron (Ex 29:4; 30:18-21; 40:12, 30-32; Le 8:6).

Figurative (Ps 26:6; 51:7; Eze 36:25). See Spiritual Purification.

PURIM. A feast instituted to commemorate the deliverance of the Jews from the plot of Haman (Es 9:20-32).

See Annual Feasts.

PURITY (1Ti 4:12; 5:22; Tit 1:15). Jesus our pattern in (1Jo 3:3). Word of God pure (Ps 19:8; 12:6; 119:140).

Of heart (Ps 24:3-5; 65:3; Pr 15:26; 20:9; 21:8; 30:12; Isa 1:18, 25; 6:7; Mal 6:11; 1Ti 1:5; 2Ti 2:21, 22; Heb 10:2). Blessedness of (M't 5:8). Prayer for (Ps 51:7; Da 12:10; Heb 9:13, 14).

Through divine discipline (Mal 3:2, 3; Joh 15:2); the blood of Christ (Heb 9:13, 14).

Enjoined (1Ti 3:9; 5:22; 2Ti 1:3; 2:21, 22; Jas 4:8; 1Pe 1:22). Meditation upon, enjoined (Ph'p 4:8). Exemplified by Paul (2Ti 1:3).

See Holiness; Spiritual Purification.

For Symbolisms of purity, see Ablutions; Color, White; Defilement; Purification.

PURPLE, a color highly esteemed in ancient times; because of its costliness, it became a mark of distinction to wear robes of purple. Royalty was so dressed. The color included various shades between crimson and violet (Ex 25:4; 26:36; 28:15; 35:6; J'g 8:26; 2Ch 2:14).

See Colors, Purple.

PURSE, finely finished leather pouch. In M't 10:9 the reference is to the Oriental girdle worn around the waist.

PURTENANCE, entrails (Le 1:9).

PURVEYOR, for Solomon (1Ki 4:7-19, 27).

PUT 1. Son of Ham (Ge 10:6).

2. Libya (Isa 66:19; Eze 27:10; 38:5; Na 3:9). Put has also been taken to signify Egypt.

PUTEOLI (little wells or **springs),** seaport of Italy, eight miles W of Naples; nearest harbor to Rome (Ac 28:13, 14). Modern Pozzuoli.

PUTIEL, the father-in-law of Eleazar the priest (Ex 6:25).

PUVAH (See Phuvah.)

PYGARG, probably a species of antelope (De 14:5).

PYRAMIDS, tombs with superstructures of pyramidal form made for the interment of royalty in Egypt. About 80 survive.

PYRRHUS (fiery red), father of Sopater (Ac 20:4).

Q

QUAIL. Miracle of, in the wilderness of Sin (Ex 16:13); at Kibroth-hattaavah (Nu 11:31, 32; Ps 105:40).

QUARANTANIA, mountain where according to tradition Satan tempted Jesus to worship him (M't 4:8-10); Tell es-Sultan, a short distance W of OT Jericho.

QUARANTINE (See Sanitation, Quarantine.)

QUARRIES (graven images), in J'g 3:19, 26 the reference is probably to graven images.

QUARTUS, a Christian in Corinth (Ro 16:23).

QUATERNION, a squad of four soldiers (Ac 12:4).

QUEEN. The wife of a king (1Ki 11:19). Crowned (Es 1:11; 2:17). Divorced (Es 1:10-22). Sits on the throne with the king (Ne 2:6). Makes feasts for the women of the royal household (Es 1:9). Exerts an evil influence in public affairs (see Jezebel). Counsels the king (Da 5:10-12). Of Sheba visits Solomon (1Ki 10:1-13). Candace, of Ethiopia (Ac 8:27).

The reigning sovereign, Athaliah. (See Athaliah).

The moon called queen of heaven (Jer 7:18; 44:7-19, 25). Worshiped (see Idolatry).

QUEEN OF HEAVEN, female deity, probably Ashtoreth, goddess of love and fertility (Jer 7:18; 44:17-25).

QUICKENING. Of the church: By the Father (Ps 71:20; 80:18; Ro 4:17; 8:11; Eph 2:1; 1Ti 6:13); by the Son (Joh 5:21; 1Co 15:45); by the Holy Spirit (Joh 6:63; Ro 8:11; 2Co 3:6; 1Pe 3:18).

QUICKSANDS, sandbanks off shores of N Africa S of Crete; very treacherous (Ac 27:17).

QUIRINIUS, governor of Syria when the emperor Augustus issued a decree for the census in which Joseph enrolled (Lu 2:2). It is quite certain that he was governor of Syria A. D. 6-9 and that a census was ordered for that period; but there is no clear evidence that he was governor and ordered a census 14 years prior to that. However, an inscription survives which states that Quirinius governed Syria twice.

QUIVER, for arrows (Ge 27:3; Isa 22:6).

QURUN HATTIN (See Hattin, Horns of; Beatitudes, Mount of.)

R

RA (See Re.)

RAAMAH. 1. Son of Cush (Ge 10:7; 1Ch 1:9).

2. A place in Arabia (Eze 27:22).

RAAMIAH (Jehovah has thundered), Israelite who returned from captivity with Zerubbabel (Ne 7:7); "Reelaiah" in Ezr 2:2.

RAAMSES, Egyptian store city built by Israelites (Ex 1:11); probably the modern San el Hagar in NE part of Delta.

RABBAH, RABBATH 1. Town in Judah (Jos 15:60); not now identifiable.

2. Capital of Ammon, represented today by Amman, capital of Jordan, 22 miles E of Jordan (Jos 13:25; 2Sa 11:1; 12:27-29; 1Ch 20:1; Jer 49:2, 3). Subsequently captured by Ptolemy Philadelphus (285-247 B. C.), who changed its name to Philadelphia; became one of the cities of the Decapolis. Twice spelled "Rabbath" (De 3:11; Eze 21:20).

RABBATH-AMMON (See Rabbah.)

RABBI. The title of a teacher (M't 23:7, 8; Joh 3:2). Ostentatiously used by the Pharisees (M't 23:7). Used in addressing John (Joh 3:26); in addressing Jesus (Joh 1:38, 49; 3:2; 6:25 [*R. V.*, M't 26:25, 49; M'k 9:5; 11:21; 14:45; Joh 4:31; 9:2; 11:8]). Jesus called Rabboni (M't 10:51; Joh 20:16). Forbidden by Jesus as a title to his disciples (M't 23:8).

RABBITH, a city in Issachar (Jos 19:20).

RABBLE, THE (Ex 12:38; Nu 11:4; M't 26:47; Ac 16:22; 17:5).

RABBONI, variant of Rabbi, the Hebrew word for Master (Joh 20:16).

RAB-MAG, an Assyrian prince, or, possibly, a second name given to Nergalsharezer (Jer 39:3, 13).

RABSARIS. 1. An Assyrian officer. Sent by Sennacherib against Jerusalem (2Ki 18:17).

2. An Assyrian prince in time of Nebuchadnezzar, or, possibly, a second name given to Nebushasban (Jer 39:3, 13).

RAB-SHAKEH, an Assyrian officer. Sent by Sennacherib against Jerusalem; undertakes by a speech in the Jews' language to cause disloyalty to Hezekiah and a surrender of the city (2Ki 18:17-36; 19:4, 8; Isa 36; 37:4, 8).

RACA (empty, worthless), term of contempt and scorn (M't 5:22).

RACE. 1. Human. Unity of (Ge 3:20; Mal 2:10; Ac 17:26).

2. Foot race. *Figurative:* Ps 19:5; Ec 9:11; 1Co 9:24; Ga 5:7; Ph'p 2:16; Heb 12:1, 2.

RACHAB (See Rahab.)

RACHAL, a city in Judah (1Sa 30:29).

RACHEL (ewe), daughter of Laban and wife of Jacob. Meets Jacob at the well (Ge 29:9-12). Jacob serves Laban fourteen years to secure her for his wife (Ge 29:15-30). Sterility of (Ge 29:31). Her grief in consequence of her sterility; gives her maid to Jacob in order to secure children in her own name (Ge 30:1-8, 15, 22-34). Later fecundity of; becomes the mother of Joseph (Ge 30:22-25); of Benjamin (Ge 35:16-18, 24). Steals the household images of her father (Ge 31:4, 14-19, 33-35). Her death and burial (Ge 35:18-20; 48:7; 1Sa 10:2).

RADDAI, son of Jesse (1Ch 2:14).

RAGAU, called also Reu. Son of Peleg and ancestor of Jesus (Ge 11:18-21; 1Ch 1:25; Lu 3:35).

RAGUEL, called also Reuel and Jethro. Moses' father-in-law (Nu 10:29).

See Jethro.

RAHAB (broad). 1. Harlot of Jericho who hid Israelite spies (Jos 2:1); mother of Boaz; great-grandmother of King David (M't 1:5; Ru 4:18-21); shining example of faith (Heb 11:31).

2. Mythical monster of the deep; enemy of Jehovah (Job 9:13 RSV; Ps 89:10); applied to Egypt (Ps 87:4; Isa 30:7; 51:9).

RAHAM (pity, love), son of Shema (1Ch 2:44).

RAHEL (See Rachel.)

RAILING, forbidden (1Co 5:11; 1Ti 6:4; 1Pe 3:9; 2Pe 2:11; Jude 9).

See Slander; Speaking Evil.

Instances of: 1Sa 25:14; 2Sa 16:7; M'k 15:29.

RAIMENT (See Dress.)

RAIMENT, CHANGES OF (See Dress.)

RAIN. Forty days of, at the time of the flood (Ge 7:4, 10-12, 17-24). The plague of, upon Egypt (Ex 9:22-26, 33, 34).

Miraculously caused by Samuel (1Sa 12:16-19); by Elijah (1Ki 18:41-45). David delivered by (2Sa 5:17-21; Isa 28:21). North wind unfavorable to (Pr 25:23). Withheld as judgment (De 11:17; 28:24; 1Ki 8:35; 2Ch 7:13; Jer 3:3; Am 4:7; Zec 14:17). The earth shall no more be destroyed by (Ge 9:8-17). Sent by God (De 11:13, 14; Job 37:6; Isa 30:23; Jer 5:24; 14:22). Contingent upon obedience (Le 26:3, 4; De 11:13, 14). Prayer for (1Ki 8:35, 36; 2Ch 6:26, 27). Answer to prayer for, promised (2Ch 7:13, 14; Zec 10:1). Withheld, in answer to prayer (Jas 5:17, 18).

In Palestine the rainy season extends from October to April; the dry season, from May to October. The early rain occurs in October and November (Ps 84:6; Isa 30:23; Jer 5:24); the latter rain in March and April (Job 29:23; Pr 16:15; Jer 3:3; 5:24; Zec 10:1). Crops are therefore planted so that they will grow during the rainy season. "Rain" is often used in the OT in a figurative sense. Abundance of rain denotes the rich blessing of Jehovah upon His people (De 28:12); lack of rain is a sign of God's displeasure (De 28:23, 24). In Canaanite religion Baal was conceived as the god of rain, and was therefore ardently worshipped.

RAINBOW. A token that the earth shall no more be destroyed by flood (Ge 9:8-16; Eze 1:28). *Symbolical:* Re 4:3; 10:1.

See Meteorology.

RAISIN, preserved grape. Given by Abigail to David (1Sa 25:18). Given to the famishing Egyptian to revive him (1Sa 30:12). Given by Ziba to David (2Sa 16:1). Given to David at Ziklag (1Ch 12:40).

RAISING, from the dead (see Dead; Resurrection).

RAKEM, a descendant of Machir, son of Manasseh (1Ch 7:16).

RAKKATH, fortified city in Naphtali (Jos 19:35); probably near Sea of Galilee on site of Tiberias.

RAKKON, a city in Dan (Jos 19:46).

RAM. 1. Son of Hezron and an ancestor of Jesus (Ru 4:19; 1Ch 2:9, 10). Called Aram (M't 1:3, 4; Lu 3:33).

2. Son of Jerahmeel (1Ch 2:25, 27).

3. An ancestor, probably of Elihu, mentioned in Job 32:2.

4. A sheep. Skins of, used for the roof of the tabernacle (Ex 26:14; 39:34). Seen in Daniel's vision (Da 8:3, 20). Used in sacrifice. (See Offerings.)

Trumpets made of the horns of. (See Trumpets.)

RAMAH (height). 1. Called Rama (M't 2:18). A city allotted to Benjamin (Jos 18:25; J'g 19:13). Attempted fortification of, by King Baasha; destruction of, by Asa (1Ki 15:17-22; 2Ch 16:1-6). People of, return from the Babylonian captivity (Ezr 2:26; Ne 7:30; 11:33). Jeremiah imprisoned in (Jer 40:1). Prophecies concerning (Isa 10:29; Jer 31:15; Ho 5:8; M't 2:18).

2. A city of Asher (Jos 19:29).

3. A city of Naphtali (Jos 19:36).

4. Called also Ramathaim-Zophim. A city in Mount Ephraim (J'g 4:5; 1Sa 1:1). Home of Elkanah (1Sa 1:1, 19; 2:11); and of Samuel (1Sa 1:19, 20; 7:17; 8:4; 15:34; 16:13). David flees to (1Sa 19:18). Samuel dies and was buried in (1Sa 25:1; 28:3).

5. See Ramoth-Gilead.

RAMATH, a city of Simeon (Jos 19:8).

RAMATH-LEHI, place where Samson slew a thousand Philistines with the jawbone of an ass (J'g 15:17).

RAMATH-MIZPEH (heights or **watchtower),** N boundary line of Gad (Jos 13:26). Also called Mizpeh, Galeed, and Jegar-Sahadutha.

RAMATH (RAMAH) OF THE SOUTH (Ramoth of the south), city in S Judah allotted to tribe of Simeon (Jos 19:8).

RAMATHAIM-ZOPHIM (See Ramah, 4.)

RAMATHITE (See Ramah.)

RAMESSES (various other spellings, e.g., Rameses, Ramses), name of 11 Egyptian pharaohs, of whom Ramesses II (c. 1301-1234 B. C.) was the most famous, many scholars holding that he was the pharaoh of the Exodus. Some of these pharaohs must have had at least indirect influence on Israelite life, but none of them is mentioned in the OT.

RAMIAH, an Israelite in the time of Ezra. Had taken a strange wife (Ezr 10:25).

RAMOTH (height). 1. An Israelite in the

time of Ezra. Had taken a strange wife (Ezr 10:29).

2. Called Ramath of the South. A place probably in the south of Simeon (Jos 19:8; 1Sa 30:27).

3. A city of Issachar, allotted to the Levites (1Ch 6:73).

4. Ramoth in Gilead. (See Ramoth-Gilead.)

RAMOTH-GILEAD. Called also Ramah (2Ki 8:29, 2Ch 22:6). A city of Gad, and a city of refuge (De 4:43; Jos 20:8; 1Ch 6:80). One of Solomon's commissaries at (1Ki 4:13). In the possession of the Syrians (1Ki 22:3). Besieged by Israel and Judah; Ahab slain at (1Ki 22:29-36; 2Ch 18). Recovered by Joram; Joram wounded at (2Ki 8:28, 29; 9:14, 15; 2Ch 22:5, 6). Elisha anoints Jehu king at (2Ki 9:1-6).

RAMS' HORNS (See Shofar; Trumpet.)

RAMS' SKINS, skins of sheep; used for clothing of shepherds and covering for tabernacle (Ex 25:5).

RANSOM. Of a man's life (Ex 21:30; 30:12; Job 36:18; Ps 49:7, 8; Pr 6:35; 13:8; Ho 13:14).

Figurative: Job 33:24; Isa 35:10; 51:10; M't 20:28; 1Ti 2:6.

See Jesus; Saviour; Redemption.

RAPACITY of the wicked (Lu 11:39; 20:14, 47; Joh 10:12; Ac 20:29; Ga 5:15; Jas 4:2; 1Pe 5:8).

RAPE. Law imposes death penalty for (De 22:25-27). Captives afflicted with (Isa 13:16; La 5:11; Zec 14:2).

Instances of: Of the servant of a Levite by Benjamites; tribe of Benjamin nearly exterminated by the army of the other tribes, as punishment for (J'g 19:22-30; 20:35). Of Tamar by Amnon; avenged in the death of Amnon at the hand of Absalom, Tamar's brother (2Sa 13:6-29, 32, 33).

RAPHA. 1. Son of Benjamin (1Ch 8:2).

2. Called also Rephaiah. A descendant of Jonathan (1Ch 8:37; 9:43).

3. An ancestor of certain Philistine warriors (2Sa 21:16, 20, 22 [marg.]; 1Ch 20:4, 6, 8, [marg.]).

RAPHU, father of spy Palti (Nu 13:9).

RAPTURE. The imminent translation or removal from earth of the Church at the second coming of Christ (M't 24:36-42; M'k 13:32; Ac 1:7, 11; 1Co 15:50-52; 1Th 4:14-18; Tit 2:13; 1Pe 3:12; Re 1:7).

Includes both living and dead (1Co 15:50-52; Ph'p 3:20, 21; 1Th 4:13-17; 1Jo 3:2). Followed by, the marriage of the Church to Christ (M't 25:1-10; 2Co 11:2; Eph 5:23, 32; Re 19:6-9); believers being rewarded (M't 25:19; 1Co 3:12-15; 2Co 5:10; 2Ti 4:8; 1Pe 5:2).

See Second Coming of Christ.

RAS SHAMRA, modern name of mound marking the site of ancient city of Ugarit, located on Syrian coast opposite island of Cyprus; an important commercial center; destroyed by Sea Peoples who overran the area c. 1200 B. C.; reached peak of prosperity in 15th-14th centuries B. C. Several hundred clay tablets forming part of scribal library were found from 1929 through 1936; personal and diplomatic correspondence; business, legal, and governmental records; veterinary texts, and, most important religious literature. These throw a great deal of light upon Canaanite religion, culture, and Hebrew literary style; and show striking similarities between Canaanite and Hebrew systems of worship. They clarify our knowledge of the world in which Israel developed.

RASHNESS (Ps 116:11; Pr 19:2). Admonitions against (Pr 25:8; Ec 5:2; 7:9). Folly of (Pr 14:29; 29:20). Tends to want (Pr 21:5).

Instances of: Moses, in slaying the Egyptian (Ex 2:11, 12; Ac 7:24, 25); when he smote the rock (Nu 20:10-12). Jephthah's vow (J'g 11:31-39). Israel's vow to destroy the Benjamites (J'g 21:1-23). Uzzah, in steadying the ark (2Sa 6:6, 7). David, in his generosity to Ziba (2Sa 16:4; w 19:26-29). Rehoboam, in forsaking the counsel of the old men (1Ki 12:8-15). Josiah, in fighting against Necho (2Ch 35:20-24). Naaman, in refusing to wash in Jordan (2Ki 5:11, 12). Peter, in cutting off the ear of Malchus (M't 26:51; M'k 14:47; Lu 22:50). James and John, in desiring to call down fire on the Samaritans (Lu 9:54). Paul, in persisting in going to Jerusalem, against the repeated admonitions of the Holy Ghost (Ac 21:4, 10-15). The centurion, in rejecting Paul's counsel (Ac 27:11).

RASOR, RAZOR. Priests of Israel were not permitted to cut their beard (Le

21:5). Nazarites could not use the razor as long as their vows were upon them (Nu 6:5).

RAVEN. A black carnivorous bird (Pr 30:17; Song 5:11). Forbidden as food (Le 11:15; De 14:14). Preserved by Noah in the ark (Ge 8:7). Fed Elijah (1Ki 17:4-6). Cared for by divine providence (Lu 12:24).

RAVISHMENT (See Rape.)

RE, RA, Egyptian sun-god. Joseph married daughter of the priest of On of the cult of Re (Ge 41:45).

READING, taught (De 6:9; 11:20).

READINGS, *Select.* Judah's Defense (Ge 44:18-34). Joseph Revealing His Identity (Ge 45:1-15). The Deliverance of the Israelites from Pharaoh (Ex 14:5-30). Song of Moses When Pharaoh and his Army Were Overthrown (Ex 15:1-19). David's Lament Over Absalom (2Sa 18:19-33). Lights and Shadows (Ru 1:1-22). Elijah's Miraculous Preservation (1Ki 17:1-16). Elisha and the Widow's Oil (2Ki 4:1-7). Naaman the Leper (2Ki 5:1-14). Esther's Triumph (Es 4:1-17; 7:1-10). The Brevity of Life (Job 14:1-10). Nature's Testimony (Job 28:1-28). God's Challenge to Job (Job 38). The Beasts of the Field (Job 39). The Righteous and the Wicked in Contrast (Ps 1). The Triumphant King (Ps 2). Man in Nature (Ps 8). Man in Extremity (Ps 18:1-19). Confidence in God (Ps 23). The King of Glory (Ps 24). The Glory of God (Ps 29). Our Refuge (Ps 46). The Majesty of God (Ps 77:13-20). The Joy of the Righteous (Ps 84). The State of the Godly (Ps 91). The New Song (Ps 98). The Majesty and Providence of God (Ps 104). In Captivity (Ps 137). The Omnipresence of God (Ps 139). Old Age (Ec 12:1-7). Christ's Kingdom Foreshadowed (Isa 35:1-10). The Omnipotence and Incomparableness of God (Isa 40:1-30). The Wrath of God (Am 9:1-6). The Majesty of God (Hab 3:3-13). Mary's Magnificat (Lu 1:46-56). The Prophetic Blessing of Zacharias (Lu 1:67-80). The Beatitudes (M't 5:1-16). God's Providence (M't 6:26-34). Wise and Foolish Builders (M't 7:21-27). The Good Samaritan (Lu 10:25-37). The Prodigal Son (Lu 15:11-32). The Raising of Lazarus (Joh 11:1-45). The Betrayal (Lu 22:47-62). The Resurrection (Lu 24:1-12). Peter at Pentecost (Ac 2:1-36). Stephen's Defense (Ac 7). Paul and Silas in Prison (Ac 16:16-40). Paul on Mars' Hill (Ac 17:22-31). Paul Before Felix (Ac 24:1-27). Paul Before Agrippa (Ac 26:1-32). Charity (1Co 13). The New Heaven and the New Earth (Re 21:1-7). The River of Life (Re 22:1-21).

REAIA, son of Micah, a Reubenite (1Ch 5:5).

REAIAH. 1. A man of Judah, son of Shobal (1Ch 4:2). Apparently called Haroeh (1Ch 2:52).

2. Ancestor of a family which returned to Jerusalem from captivity in Babylon (Ezr 2:47; Ne 7:50).

REAPING. In ancient times done either by pulling up grain by roots or cutting with a sickle. Stalks then bound into bundles and taken to threshing floor (Ps 129:7).

Laws concerning gleaning at time of reaping (Le 19:9, 10; 23:22; De 24:19, 20).

Figurative (Ps 126:6; Ho 10:12, 13; Joh 4:35-38); of deeds that produce own harvest (Pr 22:8; Ho 8:7; 1Co 9:11; Ga 6:7, 8).

REASONING. With God (Job 13:3, 17-28). God reasons with men (Ex 4:11; 20:5, 11; Isa 1:18; 5:3, 4; 43:26; Ho 4:1; Mic 6:2).

Natural understanding (Da 4:36). To be applied to religion (1Co 10:15; 1Pe 3:15). Not a sufficient guide in human affairs (De 12:8; Pr 3:5; 14:12). Of the Pharisees (Lu 5:21, 22; 20:5). Of Paul from the Scriptures (Ac 17:2; 18:4, 19; 24:25). The gospel cannot be explained by (2Co 1:18-28; 2:1-14).

See Investigation; Philosophy.

REBA, a king of Midian. Slain by the Israelites (Nu 31:8; Jos 13:21).

REBECCA (See Rebekah.)

REBEKAH. Daughter of Bethuel, grand-niece of Abraham (Ge 22:20-23). Becomes Isaac's wife (Ge 24:15-67; 25:20). Mother of Esau and Jacob (Ge 25:21-28). Passes as Isaac's sister (Ge 26:6-11). Displeased with Esau's wives (Ge 26:34, 35). Prompts Jacob to deceive Isaac (Ge 27:5-29). Sends Jacob to Laban (Ge 27:42-46). Burial place of (Ge 49:31). Called Rebecca (Ro 9:10).

REBELLION, treasonable (Pr 17:11).

Instances of: Absalom (2Sa 15-18).

Sheba (2Sa 20). Revolt of the ten tribes (1Ki 12:16-20; 2Ch 10; 13:5-12). See Sin.

RECAH, RECA, unknown place in tribe of Judah (1Ch 4:12).

RECHAB (horseman). 1. Son of Rimmon. Murders Ish-bosheth, son of Saul; put to death by David (2Sa 4:5-12).

2. Father of Jehonadab (2Ki 10:15, 23; 1Ch 2:55; Jer 35:6, 8, 16, 19). Ancestor of the Rechabites (Jer 35).

3. Father of Malchiah (Ne 3:14).

RECHABITES. A family of Kenites descended from Rechab, through Jonadab (1Ch 2:55; Jer 35:6). Enjoined by Jonadab to drink no wine (Jer 35:6). Adhere to the injunction of abstinence; perpetuation of the family promised as a reward (Jer 35).

See Abstinence, Total; Nazarites.

RECHAH, a city of unknown location (1Ch 4:12).

RECIPROCITY (Ro 15:27; 1Co 9:11; Ga 6:6).

RECONCILIATION. Between man and man (M't 5:23-26). Between Esau and Jacob (Ge 33:4, 11). Between Saul and David (1Sa 19:7). Between Pilate and Herod (Lu 23:12).

Between God and Man: Through atonement of animal sacrifices (Le 8:15; Eze 45:15). After the seventy weeks of Daniel's vision (Da 9:24).

Through Christ (Ro 5:1, 10; 11:15; 2Co 5:18-21; Eph 2:15-18; Col 1:20-22; Heb 2:17).

See Atonement; Jesus, Mission of; Propitiation; Redemption.

RECONNAISSANCE. Of Jericho (Jos 2:1-24); Beth-el (J'g 1:23); Laish (J'g 18:2-10).

RECORDER (See Occupations and Professions.)

RECREATION, Jesus takes, from the fatigues of his ministry (M'k 6:31, 32; 7:24).

RED, blood-like or blood-red color (Ex 25:5; 26:14; 35:7; Zec 1:8; Re 6:4).

RED HEIFER, ashes of red heifer were used for removal of certain types of ceremonial uncleanness (Nu 19:9).

RED SEA. The locusts which devastated Egypt destroyed in (Ex 10:19). Israelites cross; Pharaoh and his army drowned in (Ex 14; 15:1, 4, 11, 19; Nu 33:8 De 11:4; Jos 2:10; 4:23; 24:6, 7; J'g 11:16; 2Sa 22:16; Ne 9:9-11; Ps 66:6; 78:13, 53; 106:7-11, 22; 136:13-15; Isa 43:16, 17; Ac 7:36; 1Co 10:1, 2; Heb 11:29). Israelites camp by (Ex 14:2, 9; Nu 14:25; 21:4; 33:10, 11; De 1:40; 2:1-3). Boundary of the promised land (Ex 23:31). Solomon builds ships on (1Ki 9:26).

REDEEMED, THE (Isa 35:9; 51:11; M't 8:11; Re 5:9; 7:9; 14:4; 19:6).

REDEEMER (See Jesus, Saviour; Redemption).

REDEMPTION (to tear loose; a ransom), deliverance from the enslavement of sin and release to a new freedom by the sacrifice of the Redeemer, Jesus Christ. The death of Christ is the redemptive price. The word contains both the ideas of deliverance and the price of that deliverance, or ransom (Ro 3:24; Ga 3:13; Eph 1:7; 1Pe 1:18, 19).

Of Person or Property (Ex 13:13; Le 25:25-34; 27:2-33; Ro 4:3-10). Redemption money paid to priests (Nu 3:46-51). Of the firstborn (Ex 13:13; 34:20; Le 27:27; Nu 3:40-51; 18:15-17).

Of Land (Le 27:19, 20; Jer 32:7). In Hebrew society, any land which was forfeited through economic distress could be redeemed by the nearest of kin. If not so redeemed, it returned to its original owner in the year of Jubilee (Le 25:24-34).

Of Our Souls (Ps 111:9; 130:7). Through Christ (M't 20:28; M'k 10:45; Lu 2:38; Ac 20:28; Ro 3:24-26; 1Co 1:30; 6:20; 7:23; Ga 1:4; 2:20; 4:4, 5; Eph 1:7; 5:2; Col 1:14, 20-22; 1Ti 2:6; Tit 2:14; Heb 9:12, 15; 1Pe 1:18, 19; Re 5:9, 10).

See Atonement; Ransom; Redeemer.

REED. A water plant (Isa 19:6, 7; 35:7; Jer 51:32). Used as a measuring device of six cubits (Eze 40:3-8; 41:8; 42:16-19; 45:1; Re 11:1; 21:15, 16). Mockingly given to Jesus as a symbol of royalty (M't 27:29). Jesus smitten with (M't 27:30; M'k 15:19).

Figurative: Of weakness (1Ki 14:15; 2Ki 18:21; Isa 36:6; 42:3; Eze 29:6; M't 11:7; 12:20).

REELAIAH. A returned captive from Babylon (Ezr 2:2). Called Raamiah (Ne 7:7).

REFINING, the process of eliminating by fire the dross of metals. Of gold (1Ch

28:18). Of silver (1Ch 29:4). Of wine (Isa 25:6).

Figurative: Of the corrective judgments of God (Isa 1:25; 48:10; Jer 9:7; Zec 13:9; Mal 3:2, 3). Of the purity of the word of God (Ps 18:30; 119:140).

REFUGE, CITIES OF, six cities on either side of the Jordan which were set aside for the asylum of the accidental slayer (Nu 35:6, 11-32; De 4:43; 19:1-13; Jos 20); Bezer (Benjamin), Ramoth-Gilead (Gad), Golan (Manasseh), Hebron (Judah), Shechem (Ephraim), Kedesh (Naphtali).

REFUGEE SLAVES. Laws concerning (De 23:15, 16).

See Servant, Bond.

REGEM, son of Jahdai (1Ch 2:47).

REGEM-MELECH, a captive sent as a messenger from the Jews in Babylon to Jerusalem (Zec 7:2).

REGENCY (1Ki 22:47; 2Ki 15:5).

REGENERATION, spiritual change wrought in the heart of man by the Holy Spirit in which his inherently sinful nature is changed so that he can respond to God in faith and live in accordance with His will. It extends to the whole nature of man, altering his governing disposition, illumining his mind, freeing his will, and renewing his nature.

Rendered also, born, again (Joh 3:3-8; 1Pe 1:2, 3, 22, 23); of God (Joh 1:4, 12, 13, 16; Jas 1:18; 1Jo 2:27, 29; 3:9, 14; 4:7; 5:1, 4, 5, 11, 12, 18); of the Spirit (Joh 3:5, 6; Ga 4:9).

Necessity of (Jer 13:23; M't 12:33-35; 18:3; M'k 10:15; Lu 18:17; Joh 3:3, 5; Tit 3:5, 6).

Through the Holy Spirit (Eze 12:10; Joh 3:5-8; 1Co 12:13; 2Th 2:13; 1Pe 1:2, 3, 22).

Parables of (M't 13:23, 33; M'k 4:20, 26-29; Lu 13:21).

Other related terms of the beginning of the spiritual life: Circumcision of the heart (De 29:4; 30:6; Eze 44:7, 9; Ro 2:28; Col 2:11-13); change of heart (Ps 51:2, 7, 10; Jer 24:7; 31:33, 34 w Heb 8:10, 11; Jer 32:38-40; Eze 11:19, 20; 18:31; 36:26, 27, 29; Ro 12:2); new creature (2Co 5:17; Ga 6:15; Eph 4:22-24; Col 3:9, 10); spiritual cleansing (Joh 15:3; Ac 15:9; 1Co 6:11); spiritual illumination (Joh 6:44, 45; 8:12; Ac 26:18; 1Co 2:11, 12, 14-16; 2Co 4:6; Eph 5:14; Heb 10:16); spiritual quickening (Eze 37:1-14; Joh 6:57; Eph 2:1, 5, 6, 8, 10; 4:7); spiritual resurrection (Joh 5:24; Ro 6:3-13; 8:2-4; Ga 2:20).

Other scriptures related to (1Ki 8:58; Ps 36:9; 65:3; 68:18; 110:3; Pr 4:23; 12:28; 14:27; Isa 1:16, 17, 25; 4:4; 12:3; 26:12; 32:3, 4, 15, 17; 35:5, 6; 42:16; 43:7; 44:3-5; 55:1-3; Jer 17:13, 14; 24:7; 33:6; 31:3; 33:6; Eze 16:9; Lu 1:16, 17; Joh 4:10, 14; 10:9, 10; 13:8; 17:2; Ac 2:38, 47; 3:26; 11:17, 21; 16:14; Ro 7:6, 24; 15:16; 1Co 1:9, 24, 30; 3:6, 7, 9; 15:10; 2Co 1:2, 22; 2Co 3:3, 18; Ph'p 1:6; Heb 4:12; Jas 5:19, 20; 1Pe 2:3, 9; 2Pe 1:3, 4).

See Atonement; Conversion; Reconciliation; Redemption; Righteous; Salvation; Sanctification; Sin, Forgiveness of.

REGICIDE. Of Ehud (J'g 3:16-23). Of Saul (2Sa 1:16). Of Ish-bosheth (2Sa 4:5-8). Of Nadab (1Ki 15:27-29). Of Elah (1Ki 16:9-11). Of Joram (2Ki 9:24). Of Ahaziah (2Ki 9:27). Of Joash (2Ki 12:20, 21). Of Amaziah (2Ki 14:19, 20). Of Zachariah (2Ki 15:10). Of Shallum (2Ki 15:14). Of Pekahiah (2Ki 15:25). Of Pekah (2Ki 15:30). Of Sennacherib (2Ki 19:36, 37; Isa 37:37, 38).

See Homicide.

REGISTRATION, of citizens (Isa 4:3).

See Census.

REHABIAH, son of Eliezer (1Ch 23:17; 24:21; 26:25).

REHOB (broad). 1. Father of Hadadezer, king of Zobah (2Sa 8:3, 12).

2. A Levite who sealed the covenant with Nehemiah (Ne 10:11).

3. A town in northern Palestine. The limit of the investigation made by the twelve spies (Nu 13:21). Possessed by the Syrians (2Sa 10:6, 8). Called Beth-rehob (2Sa 10:6).

4. An unlocated town of Asher (Jos 19:28).

5. A Levitical city of Asher (Jos 19:30; 21:31; 1Ch 6:75). Canaanites not driven from (J'g 1:31).

REHOBOAM. Successor to Solomon as king (1Ki 11:43; 2Ch 9:31). Refuses to reform abuses (1Ki 12:1-15; 2Ch 10:1-15). Ten tribes, under leadership of Jeroboam, successfully revolt from (1Ki 12:16-24; 2Ch 10:16-19; 11:1-4). Builds fortified cities; is temporarily prosperous (2Ch 11:5-23). Invaded by king of

Egypt and despoiled (1Ki 14:25-28; 2Ch 12:1-12). Death of (1Ki 14:31; 2Ch 12:16). Genealogy and descendants of (1Ch 3; M't 1). Called Roboam (M't 1:7).

REHOBOTH (broad places). 1. A city built by Asshur (Ge 10:11).

2. A city of the Edomites (Ge 36:37; 1Ch 1:48).

3. The name given to a well dug by Isaac (Ge 26:22).

REHUM (beloved). 1. A captive who returned to Jerusalem from Babylon (Ezr 2:2). Called Nehum (Ne 7:7).

2. A chancellor who wrote a letter to Artaxerxes, influencing him against the Jews (Ezr 4:8, 9, 17, 23).

3. A Levite who repaired part of the wall of Jerusalem (Ne 3:17).

4. A Jew of the exile who signed the covenant with Nehemiah (Ne 10:25).

5. A priest who returned to Jerusalem from captivity in Babylon (Ne 12:3).

REI (friendly), an Israelite loyal to David at the time of the usurpation of Adonijah (1Ki 1:8).

REINS, inward parts; kidneys as seat of emotions (Ps 7:9; 26:2; Jer 17:10; Job 19:27).

REJECTION. Of God (1Sa 8:7; 10:19; 2Ki 17:15; Lu 7:30). See God, Rejection of.

Of Israel by God (Nu 14:12, 26-37; 2Ki 17:20; Jer 6:30; 7:29; 14:19; La 5:22). Of Saul by God (1Sa 15:23, 26).

Of Jesus, see Jesus, Rejected.

REKEM (friendship). 1. A king of the Midianites, slain by the Israelites (Nu 31:8; Jos 13:21).

2. A son of Hebron (1Ch 2:43, 44).

3. A city in Benjamin (Jos 18:27).

RELEASE. *Year of:* See Jubilee, Year of.

RELIGION. *False:* De 32:31-33.

See Idolatry; Intolerance; Teachers, False.

Family (See Family.)

National: Supported by taxes (Ex 30:11-16; 38:26). Priests supported by the State (1Ki 18:19; 2Ch 11:13-15). Subverted by Jeroboam (1Ki 12:26-33; 2Ch 11:13-15). Idolatrous established by Jeroboam (1Ki 12:26-33).

Natural (Job 12:7-16; 37:1-24; Ps 8:1-9; 19:1-6; Ac 14:17; 17:23-28; Ro 1:18-20; 10:16-18).

See Revivals.

True: As presented by, Jesus (M't 5:1-45; 6:1-34; 7:1-29; 22:26-40); Paul (Ro 8:18; 10:1-13; 12:1-21; 1Co 13:1-13; Ga 5:22-25; 1Th 5:15-23); James (Jas 1:27; 2:8-26); Peter (1Pe 1:5-9); Jude (Jude 20, 21).

See Blessings, Spiritual; Commandments; Duty; Graces; Regeneration; Repentance; Sanctification; Sin, Forgiveness of.

Instances of Conspicuously Religious Persons: Abel (Ge 4:4-8; Heb 11:4). Noah (Ge 6-9). Abraham (Ge 12:1-8; 15; 17; 18:22-33). Jacob (Ge 28:10-22; 32:24-32). Moses (Ex 3:2-22; De 32; 33). Jethro (Ex 18:12). Joshua (Jos 1). Gideon (J'g 6; 7). Samuel (1Sa 3). David (see Psalms of David). Solomon (1Ki 5:3-5; 2Ch 6). Jehu (2Ki 10:16-30). Hezekiah (2Ki 18:3-7; 19:14-19). Jehoshaphat (2Ch 17:3-9; 19; 20). Jabez (1Ch 4:9, 10). Asa (2Ch 14; 15). Josiah (2Ki 22; 23). Daniel (Da 6:4-22). The three Hebrews (Da 3). Zacharias (Lu 1:13, 67-79). Simeon (Lu 2:25-35). Anna, the prophetess (Lu 2:36, 37). The centurion (Lu 7:1-10). Cornelius (Ac 10). Eunice and Lois (2Ti 1:5).

See, for additional instances, each of the apostles, disciples, and John, Paul, Peter, Stephen; also each of the prophets.

RELIGIOUS. *Coercion* (Ex 22:20; 2Ch 15:12-15; Da 3:2-6, 29; 6:26, 27).

See Intolerance.

Revivals (Zec 8:20-23). Prayer for (Hab 3:2). Prophecies concerning (Isa 32:15; Joe 2:28; Mic 4:1-8).

See Revivals.

Testimony (Ps 18:49; 22:22; 26:12; 34:8, 9; Isa 45:24; 1Co 13:1; Re 12:11).

See Testimony, Religious.

REMALIAH (Jehovah adorns), father of Pekah, king of Israel (2Ki 15:25, 27, 30; 16:1, 5; 2Ch 28:6; Isa 7:1, 4; 8:6).

REMETH (height), city in Issachar (Jos 19:17-21); Probably Ramoth of 1Ch 6:73 and Jarmuth of Jos 21:29).

REMMON (See Rimmon, 2.)

REMMON-METHOAR (See Rimmon, 3.)

REMNANT. 1. People who survived political or military crises (Jos 12:4; 13:12).

2. Spiritual kernel of Israel who would survive God's judgment and be-

come the germ of the new people of God (Isa 10:20-23; 11:11, 12; Jer 32:38, 39; Zep 3:13; Zec 8:12).

REMORSE (Pr 1:25-27). Of the lascivious (Pr 5:7-13). Of the lost (Lu 13:28). Of the wicked (Pr 28:1; Isa 2:19; 57:20, 21; Eze 7:16-18, 25, 26).

Of Israelites (Eze 33:10). Of believers (1Jo 3:20).

Instances of: David (Ps 31:10; 38:2-6; 51). Isaiah (Isa 6:5). Jeremiah (La 1:20). Peter (M't 26:75). Judas (M't 27:3-5). The Jews (Ac 2:37). Paul (Ac 9:6).

See Conviction, of Sin; Penitents; Repentance; Sin, Confession of.

RENDING, of garments, a token of affliction (Ge 37:29, 34; 44:13; Nu 14:6; J'g 11:35; 2Sa 1:2, 11; 3:31; 13:19, 31; 15:32; 2Ki 2:12; 5:8; 6:30; 11:14; 19:1; 22:11, 19; Ezr 9:3, 5; Job 1:20; 2:12; Isa 36:22; 37:1; Jer 41:5; M't 26:65; Ac 14:14).

Figurative: Joe 2:13. Symbol of rending of a kingdom) 1Sa 15:27, 28).

RENTING. Land (M't 21:33-41; Lu 20:9-16). Houses (Ac 28:30).

RENUNCIATION (Ph'p 3:7, 8). Of self for others, exemplified, by Moses (Ex 32:32); Jesus (Ph'p 2:7); Paul (Ro 9:3; 2Co 13:7).

Of self for Christ (M't 16:25; Lu 14:26-33; 17:33; Joh 12:25). Of business for Christ (M't 4:20; 9:9; M'k 1:18-20; 2:14; Lu 5:27, 28). Of possessions for Christ (M't 19:21-29; M'k 10:21-30; Lu 18:22-30). Of one's all for Christ, illustrated by parable (M't 13:44-46).

Of the will, to the Father, exemplified by Jesus (M'k 14:36; Lu 22:42; Joh 5:30; 6:38).

See Self-denial.

REPENTANCE (Ps 34:14, 18; Isa 22:12). Exhortations to (Pr 1:22, 23; Jer 6:16-18; 7:3; 26:3; Ho 6:1; 14:1-2; Am 5:4-6; M't 3:2).

Enjoined (De 32:29; 2Ch 30:7-9; Job 36:10; Isa 22:12; 31:6; 44:22; 55:6, 7; Jer 3:4, 12-14, 19, 22; 18:11; 25:5, 6; 26:13; 35:15; Eze 12:1-5; 14:6; 18:30-32; 33:10-12, 14-16, 19; Da 4:27; Ho 10:12; 14:1, 2; Joe 1:14; 2:12, 13, 15-17; Am 4:12; Jon 3:8, 9; Hag 1:7; Zec 1:3; M't 4:17; M'k 1:4, 15; 6:12; Lu 3:3; Ac 2:38; 3:19; 8:22; 17:30; Re 2:5, 16; 3:2, 3, 19).

Gift, of God (2Ti 2:25); of Christ (Ac 5:31). Goodness of God, leads to (Ro 2:4). Tribulation leads to (De 4:30; 30:1-3; 1Ki 8:33-50; 2Ch 6:36-39; Job 34:31, 32).

Condition, of forgiveness (Le 26:40-42; De 4:29-31; 30:1-3, 8; 1Ki 8:33-50; 2Ch 6:36-39; 7:14; Ne 1:9; Job 11:13-15; 22:23; Ps 34:18; Pr 28:13; Isa 55:7; Jer 3:4, 12-14, 19; 7:5-7; i8:7, 8; 36:3; Eze 18:21-23, 27, 28, 30, 31; Am 5:6; Mal 3:7; M't 5:4; Lu 13:1-5; 1Jo 1:9); of divine favor (Le 26:40-42; 2Ch 7:14; Isa 57:15).

To be preached to all nations (Lu 24:47).

Joy in heaven over (Lu 15:1-10). Of Israel foretold (Jer 50:4, 5; Eze 11:18-20; Ho 3:5; Zec 12:10). Universal, foretold (Ps 22:27; Ro 14:11). Rewards of (Pr 1:23; Isa 59:20; Jer 7:3, 5, 7; 24:7; Eze 18:21-23, 27, 28).

The burden of the preaching, of John the Baptist (M't 3:2, 7, 8; M'k 1:4, 15; Lu 3:3); of Jesus (M't 4:17; M'k 1:15; Lu 5:32); of Peter (Ac 2:38, 40; 3:19; 8:22); of Paul (Ac 17:30; 20:21; 26:20); of the apostles (M'k 6:12).

Unavailing, to Israel (Nu 14:39-45); to Esau (Heb 12:16, 17).

Attributed to God (Ge 6:6, 7; Ex 32:14; De 32:36; J'g 2:18; 1Sa 15:11, 35; 2Sa 24:16; 1Ch 21:15; Ps 106:45; 110:4; 135:14; Jer 15:6; 18:8, 10; 26:3; 42:10; Joe 2:13; Am 7:3, 6; Jon 3:9, 10). God repents not (Nu 23:19; 1Sa 15:29; Ps 110:4; Ro 11:29).

Exemplified: By Job (Job 7:20, 21; 9:20; 13:23; 40:4; 42:6). By David (Ps 32:5; 38:3, 4, 18; 40:12; 41:4; 51:1-4; 7-17). By the Israelites (Nu 21:7; 2Ch 29:6; Jer 3:21, 22, 25; 14:7-9, 20; 31:18, 19; La 3:40, 41). By Daniel for the Jews (Da 9:5-7; 10:12). By the prodigal (Lu 15:17-20).

Instances of: Joseph's brethren, for their ill treatment of Joseph (Ge 42:21; 50:17, 18). Pharaoh, for his hardness of heart (Ex 9:27; 10:16, 17). Balaam, for his spiritual blindness (Nu 22:34 w vs 24-35). Israelites, for worshiping the golden calf (Ex 33:3, 4); for their murmuring on account of lack of bread and water, when the plague of fiery serpents came upon them (Nu 21:4-7); when rebuked by an angel for not expelling the Canaanites (J'g 2:1-5); for their idolatry, when afflicted by the Philistines (J'g

10:6-16; 1Sa 7:3-6); for asking for a king (1Sa 12:16-20); in the time of Asa, under the preaching of Azariah (2Ch 15:1-15); under the preaching of Oded (2Ch 28:9-15); under the influence of Hezekiah (2Ch 30:11). Achan, for his theft (Jos 7:29). Saul, at the reproof of Samuel for not destroying the Amalekites (1Sa 15:24 w vs 6-11). Job (Job 42:6). David, at the rebuke of Nathan, the prophet (2Sa 12:11, 13 w vs 7-14; Ps 32:5; 38:3, 4, 18; 40:12; 41:4; 51:1-4, 7-17); for numbering Israel (2Sa 24:10, 17). Psalmist (Ps 100:6; 119:59, 176; 130:1-3). See Psalms, Penitential. Rehoboam, when his kingdom was invaded, and Jerusalem besieged (2Ch 12:1-12; Isa 6:5). Hezekiah, for his pride (Isa 38:15); at the time of his sickness (2Ch 32:26); when reproved by the prophet Micah (Jer 26:18, 19). Ahab, when reproved by Elijah for his idolatry (1Ki 21:27 w 17:29). Jehoahaz (2Ki 13:4). Josiah, when he heard the law which had been discovered in the temple, by Hilkiah (2Ki 22:11-20). Manasseh, when he was carried captive to Babylon by the king of Assyria (2Ch 33:12, 13). The Jews of the captivity, at the dedication of the temple (Ezr 6:21; 9:4, 6, 10, 13, 14); for their idolatrous marriages (Ezr 10); for their oppressive usury (Ne 5:1-13); after hearing the law expounded by Ezra (Ne 9:1-3); under the preaching of Haggai (Hag 1). Jonah, after his punishment (Jon 2:2-9). The Ninevites, under the preaching of Jonah (Jon 3:5-9, 10). The Jews under the preaching of John the Baptist (M't 3:6). The woman who anointed Jesus with oil (Lu 7:37-48). The disobedient son (M't 21:29). The prodigal son (Lu 15:17-21). The publican (Lu 18:13). Peter, of his denial of Jesus (M't 26:75; M'k 14:72; Lu 22:62). The Ephesians, under the preaching of Paul (Ac 19:18).

See Conviction; Penitence; Remorse; Sin, Confession of; Sin, Forgiveness of.

REPETITION. *In Prayers:* See Prayers.

REPHAEL (God heals), a porter of the temple in the time of David (1Ch 26:7).

REPHAH (a prop), a grandson of Ephraim (1Ch 7:25).

REPHAIAH (Jehovah heals). 1. A descendant of David (1Ch 3:21).

2. A Simeonite captain (1Ch 4:42).

3. Son of Tola, of the tribe of Issachar (1Ch 7:2).

4. A descendant of Jonathan (1Ch 9:43). Called Rapha (1Ch 8:37).

5. Governor over half of Jerusalem in the time of Nehemiah (Ne 3:9).

REPHAIM (mighty), giant people who lived in Canaan even before Abraham's time (Ge 14:5; 15:20; Jos 12:4; 13:12; 17:15).

REPHAIM, VALLEY OF (vale of giants), fertile plain S of Jerusalem, three miles from Bethlehem (Isa 17:4, 5; 1Ch 14:9).

REPHIDIM (plains), encampment of Israelites in wilderness; there Moses struck a rock to secure water (Ex 17:1-7; 19:2); battle with Amalekites took place there (Ex 17:8-16).

REPORTS. *Majority and Minority:* Of spies (Nu 13:26-33; 14:6-10).

REPROBACY. Admonitions against (2Co 13:5-7; Heb 3:10-12, 17-19; 6:4-9; 12:15-17). Curses denounced against (De 28:15-68; 31:17, 18; Isa 65:12; Ho 9:12; M'k 3:29; Heb 10:26-31).

See Reprobates.

REPROBATE, moral corruption, unfitness, disqualification, disapproved (Ro 1:28; 1Co 9:27). See Reprobacy; Reprobates.

REPROBATES (Jer 6:30; Ro 1:21-32; 2Ti 3:8; 1Jo 5:16; Jude 4:13; Re 22:4). Called, men of corrupt minds (2Ti 3:8); vessels of wrath (Ro 9:22).

Moral insensibility of (Isa 22:12-14; 28:13; 29:9-12; M't 13:14, 15; 15:14; Ro 11:7, 8). Rejected of God (Ps 81:11, 12; Pr 1:24-28; Jer 6:30; 7:16; 15:1; Ho 5:6; M't 15:14; 25:8-13; Lu 13:24-28; 14:24; Joh 10:26; Ro 1:21-26, 28; 2Th 2:10, 11; Heb 3:10-12, 17-19; 6:4-8; 10:26-31). Admonitions against (Heb 12:15-17).

In Israel (Nu 14:26-48; De 1:42; Isa 6:9, 10; Heb 3:10-12; 17-19; Jude 5). In the Church (2Co 13:5-7; Heb 3:10-12, 17-19; 6:4-9; Jude 4, 13).

Instances of: Antediluvians (Ge 6:5-7). Sodomites (Ge 13:13; 19:13; Jude 7). Jannes and Jambres (2Ti 3:8). Eli's house (1Sa 3:14). Saul (1Sa 15:23; 16:14; 18:12; 28:15). Judas (Joh 17:12). Angels (Jude 6). Anti-Christ (2Th 2:7-12).

See Obduracy; Reprobacy.

REPRODUCTION (See Propagation).

REPROOF. Enjoined (Le 19:17; Ps

141:5; Pr 9:7, 8; 10:17; 26:5; M't 18:15-17; Lu 17:3; Eph 5:11; 1Th 5:14; 5:20; 2Ti 4:2; Tit 1:13; Heb 3:13). Of seniors, forbidden (1Ti 5:1, 2).

Profitable (Pr 13:18; 15:5, 31, 32; 27:5, 6; 38:23; Ec 7:5). Wise profit by (Pr 17:10; 19:25; 21:11; 25:12).

Needed, in the Church (Eph 4:15; Ph'p 3:1; 1Th 5:14; 1Ti 5:1, 2, 20; 2Ti 4:2; Tit 1:13; Heb 3:13).

Hated (Pr 12:1; 10:17; 15:10, 12; Am 5:10; Joh 7:7; Ga 4:16). See Despised, below.

Faithfulness in: Instances of: Moses, of Pharaoh (Ex 10:29; 11:8); of the Israelites (Ex 16:6, 7; 32:19-30; Nu 14:41; 20:10; 32:14; De 1:12, 26-43; 9:16-24; 29:2-4; 31:27-29; 32:15-18); of Eleazar (Le 10:16-18); of Korah (Nu 16:9-11). Israelites, of the two and one-half tribes (Jos 22:15-20); of the tribe of Benjamin (J'g 20:12, 13). Samuel, of Saul (1Sa 15:14-35). Jonathan, of Saul (1Sa 19:4, 5). Nathan, of David (2Sa 12:1-9). Joab, of David (2Sa 19:1-7; 24:3; 1Ch 21:3). The prophet Gad, of David (2Sa 24:13). Shemaiah, of Rehoboam (2Ch 12:5). A prophet of Judah, of Jeroboam (1Ki 13:1-10; 2Ch 13:8-11). Elijah, of Ahab (1Ki 18:18-21; 21:20-24); of Ahaziah (2Ki 1). Micaiah, of Ahab (1Ki 22:14-28). Elisha, of Jehoram (2Ki 3:13, 14); of Gehazi (2Ki 5:26); of Hazael (2Ki 8:11-13); of Jeroboam (2Ki 13:19). Isaiah, of Hezekiah (2Ki 20:17). Jehoash, of Jehoiada (2Ki 12:7). Azariah, of Asa (2Ch 15:2); of Uzziah (2Ch 26:17, 18). Hanani, of Asa (2Ch 16:7-9). Jehu, of Jehoshaphat (2Ch 19:2). Zechariah, of the princes of Judah (2Ch 24:20). Oded, of the people of Samaria (2Ch 28:9-11). Jeremiah, of the cities of Judah (Jer 26:8-11). Ezra, of the men of Judah and Benjamin (Ezr 10:10). Nehemiah, of the Jews (Ne 5:6-13); of the corruptions in the temple, and of the violation of the Sabbath (Ne 13). Daniel, of Nebuchadnezzar (Da 4:27); of Belshazzar (Da 5:17-24). Amos, of the Israelites (Am 7:12-17).

Jesus, of the Jews: when Pharisees and Sadducees came to him desiring a sign (M't 16:1-4; M'k 8:11, 12); of the scribes and Pharisees (M't 23; Lu 11:37-54); of the Pharisees (Lu 16); when they brought the woman to him who was taken in adultery (Joh 8:7). In his parables: Of the king's feast (Lu 14:16-24); of the two sons (M't 21:28-32); of the vineyard (M't 21:33-46; M'k 12:1-12; Lu 20:9-20); of the barren fig-tree (Lu 13:6-9); the withering of the fig tree (M't 21:17-20; M'k 11:12-14).

John the Baptist, of the Jews (M't 3:7-12; Lu 3:7-9); of Herod (M't 14:3; M'k 6:17; Lu 3:19, 20). Peter, of Simon, the sorcerer (Ac 8:20-23). Stephen, of the high priest (Ac 7:51-53). Paul, of Elymas, the sorcerer (Ac 13:9-11); of Ananias, the high priest (Ac 23:3). Paul and Silas, of the magistrates of Philippi (Ac 16:37-40).

Despised: By the Israelites (Nu 14:9, 10; Jer 26:11). By Ahab (1Ki 18:17; 21:20; 22:8). By Asa (2Ch 16:10). By Herodias, (M'k 6:18, 19). By people of Nazareth (Lu 4:28, 29). Jews (Ac 5:33; 7:54).

See One Another; Reprobacy.

REPTILES. Adders (Ge 49:17). Asps (Isa 11:8). Chameleons (Le 11:30). Cockatrices (Isa 59:5). Crocodiles (Le 11:30). Dragons (Eze 29:3). Frogs (Ex 8:2). Lizards (Le 11:30). Serpents (Ex 7:10). Tortoises (Le 11:29). Vipers (Job 20:16).

REPUTATION, GOOD (Pr 22:1; Ec 7:1).

See Character; Name.

RESEN, town founded by Nimrod (Ge 10:8-12) between Nineveh and Calah.

RESERVOIR, place where water is collected and kept for use when wanted, chiefly in large quantities. Because most of W Asia was subject to periodic droughts, and because of frequent sieges, reservoirs and cisterns were a necessity (2Ch 26:10; 18:31; Ec 2:6).

RESHEPH (a flame), grandson of Ephraim (1Ch 7:25).

RESIGNATION. *Enjoined* (Ps 4:4; 46:10; Lu 21:19; Ro 12:12; Ph'p 2:14; Col 1:10, 11; Jas 1:9, 10; 4:7; 1Pe 4:12, 13, 19). Under chastisements and afflictions (Job 5:17; Pr 3:11; 18:14; Jer 51:50; La 3:39; Mic 6:9; 1Th 3:3; 2Ti 2:3; 4:5; Heb 2:6-12; 12:5, 9; Jas 5:11, 13; 1Pe 1:6). Under bereavement (1Th 4:13-18).

Exemplified by: Aaron (Le 10:1-3). The children of Israel (J'g 10:15). Eli (1Sa 3:18). David (2Sa 12:23; 15:26;

16:10, 11; 24:14). The Shunammite (2Ki 4:26). Hezekiah (2Ki 20:19; Isa 39:8). Nehemiah (Ne 9:33). By Esther (Es 4:16). Job (Job 1:13-22; 2:9, 10; 34:31; Jas 5:11). The psalmists (Ps 39:9; 103:10; 119:75). Jeremiah (Jer 10:19; La 1:18). Daniel (Da 9:14). Micah (Mic 7:9).

In "the Lord's Prayer" (M't 6:10; Lu 11:2). By: Jesus (M't 26:39; M'k 14:36; Lu 22:42; Joh 18:11). The thief on the cross (Lu 23:40, 41). Stephen (Ac 7:59, 60). Agabus, Luke and others when Paul insisted on going to Jerusalem (Ac 21:14). Paul (Ro 5:3-5; 2Co 6:4-10; 7:4; Ph'p 1:20-24; 4:11, 12; 2Ti 4:6). Paul and Silas (Ac 16:25). Thessalonian believers (2Th 1:4). Hebrew believers (Heb 10:34).

See Affliction, Benefits of, Resignation in.

RESPECT. To the aged (Le 19:32). To rulers (Pr 25:6). To a host (Lu 14:10). To one another (Ro 12:10; Ph'p 2:3; 1Pe 2:17).

RESPECT OF PERSONS (Pr 24:23; 28:21; Jas 2:1-9). God does not have (De 10:17; 2Ch 19:7; Job 31:13-15; 34:19; Ac 10:34; 15:9; Ro 2:11, 12; 10:12; Eph 6:8, 9; Col 3:25; 1Pe 1:17).

See God, Justice of; Justice.

RESPONSIBILITY. Attempts to shift: Adam (Ge 3:12, 13); Eve (Ge 3:13); Sarah (Ge 16:5, w verse 2); Esau (Ge 27:36, w Ge 25:29-34); Aaron (Ex 32: 22-24); Saul (1Sa 15:20, 21); Pilate (M't 27:24). Assumed by the Jews for the death of Jesus (M't 27:25).

Personal (Eze 14:14-20; 18:20, 30; M't 12:37; Joh 9:41; 15:22-24; Ro 14:12; 1Co 3:8, 13-15; Ga 6:5; 1Pe 4:5; Re 2:23).

According to privilege (Eze 18:1-30; 33:1-19; M't 10:11-15; 11:20-24; 12: 41, 42; 23:31-35; 25:14-30; M'k 6:11; Lu 9:5; 10:10-15; 11:31, 32, 49-51; 13:6-9; 19:12-27; 21:1-4; Joh 3:18, 19; 12:48; 15:22, 24; Ac 17:30, 31; Ro 12:3, 6-8; Eph 4:7; 1Ti 6:20).

See Judgment According to Opportunity; Privilege.

RESPONSIVE RELIGIOUS SERVICE (De 27:14-26).

REST. Divine institution for, see Sabbath. Enjoined (Ex 16:23; 20:10; 23:12; 31:15; 24:21; 35:2; De 5:12, 14).

The annual feasts added rest days: first and last days of feasts of passover and tabernacles (Ex 12:16; Le 23:5-8, 39, 40; Nu 28:18, 25; 29:12, 35); pentecost (Nu 28:26); trumpets (Le 23:24, 25; Nu 29:1); atonement (Le 16:29-31; 23:27, 28; Nu 29:7). In sabbatic year (Ex 23:11; Le 25:1-4). In year of jubilee (Le 25:11, 12).

Recommended by Jesus (M'k 6:31, 32 w M't 8:18, 24). Heavenly (2Th 1:7). Spiritual (M't 11:29; Heb 4:1-11).

See Peace, Spiritual.

RESTITUTION. To be made for injury to life, limb, or property (Ex 21:30-36; Le 24:18); for theft (Ex 22:1-4; Pr 6:30, 31; Eze 33:15); for dishonesty (Le 6:2-5; Nu 5:7; Job 20:18; Eze 33:15; Lu 19:8).

RESTORATION. Of the Jews (see Israelites). Of all things (Ac 3:21; Re 21:1-5).

RESURRECTION (M't 22:23-32; 25: 6-7; M'k 12:18-27; Lu 14:14; 20:27-37; Heb 6:2; 11:35). First, of the dead in Christ (1Th 4:16; Re 20:4-6); at Christ's second coming (1Th 4:14, 16).

Of all the dead (Joh 5:28, 29; Ac 24:15; 1Co 15:20, 21; Re 20:13). Of saints after Christ's resurrection (M't 27:52, 53).

Job's views concerning (Job 14:12-15; 19:25-27). Psalmists understood (Ps 16:9, 10; 17:15; 49:15).

Prophecies concerning (Isa 25:8; 26:19; Da 12:2, 3, 13; Ho 13:14). Of Christ (Ps 16:9, 10).

Taught by: Jesus (M't 22:30-32; 24:31; M'k 12:25-27; Lu 20:37, 38; Joh 5:21, 25, 28, 29; 6:39, 40, 44, 54; 11:23-25); the apostles (Ac 4:1, 2; 17:18, 31, 32; 23:6, 8; 24:14, 15; 26:6-8; Ro 4:16-21; 8:10, 11, 19, 21-23; 1Co 6:14; 15:12-57; 2Co 4:14; 5:1-5; Ph'p 3:11, 21; Re 20:5, 6).

Believed in by the Pharisees (Ac 23:6, 8; 24:14, 15; 26:6-8). Denied by the Sadducees (M't 22:23-28; Ac 23:6, 8).

Error concerning (2Ti 2:18).

See Dead, Raised.

Figurative: Of regeneration (Ro 6:4; Eph 2:1, 5, 6; Col 2:12; 3:1).

Typified: Isaac (Ge 22:13 w Heb 11:19). Jonah (Jon 2:10 w M't 12:40).

Symbolical (Re 11:11). Of the restoration of Israel (Eze 37:1-14).

Of Jesus (M't 27:53; 28:2-15; M'k 16:1-11; Lu 24:1-12; Joh 20:1-18; Re 1:18).

Foretold by himself (M't 16:21; 17:9,

23; 20:19; 26:61; 27:63; M'k 8:31; 9:9, 10, 31; 10:34; Lu 9:22; 18:33; 24:7, 46; Joh 2:19-21; 10:17, 18; 14:19).

Denied by the Jews (M't 28:12-15). Raised by the power of God (Ac 2:24, 32; 3:15, 26; 4:10; 5:30; 10:40; 15:20, 30, 33, 34, 37; 17:31; Ro 4:24; 8:11; 10:9; 1Co 6:14; 15:15; 2Co 4:14; Ga 1:4; Eph 1:20; Col 2:12; 1Ti 1:10; 1Pe 1:21). For our justification (Ro 4:25; 1Pe 3:21). Earnest of general resurrection (1Co 15:12-15; 1Pe 1:3).

The theme of apostolic preaching (Ac 2:24, 31, 32; 3:15; 4:10, 33; 5:30-32; 10:40, 41; 17:2, 3, 18).

See Jesus, Resurrection of.

RETALIATION (Ps 10:2). Judicial, ordained in Mosaic law (Ex 21:23-25; Le 24:17-22; De 19:19-21). Malicious, forbidden (Le 19:18; Pr 20:22; 24:29; M't 5:38-44; 7:1, 2; Lu 9:54; Ro 12:17, 19; 1Co 6:7, 8; 1Th 5:15; 1Pe 3:9). Warning against (Pr 26:27; Isa 33:1; M't 7:1, 2).

See Avenger; Hatred; Malice; Revenger.

Instances of: Israelites on the Amalekites (De 25:17-19, w 1Sa 15: 1-9). Gideon on the princes of Succoth (J'g 8:7, 13-16); kings of Midian (J'g 8:18-21); Penuel (J'g 8:8, 17). Joab on Abner (2Sa 3:27, 30). David upon Michal (2Sa 6:21-23); on Joab (1Ki 2:5, 6); Shimei (1Ki 2:8, 9). Jews on the Chaldeans (Es 9).

RETICENCE OF JESUS (Isa 53:7; M't 26:63; 27:12, 14; M'k 14:61; 15:4, 5; Joh 19:9; 1Pe 2:23).

See Prudence, of Jesus.

RETRIBUTION (See Sin, Punishment of.)

REU (friendship), son of Peleg and ancestor of Abraham (Ge 11:18-21; 1Ch 1:25).

REUBEN (See a son!). Son of Jacob (Ge 29:32; 1Ch 2:1). Brings mandrakes to his mother (Ge 30:14). Commits incest with one of his father's concubines, and, in consequence, forfeits the birthright (Ge 35:22; 49:4; 1Ch 5:1). Adroitly seeks to save Joseph from the conspiracy of his brethren (Ge 37:21-30; 42:22). Offers to become surety for Benjamin (Ge 42:37). Jacob's prophetic benediction upon (Ge 49:3, 4). His children (Ge 46:9; Ex 6:14; 1Ch 5:3-6; Nu 16:1).

REUBENITES, the descendants of Reuben, Military enrollment of, at Sinai (Nu 1:20, 21); in Moab (Nu 26:7). Place of, in camp and march (Nu 2:10). Standard of (Nu 10:18). Have their inheritance east of the Jordan (Nu 32; De 3:1-20; Jos 13:15-23; 18:7). Assist the other tribes in conquest of the region west of the Jordan (Jos 1:12-18; 22:1-6). Unite with the other tribes in building a monument to signify the unity of the tribes on the east of the Jordan with the tribes on the west of the river; monument misunderstood; the explanation and reconciliation (Jos 22:10-34). Reproached by Deborah (J'g 5:15, 16). Taken captive into Assyria (2Ki 15:29; 1Ch 5:26).

See Israel.

REUEL (God is friend). 1. Son of Esau (Ge 36:4, 10).

2. Father-in-law of Moses (Ex 2:16-22), probably same as Jethro (Ex 3:1).

3. Father of Eliasaph (called Deuel in Nu 1:14) (Nu 2:14).

4. Benjamite (1Ch 9:8).

REUMAH, a concubine of Nahor (Ge 22:24).

REVELATION, the doctrine of God's making Himself and relevant truths known to men. Revelation is of two kinds: general and special. General revelation is available to all men, and is communicated through nature, conscience, and history. Special revelation is revelation given to particular people at particular times (although it may be intended for others as well), and comes chiefly through the Bible and Jesus Christ. God reveals himself to Moses (Ex 3:1-6, 14; 6:1-3). The law is revealed (Ex 20-35; Le 1-7); the pattern of the temple (1Ch 28:11-19). The sonship of Jesus (M't 3:17; 16:17; 17:5).

See Inspiration; Prophecy; Prophet; Word of God, Inspiration of.

REVELATION, BOOK OF THE, last book in the Bible; only NT book exclusively prophetic in character; apocalyptic; tradition says it was written by John the apostle; written on island of Patmos, where John was imprisoned for his faith, either shortly after the death of Nero or at the close of the 1st century; addressed to seven churches of the Roman province of Asia; written to correct evils in the churches and to prepare them for the events that were about to confront them. Outline: 1. Christ the critic of the churches (1:1-3:22).

2. Series of seals, trumpets, and bowls; God's judgment upon a world controlled by evil (4:1-16:21).

3. Overthrow of evil society, religion, and government in the destruction of Babylon and the defeat of the beast and his armies by Christ (17:1-21:8).

4. Establishment of the city of God, the eternal destiny of His people (21:9-22:5). Epilogue: Appeal and invitation (22:6-21).

REVELLING, any extreme intemperance and lustful indulgence, usually accompanying pagan worship (Ga 5:21; 1Pe 4:3).

REVENGE. Forbidden (Le 19:18; Pr 24:29; Ro 12:17, 19; 1Th 5:15; 1Pe 3:9). Jesus an example of forbearing (1Pe 2:23). Rebuked by Jesus (Lu 9:54, 55). Inconsistent with a Christian spirit (Lu 9:55). Proceeds from a spiteful heart (Eze 25:15). Punishment for (Eze 25:15-17; Am 1:11, 12).

Exemplified: By Simeon and Levi (Ge 34:25). By Samson (J'g 15:7, 8; 16:28-30). By Joab (2Sa 3:27). By Absalom (2Sa 13:23-29). By Jezebel (1Ki 19:2). By Ahab (1Ki 22:27). By Haman (Es 3:8-15). By the Edomites (Eze 25:12). By the Philistines (Eze 25:15). By Herodias (M'k 6:19-24). By James and John (Lu 9:54). By the chief priests (Ac 5:33). By the Jews (Ac 7:54-59; 23:12).

See Retaliation.

REVENUE, Solomon's (2Ch 9:13, 14).

See Tax.

REVERENCE. For God (Ge 17:3; Ex 3:5; 19:16-24; 34:29-35; Isa 45:9). See Fear of God. For God's house (Le 19:30; 26:2). For ministers (1Sa 16:4; Ac 28:10; 1Co 16:18; Ph'p 2:29; 1Th 5:12, 13; 1Ti 5:17; Heb 13:7, 17). See Ministers. For kings (1Sa 24:6; 26:9, 11; 2Sa 1:14; 16:21; Ec 10:20; 1Pe 2:17). See Rulers. For magistrates (Ex 22:28; 2Pe 2:10; Jude 8). See Rulers. For parents (Ex 20:12; Le 19:3; Isa 45:10). See Parents. For the aged (Le 19:32; Job 32:4-7).

REVILE, REVILER, REVILING; to revile is to address with opprobrious or contumelious language; to reproach (Ex 21:17; Zep 2:8; M'k 15:32; 1Co 6:10).

REVIVALS. *Religious:* Zec 8:20-23; Prayer for (Hab 3:2). Prophecies concerning (Isa 32:15; Joe 2:28; Mic 4:1-8; Hab 3:2).

Instances of: Under Joshua (Jos 5:2-9); Samuel (1Sa 7:1-6); Elijah (1Ki 18:17-40); Jehoash and Jehoiada (2Ki 11; 12; 2Ch 23; 24); Hezekiah (2Ki 18:1-7; 2Ch 29-31); Josiah (2Ki 22; 23; 2Ch 34; 35); Asa (2Ch 14:2-5; 15:1-14); Manasseh (2Ch 33:12-19). In Nineveh (Jon 3:4-10). At Pentecost, and post-pentecostal times (Ac 2:1-42, 46, 47; 4:4; 5:14; 6:7; 9:35; 11:20, 21; 12:24; 14:1; 19:17-20).

See Religion.

REVOLT, of the ten tribes (1Ki 12:1-24).

REWARD, A MOTIVE (Isa 40:10, 11). In Moses' choice (Heb 11:26). For valor (1Sa 17:25; J'g 1:13).

To: Repentance (Le 26:40-45; Isa 1:16-20; Ac 26:18). Obedience (Ex 20:6; Le 25:18, 19; 26:3-13; De 4:40; 6:3, 18; 11:13-16, 18-21, 26-29; 27:12-26; Jos 8:33; Isa 1:16-20; 3:10; Eph 6:1-3; Heb 12:28). Faithfulness (M't 24:45-47; 25:14-33; Lu 12:42-44; 19:12-27; 1Co 3:8; Re 2:10: 22:12). Righteous conduct (Ro 2:10; 1Pe 3:9-12). Patience (Heb 10:36). Perseverance (M't 10:22; 24:13; M'k 13:13; Ro 2:6, 7; Ga 6:9; Re 2:17, 25-28; 3:5, 11, 12, 21; 21:7). Honesty (De 25:15). Follow Christ (M't 10:32; 16:24-27; 20:1-16; 25:34-46; M'k 10:21; Lu 12:8; 2Pe 1:10, 11). Endure persecution (Lu 6:22, 23; Heb 10:34). Endure tribulation (Re 2:7, 10; 17:14-17). Love enemies (Lu 6:35). Deliver the oppressed (Jer 22:3, 4; 17:24-26). Honor parents (Ex 20:12; Eph 6:1-3). Hallow Sabbath (Jer 17:24-26). Bestow charity (De 15:9-11; 24:19). Show kindness to animals (De 24:7).

See Blessing, Contingent upon Obedience; Punishments; Righteous, Promises to; Sin, Separates from God; Wicked, Punishment of.

REZEPH (stronghold), a city destroyed by the Assyrians (2Ki 19:12; Isa 37:12).

REZIA, an Asherite (1Ch 7:39).

REZIN. 1. A king of Syria who harassed the kingdom of Judah (2Ki 15:37;

16:5-9). Prophecy against (Isa 7:1-9; 8:4-8; 9:11).

2. A returned Babylonian captive (Ezr 2:48; Ne 7:50).

REZON (nobleman), king of Damascus. An adversary of Solomon (1Ki 11:23-25).

RHEGIUM, a city of Italy. Touched by Paul on the way to Rome (Ac 28:13).

RHESA, an ancestor of Jesus (Lu 3:27).

RHODA (rose), servant or slave girl in home of Mary, John Mark's mother (Ac 12:13).

RHODES (rose), island on SW tip of Asia Minor; commercial center until crippled by Rome in 166 B. C.; famous for Colossus, a statue of Helios; Paul stopped off there (Ac 21:1).

RIBAI, a Benjamite. Father of Ittai (2Sa 23:29; 1Ch 11:31).

RIBBAND (Nu 15:38.)

RIBLAH. 1. City on boundary of Canaan and Israel, N of Sea of Galilee (Nu 34:11).

2. Important town on E bank of Orontes River 50 miles S of Hamath, in Assyrian province of Mansuate. In this place Pharaoh Necho (609 B. C.) put King Jehoahaz II of Judah in chains, and Nebuchadnezzar killed the sons of King Zedekiah of Judah (587 B. C.) and put out his eyes, and then carried him off in chains to Babylon (2Ki 25:6f; Jer 39:5-7). It is possible that the two Riblahs may be the same.

RICH, THE. Admonitions to (Jer 9:23; 1Ti 6:17-19; Jas 1:9-11). Have many friends (Pr 14:20; 19:9). Made so by God (Ec 5:19, 20). Not to trust riches for divine favor (Ps 49:16-18; Ec 7:19; Zep 1:18). Difficult to enter the kingdom (M't 19:24; M'k 10:17-27; Lu 18:24, 25).

Wicked (Job 21:7-15; Ps 73:3-9; Pr 28:8, 20, 22; Jer 5:27, 28; Lu 12:15-21; 16:19-31; Jas 2:6, 7). Licentious (Jer 5:7, 8). Deluded (Pr 11:28; 13:7; 18:11). Conceited (Pr 28:11). Proud (Ps 73:3, 6, 8, 9; Eze 28:5). Arrogant (Ps 73:8). Oppressive (Ne 5:1-13; Mic 6:10-13; Jas 2:6). Cruel to the poor (Pr 18:23). Envied (Ps 73:3-22). Hated (Job 27:19, 23). Denounced (Isa 5:8; Jer 17:11; 22:13-15; Am 6:1-6; Lu 6:24, 25; Jas 5:1-4). Unscrupulous methods of (Jer 5:26-28). Discrimination in favor of, in the church, forbidden (Jas 2:1-9).

Divine judgments against (Job 27:13-23; Ps 52:1-7; 73:18-20).

Instances of Righteous: Abraham (Ge 13:2; 24:35). Isaac (Ge 26:12-14). Solomon (1Ki 10:23; 2Ch 9:22). Jehoshaphat (2Ch 18:1). Hezekiah (2Ki 20:12, 13). Job (Job 1:3; 31:24, 25, 28). Joseph of Arimathea (M't 27:57). Zacchaeus (Lu 19:2).

See Riches.

RICHES (1Sa 2:7; Ps 37:16; 52:7; Pr 11:4; 14:24; 15:6, 16, 17; 16:8; 19:4; Ec 4:8; 5:11-14; 6:1, 2; 7:11, 12; 10:19; Isa 5:8; Jer 48:36). Delusive (Pr 11:28; Lu 12:16-21). Unstable (Pr 23:5; 27:24).

Unsatisfying to the covetous (Ec 5:10-12). A snare (De 6:10-12; 8:7-17; 31:20; 32:15; Pr 30:8, 9; Jer 5:7, 8; Ho 12:8; M't 13:22; 19:16-24; M'k 4:19; 10:17-25; Lu 16:19-26; 18:18-25; 1Ti 6:9-11, 17).

Impotent in day of calamity (Eze 7:17, 19; Zep 1:18). Fraudulently gotten, unprofitable (Pr 10:2; 21:6; 28:8; Jer 17:11).

Admonitions against the desire for (Pr 23:4; 28:20, 22; 1Ti 6:9-11, 17). The heart not to be set upon (Ps 62:10; M't 6:19-21).

Liberality with (Pr 13:7, 8). Benevolent use of, required (1Jo 3:17).

Figurative: Re 3:17, 18.

See Covetousness; Rich.

RIDDLE (hidden saying, proverb), any "dark saying" of which the meaning is not immediately clear and must be found by shrewd thought (Nu 12:8; Pr 1:6). It may be a parable (Ps 49:4); or something for men to guess (J'g 14:12-19); or just a hard question (1Ki 10:1; 2Ch 9:1).

RIGHTEOUS. Compared with: The sun (J'g 5:31; M't 13:43); stars (Da 12:3); lights (M't 5:14; Ph'p 2:15); Mount Zion (Ps 125:1, 2); Lebanon (Ho 14:5-7); treasure (Ex 19:5; Ps 135:4); jewels [*R. V.*, peculiar treasure] (Mal 3:17); gold (Job 23:10; La 4:2); vessels of gold and silver (2Ti 2:20); stones of a crown (Zec 9:16); lively stones (1Pe 2:5); babes (M't 11:25; 1Pe 2:2); little children (M't 18:3; 1Co 14:20); obedient children (1Pe 1:14); members of the body (1Co 12:20, 27); soldiers (2Ti 2:3, 4); runners in a race (1Co 9:24; Heb 12:1); wrestlers (2Ti 2:5); good servants (M't 25:21); strangers and pilgrims (1Pe 2:11); sheep (Ps 78:52; M't 25:33; Joh 10); lambs (Isa 40:11; Joh 21:15); calves of the stall (Mal 4:2); lions (Pr 28:1; Mic 5:8); eagles (Ps 103:5; Isa 40:31); doves (Ps 68:13; Isa 60:8); thirsting deer (Ps 42:1); good fishes M't 13:48); dew and showers (Mic 5: 7); watered gardens (Isa 58:11); unfailing springs (Isa 58:11); vines (Song 6: 11; Ho 14:7); branches of a vine (Joh 15:2, 4, 5); pomegranates (Song 4:13); good figs (Jer 24:2-7); lilies (Song 2:2; Ho 14:5); willows by the water courses (Isa 44:4); trees planted by rivers (Ps 1:3); cedars in Lebanon (Ps 92:12); palm trees (Ps 92:12); green olive trees (Ps 52:8; Ho 14:6); fruitful trees (Ps 1:3; Jer 17:8); corn (Ho 14:7); wheat (M't 3:12; 13:29, 30); salt (M't 5:13).

Access of, to God (Ps 31:19, 20; Isa 12:6). Few (M't 7:14; 22:14). Relation of, to God (Le 20:24-26). Righteous and wicked, circumstances of, contrasted (Job 8; Ps 17:14, 15). See below.

At the judgment (see Judgment, The). Fellowship of (see Fellowship). Hatred toward (see Persecutions). Joy of (see Joy). Perseverance of (see Perseverance).

Contrasted with the wicked (Ps 1:1-6; 11:5; 17:14, 15; 32:10; 37:17-22, 37, 38; 73:1-28; 75:10; 91:7, 8; Pr 2:21, 22; 3:32, 33; 4:16-19; 10:3, 6, 9, 11, 16, 20, 21, 23-25, 28-32; 11:3, 5, 6, 8-11, 18-21, 23, 31; 12:3, 5-7, 10, 12, 13, 21, 26; 13:5, 6, 9, 17, 21, 22, 25; 14:2, 11, 19, 22, 32; 15:6, 8, 9, 28, 29; 21:15, 18, 26, 29; 22:5, 8, 9; 24:16; 28:1, 4, 5, 13, 14, 18; 29:2, 6, 7, 27; Isa 32:1-8; 65:13, 14; Ro 2:7-10; Eph 2:12-14; Ph'p 2:15; 1Th 5:5-8; Tit 1:15; 1Pe 4:17, 18; 1Jo 3:3-17).

See Wicked, Described; Wicked, Contrasted with the Righteous.

Described (Ps 1:1-3; 15:1-5; 24:3-5; 24:3-5; 37:26, 30, 31; 84:7; 112:1-9; 119:1-3; Isa 33:15, 16; 51:1; 62:12; 63:8; Jer 17:7, 8; 31:12-14, 33, 34; Eze 18:5-9; Zec 3:2, 7, 8).

As, dead to sin (Ro 6:2, 11; Col 3:3); freed from sin (Ro 6:7, 18, 22; 1Jo 3:6, 9); good (Lu 6:45); pure (M't 5:8; 1Jo 3:3; 2Ti 2:21, 22); holy (De 7:6; Eph 1:4; 4:24; Col 1:22; 3:12; 1Pe 1:15; 2Ti 2:19; Heb 3:1); sanctified (1Co 1:2; 6:11); godly (Ps 4:3; 2Pe 2:9); wise (Ps 37:30; Pr 2:9-12); faithful (M't 24:45; 25:21, 23; Lu 19:17; Eph 1:1; Col 1:2; Re 17:14); merciful (M't 5:7); meek (M't 5:5; 2Ti 2:25); industrious (Eph 4:28; 2Jo 9); stable (M't 7:24-27; Eph 4:14); saved (Ac 2:47); saints (Ro 1:7; 1Co 1:2; Eph 1:1); chosen (1Pe 2:9; Re 17:14); spotless (Jas 1:27); separate (Ex 33:16); obedient (M't 12:50; Joh 15:14; 1Jo 2:3, 5); new creature (2Co 5:17; Eph 2:10; 4:23, 24; Col 3:9, 10); spiritually minded (Ro 8:4, 6); servants of Christ (Eph 6:6); servants of righteousness (Ro 6:19); children of light (1Th 5:5); sons of God (Ro 8:14, 16; Joh 3:2); a temple of God (2Co 6:16); beloved of God (Ro 1:7); poor in spirit (M't 5:3); hungering and thirsting after righteousness (M't 5:6); growing in grace (Ps 84:7; Eph 4:13); imitators of Christ (1Pe 4:1, 2; 1Jo 2:6); salt of the earth (M't 5:13); city set on a hill (M't 5:14); led by the spirit (Ro 8:14; Ga 5:18); filled with goodness and knowledge (Ro 15:14; Col 1:9-13); grounded in love (Eph 3:17); following Christ (M't 10:38; 16:24; M'k 8:34; Lu 9:23); rooted in Christ (Col 2:7); patient, long-suffering, joyful (Col 1:11; 1Th 1:3); peaceful, meek, gentle, patient (2Ti 2:21-25); blameless, harmless and without blemish (Eph 1:4; Ph'p 2:15); kind, tenderhearted, forgiving (Eph 4:32); hating falsehood (Pr 13:5); abhorring wickedness (Ps 101:3, 4); having renounced dishonesty (2Co 4:2); without bitterness, wrath, anger, clamor, evil speaking, malice (Eph 4:31); grieved by the wickedness of the wicked (Ps 119:158; Ac 17:16; 2Pe 2:7, 8).

Happiness of (Job 5:17-27; Pr 3:13-18; 16:20; M't 4:3-12). Satisfying (Ps 36:8; 63:5).

Under fiery trials (1Pe 4:12, 13). Under persecution (M't 5:10-12).

Promises to, and Grounds of Assurance and Comfort of: Deliverance, from temptation (1Co 10:13; 2Pe 2:9); from trouble (Job 5:19-24; 34:15, 17; 50:15; 91:15; 97:10, 11; Pr 3:25, 26; Isa 41:10-13; 43:2). Refuge in adversity (Ps 33:18, 19; 62:8; 91:1-15; Pr 14:26; Na 1:7). Strength in adversity (Ps 29:11). Security (Ps 32:6, 7; 84:11; 121:3-8; Isa 33:16). Providential care (Ge 15:1; Ex 23:22; Le 26:5, 6, 10; De 33:27; 1Sa 2:9; 2Ch 16:9; Ezr 8:22; Job 5:15; Ps 34:9, 10; 125:1-3; 145:19, 20; Pr 1:33; 2:7; 3:6; 10:3; 16:7; Isa 49:9-11; 65:13, 14; Eze

34:11-17, 22-31; Lu 12:7, 32; 21:18; 1Pe 5:7). Overruling providence (Ro 8:28; 2Co 4:17). Answer to prayer (Pr 15:29; M'k 11:23, 24; Joh 14:13, 14; Ac 10:4; 1Pe 3:12; 1Jo 3:22). Temporal blessings (Le 25:18, 19; 26:5; De 28:1-13; Ps 37:9; 128:1-6; Pr 2:21; 3:1-4, 7-10; M't 6:26-33; M'k 10:30; Lu 18:29, 30). Blessings upon their children (Ps 103:17; 112:2, 3).

Of: comfort in tribulation (Isa 25:8; 66:13, 14; M't 5:4; Joh 14:16-18; Re 21:4). Joy (Isa 35:10; 51:11). Spiritual enlightenment (Isa 2:3; Joh 8:12). Peace (Isa 26:3; Ro 2:10). Seeing God (M't 5:8). Inconceivable spiritual blessings (Isa 64:4; 1Co 2:9). The rest of faith (Heb 4:9). Wisdom (Jas 1:5). Divine help (Ps 55:22; Isa 41:10-13; Heb 13:5, 6). Divine guidance (Ps 25:12; 32:8; 37:23, 24; 48:14; 73:24; Pr 3:5, 6). Divine mercy (Ps 32:10; 103:17, 18; Mal 3:17). The divine presence (Ge 26:3, 24; 28:15; 31:3; Ex 33:14; De 31:6, 8; Jos 1:5; 1Ki 6:13; Hag 1:13; 2:4, 5; M't 28:20; Joh 14:17, 23; 2Co 6:16; 13:11; Ph'p 4:9; Heb 13:5; Jas 4:8; Re 21:3). The divine likeness (1Jo 3:2). The ministry of angels (Heb 1:14). Dwelling with Christ (Joh 14:2, 3; Col 3:4; 1Th 4:17; 5:10). Everlasting remembrance (Ps 112:6). Having names written in heaven (Lu 10:20). Resurrection (Joh 5:29; 1Co 15:48-57; 2Co 4:14; 1Th 4:16). Future glory (Ro 8:18; Col 3:4; 2Ti 2:10; 1Pe 5:4). Inheritance (M't 25:34; Ac 20:32; 26:18; Col 1:12; 3:24; Tit 3:7; Heb 9:15; Jas 2:5; 1Pe 1:4). Heavenly reward (M't 5:12; 13:43; 2Ti 4:8; Heb 11:16; Jas 1:12; 2Pe 1:11; Re 2:7, 10; 22:5, 12, 14). Of eternal life (Da 12:2, 3; M't 19:29; 25:46; M'k 10:29, 30; Lu 18:29, 30; Joh 3:15, 16, 36; 4:14; 5:24, 29; 6:39, 40; 10:28; 12:25; Ro 2:7; 6:22, 23; Ga 6:8; 1Th 4:15-17; 1Ti 1:16; 4:8; Tit 1:2; 1Jo 2:25; 5:13; Re 7:14-17).

Contingent upon Perseverance (Heb 10:36; Re 2:7, 10, 11, 17, 26-28; 3:4, 5, 10, 12, 21; 21:7).

See Adoption; Affliction, Comfort in; God, Preserver, Providence of.

For promises in particular, see specific topics.

Union of, with God (1Jo 3:24; 4:13, 15, 16; 2Jo 9).

Union of, with Christ (Joh 6:51-58; 14:20; 15:1-11; 17:21-23, 26; Ro 8:1; 12:5; 1Co 6:13-20; 10:16; 2Co 13:5; Ga 2:20; Col 1:27; 2:6, 7; 1Jo 2:6, 24, 28; 3:6, 24; 5:12, 20; 2Jo 9).

See Adoption; Communion; Fellowship, with Christ.

RIGHTEOUSNESS (Ps 15:1-5; 24:3-5; 106:3; Pr 11:5, 6, 18, 30; Ho 10:12; M't 5:20; Lu 1:75; Joh 16:8, 10; Ro 6:19-22; 8:4; Eph 4:24; Jas 1:27). Figuratively described as a garment (Job 29:14; Isa 61:10; Zec 3:4; M't 22:11-14; Re 6:11; 7:9; 19:8). Required (Isa 28:17; Ho 10:12; Mic 6:8; Zec 7:9, 10; 8:16, 17; Mal 3:3; M't 5:20; 23:23; Lu 3:10-14; 13:6-9; Ro 6:19-22; 7:4-6; 8:4; 14:17-19; 2Ti 2:22; 1Jo 3:10). Enjoined in official administration (Jer 22:3, 6).

Imputed, on account of obedience (Re 6:25; Ps 106:31; Eze 18:9); on account of faith (Ge 15:6; Ro 4:3, 5, 9, 11, 13, 20, 22, 24; Ga 3:6; Jas 2:23). Proof of regeneration (1Jo 2:29). Exalts a nation (Pr 14:34). Safeguards life (Pr 10:2, 16; 11:19; 12:28; 13:6). Winning others to, rewarded (Da 12:3).

Fruits of (Ps 1:3; M't 7:16-18; 12:35; Lu 6:43; Joh 15:4-8; 2Co 9:10; Ga 5:22, 23; Ph'p 1:11; Col 3:12-15; 1Th 1:3; Tit 2:2-6, 11, 12; 1Pe 3:8-14; 2Pe 1:5-8; 1Jo 3:7). Liberality (Ac 11:29). Peace (Isa 32:17; Jas 3:8).

Symbolized: Eze 47:12; Re 22:2.

Of God, see God, Righteousness of.

Of Jesus, see Jesus, Holiness of.

See also Sin, Fruits of; Works, Good.

RIMMON (pomegranate). 1. Father of the murderers of Ish-bosheth (2Sa 4:2, 5, 9).

2. A city S of Jerusalem (Zec 14:10). Allotted to Judah (Jos 15:32; Ne 11:29); afterward to Simeon (Jos 19:7; 1Ch 4:32). Called Remmon (Jos 19:7); and En-rimmon (Ne 11:29).

3. A city of Zebulun (1Ch 6:77). Called Remmon-methoar (Jos 19:13).

4. A rock in Benjamin (J'g 20:45, 47; 21:13).

5. A Syrian idol (2Ki 5:18).

RIMMON-METHOAR, Levitical city in Zebulun (Jos 19:13).

RIMMON-PAREZ, a camping place of the Israelites (Nu 33:19, 20).

RIMMON, ROCK OF, fortress to which 600 Benjamites fled after escaping slaughter (J'g 20:45, 47; 21:13), ne Jeba or Gibeah.

RING. Of gold (Nu 31:50). Worn as a badge of office (Ge 40:42). Given as a token (Es 3:10, 12; 8:2-10). Worn in the nose (Pr 11:22; Isa 3:21). Offerings of, to the tabernacle (Ex 35:22; Nu 31:50).

RING-STREAKED, mottled of color, characterizing Laban's sheep (Ge 30:35; 31:8, 12).

RINNAH, a son of Shimon (1Ch 4:20).

RIOT, squander in evil ways (Pr 23:20; 28:7); waste (Tit 1:6; 1Pe 4:4); revelry (Ro 13:13); luxury (2Pe 2:13).

RIPHATH, a son of Gomer (Ge 10:3; 1Ch 1:6).

RISING. *Early* (Pr 31:15). For devotions (Ps 5:3; 59:16; 63:1; 88:13; Song 7:12; Isa 26:9). Practiced by the wicked (Pr 27:14; Mic 2:1; Zep 3:7); by drunkards (Isa 5:11). Illustrates spiritual diligence (Ro 13:11, 12).

Instances of: Lot (Ge 19:23). Abraham (Ge 19:27; 21:14; 22:3). Isaac (Ge 26:31). Abimelech (Ge 20:8). Jacob (Ge 28:18; 32:31). Laban (Ge 31:55). Moses (Ex 8:20; 9:13). Joshua (Jos 3:1; 6:12, 15; 7:16). Gideon (J'g 6:38). Elkanah (1Sa 1:19). Samuel (1Sa 15:12). David (1Sa 17:20). Mary (M'k 16:2; Lu 24:1). Apostles (Ac 5:21).

See Industry.

Late: Consequences of (Pr 6:9-11; 24:33, 34).

See Idleness; Slothfulness.

RISSAH (ruins), encampment of Israelites in wilderness (Nu 33:21); site unknown.

RITHMAH (juniper), a camping place of the Israelites (Nu 33:18, 19).

RIVER, may refer to large streams (Ge 2:10-14), the Nile (Ge 41:1; 2Ki 19:24), winter torrent the bed of which is dry in summer (Am 6:14), fountain stream (Ps 119:136).

Figurative: Of salvation (Ps 36:8; 46:4; Isa 32:2; Eze 47:1-12; Re 22:1, 2). Of grief (Ps 119:136; La 3:48).

RIVER OF EGYPT, brook on SW border of Palestine flowing into Mediterranean Sea (Ge 15:18; Nu 34:5); now Wadi el Arish.

RIVERS. Names of: Abana (2Ki 5:12). Arnon (De 2:36). Chebar (Eze 1:1). Euphrates (Ge 2:14). Gozan (2Ki 17:6; 1Ch 5:26). Jordan (See Jordan). Kanah (Jos 16:8). Kishon (J'g 5:21). Of Egypt (Nile, Ex 1:22). Pharpar (2Ki 5:12). Pison (Ge 2:11). Hiddekel (Ge 2:14). Ulai (Da 8:16).

RIZPAH (hot stone). Concubine of Saul (2Sa 3:7). Guards the bodies of her sons hanged by command of David (2Sa 21:8-11).

ROADS, may refer to paths or highways; hundreds of allusions to roads in Bible; road robbers quite common (M't 11:10; Lu 10:30); Romans built highways throughout empire, some of which are still in use; used by traders, travelers, and armies; Paul used Roman roads on his missionary journeys; the statement, "All roads lead to Rome," shows how well provided the Roman empire was with roads.

ROBBERS (Pr 1:11-16). Dens of (Jer 7:11). Bands of (Ho 6:9; 7:1).

See Robbery; Theft.

ROBBERY, illegal seizure of another's property; forbidden by law (Le 19:13); highways unsafe (J'g 5:6; Lu 10:30; 2Co 11:26); houses built to resist robbers; even priests sometimes turned to pillage (Ho 6:9); denounced by prophets (Isa 61:8; Eze 22:29); withholding tithes and offerings from God's storehouse regarded as robbery (Mal 3:8).

ROBE. Of righteousness (2Ch 6:41; Isa 61:10; Re 6:11; 7:9, 13). Parable of the man who was not dressed in a wedding garment (M't 22:11). See Dress.

ROBINSON'S ARCH, remains of ancient Jerusalem masonry, named for American archaeologist Edward Robinson, who discovered it in 1838. Giant stones, projecting from SW wall of Temple enclosure, are evidently part of an arch of a bridge or viaduct that in Herod's time connected Jerusalem's western hill with the eastern hill.

ROBOAM (See Rehoboam.)

ROCK. Smitten by Moses for water (De 8:15; Ps 78:15, 16, 20). Houses in (Jer 49:16; Ob 3; M't 7:24, 25). Oil from (Job 29:6; De 32:13). Name of deity (De 32:4).

Figurative: 2Sa 22:32, 47; 23:3; Ps 18:2; 31:2; 40:2; Isa 17:10; 32:2; M't 16:18; 1Co 10:4.

ROD, branch, stick, staff; symbol of authority (Ex 4:2, 17, 20; 9:23; 14:16); chastisement symbolized by rod (Mic

5:1); Messianic ruler (Isa 11:1); affliction (Job 9:34).

ROD OF AARON (Ex 7:9, 10, 12, 15, 19, 20; 8:5, 16, 17; Nu 17:6, 8, 10; Heb 9:4).

ROD OF CORRECTION (Ps 89:32; Pr 10:13; 13:24; 22:15; 23:14; 26:3; 29:15; La 3:1).

ROD OF MOSES (Ex 4:2, 17, 20; 7:19; 8:16; 9:23; 10:13; 14:16; 17:5, 9).

RODANIM, tribe descended from Javan, son of Japheth (1Ch 1:7).

ROE (See Deer.)

ROGELIM, town near Mahanaim whose citizens assisted David (2Sa 17:27, 29; 19:31).

ROHGAH, son of Shamer (1Ch 7:34).

ROLL, sheets of papyrus or parchment (made of skin) sewn together to make long sheet of writing material which was wound around a stick to make a scroll (Isa 34:4; Jer 36; Eze 3:1-3; Re 5; 10:1-10).

ROLLER, anything that turns or revolves (Isa 17:13).

ROMAMTI-EZER (highest help), son of Heman (1Ch 25:4, 31).

ROMAN EMPIRE. City of Rome founded 753 B. C.; a monarchy until 509 B. C.; a republic from 509 to 31 B. C.; empire began in 31 B. C., fell in 5th cent. Rome extended hold over all Italy and eventually over whole Mediterranean world, Gaul, half of Britain, the Rhine-Danube rivers, and as far as Parthia. Augustus, the first Roman emperor, divided Roman provinces into senatorial, which were ruled by proconsuls (Ac 13:7; 18:12; 19:38) and imperial, ruled by governors (M't 27:2; Lu 2:2; Ac 23:24). Moral corruption was responsible for the decline and fall of the Roman Empire. Roman reservoirs, aqueducts, roads, public buildings, statues survive. Many Roman officials are referred to in the NT, including the emperors Augustus (Lu 2:1), Tiberius (Lu 3:1), Claudius (Ac 11:28), Nero (Ac 25:11, 12).

ROMANS, EPISTLE TO THE, written by Paul during his three months' stay in Corinth on his 3rd missionary journey (Ac 20:2, 3; Ro 1:1; 15:25-27). He planned to visit Spain after a brief stay in Jerusalem, and he hoped to stop off in Rome on his way to Spain (Ro 1:10, 11; 15:14-33). He had never been in Rome before, and in this epistle he clearly set forth the message of the gospel which he preached. Outline: 1. Introduction (1:1-15).

2. Sinfulness of man, including both Gentiles and Jews (1:16-3:20).

3. Justification by faith (3:21-5:21).

4. Sanctification (6-8).

5. Israel and world salvation (9-11).

6. Details of Christian conduct (12-15:13).

7. Concluding remarks, Greetings (15:14-16:27).

ROME, the capital of the Roman empire. Jews excluded from, by Claudius (Ac 18:2). Paul's visit to (see Paul). Visited by Onesiphorus (2Ti 1:16, 17). Paul desires to preach in (Ro 1:15). Abominations in (Ro 1:18-32). Christians in (Ro 16:5-17; Ph'p 1:12-18; 4:22; 2Ti 4:21).

ROOF (See House, Roof of.)

ROOM. 1. Chamber in a house (Ac 1:13).

2. Place or position in society (M't 23:6; Lu 14:7, 8; 20:46).

ROOT. Usually used in figurative sense. 1. Essential cause of something (1Ti 6:10).

2. Source or progenitor (Isa 11:10; Ro 15:12).

3. Foundation or support of something (2Ki 19:30; Job 5:3).

4. Injured roots means loss of life or vitality (Job 31:12; Isa 5:24).

ROPE. Threefold (Ec 4:12). Worn on the head as an emblem of servitude (1Ki 20:31, 32). Used in casting lots (Mic 2:5).

Figurative: Of love (Ho 11:4). Of affliction (Job 36:8). Of temptations (Ps 140:5; Pr 5:22).

ROSE (Song 2:1; Isa 35:1.)

ROSETTA STONE, inscribed basalt slab, found on Rosetta branch of the Nile, in 1799, with text in hieroglyphic, demotic, and Greek. It furnished the key for the decipherment of Egyptian hieroglyphics.

ROSH (head). 1. Son of Benjamin (Ge 46:21).

2. Chief of three nations that are to invade Israel during the latter days (Eze 38:2; 39:1 ASV).

ROW, ROWERS (See Ship.)

RUBY (Job 28:18; Pr 20:15; 31:10; La 4:7).

RUDDY, red or fair complexion (1Sa 16:12).

RUDE (untrained, ignorant of rules), technically not trained (2Co 11:6).

RUDIMENTS (first principles or elements of anything), elements (Ga 4:3, 9; 2Pe 3:10, 12), first principles (Heb 5:12), physical elements of the world (2Pe 3:10, 12).

RUE (Lu 11:42).

RUFUS. 1. Brother of Alexander and son of Simon of Cyrene who bore the cross (M'k 15:21).

2. Friend of Paul (Ro 16:13).

RUHAMAH (to be pitied), Hosea's daughter by Gomer (Ho 2:1).

RULERS. Appointed and removed by God. See Government, God in. Chastised (Da 4). See Nation.

Monarchical (see Kings.)

Patriarchal (Ge 27:29, 37). Instances of: Nimrod (Ge 10:8-10). Abraham (Ge 14:13-24; 17:6; 21:21-32). Melchizedek (Ge 14:18). Isaac (Ge 26:26-31). Judah (Ge 38:24). Heads of families (Ex 6:14). Ishmael (Ge 17:20). Esau, and the dukes of Edom (Ge 36).

Theocratic. See Government.

Ordained of God (2Ch 9:8; Ro 13:1, 2, 4; 1Pe 2:14). Appointed by God (1Sa 9:15-17; 10:1; 15:17; 16:1, 7, 13; 2Sa 7:13-16; 1Ki 14:14; 16:1-4; 1Ch 28:4, 5; 29:25; Ps 89:19-37; Da 2:21, 37; 5:21; Ac 13:22). Accountable to God (2Ch 19:6, 7).

Servants of the people (1Ki 12:7; 2Ch 10:7; Eze 34:2-4). Loyalty to, enjoined (Eze 7:26). Must not be reviled (Ex 22:28; 2Sa 16:9; 19:21; Ec 10:20: Ac 23:5; 2Pe 2:10, 11; Jude 8).

Righteous, beloved (Pr 29:2, 14). Incompetent, oppress (Pr 28:16). Corrupted, by evil counsellors (Pr 25:5); by gifts (Pr 29:4; Isa 1:23; Am 5:11, 12; Mic 7:3).

Should not drink wine (Pr 31:4, 5). Forbidden, to take bribes (Ex 23:8; Da 16:19); to respect persons (Le 19:15; De 1:17; 16:19; Pr 24:23).

Required to judge justly (Ex 18:16, 20, 21; 23:3, 6, 7, 9; Le 19:15; 24:22; De 1:16, 17; 25:1; 2Ch 9:8; Ps 82:2-4; Pr 31:9; Isa 16:5; 58:6; Jer 22:2, 3; Zec 7:9, 10; 8:16). A terror to evildoers (Pr 14:35; Ro 13:3).

Mosaic law concerning atonement for sins of (Le 4:22-26).

Character and Qualifications of (Nu 27:16, 17; 2Sa 23:4; Pr 20:8, 26, 28). Diligent (Ro 12:8). Wise (Ge 41:33; De 1:13; Ps 2:10; Pr 20:26; 28:2). Merciful (Isa 16:5; Zec 7:9).

Required, to know the law (Jos 1:8; Ezr 7:25); to fear the Lord (Ps 2:11); to be truthful (Pr 17:7); to be righteous (Ex 18:21; De 16:19; 27:19; 2Sa 23:3, 4; Pr 16:10, 12).

Duties of: To rule in righteousness (Isa 58:6; Jer 22:2, 3). To be judges (2Ch 9:8). To judge according to law (De 17:18, 19; Jos 1:7, 8). In judicial functions to make thorough investigations (De 19:18, 19).

Righteous. Instances of: Pharaoh, in his treatment of Abraham (Ge 12:15-20). Abimelech, in his treatment of Abraham (Ge 20); of Isaac (Ge 26:6-11). Joseph, in his conduct of the affairs of Egypt (Ge 41:37-57). Pharaoh, in his treatment of Jacob and his family (Ge 47:5-10; 50:1-6). Moses, in his administration of the affairs of the children of Israel (Nu 16:15). See Government, Mosaic. Samuel, in not taking reward for judgment (1Sa 12:3, 4). Saul, after the defeat of the Ammonites (1Sa 11:12, 13). Solomon, in his judgment between the two women who claimed the same child (1Ki 3:16-28); according to the testimony of the queen of Sheba (1Ki 10:6-9). Asa, in abolishing sodomy and other abominations of idolatry (1Ki 15:11-15; 2Ch 14:2-5). Jehoshaphat, in walking in the ways of the Lord (1Ki 22:41-46; 2Ch 17:3-10; 19; 20:3-30). Hezekiah, in his fear of the Lord (2Ki 18:3; 20:1-11; 2Ch 30; 31). Josiah, in repairing the temple and in other good works (2Ki 22; 23; 2Ch 34; 35). Cyrus, in emancipating the Jews (Ezr 1). Darius, in advancing the rebuilding of the temple (Ezr 6:1-12). Artaxerxes, in commissioning Ezra to restore the forms of worship at Jerusalem (Ezr 7; Ne 2; 5:14). Nehemiah (Ne 4; 5). Daniel (see Daniel). King of Nineveh, in repenting, and proclaiming a fast (Jon 3:6-9).

Wicked (Ne 9:34-37; Ps 58:2; 82:2; 94:20, 21; Ec 3:16, 17; 5:8; Isa 5:7; 28:14, 15; Ho 7:3). Oppressive (Ex 3:9; 1Sa 8:10-18; Job 35:9; Pr 28:15, 16; Am

4:1; 5:11, 12). Pervert justice (De 27:19). Cause people to mourn (Pr 29:2; Ec 4:1). A public calamity (Ec 10:16; Isa 5:22, 23). An abomination to God (Pr 17:15). Abhorred by men (Pr 21:24; 29:2). Admonitions to (Eze 34:2-4, 7-10; 45:9). Denounced (Eze 34:2-4, 7-10; Am 4:1, 2; Mic 3:1-3, 9-11; Zep 3:3). Divine judgment upon (Isa 3:14, 15; 10:1-3; 30:33; 40:23; Jer 5:28, 29; Eze 21:25, 26; Ho 5:10; Am 5:11, 12; Zep 1:8).

Instances of: Potiphar, putting Joseph into prison (Ge 39:20, w 40:15). Pharaoh, oppressing the Israelites (Ex 1-11). Adoni-bezek, torturing seventy kings (J'g 1:7). Abimelech, slaying his seventy brothers (J'g 9:1-5). Eli's sons, desecrating the sacrifices (1Sa 2:12-17); debauching themselves and the worshipers (1Sa 2:22). Samuel's sons, taking bribes (1Sa 8:1-5). Saul, sparing Agag and the best of the booty (1Sa 15:8-35); in jealousy plotting against David (1Sa 18:8-29); seeking to slay David (1Sa 19); slaying Ahimelech and the priests (1Sa 22:7-19). Hanun, maltreating David's servants (2Sa 10:4; 1Ch 19:2-5). David, numbering Israel and Judah (2Sa 24:1-9; 1Ch 21:1-7; 27:23, 24). Solomon, luxurious, and idolatrous (1Ki 11:1-13); oppressing the people (1Ki 12:4; 4:7-23). Rehoboam, making the yoke heavy (1Ki 12:8-11; 2Ch 10:1-15). Jeroboam, perverting the true worship (1Ki 12:26-33; 13:1-5; 14:16); exalting debased persons to the priesthood (1Ki 12:31; 13:33; 2Ki 17:32; 2Ch 11:14, 15; Eze 44:7, w Nu 3:10). Abijam, walking in the sins of Rehoboam (1Ki 15:3). Nadab, walking in the ways of Jeroboam (1Ki 15:26). Baasha, walking in the ways of Jeroboam (1Ki 15:33, 34). Asa, imprisoning the seer, and oppressing the people (2Ch 16:10). Zimri, walking in the ways of Jeroboam (1Ki 16:19). Omir, walking in the ways of Jeroboam (1Ki 16:25-29). Ahab, serving Baal (1Ki 16:30-33; 21:21-26); confiscating Naboth's vineyard (1Ki 21, w 1Sa 8:14; 1Ki 22:38; 2Ki 9:26). Jehoram, cleaving to the sins of Jeroboam (2Ki 3:2, 3). Hazael, committing rapine (2Ki 8:12; 10:32; 12:17; 13:3-7). Jehoram, walking in the ways of the kings of Israel (2Ki 8:18; 2Ch 21:13). Jehu, departing not from the sins of Jeroboam (2Ki 10:29). Jehoahaz, in following the sins of Jeroboam (2Ki 13:1, 2). Jehoash, in following the wicked example of Jeroboam (2Ki 13:10, 11). Jeroboam II, not departing from the sins of Jeroboam (2Ki 14:23, 24). Zachariah, Menahem, Pekahiah, and Pekah, following the sins of Jeroboam (2Ki 15:9, 18, 24, 28); conspiring against and slaying Pekahiah (2Ki 15:25). Hoshea, who conspired against Pekah (2Ki 15:30), in permitting Baal-worship (2Ki 17:1, 2, 7-18). Ahaz, burning his children in idolatrous sacrifice (2Ki 16:3; 2Ch 28:2-4). Manasseh, who committed the abominations of the heathen (2Ki 21:1-17; 2Ch 33:2-7). Amon, who followed the evil example of Manasseh (2Ki 21:19-22). Jehoahaz, who followed in the ways of his fathers (2Ki 23:32). Jehoiakim, in walking in the ways of his fathers (2Ki 23:37); and Jehoiachin (2Ki 24:9). Zedekiah, following the evil example of Jehoiakim (2Ki 24:19; 2Ch 36:12, 13); and persecuting Jeremiah (Jer 38:5, 6). Joash, slaying Zechariah (2Ch 24:2, 17-25). Ahaziah, doing evil after the house of Ahab (2Ch 22:1-9). Amaziah, worshiping the gods of Seir (2Ch 25:14). Uzziah, invading the priest's office (2Ch 26:16). Ahasuerus and Haman, decreeing the death of the Jews (Es 3). Nebuchadnezzar, commanding to destroy the wise men (Da 2:1-13); and committing the three Hebrews to the furnace (Da 3:1-23). Belshazzar, in drunkenness and committing sacrilege (Da 5:22, 23). Darius, in deifying himself (Da 6:7, 9). The princes, conspiring against Daniel (Da 6:1-9). Herod the Great, slaying the children in Bethlehem (M't 2:16-18). Herod Antipas, in beheading John the Baptist (M't 14:1-11); in craftiness and tyranny (Lu 13:31, 32; 23:6-15). Herod Agrippa, persecuting the church (Ac 12:1-19). Pilate, delivering Jesus for crucifixion (M't 27:11-26; M'k 15:15). Chief priests, elders, and all the council, seeking false witness against Jesus (M't 26:59). Ananias, commanding to smite Paul (Ac 23:2).

See Government; Judges; Kings.

RUMAH (tall place), home of Pedaiah, whose daughter Zebudah bore Jehoiakim to Josiah king of Judah (2Ki 23:36), perhaps Arumah near Shechem, or Rumah in Galilee.

RUSH (See Plants.)

RUTH, Moabitess who married a son of Elimelech and Naomi of Bethlehem (Ru 1:1-4); ancestor of Christ (M't 1:5); Book of Ruth is about her.

RUTH, BOOK OF, historical romance narrating story of Ruth, Moabitess, ancestor of David and Christ. She first married a son of Elimelech and Naomi of Bethlehem (Ru 1:1-4). When her husband died, she returned with her mother-in-law to Judah (1:7), where she married Boaz, a kinsman of Naomi (2:20-23), after a nearer kinsman of Naomi had declined to do so (4:6, 13).

RYE [spelt, *R.V.*]. A small grain grown in Egypt (Ex 9:32). Cultivated in Canaan (Isa 28:25). Used in bread (Eze 4:9).

S

SABA, SABAEANS. Saba is mentioned in Ge 10:7 and 1Ch 1:9, as a son of Cush. The Sabaeans were a merchant people who in early times lived in SW Arabia in a region bordering Ophir and Havilah. Romans called it *Arabia Felix.* Sabaean raiders killed Job's flocks and servants (Job 1:15). They were slave traders (Joe 3:8). One of the Sabaean monarchs was the famous Queen of Sheba (1Ki 10:1, 4, 10, 13; 2Ch 9:1, 3, 9, 12).

SABACHTHANI, a word in the utterance of Jesus on the cross, "My God, my God, why hast Thou forsaken me?" (M't 27:46; M'k 15:34).

SABAOTH, THE LORD OF (hosts), the same as "the Lord of hosts" (Ro 9:29; Jas 5:4); probably means that all created agencies and forces are under the command and leadership of Jehovah.

SABBATH. Signifying a rest period (Ge 2:2, 3; Le 23:25; 26:34, 35). Holy (Ex 16:23; 20:8, 11; 31:14; 35:2; De 5:12; Ne 9:14; Isa 58:13, 14; Eze 44:24). A sign (Ex 31:13, 16, 17; Eze 20:12, 13, 16, 20, 21, 24). The Lord is represented as resting on (Ge 2:2, 3; Ex 31:17; Heb 4: 4).

Rest on, enjoined (Ex 16:28-30; 23:12; 31:15; 34:21; 35:2, 3; Le 6:29-31; 19:3, 30; 23:1-3, 27-32; 26:2; De 5:12-15; 2Ch 36:21; Jer 17:21, 22, 24, 25, 27; Lu 23:56). Rest on, of servants and animals, enjoined (Ex 20:10; 23:12; De 5:14). Labor on, suspended (Ex 16:5, 23-30; 20:10; M'k 16:1; Lu 23:56).

Offerings prescribed for (Le 24:8; Nu 28:9, 10; 1Ch 9:32; 23:31; 2Ch 2:4; Eze 46:4, 5). Song for (Ps 92; 118:24).

Preparation for (Ex 16:5, 22; M't 27:62; M'k 15:42; Lu 23:54; Joh 19:31). Religious usages on (Ge 2:3; M'k 6:2; Lu 4:16, 31; 6:6; 13:10; Ac 13:14).

Worship on (Eze 46:1, 3; Ac 15:21; 16:13); enjoined (Eze 46:1, 3). Religious instruction on (M'k 6:2; Lu 4:16, 31; 6:6; 13:10; Ac 13:14, 27, 42, 44; 15:21; 17:2; 18:4). Apostles taught on (Ac 15:14-44; 17:2; 18:4).

Christ's interpretation of (M't 12:1-8, 10-13; Lu 6:1-10 w M'k 2:23-28; 13:10-17; 14:1-5; Joh 7:21-24; 9:14). Christ is Lord of (M't 2:28). Christ performed miracles on (M't 12:10-13; M'k 3:1-5; Lu 6:1-10; 13:10-17; Joh 5:5-14; 7:21-24). Christ taught on (M'k 1:21, 22; 6:2; Lu 4:16, 31; 6:6; 13:10-17).

Irksome observance of (Am 8:5). Hypocritical observance of, provokes divine displeasure (Isa 1:13; La 2:6; Eze 20:12, 13, 16, 21, 24). Enemy mock (La 1:7).

Rewards for observance of (Isa 56:2, 4-7; 58:13, 14; Jer 17:21, 22, 24, 25).

Profanation of (Ex 16:27, 28; Nu 15:32-36; Ne 10:31; 13:15, 21; Jer 17:21-23; Eze 22:8; 23:38).

Christian not to be judged regarding (Col 2:16).

Observance of by: Moses (Nu 15:32-34). Nehemiah (Ne 13:15, 21). The women preparing to embalm the body of Jesus (Lu 23:56). Paul (Ac 13:14). The disciples (Ac 16:13). John (Re 1:10).

Violations of: Punished, by death (Ex 35:2; Nu 15:32-36); by judgments (Jer 17:27).

Instances of: Gathering manna (Ex 16:27). Gathering sticks (Nu 15:32). Men of Tyre (Ne 13:16). Inhabitants of Jerusalem (Jer 17:21-23).

Christian Sabbath, called the Lord's day, the first day of the week (M't 28:1, 5, 6, 7; M'k 16:9; Joh 20:1, 11-16, 19, 26; Ac 20:7; 1Co 16:2; Re 1:10).

SABBATH, COVERT FOR THE, obscure expression found in 2Kings 16: 18; may refer to a colonnade in the temple compound.

SABBATH DAY'S JOURNEY, journey of limited extent (3,000 feet) which the scribes thought a Jew might travel on the sabbath without breaking the Law (Ac 1:12).

SABBATH, MORROW AFTER THE, expression of uncertain meaning found in Le 23:11; may refer to the ordinary weekly sabbath or the first day of the Passover on whatever day of the week it might fall.

SABBATH, SECOND AFTER THE FIRST, expression of uncertain meaning found in Le 6:1. Many explanations have been suggested.

SABBATIC YEAR, a rest recurring every seventh year. Called Year of Release (De 15:9; 31:10). Ordinances concerning (Ex 23:9-11; Le 25). Israelitish bondservants set free in (Ex 21:2; De 15:12; Jer 34:14). Creditors required to release debtors in (De 15:1-6, 12-18; Ne 10:31). Ordinances concerning instruction in the law during (De 31:10-13; Ne 8:18). Punishment to follow violation of the ordinances concerning (Le 26:34, 35, w 32-41; Jer 34:12-22).

See Jubilee.

SABEANS. A people who invaded the land of Uz (Job 1:15; Isa 43:3). Giants among (Isa 45:14). Prophecies concerning (Isa 43:3; Joe 3:8). Proverbial drunkards (Eze 23:42).

See Sheba.

SABBEUS, man who divorced foreign wife (1Esdras 9:32), "Shemaiah" in Ezr 10:31.

SABTA, SABTAH, son of Cush (Ge 10:7; 1Ch 1:9); perhaps also a place in S Arabia.

SABTECHA. Son of Cush (Ge 10:7; 1Ch 1:9).

SACAR (wages). 1. Father of Ahiam (1Ch 11:35); "Sharar" in 2Sa 23:33.

2. Son of Obed-edom (1Ch 26:4).

SACKBUT, a stringed instrument of music (Da 3:5, 7, 10, 15).

See Music, Instruments of.

SACKCLOTH. A symbol of mourning (1Ki 20:31, 32; Job 16:15; Isa 15:3; Jer 4:8; 6:26; 49:3; La 2:10; Eze 7:18; Da 9:3; Joe 1:8). Worn by Jacob when it was reported to him that Joseph had been devoured by wild beasts (Ge 37:34). Animals covered with, at time of national mourning (Jon 3:8).

See Mourning.

SACRAMENT, symbolic rite instituted by Christ setting forth the central truths of the Christian faith: death and resurrection with Christ and participation in the redemptive benefits of Christ's mediatorial death. Roman Catholic Church has seven sacraments; Protestant Church has two, baptism and the Lord's Supper.

SACRED PLACES (De 12:5, 11; 14:23; 15:20; 16:2; 17:8; Jos 9:27; 18:1; 1Ch 22:1; 2Ch 7:15; Ps 78:68).

SACRIFICES. *Figurative:* Isa 34:6; Eze 39:17; Zep 1:7, 8; Ro 12:1; Ph'p 2:17; 4:18). Of self-denial (Ph'p 3:7, 8). Of praise (Ps 116:17; Jer 33:11; Ho 14:2; Heb 13:15). Calves of the lips, signifying praise (Ho 14:2).

See Offerings.

SACRILEGE, profaning holy things. Forbidden (Le 19:8; 1Co 3:17; Tit 1:11; 1Pe 5:2).

Instances of: Esau sells his birthright (Ge 25:33). Nadab and Abihu offer strange fire (Le 10:1-7; Nu 3:4). Of Uzzah (2Sa 6:6, 7). Of Uzziah (2Ch 26:16-21). Of Korah and his company (Nu 16:40). Of the people of Beth-shemesh (1Sa 6:19). Of Ahaz (2Ch 28:24). Of money changers in the temple (M't 21:12, 13; Lu 19:45; Joh 2:14-16). Of those who profaned the holy eucharist (1Co 11:29).

SADDLE (riding seat), getting a beast ready for riding (Ge 22:3; Nu 22:21; J'g 19:10; 2Sa 16:1; 17:23). Asses were not ridden with saddles; when carrying heavy burdens they had a thick cushion on their backs.

SADDUCEES, Jewish religious sect in the time of Christ. Beliefs: acceptance only of the Law and rejection of oral tradition; denial of resurrection, immortality of the soul, spirit world (M'k 12:18; Lu 20:27; Ac 23:8); supported Maccabeans; a relatively small group, but generally held the high priesthood; denounced by John the Baptist (M't 3:7, 8) and Jesus (M't 16:6, 11, 12); opposed Christ (M't 21:12f; M'k 11:15f; Lu 19:47) and the apostolic church (Ac 5:17, 33).

SADOC. 1. Ancestor of Ezra (2Esdras 1:1).

2. Descendant of Zerubbabel and ancestor of Jesus (M't 1:14).

SAFFRON (See Plants.)

SAIL (See Ship.)

SAILOR (See Occupations and Professions.)

SAINT. 1. A member of God's covenant people Israel, whether a pious layman (2Ch 6:41; Ps 16:3) or someone like a priest who is consecrated to God (Ps 106:16; 1Pe 2:5).

2. A NT believer, belonging exclusively to God (Ac 9:13; 1Co 16:1; 2Co 1:1). The saints are the Church (1Co 1:2), people called out of the world to be God's own people. Throughout the Bible the saints are urged to live lives befitting their position (Eph 4:1; Col 1:10).

SALAH (missile, petition), called also

Sala and Shelah. Son of Arphaxad and ancestor of Joseph (Ge 10:24; 11:12-15; 1Ch 1:18, 24; Lu 3:35).

SALAMIS, a city of Cyprus. Paul and Barnabas preach in (Ac 13:4, 5).

SALATHIEL (I have asked God), son of Jeconiah, king of Judah (M't 1:12), or of Neri (Lu 3:27). He may have been the real son of Neri, but only the legal heir of Jeconiah.

SALCAH, city on NE boundary of Bashan (De 3:10; Jos 12:5; 13:11); now known as Salkhad.

SALEM (peace), name of city of which Melchizedek was king (Ge 14:18; Heb 7:1, 2); probably Jerusalem.

SALIM, place near Aenon W of Jordan (Joh 1:28; 3:23, 26; 10:40).

SALLAI. 1. A Benjamite dwelling in Jerusalem (Ne 11:8).

2. A priest who returned to Jerusalem with Zerubbabel (Ne 12:20). Called Sallu (Ne 12:7).

SALLU. 1. A Benjamite dwelling in Jerusalem (1Ch 9:7; Ne 11:7).

2. See Sallai, 2.

SALMA (strength). 1. Son of Caleb (1Ch 2:51, 54).

2. Called also Salmon. Father of Boaz (Ru 4:20, 21; 1Ch 2:11). In the lineage of Joseph (M't 1:4, 5; Lu 3:32).

SALMON (clothing), father of Boaz, the husband of Ruth (Ru 4:20, 21; 1Ch 2:11; M't 1:4, 5; Lu 3:32).

SALMONE, a promontory of Crete (Ac 27:7).

SALOME. 1. Wife of Zebedee and mother of James and John (M't 27:56; M'k 15:40; 16:1); ministered to Jesus (M'k 15:40, 41); present at the crucifixion of Jesus (M't 27:56); came to tomb to anoint body of Jesus (M'k 16:1).

2. Daughter of Herodias; as a reward for her dancing she obtained head of John the Baptist (M't 14:3-11; M'k 6:17-28). Her name is not given in the Gospels.

SALT. Lot's wife turned into a pillar of (Ge 19:26). The city of Salt (Jos 15:62). The valley of salt (2Sa 8:13; 2Ki 14:7). Salt sea (Ge 14:3; Nu 34:12; De 3:17; Jos 3:16; 12:3; 15:2). Salt pits (Zep 2:9). All animal sacrifices were required to be seasoned with (Le 2:13; Ezr 6:9; Eze 43:24; M'k 9:49). Used in ratifying covenants (Nu 18:19; 2Ch 13:5). Elisha casts, into the pool of Jericho, to purify it (2Ki 2:20, 21).

Emblematic: Of fidelity (Nu 18:19; 2Ch 13:5); of barrenness and desolation (De 29:23; J'g 9:45; Jer 17:6; Zep 2:7).

Figurative: Of the saving efficacy of the church (M't 5:13; M'k 9:49, 50; Lu 14:34). Of wise conversation (Col 4:6).

SALT, CITY OF, city in wilderness of Judah, between Nibshan and Engedi (Jos 15:62); site uncertain.

SALT, COVENANT OF, a covenant confirmed with sacrificial meals at which salt was used (Le 2:13; Nu 18:19).

SALT, VALLEY OF, valley between Jerusalem and Edom in which great victories were won over the Edomites (2Sa 8:13; 2Ki 14:7; 2Ch 25:11).

SALUTATIONS. Antiquity of (Ge 18:2; 19:1).

Were Given: By brethren to each other (1Sa 17:22). By inferiors to their superiors (Ge 47:7). By superiors to inferiors (1Sa 30:21). By all passersby (1Sa 10:3, 4; Ps 129:8). On entering a house (J'g 18:15; M't 10:12; Lu 1:40, 41, 44). Often sent through messengers (1Sa 25:5, 14; 2Sa 8:10). Often sent by letter (Ro 16:21-23; 1Co 16:21; Col 4:18; 2Th 3:17). Denied to persons of bad character (2Jo 10). Persons in haste excused from giving or receiving (2Ki 4:29; Lu 10:24).

Expressions Used as: Peace be with thee (J'g 19:20). Peace to thee, and peace to thine house, and peace unto all that thou hast (1Sa 25:6). Peace be to this house (Lu 10:5). The Lord be with you (Ru 2:4). The Lord bless thee (Ru 2:4). The blessing of the Lord be upon you, we bless you in the name of the Lord (Ps 129:8). Blessed be thou of the Lord (1Sa 15:13). God be gracious unto thee (Ge 43:29). Art thou in health? (2Sa 20:9). Hail (M't 26:49; Lu 1:28). All hail (M't 28:9).

Often perfidious (2Sa 20:9; M't 26:49). Given to Christ in derision (M't 27:29, w M'k 15:18).

Often Accompanied by: Falling on the neck and kissing (Ge 33:4; 45:14, 15; Lu 15:20). Laying hold of the beard with the right hand (2Sa 20:9). Bowing frequently to the ground (Ge 33:3). Embracing and kissing the feet (M't 28:9; Lu 7:38, 45). Touching the hem of the garment (M't 14:36). Falling prostrate on the ground (Es 8:3; M't 2:11; Lu 8:41). Kissing the dust (Ps 72:9; Isa 49:23). The Jews condemned for giving only to their own countrymen (M't 5:47). The Pharisees condemned for seeking, in public (M't 23:7; M'k 12:38).

SALU, father of Zimri (Nu 25:14).

SALVATION. Call to (De 30:19, 20; Isa 55:1-3, 6, 7; Lu 3:6; Ac 16:31; Heb 2:3).

Signifying: Gracious providence (De 32:15; Ps 68:19, 20; 91:16; 95:1; 116:13; 149:4; Isa 12:2, 3); personal deliverance from enemies (2Sa 22:36; Ps 3:8; 18:2; 37:39; Isa 1:18; 32:1-4); national deliverance from enemies (Ex 15:2; 1Ch 16:35; Ps 98:2, 3; 106:8; Isa 46:12, 13; Jer 3:23); a divine standard of righteousness (Isa 56:1); the saving power of divine truth (Isa 45:17); the light and glory of Zion (Isa 62:1); the promised Messiah (Joh 4:22); personal righteousness (2Ch 6:41; Ps 132:16); eternal life (1Th 5:8, 9; 1Pe 1:5, 9; 1Jo 5:11); everlasting (Isa 45:17; 52:10); liberty (1Sa 61:1-3; M't 11:28-30).

To be developed (Ph'p 2:12; 1Th 5:8-10; Jude 3).

From God (Ps 3:8; 36:8, 9; 37:39; 68:18-20; 91:16; 98:2, 3; 106:8; 121:1-8; Isa 46:12, 13; 51:4, 5; 63:9; Jer 3:23; 21:8; Eze 18:32; Joe 2:32; 1Pe 1:5; 1Jo 2:25). God, the rock of (De 32:15; Ps 95:1).

Through Christ (Isa 61:10; M't 1:21; Lu 19:10; 24:46, 47; Joh 3:14-17; 11:51, 52; Ac 4:12; 13:26, 38, 39, 47; 16:30, 31; Ro 5:15-21; 7:24, 25; 9:30-33; 1Co 6:11; Ga 1:4; 3:13, 14; Eph 1:9, 10, 13; 2Ti 1:9, 10; 2:10; Tit 3:5-7; Heb 2:3,10; 5:9; 7:25; 1Jo 4:9, 10; 5:11; Jude 3; Re 3:20; 5:9).

By: the atonement (1Co 1:18, 21, 24, 25; Ga 1:4; 3:8, 13, 14, 21, 26-28; Col 1:20-23, 26, 27; 1Ti 2:6; Re 5:9). His resurrection (Ro 5:10). The gospel (Ro 1:16; Jas 1:21). The grace of God (Eph 2:8, 9; Tit 2:11; 2Pe 3:15). The word of God (Jas 1:21). The power of God (1Co 1:18).

Foretold, by the prophets (Isa 29:18, 19, 24; 35:8; Lu 2:31, 32; 1Pe 1:10); by angels (Lu 2:9-14). From the seed of Abraham (Ge 12:13). Proclaimed by Christ (Lu 19:10; Joh 12:32). Preached by the apostles (Ac 11:17, 18; 16:17). Wisdom in, derived from the Scriptures (2Ti 3:15). Praise for ascribed unto God and the Lamb (Re 7:9, 10).

For Israel (Isa 45:7; 46:1, 2; Ac 13:26, 38, 39, 47; Ro 1:16). For the Gentiles (1Ki 8:41-43; Isa 52:10, 15; 56:1, 6-8; M't 21:31; 24:14; Joh 10:16; Ac 11:17, 18; 15:7-9, 11; 28:28; Ro 11:11, 12; 15:9, 16; Ga 3:8, 14; Eph 3:6, 9). For all men (M't 18:14; 22:9, 10, 14; Lu 2:10, 31, 32; Lu 3:6; 13:29, 30; 24:47; Joh 1:7; 11:51, 52; Ac 2:39; Ga 3:28; Eph 2:14, 17; Col 3:11; 1Ti 2:3, 4; 4:10; 2Pe 3:9; Re 5:9; 7:9, 10; 14:6; 22:17).

From sin (M't 1:21; M'k 2:17; Lu 5:31, 32). From spiritual hunger and thirst (Joh 4:14; 6:35; 7:37, 38).

Not by works (Ro 3:28; 4:1-25; 9:30-33; 11:6; Ga 2:16; Eph 2:8, 9; 2Ti 1:9, 10; Tit 3:5-7).

Offered and rejected (De 32:15; M't 22:3-13; 23:37; Lu 14:16-24; Joh 5:40).

See Adoption; Redemption; Regeneration; Sanctification.

Conditions of: Repentance (M't 3:2; M'k 1:4; Lu 3:8; Ac 2:38; 3:19; 2Co 7:10). Faith in Christ (M'k 16:15, 16; 28:11; Joh 3:14-18; 5:24; 6:47; 9:35; 11:25, 26; 12:36; 20:31; Ac 2:21; 16:30, 31; 20:21; Ro 1:16, 17; 3:21-30; 4:1-25; 5:1, 2; 10:4, 8-13; Ga 2:16; 3:8, 26-28; Eph 2:8; Ph'p 3:9; 2Th 2:13; 1Ti 1:15, 16; Heb 4:1, 2; 1Pe 1:9). Supreme love to Christ (Lu 14:25-27). Renunciation of the world (M't 19:16-21; Lu 14:33; 18:18-26). Choice (De 30:19, 20; Ps 65:4). Seeking (Am 5:4). Fear of God (Pr 14:27; 15:23; 16:6; Mal 4:2).

See Blessings, Contingent upon Obedience; Faith; Obedience; Repentance; Perseverance.

Plan of (Joh 17:4; Heb 6:17-20). Foreordained (Eph 1:4-6; 3:11). Described as a mystery (M't 13:11; M'k 4:11; Lu 8:10; Ro 16:25, 26; 1Co 2:7-9; Eph 1:9, 10, 13; 3:9, 10; 6:19; Col 1:26, 27; 1Ti 3:16; Re 10:7).

Includes: The incarnation of Christ (Ga 4:4, 5); the atonement by Christ (Joh 18:11; 19:28-30; Ac 3:18; 17:3; Ro 16:25, 26; 1Co 1:21-25; 2:7-9; Eph 1:7-11; 3:1-8; 6:19; Col 1:26, 27; Heb 2:9-18; 10:10); initial grace (Joh 6:37, 44, 45, 65; Eph 2:5; Tit 2:11); the election of grace (2Th 2:13, 14; 2Ti 1:9, 10); inheritance (Heb 1:14); regeneration (Joh 3:3-12).

Sets forth; Reconciliation to God through Christ (2Co 5:18, 19; Col 1:9, 19-23; Heb 2:14-18); righteousness by faith in the atonement of Christ, as opposed to righteousness by works (Ro 10:3-9; 16:25, 26; Eph 2:6-10).

Experienced by Moses (Ex 15:2) Priests clothed with (2Ch 6:41; Ps 132:16). Parables of (Lu 15:2, 4-32).

Illustrated by: A horn (Ps 18:2; Lu 1:69); a tower (2Sa 22:51); a helmet (Isa 59:17; Eph 6:17); a shield (2Sa 22:36); a lamp (Isa 62:1); a cup (Ps 116:13); clothing (2Ch 6:41; Ps 132:16; 149:4; Isa 61:10); wells (Isa 12:3); walls and bulwarks (Isa 26:1; 60:18); chariots (Hab 3:8); a victory (1Co 15:57).

Typified by the brazen serpent (Nu 21:4-9, w Joh 3:14, 15).

See Atonement; Jesus, Mission of; Redemption; Regeneration; Sanctification; Sin, Forgiveness of.

SAMARIA (watch tower). 1. City of, built by Omri (1Ki 16:24). Capital of the kingdom of the ten tribes (1Ki 16:29; 22:51; 2Ki 13:1, 10; 15:8). Besieged by Ben-hadad (1Ki 20; 2Ki 6:24-33; 7). The king of Syria is led into, by Elisha, who miraculously blinds him and his army (2Ki 6:8-23). Ahab ruled in (See Ahab; Jezebel). Besieged by Shalmaneser, king of Assyria, three years; taken; the people carried away to Halah and Habor, cities of the Medes (2Ki 17:5, 6; 18:9-11). Idolatry of (1Ki 16:32; 2Ki 13:6). Temple of, destroyed (2 Ki 10:17-28; 23:19). Paul and Barnabas preach in (Ac 15:3). Visited by Philip, Peter, and John (Ac 8:5-25).

2. Country of (Isa 7:9). Foreign colonies distributed among the cities of, by the king of Assyria (2Ki 17:24-41; Ezr 4:9, 10). Roads through, from Judaea into Galilee (Lu 17:11; Joh 4:3-8). Jesus journeys through (Joh 4:1-42); heals lepers in (Lu 17:11-19). The good Samaritan from (Lu 10:33-35). No dealings between the Jews and the inhabitants of (Joh 4:9). Expect the Messiah (Joh 4:25). Disciples made from the inhabitants of (Joh 4:39-42; Ac 8:5-8, 14-17, 25). Jesus forbids the apostles to preach in the cities of (M't 10:5).

SAMARITAN PENTATEUCH (See Samaritans.)

SAMARITANS. 1. The inhabitants of the region of Samaria (2Ki 17:26; M't 10:5; Lu 9:52; 10:33; Joh 4:9, 30, 40; Ac 8:25). After the captivity of the N kingdom colonists from Babylonia, Syria, Elam, and other Assyrian territories (2Ki 17:24-34) intermarried with remnants of Jews in Samaria; held in contempt by the Jews (Ne 4:1-3; M't 10:5; Joh 4:9-26).

2. The sect which derived its name from Samaria, a term of contempt with the Jews (Joh 8:48). Religion of the Samaritans was based on the Pentateuch alone.

SAMGAR-NEBO, a prince of Babylon. At the siege of Jerusalem (Jer 39:3).

SAMLAH (a garment), one of the ancient kings of Edom (Ge 36:36, 37; 1Ch 1:47, 48).

SAMOS (height), an island in the Aegean Sea. Touched at by Paul (Ac 20:15).

SAMOTHRACIA, an island in the Aegean Sea. Touched at by Paul (Ac 16:11).

SAMSON. A judge of Israel (J'g 16:31). A Danite, son of Manoah; miraculous birth of; a Nazarite from his mother's womb; the mother forbidden to drink wine or strong drink, or to eat any unclean thing during gestation (J'g 13:2-7, 24, 25). Desires a Philistine woman for his wife; slays a lion (J'g 14:1-7). His marriage feast and the riddle propounded (J'g 14:8-19). Wife of, estranged (J'g 14:20; 15:1, 2). Is avenged for the estrangement of his wife (J'g 15:3-8). His great strength (J'g 15:7-14; Heb 11:32). Slays a thousand Philistines with the jawbone of an ass (J'g 15:13-17); Miraculously supplied with water (J'g 15:18, 19). Cohabits with Delilah, an harlot; her machinations with the Philistines to overcome him (J'g 16:20). Is blinded by the Philistines and confined to hard labor in prison; pulls down the pillars of the temple, meets his death and slays a multitude of his enemies (J'g 16:21-31; Heb 11:32).

SAMUEL (name of God or **God has heard),** last of the judges (1Sa 7:15) and first of the prophets after Moses (2Ch 25:18; Jer 15:1), a seer (1Sa 9:9) and priest (1Sa 2:18, 27, 35); son of Elkanah and Hannah (1Sa 1:19, 20); birth the result of special providence; brought up by Eli (1Sa 3); anointed Saul (1Sa 10) and David (1Sa 16:13) as kings; possible author of Biblical books which bear his name; died at Ramah (1Sa 25:1).

SAMUEL, BOOKS OF. Historical books named after the outstanding figure of the early section. I and II Samuel were once one book; the LXX divided it into two. Author's name not given, but Jewish tradition ascribes the work to the prophet Samuel, although it tells of Samuel's death and all of the events of I Samuel 25-31 and II Samuel occurred after Samuel's death. The books of Samuel present the establishment of the kingship in Israel. Outline: 1. Samuel as Judge (1Sa 1-7).

2. Saul as King (1Sa 8-2Sa 1).

3. David as King (2Sa 2-24).

SANBALLAT (the god Sin [moongod] has given life), very influential Samaritan who tried unsuccessfully to defeat Nehemiah's plans for rebuilding the walls of Jerusalem (Ne 4:1ff; 6:1-14; 13:28).

SANCTIFICATION. Separation, setting apart, with and for God (Ex 33:16); from iniquity (2Ti 2:21).

By: God (Ex 29:44; 31:13; Le 20:8; 21:8, 15, 23; 22:9, 16; Jer 1:5; Eze 20:12; 37:28). Christ (1Co 1:2, 30; 6:11; Eph 5:25-27; Heb 2:11; 10:10, 14; 13:12). The Holy Spirit (Ro 15:16; 2Th 2:13, 14; 1Pe 13:14; 1Pe 1:2). The blood of Christ (Heb 9:14; 13:12).

By faith in Christ (Ac 26:17, 18). By the truth (Joh 17:17, 19). By confession of sin (1Jo 1:9).

Intercessory prayer for (1Th 5:23). Willed of God (1Th 4:3, 4).

The altar sanctifies the gift (Ex 29:37; 30:29; M't 23:19).

Of: the Sabbath (Ge 2:3; De 5:12; Ne 13:22). Mount Sinai (Ex 19:23). The tabernacle (Ex 29:43, 44; 30:26, 29; 40:34, 35; Le 8:10; Nu 7:1). The furniture of the tabernacle (Ex 30:26-29; Nu 7:1). The altar of burnt offerings (Ex 29:36, 37; 40:10, 11; Le 8:11, 15; Nu 7:1). The laver (Ex 30:23; Le 8:11). The temple (2Ch 29:5, 17, 19).

Of: houses (Le 27:14, 15). Land (Le 27:16-19, 22). Offerings (Ex 29:27). Material things by anointing (Ex 40:9-11).

Of the firstborn of Israelites (Ex 13:2; Le 27:26; Nu 8:17; De 15:19). Eleazar to fetch the ark (1Sa 7:1). Jesse to offer sacrifice (1Sa 16:5). Of Levites (1Ch 15:12, 14; 2Ch 29:34; 30:15). Of Levites, enjoined (1Ch 15:12; 2Ch 29:5). Of priests (1Ch 15:14; 2Ch 5:11; 30:24). Of priests, enjoined (Ex 19:22). Of Aaron and his sons (Ex 28:41; 29:33, 44; 40:13; Le 8:12, 30). Of Israel (Ex 19:10, 14). Of Israel, enjoined (Ex 19:10; Le 11:44; 20:7; Nu 11:18; Jos 3:5; 7:13; Joe 2:16). Job's children, by Job (Job 1:5).

Of the Corinthian Christians (1Co 1:2; 6:11; 7:14). Of the church (Eph 5:26; 1Th 5:23; Jude 24).

See Holiness; Purity; Sin, Forgiveness of; Spiritual Purification.

SANCTUARY (holy place). 1. The tabernacle or temple, where God established His earthly abode.

2. Judah (Ps 114:2).

3. Place of asylum (1Ki 2:28f).

4. In plural, idolatrous shrines (Am 7:9).

5. Earthly sanctuary a type of the heavenly sanctuary, in which Christ is high priest and sacrifice (Heb 10:1-18).

SAND, found in desert and shores of large bodies of water; symbolic of numberlessness, vastness (Ge 22:17; Jer 33:22; 1Ki 4:29), weight (Job 6:3), and instability (M't 7:26).

SANDAL (See Dress).

SANHEDRIM, SANHEDRIN (council), highest Jewish tribunal during Greek and Roman periods; its origin is unknown; lost its authority when Jerusalem fell to the Romans in A. D. 70; in time of Jesus it had authority only in Judaea, but its influence was recognized even in the Diaspora (Ac 9:2; 22:5; 26:12). Composed of 70 members, plus the president, who was the high priest; members drawn from chief priests, scribes, and elders (M't 16:21; 27:41; M'k 8:31; 11:27; 14:43, 53; Lu 9:22); the secular nobility of Jerusalem; final court of appeal for all questions connected with the Mosaic law; could order arrests by its own officers of justice (M't 26:47; M'k 14:43; Ac 4:3; 5:17f; 9:2); did not have right of capital punishment in time of Christ (Joh 18:31, 32).

SANITATION AND HYGIENE. Relating to: Carcasses (Le 5:2; 10:4, 5; 11:24-40; 22:4, 6; Nu 9:6, 10; 19:11-16; 31:19; De 21:22, 23). Childbirth (Le 12:3; Eze 16:4). Circumcision (see Circumcision). Contagion (Le 5:2, 3; 7:19, 21; 11: 24-40; Nu 9:6, 10; 19:11-16, 22; 31:19, 20); Leprosy (Le 13:2-59; 14:2, 3, 8, 9, 34-57; Nu 5:2-4; De 24:8). Venereal diseases (Le 15:2-33; 22:4-8).

For prevention of the spread of disease: By washing (Le 13:6, 34,53, 54, 58, 59; 14:8, 9, 46, 48, 54-57; 15:2-28; Nu 31:19, 20, 22-24; De 23:10, 11). Burning (Le 7:19; 13:51, 52, 55-57; Nu 31:19, 20, 22, 23). Isolation, *i.e.*, quarantine (Le 13:2-5, 31-33, 45, 46-50; 14:34-38; 15:19; Nu 5:2, 3; 12:10, 14, 15; 2Ki 7:3; 15:5; 2Ch 26:21; Lu 17:12). Demolishing infected houses (Le 14:39-45).

Food. Articles prescribed as: Cloven-footed, cud-chewing beasts (Le 11:2, 3; De 14:6). Aquatic animals having fins and scales (Le 11:9; De 14:9). Certain insects (Le 11:22).

Articles forbidden as: Fat (Le 3:17; 7:23-25). Blood (Le 3:17; 7:26, 27; 17:10-14; 19:26; De 12:16, 20-25; 15:22, 23). Flesh having touched any unclean thing (Le 7:19). Flesh of peace and thank offerings remaining until the second day (Le 7:15; 22:30). Flesh of vow or voluntary offerings remaining till the third day (Le 7:16, 18; 19:5-8). All beasts that are not both cloven-footed and cud-chewing (Le 11:4, 8, 26; De 14:7, 8). Aquatic animals not having fins and scales (Le 11:10-12; De 14:10). Animals dying of themselves or torn by beasts (Ex 22:31; Le 17:15; 22:8; De 14:21). Certain insects (Le 11:23). Certain creeping things (Le 11:20, 21, 28-31, 41). Certain birds (Le 11:13-18).

Gluttony: Disease resulting from (Nu 11:18-20, 31-33).

Filth: Disposition of (Ex 29:14, 34; Le 4:11, 12, 21; 6:30; 7:17, 19; 8:17, 32; 9:11; 16:27, 28; 19:6; De 23:12, 13; Heb 13:11).

Rest: Enjoined, on the Sabbath (Ex 20:9-11; 31:13-17; 34:21; 35:2; De 5:12, 14); on the first and last days of annual feasts (Ex 34:22; Le 23:3-8, 24, 25, 33-42; Nu 9:2, 3; 28:16-18, 25, 26; 29:1, 7); on the day of atonement (Le 23:26-32); in the sabbatic year (Le 25:2-7); in the jubilee (Le 25:8-12).

Women in childbirth (Le 12:2, 4, 5).

Unclean defined (Le 11:24-40; 20:2-6, 10; 27:20-23). Penalties concerning (De 28:15, 21, 22, 27, 35, 45, 59-62).

See Ablutions; Defilement; Leprosy; Purification; Uncleanness.

SANSANNAH (a palm branch), a city of Judah (Jos 15:31).

SAPH (a basin, threshold), Philistine giant slain by one of David's heroes (2Sa 21:18; 1Ch 20:4).

SAPHIR (glittering), town probably in SW Palestine (Mic 1:10-15).

SAPPHIRA (beautiful), wife of Ananias; struck dead at Peter's feet because she lied (Ac 5:1-10).

SAPPHIRE. A precious stone (Job 28:6, 16; Isa 54:11; Eze 28:13). Set in the breastplate (Ex 28:18). The color of the firmament (Eze 1:26). Seen in the foundation of the New Jerusalem in John's apocalyptic vision (Re 21:19).

SARAH (princess). 1. Called also Sarai. Wife of Abraham (Ge 11:29-31; 12:5). Near of kin to Abraham (Ge 12:10-20; 20:12). Abraham represents her as his sister, and Abimelech, king of Gerar, takes her; she is restored to Abraham by means of a dream (Ge 20:1-14). Is sterile; gives her maid, Hagar, to Abraham as a wife (Ge 16:1-3). Her jealousy of Hagar (Ge 16:4-6; 21:9-14). Her miraculous conception of Isaac (Ge 17:15-21; 18:9-15). Name changed from Sarai to Sarah (Ge 17:15). Gives birth to Isaac (Ge 21:3, 6-8). Death and burial of (Ge 23; 25:10). Character of (Heb 11:11; 1Pe 3:5, 6).

2. See Serah.

SARAPH (noble one), a descendant of Shelah (1Ch 4:22).

SARCASM. *Instances of:* Cain's self-justifying argument when God asked him where Abel was (Ge 4:9). Israelites reproaching Moses (Ex 14:11). God reproaching Israel (Nu 11:20; J'g 10:14). Balak reproaching Balaam (Nu 24:11). Joshua to descendants of Joseph (Jos 17:15). By Jotham (J'g 9:7-19); Samson (J'g 14:18). The men of Jabesh to Nahash (1Sa 11:10). Eliab to David (1Sa 17:28). Elijah to the priests of Baal (1Ki 18:27). David's reply to Michal's irony (2Sa 6:21). Ahab's reply to Ben-hadad (1Ki 20:11). Jehoash to Amaziah (2Ki 14:9, 10; 2Ch 25:18, 19). Rabshakeh to Hezekiah (2Ki 18:23, 24). Sanballat's address to the army of Samaria (Ne 4:2, 3). Zophar to Job (Job 11:12). Job to Zophar (Job 12:2, 3). Of Solomon (Pr

26:16). The persecutors of Jesus (M't 27:28, 29; Lu 23:11; Joh 19:2, 3, 5, 15). Paul (1Ti 4:7). Agrippa to Paul (Ac 26:28).

See Irony; Satire.

SARDINE (See Mineral.)

SARDIS, chief city of Lydia; famous for arts and crafts; patron of mystery cults (Re 1:11; 3:1-6).

SARDITE, descendant of Sered (Ge 46:14; Nu 26:26).

SARDIUS, a precious stone. In the breastplate (Ex 28:17; 39:10). In the garden of Eden (Eze 28:13). Seen in John's apocalyptic vision of the foundation of the New Jerusalem (Re 21:20).

Figurative: Re 4:3.

SARDONYX, a precious stone.

Figurative: In the foundation of the heavenly city (Re 21:20).

SAREPTA, Phoenician town eight miles S of Sidon (Lu 4:26; 1Ki 17:9, 10).

SARGON (the constituted king). 1. Sargon I, king and founder of early Babylonian empire (2400 B. C.). Not referred to in Bible.

2. Sargon II (722-705 B. C.), Assyrian king (Isa 20:1); successor of Shalmaneser who captured Samaria (2Ki 17:1-6); defeated Egyptian ruler So (2Ki 17:4); destroyed Hittite empire; succeeded by his son Sennacherib.

SARID (survivor), village on boundary of Zebulun (Jos 19:10, 12), probably modern Tell Shadud, N of Megiddo.

SARON (See Sharon.)

SARSECHIM, prince of Nebuchadnezzar who entered Jerusalem when it fell (Jer 39:3).

SARUCH (See Serug.)

SATAN (adversary). 1. As a common noun: enemy or adversary (1Sa 29:4; 1Ki 5:4; 11:14; Ps 38:20; 109:6).

2. As a proper noun: the chief of the fallen spirits, the grand adversary of God and man (Job 1:6, 12; 2:1; Zec 3:1); hostile to everything good. Not an independent rival of God, but is able to go only as far as God permits (Job 1:12; 2:6; Lu 22:31); basically evil; story of his origin not told, but he was originally good; fell as a star out of heaven through pride (Isa 14:12; Eze 28:12-19; Lu 10:18; 1Ti 3:6); ruler of a powerful kingdom standing in opposition to God (M't 12:26; Lu 11:18); ever seeks to defeat the divine plans of grace toward mankind (1Pe 5:8); defeated by Christ at Calvary (Ge 3:15; Joh 3:8).

Sterilizes the heart (M't 13:19, 38, 39; M'k 4:15; Lu 8:12). Causes, spiritual blindness (2Co 4:4); physical infirmities (Lu 13:16).

Devices of (2Co 2:11; 12:7; Eph 6:11, 12, 16; 1Th 2:18; 1Ti 3:6, 7).

Hymeneas and Alexander delivered to (1Ti 1:20). Contends with Michael (Jude 9). Ministers of, dissemblers (2Co 11:15).

To be resisted (Eph 4:27; Jas 4:7; 1Pe 5:8, 9). Resistance of, effectual (1Jo 2:13; 5:18). Gracious deliverance from the power of (Ac 27:18; Col 1:13). Persecutes the church (Re 2:10, 13, 14).

Christ accused of being (M't 9:34; M'k 2:22-26; Lu 11:15, 18). Paul accuses Elymas the sorcerer of being (Ac 13:10).

Called: Apollyon (Re 9:11). Beelzebub (M't 12:24; M'k 3:22; Lu 11:15). Belial (2Co 6:15). The Devil (M't 4:1; 13:39; Lu 4:2-6; Re 20:2). Lucifer (Isa 14:12). Satan (1Ch 21:1; Job 1:6; Zec 3:1; Lu 22:31; Joh 13:27; Ac 5:3; 26:18; Ro 16:20). See Titles, of the Devil.

Character of: Accuser (Job 1:6, 7, 9-12; 2:3-7); Adversary (Lu 22:31, 53; 1Pe 5:8). Deceiver of the whole world (Re 12:9). Murderer and liar (Joh 8:44; Ac 5:3). Sinned from the beginning (1Jo 3:8). Subtle (Ge 3:1; 2Co 11:3). Tempter (M't 4:3; 1Co 7:5; 1Th 3:5; 1Ti 5:15). Transforms himself into an angel of light (2Co 11:14).

Described as: Accuser of our brethren (Re 12:10). Angel of the bottomless pit (Re 9:11). Enemy (M't 13:29). Father of lies (Joh 8:44). Great dragon (Re 12:9). Old serpent (Re 12:9; 20:2). Power of darkness (Col 1:13). Prince, of this world (Joh 12:31; 14:30; 16:11); of devils (M't 12:24); of the power of the air (Eph 2:2). Ruler of the darkness of this world (Eph 6:12). Son of the morning (Isa 14:12). Spirit that worketh in the children of disobedience (Eph 2:2). The god of this world (2Co 4:4). Wicked one (M't 13:19, 38).

Instances of temptations by: Eve (Ge 3:1, 4, 5, 14, 15; 2Co 11:3). Job (Job 1:13-22; 2:7-10). David (1Ch 21:1). Jesus (M't 4:1-11; M'k 1:13; Lu 4:1-13; Joh 14:30). Judas (Joh 13:2, 27).

Kingdom of: Called gates of hell (RV hades) (M't 16:18). To be destroyed (Ge 3:15; M't 13:30; Ro 16:20; 1Jo 3:8).

Symbolized: By the serpent (Ge 3:13; 2Co 11:3). By the dragon (Re 12:3, 4).

Synagogue of (Re 2:9; 3:9).

See Demons.

Destiny of: A conquered enemy of believers (Joh 12:31; 16:9, 10; 1Jo 3:8; Col 2:15). Judged already (Joh 16:11). Under perpetual curse (Ge 3:14; Isa 65:25). To be cast out of this world (Joh 12:31); bound (Re 20:1-3); cast into lake of fire (M't 25:41; Re 20:10).

SATIRE. Hannah's song of exultation over Peninnah (1Sa 2:1-10, w 1:5-10). Of Jesus against hypocrites (M't 23:2-33; M'k 12:13-40; Lu 11:39-54).

See Irony; Sarcasm.

SATRAP, viceroy in Persian empire who ruled several small provinces (satrapies), each having its own governor. In KJV "lieutenant" in Ezr 8:36; Es 3:12; 8:9; 9:3, "prince" in Da 3:2, 3, 27; 6:1-7.

SATYR, a mythological creature, represented as half man and half goat (Le 17:7 [*R. V.*, margin]; 2Ch 11:15 [*R.V.*, margin]; Isa 13:21; 34:14).

SAUL (asked of God). 1. Called also Shaul. King of Edom (Ge 36:37, 38; 1Ch 1:48, 49).

2. King of Israel. A Benjamite, son of Kish (1Sa 9:1, 2). Sons of (1Ch 8:33). His personal appearance (1Sa 9:2; 10:23). Made king of Israel (1Sa 9; 10; 11:12-15; Ho 13:11). Dwells at Gibeah of Saul (1Sa 14:2; 15:34; Isa 10:29). Defeats the Philistines (1Sa 13; 14:46, 52). Smites the Amalekites (1Sa 15). Is reproved by Samuel for usurping the priestly functions (1Sa 13:11-14); for disobedience in not slaying the Amalekites; the loss of his kingdom foretold (1Sa 15). Dedicates the spoils of war (1Sa 15:21-25; 1Ch 26:28). Sends messengers to Jesse, asking that David be sent to him as musician and armor-bearer (1Sa 16:17-23). Defeats the Philistines after Goliath is slain by David (1Sa 17). His jealousy of David; gives his daughter, Michal, to David to be his wife; becomes David's enemy (1Sa 18). Tries to slay David; Jonathan intercedes and incurs his father's displeasure; David's loyalty to him; Saul's repentance; prophesies (1Sa 19). Hears Doeg against Ahimelech, and slays the priest and his family (1Sa 22:9-19). Pursues David to the wilderness of Ziph; the Ziphites betray David to (1Sa 23). Pursues David to En-gedi (1Sa 24:1-6). His life saved by David (1Sa 24:5-8). Saul's contrition for his bad faith (1Sa 24:16-22). David is again betrayed to, by the Ziphites; Saul pursues him to the hill of Hachilah; his life spared again by David; his confession, and his blessing upon David (1Sa 26). Slays the Gibeonites; crime avenged by the death of seven of his sons (2Sa 21:1-9). His kingdom invaded by Philistines; seeks counsel of the witch of En-dor, who foretells his death (1Sa 28:3-25; 29:1). Is defeated, and with his sons is slain (1Sa 31); their bodies exposed in Beth-shan; rescued by the people of Jabesh and burned; bones of, buried under a tree at Jabesh (1Sa 31, w 2Sa 1; 2; 1Ch 10). His death a judgment on account of his sins (1Ch 10:13).

3. Of Tarsus. See Paul.

SAVIOUR (deliverer), one who saves, delivers, or preserves from any evil or danger, whether physical or spiritual, temporal or eternal; term applied both to men (J'g 3:9, 15; 2Ki 13:5; Ne 9:27; Ob 21) and God (Ps 44:3, 7; Isa 43:11; 45:21; 60:16; Jer 14:8; Ho 13:4). In NT it is never applied to man, but only to God and Christ (Lu 1:47; 1Ti 1:1; 2:3; 4:10; Tit 1:3). Saviour is pre-eminently the title of the Son (2Ti 1:10; Tit 1:4; 2:13; 3:6; 2Pe 1:1; 1Jo 4:10).

See God, Saviour; Jesus, Saviour.

SAVOR, SAVOUR, taste (M't 5:13; Lu 14:34), smell (Joe 2:20). Also used metaphorically (2Co 2:14; Eph 5:2; Ph'p 4:18).

SAVORY MEAT, meals made by Jacob and Esau for their father Isaac prior to receiving his blessing (Ge 27:4, 9, 14, 17, 31).

SAW. Used as an instrument of torture (2Sa 12:31; Heb 11:37); for cutting stone (1Ki 7:9).

Figurative: Isa 10:15.

SCAB, disease of the skin (Le 13:2, 6-8; 14:56; 21:20; 22:22; De 28:27; Isa 3:17).

See Disease; Sanitation; Scurvy.

SCAFFOLD, platform (2Ch 6:13).

SCALE. 1. Only fish having fins and scales were permitted as food for Hebrews (Le 11:9-12).

2. Instrument for weighing (Isa 40:12; Pr 16:11; 20:23).

SCALL, a form of leprosy (Le 13:30).
See Leprosy.

SCAPEBIRD (Le 14:4-7, 53).

SCAPEGOAT, the second of two goats for which lots were cast on the Day of Atonement (Le 16:8, 10, 26). The first was sacrificed as a sin offering, but the second had the people's sins transferred to it by prayer and was then taken into the wilderness and released.

SCARLET, probably a bright rich crimson. Scarlet cloth was used for the hangings of the tabernacle (Ex 25:4), high priest's vestments (Ex 39:1), royal or expensive apparel (2Sa 1:24). Sins are "as scarlet" (Isa 1:18).
See Colors.

SCEPTER. A wand used by kings to signify favor or disfavor to those who desired audience (Es 5:2; 8:4). A symbol of authority (Nu 24:17; Isa 14:5). Made of gold (Es 4:11); of iron (Ps 2:9; Re 2:27; 12:5).
Figurative: Ge 49:10; Nu 24:17; Isa 9:4.

SCEVA, chief priest living in Ephesus whose seven sons were exorcists (Ac 19:14-17).

SCHISM (rent or division), a formal division inside a religious group (1Co 12:25).

SCHOOL. Of the prophets at Naioth (1Sa 19:20); Beth-el (2Ki 2:3); Jericho (2Ki 2:5, 15); Gilgal (2Ki 4:38); Jerusalem, probably (2Ki 22:14; 2Ch 34:22). Crowded attendance at (2Ki 6:1).
In the home (De 4:9, 10; 6:7, 9; 11:19, 20; Ps 78:5-8). Bible School (De 31:10-13).
State (2Ch 17:7-9; Da 1:3-21). Of Gamaliel (Ac 5:34; 22:3). Of Tyrannus (Ac 19:9). Schoolmaster [tutor, *R. V.*] (Ga 3:24, 25).
See Instruction; Psalms, Didactic.

SCIENCE. Observations of, and deductions from, facts (Job 26:7-14; 28; Ec 1:13-17). So-called, false (1Ti 6:20).
The key of knowledge (Lu 11:52; Ro 2:20).
See Geology; Astronomy; Philosophy.

SCOFFER, one who derides, mocks (2Pe 3:3).

SCOFFING. Of the children of Israel (2Ch 30:6-10; 36:16; Ps 78:19, 20; Ps 107:11, 12; Ho 7:5). Of unbelievers (Ps 42:3, 10; 73:8, 9, 11, 12; Pr 1:22, 25; Jer 17:15; 43:2; La 1:7; Eze 8:12; 9:9; 12:22; 2Pe 3:3, 4). Of the wicked at God's requirements (Job 21:14, 15; Isa 10:15; 57:4; Eze 11:2, 3; 33:20).
Of Christ (M't 12:24; M'k 3:22; Lu 4:23; 11:15; 16:14). Of first Christians (Ac 2:13). Of Paul (Ac 13:45; 17:18, 32).
Proverbs of (Pr 1:22, 25; 3:34; 9:12; 13:1; 14:6, 9; 19:29; 21:11, 24; 22:10; 24:9). Punishment for (Pr 3:24; 9:12; 19:29; Isa 5:18, 19, 24, 25; 29:20; Heb 10:29).
See Hatred; Malice; Unbelief.
Instances of: Ishmael (Ge 21:9). Children at Beth-el (2Ki 2:23). Ephraim and Manasseh (2Ch 30:10). Chiefs of Judah (2Ch 36:16). Sanballat (Ne 4:1). Enemies of Job (Job 30:1, 9). Enemies of David (Ps 35:15, 16). Rulers of Israel (Isa 28:14). Ammonites (Eze 25:3). Tyrians (Eze 26:2). Heathen (Eze 36:2, 3). Soldiers (M't 27:28-30; Lu 23:36). Chief priests (M't 27:41). Pharisees (Lu 16:14). The men who held Jesus (Lu 22:63, 64). Herod (Lu 23:11). People and rulers (Lu 23:35). Some of the multitude (Ac 2:13). Athenians (Ac 17:32).

SCORNERS (Ps 1:1; Pr 9:12; 21:11, 24). An abomination (Pr 24:9). Admonitions to (Pr 1:22, 23). Punishment of (Pr 19:29; Isa 29:20). Warnings against (Pr 3:34; 13:1; 14:6; 19:29; 22:10; 29:8).
See Scoffing.

SCORPION. A venomous insect common in the wilderness through which the children of Israel journeyed (De 8:15). Power over, given to the seventy (Lu 10:19). Unfit for food (Lu 11:12). Sting of in the tail (Re 9:10).
Symbolical: Re 9:3, 5, 10.
Figurative: Of enemies (Eze 2:6). Of cruelty (1Ki 12:11, 14).

SCOURGING, corporal punishment by stripes. Prescribed in the Mosaic law for fornication (Le 19:20; De 22:18); for other offenses (De 25:2). Forty stripes the maximum limit (De 25:3). Fatal (Job 9:23); of servants avenged (Ex 21:20). Foretold by Jesus as a persecution of the Christians (M't 10:17).
Of children, see Children, Correction of; Punishment.
Instances of: Of Jesus (M't 20:19; 27:26; M'k 15:15; Joh 19:1). Of Paul and

Silas (Ac 16:23). Of Paul (Ac 21:32; 22:24; 2Co 11:24, 25). Of Sosthenes (Ac 18:17).

Figurative: Of the oppressions of rulers (1Ki 12:11). Of the evil tongue (Job 5:21).

See Assault and Battery.

SCREECH OWL (See Birds.)

SCRIBE. A writer and transcriber of the law (2Sa 8:17; 20:25; 1Ki 4:3; 2Ki 12:10; 18:37; 19:2; 1Ch 24:6; 27:32; Ne 13:13; Jer 36:12). King's secretary (2Ki 12:10-12; 22:1-14; Es 3:12; 8:9). Mustering officer of the army (2Ki 25:19; 2Ch 26:11). Instructors in the law (M't 7:29; 13:52; 17:10; 23:2, 3). See Levites. Test Jesus with questions, bringing to Jesus a woman taken in adultery (Joh 8:3). Members of the council (M't 2:4). Conspire against Jesus (M't 26:3, 57; 27:41; M'k 41:1; Lu 22:66). Hypocrisy of, reproved by Jesus (M't 15:20; 9:3; 12:38; 15:1; 16:21; 20:18; 21:15).

SCRIPTURES. The word of God (Jer 30:2). Interpreted by doctors (Joh 3:10; 7:52). Inspired (2Ti 3:16).

See Word of God.

SCROLL, book made of papyrus or smoothed skins of animals sewn together to make a long strip which was wound around sticks at both ends (Isa 34:4; Jer 36; Eze 3:1-3; Re 5; 10:1-10). They varied in length from a few feet to 35 feet. The codex form of book was not used until the 2nd century A.D.

SCROLLS, DEAD SEA (See Dead Sea Scrolls.)

SCULPTURE (See Art.)

SCURVY (Le 22:22).

See Scab.

SCYTHIAN, a nomadic people, savage and uncivilized, living N and E of the Black Sea (Col 3:11).

SEA. Creation of (Ge 1:9, 10; Ps 95:5; 148:4, 5). Limits of, established by God (Ps 1:9; Job 26:10; 38:8; Ps 33:7; Jer 5:22). Calmed by Jesus (M't 8:24-26; M'k 4:37-39). Jesus walked on (M't 14:25-31). Dead, to be given up by, at the resurrection (Re 20:13).

Symbolical: In Daniel's vision (Da 7:2, 3). In John's apocalyptic vision (Re 4:6; 8:8, 9; 10:2, 5, 6, 8; 13:1; 15:2; 16:3; 21:1).

SEA, BRAZEN, the great basin in Solomon's temple where the priests washed their hands and feet preparatory to temple ministry (1Ki 7:23-26; 2Ch 4:2-6).

SEA OF GALILEE. Called Sea of Chinnereth (Nu 34:11; De 3:17; Jos 13:27). Sea of Chinneroth (Jos 12:3). Lake of Gennesaret (Lu 5:1). Sea of Tiberias (Joh 21:1).

Jesus calls disciples on shore of (M't 4:18-22; Lu 5:1-11). Jesus teaches from a ship on (M't 13:13). Miracles of Jesus on (M't 8:24-32; 14:22-33; 17:27; M'k 4:37-39; Lu 5:1-9; 8:22-24; Joh 12:1-11).

SEA OF GLASS, a glassy sea before the throne of God (Re 4:6; 15:2).

SEA OF JAZER. No such sea is known; perhaps a scribal error for "city of Jazer" (Jer 48:32).

SEA MEW (See Birds, Cuckoo.)

SEA MONSTER, any great fish of the sea (Ge 1:21; Job 7:12; in KJV "whale").

SEAL. 1. A stamp used for signifying documents. Given as a pledge (Ge 38:18). Engraved (Ex 28:11, 21, 36; 39:6, 14, 30; 2Ti 2:19). Decrees signified by (1Ki 21:8; Es 8:8). Documents sealed with: Ahab's letter (1Ki 21:8); covenants (Ne 9:38; 10:1; Isa 8:16); decrees (Es 8:8; Da 6:9); deeds (Jer 32:10). Treasures secured by (De 32:34). Lion's den made sure by (Da 6:17); sepulcher of Jesus (M't 27:66).

Circumcision a seal of righteousness (Ro 4:11).

Figurative: Of secrecy (Da 12:9; Re 5:1). Of certainty of divine approval (Joh 6:27; Ro 15:38; 2Co 1:22; Eph 1:13; 4:30; Re 7:3, 4). In John's vision (Re 6; 8:1; 10:4).

2. An amphibious animal. Skins of, according to the Revised Version, were used as a covering of the tabernacle (Ex 25:5; 26:14; 35:7, 23; 36:19; 39:34; Nu 4:25).

SEAMEN (See Mariners.)

SEASONS (Ge 1:14; 8:22; Ps 104:19; Jer 33:20; Da 2:21; M't 21:41; 24:32; M'k 12:2; Ac 1:7; 1Th 5:1).

SEAT, chair, stool, throne (1Sa 20:18; Lu 1:52).

SEBA. 1. Son of Cush (Ge 10:7; 1Ch 1:9).

2. A region in Ethiopia (Ps 72:10; Isa 43:3).

SEBAT, 11th month of the Hebrew year (Zec 1:7); corresponded to our February.

SECACAH, village in wilderness of Judah (Jos 15:61); location unknown.

SECHU, village near Ramah (1Sa 19:22).

SECOND COMING OF CHRIST, THE, Time of, unknown (M't 24:36; M'k 13:32).

Called the: Times of refreshing from the presence of the Lord (Ac 3:19). Times of restitution of all things (Ac 3:21, w Ro 8:21). Last time (1Pe 1:5). Appearing of Jesus Christ (1Pe 1:7). Revelation of Jesus Christ (1Pe 1:13). Glorious appearing of the great God and our Saviour (Tit 2:13). Coming of the day of God (2Pe 3:12). Day of our Lord Jesus Christ (1Co 1:8).

Foretold by: Prophets (Da 7:13; Jude 14). Himself (M't 25:31; Joh 14:3). Apostles (Ac 3:20; 1Ti 6:14). Angels (Ac 1:10, 11). Signs preceding (M't 24:3).

The manner of: In clouds (M't 24:30; 26:64; Re 1:7). In the glory of His Father (M't 16:27). In His own glory (M't 25:31). In flaming fire (2Th 1:8). With power and great glory (M't 24:30). As He ascended (Ac 1:9, 11). With a shout and the voice of the Archangel (1Th 4:16). Accompanied by Angels (M't 16:27; 25:31; M'k 8:38; 2Th 1:7). With His saints (1Th 3:13; Jude 14). Suddenly (M'k 13:36). Unexpectedly (M't 24:44; Lu 12:40). As a thief in the night (1Th 5:2; 2Pe 3:10; Re 16:15). As the lightning (M't 24:27). The heavens and earth shall be dissolved (2Pe 3:10, 12). They who shall have died in Christ shall rise first at (1Th 4:16). The saints alive at, shall be caught up to meet Him (1Th 4:17). Is not to make atonement (Heb 9:28, w Ro 6:9, 10, and Heb 10:14).

The purposes of, are to: Complete the salvation of saints (He 9:28; 1Pe 1:5). Be glorified in His saints (2Th 1:10). Be admired in them that believe (2Th 1:10). Bring to light the hidden things of darkness (1Co 4:5). Judge (Ps 50:3, 4, w Joh 5:22; 2Ti 4:1; Jude 15; Re 20:11-13). Reign (Isa 24:23; Da 7:14; Re 11:15). Destroy death (1Co 15:25, 26). Every eye shall see Him at (Re 1:7). Should be always considered as at hand (Ro 13:12; Ph'p 4:5; 1Pe 4:7). Blessedness of being prepared for (M't 24:46; Lu 12:37, 38).

Saints: Assured of (Job 19:25, 26). Love (2Ti 4:8). Look for (Ph'p 3:20; Tit 2:13). Wait for (1Co 1:7; 1Th 1:10). Haste unto (2Pe 3:12). Pray for (Re 22:20). Should be ready for (M't 24:44; Lu 12:40). Should watch for (M't 24:42; M'k 13:35-37; Lu 21:36). Should be patient unto (2Th 3:5; Jas 5:7, 8). Shall be preserved unto (Ph'p 1:6; 2Ti 4:18; 1Pe 1:5; Jude 24). Shall not be ashamed at (1Jo 2:28; 1Jo 4:17). Shall be blameless at (1Co 1:8; 1Th 3:13; 5:23; Jude 24). Shall be like Him at (Ph'p 3:21; 1Jo 3:2). Shall see Him as He is (1Jo 3:2). Shall appear with Him in glory at (Col 3:4). Shall receive a crown of glory at (2Ti 4:8; 1Pe 5:4). Shall reign with Him at (Da 7:27; 2Ti 2:12; Re 5:10; 20:6; 22:5). Faith of, shall be found unto praise at (1Pe 1:7).

The wicked: Scoff at (2Pe 3:3, 4). Presume upon the delay of (M't 24:48). Shall be surprised by (M't 24:37-39; 1Th 5:3; 2Pe 3:10). Shall be punished at (2Th 1:8, 9). The man of sin to be destroyed at (2Th 2:8). Illustrated (M't 25:6; Lu 12:36, 39; 19:12, 15).

See Jesus, Second Coming of.

SECOND DEATH (Re 19:20; 20:14; 21:8). Righteous exempt from (Re 2:11).

See Punishment, Eternal; Wicked, Punishment of.

SECRET. Alms to be given in (M't 6:4). Prayer to be offered in (M't 6:6). Of others not to be divulged (Pr 25:9; M't 18:15).

Belong to God (De 29:29; Ps 25:14). God knows secrets of heart (De 31:21; 1Sa 16:7; 2Sa 7:20; 2Ki 19:27; Ps 44:21; 90:8; Heb 4:12, 13).

Shall be revealed, and judged (Ec 12:14; Da 2:28; Ro 2:16; 1Co 4:5); and manifested (Da 2:47; Am 3:7; M'k 4:22; Lu 8:16, 17).

See Mystery.

SECRETARY (2Sa 8:17; 20:24; 1Ki 4:3; 2Ki 12:10-12; 18:18, 37; 22:1-14; 1Ch 27:32; Es 3:12; 8:9). Military (2Ki 25:19; 2Ch 26:11).

See Amanuensis; Scribe.

SECT (sect, party, school), religious group with distinctive doctrine: Sadducees (Ac 5:17), Pharisees (Ac 15:5; 26:5), Christians (Ac 24:5; 28:22).

SECUNDUS, a Thessalonian Christian. Accompanies Paul from Corinth (Ac 20:4-6).

SECURITY, the theological teaching which maintains the certain continuation of the salvation of those who are saved; also known as the perseverance of the saints (Joh 10:28; Ro 8:38; 39; Ph'p 1:6; 2Th 3:3; 1Pe 1:5).

For Debt: See Debt; Surety.

False: From the evils of sin. Promises peace and long life (Job 29:18). Is ignorant of God and truth (Ps 10:4; 50:21). Trusts in lies (Isa 28:15; Re 3:17). Is inconsiderate and forgetful (Isa 47:7). Relies on earthly treasures (Jer 49:4, 16). Is deceived by pride (Ob 3; Re 18:7). Puts off the evil day (Am 6:3). Leads to increased guilt (Ec 8:11). Its refuges shall be scattered (Isa 28:17). Ruin shall overtake it (Isa 47:9; Am 9:10). God is against it (Jer 21:13; Eze 39:6; Am 6:1).

See Confidence, False; Self-Deception; Self-Delusion.

SEDITION. Charged against Paul (Ac 24:5). How punished (Ac 5:36, 37).

SEDUCER, false teacher, deceiver, perhaps through the use of magical arts (2Ti 3:13).

SEDUCTION (2Ti 3:6, 13). Laws concerning (Ex 22:16, 17; De 22:23-29).

See Rape.

Instances of: Of Dinah (Ge 34:2). Tamar (2Sa 13:1-14).

SEED. Every herb, tree, and grass, yields its own (Ge 1:11, 12, 29). Each kind has its own body (1Co 15:38). Not to be mingled in sowing (Le 19:19; De 22:9).

Parables concerning (M't 13; Lu 8).

Illustrative (Ec 11:6; Ho 10:12; 2Co 9:6; Ga 6:7, 8).

Sowing of, type of burial of the body (1Co 15:36-38).

SEEDTIME (See Agriculture.)

SEEKERS. Must: have faith (Heb 11:6). Remember God's mercies (Isa 51:1). Count the cost (Lu 14:26-33).

Seeking God: Enjoined (1Ch 16:11; 22:19; Ps 105:4; Isa 26:8, 9; Hos 10:12; Joe 2:12, 13; Am 5:4-6, 8, 14; Zep 2:3; M't 6:33; Jas 4:8; Re 22:17). For salvation (Ge 49:18). To sacrifice (2Ch 11:16). The result of adversity (Ps 78:34; 83:16; Ho 5:15). Prophesied (Jer 50:4; Ho 3:5; Zec 8:20-23). Punishment for not being (2Ch 15:13; Isa 8:19). Not of self (Ro 3:11). By incorrigible sinners, vain (Am 8:12; Lu 13:24).

Promises to (Joh 6:37). Of finding God (De 4:29; 1Ch 28:9; 2Ch 15:2, 12; Pr 8:17, 34, 35; Isa 45:19, 22; Jer 29:13; Ac 17:27). Of pardon (2Ch 30:18, 19; Ps 69:32; Isa 55:6, 7; Eze 18:21-23; Ac 2:21). Of salvation (Heb 9:28). Of providential care (2Ch 26:5; Ezr 8:22; Ps 34:4; 81:10; 145:19; Isa 49:9-12, 23; M't 6:33). Of spiritual blessings (Job 8:5, 6; Ps 9:10; 22:26; 24:3-6; 40:1-4; 63:1-8; 70:4, 5; 119:2; 145:18, 19; Pr 2:3-5; 28:5; Isa 44:3, 4; 45:19, 22; 55:6, 7; 61:1-3; La 3:25, 26, 41; M't 5:6; 6:33; 7:7-11; Lu 6:21; 11:9-13; Ac 2:21; Ro 10:12, 13; Heb 7:25; Re 3:20; 21:6).

Instances of: Asa (2Ch 14:7). Jehoshaphat (2Ch 17:3, 4). Uzziah (2Ch 26:5). Hezekiah (2Ch 31:21). Josiah (2Ch 34:3). Ezra (Ezr 7:10). Job (Job 5:8). David (Ps 17:1, 2; 25:5, 15; 27:4, 8; 34:4; 40:1, 2; 63:1-8; 143:6). The psalmists (Ps 33:20; 42:1-4; 77:1-9; 84:2; 119:10; 130:5, 6). Solomon's bride for Solomon (Song 3:1-4). Daniel (Da 9:3, 4). The Magi (M't 2:1, 2). Cornelius, the Centurion (Ac 10:7, 30-33).

See Backsliders; Penitent; Sin, Confession of; Forgiveness of; Zeal.

SEEKING GOD. Commanded (Isa 55:6; M't 7:7).

Includes Seeking: His name (Ps 83:16). His word (Isa 34:16). His face (Ps 27:8; 105:4). His strength (1Ch 16:11; Ps 105:4). His commandments (1Ch 28:8; Mal 2:7). His precepts (Ps 119:45, 94). His kingdom (M't 6:33; Lu 12:31). His righteousness (M't 6:33). Christ (Mal 3:1; Lu 2:15, 16). Honor which comes from Him (Joh 5:44). Justification by Christ (Ga 2:16, 17). The city which God has prepared (Heb 11:10, 16; 13:14). By prayer (Job 8:5; Da 9:3). In His house (De 12:5; Ps 27:4).

Should Be: Immediate (Ho 10:12). Evermore (Ps 105:4). While He may be found (Isa 55:6). With diligence (Heb 11:6). With the heart (De 4:29; 1Ch 22:19). In the day of trouble (Ps 77:2).

Ensures: His being found (De 4:29; 1Ch 28:9; Pr 8:17; Jer 29:13). His favor (La 3:25). His protection (Ezr 8:22). His not forsaking us (Ps 9:10). Life (Ps 69:32; Am 5:4, 6). Prosperity (Job 8:5, 6; Ps 34:10). Being heard of Him (Ps 34:4). Understanding all things (Pr 28:5). Gifts of righteousness (Ho 10:12). Imperative upon all (Isa 8:19). Afflictions designed to lead to (Ps 78:33, 34; Ho 5:15). None, by nature, are found to be engaged in (Jas 14:2, w Ro 3:11; Lu 12:23, 30).

Saints: Specially exhorted to (Zep 2:3). Desirous of (Job 5:8). Purpose, in heart (Ps 27:8). Prepare their hearts for (2Ch 30:19). Set their hearts to (2Ch 11:16). Engage in, with the whole heart (2Ch 15:12; Ps 119:10). Early in (Job 8:5; Ps 63:1; Isa 26:9). Earnest in (Song 3:2, 4). Characterized by (Ps 24:6). Is never in vain (Isa 45:19). Blessedness of (Ps 119:2). Leads to joy (Ps 70:4; 105:3). Ends in praise (Ps 22:26). Promise connected with (Ps 69:32). Shall be rewarded (Heb 11:6).

The Wicked: Are gone out of the way of (Ps 14:2, 3, w Ro 3:11, 12). Prepare not their hearts for (2Ch 12:14). Refuse, through pride (Ps 10:4). Not led to, by affliction (Isa 9:13). Sometimes pretend to (Ezr 4:2; Isa 58:2). Rejected, when too late in (Pr 1:28). They who neglect denounced (Isa 31:1). Punishment of those who neglect (Zep 1:4-6).

Exemplified: Asa (2Ch 14:7). Jehoshaphat (2Ch 17:3, 4). Uzziah (2Ch 26:5). Hezekiah (2Ch 31:21). Josiah (2Ch 34:3). Ezr (Ezr 7:10). David (Ps 34:4). Daniel (Da 9:3, 4).

SEER (See Prophet.)

SEGUB. 1. Son of Hiel, the rebuilder of Jericho (1Ki 16:34).

2. Grandson of Judah (1Ch 2:4, 5, 21, 22).

SEIR, Horite; ancestor of inhabitants of the land of Seir (Ge 26:20; 1Ch 1:38).

SEIR, LAND OF and **MOUNT.** 1. Alternate names for the region occupied by the descendants of Edom or Esau. Originally called the land of Seir (Ge 32:3); later called Edom (Ge 36:8, 9); extends S from Moab on both sides of the Arabah c. 100 miles; mountainous; in Greek period called Idumea. Mt. Seir c. 3500 feet high. "Seir" also used for people who lived in Mt. Seir (Eze 25:8).

2. Region on border of Judah W of Kirjath-jearim (Jos 15:10).

SEIRAH, SEIRATH, town in Ephraim, probably in SE part (J'g 3:26).

SEIZIN, of real property.

See Land.

SELA, Edomite city called Petra by Greeks (2Ki 14:7; Isa 42:11); capital of the Nabateans.

SELAH (to lift up), term of uncertain meaning found frequently in Psalms; probably for instruction to singers or musicians (Ps 9:16; Hab 3:3, 9, 13).

SELA-HAMMAHLEKOTH, cliff in wilderness of Maon (1Sa 23:28).

SELED, a descendant of Jerahmeel (1Ch 2:30).

SELEUCIA, seaport of Syrian Antioch, founded by Seleucus I in 300 B. C. (Ac 13:4).

SELEUCIDS, a dynasty of rulers of the kingdom of Syria (included Babylonia, Bactria, Persia, Syria, and part of Asia Minor), descended from Seleucus I, general of Alexander the Great. It lasted from 312 to 64 B. C., when the Romans took it over. One of them, Antiochus Epiphanes, precipitated the Maccabean War by trying forcibly to Hellenize the Jews.

SELF-CONDEMNATION (1Ki 8:31, 32; Job 9:20; Pr 5:12, 13; M't 23:31; Ro 2:1; 1Jo 3:20; Re 1:7).

Parables of (M't 21:33-41; 25:24-27; M'k 12:1-12; Lu 19:21, 22).

Instances of: Achan (Jos 7:19-25). David (1Sa 24:1-15; 26:1-20; 2Sa 12:5-7; 24:17). Ahab (1Ki 20:39-42). Jonah (Jon 1:12). Those who condemned the woman (Joh 8:9).

See Self-incrimination; Remorse; Repentance.

SELF-CONFIDENCE (See Confidence, False.)

SELF-CONTROL. Of Saul (1Sa 10:27). Of David (1Sa 24:1-15; 26:1-20). Of Jesus (M't 26:62, 63; 27:12-14).

See Abstinence, Total; Graces, Christian; Patience; Tact; also, Rashness.

SELF-DECEPTION (Jas 1:26).

See Confidence, False; Security, False.

SELF-DEFENSE, accused heard in (M't 27:11-14; M'k 15:2-5; Lu 23:3; Joh 7:51; Ac 2:37-40; 22; 23; 24:10-21; 26).

See Defense.

SELF-DELUSION. A characteristic of the wicked (Ps 49:18). Prosperity frequently leads to (Ps 30:6; Ho 12:8; Lu 12:17-19). Obstinate sinners often given up to (Ps 81:11, 12; Ho 4:17; 2Th 2:10, 11).

Exhibited in thinking that: Our own

ways are right (Pr 14:12); we should adhere to established wicked practices (Jer 44:17); we are pure (Pr 30:12); we are better than others (Lu 18:11); we are rich in spiritual things (Re 3:17); we may have peace while in sin (De 29:19); we are above adversity (Ps 10:6); gifts entitle us to heaven (M't 7:21, 22); privileges entitle us to heaven (M't 3:9; Lu 13:25, 26); God will not punish our sins (Jer 5:12); Christ will not come to judge (2Pe 3:4); our lives will be prolonged (Isa 56:12; Lu 12:19; Jas 4:13).

Frequently persevered in to the last (M't 7:22; 25:11, 12; Lu 13:24, 25). Fatal consequences of (M't 7:23; 24:48-51; Lu 12:20; 1Th 5:3).

Exemplified: Ahab (1Ki 20:27, 34). Israelites (Ho 12:8). Jews (Joh 8:33, 41). Church of Laodicea (Re 3:17).

See Confidence, False; Security, False.

SELF-DENIAL (Lu 21:2-4; 1Co 6:12; 9:12, 15, 18, 19, 23, 25-27; 10:23, 24; 2Co 6:3; Ph'p 2:4-8; 3:7-9; 2Ti 2:4; Tit 2:12; Heb 13:13; Re 12:11). Parables of (M't 13:44-46; 18:8, 9; M'k 9:43).

In respect to, appetite (Pr 23:2; Da 10:3); sinful pleasures (M't 5:29, 30; 18:8, 9; M'k 9:43); carnality (Ro 6:6; 8:12, 13, 35, 36; 13:14; 1Co 9:27; Ga 5:16, 17, 24; Col 3:5; Tit 2:12; 1Pe 2:11, 12, 14-16).

Required of Christ's disciples (M't 8:19-22; 10:37-39; 16:24, 25; 19:12, 21; M'k 2:14; 8:34, 35; 10:29; Lu 5:11; 9:23, 24, 57, 58; 12:33; 14:26, 27, 33; 18:27-29, 30; Joh 12:25; 2Ti 2:4; Heb 13:13; 1Pe 4:1; 3Jo 7); for a brother's sake (Ro 14:1-22; 15:1-5; 1Co 8:10-13; 10:23-24; Ph'p 2:4); for the sake of the ministry (2Co 6:3). Christ's teachings concerning (M'k 12:43, 44; Lu 21:2-4).

Instances of: Abraham, when he accorded to Lot his preference for the grazing lands of Canaan (Ge 13:9; 17:8); in offering Isaac (Ge 22:12). Moses, in choosing suffering over pleasure (Heb 11:25); in taking no compensation from the Israelites (Nu 16:15). Samuel, in his administration of justice (1Sa 12:3, 4). The widow of Zarephath, in sharing with Elijah the last of her sustenance (1Ki 17:12-15). David, in paying for the threshing floor (2Sa 24:24). The psalmist (Ps 132:3-5). Daniel, in his abstemiousness (Da 1:8); in refusing rewards from Belshazzar (Da 5:16, 17). Esther, in risking her life for her people (Es 4:16). The Rechabites, in refusing wine or strong drink, or even to plant vineyards (Jer 35:6, 7).

Peter and other apostles, in abandoning their vocations to follow Jesus (M't 4:20; 9:9; M'k 1:16-20; 2:14; Lu 5:11, 27, 28); in forsaking all (M't 19:27; M'k 10:28; Lu 5:28). The widow, who cast all into the treasury (Lu 21:4). The early Christians, in having everything in common (Ac 2:44, 45; 4:34). Joseph, in selling his possessions and giving all to the apostles (Ac 4:36, 37). Paul (1Co 10: 23, 24; Ga 2:20; 6:14); in not counting even his life valuable to himself (Ac 20:24; 21: 13; Ph'p 3:7, 8); in laboring for his own support while he taught (Ac 20:34, 35; 1Co 4:12; 10:33); in not exercising his authority (1Co 6:12; 9:12, 15, 18, 19, 23-27).

See Cross; Humility.

SELF-EXALTATION. Christian attitude toward (2Co 10:5, 17, 18). Christ's teaching concerning (M'k 12:38). Parables of (Lu 14:7-11). Self-deception of (Ga 6:3). Punishment for (Eze 31:10-14; Ob 3, 4).

Instances of: Job (Job 12:3). Pharaoh (Ex 9:17). Korah, Dathan and Abiram (Nu 16:1-11). Sennacherib (2Ch 32:9-19). Prince of Tyre, making himself God (Eze 28:2, 9, 10). Nebuchadnezzar (Da 4:30; 5:20); Belshazzar (Da 5:22, 23). Simon the sorcerer (Ac 8:9-11). Herod, when deified by the people (Ac 12:20-23). The son of perdition (2Th 2:4).

See Pride; Self-Righteousness.

SELF-EXAMINATION. Enjoined (Ps 4:4; Hag 1:7; 1Co 11:28, 31; 2Co 13:5; Ga 6:4); by inference (Jer 17:9). Conversion as a result of (Ps 119:59; La 3:40).

Exemplified by: Job (Job 13:23); David (Ps 19:2; 26:2; 139:23, 24); the Psalmist (Ps 77:6; 119:59); the disciples (M't 26:22; M'k 14:19).

See Meditation; Repentance; Sin, Confession of.

SELF-INCRIMINATION. Under ancient customs accused persons were required to give self-incriminating testimonies of guilt of the offense charged and were, on occasions, scourged to force self-incriminating testimony whether guilty or innocent (Nu 5:11-27; 2Sa 1:10, 16; 1Ki 8:31, 32; 2Ch 6:22; Ac 22:24).

Instance of: Achan (Jos 8:19-25).

See Self-Condemnation.

SELF-INDULGENCE. Instances of: Solomon (Ec 2:10). The rich fool (Lu 12:16-20). Dives (Lu 16:19).

See Gluttony; Idleness; Slothfulness; also Self-Denial.

SELFISHNESS. Admonitions against (Da 15:9; Lu 6:32-34; Ro 14:15; 15:1-3; 1Co 10:24; Ga 6:2; Ph'p 2:4). Christ's example against (Ro 15:3; 2Co 5:15; Ph'p 2:5-8).

Unsympathetic with the unfortunate (Pr 28:27; Jas 2:15, 16; 1Jo 3:17). Judged (Pr 18:17; 24:11, 12; Hag 1:4, 9, 10).

Of: corrupt officials (Mic 3:11); priests and prophets (Eze 34:18; Zec 7:6); the opulent (Pr 11:26; M't 19:21, 22); monopolists (Pr 11:26; Isa 5:8); the self-indulgent (Ro 14:15; 2Ti 3:2-4).

Exemplified by: Cain (Ge 4:9); the children of Reuben (Nu 32:6); David's friends (Ps 38:11); the children of Israel (Hag 1:4; Mal 1:10); early Christians (Ph'p 2:20, 21).

See Liberality; Poor; Unselfishness.

SELF-RIGHTEOUSNESS. Assertive (Pr 20:6; M't 7:22, 23). Delusive (Pr 12:15; 16:2; 21:2; 28:26; Isa 28:20; 50:11; 64:6; Ho 12:8; M't 7:22, 23; 22:12, 13; Ga 6:3).

Admonitions against (De 9:4-6; 1Sa 2:9; Pr 27:2, 21; Jer 7:4; Hab 2:4; 2Co 1:9; 10:17, 18). Denounced (Job 12:2; Pr 25:14, 27; 26:12; 30:12, 13; Isa 5:21; 65:3-5; Jer 2:13, 22, 23, 34, 35; Jer 8:8; Eze 33:24-26; Am 6:13; M't 9:10-13; M'k 2:16; 8:15; Lu 5:30; 16:14, 15; 18:9-14; 22:12, 13; 23:29-31; Ro 11:19-21). Judgments against (Pr 14:12; Isa 28:17; 50:11; Jer 8:8; 49:4, 16; Zep 3:11).

Proverbs concerning (Pr 12:15; 14:12; 16:2; 20:6; 21:2; 25:14, 27; 26:12; 27:2, 21; 28:13, 26; 30:12, 13). Parables concerning (Lu 7:36-50; 10:25-37; 15:25-32; 18:9-14). Paul's instruction regarding (Ro 2:17-20; 3:27; 10:3; 11:19-21; 2Co 1:9; 10:17, 18; Ga 6:3).

Job accused of (Job 11:4; 32:1, 2; 33:8, 9; 35:2, 7, 8). Of the wicked (Ps 10:5, 6).

Instances of: Children of Israel (Nu 16:3; Ro 2:17-20; 10:3). Saul (1Sa 15:13-21). Pharisees (M't 9:10-13; M'k 2:16, 17; Lu 5:30; 7:39; 15:2; 16:14, 15; 18:9-14; Joh 9:28-41). The rich young ruler (M't 19:16-22; M'k 10:17-22; Lu 18:18-23). The lawyer (Lu 10:25-29). Church of Laodicea (Re 3:17, 18).

See Hypocrisy; Self-Exaltation.

SELF-WILL, stubbornness. Forbidden (2Ch 30:8; Ps 75:5). Proceeds from unbelief (2Ki 17:14); pride (Ne 9:16, 29); an evil heart (Jer 7:24). God knows (Isa 48:4). Exhibited in refusing to hearken to God (Pr 1:24); refusing to hearken to the messengers of God (1Sa 8:19; Jer 44:16; Zec 7:11); refusing to walk in the ways of God (Ne 9:17; Isa 42:24; Ps 78:10); refusing to hearken to parents (De 21:18, 19); refusing to receive correction (De 21:18; Jer 5:3; 7:28); rebelling against God (De 31:27; Ps 78:8); resisting the Holy Ghost (Ac 7:51); walking in the counsels of an evil heart (Jer 7:24, w Jer 23:17); hardening the neck (Ne 9:16); hardening the heart (2Ch 36:13); going backward and not forward (Jer 7:24); heinousness of (1Sa 15:23).

Ministers should be without (Tit 1:7); warn their people against (Heb 3:7-12); pray that their people may be forgiven for (Ex 34:9; De 9:27). Characteristic of the wicked (Pr 7:11; 2Pe 2:10). The wicked cease not from (J'g 2:19). Punishment for (De 21:21; Pr 29:1).

Illustrated: Ps 32:9; Jer 31:18.

Exemplified: Simeon and Levi (Ge 49:6). Israelites (Ex 32:9; De 9:6, 13). Saul (1Sa 15:19-23). David (2Sa 24:4). Josiah (2Ch 35:22). Zedekiah (2Ch 36:13).

See Obduracy.

SELVEDGE, the edge of each of the two curtains which covered the boards of the tabernacle (Ex 26:4; 36:11).

SEM (See Shem.)

SEMACHIAH (Jehovah has sustained), son of Shemaiah (1Ch 26:7).

SEMEI. Man who put away foreign wife (1 Esdras 9:33), probably same as Shimei in Ezra 10:33).

SEMEIN, ancestor of Christ (Lu 3:26).

SEMITES, a diverse group of ancient peoples whose languages are related, belonging to the Semitic family of languages; their world was the Fertile Crescent: principal Semitic peoples of ancient times: Akkadians—including Babylonians and Assyrians; Arameans; Canaanites—including Edomites, Ammonites, Moabites, Hebrews; Arabs; Ethiopians.

SENAAH, descendants of Senaah (sometimes spelled Hassenaah); returned with Zerubbabel (Ezr 2:35; Ne 7:38).

SENATE (council of elders). Chosen elders of the nation, vested with representative, judicial, and executive authority (Ex 4:29; 5:15, 19; 6:14-25; 12:21; Nu 11:16-30).

Closely associated with Moses and subsequent leaders (Ex 3:16-18; 4:29; 12:21; 17:5, 6; 18:12; 19:7; 24:1, 14; Nu 16:25; De 5:23; 27:1; 29:10; 31:9, 28; Jos 7:6; 8:10, 33; 23:2; 24:1; J'g 11:5-11; Ac 5:17, 18, 21). Made confession of sin in behalf of the nation (Le 4:15; 9:1).

Miscellany of Facts Relating to the Senate and Senators or Elders. Demands a king (1Sa 8:4-10, 19-22). Saul pleads to be honored before (1Sa 15:30). Chooses David as king (2Sa 3:17-21; 5:3; 1Ch 11:3). Closely associated with David (2Sa 12:17; 1Ch 15:25; 21:16). Joins Absalom in his usurpation (2Sa 17:4). David upbraids (2Sa 19:11). Assists Solomon at the dedication of the temple (1Ki 8:1-3; 2Ch 5:2-4). Counsels king Rehoboam (1Ki 12:6-8, 13). Counsels king Ahab (1Ki 20:7, 8). Josiah assembles, to hear the law of the Lord (2Ki 23:1; 2Ch 34:29, 31).

Legislates with Ezra in reforming certain marriages with the heathen (Ezr 10:8-14). Legislates in later times (M't 15:2, 7-9; M'k 7:1-13). Sits as a court (Jer 26:10-24). Constitutes, with priests and scribes, a court for the trial of both civil and ecclesiastical causes (M't 21:23; 26:3-5, 57-68; 27:1, 2; M'k 8:31; 14:53-65; 15:1; Lu 22:52-71; Ac 4:1-21; 6:12-15). Seeks counsel from prophets (Eze 8:1; 14:1; 20:1, 3). Corrupt (1Ki 21:8-14; Eze 8:11, 12; M't 26:14, 15; 27:3, 4).

A similar senate existed among the Egyptians (Ge 50:7); the Midianites and Moabites (Nu 22:4, 7 , 8); the Gibeonites (Jos 9:11).

SENATOR (See Occupations and Professions.)

SENEH, a rock protecting the garrison of the Philistines at Michmash (1Sa 14:4).

SENIR, Amorite name of Mt. Hermon (De 3:9; Song 4:8); also spelled "Shenir" in KJV.

SENNACHERIB (Sin [moon-god] **multiplied brothers),** king of Assyria (705-681 B. C.); son and successor of Sargon II; great builder and conqueror; invaded Judah in time of Hezekiah, but his army was miraculously destroyed (2Ki 18; 19; Isa 36; 37). Accounts of his campaigns recorded on clay prisms survive.

SENSUALITY (Ec 2:24; 8:15; 11:9). Of the glutton (Isa 22:13). Of the drunkard (Isa 56:12). Of the selfish rich (Lu 12:19, 20; 16:25).

Epicurean philosophy justifies (Isa 22:13; 1Co 15:32). Admonition against (Jas 5:5). Warning against (Jude 18, 19).

See Adultery; Drunkenness; Fornication; Gluttony; Lasciviousness; Self-Indulgence; Sodomy; also Abstinence, Total; Continence; Self-Denial; Temperance.

SENTRY (See Watchman.)

SENUAH, father of Judah, a governor of Jerusalem (Ne 11:9).

SEORIM, descendant of Aaron; head of fourth course of priests (1Ch 24:1-8).

SEPHAR, a mountain in Arabia (Ge 10:30).

SEPHARAD, an unknown place, to which the inhabitants of Jerusalem were exiled (Ob 20).

SEPHARVAIM, an Assyrian city, from which the king of Assyria colonized Samaria (2Ki 17:24, 31; 18:34; 19:13; Isa 36:19; 37:13).

SEPHARVITES, the people of Sepharvaim (2Ki 17:31).

SEPTUAGINT, translation of the OT into Greek prepared in Alexandria in second and third centuries B.C.

SEPULCHRE (See Burial.)

SEPULCHRE, CHURCH OF THE HOLY, the church professedly covering the tomb where Jesus was buried, built by Constantine in A. D. 325.

SERAH, called also Sarah. Daughter of Asher (Ge 46:17; Nu 26:46; 1Ch 7:30).

SERAIAH. 1. Called also Sheva, Shisha, and Shavsha. David's scribe (2Sa 8:17; 20:25; 1Ki 4:3; 1Ch 18:16).

2. Chief priest at time of taking of

Jerusalem (2Ki 25:18). Father of Ezra (Ezr 7:1). Slain by Nebuchadnezzar (2Ki 25:18-21; Jer 52:24-27).

3. An Israelitish captain who surrendered to Gedaliah (2Ki 25:23; Jer 40:8).

4. Son of Kenaz (1Ch 4:13, 14).

5. A Simeonite (1Ch 4:35).

6. A priest who returned from the Babylonian captivity (Ezr 2:2; Ne 12:1, 12). Called Azariah (Ne 7:7).

7. One who sealed the covenant with Nehemiah (Ne 10:2). Possibly identical with 6, above.

8. A ruler of the temple after the captivity (Ne 11:11).

9. Son of Azriel. Commanded by king Jehoiakim to seize Jeremiah (Jer 36:26).

10. A servant of Zedekiah (Jer 51:59, 61).

SERAPHIM (burning ones), celestial beings whom Isaiah saw standing before the enthroned Lord (Isa 6:2, 3, 6, 7).

SERAPIS, Graeco-Egyptian god widely worshipped in Mediterranean world; not mentioned in Bible.

SERED, son of Zebulun (Ge 46:14; Nu 26:26).

SERGEANT (See Occupations and Professions.)

SERGIUS PAULUS, a Roman deputy and convert of Paul (Ac 13:7-12).

SERMON ON THE MOUNT, the 1st of six extended discourses of Jesus given in the Gospel of Matthew (5-7). It contains Christ's instruction to His disciples for godly living in the present world.

SERPENT. Satan appears in the form of, to Eve (Ge 3:1-15; 2Co 11:3). Subtlety of (Ge 3:1; Ec 10:8; M't 10:16). Curse upon (Ge 3:14, 15; 49:17). Feeds upon the dust (Ge 3:14; Isa 65:25; Mic 7:17). Unfit for food (M't 7:10). Venom of (De 32:24, 33; Job 20:16; Ps 58:4; 140:3; Pr 23:31, 32; Ac 28:5, 6). The staff of Moses transformed into (Ex 4:3; 7:15). Fiery, sent as a plague upon the Israelites (Nu 21:6, 7; De 8:15; 1Co 10:9). The wound of, miraculously healed by looking upon the brazen, set up by Moses (Nu 21:8, 9). Charming of (Ps 58:4, 5; Ec 10:11; Jer 8:17). Mentioned in Solomon's riddle (Pr 30:19). Constriction of (Re 9:19). Sea serpent (Am 9:3). The seventy endued with power over (Lu 10:19). The apostles given power over (M'k 16:18; Ac 28:5).

Figurative: Isa 14:29; 30:6; 65:25.

SERUG. An ancestor of Abraham (Ge 11:20-23; 1Ch 1:26). Called Saruch (Lu 3:35).

SERVANT. Distinguished as bond servant (who was a slave) and hired servant.

Bond: Laws of Moses concerning (Ex 20:10; 21:1-11, 20, 21, 26, 27, 32; Le 19:20-22; 25:6, 10, 35-55; De 5:14; 15:12, 14, 18; 24:7). Manstealing forbidden (De 21:10-14; 24:7; 1Ti 1:10; Re 18:13). Fugitive, not to be returned to master (De 23:15, 16). David erroneously supposed to be a fugitive slave (1Sa 25:10). Instances of fugitive: Hagar, commanded by an angel to return to her mistress (Ge 16:9). Sought by Shimei (1Ki 2:39-41). Interceded for, by Paul (Ph'm 10-21).

Rights of those born to a master (Ge 14:14; 17:13, 27; Ex 21:4; Pr 29:21; Ec 2:7; Jer 2:14).

Bought and sold (Ge 17:13, 27; 37:28, 36; 39:17; Le 22:11; De 28:68; Es 7:4; Eze 27:13; Joe 3:6; Am 8:6; Re 18:13). Captives of war made (De 20:14; 21:10-14; 2Ki 5:2; 2Ch 28:8, 10; La 5:13); captive bond servants shared by priests and Levites (Nu 31:28-47). Thieves punished by being made (Ge 43:18; Ex 22:3). Defaulting debtors made (Le 25:39; M't 18:25). Children of defaulting debtors sold for (2Ki 4:1-7). Voluntary servitude of (Le 25:47; De 15:16, 17; Jos 9:11-21). Given as dowry (Ge 29:24, 29). Owned by priests (Le 22:11; M'k 14:66). Slaves owned slaves (2Sa 9:10). The master might marry or give in marriage (Ex 21:7-10; De 21:10-14; 1Ch 2:34, 35). Taken in concubinage (Ge 16:1, 2, 6; 30:3, 9). Used as soldiers by Abraham (Ge 14:14).

Must be circumcised (Ge 17:13, 27; Ex 12:44). Must enjoy religious privileges with the master's household (De 12:12, 18; 16:11, 14; 29:10, 11). Must have rest on the sabbath (Ex 20:10; 23:12; De 5:14). Equal status of, with other disciples of Jesus (1Co 7:21, 22; 12:13; Ga 3:28; Eph 6:8).

Social status of (M't 10:24, 25; Lu 17:7-9; 22:27; Joh 13:16).

Bond service threatened, as a national punishment, for disobedience of Israel (De 28:68; Joe 3:7, 8). Degrading influences of bondage exemplified by cowardice (Ex 14:11, 12; 16:3; J'g 5:16-18, 23).

Proverbs concerning (Pr 12:9; 13:17; 17:2; 19:10; 25:13; 26:6; 27:18, 27; 29:19, 21; 30:10, 21-23). Parables of (M't 24:45-51; Lu 12:35-48; 16:1-13).

Conspiracy by (See Conspiracy).

Cruelty to: Hagar (Ge 16:1-21; Ga 4:22-31); the Israelites (Ex 1:8-22; 2:1-4; 5:7-9; Ac 7:19, 34). Sick, abandoned (1Sa 30:13). Admonitions against (Jer 22:13).

Instances of cruelty to: Joseph (Ge 37:26-28, 36); Israelites (Ex 1:10-22; 5:7-14; De 6:12, 21). Gibeonites (Jos 9:22-27). Canaanites (1Ki 9:21). Jews in Babylon (2Ch 36:20; Es 1:1-10). Emancipation of (2Ch 36:23; Ezr 1:1-4).

Duties of: To be faithful (1Co 4:2); obedient (M't 8:9; Eph 6:5-8; Col 3:22-25; Tit 2:9, 10; 1Pe 2:18-20). To honor masters (Mal 1:6; 1Ti 6:1, 2). Warning to (Zep 1:9).

Figurative (Le 25:42, 55; Ps 116:16; Isa 52:3; M't 24:45-51; Lu 12:35-48; 16:1-13; 17:7-9; Joh 8:32-35; Ro 6:16-22; 1Co 4:1, 2; 7:21-23; Ga 5:13; 1Pe 2:16; 2Pe 2:19; Re 7:3).

Good, Instances of: Joseph (Ge 39:2-20; 41:9-57; Ac 7:10); Elisha (2Ki 2:1-6). Servants of Abraham (Ge 24); of Boaz (Ru 2:4); of Jonathan (1Sa 14:7); of Abigail (1Sa 25:14-17); of David (2Sa 12:18; 15:15, 21); of Ziba (2Sa 9); of Naaman (2Ki 5:2, 3, 13); of Nehemiah (Ne 4:16, 23); of centurion (M't 8:9); of Cornelius (Ac 10:7); Onesimus (Ph'm 11). Servants in the parable of the pounds and talents (M't 25:14-23; Lu 19:12-19).

Kindness to (Ps 123:2; Pr 29:21). Enjoined (Le 25:43; Eph 6:9). Exemplified by Job (Job 19:15, 16; 31:13, 14); by Boaz (Ru 2:4); by the centurion (M't 8:8-13; Lu 7:2-10); by Paul (Ph'm 1-21). Redeemed (Ne 5:8). Emancipated (2Ch 36:23; Ezr 1:1-4; Jer 34:8-22; Ac 6:9; 1Co 7:21). Freed men called libertines (Ac 6:9). Tact in management of (Ec 7:21).

Wicked and Unfaithful, Instances of: Jeroboam (1Ki 11:26); Gehazi (2Ki 5:20-27); Zimri (1Ki 16:9, 10; 2Ki 9:31); Onesimus (Ph'm 11).

Of Abraham and Lot (Ge 13:7). Of Abimelech (Ge 21:25). Of Ziba (2Sa 16:1-4, w 2Sa 19:26, 27). Of Absalom (2Sa 13:28, 29; 14:30). Of Shimei (1Ki 2:39). Of Joash (2Ki 12:19-21). Of Amon (2Ki 21:23). Of Job (Job 19:15, 16). In the parable of the talents and pounds (M't 25:24-30; Lu 19:20-26). In the parable of the vineyard (M't 21:33-41; M'k 12:1-9).

See Employee; Employer; Master.

Hired: Jacob (Ge 29:15; 30:26); reemployed (Ge 30:27-34; 31:6, 7, 41). Parable of laborers for a vineyard (M't 20:1-15). Of the father of the prodigal son (Lu 15:17, 19); of the prodigal son (Lu 15:5-19).

Kindness to (Ru 2:4). Treatment of, more considerable than that accorded slaves (Le 25:53). Await employment in marketplace (M't 20:1-3).

Mercenary (Job 7:2). Unfaithful (Joh 10:12, 13).

Rights of, to: Receive wages (M't 10:10; Lu 10:7; Ro 4:4; 1Ti 5:18; Jas 5:4). Daily payment of wages (Le 19:13; De 24:15). Share in spontaneous products of land in Sabbatic year (Le 25:6). Wages of, paid in portion of flocks or products (Ge 30:31, 32; 2Ch 2:10); or in money (M't 20:2, 9, 10).

Oppression of, forbidden (De 24:14; Col 4:1).

Oppressors of, punished (Mal 3:5).

See Masters; Wages.

SERVANT OF JEHOVAH, agent of the Lord like patriarchs (Ex 32:13); Moses (Nu 12:7f), prophets (Zec 1:6), and others. Chiefly used as a title for the Messiah in Isaiah 40-66. NT applies the Servant-passages to Christ (Isa 42:1-4; M't 12:16-21).

SERVICE, refers to all sorts of work from the most inferior and menial to the most honored and exalted (Le 23:7f; Nu 3:6ff).

SERVITOR (See Occupations and Professions.)

SETH, Son of Adam (Ge 4:25, 26; 5:3, 8; 1Ch 1:1; Lu 3:38). Called Sheth (1Ch 1:1).

SETHUR (hidden), one of the twelve spies (Nu 13:13).

SEVEN. Interesting facts concerning the number.

Days: Week consists of (Ge 2:3; Ex 20:11; De 5:13, 14). Noah in the ark before the flood (Ge 7:4, 10); remains in the ark after sending forth the dove (Ge 8:10, 12). Mourning for Jacob lasted (Ge 50:10); of Job (Job 2:13). The plague of bloody waters in Egypt lasted (Ex 7:25). The Israelites compassed Jericho (Jos 6:4). The passover lasted (Ex 12:15). Saul directed by Samuel to tarry at Gilgal, awaiting the prophet's command (1Sa 10:8; 13:8). The elders of Jabesh-gilead ask for a truce of (1Sa 11:3). Dedication of the temple lasted double (1Ki 8:65). Ezekiel sits by the river Chebar in astonishment (Eze 3:15). The feast of tabernacles lasted (Le 23:34, 42). Consecration of priests and altars lasted (Ex 29:30, 35; Eze 43:25, 26). Defilements lasted (Le 12:2; 13:4). Fasts of (1Sa 31:13; 2Sa 12:16, 18, 22). The firstborn of flocks and sheep shall remain with mother, before being offered (Ex 22:30). The feast of Ahasuerus continued (Es 1:5). Paul tarries at Tyre (Ac 21:4); at Puteoli (Ac 28:14).

Weeks: In Daniel's vision concerning the coming of the Messiah (Da 9:25). Ten times (Da 9:24). The period between the Passover and the Pentecost (Le 23:15).

Months: Holy convocations in the seventh month (Le 23:24-44; Nu 29; Eze 45:25).

Years: Jacob serves for each of his wives (Ge 29:15-30). Of plenty (Ge 41:1-32, 53). Famine lasted in Egypt (Ge 41:1-32, 54-56); in Canaan (2Sa 24:13; 2Ki 8:1). Insanity of Nebuchadnezzar (Da 4:32). Seven times, the period between the jubilees (Le 25:8).

Miscellany of Sevens: Of clean beasts taken into the ark (Ge 7:2). Abraham gives Abimelech seven lambs (Ge 21:28). Rams and bullocks to the number of, required in sacrifices (Le 23:18; Nu 23:1; 29:32; 1Ch 15:26; Eze 45:23). Blood sprinkling seven times (Le 4:6; 14:7); oil (14:16). Seven kine and seven ears of corn in Pharaoh's vision (Ge 41:2-7). The Israelites compassed Jericho seven times, on the seventh day sounding seven trumpets (Jos 6:4). Elisha's servant looked seven times for appearance of rain (1Ki 18:43). Naaman required to wash in Jordan seven times (2Ki 5:10). Seven steps in the temple seen in Ezekiel's vision (Eze 40:22, 26). The heat of Nebuchadnezzar's furnace intensified sevenfold (Da 3:19). The light of the sun intensified sevenfold (Isa 30:26). The threatened sevenfold punishment of Israel (Le 26:18-21). Silver purified seven times (Ps 12:6). Worshiping seven times a day (Ps 119:164). Seven chamberlains at the court of Ahasuerus (Es 1:10); seven princes (Es 1:14). Seven counsellors at the court of Artaxerxes (Ezr 7:14). Seven maidens given to Esther (Es 2:9). Symbolical of many sons (Ru 4:15; 1Sa 2:5; Jer 15:9); of liberality (Ec 11:1, 2). Seven magi (Pr 26:16). Seven women shall seek polygamous marriage (Isa 4:1). Seven shepherds to be sent forth against Assyria (Mic 5:5, 6). Seven lamps and pipes (Zec 4:2). Seven deacons in the apostolic church (Ac 6:3). Seven churches in Asia (Re 1:4, 20). Seven seals (Re 5:1). Seven thunders (Re 10:3). Seven heads and seven crowns (Re 12:3; 13:1; 17:9). Seven kings (Re 17:10). Seven stars (Re 1:16, 20; 3:1; Am 5:8). Seven spirits (Re 1:4; 3:1; 4:5; 5:6). Seven eyes of the Lord (Zec 3:9; 4:10; Re 5:6). Seven golden candlesticks (Re 1:12). Seven angels with seven trumpets (Re 8:2). Seven plagues (Re 15:1). Seven horns and seven eyes (Re 5:6). Seven angels with seven plagues (Re 15:6). Seven golden vials (Re 15:7). Scarlet colored beast having seven heads (Re 17:3, 7).

SEVEN WORDS FROM THE CROSS, the seven sentences spoken by Jesus from the cross. No one Gospel gives them all.

Father, forgive them . . . (Lu 23:34). Today . . . in paradise (Lu 23:43). Woman, behold . . . (Joh 19:26-27). My God . . . (M't 27:46, 47; M'k 15:34-36). I thirst (Joh 19:28). It is finished (Joh 19:30). Father, into thy hands . . . (M't 27:50; M'k 15:37).

SEVENEH, Egyptian town located on first cataract of Nile, known today as Aswan (Eze 29:10; 30:6 ASV).

SEVENTY. The senate of the Israelites composed of seventy elders (Ex 24:1, 9; Nu 11:16, 24, 25). Seventy disciples sent forth by Jesus (Lu 10:1-17). The Jews in captivity in Babylon seventy years (Jer 25:11, 12; 29:10; Da 9:2; Zec 1:12; 7:5). See Israel.

SEVENTY, THE, disciples sent on preaching mission by Jesus (Lu 10:1).

SEVENTY WEEKS, THE, name applied to period of time (probably 490 years) referred to in Da 9:24-27.
SHAALABBIN (haunt of foxes), town between Ir-shemesh and Aijalon (Jos 19:42).
SHAALBIM, town, probably in central Palestine, won by Danites from Amorites (J'g 1:35).
SHAALBONITE (See Shaalbim.)
SHAAPH. 1. Son of Jahdai (1Ch 2:47).
2. Son of Caleb (1Ch 2:49).
SHAARAIM (two gates). 1. Town in Judah (Jos 15:36; 1Sa 17:52).
2. Town in Simeon (1Ch 4:31); "Sharuhen" in Jos 19:6 and "Shilhim" in Jos 15:32.
SHAASHGAZ, a chamberlain of Ahasuerus (Es 2:14).
SHABBETHAI (Sabbath-born). 1. A Levite, assistant to Ezra (Ezr 10:15).
2. An expounder of the Law (Ne 8:7).
3. A chief Levite, attendant of the temple (Ne 11:16).
SHACHIA, son of Shaharaim (1Ch 8:10).
SHADDAI, name (exact meaning unknown) for God often found in OT (Ge 17:1; 28:3; 43:14; Nu 24:4, 16; Ps 68:14).
SHADOW, used literally, figuratively (1Ch 29:15; Ps 17:8; Isa 30:3), theologically (Col 2:17; Heb 8:5; 10:1).
SHADOW OF DEATH (Job 12:22; 16:16; Ps 23:4; 44:19; 107:10; M't 4:16).
SHADRACH, called also Hananiah. A Hebrew captive in Babylon (Da 1; 2:17, 49; 3).
SHAFT, shank of the golden candelabrum (Ex 25:31); used in Messianic sense in Isa 49:2.
SHAGE (wandering), father of Jonathan, one of David's guard (1Ch 11:34).
SHAHARAIM (double dawn), a Benjamite (1Ch 8:8).
SHAHAZIMAH (toward the heights), a city in Issachar (Jos 19:22).
SHALEM (safe), town near Shechem (Ge 33:18).
SHALIM, LAND OF, region probably near N boundary of Benjamin's territory (1Sa 9:4).
SHALISHA (a third part), a district bordering on Mount Ephraim (1Sa 9:4).
SHALLECHETH, one of the gates of the temple (1Ch 26:16).
SHALLUM (recompense). 1. Son of Naphtali (1Ch 7:13), "Shillem" in Ge 46:24 and Nu 26:48f.
2. Son of Shaul (1Ch 4:25).
3. Son of Sisamai (1Ch 2:40f).
4. Son of Kore; chief of gatekeepers (1Ch 9:17, 19, 31; Ne 7:45), "Meshelemiah" in 1Ch 26:1 and "Shelemiah" in 1Ch 26:14.
5. Son of Zadok (1Ch 6:12f), "Meshullam" in 1Ch 9:11 and Ne 11:11.
6. King of Israel (2Ki 15:10-15).
7. Father of Jehizkiah (2Ch 28:12).
8. Husband of the prophetess Huldah (2Ki 22:14).
9. King of Judah (1Ch 3:15), better known as Jehoahaz II.
10. Uncle of Jeremiah (Jer 32:7).
11. Father of Maaseiah (Jer 35:4).
12. Levite who divorced foreign wife (Ezr 10:24).
13. Man who divorced foreign wife (Ezr 10:42).
14. Ruler who helped build Jerusalem walls (Ne 3:12).
SHALLUN (recompense), a Jew who repaired a gate of Jerusalem (Ne 3:15).
SHALMAI, ancestor of Nethinim that returned with Zerubbabel (Ezr 2:46; Ne 7:48).
SHALMAN, either contraction of Shalmaneser or the Moabite king Salmanu (Ho 10:14).
SHALMANESER (the god Shulman is chief), title of five Assyrian kings, of whom one is mentioned in OT, another refers to an Israelitish king. 1. Shalmaneser III (859-824 B. C.); son of Ashurnasirpal; inscription left by him says that he opposed Benhadad of Damascus and Ahab of Israel, and made Israel tributary.
2. Shalmaneser V (726-722 B. C.), son of Tiglath-pileser; received tribute from Hoshea; besieged Samaria and carried N tribes into captivity (2Ki 17:3; 18:9), "Shalman" in Ho 10:14).
SHAMA (God has heard), one of David's heroes (1Ch 11:44).
SHAMARIAH, son of Rehoboam (2Ch 11:19).
SHAMBLES, meat market (1Co 10:25).
SHAME. Jesus ashamed of those who deny him (M'k 8:38; Lu 9:26). Of Adam and Eve (Ge 3:10). Destitute of, the Israelites when they worshiped the gold-

en calf (Ex 32:25); the unjust (Zep 3:5). Of the cross (Heb 12:2).

SHAMED (destruction), son of Elpaal (1Ch 8:12).

SHAMER (guard). 1. Father of Bani (1Ch 6:46).

2. Son of Heber; head of Asherite clan (1Ch 7:34).

SHAMELESSNESS (Jer 6:15; 8:12; Zep 3:5).

SHAMGAR, son of Anath; judge; slew 600 Philistines with an oxgoad (J'g 3:31; 5:6).

SHAMHUTH (desolation), David's 5th divisional commander of the army (1Ch 27:8).

SHAMIR (sharp point). 1. Town in Judah c. 13 miles SW of Hebron (Jos 15:48).

2. Town in Ephraim; home of Tola (J'g 10:1f).

3. Temple attendant (1Ch 24:24).

SHAMMA (astonishment), son of Zophah, an Asherite (1Ch 7:37).

SHAMMAH (waste). 1. Grandson of Esau (Ge 36:13, 17; 1Ch 1:37).

2. Brother of David (1Sa 16:9; 17:13); also called Shimea (1Ch 20:7), Shimeah (2Sa 13:3, 32), and Shimei (2Sa 21:21).

3. One of David's mighty men (2Sa 23:11), "Shage" in 1Ch 11:34.

4. Another of David's mighty men (2Sa 23:33); also called Shammoth (1Ch 11:27) and Shamhuth (1Ch 27:8). May be same as 3.

SHAMMAI (Jehovah has heard). 1. Son of Onam (1Ch 2:28, 32).

2. Father of Maon (1Ch 2:44, 45).

3. Son of Ezra (1Ch 4:17).

SHAMMOTH (desolation), one of David's mighty men (1Ch 11:27); apparently same as Shammah (2Sa 23:25) and Shamhuth (1Ch 27:8).

SHAMMUA (renowned). 1. Son of Zaccur; Reubenite spy (Nu 13:4).

2. Son of David and Bath-sheba (2Sa 5:14, KJV has Shammuah; 1Ch 14:4).

3. Levite; father of Abda (Ne 11:17), "Shemaiah" in 1Ch 9:16.

4. Priest (1Ch 24:14; Ne 12:6, 18), "Bilgai" in Ne 10:8.

SHAMMUAH, son of David (2Sa 5:14). Called Shimea (1Ch 3:5); Shammua (1Ch 14:4).

SHAMSHERAI (sunlike), son of Jeroham (1Ch 8:26).

SHAPHAM, chief of Gad (1Ch 5:12).

SHAPHAN (rock rabbit). 1. A scribe of king Josiah (2Ki 22:3-14; 2Ch 34:8-20). Father of Gemariah (Jer 36:10-12).

2. Father of Ahikam and grandfather of Gedaliah (2Ki 22:12; 25:22; 2Ch 34:20; Jer 26:24; 39:14; 40:5, 9, 11; 41:2; 43:6).

3. Father of Elasah (Jer 29:3).

4. Father of Jaazaniah (Eze 8:11).

SHAPHAT (he has judged). 1. Simeonite spy (Nu 13:5).

2. Father of Elisha the prophet (1Ki 19:16, 19).

3. Gadite chief in Bashan (1Ch 5:12).

4. Herdsman of David (1Ch 27:29).

5. Son of Shemaiah (1Ch 3:22).

SHAPHER, a mountain, camping place of the Israelites in the desert (Nu 33:23, 24).

SHARAI, a descendant of Bani who put away his Gentile wife (Ezr 10:40).

SHARAIM (two gates), town in Judah (Jos 15:36).

SHARAR (firm), father of one of David's mighty men (2Sa 23:33), "Sacar" in 1Ch 11:35.

SHARE, plowshare (1Sa 13:20).

SHAREZER (protect the king). 1. Son of Assyrian king Sennacherib (2Ki 19:37; Isa 37:38).

2. Contemporary of Zechariah the prophet (Zec 7:2, "Sherezer" in KJV).

SHARON. 1. Palestine coastal plain between Joppa and Mount Carmel (1Ch 27:29; Isa 35:2).

2. Suburbs of Sharon possessed by tribe of Gad (1Ch 5:16).

3. Lassharon, q.v. (Jos 12:18).

4. Figurative of fruitfulness, glory, peace (Isa 35:2; 65:10).

5. Called Saron (Ac 9:35).

SHARONITE, man of Sharon (1Ch 27:29).

SHARUHEN, Simonite town in Judah's territory (Jos 19:6). Apparently the same as Silhim (Jos 15:32) and Shaarim (1Ch 4:31). Now identified with Tell el-Farah.

SHASHAI (noble), a descendant of Bani, who put away his Gentile wife (Ezı 10:40).

SHASHAK, a Benjamite (1Ch 8:14, 25).

SHAUL (asked of Jehovah). 1. Son of Simeon (Ge 46:10; Ex 6:15; Nu 26:13; 1Ch 4:24).

2. An ancient king of Edom (1Ch

1:48, 49). Called Saul (Ge 36:37).

3. Son of Uzziah (1Ch 6:24).

SHAVEH, VALLEY OF (plain), valley where, after rescuing his nephew Lot, Abraham met the king of Sodom (Ge 14:17).

SHAVEH-KIRIATHAIM (plain of Kiriathaim), plain where Chedorlaomer smote the Emim (Ge 14:5), probably on E of Dead Sea (Nu 32:37).

SHAVING, priests and Nazirites were prohibited from shaving (Le 21:5; Nu 6:5); Hebrews generally wore beards. Shaving was often done for religious reasons, as an act of contrition (Job 1:20), consecration for Levites (Nu 6:9; 8:7), cleansing for lepers (Le 14:8f; 13:32ff); also as an act of contempt (2Sa 10:4).

SHAVSHA, David's secretary of state (1Ch 18:16), "Shisha" in 1Ki 4:3; "Seraiah" in 2Sa 8:17; "Sheva" in 2Sa 20:25.

SHEAF, a handful of grain left behind by the reaper, gathered and bound by women and children, and later taken to the threshing-floor (Jer 9:22; Ru 2:7, 15). Some sheaves were left behind for the poor (De 24:19).

SHEAL (asking), a descendant of Bani, who put away his Gentile wife (Ezr 10:29).

SHEALTIEL (I have asked God), called also Salathiel. Father of Zerubbabel and ancestor of Jesus (1Ch 3:17; Ezr 3:2, 8; 5:2; Ne 12:1; Hag 1:1, 12, 14; 2:2, 23; M't 1:12; Lu 3:27).

SHEARIAH (Jehovah esteems), son of Azel; descendant of Jonathan (1Ch 8:38; 9:44).

SHEARING HOUSE (binding house of the shepherds), place between Jezreel and Samaria where Jehu slaughtered 42 members of the royal house of Ahaziah, king of Judah (2Ki 10:12-14).

SHEAR-JASHUB (remnant shall return), symbolic name of Isaiah's oldest son (Isa 7:3; 8:18).

SHEBA (seven, an oath). 1. Son of Raamah (Ge 10:7; 1Ch 1:9).

2. Son of Joktan (Ge 10:28; 1Ch 1:22).

3. Son of Jokshan (Ge 25:3; 1Ch 1:32).

4. A Benjamite who led an insurrection against David (2Sa 20).

5. A Gadite (1Ch 5:13).

6. A city of Simeon (Jos 19:2).

7. Queen of, visits Solomon (1Ki 10:1-13; 2Ch 9:1-12). Kings of, bring gifts to Solomon (Ps 72:10). Rich in gold (Ps 72:15); incense (Jer 6:20). Merchandise of (Eze 27:22, 23; 38:13). Prophecies concerning the people of, coming into the kingdom of Messiah (Isa 60:6).

See Sabeans.

SHEBAH (seven, oath), name of well dug by Isaac's servants. Town of Beersheba named from this well (Ge 26:31-33).

SHEBAM (sweet smell), town in Reuben (Nu 32:3), called "Shibmah" in Nu 32:38; E of Dead Sea, but exact location unknown.

SHEBANIAH. 1. Trumpeter priest (1Ch 15:24).

2. Levite who signed covenant with Nehemiah (Ne 9:4, 5; 10:10).

3. Another Levite who signed covenant (Ne 10:12).

4. Priest who signed covenant (Ne 10:4).

5. Priest (Ne 12:14).

SHEBARIM (breaches), place near Ai to which Israelite soldiers were chased (Jos 7:5).

SHEBAT (See Sebat.)

SHEBER, son of Caleb (not famous spy) (1Ch 2:48).

SHEBNA. 1. A scribe of Hezekiah (2Ki 18:18, 26, 37; 19:2; Isa 36:3, 11, 22; 37:2).

2. An official of the king (Isa 22:15-19).

SHEBUEL. 1. Son of Gershom (1Ch 23:16; 26:24). Called Shubael (1Ch 24:20).

2. A singer, son of Heman (1Ch 25:4). Called Shubael (1Ch 25:20).

SHECANIAH, SHECHANIAH (dweller with Jehovah). 1. Head of tenth course of priests in days of David (1Ch 24:11).

2. Levite (2Ch 31:15).

3. Descendant of David (1Ch 3:21, 22).

4. Man who returned with Ezra (Ezr 8:3).

5. Another such man (Ezr 8:5).

6. Man who proposed to Ezra that foreign wives be put away (Ezr 10:2-4).

7. Keeper of E gate of Jerusalem in time of Nehemiah (Ne 3:29).

8. Father-in-law of Tobiah the foe of Nehemiah (Ne 6:18).

9. Chief priest who returned with Zerubbabel (Ne 12:3).

SHECHEM (shoulder). 1. Called also Sichem and Sychem, a district in the central part of the land of Caanan. Abraham dwells in (Ge 12:6). Jacob buys a piece of ground in, and erects an altar (Ge 33:18-20). The flocks and herds of Jacob kept in (Ge 37:12-14). Joseph buried in (Jos 24:32). Jacob buried in (Ac 7:16, w Ge 50:13).

2. Called also Sychar, a city of refuge in Mount Ephraim (Jos 20:7; 21:21; J'g 21:19). Joshua assembled the tribes of Israel at, with all their elders, chiefs, and judges, and presented them before the Lord (Jos 24:1-28). Joshua buried at (Jos 24:30-32). Abimelech made king at (J'g 8:31; 9). Rehoboam crowned at (1Ki 12:1). Destroyed by Abimelech (J'g 9:45); rebuilt by Jeroboam (1Ki 12:25). Men of, slain by Ishmael (Jer 41:5). Jesus visits; disciples made in (Joh 4:1-42).

3. Son of Hamor; seduces Jacob's daughter; slain by Jacob's sons (Ge 33:19; 34; Jos 24:32; J'g 9:28). Called Sychem (Ac 7:16).

4. Ancestor of the Shechemites (Nu 26:31; Jos 17:2).

5. Son of Shemidah (1Ch 7:19).

SHECHEMITES, descendants of Shechem (Nu 26:31).

SHECHINAH (See Shekinah.)

SHEDEUR (caster forth of light). Reubenite; father of Elizur (Nu 1:5; 2:10; 7:30; 10:18).

SHEEP. Offered in sacrifice, by Abel (Ge 4:4); by Noah (Ge 8:20); by Abraham (Ge 22:13). See Offerings. Required in the Mosaic offerings (see Offerings). The land of Bashan adapted to the raising of (De 32:14); Bozrah (Mic 2:12); Kedar (Eze 27:21); Nebaioth (Isa 60:7); Sharon (Isa 65:10). Jacob's management of (Ge 30:32-40). Milk of, used for food (De 32:14). Shearing of (Ge 31:19; 38:12-17; Isa 53:7); feasting at the time of shearing (1Sa 25:11, 36; 2Sa 13:23). First fleece of, belonged to priests and Levites (De 18:4). Tribute paid in (2Ki 3:4; 1Ch 5:21; 2Ch 17:11).

Figurative: 1Ch 21:17; Ps 74:1; Jer 13:20. Of backsliders (Jer 50:6). Of lost sinners (M't 9:36; 10:6). Of the righteous (Jer 50:17; Eze 34; M't 26:31; M'k 14:27; Joh 10:1-16). Of the defenselessness of ministers (M't 10:16).

Parable of the lost (M't 18:11-13; Lu 15:4-7).

SHEEPCOTE, SHEEPFOLD, enclosure for protection of sheep (Nu 32:16; J'g 5:16; 1Sa 24:3).

SHEEP GATE, an ancient gate of Jerusalem (Ne 3:1, 32; 12:39; Joh 5:2).

SHEEP MARKET, RV and RSV have "sheep gate" (Joh 5:2).

SHEEPMASTER (See Occupations and Professions.)

SHEEP-SHEARER (See Occupations and Professions.)

SHEERAH (See Sherah.)

SHEET, large piece of linen (Ac 10:11; 11:5).

SHEHARIAH, son of Jeroham; Benjamite (1Ch 8:26).

SHEKEL. A weight, equal to twenty gerahs (Ex 30:13; Nu 3:47; Eze 45:12). Used to weigh silver (Jos 7:21; J'g 8:26; 17:2, 3). Fractions of, used in currency (Ex 30:13; 1Sa 9:8; Ne 10:32). Used to weigh gold (Ge 24:22; Nu 7:14, 20-86; Jos 7:21; 1Ki 10:16); cinnamon (Ex 30:23); hair (2Sa 14:26); iron (1Sa 17:7); myrrh (Ex 30:23); rations (Eze 4:10). Fines paid in (De 22:19, 29). Fees paid in (1Sa 9:8). Sanctuary revenues paid in (Ex 30:13; Ne 10:32). Of different standards: Of the sanctuary (Ex 30:13); of the king's weight (2Sa 14:26). Corrupted (Am 8:5).

SHEKINAH (dwelling of God), the visible sign of God's presence on the ark of testimony in the Holy of holies (Ex 25:22; Le 16:2; 2Sa 6:2; 2Ki 19:14, 15; Ps 80:1; Isa 37:16; Eze 9:3; 10:18; Heb 9:5).

SHELAH (sprout). 1. Son of Judah (Ge 38:5, 11, 14, 26; 46:12; Nu 26:20; 1Ch 2:3; 4:21).

2. See Salah.

SHELANITES. Descendants of Shelah (Nu 26:20). Apparently called Shilonites (1Ch 9:5).

SHELEMIAH (friend of Jehovah). 1. Doorkeeper of tabernacle (1Ch 26:14); in previous verses of this chapter he is called "Meshelemiah."

2. Son of Cushi (Jer 36:14).

3. Man sent to arrest Jeremiah (Jer 36:26).
4. Father of man whom Zedekiah sent to Jeremiah to ask his prayers (Jer 37:3).
5. Son of Hananiah (Jer 37:13).
6. Two men who divorced foreign wives (Ezr 10:39, 41).
7. Father of Hananiah (Ne 3:30).
8. Priest; treasurer (Ne 13:13).

SHELEPH, son of Joktan (Ge 10:26; 1Ch 1:20).

SHELESH, son of Helem (1Ch 7:35).

SHELOMI (at peace), father of Ahihud, Asherite prince (Nu 34:27).

SHELOMITH, SHELOMOTH (peaceful). 1. Daughter of Dibri; her son was killed for blasphemy (Le 24:10-12, 23).
2. Cousin of Moses (1Ch 23:18).
3. Gershonite Levite (1Ch 23:9).
4. Descendant of Moses (1Ch 26:25).
5. Child of Rehoboam (2Ch 11:20).
6. Daughter of Zerubbabel (1Ch 3:19).
7. Ancestor of a family that returned with Ezra (Ezr 8:10).

SHELUMIEL (God is peace), son of Zurishaddai, and leader of Simeon in time of Moses (Nu 1:6; 2:12; 7:36, 41; 10:19).

SHEM (name, fame), son of Noah. Preserved in the ark (Ge 5:32; 6:10; 7:13; 9:18; 1Ch 1:4). His filial conduct (Ge 9:23-27). Descendants of (Ge 10:1, 21-31; 11:10-29; 1Ch 1:17-54). Called Sem (Lu 3:36).

SHEMA (fame, rumor). 1. Town in S Judah (Jos 15:26).
2. Son of Hebron (1Ch 2:44).
3. Son of Joel (1Ch 5:8).
4. Benjamite (1Ch 8:13).
5. Assistant of Ezra (Ne 8:4).
6. Hebrew name for De 6:4.

SHEMAAH (fame), father of Ahiezer and Joash, soldiers of David (1Ch 12:3).

SHEMAIAH (Jehovah has heard). 1. Simeonite prince (1Ch 4:37).
2. Reubenite (1Ch 5:4), possibly same as Shema of verse 8.
3. Chief Levite (1Ch 15:8, 11).
4. Levite scribe (1Ch 24:6).
5. Son of Obed-edom (1Ch 26:4, 6, 7).
6. Prophet who forbade Rehoboam to war against Israel (1Ki 12:22-24).
7. Descendant of David (1Ch 3:22).
8. Merarite Levite (1Ch 9:14; Ne 12:18).
9. Levite who returned from exile (1Ch 9:16). "Shammua" in Ne 11:17.
10. Levite (2Ch 17:8).
11. Levite who cleansed temple (2Ch 29:14).
12. Levite who assisted in distribution of food (2Ch 31:15).
13. Levite in days of Josiah (2Ch 35:9).
14. Levite who returned with Ezra (Ezr 8:13).
15. One whom Ezra sent back for ministers (Ezr 8:16), possibly same as preceding.
16. Priest who divorced foreign wife (Ezr 10:21).
17. Another priest who did the same thing (Ezr 10:31).
18-23. Men who played various roles in Nehemiah's rebuilding and dedication of the Jerusalem wall (Ne 3:29; 6:10ff; 10:8; 12:6, 18, 34, 35, 36, 42).
24. Father of Uriah the prophet (Jer 26:20).
25. False prophet who fought against Jeremiah (Jer 29:24-32).
26. Father of Delaiah, prince in days of Jehoiakim (Jer 36:12).

SHEMARIAH (Jehovah keeps). 1. One of David's mighty men (1Ch 12:5).
2. Son of Rehoboam, king of Judah (2Ch 11:19).
3. Man who put away foreign wife (Ezr 10:32).
4. Another man who put away foreign wife (Ezr 10:41).

SHEMEBER, king of Zeboiim, a city near the Dead Sea (Ge 14:2).

SHEMER (guard). 1. Asherite (1Ch 7:34).
2. Merarite Levite (1Ch 7:34).
3. Man who sold hill to Omri, king of Israel (1Ki 16:24).

SHEMIDA, called also Shemidah. Son of Gilead (Nu 26:32; Jos 17:2; 1Ch 7:19).

SHEMIDAITES, family descended from Shemida (Nu 26:32; Jos 17:2).

SHEMINTH, musical term of uncertain meaning possibly "octave" (1Ch 15:21; Ps 6; 12, titles).

SHEMIRAMOTH. 1. A Levite musician (1Ch 15:18, 20; 16:5).
2. A Levite sent by Jehoshaphat to

instruct the people in the law (2Ch 17:8).

SHEMUEL (name of God). 1. Simeonite (Nu 34:20).

2. Samuel; spelled "Shemuel" in KJV of 1Ch 6:33.

3. Issachar chief (1Ch 7:2).

SHEN (pointed rock), unidentified site near which Samuel erected the stone "Ebenezer" (1Sa 7:12).

SHENAZAR, son of Jeconiah (1Ch 3:18).

SHENIR, called also Senir. Amorite name of Mount Hermon (De 3:9; 1Ch 5:23; Song 4:8; Eze 27:5).

SHEOL, the OT name for the place of departed souls, corresponding to the NT word "Hades." When translated "hell" it refers to the place of punishment, but when translated "grave" the reference is to the souls of good men. It often means the place or state of the soul between death and resurrection. The clearest indication of different conditions in Sheol is in Christ's parable of the rich man and Lazarus (Lu 16:19-31).

SHEPHAM (nakedness), place in NE of Canaan, near Sea of Galilee (Nu 34:10, 11).

SHEPHATIAH (Jehovah is judge). 1. Son of David (2Sa 3:4).

2. Son of Reuel (1Ch 9:8).

3. One of David's mighty men (1Ch 12:5).

4. Simeonite prince (1Ch 27:16).

5. Son of King Jehoshaphat (2Ch 21:2).

6. Founder of family which returned with Zerubbabel (Ezr 2:4).

7. One of children of Solomon's servants whose descendants returned with Zerubbabel (Ezr 2:57).

8. One whose descendants returned with Ezra (Ezr 8:8). May be same as the preceding.

9. Son of Mahalaleel (Ne 11:4).

10. Prince who wanted Jeremiah to be put to death for prophesying (Jer 38:1).

SHEPHELAH, THE (low country), hilly country between mountains of Judah and the maritime plain S of the plain of Sharon, extending through the country of Philistia along the Mediterranean (Jos 12:8).

SHEPHER (See Shapher.)

SHEPHERD. One who cares for flocks (Ge 31:38-40; Ps 78:52, 53; Jer 31:10; Am 3:12; Lu 2:8). David the, defends his flock against a lion and a bear (1Sa 17:34, 35). Causes the flock to rest (Ps 23:2; Song 1:7; Jer 33:12). Numbers the flock (Le 27:32; Jer 33:13). Knows his flock by name (Jos 10:3-5). Keeps the sheep and goats apart (M't 25:32). Waters the flocks (Ge 29:2-10). Keeps the flocks in folds (Nu 32:16; 1Sa 24:3; 2Sa 7:8; Joh 10:1). Watch towers of (2Ch 26:10; Mic 4:8). Dogs of (Job 30:1). Was an abomination to the Egyptians (Ge 46:34). Angels appeared to (Lu 2:8-20).

Instances of: Abel (Ge 4:2). Rachel (Ge 29:9). Daughters of Jethro (Ex 2:16). Moses (Ex 3:1). David (1Sa 16:11; 2Sa 7:8; Ps 78:70).

Figurative: Ge 49:24. Of God's care (Ps 23; 78:52; 80:1). Of prophets, priests, Levites, and civil authorities (Eze 34). Of Christ (Zec 13:7; M't 26:31; Joh 10:1-16; Heb 13:20; 1Pe 2:25). Name given to Jesus (Isa 40:11; M'k 14:27; Joh 10:11; 1Pe 2:25; 5:4).

Name given to Cyrus (Isa 44:28).

SHEPHI, SHEPHO (barrenness), early descendant of Seir (Ge 36:23; 1Ch 1:40). "Shepho" in Ge, "Shephi" in 1Ch.

SHEPHUPHAN, son of Bela (1Ch 8:5).

SHERAH, daughter of Ephraim; descendants built three villages (1Ch 7:24).

SHERD (See Potsherd; Ostraca.)

SHEREBIAH. 1. Levite prominent in Ezra's time (Ezr 8:18, 24).

2. Covenanter with Nehemiah (Ne 10:12).

3. Levite who returned with Zerubbabel (Ne 12:8).

4. Chief Levite (Ne 12:24).

SHERESH, son of Machir (1Ch 7:16).

SHEREZER, man sent from Bethel to Jerusalem to inquire whether days of mourning should be continued (Zec 7:2).

SHERIFF (Da 3:2, 3).

SHESHACH, perhaps a cryptogram for "Babel" or "Babylon" (Jer 25:26; 51:41).

SHESHAI, son of Anak (Nu 13:22; Jos 15:14; J'g 1:10).

SHESHAN, a descendant of Jerahmeel (1Ch 2:31, 34, 35).

SHESHBAZZAR, Jewish prince whom Cyrus made governor and who helped lay the foundation of the temple (Ezr 1:8, 11; 5:14, 16). May be same as Zerubbabel.

SHETH (compensation). 1. Third son of Adam and Eve (1Ch 1:1).

2. Designation for Moab (Nu 24:17).

SHETHAR, a prince of Persia (Es 1:14).

SHETHAR-BOZENAI, SHETHAR BOZNAI, Persian official who tried to hinder Jews (Ezr 5:3, 6).

SHEVA. 1. David's scribe (2Sa 20:25), perhaps same as "Seraiah" in 8:17.

2. Son of Caleb (1Ch 2:49).

SHEWBREAD (Heb 9:2). Called Hallowed Bread (1Sa 21:6). Ordinance concerning (Le 24:5-9). Required to be kept before the Lord continually (Ex 25:30; 2Ch 2:4). Provided by a yearly *per capita* tax (Ne 10:32, 33). Prepared by the Levites (1Ch 9:32; 23:29). Unlawfully eaten by David (1Sa 21:6; M't 12:3, 4; M'k 2:25, 26; Lu 6:3, 4). Placed on the table of shewbread (Ex 40:22, 23). See Table of, below.

Table of: Heb 9:2. Ordinances concerning (Ex 25:23-28; 37:10-15). Its situation in the tabernacle (Ex 26:35; 40:22). Furniture of (Ex 25:29, 30; 37:16; Nu 4:7). Consecration of (Ex 30:26, 27, 29). How removed (Nu 4:7, 15). For the temple (1Ki 7:48, 50; 2Ch 4:19, 22).

SHIBAH, well from which Beer-sheba was named (Ge 26:33); in KJV "Shebah."

SHIBBOLETH (ear of grain; stream), word differently pronounced on the two sides of the Jordan, and was used by the men of Gilead to determine whether the speaker was of Ephraim or not (J'g 12:5, 6).

SHIBMAH, SIBMAH, city taken by tribe of Reuben from Moabites (Nu 32:38).

SHICRON, SHIKKERON, town on N boundary of Judah (Jos 15:11).

SHIELD, defensive armor. Different kinds of, designated as buckler, shield, target (Ps 35:2; Eze 38:4). Used by Saul (2Sa 1:21); by the Benjamites (2Ch 14:8; 17:17). Uzziah equipped the children of Israel with (2Ch 26:14). Made of brass (1Ki 14:27); of gold (2Sa 8:7; 1Ki 10:16, 17; 2Ch 9:15, 16); of wood (Eze 39:9, 10); with bosses (Job 15:26). Stored in armories (1Ki 10:17; 2Ch 11:12; 32:5, 27); in the tabernacle (2Ki 11:10; 2Ch 23:9). Covered when not in use (Isa 22:6). Painted red (Na 2:3).

See Arms.

Figurative: Of God's protection (Ge 15:1; De 33:29; 2Sa 22:3, 36; Ps 5:12; 18:2, 35; 33:20; 59:11; 84:9, 11; 89:18; Pr 30:5). Of God's truth (Ps 91:4). Of an entire army (Jer 46:3).

SHIGGAION, musical term of unknown meaning found in heading of Ps 7.

SHIGIONOTH, plural of Shiggaion. Heading of Habakkuk's psalm (Hab 3:1).

SHIHON, SHION, town on border of Issachar, near Nazareth (Jos 19:19).

SHIHOR, SIHOR, may refer to the Nile, a stream which separated Egypt from Palestine, or a branch of the Nile (Jos 13:3; 1Ch 13:5; Isa 23:3; Jer 2:18).

SHIHOR-LIBNATH, small stream on S border of Asher (Jos 19:26).

SHIKKERON (See Shicron.)

SHILHI, father-in-law of Jehoshaphat, king of Judah (1Ki 22:42; 2Ch 20:31).

SHILHIM, a city of Judah (Jos 15:32).

SHILLEM, SHILLEMITE, son of Naphtali (Ge 46:24) and his descendants (Nu 26:49); "Shallum" in 1Ch 7:13.

SHILOAH. A stream or pool (Isa 8:6). Probably identical with Siloah and Siloam, which see.

SHILOH. 1. City in Ephraim, c. 12 miles N and E of Bethel where the tabernacle remained from the time of Joshua to the days of Samuel (J'g 21:19; 1Sa 4:3); Benjamites kidnapped wives (J'g 21:15-24); residence of Eli and Samuel (1Sa 3); home of the prophet Ahijah (1Ki 14); a ruin in Jeremiah's time (Jer 7:12, 14).

2. Word of uncertain meaning regarded by many Jews and Christians as a reference to the Messiah (Ge 49:10).

SHILONI, father of Zechariah (Ne 11:5).

SHILONITE. 1. A man of Shiloh (1Ki 11:29; 12:15; 15:29; 2Ch 9:29; 10:15).

2. Used, apparently, to denote a descendant of Shelah (1Ch 9:5).

See Shelamites.

SHILSHAH, Asherite; son of Zophah (1Ch 7:37).

SHIMEA. 1. Brother of David (1Ch 20:7).

2. Son of David and Bathsheba (1Ch 3:5).

3. Merarite Levite (1Ch 6:30).

4. Gershonite Levite (1Ch 6:39). No. 1 is probably the same as "Shimma"

(1Ch 2:13 KJV), "Shamma" (1Sa 16:9), "Shimeah" (2Sa 21:21 KJV), and "Shimei" (2Sa 21:21 ASV, RSV).

SHIMEAH. 1. Brother of David (2Sa 13:3).

2. Benjamite (1Ch 8:32), "Shimeam" in 1Ch 9:38.

SHIMEAM (See Shimeah.)

SHIMEATH (fame), mother of an assassin of King Joash (2Ki 12:21; 2Ch 24:26).

SHIMEATHITES, a family of scribes (1Ch 2:55).

SHIMEI (famous). 1. Called also Shimi. Son of Gershon (Ex 6:17; Nu 3:18; 1Ch 6:17; 23:7, 10).

2. A Benjamite. Curses David; David's magnanimity toward (2Sa 16:5-13; 19:16-23, with 1Ki 2:36-46).

3. An officer of David (1Ki 1:8).

4. One of Solomon's commissary officers (1Ki 4:18).

5. Grandson of Jeconiah (1Ch 3:19).

6. Son of Zacchur (1Ch 4:26, 27).

7. A Reubenite. Son of Gog (1Ch 5:4).

8. A Merarite. Son of Libni (1Ch 6:29).

9. A Gershonite. Son of Jahath (1Ch 6:42).

10. Father of a family in Benjamin (1Ch 8:21). In AV, called Shimhi.

11. A Levite (1Ch 23:9).

12. A leader of singers in time of David (1Ch 25:17).

13. David's overseer of vineyards (1Ch 27:27).

14. A son of Heman (2Ch 29:14).

15. A Levite. Treasurer of tithes and offerings in time of Hezekiah (2Ch 31:12, 13).

16. A Levite who put away his Gentile wife (Ezr 10:23).

17. The name of two Israelites who put away Gentile wives (Ezr 10:33, 38).

18. A Benjamite. Grandfather of Mordecai (Es 2:5).

19. The ancestor of a family (Zec 12:13). Possibly identical with 1.

SHIMEON (hearing), an Israelite who put away his Gentile wife (Ezr 10:31).

SHIMHI, father of a family in Benjamin (1Ch 8:21). In *R. V.*, called Shimei.

SHIMI (See Shimei, 1.)

SHIMITE, descendant of Shimei (Nu 3:21 KJV; ASV "Shimeites").

SHIMMA, son of Jesse (1Ch 2:13 KJV), "Shammah" in 1Sa 16:9.

SHIMON, a man of Judah (1Ch 4:20).

SHIMRATH (watch), son of Shimhi (1Ch 8:21).

SHIMRI. 1. Son of Shemaiah; Simeonite (1Ch 4:37).

2. Father of Jediael and Joha, two of David's mighty men (1Ch 11:45).

3. Merarite Levite. "Simri" in KJV of 1Ch 26:10.

4. Levite who assisted in cleansing the temple (2Ch 29:13).

SHIMRITH (watchful), Moabitess; mother of Jehozabad who helped slay Joash, king of Judah (2Ch 24:26), "Shomer" in 2Ki 12:21).

SHIMROM, SHIMRON (guard). 1. Son of Issachar (Ge 46:13), "Shimrom" in KJV of 1Ch 7:1.

2. Town in N Canaan whose king fought Joshua (Jos 11:1ff), "Shimron-Meron" in Jos 12:20.

SHIMRONITES, the family of Shimron (Nu 26:24).

SHIMRON-MERON. A city conquered by Joshua (Jos 12:20). Probably identical with Shimron, 2, which see.

SHIMSHAI (sunny), scribe who tried to hinder Jews in rebuilding temple (Ezr 4:8).

SHINAB, king of Admah. Canaanite city later destroyed (Ge 14:2).

SHINAR, alluvial plain of Babylonia in which lay cities of Babel, Erech, Accad, and Calneh (Ge 10:10); tower of Babel built there (Ge 11:1-9); Amraphel, king of Shinar, invaded Canaan (Ge 14:1); Jews exiled to Shinar (Zec 5:11); Nebuchadnezzar transported Temple treasures to Shinar area (Da 1:2).

SHION, town in Issachar (Jos 19:19), KJV has "Shihon."

SHIP. Built by Noah (Ge 6:13-22); by Solomon (1Ki 9:26; 2Ch 8:17); by Jehoshaphat (1Ki 22:48; 2Ch 20:35, 36); of gopher wood (Ge 6:14); of fir wood (Eze 27:5); of bulrushes (Isa 18:2); sealed with pitch (Ge 6:15). Equipped with helm (Jas 3:4); rudder (Ac 27:40); tackling (Isa 33:23; Ac 27:19); sails (Isa 33:23; Ac 27:1, 9, 17, 40); sails embroidered (Eze 27:7); masts (Isa 33:23; Eze 27:5); oars (Jon 1:13; M'k 6:48); figurehead (Ac 28:11); anchor (Ac 27:29, 30, 40; Heb 6:19); lifeboats (Ac 27:30, 32). Used in commerce (Ac 21:3; 27:10); in commerce with Tarshish (1Ki 22:48; Isa 60:9; Jon 1:3); with Ophir (1Ki 10:11; 2Ch 8:18); with Adramyttium (Ac 27:2); for passenger traffic (Isa 60:9; Jon 1:3; Ac 20:13; 27:2, 37; 28:11); for ferriage (2Sa 19:18). Repaired by calking (Eze 27:9). Wrecked at Ezion-geber (1Ki 22:48; 2Ch 20:35-37); at Melita (Ac 27:14-44). Warships used by Chittim (Nu 24:24; Da 11:30).

See Mariners.

SHIPHI, father of Ziza (1Ch 4:37).

SHIPHMITE, patronymic of Zabdi, vineyard overseer (1Ch 27:27).

SHIPHRAH (beauty), Hebrew midwife who saved Hebrew boy babies (Ex 1:15-21).

SHIPHTAN (judicial), father of the representative of Ephraim on the committee which divided the promised land among the Israelites (Nu 34:24).

SHISHA, father of two of Solomon's secretaries (1Ki 4:3); may be identical with Seraiah (2Sa 8:17), Sheva (2Sa 20:25), and Shavsha (1Ch 18:16).

SHISHAK, Egyptian king, founder of 22nd dynasty (950-929 B. C.), gave refuge to Jeroboam (1Ki 11:40); invaded Jerusalem in reign of Rehoboam (1Ki 14:25f).

SHITRAI, a chief herder of David (1Ch 27:29).

SHITTAH TREE (See Plants.)

SHITTIM. 1. Called also Abel-shittim (Nu 33:49). A camping place of Israel (Nu 25:1; 33:49). Joshua sends spies from (Jos 2:1). Valley of (Joe 3:18). Balaam prophesies in (Mic 6:5).

2. Called also Shittah, a tree, the wood of which is fragrant. Planted and cultivated (Isa 41:19). The ark of the covenant made of (Ex 25:10); staves of the ark (Ex 25:13; 38:6); boards in the tabernacle (Ex 26:15-37); the altar of burnt offering (Ex 38:1, 6).

SHIZA, a Reubenite. Father of one of David's mighty men (1Ch 11:42).

SHOA (rich), people mentioned in association with Babylonians, Chaldeans, and Assyrians (Eze 23:23). May be Sutu of Amarna letters.

SHOBAB. 1. Grandson of Hezron (1Ch 2:18).

2. Son of David (1Ch 3:5).

SHOBACH. Captain of the host of Hadarezer. Slain by David's army (2Sa 10:16, 18). Called Shophach (1Ch 19:16, 18).

SHOBAI, a porter, whose descendants returned to Jerusalem with Zerubbabel (Ezr 2:42; Ne 7:45).

SHOBAL. 1. Chief of Horites (Ge 36:20, 23, 29).

2. Ephrathite; founder of Kirjath-jearim (1Ch 2:50, 52).

3. Grandson of Judah (1Ch 4:1, 2).

SHOBEK, a Jew who sealed the covenant with Nehemiah (Ne 10:24).

SHOBI, son of Nahash. Brought supplies to David in his flight from Absalom (2Sa 17:27).

SHOCHO, city in Judah, built by Rehoboam (2Ch 11:7); KJV has "Shoco."

SHOE. Taken off on holy ground (Ex 3:5; Jos 5:15; Ac 7:33). Put off in mourning (Eze 24:17). Of the children of Israel did not wax old (De 29:5). Loosed in token of refusal to observe the levirate marriage (De 25:9; Ru 4:7, 8). Poor sold for a pair of (Am 2:6; 8:6). Made of iron (De 33:25); of badgers' skins (Eze 16:10); latchet of (Ge 14:23; Isa 5:27; M'k 1:7); loosing of, a humble service (Lu 3:16).

SHOFAR, a trumpet of ram's horn (Jos 4:4-6). See Trumpet.

SHOHAM, a Merarite (1Ch 24:27).

SHOMER (keeper). 1. Father of Jehozabad, conspirator of Joash of Judah (2Ki 12:20, 21; 2Ch 24:25, 26).

2. Great-grandson of Asher (1Ch 7:32); "Shamer" in verse 34 KJV.

SHOPHACH, Syrian general slain by David (1Ch 19:16, 18), "Shobach" in 2Sa 10:16.

SHOPHAN, 2nd half of Atrothshophan, city of Gad (Nu 32:35).

SHORE, the land where it meets the sea (Jos 15:2; J'g 5:17; M't 13:2).

SHOSHANNIM (lilies), found in titles of Pss 45, 69, 80 and in Ps 60 in the singular; may refer to lily-shaped musical instrument or tune known as "Lilies."

SHOULDER, used both literally and figuratively. The shoulder of a sacrificed ox or sheep went to the priest as his portion (De 18:8); the sacred furniture of the tabernacle had to be carried upon the shoulders (Nu 7:6-9). "To pull away the shoulder" (Zec 7:11) is to refuse to obey.

SHOULDER PIECE. 1. Part of the ephod in which the front and the back were joined together (Ex 28:7, 8).

2. Piece of meat taken from shoulder of animal (Eze 24:4).

SHOUTING. In joy and praise (1Ch 15:28; 2Ch 15:12-14; Ezr 3:11-13; Ps 5:11; 47:1; Isa 12:6; Lu 17:15; 19:37-41; Ac 3:8, 9; Re 5:12-14).

In battle (Jos 6:20; J'g 7:18; 1Sa 17:20, 52; 2Ch 13:15).

SHOVEL, a utensil in the tabernacle (Ex 27:3; 38:3; Nu 4:14); temple (1Ki 7:40; Jer 52:18).

SHOWBREAD (See Shewbread.)

SHRINE, an idolatrous symbol of the Temple of Diana (Ac 19:24).

SHROUD, generally the dress for the dead, but also a bough (Eze 31:3), where ASV has "a forest-like shade."

SHRUB (See Plants.)

SHUA (prosperity). 1. Canaanite whose daughter became Judah's wife (Ge 38:2, 12).

2. Heber's daughter (1Ch 7:32).

SHUAH (depression). 1. Son of Abraham by Keturah (Ge 25:2; 1Ch 1:32).

2. See Shua 1.

3. Chelub's brother (1Ch 4:11).

SHUAL (fox). 1. Son of Zophah (1Ch 7:36).

2. District near Michmash (1Sa 13:17).

SHUBAEL (captive), name of two Levites (1Ch 24:20; 25:20). Also called "Shebuel."

SHUHAM. Son of Dan (Nu 26:42). Called Hushim (Ge 46:23).

SHUHITE (native of Shuah), descendant of Shuah 1 (Job 2:11; 8:1; 18:1; 25:1).

SHULAMITE (peaceful), probably native of Shunem (Song 6:13).

SHUMATHITES (garlic), family of Kirjath-jearim (1Ch 2:53).

SHUNAMMITE. 1. A person from Shunem. Abishag, the damsel who nourished David (1Ki 1:3); desired by Adonijah as wife (1Ki 2:13-25).

2. A woman who gave hospitality to Elisha, and whose son he raised to life (2Ki 4:8-37).

SHUNEM, city of Issachar (Job 19:18), 3½ miles N of Jezreel; site of Philistine encampment before battle (1Sa 28:4); home of Abishag, David's nurse (1Ki 1:3); home of woman who befriended Elisha (2Ki 4:8-37).

SHUNI, son of Gad (Ge 46:16; Nu 26:15).

SHUPHAM, SHUPHAMITE, son of Benjamin and progenitor of Shuphamites (Nu 26:39). May be same as Shephuphan of 1Ch 8:5.

SHUPPIM. 1. Son of Ir (1Ch 7:12, 15).

2. A Levite (1Ch 26:16).

SHUR (wall), a wilderness southwest of Palestine (Ge 16:7; 20:1; 25:18; Ex 15:22; 1Sa 15:7; 27:8).

SHUSHAN. 1. Capital of the Medo-Persian empire (Es 1:2, 3; 8:15).

2. King's palace at (Ne 1:1; Es 1:2, 5; 2:5, 8; 4:8, 16; 8:14, 15; 9:11, 15).

SHUSHAN-EDUTH (See Music.)

SHUTHELAH, SHUTHALHITE. Son of Ephraim (Nu 26:35, 36); descendants called "Shuthalhites" (1Ch 7:20, 21).

2. Son of Zabad; father of Ezer and Elead (1Ch 7:21).

SHUTTLE, part of weaving loom; used as a figure of the shortness of life (Job 7:6).

SIA (assembly), progenitor of Nethinim that returned with Zerubbabel (Ne 7:47); "Siaha" in Ezr 2:44.

SIAHA (See Sia.)

SIBBECAI, SIBBECHAI, one of David's mighty men, designated "Hushathite" (2Sa 21:18; 1Ch 11:29; 20:4; 27:11); slew Philistine Saph (2Sa 21:18).

SIBBOLETH (See Shibboleth.)

SIBMAH. A city of Reuben (Jos 13:19; Isa 16:8, 9; Jer 48:32). Apparently called also Shebam (Nu 32:3); and Shibmah (Nu 32:38).

SIBRAIM, place on N boundary of Palestine (Eze 47:16).

SICHEM, same as Shechem.

SICILY, island lying off the toe of Italy, visited by Paul (Ac 28:12). See Syracuse.

SICK, THE. Visiting (Ps 41:6). Visiting, a duty (M't 25:36, 43; Jas 1:27).

Figurative: Isa 1:5, 6; Ho 5:13.

See Afflicted; Affliction; Disease.

SICKLE (reaping hook), tool used for cutting grain, sometimes also for pruning (De 16:9; Joe 3:13; M'k 4:29). Used figuratively for God's judgment (Joe 3:13; Re 14:14).

SICKNESS (See Affliction; Disease.)
SIDDIM, vale of, a valley of uncertain location. Scene of the defeat of the king of Sodom (Ge 14:3, 8, 10).
SIDON. 1. Called also Zidon. Son of Canaan (Ge 10:15; 1Ch 1:13).

2. A city on the northern boundary of the Canaanites (Ge 10:19). Designated by Jacob as the border of Zebulun (Ge 49:13). Was on the northern boundary of Asher (Jos 19:28; 2Sa 24:6). Belonged to the land of Israel according to promise (Jos 13:6). Inhabitants of, dwelt in security and carelessness (J'g 18:7). Israelites failed to make conquest of (J'g 1:31; 3:3). The inhabitants of, contributed cedar for the first and second temple (1Ki 5:6; 1Ch 22:4; Ezr 3:7). Solomon marries women of (1Ki 11:1). Ahab marries a woman of (1Ki 16:31). People of, come to hear Jesus (M'k 3:8; Lu 6:17). Inhabitants of, offend Herod (Ac 12:20-23).

Commerce of (Isa 23:2, 4, 12). Seamen of (Eze 27:8). Prophecies concerning (Jer 25:15-22; 27:3-11; 47:4; Eze 28:21-23; 32:30; Joe 3:4-8). Jesus visits the region of, and heals the daughter of the Syrophenician woman (M't 15:21-28; M'k 7:24-31). Visited by Paul (Ac 27:3).
SIEGE. Offer of peace must be made to the city before beginning (De 20:10-12). Conducted by erecting embankments parallel to the walls of the besieged city (De 20:19, 20; Isa 29:3; 37:33). Battering rams used in (see Battering-rams). Distress of the inhabitants during (2Ki 6:24-29; 25:3; Isa 9:20; 36:12; Jer 19:9). Cannibalism in (2Ki 6:28, 29).

Instances of: Of Jericho (Jos 6). Rabbah (2Sa 11:1); Abel (2Sa 20:15); Gibbethon (1Ki 15:27); Tirzah (1Ki 16:17). Jerusalem, by the children of Judah (J'g 1:8); by David (2Sa 5:6, 9); by Rezin, king of Syria, and Pekah, son of Remaliah, king of Israel (2Ki 16:5); by Nebuchadnezzar (2Ki 24:10, 11; Da 1:1; 2Ki 25:1-3; Jer 52); by Sennacherib (2Ch 32:1-23). Samaria (1Ki 20:1; 2Ki 6:24; 17:5; 18:9-11).
SIEVE, sifting device for grain; made of reeds, horsehair, or strings (Isa 30:28; Am 9:9). Also used figuratively (Lu 22:31).
SIGN. A miracle to confirm faith (M't 12:38; 16:4; 24:30; M'k 8:11, 12; 13:4; Joh 2:11; 3:2; 4:48). Asked for by, and given to Abraham (Ge 15:8-17); Moses (Ex 4:1-9); Gideon (J'g 6:17, 36-40); Hezekiah (2Ki 20:8); Zacharias (Lu 1:18). Given to Jeroboam (1Ki 13:3-5).

A token of coming events (M't 16:3, 4; 24:3).

See Miracles.
SIGNAL, used in war (Isa 18:3).

See Armies; Ensigns; Trumpets.
SIGNET (See Seal.)
SIHON, king of the Amorites. His seat of government at Heshbon (Nu 21:26). The proverbial chant celebrating the victory of Sihon over the Moabites (Nu 21:26-30). Conquest of his kingdom by the Israelites (Nu 21:21-25; De 2:24-37; 3:2, 6, 8).
SIHOR (turbid), called also Shihor. A river of Egypt, given by some authorities as the Nile (Jos 13:3; 1Ch 13:5; Isa 23:3; Jer 2:18).
SILAS (asked), called also Silvanus. Sent to Paul, in Antioch, from Jerusalem (Ac 15:22-34). Becomes Paul's companion (Ac 15:40, 41; 2Co 1:19; 1Th 1:1; 2Th 1:1). Imprisoned with Paul in Philippi (Ac 16:19-40). Driven, with Paul, from Thessalonica (Ac 17:4-10). Left by Paul at Berea (Ac 17:14). Rejoins Paul at Corinth (Ac 17:15; 18:5). Carries Peter's epistle to Asia Minor (1Pe 5:12).
SILK. Wearing apparel made of (Pr 31:22; Eze 16:10, 13). Merchandise of (Re 18:12).

See Cotton; Linen.
SILLA (embankment), a place of uncertain location (2Ki 12:20).
SILOAH, SHILOAH (See Siloam.)
SILOAM, reservoir located within the city walls of Jerusalem at the S end of the Tyropoean Valley; receives water through 1,780-foot tunnel from En-rogel (Joh 9:7); constructed by Hezekiah in eighth century B. C. "Shiloah" in Isa 8:6; "Shelah" (KJV "Siloah") in Ne 3:15. Modern Birket Silwan.
SILOAM, TOWER OF, probably part of fortification system of Jerusalem wall, near pool of Siloam (Lu 13:4).
SILOAM, VILLAGE OF, not mentioned in Bible; modern village (Silwan) situated across valley E of the Spring Gihon.
SILVANUS (See Silas.)
SILVER. From Tarshish (Eze 27:12);

Refining of (Pr 17:3; 25:4; 26:23; Eze 22:18-22; Jer 6:29, 30; Zec 13:9; Mal 3:3). See Refining. Used for money (Ge 13:2; 17:12; 20:16; 23:13-16; Am 8:6; M't 10:9; 26:15; M'k 14:11; Ac 19:19). See Money. For ornamentation of, and in the manufacture of, the utensils for the tabernacle (Ex 26:19; 27:17; 35:24; 36:24; 38:25; Nu 7:13, 19, 25, 31, 37, 43, 49, 55, 61, 67, 73, 79, 85); of the temple (1Ch 28:14; 29:2-5; Ezr 5:14; 6:5; 8:26; Da 5:2). Cups made of (Ge 44:2); trumpets (Nu 10:2); cords (Ec 12:6); chains (Isa 40:19); shrines (Ac 19:24); idols (Ex 20:23; Isa 30:22; Ho 13:2); baskets, or filigree [marg., *R. V.*] (Pr 25:11); jewels (Song 1:11); see Jewels; palace (Song 8:9).

Vessels of (Nu 7:85; 1Ki 10:25; 2Sa 8:10; 2Ki 12:13; 1Ch 18:10; 2Ch 24:14; Ezr 1:6; 5:14; 6:5; 8:26; Da 5:2; 11:8).

Abundance of (1Ki 10:27; 1Ch 22:14; 29:2-7; 2Ch 1:15; Ec 2:8; Isa 2:7). Dross from (Pr 25:4; 26:23). Reprobate (Jer 6:30). Workers in (2Ch 2:14; Ac 19:24). See Smith.

See Money.

Symbolical: Da 2:32, 35.

SILVERSMITH (Ac 19:24).

See Smith.

SIMEON (hearing). 1. Son of Jacob (Ge 29:33; 35:23; Ex 1:1, 2; 1Ch 2:1). With Levi avenges upon the Shechemites the seduction of Dinah (Ge 34; 49:5-7). Jacob's denunciation of (Ge 34:30; 49:5-7). Goes down into Egypt to buy corn; is bound by Joseph, and detained (Ge 42:24, 36; 43:23). His sons (Ge 46:10; Ex 6:15; 1Ch 4:24-37). Descendants of (Nu 26:12-14). See Tribe of, below.

2. Tribe of: Military enrollment of, at Sinai (Nu 1:22, 23; 2:13); in the plains of Moab (Nu 26:14). Place of, in camp and march (Nu 2:12; 10:18, 19). Inheritance allotted to (Jos 19:1-9; J'g 1:3-17; 1Ch 4:24-43). Stood on Mount Gerizim to bless at the time of the rehearsal of the law (De 27:12). Joined with the people of Judah and Benjamin in the renewal of the passover (2Ch 15:9, w *verses* 1-15). Idolatry of (2Ch 34:6, w *verses* 1-7).

See Israel.

3. A devout man in Jerusalem. Blesses Jesus in the temple (Lu 2:25-35).

4. An ancestor of Jesus (Lu 3:30).

5. A disciple. Called also Niger (Ac 13:1).

6. Name given to Peter (Ac 15:14). See Peter.

SIMEONITE, member of tribe of Simeon.

SIMILITUDE (likeness), pattern, resemblance, similarity (Nu 12:8; 2Ch 4:3; Ps 106:20; Heb 7:15).

SIMON (hearing). 1. See Peter.

2. One of the twelve apostles. Called The Canaanite (M't 10:4; M'k 3:18); Zelotes (Lu 6:15; Ac 1:13).

3. A brother of Jesus (M't 13:55; M'k 6:3).

4. A leper. Jesus dines with (M't 26:6; M'k 14:3).

5. A man of Cyrene. Compelled to carry Jesus' cross (M't 27:32; M'k 15:21; Lu 23:26).

6. A Pharisee. Jesus dines with (Lu 7:36-44).

7. The father of Judas Iscariot (Joh 6:71; 12:4; 13:2, 26).

8. A sorcerer. Converted by Philip; rebuked by Peter (Ac 8:9-13, 18-24).

9. A tanner. Peter lodges with (Ac 9:43; 10:6, 17, 32).

SIMON MACCABEUS, Hasmonaean ruler in Palestine (143-134 B. C.).

SIMONY, ecclesiastical corruption (Ac 8:18, 19).

SIMPLE, naive; easily led into wrongdoing (Ps 19:7; 119:130; Pr 7:7).

SIMRI, Levite; doorkeeper (1Ch 26:10).

SIN. *Adamic:* Original, of Adam (Ge 3:6; Ho 6:7; Ro 5:12, 15-19).

Sin Nature: The inherited tendencies to evil (M't 7:17, 18; 12:33-35; M'k 7:20-23; Lu 6:45; Ro 6:6; 7:17, 20, 23, 25; 8:3, 5-7; Ga 5:16, 17; Eph 2:3; Jas 1:14; 4:17).

Defined: Transgression of the law (Ho 6:8; M't 5:28; 1Co 8:12; Heb 12:15; Jas 2:10, 11; 4:17; 1Jo 3:4; 5:17). Turning away from God (De 29:18; Ps 95:10). Not seeking God (2Ch 12:14). Foolish thoughts (Pr 24:9). Self-deception (Isa 42:20). That not of faith (Ro 14:23).

See Atonement; Conviction; Depravity; Regeneration; Repentance; Reprobacy; Salvation; Sanctification; Wicked, Punishment of.

Against the body (Ec 5:6); knowledge (Pr 26:11; Lu 12:47, 48; Joh 9:41; 15:22; Ro 1:21, 32; 2:17-23; Heb 10:26; Jas

4:17; 2Pe 2:21, 22). See Ignorance, Sins of. Attempts to cover, vain (Ge 3:10; Job 31:33; Isa 29:15; 59:6).

Besetting (Heb 2:1).

Christ's description of (M't 5:2-20; Joh 8:34, 44).

Deceitful (Heb 3:13). Defiles (Ps 51:2, 7; Isa 1:18; Heb 12:15; 1Jo 1:7). See Defilement. Degrees in (Lu 7:41-47; 12:47, 48). Dominion of (Ro 3:9).

Enslaves (Joh 8:34; Ro 6:16; 2Pe 2:19).

Fools mock at (Pr 14:9).

Little sins (Song 2:15).

Magnitude of (Job 22:5; Ps 25:11).

None in heaven (Re 22:3, 4).

Parable of (M't 13:24, 25, 33, 39). Paul's discussion of the responsibility for (Ro 2-9). Pleasures of (Joh 20:12-16; 21:12, 13; Lu 8:14; Heb 11:25). See Pleasures, Worldly.

Reproach to God (2Sa 12:14).

Secret sins (Ps 19:12; 44:22; 64:2; 90:8; Ec 12:14; Eze 8:12; 11:5; M't 10:26; Lu 8:17; 12:2, 3; Joh 3:20; Ro 2:16; Eph 5:12). Sinfulness of (Job 22:5; Ps 25:11; Isa 1:18; Ro 7:13).

To be hated (De 7:26; Ps 119:113).

Confession of: (1Ki 8:47; Pr 28:13). Signified by placing hands on head of offering (Le 3:2, 13; 4:4, 15, 24, 29, 33; 16:21; Nu 8:12). Illustrated in parables, of prodigal son (Lu 15:17-21); of Pharisee and publican (Lu 18:13).

To God, enjoined (Le 5:5-10; 16:21). To saints, enjoined (Jas 5:16; 1Jo 1:8-10).

To God, exemplified by Israel (Nu 14:40; J'g 10:10; 1Sa 7:6); by Saul (1Sa 15:2, 4); by David (2Sa 12:13; 24:10, 17; 1Ch 21:17); by the psalmist (Ps 32:5; 38:3, 4, 18; 40:11, 12; 41:4; 51:2-5; 69:5; 73:21, 22; 119:59, 60, 176); by the Jews (2Ch 29:6; Ezr 9:4-7, 10-15; Ne 9:2, 3, 5-38; Ps 106:6; Isa 26:13; 59:12-15; 64:5-7; Jer 3:21, 22, 25; 8:14, 15; 14:7, 20; 31:18, 19; La 3:40-42; Da 9:5, 6, 8-11, 15); by Job (Job 7:20; 9:20; 13:23; 40:4; 42:5, 6); by Isaiah (Isa 6:5); by Jeremiah (La 1:18-20); by Paul (1Co 15:9).

Consequences of: Debauched countenance (Isa 3:9). Guilty fear (Ge 3:7-10; Pr 10:24; 25:1). Depraved conscience (Pr 30:20). Privations (Jer 5:25). Trouble (Isa 57:20, 21; Jer 4:18).

Entailed upon children (Ex 20:5; 34:7; Le 26:39, 40; Nu 14:33; De 5:9; Ps 21:10; 37:28; 109:9, 10; Pr 14:11; Isa 14:20-22; 65:7; Jer 32:18; La 5:7; Ro 5:12-21). Attributed to Job's children because of Job's alleged wickedness (Job 5:4; 18:19; 21:19). Guilt of, and punishment for, not entailed upon children (De 24:16; 2Ki 14:6; 2Ch 25:4; Jer 31:29, 30; Eze 18:2-4, 20).

No escape from (Ge 3:8-19; Isa 28:18-22; Am 9:2-4; M't 23:33; Heb 2:3). See Punishment, No escape from; Wicked.

Conviction of: Produced by dreams (Job 33:14-17); by visions (Ac 9:3-9); by afflictions (Job 33:18-30; La 1:20; Lu 15:17-21); by adversity (Ps 107:4-6, 10-14, 17-20, 23-30); by the gospel (Ac 2:37); by religious testimony (1Co 14:24, 25); by the conscience (Joh 8:9; Ro 2:15); by the Holy Spirit (Joh 16:7-11). See Conviction; Repentance, Instances of.

Forgiveness of: (Ac 26:18; Eph 1:7). Promised (Ex 34:6, 7; Le 4:20, 26, 31, 35, 40-42; 5:4-13; Nu 14:18; 15:25; De 4; Ps 130:4; Isa 1:6-18; 43:25, 26; 44:21, 22; 55:6, 7; Jer 31:34; 33:8; Eze 18:21, 22; 33:14-16; M't 12:31; M'k 3:28; Heb 8:12; 10:17; Jas 5:15; 1Jo 1:7, 9). Blessedness of (Ps 32:1, 2; Ro 4:7, 8).

Instances of: Israelites (Nu 14:20; Ps 85:2, 3; 99:8; 103:12). David (2Sa 12:13; Ps 32:5). Isaiah (Isa 6:7). Man with palsy (M't 9:2, 6; M'k 2:5; Lu 5:20, 24). The prostitute (Lu 7:48; Joh 8:11). Believers (Col 2:13).

Conditions of: Repentance (M't 3:6; Lu 3:3; 13:3, 5; Ac 2:38; 3:19). Faith (Ac 10:36, 43; 13:38, 39; 26:16-18). Confession of sins (1Jo 1:7, 9). Parable of (M't 18:23-27).

Through shedding of blood (Heb 9:22). Spirit of (M't 6:12, 14, 15; 18:35; M'k 11:25).

The mission of Christ, to secure (M't 1:21; 26:28; Lu 24:47; 1Jo 2:1, 2, 12; Re 1:5).

Prayer for (Ps 19:12; 25:7, 11; 51:9; 79:9). Intercessory prayer for (1Ki 8:22-50).

Apostolic (Joh 20:23).

See Atonement; Conviction; Offerings; Repentance.

From the heart (Isa 44:20; Jer 7:24;

17:9; Eze 20:16; M't 5:28; 7:17, 18; 12:33-35; 15:8, 11, 16-19; Lu 6:45). Of the tongue (Ec 5:6). In thought (Pr 24:9). In secret (Ps 19:12; 90:8; Ec 12:14; Eze 8:12; Joh 3:20; Ro 2:16; Eph 5:12). Against conscience (Ro 14:23). Against knowledge (Lu 12:47, 48; Joh 9:41; 15:22; Ro 1:21, 32; 2:17-23; Heb 10:26; Jas 4:17; 2Pe 2:21, 22).

Fruits of (De 29:18; M'k 7:21-23; 1Co 3:3; 6:9-11; Ga 5:19-21; 1Pe 4:3; Jas 5:11). Of original sin (Ge 3:7-24; 4:9-13; Ro 5:12-21). God's anger (Jer 7:19). Moral insensibility (Pr 30:20). No peace (Isa 57:20, 21). Shame (Pr 3:35). Withholding of God's goodness (Jer 7:19).

Destruction and death (Ge 6:5-7; 1Ki 13:33, 34; Job 5:2; Ps 5:10; 94:23; Pr 5:22, 23; 10:24, 29-31; 11:18, 19, 27, 29; Isa 3:9, 11; 9:18; 14:21; Jer 14:16; 21:14; Eze 11:21; 22:31; 23:31-35; Ho 12:14; 13:9; Ro 6:23).

The same as sown (Job 4:8; 13:26; 20:11; Ps 9:15, 16; 10:2; 141:10; Pr 1:31; 11:5-7; 12:13, 14-21, 26; 22:8; Isa 50:11; Jer 4:18; 21:14; Eze 11:21; Ho 8:7; 10:13; Mic 7:13; Ro 7:5; Ga 6:7, 8).

Proverbs concerning (Pr 1:31; 3:35; 5:22, 23; 8:36; 10:24, 29-31; 11:5-7, 18, 19, 27, 29; 12:13, 14, 21, 26; 13:5, 6, 15; 22:8; 27:8; 28:1; 29:6; 30:20).

Incitement to: The devil (M't 13:24, 25, 38, 39; Joh 8:34, 44; Eph 2:1, 2; 1Jo 3:6, 8-10, 15). The fallen nature (Ga 5:16, 17; Eph 2:3; Jas 1:14, 15; 4:1-3).

Known: To God (Ge 3:11; 4:10; 18:13; Ex 16:8, 9, 12; Nu 12:2; 14:26, 27; De 1:34; 31:21; 32:34; Jos 7:10-15; Job 7:10-15; 10:14; 11:11; 13:27; 14:16, 17; 20:27; 24:23; 34:21, 22, 25; Ps 44:20, 21; 69:5; 90:8; 94:11; Ec 5:8; Isa 29:15; Jer 2:22; 16:17; 29:23; Eze 21:24; Ho 5:3; 7:2; Am 5:12; 9:1-4, 8; Hab 2:11; Mal 2:14; M't 10:26).

To Jesus (M't 26:46; Lu 6:8; Joh 4:17-19; 5:42; 6:64; 3:11; Re 2:23).

See God, Omniscient; Jesus, Omniscience of.

Love of (Job 15:16; 20:12, 13; Pr 2:14; 4:16, 17; 10:23; 16:30; 26:11; Jer 14:10; Eze 20:16; Ho 4:8; 9:10; Mic 7:3; Joh 3:19, 20; 12:43; 1Pe 3:19, 20; 2Pe 2:22).

See Reprobacy; Wicked, Described.

National, Punishment of (Ge 6:5-7; 7:21, 22; Le 26:14-38; De 9:5; Job 34:29, 30; Isa 19:4; Jer 12:17; 25:31-38; 46:28; Eze 16:49, 50; Jon 1:2).

See Government; Nations.

Instances of: The Sodomites (Ge 18:20). Egyptians (Ex 7-14); see Egypt. Israelites (Le 26:14-39; De 32:30; 2Sa 21:1; 24:1; 2Ki 24:3, 4, 20; 2Ch 36:21; Ezr 9; Ne 9:36, 37; Isa 1:21-23; 3:4, 8; 5; 59:1-15; Jer 2; 5; 6; 9; 23; 30:11-15; La 1:3, 8, 14; 4:6; Eze 2; 7; 22; 24:6-14; 28:18; 33:25, 26; 36:16-20; 39:23, 24, 44:4-14; Ho 4:1-11; 6:8-10; 7:1-7; 13; Am 2; 5; Mic 6; 7:2-6). Babylon (Jer 50:45, 46; 51); see Babylon.

See also prophecies cited in the topics Assyria; Damascus; Edom; Elam; Ethiopia; Philistines; Syria.

Not imputed: To righteous (Ps 32:2; Ro 4:6-8); to ignorant (Ro 4:15; 5:13); to redeemed (2Co 5:19).

Progressive (De 29:19; 1Ki 16:31; Ps 1:1; Isa 5:18; 30:1; Jer 9:3; 16:11, 12; Ho 13:2; 2Ti 3:13; Jas 1:14, 15). Progressiveness exemplified in Joseph's brethren, from jealousy (Ge 37:4); to conspiracy (Ge 37:18); to murder (Ge 37:20). See also Cain and Abel. Retroactive (Ps 7:15, 16; 9:15, 16; 10:2; 94:23; Pr 1:31; 5:22, 23; 8:36; 11:5, 6, 27, 29; Isa 3:9, 11; Jer 2:19; 4:8; 7:19). A root of bitterness (De 29:18; Heb 12:15).

Punishment of (Ge 2:17; 3:16-19; 4:10-14; 6:5-7; 18:20; 19:13; Ex 32:33, 34; 34:7; Le 19:8; 26:14-21; Nu 15:30, 31; 32:23; De 28:15-68; 1Ki 13:33, 34; 1Ch 21:7-27; Job 21:17; Ps 95:10, 11; Pr 1:24-32; Jer 44:2-6; Eze 18:4; M't 25:41, 46; Ro 6:23).

See Punishment; Wicked, Punishment of.

Pollution of: Typified, by the defilement caused by touching any unclean thing (Le 5:2, 3; 11:24-28, 31; 22:5); by eating any unclean thing (Le 11:41-47); by touching a dead body (Le 21:1; Nu 5:2; 9:6, 10; 19:11, 13, 16; 31:19); by leprosy (Le 13:3, 8, 11, 20, 25, 27, 30, 36, 44-46, 51, 55; 14:44; Nu 5:2, 3); by sexual impurities (Le 15:1-33; 22:4; De 23:10, 11).

Repentance for: Enjoined (2Ch 30:7-9; Job 36:10; Ps 34:14; Pr 1:22, 23; Isa 22:12; 31:6; 44:22; 55:6, 7; Jer 3:4, 12-14, 19; 6:8, 16; 18:11; 25:5; 26:13; 35:15; Eze 14:6; 18:30-32; 33:10-12; Da 4:27; Ho 6:1; 10:12; 14:1, 2; Joe 1:14;

2:12, 13, 15-18; Am 4:12; Jon 3:8, 9; Zec 1:3; M't 4:17; M'k 1:15; 6:12; Ac 2:38, 40; 3:19; 8:22; 17:30; 20:21; Jas 4:8-10; Re 2:5, 16; 3:2, 3, 19).

Gift, of God (2Ti 2:25); of Christ (Ac 5:31). Tribulation leads to (De 4:30; 1Ki 8:33-50; 2Ch 6:36-39; Ps 107:4-6, 10-14, 17-20, 23-30). Goodness of God leads to (Ro 2:4).

A condition of pardon (Le 26:40-42; De 4:29-31; 30:1-3; 2Ch 7:14; Ne 1:9; Pr 28:13; Jer 7:5-7; 36:3; Eze 18:21-23, 27, 28, 30, 31; Mal 3:7; 1Jo 1:9).

Repugnant: To God (Ge 6:6, 7; Le 18:24-30; Nu 22:32; De 25:16; 32:19; 2Sa 11:27; 1Ki 14:22; Ps 5:4-6; 10:3; 11:5; 78:59; 95:10; 106:40; Pr 3:32; 6:16-19; 11:20; 15:8, 9, 26; 21:27; Isa 43:24; Jer 25:7; 44:4, 21, 22; Hab 1:13; Zec 8:17; Lu 16:15). See God, Holiness of.

To Christ (Re 2:6, 15).

To the righteous (Ge 39:7-9; De 7:26; Job 1:1; 21:16; 22:18; Ps 26:5, 9; 84:10; 101:3, 4, 7; 119:104, 113, 128, 163; 120:2, 5-7; 139:19-22; Pr 8:13; 29:27; Jer 9:2; Ro 7:15, 19, 23, 24; 2Pe 2:7, 8; Jude 23; Re 2:2. See Holiness.

Separates from God: (De 31:17, 18; Jos 7:12; 2Ch 24:20; Job 13:24; 23:2, 8, 9; Ps 78:59, 60; Isa 59:1, 2; 64:7; Eze 23:18; Ho 9:12; Am 3:2, 3; Mic 3:4; M't 7:23; 25:41; Lu 13:27; Ro 8:7; Heb 12:14). See God, Holiness of; Wicked, Punishment of.

Works spiritual death (Ro 5:12, 21; 6:21, 23; 7:13; Eph 2:1; Jas 1:15).

By righteous, dishonors God (2Sa 12:14); a reproach (2Sa 12:14).

Against the Holy Spirit, unpardonable (M't 12:31; M'k 3:29; Lu 12:10; 1Jo 5:16, 17).

Typified: The design of the Mosaic ordinances was to impress the Israelites, and through them the consciences of all people for all time, with the offensiveness of sin. To produce this effect the Mosaic law contained numerous types of sin, the design of which was to teach that sin is repugnant to God, and that it separates from God and from the righteous. Hence, we find many object lessons about uncleanness and defilement, blemishes, separation from the congregation, atonements and atoning sacrifices, washings and purifications; all of which were designed to typify the corruption of sin and the necessity, in order to please a holy Jehovah, that sin must be purged and the heart purified.

By blemishes that disqualified animals for sacrifices (Ex 12:5; Le 1:10; 3:1, 6; 4:3, 23; 5:15; 6:6; 9:2, 3; 22:19-22; Nu 28:3, 9, 11, 19, 31; 29:2, 8, 13, 17, 20, 23, 26, 29, 32, 36). By blemishes of priests, disqualifying them from performing sacred offices (Le 21:17-23). By unclean animals (Le 11:1-47; 20:25; De 14:3-20).

Its effect, in separating the wicked from God and from the righteous, by excluding the defiled and unclean from the congregation (Le 7:20, 25, 27; 13:5, 26, 33; 15:19; 17:9, 10, 15; 18:29; 19:8; 20:3-6; Nu 5:2, 3; 19:20; De 23:10, 11).

Words for: Missing the mark (Ro 5:12). Overstepping the boundary, or trespassing (Ro 4:15). Blunder, or offense (Ro 5:15). Disobedience, or disregard (Ro 5:19). Unrighteousness (Ro 1:18). Ungodliness (Ro 1:18). Lawlessness (Tit 2:14).

SIN, Egyptian city on E arm of the Nile (Eze 30:15, 16).

SIN, WILDERNESS OF, wilderness through which the Israelites passed between Elim and Mt. Sinai (Ex 16:1; 17:1; Nu 33:11, 12).

SINA (See Sinai.)

SINAI. 1. A mountain in the peninsula E of Red Sea. Called also Sina-Hora. Children of Israel arrive at in their wanderings in the wilderness (Ex 16:1; 19:2; De 1:2). The law delivered to Moses upon (Ex 19:3-25; 20; 24:12-18; 32:15, 16; 34:2-4; Le 7:38; 25:1; 26:46; 27:34; Nu 3:1; De 4:15; 5:26; 29:1; 33:2; Ne 9:13; Ps 68:8, 17; Mal 4:4; Ac 7:30, 38).

Figurative: Ga 4:24, 25.

See Horeb; Israelites.

2. Wilderness of. Children of Israel journeyed in (Nu 10:12); kept the passover in (Nu 9:1-5); numbered in (Nu 26:64).

SINCERITY. Does not exempt from guilt (Ge 20). See Ignorance, Sins of. Forgiveness of enemies must be sincere (M't 18:35). Servants must render honest service (Eph 6:5-7). Whatsoever is done must be in (1Co 10: 31). Jesus was an example of (1Pe 2:

22). Ministers should be examples of (Tit 2:7). Opposed to fleshly wisdom (2Co 1:12).

Should characterize our love to God (2Co 8:8, 24); our love to Jesus (Eph 6:24); our service to God (Jos 24:14); our faith (1Ti 1:5); our love to one another (Ro 12:9; 1Pe 1:22; 1Jo 3:18); our whole conduct (2Co 1:12); the preaching of the gospel (2Co 2:17; 1Th 2:3-5).

A characteristic of the doctrines of the gospel (1Pe 2:2). The gospel sometimes preached without (Ph'p 1:16). The wicked devoid of (Ps 5:9; 55:21). Exhortations to (1Co 5:8; 1Pe 2:1). Blessedness of (Ps 32:2).

Exemplified: By men of Zebulun (1Ch 12:33). By Hezekiah (Isa 38:3). By Nathanael (Joh 1:47). By Paul (2Co 1:12). By Timothy (2Ti 1:5). By Lois and Eunice (2Ti 1:5).

SINEW, tendon, in contrast to bone structure (Ge 32:32; Job 40:17; Eze 37:6-8).

SINGERS (See Music.)

SINGLE EYE, eye that is clear, sound, and healthy, with the connotation generous (M't 6:22).

SINIM, an unknown land, conjectured by some authorities to be China (Isa 49:12).

SINITES, a tribe of Canaanites (Ge 10:17; 1Ch 1:15).

SINFULNESS. Universal (1Ki 8:46; 2Ch 6:36; Ps 14:3; Ec 7:20; Ro 3:23; 11:32; 1Jo 1:8, 10).

See Depravity.

SINLESSNESS (Ps. 119:3). The believer's goal (Ph'p 1:9-11; 1Th 3:13; 5:23; 1Pe 4:1, 2; 1Jo 3:6, 9; 5:18). Impossible to attain (1Jo 1:8; 10).

SIN MONEY (2Ki 12:16).

See Conscience Money.

SIN-OFFERING. Probable origin of (Ge 4:4, 7).

Was offered: For sins of ignorance (Le 4:2, 13, 22, 27). At the consecration of priests (Ex 29:10, 14; Le 8:14). At the consecration of Levites (Nu 8:8). At the expiration of a Nazarite's vow (Nu 6:14). On the day of atonement (Le 16:3, 9). Was a most holy sacrifice (Le 6:25, 29).

Consisted of: A young bullock for priests (Le 4:3; 9:2, 8; 16:3, 6). A young bullock or he-goat for the congregation (Le 4:14; 16:9; 2Ch 29:23). A male kid for a ruler (Le 4:23). A female kid or female lamb for a private person (Le 4:28, 32). Sins of the offerer transferred to, by imposition of hands (Le 4:4, 15, 24, 29; 2Ch 29:23). Was killed in the same place as the burnt-offering (Le 4:24; 6:25).

The blood of: For a priest or for the congregation, brought by the priest into the tabernacle (Le 4:5, 16). For the priest or for the congregation, sprinkled seven times before the Lord, outside the veil, by the priest with his finger (Le 4:6, 17). For a priest or for the congregation, put upon the horns of the altar of incense (Le 4:7, 18). For a ruler or for a private person put upon the horns of the altar of burnt-offering by the priest with his finger (Le 4:25, 30). In every case poured at the foot of the altar of burnt-offering (Le 4:7, 18, 30; 9:9). Fat of the inside, kidneys, etc. burned on the altar of burnt-offering (Le 4:8-10, 19, 26, 31; 9:10). When for a priest or the congregation, the skin, carcass, burned without the camp (Le 4:11, 12, 21; 6:30; 9:11). Was eaten by the priests in a holy place, when its blood had not been brought into the tabernacle (Le 6:26, 29, w 30). Aaron rebuked for burning and not eating that of the congregation, its blood not having been brought into the tabernacle (Le 10:16-18, w 9:9, 15). Whatever touched the flesh of, was rendered holy (Le 6:27). Garments sprinkled with the blood of, to be washed (Le 6:27). Laws respecting the vessels used for boiling the flesh of (Le 6:28). Was typical of Christ's sacrifice (2Co 5:21; Heb 13:11-13).

SINNER (See Wicked.)

SION. 1. A name of Mount Hermon (De 4:48).

2. See Zion.

SIPHMOTH, a city of Judah (1Sa 30:28).

SIPPAI. A Philistine giant (1Ch 20:4). Called Saph (2Sa 21:18).

SIRACH, SON OF, supposed author of Ecclesiasticus; wrote c. 190-170 B.C.

SIRAH, well, c. 1 mile N of Hebron (2Sa 3:26).

SIRION (coat of mail), Sidonian name

of Mount Hermon (De 3:9; Ps 29:6).
SISAMAI, son of Eleasah (1Ch 2:40).
SISERA. 1. Captain of army of Jabin, king of Hazor; defeated in battle by Barak; slain by Deborah (J'g 4:5; 1Sa 12:9; Ps 83:9).

2. Ancestor of Nethinim who returned with Zerubbabel (Ezr 2:53; Ne 7:55).

SISTER. 1. Full or half sister (Ge 20:12; De 27:22).

2. Wife (Song 4:9).

3. Woman of same country or tribe (Nu 25:18).

4. Blood relatives (M't 13:56; M'k 6:3).

5. Female fellow Christian (Ro 16:1; 2Jo 13).

SITNAH (hostility), well dug by Isaac between Gerar and Rehoboth (Ge 26:21).
SIVAN, name of third month of Hebrew sacred year (May-June) (Es 8:9).
SKEPTICISM (Job 21:15; 22:17; Ps 14:1; 53:1; Zep 1:12; Mal 3:14). Of Pharaoh (Ex 5:2). Of Thomas (Joh 20:25-28).

See Unbelief.

SKILL, examples of (Ex 28:3; 31:3; 35:35; 38:23; 1Ki 7:14; 1Ch 22:15; 2Ch 2:13; 26:15).
SKIN. Clothes of (Ge 3:21). For covering the tabernacle (Ex 25:5; Nu 4:8-14). Diseases of (Le 15:38, 39; De 28:27; Job 7:5). See Boils; Leprosy.
SKIRT (See Dress.)
SKULL (See Golgotha.)
SKY, clouds, firmament; also used figuratively (De 33:26).
SLANDER. Comes from the evil heart (Lu 6:45). Often arises from hatred (Ps 109:3). Idleness leads to (1Ti 5:13). The wicked addicted to (Ps 50:20). Hypocrites addicted to (Pr 11:9). A characteristic of the devil (Re 12:10). The wicked love (Ps 52:4). They who indulge in, are fools (Pr 10:18). Women warned against (Tit 2:3). Ministers' wives should avoid (1Ti 3:11). Christ was exposed to (Ps 35:11; M't 26:60). Rulers exposed to (Jude 8). Ministers exposed to (Ro 3:8; 2Co 6:8). The nearest relations exposed to (Ps 50:20). Saints exposed to (Ps 38:12; 109:2; 1Pe 4:4).

Saints should keep their tongues from (Ps 34:13, w 1Pe 3:10); should lay aside (Eph 4:31); should be warned against (Tit 3:1, 2); should give no occasion for (1Pe 2:12; 3:16); should return good for (1Co 4:13); blessed in enduring (M't 5:11); characterized as avoiding (Ps 15:1, 3).

Should not be listened to (1Sa 24:9); causes anger (Pr 25:23).

A fruit of wickedness (Ro 1:29, 30; 2Co 12:20; 2Pe 2:10). Forbidden (Ex 23:1; 1Ti 3:11; Tit 2:3; 3:2; Jas 4:11; 1Pe 2:1). Punishment for (De 19:16-21; 22:13-19; Ps 101:5; 1Co 6:10).

Instances of: Joseph, by Potiphar's wife (Ge 39:14-18). Land of Canaan misrepresented by the spies (Nu 14:36). Of Mephibosheth, by Ziba (2Sa 16:3; 19:24-30). Of David, by his enemies (Ps 31:13; 35:21; 41:5-9; 64:3; 140:3). Of Naboth, by Jezebel (1Ki 21:9-14). Of Jeremiah, by the Jews (Jer 6:28; 18:18). Of the Jews, of one another (Jer 9:4). Of Jesus, by the Jews falsely charging that he was a winebibber (M't 11:19); that he blasphemed (M'k 14:64; Joh 5:18); that he had a devil (Joh 8:48, 52; 10:20); that he was seditious (Lu 22:65; 23:5); that he was a king (Lu 23:2; Joh 18:37 w 19:1-5). Of Paul (see Paul).

Effects of: Separating friends (Pr 16:28; 17:9); deadly wounds (Pr 18:8; 26:22); strife (Pr 26:20); discord among brethren (Pr 6:19); murder (Ps 31:13; Eze 22:9).

The tongue of, is a scourge (Job 5:21); is venomous (Ps 140:3; Ec 10:11); is destructive (Pr 11:9). End of, is mischievous madness (Ec 10:13). Men shall give account for (M't 12:36).

See Accusation, False; False Witness; Falsehood; Speaking Evil.

SLAVE, SLAVERY (See Servant.)
SLAYER, THE (Nu 35:11; De 4:42; 19:3; Jos 20:3).
SLEEP. From God (Ps 127:2). Of the sluggard (Pr 6:9, 10). Of Jesus (M't 8:24; M'k 4:38; Lu 8:23). A symbol of death (Job 14:12; M't 9:24; M'k 5:39; Lu 8:52; Joh 11:11, 12; 1Th 4:14). See Death.
SLIME, a cement made of asphaltum. Valley of Siddim afforded (Ge 14:10). Used at Babel (Ge 11:3). Used in Noah's ark (Ge 6:14); ark of Moses (Ex 2:3). Inflammable (Isa 34:9).
SLING. Used for throwing stones (Pr 26:8). David slays Goliath with (1Sa 17:40-50). Dextrous use of (J'g 20:16; 2Ki 3:25; 2Ch 26:14).

SLIP, cutting from a plant (Isa 17:10).

SLOTHFULNESS. The ant, an example against (Pr 6:6-11). Character of (Pr 10:4, 5, 26; 13:4; 15:19; 18:9; 19:15, 24; 20:4; 21:25; 22:13; 23:21; 24:30-34; 26:13-16; Isa 56:10).

Results in, poverty (Pr 10:4, 5; 12:24, 27; 13:4; 15:19; 18:19; 19:15, 24; 20:4; 21:25; 23:21; 24:30-34; 26:13-16; Ec 10:18); condemnation (M't 25:26, 27).

Not to be of a Christian (Ro 12:11; 2Th 3:10-12; Heb 6:12).

See Idleness; Industry.

SLOW, always refers to the passions in the OT (Ne 9:17; Ps 103:8; 145:8).

SLUGGARD (See Idleness; Laziness; Slothful.)

SMITH, a worker in metals. Tubal-cain (Ge 4:22). Bezaleel (Ex 31:1-11). The Philistines (1Sa 13:19). Jewish, carried captive to Babylon (2Ki 24:14; Jer 24:1). The manufacturers of idols (Isa 41:7; 44:12). Genius of, from God (Ex 31:3-5; 35:30-35; Isa 54:16).

SMITING (See Assault and Battery.)

SMITING AND SCOURGING OF JESUS. Prophesied (Isa 50:6). Described (M't 20:19; 26:67, 68; 27:26, 30; M'k 10:34; 15:15, 19; Lu 22:63, 64; 23:16; Joh 18:22; 19:1).

SMOKE. *Figurative:* Isa 6:4; Ho 13:3.

SMYRNA, ancient seaport on W coast of Asia Minor 40 miles N of Ephesus; seat of important Christian church (Re 1:11; 2:8-11).

SNAIL, a crustacean. Forbidden as food (Le 11:30). Perishable (Ps 58:8).

SNARE, device for catching birds and animals (Ps 124:7); also used figuratively (Ps 91:3).

SNOUT, long projecting nose of a beast, as of a pig (Pr 11:22).

SNOW, falls in elevated areas of Palestine in January and February, but soon melts; Mt. Hermon covered with snow even in summer; used for cooling purposes. Used figuratively for righteousness and purity (Isa 1:18; Ps 51:7; M't 28:3; Re 1:14).

SNUFF, panting for wind (Jer 14:6), contempt for God's sacrifices (Mal 1:13).

SNUFFDISHES, in the tabernacle (Ex 25:38).

SNUFFERS. Provided for the lamps in the temple (1Ki 7:50; 2Ki 12:13; 25:14; Jer 52:18).

SO, king of Egypt with whom Hoshea, king of Israel, made an alliance, so bringing down the wrath of Assyria upon Israel (2Ki 17:4); not identified.

SOAP, in a modern sense was unknown in OT times, but fullers made a cleansing material compounded from vegetable alkali (Jer 2:22; Mal 3:2).

SOBERMINDEDNESS. Enjoined (Ro 12:3; 1Pe 1:13; 4:7; 5:8); upon women (1Ti 3:11; Tit 2:4, 5); upon men (Tit 2:2, 6); upon ministers (1Ti 3:2; Tit 1:8).

SOBRIETY. Commanded (1Pet 1:13; 5:8). The gospel designed to teach (Tit 2:12). With watchfulness (1Th 5:6). With prayer (1Pe 4:7). Required in ministers (1Ti 3:2, 3; Tit 1:8); wives of ministers (1Ti 3:11); aged men (Tit 2:2); young men (Tit 2:6); young women (Tit 2:4); all saints (1Th 5:6, 8). Women should exhibit in dress (1Ti 2:9). We should estimate our character and talents with (Ro 12:3). We should live in (Tit 2:12). Motive for (1Pe 4:7; 5:8).

See Temperance; Drunkenness.

SOCHO, SOCOCH, SOCOH (branches). 1. Town in Judah (Jos 15:35) NW of Adullam; identified with Khirbet Shuweikeh.

2. Another city by this name 10 miles SW of Hebron (Jos 15:48).

3. Son of Heber (1Ch 4:18).

SODI, father of Zebulun spy (Nu 13:10).

SODOM, called also Sodoma. Situated in the plain of the Jordan (Ge 13:10). The southeastern limit of the Canaanites (Ge 10:19). Lot dwells at (Ge 13:12). King of, joins other kings of the nations resisting the invasion of Chedorlaomer (Ge 14:1-12). Wickedness of the inhabitants of (Ge 13:13; 19:4-13; De 32:32; Isa 3:9; Jer 23:14; La 4:6; Eze 16:46, 48, 49; Jude 7). Abraham's intercession for (Ge 18:16-33). Destroyed on account of the wickedness of the people (Ge 19:1-29; De 29:23; Isa 13:19; Jer 49:18; 50:40; La 4:6; Am 4:11; Zep 2:9; M't 10:15; Lu 17:29; Ro 9:29; 2Pe 2:6).

Figurative: Of wickedness (De 23:17; 32:32; Isa 1:10; Eze 16:46-56).

SODOMITES, inhabitants of Sodom. Wickedness of (Ge 19:4-14). Destroyed by fire as a judgment (Ge 19:24, 25). To be judged according to opportunity (M't

11:24; Lu 10:12). A proverbial term of reproach applied to those who practice sodomy (De 23:17; 1Ki 14:24; 15:12; 22:46; 2Ki 23:7; Job 36:14; [marg.]). The word "harlot" in Ge 38:21, 22; De 23:17; Ho 4:14, is the translation of a Hebrew feminine form of the word translated elsewhere "sodomite." (See Sodomy.)

SODOMY (male temple prostitute), unnatural sexual perversion for which Sodom became noted (Ge 19:5). Forbidden by law (De 23:17); fastened itself upon Israel (1Ki 14:24) and ancient heathen world (Ro 1:26f); practiced even in temple (2Ki 23:7).

SOJOURNERS (Ge 12:10; 20:1; 21:34; 47:4; Le 18:26; 20:2; 25:40; Nu 15:15; De 26:5; J'g 17:7; Ru 1:1; Heb 11:9).

SOLDER (joint), metallic substance used to join metals together (Isa 41:7).

SOLDIERS. Military enrollment of Israel in the wilderness of Sinai (Nu 1; 2); in the plains of Moab (Nu 26). Levies of, in the ratio of one man to ten subject to duty (J'g 20:10). Dressed in scarlet (Na 2:3). Cowards, excused from duty as (De 20:8; J'g 7:3). Others exempt from service (De 20:5-9; 24:5). Come to John (Lu 3:14). Mock Jesus (M't 27:27-31; M'k 15:16-20; Lu 23:11, 36, 37). Officers concerned in the betrayal of Jesus (Lu 22:4). Crucified Jesus (M't 27:27, 31-37; M'k 15:16-24; Joh 19:23, 24). Guard the sepulchre (M't 27:65; 28:11-15). Guard prisoners (Ac 12:4-6; 28:16). Maintain the peace (Ac 21:31-35). Their duty as sentinels (Ac 12:19). Perform escort duty (Ac 21:31-33, 35; 22:24-28; 23:23, 31-33; 27:1, 31, 42, 43; 28:16).

Figurative: Of the divine protection (Isa 59:16, 17). Of the Christian (Eph 6:11-17; 2Ti 2:3). Jesus called Captain of our Salvation (Heb 2:10).

See Armies.

SOLOMON (peaceable). Son of David by Bathsheba (2Sa 12:24; 1Ki 1:13, 17, 21). Named Jedidiah, by Nathan the prophet (2Sa 12:24, 25). Ancestor of Joseph (M't 1:6). Succeeds David to the throne of Israel (1Ki 1:11-48; 2:12; 1Ch 23:1; 28; Ec 1:12). Anointed king a second time (1Ch 29:22). His prayer for wisdom, and his vision (1Ki 3:5-14; 2Ch 1:7-12). Covenant renewed in a vision after the dedication of the temple (1Ki 9:1-9; 2Ch 7:12-22). His rigorous reign (1Ki 2).

Builds the temple (1Ki 5; 6; 9:10; 1Ch 6:10; 2Ch 2; 3; 4; 7:11; Jer 52:20; Ac 7:45-47). Dedicates the temple (1Ki 8; 2Ch 6). Renews the courses of the priests and Levites, and the forms of service according to the regulations of David (2Ch 8:12-16; 35:4; Ne 12:45).

Builds his palace (1Ki 3:1; 7:1, 8; 9:10; 2Ch 7:11; 8:1; Ec 2:4); his house of the forest of Lebanon (1Ki 7:2-7); for Pharaoh's daughter (1Ki 7:8-12; 9:24; 2Ch 8:11; Ec 2:4). Ivory throne of (1Ki 7:7; 10:18-20). Porches of judgment (1Ki 7:7). Builds Millo, the wall of Jerusalem, the cities of Hazor, Megiddo, Gezer, Beth-horon, Baalath, Tadmor, store cities, and cities for chariots, and for cavalry (1Ki 9:15-19; 2Ch 9:25). Provides an armory (1Ki 10:16, 17). Plants vineyards and orchards of all kinds of fruit trees; makes pools (Ec 2:4-6); imports apes and peacocks (1Ki 10:22). Drinking vessels of his houses (1Ki 10:21; 2Ch 9:20). Musicians and musical instruments of his court (1Ki 10:12; 2Ch 9:11; Ec 2:8). The splendor of his court (1Ki 10:5-9, 12; 2Ch 9:3-8; Ec 2:9; M't 6:29; Lu 12:27).

Commerce of (1Ki 9:28; 10:11, 12, 22, 28, 29; 2Ch 1:16, 17; 8:17, 18; 9:13-22, 28). Presents received by (1Ki 10:10; 2Ch 9:9, 23, 24). Is visited by the queen of Sheba (1Ki 10:1-13; 2Ch 9:1-12). Wealth of (1Ki 9; 10:10, 14, 15, 23, 27; 2Ch 1:15; 9:1, 9, 13, 24, 27; Ec 1:16). Has seven hundred wives and three hundred concubines (1Ki 11:3, w De 17:17); their influence over him (1Ki 11:4). Marries one of Pharaoh's daughters (1Ki 3:1). Builds idolatrous temples (1Ki 11:1-8; 2Ki 23:13). His idolatry (1Ki 3:3, 4; 2Ki 23:13; Ne 13:26).

Extent of his dominions (1Ki 4:21, 24; 8:65; 2Ch 7:8; 9:26). Receives tribute (1Ki 4:21; 9:21; 2Ch 8:8). Officers of (1Ki 2:35; 4:1-19; 2Ch 8:9, 10). His purveyors (1Ki 4:7-19). Divides his kingdom into subsistence departments; the daily subsistence rate for his court (1Ki 4:7-23, 27, 28).

Military equipment of (1Ki 4:26, 28; 10:16, 17, 26, 28; 2Ch 1:14; 9:25, w De 17:15, 16). Cedes certain cities to Hiram (1Ki 9:10-13; 2Ch 8:2). Wisdom and fame of (1Ki 4:29-34; 10:3, 4, 8, 23, 24; 1Ch 29:24, 25; 2Ch 9:2-7, 22, 23; Ec 1:16; M't 12:42). Piety of (1Ki 3:5-15; 4:29; 8). Beloved of God (2Sa 12:24). Justice of, illustrated in his judgment of the two harlots (1Ki 3:16-28). Oppressions of (1Ki 12:4; 2Ch 10:4).

Reigns forty years (2Ch 9:30). Death of (2Ch 9:29-31).

Prophecies concerning (2Sa 7:12-16; 1Ki 11:9-13; 1Ch 17:11-14; 28:6, 7; Ps 132:11).

A type of Christ (Ps 45:2-17; 72).

SOLOMON, SONG OF, full title is "The song of songs which is Solomon's" (1:1); the last of the five OT poetic books in the English Bible. Also called *Canticles,* from Latin *Canticum Canticorum* (1:1). Authorship attributed by book itself and by tradition to Solomon. Outline: 1. The mutual admiration of the lovers (1:2-2:7).

2. Growth in love (2:8-3:5).

3. The marriage (3:6-5:1).

4. Longing of the wife for her absent husband (5:2-6:9).

5. The beauty of the Shulammite bride (6:10-8:4).

6. The wonder of love (8:5-8:14). There is great diversity and much overlapping among interpretations of the book. Various views are: 1. Allegorical, 2. Topical, 3. Literal, 4. Dramatic, 5. Erotic-literary, 6. Liturgical, and 7. Didactic-moral. Commonly held interpretation by Jews is that the bridegroom represents God; the Shulammite bride, the Jewish people. Many Christians hold that the bridegroom is Christ; the Shulammite bride, the Church.

SOLOMON'S POOLS, three pools near Jerusalem from which water was brought by means of aqueducts to Jerusalem (Ec 2:6). They are still in use.

SOLOMON'S PORCH, colonnade built by Solomon on E side of the temple area (Joh 10:23; Ac 3:11; 5:12).

SOLOMON'S SERVANTS, slaves used by Solomon in his temple for menial tasks; their descendants returning from Babylon under Zerubbabel (Ezr 2:55, 58; Ne 7:57, 60; 11:3).

SOLOMON'S TEMPLE (See Temple.)

SON. 1. Any human offspring regardless of sex (Ge 3:16).

2. Male descendant (2Ki 9:20; Mal 3:6).

3. Member of a guild or profession (2Ki 2:3, 5; Ne 3:8).

4. Spiritual son (1Ti 1:18).

5. Address to younger man (1Sa 3:6).

6. Follower (Nu 21:29; De 14:1).

7. Adopted son (Ex 2:10).

8. Native (La 4:2).

9. Possessor of a quality (1Sa 25:17; Lu 10:6).

10. Used of Christ in a unique sense.

SON-IN-LAW. Unjust, Jacob (Ge 30:37-42). Faithful, Peter (M'k 1:29, 30; Lu 4:38).

SON OF GOD, a title of Jesus referring to His co-equality, co-eternity, consubstantiality with the Father and the Spirit in the eternal Triune Godhead (Joh 5:18, 23, 36). Christ claimed to be eternal, co-equal and of the same substance as the Father. He is uniquely God's son. See Jesus, Son of God.

SON OF MAN. 1. A member of the order of humanity (Eze 2:1, 3, 8ff; Da 8:17).

2. Used in a Messianic sense in Da 7:13, 14. Jesus applies the term to Himself many times in the Gospels (M't 8:20; 9:6; 10:23; 11:19; 12:8, etc.). Sometimes He uses it in connection with His earthly mission, but He also uses it when describing His final triumph as Redeemer and Judge (M't 16:27f; 19:28; 24:30; 25:31). He appears to identify Himself with the Son of Man of Da 7:13, 14. See Jesus, Son of Man.

SONG. Sung at the passover (M't 26:30; M'k 14:26). Didactic (De 32). See Psalms, Didactic. Personification of the church (Song 1-8). Of Moses (Ex 15:1-19). Of Deborah and Barak (J'g 5). Of Hannah (1Sa 2:1-10). Of David (2Sa 22:2-51; 23:1-7). Of Mary (Lu 1:46-55). Of Moses and the Lamb (Re 15:3, 4). New (Ps 33:3; 40:3). Prophetic (see Psalms, Prophetic). Spiritual, singing of, enjoined (Eph 5:19; Col 3:16). Of praise (see Praise; Psalms, Thanksgiving; Thankfulness). Of redemption (Re 5:9, 10). Of the redeemed (Re 14:2, 3-5). Of thanksgiving (see Psalms, Thanksgiving; Thankfulness). War (Ex 15:1-21; Nu 21:27-30; J'g 5; 2Sa 1:19-27; 22). Solomon wrote one thousand and five (1Ki 4:32).

See Poetry; Praise; Psalms, Thanksgiving.

SONG OF DEGREES (See Music.)

SONG OF SONGS (See Solomon, Song of.)

SONG OF THE THREE HEBREW CHILDREN, an addition to the book of Daniel found in the OT Apocrypha. Author is unknown; written c. 164 B. C.

SONS OF GOD, CHILDREN OF GOD, any personal creatures of God: angelic beings (Job 1:6; 2:1; 38:7); the entire human race (Ac 17:28); the regenerate as distinguished from the unregenerate (1Jo 3:10). The "sons of God" in Ge 6:1-4 are probably human beings, with special emphasis upon man's nature as created in the image of God.

SONS OF THE PROPHETS, members of prophetic guilds or schools; gathered around great prophets like Samuel and Elijah for common worship, united prayer, religious fellowship, and instruction of the people (1Sa 10:5, 10; 2Ki 4:38, 40). In the times of Elijah and Elisha they lived together at Bethel, Jericho, and Gilgal (2Ki 2:3, 5; 4:38).

SOOTHSAYER, SOOTHSAYING, one claiming power to foretell future events (Jos 13:22; Jer 27:9), interpret dreams (Da 4:7), and reveal secrets (Da 2:27).

SOP (morsel of bread), bread to dip food from a common platter (Ru 2:14; Pr 17:1; Joh 13:26).

SOPATER, Berean Christian; companion of Paul (Ac 20:4; Ro 16:21).

SOPHERETH, a servant of Solomon, whose descendants returned from captivity to Jerusalem (Ezr 2:55; Ne 7:57).

SORCERY, divination by an alleged assistance of evil spirits. Forbidden (Le 19:26-28, 31; 20:6; De 18:9-14). Denounced (Isa 8:19; Mal 3:5).

Practiced: By the Egyptians (Isa 19:3, 11, 12); by the magicians (Ex 7:11, 22; 8:7, 18); by Balaam (Nu 22:6; 23:23, w chapters 22; 23); by Jezebel (2Ki 9:22); by the Ninevites (Na 3:4, 5); by the Babylonians (Isa 47:9-13; Eze 21:21, 22; Da 2:2, 10, 27); by Belshazzar (Da 5:7, 15); by Simon Magus (Ac 8:9, 11); by Elymas (Ac 13:8); by the damsel at Philippi (Ac 16:16); by vagabond Jews (Ac 19:13); by sons of Sceva (Ac 19:14, 15); by astrologers (Jer 10:2; Mic 3:6, 7); by false prophets (Jer 14:14; 27:9; 29:8, 9; Eze 13:6-9; 22:28; M't 24:24).

To cease (Eze 12:23, 24; 13:23; Mic 5:12).

Messages of, false (Eze 21:29; Zec 10:2; 2Th 2:9). Diviners shall be confounded (Mic 3:7). Belongs to the works of the flesh (Ga 5:20). Wickedness of (1Sa 15:23). Vainness of (Isa 44:25). Punishment for (Ex 22:18; Le 20:27; De 13:5). Divining by familiar spirits (Le 20:27; 1Ch 10:13; 2Ch 33:6; Isa 8:19; 19:3; 29:4); by entrails (Eze 21:21); by images (2Ki 23:24; Eze 21:21); by rods (Ho 4:12).

Saul consulted the Witch of Endor (1Sa 28:7-25).

Books of, destroyed (Ac 19:19).

SORE (See Diseases.)

SOREK (vineyard), valley in Philistine territory c. 8-½ miles S of Joppa (J'g 16:4).

SORREL, a color (Zec 1:8).

SORROW. God takes notice of Hagar's (Ge 21:17-20); Israelites (Ex 3:7-10).

For sin (2Co 7:10, 11). See Repentance; Sin, Confession of.

No sorrow in heaven (Re 21:4). "Sorrow and sighing shall flee away" (Isa 35:10).

Of Hannah (1Sa 1:15). Of David for Absalom (2Sa 18:33; 19:1-8). Of Mary and Martha (Joh 11:19-40). Jeremiah (La 1:12). Jesus (Isa 53:11; M't 26:37-44; M'k 14:34-42; Lu 22:42-44).

From bereavement: Of Jacob for Joseph (Ge 37:34, 35); for Benjamin (Ge 43:14).

Of the lost (M't 8:12; 13:42, 50; 22:13; 24:51; 25:30; Lu 13:28; 16:23). See Wicked, Punishment of.

See Affliction, Benefits of, Consolation in, Design of, Resignation in; Suffering.

SOSIPATER, kinsman of Paul (Ro 16:21).

SOSTHENES. 1. Chief ruler of the synagogue in Corinth (Ac 18:17).

2. A Christian with whom Paul wrote the first letter to the Corinthians (1Co 1:1).

SOTAI, a servant of Solomon whose descendants returned from captivity to Jerusalem (Ezr 2:55; Ne 7:57).

SOUL, the non-material ego of man in its ordinary relationships with earthly and physical things; the immortal part of man (M't 10:28). See Immortality; Man, a Spirit.

SOUNDING, in navigation (Ac 27:28).

SOUTH, the Negeb, an indefinite area lying between Palestine and Egypt (Ge 12:9; 13:1; 1Sa 27:8-12; 2Ch 28:18).

SOVEREIGNTY OF GOD, the supreme authority of God. He is not subject to any power or law which could be conceived as superior to or other than Himself (Isa 45:9; Ro 9:20, 21).

See God, Sovereignty of; Jesus, King.

SOWER. Parable of the (M't 13:3-8; M'k 4:3-20; Lu 8:5-8). Sowing (Ec 11:4; Isa 28:25).

Figurative: Ps 126:5; Pr 11:18; Isa 32:20; Ho 8:7; 10:12; Ga 6:7, 8.

SPAIN, westernmost peninsula of Europe. Paul hoped to visit this Roman province (Ro 15:24, 28).

SPAN, about nine or ten inches (Ex 28:16; 39:9).

SPARROW. Nests of (Ps 84:3). Two, sold for a farthing (M't 10:29; Lu 12:6).

SPEAKING OR SPEECH. *Evil* (Ps 10:8; 52:2-4; Isa 32:6, 7; Jer 20:10; Jude 8, 10).

Causes strife (Pr 15:1; 16:27, 28; 17:9; 25:23). Characteristic of man (Ro 1:29, 30; 3:13, 14). Not characteristic of a Christian (Eph 4:25, 29, 31; 5:4; Tit 3:2; Jas 1:26; 3:5, 6, 8-10; 4:11; 1Pe 2:1; 3:9, 10).

Excludes from kingdom of heaven (1Co 6:10). Hated of God (Pr 6:16-19; 8:13). Punishment for (Ps 12:3, 4; 52:12).

Forbidden (Ex 22:28; Ps 34:13; Pr 4:24; 6:16-19; M't 5:22, 37; 12:34-37; Ac 23:5; Eph 4:25, 29, 31; Tit 3:2; Jas 1:26; 3:5, 6, 8-10; 4:11; 1Pe 2:1; 3:9, 10).

Proverbs concerning (Pr 4:24; 6:16-19; 8:13; 10:11, 19, 31, 32; 11:11; 12:5, 6, 13, 17-19; 13:3; 14:25; 15:1, 4, 28; 16:27, 28; 17:4, 9, 20; 18:8, 21, 23; 19:1, 22, 23; 24:2; 25:23; 26:20-23, 28; Ec 10:11, 20). Prayers for deliverance from curse of (Ps 64:2-5; 70:3; 120:1-7).

Self-accusation: Solomon (Ec 7:22); Isaiah (Isa 6:5); Paul (Ac 23:5).

Instances of: Against Job (Job 19:18). Against Lot, those of Sodom (2Pe 2:7, 8, 10). Against Moses (Ps 106:33). Against psalmists (Ps 35:21; 41:5-9; 69:12, 26; 102:8; 119:23). Against the church, those of the circumcision (Tit 1:10, 11); false teachers (Jude 8, 10).

See Accusation, False; Blasphemy; Busybody; Falsehood; Flattery; Slander; Talebearer; Uncharitableness.

Foolish (Job 13:5; 16:3, 4; 38:2). Accountable to God (M't 12:36, 37). Forbidden (Pr 30:18). Not characteristic of a Christian (Eph 5:4).

Proverbs concerning (Pr 10:14; 12:23; 13:3; 14:3; 15:2, 7, 14; 18:6, 7, 13; 26:4, 7, 9; 29:11, 20; 30:10; Ec 5:3, 5; 10:13, 14).

See Fool.

Wise (Job 16:5; 27:4; Am 5:13; Zep 3:13; Zec 8:16; Re 14:17). As good as nails (Ec 12:11). Precious as jewels (Pr 20:16).

Edifying (Eph 4:29). Rewards of (Ps 15:1-3; 50:23; Pr 14:3; 22:11). Of the ideal woman (Pr 31:26).

Admonitions concerning, to believers (Eph 4:22, 25, 29; Ph'p 1:27; Col 4:6; Jas 1:19, 26; 3:2, 13; 1Pe 2:12; 3:15, 16). Christ's words concerning (M't 12:35, 37; Lu 6:45).

Of psalmists (Ps 37:30; 39:1; 77:12; 119:13, 27, 46, 54, 172; 141:3; 145:5-7, 11, 12).

Proverbs concerning (Pr 10:11, 13, 19-21, 31, 32; 11:12-14; 12:6, 14, 16-20, 23; 13:2, 3; 14:3; 15:1, 2, 4, 7, 23, 26, 28; 16:21, 23, 24; 17:7, 27, 28; 18:4, 20; 19:1; 20:15; 21:23; 22:11; 24:6; 25:11, 15; 26:5; 29:11; 31:26; Ec 3:7; 9:17; 10:12; 12:9-11). Prayer concerning (Ps 141:3).

See Wisdom.

SPEAR. Spears and javelins differed in weight and size, but had similar uses.

An implement of war (2Ki 11:10; Ne 4:13). Goliath's (1Sa 17:7). Saul's (1Sa 18:10, 11). Stored in the temple (2Ch 23:9). To be changed into pruning hooks (Isa 2:4; Mic 4:3). Pruning hooks to be beaten into (Joe 3:10). Thrust into Jesus' side. (Zec 12:10; Joh 19:34; 20:27; Re 1:7).

SPECKLED, mottled in color (Ge 30:25-43).

SPELT (See Rye.)

SPERMATORRHEA, a disease of the genital organs (Le 15:16).

SPICES. In the formula for the sacred oil (Ex 25:6; 35:8). Stores of (2Ki 20:13). Used in the temple (1Ch 9:29).

Exported from Gilead (Ge 37:25). Sent as a present by Jacob to Joseph (Ge 43:11). Presented by the queen of Sheba to Solomon (1Ki 10:2, 10). Sold in the markets of Tyre (Eze 27:22). Used in the embalming of Asa (2Ch 16:14). Prepared for embalming the body of Jesus (M'k 16:1; Lu 23:56; 24:1; Joh 19:39, 40).

SPIDER. Mentioned in one of Agur's riddles [*R. V.*, lizard] (Pr 30:28). Web of, figurative of the hope of the hypocrite (Job 8:14; Isa 59:5).

SPIES (Ge 42:9). Sent to investigate Canaan (Nu 13); Jaazer (Nu 21:32); Jericho (Jos 2:1). Used by David (1Sa 26:4); at the court of Absalom (2Sa 15:10; 17:1-17). Pharisees acted as (Lu 20:20). In the church of Galatia (Ga 2:4).

SPIKENARD. An aromatic plant (Song 4:13, 14). Perfume prepared from (Song 1:12). A fragrant oil from, used in anointing (M't 14:3; Joh 12:3).

SPINDLE, implement used in spinning (Ex 35:24; Pr 31:19).

SPINNING, by hand (Ex 35:25; Pr 31:19).

SPIRIT (breath, wind, spirit), the non-material ego in special relationships; the self is generally called "spirit" when the direct relationship of the individual to God is the point of emphasis (Ro 8:15, 16).

SPIRIT, HOLY (See Holy Spirit.)

SPIRITS IN PRISON, those who in the days of Noah refused his message (1Pe 3:18-20; 4:6).

SPIRITUAL ADOPTION (See Adoption, Spiritual.)

SPIRITUAL BLESSINGS (See Blessings, Spiritual; Holy Spirit; Sanctification.)

SPIRITUAL BLINDNESS (See Blindness, Spiritual.)

SPIRITUAL BOASTING (Ro 11:18-21). Incompatible, with faith (Ro 3:27; Eph 2:8-10); with humility (1Co 1:29 w 17-31; 4:6, 7; 2Co 10:12-16).

In the Lord, approved (Jer 9:24; 2Co 10:17, 18; Ga 6:14).

See Boasting, Spiritual.

SPIRITUAL DEATH, alienation from the life of God; a state of condemnation (Ro 7:9, 11; 8:5, 6, 13; Eph 4:18).

Quickening from (Joh 5:24-26; Ro 5:12, 15; Eph 2:1, 5, 6; 5:14; Col 2:13).

See Death; Second Death.

SPIRITUAL DESIRE (See Desire, Spiritual.)

SPIRITUAL DILIGENCE (See Zeal.)

SPIRITUAL GIFTS. Extraordinary gifts of the Spirit given to Christians to equip them for the service of the Church (Ro 11:29; 12:6-8; 1Co 12:4-11, 28-30; Eph 4:7-11; 1Pe 4:10, 11).

See Charisma; Holy Spirit; Tongues.

SPIRITUAL HUNGER (See Hunger, Figurative of Spiritual Desire.)

SPIRITUAL PEACE (Isa 27:5; 54:1, 10, 13; 55:2, 12; 57:19; Eze 34:25; Lu 2:14, 29; Ro 5:1; 1Co 14:33). Christ's kingdom, a kingdom of (Isa 9:6; 11:6-9, 13; Mic 5:5; Lu 1:79; Ac 10:36).

See Peace, Spiritual.

SPIRITUAL POWER (See Power, Spiritual.)

SPIRITUAL PURIFICATION (Ps 65:3; 73:1; Pr 20:9; Joh 13:8, 9).

By corrective judgments (Isa 4:3, 4). By mercy and truth (Pr 16:6). By the Holy Spirit (1Co 6:11; Tit 3:5, 6). By the blood of Christ (Heb 1:3; 9:14; 2Pe 1:9; 1Jo 1:7; Re 1:5; 7:14).

Of the Church (Eph 5:26).

Enjoined (Isa 1:16; M't 23:26; Ac 22:16; 1Co 5:7; 2Co 7:1; Heb 10:22; Jas 4:8).

Promised (Isa 1:18; Jer 33:8; Eze 36:25; Da 12:10; Zec 13:1; 1Jo 1:9). Prayer for (Ps 51:2, 7; 79:9).

See Purification; Sanctification.

SPIRITUAL UNDERSTANDING (M't 13:23; Lu 10:21, 22; Joh 7:17).

Of apostles (M't 13:16, 17; Lu 8:10; 10:23, 24). Of Peter (M't 16:16, 17). Of Mary (Lu 10:39, 42).

Lacking, in disciples (M't 15:15, 16; Lu 24:25); in Jews (M't 13:11-16; Joh 6:26, 41, 52; 9:28, 29, 39-41; 12:27-40; Ac 28:24-27); in Simon Magus (Ac 8:18-23).

Enjoined: Concerning, the import of preaching (M't 11:13-15); the import of parables (M't 13:9, 43; Lu 8:8); the character of the disciples of Jesus (Lu 14:33-35); the Holy Spirit's message to the churches (Re 2:7).

See Wisdom, Spiritual.

SPIRITUALISM (See Necromancy; Sorcery.)

SPIRITUALITY. Described as the great and enduring good (Lu 10:42); as love and devotion to God (De 6:5; Jos 22:5; 1Ki 8:23; Ps 1:2; 51:6).

Brings peace (Isa 26:3; Jer 33:6; Ro 8:6; 14:17); indifference to worldly good (1Co 7:29-31; Col 3:1-3); thirst for heavenly blessings (M't 5:6; Joh 6:27).

Is produced by the indwelling of the Holy Spirit (Joh 14:16, 17; Ro 8:4).

SPITTING. In the face, as an indignity (Nu 12:14; De 25:9; Job 30:10; M't 26:67; 27:30). Jesus used spittle in healing (M'k 7:33; 8:23).

SPOILS. Of war (Ge 14:11, 12; Nu 31:9, 10; De 2:35). Divided between the combatants and noncombatants of the Israelites, including priests and Levites (Nu 31:25-54; 1Sa 30:24). Dedicated to the Lord (1Sa 15:15; 1Ch 26:27; 2Ch 15:11).

SPOKES, rods connecting the rim of a wheel with the hub. Basins for washing of sacrifices were set on bases moving upon wheels. The spokes were part of these wheels (1Ki 7:27-33).

SPONGE (M't 27:48; M'k 15:36; Joh 19:29).

SPOONS. Of the tabernacle (Ex 25:29; Nu 4:7; 7). Of the temple (1Ki 7:50; 2Ch 4:22).

SPOT, blemish, blot (Song 4:7; Job 11:15; Le 24:19f; Pr 9:7; Jude 23).

SPOUSE (See Marriage.)

SPREAD, SPREADING, scatter, disperse (M't 21:8; M'k 1:28).

SPRING. 1. Season of, promised annual return of (Ge 8:22). Described (Pr 27:25; Song 2:11-13).

2. Of water. Hot (Ge 36:24).

Figurative: Corrupt (Pr 25:26; Jas 3:11).

See Wells.

SPRINKLING. Of blood (Le 14:7, 51; 16:14; Heb 9:13, 19, 21; 11:28; 1Pe 1:2). See Blood. Of water (Nu 8:7; Eze 36:25; Heb 9:19; 10:22).

STABLE, enclosure to lodge and feed animals (Eze 25:5).

STABILITY. Of Character (Ps 57:7; 108:1; 112:7).

Rewarded (M't 10:22; 24:13; M'k 4:20; 2Th 3:3).

Enjoined (1Co 7:20; 15:58; 2Th 2:15; Heb 10:23; 13:9; Jas 1:23-25; Re 22:11).

See Character; Decision; Perseverance.

STACHYS (head of grain), a Christian in Rome (Ro 16:9).

STACTE (drop), fragrant ingredient used in incense (Ex 30:34).

STAFF, STAVES (See Rod.)

STAIRS, steps leading to an upper chamber (1Ki 6:8; Ac 21:40) or some other elevated place (Eze 40:6; 43:17).

STAKE, tent-pin or tent-pole (Ex 27:19; Isa 33:20).

STALL, place for care of livestock, or compartment in a stable for one animal (2Ch 32:28). Solomon's barns provided stalls for 4,000 horses (2Ch 9:25).

STAMMERING (Isa 32:4; 33:19). Of Moses (Ex 4:10).

STANDARD. An ensign used by each of the tribes of Israel in camp and march (Nu 1:52; 2:2). Banners used as (Ps 20:5; Song 6:4, 10). Used in war (Jer 4:21). Used to direct the route to defensed cities (Jer 4:6); to call attention to news (Jer 50:2; 51:12).

See Armies; Banner; Ensign.

Figurative: Isa 49:22; 62:10; Jer 4:6.

STARS. Created by God (Ge 1:16; Job 26:13; Ps 8:3; 33:6; 136:7, 9; Am 5:8). Differ in splendor (1Co 15:41). Worship of, forbidden (De 4:19). Worshiped (2Ki 17:16; 21:3; 23:5; Jer 19:13; Am 5:26; Zep 1:5; Ac 7:42, 43). Constellations of (Isa 13:10); Orion (Job 9:9; Am 5:8); serpent (Job 26:13). Planets (2Ki 23:5); the morning star (Job 38:7; Re 2:28; 22:16). Darkening of (Job 9:7; Ec 12:2; Isa 13:10; 34:4; Joe 2:10; 3:15; Re 8:11, 12). Comets (Jude 13). Falling of (Da 8:10; M't 24:29; M'k 13:25; Re 6:13; 8:10; 9:1; 12:4). Guides the wise men (M't 2:2, 7, 9, 10).

Figurative: Of the deliverer (Nu 24:17). Seven stars of the seven churches (Re 1:16, 20). Crown of twelve stars (Re 12:1). Of Jesus (Re 22:16).

STATE (See Church and State; Government.)

STATECRAFT. Wisdom in (Pr 28:2). School in (Da 1:3-5). Skilled in.

Instances of: Joseph (Ge 47:15-26); Samuel (1Sa 11:12-15); Nathan (1Ki 1:11-14); Jeroboam (1Ki 12:26-33); Daniel (see Daniel).

See Government; Kings; Rulers.

STATURE, natural height of an animal body (2Sa 21:20; Isa 45:14; Lu 19:3).

STAVES, used as weapons (M't 26:47; M'k 14:43).

Symbolical: Zec 11:7-14.

STEADFASTNESS (Ps 57:7; 108:1; 112:7; Ro 14:4; 1Th 3:8; Col 1:23; Jas 1:25).

Enjoined (1Co 7:20; 15:58; 16:13; Ga 6:1; Eph 6:11, 13, 14; Ph'p 1:27; 4:1; 1Th 5:21; 2Th 2:15; 3:13; Heb 10:23; 13:9; Jas 1:25; 1Pe 5:9).

Rewards of (M't 10:22; 24:13; M'k 13:13; Re 2:7, 10, 11, 17, 25-28; 3:5, 11, 12, 21; 21:17).

See Decision; Perseverance; Stability.

STEALING (See Theft.)

STEEL. Bows of (2Sa 22:35; Job 20:24; Ps 18:34). Strength of (Jer 15:12). In each of the above references, the *R. V.* renders the translation "brass."

STELE (erect block or **shaft),** narrow, upright slab of stone with an inscription cut on it to commemorate an event, mark a grave, or give a votive likeness of a deity. Prevalent especially in Egypt and Greece.

STEPHANAS (crown), a Christian in Corinth, whose household Paul baptized (1Co 1:16; 16:15, 17).

STEPHEN (crown), a Christian martyr. Appointed one of the committee of seven to oversee power of (Ac 6:5, 8-10). False charges against (Ac 6:11-15). Defense of (Ac 7). Stoned (Ac 7:54-60; 8:1; 22:20). Burial of (Ac 8:2). Gentle and forgiving spirit of (Ac 7:59, 60).

STERILITY, of women. (See Barrenness.)

STEWARD (Ge 15:2; 43:19; 1Ch 28:1; Lu 8:3).

Figurative: The faithful steward described (Lu 12:35-38, 42). The unfaithful, described (Lu 16:1-8). See the parable of the pounds (Lu 19:12-27); of the talents (M't 25:14-30). Must be faithful (1Co 4:1, 2; Tit 1:7; 1Pe 4:10).

STEWARDSHIP, of the Gospel (1Co 9:17; Ga 2:7; Col 1:25; 1Th 2:4; 1Ti 1:11; Tit 1:3).

STICKS, used as cymbals (Eze 37:16).

STIFF-NECKED (See Impenitent; Obduracy.)

STOCK. 1. Wooden idol worshiped by apostate Israel (Isa 44:19; Jer 2:27).

2. Family (Le 25:47; Isa 40:24; Ac 13:26; Ph'p 3:5).

3. Instrument of punishment in which head, hands, and feet were fastened (2Ch 16:10; Jer 20:2; Job 13:27).

STOICISM. A Grecian philosophy, inculcating doctrines of severe morality, self-denials, and inconvenient services. Scripture analogies to: John the Baptist wears camel's hair and subsists on locusts and wild honey (M't 3:4); comes "neither eating nor drinking" (M't 11:18; Lu 7:33). Jesus requires self-denials and crosses (M't 10:38, 39; 16:24; M'k 8:34, 35; Lu 9:23-26; 14:27); the subordination of natural affection (M't 10:37; Lu 14:26). Paul teaches that the "law of the mind" is at war with the "law of the members" (Ro 7:23, w *verses* 14-24); that the body must be kept under (1Co 9:27); advises celibacy (1Co 7:1-9, 25, 26, 32, 33, 39, 40).

School of, at Athens (Ac 17:18).

See Asceticism.

STOICS (See Asceticism; Stoicism.)

STOMACHER, an article of dress (Isa 3:24).

STONES. Commandments engraved upon (Ex 24:12; 31:18; 34:1-4; De 4:13; 5:22; 9:9-11; 10:1-3). The law of Moses written upon (Jos 8:32). Houses built of (Isa 9:10; Am 5:11). Temple built of (1Ki 5:17, 18; 7:9-12; M't 24:2; Lu 19:44; 21:5, 6). Prepared in the quarries (1Ki 6:7). Hewn (Ex 34:1; De 10:1; 1Ki 5:17; 6:36; 7:9; 2Ki 12:12; 22:6; 1Ch 22:2; 2Ch 34:11; La 3:9). Sawn (1Ki 7:9). Hewers of (1Ki 5:18; 2Ki 12:12; 1Ch 22:15).

City walls built of (Ne 4:3). Memorial pillars of (Ge 28:18-22; 31:45-52; Jos 4:2-9, 20-24; 24:25; 1Sa 7:12). Great, as landmarks, Abel (1Sa 6:18); Ezel (1Sa 20:19); Zoheleth (1Ki 1:9).

Cast upon accursed ground (2Ki 3:19, 25). Used in building altars (Jos 8:31); for weighing (Le 19:36 [marg.]); for closing sepulchers (M't 27:60; M'k 15:46; 16:3). Sepulchers hewn in (M't 27:60; M'k 15:46; 16:3). Idols made of (De 4:28; 28:36, 64; 29:17; 2Ki 19:18; Isa 37:19; Eze 20:32).

Great, in Solomon's temple (1Ki 5:17, 18; 7:9-12). Magnificent, in Herod's (M'k 13:1). Skill in throwing (J'g 20:16; 1Ch 12:2). See Slings.

See Adamant; Chalcedony; Marble; Onyx; Pillars. See Precious, below.

Figurative: Ge 49:24; Zec 3:9. Of temptation, "stone of stumbling" (Isa 8:14; Ro 9:33; 1Pe 2:8). Of Christ, "a tried stone," "a precious stone," "a sure foundation" (Isa 28:16); of Christ's rejection, the rejected corner stone (Ps 118:22; M't 21:42-44; M'k 12:10; Lu 20:17, 18; Ac 4:11; 1Pe 2:4); the true foundation (Isa 28:16; M't 16:18; 1Co 3:11; Eph 2:20; Re 21:14). Of Christ, the water of life (1Co 10:4). Of the impenitent heart (Eze 36:26). Of the witness of the Spirit, the white stone (Re 2:17).

Symbolical: Of the kingdom of Christ (Da 2:34, 45).

Precious: In the breastplate and ephod (Ex28:9-21;39:6-14).Voluntaryofferings of, by the Israelites for the breastplate and ephod (Ex 35:27). Exported from Sheba (1Ki 10:2, 10; 2Ch 9:9, 10; Eze 27:22); Ophir (1Ki 10:11). Partial catalogue of (Eze 28:13). Seen in the foundation of the New Jerusalem in John's apocalyptic vision (Re 21:19, 20).

In kings' crowns (2Sa 12:30; 1Ch 20:2).

Figurative: Isa 54:11, 12.

See Agate; Amethyst; Beryl; Carbuncle; Chrysolite; Chrysoprasus; Coral; Crystal; Diamond; Emerald; Jacinth; Jasper; Ligure; Ruby; Sapphire; Sardius; Sardonyx; Topaz.

STONING, the ordinary form of capital punishment prescribed by Hebrew law (Le 20:2) for blasphemy (Le 24:16), idolatry (De 13:6-10), desecration of sabbath (Nu 15:32-36), human sacrifice (Le 20:2), occultism (Le 20:27). Execution took place outside city (Le 24:14; 1Ki 21:10, 13, Ac 7:58).

STOOL (2Ki 4:10).

Footstool: Figurative: Of the earth (Isa 66:1; M't 5:35; Ac 7:49); temple (1Ch 28:2; La 2:1); sanctuary (Ps 99:5; 132:7); enemies of Jesus (Ps 110:1; M't 22:44; M'k 12:36; Lu 20:43; Ac 2:35; Heb 1:13).

STORE CITIES, supply depots for provisions and arms (1Ki 9:15-19; 2Ch 8:4-6; 16:4).

STOREHOUSE, place for keeping treasures, supplies, and equipment (De 28:8; 1Ch 29:16; 2Ch 31:10; Mal 3:10).

STORK. Forbidden as food (Le 11:19). Nest of, in fir trees (Ps 104:17). Migratory (Jer 8:7).

Figurative: Zec 5:9.

STOVE, household stoves usually made of clay; were small and portable, burning charcoal; the well-to-do had metal stoves or braziers (Jer 36:22f RSV).

STRAIGHT, name of a street in Damascus (Ac 9:11).

Figurative: Of righteousness, "straight paths" (Isa 40:3, 4; M't 3:3; Heb 12:13).

STRAIT GATE (M't 7:13, 14; Lu 13:24).

STRAKES, archaic word for "streaks" (Ge 30:37; Le 14:37).

STRANGERS. Mosaic law relating to: Authorized bondservice of (Le 25:44, 45); usury of (De 15:3; 23:20); sale to, of flesh of animals that had died (De 14:21); forbid their being made kings over Israel (De 17:15); their eating the passover (Ex 12:43, 48); their eating things offered in sacrifice (Ex 29:33; Le 22:10, 12, 25); their blaspheming (Le 24:16); their approaching the tabernacle (Nu 1:51); their eating blood (Le 17:10); injustice to (Ex 12:49; Le 24:22; Nu 9:14; De 1:16; Jer 22:3); oppression of, forbidden (Ex 22:21; Le 23:9; De 24:14, 17; 27:19; Jer 22:3). Instances of oppression of (Eze 22:29; Mal 3:5).

Required to observe the sabbath (Ex 20:10; 23:12). Might offer oblations (Le 17:8; 22:18, 19). Were buried in separate burial places (M't 27:7).

Kindness to, required (Le 19:33, 34). Love of, enjoined (De 10:18, 19). Abhorrence of, forbidden (De 23:7). Marriage with, forbidden (De 25:5). Hospitality to (see Hospitality).

See Alms; Heathen; Proselytes; Foreigners.

STRANGLE, to deprive of life by choking. Israelites were forbidden to eat flesh from strangled animals (Le 17:12). At the Jerusalem council even Jewish Christians were forbidden to eat such meat (Ac 15:20).

STRATEGY, in war (Ge 14:14, 15; 32:7, 8; Jos 8:3-25; J'g 7:16-23; 20:29-43; 2Sa 15:32-34; w 17:7-14; Ne 6; Isa 15:1; Jer 6:5).

See Ambushes; Armies.

STRAW. Used for provender (Ge 24:32; Isa 65:25); for brick (Ex 5:7).

STRAY. Animals straying to be returned (Ex 23:4; De 22:1-3). Instance of animals straying, Kish's (1Sa 9).

STREAM OF EGYPT (See River of Egypt.)

STREETS (Pr 1:20; Na 2:4; M'k 6:56; Lu 14:21; Ac 9:11).

STRENGTH, a title given Jehovah (1Sa 15:29). Spiritual (see Power, Spiritual).

STRIFE (Ps 55:9; 80:6). Hated of God (Isa 58:4; Hab 1:3). Punishment for (Isa 41:11, 12; Ro 2:8, 9). Correction of (M't 18:15-17).

Christ brings (M't 10:34-36; Lu 12:51-53, 58, 59).

Domestic (Pr 19:13; 21:19; 25:24).

Caused by: busybodies (Pr 26:20); perversity (Pr 16:28); hatred (Pr 10:12); lusts (Jas 4:1, 2); pride (Pr 13:10); scornfulness (Pr 22:10); wrath (Pr 15:18; 29:22; 30:33); excessive indulgence in the use of intoxicating liquors (Pr 23:29, 30).

Destructive to those who are involved therein (M't 12:25; M'k 3:24, 25; Lu 11:17).

Exhortations against (Ge 13:8; 45:24; Ps 31:20; Pr 3:30; 17:14; 25:8; M't 5:25, 39-41; Ro 12:18; 13:13; 14:1, 19, 21; 16:17, 18; 1Co 4:6, 7; 2Co 12:20; Ga 5:15, 20; Ph'p 2:3, 14, 15; 1Ti 3:2, 3; 6:3-5, 20, 21; 2Ti 2:14, 23-25; Tit 3:1-3, 9; Jas 3:14-16).

Abstinence from, honorable (Pr 20:3).

Prayers concerning (Ps 55:9; 1Ti 2:8). Proverbs concerning (Pr 3:30; 6:12-14, 16-19; 10:12; 13:10; 15:18; 17:1, 14, 19; 18:6, 19; 19:13; 20:3; 21:19; 22:10; 23:29, 30; 25:8, 24; 26:17, 20, 21; 27:15; 28:25; 29:22; 30:33).

See Anger; Envy; Jealousy; Malice.

Instances of: Between Abraham and Lot's herdmen (Ge 13:6, 7); Abimelech's (Ge 21:25); Isaac's and those of Gerar (Ge 26:20-22). Laban and Jacob (Ge 31:36). Israelites (De 1:12). Jephthah and his brethren (J'g 11:2); and Ephraimites (J'g 12:1-6). Israel and Judah, about David (2Sa 19:41-43). Disciples, over who might be greatest (M'k 9:34; Lu 22:24). Jews, concerning Jesus (Joh 10:19). Christians at Antioch, about circumcision (Ac 15:2). Paul and Barnabas, about Mark (Ac 15:38, 39). Pharisees and Sadducees, concerning the resurrection (Ac 23:7-10).

Christians, at Corinth (1Co 1:10-12; 3:3, 4; 6:1-7; 11:16-21); at Philippi (Ph'p 1:15-17).

STRIKER, a pugnacious person (1Ti 3:3; Tit 1:7).

STRINGED INSTRUMENTS (See Music.)

STRIPES, wounds inflicted by scourges for punishment (Ex 21:25); authorized by Jewish law for certain offenses (De 25:2, 3) and practiced also by Romans (M't 27:26).

STRIVING WITH GOD, folly of (Job 9:3; 33:13; 40:2; Isa 45:9; Ro 9:20).

STRONG DRINK (See Wine.)

STUBBLE. *Figurative:* Of the wicked (Ex 15:7; Job 21:18; Ps 83:13; Isa 5:24; 40:24; 41:2; 47:14; Jer 13:24; Joe 2:5; Na 1:10; Mal 4:1).

STUBBORNNESS (See Obduracy.)

STUDENTS. Poverty of (2Ki 4:1). In state school (Da 1). In schools of the prophets (1Sa 19:20; 1Ki 20:35; 2Ki 2:2, 3, 5, 7, 15; 4:1).

See Instruction; School.

STUMBLING. *Figurative:* Causes of (Ps 69:6). Stone of (Isa 8:14; Ro 9:32, 33; 1Pe 2:8). Stumbling-block (Le 19:14; Ps 119:165; Isa 57:14; Jer 6:21; Eze 3:20; 7:19; 14:3, 4, 7; Zep 1:3; Lu 11:52; Ro 11:9; 14:13; 1Co 1:23; 8:9-13; Re 2:14).

See Temptation.

SUAH, an Asherite. Son of Zophah (1Ch 7:36).

SUBJECTS (See Citizen; Government; Patriotism; Rulers.)

SUBMISSION. To authority: Jesus an example of (M't 26:39, 42; M'k 14:36; Lu 22:42; Heb 5:8).

Of Paul (1Co 16:7).

See Obedience.

SUBSTITUTION (Ge 22:13; Ex 28:38). The offering for the offerer (Le 1:4; 16:21, 22). The Levites for the firstborn of the Israelites (Nu 3:12, 41, 45; 8:18). The life of Ahab for that of Ben-hadad (1Ki 20:42).

Of Christ for us (Isa 53:4-6; 1Co 5:7; 2Co 5:21; Ga 3:13; 1Pe 2:24).

See Suffering, Vicarious.

SUBURB, lands near cities used for pasturage of animals (Jos 21:2, 42; Eze 45:2).

SUCCESSION. Of priests, irregularity in (Heb 7:1-28). See Priests. Of kings (see Kings).

SUCCOTH (booths). 1. A city probably east of the Jordan. Jacob builds a house in (Ge 33:17). Allotted to Gad (Jos 13:27). People of, punished by Gideon (J'g 8:5-8, 14-16). Located near the Jordan (1Ki 7:46; 2Ch 4:17; Ps 60:6; 108:7).

2. First camping place of the Israelites on leaving Rameses (Ex 12:37; 13:20; Nu 33:5, 6).

SUCCOTH BENOTH, pagan idol brought into Samaria after Assyria had captured it (2Ki 17:24-30).

SUCHATHITES, inhabitants of Sucah or Socah (1Ch 2:55); site unknown.

SUDDEN EVENTS (Ec 9:12; Mal 3:1; M't 24:27; M'k 13:36; Lu 2:13; Ac 2:2; 9:3; 16:26).

SUETONIUS, Roman writer (c. A. D. 69-140), famous for his *Lives of the Caesars.*

SUFFERING. *For Christ:* Promised by Christ (M't 10:34-36; Lu 12:51-53, 58, 59; Ac 9:16). Fellowship with Christ on account of (Ph'p 3:10). Condition of joint heirship with Christ (Ro 8:17-22, 26)

A privilege (Ph'p 1:29). Rejoicing in (Ac 5:41; Col 1:24).

Motives for patient enduring of: future glory (Ro 8:17, 18; 2Co 4:8-12, 17, 18; 1Pe 4:13, 14); reigning with Christ (2Ti 2:12; Re 22:5).

Consolations in (2Co 1:7; Ph'p 2:27-30; 2Ti 2:12; 1Pe 5:10). Patience in (1Co 4:11-13; 2Th 1:4, 5; Jas 5:10; 1Pe 4:14).

See Affliction; Persecution.

Of Christ: Purpose of his coming (Lu 24:46, 47; Joh 6:51; 10:11, 15; 11:50-52). Reason for Christ's coming (Ro 4:25; 5:6-8; 14:15; 1Co 1:17, 18, 23, 24; 15:3; 2Co 5:14, 15; Ga 1:4; 2:20, 21; Eph 5:2, 25; 1Th 5:9, 10; Heb 2:9, 10, 14, 18; 5:8, 9; 9:15, 16, 28; 10:10, 18-20; 1Pe 2:21, 24; 1Pe 3:18; 4:1; 1Jo 3:16).

See Atonement; Jesus, Death of, Design of His Death, Sufferings of.

Vicarious (Ex 9:13-16; Joh 15:13; Ro 9:3; 1Pe 2:21-24; 1Jo 3:16).

See Jesus, Sufferings of; Penalty, Vicariously assumed; Suffering, of Christ, above.

Instance of: Goliath, for the Philistines (1Sa 17).

SUICIDE (Am 9:2; Re 9:6). Temptation to, of Jesus (M't 4:5, 6; Lu 4:9, 10, 11). Of the Philippian jailer (Ac 16:27).

See Death, Desired.

Instances of: Samson (J'g 16:29, 30). Saul and his armor-bearer (1Sa 31:4, 5; 1Ch 10:4, 5). Ahithophel (2Sa 17:23). Zimri (1Ki 16:18). Judas (M't 27:5; Ac 1:18).

SUING (M't 5:40). See Creditors; Debtors.

SUKKIM, soldiers of unknown identity who joined Shishak in his invasion of Judah (2Ch 12:3).

SUKKOTH (See Feasts.)

SULPHUR (See Minerals.)

SUMER, one of two political divisions, Sumer and Akkad, originally comprising Babylonia.

SUMMER. Season of, promised while the earth remains (Ge 8:22). Cool rooms for (J'g 3:20, 24; Am 3:15). Fruits of (2Sa 16:1, 2; Isa 16:9; 28:4; Jer 40:10, 12; 48:32; Am 8:1, 2; Mic 7:1). Drought of (Ps 32:4). Given by God (Ps 74:17). The time for labor and harvest (Pr 6:6-8; 10:5; 30:25; Jer 8:20). Snow in (Pr 26:1). Threshing in (Da 2:35). Approach of (M't 24:32; M'k 13:28; Lu 21:30).

Figurative: Jer 8:20.

SUN. Created (Ge 1:14-18; Ps 74:16; 136:7; Jer 31:35). Rising and setting of (Ec 1:5). Diurnal motion of (Ps 19:4, 6). Worship of, forbidden (De 4:19; 17:3). Worshiped (Job 31:26-28; Jer 8:2; Eze 6:4, 6; 8:16). Kings of Judah dedicate horses to (2Ki 23:11).

Miracles concerning: Darkening of (Ex 10:21-23; Isa 5:30; 24:23; Eze 32:7; Joe 2:10, 31; 3:15; Am 8:9; Mic 3:6; M't 24:29; 27:45; M'k 13:24; 15:33; Lu 21:25; 23:44, 45; Ac 2:20; Re 6:12; 8:12; 9:2; 16:8). Stands still (Jos 10:12, 13; Hab 3:11). Shadow of, goes back on Ahaz's dial (2Ki 20:11; Isa 38:8).

Does not shine in heaven (Re 21:23).

Figurative: Ps 84:11; Mal 4:2; J'g 5:31; Isa 30:26; 60:19, 20; Jer 15:9; Re 1:16; 12:1; 19:17.

SUN, WORSHIP OF. Worship of the sun found varied forms in the ancient world. Even the Israelites at times worshiped sun images (Le 26:30; Isa 17:8). Shamash was a great sun god of the ancient Middle East. Phoenicia worshiped a sun Baal, Baal-hammon. In Egypt the center of sun worship was On, or Heliopolis, where the sun was called Re.

SUN-DIAL (2Ki 20:11; Isa 38:8).

SUNSTROKE (2Ki 4:19).

SUNDAY, first day of the week, commemorating the resurrection of Jesus

(Joh 20:1-25) and the Day of Pentecost (Ac 2:1-41). For a time after the ascension of Jesus the Christians met on 7th and 1st days of the week, but as the Hebrew Christian churches declined in influence, the tendency to observe the Hebrew sabbath slowly passed. The disciples at Troas worshiped on the first day (Ac 20:7). Paul admonished the Corinthians to lay by in store as God had prospered them, doing it week by week on the first day (1Co 16:2). The term "Lord's Day" occurs in Re 1:10.

SUPEREROGATION, the doctrine of excessive and meritorious righteousness (Eze 33:12, 13; Lu 17:10).

SUPERSCRIPTION (inscription). 1. The wording on coins (M't 22:20).

2. Words written on board attached to the cross naming the crime of which the condemned was accused (M'k 15:26; Lu 23:38; Joh 19:19, 20).

SUPERSTITION (Ac 25:19 [*R. V.*, Religion]).

Instances of: Israelites, supposing that their defeat in battle with the Philistines was due to their not having brought with them the ark of the covenant (1Sa 4:3, w *verses* 10, 11). Philistines, refusing to tread the threshold of the temple of Dagon after the image of Dagon had repeatedly fallen (1Sa 5:5).

The belief of the Syrians concerning the help of the gods (1Ki 20:23). Jews, attributing their calamities to having ceased offering sacrifices to the queen of heaven (Jer 44:17-19). Nebuchadnezzar, supposing that the spirit of the gods was upon Daniel (Da 4:8, 9). The sailors who cast Jonah into the sea (Jon 1:4-16). The disciples, supposing they saw a spirit when Jesus came walking upon the sea (M't 14:26; M'k 6:49, 50). Herod, imagining that John the Baptist had risen from the dead (M'k 6:14, 16).

The Gadarenes, on account of Jesus casting devils out of the Gadarene (M't 8:34). The disciples who were frightened at the appearance of Peter (Ac 12:14, 15). The Ephesians, in their sorceries (Ac 19:13-19). The people of the island of Melita, in imagining Paul to be a god (Ac 28:6).

See Idolatry; Sorcery.

SUPERSTITIOUS, used in Ac 17:22 with the sense "very religious," as ASV and RSV have it.

SUPH, SUPHAH, KJV has "The Red Sea" for both these words (Nu 21:14; De 1:1). Suph is an unidentified region E of the Jordan; Supha, probably the region of the Red Sea.

SUPPER (See Feasts; Eucharist.)

SUPPER, LORD'S (See Lord's Supper.)

SUPPLICATION (See Prayer.)

SUR, gate of the temple (2Ki 11:6).

SURETY, SURETYSHIP. 1. One who makes himself responsible for the obligations of another is a surety (Pr 6:1; 11:15; 17:18; 20:16).

2. Guarantee; security for payment (Ge 44:32).

SURFEITING (drinking-bout), overindulgence of food or drink; dissipation (Lu 21:34).

SUSA (See Shushan.)

SUSANCHITES, colonists from Susa or Shushan planted in Samaria by Assyrians (Ezr 4:9, 10).

SUSANNA (lily). 1. Woman who ministered to Christ (Lu 8:1-3).

2. Heroine of *The History of Susanna,* in the OT Apocrypha.

SUSI, a Manassite (Nu 13:11).

SUSPICION (See Accusation, False.)

SWADDLING BAND, bands of cloth in which a newborn baby was wrapped (Lu 2:7, 12). Used figuratively in Job 38:9.

SWALLOW. Builds its nest in the sanctuary (Ps 84:3). Chattering of, figurative of the mourning of the afflicted (Isa 38:14). Migration of (Jer 8:7).

SWAN, forbidden as food (Le 11:18; De 14:16).

SWEARING (See Blasphemy; God, Name of not to be Profaned; Oath.)

SWEAT (Ge 3:19). An offense in the sanctuary (Eze 44:18). Of blood (Lu 22:44).

SWEAT, BLOODY, physical manifestation of the agony of Jesus in Gethsemane (Lu 22:44). Christ's sweat did not become blood, but became "as it were" great drops of blood.

SWEET INCENSE, made of spices (Ex 25:6).

See Incense.

SWEET SAVOR (Ge 8:21; Ex 29:18; Le 1:9; Nu 15:7; Ezr 6:10; 2Co 2:15; Eph 5:2).

SWELLING, usually "pride"; or means the flooding of Jordan in spring (Jer 12:5; 49:19; 50:44); in Ps 46:3, the tumult of a stormy sea.

SWINE. Forbidden as food (Le 11:7; De 14:8). Used for food (Isa 65:4; 66:17), for sacrifice (Isa 66:3). Wild boar (Ps 80:13). Jewels in the nose of (Pr 11:22). Viciousness of (M't 7:6). Jesus sends devils into (M't 8:28-32; M'k 5:11-14; Lu 8:32, 33). Feeding of (Lu 15:15, 16). Sow returns to her wallow (2Pe 2:22).

SWORD, THE. Probable origin of (Ge 3:24). Was pointed (Eze 21:15). Frequently had two edges (Ps 149:6).

Described as: Sharp (Ps 57:4). Bright (Na 3:3). Glittering (De 32:41; Job 20:25). Oppressive (Jer 46:16). Hurtful (Ps 144:10). Carried in a sheath or scabbard (1Ch 21:27; Jer 47:6; Eze 21:3-5). Suspended from the girdle (1Sa 17:39; 2Sa 20:8; Ne 4:18; Ps 45:3).

Was Used: By the patriarchs (Ge 34:25; 48:22). By the Jews (J'g 7:22; 2Sa 24:9). By heathen nations (J'g 7:22; 1Sa 15:33). For self-defense (Lu 22:36). For destruction of enemies (Nu 21:24; Jos 6:21). For punishing criminals (1Sa 15:33; Ac 12:2). Sometimes for self-destruction (1Sa 31:4, 5; Ac 16:27). Hebrews early acquainted with making of (1Sa 13:19). In time of war plowshares made into (Joe 3:10). In time of peace made into plowshares (Isa 2:4; Mic 4:3). Sharpened and furbished before going to war (Ps 7:12; Eze 21:9). Was brandished over the head (Eze 32:10). Was thrust through enemies (Eze 16:40). Often threatened as a punishment (Le 26:25, 33; De 32:25). Often sent as a punishment (Ezr 9:7; Ps 78:62). Was one of God's four sore judgments (Eze 14:21). Those slain by, communicated ceremonial uncleanness (Nu 19:16).

Illustrative: Of the word of God (Eph 6:17, w Heb 4:12). Of the word of Christ (Isa 49:2, w Re 1:16). Of the justice of God (De 32:41; Zec 13:7). Of the protection of God (De 33:29). Of war and contention (M't 10:34). Of severe and heavy calamities (Eze 5:2, 17; 14:17; 21:9). Of deep mental affliction (Lu 2:35). Of the wicked (Ps 17:13). Of the tongue of the wicked (Ps 57:4; 64:3; Pr 12:18). Of persecuting spirit of the wicked (Ps 37:14). Of the end of the wicked (Pr 5:4). Of false witnesses (Pr 25:18). Of judicial authority (Ro 13:4). (Drawing of,) of war and destruction (Le 26:33; Eze 21:3-5). (Putting, into its sheath,) of peace and friendship (Jer 47:6). (Living by,) of rapine (Ge 27:40). (Not departing from one's house,) of perpetual calamity (2Sa 12:10).

SYCAMINE, a tree (Lu 17:6).

SYCAMORE, a tree. Abundant in the land of Canaan (1Ki 10:27; 2Ch 1:15; 9:27; Isa 9:10). Groves of, cared for (1Ch 27:28). Destroyed by frost (Ps 78:47). Care of (Am 7:14). Zacchaeus climbs into (Lu 19:4).

SYCHAR, village ½ mile N of Jacob's well, on E slope of Mt. Ebal (Joh 4:5).

SYCHEM (See Shechem.)

SYENE, Egyptian town on border of Egypt and Ethiopia (Eze 29:10; 30:16); the present-day Aswan.

SYMBOLS AND SIMILITUDES. Trees of life and knowledge (Ge 2:9, 17; 3:3, 24; Re 22:2). Rainbow (Ge 9:12, 13). Circumcision, of the covenant of Abraham (Ge 17:11; Ro 4:11). Passover, of the sparing of the firstborn, and of the atonement made by Christ (Ex 12:3-28; 1Co 5:7). Of the divine presence, the pillar of cloud (Ex 13:21, 22; 14:19, 20; 19:9, 16); thunder on Mount Sinai (Ex 19:9, 16). Darkness, of God's inscrutability (Ex 20:21; Le 16:2; 1Ki 8:12; Ps 18:11; 97:2; Heb 12:18, 19). The smitten rock, of Christ (Ex 17:6; 1Co 10:4). The sprinkled blood, of the covenant (Ex 24:8). Wine, of the atoning blood (M't 26:27-29; M'k 14:23-25; Lu 22:17, 18, 20). The brazen serpent, of Christ (Nu 21:8, 9; Joh 3:14).

Sacrificial animals (Ge 15:8-11; Joh 1:29, 36). Waving the wave offering and heaving the heave offering (Ex 29:24-28; Le 8:27-29; 9:21). The whole system of Mosaic rites (Heb 9:9, 10, 18-23). Tabernacle (Ps 15:1; Eze 37:27; Heb 8:2, 5; 9:1-12, 23, 24). Sanctuary (Ps 20:2). Canaan, of the spiritual rest (Heb 3:11, 12; 4:5).

Salt (Nu 18:19). Offering water to drink (Ge 24:13-15, 42-44). Lapping water (J'g 7:4-8). Invitation to approach (1Sa 14:8-12). Bow-shot, by Jonathan (1Sa 20:21-37); by Joash (2Ki 13:15-19). Men meeting Saul (1Sa 10:2-7). Rain and thunder (1Sa 12:16-18). Rent altar (1Ki 13:3, 5). Rending of the veil (M't 27:51; M'k 15:38; Lu 23:45). Wounding (1Ki 20:35-40). Praying toward the temple (1Ki 8:29; Da 6:10). Harvest (2Ki 19:29). Isaiah's children (Isa 8:18). Nakedness (Isa 20:2-4). Almond rod (Jer 1:11). Sticks and staves (Eze 37:16, 17; Zec 11:7, 10, 11, 14). Food (2Ki 19:29; Isa 37:30). Shadow on Ahaz's dial (2Ki 20:8-11; Isa 38:7, 8). Cooking (Jer 1:13; Eze 4:9-15; 24:3-5). Girdle (Jer 13:1-7; Ac 21:11). Bottles (Jer 13:12; 19:1, 2, 10). Breaking of potter's vessel (Jer 19). Good and bad figs (Jer 24). Basket of fruit (Jer 24:1-3; Am 8:1, 2). Wine (Jer 25:15-17; M't 26:27; M'k 14:23; Lu 22:17). Yokes (Jer 27:2, 3; 28:10). Jeremiah's deeds of land (Jer 32:1-16). Book cast into Euphrates (Jer 51:63). Dumbness (Eze 3:26, 27; 24:27; 29:21; 33:22; Lu 1:20-22, 62-64). Siege (Eze 4:1-3). Posture (Eze 4:4-8). Unclean food (Eze 4:9-17). Ezekiel's beard (Eze 5:1-4). Change of domicile (Eze 12:3-11). Eating bread with carefulness (Eze 12:17-20). Eating and drinking in fear (Eze 12:18). Vine (Eze 15:2; 19:10-14). Death (Eze 24:16-19). Boiling pot (Eze 24:1-5). Mourning forbidden (Eze 24:15-18). Two sticks (Eze 37:15-28). Handwriting on the wall (Da 5:5, 6, 16-28). Plumb line (Am 7:7, 8). Marrying a whore (Ho 1:2-9; 3:1-4). Roll (Zec 5:2-4). Ephah (Zec 5:6-11). Jonas (M't 16:4; Lu 11:29, 30). Star in the east (M't 2:2). Smitten rock (1Co 10:4; Ex 17:6). Salt (Col 4:6). Bread (M't 26:26; M'k 14:22; Lu 22:19). Childhood (M't 18:3; M'k 10:14, 15; Lu 18:16, 17). Manna (Joh 6:31-58).

Of the Holy Spirit: Water (Joh 3:5; 7:38, 39); cleansing by (Eze 16:9; 36:25; Eph 5:26; Heb 10:22); vivifying (Ps 1:3; Isa 27:3, 6; 44:3, 4; 58:11).

Fire (M't 3:11); purifying (Isa 4:4; Mal 3:2, 3); illuminating (Ex 13:21; Ps 78:14); searching (Zep 1:12, w 1Co 2:10).

Wind (Song 4:16); incomprehensible (Joh 3:8; 1Co 12:11); powerful (1Ki 19:11, w Ac 2:2); sensible in its effects (Joh 3:8); reviving (Eze 37:9, 10, 14).

Oil (Ps 45:7); healing (Isa 1:6; Lu 10:34; Re 18:13); comforting (Isa 61:3; Heb 1:9); illuminating (Zec 4:2, 3, 11-13; M't 25:3, 4; 1Jo 2:20, 27); consecrating (Ex 29:7; 30:30; Isa 61:1).

Rain and Dew (Ps 72:6); fertilizing (Eze 34:26, 27; Ho 6:3; 10:12; 14:5); refreshing (Ps 68:9; Isa 18:4); abundant (Ps 133:3); imperceptible (2Sa 17:12, w M'k 4:26-28).

A Dove (M't 3:16).

A Voice (Isa 6:8); speaking (M't 10:20); guiding (Isa 30:21, w John 16:13); warning (Heb 3:7-11).

A Seal (Re 7:2); impressing (Job 38:14, w 2Co 3:18); earnest (Eph 1:13, 14; 4:30; 2Co 1:22).

Cloven Tongues (Ac 2:3, 6, 11).

Ablutions, a symbol of purity (see Ablutions; Purifications). For symbolisms of color (see Colors). See also Allegory; Instruction, by Symbols; Instruction, of Children; Instruction, in Religion.

SYMEON (See Simeon.)

SYMPATHY. (Ec 7:2). Enjoined (Ro 12:15; Jas 1:27; 1Pe 3:8). In Christ (Ph'p 2:1, 2).

Instances of: David with Hanun (2Sa 10:2). The Jewish maid with Naaman (2Ki 5:1-4). Job's friends (Job 2:11-13); turned against Job (Job 6:14; 22:29). Ebed-melech with Jeremiah (Jer 38:7-13). Nebuchadnezzar with Daniel (Da 6:18-23).

The four friends with the palsied man whom they took to Jesus (M'k 2:3, 4). Others with the helpless whom they brought to Jesus (M't 4:24). The good Samaritan with the man who fell among robbers (Lu 10:33-35). The Jews with Martha and Mary (Joh 11:19, 31, 33). The people of Melita with the shipwrecked mariners (Ac 28:1, 2).

See Afflicted; Afflictions; Jesus, Compassion of; Kindness; Pity; Poor.

SYNAGOGUE. 1. Primarily an assembly (Ac 13:43; Jas 2:2). Constitutes a court of justice (Lu 12:11; Ac 9:2). Had powers of criminal courts (M't 10:17; M't 23:34; Ac 22:19; 26:11); of ecclesiastical courts (Joh 9:22, 34; 12:42; 16:2).

2. Place of assembly. Scriptures read and expounded in (Ne 8:1-8; 9:3, 5; M't 4:23; 9:35; 13:54; M'k 1:39; Lu 4:15-33; 13:10; Joh 18:20; Ac 9:20; 13:5-44; 14:1; 15:21; 17:2, 10; 18:4, 19, 26).

In Jerusalem (Ac 6:9); Damascus (Ac

9:2, 20); other cities (Ac 14:1; 17:1, 10; 18:4). Built by Jairus (Lu 7:5); Jesus performed healing in (M't 12:9-13; Lu 13:11-14). Alms given in (M't 6:2).

Of Satan (Re 2:9; 3:9).

See Church.

SYNAGOGUE, MEN OF THE GREAT, or of the Great Assembly, a college of learned men supposedly organized by Nehemiah after the Return from Exile (Ne 8-10), to which Jewish tradition attributed the origination and authoritative promulgation of many ordinances and regulations.

SYNOPTIC PROBLEM (See Gospels.)

SYNTICHE, SYNTYCHE (fortunate), Christian woman at Philippi (Ph'p 4:2).

SYRACUSE, a city of Sicily. Paul visits (Ac 28:12).

SYRIA, highlands lying between the river Euphrates and the Mediterranean Sea. Called Aram, from the son of Shem (Ge 10:22, 23, Nu 23:7; 1Ch 1:17; 2:23). In the time of Abraham it seems to have embraced the region between the rivers Tigris and Euphrates (Ge 24:10, w 25:20), including Padan-aram (Ge 25:20; 28:5).

Minor kingdoms within the region: Aramzobah, called also Zobah and Zoba (1Sa 14:47; 2Sa 8:3; 10:6, 8; 1Ki 11:23; 1Ch 18:5, 9; 19:6; Ps 60 [title]); Geshur (2Sa 15:8); Aram-rehob, called also Beth-rehob (2Sa 10:6, 8); Damascus (2Sa 8:5, 6; 1Ch 18:5, 6); Hamath (2Sa 8:9, 10).

Conquest of: By David (2Sa 8:3-13); by Jeroboam (2Ki 14:25, 28); by Tiglath-pileser, king of Assyria (2Ki 16:7-9; 18:33, 34). People of, colonized in Samaria by the king of Assyria (2Ki 17:24). Confederate with Nebuchadnezzar (2Ki 24:2; Jer 39:5).

The Roman province of, included the land of Canaan (Lu 2:2, 3); and Phenicia (M'k 7:26; Ac 21:3). The fame of Jesus extended over (M't 4:24).

Paul goes to, with letters to apprehend the Christians; is converted and begins his evangelistic ministry (Ac 9:1-31). See Paul.

Paul preaches in (Ac 15:41; 18:18; 21:3; Ga 1:21). Damascus, the capital of (see Damascus.)

Wars between, and the kingdoms of Judah and Israel (see Israel). Prophecies concerning (Isa 7:8-16; 8:4-7; 17:1-3; Jer 1:15; 49:23-27; Am 1:3-5; Zec 9:1).

SYRIA-MAACHAH, called also Maachah. A small kingdom (1Ch 19:6). See Maachah, 10.

SYRIAC, language of Syria. KJV uses "Aramaic" (2Ki 18:26; Ezr 4:7; Isa 36:11; Da 2:4).

SYRIAC VERSIONS (See Texts and Versions.)

SYRIAN. 1. Language of Syria; see Syriac.

2. People of Syria (2Sa 8:5).

SYROPHENICIAN, the nationality of a woman whose daughter was cured by Jesus (M't 15:21-28; M'k 7:24-30).

SYRTIS, banks of quicksand off the coast of Libya (Ac 27:17).

T

TAANACH, called also Tanach. A city conquered by Joshua (Jos 12:21). Allotted to Manasseh (Jos 17:11; 1Ch 7:29). Canaanites not driven from (Jos 17:12; J'g 1:27). Assigned to the Levites (Jos 21:25). The scene of Barak's victory (J'g 5:19). One of Solomon's commissaries at (1Ki 4:12).

TAANATH-SHILOH (approach to Shiloh), town on NE border of Ephraim (Jos 16:6), c. 10 miles E of Shechem.

TABBAOTH (rings), family of temple servants who returned with Zerubbabel (Ezr 2:43; Ne 7:46).

TABBATH, place probably E of the Jordan between Jabesh-gilead and Succoth (J'g 7:22).

TABEAL, father of one whom the kings of Syria and Israel sought to make king in Judah instead of Ahaz (Isa 7:6. [*R. V.*, Tabeel.]).

TABEEL. 1. A Persian official in Samaria (Ezr 4:7).

2. See Tabeal.

TABERAH (burning), encampment of Israel in wilderness where fire of Lord consumed some complainers (Nu 11:1-3; De 9:22); site unidentified.

TABERNACLE. One existed before Moses received the pattern authorized on Mount Sinai (Ex 33:7-11). The one instituted by Moses was called Sanctuary (Ex 25:8); Tabernacle [*A. V.*], Tent of Meeting [*R. V.*] (Ex 27:21); Tabernacle [*A. V.*], Tent [*R. V.*] (Ex 33:7; 2Ch 5:5); of Testimony (Ex 38:21; Nu 1:50); Tent of Testimony [*R. V.*] (Nu 17:7, 8; 2Ch 24:6); Temple of the Lord (1Sa 1:9; 3:3); House of the Lord (Jos 6:24).

Pattern of, revealed to Moses (Ex 25:9; 26:30; 39:32, 42, 43; Ac 7:44; Heb 8:5). Materials for, voluntarily offered (Ex 25:1-8; 35:4-29; 36:3-7). Value of the substance contributed for (Ex 38:24-31). Workmen who constructed it were inspired (Ex 31:1-11; 35:30-35).

Description of: Frame (Ex 26:15-37; 36:20-38). Outer covering (Ex 25:5; 26:7-14; 36:14-19). Second covering (Ex 25:5; 26:14; 35:7, 23; 36:19; 39:34). Curtains of (Ex 26:1-14, 31-37; 27:9-16; 35:15, 17; 36:8-19, 35, 37); Court of (Ex 27:9-17; 38:9-16, 18; 40:8, 33).

Holy place of (Ex 26:31-37; 40:22-26; Heb 9:2-6, 8). The most holy place (Ex 26:33-35; 40:20, 21; Heb 9:3-5, 7, 8).

Furniture of (Ex 25:10-40; 27:1-8, 19; 37; 38:1-8). See Altar; Ark; Candlestick; Cherubim; Laver; Mercy Seat; Shewbread.

Completed (Ex 39:32). Dedicated (Nu 7). Sanctified (Ex 29:43; 40:9-16; Nu 7:1). Anointed with holy oil (Ex 30:25, 26; Le 8:10; Nu 7:1). Sprinkled with blood (Le 16:15-20; Heb 9:21, 23). Filled with the cloud of glory (Ex 40:34-38).

How prepared for removal during the journeyings of the Israelites (Nu 1:51; 4:5-15). How and by whom carried (Nu 4:5-33; 7:6-9). Strangers forbidden to enter (Nu 1:51). Duties of the Levites concerning (see Levites). Defilement of, punished (Le 15:31; Nu 19:13, 20; Eze 5:11; 23:38). Duties of the priests in relation to (see Priests). Israelites worship at (Nu 10:3; 16:19, 42, 43; 20:6; 25:6; 1Sa 2:22; Ps 27:4). Offerings brought to (Le 17:4; Nu 31:54; De 12:5, 6, 11-14).

Tribes encamped around, while in the wilderness (Nu 2). All males required to appear before, three times each year (Ex 23:17). Tabernacle tax (Ex 20:11-16).

Carried in front of the children of Israel in the line of march (Nu 10:33-36; Jos 3:3-6). The Lord reveals himself at (Le 1:1; Nu 1:1; 7:89; 12:4-10; De 31:14, 15).

Pitched at Gilgal (Jos 4:18, 19); at Shiloh (Jos 18:1; 19:51; J'g 18:31; 20:18, 26, 27; 21:19; 1Sa 2:14; 4:3, 4; Jer 7:12, 14); at Nob (1Sa 21:1-6); at Gibeon (1Ch 21:29). Renewed by David, and pitched on Mount Zion (1Ch 15:1; 16:1, 2; 2Ch 1:4). Solomon offers sacrifice at (2Ch 1:3-6). Brought to the temple by Solomon (2Ch 5:5, w 1Ki 8:1, 4, 5).

Symbol of spiritual things (Ps 15:1: Heb 8:2, 5; 9:1-12, 24).

See Levites; Priests; Temple.

TABERNACLES, FEAST OF, called also Feast of Ingathering. Instituted (Ex 23:16; 34:22; Le 23:34-43; Nu 29:12-40; De 16:13-16). Design of (Le 23:42, 43). The law read in connection with, every seventh year (De 31:10-12; Ne 8:18).

Observance of, after the captivity (Ezr 3:4; Ne 8:14-18); by Jesus (Joh 7:2, 14). Observance of, omitted (Ne 8:17). Penalty for not observing (Zec 14:16-19).

Jeroboam institutes an idolatrous feast to correspond to, in the eighth month (1Ki 12:32, 33; 1Ch 27:11).

TABITHA (gazelle), Christian woman in Joppa; befriended poor widows; raised from dead by Peter (Ac 9:36-43).

TABLE. 1. Table for food (J'g 1:7; 1Ki 2:7).

2. Lord's table—Lord's Supper (1Co 10:21).

3. "Serving tables" (Ac 6:2) refers to distribution of food, etc., to the Christian poor.

4. Tabernacle and Temple were provided with various tables.

5. Stone tablets on which Law was written (Ex 24:12).

6. Tables were also tablets on which messages were written (Lu 1:63).

TABLE OF SHEWBREAD, the 12 loaves of consecrated unleavened bread placed on a table in the Holy Place in the Tabernacle and Temple (Ex 25:30; Le 24:5-9).

TABLES OF THE LAW, stone tablets on which Moses wrote the 10 commandments (Ex 24:3, 4; 31:18; De 4:13; 5:22).

TABLET (See Dress.)

TABOR. 1. A mountain on the border of Issachar (Jos 19:22; J'g 8:18; Ps 89:12; Jer 46:18; Ho 5:1). Assembling place of Barak's army (J'g 4:6, 12, 14).

2. A plain [*R. V.* "oak"] of unknown location (1Sa 10:3).

3. A Levitical city in Zebulun (1Ch 6:77).

See Chisloth-tabor.

TABRET, timbrel (1Sa 10:5).

TABRIMMON, TABRIMON, father of Benhadad, king of Syria (1Ki 15:18); "Tabrimon" in KJV.

TACHE (clasp), clasp (Ec 26:6; 36:13, 18).

TACHMONITE, TACHEMONITE, family of David's chief captain (2Sa 23:8); same as Jashobeam, a Hachmonite (1Ch 11:11).

TACKLING, either hawsers (Isa 33:23) or furniture (Ac 27:19) of a ship.

TACT (Pr 15:1; 25:15). In preaching (1Co 9:19-22; 2Co 12:6). Of Gideon (J'g 8:1-3). Of Saul, in managing malcontents (1Sa 10:27; 11:7, 12-15). Nabal's wife (1Sa 25:18-37). In David's popular methods: in mourning for Abner (2Sa 3:28-37); in organizing the temple music (1Ch 15:16-24); in securing popular consent to bringing the ark to Jerusalem (1Ch 13:1-4). Joab's trick in obtaining David's consent to the return of Absalom (2Sa 14:1-22). The wise woman of Abel (2Sa 20:16-22). Solomon, in arbitrating between the harlots (1Ki 3:24-28).

Mordecai, in concealing Esther's nationality (Es 2:10). Esther, in placating the king (Es 5-7). Paul, in circumcising Timothy (Ac 16:3); in turning the preaching of adversaries to account (Ph'p 1:10-22); in stimulating benevolent giving (2Co 8:1-8; 9:1-5); in arraying the two religious factions of the Jews against each other when he was in trouble (Ac 23:6-10). The town clerk of Ephesus (Ac 19:35-41). The church council at Jerusalem (Ac 21:20-25).

TACTICS (See Armies; Strategy.)

TADMOR, city in desert NE of Damascus (1Ki 9:18; 2Ch 8:4), a fabulously rich trade metropolis later called Palmyra. Magnificent ruins have been excavated.

TAHAN. 1. Son of Ephraim (Nu 26:35).

2. A descendant of Ephraim (1Ch 7:25).

TAHAPANES, TAHPANHES, fortress city at E edge of the Nile Delta to which Jews fled after the fall of Jerusalem (Jer 2:16, KJV has "Tahapanes"; 43:7-9; 44:1; 46:14). Eze 30:18 has "Tehaphnehes."

TAHASH, son of Nahor and Reumah (Ge 22:24), KJV has "Thahash."

TAHATH (below). 1. A camping place of the Israelites (Nu 33:26, 27).

2. A Kohathite (1Ch 6:24, 37).

3. The name of two Ephraimites (1Ch 7:20).

TAHPANHES, called also Tahapanes and Tehaphnehes. A city in Egypt (Jer 2:16; 43:7-9; 44:1; 46:14; Eze 30:18).

TAHPENES, a queen of Egypt (1Ki 11:19, 20).

TAHREA, grandson of Mephibosheth (1Ch 9:41); called "Tarea" in 8:35.

TAHTIM-HODSHI, place E of Jordan in the land of the Hittites (2Sa 24:6).

TAILORING (Ex 31:2, 3, 6, 10; 39:1).

TALE, sigh (Ps 90:9), number (Ex 5:8, 18), count (1Ch 9:28), slander (Eze 22:9), idle talk (Lu 24:11), talebearing, slander (Le 19:16; Pr 11:13).

TALEBEARER. The pernicious vice of repeating damaging reports, either true or false (Ps 15:1-3; Pr 11:13; 20:19).

Separates friends (Pr 16:28; 17:9). Causes, strife (Pr 26:20); tension (Pr 18:8). Is forbidden (Le 19:16; 1Ti 5:11, 13).

See Busybody; Slander; Speaking, Evil.

Instances of: Joseph (Ge 37:2). Israelites (2Sa 3:23). Tobiah (Ne 6).

TALENT (1Ki 9:14, 28; 10:10, 14). A weight equal to three thousand shekels—about one hundred and twenty-five pounds (Ex 38:25, 26). Value of, of gold, about six thousand pounds, or twenty-nine thousand one hundred dollars; of silver, four hundred pounds, or one thousand nine hundred and forty dollars. Parables of the (M't 18:24; 25:15, 28).

TALITHA CUMI, Aramaic for "damsel, arise" (M'k 5:41).

TALKING, with God (see Communion).

TALMAI. 1. A son of Anak (Nu 13:22; Jos 15:14; J'g 1:10).

2. King of Geshur (2Sa 3:3; 13:37; 1Ch 3:2).

TALMON. A porter of the temple (1Ch 9:17). Family of, return from captivity with Zerubbabel (Ezr 2:42; Ne 7:45; 11:19; 12:25).

TALMUD, collection of Jewish tradition of the early Christian centuries; two forms: Palestinian and Babylonian.

TAMAH, temple servant whose descendants returned from captivity (Ne 7:55); "Thamah" in Ezr 2:53.

TAMAR (palm tree). 1. Wife of Er, then of Onan; mother of Perez and Zerah (Ge 38); M't 1:3 KJV "Thamar."

2. Daughter of David; abused by half-brother Amon (2Sa 13:1-33).

3. Daughter of Absalom (2Sa 14:27).

4. Unidentified borderland site in restored Israel (Eze 47:19; 48:28).

5. City in Syria, more commonly known as Tadmor, later Palmyra.

TAMBOURINE (See Timbrel.)

TAMIR (See Tadmor.)

TAMMUZ, fertility god worshiped in Mesopotamia, Syria, and Palestine; corresponded to Osiris in Egypt and Adonis of the Greeks (Eze 8:14).

TANACH (See Taanach.)

TANHUMETH, father of Seraiah (2Ki 25:23; Jer 40:8).

TANIS (See Zoar.)

TANNER, TANNING. Tanning is the conversion of skin into leather by removing the hair and soaking it in tanning solution (Ex 25:5; 26:14; Ac 10:6).

TANTALIZING (1Sa 1:6, 7; 1Ki 18:27).

TAPESTRY (Pr 7:16; 31:22). Of the tabernacle (Ex 26:1-14, 31-37; 27:9-17; 36:8-18). Gold thread woven in (Ex 39:3). In palaces (Es 1:6; Song 1:5). In groves (2Ki 23:7).

See Curtains; Embroidery.

TAPHATH, daughter of Solomon (1Ki 4:11).

TAPPUAH. 1. A city of Judah (Jos 12:17; 15:34).

2. A city in Ephraim (Jos 16:8; 17:8).

3. Son of Hebron (1Ch 2:43).

TARAH, a camping place of the Israelites (Nu 33:27, 28).

TARALAH, city of Benjamin between Irpeel and Zelah (Jos 18:27).

TAREA. A son of Micah (1Ch 8:35). Called Tahrea (1 Ch 9:41).

TARES, probably bearded darnel, a poisonous plant; resembles wheat (M't 13:25-30).

TARGET, a defensive article of armor. Used by spearmen (2Ch 14:8). Made of brass (1Sa 17:6); of gold (1Ki 10:16; 2Ch 9:15).

See Shield.

TARIFF (See Duty.)

TARPELITES, people sent as colonists to Samaria by Assyrians (Ezr 4:9, 10).

TARSHISH. 1. Son of Javan (Ge 10:4).

2. Place in W Mediterranean, perhaps in Spain or Tunisia (2Ch 9:21; 20:36, 37; Ps 72:10; Jon 1:3).

3. "Ships of Tarshish"; large, seagoing trade ships (1Ki 9:26; 10:22; 22:48; 2Ch 9:21).

4. Great-grandson of Benjamin (1Ch 7:10).

5. Persian prince (Es 1:14).

TARSUS, capital of Cilicia, in Asia Minor. Paul's birthplace (Ac 9:11; 21:39; 22:3). Paul sent to, from Jerusalem, to avoid assassination (Ac 9:30). Paul brought from, by Barnabas (Ac 11:25, 26).

TARTAK, god worshiped by Avvites, colonists in Samaria (2Ki 17:31).

TARTAN, commander-in-chief of the Assyrian army (Isa 20:1; 2Ki 18:17). A title, not a proper name.

TASKMASTER, one who burdens another with labor; overseer (Ex 1:11; 3:7; 5:6, 10, 13).

TASTE, the sense of, lost (2Sa 19:35).

TATTENAI, TATNAI, Persian governor ordered to assist Jews in rebuilding the temple (Ezr 5:3, 6; 6:6, 13).

TATTLER (See Talebearer.)

TATTOOING, forbidden (Le 19:28).

TAVERN, an inn (Ac 28:15).

TAVERNS, THREE, place, c. 33 miles SE of Rome where Paul met Roman Christians (Ac 28:15).

TAX. Poll (Ex 30:11-16; 38:26; Ne 10:32; Lu 2:1). Jesus pays (M't 17:24-27).

Land (Ge 41:34, 48; 2Ki 23:35). Land mortgaged for (Ne 5:3, 4). Priests exempted from (Ge 47:26; Ezr 7:24). Paid in grain (Am 5:11; 7:1); in provisions (1Ki 4:7-28).

Personal (1Ki 9:15; 2Ki 15:19, 20; 23:35). Resisted by Israelites (1Ki 12:18; 2Ch 10:18). World-wide, levied by Caesar. The *R. V.* changes the reading to enrolled instead of taxed (Lu 2:1-3).

Collectors of (2Sa 20:24; 1Ki 4:6; Isa 33:18; Da 11:20; M'k 2:14; Lu 3:13; 5:27); unpopular (M't 5:46; 9:11; 11:19; 18:17; 21:31; Lu 18:11); stoned (2Ch 10:18).

TEACHERS. Samuel, head of school of prophets (1Sa 19:20). Elisha, head of, at Gilgal (2Ki 4:38).

Itinerant (2Ch 17:7-9). Of public assemblies (Ne 8:1-8, 13, 18). Should receive compensation (Ga 6:6).

See Instruction; Jesus, Teacher; Ministers, Duties of.

False: Admonition against (De 13:1-3; M't 5:19; 7:15; 15:2-20; 23:2-33; Lu 11:38-52).

See Ministers, False.

TEACHING (See Instruction; Ministers, Duties of.)

TEARS (Ps 6:6; 39:12; 42:3). Observed by God (Ps 56:8; Isa 38:3-5). Wiped away (Re 7:17). None in heaven (Re 21:4).

Figurative: Ps 80:5.

TEBAH, son of Nahor (Ge 22:24).

TEBALIAH, son of Hosah (1Ch 26:11).

TEBETH, the tenth month (January) (Es 2:16; Eze 29:1).

TECHNICALITIES, legal (M't 12:2, 10; Lu 6:2, 7).

TEETH (Pr 10:26). Gnashing of (Ps 112:10; La 2:16; M't 8:12; 13:42, 50; 22:13; 24:51; 25:30; M'k 9:18; Lu 13:28).

TEHAPHNEHES (See Tahpanhes.)

TEHINNAH (entreaty), son of Eshton (1Ch 4:12).

TEIL TREE, oak (Isa 6:13).

TEKEL, weighed (Da 5:25).

TEKOA. 1. Son of Ashur (1Ch 2:24; 4:5). Some authorities interpret these passages to mean that Ashur colonized the town of Tekoah.

2. See Tekoah.

TEKOAH, called also Tekoa. A city in Judah (2Ch 11:6). Home of the woman who interceded for Absalom (2Sa 14:2, 4, 9). Rebuilt by Rehoboam (2Ch 11:6). Desert of (2Ch 20:20). People of, work on the new wall of Jerusalem (Ne 3:5, 27). Prophecy concerning (Jer 6:1). Home of Amos (Am 1:1).

See Tekoa.

TEL-ABIB (grain heap), place on Chebar river where Ezekiel lived (Eze 3:15).

TELAH (fracture), son of Rephah (1Ch 7:25).

TELAIM (lambs), place where Saul mustered army against Amalek (1Sa 15:4); may be same as Telem (Jos 15:24) in Judah.

TELASSAR, called also Thelasar. A city or district conquered by the Assyrians (2Ki 19:12; Isa 37:12).

TELEM. 1. A city of Judah (Jos 15:24).

2. A porter who put away his Gentile wife (Ezr 10:24).

TEL-HARSA, called also Tel-haresha. A place in Babylonia (Ezr 2:59; Ne 7:61).

TELL, mound or heap of ruins which marks the site of an ancient city and is composed of accumulated occupational debris, usually covering a number of archaeological or historical periods and showing numerous building levels or strata (De 13:16; Jos 18:28 RSV; Jer 30:18).

TELL EL AMARNA, city built as capital of Egypt by Akhnaton (c. 1387-1366 B. C.); more than 350 clay tablets, representing official correspondence from rulers in W Asia to Akhnaton, found there in 1887.

TEL-MELAH, Babylonian town, probably not far N of Persian Gulf (Ezr 2:59; Ne 7:61).

TEMA. 1. Son of Ishmael (Ge 25:15; 1Ch 1:30).

2. A people of Arabia, probably descendant from Tema, Ishmael's son (Job 6:19; Isa 21:14; Jer 25:23).

TEMAN. 1. Grandson of Esau (Ge 36:11).

2. Edomite chief (Ge 36:42).

3. City in NE Edom (Jer 49:7).

TEMANI, inhabitant of Teman (Ge 36:34).

TEMENI, son of Ashur (1Ch 4:6).

TEMPER (See Anger; Malice; Self-control.)

TEMPERANCE (Ph'p 4:5; Tit 1:8; 2Pe 1:6). In eating (Pr 23:1-3; 25:16). In the use of wine (1Ti 3:8; Tit 2:3).

Enjoined (Ro 13:14; Ph'p 4:5; 1Th 5:6-8; 1Ti 3:2; Tit 2:2, 3, 12; 2Pe 1:5, 6).

Practiced, by athletes (1Co 9:25, 27); by Daniel (Da 1:8, 12-16).

See Abstinence; Drunkenness; Wine.

TEMPLE. *Solomon's:* Called also Temple of the Lord (2Ki 11:10); Holy Temple (Ps 79:1); Holy House (1Ch 29:3); House of God (1Ch 29:2; 2Ch 23:9); House of the Lord (2Ch 23:5, 12; Jer 28:5); Father's House (Joh 2:16); House of the God of Jacob (Isa 2:3); House of My Glory (Isa 60:7); House of Prayer (Isa 56:7; M't 21:13); House of Sacrifice (2Ch 7:12); House of their Sanctuary (2Ch 36:17); Holy and Beautiful House (Isa 64:11); Holy Mount (Isa 27:13); Mountain of the Lord's House (Isa 2:2); Palace (1Ch 29:1, 19); Sanctuary (2Ch 20:8); Tabernacle of Witness (2Ch 24:6); Zion (Ps 20:2; 48:12; 74:2; 87:2; Isa 2:3).

Greatness of (2Ch 2:5, 6). Beauty of (Isa 64:11). Holiness of (1Ki 8:10; 9:3; La 1:10; M't 23:17; Joh 2:14-16).

David undertakes the building of (2Sa 7:2, 3; 1Ch 22:7; 28:2; Ps 132:2-5; Ac 7:46); forbidden of God because he was a man of war (2Sa 7:4-12; 1Ki 5:3; 1Ch 22:8; 28:3). Not asked for by God (2Sa 7:7). The building of, committed to Solomon (2Sa 7:13). David makes preparation of (1Ch 22; 28:14-18; 29:1-5; 2Ch 3:1; 5:1). Built by Solomon (Ac 7:47). Solomon makes levies of men for the building of (1Ki 5:13-16; 2Ch 2:2, 17, 18).

Materials for, furnished by Hiram (1Ki 5:8-18). Pattern and building of (1Ki 6; 7:13-51; 1Ch 28:11-19; 2Ch 3; 4; Ac 7:47). Time when begun (1Ki 6:1, 37; 2Ch 3:2); finished (1Ki 6:38). Site of (1Ch 21:28-30; 22:1; 2Ch 3:1); where Abraham offered Isaac (Ge 22:2, 4).

Materials prepared for (1Ki 5:17, 18). No tools used in the erection of (1Ki 6:7). Foundations of (1Ki 5:17,18; Lu 21:5).

Apartments and furnishings of: Oracle, or holy of holies, in (1Ki 6:19, 20; 8:6). Called Most Holy House (2Ch 3:8); Inner House (1Ki 6:27); Holiest of All (Heb 9:3). Description of (1Ki 6:16, 19-35; 2Ch 3:8-14; 4:22). Gold used in (2Ch 3:8-10). Contents of the holy of holies: ark (1Ki 6:19; 8:6; 2Ch 5:2-10), see Ark; cherubims (1Ki 6:23-28; 2Ch 3:10-13; 5:7, 8). See Ark; Cherubim; Veil; Mercy Seat.

Holy place (1Ki 8:8, 10). Called the Greater House (2Ch 3:5); Temple (1Ki 6:17). Description of (1Ki 6:15-18; 2Ch 3:3, 5-7, 14-17). Contents of the holy place: The table of shewbread (1Ki 7:48; 2Ch 29:18). See Shewbread, Table of. Other tables of gold and silver (1Ch 28:16; 2Ch 4:18, 19). Candlesticks and their utensils (1Ki 7:49, 50; 1Ch 28:15; 2Ch 4:7, 20-22). See Candlestick. Altar of incense and its furniture (1Ki 6:20; 7:48, 50; 1Ch 28:17, 18; 2Ch 4:19, 22). See Altar of Incense.

Porch of, called Porch of the Lord (2Ch 15:8). Dimensions of (1Ki 6:3; 2Ch 3:4). Doors of (2Ch 29:7). Overlaid with gold (2Ch 3:4). Pillars of (1Ki 7:15-22; 2Ki 11:14; 23:3; 25:17; 2Ch 3:15-17; 4:12, 13).

Chambers of (1Ki 6:5-10; 2Ki 11:2, 3). Offerings brought to (Ne 10:37-39). Treasuries in (see Treasure).

Courts of: Of the priests (2Ch 4:9); inner (1Ki 6:36); surrounded by rows of stones and cedar beams (1Ki 6:36; 7:12). Contents of the courts: Altar of burnt offering (2Ch 15:8), see Altar; the brazen sea (1Ki 7:23-37, 44, 46; 2Ch 4:2-5, 10); ten lavers (1Ki 7:38-46; 2Ch 4:6). Great court of (2Ch 4:9; Jer 19:14; 26:2). Covered place for the Sabbath and king's entry (2Ki 16:18).

Gates of: Higher gate (2Ki 15:35); new gate (Jer 26:10; 36:10); beautiful gate (Ac 3:2); eastern gate, closed on working days, open on the Sabbath (Eze 46:1, 12). Gifts received at (2Ch 24:8-11).

Uses of the temple: A dwelling place of the Lord (1Ki 8:10, 11, 13; 9:3; 2Ki 21:7; 1Ch 29:1; 2Ch 5:13, 14; 7:1-3, 16; Eze 10:3, 4; Mic 1:2); to contain the ark of the covenant (1Ki 8:21); for the offering of sweet incense (2Ch 2:4); for the continual shewbread and the burnt offerings (2Ch 2:4); for prayer and worship (1Ki 8; 2Ki 19:14, 15; 2Ch 30:27; Isa 27:13; 56:7; Jer 7:2; 26:2; Eze 46:2, 3, 9; Zec 7:2, 3; 8:21, 22; M'k 11:17; Lu 1:10; 2:37; 18:10; Ac 3:1; 22:17); prayer made toward (1Ki 8:38; Da 6:10; Jon 2:4); for an armory (2Ki 11:10; 2Ch 23:9, 10); for refuge (2Ki 11:15; Ne 6:10, 11).

Facts about: Dedication of (1Ki 8; 2Ch 5; 6; 7); services in, organized by David (1Ch 15:16; 23:24). Pillaged by Shishak (1Ki 14:25, 26); by Jehoash, king of Israel (2Ki 14:14). Repaired by Jehoash, king of Judah (2Ki 12:4-14; 2Ch 24:7-14); by Josiah (2Ki 22:3-7; 2Ch 34:8-13). Ahaz changes the pattern of the altar in (2Ki 16:10-17). Purified by Hezekiah (2Ch 29:15-19). Converted into an idolatrous shrine by Manasseh (2Ki 21:4-7; 2Ch 33:4-7). Treasures of, used in the purchase of peace: By Asa, from Ben-hadad (1Ki 15:18); by Jehoash, king of Judah, from Hazael (2Ki 12:18); by Hezekiah, from the king of Assyria (2Ki 18:15, 16). Ezekiel's vision concerning (Eze 8:16). Jews swore by (M't 23:16-22).

Destroyed by Nebuchadnezzar, and the valuable contents carried to Babylon (2Ki 24:13; 25:9-17; 2Ch 36:7, 19; Ps 79:1; Isa 64:11; Jer 27:16, 19-22; 28:3; 52:13, 17-23; La 2:7; 4:1; Ezr 1:7). Vessels of, used by Belshazzar (Da 5:2, 3).

Destruction of, foretold (Isa 66:6; Jer 27:18-22; Eze 7:22, 25; M't 24:2; M'k 13:2).

Restoration of, ordered by Cyrus (Ezr 1:7-11).

The Second: Restored by Zerubbabel (Ezr 1; 2:68, 69; 3:2-13; 4; 5:2-17; 6:3-5; Ne 7:70-72; Isa 44:28; Hag 2:3). Building of, suspended (Ezr 4); resumed (Ezr 4:24; 5; 6; Hag 1:2-9; 2:15; Zec 8:9); finished (Ezr 6:14, 15); dedicated (Ezr 6:15-18). Artaxerxes' favorable action toward (Ezr 7:11-28; 8:25-34).

Prophecies of its restoration (Isa 44:28; Da 8:13, 14; Hag 1; 2; Zec 1:16; 4:8-10; 6:12-15; 8:9-15; Mal 3:1).

Ezekiel's Vision of: Eze 37:26, 28; chapters 40-48.

Herod's: Forty-six years in building (Joh 2:20). Goodly stones of (M'k 13:1; Lu 21:5). Magnificence of (M't 24:1). Beautiful gate of (Ac 3:10). Solomon's porch (Joh 10:23; Ac 3:11; 5:12). Treasury of (M'k 12:41-44). Zacharias, officiating priest in, has a vision of an angel; receives promise of a son (Lu 1:5-23, w *verses* 57-64). Jesus brought to, according to the law and custom (Lu 2: 21-39); Simeon blesses Jesus in (Lu 2: 25-35); Anna, the prophetess, dwells in (Lu 2:36, 37). Jesus in, when a youth (Lu 2:46); taken to the pinnacle of, in his temptation (M't 4:5-7; Lu 4:9-12); teaches in (M'k 11:27-33; 12:35-44; 14:49; Joh 5:14-47; 7:14-28; 8; 10:23-38; 18:20); performs miracles in (M't 21:14, 15); drives money changers from (M't 21:12, 13; M'k 11:15-17; Lu 19:45, 46; Joh 2:15, 16).

Captains of (Lu 22:52; Ac 4:1; 5:24, 26). Judas casts down the pieces of silver in (M't 27:5).

Veil of, rent at the time of the crucifixion (M't 27:51). The disciples worship in, after the resurrection (Lu 24:53; Ac 2:46; 3:1). Peter heals the lame man at the gate of (Ac 3:1-16). Disciples preach in (Ac 5:20, 21, 42). Paul's vision in (Ac 22:17-21). Paul observes the rights of (Ac 21:26-30); is apprehended in (Ac 21:33).

Prophecies concerning its destruction, by Daniel (Da 8:11-15; 11:30, 31). Jesus foretells the destruction of (M't 24; M'k 13:2; Lu 21:6).

Figurative: Of the body of Jesus (M't 26:61; 27:40; Joh 2:19). Of the indwelling of God (1Co 3:16, 17; 2Co 6: 16). Of the Church (Eph 2:21; 2Th 2:4; Re 3:12). Of the kingdom of Christ (Re 11; 14:15, 17). Of Christ, the head of the Church, sending forth the forces of righteousness against the powers of evil (Re 15:5-8; 16:1-17).

Idolatrous: Of Dagon, at Ashdod (1Sa 5:2); of the calves, at Beth-el (1Ki 12:31, 33); of Rimmon, at Damascus (2Ki 5:18); of Baal, at Samaria (2Ki 10:21. 27); at Babylon (2Ch 36:7; Da 1:2); of

Diana, at Ephesus (Ac 19:27).

Trophies stored in (1Sa 31:10; 1Ch 10:9, 10; Da 1:2).

See Tabernacle.

TEMPORAL BLESSINGS (See Blessings.)

TEMPTATION (trial, proof), has two meanings: any attempt to entice or tempt into evil; a testing which aims at an ultimate spiritual good.

Temptation to evil (Pr 12:26; Ro 8:35-39). Called snares of death (Pr 13:14; 14:27).

Way of escape from (1Co 10:13). Christ succors in (Heb 2:18; 4:15; Re 3:10). The Lord delivers from (2Pe 2:9).

Benefits of **(Jas 1:2-4, 12; 1Pe 1:6, 7).**

Leading into: To be avoided (M't 5:29, 30; 6:9; M'k 9:42-48; Lu 17:1; Ro 14:13, 15, 21; 1Co 7:5; 8:9-13; 10:28-32). Prayer against being led into (M't 6:13; 26:41; M'k 14:38; Lu 11:4; 22:40, 46). Not to lead others into (Ro 14:13, 15, 21; 1Co 7:5; 8:9-13; 10:28-32).

Instances of leading others into: Abraham, of Pharaoh (Ge 12:18, 19); of Abimelech (Ge 20:9). Rebekah, of Jacob (Ge 27:6-14). Balak, of Balaam (Nu 22:5-7, 16, 17; 23:11-13, 25-27). Eli's sons, of Israel (1Sa 2:24, 25). Gideon, of Israel (J'g 8:27). The old prophet of Bethel, of the prophet of Judah (1Ki 13:15-19). Jeroboam, of Israel (1Ki 15:30, 34).

Resistance to: Enjoined (De 7:25, 26; Pr 1:10-19; 4:14, 15; 5:3, 8; 19:27; M't 24:42-44; 25:13; 26:41; M'k 13:21, 22, 33-37; 14:37, 38; Ro 6:12-14; 12:21; Eph 6:11, 13-17; Jas 4:7; 1Pe 5:8, 9; 1Jo 4:4). Source of resistance (Ps 17:4; 73:2-25; 94:17, 18).

Rewards to those who resist (Isa 33:15. 16; Jas 1:12; Re 3:10).

Instances of those who resisted: Joseph (Ge 39:7-12). Balaam (Nu 22:7-18, 38; 23:7-12, 18-24). David (1Sa 26:5-25). The prophet of Judah (1Ki 13:7-9). Micaiah (1Ki 22:13-28). The people of Jerusalem (2Ki 18:30-36). Job (Job 1:6-21; 2:4-10; 31:1, 5-17, 19-34, 38-40). Rechabites (Jer 35:5-9). Nehemiah (Ne 4:9). Jesus (M't 4:1-11; 26:38-42; Lu 4:1-13; Heb 4:15; 12:3, 4).

Sources of: Cherished pleasures (M't 5:29, 30; 18:7-9; M'k 9:43-45). Evil company (Ex 34:12-16: Pr 2:10-16). Harlots and carnal desires (Pr 5:1-20; 6:24-29; 7:1-27; 9:15-18; Ec 7:26). Carnal desires (Ro 7:5; Ga 5:17; Jas 1:13-15; 2Pe 2:18; 1Jo 2:16, 17). False teachers (M't 18:6, 7; Lu 17:1; 1Jo 2:26; 4:1-3; Re 2:20). Persecutions (Joh 16:1, 2). Prosperity (De 8:10-17; Lu 12:16-21). Riches (M't 19:16-24; M'k 10:17-30; 1Ti 6:9, 10). Cares, riches and pleasures (M't 13:22; Lu 8:13, 14; 21:34-38).

Satan (Ge 3:1-5; 1Ch 21:1; M'k 4:15, 17; Lu 22:3, 31, 32; 2Co 2:11; 11:3, 14, 15; 12:7; Ga 4:14; Eph 4:27; 6:11, 13-17; 1Th 3:5; 1Ti 5:15; Jas 4:7; 1Pe 5:8, 9; Re 12:10, 11, 17).

Wicked men (Pr 16:29; 28:10; Ho 7:5; Am 2:12; M't 5:19; 2Ti 3:13). See Demons; Faith, Trial of; Satan.

Warnings against yielding to (Ex 34:12-16; De 8:11-20; Pr 2:10-16; 5:1-21; 6:27, 28; 7:1-27; 9:15-18; Ec 7:26; Jer 2:25; M't 26:31, 41; M'k 14:37, 38; Lu 21:34-36; 22:40; 1Co 16:13; Eph 6:11, 13-17; Heb 12:3, 4; 1Pe 4:7; 5:8, 9; 2Pe 3:17; Re 3:2, 3).

Yielding to: Instances of: Adam and Eve (Ge 3:1-19). Sarah, to lie (Ge 12:13; 18:13-15; 20:13). Isaac, to lie (Ge 26:7). Jacob to defraud Esau (Ge 27:6-13). Balaam (Nu 22:15-22; 2Pe 2:15). Achan (Jos 7:21). David, to commit adultery (2Sa 11:2-5); to number Israel (1Ch 21). Solomon, to become an idolater through the influences of his wives (1Ki 11:4; Ne 13:26). The prophet of Judah (1Ki 13:11-19). Hezekiah (2Ki 20:12-20; Isa 39:1-4, 6, 7). Peter (M't 26:69-74; M'k 14:67-71; Lu 22:55-60).

Of Jesus (Lu 22:28). In all points as we are (Heb 4:15). By the devil (M't 4:1-11; M'k 1:12, 13; Lu 4:1-13). Before his crucifixion (M't 26:38-42).

Test of God: Design of, a test (Ps 66:10-13; 119:101, 110; Da 12:10; Zec 13:9; 1Pe 1:6, 7; 4:12); of fidelity (De 13:1-3; 2Ch 32:31; Job 1:8-22; 2:3-10); of obedience (Ge 22:1-14, De 8:2, 5; Heb 11:17).

Benefits of (Jas 1:2-4, 12; 1Pe 1:6, 7). Rewards of (Isa 33:15, 16; Lu 12:35-38; Jas 1:12; 1Jo 4:4).

See Affliction, Design of; Faith, Trial of.

TEN, used for an indefinite number (Ge 31:7; Le 26:26; Nu 14:22; Zec 8:23).

TEN COMMANDMENTS (See Commandments.)

TENANTS, evicted (M't 21:41; M'k 12:9; Lu 20:16).

TENONS (hands), projections in tabernacle boards to hold the boards in place (Ex 26:17).

TENSION (See Anxiety.)

TENT. Used for dwelling (Ge 4:20); by Noah (Ge 9:21); by Abraham (Ge 12:8; 13:18; 18:1); by Lot (Ge 13:5); by Moses (Ex 18:7); by children of Israel (Nu 24:5, 6; 2Sa 20:1; 1Ki 12:16); by the Midianites (J'g 6:5); by Cushites (Hab 3:7); by Arabians (Isa 13:20); by shepherds (Isa 38:12; Jer 6:3). Women had tents apart from men (Ge 24:67; 31:33). Used for cattle (2Ch 14:15). Manufacture of (Ac 18:3). Used as a place of worship (see Tabernacle).

TERAH. 1. Son of Nahor (Ge 11:24, 25); father of Abraham, Nahor, Haran (Ge 11:26); idolater (Jos 24:2); went as far as Haran with Abraham (Ge 11:24-32).

2. Encampment of Israelites in wilderness (Nu 33:27, 28), KJV has "Tarah."

TERAPHIM, household idols. Used by Laban, stolen by Rachel (Ge 31:19, 30-35); by Micah, stolen by the Danites (J'g 17:5; 18:14, 17-20). Condemned and disposed of by Jacob (Ge 35:2-4, w Ge 31:35-39). Destroyed by Josiah (see Idols).

TERESH, a Persian chamberlain. Plotted against Ahasuerus (Es 2:21-23; 6:2).

TERRACE, steps leading up to temple (2Ch 9:11).

TERROR, extreme fear or dread; or sometimes, the one who causes such agitation (Ge 35:5; Ps 55:4; 2Co 5:11).

TERTIUS, Paul's amanuensis in writing the book of Romans (Ro 16:22).

TERTULLUS, diminutive of Tertius; lawyer employed by Jews to state their case against Paul before Felix (Ac 24:1).

TESTAMENT. 1. Covenant (Heb 8:6-10; 9:1, 4).

2. Testamentary disposition, or will (Heb 9:16, 17).

3. Books of the Bible, containing the Old and New covenants.

TESTAMENTS OF THE TWELVE PROPHETS, apocryphal document that claims to report the last words of the 12 sons of Jacob; probably written c. 2nd cent. A. D.

TESTIMONY. *Commandments:* Those revealed to Moses (Ex 25:16; De 4:44, 45; 1Ki 2:3). Kept in the ark (Ex 25:16, 21). Engraved on tablets (Ex 31:18; 32:15; 38:21). Mercy seat was over (Ex 26:34; 30:6; 40:20).

Ark, called Ark of (Ex 25:22; 26:34; 40:3, 5, 20, 21). Tabernacle called Tabernacle of (Nu 1:50, 53; 9:19; 10:11). See Ark; Tabernacle.

See Commandments; Decalogue.

Legal (See Evidence; Witnesses).

Religious (Ps 18:49; 22:22; 26:12; 34:1-4, 8, 9; 77:12; 119:13, 26, 27, 46, 67, 71; Isa 43:10; 44:8; 45:24; 1Co 1:5, 6; 12:3; 15:15).

Required of the righteous (1Ch 16:8, 9; Ps 9:11; Isa 12:4-6; 43:10; 44:8; Jer 51:10; M't 4:21; 5:15, 16, 19, 20; M'k 4:21; 5:19, 20; Lu 8:16, 39; 24:48; Joh 15:27; Ac 1:8, 22; 3:15; 5:32; 13:31; Ro 10:9, 10; Eph 5:19; 2Ti 1:8; 1Pe 3:15; 5:12).

Concerning God's, faithfulness (Ps 73:23-26, 28; 89:1); glory (Ps 145:11, 12); merciful providences (Ps 40:1-3; 54:7; 91:2-13; Da 4:2, 3; Ac 14:15-17); righteousness (Ps 35:28; 71:16); salvation (Ps 30:1-6; 40:1-3; 62:1, 2; 66:16-20; 71:15, 18; Ga 2:20; Ph'p 3:4-14; Tit 3:3-7; Heb 2:3, 12); words (Ps 119:172); works (Ps 71:17, 24; 145:4-7, 10-12; Jer 51:10; Ac 2:11).

Concerning confidence in God (Ps 16:5-9; 18:2, 3, 35, 36; 23:1-6; 26:6, 7; 27:1-6, 13; 28:6-8; 30:1-6). Rewards of (M't 10:32; Lu 12:8). Victory by (Re 12:11).

Exemplified by: Job (Job 19:25-27). The psalmist (Ps 35:28; 40:1-3, 9; 57:7-9; 116:1-19). Nebuchadnezzar (Da 4:34-37). The woman of Sychar (Joh 4:28-30, 39, 41, 42). The blind man whom Jesus healed (Joh 9:17, 30-33). The apostles to the resurrection of Jesus (Ac 4:33; 1Jo 1:1-4). The disciples at Pentecost (Ac 2:4-11). Peter (Ac 4:18-20; 2Pe 1:16; 5:1, 12). John (Ac 4:18-20; 1Jo 1:1-4). Paul concerning, his conversion (Ac 22:1-16; 26:12-23); his devotion to Christ (1Co 13:1; Ph'p 3:4-14); his confidence in Christ (2Co 4:13, 14; 5:1; 2Ti 1:12); his hope of the crown of righteousness

(2Ti 4:7, 8); his hope of eternal life (Tit 1:1, 2). Timothy (1Ti 6:12).

TETRARCH, petty prince, ruler of a small district (M't 14:1; Lu 3:1; 9:7; Ac 13:1).

TEXTS AND VERSIONS (Old Testament). The original manuscripts of the OT have all been destroyed; the oldest manuscripts that survive are the famous Dead Sea Scrolls found in 1947 and later in caves along the Dead Sea, dating from 250 B. C. to c. A. D. 70; all the OT books except Esther are represented, most of them in fragmentary form. The oldest versions of the OT are: (1) Greek, Septuagint (250-100 B. C.), versions made in the 2nd cent. A. D. by Aquila, Theodotion, and Symmachus, and a translation made by Origen c. A. D. 240; (2) Aramaic (1st to 9th cent. A. D.); (3) Syriac (2nd or 3rd cent. A. D.); (4) the Latin (3rd and 4th centuries A. D.); (5) Coptic, Ethiopic, Gothic, Armenian, Georgian, Slavonic, Arabic (2nd to 10th centuries).

TEXTS AND VERSIONS (New Testament). Greek manuscripts whether of a portion or of the whole of the NT total nearly 4700. Of these c. 70 are papyri, 250 uncials, 2500 minuscules, and 1800 lectionaries; the earliest is a fragment of the Gospel of John and dates c. A. D. 125. The oldest NT versions are (1) Latin (2nd to 4th centuries), (2) Syriac (2nd to 6th centuries), (3) Coptic (2nd and 3rd centuries), (4) Gothic, Armenian, Georgian, Ethiopic, Arabic, Persian, Slavonic (4th to 9th centuries). A great deal of evidence for the text of the NT is also found in the writings of the early Church Fathers, principally in Greek, Latin, and Syriac.

THADDAEUS, one of the 12 apostles (M't 10:3; M'k 3:18). This name does not appear in Lu 6:16 and Ac 1:13, where the name "Judas, son of James" (RSV) occurs instead. Little is known about him.

THAHASH, son of Nahor (Ge 22:24).

THAMAH, called also Tamah. One of the Nethinim (Ezr 2:53; Ne 7:55).

THAMAR (See Tamar, 1.)

THANKFULNESS. *To God.* (Commanded or required (Ge 35:1; Ex 12:14, 17, 42; 13:3, 8-10, 14-16; 16:32; 34:26; Le 19:24; 23:14; De 12:18; 16:9-15; 26:10; J'g 5:11; Ps 50:14, 15). Enjoined (Ps 48:11; 106:1; Pr 3:9, 10; Ec 7:14; Isa 48:20; Joe 2:26; Ro 2:4; 15:27; Eph 1:16; 5:4, 19, 20; Ph'p 4:6; Col 1:12; 2:7; 3:15-17; 4:2; 1Th 5:18; Heb 13:15; Jas 1:9). Exhorted (Ps 98:1; 105:1, 5, 42-45; 107:1, 2, 15, 22, 42, 43; 118:1, 4; Col 3:15; 1Ti 2:1; 4:3-5).

Jesus set an example of (M't 11:25; 15:36; 26:27; M'k 8:6, 7; 14:23; Lu 22:17, 19; Joh 6:11, 23; 11:41).

Should be offered, to God (Ps 30:4; 50:14; 75:1; 92:1; 97:12; 106:1; 118:1; 2Co 9:11; Eph 5:4, 19, 20; Ph'p 4:6; Col 1:12; 2:7; 3:15-17; 4:2; 1Th 5:18; 1Ti 2:1; Heb 13:15); through Christ (Ro 1:8; Col 3:17; Heb 13:15); in the name of Christ (Eph 5:20); in behalf of ministers (2Co 1:11); in private worship (Da 6:10); in public worship (1Ch 23:30; 25:3; Ne 11:17; Ps 35:18); in everything (1Th 5:18); upon the completion of great undertakings (Ne 12:31, 40); before taking food (M't 14:19; M'k 8:9; Lu 24:30; Joh 6:11; Ac 27:35); always (Eph 1:16; 5:20; 1Th 1:2); as the remembrance of God's holiness (Ps 30:4; 97:12).

For: the goodness and mercy of God (Ps 68:19; 79:13; 89:1; 100:4; 106:1; 107:1; 116:12-14, 17; 136:1-3; Isa 63:7); the gift of Christ (2Co 9:15); Christ's power and reign (Re 11:17); the reception and effectual working of the word of God in others (1Th 2:13); deliverance, from adversity (Ps 31:7, 21; 35: 9, 10; 44:7, 8; 54:6, 7; 66:8, 9, 12-16, 20; 98:1); through Christ, from indwelling sin (Ro 7:23-25); providential deliverance (Ex 12:14, 17, 42; 13:3, 8-10, 14-16; J'g 5:11; Ps 105:1-45; 107:1, 2, 15, 22, 42, 43; 136:1-26; Joe 2:26); victory over death and the grave (1Co 15:57); wisdom and might (Da 2:23); the triumph of the gospel (2Co 2:14); the conversion of others (Ro 6:17); faith exhibited by others (Ro 1:8; 2Th 1:3); love exhibited by others (2Th 1:3); the grace bestowed on others (1Co 1:4; Ph'p 1:3-5; Col 1:3-6); the zeal exhibited by others (2Co 8:16); nearness of God's presence (Ps 75:1); appointment to the ministry (1Ti 1:12); willingness to offer our property for God's service (1Ch 29:6-14); the supply of our bodily wants (Ro 14:6, 7; 1Ti 4:3, 4); all men (1Ti 2:1); all things (2Co 9:11; Eph 5:20);

temporal blessings (Ro 14:6, 7; 1Ti 4:3-5).

Should be accompanied by intercession for others (1Ti 2:1; 2Ti 1:3; Ph'm 4). Should always accompany prayer (Ne 11:17; Ph'p 4:6; Col 4:2). Should always accompany praise (Ps 92:1; Heb 13:15). Expressed in psalms (1Ch 16:7). Ministers appointed to offer, in public (1Ch 16:4, 7; 23:30; 2Ch 31:2).

Saints exhorted to (Ps 105:1; Col 3:15); resolve to offer (Ps 18:49; 30:12); habitually offer (Da 6:10); offer sacrifices of (Ps 116:17); abound in the faith with (Col 2:7); magnify God by (Ps 69:30); come before God with (Ps 95:2); should enter God's gates with (Ps 100:4). Of hypocrites, full of boasting (Lu 18:11). The wicked averse to (Ro 1:21).

Of the heavenly host (Re 4:9; 7:11, 12; 11:16, 17).

Cultivated, by Feast of Tabernacles (De 16:9-15); by thank offering (Ex 34:26; Le 19:24; 23:14; De 12:18; 26:10; Pr 3:9, 10); by songs (1Ch 16:7-36; Ps 95:2; 100).

Instances of: Eve (Ge 4:1, 25). Noah (Ge 8:20). Melchizedek (Ge 14:20). Lot (Ge 19:19). Abraham (Ge 12:7). Sarah (Ge 21:6, 7). Abraham's servant (Ge 24:27). Isaac (Ge 26:22). Leah (Ge 29:32-35). Rachel (Ge 30:6). Jacob (Ge 32:10; 35:3, 7; 48:11, 15, 16). Joseph (Ge 41:51, 52). Moses (Ex 15:1-18). Miriam (Ex 15:20-22). Jethro (Ex 18:10). Israel (Ex 4:31; 15:1-21; Nu 21:17; 31:49-54; 1Ch 29:22). Deborah (J'g 5). Hannah (1Sa 1:27, 28; 2:1-10). Samuel (1Sa 7:12). David (2Sa 6:21; 1Ch 29:13). Solomon (1Ki 8:15, 56; 2Ch 6:4). Queen of Sheba (1Ki 10:9). Hiram (2Ch 2:12). Jehoshaphat's army (2Ch 20:27, 28). Ezra (Ezr 7:27). The Levites (2Ch 5:12, 13; Ne 9:4-38). The Jews (Ne 12:31, 40, 43).

The Psalmist (Ps 9:1, 2, 4; 13:6; 22:23-25; 26:7; 28:7; 30:1, 3, 11, 12; 31:7, 21; 35:9, 10, 18; 40:2, 3, 5; 41:11, 12; 44:7, 8; 54:6, 7; 56:12, 13; 59:16, 17; 66:8, 9, 12-16, 20; 68:19; 71:15, 23, 24; 79:13; 89:1; 92:1, 2, 4; 98:1; 100:4; 102:18-20; 104:1; 116:12-14, 17; 119:65, 108; 136:1-26).

Isaiah (Isa 63:7). Daniel (Da 2:23; 6:22). Nebuchadnezzar (Da 4:2, 34). The mariners (Jon 1:16). Jonah (Jon 2:9). The shepherds (Lu 2:20). Simeon (Lu 2:28). Anna (Lu 2:38).

Those whom Jesus healed: The man with palsy (Lu 5:25); the demoniac (Lu 8:39); the woman bent with infirmity (Lu 13:13); one of the ten lepers (Lu 17:15, 16); blind Bartimaeus (Lu 18:43); the centurion for his son (Joh 4:53).

The lame man healed by Peter (Ac 3:8). Early Christians (Ac 2:46, 47).

Paul (Ac 27:35; 28:15; Ro 1:8; 6:17; 1Co 1:4; 2Co 2:14; Ph'p 1:3-5; Col 1:3-6; 2Th 1:3; 1Ti 1:12).

See Joy; Praise; Psalms; Worship.

Of Man to Man. The Israelites, to Joshua (Jos 19:49, 50). The spies, to Rahab (Jos 6:22-25). Saul, to the Kenites (1Sa 15:6). Naomi, to Boaz (Ru 2:19, 20). David, to the men of Jabesh-gilead (2Sa 2:5-7); to Hanun (2Sa 10:2); to Barzillai (1Ki 2:7). Paul, to Phebe (Ro 16:1-4); to Onesiphorus (2Ti 1:16-18). The people of Melita, to Paul (Ac 28:10).

THANK OFFERINGS (See Offerings.)

THANKSGIVING. By Jesus (M't 11:25; 15:36; 26:27; M'k 8:6, 7; 14:23; Lu 22:17, 19; Joh 6:11, 23; 11:41).

For food: commonly called "grace" (1Sa 9:13; M't 14:19; 15:36; M'k 6:41; 8:6, 7; Lu 9:16; 24:30; Joh 6:11, 23; Ac 27:35; Ro 14:6; 1Co 10:30, 31; 1Ti 4:3-5).

Instances of: Jesus (M't 14:19; M'k 8:6, 7). Paul (Ac 27:35).

See Praise; Prayer, Before Taking Food; Thankfulness.

THARA (See Tarah.)

THARSHISH. 1. Son of Bilhan (1Ch 7:10. [R. V., Tarshish.])

2. See Tarshish, 2.

THEATER, place for dramatic performances (Ac 19:29, 31).

THEBES (town, village), capital of Egypt during 18th dynasty called "No" in the Bible; on E bank of Nile; famous for temples; cult center of god Amon (Jer 46:25); denounced by prophets (Jer 46:25; Eze 30:14-16).

THEBEZ, city in Ephraim c. halfway from Beth-Shean to Shechem; Abimelech, son of Gideon, slain there (J'g 9:50; 2Sa 11:21).

THEFT (Ps 119:61; Pr 21:7; Na 3:1; M't

6:19, 20; 15:19; M'k 7:21, 22; Ro 2:21; Re 9:21).

Forbidden (Ex 20:15; Le 19:11, 13; De 5:19; 23:24, 25; Ps 62:10; M't 19:18; Lu 18:20; Ro 13:9; Eph 4:28; Tit 2:10; 1Pe 4:15). Restitution for things stolen required of the penitent (Ezr 35:15). Penalty for (Ex 21:16; 22:1-4, 10, 12-15; Le 6:2-5; Pr 6:30, 31; Zec 5:3; M't 27:38, 44; M'k 15:27).

Instances of: Rachel, of the household gods (Ge 31:19, 34, 35). Achan (Jos 7:11). Micah (J'g 17:2). The spies of Laish (J'g 18:14-27). Israelites (Eze 22:29; Ho 4:1, 2). Judas (Joh 12:6).

See Dishonesty; Thieves.

THELASAR, called also Telassar. A city or district conquered by the Assyrians (2Ki 19:12; Isa 37:12).

THEOCRACY. Established (Ex 19:8; 24:3, 7; De 5:25-29; 33:2-5; J'g 8:23; 1Sa 12:12). Rejected by Israel (1Sa 8:7, 19; 10:19; 2Ch 13:8).

See God, Sovereign; Government.

THEOLOGY (See God.)

THEOPHANY, visible appearance of God, generally in human form (Ge 3:8; 4; 28:10-17).

THEOPHILUS, man to whom Gospel of Luke and Acts of the Apostles are addressed (Lu 1:3; Ac 1:1). Nothing is known of him.

THESSALONIANS, EPISTLES TO, written by Paul in Corinth c. A. D. 51 during Paul's 2nd missionary journey, not long after he had founded the church. First epistle written to encourage the Thessalonians' growth as Christians and to settle a question that was troubling them, whether those of their number who had died would miss some of the blessings of the second coming of Christ. Outline: 1. Conversion of the Thessalonians (1:1-10).

2. The ministry of Paul at Thessalonica (2).

3. Paul's concern and prayer for the church (3).

4. Problems of the church: moral instruction, the Lord's coming, ethical duties (4:1-5:22).

5. Conclusion (5:23-28).

Second Thessalonians was written to correct some misconceptions concerning the second coming of Christ. Outline: 1. Comfort in persecution (1).

2. Signs of the day of Christ: apostasy, revelation of the man of sin, preservation of God's people (2).

3. Spiritual counsel (3).

THESSALONICA, a city of Macedonia. Paul visits (Ac 17:1; Ph'p 4:16). People of, persecute Paul (Ac 17:5-8, 11, 13). Men of, accompany Paul (Ac 20:4; 27:2). Paul writes to Christians in (1Th 1:1; 2Th 1:1). Demas goes to (2Ti 4:10).

THEUDAS, Jew who led rebellion against Rome (Ac 5:36, 37).

THICKET (1Sa 13:6; Jer 4:7).

THIEF, THIEVES, in Mosaic law punishment of thieves was very severe (Ex 22:1-4).

Penalty for (De 24:7; Pr 6:30, 31; Eze 18:10, 13; Zec 5:3; M't 27:38, 44; M'k 15:27).

Collusion with (Ps 50:18). Excluded from the kingdom of God (1Co 6:10). Desecrated the temple (M't 21:13; M'k 11:17, Lu 19:45, 46). Ingnominious (Jer 2:26). Worship of, offensive to God (Jer 7:9, 10).

Christ to come again as (Re 3:3).

Figurative (Ob 5; Joh 10:1).

See Theft.

THIGH, to put one's hand under the thigh of another was to enhance the sacredness of an oath (Ge 24:2, 9; 47:29).

THIMNATHAH, town on N boundary of Judah three miles SW of Bethshemesh (Jos 19:43). Modern Tibnah.

THIRST, figurative of the ardent desire of the devout mind (Ps 42:1-4; 63:1; 143:6; Isa 55:1; Am 8:11-13; M't 5:6; Joh 4:14, 15; 7:37; Re 21:6; 22:17).

See Desire, Spiritual; Diligence; Hunger, Spiritual; Zeal.

THISTLE, exists in many varieties in Palestine. Used figuratively for trouble, desolation, judgment, wickedness (Nu 33:55; Pr 24:31; 15:19; Isa 5:6; 2Co 12:7).

THOMAS (twin), called Didymus. One of the twelve apostles (M't 10:3; M'k 3:18; Lu 6:15). Present at the raising of Lazarus (Joh 11:16). Asks Jesus the way to the Father's house (Joh 14:5). Absent when Jesus first appeared to the disciples after the resurrection (Joh 20:24). Skepticism of (Joh 20:25). Sees Jesus after the resurrection (Joh 20:26-29; 21:1, 2). Dwells with the other apostles in

Jerusalem (Ac 1:13, 14). Loyalty of, to Jesus (Joh 11:16; 20:28).

THOMAS, GOSPEL OF, Gnostic gospel consisting entirely of supposed sayings of Jesus; dated c. A. D. 140; found at Naj Hamadi in Egypt in 1945.

THORN. The ground cursed with (Ge 3:18). Used as an awl (Job 41:2); for fuel (Ps 58:9; 118:12; Ec 7:6). Hedges formed of (Ho 2:6; Mic 7:4). Crown of, mockingly put on Jesus' head (M't 27:29; M'k 15:17; Joh 19:2, 5).

Figurative: Of afflictions (Nu 33:55; 2Co 12:7). Of the adversities of the wicked (Pr 22:5). Of the evils that spring from the heart to choke the truth (M't 13:7, 22).

THORN IN THE FLESH, Paul's description of a physical ailment from which he prayed to be relieved (2Co 12:7). What it was is not known.

THOUGHTS, GOD'S (Ps 40:5, 17; 139:17; Isa 55:9; Jer 29:11).

THOUSAND, often used symbolically in the Bible. In OT sometimes means "many" (1Sa 21:11; 2Ch 15:11), "family" (Nu 10:4).

THOUSAND YEARS, the millennium (Re 20:1-4).

THRACE, kingdom and later a Roman province, in SE Europe, E of Macedonia (2Macc 12:35).

THREAD (Ge 14:23; J'g 16:21; Song 4:3).

THREATENINGS of God against the wicked (Le 26:16; Jos 23:15; 1Sa 12:25; 1Ki 9:7; Ps 7:12; Isa 14:23; 66:4; Mal 3:5).

THREE HOLY CHILDREN, SONG OF, apocryphal additions to the OT book of Daniel; probably written in first century B.C.

THREE TAVERNS, a town in Italy. Roman Christians meet Paul in (Ac 28:15).

THRESHING. By beating (Ru 2:17); by treading (De 25:24; Isa 25:10; Ho 10:11; 1Co 9:9; 1Ti 5:18). With instruments of wood (2Sa 24:22); of iron (Am 1:3); with a cart wheel (Isa 28:27, 28). Floors for (Ge 50:10, 11; J'g 6:37; Ru 3:2-14; 1Sa 23:1; 2Sa 6:6; Ho 9:2; Joe 2:24). Floor of Araunah bought by David for a place of sacrifice (2Sa 24:16-25). Floor for, in barns (2Ki 6:27).

THRESHING FLOOR, place where grain was threshed, usually clay soil packed to a hard, smooth surface (De 25:4; Isa 28:27; 1Co 9:9).

THRESHOLD, piece of wood or stone at the bottom of a door, which has to be crossed on entering a house.

THRONE. Of Pharaoh (Ge 41:40; Ex 11:5). Of David (1Ki 2:12, 24; Ps 132:11, 12; Isa 9:7; Jer 13:13; 17:25; Lu 1:32). Of Solomon (1Ki 2:19; 2Ch 9:17-19). Of ivory (1Ki 10:18-20). Of Solomon, called The Throne of the Lord (1Ch 29:23). Of Herod (Ac 12:21). Of Israel (1Ki 8:20; 10:9; 2Ch 6:10).

Abdicated by David (1Ki 1:32-40).

Figurative: Anthropomorphic use of: Of God (2Ch 18:18; Ps 9:4, 7; 11:4; 47:8; 89:14; 97:2; 103:19; Isa 6:1; 66:1; M't 5:34; 23:22; Heb 8:1; 12:2; Re 14:3, 5); of Christ (M't 19:28; 25:31; Ac 2:30; Re 1:4; 3:21; 4:2-10; 7:9-17; 19:4; 21:5; 22:3).

THUMB. Blood put on, in consecration (Ex 29:20; Le 8:23); in purification (Le 14:14, 25). Oil put on (Le 14:17, 28). Of prisoners cut off (J'g 1:6, 7). See Hand.

THUMMIM (See Urim.)

THUNDER. Sent as a plague upon the Egyptians (Ex 9:23-34); the Philistines, in battle with the children of Israel (1Sa 7:10). Sent as a judgment (Isa 29:6). On Sinai (Ex 19:16; Ps 77:18; Heb 12:18, 19). A token of divine anger (1Sa 12:17, 18). A manifestation of divine power (Job 26:14; Ps 77:18). Sons of Zebedee called sons of (M'k 3:17).

THUNDER, SONS OF, title given James and John by Jesus (M'k 3:17).

THUTMOSE (also Tuthmosis, Thotmes), name of four kings of Egypt of 18th dynasty, centering in Thebes. Under their rule Egypt attained her greatest power.

THYATIRA, city in Roman province of Asia, on boundary of Lydia and Mysia; noted for weaving and dyeing (Ac 16:14; Re 2:18-29).

THYINE, an aromatic wood (Re 18:12).

TIAMAT, mythical monster in Babylonian-Assyrian creation story.

TIBERIAS, city on W shore of Sea of Galilee; built by Herod Antipas, and named for the emperor Tiberius; famous health resort; after A. D. 70 it became a center of rabbinic learning. Modern Tabariyeh.

TIBERIAS, SEA OF (See Sea of Galilee.)
TIBERIUS, second Roman emperor (A. D. 14-37); reigning emperor at time of Christ's death (Lu 3:1).
TIBHATH, city of Zobah, E of Anti-Lebanon Mountains (1Ch 18:7-9); "Betah" in 2Sa 8:8.
TIBNI, son of Ginath; unsuccessful competitor for throne of Israel (1Ki 16:21).
TIDAI, king of Goiim; confederate of Chedorlaomer (Ge 14:1-17).
TIGLATH-PILESER, famous Assyrian king (1114-1074 B. C.); great conqueror; received tribute from King Azariah of Judah and King Menahem of Samaria (2Ki 15:19, 20); Ahaz secured his help against Pekah of Israel and Rezin of Syria; deported Transjordanian Israelites (1Ch 5:6, 26); Ahaz gave tribute to him (2Ch 28:20, 21).
TIGRIS (arrow), one of the two great rivers of the Mesopotamian area; 1,150 miles long ("Hiddekel" Da 10:4).
TIKVAH. 1. Father-in-law of the prophetess Huldah (2Ki 22:14).
2. Father of Jahaziah (Ezr 10:15).
TILE, slab of burnt clay used for writing and roofing (Eze 4:1-8; Lu 5:19).
TILE, brick (Eze 4:1; Lu 5:19).
TILGATH-PILNESER (See Tiglath-Pileser.)
TILON, son of Shimon (1Ch 4:20).
TIMBREL, called also Tabret, an instrument of music of the tambourine sort. Used by Miriam (Ex 15:20); by Jephthah's daughter (J'g 11:34). Used in religious service (2Sa 6:5; 1Ch 13:8; Ps 68:25; 81:2; 149:3; 150:4). Used in dances (Job 21:12). See Music, Instruments of.
TIME. In the early Biblical period time was marked by sunrise and sunset, phases of the moon, and location of a few constellations; but there were no names for days and months, and no accurate knowledge of years. Ancient people had no method of reckoning long periods of time. They dated from great and well-known events, like the founding of Rome (753 B. C.), the beginning of the Olympian games (766 B. C.), the founding of the Seleucid dynasty (312 B. C.), the Exodus, the Babylonian Exile, the earthquake (Am 1:1). The starting point in the Maccabean age was the beginning of the Seleucid era (312 B. C.). The year was lunar (354 days, 8 hours, 38 seconds), divided into 12 lunar months, with seven intercalary months added over 19 years. The Hebrew month began with the new moon. Early Hebrews gave the months names; later they used numbers; and after the Exile they used Babylonian names. The sacred year began with Nisan (March-April); the secular year, with Tishri (September-October). Months were divided by the Jews into weeks of seven days, ending with the Sabbath (Ex 20:11; De 5:14, 15). Days were divided into 24 hours of 60 minutes of 60 seconds. The Roman day began at midnight and had 12 hours (Joh 11:9); the Hebrew day was reckoned from sunset. Night was divided into watches. At first the Hebrews had three watches; in the time of Christ there were four. Various kinds of clocks were used; sundials, shadow clocks, water clocks.
TIMES, OBSERVER OF, person who has a superstitious regard for days regarded as lucky or unlucky, as decided by astrology (De 18:9-14).
TIMEUS, TIMAEUS, father of Bartimaeus (M'k 10:46).
TIMNA (holding in check). 1. Concubine of Eliphaz (Ge 36:12).
2. Sister of Lotan (Ge 36:22).
3. Chieftain of Edom (Ge 36:40), KJV has "Timnah."
4. Son of Eliphaz (1Ch 1:36).
TIMNAH. In KJV eight times "Timnath" (Ge 38:12-14; J'g 14:1-5), once "Thimnathah" (Jos 19:43). 1. Town on border of Judah c. three miles SW of Beth-Shemesh (Jos 15:10); site of Tibnah.
2. Town in hill country of Judah (Jos 15:57). Location unknown.
TIMNATH. 1. A city given by some authorities as identical with Timnah, 2 (Ge 38:12-14).
2. Home of Samson's wife (J'g 14:1, 2, 5; 15:6). Believed by some authorities to be identical with the preceding.
TIMNATH-HERES (See Timnath-serah.)
TIMNATH-SERAH, a city, called also Timnath-heres. Given to Joshua (Jos 19:50). Joshua buried in (Jos 24:30; J'g 2:9).

TIMNITE, native of Timnah (J'g 15:3-6).
TIMON, one of seven deacons (Ac 6:5).
TIMOTHEUS (See Timothy.)
TIMOTHY (honoring God), called also Timotheus, the companion of Paul. Parentage of (Ac 16:1). Reputation and Christian faith of (Ac 16:2; 1Co 4:17; 16:10; 2Ti 1:5; 3:15). Circumcised; becomes Paul's companion (Ac 16:3; 1Th 3:2). Left by Paul at Berea (Ac 17:14). Rejoins Paul at Corinth (Ac 17:15; 18:5). Sent into Macedonia (Ac 19:22). Rejoined by Paul; accompanies Paul to Asia (Ac 20:1-4). Sent to the Corinthians (1Co 4:17; 16:10, 11; see postscript to 1Co). Preaches to the Corinthians (2Co 1:19). Sent to the Philippians (Ph'p 2:19, 23). Sent to the Thessalonians (1Th 3:2, 6). Left by Paul in Ephesus (1Ti 1:3).

Confined with Paul in Rome (Ph'p 2:19-23; Ph'm 1; Heb 13:23; with the postscripts to Philippians, Philemon, and Hebrews).

Ordained bishop of the Ephesians (see postscript to 2Ti). Joins Paul in the Epistle to the Philippians (Ph'p 1:1); to the Colossians (Col 1:1, 2); to the Thessalonians (1Th 1:1; 2Th 1:1); to Philemon (Ph'm 1). Acts as Paul's amanuensis in writing the first letter to the Corinthians (see postscript to 1Co); in writing the letter to the Hebrews (see postscript to Hebrews).

Zeal of (Ph'p 2:19-22; 1Ti 6:12). Power of (1Ti 4:14; 2Ti 1:6). Paul's love for (1Co 4:17; Ph'p 2:22; 1Ti 1:2, 18; 2Ti 1:2-4). Paul writes to (1Ti 1:1, 2; 2Ti 1:1, 2).
TIMOTHY, EPISTLES TO (See Pastoral Epistles.)
TIN (Nu 31:22; Eze 22:18, 20; 27:12).
TINKLING, sound of small bells worn by women on chain fastened to anklets (Isa 3:16).
TIPHSAH. 1. City on Euphrates (1Ki 4:24).

2. Town, apparently not far from Tirzah (2Ki 15:16); possibly modern Tappuah.
TIRAS, son of Japheth (Ge 10:2; 1Ch 1:5).
TIRATHITE, family of scribes in Jabez (1Ch 2:55).
TIRE (headdress), ornamental headdress (Eze 24:17, 23; Isa 3:20 KJV "bonnet"; 61:10, KJV "ornaments").
TIRHAKAH, Egyptian king, 3rd of the 25th dynasty; defeated by Sennacherib (2Ki 19:9; Isa 37:9), and later by Esarhaddon and Assurbanipal.
TIRHANAH, son of Caleb and Maacah (1Ch 2:48).
TIRIA, son of Jehaleleel (1Ch 4:16).
TIRSHATHA (revered), title of governor of Judah under Persians (Ezr 2:63; Ne 7:65, 70; 8:9; 10:1).
TIRZAH. 1. A daughter of Zelophehad (Nu 26:33; 36:11; Jos 17:3). Special legislation in regard to the inheritance of (Nu 27:1-11; 36; Jos 17:3, 4).

2. A city of Canaan. Captured by Joshua (Jos 12:24). Becomes the residence of the kings of Israel (1Ki 14:17; 15:21, 33; 16:6, 8, 9, 15, 17, 23). Royal residence moved from (1Ki 16:23, 24). Base of military operations of Menahem (2Ki 15:14, 16). Beauty of (Song 6:4).
TISHBITE, designation of Elijah (1Ki 17:1); probably to be identified with modern el-Istib, little W of Mahanaim.
TITHES. Paid by Abraham to Melchizedek (Ge 14:20; Heb 7:2-6). Jacob vows a tenth of all his property to God (Ge 28:22).

Mosaic laws instituting (Le 27:30-33; Nu 18:21-24; De 12:6, 7, 17, 19; 14:22-29; 26:12-15). Customs relating to (Ne 10:37, 38; Am 4:4; Heb 7:5-9). Tithe of tithes for priests (Nu 18:26; Ne 10:38). Stored in the temple (Ne 10:38, 39; 12:44; 13:5, 12; 2Ch 31:11, 12; Mal 3:10).

Payment of, resumed in Hezekiah's reign (2Ch 31:5-10). Under Nehemiah (Ne 13:12). Withheld (Ne 13:10; Mal 3:8).

Customary in later times (M't 23:23; Lu 11:42; 18:12). Observed by idolaters (Am 4:4, 5).

See Alms; Beneficence; Giving; Liberality; Tax.
TITLE, to real estate. (See Land.)
TITLES AND NAMES: *Of Christ.* Adam, Second (1Co 15:45). Almighty (Re 1:8). Amen (Re 3:14). Alpha and Omega (Re 1:8; 22:13). Advocate (1Jo 2:1). Angel (Ge 48:16; Ex 23:20, 21). Angel of the Lord (Ex 3:2; J'g 13:15-18). Angel of God's presence (Isa 63:9).

Apostle (Heb 3:1). Arm of the Lord (Isa 51:9; 53:1). Author and Finisher of our faith (Heb 12:2). Blessed and only Potentate (1Ti 6:15). Beginning of the creation of God (Re 3:14). Branch (Jer 23:5; Zec 3:8; 6:12). Bread of Life (Joh 6:35, 48). Captain of the Lord's hosts (Jos 5:14, 15). Captain of salvation (Heb 2:10). Chief Shepherd (1Pe 5:4). Christ of God (Lu 9:20). Consolation of Israel (Lu 2:25). Chief Corner-stone (Eph 2:20; 1Pe 2:6). Commander (Isa 55:4). Counsellor (Isa 9:6). David (Jer 30:9; Eze 34:23). Day-spring (Lu 1:78). Deliverer (Ro 11:26). Desire of all nations (Hag 2:7). Door (Joh 10:7). Elect of God (Isa 42:1). Emmanuel (Isa 7:14, with M't 1:23). Eternal life (1Jo 1:2; 5:20). Everlasting Father (Isa 9:6). Faithful witness (Re 1:5; 3:14). First and Last (Re 1:17; 2:8). First-begotten of the dead (Re 1:5). First-born of every creature (Col 1:15). Forerunner (Heb 6:20). God (Isa 40:9; Joh 20:28). God blessed for ever (Ro 9:5). God's fellow (Zec 13:7). Glory of the Lord (Isa 40:5). Good Shepherd (Joh 10:14). Great High Priest (Heb 4:14). Governor (M't 2:6). Head of the Church (Eph 5:23; Col 1:18). Heir of all things (Heb 1:2). Holy One (Ps 16:10, w Ac 2:27, 31). Holy One of God (M'k 1:24). Holy One of Israel (Isa 41:14). Horn of salvation (Lu 1:60). I am (Ex 3:14, w Joh 8:58). Jehovah (Isa 26:4). Jesus (M't 1:21; 1Th 1:10). Judge of Israel (Mic 5:1). Just One (Ac 7:52). King (Zec 9:9, w M't 21:5). King of Israel (Joh 1:49). King of the Jews (M't 2:2). King of saints (Re 15:3). King of Kings (1Ti 6:15; Re 17:14). Law-giver (Isa 33:22). Lamb (Re 5:6, 12; 13:8, 21:22; 22:3). Lamb of God (Joh 1:29, 36). Leader (Isa 55:4). Life (Joh 14:6; Col 3:4; 1Jo 1:2). Light of the world (Joh 8:12). Lion of the tribe of Judah (Re 5:5). Lord of glory (1Co 2:8). Lord of all (Ac 10:36). Lord our righteousness (Jer 23:6). Lord God of the holy prophets (Re 22:6). Lord God Almighty (Re 15:3). Mediator (1Ti 2:5). Messenger of the covenant (Mal 3:1). Messiah (Da 9:25; Joh 1:41). Mighty God (Isa 9:6). Mighty One of Jacob (Isa 60:16). Morning-star (Re 22:16). Nazarene (M't 2:23). Offspring of David (Re 22:16). Only-begotten (Joh 1:14). Our Passover (1Co 5:7). Plant of renown (Eze 34:29). Prince of life (Ac 3:15). Prince of peace (Isa 9:6). Prince of the kings of the earth (Re 1:5). Prophet (Lu 24:19; Joh 7:40). Ransom (1Ti 2:6). Redeemer (Job 19:25; Isa 59:20; 60:16). Resurrection and life (Joh 11:25). Rock (1Co 10:4). Root of David (Re 22:16). Root of Jesse (Isa 11:10). Ruler of Israel (Mic 5:2). Saviour (2Pe 2:20; 3:18). Servant (Isa 42:1; 52:13). Shepherd and Bishop of Souls (1Pe 2:25). Shiloh (Ge 49:10). Son of the blessed (M'k 14:61). Son of God (Lu 1:35; Joh 1:49). Son of the Highest (Lu 1:32). Son of David (M't 9:27). Son of man (Joh 5:27; 6:37). Star (Nu 24:17). Sun of righteousness (Mal 4:2). Surety (Heb 7:22). True God (1Jo 5:20) True Light (Joh 1:9). True Vine (Joh 15:1). Truth (Joh 14:6). Way (Joh 14:6). Wisdom (Pr 8:12). Witness (Isa 55:4). Wonderful (Isa 9:6). Word (Joh 1:1; 1Jo 5:7). Word of God (Re 19:13). Word of Life (1Jo 1:1).

Titles and Names of the Church. Assembly of the saints (Ps 89:7). Assembly of the upright (Ps 111:1). Body of Christ (Eph 1:22, 23; Col 1:24). Branch of God's planting (Isa 60:21). Bride of Christ (Re 21:9). Church of God (Ac 20:28). Church of the Living God (1Ti 3:15). Church of the first-born (Heb 12:23). City of the Living God (Heb 12:22). Congregation of saints (Ps 149:1). Congregation of the Lord's poor (Ps 74:19). Dove (Song 2:14; 5:2). Family in heaven and earth (Eph 3:15). Flock of God (Eze 34:15; 1Pe 5:2). Fold of Christ (Joh 10:16). General assembly of the first-born (Heb 12:23). Golden candlestick (Re 1:20). God's building (1Co 3:9). God's husbandry (1Co 3:9). God's heritage (Joe 3:2; 1Pe 5:3). Habitation of God (Eph 2:22). Heavenly Jerusalem (Ga 4:26; Heb 12:22). Holy city (Re 21:2). Holy mountain (Zec 8:3). Holy hill (Ps 15:1). House of God (1Ti 3:15; Heb 10:21). House of the God of Jacob (Isa 2:3). House of Christ (Heb 3:6). Household of God (Eph 2:19). Inheritance (Ps 28:9; Isa 19:25). Israel of God (Ga 6:16). King's daughter (Ps 45:13). Lamb's wife (Re 19:7; 21). Lot of God's inheritance (De 32:9). Mount Zion (Ps

2:6; Heb 12:22). Mountain of the Lord's house (Isa 2:2). New Jerusalem (Re 21:2). Pillar and ground of the truth (1Ti 3:15). Sanctuary of God (Ps 114:2). Spiritual house (1Pe 2:5). Spouse of Christ (Song 4:12; 5:1). Sought out, a city not forsaken (Isa 62:12). Temple of God (1Co 3:16, 17). Temple of the Living God (2Co 6:16). Vineyard (Jer 12:10; M't 21:41).

Titles and Names of the Devil. Abaddon (Re 9:11). Accuser of our brethren (Re 12:10). Adversary (1Pe 5:8). Angel of the bottomless pit (Re 9:11). Apollyon (Re 9:11). Beelzebub (M't 12:24). Belial (2Co 6:15). Crooked serpent (Isa 27:1). Dragon (Isa 27:1; Re 20:2). Enemy (M't 13:39). Evil spirit (1Sa 16:14). Father of lies (Joh 8:44). Great red dragon (Re 12:3). Leviathan (Isa 27:1). Liar (Joh 8:44). Lying spirit (1Ki 22:22). Murderer (Joh 8:44). Old serpent (Re 12:9; 20:2). Piercing serpent (Isa 27:1). Power of darkness (Col 1:13). Prince of this world (Joh 14:30). Prince of the devils (M't 12:24). Prince of the power of the air (Eph 2:2). Ruler of the darkness of this world (Eph 6:12). Satan (1Ch 21:1; Job 1:6). Serpent (Ge 3:4, 14; 2Co 11:3). Spirit that worketh in the children of disobedience (Eph 2:2). Tempter (M't 4:3; 1Th 3:5). The god of this world (2Co 4:4). Unclean spirit (M't 12:43). Wicked one (M't 13:19, 38).

Titles and Names of the Holy Ghost. Breath of the Almighty (Job 33:4). Comforter (Joh 14:16, 26; 15:26). Eternal Spirit (Heb 9:14). Free Spirit (Ps 51:12). God (Ac 5:3, 4). Good Spirit (Ne 9:20; Ps 143:10). Holy Spirit (Ps 51:11; Lu 11:13; Eph 1:13; 4:30). Lord, The (2Th 3:5). Power of the Highest (Lu 1:35). Spirit, The (M't 4:1; Joh 3:6; 1Ti 4:1). Spirit of the Lord God (Isa 61:1). Spirit of the Lord (Isa 11:2; Ac 5:9). Spirit of God (Ge 1:2; 1Co 2:11; Job 33:4). Spirit of the Father (M't 10:20). Spirit of Christ (Ro 8:9; 1Pe 1:11). Spirit of the Son (Ga 4:6). Spirit of life (Ro 8:2; Re 11:11). Spirit of grace (Zec 12:10; Heb 10:29). Spirit of prophecy (Re 19:10). Spirit of adoption (Ro 8:15). Spirit of wisdom (Isa 11:2; Eph 1:17). Spirit of counsel (Isa 11:2). Spirit of might (Isa 11:2). Spirit of understanding (Isa 11:2). Spirit of knowledge (Isa 11:2). Spirit of fear of the Lord (Isa 11:2). Spirit of truth (Joh 14:17; 15:26). Spirit of holiness (Ro 1:4). Spirit of revelation (Eph 1:17). Spirit of judgment (Isa 4:4; 28:6). Spirit of burning (Isa 4:4). Spirit of glory (1Pe 4:14). Seven Spirits of God (Re 1:4).

Titles and Names of Ministers. Ambassadors for Christ (2Co 5:20). Angels of the Church (Re 1:20; 2:1). Apostles (Lu 6:13; Eph 4:11; Re 18:20). Apostles of Jesus Christ (Tit 1:1). Bishops (Ph'p 1:1; 1Ti 3:1; Tit 1:7). Deacons (Ac 6:1; 1Ti 3:8; Ph'p 1:1). Elders (1Ti 5:17; 1Pe 5:1). Evangelists (Eph 4:11; 2Ti 4:5). Fishers of men (M't 4:19; M'k 1:17). Laborers (M't 9:38, with Ph'm 1; 1Th 2:2). Messengers of the Church (2Co 8:23). Messengers of the Lord of hosts (Mal 2:7). Ministers of God (2Co 6:4). Ministers of the Lord (Joe 2:17). Ministers of Christ (Ro 15:16; 1Co 4:1). Ministers of the sanctuary (Eze 45:4). Ministers of the gospel (Eph 3:7; Col 1:23). Ministers of the word (Lu 1:2). Ministers of the New Testament (2Co 3:6). Ministers of the Church (Col 1:24, 25). Ministers of righteousness (2Co 11:15). Overseers (Ac 20:18). Pastors (Jer 3:15; Eph 4:11). Preachers (Ro 10:14; 1Ti 2:7). Servants of God (Tit 1:1; Jas 1:1). Servants of the Lord (2Ti 2:24). Servants of Jesus Christ (Ph'p 1:1; Jude 1). Servants of the Church (2Co 4:5). Shepherds (Jer 23:4). Soldiers of Christ (Ph'p 2:25; 2Ti 2:3). Stars (Re 1:20; 2:1). Stewards of God (Tit 1:7). Stewards of the grace of God (1Pe 4:10). Stewards of the mysteries of God (1Co 4:1). Teachers (Isa 30:20; Eph 4:11). Watchmen (Isa 62:6; Eze 33:7). Witnesses (Ac 1:8; 5:32; 26:16). Workers together with God (2Co 6:1).

Titles and Names of Saints. Believers (Ac 5:14; 1Ti 4:12). Beloved of God (Ro 1:7). Beloved brethren (1Co 15:58; Jas 2:5). Blessed of the Lord (Ge 24:31; 26:29). Blessed of the Father (M't 25:34). Brethren (M't 23:8; Ac 12:17). Brethren of Christ (Lu 8:21; Joh 20:17). Called of Jesus Christ (Ro 1:6). Children of the Lord (De 14:1). Children of God (Joh 11:52); 1Jo 3:10). Children of the Living God (Ro 9:26). Children of the Father

(M't 5:45). Children of the Highest (Lu 6:35). Children of Abraham (Ga 3:7). Children of Jacob (Ps 105:6). Children of promise (Ro 9:8; Ga 4:28). Children of the free-woman (Ga 4:31). Children of the kingdom (M't 13:38). Children of Zion (Ps 149:2; Joe 2:23). Children of the bride-chamber (M't 9:15). Children of the light (Lu 16:8; Eph 5:8; 1Th 5:5). Children of the day (1Th 5:5). Children of the resurrection (Lu 20:36). Chosen generation (1Pe 2:9). Chosen ones (1Ch 16:13). Chosen vessels (Ac 9:15). Christians (Ac 11:26; 26:28). Dear children (Eph 5:1). Disciples of Christ (Joh 8:31; 15:8). Elect of God (Col 3:12; Tit 1:1). Epistles of Christ (2Co 3:3). Excellent, The (Ps 16:3). Faithful brethren in Christ (Col 1:2). Faithful, The (Ps 12:1). Faithful of the land, The (Ps 101:6). Fellow-citizens with the saints (Eph 2:19). Fellow-heirs (Eph 3:6). Fellow-servants (Re 6:11). Friends of God (2Ch 20:7; Jas 2:23). Friends of Christ (Joh 15:15). Godly, The (Ps 4:3; 2Pe 2:9). Heirs of God (Ro 8:17; Ga 4:7). Heirs of the grace of life (1Pe 3:7). Heirs of the kingdom (Jas 2:5). Heirs of promise (Heb 6:17; Ga 3:29). Heirs of salvation (Heb 1:14). Holy brethren (1Th 5:27; Heb 3:1). Holy nation (Ex 19:6; 1Pe 2:9). Holy people (De 26:19; Isa 62:12). Holy priesthood (1Pe 2:5). Joint-heirs with Christ (Ro 8:17). Just, The (Hab 2:4). Kings and priests unto God (Re 1:6). Kingdom of priests (Ex 19:6). Lambs (Isa 40:11; Joh 21:15). Lights of the world (M't 5:14). Little children (Joh 13:33; 1Jo 2:1). Lively stones (1Pe 2:5). Members of Christ (1Co 6:15; Eph 5:30). Men of God (De 33:1; 1Ti 6:11; 2Ti 3:17). Obedient children (1Pe 1:14). Peculiar people (De 14:2; Tit 2:14; 1Pe 2:9). Peculiar treasure (Ex 19:5; Ps 135:4). People of God (Heb 4:9; 1Pe 2:10). People near unto God (Ps 148: 14). People saved by the Lord (De 33:29). Pillars in the temple of God (Re 3:12). Ransomed of the Lord (Isa 35:10). Redeemed of the Lord (Isa 51:11). Royal priesthood (1Pe 2:9). Salt of the earth (M't 5:13). Servants of Christ (1Co 7:22; Eph 6:6). Servants of righteousness (Ro 6:18). Sheep of Christ (Joh 10:1-16; 21:16). Sojourners with God (Le 25: 23; Ps 39:12). Sons of God (Joh 1:12; Ph'p 2:15; 1Jo 3:1, 2). The Lord's freemen (1Co 7:22). Trees of righteousness (Isa 61:3). Vessels unto honor (2Ti 2:21). Vessels of mercy (Ro 9:23). Witnesses for God (Isa 44:8).

Titles and Names of the Wicked. Adversaries of the Lord (1Sa 2:10). Children of Belial (De 13:13; 2Ch 13:7). Children of the devil (Ac 13:10; 1Jo 3:10). Children of the wicked one (M't 13:38). Children of hell (M't 23:15). Children of base men (Job 30:8). Children of fools (Job 30:8). Children of strangers (Isa 2:6). Children of transgression (Isa 57:4). Children of disobedience (Eph 2:2; Col 3:6). Children in whom is no faith (De 32:20). Children of the flesh (Ro 9:8). Children of iniquity (Ho 10:9). Children that will not hear the law of the Lord (Isa 30:9). Children of pride (Job 41:34). Children of this world (Lu 16:8). Children of wickedness (2Sa 7:10). Children of wrath (Eph 2:3). Children that are corrupters (Isa 1:4). Cursed children (2Pe 2:14). Enemies of God (Ps 37:20; Jas 4:4). Enemies of the cross of Christ (Ph'p 3:18). Enemies of all righteousness (Ac 13:10). Evil doers (Ps 37:1; 1Pe 2:14). Evil men (Pr 4:14; 2Ti 3:13). Evil generation (De 1:35). Evil and adulterous generation (M't 12:39). Fools (Pr 1:7; Ro 1:22). Froward generation (De 32:20). Generation of vipers (M't 3:7; 12:34). Grievous revolters (Jer 6:28). Haters of God (Ps 81:15; Ro 1:30). Impudent children (Eze 2:4). Inventors of evil things (Ro 1:30). Lying children (Isa 30:9). Men of the world (Ps 17:14). People laden with iniquity (Isa 1:4). Perverse and crooked generation (De 32:5; M't 17:17; Ph'p 2:15). Rebellious children (Isa 30:1). Rebellious people (Isa 30:9; 65:2). Rebellious house (Eze 2:5, 8; 12:2). Reprobates (2Co 13:5-7). Scornful, The (Ps 1:1). Seed of falsehood (Isa 57:4). Seed of the wicked (Ps 37:28). Seed of evil doers (Isa 1:4; 14:20). Serpents (M't 23:33). Servants of corruption (2Pe 2:19). Servants of sin (Joh 8:34; Ro 6:20). Sinful generation (M'k 8:28). Sinners (Ps 26:9; Pr 1:10). Sons of Belial (1Sa 2:12; 1Ki 21:10). Sottish children (Jer 4:22). Strange children (Ps 144:7). Stubborn and rebellious generation (Ps

78:8). Transgressors (Ps 37:38; 51:13). Ungodly, The (Ps 1:1). Ungodly men (Jude 4). Unprofitable servants (M't 25:30). Untoward generation (Ac 2:40). Vessels of wrath (Ro 9:22). Wicked of the earth (Ps 75:8). Wicked transgressors (Ps 59:5). Wicked servants (M't 25:26). Wicked generation (M't 12:45; 16:4). Wicked ones (Jer 2:33). Wicked doers (Ps 101:8; Pr 17:4). Workers of iniquity (Ps 28:3; 36:12).

TITTLE (horn), small, horn-shaped mark used to indicate accent in Hebrew (M't 5:18; Lu 16:17).

TITUS, a Greek companion of Paul. Paul's love for (2Co 2:13; 7:6, 7, 13, 14; 8:23; Tit 1:4). With Paul in Macedonia (2Co 7:5, 6; see postscript to 2 Corinthians). Affection of, for the Corinthians (2Co 7:15). Sent to Corinth (2Co 8:6, 16-22; 12:17, 18). Character of (2Co 12:18). Paul's amanuensis in writing to the Corinthians (see postscript to 2 Corinthians). Accompanies Paul to Jerusalem (Gal 2:1-3). Compare Acts 15:1-29. Left by Paul in Crete (Tit 1:5); to rejoin him in Nicopolis (Tit 3:12). Ordained bishop of the Cretians (see postscript to Titus). Paul writes to (Tit 1:1-4). With Paul in Rome (2Ti 4:10, w postscript to 2Ti). Goes to Dalmatia (2Ti 4:10).

TITUS, EPISTLE TO (See Pastoral Epistles.)

TITUS, FLAVIUS VESPASIANUS, Roman emperor (A. D. 79-81); captured and destroyed Jerusalem in A. D. 70.

TITUS JUSTUS (See Justus.)

TIZITE, designation of Toha, one of David's soldiers (1Ch 11:45).

TOAH, ancestor of Samuel (1Ch 6:34); "Nahath" in 1Ch 6:26 and "Tohu" in 1Sa 1:1.

TOB, district in Syria, extending NE from Gilead, to which Jephthah fled (J'g 11:1-3).

TOB-ADONIJAH (Jehovah is good). A Levite sent by Jehoshaphat to instruct the people in the law (2Ch 17:8).

TOBIAH (Jehovah is good). 1. Ancestor of a family of Babylonian captives (Ezr 2:60; Ne 7:62).

2. An enemy of the Jews in the time of Nehemiah. Opposes the rebuilding of the wall of Jerusalem (Ne 2:10, 19; 4:3, 7, 8). Conspires to injure and intimidate Nehemiah (Ne 6:1-14, 19). Subverts nobles of Judah (Ne 6:17, 18). Allies himself with Eliashib, the priest (Ne 13:4-9).

TOBIJAH. 1. A Levite sent by Jehoshaphat to instruct the people in the law (2Ch 17:8).

2. A captive in Babylon (Zec 6:10, 14).

TOBIT, BOOK OF (See Apocrypha.)

TOCHEN (a measure), a city in Simeon (1Ch 4:32).

TOE. Anointed in consecration (Ex 29:20; Le 8:23, 24); in purification (Le 14:14, 17, 25, 28). Of prisoners of war cut off (J'g 1:6, 7). Six, on each foot (2Sa 21:20; 1Ch 20:6).

TOGARMAH. Son of Gomer (Ge 10:3; 1Ch 1:6). Descendants of (Eze 27:14; 38:6).

TOHU, ancestor of Samuel (1Sa 1:1).

TOI, king of Hamath who congratulated David for victory over Hadadezer (2Sa 8:9-11).

TOKEN. A sign (Ex 3:12). Sun and moon for time and seasons (Ge 1:14). The mark of Cain (Ge 4:15). Rainbow, that the world might no more be destroyed by a flood (Ge 9:12-17). Circumcision, of the covenant of Abraham (Ge 17:11). Presents (Ge 21:27, 30). Miracles of Moses, of the divine authority of his missions (Ex 4:1-9). Blood of the pascal lamb (Ex 12:13). The Passover (Ex 13:9). Consecration of the firstborn (Ex 13:14-16). The Sabbath (Ex 31:13, 17); a fringe (Nu 15:38-40). Scarlet thread (Jos 2:18, 21). Cover of the altar (Nu 16:38-40). Aaron's rod (Nu 17:10). Memorial stones (Jos 4:2-9). Dew on Gideon's fleece (J'g 6:36-40). Prayer for tokens of mercy (Ps 86:17).

See Miracles.

TOLA. 1. Son of Issachar (Ge 46:13).

2. Judged Israel 23 years (J'g 10:1, 2).

TOLAD, city of Simeon (1Ch 4:29).

TOLERATION, religious (Mic 4:4, 5; M'k 9:38-40; Lu 9:49, 50; Ac 17:11, 28:31; Ro 14; 1Co 10:28-32).

See Intolerance.

TOLL (See Tribute; Tax.)

TOMB, a burial place or sepulchre. Most Hebrew burying sites were unmarked; some kings were buried in a vault in Jerusalem (2Sa 2:32; Ne 2:3);

tombs of NT times were either caves or else were dug into stone cliffs; doors were circular, weighing from one to three tons (Lu 24:2; Joh 20:1).

TOMBSTONE, at Rachel's grave (Ge 35:20).

See Pillars.

TONGS, snuffers (Ex 25:38; Nu 4:9), instrument for taking hold of something (Isa 6:6; 44:12).

TONGUE. Language (Ge 10:5, 20; Isa 66:18; Re 7:9). Confusion of (Ge 11:1-9). Gift of (Ac 2:1-18, 33; 10:46; 19:6; 1Co 12:10, 28, 30; 14).

Loquacious (Pr 10:8, 19). Restrained by wisdom (Pr 17:27; 21:23; Ec 3:7). Hasty (Pr 29:20).

An evil (see Speaking, Evil; Slander).

TONGUES, CONFUSION OF, punishment by God for arrogant attempt to build tower reaching to heaven (Ge 11:1-9).

TONGUES OF FIRE, one of phenomena which occurred at outpouring of Holy Spirit on day of Pentecost; Symbolic of Holy Spirit who came in power on the Church (Ac 2:3).

TONGUES, GIFT OF, a spiritual gift mentioned in M'k 16:17; Ac 2:1-13; 10:44-46; 19:6; 1Co 12, 14. The gift appeared on the day of Pentecost with the outpouring of the Holy Spirit on the assembled believers (Ac 2:1-13). The phenomenon appeared again in the home of Cornelius (Ac 10:44-11:17), at Ephesus (Ac 19:6), and in the church at Corinth (1Co 12, 14). Instruction regarding the use of tongues is given by Paul in 1Co 12-14.

TOOLS. The following kinds are mentioned in the Bible: cutting, boring, forks and shovels, carpentry, drawing, measuring, tilling, metal-working, stone-working.

TOOTH. Both human and animal teeth are mentioned (Nu 11:33; De 32:24); figurative use is common: cleanness of teeth, famine (Am 4:6), gnashing of teeth, rage and despair (Job 16:9), oppression (Pr 30:14), plenty (Ge 49:12).

TOPAZ. A precious stone (Eze 28:13; Re 21:20). In the breastplate (Ex 28:17; 39:10). Ethiopian, celebrated (Job 28:19).

TOPHEL (cement), place in wilderness where Moses addressed Israelites (De 1:1); may be modern el-Tafeleh, 15 miles SE of Dead Sea.

TOPHET, called also Topheth. A place in the valley of the sons of Hinnom (2Ki 23:10). Jewish children passed through the fire to Molech in (2Ki 23:10; Jer 7:31, 32; 19:6, 11-14; 32:35. See also 2Ch 28:3; 33:6). Destroyed by Josiah (2Ki 23:10). Horror of (Isa 30:33).

TOPOGRAPHY, of Canaan (Jos 13:15-33; 15; 18:9).

TORAH (instruction, law), divine law; the Pentateuch; the entire Jewish Scriptures (Joh 10:34).

TORCHES (J'g 7:16; 15:4; Na 2:3; Joh 18:3).

TORMENTOR, probably jailer (M't 18:34).

TORMENTS, of the wicked (Lu 16:23-28; Re 14:10, 11).

See Wicked, Punishment of.

TORTOISE (Le 11:29).

TOTAL ABSTINENCE (See Abstinence.)

TOU (See Toi.)

TOW, short fibers of flax or hemp (J'g 16:9; Isa 1:31; 43:17).

TOWEL, cloth for wiping and drying (Joh 13:4, 5).

TOWER. Of Babel (Ge 11:1-9). Of Edar (Ge 35:21). Of Penuel (J'g 8:8, 9, 17). Of Shechem (J'g 9:46, 49). Of Meah (Ne 3:1; 12:39). Of Hananeel (Ne 3:1; 12:39; Jer 31:38; Zec 14:10). Of David (Song 4:4). Of Syene (Eze 29:10). Of Siloam (Lu 13:4). In the walls of Jerusalem (2Ch 26:9; 32:5; Ne 12:38, 39). Of other cities (2Ch 14:7).

In the desert (2Ch 26:10). For watchmen or sentinels (2Ki 9:17; 18:8). As fortress (M't 21:33).

Parable of (Lu 14:28, 29).

See Forts.

Figurative: Of divine protection (2Sa 22:3, 51; Ps 18:2; 61:3; 144:2; Pr 18:10).

TOWN, in ancient times large cities had towns or villages surrounding them for protection (Nu 21:25, 32; Jos 15:45-47); sometimes it means an unwalled town (De 3:5; 1Sa 16:4).

TOWN CLERK, official in Graeco-Roman cities of the 1st century, as at Ephesus (Ac 19:35).

TRACHONITIS (rough region), area of

c. 370 sq. miles S of Damascus; tetrarchy of Philip (Lu 3:1).

TRADE AND TRAVEL. Trade in the OT. Ur of the Chaldees a trading port; Egypt, from earliest times, a great trading nation (Ge 37:25); first organized commerce of Hebrew people was under Solomon, who formed a partnership with the great mercantile cities of Tyre and Sidon (1Ki 9:27, 28; 10:11); after the death of Solomon Israel again became an agricultural nation. Trade in the NT. Jewish trade and commerce have small place in the Gospels. All through NT times trade, in the wider sense of the word, was in the hands of Rome and of Italy. Travel. Motives for travel: trade, colonization, exploration, migration, pilgrimage, preaching, courier service, exile. Travel had serious hazards (2Co 11:25-27; Ac 27, 28); was facilitated by wonderful Roman roads, some of which still are used. Regular passenger service by land or sea was unknown.

TRADE GUILDS, societies of tradesmen organized chiefly for purpose of social intercourse (Ac 19); not trade unions in the modern sense.

TRADITION, the decisions and minor precepts taught by Paul (1Co 11:2; 2Th 2:15; 3:6).

Commandments of men (M't 12:1-8; 15:2-6; M'k 7:3-9; Lu 6:1-11; Col 2:8; 1Pe 1:18). Not authoritative (M't 15:3-20; 1Ti 1:4; 4:7).

TRAFFIC, suspended on the Sabbath (Ne 13:15-22).

TRAIN. 1. Retinue of a monarch (1Ki 10:2).

2. Skirt of a robe (Isa 6:1).

3. To discipline (Tit 2:4 RSV).

TRAITOR. Judas (M't 26:14-16, 46-50; M'k 14:10, 11, 43-45; Lu 22:3-6, 21-23, 47, 48; Joh 13:2, 27-30; 18:2-8, 13).

See Treason.

TRAJAN. Roman emperor (A.D. 98-117); able soldier; progressive ruler.

TRAMP (Pr 6:11 [*R.V.* marg.]).

TRANCE (a throwing of the mind out of its normal state), mental state in which the senses are partially or wholly suspended and the person is unconscious of his environment while he contemplates some extraordinary object (Ac 10:9-16; 22:17-21).

TRANSFIGURATION. Of Moses (Ex 34:29-35). Of Jesus (M't 17:2-9; M'k 9:2-10; Lu 9:29-36; 2Pe 1:16-18). Of Stephen (Ac 6:15).

TRANSGRESSION, breaking of a law (Pr 17:19; Ro 4:15). See Sin.

TRANSJORDAN, TRANS-JORDAN, large plateau E of Jordan, comprised in modern Hashemite Kingdom of Jordan; in NT times, the Peraea and the Decapolis; in OT times, Moab, Ammon, Gilead, and Bashan. Associated with Moses; Joshua; the tribes Reuben, Gad, and Manasseh; David; Nabataeans.

TRANSLATION, removal from earth to heaven. Of Enoch (Ge 5:24; Heb 11:5). Of Elijah (2Ki 2:1-12). Of Jesus (M'k 16:19; Lu 24:51; Ac 1:9-11). Desired by Paul (2Co 5:4).

TRANSPORTATION, in ancient times done chiefly by camels, donkeys, horses, and boats.

TRAP (Jos 23:13; Job 18:10; Jer 5:26).

TRAVAIL, pangs of childbirth (Ge 35:16; 38:27; 1Sa 4:19), trouble (Isa 23:4; 54:1), to be weak or sick (Jer 4:31), weariness (Ex 18:8).

TRAVEL (See Trade and Travel.)

TREACHERY (Jer 9:8). Of Rahab to her people (Jos 2). Of the man of Beth-el (J'g 1:24, 25). Of Jael (J'g 4:18-21). Of Shechemites (J'g 9:23). Of Joab (2Sa 3:26, 27). Of Baanah and Rechab (2Sa 4:6). Of David to Uriah (2Sa 11). Of Joab to Amasa (2Sa 20:9, 10). Of Jehu (2Ki 10:18-28). Of the enemies of Nehemiah (Ne 6).

See Conspiracy; Treason.

TREASON. *Instances of:* Of Aaron and Miriam against Moses (Nu 12:1-11). Of Korah, Dathan and Abiram against Moses and Aaron (Nu 16:1-33). Of Rahab against Jericho (Jos 2). Of the betrayer of Beth-el (J'g 1:24, 25). Of the Shechemites against Abimelech (J'g 9:22-25). Of the Ephraimites against Jephthah (J'g 12:1-4). Of the Israelites against Saul (1Sa 10:27), against Rehoboam (1Ki 12:16-19). Of the Egyptian servant against the Amalekites (1Sa 30:15, 16). Of Abner against Ish-bosheth (2Sa 3:6-21). Of Jehoiada against Athaliah (2Ki 11:14-16). Of Absalom against his father (see Absalom).

Death penalty for (Es 2:23).

Jesus falsely accused of (M't 27:11, 29,

30; Lu 23:2, 3, 38; Joh 19:12, 14, 15, 19). Paul falsely accused of (Ac 17:7).

David's amnesty of the traitors (2Sa 19:16-23); to Amasa (2Sa 19:13).

See Conspiracy; Treachery.

TREASURE. 1. A thing of highly estimated value. Money (Ge 42:25, 27, 28, 35; 43:23, w *verses* 18, 21, 22). Precious stones (1Ch 29:8).

Jesus forbids the hoarding of (M't 6:19; 19:21; Lu 12:33). Hidden (M't 13:44).

Figurative: Of the graces of the spirit (Pr 21:20; Isa 33:6). Of spiritual understanding (M't 13:52; Col 2:3). Of the object of the affections (M't 6:21; Lu 12:34). Of spiritual calling (2Co 4:6, 7).

Gospel called (2Co 4:7). Parable of (M't 13:44).

TREASURE CITIES, built for the storage of the king's substance (Ex 1:11; 1Ki 9:19; 2Ch 8:4, 6).

TREASURE-HOUSES. Of kings (2Ki 20:13; 1Ch 27:25; 2Ch 32:27, 28; Ezr 1:7, 8; Es 3:9). Records preserved in (Ezr 5:17; 6:1). Treasurer in charge of (Ezr 7:20, 21).

Heathen temples used for (Da 1:2).

Tabernacle used for (Nu 31:54; Jos 6:19, 24). Solomon's temple used for (1Ki 7:51; 2Ki 12:4-14, 18; 22:4, 5; 1Ch 28:11, 12; M't 27:6; M'k 12:41, 43; Lu 21:1; Joh 8:20). Under the charge of the Levites (1Ch 26:20). Chambers provided in the temple for various kinds of offerings (Ne 10:38, 39; 13:5, 9, 12; Mal 3:10). Priests and Levites in charge of (1Ch 9:26; 26:20-28; Ne 12:44; 13:13).

TREASURER, one trusted with charge of treasure or treasures.

TREATY. Between nations: Israelites and Gibeonites (Jos 9:3-15); Judah and Syria (1Ki 15:19). Cession of territory by (1Ki 9:10-14; 20:34). Sacredness of (Jos 9:16-21, w chapter 2:8-21).

Reciprocity (1Ki 5:1-12). With idolatrous nations forbidden (Ex 34:12, 15).

TREE. Palestine in ancient times far more wooded than today; over 25 different kinds of trees have been identified as having grown in the Holy Land; trees venerated by heathen people; Hebrews forbidden to plant a tree near a sacred altar (De 16:21).

Known by its fruits (M't 7:17-19; Lu 6:43, 44).

Symbolical (Da 4:10-12). See Tree, of Knowledge, of Life, below.

TREE OF KNOWLEDGE, special tree in garden of Eden, set apart by the Lord as an instrument to test the obedience of Adam and Eve (Ge 2:9, 17; 3:3-6, 11, 12, 17).

TREE OF LIFE, another special tree in the garden of Eden; its fruit conferred immortality on persons eating it (Ge 2:9; 3:22, 25; Re 22:2).

TRENCH, rampart, intrenchment (2Sa 20:15; 1Sa 17:20; 26:5).

TRESPASS (Ex 22:9). Of an ox (Ex 21:28-36). Of a brother (M't 18:15-18; Lu 17:3, 4). Creditor shall not enter debtor's house to take a pledge (De 24:10). See Sin.

TRESPASS OFFERING, sacrifice of a ram for the purpose of expiation of sins against others; in addition to the sacrifice, restitution had to be made (Le 5:16; 6:5; Nu 5:7, 8).

TRES TABERNAE (See Three Taverns.)

TRIAL. Before court (Le 24:10-14). Right of (Joh 7:51; Ac 16:37-39; 22:25-30).

See Court; Justice; Prisoners.

TRIAL OF JESUS, betrayed by Judas into the hands of the Jewish religious leaders, Jesus was first brought before Annas, former high priest, and father-in-law of the current high priest Caiaphas, for a brief examination (Joh 18:13); then at cock-crowing time He appeared before the Sanhedrin in the palace of Caiaphas, where He was questioned and had indignities heaped upon Him (M'k 14:60-65; Lu 22:63-64); at dawn He appeared before the Sanhedrin again and was condemned to death (Lu 22:66-70); next He was brought by the Sanhedrin before Pilate, who after an examination pronounced Him innocent (Joh 18:33-38), but the Jews would not hear of His being released, and Pilate therefore sent Him to Herod Antipas, who was also present for the Passover, on the plea that He belonged to Herod's jurisdiction. Herod, however, merely mocked Jesus and returned Him to Pilate uncondemned (Lu 23:2-12); Pilate then gave the Jews the opportunity of choosing for release either Barabbas or Jesus, and the Jews chose Barabbas; another attempt by Pilate to have Jesus released met with failure, for the Jews threatened him if he did not carry out their wishes; after the Roman soldiers scourged and mocked Him, Jesus was crucified (M'k 15:16-20).

See Jesus, Trial of.

TRIBE, TRIBES, the tribes of Israel were descended from the 12 sons of Jacob, with Joseph's sons, Ephraim and Manasseh forming two, while no tribal territory was allotted to Levi (Ge 48:5; Nu 26:5-51; Jos 13:7-33; 15-19). The leaders of the tribes are called by various names: princes, rulers, heads, chiefs (Ex 34:31; Nu 1:16; Ge 36:15ff); before the Israelites entered the promised land two tribes, Reuben and Gad, and half of Manasseh chose to settle on the E side of the Jordan (Nu 32:33). During the period of the Judges in Israel the tribes were each one a law unto themselves. When David became king over the whole land the 12 tribes were unified. He appointed a captain over each tribe (1Ch 27:16-22). The captivities wiped out tribal distinctions.

TRIBULATION, GREAT TRIBULATION, a period of suffering sent from God upon earth at the end time because of its awful wickedness (Da 12:1; M't 24:21).

TRIBUTE. From conquered nations (Jos 16:10; J'g 1:30-33; 2Ki 15:19; 23:35; M't 17:24-27; 22:15-22; Lu 2:1-5). By Arabians to Solomon (2Ch 9:14); to Jehoshaphat (2Ch 17:11).

See Duty; Tax.

TRINITY, HOLY (Isa 11:2, 3; 42:1 w M't 12:18; Isa 48:16). God speaks of self as us (Ge 1:26; 3:22; Isa 6:3, 8). Three persons of Godhead referred to in same passage, sometimes in same sense (Isa 42:1 w M't 12:18; M't 3:16; 28:19; Lu 3:22; Joh 3:34, 35; 14:16, 17, 26 w 15:26 & 16:7, 13-15; Ac 1:2, 4, 5; 2:33; 10:36-38; Ro 1:3, 4; 8:9-11, 26, 27; 1Co 12:3-6; 2Co 1:21, 22; 5:5; 13:14; Ga 4:4, 6; 2Th 2:13, 14, 16; 1Ti 3:16; Tit 3:4-6; Heb 9:14; 1Pe 1:2; 3:18; 1Jo 5:6,. 7). Tri-holiness of God suggests (Isa 6:3; Re 4:8).

God and Holy Spirit (Isa 42:1; 48:16; 63:9, 10; 1Co 2:10, 11; 6:19). Christ and Holy Spirit (Isa 61:1-3 w Lu 4:18; M't 1:18, 20; 12:28; 28:19; Lu 1:35; 4:1, 14; Joh 1:32, 33; 7:39; 20:22; 1Co 8:6; 2Co 3:17; Ph'p 1:19; Col 2:2).

See Angel of the Lord; God; Holy Spirit; Holy Trinity; Jesus.

TRIUMPH (to lead in triumph), celebration of victory; in Roman times a magnificent procession in honor of a victorious general (2Co 2:14; Col 2:15).

TRIUMPHAL ENTRY OF JESUS. Into Jerusalem (Ps 118:26; Zec 9:9; M't 21:5, 8-10; M'k 11:7-11; Lu 19:35-38; Joh 12:12, 13).

TROAS, a chief city and port of the Roman Province of Asia, on the Aegean coast, c. 10 miles from the ruins of ancient Troy; known as Alexandria Troas (Ac 16:8; 20:5; 2Co 2:12). This general area is also sometimes called Troas.

TROGYLLUM, promontory thrusting SW from Asian mainland N of Miletus, opposite island of Samos (Ac 20:15).

TROPHIES. Goliath's head and armor (1Sa 17:54; 21:9); Saul's (1Sa 31:8-10). Placed in temples. See Temples.

TROPHIMUS (nourishing), an Ephesian companion of Paul. Accompanies Paul from Greece to Asia (Ac 20:4). With Paul in Jerusalem; made the occasion of an attack on Paul (Ac 21:27-30). Left ill at Miletus (2Ti 4:20).

TROUBLE. Being Anxious: Forbidden (M't 6:25-34; Ph'p 4:6). Remedy (Joh 16:6, 7; 1Pe 5:7).

See Affliction; Anxiety; Suffering.

Instances of: Israelites at the Red Sea (Ex 14:10-12); about water (Ex 15:23-25; 17:2, 3; Nu 20:1-13); food (Ex 16:2, 3; Nu 11:4-33). When Moses tarried in the mount (Ex 32:1). When the spies brought their adverse report (Nu 13:28, 29, 31-33; 14:1-4, w *verses* 4-12). Elijah, under the juniper tree and in the cave (1Ki 19:4-15). The disciples, as to how the multitude could be fed (M't 14:15; M'k 6:37); in the tempest, when Jesus was asleep in the ship (M't 8:23-26; M'k 4:36-39; Lu 8:22-24); when Jesus was crucified (Lu 24:4-9, 24-31, 36-40). Mary at the sepulchre (Joh 20:11-17). The people in the shipwreck (Ac 27:22-25, 30-36).

TRUCE, in battle (2Sa 2:26-31).

TRUMPET. Made of ram's horn (Jos 6:4-6, 8, 13); of silver (Nu 10:2). Uses of, prescribed by Moses (Nu 10:1-10). Used in war (Job 39:24, 25; Jer 4:19; 6:1, 17; 42:14; 51:27; Eze 7:14; Am 2:2; 3:6; Zep 1:16; 1Co 14:8). To summon soldiers, by Phinehas (Nu 31:6); by Ehud (J'g 3:27); by Gideon (J'g 6:34); by Saul (1Sa 13:3); by Joab (2Sa 2:28; 18:16; 20:22); by Absalom (2Sa 15:10); by Sheba (2Sa 20:1); by Nehemiah (Ne 4:18, 20). By Gideon's soldiers (J'g 7:8-22). In war, of Abijah (2Ch 13:12, 14). In the siege of Jericho (Jos 6:4-20).

Sounded in time of danger (Eze 33:3-6; Joe 2:1).

Used at Sinai (Ex 19:13-19; 20:18; Heb 12:19); on the great day of atonement (Isa 27:13); at the jubilee (Le 25:9); at the bringing up of the ark (2Sa 6:5, 15; 1Ch 13:8; 15:28); the anointing of kings (1Ki 1:34, 39; 2Ki 9:13; 11:14); dedication of Solomon's temple (2Ch 5:12, 13; 7:6); in worship (1Ch 15:24; 16:42; 25:5; Ps 81:3, 4); at Jehoshaphat's triumph (2Ch 20:28); at the foundation of the second temple (Ezr 3:10, 11); at the dedication of the wall (Ne 12:35, 41).

Figurative: Isa 27:13; Eze 33:3; Joe 2:1; Zec 9:14; M't 6:2.

Symbolical: M't 24:31; 1Co 15:52; 1Th 4:16; Re 1:10; 4:1; 8; 9:1-14; 10:7; 11:15.

See Music, Instruments of.

TRUMPETS, FEAST OF: When and how observed (Le 23:24, 25; Nu 29:1-6). Celebrated after the captivity with joy (Ne 8:2, 9-12).

See Feasts.

TRUST (See Faith.)

TRUSTEE. Mosaic law concerning (Ex 22:7-13; Le 6:2-7). The parable of the pounds (M't 25:14-28; Lu 19:12-27).

See Steward.

TRUTH (Ps 85:10, 11). Precious (Pr 23:23). Preserves (Ps 46:11; 61:7; 91:4; Pr 20:28). Purifies (Pr 16:6; 1Pe 1:22). Sanctifies (Joh 17:17, 19; 2Th 2:13). Brings freedom (Joh 8:32).

Reaches unto the clouds (Ps 57:10; 108:4). Endures forever (Ps 100:5; 117:2). Ways of the Lord in (Ps 25:10).

The foundation of which Christ is the corner stone (Eph 2:20).

Came by Jesus Christ (Joh 1:17; 8:45; 14:6; 18:37, 38; Eph 2:20). Revealed to the righteous (Ps 57:3; 86:11).

Word of God called word of (Joh 17:17; Eph 1:13; Col 1:5; 2Ti 2:15; Jas 1:18); scripture of (Da 10:21).

Acceptance of necessary to salvation (2Th 2:12, 13; 1Ti 2:4; 2Ti 2:25; 3:7; Heb 10:26).

Rejection of, brings condemnation (2Th 2:10-12; Tit 1:14).

To be taught by parents to children (Isa 38:19). Church is pillar of (1Ti 3:15).

Believers should worship God in (Joh 4:24 w Ps 145:18); serve God in (Jos 24:14; 1Sa 12:24); walk before God in (1Ki 2:4; 2Ki 20:3); keep religious feasts with (1Co 5:8); esteem, as inestimable (Pr 23:23); love (Zec 8:19); rejoice in (1Co 13:6); speak, to one another (Zec 8:16; Eph 4:25); execute judgment with (Zec 8:16); meditate upon (Ph'p 4:8); bind, about the neck (Pr 3:3); write upon the tables of the heart (Pr 3:3).

The fruit of the Spirit is in (Eph 5:9).

Ministers should speak (2Co 12:6; Ga 4:16); teach in (1Ti 2:7); approve themselves by (2Co 6:7, 8); preach (2Co 4:2; 2Ti 2:15). Kings are preserved by (Pr 20:28).

They who speak, show forth righteousness (Pr 12:17); are the delight of God (Pr 12:22); will be established forever (Pr 2:1).

The wicked destitute of (Da 9:13; Ho 4:1; 1Ti 6:5); resist (2Ti 3:8; 4:4); turn away from (2Ti 4:4); speak not (Jer 9:5); uphold not (Isa 59:14, 15); plead not for (Isa 59:4); are not valiant for (Jer 9:3); punished for want of (Jer 9:5, 9; Ho 4:1, 3). See Wicked.

The Gospel as: Came by Christ (Joh 1:17). Is in Christ (1Ti 2:7). John bare witness to (Joh 5:33). Is according to godliness (Tit 1:1). Is sanctifying (Joh 17:17, 19). Is purifying (1Pe 1:22). Is part of the Christian armor (Eph 6:14). Revealed abundantly to saints (Jer 33:6). Abides continually with saints (2Jo 2). Should be acknowledged (2Ti 2:25). Should be believed (2Th 2:12, 13; 1Ti 4:3). Should be obeyed (Ro 2:8; Ga 3:1). Should be loved (2Th 2:10). Should be manifested (2Co 4:2). Should be rightly divided (2Ti 2:15). The Church is the pillar and ground of (1Ti 3:15). The devil is devoid of (Joh 8:44).

Of the Gospel (2Ti 4:3, 4; Tit 1:1, 14; 2:1; Jas 1:18, 21, 23, 25; 2:13; 5:19; 1Pe

1:22-25; 2:2, 8; 3:1; 5:12; 2Pe 1:12). See Doctrines of Jesus; God, Truth.

Of God: Is one of His attributes (De 32:4; Isa 65:16); He keeps, forever (Ps 146:6); abundant (Ex 34:6); inviolable (Nu 23:19; Tit 1:2); enduring to all generations (Ps 100:5). Exhibited in His ways (Re 15:3); works (Ps 33:4; 111:7; Da 4:37); judicial statutes (Ps 19:9); word (Ps 119:160; Joh 17:17); fulfillment of promises in Christ (2Co 1:20); fulfillment of His covenant (Mic 7:20); dealings with saints (Ps 25:10); deliverance of saints (Ps 57:3); punishment of the wicked (Re 16:7). Is a shield and buckler to saints (Ps 91:4). We should confide in (Ps 31:5; Tit 1:2). Plead in prayer (Ps 89:49). Pray for its manifestation to ourselves (2Ch 6:17). Pray for its exhibition to others (2Sa 2:6). Make known, to others (Isa 38:19). Magnify (Ps 71:22; 138:2). Is denied by the devil (Ge 3:4, 5); the self-righteous (1Jo 1:10); unbelievers (1Jo 5:10).

Often linked with His mercy (Ps 85:10, 11; 93:3; 100:5).

Attribute: Of God (Ex 34:6; De 32:4; Ps 31:5; 40:10, 11; 71:22; 86:15; 89:14; 115:1; 117:2; 138:2; 146:6; Isa 25:1; 65:16; Jer 4:2; 5:3). Exhibited, in His government (Ps 119:151); in His judgments (Ps 96:13; Ro 2:2); in His word (Joh 17:19); in His works (Ps 111:7, 8; Da 4:37).

Of Christ (Joh 1:14; 14:6).

Of the Holy Spirit (Joh 14:17; 16:13; 1Jo 5:7).

Grace of the Righteous (Ps 51:6; Pr 3:3; Joh 3:21; 3Jo 3).

Righteous, should be girded with (Eph 6:14); should know (1Ti 4:3; 1Jo 2:21; 3:19; 4:6); should walk in (2Jo 4; 3Jo 4); should obey (Ro 2:8); should love (Zec 8:19; 2Th 2:10); should rejoice in (1Co 13:6); should meditate upon (Ph'p 4:8).

TRUTHFULNESS. Commended (Pr 12:17, 19). Enjoined (Zec 8:16; Eph 4:25; Col 3:9). Magistrates should be men of (Ex 18:21). Fearlessness in (2Co 12:6; Ga 4:16). Of Job (Job 27:4; 36:4).

Wicked, lack (Jer 9:5). Satan, devoid of (Joh 8:44). See Satan; wicked.

TRYPHENA (dainty), Christian woman friend of Paul's in Rome (Ro 16:12).

TRYPHOSA (delicate), another Christian woman friend of Paul's in Rome (Ro 16:12).

TUBAL, son of Japheth (Ge 10:2; 1Ch 1:5). Descendants of, become a nation (Isa 66:19; Eze 27:13; 32:26; 38:2, 3; 39:1).

TUBAL-CAIN, son of Lamech and Zillah; worker in brass and iron (Ge 4:22).

TUMOR, a morbid swelling (1Sa 5:6, 9, 12; 6:4, 5, 11, 17).

See Boil.

TUNIC, shirt-like garment worn by men and women under other clothes in Bible times.

TURBAN, man's brimless headdress formed by winding cloth around head or a tight-fitting cap.

TURTLE, TURTLEDOVE, bird found in Palestine and used by poor people for sacrifice (Le 12:6-8; Lu 2:24).

TUTOR (2Ki 10:1; Ac 22:3; Ga 4:1, 2).

TWELVE, THE (See Apostles.)

TWILIGHT (1Sa 30:17; 2Ki 7:5; Job 3:9; Eze 12:6).

TWINS. Jacob and Esau (Ge 25:24-26). Pharez and Zarah (Ge 38:27-30).

TYCHICUS (fortuitous), an Asian companion of Paul. Accompanies Paul from Greece to Asia (Ac 20:4). With Paul in Nicopolis (Tit 3:12, w postscript to Titus). With Paul in Rome (Eph 6:21, 22; Col 4:7, 8, w postscripts to Ephesians and Colossians). Paul's amanuensis in writing to the Ephesians and Colossians (see the postscripts to Ephesians and Colossians). Sent to Ephesus (Eph 6:21, 22; 2Ti 4:12). Sent to Colosse (Col 4:7, 8).

TYPES. *Miscellaneous:* Bride, a type of the Church (Re 21:2, 9; 22:17). The sanctuary a type of the heavenly sanctuary (Ex 40:2, 24; Heb 8:2, 5; 9:1-12). The saving of Noah and his family, of the salvation through the gospel (1Pe 3:20, 21).

Defilement a type of sin (see Defilement; Purification). Leaven a type of sin (see Leaven). Ablutions were (see Ablutions).

See Allegory; Parables; Symbols.

Of Sin (See Blemish; Defilement; Leaven.)

Of the Saviour: Col 2:17; Heb 9:7-15, 18-28; 10:1-10. High priest, typical of the mediatorship (Ex 28:1, 12, 29, 30,

38; Le 16:15; Zec 6:12, 13, w Heb 5; 8:2; 10:21). The institutions ordained by Moses (M't 26:54; Lu 24:25-27, 44-47; Col 2:14-17; Heb 10:1-14). The sacrifices (Le 4:2, 3, 12; Heb 9:7-15, 18-25; 10:1-22, 29; 13:11-13; 1Pe 1:19, Re 5:6). The morning and evening sacrifice (Joh 1:29, 36). The red heifer (Nu 19:2-6, w Heb 9:13, 14). The paschal lamb (1Co 5:7). The brazen altar (Ex 27:1, 2, w Heb 13:10). The laver of brass (Ex 30:18-20, w Zec 13:1; Eph 5:26, 27). Mercy seat (Ex 25: 17-22, w Heb 4:16). The veil (Ex 40:21; 2Ch 3:14, w Heb 10:20). Manna (Joh 6:32-35; 1Co 10:3). Cities of refuge (Nu 35:6, w Heb 6:18). Brazen serpent (Nu 21:9; Joh 3:14, 15). Tree of life (Ge 2:9, w Joh 1:4; Re 22:2).

Adam (Ro 5:14; 1Co 15:45). Abel (Ge 4:8, 10, w Heb 12:24). Noah (Ge 5:29, w 2Co 1:5). Melchizedek (Heb 7:1-17). Moses (De 18:15, 18; Ac 3:20, 22; 7:37; Heb 3:2-6). David (2Sa 8:15; Ps 89:19, 20; Eze 37:24; Ph'p 2:9). Eliakim (Isa 22:20-22; Re 3:7). Jonah (Jon 1:17, w M't 12:40).

TYRANNUS (tyrant), Greek teacher in whose school Paul preached after he was expelled from the synagogue (Ac 19:9).

TYRANNY (See Government, Tyrannical.)

TYRE (rock). 1. Kingdom of; Hiram, king of (1Ki 5:1; 2Ch 2:3). Sends material to David for his palace (2Ch 2:3). Men and materials sent from, to Solomon, for the erection of the temple and his castles (1Ki 5:1-11; 9:10, 11; 2Ch 2:3-16).

See Hiram.

2. City of. Situated on the shore of the Mediterranean. On the northern boundary of Asher (Jos 19:29). Pleasant site of (Ho 9:13). Fortified (Jos 19:29; 2Sa 24:7). Commerce of (1Ki 9:26-28; 10:11; Isa 23; Eze 27; 28:1-19; Zec 9:2; Ac 21:3). Merchants of (Isa 23:8). Antiquity of (Isa 23:7). Riches of (Isa 23:8; Zec 9:3). Besieged by Nebuchadnezzar (Eze 26:7; 29:18).

Jesus goes to the coasts of (M't 15:21). Heals the daughter of the Syrophenician woman near (M't 15:21-28; M'k 7:24-31). Multitudes from, come to hear Jesus, and to be healed of their diseases (M'k 3:8; Lu 6:17). Herod's hostility toward (Ac 12:20-23). Paul visits (Ac 21:3-7).

To be judged according to its opportunity and privileges (M't 11:21, 22; Lu 10:13, 14).

Prophecies relating to (Ps 45:12; 87:4; Isa 23; Jer 25:22; 27:1-11; 47:4; Eze 26-28; Joe 3:4-8; Am 1:9, 10; Zec 9:2-4).

TYROPEON VALLEY, valley in Jerusalem separating W and E hills and joining Kidron and Hinnom valleys on the S.

U

UCAL, obscure word; usually taken as son or pupil of Agur (Pr 30:1).

UEL (will of God), an Israelite who divorced his Gentile wife (Ezr 10:34).

UGARIT, ancient city on N Syrian coast, 40 miles SW of Antioch; also called Ras Shamra; great commercial and religious center; hundreds of tablets known as "Ras Shamra Tablets" discovered there.

UKNAZ, son of Jephunneh (1Ch 4:15), KJV has "even Kenaz."

ULAI, river in Elam near Susa on whose bank Daniel saw vision (Da 8:2, 16).

ULAM. 1. Son of Sheresh (1Ch 7:16, 17).

2. Son of Eshek (1Ch 8:39, 40).

ULLA, an Asherite (1Ch 7:39).

UMMAH, a city of Asher (Jos 19:30).

UNBELIEF. Hardens the heart (Ps 95:8-11 w Heb 3:12, 16-19; Ac 19:9). Rejects Christ (Isa 53:1-3 w Joh 12:38; M'k 6:3, 6; Joh 1:11; 5:38, 40, 44, 46, 47; 10:25, 26). Displeases God (Ps 78:19-22; Heb 11:6). Makes God a liar (1Jo 5:10). Leads to defeat (Isa 7:9); destruction (Ro 11:20; 2Th 2:12); reproof (Joh 16:8, 9); damnation (Ro 14:23); rejection (1Pe 2:7, 8); instability (Jas 1:6, 7). Caused by spiritual blindness (Isa 6:9, 10; M't 13:13-15, 58; Lu 13:34; 19:41, 42; Joh 12:37, 39, 40, 47). Characteristic of all mankind (Ro 11:20, 30-32; 2Th 3:2).

Admonitions against (Ac 13:40, 41; 2Co 6:14-16; Heb 3:12; 16-19; 4:1-3, 6, 11; 12:25). Illustrated (Ro 10:6, 7, 16; 2Pe 3:4). At Christ's second coming (Lu 18:8).

Parable of (M'k 4:24, 25; Lu 8:12, 18; 14:16-24). The spirit of the antichrist (1Jo 2:22, 23; 4:3).

Does not nullify the faith of God (Ro 3:3); but allows him to extend his mercy (Ro 11:20, 30-32).

Used as excuse, by Moses (Ex 4:1).

UNBELIEVERS. Are spiritually blind (Joh 14:17; 1Co 2:14; 2Pe 3:4-7). Are impure (Tit 1:15). Make God a liar (1Jo 5:10). Will not be convinced (Lu 16:31; 22:67; Joh 4:48; 12:37-40). God's forbearance toward (Ro 10:16, 21). Shall be destroyed (Jer 5:12-14; M't 10:14, 15; Lu 12:46; Joh 8:24; 12:48; Ac 13:41; 1Co 1:18; 2Th 2:11, 12; Jude 5-7; Re 21:8). Tongues a sign to (1Co 14:22).

Instances of: Eve (Ge 3:4-6). Moses (Nu 11:21-23); and Aaron (Nu 20:12). Israelites (De 9:23; 2Ki 17:14; Ps 78; 106:7, 24; Isa 58:3; Mal 1:2, 7; Ro 31:32). Naaman (2Ki 5:12). Samaritan lord (2Ki 7:2). Disciples (M't 17:17; Lu 24:11, 25). Zacharias (Lu 1:20). Chief priests (M't 21:32; Lu 22:67). The Jews (M't 11:16-19; M'k 1:45; 2:6-11; 8:11, 12; 15:29-32; Lu 7:31-35; Joh 5:38, 40, 43, 46, 47; Ac 22:18; 28:24). Disciples (M't 17:20; M'k 4:38, 40; 16:14, 16; Lu 24:11, 21, 25, 26, 36-45; Joh 6:36, 60-62, 64, 66, 70, 71). Father of child possessed with a spirit confesses (M'k 9:24). Brethren of Christ (Joh 7:5). Thomas (Joh 20:25). Jews of Iconium (Ac 14: 2). Thessalonian Jews (Ac 17:5). Jews in Jerusalem (Ro 15:31). Ephesians (Ac 19:9). Saul (1Ti 1:13). People of Jericho (Heb 11:31).

UNBELIEVING ISRAELITES. Destroyed (Nu 14:11, 13-39; 32:11; De 1:34, 35; Ps 95:11; 106:26; 1Co 10:5, 10; Heb 3:17; Jude 5).

UNBLEMISHED. Offerings must be (Ex 12:5; Le 22:21; Eph 5:27; 1Pe 1: 19).

UNCHARITABLENESS (Isa 29:21). Admonitions against (M't 7:1-5; Lu 6:37-42; 12:57; Joh 7:24; 8:7; Ro 2:1; 14:1-15; 1Co 4:3-5, 7; 13:1-6). Forbidden (Jas 4:11, 12).

See Accusations, False; Charitableness; Slander; Speaking, Evil; Talebearer.

Instances of: The Israelites toward Moses, charging him with having made them abhorred by the Egyptians (Ex 5:21); charging him with bringing them out of Egypt to die (Ex 14:11, 12); in murmuring against Moses (see Murmuring, Instances of).

The tribes west of Jordan toward the two and a half tribes (Nu 32:1-33; Jos 22:11-31). Of Eli toward Hannah (1Sa 1:14-17).

Eliab toward David, charging him with presumption, when he offered to fight Goliath (1Sa 17:28). Princes of Ammon toward David, when he sent commissioners to convey his sympathy to Hanun (2Sa 10:3). Bildad toward Job (Job 8). Eliphaz toward Job (Job 15; 22; 42:7, 8). Zophar toward Job (Job 11:1-6; 20). Nathanael, when he said, "Can any good thing come out of Nazareth," (Joh 1:46). The Jews, charging Paul with teaching contrary to the law and against the temple (Ac 21:28).

UNCIAL LETTERS, large letters, like capitals. Early Greek manuscripts of NT written in uncials.

UNCIRCUMCISED. 1. One who has not submitted to Jewish rite of circumcision.

2. Gentiles (Ge 34:14; J'g 14:3; Ro 4:9).

3. One whose heart is not open to God (Jer 4:4; 6:10; Ac 7:51).

UNCLE. 1. Brother of one's father or mother (2Ki 24:17).

2. Any kinsman on father's side (Le 10:4; Am 6:10).

UNCLEAN, UNCLEANNESS. 1. Two kinds of uncleanness: moral and ceremonial.

2. Foods regarded as unclean in OT: animals that did not chew the cud and part the hoof; animals and birds which eat blood or carrion; anything strangled or that died of itself (Le 11:1-8, 26-28); water creatures without scales and fins (Le 11:9-12); insects without hind legs for jumping (Le 11).

3. Other forms of ceremonial uncleanness: contact with the dead (Le 11:24-40; 17:15; Nu 19:16-22); leprosy (Le 13; 14; Nu 5:2); sexual discharge (Le 15:16-33); childbirth (Le 12:6-8). In Christianity uncleanness is moral, not ceremonial.

UNCLOTHED. *Figurative:* M't 22:11; 2Co 5:3; Re 3:17; 16:15.

UNCTION (anointing), act of anointing (1Jo 2:20, 27).

UNDEFILED, any person or thing not tainted with moral evil (Ps 119:1; Heb 7:26; 13:4; 1Pe 1:4).

UNDERSETTERS, supports of the laver in Solomon's temple (1Ki 7:30, 34).

UNFAITHFULNESS. Unfaithful in little, unfaithful in much (Lu 16:10). Brings spiritual bankruptcy (M't 13:12; 25:29); destruction (Joh 15:2): damnation (Lu 19:12-27; M't 25:41-46). God rewards accordingly (Pr 24:11, 12; M't 25:8-13, 24-30, 41-46).

Denounced: In parables, of the vineyard (Isa 5:1-7; M't 21:33-43; M'k 12:1-9); of the empty vine (Ho 10:1, 2); of the slothful servant (M't 25:24-30; Lu 19:20-27).

Illustrated: By the unfruitful tree (M't 3:10; M'k 11:13, 14); by the unfruitful branch (Joh 15:2, 4, 6); by blindness (2Pe 1:8, 9).

See Sin, Fruits of; Unfruitfulness. See also Righteousness, Fruits of.

Of Friends: See Friends, False.

UNFRUITFULNESS (Isa 5:2).

Punished (M't 3:10 w Lu 3:9; M't 7:19; 13:3-7 w M'k 4:3-7, 14-19 & Lu 8:4-14; M't 21:19, 20 w M'k 11:13; Lu 3:9; 13:6-9; Joh 15:2, 4, 6).

See Sin, Fruits of; Unfaithfulness. See also Righteousness, Fruits of.

UNGODLY. To be avoided (Ps 1:1). Seem to materially prosper (Ps 73:11). Judged (Ps 1:6; 3:7; 2Pe 3:7). Christ died for (Ro 5:6); therefore God justifies (Ro 4:5). Law made for (1Ti 1:9).

See Wicked.

UNICORN, fabulous animal; horned; strong; wild; difficult to catch; may be wild ox (Nu 23:22; 24:8; De 33:17; Job 39:9f; Ps 29:6).

UNION, advantages of (Pr 15:22; Ec 4:9-12).

Of the Righteous: See Unity, of the Righteous; of the righteous with Christ: see Righteous, Unity of, with Christ.

UNITY. *Of the Godhead.* See God, Unity of.

Of the righteous. Advantages of (Pr 15:22; Ec 4:9-12). Fraternal (M't 23:8). Of the righteous (Ps 133:1; Isa 52:8; Ac 4:32).

Enjoined among Christians (Ro 12:16; 14:19; 15:5, 6; 1Co 1:10; 2Co 13:11; Eph 4:3; Ph'p 1:27; 2:2; 3:16, 17; 1Pe 3:8). Christ's prayer for, of the church (Joh 17:11, 21-23).

See Communion; Fellowship; One Another.

UNKNOWN GOD, inscription on an altar at Athens dedicated to an unknown god that worshipers did not want to overlook (Ac 17:23).

UNKNOWN TONGUE, charismatic

gift of speaking in tongues (1Co 14:2, 4, 13, 14, 19, 27).

UNLEARNED, illiterate (Ac 4:13; 2Pe 3:16); non-professional (1Co 14:16, 23f).

UNLEAVENED, unmixed with yeast (1Co 5:7, 8).

UNLEAVENED BREAD, bread made without yeast (Ex 12:8).

UNLEAVENED BREAD, FEAST OF (See Feasts.)

UNNI. 1. Levite; musician (1Ch 15:18, 20).

2. Levite; musician (Ne 12:9). "Unno" is the correct spelling.

UNPARDONABLE SIN. Blasphemy against the Holy Spirit (M't 12:31, 32; M'k 3:28, 29; Lu 12:10), probably the sin of decisively and finally rejecting the testimony of the Holy Spirit regarding the person and work of Jesus Christ.

Instances of: Israel (Nu 14:26-45). Eli's house (1Sa 3:14).

UNSELFISHNESS. Royal law (Jas 2:8). Enjoined (Ro 12:10; 15:1; 1Co 10:24; Ga 6:2; Ph'p 2:3, 4). Love inspires (1Co 13:4, 5).

Jesus: An example of (Ro 15:3; 2Co 8:9). His love inspires (2Co 5:14, 15).

Instances of: Abraham (Ge 13:9; 14:23, 24). King of Sodom (Ge 14:21). Children of Heth (Ge 23:6, 11). Judah (Ge 44:33, 34). Moses (Nu 11:29; 14:12-19). Gideon (J'g 8:22, 23). Saul (1Sa 11:12, 13). Jonathan (1Sa 23:17, 18). David (1Sa 24:17; 2Sa 15:19, 20; 23:16, 17; 1Ch 21:17; Ps 69:6). Araunah (2Sa 24:22-24). Nehemiah (Ne 5:14-18). Jews (Es 9:15). Daniel (Da 5:17). Jonah (Jon 1:12, 13). Joseph (M't 1:19). The disciples (Ac 4:34, 35). Priscilla and Aquila (Ro 16:3, 4). Paul (1Co 10:33; Ph'p 1:18; 4:17; 2Th 3:8). Philemon (Ph'm 13, 14). Onesiphorus (2Ti 1:16-18).

See Charitableness; Fellowship; Fraternity; Selfishness.

UNWORTHINESS (M't 10:37; 22:8; Ac 13:46).

UNTEMPERED MORTAR, mortar made of clay instead of slaked lime.

UPHARSIN, "divisions" or "divided" (Da 5:24-28).

UPHAZ, place where gold was obtained (Jer 10:9; Da 10:5); location unknown. Perhaps "Ophir" should be read.

UPPER CHAMBER, UPPER ROOM. room built on wall or roof of a house; scene of our Lord's last supper (M'k 14:15; Lu 22:12).

UPRIGHTNESS (See Righteousness.)

UR (flame), father of Eliphal (1Ch 11:35).

UR OF THE CHALDEES, city in S Mesopotamia, c. 140 miles SE of old Babylon; early home of Abraham (Ge 11:28, 31; 15:7; Ne 9:7).

URBANE (polite), Roman Christian (Ro 16:9).

URI (fiery). 1. Father of Bezaleel (Ex 31:2; 35:20; 38:22; 1Ch 2:20; 2Ch 1:5).

2. Father of Geber (1Ki 4:19).

3. Temple porter who divorced foreign wife (Ezr 10:24).

URIAH, URIAS (Jehovah is light). 1. Hittite; husband of Bathsheba (2Sa 11:3).

2. High priest during reign of Ahaz of Judah, for whom he built a pagan altar in the temple (2Ki 16:10-16).

3. Priest who aided Ezra (Ne 8:4).

4. Father of Meremoth (Ezr 8:33; Ne 3:4).

5. Son of Shemaiah, a prophet of Kirjath-jearim (Jer 26:20-23).

URIEL (God is light). 1. Kohathite Levite (1Ch 6:24).

2. Chief of Kohathites who assisted in bringing the ark from house of Obed-Edom (1Ch 15:5, 11).

3. Father of Michaiah, wife of Rehoboam (2Ch 13:2).

URIJAH (Jehovah is light). 1. A priest in the time of Ahaz. Builds a new altar for Ahaz (2Ki 16:10-16). Probably identical with Uriah, witness to a prophecy of Isaiah (Isa 8:2).

2. See Uriah, 2.

3. A priest. Assistant to Ezra (Ne 8:4). Called in *R. V.*, Uriah.

4. A prophet in the time of Jehoiakim. Prophesies against Judah (Jer 26:20). Fled to Egypt; taken; slain by Jehoiakim (Jer 26:21-23).

URIM AND THUMMIM, signifying light and perfection. In the breastplate (Ex 28:30; Le 8:8). Eleazar to ask counsel for Joshua, after the judgment of (Nu 27:21). Priests only might interpret (De 33:8; Ezr 2:63; Ne 7:65). Israelites consult (J'g 1:1; 20:18, 23). Withheld answer from King Saul (1Sa 28:6).

USURPATION. *Of Political Functions:*

By Absalom (2Sa 15:1-12). By Adonijah (1Ki 1:5-9). By Baasha (1Ki 15:27, 28). By Zimri (1Ki 16:9, 10). By Jehu (2Ki 9:11-37). By Athaliah (2Ki 11:1-16). By Shallum (2Ki 15:10).

In Ecclesiastical Affairs: By Saul, in assuming priestly functions (1Sa 13:8-14). By Solomon, in thrusting Abiathar out of the priesthood (1Ki 2:26, 27). By Uzziah, in assuming priestly offices (2Ch 26:16-21). By Ahaz (2Ki 16: 12, 13).

See Church and State, State Superior to the Church; Government, Ecclesiastical.

Of Executive Power: In ordering Naboth's death and confiscation of his vineyard (1Ki 21:7-19). In the scheme of Joseph to dispossess the Egyptians of their real and personal property (Ge 47:13-26). Of Pharaoh, making bond-servants of the Israelites (Ex 1:9-22). Moses accused of (Nu 16:3).

USURY, interest, not necessarily unreasonable exaction, but all income from loans. Forbidden (Ex 22:25; Le 25:35-37; De 23:19; Ps 15:5; Pr 28:8; Jer 15:10; Eze 18:8, 13, 17; 22:12). Exaction of, rebuked (Ne 5:1-13). Authorized, of strangers (De 23:20). Exacted by Jews (Eze 22:12).

Just men innocent of the vice of requiring (Eze 18:8).

See Interest; Money.

UTHAI. 1. Son of Ammihud (1Ch 9:4).

2. Man who returned with Ezra (Ezr 8:14).

UZ. 1. Son of Nahor (Ge 22:21), KJV has "Huz."

2. Son of Aram (Ge 10:23; 1Ch 1:17).

3. Son of Dishan (Ge 36:28).

4. Country in which Job lived (Job 1:1); site uncertain.

UZAI, father of Palal (Ne 3:25).

UZAL, son of Joktan (Ge 10:27; 1Ch 1:21); founded Uzal, capital of Yemen.

UZZA (strength). 1. Son of Shimei (1Ch 6:29).

2. Son of Ehud (1Ch 8:7).

3. Owner or caretaker of garden in which Manasseh and Amon were buried (2Ki 21:18, 26).

4. One whose children returned under Zerubbabel (Ezr 2:49; Ne 7:51).

UZZA, GARDEN OF, garden in which Manasseh and his son were buried (2Ki 21:18, 26).

UZZAH (strength), son of Abinadab; slain for touching the Ark to steady it when the oxen carrying it stumbled (2Sa 6:3-8; 1Ch 13:6-11).

UZZEN-SHERAH, town built by Ephraim's daughter Sheerah (1Ch 7:24).

UZZI (strong). 1. Descendant of Aaron (1Ch 6:5, 51; Ezr 7:4).

2. Grandson of Issachar (1Ch 7:2, 3).

3. Benjamite (1Ch 7:7).

4. Father of Elah (1Ch 9:8).

5. Overseer of Levites (Ne 11:22).

6. Priest in family of Jedaiah (Ne 12:19).

UZZIA (Jehovah is strength), one of David's mighty men (1Ch 11:44).

UZZIAH (Jehovah is strength). 1. Called Azariah. King of Judah (2Ki 14:21; 15:1, 2; 2Ch 26:1, 3). Rebuilds Elath (2Ki 14:22; 2Ch 26:2). Reigns righteously (2Ki 15:3; 2Ch 26:4, 5). Defeats the Philistines (2Ch 26:6, 7). Takes tribute from the Ammonites; strengthens the kingdom (2Ch 26:8). Strengthens the fortifications of Jerusalem (2Ch 26:9). Promotes cattle raising and agriculture (2Ch 26:10). Military establishment of (2Ch 26:11-15). Is presumptuous in burning incense; stricken with leprosy; quarantined (2Ch 26:16-21; 2Ki 15:5). Jotham regent during quarantine of (2Ki 15:5; 2Ch 26:21). Death of (2Ki 15:7; 2Ch 26:23). History of, written by Isaiah (2Ch 26:22; Isa 1:1). Earthquake in the reign of (Am 1:1; Zec 14:5).

2. Son of Uriel (1Ch 6:24).

3. Father of Jehonathan (1Ch 27:25).

4. A priest. Puts away his Gentile wife (Ezr 10:21).

5. Father of Athaiah (Ne 11:4).

UZZIEL, UZZIELITE (God is strength). 1. Kohathite Levite (Ex 6:18, 22; Le 10:4).

2. Son of Ishi; Simeonite (1Ch 4:42).

3. Head of Benjamite family (1Ch 7:7).

4. Son of Heman (1Ch 25:4).

5. Levite who helped in cleansing temple (2Ch 29:14-19).

6. Son of Harhaiah (Ne 3:8). Anyone descended from Uzziel, the Levite, was known as an Uzzielite (Nu 3:27; 1Ch 15:10; 26:23).

V

VAGABOND (to wander), word used in curse pronounced upon Cain (Ge 4:12, 14), imprecatory prayer of David (Ps 109:10), and professional exorcists (Ac 19:13).

VAIL. *Of the ark.* A covering (Ex 35:12; 39:34; 40:21; Nu 4:5).

Of the tabernacle. Hangings used to divide the holy of holies from the holy place (Ex 26:31-33; 35:12; 39:34; 40:21). Called, the second vail (Heb 9:3). Ordinances prescribing (Ex 26:31-33). Made by Bezaleel and Aholiab (Ex 36:35, 36).

A type of the humanity or body of Christ (Heb 10:20).

Figurative (Heb 6:19).

Of the temple (2Ch 3:14). Rent at the time of the crucifixion of Christ (M't 27:51; M'k 15:38; Lu 23:45).

VAJEZATHA (son of the atmosphere), son of Haman (Es 9:9).

VALE, VALLEY, low-lying ground; plain, ravine, gorge, a wadi (De 34:6; Jos 10:40; Lu 3:5).

Mentioned in Scripture: Achor (Jos 7:24; Isa 65:10; Ho 2:15). Ajalon (Jos 10:12). Baca (Ps 84:6). Berachah (2Ch 20:26). Bochim (J'g 2:5). Charashim (1Ch 4:14). Elah (1Sa 17:2; 21:9). Eshcol (Nu 32:9; De 1:24). Gad (2Sa 24:5). Gerar (Ge 26:17). Gibeon (Isa 28:21). Hebron (Ge 37:14). Hinnom or Tophet (Jos 18:16; 2Ki 23:10; 2Ch 28:3; Jer 7:32). Jehoshaphat or decision (Joe 3:2, 14). Jericho (De 34:3). Jezreel (Ho 1:5). Jiphthah-el (Jos 19:14, 27). Keziz (Jos 18:21). Lebanon (Jos 11:17). Megiddo (2Ch 35:22; Zec 12:11). Moab where Moses was buried (De 34:6). Passengers or Hamon-gog (Eze 39:11). Rephaim or giants (Jos 15:8; 18:16; 2Sa 5:18; Isa 17:5). Salt (2Sa 18:13; 2Ki 14:17). Shaveh or king's dale (Ge 14:17; 2Sa 18:18). Shittim (Joe 3:18). Siddim (Ge 14:3, 8). Sorek (J'g 16:4). Succoth (Ps 60:6). Zared (Nu 21:12). Zeboim (1Sa 13:18). Zephathah (2Ch 14:10). To be filled with hostile chariots, threatened as a punishment (Isa 22:7).

VALLEY GATE, gate in Jerusalem walls (Ne 2:13; 3:13; 12:31, 38); location uncertain.

VALOR (See Courage.)

VANIAH, man who divorced foreign wife (Ezr 10:36).

VANITY. A consequence of the fall (Ro 8:20). Every man is (Ps 39:11). Every state of man is (Ps 62:9). Man at his best estate is (Ps 39:5). Man is like to (Ps 144:4). The thoughts of man are (Ps 94:11). The days of man are (Job 7:16; Ec 6:12). Childhood and youth are (Ec 11:10). The beauty of man is (Ps 39:11; Pr 31:30). The help of man is (Ps 60:11; La 4:17). Man's own righteousness is (Isa 57:12). Worldly wisdom is (Ec 2:15, 21; 1Co 3:20). Worldly pleasure is (Ec 2:1). Worldly anxiety is (Ps 39:6; 127:2). Worldly labor is (Ec 2:11; 4:4). Worldly enjoyment is (Ec 2:3, 10, 11). Worldly possessions are (Ec 2:4-11). Treasures of wickedness are (Pr 10:2). Heaping up riches is (Ec 2:26; 4:8). Love of riches is (Ec 5:10). Unblessed riches are (Ec 6:2). Riches gotten by falsehood are (Pr 21:6). All earthly things are (Ec 1:2). Foolish questions are (1Ti 1:6, 7; 6:20; 2Ti 2:14, 16; Tit 3:9). The conduct of the ungodly is (1Pe 1:18). The religion of hypocrites is (Jas 1:26). The worship of the wicked is (Isa 1:13; M't 6:7). Lying words are (Jer 7:8). False teaching is but (Jer 23:32). Mere external religion is (1Ti 4:8; Heb 13:9). Almsgiving without charity is (1Co 13:3). Faith without works is (Jas 2:14). Idolatry is (Jer 18:15). Wealth gotten by, diminishes (Pr 13:11).

Saints hate the thoughts of (Ps 119:113); pray to be kept from (Ps 119:37; Pr 30:8); avoid (Ps 24:4); avoid those given to (Ps 26:4).

The wicked especially characterized by (Job 11:11); though full of, affect to be wise (Job 11:21); love (Ps 4:2); imagine (Ps 2:1; Ac 4:25; Ro 1:21); devise (Ps 36:4 [see marg.]); speak (Ps 10:7; 12:2; 41:6); count God's service as (Job 21:15; Mal 3:14); allure others by words of (2Pe 2:18); walk after (Jer 2:5); walk in (Ps 39:6; Eph 4:17); inherit (Jer 16:19); reap (Pr 22:8; Jer 12:13); judicially given up to (Ps 78:33; Isa 57:13).

Fools follow those given to (Pr 12:11). Following those given to, leads to poverty (Pr 28:19). All should know and acknowledge (De 4:35).

See Pride.
VASHNI (weak), eldest son of Samuel (1Ch 6:28); in 1Sa 8:2 Joel is named as Samuel's first-born. The Hebrew text is probably corrupt here.
VASHTI (beautiful woman), wife of Ahasuerus; queen of Persia; divorced (Es 1:19).
VEDAN. A place whose merchants traded with Tyre (Eze 27:19). In KJV called Dan.
VEGETARIANS, persons who eat no flesh (Ro 14:2).
VEGETATION. Created the third day (Ge 1:11; 2:5). For food (Ge 1:29, 30).
VEIL. 1. Fabric used for concealment or for protection against elements (Ge 24:65; 1Co 11:4-16).
2. In tabernacle and temple a beautiful, hand-woven veil separated the holy place from the holy of holies (Ex 26:31-37). See Vail.
3. Worn by Rebekah (Ge 24:65); by Tamar (Ge 38:14, 19); by Moses, to screen his face when he descended from Mount Sinai (Ex 34:33, 35; 2Co 3:13-16).
VEIN (source), mine (Job 28:1).
VENERATION, for parents (Ge 48:15, 16).
See Old Age; Parents; Reverence.
VENGEANCE, any punishment meted out in the sense of retribution (J'g 15:7; Jer 11:20; 20:12). It belongs to God (De 32:35, 36; Ps 94:1; Lu 18:7, 8; Ro 12:19; 2Th 1:6; Heb 10:30; Re 6:10).
Instance of: Sons of Jacob on Hamor and Shechem (Ge 34:20-31).
See Judgments; Revenge; Retaliation.
VENISON (game of any kind), any game taken in hunting (Ge 25:28; 27:5ff).
VENTRILOQUISM (Isa 29:4). Divination by (Ac 16:16).
VERDICT, against Jesus (M't 26:66; 27:24-26; M'k 15:15; Lu 23:24; Joh 19:16).
See Courts.
VERMILION, brilliant red color (Jer 22:14; Eze 23:14).
VERSIONS OF THE SCRIPTURES (See Texts and Versions.)
VESSEL, any material thing which may be used for any purpose, whether it be a tool, implement, weapon, or receptacle (Ho 13:15). In the NT it is sometimes applied to persons (Ro 9:20-24; 2Ti 2:20, 21).
VESTMENTS. Of priests (see Priests).
VESTRY, place where royal or ceremonial vestments were kept (2Ki 10:22).
VESTURE, archaic word for garments (Ge 41:42; De 22:12; Ps 22:18). Sometimes used metaphorically (Ps 102:26; Heb 1:12).
VIA DOLOROSA, traditional route which our Lord traveled on the day of His crucifixion from the judgment seat of Pilate to the place of His crucifixion (M't 27:26, 31, 33).
VIAL, flask or bottle (1Sa 10:1); shallow bowl or basin (Re 5:8; 21:9).
VICARIOUS DEATH: The ram for Isaac (Ge 22:13). Jesus for sinners (see Jesus, Death of, Mission of, Sufferings of).
See Atonement; Sufferings, Vicarious; Jesus, Saviour.
VICEGERENCY. Of Elisha, in miraculously rewarding the Shunammite (2Ki 4:16, 17); in cursing Gehazi (2Ki 5:27). Of the apostles (M't 16:19; 18:18; Joh 20:23).
VICTORIES. In battle, from God (Ps 55:18; 76:5, 6). Celebrated in song (J'g 5; 2Sa 22); by women (1Sa 18:6, 7; 2Sa 1:20).
See Armies; War, God in.
VICTUAL, food.
VIGILANCE. *Instance of:* King of Jericho (Jos 2:1-3).
See Watchman.
VILLAGE. Villages were usually grouped around a fortified town to which the people could flee in time of war (2Ch 8:18).
VINE. Degeneracy of (Jer 2:21). Fable of (J'g 9:12, 13). Pruned (Isa 5:6; Joh 15:1-5). Parables of (Ps 80:8-14; Eze 17:6-10; 19:10-14).
Symbolical: Joh 15:1-5.
See Vineyard.
VINEGAR, a sour wine. Forbidden to Nazarites (Nu 6:3). Used with food (Ru 2:14; Ps 69:21; Pr 10:26; 25:20). Offered to Christ on the cross (M't 27:34, 48; Joh 19:29, w Mark 15:23).
VINEYARDS. Origin and antiquity of (Ge 9:20). The design of planting (Ps 107:37; 1Co 9:7). Frequently walled or fenced with hedges (Nu 22:24; Pr 24:31; Isa 5:2, 5). Cottages built in, for the

keepers (Isa 1:8). Provided with the apparatus for making wine (Isa 5:2; M't 21:33). The stones carefully gathered out of (Isa 5:2).

Laws Respecting: Not to be planted with different kinds of seed (De 22:9). Not to be cultivated during the sabbatical year (Ex 23:11; Le 25:4). The spontaneous fruit of, not to be gathered the sabbatical or jubilee year (Le 25:5, 11). Compensation in kind to be made for injury done to (Ex 22:5). Strangers entering, allowed to eat fruit of, but not to take any away (De 23:24). The gleaning of, to be left for the poor (Le 19:10; De 24:21). The fruit of new, not to be eaten for three years (Le 19:23). The fruit of new, to be holy to the Lord in the fourth year (Le 19:24). The fruit of new, to be eaten by the owners from the fifth year (Le 19:25). Planters of, not liable to military service till they had eaten of the fruit (De 20:6). Frequently let out to husbandmen (Song 8:11; M't 21:33). Rent of, frequently paid by part of the fruit (M't 21:34). Were often mortgaged (Ne 5:3, 4). Estimated rent of (Song 8:11; Isa 7:23). Estimated profit arising from, to the cultivators (Song 8:12). The poor engaged in the culture of (2Ki 25:12; Isa 61:5). Members of the family often wrought in (Song 1:6; M't 21:28-30). Mode of hiring and paying laborers for working in (M't 20:1, 2). Of the kings of Israel superintended by officers of state (1Ch 27:27).

The Vintage or Ingathering of: Was a time of great rejoicing (Isa 16:10). Sometimes continued to the time of sowing seed (Le 26:5). Failure in, occasioned great grief (Isa 16:9, 10). Of red grapes particularly esteemed (Isa 27:2). The produce of, was frequently destroyed by enemies (Jer 48:32). The whole produce of, often destroyed by insects (De 28:39; Am 4:9). In unfavorable seasons produced but little wine (Isa 5:10; Hag 1:9, 11). The wicked judicially deprived of the enjoyment of (Am 5:11; Zep 1:13). The Rechabites forbidden to plant (Jer 35:7-9). Of the slothful man neglected and laid waste (Pr 24:30, 31).

Illustrative: Of the Jewish Church (Isa 5:7; 27:2; Jer 12:10; M't 21:23).

VINEYARDS, PLAIN OF THE, Abel-cheramim, village of the Ammonites E of Jordan (J'g 11:33).

VINTAGE (Le 26:5; J'g 8:2; Isa 16:10; 24:13; 32:10; Jer 48:32; Mic 7:1).

VIOL, an instrument of music (Isa 5:12).
See Music, Instruments of; Psaltery.

VIPER. A serpent (Job 20:16; Isa 30:6; 59:5). Fastens on Paul's hand (Ac 28:3).
See Serpent.

Figurative: M't 3:7; 23:33; Lu 3:7.

VIRGIN. Proofs of (De 22:13-21). Dowry of (Ex 22:17). Character of, to be protected (De 22:17-21, 23, 24). Betrothal of, a quasi marriage (De 22:23, 24). Distinguishing apparel of (2Sa 13:18). Priests might marry none but (Le 21:14). Mourn in the temple (La 1:4; 2:10). Virginity of, bewailed (J'g 11:37-39). Parable of the wise and foolish (M't 25:1-13). Mother of Jesus a (Isa 7:14; M't 1:23; Lu 1:27). Advised by Paul not to marry (1Co 7).

Figurative: Of the Church (Isa 62:5; Jer 14:17; 31:4, 13; 2Co 11:2). Of personal purity (1Co 7:25, 37; Re 14:4).

VIRGIN BIRTH, the NT teaching that Jesus Christ entered into the stream of human life without the mediation of an earthly father, born not of sexual intercourse but as a result of the supernatural overshadowing of the Holy Spirit (M't 1:18-25; Lu 1:26-2:7).

VIRGINITY (See Virgin.)

VIRTUE, righteousness, goodness, chastity (Pr 31:10f); power (M'k 5:30; Lu 6:19; 8:46).

VISION, a mode of revelation (Nu 12:6; 1Sa 3:1; 2Ch 26:5; Ps 89:19; Pr 29:18; Jer 14:14; 23:16; Da 1:17; Ho 12:10; Joe 2:28; Ob 1; Hab 2:2; Ac 2:17).

Of Abraham, concerning his descendants (Ge 15:1-17). Of Jacob, of the ladder with ascending and descending angels (Ge 28:12); at Beer-sheba (Ge 46:2). Of Joshua, of the captain of the Lord's host (Jos 5:13-15). Of Moses, of the burning bush (Ex 3:2); of the glory of God (Ex 24:9-11; 33:18-23).

Of the Israelites of the manifestation of the glory of God (Ex 24:10, 17; Heb 12:18-21). Of Balaam, in a trance (see Balaam). Of Elisha, at the translation of Elijah (2Ki 2:11). Of Elisha's servant, of the chariots of the Lord (2Ki 6:17). Of Micaiah, of the defeat of the Israelites; of the Lord on his throne; and of a lying spirit (1Ki 22:17-23; 2Ch 18:16-22). Of David, of the angel of the Lord by the threshing floor of Ornan (1Ch 21:15-18). Of Job, of a spirit (Job 4:12-16). Of Isaiah, of the Lord and his glory in the temple (Isa 6), of the valley of vision (Isa 22). Of Jeremiah, of an almond rod (Jer 1:11); of the seething pot (Jer 1:13).

Of Ezekiel, of the glory of God (Eze 1:3, 12-14; 3:23); of the roll (Eze 2:9); of the man of fire (Eze 8; 9); of the coals of fire (Eze 10:1-7); of the dry bones (Eze 37:1-14); of the city and temple (Eze 40-48); of the waters (Eze 47:1-12).

Of Daniel, of the four beasts (Da 7); of the Ancient of days (Da 7:9-27); of the ram and the he goat (Da 8); of the angel (Da 10).

Of Amos, of grasshoppers (Am 7:1, 2); of fire (Am 7:4); of a plumb line (Am 7:7, 8); of summer fruit (Am 8:1, 2); of the temple (Am 9:1).

Of Zechariah, of horses (Zec 1:8-11); of horns and carpenters (Zec 1:18-21); of the high priest (Zec 3:1-5); of the golden candlestick (Zec 4); of the flying roll (Zec 5:1-4); of the mountains and chariots (Zec 6:1-8).

Of Zacharias, in the temple (Lu 1:13-22). Of John the Baptist, at the baptism of Jesus (M't 3:16; M'k 1:10; Lu 3:22; Joh 1:32-34). Peter, James, and John, of the transfiguration of Jesus and the appearance of Moses and Elijah (M't 17:1-9; Lu 9:28-36). Of the people, of the tongues of fire at Pentecost (Ac 2:2, 3). Of Stephen, of Christ (Ac 7:55, 56). Of Paul, of Christ, on the way to Damascus (Ac 9:3-6; 1Co 9:1); of Ananias (Ac 9:12); of a man of Macedonia, saying, "Come over into Macedonia, and help us" (Ac 16:9); in Corinth (Ac 18:9, 10); in a trance (Ac 22:17-21); of paradise (2Co 12:1-4). Of Ananias, of Christ (Ac 9:10-12). Of Cornelius, the centurion, of an angel (Ac 10:3). Of Peter, of the sheet let down from heaven (Ac 10:9-18).

Of John on the Isle of Patmos (the Book of Revelation).

Of Christ and the golden candlesticks (Re 1:10-20); the open door (Re 4:1); a rainbow and throne (Re 4:2, 3); twenty-four elders (Re 4:4); seven lamps (Re 4:5); sea of glass (Re 4:6); four living creatures (Re 4:6-8); book with seven seals (Re 5:1-5); golden vials (Re 5:8); of the six seals (Re 6); four horses (Re 6:2-8); earthquake and celestial phenomena (Re 6:12-14); four angels (Re 7:1); sealing of the one hundred and forty-four thousand (Re 7:2-8); of the seventh seal and seven angels (Re 8-11); of the censer (Re 8:5); hail and fire (Re 8:7); mountain cast into the sea (Re 8:8, 9); falling star (Re 8:10, 11; 9:1); the third part of sun and moon and stars darkened (Re 8:12); bottomless pit (Re 9:2); locusts (Re 9:3-11); four angels loosed from the Euphrates (Re 9:14); army of horsemen (Re 9:16-19); angel having a book (Re 10:1-10); seven thunders (Re 10:3, 4); measurement of the temple (Re 11:1, 2); two witnesses (Re 11:3-12); court of the Gentiles (Re 11:2); two olive trees and two candlesticks (Re 11:4); the beast out of the bottomless pit (Re 11:7); fall of the city (Re 11:13); second and third woes (Re 11:14); a woman clothed with the sun; birth of the man child (Re 12); a red dragon (Re 12:3-17); war in heaven (Re 12:7-9); the beast rising out of the sea (Re 13:1-10); the beast coming out of the earth (Re 13:11-18); the Lamb on Mount Zion (Re 14:1-5); the angel having the everlasting gospel (Re 14:6, 7); the angel proclaiming the fall of Babylon (Re 14:8-13); the Son of man with a sickle (Re 14:14-16); angel reaping the harvest (Re 14:14-20); angel coming out of the temple (Re 14:17-19); an angel having power over fire (Re 14:18); the vine and the winepress (Re 14:18-20); angels with the seven last plagues (Re 15); sea of glass (Re 15:2); temple opened (Re 15:5); the plague upon the men who had the mark of the beast (Re 16:2); sea turned into blood (Re 16:3); the seven angels with the seven vials of the wrath of God (Re 16; 17); destruction of Babylon (Re 18); of the multitude praising (Re 19:1-9); of him who is faithful and true riding a white horse (Re 19:11-16); angel in the sun (Re 19:17-21); Satan bound a thousand years (Re 20:1-3); thrones of judgment, and the resurrection, and the loosing of Satan (Re 20:1-10); great white throne (Re 20:11); opening of the book of life (Re 20:12); death and hell (Re 20:14); New Jerusalem (Re 21); river of life (Re 22:1); tree of life (Re 22:2).

See Dream.

VISITATION, divine visit for purpose of rewarding or punishing people for their deeds (Jer 10:15; Lu 19:44; 1Pe 2:12).

VISITORS (See Guests.)

VOICE, OF GOD (Eze 1:24, 28; 10:5; Joh 5:37; 12:28-30; Ac 7:31; 9:4, 7; 26:14, 15).

See Anthropomorphisms.

VOLCANOES (De 4:11; 5:23; J'g 5:5, Ps 97:5; 104:32; 144:5; Isa 34:9, 10; 64:1-3; Jer 51:25; Mic 1:4; Na 1:5, 6).

See Earthquake; Mountain.

VOLUPTUOUSNESS (See Lasciviousness; Sensuality.)

VOPSHI, father of Nahbi (Nu 13:14).

VOWS (Ps 22:25; 61:8; 65:1). Heard of God (Ps 61:5). Obligatory (Nu 30:2; De 23:21-23; Job 22:27; Ps 50:14; 56:12; 66:13, 14; 76:11; Ec 5:4, 5; Na 1:15). In affliction (Ps 116:14-19). Rash (Pr 20:25; Ec 5:6); by Jephthah (J'g 11:29-40); by Israelites (J'g 29:7-11).

Mosaic laws concerning (Le 23:37, 38; Nu 29:39). Must be voluntary (Le 22:18-25; Nu 15:2-16). Must be performed (Le 5:4-13; Nu 30:2-16). See Obligatory, above. Estimation of the redemption price of things offered in vows, to be made by the priest, according to age and sex of the person making the offering (Le 27:1-13). The redemptive price of the offering of real estate, to be valued by the priest (Le 27:14, 15); of a field (Le 27:16-25).

Of women (Nu 30:3-16). Of Nazarites (Nu 6:1-21). Unintentional (Le 5:4-5). Offerings devoted under (Le 5:6-13; 7:16-18; 27:1-25; Nu 15:2-16). Things offered in, must be perfect (Le 22:18-25).

Edible things offered in, to be eaten the same day they were offered (Le 7:16-18). Things offered in, to be brought to the tabernacle or temple (De 12:6, 11, 17, 18, 26); belonged to the priests (Nu 18:14).

Things forbidden to be offered in: Receipts of the whore and price of a dog (De 23:18); a minor, of himself (M'k 7:11-13).

See Contract; Covenant.

Instances of: Of Jacob (Ge 28:20-22). Of the mother of Micah, in the dedication of silver for the making of an idol (J'g 17:2, 3). Of Hannah, to consecrate unto the Lord the child for which she prayed (1Sa 1:11, w *verses* 27, 28). Of Elkanah (1Sa 1:21). Of Absalom (2Sa 15:7, 8). Of Job, not to entertain thoughts of fornication (Job 31:1). Of David (Ps 132: 2). Of Ananias and Sapphira, in the dedication of the proceeds of the sale of their land (Ac 5:1-11). Of the Jews, to slay Paul (Ac 23:12-15). Of Jephthah, and of the Israelites (see Rash Vows, above).

See Nazarite.

VULGATE, Latin version of the Bible, prepared by Jerome in 4th century.

VULTURE, name given to several kinds of large birds of prey, usually feeding on carrion; unclean for the Jews (Le 11:14; De 14:13).

W

WADI, valley which forms the bed of a stream during the winter, but which dries up in hot season (Ge 26:19).

WAFERS, thin cakes (Ex 16:31; 1Ch 23:29).

WAGES. Of Jacob (Ge 29:15-30; 30:28-34; 31:7, 41). Parable concerning (M't 20:1-15).

Laborer entitled to (De 25:4; M't 10:10; Lu 10:7; Ro 4:4). Must be just (Col 4:1). Must be paid promptly (Le 19:13; De 24:15). Withholding of, denounced (Jer 22:13; Mal 3:5; Jas 5:4).

Wasting of, denounced (Hag 1:6). Contentment with, enjoined (Lu 3:14).

Figurative (Ro 6:23).

WAGON, vehicle with wheels used for carrying goods as well as persons (Ge 45:19, 21; 46:5).

WAIL, in ancient funeral processions wailing relatives and hired mourners and musicians preceded body to grave (Jer 9:17-21; Am 5:16; M't 9:23). Of the wicked (M't 13:42).

WAITING. Upon God: As the God of providence (Jer 14:22); as the God of salvation (Ps 25:5); as the giver of all temporal blessings (Ps 104:27, 28; 145:15, 16).

For mercy (Ps 123:2); pardon (Ps 39:7, 8); the consolation of Israel (Lu 2:25); salvation (Ge 49:18; Ps 62:1, 2); guidance and teaching (Ps 25:5); protection (Ps 33:20; 59:9, 10); the fulfillment of his word (Hab 2:3); the fulfillment of his promises (Ac 1:4); hope of righteousness by faith (Ga 5:5); coming of Christ (1Ch 1:7; 1Th 1:10). Is good (Ps 52:9). God calls us to (Zep 3:8). Exhortations and encouragements to (Ps 27:14; 37:7; Ho 12:6).

Should be with the soul (Ps 62:1, 5); with earnest desire (Ps 130:6); with patience (Ps 37:7; 40:1); with resignation (La 3:26); with hope in his word (Ps 130:5); with full confidence (Mic 7:7); continually (Ho 12:6); all the day (Ps 25:5); specially in adversity (Ps 59:1-9; Isa 8:17); in the way of his judgments (Isa 26:8). Saints resolve on (Ps 52:9; 59:9). Saints have expectation from (Ps 62:5). Saints plead, in prayer (Ps 25:21; Isa 33:2). The patience of saints often tried in (Ps 69:3).

They who engage in, wait upon him only (Ps 62:5); are heard (Ps 40:1); are blessed (Isa 30:18; Da 12:12); experience his goodness (La 3:25); shall not be ashamed (Ps 25:3; Isa 49:23); shall renew their strength (Isa 40:31); shall inherit the earth (Ps 37:9); shall be saved (Pr 20:22; Isa 25:9); shall rejoice in salvation (Isa 25:9); shall receive the glorious things prepared by God for them (Isa 64:4). Predicted of the Gentiles (Isa 42:4; 60:9). Illustrated (Ps 123:2; Lu 12:36; Jas 5:7).

Exemplified: Jacob (Ge 49:18); David (Ps 39:7); Isaiah (Isa 8:17); Micah (Mic 7:7); Joseph (M'k 15:43).

WALKING. With God: According to his commands (De 5:33; Ps 1; Jer 7:23); in his ways (De 28:9; Jos 22:5); in the old paths (Jer 6:16); as taught by him (1Ki 8:36; Isa 2:3; 30:21); uprightly (Pr 2:7); in his statutes and judgments (Eze 37:24); in newness of life (Ro 6:4); not after the flesh, but after the Spirit (Ro 8:1; Ga 5:16); honestly, as in the day (Ro 13:13); by faith, not by sight (2Co 5:7); in love, following Christ (Eph 5:2); worthy of the Lord (Col 1:10); in Christ (Col 2:6); by the gospel rule (Ph'p 3:16); in the light, as God is (1Jo 1:7); in white raiment (Re 3:4); in the light of heaven (Re 21:24).

Instances of: Enoch (Ge 5:24); Noah (Ge 6:9).

WALLS, of the cities. Of Bashan, destroyed by the Israelites (De 3:5, 6). Of Jericho (Jos 2:15; 6). Of Jerusalem (see Jerusalem). Of Babylon (Jer 51:44); broad (Jer 51:58). Of Beth-shan (1Sam 31:10). Of Rabbah (2Sa 11:20). Of Abel (2Sa 20:15, 21).

Houses built upon (Jos 2:15). Double (2Ki 25:4; Isa 22:11). Sentinels on (see Watchman).

Figurative: Of the new Jerusalem (Re 21:12, 14, 17-21).

WAR. Divine approval of (2Sa 22:35). Civil (J'g 12:1-6; 20; 2Sa 2:12-31; 3:1; 20; 1Ki 14:30; 16:21; Isa 19:2); forbidden (2Ch 11:4); averted (Jos 22:11-34).

Enemy harangued by general of opposing side (2Ki 18:19-36; 2Ch 13:4-12). Of extermination (Nu 31:7-17; De 2:33, 34; 3:6; 20:13-18; Jos 6:21, 24; 8:24, 25; 10:2-40; 11:11-23; 1Sa 15:3-9; 27:8-11).

God in (Ex 14:13, 14; De 1:30; 3:21, 22; 7:17-24; 20:1, 4; 31:6-8, 23; 32:29, 30; Jos 1:1, 5-7, 9; J'g 1:2; 6:16; 7:9; 11:29; 1Sa 17:45-47; 19:5; 30:7, 8; 2Sa 5:22-24; 22:18; 1Ki 20:28; Ps 18:34; 76:3; Jer 46:15; Am 5:8, 9; Zec 10:5). God uses, as a judgment (Ex 23:24; Le 26:17, 31-39; De 28:25-68; 32:30; J'g 2:14; 2Ki 15:37; 1Ch 5:22, 26; 21:12; 2Ch 12:1-12; 15:6; 24:23, 24; 33:11; 36; Job 19:29; Ps 44:9-16; 60:1-3; 105:25; Isa 5:1-8, 25-30; 9:8-12; 13:3, 4, 9; 19:2; 34:2-6; 43:28; 45:7; Jer 12:7, 12; 46:15-17, 21; 47:6, 7; 48:10; 49:5; 50:25; Eze 23:22-25; Am 3:6; 4:11; Zep 1:7-18; Zec 8:10; 14:2).

Repugnant to God (1Ch 22:8, 9; Ps 68:30; 120:6, 7; Re 13:10). God sends panic in (Ex 15:14-16); threatens defeat in (De 32:25; 1Sa 2:10; 2Ch 18:12-16; Isa 30:15-17; Eze 15:6-8; 21:9-17); inflicts defeat in (Jos 7:12, 13; 2Ch 12:5-8; 24:23, 24; Ps 76:3; 78:66; 79:10; Isa 5:25; Jer 46:15, 16).

Councils of (Jos 22:10-34; J'g 7:10, 11; 2Sa 16:20; 17:1-15; Ps 48:4-7; Pr 11:14; 20:18). Wisdom required in (Pr 21:22; 24:6; Ec 9:14-18; Lu 14:31, 32).

Tumult of (Am 2:2). Slain in, neglected (Isa 14:19; 18:6). Evils of (2Sa 2:26; Ps 46:8; 79:1-3; 137:9; Isa 3:5, 25, 26; 5:29, 30; 6:11, 12; 9:5, 19-21; 13:15, 16; 15; 16:9, 10; 18:6; 19:2-16; 32:13, 14; 33:8, 9; 34:7-15; Jer 4:19-31; 5:16, 17; 6:24-26; 7:33, 34; 8:16, 17; 9:10-21; 10:20; 13:14; 14:18; 15:8, 9; 19:7-9; 25:33; 46:3-12; 47:3; 48:28, 33; 51:30-58; La 1-5; Eze 33:27; 39:17-19; Ho 10:14; 13:16; Joe 2:2-10; Am 1:13; 6:9, 10; 8:3; Na 2:10; 3:3, 10; Zec 14:2; Lu 21:20-26; Re 19:17, 18).

To cease (Ps 46:9; Isa 2:4; Mic 4:3).

Wars and rumors of (M't 24:6; M'k 13:7; Lu 21:9).

See Armies; Arms; Fort; Soldiers; Strategy; Tower; Watchman.

Figurative: Warfare of saints: Is not after the flesh (2Co 10:3). Is a good warfare (1Ti 1:18, 19). Called the good fight of faith (1Ti 6:12).

Is against the devil (Ge 3:15; 2Co 2:11; Eph 6:12; Jas 4:7; 1Pe 5:8; Re 12:17); the flesh (Ro 7:23; 1Co 9:25-27; 2Co 12:7; Ga 5:17; 1Pe 2:11); enemies (Ps 38:19; 56:2; 59:3); the world (Joh 16:33; 1Jo 5:4, 5); death (1Co 15:26, w Heb 2:14, 15).

Often arises from the opposition of friends or relatives (Mic 7:6; M't 10:35, 36). To be carried on under Christ, as our Captain (Heb 2:10); under the Lord's banner (Ps 60:4); with faith (1Ti 1:18, 19); with a good conscience (1Ti 1:18, 19); with steadfastness in the faith (1Co 16:13; 1Pe 5:9, w Heb 10:23); with earnestness (Jude 3); with watchfulness (1Co 16:13; 1Pe 5:8); with sobriety (1Th 5:6; 1Pe 5:8); with endurance of hardness (2Ti 2:3, 10); with self-denial (1Co 9:25-27); with confidence in God (Ps 27:1-3); with prayer (Ps 35:1-3; Eph 6:18); without earthly entanglements (2Ti 2:4). Mere professors do not maintain (Jer 9:3).

Saints are all engaged in (Ph'p 1:30); must stand firm in (Eph 6:13, 14); exhorted to diligence in (1Ti 6:12; Jude 3); encouraged in (Isa 41:11, 12; 51:12; Mic 7:8; 1Jo 4:4); helped by God in (Ps 118:13; Isa 41:13, 14); protected by God in (Ps 140:7); comforted by God in (2Co 7:5, 6); strengthened by God in (Ps 20:2; 27:14; Isa 41:10); strengthened by Christ in (2Co 12:9; 2Ti 4:17); delivered by Christ in (2Ti 4:18); thank God for victory in (Ro 7:25; 1Co 15:57).

Armor for: a girdle of truth (Eph 6:14); the breastplate of righteousness (Eph 6:14); preparation of the gospel (Eph 6:15); shield of faith (Eph 6:16); helmet of salvation (Eph 6:17; 1Th 5:8); sword of the Spirit (Eph 6:17); called armor of God (Eph 6:11); called armor of righteousness (2Co 6:7); called armor of light (Ro 13:12); not carnal (2Co 10:4); mighty through God (2Co 10:4, 5); the whole, is required (Eph 6:13); must be put on (Ro 13:12; Eph 6:11); to be on right hand and left (2Co 6:7).

Victory in, is from God (1Co 15:57; 2Co 2:14); through Christ (Ro 7:25; 1Co 15:57; 2Co 12:9; Re 12:11); by faith (Heb 11:33-37; 1Jo 5:4, 5); over the devil (Ro 16:20; 1Jo 2:14); over the flesh (Ro 7:24, 25; Ga 5:24); over the world (1Jo 5:4, 5); over all that exalts itself (2Co 10:5); over death and the grave (Isa

25:8; 26:19; Ho 13:14; 1Co 15:54, 55); triumphant (Ro 8:37; 2Co 10:5).

They who overcome in, shall eat of the hidden manna (Re 2:17); eat of the tree of life (Re 2:7); be clothed in white raiment (Re 3:5); be pillars in the temple of God (Re 3:12); sit with Christ in his throne (Re 3:21); have a white stone, and in it a new name written (Re 2:17); have power over the nations (Re 2:26); have the name of God written upon them by Christ (Re 3:12); have God as their God (Re 21:7); have the morning star (Re 2:28); inherit all things (Re 21:7); be confessed by Christ before God the Father (Re 3:5); be sons of God (Re 21:7); not be hurt by the second death (Re 2:11); not have their names blotted out of the book of life (Re 3:5).

Symbolized by a red horse (Re 6:4).

In Heaven: Symbolical (Re 12:7).

WARFARE (See War.) Spiritual (see Figurative, under War.)

WAR SONGS. Celebrating, the destruction of Pharaoh's army (Ex 15:1-21); victory over Sihon, king of the Amorites (Nu 21:24-30); victory over Sisera (J'g 5).

David's lament over the defeat of Saul (2Sa 1:19-27). Celebrating David's victories over his enemies and his deliverance from Saul (2Sa 22).

WARNING (See Wicked, Warned.)

WARRIORS (Nu 32:17; Jos 4:13; 1Ch 8:40; 12:2, 8, 21; 2Ch 14:8; 17:18; 25:5; 26:13).

WASHING. Of hands, a token of innocency (De 21:6; Ps 26:6; 73:13; M't 27:24).

See Ablution; Purification.

Figurative: Of regeneration (Ps 51:7; Pr 30:12; Isa 1:16; 4:4; Zec 13:1; 1Co 6:11; Eph 5:26; Tit 3:5).

WASTE PLACES, restored (Isa 35:1; 41:19; 44:26; 49:19; 51:3; 52:9; 58:12; 61:4; Eze 36:10).

WATCH, man or group of men set to guard a city, crops, etc (Ne 4:9; M't 27:62-66).

WATCHES OF THE NIGHT, divisions into which hours of the night were divided. Jews had a threefold division; Romans, fourfold (J'g 7:19; M'k 6:48).

WATCHFULNESS (Ps 102:7; Hab 2:1; 1Co 9:27). Over the tongue (Ps 39:1; 141:3; Jas 3:5-8).

With prayer (Ne 4:9; M't 26:41; M'k 13:33; Eph 6:18; Col 4:2; 1Pe 4:7).

Enjoined (De 4:15; 6:17; Jos 22:5; 23:11; 1Ki 2:3, 4; 8:25; 2Ch 19:7; Job 36:18-21; Pr 8:34; 16:17; Na 2:1; M't 18:10; 24:42-51; 25:13; M'k 4:24; 13:32-37; Lu 8:18; 11:35; 12:35-40; 17:3; 21:34-36; Ro 11:20; 1Co 10:12; 11:28; 16:13; Ga 6:1; Eph 5:15; Col 2:8; 1Th 5:4, 6, 21; Heb 2:1; 1Pe 5:8; 2Pe 1:19; 1Jo 5:18).

Upon Israel (De 27:9). Upon young men (Ps 119:9; Pr 4:23-27). Upon married men (Mal 2:15). Upon ministers (Ac 20:28-31; 1Co 3:10; Col 4:2; 1Ti 4:16; 2Ti 4:5).

Over motives (M't 6:1-5). Over conscience (Lu 11:35). Over the heart (Pr 4:23; 28:26).

Against: hypocrisy (M't 16:6); apostasy (2Jo 8); lethargy (Ro 13:11; 1Pe 1:13, 17); backsliding (De 4:9, 23; Heb 3:12; 12:15; Jude 20, 21; Re 3:2, 3, 11); worldliness (1Co 7:29-31); covetousness (M't 24:42-47; M'k 13:33-37; Lu 12:15, 35-40); idolatry (Ex 23:13; De 4:23; 11:16; 12:13); evil associations (Ex 34:12; Ph'p 3:2; 2Pe 3:17); false teachers (M't 7:15; M'k 13:22, 23; Ac 20:28-31; 1Jo 4:1); deceivers (M't 24:4).

See Temptation.

WATCHMAN, a sentinel. On the walls of cities (Song 3:3; 5:7); of Jerusalem (2Sa 13:34; 18:24, 25; Ne 4:9; 7:3; Isa 52:8; 62:6); of Babylon (Jer 51:12). On towers (2Ki 9:17; 2Ch 20:24; Isa 21:5-12; Jer 31:6). At the gates of the temple (2Ki 11:6, 7). Alarm of, given by trumpets (Eze 33:3-6). Unfaithfulness in the discharge of duty of, punished by death (Eze 33:6; M't 28:14; Ac 12:19).

WATER. Creation of (Ps 148:4, 5). Covered the whole earth (Ge 1:9). Daily allowance of (Eze 4:11). City waterworks (2Ki 20:20). Vision of, by Ezekiel (Eze 47:1-5). Of separation (Nu 19:2-22). Libation of (1Sa 7:6). Irrigation with (see Irrigation). Miraculously supplied to the Israelites (Ex 17:1, 6; Nu 20:11); to Samson (J'g 15:19); to Jehoshaphat's army (2Ki 3:16-20). Purified by Elisha (2Ki 2:19-22). Red Sea divided (Ex 14:21, 22); the river Jordan (Jos 3:14-17; 2Ki 2:6-8, 14). Jesus walks on (M't 14:25). Changed to wine (Joh 2:1-11); to blood (Re 16:3-5).

Figurative: Water of life (Joh 4:14; 7:37-39; Re 21:6; 22:17). Of affliction (2Sa 22:17; Ps 69:1; Isa 30:20; 43:2). Of salvation (Isa 12:3; 49:10; 55:1; Eze 36:25; Joh 4:10; 7:38). Domestic love (Pr 5:15).

Symbolical: Isa 8:7; Re 8:11; 12:15; 16:4; 17:1, 15.

WATER OF BITTERNESS, water mingled with dust which a woman suspected of unfaithfulness was expected to drink to prove her innocence (Nu 5:12-31).

WATER OF JEALOUSY (See Water of Bitterness.)

WATER OF SEPARATION, water for removal of impurity (Nu 19:9, 13, 20, 21; 31:23).

WATERPOT, earthen jars for carrying or holding water (Joh 4:28).

WATERSPOUT, cataract (Ps 42:7).

WAVE OFFERING, sacrificial portion waved before the Lord.

WAX (Ps 22:14; 68:2; 97:5; Mic 1:4).

WAY. *Figurative:* Of holiness (Ps 16:11; Isa 35:8, 9; Jer 6:16; Ho 14:9). Of righteousness, narrow (M't 7:14). Of sin, broad (M't 7:13). Jesus the (Joh 14:6; Heb 9:8). Doctrines taught by Christ (Ac 9:2; 19:23; 22:4; 24:14, 22).

WAYFARING MAN, traveler (J'g 19:17; 2Sa 12:4; Isa 33:8; 35:8).

WAYS, DIVINE (Ps 18:30; 145:17; Isa 55:9; Da 4:37; Ho 14:9; Hab 3:6; Ro 11:33; Re 15:3).

WEAK. Duty of the strong to (Job 4:3, 4; Isa 35:3-7; M't 25:35, 40; Ro 14:1-23; 15:1-3; 1Co 8:7-13; 9:22; 2Co 11:29; Ga 6:1, 2; Jas 5:19, 20).

See Kindness.

WEALTH, abundance of possessions whether material, social, or spiritual. In early history of Israel wealth consisted largely of flocks and herds, silver and gold, brass, iron, and clothing (Jos 22:8). God taught Israel that He was the giver of their wealth (De 8:18); taught them to be liberal (Pr 11:24). Jesus did not condemn wealth, but stressed the handicap of wealth to one wanting to enter the kingdom of God (M't 19:24; Lu 16:19-31).

WEAN, WEANING, to wean is to accustom a child to depend upon other food than its mother's milk; celebrated by a feast (Ge 21:8) and with an offering (1Sa 1:24).

WEAPONS (See Armor; Arms.)

WEASEL, a small, carnivorous animal, allied to the ferret; for Israelites, unclean (Le 11:29).

WEATHER. There is no Hebrew word corresponding to "weather," but the Israelites were keenly aware of weather phenomena. The great topographical diversity of Palestine assures a variety of weather on a given day: on the top of Mt. Hermon (9,000 feet above sea level) there is snow on the ground the year round; while at Jericho in summer (1,300 feet below sea level) the heat is very oppressive, and the region around the Dead Sea (3,000 feet below sea level) is intolerable. On the coast even the hottest summer day is made bearable by refreshing breezes from the Mediterranean. Signs of (M't 16:2, 3). Sayings concerning (Job 37:9, 17, 22).

WEAVING (Isa 19:9; 38:12). Bezaleel skilled in (Ex 35:35). Wrought by women (2Ki 23:7). Of the ephod (Ex 28:32, 39:22). Of coats (Ex 39:27).

Weaver's shuttle (Job 7:6); beam (J'g 16:14; 2Sa 21:19; 1Ch 11:23).

WEDDING, a joyous occasion, celebrated with music, feasting, drinking of wine, joking; after the Exile written contracts were drawn up and sealed; bridegroom went to bride's home with friends and escorted her to his own house (M't 25:7); festive apparel expected of guests; festivities lasted one or two weeks (Ge 29:27; J'g 14:12).

WEDGE, literally "tongue" (Jos 7:21, 24). Occurrence of word in Isa 13:12 is an error. ASV properly renders "golden wedge" as "pure gold."

WEEDING (M't 13:28).

WEEK (See Calendar; Time.)

WEEKS, FEAST OF, Pentecost, celebrated 50 days after sheaf waving on 16th Nisan (Ex 34:18-26).

WEEPING (Ro 12:15; 1Co 7:30). In perdition (M't 8:12; 22:13; 24:51; 25:30). None in heaven (Re 7:17). Penitential (Jer 50:4; Joe 2:12). Instances of penitential: The Israelites (J'g 2:4, 5). Peter (M't 26:75; M'k 14:72; Lu 22:62). While doing good (Ps 126:5, 6). For others (Jer 9:1). On account of tribulation (Jer 22:10; Am 5:16, 17).

Instances of: Of Abraham for Sarah (Ge 23:2). Of Esau (Ge 27:38). Of Jacob and Esau (Ge 33:4). Of Jacob (Ge 37:35). Of Joseph (Ge 42:24; 43:30; 45:2, 14; 46:29; 50:1, 17). Of Hannah (1Sa 1:7). Of Jonathan and David (1Sa 20:41). Of David (2Sa 1:17; 3:32; 13:36; 15:23, 30; 18:33). Of Hezekiah (2Ki 20:3; Isa 38:3). Of Jesus, over Jerusalem (Lu 19:41); at the grave of Lazarus (Joh 11:35). Of Mary, when she washed the feet of Jesus (Lu 7:38; Joh 11:2, 33). Of Mary Magdalene (Joh 20:11). Of Paul (Ac 20:19; Ph'p 3:18).

WEIGHTS AND MEASURES. Balances were used for scales (Le 19:36; Pr 16:11) and stones for weights (Le 19:36). Some Biblical measures: 1. *Liquid. Log* equals ⅔ pint; *hin* equals 12 logs, or one gallon; *bath* equals six *hins*, or six gallons; *cor* equals 10 *baths*, or 60 gallons.

2. *Dry. Cab* equals two plus pints; *omer* equals 1⅘ *cabs*, or four pints; *seah* equals 3⅓ *omers*, or ⅕ bushel; *ephah* equals three *seahs*, or ⅗ bushel; *homer* equals 10 *ephahs*, or 6¼ bushels.

3. *Length. Finger* equals ¾ inches; *palm* equals four fingers, or three inches; *span* equals three *palms*, or nine inches; *cubit* equals two *spans*, or 18 inches; *fathom* equals four *cubits*, or six feet.

4. *Weights. Gerah* equals nine grains; *beqa* equals 10 *gerahs*, or 88 grains; *shekel* equals two *beqas*, or .4 ounce; *maneh* equals 50 *shekels*, or 20 ounces; *talent* equals 60 *manehs*, or 75.5 pounds.

WELLS. The occasion of feuds: Between Abraham and Abimelech (Ge 21:25-30); between Isaac and Abimelech (Ge 26:15-22, 32, 33). Of Jacob (Joh 4:6). Of Solomon (Ec 2:6). Of Uzziah (2Ch 26:10). Of Hezekiah (see Gihon). At Haran (Ge 24:16).

Figurative: Of salvation (Isa 12:3; Joh 4:14). Without water (Jer 15:18; 2Pe 2:17).

See Spring.

WEN, a tumor (Le 22:22).

WEST, used figuratively with "east" to denote great distance (Ps 103:12).

WHALE. 1. Any large sea animal (Ge 1:21; Eze 32:2).

2. Sea monster (M't 12:40). Great fish in Jonah 1:17.

WHEAT (Re 6:6). Grown in Palestine (1Ki 5:11; Ps 81:16; 147:14). Offerings of (Nu 18:12). Prophecy of the sale of a measure of, for a penny (Re 6:6).

Parables of (M't 13:25; Lu 16:7). Winnowing of (M't 3:12; Lu 3:17). Ground in a mortar (Pr 27:22). Chaff of (Jer 23:28; M't 3:12; Lu 3:17). Growth of, figurative of vicarious death (Joh 12:24).

Figurative: Of God's mercy (Ps 81:16; 147:14). Of self-righteousness (Jer 12:13).

WHEEL. Potter's (Jer 18:3).

Figurative: Pr 20:26; Ec 12:6.

Symbolical: Eze 1:15-21; 3:13; 10:9-19; 11:22.

WHELP, the young of a dog or a beast of prey; a cub (Ge 49:9; De 33:22; Jer 51:38; Na 2:11, 12).

WHIP (1Ki 12:11; Pr 26:3; Na 3:2).

WHIRLWIND. Destructive (Pr 1:27). From the south in the land of Uz (Job 37:9); in the valley of the Euphrates (Isa 21:1); in the land of Canaan (Zec 9:14). From the north (Eze 1:4). Elijah translated in (2Ki 2:1, 11); God answered Job in (Job 38:1).

See Meteorology.

Figurative: Of the judgment of God (Jer 23:19; 30:23). Of the fruits of unrighteousness (Ho 8:7). Of divine judgments (Eze 1:4).

WHISPER (See Busybody; Slander; Talebearer.)

WHISPERER, a slanderer (Ro 1:29; 2Co 12:20).

See Slander; Speaking, Evil.

WHITE (See Color.)

WHORE, prostitute or harlot; whoredom, a capital crime (Ge 38:24); often used figuratively for apostasy and idolatry (Ex 34:15f; Le 17:7; De 31:16; J'g 2:17; 1Ch 5:25; Ho 1:2).

WHOREDOM, licentious rites of, in idolatrous worship (Le 19:29; De 31:16; J'g 2:17; 2Ki 9:22).

See Idolatry.

Figurative: Eze 16; 23; Re 17:1-6.

WHOREMONGER (Re 21:8; 22:15).

See Adultery; Sensuality.

WHOSOEVER, Of Condemnation (Ex 32:33; De 18:19; M't 5:22; Joh 8:34; Ro 2:1; 1Jo 2:23; 3:4, 10, 15; 2Jo 9).

Of Salvation (Lu 12:8; Joh 4:14; Ac 10:43; 1Jo 5:1; Re 22:17).

WICKED. Compared with: Abominable branches (Isa 14:19); ashes under the feet (Mal 4:3); bad fishes (M't 13:48); beasts

(Ps 49:12; 2Pe 2:12); the blind (Zep 1:17; M't 15:14); brass and iron (Jer 6:28; Eze 22:18); briers and thorns (Isa 55:13; Eze 2:6); bulls of Bashan (Ps 22:12); carcases trodden under feet (Isa 14:19); chaff (Job 21:18; Ps 1:4; M't 3:12); clouds without water (Jude 12); corn blasted (2Ki 19:26); corrupt trees (Lu 6:43); deaf adders (Ps 58:4); dogs (Pr 26:11; M't 7:6; 2Pe 2:22); dross (Ps 119:119; Eze 22:18, 19); early dew that passeth away (Ho 13:3); evil figs (Jer 24:8); fading oaks (Isa 1:30); fiery oven (Ps 21:9; Ho 7:4); fire of thorns (Ps 118:12); fools building upon sand (M't 7:26); fuel of fire (Isa 9:19); garden without water (Isa 1:30); goats (M't 25:32); grass (Ps 37:2; 92:7); grass on the housetop (2Ki 19:26); green bay tree (Ps 37:35); green herbs (Ps 37:2); heath in the desert (Jer 17:6); horses rushing into the battle (Jer 8:6); idols (Ps 115:8); lions greedy of prey (Ps 17:12); melting wax (Ps 68:2); morning clouds (Ho 13:3); moth-eaten garments (Isa 50:9; 51:8); passing whirlwinds (Pr 10:25); potsherds (Pr 26:23); raging waves of the sea (Jude 13); reprobate silver (Jer 6:30); scorpions (Eze 2:6); serpents (Ps 58:4; M't 23:33); smoke (Ho 13:3); stony ground (M't 13:5); stubble (Job 21:18; Mal 4:1); swine (M't 7:6; 2Pe 2:22); tares (M't 13:38); troubled sea (Isa 57:20); visions of the night (Job 20:8); wandering stars (Jude 13); wayward children (M't 11:16); wells without water (2Pe 2:17); wheels (Ps 83:13); whited sepulchers (M't 23:27); wild ass's colts (Job 11:12).

God is angry with (Ps 5:5, 6; 7:11; Ro 9:13; 1Co 10:5). Spirit of God withdrawn from (Ge 6:3; Ho 4:17-19; Ro 1:24, 26, 28). Hate the righteous (M't 5:11, 12; Lu 6:22, 23). Worship of, offensive to God (Ps 50:16, 17; Isa 1:10-15).

Present and future state of the wicked and righteous contrasted (Job 8; Ps 49. See below).

Prosperity of (Job 5:3-5; 12:6; 15:21, 23, 27, 29; 20:5, 22; 21:7-13; Ps 37:1, 35, 36; 49:10-15; 73:3-22; 92:6, 7; Ec 8:12, 13; Jer 12:1, 2; Hab 1:3, 4, 13-17; Mal 3:15). Hate reproof (1Ki 22:8; 2Ch 18:7). God's mercy to (Job 33:14-30); love for (De 5:29; 32:29; M't 18:11-14; Joh 3:16, 17; Ro 5:8; 1Jo 3:16; 4:9, 10). Dread God (Job 18:11). Eliphaz's exhortation to (Job 22:21-30). Temporal punishment of (Job 15:20-35; 18:5-21; 20:5-29; 21:7-33; 24:2-24; 27:13-23; Jer 5:25; Eze 11:10; 12:19, 20; Zec 14:17-19). False hope of (Job 8:13-18).

Gospel invitation to, illustrated by the parables of the householder (M't 20:1-16); and marriage supper (M't 22:1-14).

Warned (Jer 7:13-15, 23-25; 25:4-6; 26:2-7, 12, 13; 29:17-19; Eze 33:8; Da 4:4-27; 5:4-29, Zep 2:1, 2; Lu 3:7-9; 1Co 10:11; Jude 4-7; Re 3:1-3, 16-19). Terrors of, at the judgment (Re 1:7). Death of (Ps 49:14; 73:4).

See Impenitence; Obduracy; Penitence; Reprobacy; Seekers; Sin, Confession of.

Contrasted with the righteous (Ps 1:1-6; 11:5; 17:14, 15; 32:10; 37:17-22, 37, 38; 73:1-28; 75:10; 91:7, 8; 107:33-38; 125:5; Pr 2:21, 22; 3:32, 33; 4:16-19; 10:3, 6, 9, 11, 16, 20, 21, 23-25, 28-32; 11:3, 5, 6, 8-11, 18-21, 23, 31; 12:2, 3, 5-7, 10, 12, 13, 21, 26; 13:5, 6, 9, 17, 21, 22, 25; 14:2, 11, 19, 22, 32; 15:6, 8, 9, 28, 29; 21:15, 18, 26, 29; 22:5, 8, 9; 24:16; 28:1, 4, 5, 13, 14, 18; 29:2, 6, 7, 27; Isa 32:1-8; 65:13, 14; Mal 3:18; Ro 2:7-10; Eph 2:12-14; Ph'p 2:15; 1Th 5:5-8; Tit 1:15; 1Pe 4:17, 18; 1Jo 1:6, 7; 3:3-17).

Described as: (Job 8:13-17; 15:16, 20-35; Ps 10:4-11; 36:1-4; 73:4-12; Isa 59:2-8; Jer 2:22-25). Abomination (Pr 13:9; 15:9; Ho 9:10). Alienated (Col 1:21). Beasts (Ps 49:20); dogs (Ps 59:6; Ec 3:18); horse rushing into battle (Jer 8:6). Blind (Eze 12:2). Carnal (Ro 8:5, 7, 8; 9:8). Children of the devil (Joh 3:44; Ac 13:10; 1Jo 3:10). Perverse (Jer 9:6; Ro 1:21; 2:4, 5; Ph'p 2:15). Despising God (Job 21:14; Ro 11:28). Contentious (Ro 2:8). Corrupt (Ps 53:1; 73:8; Isa 59:3; Jer 2:22; Eze 16:47; 20:16; Mic 7:2-4; Tit 1:15). Loving darkness (Joh 3:19, 20). Dead in sin (Eph 2:1-3; 1Jo 3:14). Delighting, in lies (Ps 62:4); in frowardness (Pr 2:13-19). Defiled (Tit 1:15, 16). Depraved (Isa 1:4-6; Jer 17:9; 30:12-15; Ro 1:20-32; 3:10-18; 1Ti 1:9, 10; 2Ti 3:2-9, 13; Tit 3:2; 2Pe 2:10, 12-19; Jude 12, 13). Destitute, of faithfulness (Ps 5:9); of the love of God (Joh 5:42). Devilish (1Jo 3:8). Devisers of mischief (Ps 52:1-4; 64:3-6; Pr 4:16; 6:12-15; 10:23; Isa 32:6, 7; Jer 4:22). Enemies (Ro 5:10; Col 1:21). Filthy (Ezr 9:11). In the gall of bitterness (Ac 8:23).

Uncircumcised (Isa 52:1; Jer 6:10; Eze 28:10; 31:18; 32:19-32). Uncircumcised of heart (Le 26:41; Eze 44:7; Ac 7:51); of lips (Ex 6:12).

Disobedient (Jer 11:8; Tit 1:16). Alienated from God (Col 1:21). Full of gall and venom (De 32:32, 33; Ps 58:3-5). Grievous sinners (Ge 13:13; 18:20; Job 22:5; Isa 1:4-6).

Hating, correction (Pr 15:10; Am 5:10); instruction (Ps 50:17; Pr 1:29, 30); the light (Joh 3:20).

Being in moral darkness (M't 4:16; 6:23; Lu 1:79; Eph 4:17, 18). Not knowing the way of the Lord (Jer 5:4). Lewd (Jer 11:15). Lost (M't 18:11; Lu 19:10). Loving wickedness (Ps 7:14; Jer 14:10; Ho 4:8; Mic 3:2). Malicious toward the righteous (Ps 37:12; 94:3-8; 140:9). Mocking sin (Ps 14:9). Obdurate (Ps 10:4, 11; Pr 1:29, 30; Isa 26:10, 11; Eze 3:7). Outsiders (M'k 4:11). Past feeling (Eph 4:19). Progressing in wickedness (Isa 30:1, 10, 11; Jer 9:3; 2Ti 3:13). Rebellious (De 9:24). Sensual (Ph'p 3:19; Jude 19). Servants of sin (Jo 8:34). Shameful (Eph 5:11, 12). Shameless (Jer 6:15; 8:12; Zep 3:5). Unscrupulous (Job 24:2-24; Ps 10:4-10; Isa 5:18-23; Jer 5:26-28; 9:2-6). Sold to work iniquity (1Ki 21:20). Stiff-necked (De 9:13; Ac 7:51). A troubled sea (Isa 57:20, 21 w Jas 1:6, 7). Under condemnation (Joh 3:18, 19). Unclean (Ezr 9:11; Job 14:4; Hag 2:14). Ungodly (Ro 5:6); without strength (Ro 5:6). Vomit (Le 18:25; see Re 3:16).

Wretched, miserable, poor, blind, naked (Re 3:17, 18).

Happiness of: Sensual (Isa 22:13; 56:12). Limited to this life (Lu 16:25). Ends suddenly (Job 21:12, 13; Lu 12:19, 20).

Hope of: Shall perish (Job 8:13; 11:20; 27:8; Pr 10:28).

Miscellany concerning: Hate reproof (1Ki 22:8; 2Ch 18:7). God's mercy to (Job 33:14-30). God's love for (De 5:29; 32:29; M't 18:12-14; Joh 3:16, 17; Ro 5:8; 1Jo 4:9, 10).

Gospel invitation to, illustrated by the parables of the householder (M't 20:1-16); and marriage supper (M't 22:1-14).

Terrors of, at the judgment (Re 1:7). Death of (Ps 49:14; 73:3, 4, 17-19).

Prayers of: Abominable to God (Pr 15:8, 29; 21:27; 28:9). Not answered (De 1:45; 1Sa 28:6; 2Sa 22:42; Job 27:9; 35:12, 13; Ps 18:41; 66:18; Pr 1:24-28; 21:13, 27; Isa 1:15; 59:2; Jer 11:11; 14:12; 18:17; La 3:8, 44; Eze 8:18; 20:3, 31; Ho 5:6; Mic 3:4; Zec 7:13; Mal 1:9; 2:11-13; Joh 9:31; Jas 1:6, 7; 4:3; 1Pe 3:7). On behalf of, not answered (De 3:26; Jer 15:11).

Prosperity of (Job 12:6; 21:7-13; Ps 73:3-12; Jer 12:1, 2; Mal 3:15). Brief (Job 5:3-5; 15:21, 23, 27, 29; 20:5, 22, 23; 21:17, 18; 24:24; Ps 37:35, 36; 49:10-14; 73:18, 19; 92:7; Ec 8:12, 13).

Punishment of (Ge 4:7; Ex 20:5; 34:7; Nu 32:33; 1Sa 3:11-14; 2Sa 3:39; 7:14; 22:27, 28; 23:6, 7; 1Ki 21:20, 21; Job 8:20, 22; 11:20; 18:5-21; 19:29; 21:7-33; 27:13-23; 36:12, 17; Ps 3:7; 5:5; 18:14, 26, 27; 36:12; Ps 37:1, 2, 9, 10, 17, 20, 22, 34-38; 64:7, 8; 73:18-20, 27; 91:8; 97:3; 107:17, 33, 34; 119:21, 118, 119, 155; 129:4; 146:9; 147:6; Pr 3:3; 10:3, 6-8, 14, 24, 25, 27-31; 11:3, 5-8, 19, 21, 23, 31; 13:2, 5, 6, 9, 21, 25; 14:12, 19, 32; 16:4, 5; 22:5, 23; 26:10; Ec 8:12, 13; Isa 3:11; 26:21; Jer 21:14; 36:31; La 3:39; Eze 3:18-20; 18:1-32; 33:7-20; Ho 14:9; Am 3:2; Mic 2:3; 6:13; M't 15:13 w Joh 15:2; Ro 1:18; 2:5, 8, 9; Col 3:25; 1Th 1:10; 1Pe 3:12; 2Pe 2:3-9, 12-17; Jude 5-7; Re 14:10, 11).

By: Chastisements (Ps 89:32; 1Co 5:5; 1Ti 1:20). Judgments (Ex 32:35; Le 26:14-39; De 11:26-28; 28:15-68; 30:15, 18, 19; Job 20:5-29; Ps 11:6; 21:9, 10; 39:11; 75:8; 78:49-51; Isa 5:11-14, 24; 9:18; 10:3; 13:9, 11, 14-22; 24:17, 18; 28:18-22; 65:12-15; Jer 5:25; 8:12-14, 20-22; 14:10, 12; 25:31; 44:2-14, 23-29; 49:10; La 3:39; 4:22; 5:16, 17; Eze 5:4, 8-17; 9:5-7, 10; 20:8; 22:14, 20, 21, 31; 24:13, 14; Ho 2:9-13; 5:4-6, 9; 9:7, 9, 15; Joe 2:1, 2; 3:13-16; Am 5:18-20; Lu 12:46; 1Co 10:5-11; 1Ti 5:24; Heb 10:26-31; 1Pe 4:17, 18). Sorrow (Ge 3:16-19; Job 15:20-24; Ps 32:10; Ec 2:26; Isa 50:11). Trouble (Isa 48:22; 57:20, 21). Being rejected of the Lord (1Ch

28:9; 2Ch 15:2; M't 10:33; M'k 8:38; Lu 9:26; 13:27, 28 w M't 7:23; Joh 8:21; 2Ti 2:12, 13; Heb 6:8). Being excluded from the kingdom of heaven (1Co 6:9, 10; Ga 5:19-21; Eph 5:5; Re 21:27; 22:19). Being blotted from God's book (Ex 32:33). Destruction (Ge 6:3, 7, 12, 13; Nu 15:31; De 7:9, 10; 1Sa 12:25; 1Ch 10:13, 14; Job 4:8, 9; 31:3; Ps 2:9; 7:11-13; 9:5, 17; 34:16, 21; 52:5; 55:19, 23; 92:7, 9; 94:13, 23; 101:8; 104:35; 106:18, 43; 145:20; Pr 2:22; 12:7; 21:12, 15, 16; 24:20; Isa 11:4; 13:8; 64:5-7; Jer 13:14, 16, 22; Eze 25:7; Ho 7:12, 13; Am 8:14; Na 1:2, 8-10; Zep 1:12-18; Zec 5:2-4; Mal 4:1; M't 3:10, 12 w Lu 3:17; M't 7:13, 19; 10:28 w Lu 12:4, 5; M't 21:41, 44 w M'k 12:1-9 & Lu 20:16, 18; M't 24:50, 51; Lu 9:24, 25 w M't 16:26 & M'k 8:36; Lu 19:27; Joh 5:29; Ac 3:23; Ro 2:12; 9:22; 1Co 3:17; Ph'p 3:19; 1Th 5:3; 2Th 2:8-10). Sudden destruction (Pr 6:15; 24:22; 28:18; 29:1). Everlasting destruction (2Th 1:9). Everlasting contempt (Da 12:2). Everlasting fire (Isa 28:18-22; M't 18:8, 9; 25:41; M'k 9:43; Re 20:15; 21:8). Death (Ge 2:17; Ps 1:4-6; Pr 16:25; 19:16; Ho 13:1, 3; Am 9:1-5, 10; Ro 5:12, 21; 6:16, 21; 8:2, 6, 13; 1Co 15:21, 22; 2Co 7:10; Ga 6:8; 1Jo 3:14, 15; Jas 1:15; 5:20; Re 2:22, 23). The second death (Re 21:8). The damnation of hell (M't 23:33; M'k 16:16; Joh 3:15, 16, 18, 36). Being cast into outer darkness (M't 8:12; 22:13; 25:30).

The last judgments (Re 6:15-17; 9:4-6, 15, 18; 11:18; 16:2-21; 18:5; 19:15, 17-21; 20:10, 15; 21:8, 27; 22:19).

Everlasting (M't 25:46; Re 14:10, 11; 20:10).

Degrees in (M't 10:15; 11:22, 24; M'k 12:40).

No escape from (Job 34:22; 1Th 5:3; Heb 2:3).

Set forth in parables of: the tares (M't 13:24-30, 38-42, 49, 50); the talents (M't 25:14-30); the barren fig tree (Lu 13:6-9); the man who built his house on the sand (M't 7:26, 27; Lu 6:49); Lazarus and the rich man (Lu 16:22-28). Woes denounced against (Isa 5:8, 11, 18-23; M't 26:24; M'k 14:21; Lu 11:52; 17:1, 2; 22:22; Jude 11).

God has no pleasure in the death of (Eze 18:23; 33:11).

See Punishment.

Warned (Jer 7:13-15, 23-25; 25:4-6; 26:2-7, 12, 13; 29:17-19; Eze 33:8; Da 4:4-27; 5:4-29; Zep 2:1, 2; Lu 3:7-9; 1Co 10:11; Re 3:1-3, 16-19).

See Judgments; Hell; Punishment.

WIDOW (Job 22:5, 9; 1Ti 5:3-6, 9-12, 16). High priest forbidden to marry (Le 21:14). Supported by father, when daughter of priest (Le 22:13). Vows of, binding (Nu 30:9). Entitled to glean in orchards and harvest fields (De 24:19-21).

Levirate marriage of (De 25:5-10). Marriage of, authorized (Ro 7:3; 1Co 7:39; 1Ti 5:14). Marriage of discouraged (1Co 7:8, 9).

Kindness to, exemplified by Job (Job 29:13; 31:16, 22). God, the friend of (De 10:18; Ps 68:5; 146:9; Pr 15:25; Jer 49:11).

Care of, in the Christian churches (Ac 6:1-7; 1Ti 5:9, 16). Care of, enjoined (De 14:28, 29; 16:11, 14; Isa 1:17; Jer 7:6, 7; 1Ti 5:3; Jas 1:27).

Neglected (Ac 6:1). Oppressed (Job 24:3, 21; Ps 94:6; Isa 1:23; Eze 22:7; M't 23:14; M'k 12:40; Lu 20:47). Oppression of, forbidden (Ex 22:22-24; De 24:17; 27:19; Isa 10:2; Jer 22:3; Zec 7:10; Mal 3:5).

Widow's dowry: See Dowry.

Instances of: Naomi (Ru 1:3). Ruth (Ru 1-4). The widow of Zarephath, who sustained Elijah during a famine (1Ki 17). The woman whose sons Elisha saved from being sold for debt (2Ki 4:1-7). Anna (Lu 2:36, 37). The woman who gave two mites in the temple (M'k 12:41-44; Lu 21:2); of Nain, whose only son Jesus raised from the dead (Lu 7:11-15).

See Woman; Marriage, Levirate.

WIFE (Pr 30:23). Called: Help (Ge 2:18, 20); desire of the eyes (Eze 24:10).

Compared to fruitful vine (Ps 128:3).

The judgment denounced against Eve (Ge 3:16).

Contentious (Pr 19:13; 21:9, 19; 25:24). Instances of, Zipporah (Ex 4:25).

Unfaithful (Nu 5:12-31). Instances of, Potiphar's (Ge 39:7); Bath-sheba (2Sa 11:2-5).

Tactful, Abigail (1Sa 25:3, 14-34); Esther (Es 5:5-8; 7:1-4). Prudent (Pr 19:14). Loyal, Jacob's (Ge 31:14-16). Virtuous (Pr 12:4; 31:10-12). Incorruptible, Vashti (Es 1:10-12). Wise (Pr 14:1).

Beloved, by Isaac (Ge 24:67); by Jacob (Ge 29:30). Hated (Ge 29:31-33).

Taking of, commended (Pr 18:22; 1Co 7:2; 1Ti 5:14). Bought (Ge 29:18-30; 31:41; Ex 21:7-11; Ru 4:10). Obtained by kidnapping (J'g 21:21). Procured (Ge 24; 34:4-10; 38:6).

Duty of husband to (1Co 7:2-5, 27; Eph 5:25, 28, 31, 33; Col 3:19; 1Pe 3:7). Relation of, to husband (Ge 2:18, 23, 24; 1Co 7:2-5, 10, 11, 13, 39; 11:3, 8, 9, 11, 12).

Duty of, to husband: To be obedient (1Co 14:34, 35; Eph 5:22, 24; Col 3:18; Tit 2:5; 1Pe 3:1, 6); to be affectionate (Tit 2:4); to be faithful (Tit 3:11).

Domestic duties of (Ge 18:6; Pr 31:13-27).

Vows of (Nu 30:6-16).

Instances of evil influence of, upon husbands: Eve (Ge 3:6, 12). Solomon's wives (1Ki 11:1-8; Ne 13:26). Jezebel (1Ki 21:25; 2Ki 9:30-37). Haman's (Es 5:14). Herodias (M't 14:3, 6-11; M'k 6:17, 24-28).

See Husband; Marriage; Parents; Widow; Women.

WILDERNESS. Wandering of the Israelites in (see Israel). Typical of the sinner's state (De 32:10). Jesus' temptation in (M't 4:1; M'k 1:12, 13; Lu 4:1).

See Desert.

WILL. *The Mental Faculty:* Freedom of, recognized by God (Ge 4:6-10; De 5:29; 1Ki 20:42; Isa 1:18-20; 43:26; Jer 36:3, 7; Joh 7:17).

See Blessings, Contingent on Obedience; Choice; Contingencies.

WILL. *Of God.* The supreme rule of duty (M't 6:10; 12:50 w M'k 3:35; M't 26:39, 42; M'k 14:36; Lu 22:42; Joh 4:34; 5:30; 6:38-40; Ro 12:2; Eph 5:17). Plans of the righteous subject to (Ac 18:21; Ro 1:10; 15:32; 1Co 4:19; 16:7; Heb 6:3; Jas 4:15). "Lord's prayer" concerns (M't 6:10; Lu 11:2). See Agency.

Reasons for wanting to know: Love for God (Joh 14:15, 21, 23, 24); desire to please God (1Jo 3:22). Blessings in this life (1Pe 3:10-12); rewards in future life (1Co 3:10-15; 2Ti 4:8; Heb 10:35). Avoid chastisement (1Co 3:16, 17; 11:31, 32; 1Pe 4:17). Good example to other believers (1Co 4:16; 1Th 1:7; 2Th 3:9; Heb 13:7). Not be ashamed at Second Coming (1Jo 2:28). Glorify God (1Co 10:31; Col 3:17, 23; Heb 12:10; 2Pe 1:4).

Defined: God's purpose (2Ti 1:9 w Eph 1:9); God's plan (1Co 12:11; 2Co 1:15; Jas 3:4); God's will (Ac 27:12; Eph 1:11). See Supreme Rule of duty, above.

Obligation to know (Eph 5:15-17).

How God reveals: Through His Word (Ps 119:105; 2Ti 3:16, 17). Through control of thoughts, indirectly (2Co 7:8-11; 12:7; 1Pe 1:6, 7; 4:12, 13; Jas 1:2-4); directly (Pr 16:1, 9; 21:1 w 17:17; Eph 2:13); through Satan (Job 1:12; 2:6). Through control of circumstances (Pr 16:9; 20:24; Ac 2:23; 4:28; Eph 1:11). Until revelation complete, through dreams (Ge 20:3, 6; 31:11, 24; 1Ki 3:5; M't 2:12-13); and visions (Ge 15:1; Zec 1:7, 8; Ac 10:10, 11).

Prerequisites: Spiritual maturity (Isa 55:8, 9; 1Co 2:7; Eph 4:14; Col 1:9; 1Ti 3:6; Heb 5:13, 14; 13:21); through the teaching ministry of the Holy Spirit (Joh 16:13, 14; 1Co 2:12-14; 1Jo 2:27); through application in testings (Ph'p 3:15; Heb 5:14; 12:7, 11; Jas 1:2-5). Yieldedness or self-denial (Ro 6:13, 19; 12:1; 1Pe 2:9; Re 1:6); discipleship (M't 16:24; M'k 8:34; Lu 9:23). Desire to, know God's will (Joh 7:17); do it (M'k 4:24, 25; Ac 10:22, 35, 44, 47; 1Jo 2:11). Willingness to obey daily (M't 16:24; M'k 8:34; Lu 9:23; Ro 6:16; Ph'p 2:13; 2Pe 2:19). Faith (Ps 37:5; Pr 3:5, 6; Ro 14:23; 2Co 5:7; Ph'p 2:13; Heb 11:17, 27). Patience (Ps 37:7; Jas 1:5, 6). Common sense (Tit 2:12). Peace of God (Col 3:15); a clear conscience (Ro 14:23).

A Testament: Of Abraham (Ge 25:5, 6). Jacob (Ge 48:49). David (1Ki 2:1-9). Jehoshaphat (2Ch 21:3). May not be annulled (Ga 3:15). In force after death only (Heb 9:16, 17).

See Testament.

WILLFULNESS (See Obduracy; Self-Will.)

WILLOW, type of tree growing along brook or near water; several species in Palestine; symbol of joy (Le 23:40; Job 40:22), sorrow (Ps 137:2).

WILLOWS, BROOK OF THE, brook on boundary of Moab (Isa 15:7).

WILLS, statements, oral or written in form, to which law courts give effect, by which property may be disposed of after death (Heb 9:16, 17).

WIMPLE (Isa 3:22).

WIND, blasting (2Ki 19:7, 35).

East: Hot and blasting in Egypt (Ge 41:6); in the valley of the Euphrates (Eze 19:12); in Canaan (Ho 13:15; Lu 12:55); at Nineveh (Jon 4:8); tempestuous in Uz (Job 27:21).

West: Took away the plague of locusts from the land of Egypt (Ex 10:19).

North: Free from humidity in Canaan (Pr 25:23).

South: Soothing (Job 37:17); tempestuous (Job 37:9); purifying (Job 37:21).

Figurative: Ho 4:19. Of the judgments of God (Jer 22:22; Ho 13:15; M't 7:25). Of the Spirit (Joh 3:8). Of heresy (Eph 4:14).

WINDOW (Ge 6:16; 26:8; Jos 2:15, 21; 1Ki 6:4; Eze 40:16-36; Ac 20:9).

WINE (Ps 4:7; Isa 25:6; 56:12; Jer 40:10, 12; Ho 2:8, 22; 7:14; Joe 1:5; 2:24; Am 6:6; Hab 2:5: Zec 9:17; 10:7).

Made from grapes (Ge 40:11; 49:11; Isa 25:6; Jer 40:10, 12); from pomegranates (Song 8:2). Kept in jars (Jer 13:12; 48:12; in skins (Jos 9:4, 13; Job 32:19; M't 9:17; Lu 5:37, 38); in bottles (Jos 9:4, 13; Job 32:19; Jer 13:12; 48:12; M't 9:17; Lu 5:37, 38). Cellars for (1Ch 27:27). Storehouses for (2Ch 32:8). Plentiful in Canaan (De 33:28; 2Ki 18:32). New (Hag 1:11; M'k 2:22; Lu 5:37-39). Old (Lu 5:39).

Medicinal use of (Pr 31:6, 7); recommended by Paul to Timothy (1Ti 5:23). Used at meals (M't 26:27-29; M'k 14:23). Made by Jesus at the marriage feast in Cana (Joh 2:9, 10). Sacramental use of (M't 26:27-29; Lu 22:17-20).

Forbidden, to priests while on duty (Le 10:9; Eze 44:21); to Nazarites (Nu 6:2, 3; see Nazarite); to kings (Pr 31:4).

Abstinence from, of Daniel (Da 1:5, 8, 16; 10:3); of courtiers of Ahasuerus (Es 1:8); of the Rechabites (Jer 35:6, 8, 14, 16); of Timothy (1Ti 5:23). Samson's mother forbidden to drink (J'g 13:4, 5). Denied to the Israelites in the wilderness, that they might know that the Lord was their God (De 29:6).

Offered with sacrifices (Ex 29:40; Le 23:13; Nu 15:5, 10; 18:12; 28:7, 14; De 14:23; Ne 10:39; 28:7, 14). Given by Melchizedek to Abraham (Ge 14:18).

Fermented (Le 10:9; Nu 6:3; 28:7; De 14:26; 29:6; Pr 23:31, 32; M'k 2:22). Refined (Isa 25:6; Jer 48:11). Of staggering (Ps 60:3). Inflames the eyes (Ge 49:12). Commerce in (Re 18:13). Banquets of (Es 5:6). Children sold for (Joe 3:3).

Given to Jesus at the crucifixion (M't 27:48; M'k 15:23; Lu 23:36; Joh 19:29). Jesus accused of drinking (M't 11:19; Lu 7:34). Intoxication from, falsely charged against apostles (Ac 2:13).

Intoxication from the use of (Ps 60:3, 7; 104:15; Pr 4:17; 31:6, 7; Jer 23:9; Joe 1:5; Hab 2:5; Zec 10:7). Vanity of (Ec 2:3, 11).

Instances of Intoxication From: Noah (Ge 9:21); Lot (Ge 19:32); Joseph and his brethren (Ge 43:34); Nabal (1Sa 25:36); Amnon (2Sa 13:28, 29); Ahasuerus (Es 1:10); kings of Israel (Ho 7:5); falsely charged against the disciples (Ac 2:13).

Figurative: Of the divine judgments (Ps 60:3; 75:8; Jer 51:7). Of the joy of wisdom (Pr 9:2, 5). Of the joys of religion (Isa 25:6; 55:1; Joe 2:19). Of abominations (Re 14:8; 16:19).

Symbolical: Of the blood of Jesus (M't 26:28; M'k 14:23, 24; Lu 22:20; Joh 6:53-56).

Admonitions against: use as a beverage (Le 10:9; Nu 6:3; J'g 13:4; Pr 20:1; 21:17; 23:29-32; 31:4, 5; Isa 5:11, 22; 24:9; 28:1, 3, 7; 35:2-10, 14, 18, 19; Jer 23:9; Eze 44:21; Ho 4:11; Lu 1:15; Ro 14:21); the immoderate use of (Eph 5:18; Tit 2:3). See Abstinence; Drunkenness.

See Vine; Vineyard.

WINEBIBBER, Jesus falsely accused of being a (M't 11:19; Lu 7:34).

WINE PRESS (Nu 18:27, 30; De 15:14; J'g 6:11). In vineyards (Isa 5:2; M't 21:33; M'k 12:1). Trodden with joy and shouting (Jer 48:33).

Figurative: Treading the, of the sufferings of Christ (Isa 63:2, 3); of the judgments of God (La 1:15; Re 14:19, 20).

WINESKIN, made of tanned whole skins of animals (M't 9:17).

WING, often used figuratively (Ps 18:10; 55:6; 68:13; Pr 23:5; M't 23:37).

WINNOWING, separating kernels of threshed grain from chaff; done by shaking bunches of grain into breeze-stirred air so that the kernels fall to the ground, while the chaff is blown away by the wind (Ru 3:2; Isa 30:24).

WINTER. Annual return of, shall never cease (Ge 8:22). Plowing in, in Canaan (Pr 20:4 [marg.]). Rainy season in, in Canaan (Song 2:11). Shipping suspended in, on the Mediterranean Sea (Ac 27:12; 28:11). Paul remains one, at Nicopolis (Tit 3:12). Summer and winter houses (Jer 36:22; Am 3:15).

See Meteorology.

WINTERHOUSE. The wealthy had separate residences for hot and cold seasons (Am 3:15).

WISDOM (Job 32:9; Ps 2:10; 90:12; Pr 2:1-20; 4:18-20; 7:4; 9:1-6; 10:13, 21, 23; 12:1, 8, 15; 13:14-16; 14:6-8, 16, 18, 33; 15:2, 7, 14, 33; 16:16, 20-24; 17:10, 24; 18:15; 19:8, 20; 21:11; Ec 8:1, 5; 9:13-18; 10:12; 12:11; Isa 11:9; 29:24; M't 11:19; Lu 1:17; 7:35; 21:15; Jas 1:5).

Commended (Pr 3:13-26; 24:3-7; Ec 7:11, 12, 19; 10:10). Is above value (Job 28:12-19; Pr 3:13-15; 16:16).

Personified (Pr 1:20-33; 8:1-36; 9:1-18).

Spiritual (De 32:29; Job 5:27; 8:8, 10; 12:2, 3, 7-13, 16, 17, 22).

The fear of the Lord is the beginning of (Ps 111:10; Pr 1:7; 9:10; Isa 33:6). Is revealed to the obedient (Ps 107:43; Pr 28:5, 7; 29:3; Ec 8:5; Da 12:3, 4, 10; Ho 6:3, 6; 14:9; M't 6:22, 23; Lu 11:34-36; Joh 7:17; 10:4, 14; 1Co 2:6-10; 8:3; 1Jo 4:6). Exemplified (Ps 9:10; 76:1; Pr 1:5; 11:12; M't 7:24, 25; 25:1-13; M'k 12:32-34; Ac 6:10; Ro 15:4; 1Co 13:11; Ph'p 3:7, 8, 10; 1Th 5:4, 5; Jas 3:13). Parable of (M't 25:1-13).

Exhortations to attain to (Pr 2:1-20; 4:4-13, 18-20; 22:17-21; 23:12, 19, 23; 24:13, 14; Ro 16:19; 1Co 8:3; 14:20; 2Co 8:7; Eph 5:15-17; Col 3:10, 16; 2Pe 3:18).

See Knowledge; Speaking, Wisdom in.

From God (Ex 4:12; 8:4, 10; De 4:5, 6, 35, 36; 29:4; 1Ch 22:12; Ne 9:20; Job 4:3; 11:5, 6; 22:21, 22; 28:20-28; 32:7, 8; 33:16; 35:10, 11; 36:22; 38:36, 37; Ps 16:7; 19:1, 2; 25:8, 9, 12, 14; 32:8; 36:9; 51:6; 71:17; 94:12; 112:4; 119:130; Pr 1:23; 2:6, 7; 3:5, 6; Ec 2:26; Isa 2:3; 11:1-3; 30:21; 42:6, 7, 16; 48:17; 54:13; Jer 9:23, 24; 24:7; Da 1:17; 2:21-23; 11:32, 33; M't 11:25-27; 13:11; 16:16, 17; Lu 1:76-79; 12:11, 12; 21:15; 24:32, 45; Joh 1:1, 4, 5, 7-9, 11; 6:45; 8:12, 31, 32; 9:5, 39; 12:49; 14:7; 16:13, 14; 17:3, 6-8, 25, 26; 18:37; Ro 1:19, 20; 1Co 1:30; 2:9-14; 12:8; 2Co 4:6; 3:15; Ga 4:9; Eph 4:11-13; Ph'p 3:15; Col 1:26-28; 1Ti 2:4; 2Ti 1:7; 3:15; Jas 3:17; 2Pe 1:2-5, 8, 12; 3:18; 1Jo 2:20, 27; 5:20). See God, Wisdom of.

Exemplified: Of Joseph (Ge 41:16, 25-39; Ac 7:10). Of Moses (Ac 7:22). Of Bezaleel (Ex 31:3-5; 35:31-35; 36:1). Of Aholiab (Ex 31:6; 35:34, 35; 36:1); of other skilled artisans (Ex 36:2); of women (Ex 35:36). Of Hiram (1Ki 7:14; 2Ch 2:14). Of Solomon (1Ki 3:12, 16-28; 4:29-34; 5:12; 10:24). Of Ethan, Heman, Chalcol, and Darda (1Ki 4:31). Of the princes of Issachar (1Ch 12:32). Of Ezra (Ezr 7:25). Of Daniel (Da 1:17; 5:14). Of Paul (2Pe 3:15). Of the Magi (M't 2:1-12).

Prayer for (Nu 27:21; J'g 20:18, 23, 26-28; 1Ki 3:7, 9; 8:36; 2Ch 1:10; Job 34:32; Ps 5:8; 25:4, 5; 27:11; 31:3; 39:4; 43:3; 86:11; 90:12; 119:12, 18, 19, 26, 27, 33, 34, 66, 68, 73, 80, 124, 125, 135, 144, 169, 171; 139:24; Eph 1:16-19; 3:14-19; 6:18-20; Ph'p 1:9; Col 1:9, 10; 2:1-3; 4:2-4; 2Ti 2:7; Jas 1:5). To be possessed in humility (Jer 9:23, 24; Jas 3:13). See Desire, Spiritual. Solomon's prayer for, see Solomon.

Promised (Joh 8:22). Opportunity to obtain, forfeited (Pr 1:24-31). Shall become universal.

Worldly (Job 4:18-21; 5:13; 11:2, 12; 37:24).

Desired, by Eve (Ge 3:6, 7). Misleading (Pr 21:30; Isa 47:10; 1Co 8:1, 2); ending in death (Pr 16:25). Folly of (Ec 2:1-26; 7:11-13, 16-25; 8:1, 16, 17; Jer 8:7-9; 49:7; M't 6:23; Ro 1:21-23). Increases sorrow (Ec 1:18; Isa 47:10, 11). Denounced (2Co 1:12). Woe denounced against (Isa 5:21). Shall perish (Isa 29:14-16). Illustration of (M't 7:24-27; Lu 16:18).

Council of others enjoined (Pr 15:22; 20:18; 24:3-7). Wise application of, profitable (Ec 10:10; Isa 28:24-29).

Admonitions against (Pr 3:7; Col 2:8; 1Ti 6:20, 21). Admonitions against glorying in (Jer 9:23, 24).

Heavenly things not discerned by (M't 11:25; Lu 10:21). Gospel not to be preached with (1Co 1:17-26; 2:1-14). To be renounced in order to attain spiritual wisdom (1Co 3:18-20).

Of God, see God, Wisdom of. Of Jesus, see Jesus, Wisdom of.

WISDOM OF JESUS, SON OF SIRACH (See Apocrypha.)

WISDOM OF SOLOMON (See Apocrypha.)

WISE MEN. 1. Men of understanding and skill in ordinary affairs (Pr 1:5; Job 15:2; Ps 49:10); came to be recognized as a distinct class, listed with priests and prophets in Jer 18:18, and also found outside Palestine (Ge 41:8; Ex 7:11; Da 2:12-5:15).

2. The magi (M't 2:1ff); astrologers; came from East; number and names are legendary.

WITCH, one (usually a woman) in league with evil spirits who practices the black art of witchcraft; condemned by law (Ex 22:18; De 18:9-14; 1Sa 28:3, 9; 2Ki 23:24; Isa 8:19; Ac 19:18, 19).

Masculine of Witch, usually Wizard.

WITCHCRAFT (1Sa 15:23; 2Ki 9:22; Na 3:4). Law concerning (Ex 22:18; Le 19:31; 20:6, 7).

Witch of Endor (1Sa 28:7-25). Witches, to be destroyed (Mic 5:12); destroyed (1Sa 28:3, 9).

See Sorcery.

WITHE, strong, flexible willow or other twig (J'g 16:7-9).

WITHERED HAND, hand wasted away through some form of atrophy (M'k 3:1-6).

WITNESS (Le 5:1; Pr 18:17). Qualified by oath (Ex 22:11; Nu 5:19, 21; 1Ki 8:31, 32); by laying hands on the accused (Le 24:14). Two necessary to establish a fact (Nu 35:30; De 17:6; 19:15; M't 18:16; Joh 8:17; 2Co 13:1; 1Ti 5:19; Heb 10:28). Required to cast the first stone in executing sentence (De 13:9; 17:5-7; Ac 7:58).

To the transfer of land (Ge 21:25-30; 23:11, 16-18; Ru 4:1-9; Jer 32:9-12, 25, 44). To marriage (Ru 4:10, 11; Isa 8:2, 3). Incorruptible (Ps 15:4). Corrupted by money (M't 28:11-15; Ac 6:11, 13).

Figurative: Of instruction in righteousness (Re 11:3).

See Courts; Evidence; Falsehood; False Witness; Holy Spirit; Testimony; Testimony, Religious.

WITNESS OF THE SPIRIT, direct, immediate, personal communication by the Holy Spirit that we are children of God (Ro 8:15, 16) or some other truth (Ac 20:23; 1Ti 4:1).

WITNESSING FOR CHRIST (Lu 2:17, 38; 24:48; Ac 1:8; 10:39; 22:15; 23:11; 26:22).

Of John the Baptist (Joh 1:15; 3:26). Of the apostles (Joh 15:27; 19:35; Ac 10:39-43; 1Jo 1:1-5); to his resurrection (Ac 1:22; 2:32; 3:15; 4:33; 5:32; 1Co 15:3-8).

WIZARD, magician or sorcerer, male or female (Le 19:31; 20:6, 27; 1Sa 28:3, 9; Isa 8:19).

WOLF, ravenous (Ge 49:27; Jer 5:6; Eze 22:27; Zep 3:3; Joh 10:12).

Figurative: Of the enemies of the righteous (M't 7:15; 10:16; Joh 10:12; Ac 20:29). Of the reconciling power of the gospel (Isa 11:6).

WOMEN. Creation of (Ge 1:27; 2:21, 22). Named (Ge 2:23). Fall of, and curse upon (Ge 3:1-16; 2Co 11:3; 1Ti 2:14). Promise to (Ge 3:15).

Had separate apartments in dwellings (Ge 24:67; 31:33; Es 2:9, 11). Veiled the face (Ge 24:65; see Veil).

Vows of (Nu 30:3-16). When jealously charged with infidelity, guilt or innocence to be determined by trial (Nu 5:12-31).

Took part in ancient worship (Ex 15:20, 21; 38:8; 1Sa 2:22); in choir (1Ch 25:5, 6; Ezr 2:65; Ne 7:67). Worshiped in separate compartments (Ex 38:8; 1Sa 2:22). Consecrated jewels to tabernacle (Ex 35:22); mirrors (Ex 38:8). Required to attend reading of the law (De 31:12; Jos 8:35). Ministered in the tabernacle (Ex 38:8; 1Sa 2:22).

Purifications of: After menstruation (Le 15:19-33; 2Sa 11:4); childbirth (Le 12; Lu 2:22). Difference in ceremonies made between male and female children (Le 12).

Religious privileges of, among early Christians (Ac 1:14; 12:12, 13; 1Co 11:5; 14:34; 1Ti 2:11).

Domestic duties of (Ge 18:6; Pr 31:15-19; M't 24:41). Cooked (Ge 18:6); spun (Ex 35:25, 26; 1Sa 2:19; Pr 31:19-24); embroidered (Pr 31:22). Made garments (1Sa 2:19; Ac 9:39). Gleaned (Ru 2:7, 8, 15-23). Kept vineyards (Song 1:6). Tended flocks and herds (Ge 24:11, 13, 14, 19, 20; 29:9; Ex 2:16). Worked in fields (Isa 27:11; Eze 26:6, 8). Was doorkeeper (M't 26:69; Joh 18:16, 17; Ac 12:13, 14).

Forbidden to wear men's costume (De 22:5). Wore hair long (1Co 11:5-15). Rules for dress of Christian (1Ti 2:9, 10; 1Pe 3:3, 4). Ornaments of (Isa 3:16-23; Jer 2:32).

Weaker than men (1Pe 3:7). Are timid (Isa 19:16; Jer 50:37; 51:30; Na 3:13); affectionate (2Sa 1:26); tender to her offspring (Isa 49:15; La 4:10); mirthsome (J'g 11:34: 21:21; Jer 31:13; Zec 9:17); courteous to strangers (Ge 24:17).

Could not marry without consent of parents, father (Ge 24:3, 4; 34:6; Ex 22:17; Jos 3:16, 17; 1Sa 17:25; 18:17-27). Not to be given in marriage considered a calamity (J'g 11:37; Ps 78:63; Isa 4:1). Sold for husband's debts (M't 18:25). Taken captive (Nu 31:9, 15, 17, 18, 35; La 1:18; Eze 30:17, 18). Shrewd (2Sa 20:16-22). Good wife, of the Lord (Pr 18:22; 19:13, 14).

Fond of self-indulgence (Isa 32:9-11); of ornaments (Jer 2:32). Subtle and deceitful (Pr 6:24-29, 32-35; 7:6-27; Ec 7:26). Silly, and easily led into error (2Ti 3:6). Zealous in promoting superstition and idolatry (Jer 7:18; Eze 13:17, 23). Active in instigating iniquity (Nu 31:15, 16; 1Ki 21:25; Ne 13:26). Guilty of sodomy (2Ki 23:7; Ro 1:26). See Wicked, below.

Punishment to be inflicted on men for seducing, when betrothed (De 22:23-27). Punishment for seducing, when not betrothed (Ex 22:16, 17; De 22:28, 29). Protected during menstruation (Le 18:19; 20:18). Treated with cruelty in war (De 32:25; La 2:21; 5:11).

Virtuous, held in high estimation (Ru 3:11; Pr 11:16, 22; 12:4; 14:1; 31:10-30). See Good, below.

As rulers (Isa 3:12); Deborah (J'g 4:4); Athaliah (2Ki 11:1-16; 2Ch 22:2, 3, 10-12; 23:1-15); Queen of Sheba (1Ki 10:1-13; 2Ch 9:1-9, 12); Candace (Ac 8:27); Persian queen sat on throne with the king (Ne 2:6).

Patriotic: Miriam (Ex 15:20); Deborah (J'g 4:4-16; 5); women of Israel (1Sa 18:6); of Thebez (J'g 9:53, 54); of Abel (2Sa 20:16-22); Esther (Es 4:4-17; 5:1-8; 7:1-6; 8:1-8); of the Philistines (2Sa 1:20). Aid in defensive operations (J'g 9:53).

Influential in public affairs: Bathsheba (1Ki 1:15-21); Jezebel (1Ki 21:7-15, 25); Athaliah (2Ki 11:1, 3; 2Ch 21:6; 22:3); the queen of Babylon (Da 5:9-13); Pilate's wife (M't 27:19).

As poets: Miriam (Ex 15:21); Deborah (J'g 5); Hannah (1Sa 2:1-10); Elisabeth (Lu 1:42-45); Mary (Lu 1:46-55).

As prophets: Miriam (Ex 15:20, 21; Mic 6:4); Deborah (J'g 4:4, 5); Huldah (2Ki 22:14-20; 2Ch 34:22-28); Noadiah (Ne 6:14); Anna (Lu 2:36-38), Philip's daughters (Ac 21:9). False prophets (Eze 13:17-23).

In business (1Ch 7:24; Pr 31:14-18, 24). Property rights of: In inheritance (Nu 27:1-11; 36; Jos 17:3-6; Job 42:15); to sell real estate (Ru 4:3-9).

First to sin (Ge 3:6). Last at the cross (M't 27:55, 56; M'k 15:40, 41). First at the sepulcher (M'k 15:46, 47; 16:1-6; Lu 23:27, 28, 49, 55, 56; 24:1-10). First to whom the risen Lord appeared (M'k 16:9; Joh 20:14-18).

Converted by preaching of Paul (Ac 16:14, 15; 17:4, 12, 34).

Paul's precepts concerning (1Co 11:3-15; 14:34, 35; Eph 5:22-24; Col 3:18; 1Ti 2:9-12; 3:11; 5:1-16; Tit 2:3-5).

Social status of: In Persia (Es 1:10-22; Da 5:1-12); in Roman empire (Ac 24:24; 25:13, 23; 26:30).

See Widow; Wife. See also Husbands; Parents.

Good (Pr 12:4; 31:10-31; 1Ti 2:9, 10; 3:11; 5:3-16; Tit 2:3-5). Virtuous (Ru 3:11; Pr 11:16, 22; 12:4; 14:1). Affectionate (2Sa 1:26); to offspring (Isa 49:15). Illustrated by the five wise virgins (M't 25:1-10).

Instances of: Deborah, a judge, prophetess, and military leader (J'g 4:5). Mother of Samson (J'g 13:23). Naomi (Ru 1:2; 3:1; 4:14-17). Ruth (Ru 1:4, 14-22 & chps 2-4). Hannah, the mother of Samuel (1Sa 1:9-18, 24-28). Widow of Zarephath, who fed Elijah during the famine (1Ki 17:8-24). The Shunammite, who gave hospitality to Elisha (2Ki 4:8-38). Vashti (Es 1:11, 12). Esther (Es 4:15-17; 5:1-8; 7:1-6; 8:1-8). Mary (Lu 1:26-38). Elisabeth (Lu 1:6, 41-45). Anna (Lu 2:37). The widow who cast her mite into the treasury (M'k 12:41-44; Lu 21:2-4). Mary and Martha (M'k 14:3-9; Lu 10:42; Joh 11:5). Mary Magdalene

(M'k 16:1; Lu 8:2; Joh 20:1, 2, 11-16). Pilate's wife (M't 27:19). Dorcas (Ac 9:36). Lydia (Ac 16:14). Priscilla (Ac 18:26). Phebe (Ro 16:1, 2). Julia (Ro 16:15). Mary (Ro 16:6). Lois and Eunice (2Ti 1:5). Philippians (Ph'p 4:3).

Figurative: Of the church of Christ (Ps 45:2-15; Ga 4:26; Re 12:1). Of saints (M't 25:1-4; 2Co 11:2; Re 14:4).

Wicked (2Ki 9:30-37; 23:7; Jer 44:15-19, 25; Eze 8:14; Ro 1:26). Zeal of, in licentious practices of idolatry (2Ki 23:7; Ho 4:13, 14); in promoting superstition and idolatry (Jer 7:18; Eze 13:17, 23). Careless (Isa 32:9-11). Contentious (Pr 27:15, 16). Fond of self-indulgence (Isa 32:9-11); ornamentation (Jer 2:32). Idolatrous (Nu 31:15, 16; 2Ki 23:7; Ne 13:26; Jer 7:18). Tattling (1Ti 5:11-13). Haughty and vain (Isa 3:16). Odious (Pr 30:23). Guileful and licentious (Pr 2:16-19; 5:3-20; 6:24-29, 32-35; 7:6-27; Ec 7:26; Eze 16:32; Ro 1:26). Commits forgery (1Ki 21:8). Subtle and deceitful (Pr 6:24-29, 32-35; 7:6-27; Ec 7:26). Silly and wayward (2Ti 3:6). Illustrated by the five foolish virgins (M't 25:1-12).

Active in instigating iniquity (Nu 31:15, 16; 1Ki 21:25; Ne 13:26). Guilty of sodomy (2Ki 23:7; Ro 1:26).

Instances of Wicked: Eve, in yielding to temptation and seducing her husband (Ge 3:6; 1Ti 2:14). Sarah, in her jealousy and malice toward Hagar (Ge 21:9-11, w *verses* 12-21). Lot's wife, in her rebellion against her situation, and against the destruction of Sodom (Ge 19:26; Lu 17:32). The daughters of Lot, in their incestuous lust (Ge 19:31-38). Rebekah, in her partiality for Jacob, and her sharp practice to secure for him Isaac's blessing (Ge 27:11-17). Rachel, in her jealousy of Leah (Ge 30:1); in stealing images (31:19, 34). Leah in her imitation of Rachel in the matter of children (Ge 30:9-18). Dinah, in her fornication (Ge 34:1, 2). Tamar, in her adultery (Ge 38:14-24). Potiphar's wife, in her lascivious lust and slander against Joseph (Ge 39:7-20). Zipporah, in her persecution of Moses on account of his religious obligations (Ex 4:25, 26). Miriam, in her sedition with Aaron against Moses (Nu 12). Rahab, in her harlotry (Jos 2:1). Delilah, in her conspiracy against Samson (J'g 16:4-20). Peninnah, the wife of Elkanah, in her jealous taunting of Hannah (1Sa 1:4-8). The Midianitish woman in the camp of Israel, taken in adultery (Nu 25:6-8). Michal, in her derision of David's religious zeal (2Sa 6:16, 20-23). Bath-sheba, in her adultery, in becoming the wife of her husband's murderer (2Sa 11:4, 5, 27; 12:9, 10). Solomon's wives, in their idolatrous and wicked influence over Solomon (1Ki 11:1-11; Ne 13:26). Jezebel, in her persecution and destruction of the prophets of the Lord (1Ki 18:4, 13); in her persecution of Elijah (1Ki 19:2); in her conspiracy against Naboth, to despoil him of his vineyard (1Ki 21:1-16); in her evil counsels to, and influence over, Ahab (1Ki 21:25, w *verses* 17-27, and 2Ki 9:30-37). The cannibal mothers of Samaria (2Ki 6:28, 29). Athaliah, in destroying the royal household and usurping the throne (2Ki 11:1-16; 2Ch 22:10, 12; 23:12-15). The sodomites of Judah (2Ki 23:7). Noadiah, a false prophetess, in troubling the Jews when they were restoring Jerusalem (Ne 6:14). Haman's wife, in counseling him to hang Mordecai (Es 5:14; 6:13). Job's wife, in counseling him to curse God (Job 2:9; 19:17). The idolatrous wife of Hosea (Ho 1:2, 3; 3:1). Herodias, in her incestuous marriage with Herod (M't 14:3, 4; M'k 6:17-19; Lu 3:19); compassing the death of John the Baptist (M't 14:6-11; M'k 6:24-28). The daughter of Herodias, in her complicity with her mother in securing the death of John the Baptist (M't 14:8; M'k 6:18-28). Sapphira, in her blasphemous falsehood (Ac 5:2-10). The woman taken in adultery and brought to Jesus in the temple (Joh 8:1-11).

Figurative: Of backsliding (Jer 6:2; Re 17:4, 18). Of the wicked (Isa 32:9, 11; M't 25:1-13).

Symbolical: Of wickedness (Zec 5:7, 8; Re 17; 19:2).

See Widow; Wife.

WONDERFUL, a name of the Messiah (Isa 9:6; See J'g 13:18).

See Jesus, Names of.

WOOL. Used for clothing (Le 13:47-52, 59; Pr 31:13; Eze 34:3; 44:17). Prohibited in the priest's temple dress (Eze 44:17). Mixing of, with other fabrics forbidden (Le 19:19; De 22:11). Fleece of (J'g 6:37). First fleece of, belonged to the priests (De 18:4).

WORD, a title of Jesus (Joh 1:1, 14; 1Jo 5:7; Re 19:13).

See Jesus, Names of.

WORD OF GOD. Written, *i.e.*, The Bible. Called: Book (Ps 40:7; Re 22:19); Book of the Lord (Isa 34:16); Book of the Law (Ne 8:3; Ga 3:10); Holy Scriptures (Ro 1:2; 2Ti 3:15); Law of the Lord (Ps 1:2; Isa 30:9); Oracles of God (Ro 3:2; 1Pe 4:11); Scriptures (1Co 15:3); Scriptures of Truth (Da 10:21); Sword of the Spirit (Eph 6:17); The Word (Jas 1:21-23; 1Pe 2:2); Word of God (Lu 11:28; Heb 4:12); Good Word of God (Heb 6:5); Word of Christ (Col 3:16); Word of Life (Ph'p 2:16); Word of Truth (Pr 22:21; Eph 1:13; 2Ti 2:15; Jas 1:18).

Compared to: a lamp (Ps 119:105; Pr 6:23); fire (Jer 23:29); seed (M't 13:38, 18-23, 37, 38; M'k 4:3-20, 26-32; Lu 8:5-15); to a two-edged sword (Heb 4:12).

To be publicly read (Ex 24:7; De 31:11-13; Jos 8:33-35; 2Ki 23:2; 2Ch 17:7-9; Ne 8:1-8, 13, 18; Isa 2:3; Jer 36:6; Ac 13:15, 27; Col 4:16; 1Th 5:27). Instruction of, to be desired (Ps 119:18, 19). The people stood and responded saying "Amen" (Ex 24:7; De 27:12-26; Ne 8:5, 6). Expounded (Ne 8:8); by Jesus (Lu 4:16-27; 24:27, 45; Joh 2:22); by the apostles (Ac 2:16-47; 8:32, 35; 17:2; 28:23). Searched (Ac 17:11).

Searching of, enjoined (Isa 34:16; Joh 5:39; 7:52). To be studied (2Ti 2:15; 1Pe 2:2, 3). Various portions to be compared (2Pe 2:20). Obeyed (Re 4:5, 6; 29:29; Ps 78:1, 7; Isa 34:16; Eze 44:5; Hab 2:2; M't 7:24, 25; Lu 6:47, 48; 11:28; Ro 16:26; 1Co 11:2; 1Th 4:1, 2; 2Th 2:14, 15; Heb 2:1-3; Jas 1:25; 2Pe 3:1, 2; Jude 3, 17; Re 1:3). Believed (M'k 1:15; 1Jo 5:11, 13).

Longing for (Ps 119:20, 131; Am 8:11-13). Walking after (Ps 119:30). Psalm of (Ps 119).

To be: in the heart (De 30:11-14; Job 22:22; Ps 37:31; 40:8; 119:11; Pr 6:20, 21; Isa 51:7; Eze 3:10; Ro 10:6-8); meditated upon (Jos 1:8; Ps 1:2; 119:15, 23, 48, 78, 97, 99, 148); worn on the hand and forehead (Ex 13:9; De 6:8; 11:18); posted, on the door posts (De 6:9; 11:20); in public places (De 27:2, 3, 8; Jos 8:32); studied by rulers (De 17:18, 19; Jos 1:8); taught to children (De 6:7; 11:19; 21:12, 13; Ps 78:5); in the side of the ark of the covenant (Ex 25:21; De 21:26); read in public assemblies (De 31:11; see above); taught in the Psalms (De 31:19, 21; Ps 119:54); used for teaching and admonishing one another (1Co 10:11; Col 3:16); instruction (2Ti 3:16, 17).

Not to be: added to nor taken from (De 4:2; 12:32; Pr 30:6; Re 22:18, 19); handled deceitfully (2Co 4:2); broken (Joh 10:35).

Nature of: Comforting (Ps 119:28, 50, 52, 76, 83, 92). Delight of the righteous (Job 23:12; Ps 1:2; 119:16, 24, 35, 77, 103, 143, 162, 174). Desired, more than gold (Ps 119:72, 127). Edifying (Ps 119:98, 99, 104, 130; Ac 20:32; Ro 4:23, 24; 15:4; 1Ti 4:6; 1Jo 2:7, 8, 12, 14, 21). Effective (Isa 55:11). Enduring, forever (Ps 119:89, 138, 152; Isa 40:8; M'k 13:31; Lu 16:17; 1Pe 1:23-25). Full, of hope (Ps 119:81; Col 1:5); of joy (Jer 15:16; 1Jo 1:4).

Inspired (Ex 19:7; 20:1; 24:3, 4, 12; 31:18; 32:16; 34:27, 32; Le 26:46; De 4:5, 10, 14; 2Ki 17:13; 2Ch 33:18; Ps 99:7; 147:19; Isa 34:16; 59:21; Jer 30:2; 36:1, 2, 27, 28, 32; 51:59-64; Eze 11:25; Da 10:21; Ho 8:12; Zec 7:12; Ac 1:16; 28:25; Ro 3:1, 2; 1Co 2:12, 13; 14:37; Eph 6:17; 1Th 2:13; 2Ti 3:16, 17; Heb 1:1, 2; 3:7, 8; 5:12; 2Pe 1:21; 3:2, 15; Re 1:1, 2, 11, 17-19; 2:7; 22:6-8).

Living (Heb 4:12). Loved (Ps 119:47, 48, 70, 97, 111, 113, 119, 159, 163, 167). Part of the Christian armor (Eph 6:17). Perfect (Ps 19:7; Jas 1:24). Powerful (Lu 1:37; Heb 4:12). Praiseworthy (Ps 56:4). Pure (Ps 12:6; 19:8; 119:140; Pr 30:5). Quickening (Ps 119:25, 93; Jas 1:18; 1Pe 1:23). Restraining (Ps 17:4; 119:11). Revered (Ps 119:161; 138:2).

Sanctifying (Joh 15:3; 17:17, 19; Eph 5:26; 1Ti 4:5). Spirit and life (Joh 6:63). Spiritual food, bread (De 8:3; M't 4:4). Standard of righteous (Ps 119:138, 144, 172; Isa 8:20). Trustworthy (Ps 19:7, 9; 33:4, 6; 93:5; 111:7, 8; 119:86). Truth (Ps 119:142, 151, 160; 1Th 2:13; Jas 1:18). Wonderful (Ps 119:129).

Bears the test of criticism and experience (2Sa 22:31; Ps 18:30). Cleanses life of youth (Ps 119:9). Convicts of sin (2Ki 22:9-13; 2Ch 17:7-10; 34:14-33). Gives peace (Ps 119:165). Inspires faith (Ro 10:17; Heb 11:3). Makes, free (Ps 119:45; Joh 8:32); wise (Ps 119:99; 2Ti 3:15). Rejoices the heart (Ps 119:111; Jer 15:16). Spirit of, gives life (2Co 3:6). Standard of judgment, the world to be judged by (Joh 12:48; Ro 2:16). Works salvation (1Th 2:13; 1Pe 1:23).

Ignorance of (M't 22:29; M'k 12:24). Rejected by the wicked (Pr 13:13; Isa 28:13; 30:9; Jer 8:9; Ho 8:12; M'k 7:9, 13; Ac 13:46). Disbelief in (Ps 50:16, 17; Isa 30:9; Jer 6:10; Lu 16:31; 24:25; Joh 5:46, 47; 8:37; 2Ti 4:3, 4; 1Pe 2:8; 2Pe 3:15, 16).

Fulfilled by Jesus (M't 5:17; Lu 24:27; Joh 19:24). Testify of Jesus (Joh 5:39; 20:31; Ac 10:43; 18:28; 1Co 15:3; Heb 10:7). See Jesus, Prophecies Concerning.

Rejection of (Ps 50:16, 17; Pr 1:29; 13:13; Isa 5:24; 28:9-14; 30:9-11; 53:1; Jer 6:10; 8:9; Ho 8:12; Am 2:12; Mic 2:6; Lu 16:31; 24:25; Joh 3:20; 5:46, 47; 8:37, 45; 1Co 1:18, 22, 23; 2Ti 4:3, 4; 1Pe 2:8; 2Pe 3:15, 16; Re 22:19).

See Commandments.

WORDS. Of Jesus: Gracious (Lu 4:22); spirit and life (Joh 6:63); eternal life (Joh 6:68); shall judge (Joh 12:47, 48). Of the wise: As goads, and as nails well fastened (Ec 12:11); gracious (Ec 10:12). Spoken in season (Pr 15:23; Isa 50:4). Fitly spoken, like apples of gold in filigree of silver (Pr 25:11). Of the perfect man, gentle (Jas 3:2).

Should be acceptable to God (Ps 19:14).

Of the teacher, should be plain (1Co 14:9, 19). Unprofitable, to be avoided (2Ti 2:14). Unspeakable, heard by Paul in paradise (2Co 12:4). Vain, not to be regarded (Ex 5:9; Eph 5:6); like a tempest (Job 8:2). Without knowledge, darken counsel (Job 38:2). Idle, account must be given for in the day of judgment (M't 12:36, 37). Hasty, folly of (Pr 29:20). In a multitude of, is sin (Pr 10:19). Fool known by the multitude of (Ec 5:3); will swallow himself (Ec 10:12-14). Seditious, deceive the simple (Ro 16:18). Deceitful, are a snare to him who utters them (Pr 6:2). Of the hypocrite, softer than oil (Ps 55:21). Of the talebearer, wounds to the soul (Pr 18:8).

See Busybody; Slander; Speaking, Evil; Talebearer.

WORK (See Industry; Labor.)

WORKS, GOOD (2Co 9:8; Eph 2:10; Ph'p 2:13; Col 1:10; 1Th 1:3, 7, 8; 2Th 2:17; 1Ti 2:10; 2Ti 2:21; Jas 1:22-27; 3:17, 18).

Jesus an example of (Joh 10:32; Ac 10:38). Holy women should manifest (1Ti 2:10; 5:10). God remembers (Ne 13:14, w Heb 6:9, 10). Shall be brought into judgment (Ec 12:14, w 2Co 5:10). In the judgment, will be an evidence of faith (M't 25:34-40, w Jas 2:14-20). Ministers should be patterns of (Tit 2:7). Ministers should exhort to (1Ti 6:17, 18; Tit 3:1, 8, 14). God is glorified by (Joh 15:8). Designed to lead others to glorify God (M't 5:16; 1Pe 2:12). A blessing attends (Jas 1:25). Of the righteous, are manifest (1Ti 5:25).

Parables relating to: The talents and pounds (M't 25:14-29; Lu 19:12-27); of the laborers in the vineyard (M't 20:11-15); the two sons (M't 21:28-31); of the barren fig tree (Lu 13:6-9).

In altruistic service (Eze 18:7, 8; M't 10:42; 25:35-46; Jas 1:27). Manifest faith (Ps 37:3; M't 19:16-21; Ro 2:13; Ga 6:4; Jas 2:14-26).

Enjoined upon (Ps 37:3; M't 3:8; Joh 15:2-8, 14); ministers (Tit 2:7); women professing godliness (1Ti 2:10); widows (1Ti 5:10); other Christians (M't 5:16; Col 3:13; Tit 3:1, 2, 8, 14; Heb 10:24; Jas 1:22-27; 3:13; 1Pe 2:12); the rich (1Ti 6:18).

To be done without ostentation (M't 6:1-4). Emulation in, enjoined (Heb 10:14). Zeal in, required (Tit 2:14). Remembered by God (De 6:25; 24:13; Ps 106:30, 31; Jer 22:15, 16; Eze 18:5-9; M't 6:1-4; 18:5; 25:34-36; Joh 15:2-8, 14; Ac 10:14, 38; Heb 6:9, 10; Re 14:13; 22:14).

Glorifies God (M't 25:34-46; Joh 15:2-8, 14; 1Co 3:6-9; Ph'p 1:11; Heb 13:21). Scriptures given for (2Ti 3:16, 17); Christ died for (Tit 2:14).

Insufficient for salvation (Ps 49:7, 8; 127:1, 2; Ec 1:14; Isa 13:14; 57:12; 64:6; Eze 7:19; 33:12-19; Da 9:8; M't 5:20; Lu 17:7-10; 18:9-14; Ac 13:39; Ro 3:20-21; 4:1-25; 8:3; 9:16, 31, 32; 11:6; 1Co 13:1-3; Ga 2:16, 21; 3:10-12, 21; 4:9-11; 5:2, 4, 6, 18; 6:15; Eph 2:8, 9; Ph'p

3:3-9; Col 2:20-23; 2Ti 1:9; Tit 3:4, 5; Heb 4:3-10; 6:1, 2; 9:1-14; Jas 2:10, 11). Hypocritical (M't 6:1-4).

Under the law (Le 18:5; Eze 20:11, 13, 20; Lu 10:28; Ro 10:5; Ga 3:12).

WORKS OF GOD. In creation (Job 9:8, 9; Ps 8:3-5; 89:11; 136:5-9; 139:13, 14; 148:4, 5; Ec 3:11; Jer 10:12); good (Ge 1:10, 18, 21, 25). Faithful (Ps 33:4). Wonderful (Ps 26:7; 40:5). Incomparable (Ps 86:8). In his overruling providence in the affairs of men (Ps 26:7; 40:5; 66:3; 75:1; 111:2, 4, 6; 118:17; 145:4-17). See also God, Works of.

WORLD. 1. Universe (Joh 1:10).

2. Human race (Ps 9:8; 96:13; Ac 17:31).

3. Unregenerate humanity (Joh 15:18; 1Jo 2:15).

4. Roman Empire (Lu 2:1).

WORLDLINESS (Ec 1:8; 8:15; Isa 56:12; Joh 15:19; Tit 3:3; 2Pe 2:12-15, 18, 19).

Proverb of, "Eat and drink, for tomorrow we die" (Ec 2:24; Isa 22:13; Lu 12:19; 1Co 15:32). Tends to poverty (Pr 21:17; Hag 1:6). Fatal to spirituality (Ga 6:8; Ph'p 3:19; 1Ti 5:6). Chokes the Word (M't 13:22; M'k 4:19; Lu 8:14).

Leads, to the rejection of the gospel (M't 22:2-6; Lu 14:17-24); to the rejection of Christ (Joh 5:44; 12:43): to moral insensibility (Isa 22:13; 32:9-11; 47:7-9); to death (Pr 14:12, 13).

Prosperity of, short (Job 20:4-29; 21:11-15; Ps 49:16-18; Isa 24:7-11; 28:4). Prayer regarding (Ps 73:2-22). Parable of (Lu 16:1-13, 19-25). Vanity of (Ec 2:1-12; 6:11, 12).

Admonitions against (Pr 23:20, 21; 27:1, 7; Ec 7:2-4; 11:9, 10; Ho 9:1, 11, 13; Am 6:3-7; 8:10; Mic 2:10; 6:14; M't 6:19, 25-34; 16:26; 24:28; M'k 8:36, 37; Lu 17:26-29, 33; 21:34; Joh 12:25; Ro 12:2; 1Co 7:29-31; 10:6; Col 3:2, 5; 2Ti 2:4, 22; 3:2-9; Tit 2:12; Jas 2:1-4; 4:4, 9; 5:5; 1Pe 1:14, 24; 2:11; 4:1-4; 1Jo 2:15-17). Denounced (Isa 5:11, 12; 47:8, 9; Jude 11-13, 16, 19).

Moses' choice against (Heb 11:24-26).

Instances of: Antediluvians (M't 24:38, 39; Lu 17:26, 27). Sodomites (Lu 17:28, 29). Esau (Ge 25:31-34; Heb 12:16). Jacob (Ge 25:31-34; 27:36; 30:37-43). Judah (Ge 37:26, 27). Israelites (1Sa 8:19, 20). Balaam (2Pe 2:15: Jude 11 w Nu 22; 23; 24). Eli's sons (1Sa 2:12-17). Gehazi (2Ki 5:20-27). Herod (M't 14:6, 7). The disciples (M't 18:1-4; M'k 9:34; Lu 9:46-48). The rich fool (Lu 12:16-21). Dives (Lu 16:19-25). The worldly steward (Lu 16:1-13). Cretans (Tit 1:12).

See Worldly Pleasure

WORLDLY CARE (See Anxiety.)

WORLDLY PLEASURE (Job 20:12; Ec 7:4; Isa 22:13; 2Ti 3:4; Tit 3:3).

Eschewed by Moses (Heb 11:25). To be eschewed by the righteous (1Pe 4:3, 4). Brings poverty (Pr 21:17). Chokes righteousness (Lu 8:14). Leads to, suffering (Isa 47:8, 9; 2Pe 3:13); spiritual death (1Ti 5:6). Denounced (Isa 5:11, 12; Jas 5:5). Folly of (Ec 1:17; 2:1-13).

See Worldliness.

WORLDLY WISDOM. Desired by Eve (Ge 3:6, 7). Misleading (Isa 47:10). Increases sorrow (Ec 1:18). Shall perish (Isa 29:14). Heavenly things not discerned by (M't 11:25; Lu 10:21). Gospel not to be preached with (1Co 1:17-26; 2:1-14). To be renounced in order to attain spiritual wisdom (1Co 3:18-20).

Admonitions against (Col 2:8; 1Ti 6:20, 21). Admonitions against glorying in (Jer 9:23, 24).

WORM, creeping, boneless animal (Ex 16:24; Isa 51:8; Ac 12:23); used metaphorically of man's insignificance (Job 25:6; Isa 41:14).

WORMWOOD, bitter plant which grows in wastelands (De 29:18); symbolic of bitter experience (Pr 5:4).

WORSHIP. To be rendered to God only (Ex 20:3; De 5:7; 6:13; M't 4:10; Lu 4:8; Ac 10:26; 14:15; Col 2:18; Re 19:10; 22:8). Not needed by God (Ac 17:24, 25).

Divine presence in (Ex 29:42, 43; 40:34, 35; Le 19:30: Nu 17:4; 1Ki 8:3-11; 2Ch 5:13, 14; Ps 77:13; 84:4; Isa 56:7; M't 18:20; Ac 2:1-4; Heb 10:25).

Origin of (Ge 4:26). Of Jesus (see Jesus, Worship of).

Acceptable to God (Ge 4:4; 8:21). Of the wicked, rejected (Ge 4:5, 7). See Prayer, of the Wicked. "Iniquity of the holy things" (Ex 28:38).

Sanctuary instituted for (Ex 25:8, 22; 29:43; 40:34, 35; Nu 17:4). Summons to (Ps 95:6; Isa 2:3; Mic 4:2).

Enjoined (Ge 35:1; Ex 15:1; 23:17, 18;

34:23; De 12:5-7, 11, 12; 16:6-8; 31:11-13; 33:19; 2Ki 17:36; 1Ch 16:29; Ne 10:39; Ps 29:2; 45:11; 76:11; 96:8, 9; 97:7; 99:5; Isa 12:5, 6; 49:13; 52:9; Jer 31:11, 12; Joe 1:14, 15; 2:15-17; Na 1:15; Hag 1:8; Zec 14:16-18; M't 8:4; M'k 1:44; Lu 4:8; 5:14; 1Ti 2:8; Heb 10:25; 12:28; Re 14:7; 19:10).

Attitudes in: Bowing (Ex 34:8; 2Ch 20:18). Prostration (Ge 17:3; M'k 3:11).

Prayer in (see Prayer).

Benedictions pronounced (see Benedictions).

With music (2Ch 5:13, 14; Ezr 3:10, 11; Ps 100:1, 2; 126:1-3; Isa 30:29; 38:20). Rendering praise (Ps 22:22; 138:2; 149:1); thanksgiving (Ps 35:18; 100:4; 116:17).

In spirit and in truth (Joh 4:23, 24; 1Co 14:15; Ph'p 3:3). Renews strength (Isa 40:31). Loved by God's people (Ps 27:4; 84:1-4, 10; Zec 8:21). Reward of (Ps 65:4; 92:13, 14; 122:1).

Preparation for (Ex 19:10-13, 21-24; 20:24, 25; 30:19, 21; Le 10:3; Ps 26:6; Isa 56:6, 7; Zep 3:18; Mal 3:3, 4). Requirements of (Ps 24:3-6; 51:18, 19).

Proprieties in (Ec 5:1, 2; 1Co 11:13, 20-22; 14:2-19). Reverence in (Ex 3:5; 19:10-12, 21-24; 24:1, 2; Ec 5:1; Hab 2:20).

Private (M't 6:6; 14:23; Lu 6:12).

At night (Isa 30:29; Ac 16:25). Jesus prays at night (Lu 6:12). In the temple (Jer 26:2; Lu 18:10; 24:53; Ac 3:1). In the heavenly temple (Re 11:1). In private homes (Ac 1:13, 14; 5:42; 12:12; 20:7-9; Ro 16:5; 1Co 16:19; Col 4:15; Ph'm 2). Anywhere (Joh 4:21-24). To become universal (Isa 45:23; Ro 14:11; Ph'p 2:10).

Of hypocrites, repugnant to God (Isa 1:11-15; 29:13-16; Ho 6:6; Am 5:21-24). Of the wicked, rejected (Ge 4:5, 7).

Family (De 16:11, 14). Of Abraham (Ge 12:7, 8; 13:4, 18). Of Jacob (Ge 35:2, 3). Of Job (Job 1:5). Of the Philippian jailer (Ac 16:34).

National (Re 15:4). The whole nation required to assemble for, including men, women, children, servants, and strangers (De 16:11; 31:11-13); in Mount Gerizim and Mount Ebal (Jos 8:32-35). The word of God read in public assemblies (Ex 24:7; De 27:12-26; 31:11-13; Jos 8:33-35; 2Ki 23:1-3; Ne 8:1-8, 13-18; M't 21:23; Lu 4:16, 17).

Of angels, forbidden (Re 19:10; 22:8, 9).

See Afflictions, Prayer in; Blasphemy; Children; Church; Consecration; Dedication; Idolatry; Instruction, in Religion; Levites; Minister; Music; Offering; Praise; Prayer; Preaching; Priest; Psalms; Religion; Sacrilege; Servant; Stranger; Tabernacle; Temple; Thanksgiving; Women; Word of God; Young Men.

Instances of: Israel (Ex 15:1, 2; Ps 107:6-8, 32). Moses (Ex 34:8). Solomon (2Ch 7:11). Priests and Levites (2Ch 30:27). Psalmists (Ps 5:7; 42:4; 48:9; 55:14; 63:1, 2; 66:4, 13, 14; 89:7; 93:5; 103:1-4; 116:12-14, 17; 119:108; 132:7, 13, 14). Isaiah (Isa 49:13; 52:9).

WORSHIPPERS, examples of (Ge 22:5; 24:26; Ex 34:8; Jos 5:14; J'g 7:15; 1Sa 1:28; 2Sa 12:20; 2Ch 7:3; Ne 8:6; Job 1:20; Re 4:10; 7:11; 11:16).

WOUNDS, treatment of (Pr 20:30; Isa 1:6; Lu 10:34).

WRATH. 1. Anger of men (Ge 30:2; 1Sa 17:28); may be evil (2Co 12:20) or reaction to evil (1Sa 20:34); work of the flesh (Ga 5:20). See Anger.

2. Anger of God—reaction of righteous God against sinful people and evil in all forms (De 9:7; Isa 13:9; Ro 1:18; Eph 5:6; Re 14:10, 19). See Anger of God.

WREATHS (Ex 28:14; 1Ki 7:17; 2Ch 4:12).

WRESTLE. To contend by grappling with an opponent (Ge 32:24, 25); used figuratively (Ge 30:8; Eph 6:12).

WRITING, invented in Mesopotamia, probably by Sumerians, at least as early as 2500 B. C.; they had a primitive, nonalphabetic linear writing, not phonetic but pictographic, ideas being recorded by means of pictures of sense-symbols, rather than by sound-symbols. The next stage in the history of writing was the introduction of the phonogram, or the type of sign which indicates a sound, and afterward came alphabetic scripts. Egyptians first developed an alphabetic system of writing. Hebrews derived their alphabet from Phoenicians. Semitic writing dating between 1900 and 1500 B. C. has been found at Serabit el-Khadim in Sinai. Greeks received their alphabet from Phoenicians and Aramaeans. Writing first mentioned in

Bible in Ex 17:14. Ten Commandments written with finger of God (Ex 31:18; 32:15, 16). Ancient writing materials: clay, wax, wood, metal, plaster (De 27:2, 3; Jos 8:32; Lu 1:63); later, parchment (2Ti 4:13) and papyrus (2Jo 12). Instruments of writing: reed, on papyrus and parchment; stylus, on hard material (Ex 32:4).

See Books; Engraving; Ink; Inkhorn; Letters; Pen; Tables of Stone.

X,Y

XERXES, king of Persian Empire from 486-465 B. C.; same as Ahasuerus, mentioned in Ezra, Esther and Daniel.

YAHWEH (See Yhwh below.)

YARMUK, WADI EL, stream six miles SE of Sea of Galilee flowing into Jordan; marked S boundary of kingdom of Bashan.

YARN, found in KJV of 1Ki 10:28 and 2Ch 1:16; correctly rendered in RSV by the proper name "Kue," the old Assyrian name given to Cilicia, in SE Asia Minor.

YEAR (Ge 1:14). Divided into months (Ex 12:2; Nu 10:10; 28:11). See Months.

Annual feasts (Le 25:5). See Feasts.

Redemption of houses sold, limited to one (Le 25:29, 30). Land to rest one, in seven (Le 25:5). Of release (De 15:9).

Age computed by: Of Abraham (Ge 25:7); of Jacob (Ge 47:9). See Longevity.

A thousand, with the Lord as one day (Ps 90:4; 2Pe 3:8). Satan to be bound a thousand (Re 20:2-4, 7).

See Jubilee, Year of; Millennium; Time.

YHWH, the Hebrew name for God, Jehovah; known as tetragrammaton, four consonants standing for ancient Hebrew name for God, Yahweh.

YODH, 10th letter of Hebrew alphabet, pronounced much like English "y."

YOKE, wooden frame for joining two draft animals; a wooden bar held on neck by thongs around neck (Nu 19:2; De 21:3). Yoke of oxen is a pair (1Sa 14:14; Lu 14:19).

Figurative of: Oppression (Le 26:13; 1Ki 12:4; 2Ch 10:4, 9-11; Isa 9:4; 10:27; Jer 28:2, 4, 10; 30:8); the bondage of sin (La 1:14); burdensome ordinances (Ac 15:10; Ga 5:1); discipleship to Christ (M't 11:29, 30); discipline (La 3:27).

Removal of, figurative of deliverance (Ge 27:40; Jer 2:20; M't 11:29, 30).

YOKEFELLOW (yoked together), person united to another by close bonds, as in marriage or labor (Ph'p 4:3).

YOM KIPPUR, Hebrew for "Day of Atonement." (See Feasts.)

YOUNG MEN. Wise, exemplified in Moses' wise choice (Ex 24:3-5; Heb 11: 24-26). Wise, a comfort to parents (Pr 10:1; 15:20; 29:3). Foolish, a sorrow to parents (Pr 10:1; 17:25; 19:13, 26; 28:7). Wise and foolish, contrasted (Pr 10:1; 13:1; 15:20). Glory of, their strength (Pr 20:29).

Admonitions to (Pr 3:1-5; 4:20-27; 6:1-5, 20-25; 19:27; 23:15-23, 25, 26; 24:1-12, 15-34; 27:11). Against lust (2Ti 2:22, 23). Against wine (Pr 23:20, 21, 29-35). Against loving the world (1Jo 2:13-17). Against the snares of the harlot (Pr 5:3-14; 6:24-35; 7:1-27; 23:27, 28; 31:1-3). Against the enticements of sinners (Pr 1:10-16). Against evil companions (Pr 2:12-15; 4:14, 15; 24:1, 2).

Exhortations to: Be sober-minded (Tit 2:6). Be an example of piety (1Ti 4:12). Keep the heart with all diligence (Pr 4:23). Take heed to their ways (Ps 119:9). Seek wisdom (Pr 2:1-8; 3:13-23; 4:5-13; 24:13, 14). Obey parents (Pr 6:20-23; 23:22-26). Obey the Lord (Pr 3:5-12). Praise the Lord (Ps 148:12, 13).

Folly of: Exemplified, by Esau (Ge 25:31-34; Heb 12:16, 17); Rehoboam's counselors (1Ki 12:8-11); Rehoboam (1Ki 12:13, 14); the rich young ruler (M't 19:16-22; M'k 10:17-22; Lu 18:18-23); the prodigal (Lu 15:11-32).

Instances of Religious: See Joseph; Joshua; Samuel; David; Solomon; Uriah.

See also Children; Parents.

Z

ZAANAIM, called also Zaanannim. A plain near Kedesh (Jos 19:33; J'g 4:11).

ZAANAN, called also Zenan. A place of uncertain location (Jos 15:37; Mic 1:11).

ZAANANNIM (See Zaanaim.)

ZAAVAN (not quiet), called also Zavan. A son of Ezer (Ge 36:27; 1Ch 1:42).

ZABAD (Jehovah has given). 1. Son of Nathan (1Ch 2:36, 37).

2. An Ephraimite (1Ch 7:21).

3. One of David's valiant men (1Ch 11:41).

4. An assassin of King Joash (2Ch 24:26; 25:3, 4). Called Jozachar in 2Ki 12:21.

5. Three Israelites who divorced their Gentile wives (Ezr 10:27, 33, 43).

ZABBAI. 1. Son of Bebai (Ezr 10:28).

2. Father of Baruch (Ne 3:20).

ZABBUD (given), a returned exile (Ezr 8:14).

ZABDI (God has given). 1. Father of Carmi (Jos 7:1, 17, 18).

2. A Benjamite (1Ch 8:19).

3. David's storekeeper (1Ch 27:27).

4. Son of Asaph (Ne 11:17).

ZABDIEL (God has given). 1. Father of Jashobeam (1Ch 27:2).

2. An overseer of one hundred and twenty-eight mighty men of valor, who dwelt in Jerusalem (Ne 11:14).

ZABUD (bestowed), a chief officer of Solomon (1Ki 4:5).

ZABULON (See Zebulun.)

ZACCAI, a Jew whose descendants returned from exile (Ezr 2:9; Ne 7:14).

ZACCHAEUS (pure), chief publican; climbed sycamore tree to see Jesus, and became His disciple (Lu 19:8).

ZACCHUR. A Simeonite (1Ch 4:26). See Zaccur.

ZACCUR (remembered). 1. Father of Reubenite spy, Shammua (Nu 13:4).

2. Simeonite (1Ch 4:26), "Zacchur" in KJV.

3. Son of Merari (1Ch 24:27).

4. Son of Asaph; musician (1Ch 25:1, 2; Ne 12:35).

5. Son of Imri who helped rebuild walls of Jerusalem (Ne 3:2).

6. Man who sealed covenant with Nehemiah (Ne 10:12).

7. Father of Hanan (Ne 13:13).

ZACHARIAH (Jehovah has remembered). 1. Son of Jeroboam, and last of the house of Jehu (2Ki 10:30; 14:29; 15:8-12).

2. Grandfather of Hezekiah (2Ki 18:2; 2Ch 29:1).

ZACHARIAS (Jehovah has remembered). 1. Father of John the Baptist (Lu 1:5); righteous priest; angel announced to him he would have a son (Lu 1:5-80).

2. Son of Barachias; slain between altar and temple (M't 23:35; Lu 11:51).

ZACHER (memorial), son of Jehiel (1Ch 8:31; 9:37).

ZADOK (righteous). 1. High priest in time of David's reign (2Sa 19:11; 20:25; 1Ch 15:11; 16:39). Removes the ark from Jerusalem at the time of Absalom's usurpation; returns with it at David's command (2Sa 15:24-36; 17:15, 17-21). Stands aloof from Adonijah at the time of his attempted usurpation (1Ki 1:8, 26). Summoned by David to anoint Solomon (1Ki 1:32-40, 44, 45). Performs the function of high priest after Abiathar was deposed by Solomon (1Ki 2:35; 1Ch 29:22).

2. Father of Jerusha (2Ki 15:33; 2Ch 27:1).

3. Son of Ahitub (1Ch 6:12).

4. A man of valor (1Ch 12:28).

5. Son of Baana (Ne 3:4).

6. A priest (Ne 3:29).

7. A returned exile (Ne 10:21).

8. Son of Meraioth (Ne 11:11).

9. A treasurer of the temple (Ne 13:13).

ZAHAM (odious fool), grandson of Solomon (2Ch 11:19).

ZAIR (small), village E of Dead Sea where Joran smote Edomites (2Ki 8:21).

ZALAPH (caper-plant), father of man who helped Nehemiah repair walls (Ne 3:30).

ZALMON (dark). 1. One of David's mighty men (2Sa 23:28), called "Ilai" in 1Ch 11:29.

2. Forest near Shechem (J'g 9:48).

ZALMONAH (gloomy), encampment of Israelites in wilderness, SE of Edom (Nu 33:41, 42).

ZALMUNNA (deprived of shade), king of Midian (J'g 8:5-21; Ps 83:11).

ZAMZUMMIM (murmurers), race of giants (De 2:20); lived E of Jordan; called Rephaim (2Sa 5:18, 22); may be same as "Zuzims" (Ge 14:5).

ZANOAH (rejected). 1. A city of western Judah (Jos 15:34; Ne 3:13; 11:30).

2. A city of eastern Judah (Jos 15:56).

3. A descendant of Caleb (1Ch 4:18).

ZAPHENATH-PANEAH (one who furnishes the sustenance of the land), name given to Joseph by Pharaoh (Ge 41:45).

ZAPHON (north), territory E of Jordan assigned to Gad (Jos 13:27); modern Amateh.

ZARA, Greek for Hebrew Zerah, mentioned in ancestry of Christ (M't 1:3).

ZARAH, called also Zerah and Zara. Son of Judah and Tamar (Ge 38:30; 46:12; Nu 26:20; 1Ch 2:4, 6; Ne 11:24).

ZAREAH, a city of Judah (Ne 11:29). See Zorah.

ZAREATHITE (See Zorah.)

ZARED, called also Zered. A brook (Nu 21:12; De 2:13, 14)

ZAREDA (See Zarethan.)

ZAREPHATH (refinement), a city between Tyre and Sidon. Elijah performs two miracles in (1Ki 17:8-24). Called Sarepta in Lu 4:26.

ZARETHAN, place near Bethshean and Adam (Jos 3:16); KJV has "Zaretan"; "Zeredah" in 2Ch 4:17. Exact site not ascertained.

ZARETH-SHAHAR (the glory of dawn), a city in Reuben (Jos 13:19).

ZARHITES, THE (those who shine), descendants of Zerah, son of Judah (Nu 26:13, 20; Jos 7:17; 1Ch 27:11, 13).

ZARTANAH, city in Jordan valley (1Ki 4:12); location uncertain.

ZARTHAN. 1. Place between Succoth and Adam (1Ki 7:46); "Zeredathah" in 2Ch 4:17.

2. Place of uncertain location (Jos 3:16).

ZATTHU (See Zattu.)

ZATTU. 1. One whose descendants returned with Zerubbabel (Ezr 2:8; 10:27; Ne 7:13).

2. Probably identical with Zatthu. One who sealed the covenant with Nehemiah (Ne 10:14).

ZAVAN (See Zaavan.)

ZAZA, son of Jonathan (1Ch 2:33).

ZEAL. Without love, unprofitable (1Co 13:3).

Without knowledge (Nu 11:27, 28; J'g 11:30, 31, 34, 35; Ec 7:16; M't 8:19, 20; Lu 9:57, 58; Joh 16:2; Ac 21:20; Ro 10:2, 3; Ga 1:13, 14). Wisdom of (Pr 11:30).

Required (Isa 62:6, 7; M't 5:13-16; M'k 4:21, 22; Lu 8:16, 17; Ac 10:42; 1Co 15:58; Tit 2:14; 3:1.

Enjoined (Jos 24:15, 16; Ezr 7:23; Ps 60:4; 96:2; Ec 9:10; Isa 60:1; Hag 2:4; Ro 12:11; 1Co 7:29-35; Ga 6:9; Eph 5:15, 16; 6:10-20; Ph'p 1:27, 28; Col 4:5; 2Th 3:13; Heb 12:1, 2; 13:13-15; 1Pe 2:2; 2Pe 1:10, 11; 3:14; Jude 3, 22, 23; Re 3:19).

Expected (Hab 5:2; Zec 4:20, 21; 2Co 4:8-10, 13, 16-18; Ga 4:18; Ph'p 2:15).

Rewards of (Da 12:3; M't 25:21, 23; Lu 19:17-19; Jas 5:20).

Exemplified in the following instances: Moses (Ex 2:12; 11:8; 32:19, 20, 31, 32; Nu 10:29; 11:29; De 9:18, 19). Phinehas (Nu 25:7-13; Ps 106:30). Joshua (Nu 11:27-29; Jos 7:6; 24:14-16). Gideon (J'g 6:11-32). Jephthah (J'g 11:30, 31, 34-39). Samuel (1Sa 12:23; 15:11, 35; 16:1). David (1Sa 17:26; 2Sa 6; 7:2; 8:11, 12; 24:24; 1Ch 29:17; Ps 40:8-10; 42:1, 2; 51:13; 69:7-9; 71:17, 18). Solomon (1Ki 8:31-53; 2Ch 6:22-42). Elijah (1Ki 19:10). Obadiah (1Ki 18:3, 4). Micaiah (1Ki 22:14). Jehu (2Ki 9:10). Jehoiada (2Ki 11:4-17; 2Ch 23:1-17). Asa (1Ki 15:11-15; 2Ch 14:1-5, 15). Israelites (2Ch 15:15; Eze 9:4). Jehoshaphat (2Ch 17:3-10; 19). Isaiah (Isa 6:8; 62:1). Hezekiah (2Ch 30:31; Isa 37:1). Josiah (2Ki 22:23; 2Ch 34:3-7, 29-33). Priests (Eze 44:15). Ezra (Ezr 7:10; 9:10; Ne 8:1-6, 13, 18). Nehemiah (Ne 4; 5; 13:7-9, 15-28). Job (Job 16:19). Psalmist (Ps 119:53, 126, 136, 139, 158). Jeremiah (Jer 9:1-3; 13:17; 18:20; 20:9; 25:3, 4; 26:12-15). Three Hebrews (Da 3:17, 18). Habakkuk (Hab 1:2-4). Old Testament roster (Heb 11).

Jesus (M't 23:27; Lu 19:41; Joh 4:34, 35; 9:4). Anna (Lu 2:38). Andrew and Philip (Joh 1:41-46). Apostles (M'k 16:20; Ac 4:31, 33; 5:21, 25, 29-32, 41, 42; 8:4, 25, 30, 35, 40; 11:19, 20, 24, 26). Two blind men proclaiming the miracle of healing, contrary to the injunction of Jesus (M't 9:30, 31). The restored leper

(M'k 1:44, 45). Man healed of demons (M'k 5:19, 20). Peter (M't 16:22; M'k 14:29-31; Lu 22:33; Ac 2:14-40; 3:12-26; 4:2, 8-12, 18-20; 5:29-32; 2Pe 1: 12-15). Samaritan woman (Joh 4:28-30, 39).

Paul: For the evangelization of the Jews (Ro 9:1-3; 10:1; 11:14); in his ministry (Ac 9:20-29; 14:1-28; 15:25, 26; 17:16, 17, 22-31; 19:8-10; 20:18-24, 26, 27, 31, 33, 34; 21:13; 24:14-25; 26:1-29; 28:23, 30, 31; Ro 1:1, 8, 9, 14, 15; 15:15-32; 1Co 4:1-21; 9:12-27; 2Co 1:12, 17-19; 5:9, 11, 13, 14, 20; 6:3-11; 11:16-33; 12:10-21; Ga 1:15, 16; 2:2; 4:19; Eph 6:20; Ph'p 1:18, 20, 24, 25, 27; 2:16, 17; 3:4-16; Col 1:28, 29; 2:1, 5; 1Th 1:5, 6; 2:2-6, 8-11; 2Th 3:7-9; 2Ti 1:3, 7, 11-13); in his piety (1Co 4:12; 10:33; 15:31; 2Co 4:8-18; 11:22-33; 12:10; Ph'p 3:4-16; 4:11, 12, 17; 2Ti 3:10, 11); in providing self-support (Ac 20:33, 34; 1Co 4:12; 2Co 11:7-12; 2Th 3:7-9); in suffering for Christ (Ac 21:13; 2Co 6:4, 5, 8-10; 11:22-33; 12:10, 14, 15, 21; 2Ti 2:9, 10; 3:10, 11).

Paul and Barnabas (Ac 14:14, 15). Timothy (Ph'p 2:22). Phoebe (Ro 16:1, 2). Epaphroditus (Ph'p 2:26, 30). Corinthians (1Co 14:12; 2Co 7:11; 9:2). Thessalonians (1Th 1:2-8). Ephesians (Re 2:2, 3, 6). Christian Jews (Heb 10:34). John (Ac 4:8-12, 13, 18-20; 3Jo 4; Re 5:4).

In Punishing the Wicked: Moses and Levites (Ex 32:20, 26-29). Phinehas (Nu 25:11-13; Ps 106:30, 31). Israelites (Jos 22:11-20; J'g 20). Samuel (1Sa 15:33). David (2Sa 1:14; 4:9-12). Elijah (1Ki 18:40). Jehu (2Ki 10:15-28). Jehoiada (2Ki 11:18). Josiah (2Ki 23:20).

In Reproving Iniquity: See Reproof, Faithfulness in.

ZEALOT (zealous one), member of Jewish patriotic party started to resist Roman aggression; violent; fanatical; Simon the Zealot, an apostle (Lu 6:15; Ac 1:13).

ZEBADIAH (Jehovah has bestowed). 1. Benjamite (1Ch 8:15).

2. Another Benjamite (1Ch 8:17).

3. Ambidextrous Benjamite soldier of David (1Ch 12:1, 2, 7).

4. Korahite door keeper (1Ch 26:2).

5. Son of Asahel (1Ch 27:7).

6. Levite sent by Jehoshaphat to teach law to residents of Judah (2Ch 17:8).

7. Son of Ishmael; head of Jehoshaphat's affairs (2Ch 19:11).

8. Son of Michael; returned with Ezra (Ezr 8:8).

9. Son of Immer; priest who divorced foreign wife (Ezr 10:20).

ZEBAH (sacrifice), king of Midian defeated and slain by Gideon (J'g 8:10, 12, 18, 21; Ps 83:11).

ZEBAIM (gazelles), native dwelling place of "sons of Pochereth" who returned with Zerubbabel (Ezr 2:25; Ne 7:59).

ZEBEDEE, father of James and John (M't 4:21; 20:20; 27:56; M'k 1:20).

ZEBINA (purchased), son of Nebo (Ezr 10:43).

ZEBOIM (hyena). 1. Called also Zeboiim. One of the cities in the valley of Siddim (Ge 10:19; 14:2, 8; De 29:23; Ho 11:8).

2. A city and valley in Benjamin (1Sa 13:18; Ne 11:34).

ZEBUDAH (given), wife of Josiah, king of Judah (2Ki 23:36).

ZEBUL (dwelling), an officer of Abimelech (J'g 9:28-41).

ZEBULONITE (See Zebulun.)

ZEBULUN (habitation). 1. Son of Jacob and Leah (Ge 30:20; 35:23; 46:14; 49:13; Ex 1:3; 1Ch 2:1). Descendants of (Ge 46:14; Nu 26:26, 27). Called also Zabulun.

2. Tribe of. Place of, in march and camp (Nu 2:3, 7; 10:14, 16). Territory awarded to (Ge 49:13; Jos 19:10-16; M't 4:13). Aboriginal inhabitants of the territory of, not expelled (J'g 1:30). Levitical cities of (Jos 21:34, 35; 1Ch 6:77). Moses' benediction upon (De 33:18, 19). Loyalty of, in resisting the enemies of Israel: with Barak against Sisera (J'g 4:6, 10; 5:14, 18); with Gideon against the Midianites (J'g 6:35); with David when made king over Israel (1Ch 12:33, 38-40). Joins with Hezekiah in renewing the passover (2Ch 30:11, 18). Conquest of, by Tiglath-pileser; carried to Assyria into captivity (2Ki 15:29; Isa 9:1). Jesus dwelt in the land of (M't 4:15). Twelve thousand sealed (Re 7:8).

See Israel.

ZEBULUNITE (See Zebulun.)

ZECHARIAH (Jehovah remembers). 1. Reubenite chief (1Ch 5:7).

2. Korhite, son of Meshelemiah (1Ch 9:21; 26:2, 14).

3. Benjamite (1Ch 9:37).

4. Levite; musician (1Ch 15:20; 16:5).

5. Priest; trumpeter (1Ch 15:24).

6. Levite (1Ch 24:25).

7. Merarite Levite (1Ch 26:11).

8. Manassite chief; father of Iddo (1Ch 27:21).

9. Prince who taught in cities of Judah (2Ch 17:7).

10. Father of prophet Jahaziel (2Ch 20:14).

11. Son of Jehoshaphat; killed by Jehoram (2Ch 21:2-4).

12. Son of Jehoiada, the high priest; stoned (2Ch 24:20-22).

13. Prophet in reign of Uzziah (2Ch 26:5).

14. Father of Abijah (2Ch 29:1).

15. Levite; son of Asaph (2Ch 29:13).

16. Kohathite who assisted in repair of temple in days of Josiah (2Ch 34:12).

17. Temple ruler (2Ch 35:8).

18. Man who returned with Ezra (Ezr 8:3).

19. Another man who returned with Ezra (Ezr 8:11).

20. Adviser of Ezra (Ne 8:4; Ezr 8:15, 16).

21. Man who divorced foreign wife (Ezr 10:26).

22. Judahite (Ne 11:4).

23. Another Judahite (Ne 11:5).

24. Son of Pashhur; aided rebuilding of walls (Ne 11:12).

25. Son of Iddo; priest (Ne 12:16).

26. Priest; son of Jonathan; trumpeter (Ne 12:35, 41).

27. Son of Jeberechiah (Isa 8:2).

28. Prophet; son of Berechiah and grandson of Iddo (Zec 1:1); returned with Zerubbabel; contemporary with Haggai.

ZECHARIAH, BOOK OF. The author a contemporary of Haggai; began to prophesy in 520 B. C.; deals with destiny of God's people. Contents:

1. Series of eight symbolic night-visions (1-6).

2. Prophecies spoken two years later than the above; exhortations and warnings (7, 8).

3. Judgment and mercy; the coming day of the Lord (9-14).

ZEDAD (a siding), a place near Hamath (Nu 34:8; Eze 47:15).

ZEDEKIAH (Jehovah is righteous). 1. Made king of Judah by Nebuchadnezzar (2Ki 24:17, 18; 1Ch 3:15; 2Ch 36:10; Jer 37:1). Throws off his allegiance to Nebuchadnezzar (2Ki 24:20; 2Ch 36:13; Jer 52:3; Eze 17:12-21). Forms an alliance with the king of Egypt (Eze 17:11-18). The allegiance denounced by Jeremiah (2Ch 36:12; Jer 21; 24:8-10; 27:12-22; 32:3-5; 34; 37:7-10, 17; 38:14-28); by Ezekiel (Eze 12:10-16; 17:12-21). Imprisons Jeremiah on account of his denunciations (Jer 32:2, 3; 37:15-21; 38:5-28). Seeks the intercession of Jeremiah with God in his behalf (Jer 21:1-3; 37:3; 38:14-27). Wicked reign of (2Ki 24:19, 20; 2Ch 36:12, 13; Jer 37:2; 38:5, 19, 24-26; 52:2). Nebuchadnezzar destroys the city and temple, takes him captive to Babylon, blinds his eyes, slays his sons (2Ki 25:1-10; 2Ch 36:17-20; Jer 1:3; 32:1, 2; 39:1-10; 51:59; 52:4-30).

2. Grandson of Jehoiakim (1Ch 3:16).

3. A false prophet (Jer 29:21-23).

4. A prince of Judah (Jer 36:12).

5. A false prophet. Prophesies to Ahab victory over the Syrians, instead of defeat (1Ki 22:11; 2Ch 18:10). Smites Micaiah, the true prophet (1Ki 22:24; 2Ch 18:23).

ZEEB (wolf), a prince of Midian (J'g 7:25; 8:3; Ps 83:11).

ZELAH, a city in Benjamin. Saul buried in (Jos 18:28; 2Sa 21:14).

ZELEK (a fissure), an Ammonite (2Sa 23:37; 1Ch 11:39).

ZELOPHEHAD, grandson of Gilead. His daughters petition for his inheritance (Nu 27:1-11; 36; Jos 17:3-6; 1Ch 7:15).

ZELOTES (See Zealot.)

ZELZAH, a city of Benjamin (1Sa 10:2).

ZEMARAIM. 1. Town c. four miles N of Jericho assigned to tribe of Benjamin (Jos 18:22).

2. Mountain in Ephraim upon which King Abijah rebuked King Jeroboam (2Ch 13:4).

ZEMARITES, a tribe descended from Canaan (Ge 10:18; 1Ch 1:16).

ZEMIRA, grandson of Benjamin (1Ch 7:8).

ZENAN, a city of Judah (Jos 15:37).

ZENAS, a Christian believer and lawyer (Tit 3:13).

ZEPHANIAH (hidden of Jehovah). 1. Ancestor of prophet Samuel (1Ch 6:36).

2. Author of book of Zephaniah (Zep 1:1); of royal descent; principal work done in Josiah's reign; contemporaries were Nahum and Habakkuk.

3. Priest, son of Maaseiah (2Ki 25:18-21; Jer 21:1); slain by Nebuchadnezzar.

4. Father of a Josiah to whom God sent the prophet Zechariah (Zec 6:10).

ZEPHANIAH, BOOK OF, 9th of the Minor Prophets and the last before the 70 years' captivity of Judah; denounced evils of his time; prophecy dated in reign of Josiah (639-608 B. C.). Outline:

1. Judgment of Judah and Jerusalem (1-2:3).
2. Judgment on Philistia, Moab, Ammon, Assyria (2:4-15).
3. Judgment on Jerusalem (3:1-8).
4. Effects of judgment (3:9-13).
5. Restoration of Israel (3:14-20).

ZEPHATH (watch-tower), Canaanite city c. 22 miles SW of S end of Dead Sea; destroyed by tribes of Judah and Simeon and renamed "Hormah" (J'g 1:17).

ZEPHATHAH (watch-tower), valley near Mareshah in W part of Judah (2Ch 14:10).

ZEPHI (watch-tower), grandson of Esau (1Ch 1:36); "Zepho" in Ge 36:11, 15.

ZEPHO (See Zephi.)

ZEPHON (watching), Gadite from whom family of Zephonites descended (Nu 26:15); "Ziphion" in Ge 46:16.

ZEPHONITES (See Zepho.)

ZER, a city in Naphtali (Jos 19:35).

ZERAH (rising). 1. Son of Reuel (Ge 36:13, 17; 1Ch 1:37).

2. Father of Jobab (Ge 36:33; 1Ch 1:44).

3. See Zarah.

4. Son of Simeon (Nu 26:13; 1Ch 4:24).

5. A Gershonite (1Ch 6:21).

6. A Levite (1Ch 6:41).

7. King of Ethiopia (2Ch 14:9-15).

ZERAHIAH (Jehovah is risen). 1. Levite in ancestry of Ezra (1Ch 6:6, 51).

2. Leader of 200 who returned with Ezra (Ezr 8:4).

ZERED, valley between Moab and Edom; encampment of Israel in wilderness wanderings (Nu 21:12, KJV has "Zared"; De 2:13, 14).

ZEREDA, birthplace of Jeroboam of Ephraim (1Ki 11:26); site unknown.

ZEREDATHAH, in Manasseh (2Ch 4:17).

ZERERATH, part of valley of Jezreel to which Midianites fled from Gideon (J'g 7:22).

ZERESH (golden), wife of Haman the Agagite (Es 5:10, 14; 6:13).

ZERETH (splendor), son of Ashur (1Ch 4:7).

ZERI, son of Jeduthun (1Ch 25:3).

ZEROR, Benjamite; great-grandfather of King Saul (1Sa 9:1).

ZERQA, modern name for ancient river Jabbok. Also "Zerka."

ZERUAH (leprous), mother of Jeroboam (1Ki 11:26).

ZERUBBABEL (shoot of Babylon), called also Shesh-bazzar. Directs the rebuilding of the altar and temple after his return from captivity in Babylon (Ezr 3:2-8; 4:2, 3; 5:2, 14-16; Hag 1:12-14). Leads the emancipated Jews back from Babylon (Ezr 1:8-11; 2; Ne 12). Appoints the Levites to inaugurate the rebuilding of the temple (Ezr 3:2-8). Prophecies relating to (Hag 2:2; Zec 4:6-10). Called Zorobabel in the genealogy of Joseph (M't 1:12; Lu 3:27).

ZERUIAH. Sister of David (1Ch 2:16). Mother of three of David's great soldiers (1Ch 2:16; 2Sa 2:18; 3:39; 16:9-11; 17:25).

ZETHAM (olive tree), a son of Laadan (1Ch 23:8; 26:22).

ZETHAN (olive tree), son of Bilhan (1Ch 7:10).

ZETHAR, chamberlain of Xerxes (Es 1:10).

ZEUS, chief of Greek gods, corresponding to Roman Jupiter (Ac 14:12, 13; 19:35). See also RSV.

ZIA, a Gadite (1Ch 5:13).

ZIBA (plant), member of Saul's household staff (2Sa 9:2); appointed by David to work for Mephibosheth; slandered Mephibosheth (2Sa 19:24-30).

ZIBEON (hyena). 1. A Hivite (Ge 36:2, 14).

2. Son of Seir (Ge 36:20, 24, 29; 1Ch 1:38, 40).

ZIBIA (gazelle), early descendant of Benjamin (1Ch 8:9).

ZIBIAH (gazelle), woman of Beersheba who married King Ahaziah; mother of King Joash (2Ki 12:1; 2Ch 24:1).

ZICHRI. 1. Son of Izhar (Ex 6:21).

2. Three Benjamites (1Ch 8:19, 23, 27).

3. A Levite (1Ch 9:15).

4. Two chiefs in the days of David (1Ch 26:25; 27:16).

5. Father of Amasiah (2Ch 17:16).

6. Father of Elishaphat (2Ch 23:1).

7. An Ephraimite (2Ch 28:7).

8. Father of Joel (Ne 11:9).

9. A priest (Ne 12:17).

ZIDDIM (sides), a city in Naphtali (Jos 19:35).

ZIDKIJAH, a chief prince of the exiles who returned to Jerusalem (Ne 10:1).

ZIDON (fishery), in KJV usually Zidon in OT, and always Sidon in NT; Canaanite city 22 miles N of Tyre (Ge 10:15, 19); chief gods were Baal and Ashtoreth (1Ki 11:5, 33; 2Ki 23:13); father of Jezebel a king of Zidon (1Ki 16:31); modern Saida.

ZIDONIANS (See Zidon.)

ZIF, 2nd month of old Hebrew calendar, corresponding to Iyyar in later Jewish calendar (1Ki 6:1, 37).

ZIGGURAT (pinnacle), temple tower of the Babylonians, consisting of a lofty structure in the form of a pyramid, built in successive stages, with staircases on the outside and a shrine at the top.

ZIHA. 1. Head of family of Nethinim that returned with Zerubbabel (Ezr 2:43; Ne 7:46).

2. Ruler of Nethinim (Ne 11:21).

ZIKLAG. A city within the territory allotted to the tribe of Judah (Jos 15:31). Reallotted to the tribe of Simeon (Jos 19:5). David dwells at (1Sa 27:5, 6; 2Sa 1:1; 1Ch 12:1). Amalekites destroy (1Sa 30). Inhabited by the returned exiles of Judah (Ne 11:28).

ZIKRI. 1. Levite; cousin of Aaron and Moses (Ex 6:21).

2. Benjamite; son of Shashak (1Ch 8:23).

3. Benjamite of family of Shemei or Shema (KJV "Shimhi") (1Ch 8:19).

4. Benjamite; son of Jeroham (1Ch 8:27).

5. Ancestor of Mattaniah who returned from captivity (1Ch 9:15); "Zabdi" in Ne 11:17.

6. Descendant of Eliezer (1Ch 26:25).

7. Father of Eliezer; Reubenite (1Ch 27:16).

8. Father of Amasiah; soldier (2Ch 17:16).

9. Father of Elishaphat (2Ch 23:1).

10. Ephraimite; killed son of Ahaz (2Ch 28:7).

11. Father of Joel, the overseer of Benjamites (Ne 11:9).

12. Descendant of Abijah; priest (Ne 12:17).

ZILLAH (shadow), wife of Lamech (Ge 4:19, 22, 23).

ZILPAH. Leah's handmaid (Ge 29:24). Mother of Gad and Asher by Jacob (Ge 30:9-13; 35:26; 37:2; 46:18).

ZILTHAI (shadow of Jehovah). 1. A Benjamite (1Ch 8:20).

2. A captain of Manasseh (1Ch 12:20).

ZIMMAH. 1. A son of Jahath (1Ch 6:20).

2. Two Gershonites (1Ch 6:42; 2Ch 29:12).

ZIMRAN, son of Abraham (Ge 25:2; 1Ch 1:32).

ZIMRI. 1. Prince of Simeon; slain by Phinehas, grandson of Aaron, for committing adultery with Midianite woman (Nu 25:14).

2. 5th king of N kingdom; murdered King Elah; ruled seven days (c. 876 B.C.); overthrown by Omri (1Ki 16:8-20).

3. Son of Zerah; grandson of Judah (1Ch 2:6).

4. Benjamite; father of Moza (1Ch 8:36; 9:42).

5. Unknown tribe in East (Jer 25:25).

ZIN, a desert S of Judah (Nu 13:21; 20:1; 27:14; 33:36; 34:3, 4; De 32:51; Jos 15:1, 3).

ZINA. A son of Shimei (1Ch 23:10). Called Zizah in *verse* 11.

ZION (citadel), called also Sion, stronghold of Jerusalem. Taken from the Jebusites by David (2Sa 5:6-9; 1Ch 11:5-7). Called thereafter "the city of David" (2Sa 5:7, 9; 6:12, 16; 1Ki 8:1; 1Ch 11:5, 7; 15:1, 29; 2Ch 5:2). Ark of the covenant placed in (2Sa 6:12, 16; 1Ki 8:1; 1Ch 15:1, 29; 2Ch 5:2); removed from, to Solomon's temple on

Mount Moriah (1Ki 8:1; 2Ch 5:2, w 2Ch 3:1).

Collectively, the place, the forms, and the assemblies of Israelitish worship (2Ki 19:21, 31; Ps 9:11; 48:2, 11, 12; 74:2; 132:13; 137:1; Isa 35:10; 40:9; 49:14; 51:16; 52:1, 2, 7, 8; 60:14; 62:1, 11; Jer 31:6; 50:5; La 1:4; Joe 2:1, 15; M't 21:5; Joh 12:15; Ro 9:33; 11:26; 1Pe 2:6). Name of, applied to Jerusalem (Ps 87:2, 5; 149:2; Song 3:11; Isa 33:14, 20; Jer 9:19; 30:17; Zech 9:13). Called the city of God (Ps 87:2, 3; Isa 60:14). Restoration of, promised (Isa 51:3, 11, 16; 52:1, 2, 7, 8; 59:20; 60:14; Ob 17, 21; Zep 3:14, 16; Zec 1:14, 17; 2:7, 10; 8:2, 3; 9:9, 13). Name of, applied to the city of the redeemed (Heb 12:22; Re 14:1).

See Church; Jerusalem.

ZIOR (smallness), town in S Judah probably near Hebron (Jos 15:54).

ZIPH. 1. City in Negeb, probably c. four miles S by E from Hebron (Jos 15:55).

2. Wilderness named from above city where David hid (1Sa 23:14-24; 26:1, 2).

3. City in W Judah (2Ch 11:8).

4. Calebite family name (1Ch 2:42).

5. Judahite (1Ch 4:16).

ZIPHAH, a son of Jehaleleel (1Ch 4:16).

ZIPHIMS (See Ziphites.)

ZIPHION. A son of Gad (Ge 46:16). Called Zephon in Nu 26:15.

ZIPHITES, inhabitants of Ziph (1Sa 23:19; 26:1-5).

ZIPHRON, a place in the N of Palestine (Nu 34:9).

ZIPPOR (bird), father of Balak (Nu 22:2, 4, 10, 16; 23:18; Jos 24:9).

ZIPPORAH (bird). Wife of Moses (Ex 2:16-22). Reproaches Moses (Ex 4:25, 26). Separates from Moses, is brought again to him by her father (Ex 18:2-6). Miriam and Aaron upbraid Moses concerning (Nu 12:1).

ZITHRI (my protection), Kohathite Levite; cousin of Aaron and Moses (Ex 6:22).

ZIV (See Zif.)

ZIZ (shining), cliff near W side of Red Sea on way fron Engedi to Tekoa (2Ch 20:16).

ZIZA (abundance). 1. Simeonite; son of Shiphi (KJV "Ziphi") (1Ch 4:37-41).

2. Son of Rehoboam and brother of Abijah, kings of Judah (2Ch 11:20).

ZIZAH, son of Shimei (1Ch 23:11); called "Zina" in preceding verse.

ZOAN, a city in Egypt. Built seven years after Hebron in the land of Canaan (Nu 13:22). Prophecies concerning (Eze 30:14). Wise men from, were counselors of Pharaoh (Isa 19:11, 13). Princes of (Isa 30:4).

ZOAR (little). A city of the Moabites, near the Jordan (Ge 13:10). Territory of (De 34:3; Isa 15:5; Jer 48:34). King of, fought against Chedorlaomer (Ge 14:2, 8). Not destroyed with Sodom and Gomorrah (Ge 19:20-23, 30).

ZOBA (See Zobah.)

ZOBAH, called also Zoba; Aram-zobah; Hamath-zobah. A kingdom in the N of Palestine (1Sa 14:47). Conquest of, by David (2Sa 8:3-8, 12; 1Ki 11:23, 24; 1Ch 18:2-9). Its inhabitants mercenaries of the Ammonites against David (2Sa 10:6-19; 1Ch 19:6-19). David writes a psalm after the conquest of (see title of Ps 60). Invaded by Solomon (2Ch 8:3).

ZOBEBAH, daughter of Coz (1Ch 4:8).

ZODIAC, signs of (Job 38:32 [*R. V.* marg.]).

ZOHAR. 1. Hittite; father of Ephron from whom Abraham purchased field of Machpelah (Ge 23:8; 25:9).

2. Son of Simeon, 2nd son of Jacob (Ge 46:10; Ex 6:15); "Zerah" in Nu 26:13 and 1Ch 4:24.

ZOHELETH (serpent), stone or ledge by En-rogel (1Ki 1:9).

ZOHETH, son of Ishi (1Ch 4:20).

ZOPHAH, son of Helem (1Ch 7:35, 36).

ZOPHAI, ancestor of Samuel the prophet (1Ch 6:26); "Zuph" in *verse* 35.

ZOPHAR, one of Job's three friends (Job 2:11; 11; 20; 42:7-9).

ZOPHIM (watchers). 1. A place on the top of Pisgah (Nu 23:14).

2. A city on Mount Ephraim (1Sa 1:1).

ZORAH, called also Zareah and Zoreah. A city of Dan or Judah (Jos 15:33; 19:41). The city of Samson (J'g 13:2, 24, 25; 16:31). Representatives of the tribe of Dan sent from, to spy out the land with a view to its conquest (J'g 18). Fortified by Rehoboam (2Ch 11:10). Repeopled after the captivity (Ne 11:29).

ZORATHITES, inhabitants of Zorah (1Ch 2:53); (KJV has Zoreathites).

ZOREAH (See Zorah.)

ZORITES, Judahite family (1Ch 2:54).

ZOROBABEL, called also Zerubbabel and Shesh-bazzar. An ancestor of Joseph (M't 1:12, 13; Lu 3:27).
See Zerubbabel.

ZUAR (small), father of Nethaneel (Nu 1:8; 2:5; 7:18, 23; 10:15).

ZUPH (honeycomb). 1. Ancestor of the prophet Samuel (1Ch 6:35); "Zophai" in 1Ch 6:26.
2. District in Benjamin, near N border (1Sa 9:5); location unknown.

ZUR (rock). 1. King of Midian slain by Israel (Nu 25:15; 31:8).
2. Son of Jeiel (1Ch 8:30, 33).

ZURIEL (whose rock is God), son of Abihail, prince of Merarite Levites in wilderness (Nu 3:35).

ZURISHADDAI (whose rock is the almighty), father of Shelumiel (Nu 1:6; 2:12; 7:36, 41; 10:19).

ZUZIM, primitive race of giants, defeated by Chedorlaomer and allies (Ge 14:5); erroneously called "Zuzims" in KJV.